Microsoft® Official Academic Course

Microsoft Office 2010

WILEY

EDITOR	Bryan Gambrel
DIRECTOR OF SALES	Mitchell Beaton
EXECUTIVE MARKETING MANAGER	Chris Ruel
ASSISTANT MARKETING MANAGER	Debbie Martin
MICROSOFT STRATEGIC RELATIONSHIPS MANAGER	Colin Klein of Microsoft Learning
EDITORIAL PROGRAM ASSISTANT	Jennifer Lartz
CONTENT MANAGER	Kevin Holm
PRODUCTION EDITOR	Jill Spikereit
CREATIVE DIRECTOR	Harry Nolan
COVER DESIGNER	Jim O'Shea
INTERIOR DESIGNER	Amy Rosen
PHOTO EDITORS	Sheena Goldstein, Jennifer MacMillan
PRODUCT DESIGNER	Tom Kulesa
CONTENT EDITOR	Wendy Ashenberg
MEDIA SPECIALIST	Jennifer Mullin

This book was set in Garamond by Aptara, Inc. and printed and bound by Courier Kendallville. The covers were printed by Lehigh Phoenix.

Founded in 1807, John Wiley & Sons, Inc. has been a valued source of knowledge and understanding for more than 200 years, helping people around the world meet their needs and fulfill their aspirations. Our company is built on a foundation of principles that include responsibility to the communities we serve and where we live and work. In 2008, we launched a Corporate Citizenship Initiative, a global effort to address the environmental, social, economic, and ethical challenges we face in our business. Among the issues we are addressing are carbon impact, paper specifications and procurement, ethical conduct within our business and among our vendors, and community and charitable support. For more information, please visit our website: www.wiley.com/go/citizenship.

ISBN 978-0-470-90850-1

Printed in the United States of America

10 9 8 7 6 5 4 3 2 1

Foreword from the Publisher

Wiley's publishing vision for the Microsoft Official Academic Course series is to provide students and instructors with the skills and knowledge they need to use Microsoft technology effectively in all aspects of their personal and professional lives. Quality instruction is required to help both educators and students get the most from Microsoft's software tools and to become more productive. Thus our mission is to make our instructional programs trusted educational companions for life.

To accomplish this mission, Wiley and Microsoft have partnered to develop the highest quality educational programs for Information Workers, IT Professionals, and Developers. Materials created by this partnership carry the brand name "Microsoft Official Academic Course," assuring instructors and students alike that the content of these textbooks is fully endorsed by Microsoft, and that they provide the highest quality information and instruction on Microsoft products. The Microsoft Official Academic Course textbooks are "Official" in still one more way—they are the officially sanctioned courseware for Microsoft IT Academy members.

The Microsoft Official Academic Course series focuses on *workforce development*. These programs are aimed at those students seeking to enter the workforce, change jobs, or embark on new careers as information workers, IT professionals, and developers. Microsoft Official Academic Course programs address their needs by emphasizing authentic workplace scenarios with an abundance of projects, exercises, cases, and assessments.

The Microsoft Official Academic Courses are mapped to Microsoft's extensive research and job-task analysis, the same research and analysis used to create the Microsoft Office Specialist (MOS) exams. The textbooks focus on real skills for real jobs. As students work through the projects and exercises in the textbooks, they enhance their level of knowledge and their ability to apply the latest Microsoft technology to everyday tasks. These students also gain resume-building credentials that can assist them in finding a job, keeping their current job, or in furthering their education.

The concept of lifelong learning is today an utmost necessity. Job roles, and even whole job categories, are changing so quickly that none of us can stay competitive and productive without continuously updating our skills and capabilities. The Microsoft Official Academic Course offerings, and their focus on Microsoft certification exam preparation, provide a means for people to acquire and effectively update their skills and knowledge. Wiley supports students in this endeavor through the development and distribution of these courses as Microsoft's official academic publisher.

Today educational publishing requires attention to providing quality print and robust electronic content. By integrating Microsoft Official Academic Course products, *WileyPLUS*, and Microsoft certifications, we are better able to deliver efficient learning solutions for students and teachers alike.

Joseph Heider
General Manager and Senior Vice President

www.wiley.com/college/microsoft
or call the MOAC Toll-Free Number: 1+(888) 764-7001 (U.S. & Canada only)

Welcome to the Microsoft Official Academic Course (MOAC) program for Microsoft Office 2010. MOAC is the collaboration between Microsoft Learning and John Wiley & Sons, Inc. publishing company. Microsoft and Wiley teamed up to produce a series of textbooks that deliver compelling and innovative teaching solutions to instructors and superior learning experiences for students. Infused and informed by in-depth knowledge from the creators of Microsoft Office and Windows, and crafted by a publisher known worldwide for the pedagogical quality of its products, these textbooks maximize skills transfer in minimum time. Students are challenged to reach their potential by using their new technical skills as highly productive members of the workforce.

Because this knowledgebase comes directly from Microsoft, architect of Office 2010 and creator of the Microsoft Office Specialist (MOS) exams (http://www.microsoft.com/learning/en/us/certification/mos.aspx), you are sure to receive the topical coverage that is most relevant to your personal and professional success. Microsoft's direct participation not only assures you that MOAC textbook content is accurate and current; it also means that students will receive the best instruction possible to enable their success on certification exams and in the workplace.

THE MICROSOFT OFFICIAL ACADEMIC COURSE PROGRAM

The *Microsoft Official Academic Course* series is a complete program for instructors and institutions to prepare and deliver great courses on Microsoft software technologies. With MOAC, we recognize that, because of the rapid pace of change in the technology and curriculum developed by Microsoft, there is an ongoing set of needs beyond classroom instruction tools for an instructor to be ready to teach the course. The MOAC program endeavors to provide solutions for all these needs in a systematic manner in order to ensure a successful and rewarding course experience for both instructor and student—technical and curriculum training for instructor readiness with new software releases; the software itself for student use at home for building hands-on skills, assessment, and validation of skill development; and a great set of tools for delivering instruction in the classroom and lab. All are important to the smooth delivery of an interesting course on Microsoft software, and all are provided with the MOAC program. We think about the model below as a gauge for ensuring that we completely support you in your goal of teaching a great course. As you evaluate your instructional materials options, you may wish to use the model for comparison purposes with available products.

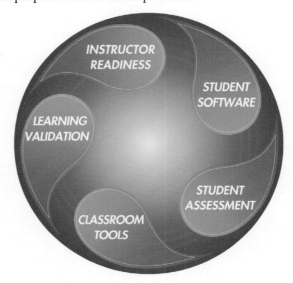

www.wiley.com/college/microsoft
or call the MOAC Toll-Free Number: 1+(888) 764-7001 (U.S. & Canada only)

PEDAGOGICAL FEATURES

The MOAC textbooks for Microsoft Office 2010 are designed to teach students the core principles of Microsoft Office needed for on-the-job success. Many pedagogical features have been developed specifically for *Microsoft Official Academic Course* programs. Unique features of our task-based approach include a Lesson Skill Matrix that correlates skills taught in each lesson to the MOS objectives; Workplace and Internet Ready exercises; and three levels of increasingly rigorous lesson-ending activities: Competency, Proficiency, and Mastery Assessment.

Presenting the extensive procedural information and technical concepts woven throughout the textbook raises challenges for the student and instructor alike. The Illustrated Book Tour that follows provides a guide to the rich features contributing to *Microsoft Official Academic Course* program's pedagogical plan. Following is a list of key features in each lesson designed to prepare students for success on the certification exams and in the workplace:

- Each lesson begins with a **Lesson Skill Matrix**. Providing a list of skills covered in the lesson.
- Each lesson features a real-world **Business Case** scenario that places the software skills and knowledge to be acquired in a real-world setting.
- **Software Orientation** provides an overview of the software features students will be working with in the lesson. The orientation will detail the general properties of the software or specific features, such as a ribbon or dialog box; and it includes a large, labeled screen image.
- Concise and frequent **Step-by-Step** instructions teach students new features and provide an opportunity for hands-on practice. Numbered steps give detailed step-by-step instructions to help students learn software skills. The steps also show results and screen images to match what students should see on their computer screens.
- **Illustrations** provide visual feedback as students work through the exercises. The images reinforce key concepts, provide visual clues about the steps, and allow students to check their progress.
- When the text instructs a student to click a particular button, **button images** are shown in the margin or in the text.
- Important technical vocabulary is listed in the **Key Terms** section at the beginning of the lesson. When these terms are used later in the lesson, they appear in bold italic type with yellow highlighter and are defined. The Glossary contains all of the key terms and their definitions.
- Engaging point-of-use **Reader aids**, located throughout the lessons, tell students why this topic is relevant (*The Bottom Line*), provide students with helpful hints (*Take Note*), or show alternate ways to accomplish tasks (*Another Way*), or point out things to watch out for or avoid (*Troubleshooting*). Reader aids also provide additional relevant or background information that adds value to the lesson.
- The **New Feature** icon appears near any software feature that is new to Office 2010.
- Each lesson ends with a **Skill Summary** recapping the skills covered in the lesson.
- The **Knowledge Assessment** section provides a total of 20 questions from a mix of True/False, Fill in the Blank, Matching, or Multiple Choice, testing students on concepts learned in the lesson.

- **Competency, Proficiency, and Mastery Assessment** sections provide progressively more challenging lesson-ending activities.
- **Internet Ready** projects combine the knowledge that students acquire in a lesson with Web-based task research.
- **Workplace Ready** features preview how Microsoft Office 2010 applications are used in real-world situations.
- The student companion website contains the **online files** needed for each lesson. These data files are indicated by the @ icon in the margin of the textbook.

Illustrated Book Tour

LESSON FEATURES

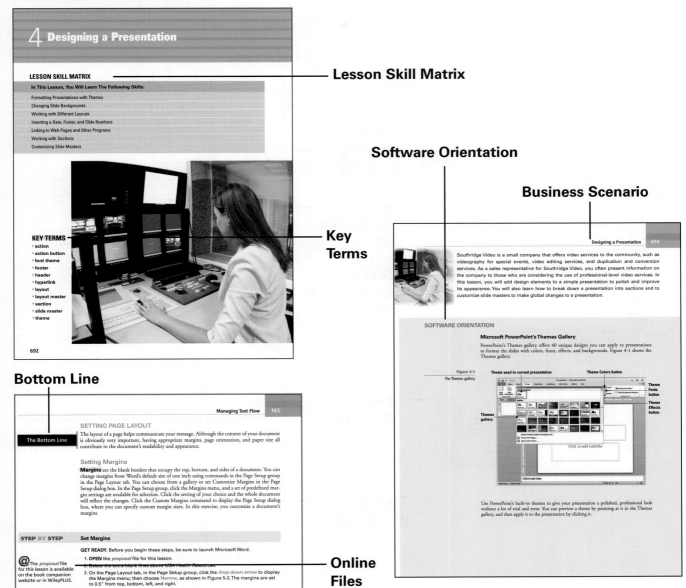

Lesson Skill Matrix

Software Orientation

Business Scenario

Key Terms

Bottom Line

Online Files

Step-by-Step Exercises

Trouble-shooting Reader Aid

Another Way Reader Aid

Screen Images with Callouts

Easy-to-Read Tables

Take Note Reader Aid

Cross Reference Reader Aid

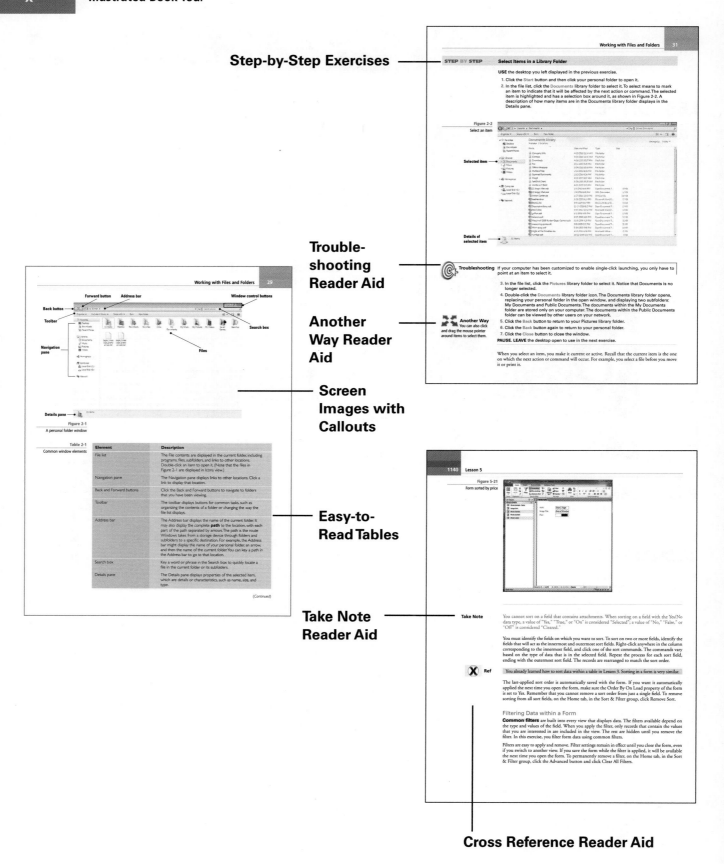

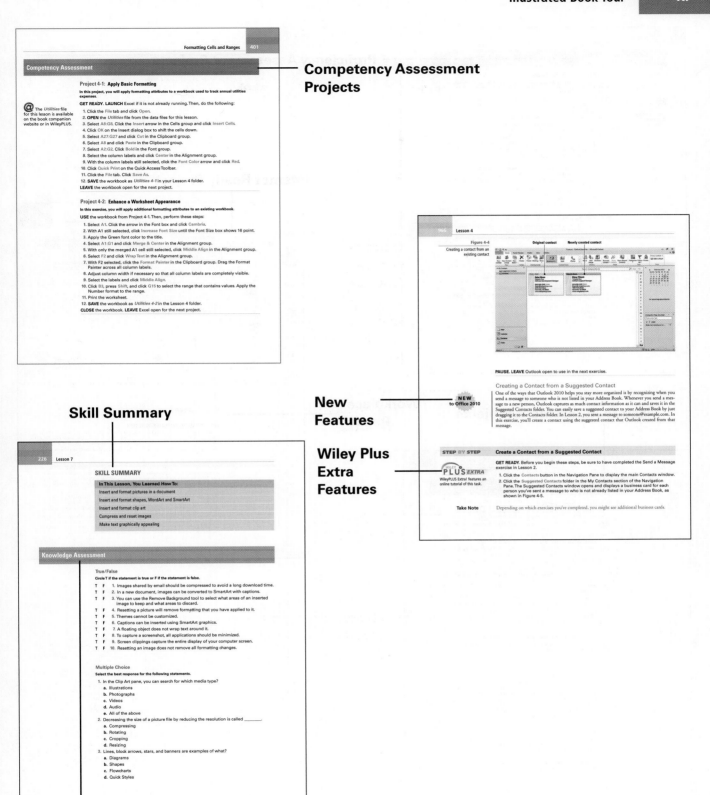

Competency Assessment Projects

Skill Summary

New Features

Wiley Plus Extra Features

Knowledge Assessment Questions

Proficiency Assessment Projects

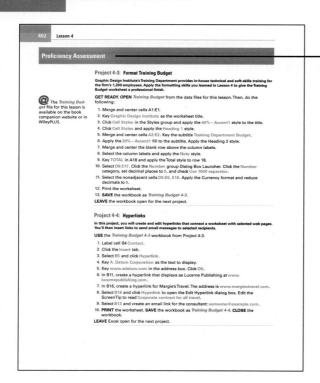

Internet Ready Project

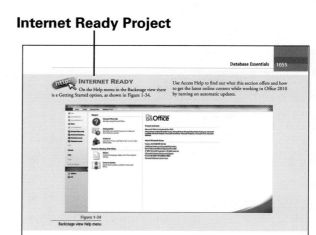

Mastery Assessment Projects

Workplace Ready

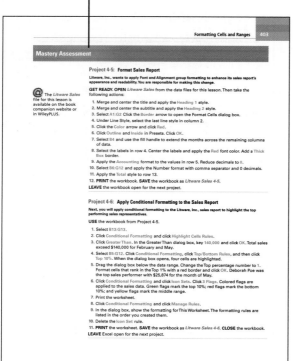

Conventions and Features Used in This Book

This book uses particular fonts, symbols, and heading conventions to highlight important information or to call your attention to special steps. For more information about the features in each lesson, refer to the Illustrated Book Tour section.

NEW to Office 2010 — This icon indicates a new or greatly improved Windows feature in this version of the software.

The Bottom Line — This feature provides a brief summary of the material to be covered in the section that follows.

CLOSE — Words in all capital letters indicate instructions for opening, saving, or closing files or programs. They also point out items you should check or actions you should take.

Take Note — *Take Note* reader aids, set in red text, provide helpful hints related to particular tasks or topics.

 Another Way — *Another Way* provides an alternative procedure for accomplishing a particular task.

Ⓧ Ref — These notes, set in gray shaded boxes, provide pointers to information discussed elsewhere in the textbook or describe interesting features that are not directly addressed in the current topic or exercise.

ALT + Tab — A plus sign (+) between two key names means that you must press both keys at the same time. Keys that you are instructed to press in an exercise will appear in the font shown here.

Key terms — Key terms appear in bold italic with highlighting.

Key My Name is — Any text you are asked to key appears in color.

Click OK — Any button on the screen you are supposed to click on or select will also appear in color.

BudgetWorksheet1 — The names of data files will appear in bold, italic, and red for easy identification.

Instructor Support Program

The *Microsoft Official Academic Course* programs are accompanied by a rich array of resources that incorporate the extensive textbook visuals to form a pedagogically cohesive package. These resources provide all the materials instructors need to deploy and deliver their courses. The following resources are available online for download.

- The **Instructor's Guide** contains Solutions to all the textbook exercises as well as chapter summaries and lecture notes. The Instructor's Guide and Syllabi for various term lengths are available from the Instructor's Book Companion site (www.wiley.com/college/microsoft).

- The **Solution Files** for all the projects in the book are available online from our Instructor's Book Companion site (www.wiley.com/college/microsoft).

- The **Test Bank** contains hundreds of questions organized by lesson in multiple-choice, true-false, short answer, and essay formats and is available to download from the Instructor's Book Companion site (www.wiley.com/college/microsoft). A complete answer key is provided.

  This title's test bank is available for use in Respondus' easy-to-use software. You can download the test bank for free using your Respondus, Respondus LE, or StudyMate Author software.

  Respondus is a powerful tool for creating and managing exams that can be printed to paper or published directly to Blackboard, WebCT, Desire2Learn, eCollege, ANGEL, and other eLearning systems.

- A complete set of **PowerPoint Presentations** is available on the Instructor's Book Companion site (www.wiley.com/college/microsoft) to enhance classroom presentations. Tailored to the text's topical coverage and Skills Matrix, these presentations are designed to convey key Microsoft Office 2010 concepts addressed in the text.

  All **images** from the text are on the Instructor's Book Companion site (www.wiley.com/college/microsoft). You can incorporate them into your PowerPoint presentations, or create your own overhead transparencies and handouts.

  By using these visuals in class discussions, you can help focus students' attention on key elements of Office 2010 and help them understand how to use it effectively in the workplace.

- The **MSDN Academic Alliance** is designed to provide the easiest and most inexpensive developer tools, products, and technologies available to faculty and students in labs, classrooms, and on student PCs. A free three-year membership is available to qualified MOAC adopters.

  Note: Microsoft Access 2010 can be downloaded from MSDN AA for use by students in this course.

- **Office Grader** automated grading system allows you to easily grade student data files in Word, Excel, PowerPoint, or Access format, against solution files. Save tens or hundreds of hours each semester with automated grading. More information on OfficeGrader is available from the Instructor's Book Companion site (www.wiley.com/college/microsoft).

- The **Student Data Files** are available online on both the Instructor's Book Companion Site and for students on the Student Book Companion Site.

- When it comes to improving the classroom experience, there is no better source of ideas and inspiration than your fellow colleagues. The **Wiley Faculty Network** connects teachers with technology, facilitates the exchange of best practices, and helps to enhance instructional efficiency and effectiveness. Faculty Network activities include technology training and tutorials, virtual seminars, peer-to-peer exchanges of experiences and ideas, personal consulting, and sharing of resources. For details visit www.WhereFacultyConnect.com.

WILEYPLUS

Broad developments in education over the past decade have influenced the instructional approach taken in the Microsoft Official Academic Course programs. The way that students learn, especially about new technologies, has changed dramatically in the Internet era. Electronic learning materials and Internet-based instruction is now as much a part of classroom instruction as printed textbooks. WileyPLUS provides the technology to create an environment where students reach their full potential and experience academic success that will last a lifetime.

WileyPLUS is a powerful and highly integrated suite of teaching and learning resources designed to bridge the gap between what happens in the classroom and what happens at home and on the job. WileyPLUS provides instructors with the resources to teach their students new technologies and guide them to reach their goals of getting ahead in the job market by having the skills to become certified and advance in the workforce. For students, WileyPLUS provides the tools for study and practice that are available to them 24/7, wherever and whenever they want to study. WileyPLUS includes a complete online version of the student textbook; Power-Point presentations; homework and practice assignments and quizzes; image galleries; test bank questions; gradebook; and all the instructor resources in one easy-to-use website.

New to WileyPLUS for Office 2010 are:

- In addition to the hundreds of questions included in the WileyPLUS courses that are not included in the testbank or textbook, we've added over a dozen additional projects that can be assigned to students.
- Many more animated tutorials, videos, and audio clips to support students as they learn the latest Office 2010 features.

MSDN ACADEMIC ALLIANCE

Free Three-Year Membership Available to Qualified Adopters!

The Microsoft Developer Network Academic Alliance (MSDN AA) is designed to provide the easiest and most inexpensive way for universities to make the latest Microsoft developer tools, products, and technologies available in labs, classrooms, and on student PCs. MSDN AA is an annual membership program for departments teaching Science, Technology, Engineering, and Mathematics (STEM) courses. The membership provides a complete solution to keep academic labs, faculty, and students on the leading edge of technology.

Software available in the MSDN AA program is provided at no charge to adopting departments through the Wiley and Microsoft publishing partnership.

As a bonus to this free offer, faculty will be introduced to Microsoft's Faculty Connection and Academic Resource Center. It takes time and preparation to keep students engaged while giving them a fundamental understanding of theory, and the Microsoft Faculty Connection is designed to help STEM professors with this preparation by providing articles, curriculum, and tools that professors can use to engage and inspire today's technology students.

Contact your Wiley rep for details.

For more information about the MSDN Academic Alliance program, go to: **msdn.microsoft.com/academic/**

IMPORTANT WEB ADDRESSES AND PHONE NUMBERS

To locate the Wiley Higher Education Rep in your area go to www.wiley.com/college, select Instructors under Resources, and click on the Who's My Rep link, or call the MOAC toll-free number: 1 + (888) 764-7001 (U.S. and Canada only).

To learn more about becoming a Microsoft Certified Professional and exam availability, visit www.microsoft.com/learning/mcp.

BOOK COMPANION WEBSITE

The students' book companion site for the MOAC series, www.wiley.com/college/microsoft, includes any resources, exercise files, and web links that will be used in conjunction with this course.

WILEY DESKTOP EDITIONS

Wiley MOAC Desktop Editions are innovative, electronic versions of printed textbooks. Students buy the desktop version for 50% off the U.S. price of the printed text and get the added value of permanence and portability. Wiley Desktop Editions provide students with numerous additional benefits that are not available with other e-text solutions.

Wiley Desktop Editions are NOT subscriptions; students download the Wiley Desktop Edition to their computer desktops. Students own the content they buy and keep it for as long as they want. Once a Wiley Desktop Edition is downloaded to the computer desktop, students have instant access to all of the content without being online. Students can also print the sections they prefer to read in hard copy. Students also have access to fully integrated resources within their Wiley Desktop Edition. From highlighting their e-text to taking and sharing notes, students can easily personalize their Wiley Desktop Edition as they are reading or following along in class.

COURSESMART

CourseSmart goes beyond traditional expectations providing instant, online access to the textbooks and course materials you need at a lower cost option. You can save time and hassle with a digital eTextbook that allows you to search for the most relevant content at the very moment you need it. To learn more go to: www.coursesmart.com.

Office 2010 Professional Six-Month Trial Software (Available in Some Editions)

Some editions of the MOAC Office 2010 series come with six-month trial editions of Office 2010 Professional. If your book included a trial, there would have been a CD glued into the front or back cover of your book. This section pertains only to those editions that came with an Office 2010 Professional trial.

STEP BY STEP **Installing the Microsoft Office System 2010 Six-Month Trial**

1. Insert the trial software CD-ROM into the CD drive on your computer. The CD will be detected, and the Setup.exe file should automatically begin to run on your computer.
2. When prompted for the Office Product Key, enter the Product Key provided with the software, and then click Next.
3. Enter your name and organization user name, and then click Next.
4. Read the End-User License Agreement, select the *I Accept the Terms in the License Agreement* check box, and then click Next.
5. Select the install option, verify the installation location or click Browse to change the installation location, and then click Next.
6. Verify the program installation preferences, and then click Next.

Click Finish to complete the setup.

UPGRADING MICROSOFT OFFICE PROFESSIONAL 2010 SIX-MONTH TRIAL SOFTWARE TO THE FULL PRODUCT

You can convert the software into full use without removing or reinstalling software on your computer. When you complete your trial, you can purchase a product license from any Microsoft reseller and enter a valid Product Key when prompted during setup.

UNINSTALLING THE TRIAL SOFTWARE AND RETURNING TO YOUR PREVIOUS OFFICE VERSION

If you want to return to your previous version of Office, you need to uninstall the trial software. This should be done through the Add or Remove Programs icon in Control Panel (or Uninstall a program in the Control Panel of Windows Vista).

STEP BY STEP **Uninstall Trial Software**

1. Quit any programs that are running.
2. In Control Panel, click Programs and Features (Add or Remove Programs in Windows XP).
3. Click Microsoft Office Professional 2010, and then click Uninstall (Remove in Windows XP).

Take Note If you selected the option to remove a previous version of Office during installation of the trial software, you need to reinstall your previous version of Office. If you did not remove your previous version of Office, you can start each of your Office programs either through the Start menu or by opening files for each program. In some cases, you may have to re-create some of your shortcuts and default settings.

www.wiley.com/college/microsoft
or call the MOAC Toll-Free Number: 1+(888) 764-7001 (U.S. & Canada only)

STUDENT DATA FILES

All of the practice files that you will use as you perform the exercises in the book are available for download on our student companion site. By using the practice files, you will not waste time creating the samples used in the lessons, and you can concentrate on learning how to use Microsoft Office 2010. With the files and the step-by-step instructions in the lessons, you will learn by doing, which is an easy and effective way to acquire and remember new skills.

Copying the Practice Files

Your instructor might already have copied the practice files before you arrive in class. However, your instructor might ask you to copy the practice files on your own at the start of class. Also, if you want to work through any of the exercises in this book on your own at home or at your place of business after class, you may want to copy the practice files.

STEP BY STEP   **Copy the Practice Files**

OPEN Internet Explorer.

1. In Internet Explorer, go to the student companion site: www.wiley.com.
2. Search for your book title in the upper-right hand corner.
3. On the Search Results page, locate your book and click on the Visit the Companion Sites link.
4. Select Student Companion Site from the pop-up box.
5. In the left-hand column, under "Browse by Resource" select Student Data Files.
6. Now select Student Data Files from the center of the screen.
7. On the File Download dialog box, select Save to save the data files to your external drive (often called a ZIP drive or a USB drive or a thumb drive) or a local drive.
8. In the Save As dialog box, select a local drive in the left-hand panel that you'd like to save your files to; again, this should be an external drive or a local drive. Remember the drive name that you saved it to.

Acknowledgments

We'd like to thank the many reviewers who pored over the manuscript, providing invaluable feedback in the service of quality instructional materials.

Access 2010

Tammie Bolling, *Tennessee Technology Center—Jacksboro*
Mary Corcoran, *Bellevue College*
Trish Culp, *triOS College—Business Technology Healthcare*
Jana Hambruch, *Lee County School District*
Aditi Mukherjee, *University of Florida—Gainesville*

Excel 2010

Tammie Bolling, *Tennessee Technology Center—Jacksboro*
Mary Corcoran, *Bellevue College*
Trish Culp, *triOS College—Business Technology Healthcare*
Dee Hobson, *Richland College*
Christie Hovey, *Lincoln Land Community College*
Ralph Phillips, *Central Oregon Community College*
Rajeev Sachdev, *triOS College—Business Technology Healthcare*

Outlook 2010

Mary Harnishfeger, *Ivy Tech State College—Bloomington*
Sandra Miller, *Wenatchee Valley College*
Bob Reeves, *Vincennes University*
Lourdes Sevilla, *Southwestern College—Chula Vista*
Phyllis E. Traylor, *St. Philips College*

PowerPoint 2010

Natasha Carter, *SUNY—ATTAIN*
Dr. Susan Evans Jennings, *Stephen F. Austin State University*
Sue Van Lanen, *Gwinnett Technical College*
Carol J. McPeek, *SUNY—ATTAIN*
Michelle Poertner, *Northwestern Michigan College*
Tim Sylvester, *Glendale Community College (AZ)*

Project 2010

Tatyana Pashnyak, *Bainbridge College*
Debi Griggs, *Bellevue College*

Word 2010

Portia Hatfield, *Tennessee Technology Center—Jacksboro*
Terri Holly, *Indian River State College*
Pat McMahon, *South Suburban College*
Barb Purvis, *Centura College*
Janet Sebesy, *Cuyahoga Community College*

We would also like to thank Lutz Ziob, Jason Bunge, Ben Watson, David Bramble, Merrick Van Dongen, Don Field, Pablo Bernal, Colin Klein, and Wendy Johnson at Microsoft for their encouragement and support in making the Microsoft Official Academic Course program the finest instructional materials for mastering the newest Microsoft technologies for both students and instructors. Finally, we would like to thank Lorna Gentry of Content LLC for development editing and Jeff Riley and his team at Box Twelve Communications for technical editing.

About the Authors

LINDA SILVA

Linda has been teaching for seventeen years and has been working at El Paso Community College for more than thirty years. She is currently a full-time faculty member of the Administrative Assistant program—of which she was formerly the district-wide coordinator—and teaches part-time in the Business program. El Paso Community College has five campuses to serve the educational needs of the community population; it also has been recognized as the fastest-growing community college in Texas and the largest grantor of associate degrees to Hispanic students in the nation. Linda believes that EPCC is "the best place to start" and "the best place to continue."

The Administrative Assistant program has adopted textbooks from the MOAC series; the students enrolled in the program are required to take Microsoft application software courses (Word, Excel, PowerPoint, Access, and Outlook), which prepare them for the Microsoft Office Specialist exam. Linda's students have successfully passed the exams—one of them passed the MOS Excel 2007 exam with a perfect score of 1,000. Linda takes the exams ahead of her students and challenges them to beat her score.

Linda enjoys the art of innovative teaching, and when she is not teaching enjoys taking on new and exciting challenges.

CATHERINE BINDER, ED.D.

Catherine Binder has over 15 years experience teaching computer technology courses—ranging from Microsoft Office and computer repair to networking and web development. She has developed curricula for Microsoft Office, operating systems, and networking courses at more than a dozen schools. Her specialty has been in revising existing curricula for use in entirely online and online/classroom hybrid course formats. She has her MOS, MCT, MCP, MCSE, A+, and ICW certifications. She was previously the department chair for Networking and Digital Lifestyle at the Katherine Gibbs School and currently resides in Fredericksburg, Pennsylvania.

FAITHE WEMPEN

Faithe Wempen, MA, is a Microsoft Office Master Instructor and an A_Certified PC technician and has authored over 100 books on Microsoft applications and operating systems. Her first book was *Abort, Retry, Fail: 101 MS-DOS Error Messages*. More recent titles include *Microsoft Office 2010 for Seniors for Dummies* and *The PowerPoint 2010 Bible*.

Faithe's online courses in Office applications have educated over a quarter of a million students for clients including CNET, Hewlett Packard, and Sony. Her articles on maximizing Office productivity have appeared in *Microsoft Office PRO* and *Microsoft Office Power User* magazines, as well as on TechRepublic.com and CertCities.com. She also spent eight years as an adjunct instructor of Computer Technology at Indiana University/Purdue University at Indianapolis (IUPUI), specializing in teaching PC hardware, operating systems, and Office applications.

CHRISTY PARRISH

Christy Parrish has spent the last 20 years developing, designing, and delivering corporate training programs. She has written several books on Microsoft Office and other productivity software packages. As a freelance author, she has also written a magazine series and hundreds of online articles on a wide variety of topics. Christy is also a member of her community artists group and is recognized for her unique photographic skills that are on display at various galleries. She is married and has two sons who both share her love of writing and art.

KEITH HOELL

Keith Hoell is a professor and Chair of Business and Technology at Briarcliffe College in Long Island, New York. An experienced academic technology professional, he has served as an instructor, dean, and technology consultant for several schools. He has a broad range of experience in various areas of technology, including database management, network administration, and Internet technologies. He also served on the Microsoft Official Academic Curriculum (MOAC) Advisory Board and helped develop other MOAC textbooks.

Besides his interest in technology, he is also an avid runner, having run in several marathons including New York and Boston.

Brief Contents

PART IV   Microsoft® PowerPoint® 2010

PART V   Microsoft® Outlook® 2010

PART VI   Microsoft® Access® 2010

Contents

PART I Microsoft® Windows® 7

1 Windows Basics 3

2 Working with Files and Folders 27

PART II   Microsoft® Word® 2010

1   Understanding Word   55

2 Basic Editing 85

3 Character Formatting   114

4 Paragraph Formatting   133

5   Managing Text Flow   163

6 Creating Tables 183

7 Using Illustrations and Graphics 202

8 Working with Themes, Quick Parts, Page Backgrounds, and Headers and Footers 231

9 Applying References and Hyperlinks 256

10   Advanced Features   276

PART III   Microsoft® Excel® 2010

1   Overview   303

2   Using Backstage   324

3 Working with Microsoft Excel 2010   343

4 Formatting Cells and Ranges 368

5 Formatting Worksheets 405

6 Managing Worksheets 437

7 Working with Data 459

8 Using Basic Formulas and Functions 483

9   Using Advanced Formulas and Securing Workbooks   521

10 Creating and Modifying Charts 540

PART IV   Microsoft® PowerPoint® 2010

1 PowerPoint Essentials 569

2 Presentation Basics 603

3 Working with Text 641

4 Designing a Presentation 692

5 Adding Tables, Charts, and SmartArt Graphics to Slides 724

6 Adding Graphics and Multimedia to a Presentation 752

7 Delivering a Presentation 799

PART V   Microsoft® Outlook® 2010

1 Getting to Know Outlook   837

2 E-mail Basics   867

4 Working with Contacts 961

5 Outlook Calendar 995

PART VI   Microsoft® Access® 2010

1 Database Essentials 1027

4 Modify Tables and Fields 1104

5 Create Forms 1128

6 Create Reports 1150

7 Create and Modify Queries   1171

Microsoft® Windows® 7

LESSON SKILL MATRIX

In This Lesson, You Will Learn The Following Skills:.

Log on to Windows 7.

Use the mouse to identify desktop items.

Open and close the Start menu.

Identify items on the Start menu.

Select Start menu settings.

Search from the Start menu.

Minimize, maximize, and resize a window.

Access Help and Support.

Shut down Windows 7.

KEY TERMS

- background
- button
- context menu
- desktop
- files
- filter
- folders
- gadgets
- icon
- index
- indexed locations
- maximize
- menu
- minimize

- **mouse**
- **mouse pointer**
- **offline files**
- **panes**
- **Recycle Bin**
- **restore down**
- **ScreenTip**
- **search results**
- **select**
- **shortcuts**
- **sidebar**
- **Start button**
- **Start menu**
- **syntax**
- **taskbar**

Northwind Traders is a small company that helps Inuit artists in Alaska market their work to customers around the globe. Originally, the owner was able to use a paper filing system for tasks such as invoicing and storing information about artists and buyers. Now that the business has grown, the owner has invested in a personal computer running the Windows 7 operating system. In this lesson, you will learn how to log on to Windows 7 and use your mouse to identify screen elements. You will open and close the Start menu, learning how to identify and select items on the menu. You will also learn how to search for items on your computer from the Start menu. Finally, you will learn how to minimize, maximize, and restore windows; get help while using Windows 7; and shut down your computer.

GETTING STARTED WITH WINDOWS 7

The Bottom Line

To use your personal computer (PC), you must be able to use Windows 7. Windows 7 is an operating system, which is the software that controls the way your computer communicates with you—the user—and with the other parts of the computer, such as the screen, the keyboard, and the printer. Once you log on to Windows 7, you can use it to access and manage information. In this section, you learn how to log on to your computer and practice using the mouse.

Logging on to Windows 7

To access the information on your computer, you must log on to your account.

STEP BY STEP   **Log on to Windows 7**

GET READY. Before you begin these steps, make sure your computer is turned on. The Welcome screen should be displayed, as shown in Figure 1-1.

Troubleshooting Your Welcome screen will not look exactly the same as the screen in Figure 1-1. The names on your Welcome screen will be the names of the users authorized to use your computer, and the pictures will be those assigned to each user account.

1. Move the mouse so that the mouse pointer touches your name on the Welcome screen.
2. Press and release the left mouse button one time. This is called a click. Either the Windows desktop or the Password screen displays.
3. If the Password screen displays, click in the password box, type your password, and then press **Enter**.

   A password is a string of characters, such as a word or phrase that protects your account from unauthorized access. When you type the password, black dots display in the password box to hide the actual password from anyone who might be looking over your shoulder.

   The Windows 7 desktop displays. It should look similar to Figure 1-2.

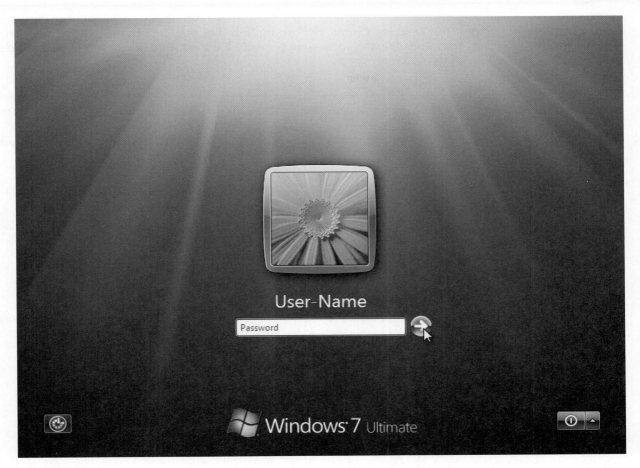

Figure 1-1

Windows 7 Welcome screen

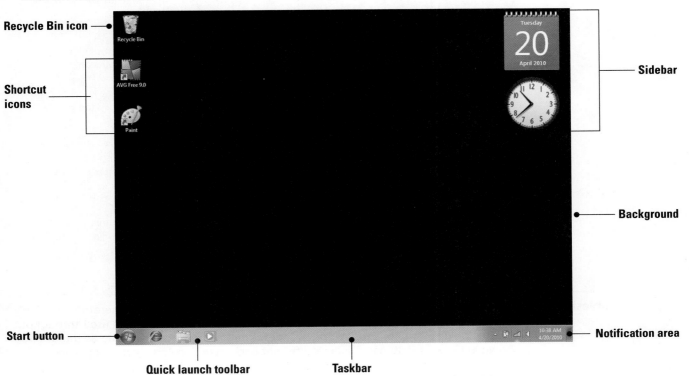

Figure 1-2

Windows 7 desktop

Troubleshooting If the Welcome Center window displays, click the Close button (the white X on the red background) in the upper-right corner of the window to close it so you can get a clear view of the desktop.

Troubleshooting If you do not know your password, consult your instructor or your system administrator.

4. Take a moment to identify the elements of the desktop that are shown in Figure 1-2. Refer to Table 1-1 for a description of each element.

Table 1-1

Common desktop elements

Element	Description
Taskbar	The **taskbar** usually runs across the bottom of the desktop (although it can be moved to the top, left side, or right side). It displays buttons and icons to let you access the features that you use most frequently. A **button** is an element that you can click to select a command or action.
Start button	The **Start button** is a round button with the Microsoft Windows logo on it. You click the Start button to open the **Start menu**, which provides access to everything stored on your computer. A **menu** is a list of choices.
Sidebar	The **sidebar** is a vertical bar usually located along the right side of the desktop. It displays **gadgets**, which are programs or tools designed to provide information at a glance. A clock, a slideshow, and an Internet news feed are the default gadgets.
Quick Launch Toolbar	The Quick Launch Toolbar is an area of the taskbar that displays **shortcuts** to frequently used programs. A shortcut is a link to a program, feature, or command.
Recycle Bin icon	The Recycle Bin icon represents the **Recycle Bin**, a folder where deleted items are stored until you remove them permanently or restore them to their original location.
Shortcut icons	Shortcut icons on the desktop let you quickly access programs, folders, and files that you use most often. The arrow in the lower-left corner indicates that the icon is a shortcut. Your computer setup determines which shortcut icons show on your desktop. Many programs create icons on the desktop during installation, or you can create your own shortcut icons on the desktop, on the taskbar, and in folders.
Background	The **background** is the broad, empty area where windows open and display content. By default, the background displays a picture that you select when you first set up your user account, but you can change it at any time to a different picture, or to a solid color, like the one shown in Figure 1-2.
Notification area	At the right end of the taskbar is the notification area, where the time and information about the programs running on your computer displays.

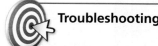

Troubleshooting As you will discover, Windows 7 can be easily customized and changed. Therefore, it is likely that the way your screen looks will often be different from the figures used throughout this book. For example, your Windows 7 desktop may not look the same as the desktop shown in Figure 1-2. It may display a different background, colors, or desktop icons.

PAUSE. LEAVE the desktop displayed to use in the next exercise.

As you have seen, in Windows 7, the logon procedure always starts from the Welcome screen. However, the actual steps may vary, depending on how your system is set up:

- On some systems, you simply click your username to log on.
- If your account has a password, you must key it when you reach the password screen to log on.

Also, because it is easy to customize Windows 7, you will find that your screen may frequently look different from the screens used to illustrate this book.

The **mouse** is a device attached to your computer that lets you input commands. The **mouse pointer** is an icon that moves on the screen when you move the mouse on your desk. On the desktop, it usually looks like an arrow pointing up and to the left.

The **desktop** is the main work area that displays when Windows 7 is running.

In the next section, you practice using the mouse while you familiarize yourself with the main components of the Windows 7 desktop.

Using the Mouse to Identify Desktop Items

In Windows 7, you use a mouse to point to and select items. The mouse pointer moves on the screen when you move the mouse on your desk.

STEP BY STEP   **Use the Mouse to Identify Desktop Items**

USE the desktop you left displayed in the previous exercise.

1. Move the mouse on your desk or on a mouse pad on your desk so that the mouse pointer moves on the desktop. If you move the mouse to the left or right, the mouse pointer moves to the left or right. If you move the mouse away from yourself toward the back of your desk, the mouse pointer moves toward the top of the desktop. If you move the mouse toward yourself, the mouse pointer moves toward the bottom of the desktop.

Take Note   If the mouse reaches the edge of your desk or mouse pad before the mouse pointer is in the correct spot on the desktop, you can pick up the mouse and reposition it without moving the pointer on the screen.

2. Move the pointer so that it is touching the Recycle Bin icon. This is called "pointing to the Recycle Bin." Notice that the icon is highlighted, as shown in Figure 1-3. An **icon** is a small picture that represents an item or command.

Figure 1-3

Point to the Recycle Bin icon

Mouse pointer

Highlighted icon ——

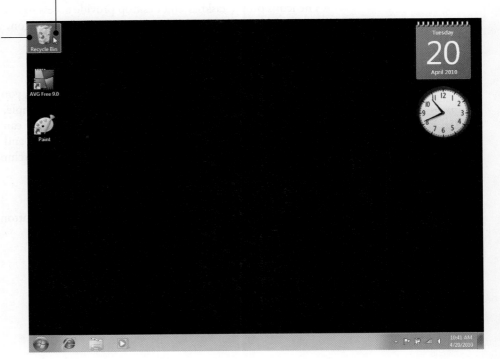

Troubleshooting If the mouse pointer changes to a hand with a pointing finger and the text label is underlined when you point to the Recycle Bin icon, it means your computer has been set to enable single-click launching of icons. If so, when you point at an icon, it becomes selected, and when you click it, it opens. If pointing selects the Recycle Bin icon, skip step 3. If you accidentally click the Recycle Bin icon, the folder window opens. Click the Close button in the upper-right corner to close it, and continue with step 4.

3. Click the Recycle Bin icon. This selects the Recycle Bin icon, which means it is marked as the item the next action or command will affect. Notice the highlight that displays around the icon, even if you move the mouse away from the icon.

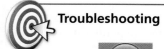

Another Way
You can also cancel a selection by pressing the Esc key on your keyboard.

4. Click a blank area of the desktop. This cancels the selection. The Recycle Bin icon is no longer highlighted.
5. Move the mouse on your desk so that the pointer is touching the Start button at the left end of the taskbar at the bottom of the screen.

Troubleshooting The taskbar is usually positioned across the bottom of the desktop, but you can move it to any side of the screen. If you do not see the taskbar at the bottom of the screen, look for it at the top, left, or right. If it does not display at all, it may be hidden. If so, move the mouse pointer to the side of the desktop where you think the taskbar is positioned (try the bottom first). It should display.

6. Use the mouse to point to the current date and time in the lower-right corner of the desktop, at the right end of the taskbar.

PAUSE. LEAVE the desktop open to use in the next exercise.

In this exercise, you practiced using the mouse to point at and identify different items on the desktop and to **select** a desktop icon. Sometimes when you point at an item on the desktop, a **ScreenTip** displays information about the item. A ScreenTip is a pop-up balloon that displays information about the item you are pointing at on the screen.

You can think of the Windows 7 desktop as similar to the top of your actual desk. On your desk, you might have an open folder or file and some papers such as a letter or report that you are reading or editing. You might also have pictures of your family or friends, a clock, a calendar, and a calculator. You can have all of these things on your Windows 7 desktop too, so that you can access them quickly and easily while you work.

The icons on the taskbar and desktop provide access to frequently used programs, features, and commands. For example, when you click the Start button, you open the Start menu.

USING THE START MENU

The Bottom Line

The Start menu is often the first element you use when you sit down at your computer because it provides access to all of your information. For example, from the Start menu you can start programs such as a word processor or database or you can locate files such as letters you have written. In this section, you use your mouse to open and close the Start menu. You practice selecting and locating items on the Start menu and searching from the Start menu.

Opening and Closing the Start Menu

To open or close the Start menu, point to the Start button on the desktop and then click the left mouse button.

STEP BY STEP   **Open and Close the Start Menu**

USE the desktop you left displayed in the previous exercise.

1. Use your mouse to point to the Start button in the lower-left corner of the desktop.

2. Click the Start button. The Start menu opens, as shown in Figure 1-4. Take a moment to use the figure to locate the parts of the Start menu on your screen. (Of course, because Windows 7 is easily customized, your Start menu probably does not look exactly the same as the one in the figure.)

Figure 1-4

Windows 7 Start menu

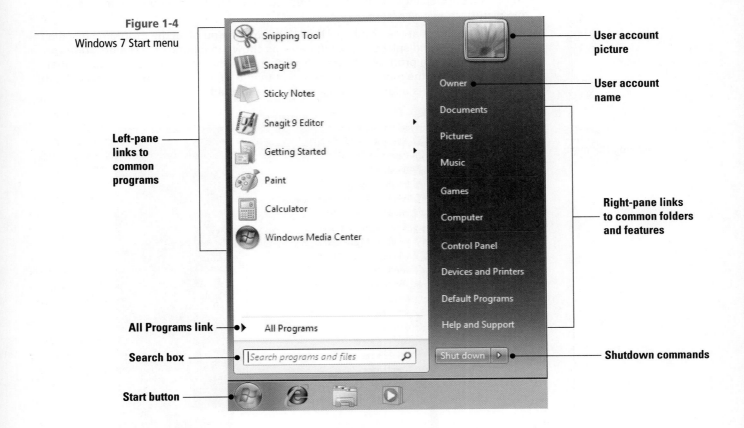

3. Click the Start button again. The Start menu closes.

PAUSE. LEAVE the desktop open to use in the next exercise.

You may have noticed that the Start menu is divided into two main sections, which are called **panes**. The left pane is a menu of links to commonly used programs; the right pane is a menu of links to commonly used features and folders. Your user account name and picture display at the top of the right pane. A **folder** is a place where you can store items such as files and other folders. A **file** is a set of information stored with a single name. The tools you need to end your Windows session and shut off your computer are at the bottom of the right pane, and the tools you need to search your computer to find information are at the bottom of the left pane.

Identifying Items on the Start Menu

Most items on the Start menu are links to the programs, folders, and files that you use most often. Simply click a link to access the feature you need.

Identify Items on the Start Menu

USE the desktop you left displayed in the previous exercise.

1. Click the Start button to open the Start menu.
2. Point to the word Documents near the top of the right pane. It should highlight, and a ScreenTip should display. The highlighted item is often called the current or active item, which means that it is the item that the next command will affect.
3. Point to the word Computer in the right pane. You might notice that the picture at the top of the pane changes depending on the current item. When you point at Computer, the picture shows a computer system.
4. Click All Programs at the bottom of the left pane. A menu of all the programs installed on your computer displays in the left pane, as shown in Figure 1-5. (The programs on your computer are probably different from the ones shown in the figure.) Notice that each program on the menu has an icon next to it to represent the program type. If an item on the menu is a folder, it has a folder icon instead.

Figure 1-5

All Programs menu

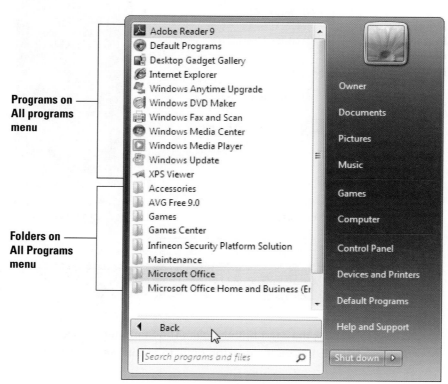

Programs on All programs menu

Folders on All Programs menu

Adobe Reader 9
Default Programs
Desktop Gadget Gallery
Internet Explorer
Windows Anytime Upgrade
Windows DVD Maker
Windows Fax and Scan
Windows Media Center
Windows Media Player
Windows Update
XPS Viewer
Accessories
AVG Free 9.0
Games
Games Center
Infineon Security Platform Solution
Maintenance
Microsoft Office
Microsoft Office Home and Business (Er

Owner
Documents
Pictures
Music
Games
Computer
Control Panel
Devices and Printers
Default Programs
Help and Support

◄   Back

Search programs and files

Shut down ▷

5. Click the Accessories folder on the All Programs menu. The folder opens—or expands—to display its contents, as shown in Figure 1-6.

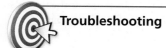

Troubleshooting   Sometimes there are too many items on the All Programs menu to display within the Start menu pane. In that case, a scrollbar displays along the right edge of the pane. You can drag the scrollbar up or down to see additional items on the menu.

6. Click Calculator on the Accessories menu. The Calculator displays on the desktop and the Start menu closes. (Notice that a button representing the window displays on the taskbar.) The Calculator is one of the accessory tools that come with Windows to help make your work easier. You can use the calculator to perform basic mathematical functions.

Figure 1-6

Expand the Accessories folder

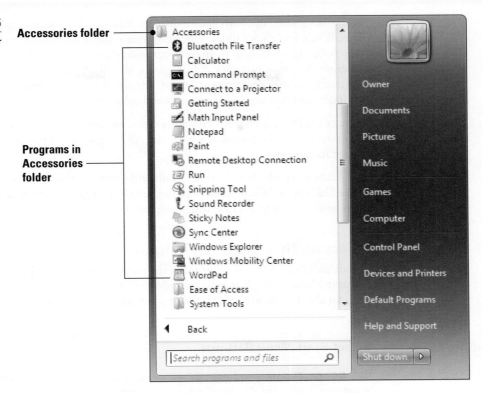

7. On the Calculator keypad, click **5**, click *****, click **3**, and then click **=**. The result—15— shows in the Calculator display, as shown in Figure 1-7.

8. Click the **Close** button in the top right corner of the Calculator (the white X on a red background).

PAUSE. LEAVE the desktop open to use in the next exercise.

Figure 1-7

Calculator

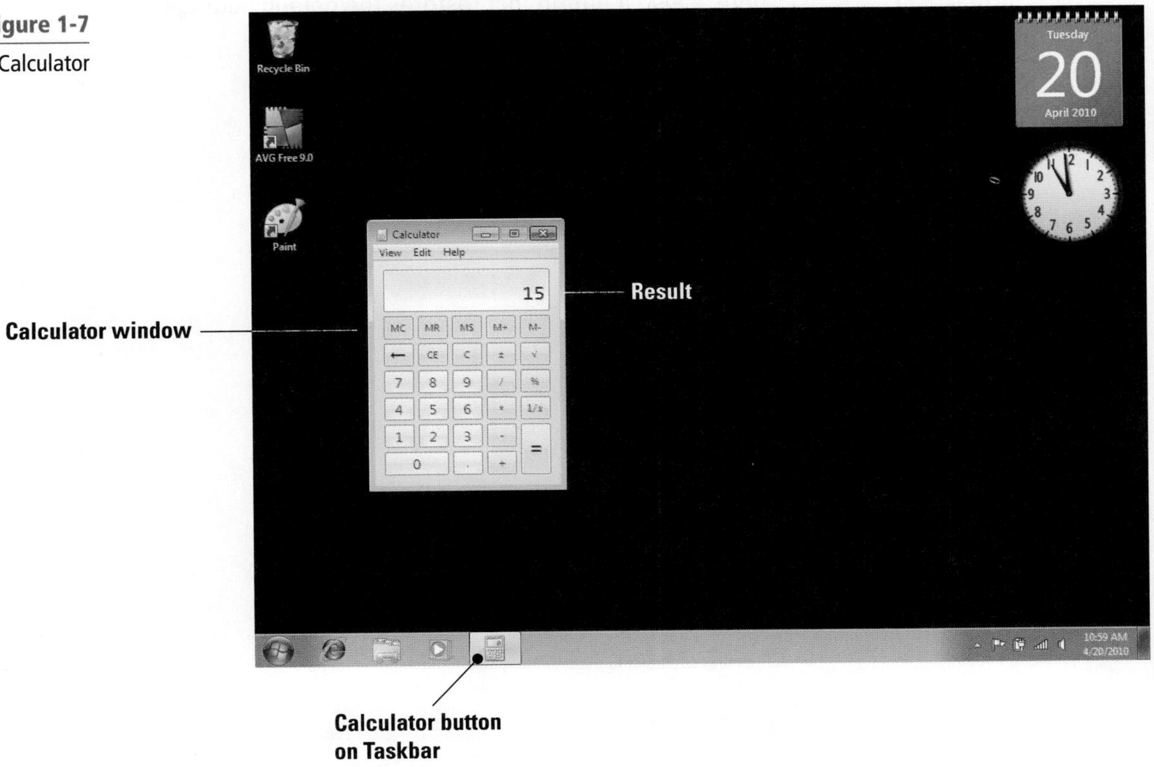

Calculator window

Result

Calculator button on Taskbar

As you have seen, the Start menu displays links to the features and folders that you use most often. When you click a link on the Start menu, the feature starts or the folder opens. If there is a right-pointing arrow next to an item, it means that when you click the item a menu will display. For example, when you click All Programs, the All Programs menu displays. When you click a program icon, the program starts and displays in its program window and the Start menu closes. A button representing the open window displays on the taskbar.

Some of the items on the All Programs menu are organized into folders, such as Accessories and Maintenance. When you click a folder on All Programs, the folder expands on the menu so you can see its contents.

The Accessories folder stores useful tools and programs that come with Windows 7. In addition to the Calculator, Windows Accessories usually include WordPad, a basic word processing program, and Paint, a graphics editing program. Other accessory programs may be available as well.

Selecting Start Menu Settings

The default Start menu settings make the most commonly used items available. In the Customize Start Menu dialog box, you can select the way links, icons, and menus display and behave. You can also set the number of recent programs you want on the menu.

STEP BY STEP   **Select Start Menu Settings**

GET READY. Before you begin these steps, start your computer and log on to your Windows 7 account. Close all open windows so you can see the desktop.

1. Right-click a blank area of the taskbar to display a shortcut menu and then click Properties. The Taskbar and Start Menu Properties dialog box displays.

2. Click the Start Menu tab and then click the Customize . . . button. The Customize Start Menu dialog box displays, as shown in Figure 1-8. The list at the top of the dialog box includes items such as links, icons, and programs that are available to display in the right pane of the Start menu, as well as options that control how each item opens. Other elements in the dialog box let you set the number of recently used programs that will display in the left pane and select the Internet and email programs to display. There is also a button that restores the default settings.

Figure 1-8

Customize Start Menu dialog box

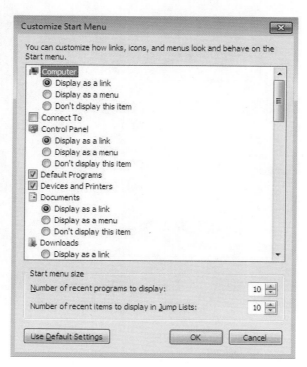

Troubleshooting If the Customize Classic Start Menu dialog box displays, click Cancel to return to the Taskbar and Start Menu Properties dialog box, click the Start menu option button, and then click the Customize button.

Another Way
To open the Taskbar and Start Menu dialog box with the Start Menu tab active, click the Start button, right-click a blank area of the Start menu, and click Properties.

3. Click to select the Recent Items check box and then click OK to return to the Start Menu tab of the Taskbar and Start Menu Properties dialog box.

4. If necessary, click to select the Store and display recently opened programs in the Start menu check box and the Store and display recently opened items in the Start menu and the taskbar check box.

5. Click OK in the Taskbar and Start Menu Properties dialog box.

6. Click the Start button to display the Start menu with the default settings. It should look similar to Figure 1-9, although the specific programs and item names on your computer may be different from the ones in the figure. Notice that nine recently used programs are listed in the left pane and links to standard folders are in the right pane. In the right pane, all but Recent Items are set to display as links, which means when you click the item, the folder window opens. Recent Items is set to display as a menu, which means when you point to it or click it, a menu of recently used items displays.

Figure 1-9

Default Start menu

Pinned items

Recently used programs

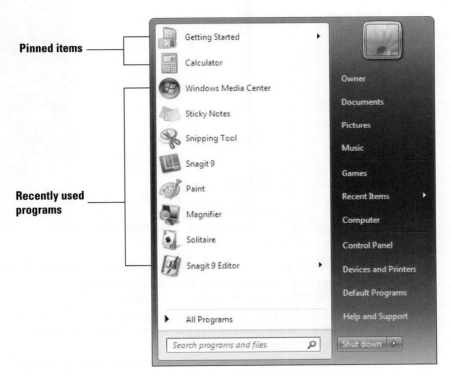

7. Right-click a blank area of the Taskbar and then click Properties. Click the Start Menu tab and then click the Customize . . . button to display the Customize Start Menu dialog box again. In the list at the top of the dialog box, you can select which items to display in the right pane and how you want the items to behave.

8. Under Computer, click the Display as a menu option button. This changes the way the item opens, from a link to a menu.

9. Click to clear the Default Programs check boxes. This removes the item from the right pane of the Start menu.

Take Note

Using smaller icons lets you fit more items on the Start menu. Clicking an Apply button in a dialog box applies the current options but leaves the dialog box open so that you can make additional changes.

10. Scroll down the list, noting the available options. At the bottom of the list, click to clear the Use Large Icons check box.

11. Under Start menu size, click the down increment arrow to change the Number of recent programs to display to 4.

12. Click OK and then click OK in the Taskbar and Start Menu Properties dialog box.

13. Click the Start button. The Start menu should look similar to Figure 1-10. In the left pane, notice that only four recently used programs are listed and that the icons are smaller. In the right pane, notice that the Connect To and Default Programs items do not display and that Computer is now a menu. Point to Computer and notice that a menu of computer components, such as storage devices, displays.

Figure 1-10

Customized Start menu

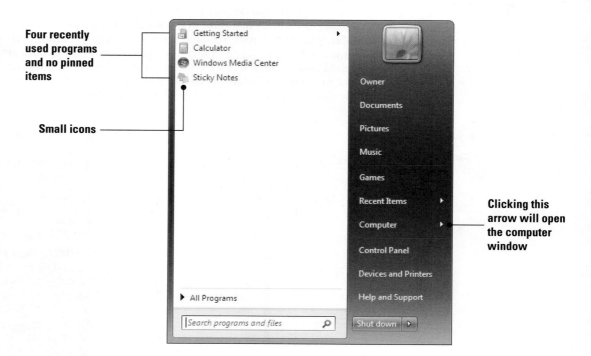

Four recently used programs and no pinned items

Small icons

Clicking this arrow will open the computer window

14. Press Esc two times to cancel the Computer menu and the Start menu.

15. Right-click a blank area of the Taskbar and then click Properties. Click the Start Menu tab and then click the Customize button.

16. Click the Use Default Settings button to restore the default settings and then click OK. Click OK in the Taskbar and Start Menu Properties dialog box to apply the changes and close the dialog box.

PAUSE. LEAVE the desktop displayed to use in the next exercise.

You can easily use the options in the Customize Start Menu dialog box to control the items that display in both the left and right panes of the Start menu. As you have seen, you can also select to display items in the right pane as menus instead of as links.

You might prefer using a menu if you want to go directly to an item stored in the main folder rather than having to navigate through folder windows. For example, if you frequently access a particular storage device, such as a flash drive, you can set Computer to display as a menu. Then, instead of opening the Computer folder and navigating to the flash drive, you can just select the flash drive from the Computer menu.

In addition to selecting items to display in the right pane, you may have noticed options for controlling general Start menu behavior, including the following:

- **Enable context menus and dragging and dropping: Context menu** is another term for shortcut menu. This option is selected by default. If you deselect this option, no shortcut menus display when you right-click a Start menu item, and you cannot drag an item to pin or unpin it to the Start menu.

- **Highlight newly installed programs:** This option is selected by default, so that when a new program is installed on your computer, the All Programs menu and the items on the All Programs menu are highlighted. If you deselect this option, newly installed programs are not highlighted.

- **Open submenus when I pause on them with the mouse pointer:** This option is selected by default. If you deselect this option, you must click an item to open a menu.

- **Sort All Programs menu by name:** This option is selected by default. Deselect this option if you want to arrange items on the All Programs menu in a different order, not alphabetically by name. You can drag the items to reposition them on the menu.

Searching from the Start Menu

The Search box on the Start menu is a quick tool to use to find a program, file, or folder when you are not sure where the item is stored. From the Start menu, Windows 7 searches the **indexed location** on your computer. An indexed location is one that is included in the Windows 7 **index**, which is a collection of information about the items stored on your computer. Windows 7 uses the index to increase the speed and accuracy of a search. In this exercise, you learn how to search from the Start menu using text and keywords.

STEP BY STEP   **Search from the Start Menu**

GET READY. Before you begin these steps, start your computer and log on to your Windows 7 account. Close all open windows so you can see the desktop.

1. Click the Start button and then navigate to the data files for this lesson.

2. Click the Start button to display the Start menu. In the Search box at the bottom of the left pane, type the letter c. As soon as you start typing characters into the Search box, Windows 7 starts looking for matching items. In this case, it starts searching for any item named with a word starting with the letter C. The text you type does not have to be the name of an item; it can be in the contents of the item or in a property. Windows 7 displays the search results in the left pane of the Start menu, organized by type. The search results are all of the items that match the criteria that you are looking for, which in this case is the text in the Search box. Your Start menu should look similar to Figure 1-11. However, the search results depend on the contents of your computer, so you may not have the exact items in the figure.

Figure 1-11

Search from the Start menu

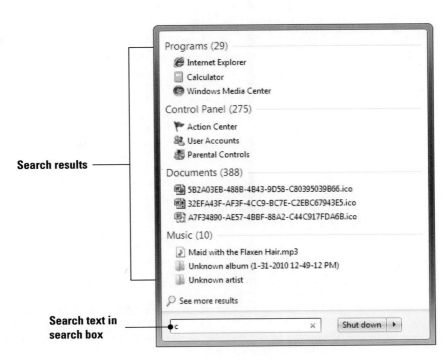

Search results

Search text in
search box

3. Type the letter **o**, so the text Co displays in the Search box. Windows 7 filters the search to find items with the text Co in the name, contents, or properties. To **filter** means to find items that meet certain criteria and exclude those that do not. In this case, the criteria are the text Co. Now, the search results listed should include the two folders Contoso and Company Info, as shown in Figure 1-12.

Figure 1-12

Filter the search to Co

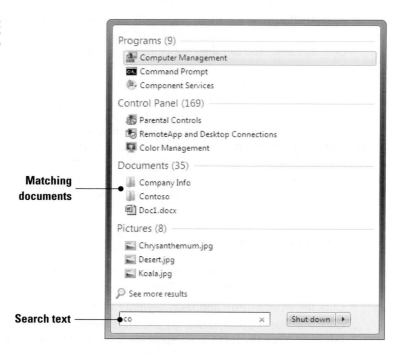

Matching documents →

Search text →

4. Type **ntoso** to complete the word Contoso in the Search box. Now, the search results should look similar to Figure 1-13, with only the exact match Contoso and its contents displayed.

Figure 1-13

Filter the search to Contoso

Matching folder →

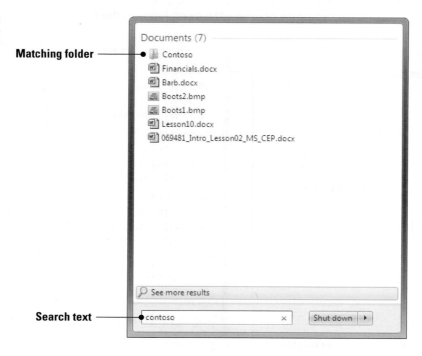

Search text →

@ The *Barb* and *Financials* files are available on the book companion website or in WileyPLUS.

Take Note

5. Press **Backspace** to delete the text in the Search box and then type **Dear**. The *Barb* and *Financials* documents should display in the search results. The text Dear is not part of either file's name or properties, but because both are letters, it is in the file contents as part of the salutation. You may have other letter documents that also display in the search results.

You can open the *Financials* and *Barb* documents in a word processor such as WordPad or Microsoft Office Word to see the contents.

6. Press **Esc** two times to close the Start menu.

PAUSE. LEAVE the desktop displayed to use in the next exercise.

As mentioned earlier, the Search box on the Start menu is a quick tool to use to find a program or an item stored in an indexed location. By default, indexed locations include your personal folder and its contents; email; **offline files**, which are copies of network files that you store locally on your computer; and web sites stored in your web browser's history.

When you search for items, Windows 7 automatically filters the **search results** based on the information you provide. Using a Search box, text is the only information you can provide. As you have seen, if you know the item's name, you can type it and quickly locate the item wherever it is stored. If you do not know the item's name, you can use text that is in the contents of the item. If you are not sure of the item's contents, you can key text that is in a property, such as a keyword in the Tags or Comments property.

When you search using text other than the item's name, Windows 7 may not be able to find the exact item you need, but it will narrow the search results so you can find the item more easily.

You can also use standard search syntax to instruct Windows 7 to look for the search text in a particular property only. **Syntax** is the way words are arranged. To specify a property, type the property, a colon, and then the search text. So, to look for files named March, type Name:March in the Search box. To look for files with a tag March, type Tag:March.

RESIZING A FOLDER WINDOW

The Bottom Line

When you open a folder in Windows 7, its contents display with elements designed to help you navigate and manage your data in Windows. In this section, you practice resizing windows on your desktop.

Minimizing, Maximizing, and Restoring a Window

Sometimes you need to quickly change the size or position of a window on the desktop. Minimize the window to temporarily remove it from the desktop, maximize it to increase its size to fill the desktop, and then restore it back to its original size and position.

STEP BY STEP   **Minimize, Maximize, and Restore a Window**

USE the desktop you left displayed in the previous exercise.

1. Click the **Start button** and then click **Paint** in the left pane of the Start menu. The Paint program window opens.

2. Click the **Minimize** button in the upper-right corner of the window. The window is reduced to a button on the taskbar, as shown in Figure 1-14.

3. Click the **Paint** taskbar button. The Paint window opens.

4. Click the **Maximize** button in the upper-right corner of the window. The window expands to fill the desktop, as shown in Figure 1-15. Notice that some of the colors in the window change to indicate it is maximized and that the Maximize button is now replaced by the Restore Down button.

5. Click the **Minimize** button to once again reduce the window to a taskbar button.

Figure 1-14

Minimize a window

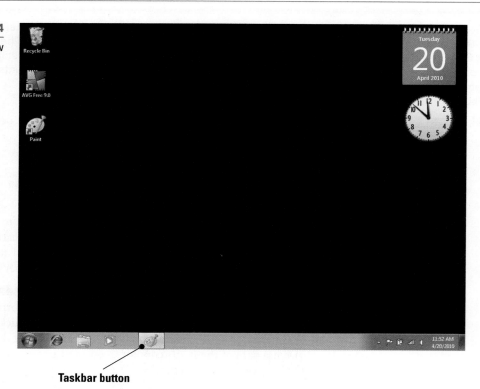

Taskbar button

Figure 1-15

Maximize a window

6. Click the taskbar button to return the window to its previous size and position—in this case, maximized.

7. Click the Restore Down button in the upper-right corner of the window. The window returns to the size and position it had before you maximized it in step 4.

8. Click the Close button to close the Paint window.

PAUSE. LEAVE the desktop open to use in the next exercise.

Restore down button

When you **minimize** a window, you reduce it to a taskbar button. A minimized window is not closed. It remains running on your computer in a minimized state. When you **maximize** a window, you expand it to fill the desktop. You cannot see other items on the desktop behind it, but they are still there. When you **restore down** a window, it returns to its previous size and position. These commands become more and more useful as you start working with multiple windows at the same time, because they enable you to juggle many tasks at once. For example, you might be writing a letter with a word processing program in one window and need to look up a name and address in your contacts list at the same time. You can easily manipulate the windows so that you can access the information you need, when you need it.

Click the Start button and then click Computer. The Computer folder displays; it is divided into two sections:

- **Hard Disk Drives:** Lists the hard disks that are fixed inside your computer or attached externally.
- **Devices with Removable Storage:** Shows devices such as digital video disc (DVD) or compact disc (CD) drives, as well as universal serial bus (USB) devices such as flash drives, scanners, or cameras that are currently connected to your computer.

A drive is a device that reads and writes data on storage media, such as a CD or DVD. In Windows 7, each drive is assigned a drive letter to help you identify it as part of your computer system. For example, the main hard disk drive is called drive C: or Local Disk (C:). See Table 1-2 for information about different types of storage devices.

Table 1-2

Disk drives and storage devices

Device name	Description
Hard disk	A device that contains one or more inflexible platters coated with material on which data can be recorded magnetically. Most personal computers have at least one primary hard disk fixed inside the computer. It is usually called drive C: or Local Disk (C:) and is the location where files and programs are typically stored. Some hard disks are attached externally to a computer. External drives can be removed and stored in a different location to safeguard data or can be attached to a different computer to transfer data.
Hard disk drive	The device that reads data from and writes data to a hard disk.
DVD drive	Reads data on DVDs or CDs. If the drive is a DVD burner, it can also write data on a DVD or CD. DVD burners may be labeled RW, which stands for "read and write." DVDs can store a large amount of data, making them suitable for storing videos, pictures, and music, as well as data.
CD drive	Reads data on a compact disk. If the drive is a CD burner, it can write data on a CD. A CD burner may be labeled RW, which stands for "read and write." Although they do not have as large a capacity as DVDs, CDs are suitable for storing music and pictures, as well as data.
Flash drive	A small storage device that plugs into a USB port on the computer. Flash drives can be moved from one computer to another, making it easy to share and transport information. Flash drives may also be called memory keys, key drives, pen drives, or thumb drives.
Network drive	Any type of drive that is connected to a network and that can be accessed by users on the network. A network drive makes it possible for people to share files and folders stored on that drive.
Other	Includes scanners, digital cameras, and digital video camcorders, which can be attached to a USB port. Data from the attached device can be transferred to the computer. A scanner is a device that converts a printed image to a digital file. A digital camera is a camera that records and stores pictures in digital format. A digital video camcorder records and stores video in digital format.

ACCESSING HELP AND SUPPORT

The Bottom Line

When you have a question about a feature in Windows 7, you can find useful information in the Help and Support Center. Access the Help and Support Center from the Start menu and use the home page to locate basic information about your computer or Windows 7.

STEP BY STEP   **Access Help and Support**

USE the desktop you left open in the previous exercise.

1. Click the Start button and then click Help and Support near the bottom of the right pane on the Start menu. The Windows Help and Support home page displays in a window, as shown in Figure 1-16. Notice that some elements in the window are the same as in a folder window, including the Back and Forward buttons, the Search box, and a toolbar.

Figure 1-16

Windows Help and Support home page

Back button

Forward button

Search box

Window control buttons

Toolbar

Scrollbar

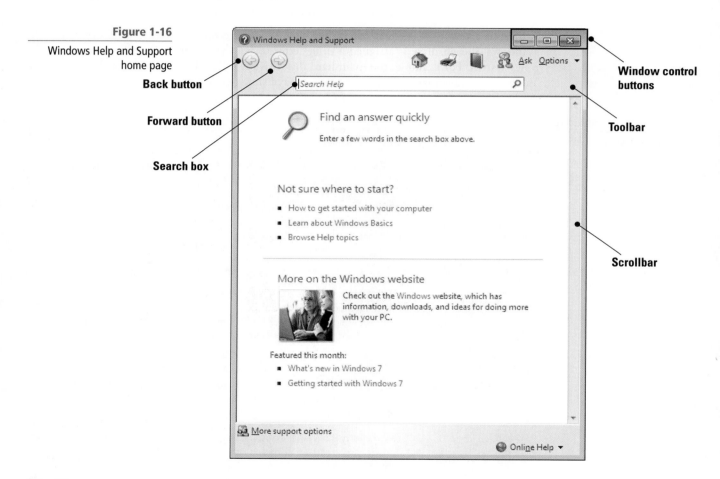

Another Way

You can also open Help and Support from many locations in Windows 7 simply by clicking the Help button.

For example, in the Documents window, click the Help button to open the Managing your documents Help and Support topic page.

2. Click Learn about Windows Basics under the heading Not sure where to start? A page listing all of the Windows Basics topics displays. The topics are grouped under headings, and each topic is a link to a page of specific help information.

3. Click The Start menu (overview) under the heading Desktop fundamentals. A page of information about the Start menu displays.

4. Drag the vertical scroll box down slowly so you can review the information about the Start menu.

5. Click the Back button to return to the previous page and then click Working with windows. A page of information about how to work with windows displays. You can also scroll down in this page.

6. Click the Help and Support home button on the toolbar. The home page displays. The Help and Support home button is available on all pages within Help and Support.

7. Click Browse Help topics to display the Contents page. Each item on the page is a link to a main topic.

8. Click Getting started with Windows 7 to go to the Getting started with Windows 7 page, as shown in Figure 1-17. Note that you must be connected to the Internet to access this page. Scroll down the page to see links to specific topics, including Tabs you can click on to access other types of helpful information.

Figure 1-17

Getting Started Help topic

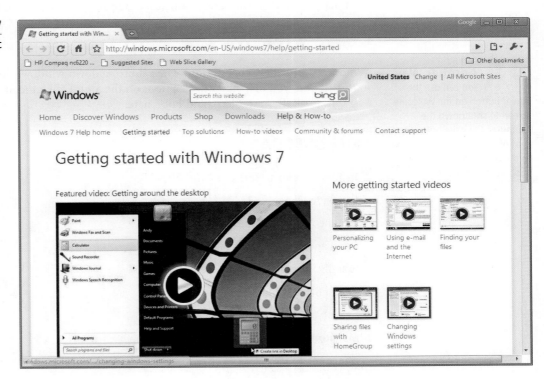

9. Click the Close button in the Help and Support window.

PAUSE. LEAVE your desktop open to use in the next exercise.

The Help and Support Center is full of information to help you accomplish any Windows task. It is organized as a series of linked pages that you can browse through in any order. Some pages provide information, and some walk you through specific steps. The color of text helps identify the type of link:

- **Blue text:** Links to another topic or to a specific task. The link may go to a location on a different page, on the same page, or in a different window. It may even go to a location on the Internet.

- **Green text:** Links to a definition. When you click the link, a definition displays in a ScreenTip.

- **Violet text:** Indicates a link that has already been used at least once. This can help you identify pages you have already accessed.

SHUTTING DOWN WINDOWS 7

The Bottom Line

When you are finished using your computer, you should shut it down. Shutting down insures that your data is saved and your computer system is secure. It also saves energy. In this section, you learn how to shut down Windows 7.

When you want to shut down Windows anwd turn off all of your computer components, use the Shut down command.

STEP BY STEP   **Shut Down Windows 7**

1. Close all open windows.
2. Click the Start button and then, at the bottom-right, click the Shut down button. Your session ends, closing all open windows, and your computer turns off. If necessary, manually turn off your display.

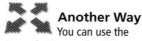 **Another Way**
You can use the Power button on the Welcome screen to shut down the computer. Click the button to shut off or click the arrow next to the button to display a menu of shutdown options.

Windows 7 provides other options when shutting down windows. In addition to those covered in this section, you may find other options on the Shut Down menu useful, such as Switch user, Log Off, Lock, Restart, Sleep, and Hibernate.

SKILL SUMMARY

In This Lesson, You Learned How To:
Log on to Windows 7
Use the Mouse to Identify Desktop Items
Open and Close the Start Menu
Identify Items on the Start Menu
Select Start Menu Settings
Search from the Start Menu
Minimize, Maximize, and Restore a Window
Access Help and Support
Shut Down Windows 7

Knowledge Assessment

Multiple Choice

Select the best response for the following questions.

1. To access information on your computer, you must log on to which of the following?
   a. Internet Explorer
   b. User Account
   c. Outlook
   d. Microsoft Office
2. An icon is a small picture that represents which of the following?
   a. Item
   b. Command
   c. Both a and b
   d. None of the above

3. How many items can be selected at one time in a file list?
   a. One
   b. Two
   c. Three or more
   d. None

4. Which of the following is selected by default in Windows 7?
   a. Sort All Programs menu
   b. Sort All Documents menu
   c. Both a and b
   d. None of the above

5. When does the Restore Down button display?
   a. Always
   b. When a window is maximized
   c. When a window is minimized
   d. Both b and c

6. Which of the following actions can you take to open Help and Support from many locations in Windows 7?
   a. Click the Learn about Windows basics link
   b. Click the Help button
   c. Click a link that displays violet text
   d. None of the above

7. Which of the following refers to the way words are arranged?
   a. Reference
   b. Index
   c. List
   d. Syntax

8. The Customize Start Menu dialog box is used to control items displayed in which pane of the Start menu?
   a. Left pane
   b. Right pane
   c. Both a and b
   d. None of the above

9. The primary way to get help and support for Windows 7 tasks is through which of the following methods?
   a. Call Microsoft on the telephone
   b. Send a letter to the Microsoft Help and Support center
   c. Use the Help and Support option on the Start menu
   d. Send an email to the Microsoft Help and Support center

10. An area where you can key search text is known as which of the following?
   a. Search results
   b. Search pane
   c. Search menu
   d. Search box

Fill in the Blank

Complete the following sentences by writing the correct word or words in the blanks provided.

1. The _____ screen lists the names of all of the people authorized to use the computer.

2. Another term for a shortcut menu is a(n) _____ menu.

3. The _____ is the main work area that displays when Windows 7 is running.

4. A(n) _____ is a collection of information about items stored on a computer; used to increase the speed and accuracy of a search.

5. Items matching specified _____ are displayed in the search results.

6. _____ down a window to return it to its previous size and position.

7. _____ a window to reduce it to a button on the taskbar.

8. _____ a window to increase its size to fill the desktop.

9. Windows 7 looks for _____ text to locate programs, files, and folders stored on your computer.

10. The top of the Start menu's left pane displays _____ items.

Competency Assessment

Project 1-1: Identify Disk Drives

Use Windows 7 to learn about your computer system.

GET READY. Have a piece of paper and pen on hand to write down information about your computer.

1. Turn on your computer and monitor.

2. On the Welcome screen, click your username.

3. If necessary, key your password in the Password box and then press Enter to display the desktop.

4. Click the Start button to open the Start menu.

5. Click Computer on the right pane of the Start menu to display the Computer folder window.

6. Click to select the icon representing your hard disk drive, which is usually named Local Disk (C:).

7. Count how many devices with removable storage you have and write the number on a piece of paper. If you can identify the type of drive, write that information down as well. For example, write down the letter of the CD drive, DVD drive, or network drive.

8. Click the Close button to close the Computer window.

PAUSE. LEAVE the desktop displayed to use in the next project.

Project 1-2: Proper Shut Down

Use Help and Support to find out how to turn off your computer properly.

USE the desktop that is displayed from the previous project.

1. Click the Start button to open the Start menu.

2. Click Help and Support to open the Help and Support home page.

3. Click Learn about Windows Basics to display the list of topics.

4. Click Turning off your computer properly to display the help topic.

5. Read the information on the help page.

6. Click Change what happens when you press the power button on your computer. Read the answer and then write the explanation in your own words on the piece of paper.

7. Click the Close button to close the Help and Support window.

PAUSE. LEAVE the desktop displayed to use in the next project.

Project 1-3: Find Program Files

While you were on vacation, a temporary worker deleted all of the program shortcuts from your Start menu. In this project, you will search from the Start menu for the Notepad, WordPad, and Paint programs.

USE the desktop that is displayed from the previous project.

1. Click Start to open the Start menu.
2. In the Search box at the bottom of the left pane of the Start menu, type WordPad. The program name should display in the search results in the left pane of the Start menu. Be careful not to press Enter after keying WordPad in the Search box. If you do press Enter, the WordPad program launches.
3. Delete the text WordPad from the Search box and type Notepad. View the search results.
4. Delete the text Notepad from the Search box and type Paint. View the search results.
5. Press Esc two times to close the Start menu.

PAUSE. LEAVE the desktop displayed to use in the next project.

Project 1-4: Explore Sample Windows 7 Folders

Explore the picture and music samples that come with Windows 7.

USE the desktop that is displayed from the previous project.

1. Use the Start menu to open the Pictures folder.
2. Select the Sample Pictures shortcut.
3. Double-click the Sample Pictures shortcut to open the Sample Pictures folder.
4. Maximize the window so you can see all of the picture files.
5. Click the Desert picture. If the Desert picture is not available, select a different picture.
6. Minimize the window.
7. Maximize the window and then restore it.
8. In the Navigation pane, click Music to open the Music folder.
9. Click the Sample Music shortcut icon to select it.
10. Double-click the Sample Music shortcut to open the Sample Music folder.
11. Click the Back button.
12. Close the folder window.

PAUSE. LEAVE the desktop displayed to use in the next project.

Project 1-5: Show Off Windows 7

You recently hired an assistant who has never used a personal computer before. In this project, give him a tour of some of the basic features of Windows 7.

USE the desktop that is displayed from the previous project.

1. Open your personal folder and select all items in the file list at the same time.
2. Maximize and then minimize the window.
3. Open the window and then restore it.

4. From the Start menu, type the word games. View the search results.

5. Press Esc two times to close the Start menu.

6. Open the Recycle Bin window and then close it.

7. Log off and then log back on.

PAUSE. LEAVE the desktop displayed to use in the next project.

Project 1-6: New Computer

You just purchased a new computer and want to personalize it for your home. In this project, you will customize the Start menu by adding shortcuts, then restore the Start menu's default settings.

USE the desktop that is displayed from the previous project.

1. Click the Start button, right-click a blank area of the Taskbar, and then click Properties.

2. Customize the Start menu to display Computer, Control Panel, and Personal folder as menus.

3. Set the number of recent programs to display to 3.

4. Restore the Start menu's default settings.

STOP. Log off your Windows 7 user account.

 INTERNET READY

As mentioned at the beginning of this lesson, Northwind Traders is a small, growing company that helps Inuit artists in Alaska market their work to customers around the globe. To prepare for a press release announcing the company's expansion, use Internet search tools to locate information about the history of Inuit art. For example, you might find out the types of traditional Inuit art created over the years, as well as the type of art created by contemporary artists. Use the information you find to write a paragraph that you can include in the press release that summarizes the evolution of Inuit art from the past to the present.

Working with Files and Folders 2

LESSON SKILL MATRIX

In This Lesson, You Will Learn The Following Skills:

Open and close a folder window.

Select items in a folder.

Create and rename a folder.

Delete files and folders.

Use the Recycle Bin.

Browse through recently opened windows.

Use the Navigation pane.

Open and arrange multiple windows.

Change the active window.

Move files and folders.

Copy to a different folder.

Copy to a storage device.

KEY TERMS

- cascade
- Clipboard
- collapsed
- destination location
- expanded
- insertion point
- path
- program
- shortcut menu
- source location
- stacks
- subfolder
- tiles

Southridge Video is a video production company that develops and produces training videos and webcasts for a variety of clients. Whenever the company adds a new client, the account manager uses Windows 7 to set up a folder so there is a place to store files and other information related to the client. In this lesson, you will learn how to work with files and folders. You will use Windows 7 to open, close, and select items in a folder. You will learn to create and rename folders. You will learn how to delete files and folders and how to use the Recycle Bin so you can restore or permanently remove deleted items. You will learn to navigate through windows and to use multiple windows. Finally, you will learn how to move and copy files and folders.

USING A FOLDER WINDOW

The Bottom Line

Imagine an office without file folders or desk drawers. Letters, reports, telephone lists, and other printed information might be strewn willy-nilly on the desk, chair, and even the floor! You would never be able to find anything when you needed it. With Windows 7, you organize your electronic data in much the same way as you would organize an office. You create folders on your computer in which you can store information. When you open a folder, its contents display in a window that also has elements designed to help you manage your data and navigate in Windows. These folders are now located within a Libraries folder in Windows 7. In this section, you will open and close folders that come with Windows 7 and practice selecting items in a folder.

Opening and Closing a Library Folder Window

You can easily open a folder that is listed on the Start menu by clicking it. If the icon is on the desktop, you double-click to open it. To close a window, click its Close button.

STEP BY STEP   **Open and Close a Library Folder Window**

USE the desktop you left displayed in the previous exercise.

1. Click the Start button to open the Start menu.
2. Click your user account name at the top of the right pane of the Start menu. Your personal folder window opens. It should look similar to the one in Figure 2-1, although the name and the contents may be different, depending on your username and the items stored in the folder. Notice that a button representing the window displays on the taskbar.
3. Take a moment to identify the elements of a folder window, as shown in Figure 2-1. Refer to Table 2-1 for descriptions of each element.
4. Click the Close button in the upper-right corner of the window. The window closes.
5. Point to the Recycle Bin icon on the desktop and then press and release the left mouse button twice in rapid succession. This is called a double-click. The Recycle Bin folder window opens. Notice that it has many of the same common elements as your personal folder window. The Recycle Bin folder contains items you have deleted but have not yet removed permanently.

Troubleshooting If your computer has been customized to enable single-click launching, you only have to click the Recycle Bin icon once to open the folder window.

6. In the Navigation pane, click Documents. Notice that the Documents folder is now listed with a Libraries folder. The Documents library folder opens, replacing the Recycle Bin folder in the window on your desktop.

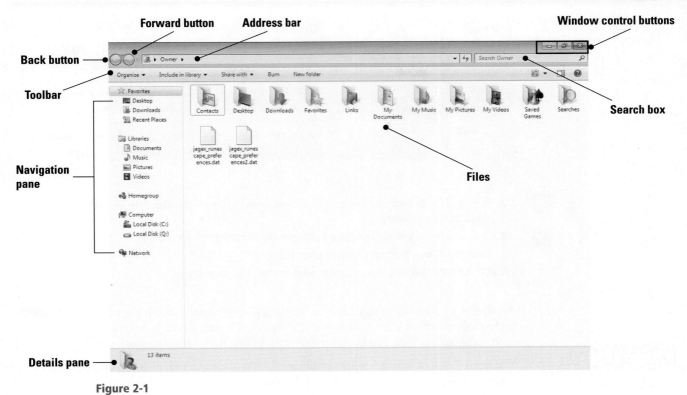

Figure 2-1

A personal folder window

Table 2-1

Common window elements

Element	Description
File list	The File contents are displayed in the current folder, including programs, files, subfolders, and links to other locations. Double-click an item to open it. (Note that the files in Figure 2-1 are displayed in Icons view.)
Navigation pane	The Navigation pane displays links to other locations. Click a link to display that location.
Back and Forward buttons	Click the Back and Forward buttons to navigate to folders that you have been viewing.
Toolbar	The toolbar displays buttons for common tasks, such as organizing the contents of a folder or changing the way the file list displays.
Address bar	The Address bar displays the name of the current folder. It may also display the complete **path** to the location, with each part of the path separated by arrows. The path is the route Windows takes from a storage device through folders and subfolders to a specific destination. For example, the Address bar might display the name of your personal folder, an arrow, and then the name of the current folder. You can key a path in the Address bar to go to that location.
Search box	Key a word or phrase in the Search box to quickly locate a file in the current folder or its subfolders.
Details pane	The Details pane displays properties of the selected item, which are details or characteristics, such as name, size, and type.

(Continued)

Table 2-1 (*contd.*)

Common window elements

Element	Description
Window control buttons	The three window control buttons let you control the size and position of the window on the desktop. Click the Minimize button to reduce the window to a button on the taskbar. Click the Maximize button to expand the window to fill the desktop. When the window is maximized, the Restore Down button displays. Click the Restore Down button to return the window to its previous size and location on the desktop. Click the Close button to close the window.

7. Click the Back button. The previously opened folder—the Recycle Bin—displays in place of Documents.

8. Click the Forward button. The Documents library folder displays.

9. Click the Close button to close the window.

PAUSE. LEAVE the desktop open to use in the next exercise.

Recall that a folder is a storage location within a library, where you can keep files, **subfolders**—folders stored within other folders—and links. Most library folder windows have the same common elements, so once you learn how to work in one folder you can work in any folder.

Windows 7 comes with a few special library folders already set up to help you get started and to organize system information. Table 2-2 describes some of the special folders.

Table 2-2

Windows 7 folders

Folder Name	Description
Personal	Each user account has a personal folder, named with the username assigned to the account. It displays at the top of the right pane on the Start menu. The personal folder contains files that belong only to the assigned user and that are not shared with other people using the same computer. By default, it displays frequently used folders so that you can quickly access your stored data, including documents, pictures, and music.
Documents	The Documents folder is the default folder for storing document files, such as letters, presentations, reports, and spreadsheets. Many programs use Documents as the default storage location for new documents, which means they automatically store new files in Documents unless you specify a different location.
Computer	The Computer folder provides access to drives and other storage devices as well as to network locations connected to your computer.
Pictures	The Pictures folder is set up to store and display digital pictures. Many graphics and photo editing programs use Pictures as the default storage location for picture files.
Music	The Music folder is set up to store and organize digital music. Many digital music players use Music as the default storage location for music files.
Recycle Bin	The Recycle Bin folder stores items you have deleted but have not yet removed permanently from your computer. You can restore items from the Recycle Bin if you realize you deleted them in error or you can empty the Recycle Bin to remove the items permanently.

Selecting Items in a Library Folder

To perform any type of command or action on an item, you must first select it. For example, you must select a file to move it. You can select one or more items by using your mouse.

STEP BY STEP Select Items in a Library Folder

USE the desktop you left displayed in the previous exercise.

1. Click the **Start** button and then click your personal folder to open it.
2. In the file list, click the **Documents** library folder to select it. To select means to mark an item to indicate that it will be affected by the next action or command. The selected item is highlighted and has a selection box around it, as shown in Figure 2-2. A description of how many items are in the Documents library folder displays in the Details pane.

Figure 2-2
Select an item

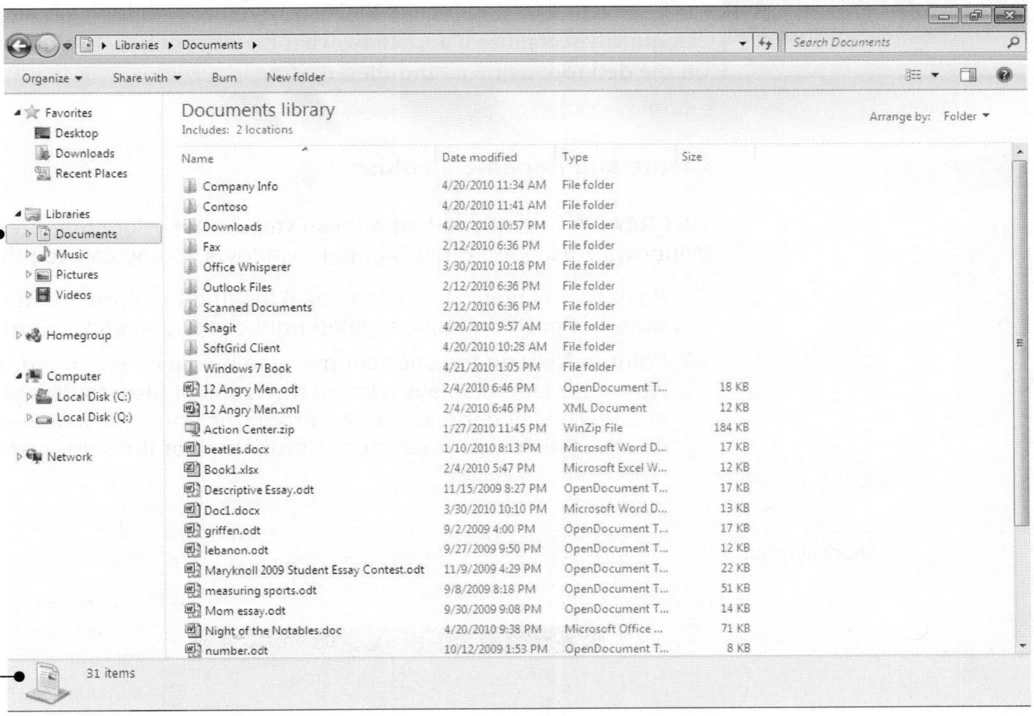

Selected item
Details of selected item
Libraries ▸ Documents ▸
Search Documents
Organize ▾
Share with ▾
Burn
New folder
Favorites
Desktop
Downloads
Recent Places
Libraries
Documents
Music
Pictures
Videos
Homegroup
Computer
Local Disk (C:)
Local Disk (Q:)
Network
Documents library
Includes: 2 locations
Arrange by: Folder ▾
Name
Date modified
Type
Size
Company Info 4/20/2010 11:34 AM File folder
Contoso 4/20/2010 11:41 AM File folder
Downloads 4/20/2010 10:57 PM File folder
Fax 2/12/2010 6:36 PM File folder
Office Whisperer 3/30/2010 10:18 PM File folder
Outlook Files 2/12/2010 6:36 PM File folder
Scanned Documents 2/12/2010 6:36 PM File folder
Snagit 4/20/2010 9:57 AM File folder
SoftGrid Client 4/20/2010 10:28 AM File folder
Windows 7 Book 4/21/2010 1:05 PM File folder
12 Angry Men.odt 2/4/2010 6:46 PM OpenDocument T... 18 KB
12 Angry Men.xml 2/4/2010 6:46 PM XML Document 12 KB
Action Center.zip 1/27/2010 11:45 PM WinZip File 184 KB
beatles.docx 1/10/2010 8:13 PM Microsoft Word D... 17 KB
Book1.xlsx 2/4/2010 5:47 PM Microsoft Excel W... 12 KB
Descriptive Essay.odt 11/15/2009 8:27 PM OpenDocument T... 17 KB
Doc1.docx 3/30/2010 10:10 PM Microsoft Word D... 13 KB
griffen.odt 9/2/2009 4:00 PM OpenDocument T... 17 KB
lebanon.odt 9/27/2009 9:50 PM OpenDocument T... 12 KB
Maryknoll 2009 Student Essay Contest.odt 11/9/2009 4:29 PM OpenDocument T... 22 KB
measuring sports.odt 9/8/2009 8:18 PM OpenDocument T... 51 KB
Mom essay.odt 9/30/2009 9:08 PM OpenDocument T... 14 KB
Night of the Notables.doc 4/20/2010 9:38 PM Microsoft Office ... 71 KB
number.odt 10/12/2009 1:53 PM OpenDocument T... 8 KB
31 items

Troubleshooting If your computer has been customized to enable single-click launching, you only have to point at an item to select it.

3. In the file list, click the **Pictures** library folder to select it. Notice that Documents is no longer selected.
4. Double-click the **Documents** library folder icon. The Documents library folder opens, replacing your personal folder in the open window, and displaying two subfolders: My Documents and Public Documents. The documents within the My Documents folder are stored only on your computer. The documents within the Public Documents folder can be viewed by other users on your network.
5. Click the **Back** button to return to your Pictures library folder.
6. Click the **Back** button again to return to your personal folder.
7. Click the **Close** button to close the window.

PAUSE. LEAVE the desktop open to use in the next exercise.

Another Way You can also click and drag the mouse pointer around items to select them.

When you select an item, you make it current or active. Recall that the current item is the one on which the next action or command will occur. For example, you select a file before you move it or print it.

The easiest way to select an item is to click it. When you want to select more than one item, you combine the click with a key press. Press and hold the following keys while you click:

- **Ctrl:** Allows you to select items that *are not* adjacent to one another.
- **Shift:** Allows you to select items that *are* adjacent to one another.

To cancel a selection, click a blank area in the window or press Esc.

CREATING AND RENAMING A FOLDER

The Bottom Line

You use folders in Windows 7 to store your computer files just as you use folders to store printed files in a filing cabinet. Every file on your computer is stored in a folder, so it is important to know how to create and name folders. By giving each folder a unique and descriptive name, you can quickly recognize it and know what files it contains. In this exercise, you create a new folder on the desktop, name it, and then rename it.

STEP BY STEP   **Create and Rename a Folder**

GET READY. Before you begin these steps, start your computer and log on to your Windows 7 account. Close all open windows so you can see the desktop.

1. Point to any blank area of the desktop and then press and release the right mouse button. Recall that this is called right-clicking. A shortcut menu displays.

2. Point to New on the shortcut menu to display a submenu, as shown in Figure 2-3. The New submenu displays a list of the types of files, folders, and other items that you can create. The list depends on the programs you have installed on your computer, so the one you see on your desktop is probably not the same as the one in the figure.

Figure 2-3

Shortcut menu

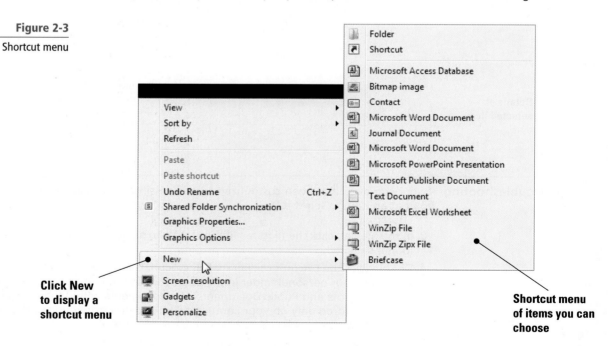

Click New to display a shortcut menu

Shortcut menu of items you can choose

3. Click Folder at the top of the New submenu. Windows 7 creates a new folder on the desktop, as shown in Figure 2-4. The default name—New Folder—is selected. In Windows 7, and most programs that run on Windows 7, selected text is replaced when you key new text.

4. Type Accounts and then press Enter. The new folder is renamed Accounts.

5. Right-click the Accounts folder icon and then click Rename on the shortcut menu. The folder name—Accounts—is selected.

Figure 2-4

New folder with default name

Figure 2-4

New folder with default name

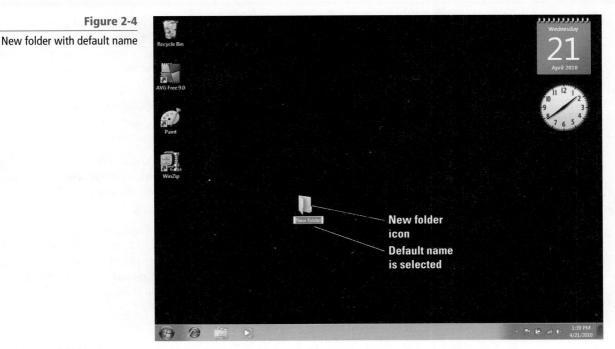

New folder
icon

Default name
is selected

**Another Way**
To display a
shortcut menu by using the
keyboard, select an item and
then press Shift + F10.

6. Move the mouse pointer to the left of the first character in the name—*A*—and click.
   The text is deselected, and an insertion point displays to the left of the folder name, as
   shown in Figure 2-5.

Figure 2-5

Renaming a folder

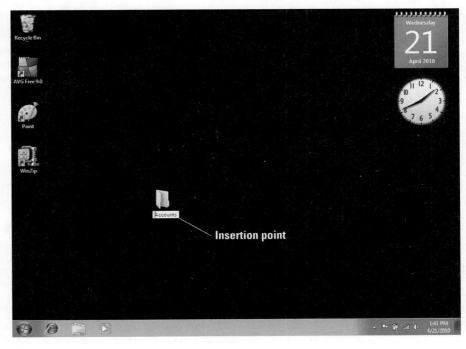

Insertion point

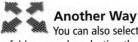**Another Way**
You can also select
a folder name by selecting the
folder icon and then clicking
the folder name.

7. Type **Active**, press the **spacebar** to insert a space, and then press **Enter**. The folder
   name changes to Active Accounts. This name is more descriptive than just Accounts.

PAUSE. LEAVE the desktop displayed to use in the next exercise.

You can create folders in any storage location on your computer, including disk drives, removable devices, and in other folders. Where you create a folder is important, because it helps

you stay organized. If you use a folder often, you may want it on the desktop so you can access it quickly at any time. Sometimes, you might create a **subfolder**, which is a folder within another folder. For example, if you work for a company that has many clients, you might have a folder for each client. In a client's folder, you might have a folder for storing correspondence and a folder for storing invoices.

Using a descriptive name for a folder helps you identify the folder contents at a glance. For example, if you name a folder Information, you cannot tell what information it contains. If you name the folder Regional Sales Information, you know exactly what the folder contains.

A **shortcut menu** is a list of commands or options relevant to the current task that displays when you right-click an item. The list that appears depends on which **programs** are installed on your computer. Programs, sometimes called applications, are sets of instructions that a computer uses to perform tasks, such as word processing or photo editing.

A folder name can have up to 260 characters, but that includes the complete path to the folder. There are nine characters that you cannot use in a folder name: \ / ? : * " >< |. If you try to key these characters in a folder name, Windows 7 displays a ScreenTip to remind you that they are unavailable. You can begin typing a folder name at the **insertion point**. An insertion point is a blinking vertical bar that indicates the location where text will be inserted.

DELETING FILES AND FOLDERS

The Bottom Line

Over time, you will accumulate many files and folders on your computer. Some may continue to be useful, others you may not need anymore. To keep your computer from getting cluttered with unnecessary information, you can delete the files and folders that you no longer need. Deleting sends items to the Recycle Bin. In this section, you delete files and folders.

STEP BY STEP **Delete Files and Folders**

 The *Schedule* file is available on the book companion website or in WileyPLUS.

USE the desktop you left displayed in the previous exercise.

1. Navigate to the data files for this lesson, right-click the *Schedule* file, and then click Delete on the shortcut menu. Windows 7 displays a confirmation dialog box, as shown in Figure 2-6, asking if you are sure you want to move the file to the Recycle Bin.

Figure 2-6

Delete confirmation dialog box

Delete File

Are you sure you want to move this file to the Recycle Bin?

schedule.docx
Type: Microsoft Word Document
Authors: Dawna Walls
Size: 10.5 KB
Date modified: 3/18/2008 12:00 PM

Yes   No

Troubleshooting If the confirmation dialog box does not display, someone customized the Recycle Bin settings on your computer so that deleted items are automatically moved to the bin without confirmation. To change this setting, right-click the Recycle Bin icon on the desktop and click Properties. In the Recycle Bin Properties dialog box, click to select the Display delete confirmation dialog check box and then click OK.

2. Click Yes to delete the file. Windows 7 deletes the *Schedule* file from the data folder.

3. Click the Tailspin Toys Account folder to select it.

4. Press Delete on your keyboard. This is an alternative method of deleting an item. Windows 7 displays the confirmation dialog box.

5. Click Yes to delete the folder.

Take Note   You can delete more than one item at a time. Simply select all the items to delete and then press Delete on your keyboard. Or, right-click the selection and click Delete. The confirmation dialog box lists the number of items you have selected.

PAUSE. LEAVE the desktop displayed to use in the next exercise.

When you delete a folder, note that all items in the folder are deleted as well. For that reason, it is a good idea to open and check the contents of a folder before you delete it.

USING THE RECYCLE BIN

The Bottom Line

The Recycle Bin folder that comes with Windows 7 is the storage location for items that you delete. Items stay in the Recycle Bin until you remove them permanently or restore them to their original location. In this section, you open the Recycle Bin and restore a deleted folder. You then permanently remove a deleted file.

STEP BY STEP   **Use the Recycle Bin**

USE the desktop you left displayed in the previous exercise.

1. On the desktop, double-click the Recycle Bin icon to open the Recycle Bin folder window. It should look similar to Figure 2-7. If you or someone else using your computer has deleted other items, they may be listed in the Recycle Bin as well.

Figure 2-7

Items in the Recycle Bin

Deleted file   Deleted folder

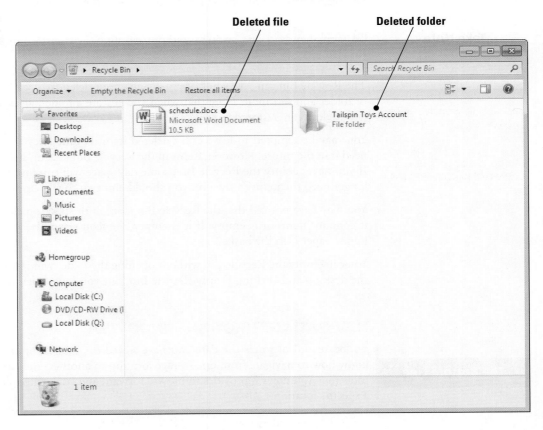

2. Click the Tailspin Toys Account folder to select it.
3. On the Recycle Bin window toolbar, click Restore this item. Windows 7 removes the folder from the Recycle Bin and restores it to its original storage location—in this case, the data folder.

Troubleshooting If you see the Restore all items button instead of the Restore this item button, it means you did not select an item to restore.

4. Click the **Minimize** button in the Recycle Bin window. The Tailspin Toys Account folder should display in the data folder.

Troubleshooting The restored folder icon may not display in the same place on the desktop where it displayed before it was deleted. If you don't see it right away, look for it in a line with other icons.

5. Delete the Tailspin Toys Account folder to send it back to the Recycle Bin.
6. Click the **Recycle Bin** window taskbar button to restore the window. 
7. On the Recycle Bin window toolbar, click **Empty the Recycle Bin**. Windows 7 displays a confirmation dialog box, as shown in Figure 2-8, asking if you are sure you want to permanently delete the items.

Figure 2-8

Delete confirmation dialog box

8. Click **Yes** to permanently delete the items. The Recycle Bin folder is now empty.
9. Close the Recycle Bin folder window.

PAUSE. LEAVE the desktop displayed to use in the next exercise.

Take Note   To permanently delete an item without emptying the entire bin, right-click the item in the Recycle Bin and click Delete on the shortcut menu.

The Recycle Bin can save you from many an errant deletion, because you can always locate a file or folder and restore it. Note that when you restore a folder, all of the items in the folder that were deleted are restored as well.

You may be tempted to leave every deleted item in your Recycle Bin forever, just in case you need it in the future. However, items in the Recycle Bin take up storage space on your disk drive. If you never empty the Recycle Bin, some day space will run low. Once you are certain you no longer need the items in the bin, you should empty it to free up space.

You may have noticed that the Recycle Bin icon on the desktop changes depending on whether it contains items or is empty. If it is empty, the icon resembles an empty basket. If it contains items, paper is in the basket.

You can empty the Recycle Bin without opening the folder window by right-clicking the icon on the desktop and clicking Empty Recycle Bin, but you must open the window to restore items.

NAVIGATING THROUGH WINDOWS

The Bottom Line   To locate and organize the data you have stored on your computer system, it is important to know how to navigate from one storage location to another. You can use the many navigational tools that Windows 7 provides to browse forward and back through folders or jump directly to a specific location.

Browsing through Recently Opened Windows

Use the Forward and Back buttons on a window's toolbar to browse through windows you have opened recently. Click the Back button to view the previous window. Click the Forward button to return to the window that was open before you clicked Back. Use the Recent Pages drop-down menu to select from a list of recently opened windows.

STEP BY STEP   **Browse through Recently Opened Windows**

USE the desktop you left displayed in the previous exercise.

1. Click **Start** and then click **Computer** to open the Computer folder window. Recall that the Computer window displays components of your computer system, such as disk drives and other devices.

2. In the file list, double-click the **Local Disk (C:)** icon to change to the folder that displays the contents of your hard disk drive.

 Troubleshooting By default, Windows 7 replaces the contents of the current window with the next folder that you open, but it can be customized to open each folder in a separate window. If the Local Disk (C:) folder opens in a new, separate window, your system has been customized. To restore the default settings, click Organize on the window's toolbar, click Folder and Search options, click the Restore Defaults button, and then click OK.

3. In the file list, double-click the **Program Files** folder to change to the Program Files folder. The Program Files folder is where Windows 7 stores the files for the programs installed on your computer. It should look similar to Figure 2-9, although the specific contents depend on the programs you have installed.

Figure 2-9

Program Files folder

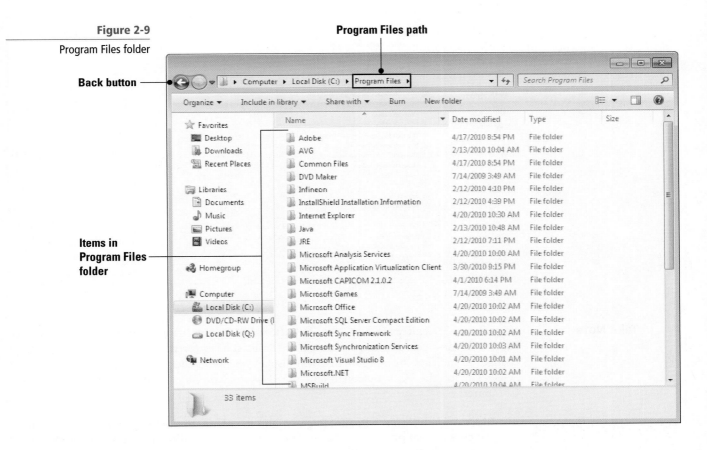

4. Click the **Back** button on the Program Files window toolbar. The previous folder displays—in this case, the Local Disk (C:) window. Notice that once you click Back, the Forward button becomes available as well.

5. Click the **Forward** button on the window toolbar. The folder that was open before you clicked Back displays again—in this case, Program Files. Now only the Back button is available, because there are no other folders to go forward to.

6. Scroll down to the Windows Photo Viewer folder and double-click it to change to the folder where the files for the Windows Photo Viewer program are stored. Windows Photo Viewer comes with Windows 7. It is a program for viewing and organizing pictures.

7. Click the **Back** button on the window toolbar to return to the previous folder (Program Files) and then click the **Back** button again to return to folder open prior to that—Local Disk (C:).

8. Click the **Forward** button to change to the Program Files folder and then click the **Forward** button again to change to the Windows Photo Viewer folder.

9. Click the **Recent Pages** drop-down arrow to the right of the Forward button. A menu of all the locations you have viewed during the current session displays, as shown in Figure 2-10. A check mark indicates the current location.

Figure 2-10

Recent Pages menu

Recent Pages drop-down arrow

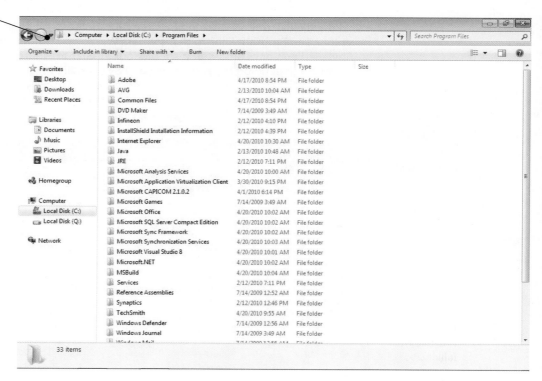

Take Note   You can use ScreenTips to help identify buttons on the window toolbar, including the Recent Pages drop-down arrow. You'll notice that the ScreenTip for the Back and Forward buttons changes to indicate the window that will display when you click the button. For example, the ScreenTip for the Back button might say Back to Computer if the previous window was Computer.

10. Click **Computer** on the Recent Pages menu to change to the Computer folder. When you click a location on the Recent Pages menu, you go directly to that folder instead of browsing through all previously opened folders.

PAUSE. LEAVE the Computer folder open to use in the next exercise.

Browsing lets you easily move back and forth among the folders you have been using. However, it may not be convenient when you need to access a completely different storage location. In the next section, you practice navigating using the options in the Navigation pane.

Using the Navigation Pane

The Favorite Links in the Navigation pane let you quickly open common folders, such as Documents or Pictures. You can expand the Folders list to access any location on your system.

STEP BY STEP   **Use the Navigation Pane**

USE the Computer folder you left open in the previous exercise.

1. In the Libraries list in the Navigation pane, click Pictures to change to the Pictures folder.

2. Click Music to change to the Music folder.

 Troubleshooting To see more items in the Folders list, increase the height of the current window by dragging a top or bottom window border or by maximizing the window.

3. Click Documents to change to the Documents folder.

4. Arrowheads display to the left of items that contain subfolders or files, as shown in Figure 2-11. A solid black arrowhead—the collapse arrow—indicates that the folder is expanded, which mean that the contents of the folder display in the list. A clear arrowhead—the expand arrow—indicates that the folder is collapsed, which means its contents are hidden.

Figure 2-11
Folders list

5. Click your Computer folder in the Navigation pane. Clicking an item in the Navigation pane makes that item current. The contents display in the File list area of the window.

6. Click the collapse arrow to the left of your Computer folder. The folder collapses in the Navigation pane to hide its subfolders, but it is still current, and its contents still display on the right, in the window's File list. Once the folder is collapsed, the arrow changes to an expand arrow.

7. Click the expand arrow to the left of Computer in the Navigation pane. The list expands to display the contents of the Computer folder in the Navigation pane. The arrow changes to a collapse arrow, as shown in Figure 2-12.

Figure 2-12

Collapse and expand
the Folders list

Figure 2-12

Collapse and expand the Folders list

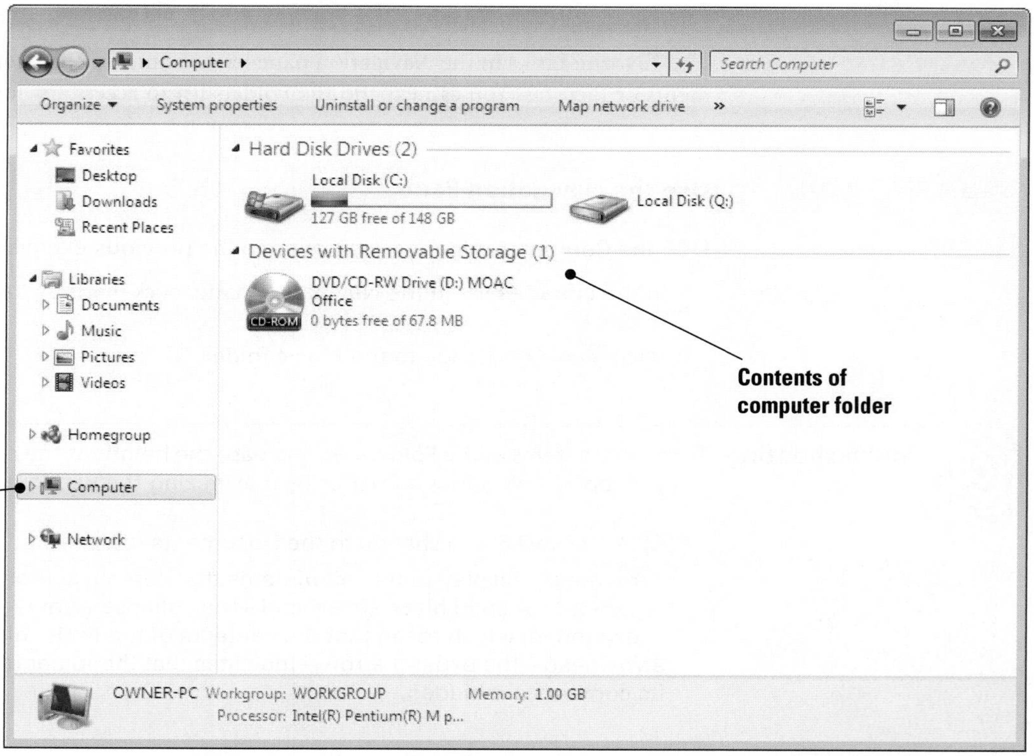

Take Note

You can change the width of the Navigation pane by dragging the border between the pane and the File list. For example, to make the pane wider, drag the border to the right. To make the pane narrower, drag the border to the left.

8. Click Local Disk (C:) in the Navigation pane to make it current.
9. Click the expand arrow to the left of Favorites. The Folders list expands, but the current folder is still Local Disk (C:).
10. Click the collapse arrow to the left of Favorites and then click Music. Music is now the current folder.

PAUSE. LEAVE the Music folder open to use in the next exercise.

The Navigation pane is useful because you can see the entire storage system of your computer while working with the contents of a specific folder. You can easily move among the many storage locations without browsing through multiple folders, simply by expanding the folder list and then clicking the location you want to make current. The contents of an **expanded** folder are displayed in a list. A clear arrowhead—the expand arrow—indicates that the folder is **collapsed**, which means its contents are hidden.

You can also work with folders in the Navigation pane in much the same way you work with them in their storage locations. For example, you can rename a folder or delete it. Simply right-click the folder in the Navigation pane to display a shortcut menu and then select the command you want to use.

USING MULTIPLE WINDOWS

The Bottom Line

Although by default each folder opens in the same window, sometimes you might want to work with more than one window at once. For example, you might want to compare the contents of two folders or copy or move an item from one folder to another or from a folder to a removable device. Or, you might want to use the Calculator while you view an invoice document. You can open a new window at any time. In this section, you open multiple windows, arrange windows on the desktop, and change the active window.

Opening and Arranging Multiple Windows

There is no limit to the number of windows you can have open at once. To open additional windows, simply click the Start button and select the window you want to open. You can arrange multiple windows so that you can see each window in its entirety or so that they overlap evenly. In this section, you practice arranging multiple windows.

STEP BY STEP   **Open and Arrange Multiple Windows**

USE the Music folder you left open in the previous exercise.

1. Click the **Start** button and then click your personal folder. It opens in a new window, overlapping the Music window, which was already open.

2. Click the **Start** button again and then click **Computer** to open the Computer folder in a new window. Now three windows are open, as shown in Figure 2-13. (The size and position of the three windows on your screen may differ from the illustration.)

Figure 2-13

Three windows open at once

3. Right-click a blank area of the Windows taskbar. A shortcut menu displays.

4. Click **Cascade Windows** on the shortcut menu. Windows 7 cascades the open windows, which means that they overlap one another in an orderly fashion, starting in the upper-left corner of the desktop, as shown in Figure 2-14. The active window, which is on top, displays in its entirety, and only the top and left of the other windows are visible.

Figure 2-14
Cascading windows overlap

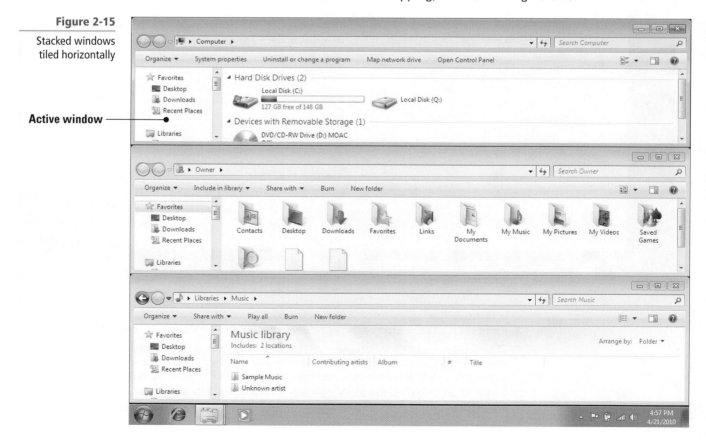

Active window

5. Right-click a blank area of the taskbar and click **Show Windows Stacked**. Windows 7 stacks the windows, or tiles them horizontally, which means they are sized to display one above the other without overlapping, as shown in Figure 2-15.

Figure 2-15

Stacked windows tiled horizontally

Active window

6. Right-click a blank area of the taskbar and click Show Windows Side by Side. Windows 7 tiles the window vertically, which means they are sized to display next to each other without overlapping, as shown in Figure 2-16.

Figure 2-16

Side-by-side windows tiled vertically

Active window

7. Right-click a blank area of the taskbar and click Undo Show Side by Side. Windows 7 restores the windows to the previous arrangement, in this case stacked vertically.

PAUSE. LEAVE the three windows stacked vertically to use in the next exercise.

Three basic options are available for arranging windows on the desktop:

- **Cascade:** Overlaps the windows evenly, with the active window on top.
- **Stack:** Aligns the windows horizontally one above the other. Each window displays in its entirety. If there are only two or three windows, each window extends across the width of the screen. If there are more than three windows, they are sized to fit so that none of them overlap.
- **Tile:** Arranges the windows so that no window overlaps another window.
- **Side by side:** Tiles the windows vertically next to each other. Each window displays in its entirety, extending from the top of the screen to the bottom.

Keep in mind that the more windows you have open, the smaller each one displays when tiled or stacked. You can exclude a window from an arrangement by minimizing it before selecting the command to cascade, stack, or arrange side by side.

The next time you open a window, it displays in its previous size and position on the desktop, even if it is the only open window. You can move or resize the window, or maximize it, if you want.

Changing the Active Window

No matter how many windows are open, only one can be active, or current. You can easily change the active window.

USE the stacked windows you left open in the previous exercise.

1. Click anywhere in the Music window. Clicking a window makes it active. Notice that the Close button in the active window is red, and that the window's taskbar button appears pressed in. In addition, the window's border and background are brighter.

2. Right-click a blank area of the taskbar and click Cascade Windows. When the windows are cascaded, it may be difficult to click in the one you want to make active.

3. Click the taskbar button for your personal folder. Clicking a taskbar button makes the window active. Notice that the active window moves in front of the other open windows.

4. Press and hold Alt and then press Tab. A pane opens in the middle of the desktop, displaying previews of each open window, as shown in Figure 2-17. A selection rectangle displays around one preview, and the window name displays at the top of the pane.

Figure 2-17

Alt + Tab switching

Selected preview

5. While continuing to hold down Alt, press Tab again, and the selection rectangle moves to the next preview. Press Tab until the selection rectangle is around Computer, then release Tab and Alt. Computer becomes the active window. This procedure is called Alt +Tab switching, and you can use it to cycle through all open windows.

6. Close the Computer window. Make your personal folder active and then close it. Make Music active and then close it.

PAUSE. LEAVE the desktop displayed to use in the next exercise.

You can only work in the active window, no matter how many windows are open at the same time. Windows 7 provides many tools for changing the active window:

- The easiest way to make a window active is to click in it.
- You can click a taskbar button to make its window active.
- Use Alt + Tab switching to cycle through all open windows. Release both the Alt key and the Tab key when the window you want to make active is selected.

Take Note

On some systems, the Quick Launch toolbar on the taskbar displays a Switch between Windows button.

When you click the button, Windows 7 displays a 3D view of all open windows. You can click a window to make it active.

MOVING FILES AND FOLDERS

The Bottom Line

You can move a file or folder from one storage location to another. This is useful for reorganizing your storage system. In addition, you can move a file or folder to a removable disk to give to someone else or to take to a different computer, or you can move a file or folder to a network drive so others can access it. You can move items by using the Cut and Paste commands or by dragging them to the new location.

STEP BY STEP   Move Files and Folders

USE the desktop you left displayed in the previous exercise.

1. Click **Start** and then click **Documents** to open the Documents library. Click the **Minimize** button to minimize the Documents window.

2. Right-click a blank area of the desktop, point to New on the shortcut menu, and then click **Folder**.

Take Note   Note that only one item can be stored on the Clipboard at a time. Each item that you cut—or each item that you copy—replaces the item currently on the Clipboard.

3. Type **Alpine Files** and then press **Enter** to rename the new folder.

Take Note   When you move a folder, any items stored in the folder also are moved.

4. Right-click the **Alpine Files** folder and click **Cut** on the shortcut menu. The Cut command moves an item from its source location and places it in the Clipboard. A source location is the location where the item was originally stored. The **Clipboard** is a temporary storage area that can hold one item at a time.

5. Click the **Documents** taskbar button to restore the window.

6. Right-click a blank area of the Name list in the Documents library window and click **Paste** on the shortcut menu. The Paste command copies the item from the Clipboard to its destination location, which is the new storage location. (The destination is sometimes called the target.) In this case, Windows 7 pastes the Alpine Files folder into the Documents window.

7. Right-click a blank area of the Name list, point to New, and then click **Folder**. Type **Ad Text** and press **Enter** to rename the new folder.

8. Drag the **Ad Text** folder icon onto the Alpine Files folder icon, as shown in Figure 2-18. Notice that when you drag the item over a potential destination, it displays an arrow and the message Move to destination name.

Figure 2-18

Drag an item to move it

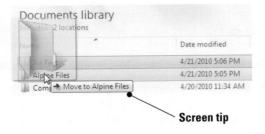

Screen tip

9. When the ScreenTip message displays Move to Alpine Files, release the mouse button. Windows 7 moves the file. Notice that the Ad Text file icon no longer displays in the Documents file list.

10. Double-click the **Alpine Files** folder icon to open it. The Ad Text folder displays in the File list.

PAUSE. LEAVE the Alpine Files folder open to use in the next exercise.

 **Another Way**
You can use the Folders list in the Navigation pane to move folders. Expand the Folders list so you can see both the original location and the destination, then drag the item from the original location to the destination. You can also drag items from the File list to a folder in the Folders list, and vice versa. Alternatively, right-click the item that you want to move and then click Cut. Then right-click the destination and click Paste.

As you have just seen, moving an item deletes it from its original **source location** and places it in a new **destination location**. As with most tasks, Windows 7 provides multiple options for moving files and folders. Each has benefits for use in different situations. As you become more comfortable working with Windows 7, you will be able to select the method that works best for you.

The Cut commands and the Paste commands combine to provide a versatile method for moving files and folders, because once an item is cut to the Clipboard, you can navigate away from the source to locate the destination. Each item stays on the Clipboard until you cut—or you can also copy—another item. That means that you can paste an item from the Clipboard as many times as you want, into many different locations. In addition, Cut and Paste are available on shortcut menus, so they are easily accessible from any location.

The drag and drop method is useful when you can see both the source and the destination locations on the screen at the same time. For example, you can move an item to a subfolder in the same folder you used in the previous exercise. You can also stack or arrange windows side by side so you can drag items from one window to another or use the folders list in the Navigation pane. Dragging is quick and easy and does not require any menus or commands.

You can move multiple items at the same time using either the Cut command with the Paste command or the drag and drop methods. Simply select all of the items you want to move and then move the items.

Both the Clipboard and drag and drop methods are also used in programs that run on Windows 7 to move selected data, such as text, graphics, and even formulas in a spreadsheet. So, once you learn to move files and folders in Windows 7, you will be able to transfer that knowledge to your application programs.

MANAGING FILES AND FOLDERS

The Bottom Line

You copy files and folders from one location to another in order to have multiple versions of the same item available. Copying does not delete the original file—it simply creates an exact replica that can be stored for safekeeping, shared with someone else, or taken to a different computer. The methods for copying are similar to those for moving. You can use the Copy and Paste commands or you can press and hold Ctrl while dragging an item to the new location.

Copying to a Different Folder

You can easily copy a file or folder to a different folder on your computer. You—or others—can edit the copy while the original remains unchanged in its original location. In this exercise, you will copy a file—supplied with this book—from the data files storage location to the Alpine Files folder. You will then create a new folder and copy two files into it.

STEP BY STEP   **Copy to a Different Folder**

@ The *Alpine_Photo1* file is available on the book companion website or in WileyPLUS

USE the Alpine Files folder you left open in the previous exercise.

1. Navigate to the *Alpine_Photo1* file in the data files for this lesson.
2. Right-click the *Alpine_Photo1* file icon and then click Copy on the shortcut menu. This copies the item to the Clipboard, leaving the original file in its source location.
3. Navigate to the Alpine Files folder and double-click the folder to open it.
4. Right-click a blank area of the Name list and then click **Paste** on the shortcut menu. Windows 7 pastes a copy of the *Alpine_Photo1* file into the Alpine Files folder.
5. In the Alpine Files folder, create a new folder named *Files for Review*.
6. Right-click the *Ad Text* folder in the Alpine Files folder and then click **Copy** on the shortcut menu.
7. Right-click the **Files for Review** folder icon and then click **Paste** on the shortcut menu. Windows 7 pastes a copy of the Ad Text folder into the Files for Review folder.
8. Double-click the **Files for Review** folder to open it. The copied Ad Text folder displays.
9. Click **Start**, click **Documents**, and then double-click the **Alpine Files** folder to open it.
10. Right-click a blank area of the taskbar and click **Show Windows Stacked** on the shortcut menu. With the windows stacked on the screen, you can see both copies of the Ad Text folder.
11. Press and hold **Ctrl** and drag the *Alpine_Photo1* file from the Alpine Files folder window to the Files for Review folder window. A plus sign displays with the icon as you drag, and the ScreenTip indicates that you are copying—not moving—the item. Also, a vertical bar indicates the location where the copied file will be inserted.

12. Release the mouse button to copy the file into the Files for Review folder. Now both the AdText folder and *Alpine_Photo1* files are stored in the Alpine Files folder and in the Files for Review folder.

13. Close the Files for Review window.

PAUSE. LEAVE the Alpine Files folder open to use in the next exercise.

The same rules apply to the Clipboard when you copy and when you cut:

- Only one item can be stored on the Clipboard at a time. As long as the item is on the Clipboard, you can paste it into many different locations.
- You can copy multiple items at the same time by using either the Cut and Paste commands or the drag and drop method. Simply select all items you want to copy before performing the copy action.
- Both the Clipboard and drag and drop methods are used in programs that run on Windows 7 to copy selected data.

When you copy files and folders, be careful that you do not clutter your computer with too many copies of the same item, because you may have trouble keeping track of which item is which. It is a good idea to rename copied items so you can tell them apart.

Copying a file to a different folder on the same computer is not a good way to back up your data. To *back up* means to create a copy of data for safekeeping. A mechanical failure that causes the drive to stop working, or a disaster such as a fire or flood, would affect both files. To keep a copy safe, you must copy it to a remote location, such as to a network or to a removable device so you can physically take it to a different location, such as a safe. In the next section, you copy items to a removable storage device.

Copying to a Storage Device

When you want to create a copy of a file or folder that you physically take away from your computer, you can copy it to a removable storage device. This is useful for keeping a copy safe in a different location, creating a copy you can use on your home computer, or giving a copy to someone else. Use the Send to command to quickly copy an item to a storage device.

| STEP BY STEP | **Copy to a Storage Device** |

GET READY. Before you begin these steps, insert a removable storage device into your computer. For example, insert a CD or DVD into a compatible drive, insert a floppy disk into a floppy disk drive, or plug a flash drive into a USB port. You may also use an external hard drive attached to a USB port or a network drive. If an AutoPlay window displays, click the Close button.

1. Right-click the **Files for Review** folder in the Alpine Files folder window.

2. Point to Send to on the shortcut menu. A menu of available locations displays, as shown in Figure 2-19. (The locations on your computer will be different from those in the illustration, depending on the number and type of devices you have available.)

3. On the menu, click the device in which you have inserted the removable media. Windows 7 copies the folder and opens a window for the device.

 **Troubleshooting** Some devices, such as CD and DVD drives, may prompt you to prepare or format the disk before copying the items. Click OK or Next, or press Enter to continue.

4. In the device window, double-click the **Files for Review** folder to open it. Notice that when you copy a folder, all items in the folder are copied as well.

5. Close the device window. Remove the media and label it **Files for Review**, with your name.

STOP. Log off and shut down your computer.

Figure 2-19

Send to menu

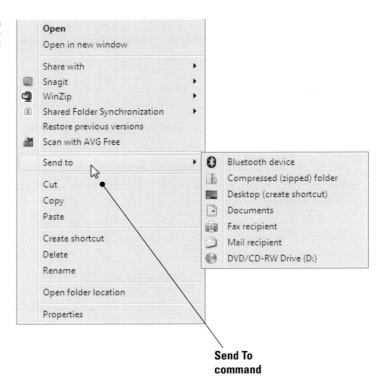

Send To
command

You can also use the Copy command with the Paste command and you can use the drag and drop method to copy or move items to a removable or network device. Also, most CD and DVD drives come with their own software programs that you can use to transfer data—including music, pictures, and videos—onto a disk.

SKILL SUMMARY

In This Lesson, You Learned How To:
Open and Close a Folder Window
Select Items in a Folder
Create and Rename a Folder
Delete Files and Folders
Use the Recycle Bin
Browse through Recently Opened Windows
Use the Navigation Pane
Open and Arrange Multiple Windows
Change the Active Window
Move Files and Folders
Copy to a Different Folder
Copy to a Storage Device

Knowledge Assessment

Fill in the Blank

Complete the following sentences by writing the correct word or words in the blanks provided.

1. A(n) _____ menu is a list of commands or options relevant to the current task that displays when you right-click an item.
2. A menu that opens off of another menu is called a(n) _____.
3. By _____ windows, you tile them horizontally so that they display one above the other without overlapping.
4. The blinking vertical bar that indicates the location where text will be inserted is called the insertion _____.
5. Arranging windows to overlap one another in an orderly fashion, starting in the upper-left corner of the desktop, is also known as _____ the windows.
6. You must _____ an item to indicate that it will be affected by the next action or command.
7. You can have as many _____ as you want open at the same time.
8. You can _____, or display, the contents of a folder in a list or menu by clicking an arrow next to the folder name.
9. You can have _____ active window(s) at a time.
10. Pressing the _____ button displays the previously viewed folder.

True/False

Circle T if the statement is true or F if the statement is false.

T   F   1. There is no limit to the length of a folder name.

T   F   2. You can only delete one item at a time using Windows 7.

T   F   3. You cannot use a question mark in a folder name.

T   F   4. You can only select one item at a time in a file list.

T   F   5. You can hide the contents of a folder in a list or menu by clicking the collapse arrow next to the folder name.

T   F   6. Stacking a window changes the active window.

T   F   7. The Send To command can be used to quickly copy a file or folder to a storage device.

T   F   8. The new storage location for a moved or copied file is the destination location.

T   F   9. When you delete a file, it is permanently erased from your computer.

T   F   10. Items in the Recycle Bin are stored in your computer's memory, so they do not take up any storage space on your disk drive.

Competency Assessment

Project 2-1: Prepare for Family Photos

A relative plans to send you family photos in digital format so you can select one to use for a New Year's Card. In this exercise, you will prepare a folder for storing the digital files. When the relative fails to send the photos, you delete the folder.

GET READY. Before you begin these steps, start your computer and log on to your Windows 7 account. Close all open windows so you can see the desktop.

1. Right-click a blank area of the desktop to display the shortcut menu.
2. Point to New on the shortcut menu to display a submenu.
3. Click Folder on the submenu to create a new folder.

4. Type **Card Photos** and then press **Enter** to rename the folder.

5. Right-click the **Card Photos** folder icon and then click **Rename**.

6. Type **NY Card Photos** and then press **Enter**.

7. Right-click a blank area of the desktop and then click **Undo Rename** to restore the name to Card Photos.

8. Double-click the **Card Photos** folder to open it.

9. Close the Card Photos folder and then press **Delete**. Click **Yes** in the confirmation dialog box.

10. Double-click the **Recycle Bin** icon on the desktop to open it.

11. Click **Empty the Recycle Bin** on the toolbar and then click Yes in the confirmation dialog box to permanently delete all items.

12. Close the Recycle Bin folder window.

PAUSE. LEAVE the desktop displayed to use in the next project.

Project 2-2: Explore Sample Windows 7 Folders

Explore the music and picture samples that come with Windows 7.

1. Use the Start menu to open the Music folder.

2. Double-click the **Sample Music** shortcut to open the Sample Music folder.

3. Click the **Kalimba** music file. If the Kalimba file is not available, select a different file. Write down the filename, date, author, and size.

4. In the Navigation pane, click **Pictures** to open the Pictures folder.

5. Double-click the **Sample Pictures** shortcut to open the Sample Pictures folder.

6. Click the first picture in the file list.

7. Click the **Back** button.

8. Close the folder window.

PAUSE. LEAVE the desktop displayed to use in the next project.

Proficiency Assessment

Project 2-3: Potential Clients

Your manager asks you to prepare folders for storing information about two potential clients. The clients never sign a contract, so you must then delete the folders.

1. Right-click a blank area of the desktop, point to New on the shortcut menu, and then click **Folder**.

2. Type **Potential Clients** and then press **Enter**.

3. Open the Potential Clients folder.

4. Right-click a blank area of the folder window, point to New, and then click **Folder**.

5. Type **Trey Research** and then press **Enter**.

6. Right-click a blank area of the folder window, point to New, and then click **Folder**.

7. Type **Contoso, Inc.** and then press **Enter**.

8. Right-click the **Contoso, Inc.** folder icon and then click **Rename**.

9. Type **Contoso, Ltd.** and then press **Enter**.

10. Right-click the **Trey Research** folder icon and then click **Delete**. Click **Yes** in the confirmation dialog box to send the folder to the Recycle Bin.

11. Right-click the **Contoso, Ltd.** folder icon and then click **Delete**. Click **Yes** in the confirmation dialog box to send the folder to the Recycle Bin.

12. Close the Potential Clients folder.

13. Right-click the Potential Clients folder icon on the desktop and then click Delete. Click Yes in the confirmation dialog box to send the folder to the Recycle Bin.

14. Double-click the Recycle Bin icon on the desktop to open it. Click Empty the Recycle Bin on the toolbar and then click Yes in the confirmation dialog box to permanently delete all items.

15. Close the Recycle Bin folder window.

PAUSE. LEAVE the desktop open to use in the next project.

Project 2-4: Catalog Photo

@ The *Catalog_Photo* file is available on the book companion website or in WileyPLUS.

An equipment manufacturer has submitted a picture for use in an Alpine Ski House catalog. In this project, you must locate the picture in the data files and copy it to the Design Project folder.

1. Navigate to the *Catalog_Photo* file in the data files for this lesson, right-click it, and then click Copy on the shortcut menu.

2. In the Navigation pane click Documents to display the contents of the Documents folder in the File list.

3. Right-click a blank area of the File list and then click Paste on the shortcut menu to paste the *Catalog_Photo* file into the Documents folder.

4. Click the Close button in the upper-right corner of the Documents window to close it.

PAUSE. LEAVE the desktop open to use in the next project.

Mastery Assessment

Project 2-5: Telephone List

@ The *Phone List* file is available on the book companion website or in WileyPLUS.

You are working on a design project with four coworkers, and you want to be able to contact them even when you are working at home. In this project, you copy a telephone list to a removable device so you can take it home.

GET READY. Before you begin these steps, start your computer and log on to your Windows 7 account. Insert a blank disk such as a CD, DVD, or floppy into the appropriate drive. Close all open windows so you can see the desktop.

1. Click Start and then click Documents to open the Documents folder window.

2. Navigate to the location of the data files for this lesson and right-click the *Phone List* file.

3. Point to the Send To command, and then click the name of the device in which you have inserted a disk.

4. When the drive is finished copying the file to the disk, remove the disk and label it with your name, the date, and the filename—Phone List.

5. Close the Documents window.

PAUSE. LEAVE the desktop displayed to use in the next project.

Project 2-6: Telephone List

@ The *Phone List* file is available on the book companion website or in WileyPLUS.

To keep your design project organized, you must keep all files in the same storage location. In this project you create a folder for storing the files, you locate and copy the Phone List text file into the folder, and then move the entire folder to your Documents folder.

1. Navigate to the *Phone_List* text file in the data files for this lesson, right-click the file, and click Copy. Then, to paste the file into the Documents folder, navigate to your Documents folder, right-click the Files list area, and click Paste. Close the Documents folder window.

2. Right-click a blank area of the desktop, point to New on the shortcut menu, and then click Folder on the submenu to create a new folder.

3. Type **Design Project** and then press **Enter** to rename the folder.

4. Right-click the **Design Project** icon on the desktop and then click **Cut** on the shortcut menu to move the folder to the Clipboard.

5. Click the **Start** button and then click **Documents**.

6. Right-click a blank area of the File list in the Documents window and then click **Paste** on the shortcut menu to paste the Design Project folder from the Clipboard into the Documents folder.

7. Double-click the **Design Project** folder icon to open it.

8. Click the **Start** button and then click **Documents** to open the Documents folder window.

9. Right-click a blank area of the taskbar and click **Show Windows Stacked** to tile the Documents window and the Design Project window horizontally on the desktop.

10. Click the *Phone List* file icon in the Documents window, drag it to the **Design Project** window, and then drop it in the File list area.

11. Close the Documents window.

12. Close the Design Project window.

13. Navigate to the Documents folder, right-click on the **Design Project** folder, and click **Delete** on the shortcut menu.

STOP. Log off and shut down your computer.

 ## INTERNET READY

Southridge Video develops and produces digital videos. The technical director wants all employees to understand the different types of digital video file formats that might be used.

In this exercise, use web search tools to locate definitions for at least five digital video formats. Create a text file and use Notepad to record the file format names, extensions, and definitions. Save the file with a descriptive filename.

Microsoft® Word® 2010

LESSON SKILL MATRIX

In This Lesson, You Will Learn The Following Skills:

Starting Word

Working with Onscreen Tools

Opening Backstage View

Using the Microsoft Word Help Button

Creating a Document

Saving a Document

Previewing and Printing a Document

Closing a Document and Closing Word

KEY TERMS

- AutoComplete
- Backstage view
- badges
- Block Style
- command
- Connection Status menu
- dialog box
- dialog box launcher
- groups
- I-beam
- insertion point
- KeyTips
- menu
- Mini toolbar
- mixed punctuation

- nonprinting characters
- open punctuation
- Preview
- Print
- Quick Access Toolbar

- Redo
- Ribbon
- Save
- Save As
- ScreenTip

- settings
- shortcut menu
- tabs
- Undo
- Word Wrap

Tech Terrace Real Estate works with clients to buy, sell, and rent homes in a neighborhood that borders a local university. The company's agents regularly create letters, sales data, and other real estate information to be mailed to current and prospective clients. Microsoft Word is the perfect tool for this task. In this lesson, you learn how to navigate the Word window and use basic Word features to create and manage documents such as those used by Tech Terrace Real Estate.

SOFTWARE ORIENTATION

Microsoft Word's Opening Screen

Before you begin working in Microsoft Word, you need to acquaint yourself with the primary user interface (UI). When you first launch Microsoft Word, you will see a screen similar to that shown in Figure 1-1.

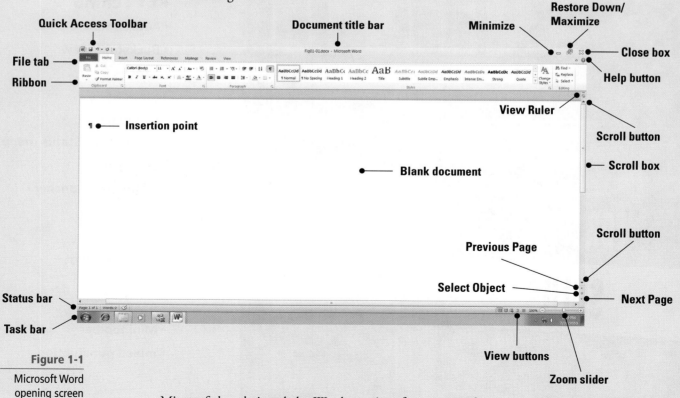

Figure 1-1

Microsoft Word opening screen

Microsoft has designed the Word user interface to provide easy access to the commands you need most often when creating and editing documents. (Note that your screen may vary somewhat from the one shown here, depending on your program's settings.) Use Figure 1-1 as a reference throughout this lesson as well as the rest of this book.

STARTING WORD

The Bottom Line

Microsoft Word is a word processing tool for creating different types of documents that are used in the work environment. When you first launch Word, a new blank document appears on your screen.

Starting Word

In this exercise, you learn how to start Word to produce a blank document.

When you start your computer, the screen you see is called the Windows desktop. From the desktop, you can launch Word by clicking the Word program icon or by choosing Microsoft Word from the Start menu. When Word is launched, the program opens with a blank document. The blinking **insertion point** in the upper-left corner of this document is where you will begin creating your text. When you place your cursor near it, the insertion point changes to a large "I," which is called the **I-beam**.

Take Note

If your computer is running an operating system other than Windows 7, such as Windows Vista or XP, you will be able to complete the lessons in this book, but some screenshots and steps might appear slightly different.

STEP BY STEP   **Start Word**

WileyPLUS Extra! features an online tutorial of this task.

GET READY. Before you begin these steps, be sure to turn on and/or log on to your computer.

1. On the Windows task bar, click the **Start** button, then click **All Programs**. A menu of installed programs appears.
2. Click the **Microsoft Office** folder.
3. Next click **Microsoft Word 2010** (see Figure 1-2). Word opens and a new blank document appears.

PAUSE. LEAVE the document open to use in the next exercise.

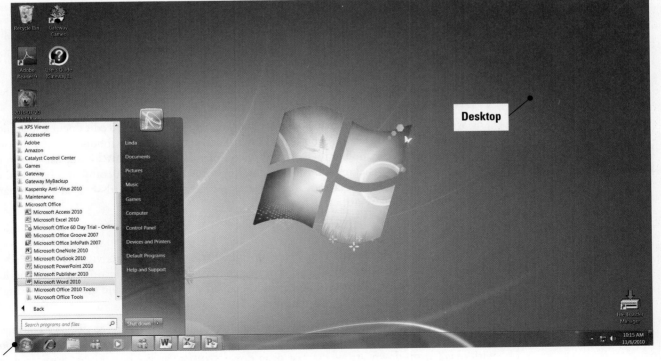

Figure 1-2

Starting Word

Another Way

To launch Word 2010 using Windows 7, click the Start 🟦 button; then, in the Search Programs and Files box, key Microsoft Word 2010; and finally, click or press Enter. You can also search for a program or file by clicking the Start button and then keying the first two characters of the program or filename into the Search box; files and programs beginning with those letters will appear in the Start menu, as shown in Figure 1-3. You can also pin Word 2010 to the Start menu and task bar, so that it is always visible.

Another Way

When Office was installed on your computer, a shortcut icon  may have been added to the Start menu or to your desktop. Double-click the shortcut icon on your desktop to start Word without having to go through the Start menu.

Figure 1-3

Launching Word using Windows 7

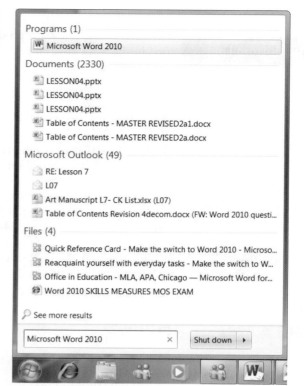

Take Note   Windows 7 is a descendant of Windows Vista, and it is the latest Microsoft operating system. Windows 7 is for PC users at home, work, and school. It is a powerful tool that controls the user interface, storage devices, other software, peripheral devices, networks/security, system resources, and task scheduling. Microsoft has made Windows 7 quick to respond and customizable to accommodate your needs.

WORKING WITH ONSCREEN TOOLS

The Bottom Line   The Word 2010 window has many onscreen tools to help you create and edit documents quickly and efficiently. In this section, you learn how to locate and use the Ribbon, the Mini toolbar, and the Quick Access Toolbar to access Word commands. A **command** is an instruction that you give to Word by clicking a button or entering information into a command box. You also learn how to use KeyTips, a tool that replaces some of the keyboard shortcuts from earlier versions of Microsoft Word.

Using the Ribbon

In Word 2010, the **Ribbon** is divided into eight **tabs**, or areas of activity. In turn, each tab contains several **groups**, or collections of related Word commands. In this exercise, you learn to use the Ribbon by making tabs active, hiding and displaying command groups, and using the dialog box launcher and drop-down arrows.

In all Office 2010 programs, the Ribbon is contextual, which means it displays commands related to the type of document or object that you have open and on screen. Command boxes with small drop-down arrows have a drop-down **menu,** or list of options, associated with them; you click the drop-down arrow to produce this menu. Most groups have a **dialog box launcher**—a small arrow in the lower-right corner of the group—that you click to launch a **dialog box** that displays additional options or information you can use to execute a command.

STEP BY STEP   **Use the Ribbon**

USE the document that is open from the previous exercise.

1. The Ribbon is located at the top of the Word screen. In your newly opened document, the Home tab is the active tab on the Ribbon, as shown in Figure 1-4. Note how the Ribbon is divided into groups.

Tabs   **Drop-down arrows**

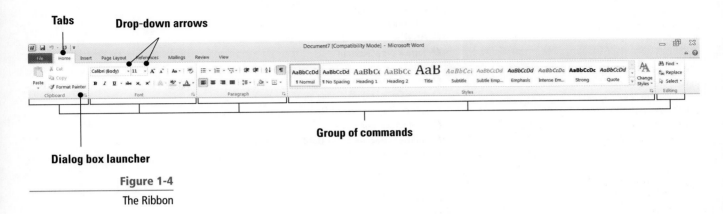

Group of commands

Dialog box launcher

Figure 1-4

The Ribbon

2. Review the other tabs on the Ribbon. Click the Page Layout tab to make it the active tab. Notice that the groups of commands change.

3. Click the Home tab.

4. Click the dialog box launcher in the lower-right corner of the Font group. The Font dialog box, as shown in Figure 1-5, appears. Click Cancel to close the dialog box.

Figure 1-5

Font dialog box

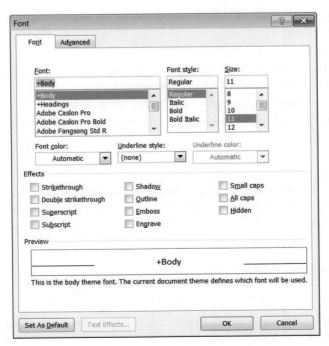

5. Click the drop-down arrow on the Font command box in the Font group to produce a menu of available fonts, as shown in Figure 1-6.

Figure 1-6

Font menu

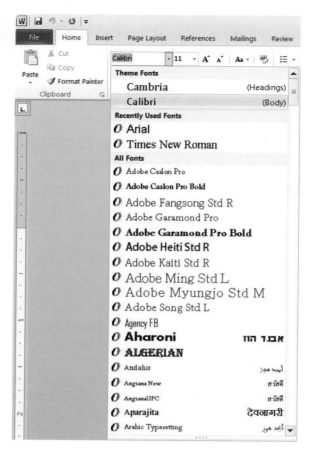

6. Click the arrow again to close the menu.
7. Double-click the Home tab. Notice the command groups are hidden to give you more screen space to work on your document.
8. Double-click Home again to redisplay the groups.

PAUSE. LEAVE the document open to use in the next exercise.

Using the Mini Toolbar

In this exercise, you learn to use the **Mini toolbar**, a small toolbar with popular commands that appears when you point to selected text. You also learn to display the **shortcut menu**, which contains a list of useful commands.

Use the Mini Toolbar

USE the document that is open from the previous exercise.

1. Key mini toolbar and drag the mouse pointer over the word "toolbar" to select it. Notice that a faint image of the Mini toolbar appears once the word is selected, as shown Figure 1-7.

Figure 1-7

Faint version of the
Mini toolbar

2. Point to the Font command on the Mini toolbar. Notice the toolbar brightens.

3. Click the drop-down arrow on the Font command box. A font menu appears. Press Esc twice to exit the command box and close the Mini toolbar.

4. Now, position the insertion point on the selected text and right-click; the Mini toolbar appears, accompanied by a shortcut menu that displays a variety of commonly used commands (see Figure 1-8).

Figure 1-8

Mini toolbar and shortcut menu

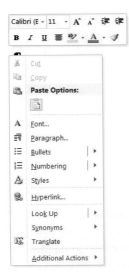

5. Click in a blank part of the document, then drag the mouse pointer over the text you typed at the beginning of the exercise. Finally, press the Delete key to remove the text.

PAUSE. LEAVE the document open to use in the next exercise.

Using the Quick Access Toolbar

The **Quick Access Toolbar** contains the commands that users access most often, such as Save, Undo, and Redo. You can customize the contents of the Quick Access Toolbar by clicking the drop-down arrow on the right side of the toolbar and choosing options from the menu that appears. In this exercise, you learn to use the commands on the Quick Access Toolbar. You also learn to customize the toolbar by changing its position in relation to the Ribbon.

STEP BY STEP   **Use the Quick Access Toolbar**

USE the document that is open from the previous exercise.

1. Click the Save ⊟ button on the Quick Access Toolbar.

2. The Save As dialog box appears. For now, you are reviewing the Save As dialog box. Later in the lesson, you will learn to save a document using this box.

3. Click Cancel.

4. Click the drop-down arrow at the Customize Quick Access Toolbar button. A menu appears, as shown in Figure 1-9.

Figure 1-9

Customizing the Quick
Access Toolbar

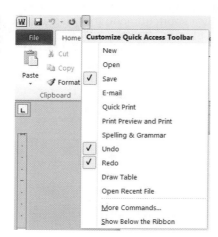

5. Click Show Below the Ribbon. The toolbar is moved.
6. Click the drop-down arrow at the Customize Quick Access Toolbar button again. Click Show Above the Ribbon to return the toolbar to its original position.

PAUSE. LEAVE the document open to use in the next exercise.

Clicking the **Save** 💾 button in the Quick Access Toolbar quickly saves an existing document. When saving a document for the first time, you will need to specify the filename and target location, such as your USB flash drive. The **Save As** dialog box will save a document in a specific format. The **Undo** command lets you cancel or undo your last command or action. You can click the Undo command as many times as necessary to undo previously executed commands. Also, if you click the arrow beside the Undo command, a menu of actions you can undo appears. Clicking the **Redo** command repeats your last action. Note that commands on the Quick Access Toolbar are not available if their button is dimmed.

Using KeyTips

In Word 2010, **KeyTips** replace some keyboard shortcuts used in previous versions of Word. Every command on the Ribbon and the Quick Access Toolbar has a KeyTip. To display Key-Tips, press the Alt key; KeyTips then appear as small letters and numbers hovering over their associated commands. The small square labels that contain this information are called **badges**. In this exercise, you learn to display and use KeyTips.

STEP BY STEP   **Use KeyTips**

USE the document that is open from the previous exercise.

1. Press the **Alt** key. KeyTips appear on the Ribbon and Quick Access Toolbar to let you know which key to use to access specific commands or tabs. (See Figure 1-10.)

Figure 1-10

KeyTips

2. Press **H** to activate the Home tab.

3. Press **A** for alignment, then **C** to center the insertion point.

4. Press the **Alt** key again.

5. Press **H** to activate the Home tab.

6. Press **A** for alignment, then **L** to align the insertion point to the left.

PAUSE. LEAVE the document open to use in the next exercise.

Take Note
Shortcut keys are keys or combinations of keys pressed together to perform a command. Shortcut keys provide a quick way to give commands without having to take your hands from the keyboard. Keyboard shortcuts from previous versions of Word that began with Ctrl have remained the same. However, those that began with Alt are now different and require the use of KeyTips.

SOFTWARE ORIENTATION

Backstage Opening Screen

Before you begin working in Backstage view, you need to be familiar with Microsoft's Office new user interface (UI). When you first launch Microsoft Word and click the File tab, you should see a screen similar to that shown in Figure 1-11. This is what is known as Backstage view.

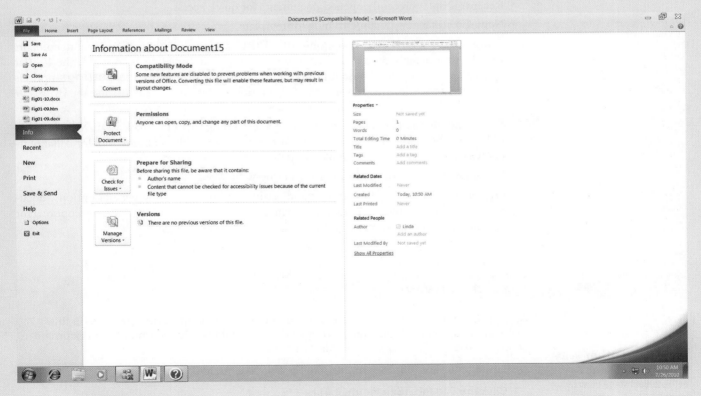

Figure 1-11

Backstage view

Use Figure 1-11 as a reference throughout this lesson as well as the rest of this book.

OPENING BACKSTAGE VIEW

Backstage view offers quick access to commands for performing many file management tasks—such as opening, closing, saving, printing, and sharing Word documents—all displayed in a single navigation pane that can be customized to meet your needs.

NEW to Office 2010

In Backstage view, commands enable you to work with document properties, grant permissions, save documents in PDF or other formats, share documents, and work with templates. Accessibility Checker can be used to check whether your document can be read by individuals with a disability. You can also print and preview a document in one action in Backstage view.

Here is a brief overview of the commands that appear in the Backstage view navigation pane:

- **Save:** Saves the current document using the new Word format.
- **Save As:** Saves a document in a specific format (Word 97-2003, PDF, TXT, RTF, HTM, and so on) and enables you to save documents in multiple locations, such as a USB flash drive, hard drive, network location, desktop, CD, or DVD.
- **Open:** Opens an existing document from any target location; if you open a document created in an earlier version of Word, Compatibility Mode automatically activates (the title bar indicates when Compatibility Mode is active).
- **Close:** Closes an open document (the program remains open).
- **Info:** The options in this group (shown open in Figure 1-11) prepare and mark documents as final so that no changes can be made to them; protect documents with a password or restricted permissions; add a digital signature; inspect the document for sensitive information; check document accessibility and compatibility; manage different versions of a document; and prepare documents for distribution.
- **Recent:** Displays recently opened documents for quick access.
- **New:** Creates a new document, blog, or template.
- **Print:** Offers several sets of options—the **Print** options enable you to send documents straight to a default printer and choose the number of copies to be printed; the Printer options enable you to choose a printer and set printer properties; the **Settings** options enable you to set document properties (orientation, collation, and so on); and the **Preview** screen enables you to visually check your document for errors before printing.
- **Save & Send:** Shares documents by saving and sending them in email, PDF, XPS, or other formats, or by saving them to a document management service (a useful tool for collaborating with others and publishing blog posts).
- **Help:** Provides support and tools for working with Word.
- **Options:** Provides Word document and setting options, including general options, document proofing options, save options, language preferences, editing options, and options for managing add-ins and templates and for keeping documents secure.

STEP BY STEP   **Use Backstage View**

As you begin this exercise, you should acquaint yourself with Backstage view. In this exercise, you access Backstage view by clicking the File tab. To return to your document screen, press the Esc key or click the Home tab.

Another Way
You can also activate Backstage view by pressing Alt+F.

USE the document that is open from the previous exercise.

1. Click the File tab. (See Figure 1-11.)
2. Notice that the Info command is the default command with available options.
3. Point to other commands with the arrow to view more options.
4. Press the Esc key or click the Home tab to exit Backstage view.

PAUSE. LEAVE the document open to use in the next exercise.

USING THE MICROSOFT WORD HELP BUTTON

The Bottom Line

Microsoft Word has options for accessing the Help features installed and available on your computer. If you are connected to the Internet, you also can choose to use Microsoft's online Help features.

Take Note

When you hover over a command on the Ribbon, a **ScreenTip** will appear displaying the name of the command and additional information about the command. You also can click the Help button to get more information and advice.

Using the Help Button

Microsoft Word Help works much like an Internet browser and has many of the same buttons, such as Back, Forward, Stop, Refresh, Home, and Print. A quick way to find Help information is to key a word or words into the search box and then click the Search button. Word will display a list of related topics as links. In this exercise, you learn to open Word Help, to choose between online and offline Help content, and to use Help by keying in search words, browsing help topics, or choosing a topic from the Table of Contents.

The **Connection Status menu** in the lower-right corner of Word Help lets you determine whether the Help screen displays content available at Office Online (you must be connected to the Internet to access this content, which offers the most up-to-date help available) or only those topics currently installed on your computer. The Search drop-down menu enables you to specify the scope of topics you want to search, including All Word, Word Help, Word Templates, Word Training, or Developer References. You can print Help information within the Word Help main window by clicking the Print button.

STEP BY STEP   **Use the Help Button**

USE the document that is open from the previous exercise.

1. Make sure you are connected to the Internet.
2. Click the Microsoft Word Help ② button in the upper-right corner of the screen. The Word Help window appears, as shown in Figure 1-12. In the upper-right corner, click the Maximize 🔲 button to expand the window. In Figure 1-12, the Connection Status command in the lower-right corner of the window indicates that Word is connected to Office.com. If your Connection status is set to Offline, your screen will look different.

Figure 1-12

Word Help window when online

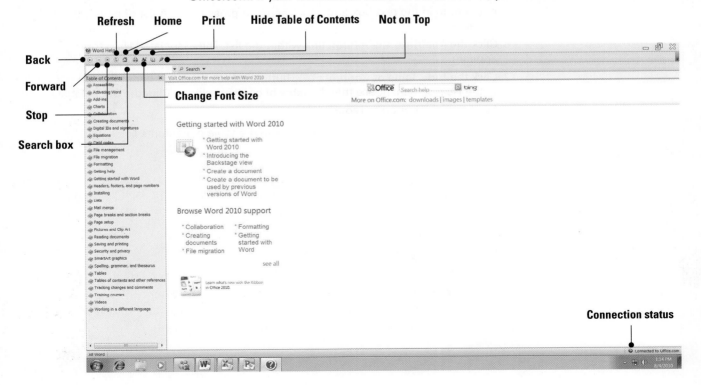

3. Click the Connection Status button to produce the Connection Status menu.

4. Click Show content only from this computer. Word Help appears, as shown in Figure 1-13.

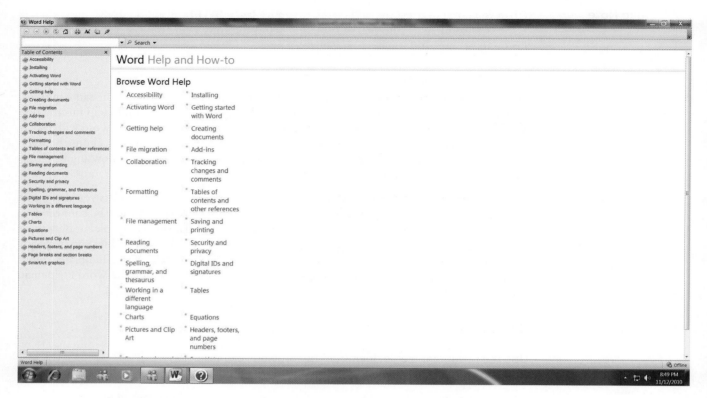

Figure 1-13

Word Help window when offline

5. Key ribbon in the text box and click Search or press Enter. A list of possible topics appears.

6. Click the Minimize the Ribbon link within the list. The associated Help topic appears.

7. Click the Hide Table of Contents 🕮 button in the command bar at the top of the Help screen; notice that the table of contents closes. Click the Show Table of Contents 🔷 button to reopen it.

8. Click the Getting started with Word link in the table of contents list.

9. Click the **What's new in Word 2010** link; the text for the topic appears in the window, as shown in Figure 1-14. Review the content.

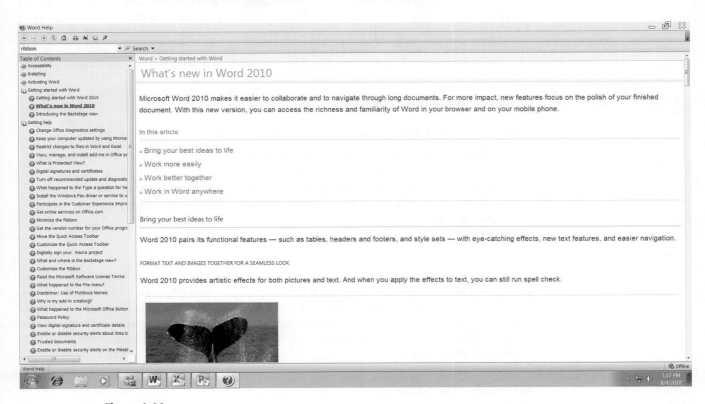

Figure 1-14

Word Help with table of contents and help topic displayed

10. Click the **Home**  button.

11. Click the **Close** button to close Microsoft Word Help.

12. Press **F1** to activate Microsoft Word Help again.

13. Change the Connection Status from Offline to **Show Content from Office.com**, then click the **Introducing the Backstage view** link. Click the **Maximize** button and review the content.

14. Click the **Close** button to close Microsoft Word Help.

PAUSE. LEAVE the document open to use in the next exercise.

 **Another Way**
The Word Help button also appears in some dialog boxes and ScreenTips for quick access to context-related help.

CREATING A DOCUMENT

The Bottom Line

When you start keying text at the insertion point in an open document, you have begun to create a Word document. As you type, Word inserts the text to the left of the insertion point and uses the program's defaults for margins and line spacing. Word also has a number of tools and automatic features to make creating a document easier, including nonprinting characters, AutoComplete, and Word Wrap.

When you key text into a new document, it will be inserted to the left of the insertion point and the document will be created using Word's defaults for margins and line spacing. The margin defaults are set to one-inch top, bottom, left, and right margins; the line spacing is set to 1.15; and the spacing after is set to 10 points.

Displaying Nonprinting Characters

When documents are formatted, Word inserts **nonprinting characters**, which are symbols for certain formatting commands, such as paragraphs (¶), indents and tabs (→), and spaces (•) between words. These symbols can help you create and edit your document. By default, these symbols are hidden. To display them, you click the Show/Hide button in the Paragraph group of the Home tab. In this exercise, you learn to display nonprinting characters in Word.

STEP BY STEP   **Display Nonprinting Characters**

USE the document that is open from the previous exercise.

1. On the Home tab, in the Paragraph group, click the Show/Hide (¶) button to display the nonprinting characters in the document.
2. Click the Show/Hide (¶) button again to hide the nonprinting characters.
3. Press Ctrl+Shift+* to once again display the nonprinting characters. This time, leave Show/Hide on.

PAUSE. LEAVE the document open to use in the next exercise.

After you create your first document, you will see the filename on the document title bar. Word names the file Document1 and displays it in Compatibility Mode format. Word assigns chronological numbers to all subsequent files that you open in that session. When you save and name your documents, the name you've assigned replaces the document number name originally assigned by Word. When you close and reopen Word, the program begins its chronological numbering at number 1 again.

Using AutoComplete

The **AutoComplete** command automatically completes the text of the current date, day of the week, and month. When you key the first four characters of the day of the week, a Screen-Tip appears with a suggestion for the completed text; press Enter to accept the suggestion. AutoComplete reduces the amount of time spent keying content or phrases in a document. In this exercise, you learn to use Word's AutoComplete feature.

STEP BY STEP   **Use AutoComplete**

USE the document open from the previous exercise.

1. Key August; as you key the first four characters, a ScreenTip appears. Press Enter to accept the suggested text.
2. Key Monday using the same process.
3. Click the Undo 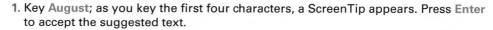 button. Make sure the insertion point is positioned after August.

PAUSE. LEAVE the document open to use in the next exercise.

 **Another Way**
To use Auto-Complete, you can also key the first four characters of the current date and then press Enter or F3.

Keying Document Text

Keying document text is easy in Word. Word sets default margins and line-spacing measurements for newly created documents, and **Word Wrap** automatically wraps text to the next line as it reaches the right margin. To separate paragraphs and create blank lines, all you need to do is press Enter. In this lesson, you create a letter using the Block Style format with mixed punctuation. Be sure to key the document exactly as shown in the steps that follow.

When sending professional correspondence to customers, it is good business practice to ensure the document is in an acceptable format and error free. The Block Style letter format has open or mixed punctuation and is common to many business documents. **Block Style** format aligns text along the left margin, including the date, inside address, salutation, body of the letter, closing, and signature. **Open punctuation** requires no punctuation after the salutation or the closing, whereas **mixed punctuation** requires a colon after the salutation and a comma after the closing.

STEP BY STEP   **Create a Document**

USE the document that is open from the previous exercise.

1. The insertion point should be positioned at the end of the word "August." Press the **spacebar** once and key **25, 20XX**. Press **Enter** twice.

2. Key the delivery address as shown:

   Ms. Miriam Lockhart (Press **Enter** once.)

   764 Crimson Avenue (Press **Enter** once.)

   Boston, MA 02136 (Press **Enter** twice.)

3. Key **Dear Ms. Lockhart.**

4. Press **Enter** once.

5. Key the following text and press **Enter** once after each paragraph.

   We are pleased that you have chosen to list your home with Tech Terrace Real Estate. Our office has bought, sold, renovated, appraised, leased, and managed more homes in the Tech Terrace neighborhood than anyone and now we will be putting that experience to work for you.

   Our goal is to sell your house quick for the best possible price.

   The enclosed packet contains a competitive market analysis, complete listing data, a copy of the contracts, and a customized house brochure. Your home has been input into the MLS listing and an Internet ad is on our website. We will be contacting you soon to determine the best time for an open house.

   We look forward to working with you to sell your home. Please do not hesitate to call if you have any questions.

6. Press **Enter** once.

7. Key **Sincerely,.**

8. Press **Enter** twice.

9. Key **Steve Buckley.** Your document should appear as shown in Figure 1-15.

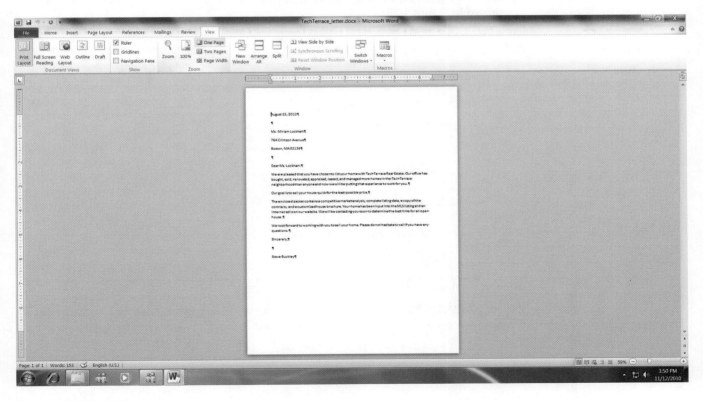

Figure 1-15

Block Style format with mixed punctuation

PAUSE. LEAVE the document open to use in the next exercise.

Take Note   To create a new blank document, click the File tab and then click the New command. "Blank document" will already be selected, so all you need to do is click Create. You can also open a new blank document using the keyboard shortcut Ctrl+N.

It is always important to save your document before closing the program. However, if you close the document or Word by accident, a prompt will appear, asking if you want to save your document. Choose Yes to save and close, No to close without saving, or Cancel to stop the Close command. The Spelling & Grammar commands will be discussed in Lesson 10.

SAVING A DOCUMENT

The Bottom Line   By default, newly created documents are saved with a specific filename closely related to the content of the document. After editing an existing document, you can choose to save that document with a new filename in a specific target location. In some cases, you may want to save the original and edited documents in the same target location but with different filenames. Keeping the original document will allow you to reference it at a future date.

Saving a Document for the First Time

When saving a document for the first time, you must specify a filename, the file type, and a target location where the document will be stored. The filename should help users find and identify the file, and the file location should be convenient for the file's future users. You can save files to portable storage devices such as CDs, DVDs, and USB flash drives, to your computer's desktop or hard drive, or to a network location. In this exercise, you learn to save a document with a specific filename to your USB flash drive.

STEP BY STEP   **Save a Document for the First Time**

USE the document that is open from the previous exercise.

1. If necessary, connect your USB flash drive to one of the USB ports on your computer.
2. Click the **File** tab, then click the **Save** command. The Save As dialog box opens, as shown in Figure 1-16.

Figure 1-16

Save As dialog box

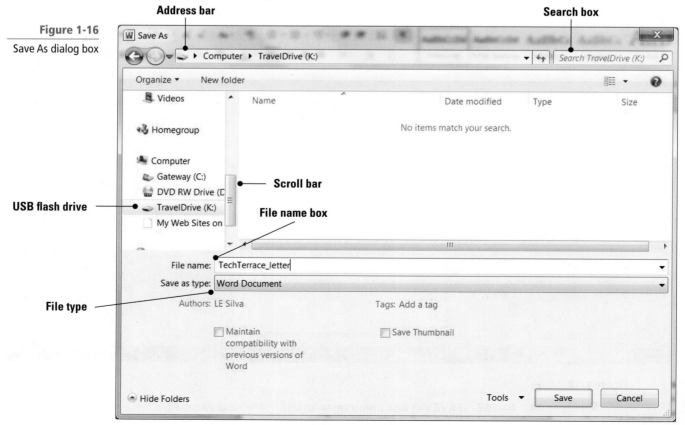

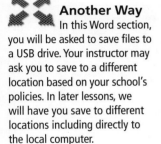

Another Way
In this Word section, you will be asked to save files to a USB drive. Your instructor may ask you to save to a different location based on your school's policies. In later lessons, we will have you save to different locations including directly to the local computer.

3. In the Windows 7 environment, the Documents Library is the default location for saving new files. Change the target location from the default to your USB flash drive by using the vertical scroll bar and scrolling down until you see your USB flash drive. Storage devices are given a specific letter identified by the operating system. The USB flash drive labeled as TravelDrive (K:) in Figure 1-16 may have a different assignment on your computer; consequently, you will need to check with your instructor for the correct path.

4. Click your USB flash drive and note the address bar and the path of the location where your file will be saved.

5. Key *TechTerrace_letter* in the File name text box and click Save.

6. If prompted to save in one of the new file formats, click the OK button. This action will allow you to use the new features in Word.

PAUSE. LEAVE the document open to use in the next exercise.

Take Note   When opening an existing document in Word 2010, it will open in one of the three modes: Word 2010, Word 2007 Compatibility Mode, or Word 97-2003 Compatibility Mode.

 Ref   It is a common business practice to send documents as an attachment via email. When documents are opened as an attachment, they open in Protected view.

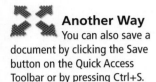

Another Way
You can also save a document by clicking the Save button on the Quick Access Toolbar or by pressing Ctrl+S.

Saving a Document in a Folder

Folders help you organize the documents you create in Word. In this exercise, you create a new folder on your USB flash drive and save the document in that folder with its original filename. Always remember to check the full location path listed in the Save As address bar to be certain that you have identified the right target location.

STEP BY STEP   **Save a Document in a Folder**

USE the document that is open from the previous exercise.

1. Click the File tab, then click Save As. The Save As dialog box opens.

2. Click New folder and key Word 2010. Press Enter.

3. In the main pane of the dialog box, double-click the Word 2010 folder; notice the address bar displays your USB flash drive followed by Word 2010, as shown in Figure 1-17. Note also that the USB flash drive TravelDrive (K:) in Figure 1-17 may not appear on your screen; therefore, you will need to check with your instructor for the correct path.

4. Key *TechTerrace* in the File name box.

5. Click Save to close the dialog box.

PAUSE. LEAVE the document open to use in the next exercise.

 **Troubleshooting**   AutoRecover is a feature that automatically saves your data at scheduled intervals. This makes it possible to recover some of your work if a problem occurs. However, this useful option is not a substitute for frequently saving your documents as you work. You should always click the Save button regularly to avoid losing work in case of a power outage or computer crash.

Saving a Document with a Different Name

You can use the Save As command to save a copy of your document with a new filename, to save the document in a new target location, or to save the document as a different file type. In this exercise, you learn to save an existing document with a new filename in the Word 2010 folder.

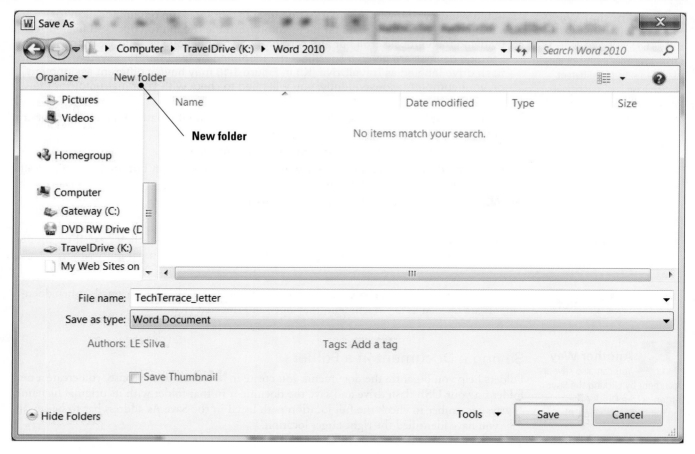

New folder

Figure 1-17

Save As dialog box in
a specific folder

STEP BY STEP   **Save Document in a Folder with a Different Name**

USE the document that is open from the previous exercise.

1. Click the File tab and then click the Save As command to open the Save As dialog box.
2. In the main pane of the dialog box, double-click the Word 2010 folder.
3. Key *TechTerrace2* in the File name box.
4. Click Save.

PAUSE. LEAVE the document open to use in the next exercise.

Another Way
The Save As dialog
box can also be opened by
pressing F12. To locate your
USB flash drive, click the
drop-down arrow beside the
address bar at the top of the
dialog box, then scroll through
the listings and click the flash
drive.

Showing File Extensions

Word gives you the option of saving your document in a number of formats (see Figure 1-18),
including as a Word template, as a Web page, in Rich Text Format, and as a PDF (Portable
Document Format) file, which safeguards the document and preserves the intended formatting
for viewing and printing. A document's file type is embedded in the filename as a file extension.
File extensions are associated with certain programs. (The Save as type drop-down list shows
the file type formats available in Windows 7, and Table 1-1 provides a description for some of
the file extensions.) In this exercise, you learn how to display file extensions in Windows 7 and
in Windows XP.

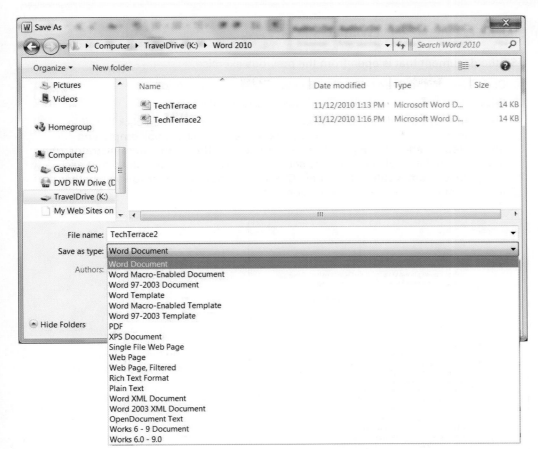

Figure 1-18

File type formats

Table 1-1

File Extensions

File Type	Description
Word Document (*.docx)	Used for Microsoft Word 2007 and 2010.
Word 97-2003 (*.doc)	Used for Microsoft Word 97-2003.
Word Template (*.dotx)	Template for Microsoft Word 2007 and 2010.
Word 97-2003 Template (*.dot)	Template for Microsoft Word 97-2003.
PDF (*.pdf)	Portable Document Format, which preserves the intended formatting of a file for later viewing and printing. PDF files open with Adobe Acrobat Viewer and can be edited using Adobe Acrobat.
XPS Document (*.xps)	XPS is a file format that preserves document formatting and enables file sharing.
Web Page (*.htm,*.html)	Both extensions denote HTML files, which stands for Hypertext Markup Language.
Rich Text Format (*.rtf)	RTF documents are opened with text editor programs such as Notepad, WordPad, and Microsoft Word. Only limited formatting is allowed.
Plain Text (*.txt)	Plain text documents are associated with Notepad, WordPad, and Microsoft Word. The .txt extension does not permit formatting other than spaces and line breaks.
OpenDocument Text (*.odt)	Used by some word processing applications such as OpenOffice.org and Google.docs. Some formatting may be lost when files are saved in this format.

STEP BY STEP **Show File Extensions in Windows 7**

USE the document that is open from the previous exercise.

1. Click Start. In the Search box, key Show hidden files and folders.
2. Click Show hidden files and folder under the Control Panel.
3. The Folder Options dialog box appears. Click the View tab, then click the Hide extensions for known file types check box to leave the check box empty and unselected, as shown in Figure 1-19. In some cases, the system administrator who manages the lab environment may set up the computers in the lab so that each computer system displays the same. Check with your instructor to see whether the file extensions will display on your computer.

Figure 1-19

Folder Options dialog box

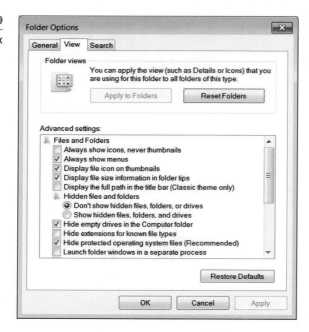

4. Click OK to close the Control Panel.

PAUSE. The Word program is still open from the previous exercise.

STEP BY STEP **Show File Extensions in Windows XP**

1. Click Start on the Windows task bar.
2. Click Control Panel.
3. Double-click Folder Options.
4. Click the View tab, then click the Hide extensions for known file types check box to leave it unselected.
5. Click OK to close the Control Panel.

PAUSE. The Word program is still open from the previous exercise.

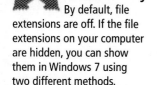

Another Way
By default, file extensions are off. If the file extensions on your computer are hidden, you can show them in Windows 7 using two different methods. Either choose Start > Control Panel > Appearance and Personalization > Folder Options or choose Start, key "folder options" in the Search box, and press Enter.

Choosing a Different File Format

The file format you choose can enable users working in an earlier version of Word to open and edit your document without losing its text formatting. In this exercise, you learn to save a document in a format compatible with an earlier version of Word.

STEP BY STEP	**Choose a Different File Format**

USE the document that is open from the previous exercise.

1. Click the File tab, then click Save As to open the Save As dialog box.
2. In the Save As type box, click the drop-down arrow and choose Word 97-2003 Document (*.doc). You should see the .doc extension in the File name box.
3. Key *TechTerrace2_97-2003* in the File name box. Select your USB flash drive and click Save.
4. Now you will save the document as another file type. Click the File tab and click Save As. In the Save As type box, click the drop-down arrow and choose PDF (*.pdf), then click Save. The USB flash drive is already opened and the document will save with the same filename. If the Adobe Reader opens the document, click the Close ▬x▬ button.

PAUSE. LEAVE Word open for the next exercise.

Take Note   PDF is a popular save-as format for documents. This file type preserves document formatting so users can view the document, but they can't change or copy it. In order to save in PDF format, you must download the appropriate add-in from microsoft.com.

Converting a Document

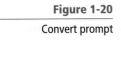

NEW to Office 2010

Compatibility Mode enables you to work in a document created in an earlier version of Word without saving the file in a different file format. In this exercise, you learn to use the Convert command to clear the compatibility options and convert a document to the Word 2010 file format.

STEP BY STEP	**Convert a Document**

USE the document that is open from the previous exercise.

1. With the *TechTerrace2_97-2003.doc* document open, click the File tab.
2. In the main pane of the Info command, click Convert, then click OK to confirm the conversion, as shown in Figure 1-20. Converting the document clears the Compatibility Mode on the title bar and upgrades your document to Word 2010 format, which allows you to access Word's new features.

Figure 1-20

Convert prompt

The check box skips this step for future conversions.

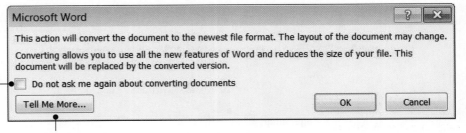

Opens the Word Help screen

3. To save the document in the Word 2010 file format, click the File tab.
4. Click Save As. Then in the File name box, key *TechTerrace_update*. The filename displays the .docx extension.

PAUSE. LEAVE the document open for the next exercise.

PREVIEWING AND PRINTING A DOCUMENT

The Bottom Line

The Print command is located on the File tab in Backstage view. There are three groups of printing options available, which enable you to print the document (either to a file or to a printer) and to choose a specific printer, the number of copies to be printed, the document's orientation, and other print settings. The Preview pane gives you an opportunity to see what your printed document will look like so you can correct errors before printing.

Previewing in Backstage

NEW to Office 2010

Before printing your document, you need to preview its contents so you can correct any text or layout errors. In this exercise, you learn to use Backstage view to preview your document.

The Print command feature includes three sets of options: Print, Printer, and Settings. Choosing the Print command automatically prints the document to the default printer. Use the selection arrow to change the number of copies to be printed. The Printer options enable you to select a printer, print to file, or change printer properties. Use the Settings options to print only specific pages or selections of the document, collate the document, and so on.

The Preview screen to the right of the Print options settings enables you to view your document as it will appear when it is printed, so you can make any necessary changes, such as changing the margins or orientation, before printing. The Preview screen lets you preview every page by clicking on the right and left arrows to page through multiple-page documents.

STEP BY STEP   **Use Print Preview**

USE the document that is open from the previous exercise.

1. Click the **File** tab, then click **Print** in the Backstage view navigation pane. The Print options and Print Preview screen appears, as shown in Figure 1-21.

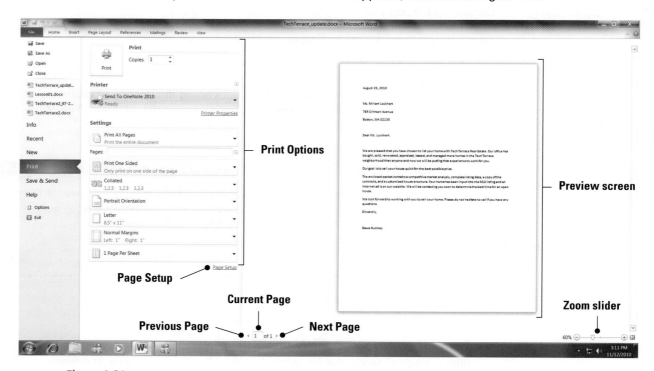

Figure 1-21

Print options and Print Preview screen

2. Click the **plus symbol (+)** on the **Zoom** slider located on the bottom-right of your screen until the zoom level changes to **100%**.

3. Press the **Esc** key or click the **Home** tab to close Backstage.

4. Click the **File** tab, then click **Save**. Your document will be saved with the same filename on your USB flash drive.

PAUSE. LEAVE the document open to use in the next exercise.

Ref   You will learn more about Page Setup in Lesson 5.

Choosing a Printer

If your computer is connected to multiple printers, you may need to choose a destination printer for your document. If your printer is already set up to print, as is the case in most classroom environments, you will not need to complete this exercise. Otherwise, follow this exercise to choose a printer.

Take Note   Before printing your document, check with your instructor.

STEP BY STEP   **Choose a Printer**

USE the document that is open from the previous exercise.

1. Click the **File** tab, then click **Print**.
2. In the Printer selection area, click the **drop-down arrow** to produce a list of all printers connected to your computer.
3. Select a printer, then click the **Printer** icon. (See Figure 1-22.)

Figure 1-22

Print options

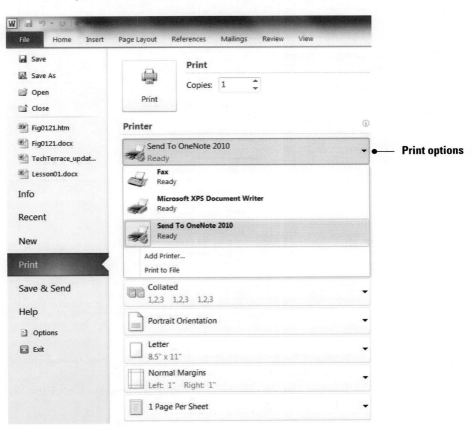

PAUSE. LEAVE the document open to use in the next exercise.

Setting Print Options

Print Settings options enable you to select the number of copies to be printed; to print only selected content, the current page, or a custom range; and to select from a number of other options for printing properties, collation, and page layout. Changes to Settings options apply to the current document. In this lesson, you learn how to change the Settings options before printing.

STEP BY STEP   **Print Settings**

USE the document that is open from the previous exercise.

1. Click the File tab, then click Print. Click the drop-down arrow on Print All Pages to produce the menu shown in Figure 1-23.

Figure 1-23

Print Settings

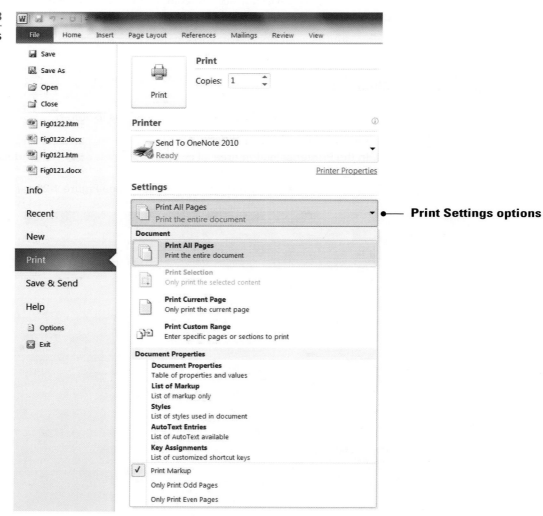

Print Settings options

2. Select Print Current Page, then click the Print icon. Selecting this option prints the current page.

3. In the Copies section of the Print options area, click the up arrow to select 2, then click the Print icon.

4. Click OK to print two copies of the letter.

5. Place your insertion point at the beginning of the third paragraph, then hold down the left mouse button and drag to the end of the paragraph to select it.

6. Click the File tab, then click Print. Click the Print All Pages drop-down arrow, then change the number of copies from 2 to 1 by clicking the down arrow. Next, click the Print icon.

PAUSE. LEAVE the document open to use in the next exercise.

Another Way
You can also print a document by pressing Ctrl+P.

CLOSING A DOCUMENT AND CLOSING WORD

The Bottom Line

Closing a document removes it from the screen. It is a good idea to close a document before exiting a program or turning off your computer. Saving your work before closing will allow you to continue working on your document at a later date.

STEP BY STEP | **Close a Document and Close Word**

USE the document that is open from the previous exercise.

1. Click the **File** tab.
2. Click the **Exit** button to close both the document and Microsoft Word.

STOP.

Another Way
The shortcut for closing a document is Ctrl+W. To close the program, you can simply click the Close ⊗ button.

SKILL SUMMARY

In This Lesson, You Learned How To:
Start Word
Work with onscreen tools
Open Backstage view
Use the Microsoft Word help button
Create a document
Save a document
Preview and print a document
Close a document and close Word

Knowledge Assessment

True/False

Circle T if the statement is true or F if the statement is false.

T F   1. When you start Word, a new blank document appears.

T F   2. The Undo button is on the Mini toolbar.

T F   3. Quick-printing a document sends the document straight to the printer.

T F   4. The File tab is used to save and print files.

T F   5. The Zoom slider is located in Backstage view in the Info command.

T F   6. You can hide the Ribbon by double-clicking the active tab.

T F   7. Saving a document in a PDF format will allow users to edit the document.

T F   8. Previewing and printing can be completed by accessing Backstage.

T F   9. You can close a document using keyboard shortcuts and KeyTips.

T F 10. The Help command cannot be accessed in dialog boxes.

Multiple Choice

Select the best response for the following statements.

1. The first screen you see when you start your computer is called the:
   a. Word screen.
   b. Windows 7 screen.
   c. desktop.
   d. screen saver.

2. When you select text, the faint image that appears is called a(n):
   a. I-beam.
   b. Mini toolbar.
   c. insertion point.
   d. All of the above

3. The _____ contains the commands you use most often, such as Save, Undo, and Redo.
   a. Quick Access Screen
   b. Quick toolbar
   c. Quick Access Toolbar
   d. Quick command

4. Letters and numbers that appear on the Ribbon when you press the Alt key are called:
   a. key trips.
   b. KeyTips.
   c. key pads.
   d. key shortcut tips.

5. The _____ lets you choose between the Help topics available online and the Help topics installed on your computer offline.
   a. Connection Status menu
   b. Connecting Status menu
   c. Connection Status Online menu
   d. Connection Status Offline menu

6. Which command would you use to save a document for the first time?
   a. Save
   b. Save As
   c. Save for the first time
   d. Either a or b

7. When you open new documents in Word, the program names them with a(n) _____ determined by the number of files opened during that session.
   a. chronological number
   b. odd number
   c. even number
   d. decimal number

8. Which of the following options would you use when saving a document with a new filename?
   a. Save
   b. Save As
   c. Ctrl+S
   d. Either a or b

9. Which of the following is an acceptable format for a business letter?

   a. Block style with mixed punctuation

   b. Semi-block style

   c. All text keyed to the left of the margin

   d. Block style with open punctuation

   e. Both a and d

10. Which of the following allows you to access the Help command?

   a. F1

   b.

   c. some dialog boxes

   d. All of the above

Competency Assessment

Project 1-1: Typing a Business Letter

You work for Proseware, Inc. and need to send a follow-up letter regarding price quotes. Key the letter in block style with mixed punctuation.

GET READY. LAUNCH Word if it is not already running.

1. Click the **File** tab, then click **Save As**. In the File name box, key *quotes*. Change the target location to the lesson folder on your USB flash drive and click **OK**.

2. At the insertion point, key **January 10, 20XX**.

3. Press **Enter** twice to create two blank lines.

4. Key the recipient's address as shown:

   Mr. David Pacheco (**Press Enter** once.)

   A. Datum Corporation (**Press Enter** once.)

   2133 Montana (**Press Enter** once.)

   El Paso, TX 79938 (**Press Enter** twice.)

5. Key the salutation **Dear Mr. Pacheco:**.

6. Press **Enter** once.

7. Key the body of the letter:

   It was our pleasure meeting with you last week to discuss quotes for the components you requested. As agreed upon, the specifications discussed will be provided to you once we receive final approval from you.

8. Press **Enter** once.

9. Key **At Proseware, Inc., we appreciate your business**.

10. Press **Enter** once.

11. Key the closing **Sincerely,**.

12. Press the **Enter** key twice.

13. Key **Joe Villanueva**.

14. Proof your document carefully.

15. Click the **File** tab, then click **Save**. The updated version of the letter will be saved with the same filename in the lesson folder on your USB flash drive.

PAUSE. LEAVE the document open for the next project.

Project 1-2: Printing a Document

After proofing the letter you just wrote, you are ready to print copies of the document.

GET READY. LAUNCH Word if it is not already running.

1. Use the *quotes* document you created in Project 1-1.
2. Click the File tab, then click Print. In the Copies section of the Print options area, click the up arrow to change the number of copies from 1 to 2.
3. Click the Print icon.
4. Click the File tab, then click Save.
5. Click the File tab, then click Close.

PAUSE. LEAVE Word open for the next project.

Proficiency Assessment

Project 1-3: Creating a Job Responsibilities Document

Your supervisor, Leonard Lachmann, has asked you to key your job duties and responsibilities into a new document.

GET READY. LAUNCH Word if it is not already running.

1. Click the File tab, then click the New command. Blank document is selected. Click Create to open a new blank document.
2. Click the File tab, then click Save As. In the File name box, key *jobresponsibilities*. Change the target location to the lesson folder on your USB flash drive and click OK.
3. Key October 4, 20XX. Press Enter twice.
4. Key Duties & Responsibilities: Press Enter once.
5. Key the following paragraphs and press Enter once after each paragraph:

   Manage a variety of user experience functions, including programming and promotions

   Manage the online customer experience by creating new site features and maintaining site usability

   Define the website's look and feel

   Partner with the Director of Technology on project planning

   Analyze site usage, feedback, and research

   Improve website experience and performance

   Manage a team of seven user-experience specialists, including graphic designers, information architects, copywriters, and developers

6. Proof your document carefully.
7. Click the File tab, then Save. The updated file will be saved with the same filename in the lesson folder on your USB flash drive.

PAUSE. LEAVE the document open for the next project.

Project 1-4: Saving in Different Formats

Now, you want to save your job responsibilities document in several different file formats.

GET READY. LAUNCH Word if it is not already running.

1. Use the *jobresponsibilities* document that is open from Project 1-3.
2. Click the File tab, then click Save As. In the Save As type box, click the drop-down arrow and choose Rich Text Format (*.rtf). Change the target location to the lesson folder on your USB flash drive and click Save.

3. Click the File tab, then Save As. In the Save As type box, click the drop-down arrow and choose XPS Document (*.xps). Your USB flash drive is already identified as the target location. Click Save. The XPS Viewer will open by default; click the Close button.

4. Click the File tab and close the jobresponsibilities.XPS document.

5. Convert the jobresponsibilities.rtf document to the Word 2010 file format. To do so, click the File tab, then click Convert. Click OK.

6. Click the File tab, then Save As. In the File name box, key *jobresponsibilities_update*. Click Save. The document is saved on your USB flash drive with a new filename.

7. Click the File tab, then **CLOSE** the document.

PAUSE. LEAVE Word open for the next project.

Mastery Assessment

@ The *menu* file for this lesson is available on the book companion website or in WileyPLUS.

Project 1-5: Saving a Word Document as a Web Page

Your coworker at the Grand Coffee Shop has been working on a new menu for the shop. She asks you to review it before saving it as a Web page.

GET READY. LAUNCH Word if it is not already running.

1. Click the File tab, then Open. Change the target location from the default to your USB flash drive.

2. **OPEN** *menu* from the data files for this lesson.

3. **SAVE** the document *menu* as a Web Page (*.htm) file in the lesson folder on your USB flash drive. Then, **CLOSE** the file.

PAUSE. LEAVE Word open for the next project.

@ The *schedulememo* file for this lesson is available on the book companion website or in WileyPLUS.

Project 1-6: Completing a Memo

You need to open and complete a partially composed memo to the members of your neighborhood's welcoming committee.

GET READY. LAUNCH Word if it is not already running.

1. **OPEN** *schedulememo* from the data files for this lesson.

2. Leave two blank lines after the subject line and key the following:

Thank you for volunteering to be on the New Neighbor Welcoming Committee. Enclosed is the meeting and refreshment schedule for the next six months. See you in January!

Committee Members:

Mary Baker

Josie Camacho

Brian Clark

Dorothy Martinez

Hazel Loera

3. **SAVE** the document as *deschedulememo* in both Word 2010 file format and PDF file format in the lesson folder on your USB flash driver.

STOP. Close Word.

 **INTERNET READY**

an online short course or a demo explaining the new features. Browse these or other topics in Word Help online.

Use Word Help to access online information about What's New in Word 2010. "Up to Speed with Word 2010" provides

Workplace *Ready*

SAVING A LETTER IN AN EARLIER VERSION OF WORD

You work for Tech Terrace Real Estate, where your job responsibilities include emailing home price listings to customers. You are aware that several customers have not upgraded from Office 2003; therefore, you would need to save the price documents as Word 97-2003 files or as PDF files so that these customers can open the documents.

Prepare a Block style letter to customers showing the price listing for five homes around town. Proof the letter carefully, then save it as a Word 97-2003 document and as a PDF.

LESSON SKILL MATRIX

In This Lesson, You Will Learn The Following Skills:

Changing and Organizing Document Views

Navigating and Searching through a Document

Selecting, Replacing, and Deleting Text

Cutting, Copying, and Pasting Text

KEY TERMS

- copy
- cut
- Go To
- gridlines
- multi-selection
- Navigation Pane
- paste
- replace
- rulers
- scroll bar
- scroll box
- scroll buttons
- thumbnails
- wildcards

Star Bright Satellite Radio is the nation's leading satellite radio company. The company sells its subscription service to automobile owners, home listeners, and people on the go with portable satellite radios. The public relations department is responsible for promoting a favorable image of Star Bright Satellite Radio to the media, potential customers, and current customers. Microsoft Word 2010 is the perfect tool for viewing and searching through the department's many documents. In this lesson, you learn to navigate and view a document in Word.

SOFTWARE ORIENTATION

The View Tab

Word offers several different ways to view a document, locate text or objects quickly, and manipulate windows. After opening a document, you can access related commands on the View tab, shown in Figure 2-1. Use this figure as a reference throughout this lesson as well as the rest of the book.

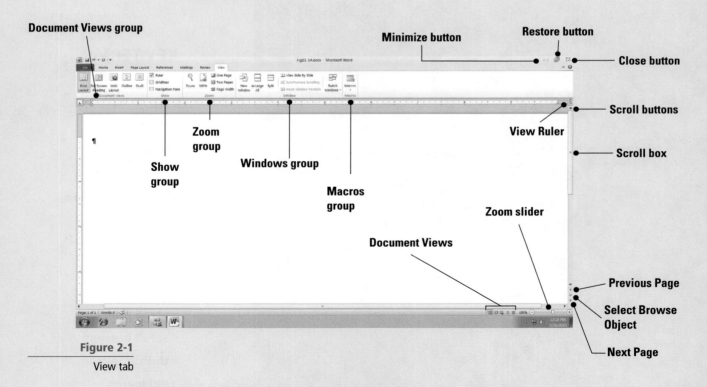

Figure 2-1

View tab

Word provides options to change a document's onscreen appearance by viewing the document in Full Screen, Web Layout, Outline, and Draft views. Adding horizontal rulers, vertical rulers, or gridlines; increasing or decreasing the document's page size; arranging the document windows; viewing the document side by side; or splitting the document can also change the view on the screen. In addition, the Navigation Pane provides options for browsing and conducting a search in a document.

CHANGING AND ORGANIZING DOCUMENT VIEWS

Word has a variety of options for opening an existing document and viewing a document. You can enable features to show gridlines, thumbnails, and rulers to help in navigating the document or you can zoom in or out. Word also allows you to open and arrange multiple document windows. You will learn about all of these features in this section.

Opening an Existing Document

Word enables you to open existing files in one of three forms: as an original document, as a copy of a document, or as a read-only document. In this exercise, you learn to open a document using the Open dialog box.

Clicking the Open command in the File tab produces the Open dialog box. You can use commands in the Open dialog box to open existing documents from target locations such as a USB flash drive, hard drive, network location, desktop, CD, DVD, or portable device. For the purpose of these exercises, the instructions assume that all data files are stored on your USB flash drive.

 Ref   Opening and saving documents in Compatibility Mode was covered in Lesson 1.

Open an Existing Document

GET READY. Before you begin these steps, be sure to turn on and/or log on to your computer and start Word.

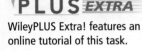

WileyPLUS Extra! features an online tutorial of this task.

1. Connect your USB flash drive to one of the USB ports on your computer.
2. Click the **File** tab.
3. Click **Open**. The Open dialog box appears. (See Figure 2-2, but note that your screen will not be identical to the figure.)

Figure 2-2

Open dialog box

Scroll bar – scroll down to locate your USB flash drive.

@ The *proposal* file for this lesson is available on the book companion website or in WileyPLUS.

4. Scroll down and locate the data files for this lesson on your USB flash drive. Double-click the **Lesson 2** folder to open it.
5. Locate and click *proposal* once.
6. Click the **Open** button. The document appears, as shown in Figure 2-3.

Address bar displays target location for data.

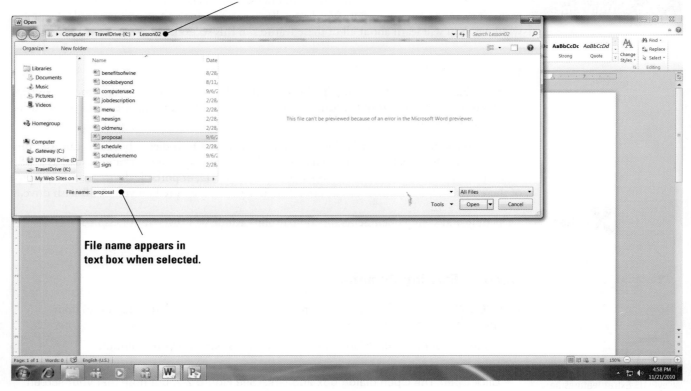

File name appears in text box when selected.

Another Way
To open a document quickly, double-click the filename.

PAUSE. LEAVE the document open to use in the next exercise.

Changing Document Views

The View tab on the Ribbon has groups of commands for Document Views, Show, Zoom, Window, and Macros. In this section, you learn to use the Document Views command group to change the way Word displays your document.

Word has five Document View options:

- **Print Layout** is the default view. It displays the document as it will look when printed and enables you to use the Ribbon to create and edit your document.
- **Full Screen Reading** view is made for reading documents onscreen. Options are available for customizing this view.
- **Web Layout** view shows how the document would look as a Web page.
- **Outline** view displays the document as an outline and offers an outline tab with commands for creating and editing outlines.
- **Draft** view is strictly for editing text. Advanced elements such as charts, graphs, pictures, and other objects are hidden in this view.

STEP BY STEP   **Change Document Views**

USE the document that is open from the previous exercise.

1. Click the View tab to see the command groups that are available.
2. In the Document Views group, click the Full Screen Reading button to change to Full Screen Reading view, as shown in Figure 2-4.

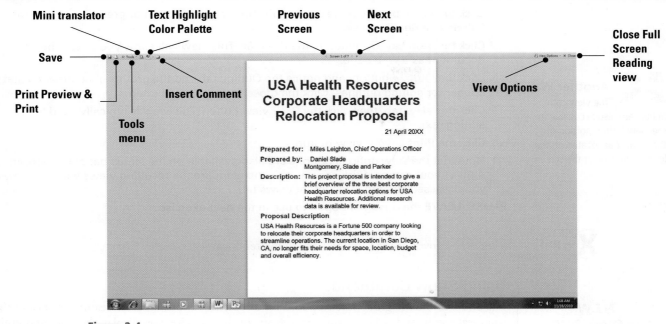

Figure 2-4

Full Screen Reading view

3. Click the **View Options** button in the upper-right corner of the screen to produce the View Options menu, as shown in Figure 2-5.

Figure 2-5

View Options menu

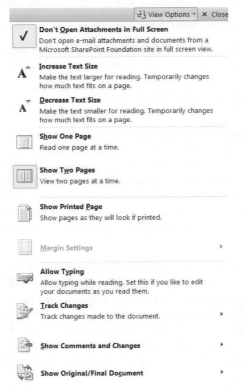

4. Choose **Increase Text Size**. The text size increases for better onscreen reading.

5. Click **View Options** again, then click **Show Two Pages**. Two pages of the document are displayed.

6. Click the **Close** button in the upper-right corner of the screen or press **Esc** to turn off Full Screen Reading view.

7. Click the **Web Layout** button in the View tab. This view will allow you to see the document as a Web page.

8. Click the **Outline** button, and notice the Outline tab and the groups of commands that appear for editing outlines. Click the **Close Outline View** button.

9. Click the **View** tab, then click the **Draft** view button. This view is typically used for editing text.

10. Click the **Print Layout** view button.

11. Note that the View options buttons are also available on the status bar at the bottom right of your screen. Click each button and compare the resulting views with the views you accessed from the Document Views tab.

PAUSE. LEAVE the document open to use in the next exercise.

Another Way
The view commands are also accessible in the View button portion of the status bar, located on the lower-right side of the screen.

 Ref

Lesson 12 covers using Outline View in master documents.

Using Show Commands

NEW to Office 2010

The Show command group offers options for displaying various onscreen features that can help you create, edit, and navigate your document. In this exercise, you display the ruler and gridlines. You also use the Navigation Pane to browse by headings and by page and to search for text.

Rulers are measuring tools to align text, graphics, and other elements used within a document. The top and bottom margins of a document can be easily adjusted manually using the vertical scroll bar. The horizontal ruler can be used to change a document's first-line indent,

hanging indent, and left and right indents. The markers display on the ruler as hanging

indent   , left indent   , and right indent   . Manual tab settings can be set on the

horizontal ruler without launching the dialog box.

Gridlines provide a grid of vertical and horizontal lines that help you align graphics and other objects in your documents. Gridlines are displayed only in Print Layout view.

 Ref

Tabs are discussed in greater detail in Lesson 4.

NEW to Office 2010

The **Navigation Pane** appears in the left side of the window when you select its command in the Show group. The Navigation Pane has three tabs. The first tab, Browse Headings in your document, displays the structure of your document by levels based on the document's headings. The second tab, Browse Pages in your document, displays **thumbnails—** tiny images of your document pages. The third tab, Browse the results from the current search, displays a list of search results when you have used the Navigation Pane's search tool (marked by a search box and magnifying glass icon) to look for particular text or objects in your document.

The search box lists the text or objects found in the document in the order those elements appear in the document. For example, the search boxes may indicate that the first instance of a word appears on page five, the next instance appears on page eight, and so on. The document appears highlighted in yellow and the text is bolded in the *Browse the results from the current search* tab. In the first tab, *Browse the headings in your document*, the section that has the found instance will appear highlighted. In the second tab, *Browse Pages in your document*, the thumbnail instances found will appear highlighted in yellow. To clear the search box, click the X in that box.

In this exercise, you learn to use show commands. The Navigation Pane will be discussed later in this lesson.

STEP BY STEP	**Use Show Commands**

USE the document that is open from the previous exercise.

1. In the Show command group, click the **Ruler** check box to insert a check mark and activate the command. The horizontal and vertical rulers appear.

2. Click the **Gridlines** check box. A grid appears behind text on the page, as shown in Figure 2-6.

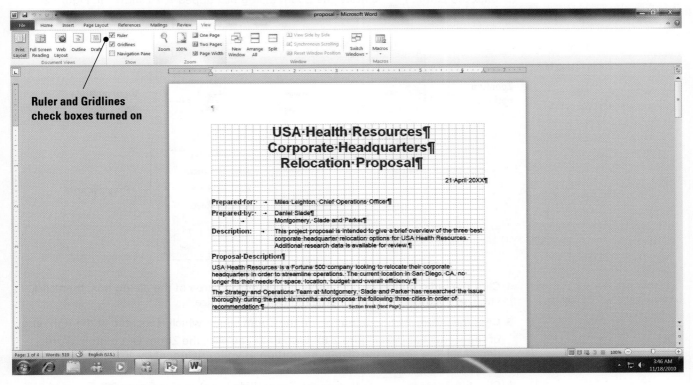

Figure 2-6

Gridlines and rulers

 Another Way
You also can display the Ruler by clicking the View Ruler icon that is located on the right side of the screen above the vertical scroll bar.

3. Click the **Gridlines** check box to remove check marks.

4. Click the **Ruler** check box to remove the rulers from view.

PAUSE. LEAVE the document open to use in the next exercise.

Using Zoom

The Zoom group of commands lets you zoom in to get a closer view of a page or zoom out to see more of the document at a smaller size. These commands also enable you to determine how many document pages Word displays within a single screen. In this exercise, you use the Zoom commands to view one or two pages; you also use the Zoom slider in the status bar to increase or decrease the size of the displayed image.

Within the Zoom group, the Page Width button expands your document to fit the width of the window. The Zoom button launches the Zoom dialog box, where you have more options for zooming in and out. For instance, you can enter a specific number in the percent box to modify the view. Similarly, in the Zoom to section, you can expand the document by clicking a specific zoom amount up to 200%. The preview area shows how the document will appear on screen. The Zoom slider can also be used to zoom in and out; this slider is located in the bottom right of your screen on the status bar.

| STEP BY STEP | Use Zoom |

USE the document that is open from the previous exercise.

1. Click the **One Page** button in the Zoom command group to display one entire page on the screen.

2. Click the **Two Pages** button to switch to a display of two pages.

3. Click the **Zoom** button. The Zoom dialog box appears, as shown in Figure 2-7.

Figure 2-7

Zoom dialog box

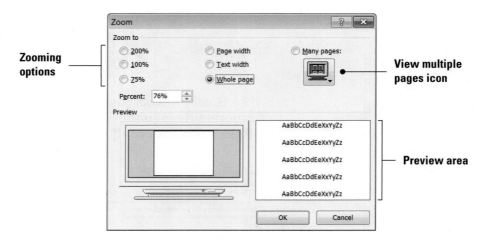

Zooming options

View multiple pages icon

Preview area

4. Click the radio button beside 200% in the Zoom to area of the dialog box, then click **OK**. The document image enlarges to twice its full size.

5. Click the **Zoom Out** button on the Zoom slider, which is located at the right end of the status bar (see Figure 2-8). Each time you click the Zoom Out button, Word decreases the size of the displayed portion of your document by 10%. Click until the Zoom Out indicator displays **60%**.

6. Click the **Zoom In** button on the Zoom Slider, as shown in Figure 2-8. Zoom to **80%**.

Figure 2-8

The Zoom In and Zoom Out buttons on the Zoom slider

Zoom slider

Zoom Out   Zoom In

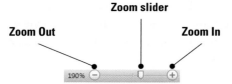

7. Drag the Zoom slider all the way to the left; Word reduces the document to thumbnail size.

8. Now, in the Zoom command group on the View tab, click the **Page Width** button. The document display expands to the width of the window.

9. Finally, in the Zoom command group, click the **100%** button to return document to its normal size.

PAUSE. LEAVE the document open to use in the next exercise.

Another Way
You can also click the percentage displayed to the left of the Zoom slider to open the Zoom dialog box.

Changing Window Views

The commands in the Window command group enable you to open and arrange multiple document windows. In this exercise, you learn to manipulate your screen by creating a second document in a new window, arranging multiple open documents on one screen, splitting a single document to view different parts, viewing multiple documents side by side, and switching between windows.

The commands in the Window command group are as follows:

- The **New Window** button opens a new window displaying the current document; this window shows the document name in the title bar followed by the number 2. Each new window you open in the same document receives a chronologically numbered name.

- The **Arrange All** button displays two or more windows on the screen at the same time. This is useful when comparing documents or when using information from multiple documents.

- The **Split** command divides one document window into two windows that scroll independently. This enables you to view two parts of a single document at the same time.

- The **View Side by Side** button allows you to view two documents next to each other. When you are viewing documents side by side, you can use the **Synchronous Scrolling** command to link the scrolling of the two documents so that you move through both at the same time. The **Reset Window Position** command repositions two side-by-side documents to appear equally sized on the screen.

- The **Switch Windows** button allows you to select which document will be the active document (the document that is ready for editing). The name of the active document appears on the title bar.

On occasion, you may need to move a window out of the way without exiting the associated application. This is where the three buttons in the upper-right corner of the Word screen come in handy. The Minimize button ▬ minimizes the window display—in other words, the window disappears and is replaced with an icon on the status bar. The Restore button 🗗 returns a document to its previous size by minimizing or maximizing its display. Finally, the Close button ✕ closes the window.

STEP BY STEP   **Change Window Views**

USE the document that is open from the previous exercise.

1. In the Window command group, click the New Window button. A new window with *proposal:2* in the document title bar appears and becomes the active document.

2. In the Window command group, click the Switch Windows button. A menu of open windows appears, as shown in Figure 2-9.

Figure 2-9

Switch Windows button and menu

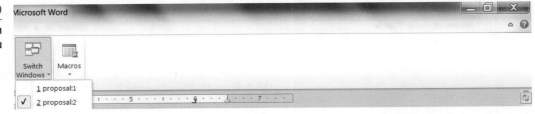

3. In the Switch Windows drop-down menu, click *proposal:1*. The original document becomes the active document.

4. Click the Arrange All button. Word displays the two windows, one above the other, on your screen, as shown in Figure 2-10.

5. Click the View Side by Side button to arrange the windows beside each other on the screen.

6. Note that Synchronous Scrolling is on by default. Place your insertion point on the slider in the vertical scroll bar and press the left mouse button as you move the slider up and down to scroll through the documents; notice that both scroll simultaneously.

7. On the document title bar, click the *proposal:2* document; this now becomes the active document.

8. Click the Synchronous Scrolling button to turn off that feature. Place your insertion point on the vertical scroll bar and scroll down; notice that the *proposal:2* document is now scrolling independently.

Document Title bar

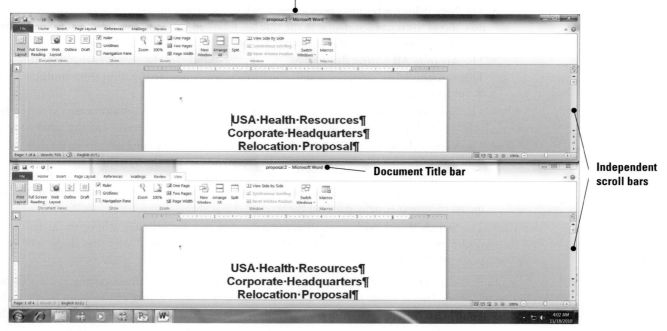

Independent scroll bars

Figure 2-10

Two windows displayed using the Arrange All command

9. Click the **Close** button to close the *proposal:2* document.

10. Click the **Maximize** button on the *proposal:1* document to fill the screen.

11. Click the **Split** button. Notice you now have a horizontal split bar and a double-sided arrow. Position the split bar below Relocation Proposal and click the mouse button. The document window splits in two and the **Split** button changes to a **Remove Split** button (see Figure 2-11).

Figure 2-11

Split window and Remove Split button

Split changes to Remove Split

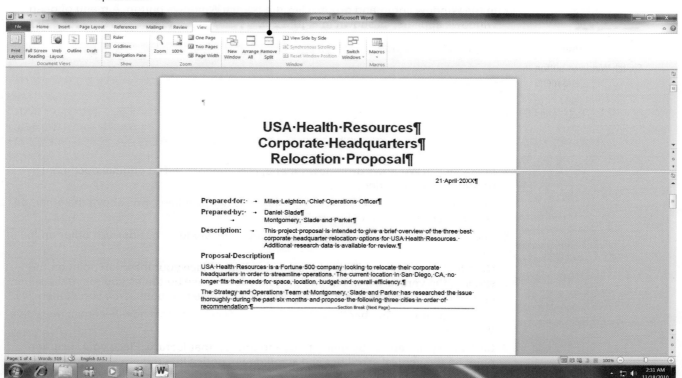

12. Click **Remove Split**.

13. Click the **Minimize** button, as shown in Figure 2-12. The document minimizes to become an icon in the Windows task bar at the bottom of the screen, and the desktop appears.

Figure 2-12

Document minimized to task bar

14. Click the *proposal* document's icon in the task bar to maximize the document back on the screen.

15. Click the **Restore** button to return the document to its minimized view.

16. Position the mouse pointer on the lower-right corner of the document window where you see the pattern of dots. Your mouse pointer becomes a double-sided arrow, or handle, as shown in Figure 2-13.

Figure 2-13

The double-sided arrow is a resize handle.

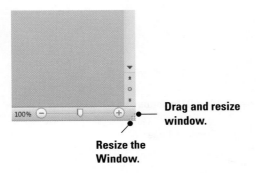

Drag and resize window.

Resize the Window.

17. Click and drag the handle toward the middle of the screen to decrease the size of the window.

18. Click the sizing corner again and drag it to the lower-right corner of the Word screen to increase the size of the window. Drag until the window fills the screen.

PAUSE. LEAVE the document open to use in the next exercise.

NAVIGATING AND SEARCHING THROUGH A DOCUMENT

The Bottom Line

As you already learned, the Navigation Pane contains commands for moving and searching through a document. You also can use Find command options, the mouse, scroll bars, and various keystroke and keyboard shortcut commands to navigate through Word documents. In this section, you practice using the mouse and scroll bar, keystroke commands, the Navigation Pane, and a number of command group commands to move quickly through a document; search for specific text, graphics, or other document elements; and remove or replace those elements.

Scroll bars allow a user to move up or down or side to side within a document. In Word, a vertical scroll bar appears on the right side of the document window, as shown in Figure 2-14; if the window view is larger than the viewing area, a horizontal scroll bar also appears at the bottom of the window to allow you to scroll left and right across the width of the document. You can click the **scroll buttons** to move up or down one line at a time, or you can click and hold a scroll button to scroll more quickly. You can also click and drag the **scroll box** to move through a document even faster or just click the scroll box to see a ScreenTip displaying your position in the document.

At the bottom of the vertical scroll bar, you can click the Previous Page button to move back to the previous page or click the Next Page button to move to the following page. Clicking the Select Browse Object button produces a pop-up menu displaying a number of different command buttons that enable you to jump to a new location within the document. In addition to Go To and Find, the commands in this box enable you to browse by field, endnote, footnote, comment, section, page, edits, headings, graphic, or tables.

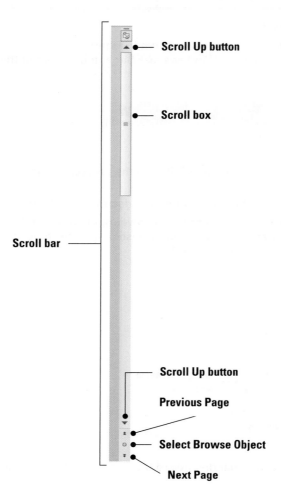

Figure 2-14

Scroll bar, scroll box, and scroll
buttons

Scroll Up button

Scroll box

Scroll bar

Scroll Up button

Previous Page

Select Browse Object

Next Page

Using the Mouse and Scroll Bar to Navigate

Using the mouse in combination with the scroll bar is a simple way to scroll through a document.

| STEP BY STEP | **Use the Mouse and Scroll Bar to Navigate** |

USE the document that is open from the previous exercise.

1. Click the Scroll Down button to scroll down one line at a time.
2. Click and hold the Scroll Down button until you scroll all the way to the end of the document.
3. Position the mouse pointer on the scroll box. Click and hold to see a ScreenTip identifying your current location in the document (see Figure 2-15).
4. Drag the scroll box all the way to the top of the scroll bar; the view quickly scrolls to the beginning of the document.
5. Click the Select Browse Object button. A menu appears with various commands you can use to browse for specific text or elements within your document (see Figure 2-16).

Figure 2-15

Scroll box ScreenTip

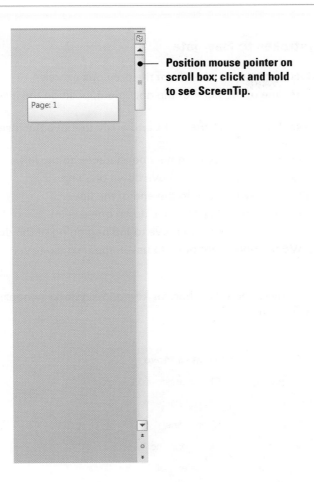

Page: 1

Position mouse pointer on scroll box; click and hold to see ScreenTip.

Figure 2-16

Select Browse Object menu

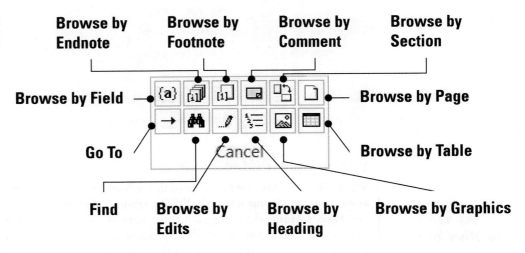

Browse by Endnote

Browse by Footnote

Browse by Comment

Browse by Section

Browse by Field

Browse by Page

Go To

Browse by Table

Cancel

Find

Browse by Edits

Browse by Heading

Browse by Graphics

6. Move the mouse pointer over each button to see its name appear in the display box.

7. Click in a **blank space** in the document to remove the menu.

PAUSE. LEAVE the document open to use in the next exercise.

Using Keystrokes to Navigate

The arrow keys and other keyboard commands can also help you move through a document.

Use Keystrokes to Navigate

USE the document that is open from the previous exercise.

1. In the first line of the body of the document, position the insertion point before the U in USA.

2. On the keyboard, press the **Right arrow** key to move the insertion point one character to the right.

3. Press the **Left arrow** key to move one character to the left.

4. Press the **Down arrow** key to move down one line.

5. Press the **End** key to move to the end of the line.

6. Press the **Page Down** key to move down one screen.

7. Press the **Ctrl+Home** keys to move to the beginning of the document.

PAUSE. LEAVE the document open to use in the next exercise.

Table 2-1 lists these and other shortcut keys and keystroke commands you can use to navigate through a document.

Table 2-1

Keyboard shortcuts for navigating a document

Shortcut Key	Related Move
Left arrow	One character to the left
Right arrow	One character to the right
Up arrow	Up one line
Down arrow	Down one line
End	To the end of the line
Home	To the beginning of the line
Page up	Up one screen
Page down	Down one screen
Ctrl+Page down	Down one page
Ctrl+Page up	Up one page
Ctrl+Home	To beginning of the document
Ctrl+End	To end of the document

Searching within a Document

NEW to Office 2010

Word's Find command is now located in the Navigation Pane in the Show group on the View tab, as well as on the Home tab in the Editing group. Either of these approaches will open the Navigation Pane. By using the Navigation Pane, you can easily locate specific text, graphics, objects, and equations within a document. The document will contain highlighted text, and the Navigation Pane will display the results in a yellow border. The third tab, Browse the results from your current search, will place the results in the order they appear in the document. In this exercise, you learn to use the Navigation Pane to search for every occurrence of a specific word within a document.

In the Home tab on the Editing group, the drop-down arrow by the Find button displays a menu that contains the Find, Advanced Find, Replace, and Go To commands. The Find command opens the Navigation Pane; the Advanced Find command opens the Find and Replace dialog box with Find as the active tab; the Replace command opens the Find and Replace dialog box with Replace as the active tab; and the Go To command opens the same dialog box with Go To as the active tab.

Figure 2-17

Navigation Pane displaying
additional options

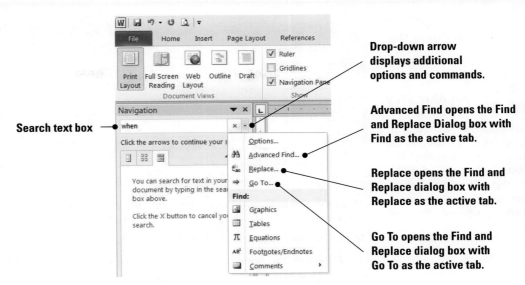

Search text box

Drop-down arrow
displays additional
options and commands.

Advanced Find opens the Find
and Replace Dialog box with
Find as the active tab.

Replace opens the Find and
Replace dialog box with
Replace as the active tab.

Go To opens the Find and
Replace dialog box with
Go To as the active tab.

To highlight every occurrence of a particular word or phrase in your document, you must activate Advanced Find. To do so, click the drop-down arrow by the Search text box, as shown in Figure 2-17, then click Advanced Find. The Find and Replace dialog box opens; within that box, key your desired word or phrase, then click the drop-down arrow on the Reading Highlight button and select Highlight All. When you close the Find and Replace dialog box, each instance of your desired word or phrase is highlighted in the document. To clear all occurrences of highlighted text, return to the Advanced Find options, click the Reading Highlight button, and then select Clear Highlighting.

STEP BY STEP   **Use the Navigation Pane to Search for Text in a Document**

USE the document that is open from the previous exercise.

1. Click the View tab; then, in the Show command group, click the Navigation Pane check box. The Navigation Pane opens.
2. Key relocation in the Search text box; the text is highlighted in the document and in the Browse Headings, Browse Pages, and Browse Results tabs of the Navigation Pane.
3. Click the third tab, Browse the results from your current search. Note that the found text is bolded, and it appears in the order of its occurrence in the document.
4. Click the first tab, Browse the headings in your document, and note highlighted headings. Then click the second tab, Browse the pages in your document, and note the highlighted found text in the thumbnails.
5. Click the Browse the pages in your document tab and click each thumbnail. Use the scroll bar to navigate to thumbnail four, then click that thumbnail.
6. Click the X in the Search text box to end your search. Press Ctrl+Home to move the insertion point to the beginning of the document.
7. Click the magnifying glass icon on the right side of the Navigation Pane box to produce a list of available options.
8. Click the Advanced Find button. The Find and Replace dialog box opens.
9. The word "relocation" should be in the Find what text box; click the Find Next button. Click the Reading Highlight button to Highlight All instances of this word. Then click Close (see Figure 2-18).

Figure 2-18

Reading Highlight

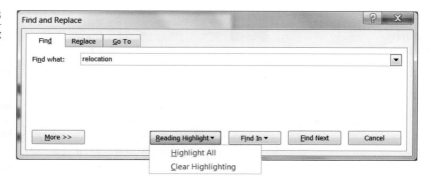

Another Way
To open the Navigation Pane using the keyboard, press Ctrl+F. You can also click the Navigation Pane button in the Show group of the View tab, or you can click the drop-down arrow in the Editing group on the Home tab.

Take Note

10. In the Show command group, click the Navigation Pane check box to turn off this pane.

To end your search, click the X in the text box.

11. **SAVE** the document as *proposal_1* in the lesson folder of your USB flash drive.

PAUSE. LEAVE the document open to use in the next exercise.

For more search options, click the More>> button in the Find and Replace dialog box. In the Search Options area that appears, you can choose additional criteria to refine the search process—for example, you can opt to match case or whole words only. You can also use **wildcard** characters to find words or phrases that contain specific letters or combinations of letters. Simply key a question mark (?) to represent a single character—for example, keying **b?t** will find *bat, bet, bit,* and *but.* Similarly, key an asterisk (*) to represent a string of characters—for example, **m*t** will find *mat, moment,* or even *medium format.*

Within the Find and Replace dialog box, you can click the Format button to find text with specific formatting, such as a particular font, paragraph setting, or style. You can also click the Special button to find special elements in a document, such as fields, footnote marks, or section breaks.

Replacing Text in a Document

Located on the Home tab in the Editing group, the Replace command opens the Find and Replace dialog box. You can use the Replace command to replace one word or phrase with another. You can also use the Find and Replace command to search for and **replace** formatting—such as a specific font color, bolding, or italics. It is also possible to search for and replace special characters and document elements such as page breaks and tabs. In this exercise, you learn to search for and replace a word with a particular type of formatting.

STEP BY STEP   **Replace Text in a Document**

USE the document that is open from the previous exercise.

1. Place the insertion point at the beginning of the document by pressing Ctrl+Home.

2. Click the Home tab to make it active. In the Editing group, click the Replace button; the Find and Replace dialog box opens.

3. Click the More>> button to review the options, then click the <<Less button to hide them.

4. In the Find what box, key Montgomery, Slade and Parker. (If "relocation" appears in the Find what box, select it and press Delete, then key in the new search string.)

5. In the Replace with box, key Becker, Steele and Castillo.

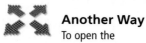

Another Way
To open the Replace tab in the Find and Replace dialog box using the keyboard, press Ctrl+H.

6. Click Find Next. Word searches for the first occurrence of the phrase Montgomery, Slade and Parker and highlights it.

7. Click Replace All. Word searches for all occurrences of the phrase Montgomery, Slade and Parker and replaces them with Becker, Steele and Castillo. Word then displays a message revealing how many replacements were made, as shown in Figure 2-19.

Navigation Pane

Drop-down arrow retains information from previous search.

Drop-down arrow retains information from previous replacement.

Find Next button

More>> button: additional features available

Replace All will replace all found instances in document.

Prompt displaying the number of replacements made in document.

Replace will replace only one found instance.

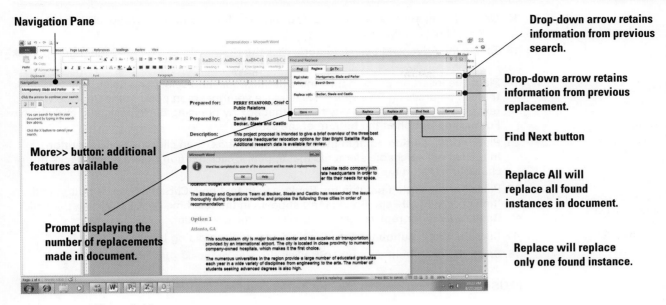

Figure 2-19

Find and Replace message

8. Click **OK**.

9. Position the insertion point at the beginning of the document. Click the **View** tab; then, in the Show command group, click the **Navigation Pane** check box. Click the drop-down arrow or magnifier so that the ScreenTip displays Find Options and additional search commands, then click **Replace**. In the Find what text box, key **Becker, Steele and Castillo**; then, in the Replace with text box, key **Montgomery, Slade and Parker**. Keep your insertion point in the Replace text box.

10. Click the **More>>** button to expand the dialog box to include additional search and replace options (see Figure 2-20).

11. Click the **Format** button and select **Font** from the drop-down list; the Find Font dialog box appears. In the Font area, use the scroll bar to scroll to Garamond, and then click to select it. In the Font Style area, select **Bold Italics**, size **14**. Click the **Font Color** drop-down arrow, then select **dark red** in the Standard Colors chart and click **OK**. Below the Replace With text box, you will see the format selections. Click **Replace All**; two replacements will be completed. Click **OK**, then **Close**.

Figure 2-20

Find and Replace dialog box with Search Options

<< Less button will display less options.

Options to control how search will be conducted

Removes formatting in the Find what and Replace with text boxes

Replace formatting displayed

Format button with options to select

Special button with options to select

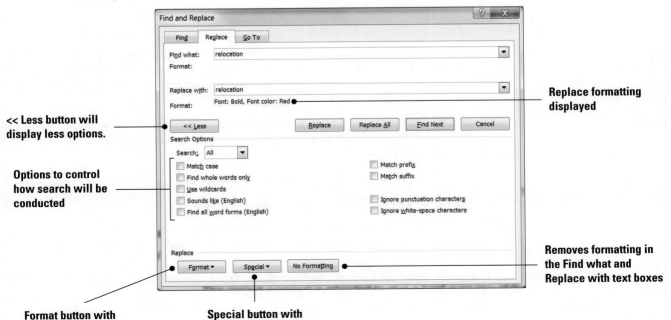

12. On the Navigation Pane, click the X, or on the Show command group, click the check box for Navigation Pane.

13. To use the Advanced Search feature, click the Home tab, and in the Editing group, click Replace.

14. Place the insertion point in the Find what text box, and select and delete any text in the box by pressing Backspace. Next, place your insertion point in the Replace with text box, select and delete any text in that box by pressing Backspace, and click the No Formatting button at the bottom of the screen.

15. Place your insertion point in the Find what text box, then click the Special button. In the list of searchable elements that appears, click Section Break; Word places the characters (^b) in the text box.

16. Place your insertion point in the Replace with text box. Click the Special button and then click Manual Page Break; (^m) appears in the text box. Click Find Next, then click Replace All. Four replacements are made in the document.

17. Click the Close button to close the Find and Replace dialog box.

18. **SAVE** the document on your USB flash drive as *proposal_update*, then **CLOSE** the document.

PAUSE. LEAVE Word open to use in the next exercise.

 Ref

Take Note

Section breaks are covered in Lesson 5.

You can use the Find and Replace tool to replace specific punctuation within a document. For instance, say you pressed the spacebar twice at the end of each sentence and you would like to replace each set of two spaces with only one space. In the Find What text box, press the **spacebar** twice; then, in the Replace with text box, press the **spacebar** once and click the Replace All button. Upon doing this, Word replaces all instances of double spacing with single spaces.

When replacing text, you can confirm each replacement to make sure it is correct by clicking Replace instead of Replace All.

 Troubleshooting If you experience problems when using the Replace command to replace formatting or one of the special elements, display the Find and Replace dialog box again. Review the Find what text box for correct spelling or correct element. Below the Replace with text box is the Formatting to replace text. For instance, if you are replacing search text with a color and bold as the style, below the Replace with text box, you will see *Font: Bold, Font color: Red* (see Figure 2-20).

Using the Go To Command to Navigate a Long Document

The *booksbeyond* file for this lesson is available on the book companion website or in WileyPLUS.

In a longer document, you may need to move through the document more quickly than is possible by scrolling. The **Go To** command and Select Browse Object button provide ways to navigate through longer documents quickly. In this exercise, you learn to use the Go To command to move through a lengthy document.

Using the Go To command will jump to a specific page, table, graphic, equation, or other item in your document. To go to the next or previous item of the same type, leave the Enter box empty, then click Previous or Next.

STEP BY STEP **Use the Go To Command**

OPEN the *booksbeyond* document from the lesson folder.

1. On the Home tab, in the Editing group, click the drop-down arrow next to the Find button, then click Go To.

2. The Go To tab of the Find and Replace dialog box is displayed, as shown in Figure 2-21.

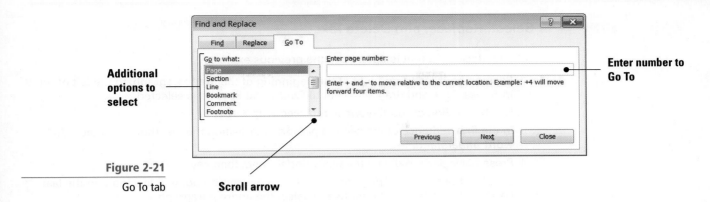

Additional options to select

Enter number to Go To

Figure 2-21

Go To tab

Scroll arrow

3. In the Go to what box, Page is selected by default. In the Enter page number box, key 6, then click Go To. The insertion point moves to page 6 of the document.

4. In the Go to what box, select **Line**. In the Enter line number box, key **23**, then click **Go To**. The insertion point moves to line 23 in the document.

5. In the Go to what box, scroll down and select **Field**. In the Enter field name box, Any Field displays. Click **Next**. The insertion point moves to the field. Click **Close**.

6. In the bottom-right corner of the vertical scroll bar, locate and click the **Select Browse Object** command, then click the **Go To** command. The Find and Replace dialog appears.

7. Click the **Select Browse Object** command, then click the Find command and key **books**. Click **Find Next** until all occurrences are found. A prompt will appear when Word has finished searching. Click **OK**.

8. Click the **Cancel** button to close the Find and Replace dialog box.

PAUSE. LEAVE the document open to use in the next exercise.

Another Way
To open the Go To tab in the Find and Replace dialog box using the keyboard, press Ctrl+G or use the Select Browse Object command.

Take Note   Word keeps track of the last three locations where you keyed or edited text. To go to a previous editing location in your document, press Shift+F5.

SELECTING, REPLACING, AND DELETING TEXT

The Bottom Line   Word offers a number of tools for selecting, deleting, and replacing text. You also can apply formatting to selected text. In this exercise, you use the mouse and keyboard to select text and delete it or replace it with new text.

Selecting, Replacing, and Deleting Text

You can delete text in Word documents by pressing the Backspace key to delete characters to the left of the insertion point, pressing the Delete key to delete characters to the right of the insertion point, or selecting text and pressing either the Delete key or Backspace key. In this exercise, you learn to select and delete text and to key in replacement text. You also practice using the Undo and Redo buttons in the Quick Access Toolbar.

The **multi-selection** feature of Word enables you to select multiple text items that are not adjacent. For example, to select every other line in a paragraph, select the first line, then press and hold the Ctrl key as you select the other lines by clicking the left mouse button. To replace text in a Word document, simply select the text, then key new text. To cancel a selection, click in any blank area of the document screen.

STEP BY STEP   **Select, Replace, and Delete Text**

USE the document that is open from the previous exercise.

1. Position your insertion point at the beginning of the first paragraph, to the left of the *B* in *Books*. Click and drag across until Books and Beyond is selected.

2. Key B & B. *Books and Beyond* is replaced with *B & B*.

3. In the first sentence of the second paragraph, position the insertion point after the word *understand*.

4. Press Backspace to delete the word *understand*, then key realize.

5. Scroll to the bottom of page one. Position the insertion point in any word in the last paragraph. Triple-click the mouse to select the entire paragraph.

6. Click in a blank part of the page, such as the margin, to deselect the paragraph. Then place your insertion point at the beginning of the last paragraph on the first page, beginning with *I understand if I have . . .* and click.

7. Move the pointer to the end of the sentence (*HR Department.*), press the Ctrl key, and click. The sentence is now selected.

8. Press Backspace to delete the sentence.

9. Click the Undo ↶ button in the Quick Access Toolbar to undo the action.

10. Click the Redo ↷ button in the Quick Access Toolbar to redo the action.

11. **SAVE** the document as *booksbeyond_updates* in the lesson folder on your USB flash drive.

PAUSE. LEAVE the document open to use in the next exercise.

Another Way
The Select button in the Editing command group of the Home tab lets you select all text in a document, select objects behind text, or select text with similar formatting.

As you've seen, when you position the mouse pointer to the left of the margin, it changes to a selection arrow that enables you to click to select the entire line to the right of the pointer. You then can drag down to continue selecting adjacent words, lines of text, or entire paragraphs. Table 2-2 lists this and other techniques for selecting text with the mouse.

Table 2-2

Selecting text with the mouse

To Select	Do This
Any amount of text	Click and drag across the text
A word	Double-click the word
A line	Click in the left margin with the mouse pointer
Multiple lines	Click and drag in the left margin
A sentence	Hold Ctrl and click anywhere in the sentence
A paragraph	Double-click in the left margin or triple-click in the paragraph
The entire document	Triple-click in the left margin

You also can use keyboard commands to select text. Table 2-3 shows various keyboard shortcuts you can press to select text.

Table 2-3

Selecting text with the keyboard

To Select	Key This
One character to the right	Shift+Right Arrow
One character to the left	Shift+Left Arrow
To the end of a word	Ctrl+Shift+Right Arrow
To the beginning of a word	Ctrl+Shift+Left Arrow
To the end of a line	Shift+End
To the beginning of a line	Shift+Home
To the end of a document	Ctrl+Shift+End
To the beginning of a document	Ctrl+Shift+Home
The entire document	Ctrl+A
To the end of a paragraph	Ctrl+Shift+Down Arrow

CUTTING, COPYING, AND PASTING TEXT

The Bottom Line

It is often necessary to copy or remove text from one location in a document and place it in another. When you **cut** text, Word removes it from the original location and places the deleted text in the Clipboard collection. When you **copy** text, Word places a duplicate copy in the Clipboard. The **Paste** command then pastes text from the Clipboard to a new location in either the original document or a new document. In this exercise, you learn two different ways to copy and move text—using the Clipboard and using the mouse.

NEW to Office 2010

Entries placed in the Clipboard can be placed anywhere in a document by positioning the insertion point in the new location then selecting one of the three Paste options shown in Table 2-4 and Figure 2-22.

Table 2-4

Paste option descriptions

Paste Option	Description	Sample Item Placed on Clipboard	How Item Displays When Pasted
Keep source formatting	Keeps the selected text with the original format, including hyperlinks	**FORMATTING** **WILEYPLUS.COM**	**FORMATTING** **WILEYPLUS.COM**
Merge formatting	If the text contains fonts of different sizes and colors, the paste will produce black text with Calibri (Body) 12-point formatting	Paste	Paste
Keep text only	Regardless of its font, size, and formatting, when pasted, the text will appear in 10-point Calibri (Body).	**College**	College

Copying and Moving Text with Clipboard Commands

The Clipboard enables you to cut or copy multiple items and paste them into any Office document. In this exercise, you learn to use the Clipboard command group on the Home tab to copy and move text.

Figure 2-22

Paste options

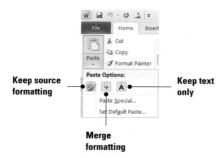

Keep source formatting

Keep text only

Merge formatting

Collected items stay on the Clipboard until all Office programs are closed or you click the Clear All button in the Clipboard task pane. The Clipboard holds up to 24 items; if another item is added, the first item is deleted from the Clipboard and the latest item is placed at the top of the list. Each entry in the Clipboard includes an icon representing the source Office program and a portion of copied text or a thumbnail of a copied graphic. By default, when text is selected, a message appears on the status bar showing how many words are selected and the total number of words in the document.

STEP BY STEP   ## Use the Clipboard to Copy and Move Text

USE the document that is open from the previous exercise.

1. Select the **first paragraph** of the document.
2. On the Home tab, in the Clipboard group, click the **Cut** button.
3. Click to place the insertion point in front of the first character of the sentence that begins "*Only the president . . .*"
4. Click the **Clipboard** command group dialog box launcher to display the Clipboard task pane.
5. In the list of cut items, move your mouse pointer to the text you cut in step 2, and click the drop-down arrow to produce the menu shown in Figure 2-23.

Figure 2-23

Clipboard task pane options

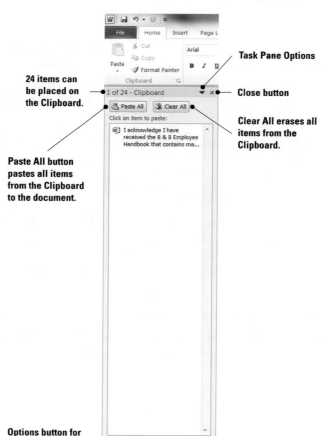

24 items can be placed on the Clipboard.

Task Pane Options

Close button

Clear All erases all items from the Clipboard.

Paste All button pastes all items from the Clipboard to the document.

Options button for displaying the Clipboard

Another Way

To copy an item to the Clipboard using the keyboard, select the item, then press Ctrl+C. To cut a selected item using the keyboard, press Ctrl+X. To paste the item most recently collected on the Clipboard, click to locate the insertion point, then press Ctrl+V on the keyboard. To produce a pop-up menu containing Cut, Copy, and Paste commands, right-click in the document.

6. Click **Paste** to insert the text into the document in the new location.

7. Click the **Close** button on the Clipboard task pane.

PAUSE. LEAVE the document open to use in the next exercise.

Take Note   Your Clipboard task pane may look different depending on how many items have been collected.

The Options drop-down arrow at the bottom of the Clipboard task pane offers multiple options for displaying the Clipboard. Table 2-5 describes these options.

Table 2-5

Options for displaying
the Clipboard

Option	Description
Show Office Clipboard Automatically	Automatically displays the Clipboard when copying.
Show Office Clipboard When Ctrl+C Pressed Twice	Automatically displays the Clipboard when you press Ctrl+C twice.
Collect Without Showing Office Clipboard	The Clipboard is not displayed when copying or cutting text.
Show Office Clipboard Icon on Taskbar	Displays the Clipboard icon in the status area of the system task bar when the Clipboard is active. Turned on by default.
Show Office Near Taskbar When Copying	Displays the "collected item" message when copying items to the Clipboard. Turned on by default.

Using the Mouse to Copy or Move Text

To move a selection of text, use your mouse to drag and drop the selection in a new location. Hold the Ctrl key while you drag to copy the text. When you are moving text by dragging, the pointer shows a box, and when you are copying text by dragging, the pointer shows a box with a plus sign (+). Text that you move or copy using the mouse is not stored in the Clipboard collection.

STEP BY STEP   **Use the Mouse to Copy or Move Text**

USE the document that is open from the previous exercise.

1. Select the second paragraph on the first page, beginning with "*I acknowledge I have received . . .*"

2. Press the **Ctrl** key as you click, then drag the selected phrase and drop it above the last paragraph on the first page. The pointer shows a plus sign (+) as you drag, indicating that you are copying the selected text.

3. Click **Undo**.

4. Select the third paragraph, beginning with "*Only the president . . .*" Hold the left mouse button, and drag and drop the selected text to position it above the second paragraph on the first page. Notice the phrase is moved to the new location. Click **Undo**.

5. **SAVE** the document in the lesson folder on your USB flash drive.

CLOSE Microsoft Word.

 **Troubleshooting**   By default, drag-and-drop editing is turned on so that you can drag the pointer to move and copy text. This option can be turned on or off in Backstage view. To do so, click the File tab, then click Word Options. Click Advanced and, under Editing options, select or clear the Allow Text to Be Dragged and Dropped check box.

SKILL SUMMARY

In This Lesson, You Learned How To:
Change and organize document views
Navigate and search through a document
Select, replace, and delete text
Cut, copy, and paste text

Knowledge Assessment

True/False

Circle T if the statement is true or F if the statement is false.

T   F   1. The New Window command launches a new window that contains the current document.

T   F   2. By selecting text, the user has the ability to change the font and font size, bolding, and deleting text.

T   F   3. Full Screen Reading view displays the document as it will look when printed.

T   F   4. The Zoom slider is located in the View menu.

T   F   5. The Synchronous Scrolling button is used when viewing documents side by side.

T   F   6. The Switch Windows command allows you to toggle between documents.

T   F   7. Double-clicking a word in a document will select the word.

T   F   8. When you key text in the search box while in the Navigation Pane, Word highlights this text by bolding the results in the document.

T   F   9. The Arrange All command places all open documents in a separate window on the screen.

T   F   10. You can use the Navigation Pane to search for words or phrases in a document.

Multiple Choice

Select the best response for the following statements.

1. Which Word feature enables you to select multiple pieces of text that are not next to each other?
   a. Multi-selection feature
   b. Multi-task feature
   c. Multi-select all text feature
   d. Ctrl+A feature

2. _____ are reduced-size versions of images.
   a. Thumbdrives
   b. Thumb documents
   c. Thumbnails
   d. Preview panes

3. The Split command will split a document:
   a. vertically.
   b. in a new window.
   c. side by side.
   d. horizontally.

4. In what view is Synchronous Scrolling active?
   a. Split
   b. Arrange All
   c. New Window
   d. View Side by Side

5. When Heading Styles have been applied to a document, the user has the option to navigate through the document using which tab on the Navigation Pane?
   a. Browse the headings
   b. Browse the pages
   c. Browse the results from your current search
   d. None of the above

6. Commands for replacing text with formatted text are located in the:
   a. Find and Replace dialog box.
   b. Advanced Options in the Navigation Pane.
   c. dialog box that opens when you press Ctrl+H.
   d. All of the above

7. The keyboard shortcut for finding text is:
   a. Ctrl+H.
   b. Ctrl+F.
   c. Ctrl+G.
   d. Ctrl+5.

8. The Replace command can be opened using:
   a. the Find and Replace dialog box.
   b. Ctrl+H.
   c. Advanced Options in the Navigation Pane.
   d. All of the above

9. Which wildcard would you use to find a single character?
   a. ?
   b. *
   c. **
   d. ??

10. The Go To command allows you to navigate by page, text, graphics, equations, or tables by initiating the:
    a. Select Browse Object command.
    b. F5 shortcut key.
    c. Find and Replace dialog box.
    d. All of the above.

Project 2-1: Updating a Sign

The Grand Street Coffee Shop places a sign on the door and near the order counter listing the featured coffees of the day. You need to update today's sign.

GET READY. LAUNCH Word if it is not already running.

1. Click the File tab and choose Open.
2. Click the location of the data files for this lesson.
3. Locate and open the *sign* document.
4. Click the File tab, then Save as. In the File name box, key *newsign.*
5. Click Save.
6. Position the I-beam before the *M* in *Morning Blend*. Drag over the words to select *Morning Blend*.
7. Key Grand Street Blend.
8. Click the Home tab. In the Editing group, click Replace.
9. Place the insertion point in the Find What text box and key Kona Blend.
10. Click in the Replace With text box and key Hawaiian Blend.
11. Click the More >> button.
12. Click the Format button and select Font. In the Font text box, click the scroll bar down arrow and select Comic Sans MS; for the Style, select Bold Italics; for the font size, select 26; and for the font color, select dark blue in the Standard Colors. Click OK, then click the << Less button.
13. Click Find Next, then the Replace button. Click OK, then Close.
14. Position the I-beam before the *T* in *Try Me* and click to place the insertion point.
15. Key $1 and press the spacebar.
16. In the next line, double-click the word Mocha to select it.
17. Key White Chocolate.
18. Click the View tab. In the Zoom group, click One Page.
19. Click Page Width.
20. Click the File tab and choose Save As from the menu.
21. Locate your USB flash drive.
22. **SAVE** the document in the lesson folder on your USB flash drive.
23. Click the File tab. Point to Print preview, then click Print.
24. Click the File tab and select Close.

PAUSE. LEAVE Word open for the next project.

@ The *sign* file for this lesson is available on the book companion website or in WileyPLUS.

Project 2-2: Editing a Job Description

Star Bright Satellite Radio is hiring. Edit the job description so that it can be sent to the human resources department for processing and posting.

GET READY. LAUNCH Word if it is not already running.

1. Click the File tab and choose Open.
2. Click the location of the data files for this lesson. Locate and click *jobdescription* one time to select it. Click Open.
3. Click the File tab, then Save as. In the File name box, key *updatedjobdescription*.
4. In the second line of the document, position the I-beam before the *D* in *Date* and click to place the insertion point.

@ The *jobdescription* file for this lesson is available on the book companion website or in WileyPLUS.

5. Beginning at the *D*, click and drag down and to the right until Date Posted and the line below it, *5/15/10*, is selected.

6. Press **Backspace** to delete both lines.

7. In the Duties & Responsibilities heading, position the insertion point before the *&*. Press **Shift** and then press the **Right arrow** key to select *&*.

8. Key **and**. The *&* is replaced with the word *and*.

9. Position the mouse pointer in the left margin beside the line in the first bulleted list that reads *Define the web site's look and feel*. Click to select the line.

10. Press the **Delete** key to delete the line.

11. In the *Education and/or Experience* heading, position the I-beam to the right of the letter r in *or*.

12. Press **Backspace** three times to delete the *r*, *o*, and */*.

13. In the first line of the bulleted list that begins *College degree required* . . ., click to position the insertion point after m*aster's degree*.

14. Press the **spacebar** and key **preferred**.

15. Click the **View** tab. In the Zoom command group, click **Zoom**, click **75%**, and click **OK**. Click **Page Wide**, then click **100%** on the Zoom command group.

16. Save the document in the lesson folder on your USB flash drive.

17. **CLOSE** the file.

PAUSE. LEAVE Word open for the next project.

Proficiency Assessment

Project 2-3: Creating a Schedule

You are chair of the New Neighbor Welcoming Committee in your neighborhood. The group meets monthly at a committee member's house. A different committee member is responsible for bringing refreshments to each meeting. Use Word to create a schedule to share with members, then view the document in different views.

GET READY. LAUNCH Word if it is not already running.

@ The *schedule* file for this lesson is available on the book companion website or in WileyPLUS.

1. **OPEN** *schedule* from the data files for this lesson. Save the file as *updatedschedule* in the lesson folder of your USB flash drive.

2. For the May 11 meeting details, key **D. Lorenzo, 7501 Oak, 8 p.m.** Beside *refreshments*, key **S. Wilson**.

3. The June 15 meeting details are **R. Mason, 7620 Oak, 8 p.m.**, and **J. Estes** is bringing the refreshments.

4. View the document in a **New Window**. Then click **Switch windows**.

5. Click **Web Layout**, then click **Draft** view.

6. Click the **Split** button, and position the split under the second title, *Meeting and Refreshment Schedule*. Click **Remove Split**.

7. Close *updatedschedule*.

8. **SAVE** the document in the lesson folder on your USB flash drive, then **CLOSE** the file.

PAUSE. LEAVE Word open for the next project.

Project 2-4: Finding and Replacing Text

In this exercise, you find and replace text using the Format and Special buttons.

GET READY. LAUNCH Word if it is not already running.

@ The *computeruse2* file for this lesson is available on the book companion website or in WileyPLUS.

1. **OPEN** *computeruse2* from the data files for this lesson.
2. **SAVE** the document as *computer_update* in the lesson folder on your USB flash drive.
3. Use the Advanced Find command to find all occurrences of the word attorney and highlight them.
4. Use the Find and Replace dialog box to replace all paragraph marks in the document with manual line breaks. Then place your insertion point at the beginning of the document.
5. Open the Navigation Pane and use the search box to find the word section in the document. Review the second and third tabs to see the found text.
6. Use the Select Browse Object button in the scroll bar, go to page 4, and then go to line 25.
7. **SAVE** the document in the lesson folder on your USB flash drive, then **CLOSE** the document.

PAUSE. LEAVE Word open for the next project.

Mastery Assessment

Project 2-5: Fixing the Coffee Shop Menu

A co-worker at the Grand Coffee Shop has been working on a new menu for the coffee shop. She asks you to take a look at it before she sends it to a graphic designer. You find the old menu file and decide to compare the two.

GET READY. LAUNCH Word if it is not already running.

@ The *menu* file for this lesson is available on the book companion website or in WileyPLUS.

@ The *oldmenu* file for this lesson is available on the book companion website or in WileyPLUS.

1. **OPEN** *menu* from the data files for this lesson.
2. **OPEN** *oldmenu* from the data files for this lesson.
3. View the two files side by side to compare them.
4. Find and insert the two items that are missing from the new menu.
5. Find and change five pricing errors on the new menu.
6. **SAVE** the corrected menu as *newmenu* in the lesson folder on your USB flash drive, then CLOSE the file.
7. **CLOSE** the *oldmenu* file.

PAUSE. LEAVE Word open for the next project.

Project 2-6: Creating a Memo

Create a memo to committee members to include with the schedule you created in Project 2-3.

GET READY. LAUNCH Word if it is not already running.

@ The *schedulememo* file for this lesson is available on the book companion website or in WileyPLUS.

1. **OPEN** *schedulememo* from the data files for this lesson.
2. Place your insertion point on the second paragraph mark after the subject line and key the following:

Thank you for volunteering to be on the New Neighbor Welcoming Committee. Enclosed please find the meeting and refreshment schedule for the next six months. See you in January!

Committee Members:

3. **SAVE** the file as *deschedulememo*.

4. **OPEN** the *updatedschedule* document you saved in Project 2-3.

5. Display both documents on your screen using the Arrange All command. Scroll through the meeting schedule document to see the names of the committee members. Key the names of the eight committee members below the *Committee Members* heading in the memo.

6. **SAVE** the *deschedulememo* document in the lesson folder on your USB flash drive, then CLOSE the file.

7. **CLOSE** the *updatedschedule* document without saving.

STOP. CLOSE Word.

 **INTERNET READY**

Locate the closest satellite company in your area and find information about the company. Prepare a three-page report for your instructor and apply the features learned in this lesson. Prepare a fourth page on which you describe what you have learned in this lesson, and submit the completed document to your instructor.

Workplace *Ready*

VIEWING A LONG DOCUMENT

As a student at your local community college, you are learning the new features in Word 2010. Your instructor has asked you to visit one of the administrative areas and discuss the new features with an administrative assistant. Your task is to request a lengthy document and demonstrate the new Navigation Pane and how quickly and easily text, graphics, tables, and equations can be located in a document. Prepare a report to your instructor on your findings.

3 Character Formatting

LESSON SKILL MATRIX

In This Lesson, You Will Learn The Following Skills:

Formatting Characters Manually

Using the Format Painter

Formatting Text with Styles

Removing Text Formatting

KEY TERMS

- character
- character styles
- font
- monospace
- paragraph styles
- point size
- proportional space
- sans serif
- serif
- Text Effects

With more than 20 million members and 2,600 facilities, the YMCA ("the Y") is the nation's largest community service organization. Health and fitness programs offered at the Y include group exercises for adults and youth, family time, sports and recreation, and group interests for senior citizens. The staff and volunteers at the Y need to create various types of documents for announcing and advertising programs throughout the year and for organizing and registering members for participation in these programs. Microsoft Word is a great tool for creating professional-looking documents that will capture attention. In this lesson, you learn how to use character formatting to create professional-looking documents.

SOFTWARE ORIENTATION

The Font Group

As you learn to format text, it is important to become familiar with the Font group of commands. The Font group, shown in Figure 3-1, is displayed in the Home tab of the Ribbon.

Figure 3-1

The Font group

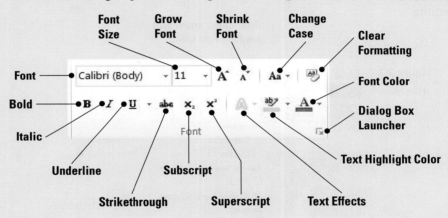

The Font group contains commands for changing the appearance of text. Refer to this figure throughout this lesson as well as the rest of the book.

FORMATTING CHARACTERS MANUALLY

The Bottom Line

Formatting characters makes your text more appealing and more readable.

Changing Fonts and Font Sizes

A **character** is any single letter, number, symbol, or punctuation mark. A **font** is a set of characters that have the same design. Each font has a unique name, such as Garamond or Arial. Microsoft Word has a variety of fonts and font sizes to help you communicate your intended message in a document. In this exercise, you use commands from the Font command group and the Mini toolbar to apply a specific font and font size to selected text.

Font sizes are measured in points. **Point size** refers to the height of characters, with one point equaling approximately 1/72 of an inch. Point sizes range from the very small 8-point size to 72 points or higher. Below are a few examples of fonts and sizes.

This is an example of Garamond 10 point.

This is an example of Arial 14 point.

This is an example of Juice ITC 18 point.

The Font group in the Home tab contains menus for changing both font type and font size. You can also access the same commands using the Mini toolbar or by right-clicking to access a shortcut menu. To change text font or size using any of these tools, you first must select the text.

Another way to change the size of text is to select the text and click the Grow Font **A** button to increase the font size or the Shrink Font **A** button to decrease the size.

STEP BY STEP   **Change Fonts and Font Sizes**

GET READY. Before you begin these steps, be sure to LAUNCH Microsoft Word.

1. Connect your USB flash drive to one of the USB ports on your computer.
2. Click the **File** tab, then click **Open**. The Open dialog box appears.
3. Use the vertical scroll bar to scroll down and locate the data files for this lesson on your USB flash drive. Double-click the **Lesson 3** folder to open it.
4. Locate and open the file named *class_descriptions*.
5. Within the document, select **Preston Creek Family YMCA**.
6. In the Font group of the Home tab, click the Font **drop-down arrow** to display the Font menu. The menu appears, as shown in Figure 3-2.

WileyPLUS Extra! features an online tutorial of this task.

@ The *class_descriptions* file is available on the book companion website or in WileyPLUS.

Drop-down arrow will produce Font menu.

Figure 3-2

Font menu

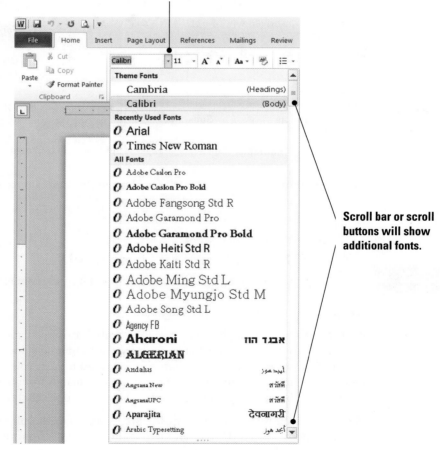

Scroll bar or scroll buttons will show additional fonts.

7. Scroll down the list and position the mouse pointer on Arial. Notice that as you point to each font in the list, the selected text changes with a live preview of what it would look like in that font.
8. Click **Arial**.

9. With the text still selected, click the **drop-down arrow** on the Font Size menu. The menu appears, as shown in Figure 3-3.

Figure 3-3

Font Size menu

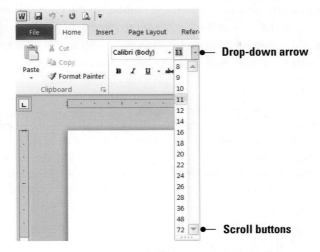

10. Click **18**.
11. Select **Group Exercise Class Descriptions**.
12. Click the **drop-down arrow** to open the Font menu, then select **Arial**.
13. With the text still selected, open the Font Size menu and select **14**.
14. Select the remainder of text in the document. Point to the selected text to display the Mini toolbar. Click the **drop-down arrow** on the Font menu on the Mini toolbar and choose **Calibri** (see Figure 3-4).

Figure 3-4

Font menu on the Mini toolbar

The Font menu

Mini toolbar contains some commands from the Font and Paragraph groups.

15. With text still selected, click the **Font Size** menu on the Mini toolbar and choose **12**.
16. Click in a **blank area** of the document to deselect.

17. Select **Preston Creek Family YMCA**. In the Font group, click the Grow Font **A˄** button once to increase the size of the text.

18. Click the Grow Font **A˄** button two more times until the point size is **24**. Notice that each time you click the button, the number in the Font Size menu changes.

19. Click in a blank area of the document to deselect.

20. **SAVE** the document as *classes* in the lesson folder on your USB flash drive.

PAUSE. LEAVE the document open to use in the next exercise.

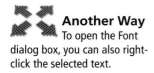

Another Way
To open the Font dialog box, you can also right-click the selected text.

Take Note   Courier is an example of a **monospaced** font, which means all its characters take up the same amount of horizontal space. Times New Roman is an example of **proportional** font, because the horizontal spacing varies. There are two types of proportional fonts: serif and sans serif. **Serif** fonts have small lines at the beginning and end of characters and are usually used with large amounts of text. A **sans serif** font is one that does not have the small line extensions on its characters. Times New Roman is an example of a serif font, whereas Arial and Calibri are sans serif fonts.

Applying Character Attributes

In addition to changing the font and font size of text, you can change the appearance of characters to apply emphasis to text. In this exercise, you learn how to apply character attributes such as bolding, italics, font colors, and outlines to selected text in Word documents.

The Font group in the Home tab includes the commands for applying bold, italic, and underline attributes to draw attention to words or phrases in your document. You can use these attributes one at a time, such as **Bold**, or together, such as **Bold Underline**. Select the text to apply one or more of the character attributes using the Font command group, the Mini toolbar, or keyboard shortcuts or by right-clicking to access a shortcut menu.

Click the Font command group dialog box launcher to open the Font dialog box with more options for formatting characters. In this dialog box, you can specify a font color, underline style, and a variety of other effects, such as small caps, strikethrough, superscript, and shadow.

NEW to Office 2010

New to the Font command group is **Text Effects**. Text Effects add a distinctive appearance to selected text, such as outline, shadow, glow, and reflection. To add Text Effects to selected text, click the drop-down arrow on the Text Effects button, then select from the available options on the menu. To remove effects, select the affected text, then click the Clear Formatting button on the Font group.

STEP BY STEP   **Apply Character Attributes**

USE the document that is open from the previous exercise.

1. Select the title of the document, **Preston Creek Family YMCA**. In the Font command group, click the Bold **B** button.

2. Select the subtitle, **Group Exercise Class Descriptions**, and click the Italic **I** button.

3. Select **Active Older Adults** and click the Bold **B** button.

4. With the text still selected, click the Underline **U** ▾ button.

Another Way
You also can select text and then press the keyboard shortcut Ctrl+B to apply bolding.

Another Way
You also can use the keyboard shortcut Ctrl+I to apply italics to selected text.

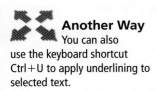

Another Way
You can also use the keyboard shortcut Ctrl+U to apply underlining to selected text.

5. With the text still selected, click the drop-down arrow beside the Underline button. A menu of underlining choices appears, as shown in Figure 3-5.

Drop-down arrow produces the Underline menu.

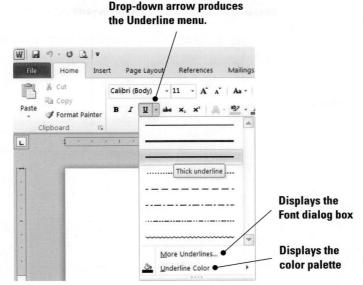

Thick underline

Displays the Font dialog box

Displays the color palette

More Underlines...

Underline Color

Figure 3-5

Underline menu

6. Click Thick Underline, the third line down in the menu.
7. Select the title, Preston Creek Family YMCA. In the Font group, click the dialog box launcher. The Font dialog box appears, as shown in Figure 3-6.
8. In the Effects section, click the Small Caps check box to insert a check mark.
9. Click the drop-down arrow on the Font Color menu. A menu of colors appears. A ScreenTip will appear when you place your insertion point over the colors; click red from the Standard Colors section at the bottom.

Figure 3-6

Font dialog box

Font dialog box launcher

Font style   **Font Size**

Font

Effects

Preview

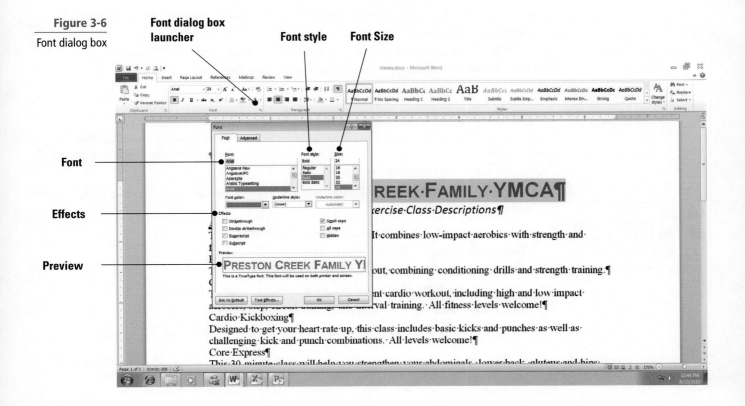

10. Click the Text Effects button at the bottom of the dialog box. The Format Text Effects dialog box opens, as shown in Figure 3-7.

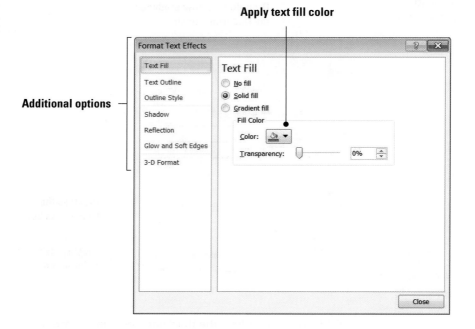

11. In the Fill Color options area, click the Color drop-down arrow. From the Standard colors menu that appears, select dark blue.

12. In the directory in the left pane of the dialog box, click Text Outline, then select Solid line in the options that appear in the right pane.

13. In the Outline Style category, change the width from .75 to 1.5 pt. Click Close to close the Format Text Effects dialog box. Each character in the selected text will now have a noticeable solid-colored outline.

14. In the Font dialog box, click the Small Caps check box to remove the check mark.

15. Click OK, then deselect the text.

16. SAVE the document as *classes_1* in the lesson folder on your USB flash drive.

PAUSE. LEAVE the document open to use in the next exercise.

Changing Case

When you need to change the case (capitalization) of text, Word provides several options and an easy way to choose the one you want. In this exercise, you learn to use the commands in Word's Change Case menu to change capitalization.

The Change Case menu in the Font group has five options for changing the capitalization of text:

Another Way
Click the Font Color
A ▾ button on the Ribbon to launch a menu of colors.

- **Sentence case:** Capitalizes the first word in each sentence
- **lowercase:** Changes all characters to lowercase
- **UPPERCASE:** Changes all characters to capital letters
- **Capitalize Each Word:** Capitalizes the first character of each word
- **tOGGLE cASE:** Changes each character to its opposite case

STEP BY STEP   **Change Case**

USE the document that is open from the previous exercise.

1. Select the title, **Preston Creek Family YMCA**. In the Font group, click the **Change Case** **Aa ▾** button. A menu of case options appears, as shown in Figure 3-8.

Figure 3-8

Change Case menu

Click on the drop-down arrow to display the Change Case menu.

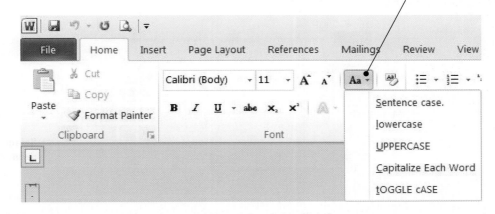

2. Click **UPPERCASE**. All letters are capitalized.
3. With the text still selected, click the **Change Case** **Aa ▾** button again and select **lowercase**.
4. With the text still selected, click the **Change Case** **Aa ▾** button again, then click **Capitalize Each Word**.
5. Select **Ymca**. Click the **Change Case** **Aa ▾** button again and choose **UPPERCASE**.
6. Click in a blank area of the document to deselect the text.
7. **SAVE** the document as *classes_2* in the lesson folder on your USB flash drive.

PAUSE. LEAVE the document open to use in the next exercise.

Highlighting Text

The Highlighting tool in the Font group enables you to apply a highlighting color across text to stress the importance of that text and draw attention to it quickly. In this exercise, you learn to use Word's Text Highlighting feature to add highlighting color to selected text.

To highlight text, first select the text you want to emphasize, then click the Text Highlight Color button in the Font group and select the color of your choice. To remove highlighting, select the highlighted text and choose No Color from the Text Highlight Color menu.

STEP BY STEP   **Highlight Text**

USE the document that is open from the previous exercise.

1. In the Font group, click the **Text Highlight Color** **aby ▾** button. Place your insertion point within the document, and notice that Highlighting is turned on and the pointer changes to a highlighter pen icon.
2. Under the Core Express heading in your document, select the last sentence, **This new class is open to all fitness levels!** When you release the mouse button, the text is highlighted in yellow.

3. Click the Text Highlight Color ![aby] ▾ button again to turn off Highlighting.

4. Select the text you highlighted in step 2. Click the drop-down arrow beside the Text Highlight Color ![aby] ▾ button. A menu of colors appears, as shown in Figure 3-9. Click turquoise (the third color from the left in the top row of the menu). Notice the highlight color in the text and the Text Highlight Color ![aby] ▾ button in the Ribbon has changed to turquoise.

Figure 3-9

Text Highlight Color menu

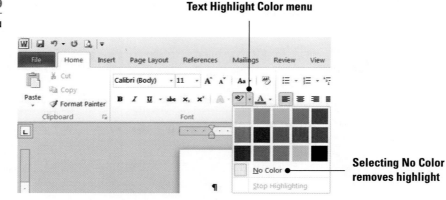

Text Highlight Color menu

Selecting No Color removes highlight

5. Select the text again. Click the Text Highlight Color ![aby] ▾ button again to remove the highlight color by selecting No Color.

6. **SAVE** the document with the same filename in the lesson folder on your USB flash drive.

PAUSE. LEAVE the document open to use in the next exercise.

USING THE FORMAT PAINTER

The Bottom Line

To format your text so that it has the look and feel you want, you may need to copy existing formatting. The Format Painter helps you copy formats to use in other areas of the document without having to repeat the same steps.

Using the Format Painter

The Format Painter command is located in the Clipboard group on the Home tab. It is used to copy attributes and other formatting from one block of text and apply them to other selected text within the document. When you activate Format Painter, the mouse pointer becomes a paintbrush. Clicking once on the Format Painter button enables you to copy and apply the format once; double-clicking allows you to apply the copied format to as many locations as you wish. In this exercise, you learn to use the Format Painter to copy and apply formatting to selected text.

STEP BY STEP   **Use the Format Painter**

USE the document that is open from the previous exercise.

1. Select the Active Older Adults heading.

2. On the Home tab, in the Clipboard group, click the Format Painter ![Format Painter] button once; Format Painter copies the formatting from your selected text, and the pointer changes to a paintbrush icon when you point to text.

3. Use the paintbrush pointer to select the next heading, Boot Camp. The copied format is applied, and the Format Painter is turned off.

4. With Boot Camp still selected, double-click the Format Painter ✒ Format Painter button. Notice the status bar message "Use the mouse to apply the previously copied paragraph formatting onto other text, or press Esc to cancel." Notice also that the mouse pointer becomes a paintbrush icon when you place it over text. You will now be able to apply the same formatting to several items in the document.

5. Select the next heading, Cardio Combo. The copied format is applied.

6. Select the next heading, Cardio Kickboxing. The copied format is applied again.

7. Select the remaining headings to apply the copied format. When you are finished with the last heading, click the Format Painter ✒ Format Painter button to turn it off.

8. **SAVE** the document as *classes_3* in the lesson folder on your USB flash drive.

PAUSE. LEAVE the document open to use in the next exercise.

Another Way
The Format Painter button is also available on the Mini toolbar. In addition, to repeat the last Format Painter action, you can press the F4 shortcut key.

FORMATTING TEXT WITH STYLES

The Bottom Line

Word provides predefined Quick Styles for formatting documents instantly with a number of character and paragraph attributes. Modifications can be made to existing styles, or new styles can be created and placed in the Quick Styles list, current document, or template. In this exercise, you learn to apply a style and to modify an existing style.

The Styles window lists the same Quick Styles displayed in the Styles Gallery. When you point to a style in the list, a ScreenTip displays the style's properties.

When you choose **paragraph styles**, the formats are applied instantly to all text in the paragraph where the insertion point is located, whether or not that text is selected. Styles created for paragraphs are marked in the Styles window by a paragraph mark to the right of the style name.

Character styles are applied to individual characters or words that you select. Character styles have a lowercase letter *a* beside them.

Sometimes, a style can be used for either paragraphs or characters. These linked styles have a paragraph symbol as well as a lowercase *a* beside them. Select the text to which you want to apply a linked style.

Applying Styles

In this exercise, you learn to use Word's Quick Styles to apply paragraph styles and character styles to selected text and paragraphs within your document.

STEP BY STEP **Apply a Style**

USE the document that is open from the previous exercise.

1. Select the Active Older Adults heading. In the Styles command group on the Home tab, click Heading 1. The style is applied to the heading.

2. Use multi-selection to select all the headings, then click Heading 1. The Heading 1 style is applied to all the remaining headings.

3. In the second sentence of the Active Older Adults description, select low-impact. In the Styles group, click the dialog box launcher. The Styles window appears, as shown in Figure 3-10.

Figure 3-10

Styles window

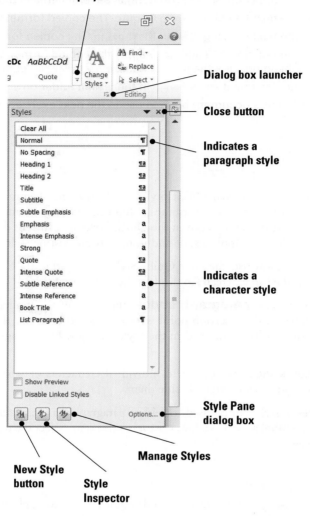

Clicking the More down arrow displays a menu.

Dialog box launcher

Close button

Indicates a paragraph style

Indicates a character style

Style Pane dialog box

Manage Styles

New Style button

Style Inspector

4. Point to Subtle Emphasis in the Styles list. Notice a ScreenTip appears and the lowercase *a* to the right of the style name becomes an arrow. Click Subtle Emphasis. The style is applied to the selected text.

5. In the Boot Camp description, select challenging and click Subtle Emphasis in the Styles window.

6. In the Core Express description, select strengthen and click Subtle Emphasis in the Styles window.

7. In the Indoor Cycling description, select high-energy and click Subtle Emphasis in the Styles window.

8. In the Yoga description, select breathing and relaxation and click Subtle Emphasis in the Styles window. Deselect the text. Click the X to close the Styles window.

9. **SAVE** the document as *classes_4* in the lesson folder on your USB flash drive.

PAUSE. LEAVE the document open to use in the next exercise.

Modifying Styles

You can make modifications to an existing style using the Modify Style dialog box. Word also gives you the option of where to place changes made to styles, such as adding them to the Quick List, current document, or applying them to new documents based on a template. In this exercise, you learn to use the Modify Style options to modify styles in Word.

To change an existing style, right-click the style's name in the Style window, then click Modify, as shown in Figure 3-11. Character attributes can be applied to a style by clicking on the Bold **B** button, Italics *I* button and/or the Underline **U** ▾ button. Similarly, clicking the drop-down arrow for Font and Font Size allows you to adjust both of these settings.

The Modify Styles dialog box has options for where to place the new modified style. The modified style can be placed on the Quick Style list so you can access it quickly. Selecting the option to *save the style only in this document* will affect only the current document. Selecting the option for *new documents based on a template* ensures that the same style is applied. For instance, say you are writing a group research paper and would like uniformity for the paper. Providing everyone within the group with a copy of the template would ensure consistency in the formatting of the paper. All styles within the document update automatically.

STEP BY STEP   **Modify Styles**

USE the document that is open from the previous exercise.

1. Under Change Styles in the Style group, click the **drop-down arrow** to display the Styles window. Select **Subtle Emphasis**, then right-click to display the Subtle Emphasis menu, as shown in Figure 3-11.

Figure 3-11

Subtle Emphasis menu

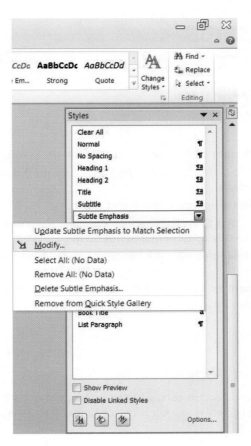

2. Click **Modify**. The Modify Style dialog box appears, as shown in Figure 3-12.

3. Click the **Bold** **B** button.

4. Click the **Font Color drop-down arrow**, then select **red** in the Standard Colors section. Notice the preview in the dialog box changes.

5. Click the **Add to Quick Style List** check box to clear it. The modifications you just made will apply to this document and not on the Style list, as shown in Figure 3-12.

Figure 3-12

Modify Style dialog box displaying Subtle Emphasis

Existing Style name appears in text box.

Character Attribute

Font Size menu

Font menu

Font color

Preview area

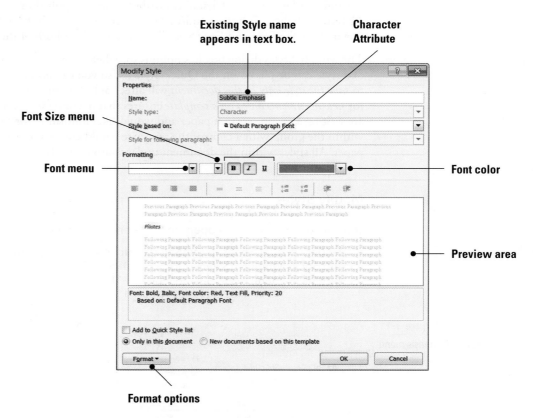

Format options

6. Click **OK**.

7. Select **Heading 1**, right-click to display the Heading 1 menu, then click **Modify**.

8. In the Modify Style dialog box, click the **Font Color drop-down arrow**. From the drop-down menu, choose **red**.

9. Open the Font Size drop-down menu and select **14**.

10. Click the **Add to Quick Style list** check box to clear the check mark. The modifications made will apply to this document and not on the Style list.

11. Click **OK**. All the headings with the Heading 1 style update automatically to the new color and size.

12. **SAVE** the document as *classes_5* in the lesson folder on your USB flash drive. CLOSE the file.

STOP. CLOSE Word.

REMOVING TEXT FORMATTING

The Bottom Line

When you are formatting documents, sometimes you need to try a few different options before you get the appearance you want. Clearing unwanted formatting is easy using Word's Clear Formatting button.

Using the Clear Formatting Button

The Clear Formatting button is located in the More area of the Styles group. Click the drop-down arrow to display a menu that lets you clear formatting from selected text. In this exercise, you learn to use the Clear Formatting button.

STEP BY STEP | **Use the Clear Formatting Button**

USE the document that is open from the previous exercise.

1. Select **Active Older Adults**. In the Styles group, click the **More drop-down arrow**, then click **Clear Formatting** . The formatting is removed and only plain text remains.

2. Press and hold **Ctrl** and select **Boot Camp**; continue to hold the **Ctrl** key to select the remaining headings, then click the **Clear Formatting** button in the Styles group. (By holding the **Ctrl** key, you can use multi-selection to select nonadjacent text.) Deselect all text and click the **X** to close the Style window.

3. **SAVE** the document as *classes_6* in the lesson folder on your USB flash drive.

CLOSE Word.

Another Way
To remove formatting you can also click Clear Formatting on the Font group.

X **Ref**   Refer to Lesson 2 for more information about multi-selection.

SKILL SUMMARY

In This Lesson, You Learned How To:
Formatting Characters Manually
Using the format painter
Formatting text with styles
Removing text formatting

Knowledge Assessment

True/False

Circle T if the statement is true or F if the statement is false.

T F 1. Toggle Case changes each character to its opposite case.

T F 2. Applying bolding to text gives it special emphasis.

T F 3. The Format Painter is found on the Mini toolbar.

T F 4. The default color for Text Highlighting is pink.

T F 5. The Shrink Font button increases point size.

T F 6. The Clear Formatting button clears text from one location and lets you apply it in another location.

T F 7. You can only highlight text with the colors yellow or turquoise.

T F 8. The Font dialog box has an option to display the underline menu.

T F 9. To apply a Quick Style, select the text, then select the style from the Style group.

T F 10. Quick Styles cannot be modified.

Multiple Choice

Select the best response for the following statements.

1. When measuring point size, one point is equal to a character height of:
   a. 1/10 of an inch.
   b. 1/12 of an inch.
   c. 1/72 of an inch.
   d. 1/18 of an inch.

2. The Underline button in the Font group contains options to underline selected text with a(n):
   a. thick underline.
   b. double underline.
   c. dotted underline.
   d. All of the above

3. A _____ is a set of characters that have the same design.
   a. point size
   b. Font
   c. paragraph style
   d. a and b

4. If you key a paragraph in uppercase and need to change it to sentence case without having to rekey the paragraph, which option would you would use?
   a. Change Case
   b. Change Size of Case
   c. Sentence Case
   d. Toggle Case

5. The _____ makes text look like it was marked with a fluorescent-colored pen.
   a. Highlighter tool
   b. Highlighting Text tool
   c. Highlighting Color tool
   d. Shading Text tool

6. The _____ lets you copy the format of text and apply those attributes to different text.
   a. Formatter
   b. Copy Special
   c. Format Painter
   d. Both a and b

7. The _____ feature removes all formatting from the selected text.
   a. Formatting Cleared
   b. Erase Formatting
   c. Remove Formatting
   d. Clear Formatting

8. Tiny lines at the ends of characters are known as:
   a. serifs.
   b. sans serifs.
   c. monospaces.
   d. proportional lines.

9. To increase the point size of selected text, click the:
   a. Increase font button.
   b. Grow font button.
   c. Enlarge font button.
   d. Enhance font button.

10. Changing the font and font size of selected text can be completed using:
    a. the Font dialog box.
    b. the Mini toolbar.
    c. the Font group of the Home tab.
    d. All of the above

Competency Assessment

Project 3-1: Formatting a Sales Letter

Star Bright Satellite Radio will be sending sales letters to people who have just purchased new vehicles equipped with their radios. Add some finishing formatting touches to this letter.

GET READY. LAUNCH Word if it is not already running.

@ The *letter* file for this lesson is available on the book companion website or in WileyPLUS.

1. **OPEN** the *letter* document from the data files for this lesson.
2. **SAVE** the document as *sales_letter* in the lesson folder on your USB flash drive.
3. In the second paragraph, select the first sentence, Star Bright Satellite. . . .
4. In the Font group on the Home tab, click the Bold button.
5. In the second paragraph, select the fifth sentence, Star Bright also broadcasts. . . .
6. In the Font group, click the Italic button.
7. In the fourth paragraph, select the first sentence, Star Bright is only $10.95 a month.
8. In the Font group, click the Bold button.
9. In the second sentence of the fourth paragraph, select Subscribe.
10. In the Font group, click the Change Case drop-down arrow, then click UPPERCASE.
11. With the word still selected, click Bold, then deselect the text.
12. **SAVE** the document in the lesson folder on your USB flash drive, then **CLOSE** the document.

PAUSE. LEAVE Word open for the next project.

Project 3-2: Formatting a Flyer

GET READY. LAUNCH Word if it is not already running.

@ The *volunteercoaches* file for this lesson is available on the book companion website or in WileyPLUS.

1. **OPEN** *volunteercoaches* from the data files for this lesson.
2. **SAVE** the document as *volunteers* in the lesson folder on your USB flash drive.
3. Select We Need You! Click the drop-down arrow in the Font menu, then click Arial Black.
4. Click the drop-down arrow in the Font Size menu, then click 48.
5. Select Volunteer Coaches Needed For Youth Sports. Click the drop-down arrow in the Font menu, then click Arial Black.
6. Click the drop-down arrow in the Font Size menu, then click 18.
7. Select Sports include and the four lines below it. Click the drop-down arrow in the Font menu, then click Calibri. Click the drop-down arrow in the Font Size menu, then click 18.
8. Select the four sports listed, then click the Italic button.

9. Select the three lines of contact information, beginning with *Contact Patrick Edelstein . . .* Click the drop-down arrow in the Font menu, then click Arial Black. Click the drop-down arrow in the Font Size menu, then click 11.

10. Select YMCA. Click the drop-down arrow in the Font Color button, then choose red from the Standard Colors section.

11. With the text still selected, click the Bold button. Click the drop-down arrow in the Font menu, then click Arial Black. Click the drop-down menu in the Font Size menu, then click 36. Deselect the text.

12. **SAVE** the document in the lesson folder on your USB flash drive, then **CLOSE** the file.

LEAVE Word open for the next project.

Proficiency Assessment

Project 3-3: Creating a Flyer

The Grand Street Coffee Shop has decided to install a wireless Internet service for customers. To announce the news, create a flyer for distribution in the coffee shop.

GET READY. LAUNCH Word if it is not already running.

1. **OPEN** *wireless* from the data files for this lesson.

@ The *wireless* file for this lesson is available on the book companion website or in WileyPLUS.

2. **SAVE** the document as *WiFi* in the lesson folder on your USB flash drive.

3. Follow the instructions in Figure 3-13 to format the document.

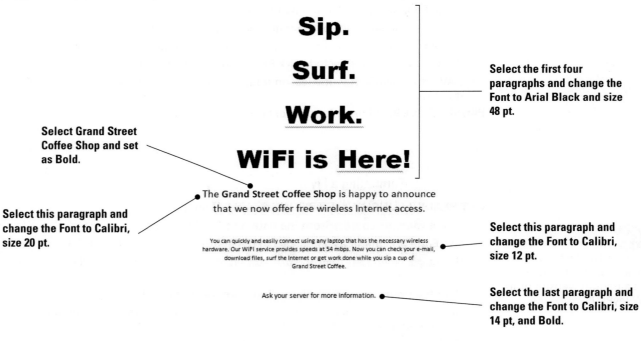

Select the first four paragraphs and change the Font to Arial Black and size 48 pt.

Select Grand Street Coffee Shop and set as Bold.

Select this paragraph and change the Font to Calibri, size 20 pt.

Select this paragraph and change the Font to Calibri, size 12 pt.

Select the last paragraph and change the Font to Calibri, size 14 pt, and Bold.

Sip.

Surf.

Work.

WiFi is Here!

The Grand Street Coffee Shop is happy to announce that we now offer free wireless Internet access.

You can quickly and easily connect using any laptop that has the necessary wireless hardware. Our WiFi service provides speeds at 54 mbps. Now you can check your e-mail, download files, surf the Internet or get work done while you sip a cup of Grand Street Coffee.

Ask your server for more information.

4. **SAVE** the document in the lesson folder on your USB flash drive, then **CLOSE** the file.

LEAVE Word open for the next project.

Project 3-4: Formatting Nutritional Information

Customers of the Grand Street Coffee Shop have asked about the nutritional makeup of some of the blended coffee items on the menu. Format a document you can post or make available for customers to take with them.

GET READY. LAUNCH Word if it is not already running.

@ The *nutritioninfo* file for this lesson is available on the book companion website or in WileyPLUS.

1. **OPEN** *nutritioninfo* from the data files for this lesson.
2. SAVE the document as *nutrition* in the lesson folder on your USB flash drive.
3. Select Grand Street Coffee Shop. On the Font menu, click Juice ITC.
4. With the text still selected, change the font size to 28.
5. Click the Font Color menu and select dark blue in the Standard Colors section.
6. Select Nutritional Information.
7. In the Font group, click the dialog box launcher. In the Effects section, click the Small Caps box and change the font size to 12 and the font color to dark blue. Click OK.
8. Select Brewed Coffee, Caffé Latte, Caffé Mocha, Cappuccino, and White Chocolate Mocha, then click the Font dialog box launcher. Click the All Caps box, change the font size to 12, make the text both Bold and Italic, and change the font color to dark blue. Click OK.
9. Select the three lines of text under the *Brewed Coffee* heading. Click Italic on the Font group. Use the Format Painter to copy the format to the text under each heading.
10. **SAVE** the document in the lesson folder on your USB flash drive, then CLOSE the file.

LEAVE Word open for the next project.

Mastery Assessment

Project 3-5: Formatting a Resume

Your friend Mike asks you to help him with his resume. Format the resume so that it looks professional.

GET READY. LAUNCH Word if it is not already running.

@ The *resume* file for this lesson is available on the book companion website or in WileyPLUS.

1. **OPEN** *resume* from the data files for this lesson.
2. **SAVE** the document as *mzresume* in the lesson folder on your USB flash drive.
3. Format the resume to the following specifications:
   - Format Mike's name with Cambria, 24 pt., bold.
   - Change his address, phone, and email information to Times New Roman 9 pt.
   - Change the main headings by bolding and italicizing; change the font to Cambria and the font size to 16.
   - For job titles, apply Times New Roman, 12 pt., small caps, and bold.
   - Italicize the sentence or sentences before the bulleted lists.
   - For places and years of employment, as well as the college name, apply Times New Roman, 12 pt., and small caps.
4. **SAVE** the document in the lesson folder on your USB flash drive, then **CLOSE** the file.

LEAVE Word open for the next project.

Project 3-6: Formatting References

Your friend Mike liked your work on his resume so much that he asks you to format his reference list with the same design as his resume.

GET READY. LAUNCH Word if it is not already running.

1. **OPEN** *references* from the data files for this lesson.
2. **SAVE** the document as *mzreferences* in the lesson folder on your USB flash drive.
3. **OPEN** *mzresume* from the data files for this lesson.
4. View the documents side by side and compare the fonts, styles, sizes, and attributes of both. Update the *mzreferences* document by changing the font, styles, size, and attributes to match those in the *mzresume* document.
5. **SAVE** the document and **CLOSE** the file.

CLOSE Word.

The *references* file for this lesson is available on the book companion website or in WileyPLUS.

INTERNET READY

Search the Internet for information on the national YMCA or your local YMCA. Create a flyer listing some of the programs available that are available in the summer. Prepare a letter for the newsletter in which you solicit volunteers to assist with the upcoming scheduled events for the summer. All members of the YMCA will receive a copy of this flyer and letter. For the letter, use Times New Roman font with a size of 12 points. For the flyer, apply whatever text effects, font colors, text highlight colors, and font styles you think make your document interesting and attractive.

Workplace *Ready*

APPLYING CHARACTER FORMATTING

At your college, visit the department that posts job opportunities for college students seeking part-time employment. Determine how you can improve the posting document's appearance by applying different character attributes and by using the Styles available in Word.

Write a letter to the director indicating the research you completed and recommending specific changes to the advertisement's text formatting and layout that you believe will better attract potential students. Submit your letter to your instructor.

LESSON SKILL MATRIX

In This Lesson, You Will Learn The Following Skills:

Formatting Paragraphs

Setting Line Spacing in Text and Between Paragraphs

Creating and Formatting a Bulleted List

Creating a Numbered List

Setting and Modifying Tabs

KEY TERMS

- alignment
- first-line indent
- hanging indent
- horizontal alignment
- indent
- leaders
- line spacing
- negative indent
- vertical alignment

You are employed at Books and Beyond, an independent used bookstore. Your job responsibilities include receiving and assessing used books, issuing trade credit, stocking the bookshelves, and placing special orders. Because you have good computer skills, you are also responsible for creating and modifying documents as needed. Currently, you are working on the store's employee handbook. In this lesson, you learn how to use Word's formatting features to change the appearance of paragraphs. In particular, you learn to set indents, change alignment and line spacing, create numbered and bulleted lists, set tabs, and use shading and borders.

SOFTWARE ORIENTATION

The Indents and Spacing Tab in the Paragraph Dialog Box

The Paragraph dialog box contains Word's commands for changing paragraph alignment, indentation, and spacing. The Indents and Spacing tab of the Paragraph dialog box is shown in Figure 4-1. Use this figure as a reference throughout this lesson as well as the rest of this book.

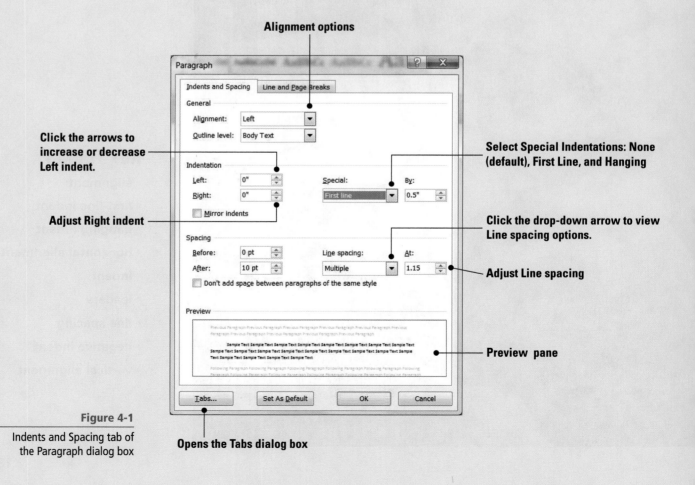

Figure 4-1

Indents and Spacing tab of the Paragraph dialog box

FORMATTING PARAGRAPHS

Paragraph formatting is an essential part of creating effective, professional-looking documents in Word. Word's paragraph formatting feature enables you to determine paragraph alignment, indentation, and spacing between paragraphs. Word's formatting features also enable you to add shading and borders to further enhance paragraph text and to remove paragraph formatting altogether.

Setting Indents

Indents can be used to set paragraphs off from other text in your documents. Word documents can include first-line indents, hanging indents, and negative indents. The commands for indenting paragraphs are available in the Paragraph command group on the Home tab, as well as in the Paragraph command group of the Page Layout tab. Both command groups have dialog box launchers that give you access to additional commands. In this exercise, you learn to set indents using the dialog box and the ruler.

An **indent** is a blank space inserted between text and the left or right margin. A **first-line indent** inserts blank space between the left margin and the first line of the paragraph (one-half inch is the default setting for this indent). A **hanging indent**, common in legal documents, begins the first full line of text in a paragraph at the left margin; all of the remaining lines in the paragraph are then indented from the left margin. A **negative indent** extends paragraph text into the left margin. You can indent paragraphs from the left margin, the right margin, or both, and you can set the sizes of indents using Word's paragraph-formatting tools. You can also drag the markers on the ruler to set indents. Table 4-1 shows the various indent markers as they appear on the ruler.

Table 4-1

Types of Indents on the Ruler

Indent Option	Associated Marker on the Ruler
First-line indent	
Hanging indent	
Left indent	
Right indent	
Negative indent	

STEP BY STEP   **Set Indents**

GET READY. Before you begin these steps, be sure to launch Microsoft Word.

1. Connect your USB flash drive to one of the USB ports on your computer.
2. Click the File tab, then click Open. The Open dialog box appears.
3. Use the vertical scroll bar to scroll down and locate the data files for this lesson on your USB flash drive. Double-click the data files folder for this lesson to open it.
4. Locate and **OPEN** the file named *acknowledgement*.
5. Click the View tab. Then, in the Show group, click the check box that displays the Ruler.
6. Click to place the insertion point at the beginning of the first paragraph.
7. On the Home tab, in the Paragraph group, click the drop-down arrow to display the Paragraph dialog box. The Indents and Spacing tab is the active tab.

8. In the Indentation section of this tab, change the Special selection by clicking the drop-down arrow and selecting First line. The By box lists 0.5 inches by default, as shown in Figure 4-2. Click OK.

Figure 4-2

Paragraph dialog box

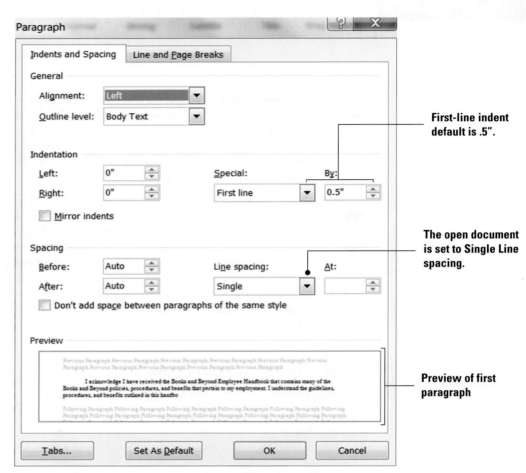

9. Figure 4-3 displays the paragraph with the first-line indent you just set.

Figure 4-3

Ruler with first-line indent marker on first paragraph

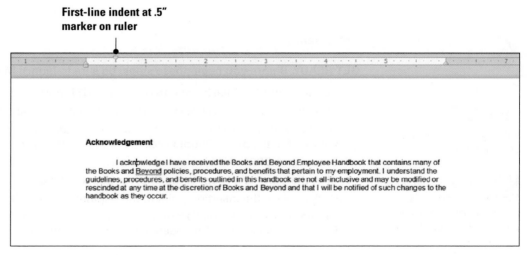

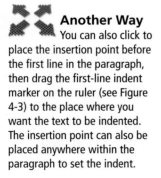

Another Way
You can also click to place the insertion point before the first line in the paragraph, then drag the first-line indent marker on the ruler (see Figure 4-3) to the place where you want the text to be indented. The insertion point can also be placed anywhere within the paragraph to set the indent.

10. Click to place the insertion point in the second paragraph.

11. On the horizontal ruler, press and hold the left mouse button and drag the hanging indent  marker to **0.5** inches. As you move the hanging indent marker, notice that the first-line indent marker moves with it. Now drag the first-line indent marker back to the left margin as shown in Figure 4-4.

Figure 4-4

Ruler with hanging indent marker on second paragraph

First-line indent at left margin

Hanging indent at .5" on the ruler

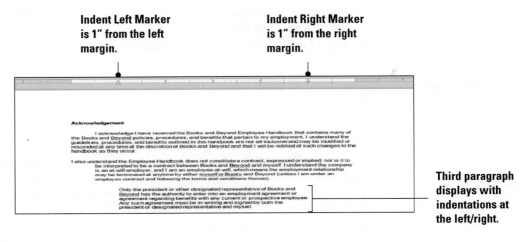

Troubleshooting If the horizontal ruler is not visible along the top of the document, click the View Ruler button at the top of the vertical scroll bar to display it, or click the View tab and choose Ruler from the Show command group.

12. Place the insertion point in the third paragraph.

Another Way
You can also click to place the insertion point on the hanging indent marker on the ruler (see Figure 4-4), then drag the marker to set the hanging indent.

13. On the Page Layout tab, in the Paragraph group, click the **up arrow** next to **Indent Left** ten times to indent the left side of the paragraph to **1 inch** on the ruler.

14. Click the **up arrow** next to Indent Right ten times to indent the right side of the paragraph to **1 inch** on the ruler (see Figure 4-5). Notice the paragraph has moved in 1 inch from both the left and the right margin and the paragraph is indented on both sides.

Figure 4-5

Ruler with left and right indent markers

Indent Left Marker is 1" from the left margin.

Indent Right Marker is 1" from the right margin.

Third paragraph displays with indentations at the left/right.

Another Way
To indent the first line of a paragraph, click in front of the line and press Tab. To indent an entire paragraph, select the whole paragraph and press Tab.

15. Place the insertion point in the last paragraph.

Figure 4-6

Ruler with negative indent

16. On the ruler, press and hold the left mouse button and drag the left indent marker into the left margin at –0.5 inches, as shown in Figure 4-6.

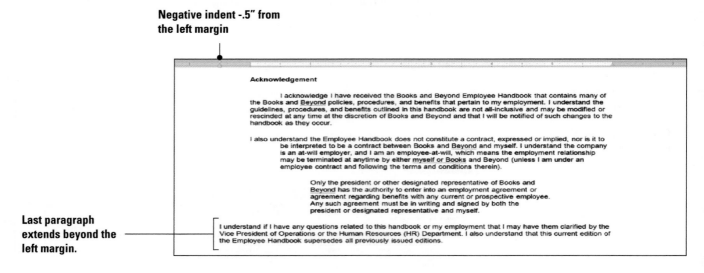

Negative indent -.5" from
the left margin

Last paragraph
extends beyond the
left margin.

Figure 4-7

Sample document displaying
several indentations

17. Your document should look similar to the one shown in Figure 4-7.

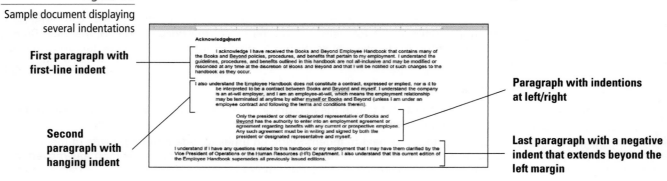

First paragraph with
first-line indent

Second
paragraph with
hanging indent

Paragraph with indentions
at left/right

Last paragraph with a negative
indent that extends beyond the
left margin

18. **SAVE** the document as *handbook_acknowledgement* in the lesson folder on your USB flash drive, then **CLOSE** the file.

PAUSE. LEAVE Word open for the next exercise.

Take Note   Changing paragraph indents can be completed using the Ruler or the Paragraph dialog box on the Home and Page Layout tabs.

Changing Alignment

Paragraph **alignment** refers to how text is positioned between a document's margins. By default, text is left-aligned at the top of the page. However, as you continue to format a document, you may need to change your text's horizontal or vertical alignment. In this exercise, you learn to align text left, center, right, and justified and to vertically center text in the document.

Horizontal alignment refers to how text is positioned between the left and right margins. There are four types of horizontal alignments: left align, center, right align, or justify. Horizontal alignment can be changed in the Paragraph group, which can be accessed on both the Home tab and the Page Layout tab. Also, when the Paragraph dialog box is open and the Indents and Spacing tab is active, you can change alignment in the General section of the tab. Alternatively, you can use various shortcut keys, as shown in Table 4-2.

Table 4-2

Horizontal Alignment Options

Option	Button	Shortcut Keys	Description
Align left		Ctrl+L	Lines up text flush with the left margin, leaving a ragged right edge
Center		Ctrl+E	Centers text between the left and right margins, leaving ragged edges on both sides
Align right		Ctrl+R	Lines up text flush with the right margin, leaving a ragged left edge
Justify		Ctrl+J	Lines up text flush on both the left and right margins, adding extra space between words as necessary for a clean look

Another Way To access the Paragraph dialog box using the shortcut method, place the insertion point in the paragraph, then right-click and select Paragraph from the menu that appears.

Vertical alignment refers to how text is positioned between the top and bottom margins of the page. Text can be aligned vertically at the top margin, at the center of the page, or at the bottom of the page, or it can be justified. Top-of-the-page vertical alignment is the default when launching Word. Centered vertical alignment places the text evenly between the top and bottom margins. Bottom vertical alignment places text next to the bottom margin of the document. Finally, justified vertical alignment aligns text evenly between the top, bottom, left, and right margins. (See Table 4-3.)

There are two ways to set vertical alignment.

- From the Page Layout tab, in the Page Setup group, launch the Page Setup dialog box. From the Layout tab, under the Page group, you will find the Vertical Alignment pull-down menu.
- From the File tab, select Print and then Page Setup. This launches the Page Setup dialog box also. From the Layout tab, under the Page group, you will find the Vertical Alignment pull-down menu.

Table 4-3

Vertical Alignment Options

Option	Description
Top vertical alignment	Aligns text at the top margin
Centered vertical alignment	Aligns text between the top and bottom margins
Bottom vertical alignment	Aligns text at the bottom margin
Justified vertical alignment	Aligns text equally between the top, bottom, left, and right margins

STEP BY STEP   **Change Alignment**

OPEN *introduction* from the data files from this lesson.

The *introduction* file for this lesson is available on the book companion website or in WileyPLUS.

1. Click to place the insertion point in the first paragraph.
2. On the Home tab, in the Paragraph group, click the **Justify**  button. The paragraph is justified between the left and right margins.
3. Place the insertion point in the second paragraph.
4. On the Home tab, in the Paragraph group, click the **drop-down arrow** to launch the Paragraph dialog box. The Indents and Spacing tab should be selected.
5. In the Alignment list under General, click the **drop-down arrow**, then click **Centered**. Click **OK**. The paragraph is centered between the left and right margins.
6. Place the insertion point in the third paragraph.

7. Press **Ctrl+R** to align the text on the right. The right side of the paragraph is now even, while the left is uneven.

8. On the Page Layout tab, in the Page Setup group, click the drop-down arrow to open the Page Setup dialog box. Then, click the Layout tab.

9. In the Vertical alignment list under Page, click the drop-down arrow and select Center.

10. In the Apply To list under Preview, Whole document is selected, as shown in Figure 4-8.

Figure 4-8

Page Setup dialog box

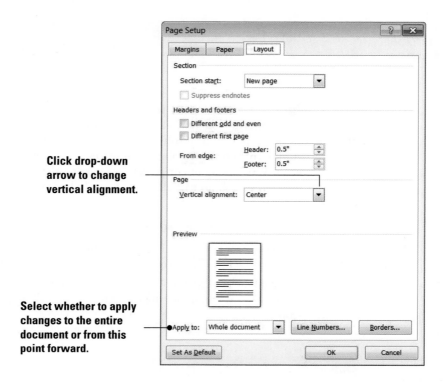

Click drop-down arrow to change vertical alignment.

Select whether to apply changes to the entire document or from this point forward.

11. Click **OK**. The text is centered between the top and bottom margins, as shown in Figure 4-9.

Figure 4-9

Horizontal and vertical alignments

Paragraph Justified

Text Centered

Text Align Right

Text Align Left

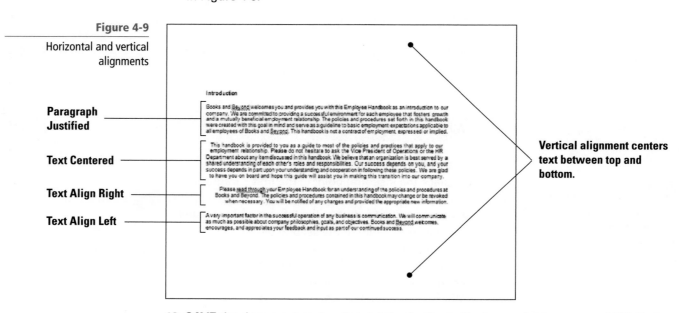

Vertical alignment centers text between top and bottom.

12. **SAVE** the document as *handbook_introduction* in the lesson folder on your USB flash drive, then **CLOSE** the file.

PAUSE. LEAVE Word open for the next exercise.

Shading a Paragraph

In this exercise, you learn to use Word's Shading feature to color the background behind selected text or paragraphs.

To apply shading to a paragraph, click the Shading button in the Paragraph group. To choose another color, click the drop-down arrow next to the Shading button, and choose a color in the current theme or a standard color from the Shading menu (place your insertion point over a color to see a ScreenTip with the color's precise name). To remove shading, click No Color.

Click More Colors to open the Colors dialog box, where additional options are available. You can choose standard colors in the Standard tab, or you can create a custom color from the Custom tab.

STEP BY STEP   **Shade a Paragraph**

OPEN the *diversity* file from the data files for this lesson.

@ The *diversity* file for this lesson is available on the book companion website or in WileyPLUS.

1. Place the insertion point in the first paragraph.
2. On the Home tab, in the Paragraph group, click the **drop-down arrow** next to the Shading ⬛ · button to display the menu shown in Figure 4-10.

Figure 4-10

Shading menu

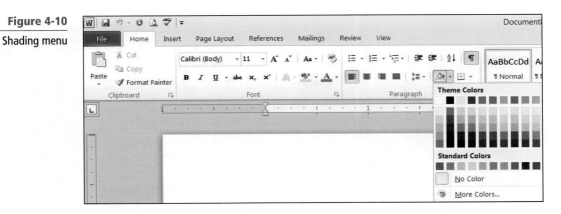

3. In the Theme Colors palette, click the color in the third row of the last column (**Orange, Accent 6, Lighter 40%**), as shown in Figure 4-11.

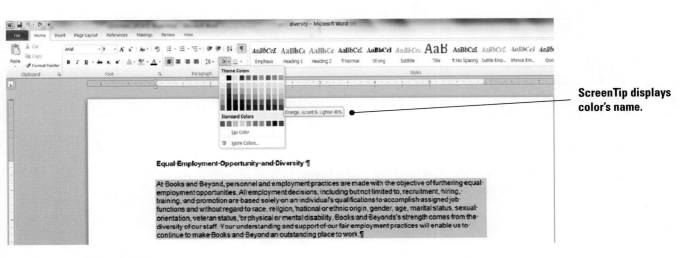

ScreenTip displays color's name.

Figure 4-11

Shaded paragraph

4. **SAVE** the document as *handbook_diversity* in the lesson folder on your USB flash drive.

PAUSE. LEAVE the document open to use in the next exercise.

Placing a Border around a Paragraph

Like shading, borders can add interest and emphasis to paragraphs. Borders can be formatted with a variety of styles, colors, and widths. In this exercise, you use Word's Border options to apply a border to a paragraph in your document.

You can apply a border to a paragraph by clicking the Border button in the Paragraph group on the Home tab. To change the border style, click the drop-down arrow next to the Border button.

For additional options, click the Borders and Shading option on the Border menu to display the Borders tab of the Borders and Shading dialog box. You can choose a number of border colors and styles in this dialog box, or you can remove a border completely. This dialog box also contains tabs for page border options and shading.

STEP BY STEP   **Place a Border around a Paragraph**

USE the document that is open from the previous exercise.

1. Place the insertion point in the second paragraph.
2. On the Home tab, in the Paragraph group, click the drop-down arrow next to the Border ⊞ ▾ button to display the menu shown in Figure 4-12.

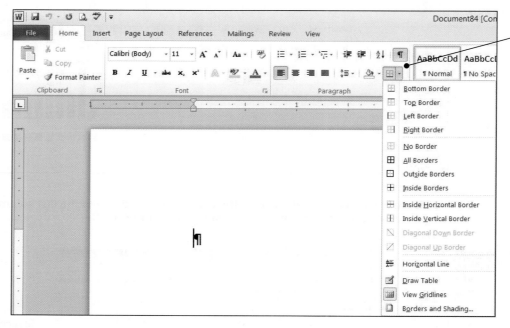

Click drop-down arrow to display Border menu.

Figure 4-12

Border menu

3. Click Outside Borders on the menu.
4. Your document should look similar to Figure 4-13.

Figure 4-13

Shading and border

Paragraph with shading

Border around paragraph

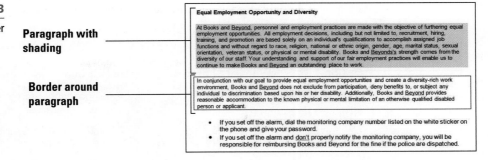

Another Way
The Borders and Shading dialog box can be accessed by clicking the drop-down arrow next to the Border button, then clicking Borders and Shading.

5. **SAVE** the document with the same filename in the lesson folder on your USB flash drive then CLOSE the file.

PAUSE. LEAVE Word open for the next exercise.

Take Note   Borders can also be added to pages, sections, tables, cells, graphic objects, and pictures.

Clearing the Formats from a Paragraph

After formatting your document, you may decide that you no longer want any formatting in a paragraph or that you want to begin again. The Clear Formatting command provides an easy way to change a paragraph back to plain text. When you execute this command, all formatting is removed, and the font and font size revert to the original document settings. To clear formatting in a paragraph, select the paragraph(s) then on the **Home** tab, in the **Font** group, click the **Clearing Formatting** button.

Ⓧ Ref   You can also clear formatting in the Styles group by clicking the More button. For more information, see Lesson 3.

SETTING LINE SPACING IN TEXT AND BETWEEN PARAGRAPHS

The Bottom Line

In Word, you can determine how much space separates lines of text, and you also can set the spacing between paragraphs. By default, Word sets line spacing (the space between each line of text) to 1.15. Line spacing is paragraph based and can be customized by specifying a point size. Paragraph spacing, which affects the space above and below paragraphs, is set to 10 points after each paragraph by default. The higher the point size is, the greater the space between paragraphs is. In this exercise, you learn to set both line and paragraph spacing.

Setting Line Spacing

Line spacing is the amount of space between the lines of text in a paragraph. In this exercise, you learn to set line spacing using a number of Word paragraph formatting tools.

Line spacing options are available in the Home tab within the Paragraph group by using the Line and Spacing button. The line spacing options can also be accessed through the Indents and Spacing tab of the Paragraph dialog box. The Paragraph formatting tools can also be accessed in the Page Layout tab within the Paragraph group by launching the Paragraph dialog box. Table 4-4 provides additional information regarding line spacing options and descriptions.

Table 4-4

Line Spacing Options

Option	Keyboard Shortcut	Description
Single	Ctrl+1	Default option that accommodates the largest font in a line, plus a small amount of extra space.
1.5	Ctrl+5	One-and-one-half times the amount of space used in single spacing.
Double	Ctrl+2	Twice the amount of space used in single spacing.
At least		Sets the spacing at the minimum amount needed to fit the largest font on the line.
Exactly		Sets the spacing at a fixed amount that Word does not adjust.
Multiple		Sets the spacing at an amount that is increased or decreased from single spacing by a percentage that you specify. Setting the line spacing to 1.3, for example, increases the space by 30%.

STEP BY STEP   **Set Line Spacing in a Paragraph**

OPEN the *handbook_introduction* document you completed earlier in this lesson.

1. Place the insertion point in the first paragraph.
2. On the Home tab, in the Paragraph group, click the Line and Paragraph Spacing button to display the Line Spacing menu, as shown in Figure 4-14.

Figure 4-14

Line Spacing menu

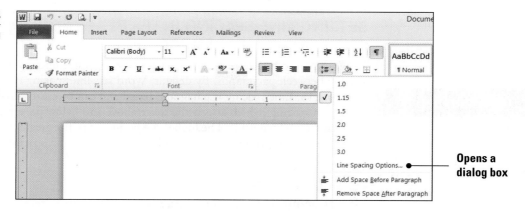

Opens a dialog box

3. Select 2.0 to double-space the selected text.
4. Place the insertion point in the second paragraph.
5. On the Home tab, in the Paragraph group, click the drop-down arrow next to the Line and Paragraph Spacing button to display the menu.
6. To set more precise spacing measurements, click Line Spacing Options to display the Indents and Spacing tab of the Paragraph dialog box.

7. In the Line Spacing section, click the **drop-down arrow** and select **Exactly** in the Line Spacing list. In the At list, click the **up** arrow until it reads **14 pt**. The line spacing is increased.

8. Click **OK**.

9. **SAVE** the document as *handbook_introduction_1* in the lesson folder on your USB flash drive.

PAUSE. LEAVE the document open to use in the next exercise.

Setting Paragraph Spacing

Paragraphs are usually separated by a blank line in Word documents. When you press the Enter key at the end of a paragraph, Word adds the designated space above or below the paragraph. By default, the spacing after a paragraph is set to 10 points and the spacing before paragraphs is set to zero, but you can change these settings for a single paragraph or for an entire document. In this exercise, you learn to set paragraph spacing.

To increase or decrease paragraph spacing, click the Before and After up or down arrows in the Indents and Spacing tab of the Paragraph dialog box. The Paragraph dialog box can be accessed using the dialog box launcher in the Paragraph group of the Home tab, the dialog box launcher in the Paragraph group of the Page Layout tab, or by right-clicking and selecting Paragraph from the menu that appears.

Paragraph spacing can also be changed in the Paragraph group on the Home tab by clicking the Line Spacing button to Add Space Before or After Paragraph or Remove Space Before or After Paragraph.

STEP BY STEP   **Set Spacing around a Paragraph**

USE the document that is open from the previous exercise.

1. Place the insertion point in the third paragraph.

2. On the Home tab, in the Paragraph group, click the **drop-down arrow** to display the Paragraph dialog box. The Indents and Spacing tab is the active tab.

3. In the Spacing section, click the **up arrow** next to Before until it reads **24 pt**.

4. Click the **up arrow** next to After until it reads **24 pt**.

5. Click **OK**. Notice the spacing between the paragraphs.

6. With the insertion point still in the third paragraph, click the **drop-down arrow** next to the Line and Paragraph Spacing ↕≡ button in the Paragraph group to display the Line Spacing menu.

7. Click **Remove Space Before Paragraph**.

8. **SAVE** the document as *handbook_introduction_2* in the lesson folder on your USB flash drive, then CLOSE the file.

PAUSE. LEAVE Word open for the next exercise.

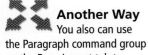
Another Way
You also can use the Paragraph command group on the Page Layout tab to change paragraph spacing.

CREATING AND FORMATTING A BULLETED LIST

The Bottom Line

Bulleted lists are an effective way to format lists of items that don't have to appear in any specific order. (Use numbered lists for items that fall in a set order.) Items in a bulleted list are marked by small icons—dots, diamonds, and so on. In Word, you can create bulleted lists from scratch, change existing text into a bulleted list, choose from a number of bullet styles, create levels within a bulleted list, and insert a symbol or picture as a bullet.

Creating a Bulleted List

By creating and formatting a bulleted list, you can draw attention to major points in a document. In this exercise, you learn to create and format such a list.

STEP BY STEP   **Create a Bulleted List**

OPEN *alarm* from the data files for this lesson.

@ The *alarm* file for this lesson is available on the book companion website or in WileyPLUS.

WILEY PLUS *EXTRA*

WileyPLUS Extra! features an online tutorial of this task.

1. Select the two sentences below the phrase Please keep in mind:.
2. On the Home tab, in the Paragraph group, click the Bullets :≡ ▾ button. Notice that a solid circle appears before the selected paragraph.
3. Click to place the insertion point at the end of the second bulleted sentence.
4. Press Enter. Word automatically continues the bulleted list by supplying the next bulleted line.
5. Beside the new bullet, key If you do not know your four-digit code and password, please get it from the HR department.
6. Select the entire bulleted list.
7. To change the format of the bulleted list, click the drop-down arrow next to the Bullets :≡ ▾ button to display the menu shown in Figure 4-15. The bulleted items may not match your screen.

Figure 4-15

Bullet formatting options

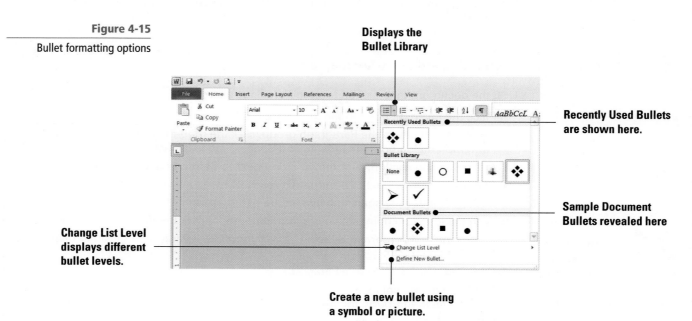

Displays the
Bullet Library

Recently Used Bullets
are shown here.

Sample Document
Bullets revealed here

Change List Level
displays different
bullet levels.

Create a new bullet using
a symbol or picture.

Take Note   To change a bulleted list to a numbered list (or vice versa), select the list and then click either the Bullets button or the Numbering button. If you wish to remove one of the bullets from the Library, complete this process in the Bullet Library section of the Bullet drop-down menu by selecting the bullet and right-clicking to remove it.

8. Click the hollow circle in the Bullet Library.
9. Place the insertion point in the second bulleted item.

10. Click the **drop-down arrow** next to the Bullets ⸬≡ ▾ button, point to Change List Level, and note the levels that appear (see Figure 4-16). When you point to the Level List, a ScreenTip will appear displaying the level.

Figure 4-16

Change List Level

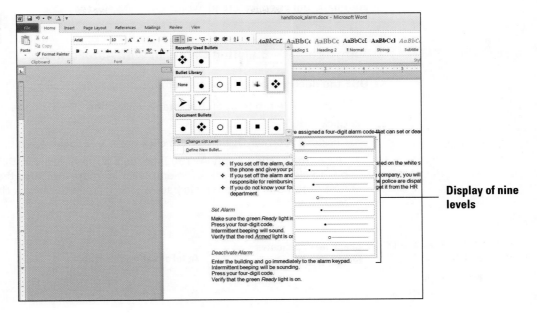

Display of nine levels

11. Click to select **Level 2**. The Bullet item is demoted from Level 1 to Level 2.
12. Place the insertion point in the third bulleted item.
13. Click the **drop-down arrow** next to the Bullets ⸬≡ ▾ button, then point to Change List Level to produce a menu of list-level options.
14. Click to select **Level 3**. Your document should look similar to the one shown in Figure 4-17.

Figure 4-17

Bullet levels

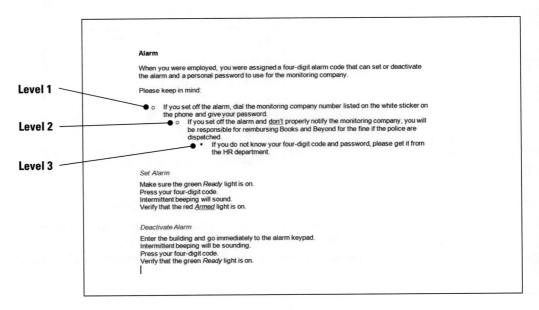

15. **SAVE** the document as *handbook_alarm* in the lesson folder on your USB flash drive.
PAUSE. LEAVE Word open for the next exercise.

Turning Automatic Bulleting On and Off with AutoFormat

After you have clicked the Bullet button to create a bulleted list, Word's AutoFormat feature automatically continues the bulleted format. In this exercise, you learn how to turn off this automatic bulleting feature in Word.

STEP BY STEP   **Turn Automatic Bulleting On or Off with AutoFormat**

USE the document that is open from the previous exercise.

1. Click the **File** tab to open Backstage view, then click **Options**.
2. Click **Proofing**.
3. Click **AutoCorrect Options**, then click the **AutoFormat As You Type** tab.
4. Under the section Apply As You Type, select the **Automatic Bulleted Lists** check box to clear its check mark (an empty check mark indicates the feature is off). To turn Automatic Bulleted Lists back on, click again to place a check mark in the box (see Figure 4-18).

Figure 4-18

AutoCorrect dialog box displaying the AutoFormat As You Type tab

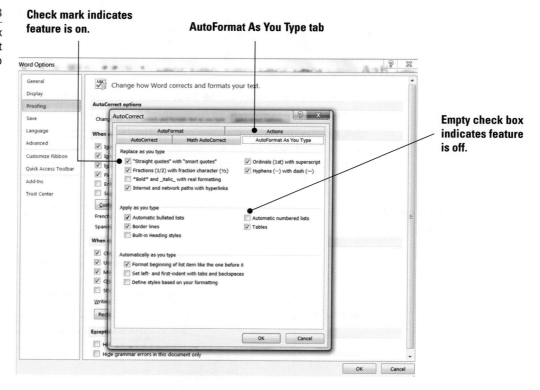

5. Click **OK** to close the AutoCorrect dialog box, then click **OK** to close the Word Options dialog box.

PAUSE. LEAVE the document open to use in the next exercise.

CREATING A NUMBERED LIST

| The Bottom Line | You can quickly add numbers to existing lines of text to create a list, or Word can automatically create a numbered list as you key. |

Creating a Numbered List

In this exercise, you learn how to create and format a numbered list in Word.

STEP BY STEP   **Create a Numbered List**

USE the *handbook_alarm_update* document from the previous exercise.

1. Select the four sentences under the Set Alarm heading.
2. On the Home tab, in the Paragraph group, click the **drop-down arrow** next to the Numbering ⬚ ▾ button to display the Numbering Library shown in Figure 4-19.

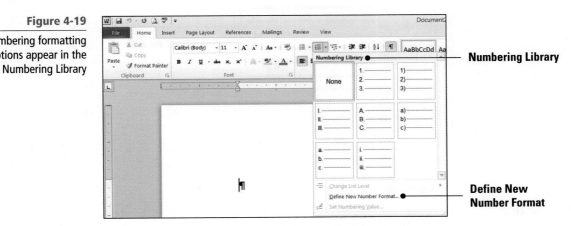

Figure 4-19

Numbering formatting options appear in the Numbering Library

3. Click the **second option** after None in the first row, second column. The rows are numbered 1., 2., 3., . . .
4. Place the insertion point at the end of item number 4 and press **Enter**. Notice that Word automatically numbers the next line sequentially.
5. In the new numbered line, key **Leave the premises immediately**.
6. Select the four sentences under the Deactivate Alarm heading.
7. On the Home tab, in the Paragraph group, click the **drop-down arrow** next to the Numbering ⬚ ▾ button.
8. Select the **numbered list** in the first column, third row. The four sentences are numbered with lowercase letters: a., b., c., d.
9. Select the **numbered list** under the *Set Alarm* heading.
10. To change the format of the numbered list, click the **drop-down arrow** next to the Numbering ⬚ ▾ button, then click **Define New Number Format**. The Define New Number Format dialog box appears.

11. Click the drop-down arrow under the Number style section and select uppercase roman numerals (see Figure 4-20). The format for the selected text changed to uppercase roman numerals.

Figure 4-20

Define New Number Format dialog box

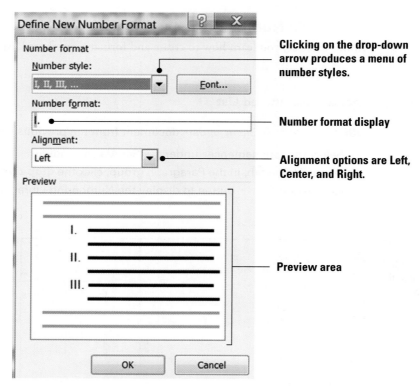

Clicking on the drop-down arrow produces a menu of number styles.

Number format display

Alignment options are Left, Center, and Right.

Preview area

12. Click **OK**.

Take Note   To change the formatting of list numbers, click any number to select the entire list. If you select the text as well, the formatting of both the text and the numbering will change.

13. **SAVE** the document as *alarm_update* in the lesson folder on your USB flash drive, then **CLOSE** the file.

PAUSE. LEAVE Word open to use in the next exercise.

Take Note   The same process used in Backstage for turning automatic bulleting on and off in Word's AutoFormat feature is applied the same way for the Automatic Numbering List.

STEP BY STEP   **Create an Outline-Style List**

@ The *outline* file for this lesson is available on the book companion website or in WileyPLUS.

OPEN *outline* from the data files for this lesson.

1. Position the insertion point on the blank line after the Discussion Outline heading.
2. On the Home tab, in the Paragraph group, click the Multilevel List button. A menu of list formats appears. Notice that when you position the mouse pointer over the formats, they enlarge and expand.

STOP. CLOSE the document without saving.

SOFTWARE ORIENTATION

Tab Dialog Box

Tabs in Word insert blank spaces before or within text and paragraphs. You will use the Tabs dialog box, shown in Figure 4-21, to set and clear tabs in Word. Use this figure as a reference throughout the remainder of this lesson as well as the rest of the book.

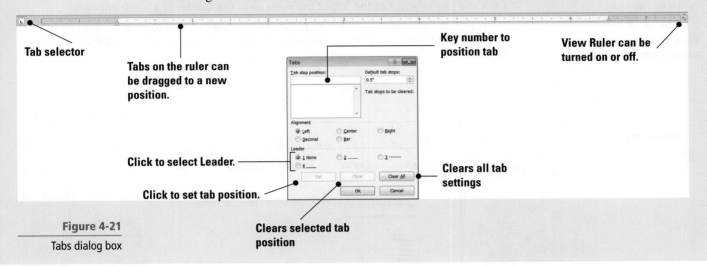

Tab selector

Tabs on the ruler can be dragged to a new position.

Key number to position tab

View Ruler can be turned on or off.

Click to select Leader.

Click to set tab position.

Clears all tab settings

Clears selected tab position

Figure 4-21

Tabs dialog box

SETTING AND MODIFYING TABS

The Bottom Line

As you previously learned, you can use the ruler to set tabs. To be more precise, you can also use the options available in the Tabs dialog box.

Take Note

To view Tabs as they are being set, display nonprinting characters, as discussed in Lesson 1.

Setting Tabs on the Ruler

By default, left-aligned tab stops are set every half-inch on the ruler. To set a tab at a different position on the ruler, you can click the tab selector at the left end of the ruler, then position the insertion point on the ruler and click. A ScreenTip will appear showing the type of tabs at the tab selector. In this exercise, you learn to set tabs on Word's ruler.

Table 4-5 lists the types of tabs available in Word and their descriptions. To view tabs on the ruler, place your insertion point over the text.

After tabs are set, press the Tab key; the insertion point will stop at the position set. To move a tab stop to a different position on the ruler, click and drag it left or right to a new position.

Table 4-5

Tab Stops on the Ruler

Name	Button	Description
Left tab	**L**	Left-aligns text at the tab place indicated on the horizontal ruler
Center tab	**⊥**	Centers text at the place indicated on the horizontal ruler
Right tab	**⅃**	Right-aligns text at the place indicated on the horizontal ruler
Decimal tab	**⊥·**	Aligns numbers around a decimal point at the place indicated on the horizontal ruler
Bar tab	**|**	Inserts a vertical bar line at the place indicated on the horizontal ruler

STEP BY STEP   Set Tabs on the Ruler

 The *perdiem* file for this lesson is available on the book companion website or in WileyPLUS.

WileyPLUS Extra! features an online tutorial of this task.

OPEN *perdiem* from the data files for this lesson.

1. On the Home tab in the Paragraph group, click the Show/Hide (¶) button to show nonprinting characters.
2. Place the insertion point on the line below the Meals & Incidentals Breakdown heading.
3. Click the tab selector at the left of the ruler until the Center ⊥ tab appears.

    A ScreenTip will appear when you place your pointer over the tab selector. The tab selector and horizontal ruler are shown in Figure 4-22, displaying the different types of tabs.

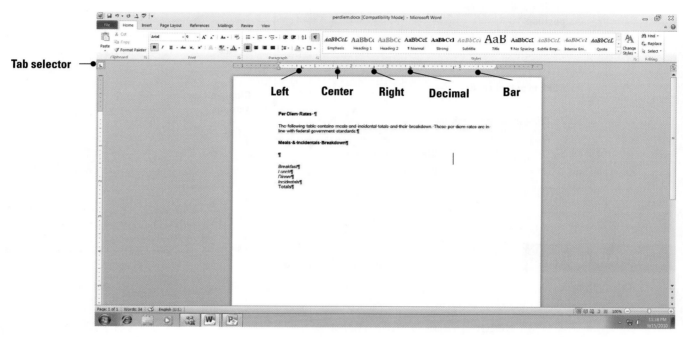

Figure 4-22

Tab selector and horizontal ruler with tab sets

Troubleshooting   If the horizontal ruler is not visible, click the View Ruler button at the top of the vertical scroll bar.

4. Click the ruler at the 2.5-inch mark to set a Center ⊥ tab.

5. Click the ruler at the 4-inch mark to set a Center ⊥ tab.

6. Press Tab and key Chicago.

7. Press Tab and key New York.

8. Select the list of words starting with *Breakfast* and ending with *Totals*.

9. Click the tab selector until the Right ⌐ tab appears.

10. Click the ruler at the 1-inch mark to set a Right ⌐ tab.

11. Deselect and place the insertion point in front of each word and press Tab to align it at the Right tab. Your document should look similar to the one shown in Figure 4-23.

Figure 4-23

Right tab formatting

Right tab setting

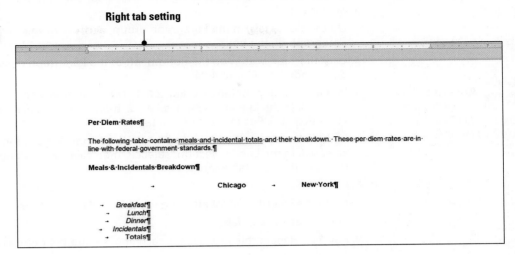

12. **SAVE** the document as *handbook_perdiem* in the lesson folder on your USB flash drive.

PAUSE. LEAVE the document open to use in the next exercise.

Using the Tabs Dialog Box

The Tabs dialog box is useful for setting tabs at precise locations on the ruler, clearing all tabs, and setting tab leaders. Tab **leaders** are symbols such as dotted, dashed, or solid lines that fill the space before a tab (see Figure 4-24). In this exercise, you practice setting tabs and leaders using the Tabs dialog box.

Figure 4-24

Tabs dialog box

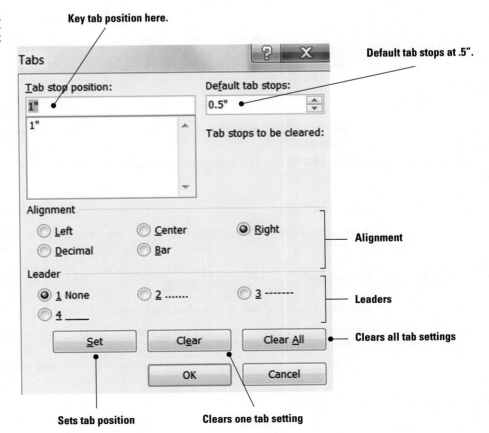

USE the document that is open from the previous exercise.

1. Select the list of words starting with Breakfast and continuing to the end of the document.

2. On the Home tab, in the Paragraph group, click the drop-down arrow to launch the Paragraph dialog box.

3. Click the Tabs button on the bottom left of the Paragraph dialog box to display the Tabs dialog box (see Figure 4-24).

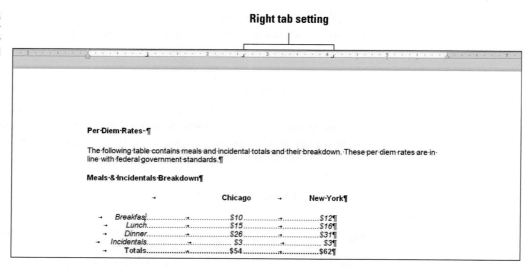

Another Way
To open the Tabs dialog box, double-click any tab stop on the ruler.

4. In the Tab stop position box, key 2.6. In the Alignment section, Right is already selected. In the Leader section, select 2, then click Set. After setting individuals tabs, you must click Set to position the tab setting.

5. In the Tab stop position box, key 4.1. In the Alignment section, Right is already selected. In the Leader section, select 2, then click Set. Setting a leader provides a guide to the next tab setting.

6. Click OK.

7. Place the insertion point after the word Breakfast and press Tab.

8. Key $10 and press Tab.

9. Key $12. Repeat this process for each line, keying the numbers shown in Figure 4-25.

Figure 4-25

Tabs and tab leaders formatting

Right tab setting

Per·Diem·Rates··¶

The·following·table·contains·meals·and·incidental·totals·and·their·breakdown.·These·per·diem·rates·are·in· line·with·federal·government·standards.¶

Meals·&·Incidentals·Breakdown¶

	Chicago	New·York¶
Breakfast	$10	$12¶
Lunch	$15	$16¶
Dinner	$26	$31¶
Incidentals	$3	$3¶
Totals	$54	$62¶

10. **SAVE** the document as *handbook_perdieum_1* in the lesson folder on your USB flash drive.

PAUSE. LEAVE the document open to use in the next exercise.

Moving Tabs

Tabs can be placed in a new position on the ruler by dragging with the mouse pointer.

STEP BY STEP   **Move Tabs**

USE the document that is open from the previous exercise.

1. Select the block of text beginning with Breakfast . . . and ending with . . . $62. Include the nonprinting character (¶).

2. Position the mouse pointer at 4.1" on the ruler until you see the Right Tab ScreenTip.

3. Press and hold the left mouse button and drag on the ruler to 5.1″. Release the left mouse button. Notice the Right tab setting for the five lines is positioned at 5.1″ on the ruler.

4. Select New York. Drag the Center tab setting and position it at 5″ on the ruler.

5. **SAVE** the document as *handbook_perdiem_2* in the lesson folder on your USB flash drive.

PAUSE. LEAVE the document open to use in the next exercise.

Clearing Tabs

Tabs can be removed by dragging off the ruler, or you can use the Tabs dialog box to clear one or all tabs. To remove a tab stop from the ruler, click and drag it off the ruler. When you release the mouse button, the tab stop disappears. Or, open the Tabs dialog box, where you can choose to clear one tab or all tabs. In this exercise, you practice clearing tabs from your Word document.

STEP BY STEP	Clear Tabs

USE the document that is open from the previous exercise.

1. Place the insertion point on the last line (Totals).
2. Move your mouse pointer to the tab stop at 5.1″ on the ruler.
3. Press and hold the mouse button and drag it off the ruler. Release the mouse button to remove the tab stop.
4. On the Home tab, in the Paragraph group, click the drop-down arrow to launch the Paragraph dialog box.
5. Click the Tabs button on the bottom left of the dialog box to display the Tabs dialog box.
6. In the Tab stop position list, click 2.6″, then click Clear to clear that tab.
7. Click the Clear All button to clear all tabs on that line.
8. Click OK to close the Tabs dialog box.
9. Select all the text on the Totals line and press the Delete button to delete it.
10. **SAVE** the document with the same filename, then **CLOSE** the file.

STOP. EXIT Word.

SKILL SUMMARY

In This Lesson, You Learned How To:
Format paragraphs
Set line spacing in text and between paragraphs
Create and format a bulleted list
Create a numbered list
Set and modifying tabs

Knowledge Assessment

True/False

Circle T if the statement is true or F if the statement is false.

T   F   1. Pressing the Enter key will indent the first line of a paragraph.

T   F   2. An indent is the space between a paragraph and the document's left and/or right margin.

T   F   3. You can use the ruler to set tabs.

T   F   4. A bar tab inserts a vertical bar line at the place indicated on the vertical ruler.

T   F   5. Tab leaders are dotted, dashed, or solid lines that fill the space before a tab.

T   F   6. The Clear Formatting command will only clear the fonts applied to the selected text.

T   F   7. Horizontal alignment refers the position of text with regard to the top and bottom margins of a document.

T   F   8. Centered vertical alignment aligns text between the top and bottom margin.

T   F   9. Indents can be changed using the markers on the ruler.

T   F   10. The shortcut to double-space a paragraph is Ctrl+2.

Multiple Choice

Select the best response for the following statements.

1. Which of the following is not a type of indent?
   a. Hanging
   b. Negative
   c. Positive
   d. First-line

2. Which word(s) refers to how text is positioned between the top and bottom margins of the page?
   a. Horizontal alignment
   b. Vertical alignment
   c. Justified
   d. Line spacing

3. Which line spacing command sets the spacing at a fixed amount that Word does not adjust?
   a. Exactly
   b. Double
   c. Multiple
   d. At least

4. Where is the View Ruler button located?
   a. In the Tabs dialog box
   b. At the top of the vertical scroll bar
   c. In the Paragraph group
   d. All of the above

5. What does dragging a tab off the ruler do?
   a. Moves it to another position
   b. Turns it into a left-aligned tab
   c. Clears it
   d. Hides it from view

6. Bullets can be defined by adding a:
   a. symbol.
   b. box.
   c. picture.
   d. Both a and c

7. Which property of borders can be changed in the Borders tab of the Borders and Shading dialog box?
   a. Color
   b. Width
   c. Style
   d. All of the above

8. The inverted L ⌐ sets which tab on the ruler?
   a. Left
   b. Right
   c. Center
   d. Decimal

9. Which tab setting would you use to align a list of currency values?
   a. Decimal
   b. Center
   c. Right
   d. Decimal with leaders

Competency Assessment

Project 4-1: Lost Art Photos

You are employed in the marketing department at Lost Art Photos and have been asked to format a promotional document.

GET READY. LAUNCH Word if it is not already running.

1. **OPEN** *photos* from the data files for this lesson.
2. **SAVE** the document as *lost_art_photos* in the lesson folder on your USB flash drive.
3. **SELECT** the document's title.
4. On the Home tab, in the Paragraph group, click **drop-down arrow** on the Border ⊞ ▾ button.
5. Scroll down and click **Borders and Shading** to open the Borders and Shading dialog box.
6. In the Setting list, click **Shadow**. On the Width list, click **3 pt**.
7. Click **OK** to close the Borders and Shading dialog box.
8. On the Home tab, in the Paragraph group, click the **drop-down arrow** next to the Shading ⬛ ▾ button.

@ The *photos* file for this lesson is available on the book companion website or in WileyPLUS.

9. Under Theme Colors, click the color that is labeled Olive Green, Accent 3, Lighter 60%.

10. Select the first paragraph.

11. On the Home tab, in the Paragraph group, click the Line Spacing ↕≡ button.

12. Click 1.0 on the menu.

13. Select Affordable Prints.

14. Click the down arrow next to the Border ⊞ ▾ button.

15. Click Outside Borders from the selection.

16. Click the drop-down arrow next to the Shading ▨ ▾ button.

17. Click the color that is labeled Olive Green, Accent 3, Lighter 40%.

18. Double-click the Format Painter ⬥ Format Painter to copy the formatting of *Affordable Prints* to each of the other headings: *Quality Product, Options, Options, Options,* and *Satisfaction Guaranteed*. Click the Format Painter to turn it off.

19. **SAVE** the document in the lesson folder on your USB flash drive, then **CLOSE** the file.

LEAVE Word open for the next project.

Project 4-2: **General Performance Expectation Guidelines**

In your job at Books and Beyond, you continue to work on documents that will be part of the employee handbook.

GET READY. LAUNCH Word if it is not already running.

@ The *guidelines* file for this lesson is available on the book companion website or in WileyPLUS.

1. **OPEN** *guidelines* from the data files for this lesson.

2. SAVE the document as *handbook_guidelines* in the lesson folder on your USB flash drive.

3. Select the two lines that begin Verbal discussion . . . and Written warning . . . .

4. On the Home tab, in the Paragraph group, click the drop-down arrow next to the Bullets ▤ ▾ button and select the solid circle.

5. Place the insertion point after the second sentence in the list and press Enter.

6. Key Termination as the third bulleted item.

7. Select the first, second, third, and last paragraph in the document.

8. On the Home tab, in the Paragraph group, and click the Justify ▤ button.

9. With the paragraphs still selected, apply the first-line indent by launching the Paragraph dialog box. On the Home tab, in the Paragraph group, click the drop-down arrow to launch the *Paragraph* dialog box. Under Special, select the drop-down arrow and select First Line Indent ▽. Click OK to close the Paragraph dialog box.

10. **SAVE** the document in the lesson folder on your USB flash drive, then **CLOSE** the file.

LEAVE Word open for the next project.

Proficiency Assessment

Project 4-3: **PTA Officers**

You are a volunteer at the local elementary school and have been asked to format a PTA document that lists the officers for the upcoming school year.

GET READY. LAUNCH Word if it is not already running.

@ The *pta* file for this lesson is available on the book companion website or in WileyPLUS.

1. **OPEN** *pta* from the data files for this lesson.

2. **SAVE** the document as *pta_officers* in the lesson folder on your USB flash drive.

3. Use the Tabs dialog box to format the document as shown in Figure 4-26.

Figure 4-26

Formatted PTA document tabs

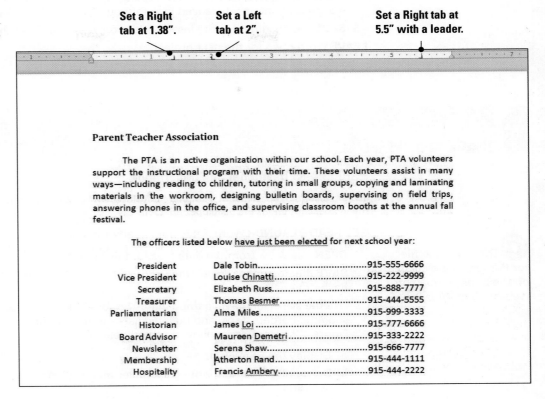

4. **SAVE** the document in the lesson folder on your USB flash drive, then **CLOSE** the file. **LEAVE** Word open for the next project.

Project 4-4: Phone List

Create a list of numbers that you call frequently to keep beside your phone.

GET READY. LAUNCH Word if it is not already running.

1. **CREATE** a new Word document.
2. **SAVE** the document as *phone_list* in the lesson folder on your USB flash drive.
3. Create a list of phone numbers and title it Numbers To Post. Create a numbered list and apply tab settings as shown in Figure 4-27.

Figure 4-27

Phone list

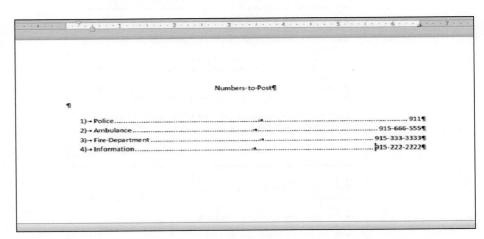

4. Create a Right tab setting at 6.5" with dot leaders, then key the phone number beside each name. The phone numbers should align evenly between the left and right margins. Maintain a balanced look for your document.
5. **SAVE** the document in the lesson folder on your USB flash drive, then **CLOSE** the file.

LEAVE Word open for the next project.

Mastery Assessment

Project 4-5: Developer Job Description

You are a content specialist at a software development company. Your supervisor asks you to format the job description for the developer position.

The *developer* file for this lesson is available on the book companion website or in WileyPLUS.

GET READY. LAUNCH Word if it is not already running.

1. **OPEN** *developer* from the data files for this lesson.
2. **SAVE** the document as *developer_description* in the lesson folder on your USB flash drive.
3. Use the skills you have learned in this lesson—such as alignment, line spacing, shading, borders, tabs, and bulleted lists—to format the document as shown in Figure 4-28. Be sure to follow these guidelines:
   a. Display the Show/Hide.
   b. Delete all of the nonprinting character marks (¶) in the document where a blank line appears.
   c. For the title, apply the shading Orange, Accent 6, Lighter 40% and set the paragraph Spacing After to 24 pts.
   d. Select the headings Position Title, Position Objective, and Reports To and apply the shading to Orange, Accent 6, Lighter 80%.

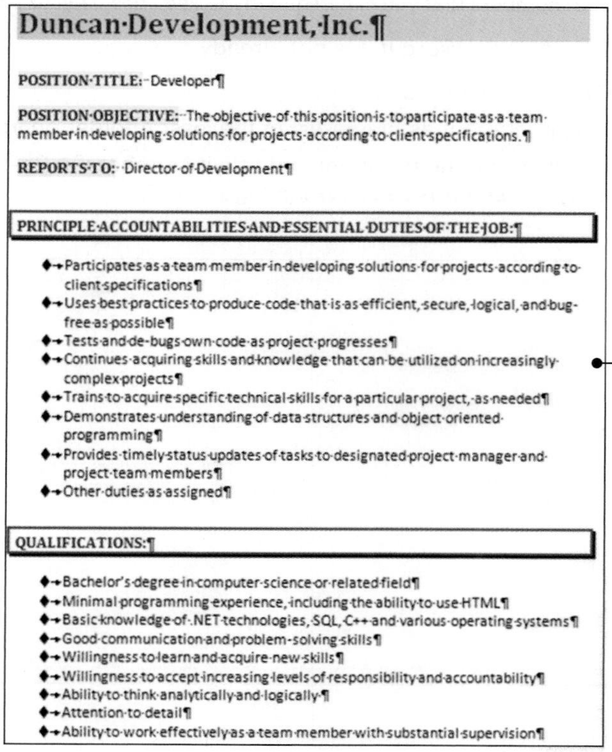
Duncan·Development,·Inc.¶

POSITION·TITLE:··Developer¶

POSITION·OBJECTIVE:··The·objective·of·this·position·is·to·participate·as·a·team·member·in·developing·solutions·for·projects·according·to·client·specifications.¶

REPORTS·TO:··Director·of·Development¶

PRINCIPLE·ACCOUNTABILITIES·AND·ESSENTIAL·DUTIES·OF·THE·JOB:¶

- Participates·as·a·team·member·in·developing·solutions·for·projects·according·to·client·specifications¶
- Uses·best·practices·to·produce·code·that·is·as·efficient,·secure,·logical,·and·bug-free·as·possible¶
- Tests·and·de-bugs·own·code·as·project·progresses¶
- Continues·acquiring·skills·and·knowledge·that·can·be·utilized·on·increasingly·complex·projects¶
- Trains·to·acquire·specific·technical·skills·for·a·particular·project,·as·needed¶
- Demonstrates·understanding·of·data·structures·and·object·oriented·programming¶
- Provides·timely·status·updates·of·tasks·to·designated·project·manager·and·project·team·members¶
- Other·duties·as·assigned¶

QUALIFICATIONS:¶

- Bachelor's·degree·in·computer·science·or·related·field¶
- Minimal·programming·experience,·including·the·ability·to·use·HTML¶
- Basic·knowledge·of·.NET·technologies,·SQL,·C++·and·various·operating·systems¶
- Good·communication·and·problem-solving·skills¶
- Willingness·to·learn·and·acquire·new·skills¶
- Willingness·to·accept·increasing·levels·of·responsibility·and·accountability¶
- Ability·to·think·analytically·and·logically·¶
- Attention·to·detail¶
- Ability·to·work·effectively·as·a·team·member·with·substantial·supervision¶

Figure 4-28

Developer job description

Follow the steps in Project 4-5 to create a matching document.

e. Select the headings, Principle Accountabilities and Essential Duties of the Job and Qualifications and apply a border with the **Shadow setting**; Width: 2¼"; Color: **Orange, Accent 6, Darker 50%**.

f. Set the paragraph Spacing After to 12 pts. after each paragraph headings: Position Title and Position Objective.

g. For the Reports To heading, set the paragraph Spacing After to 24 pts. after Director of Development.

h. Under the heading, Principle Accountabilities and Essential Duties of the Job apply the solid diamond bullets to the paragraphs.

i. At the beginning of the first bulleted item under Principle Accountabilities and Essential Duties of the Job and Qualifications set the paragraph Spacing Before to 12 pts.

j. After the last bulleted item under *Principle Accountabilities* and *Essential Duties of the Job*, set the Spacing After to 18 pts.

4. **SAVE** the document in the lesson folder on your USB flash drive, then **CLOSE** the file.

LEAVE Word open for the next project.

Project 4-6: Rabbit Show

You are a volunteer at the annual Falls Village Fair, and you have been assigned to work on a document about one of the exhibits. The person who created the document was not as familiar with line spacing, tabs, and lists as you are, so you need to format the document as shown in Figure 4-29.

GET READY. LAUNCH Word if it is not already running.

1. **OPEN** *rabbit* from the data files for this lesson.

@ The *rabbit* file for this lesson is available on the book companion website or in WileyPLUS.

2. **SAVE** the document as *rabbit_show* in the lesson folder on your USB flash drive.

3. Make any adjustments necessary to format the tabs, line spacing, and lists as shown in Figure 4-29, following these guidelines:

a. On the title, remove the first-line indent and make sure the alignment is set to Center.

b. Select the first six lines under the heading, remove the first-line indent, then remove all existing tab settings and reset the tab settings to a Right tab at **2"** and **6"** with leaders.

Figure 4-29

Rabbit Show

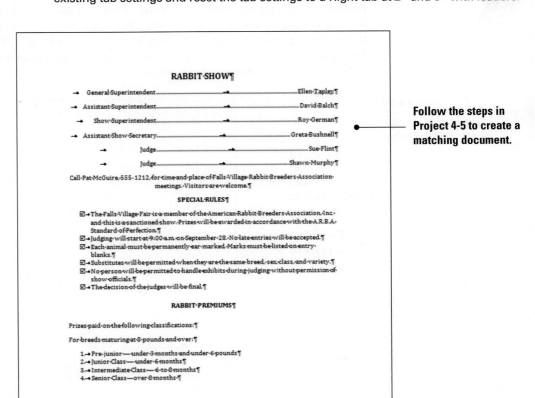

Follow the steps in Project 4-5 to create a matching document.

    c. Remove extra paragraph mark before and after Call Pat . . . and center.

    d. Remove all formatting, tabs, and indents. Apply a bullet using a check mark within a box under the heading Special Rules.

    e. Remove the nonprinting character mark before the heading RABBIT PREMIUMS. Change the paragraph spacing by setting the Spacing Before/After to 18 pts.

    f. Select the items under RABBIT PREMIUMS and clear formatting. Beginning with Pre-Junior and ending with Senior Class . . . , apply the numbering list 1., 2., 3., 4.

4. Adjust the text so that it all fits on one page.

5. **SAVE** the document in the lesson folder on your USB flash drive, then **CLOSE** the file.

CLOSE Word.

 INTERNET READY

Many online resources can provide you with solutions to challenges that you might face during a typical workday. Search the Microsoft website for Work Essentials—a place where you can find information on how to use Microsoft Word efficiently to perform typical business tasks and activities. Explore the resources and content that Work Essentials offers and write a short paragraph about one particular tool or solution that could be useful on the job and how you could use it to be more productive.

Workplace *Ready*

SALES REPORT

Your manager has asked you to assist in preparing a memorandum to the regional director in reference to the third-quarter sales report. Prepare a memorandum demonstrating skills you learned from this lesson in setting tabs. A memorandum is an interoffice communication within an organization (see Figure 4-30). Add two paragraphs with three sentences within both paragraphs explaining the sales report. Create appropriate headings and tab settings for figures. Save and print one copy for your instructor.

Figure 4-30

Sample memorandum
format with tab settings

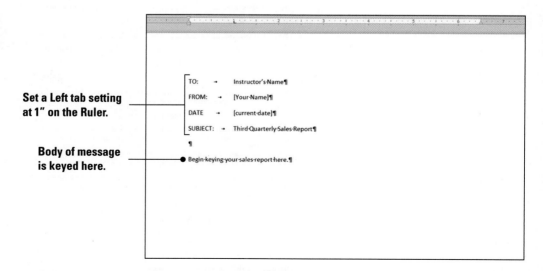

LESSON SKILL MATRIX

In This Lesson, You Will Learn The Following Skills:

Setting Page Layout

Working with Breaks

Controlling Pagination

Setting Up Columns

Inserting a Blank Page into a Document

KEY TERMS

- columns
- hyphenation
- landscape orientation
- margins
- page break
- portrait orientation
- orphan
- section break
- widow

As a marketing associate for First Bank, you are involved in a wide variety of marketing and communications projects. In particular, you are responsible for creating and maintaining marketing collateral—brochures, posters, and other printed product information—that supports the sale of a product. It is time to update the personal Checking Choices document that your bank provides to people interested in opening new accounts. Word is a great tool for producing documents such as this. In this lesson, you will learn to work with page layout, control paragraph behavior, work with section and page breaks, create and format columns, and insert a blank page.

SOFTWARE ORIENTATION

Page Layout Tab

The Page Layout tab contains groups of commands that will produce a formatted document's layout for the entire document or sections of the document. Commands in the Page Setup group allow you to set margins, change the document's orientation, and adjust the paper size for the entire document or sections in the document. Inserting section breaks into the document enables you to change the page setup for an existing section in the document without affecting the other pages in the document. The hyphenation command provides options to hyphenate words in a document automatically or manually, and the nonbreaking space wraps text to the next to avoid breaks at the right margin to create a uniform look.

Figure 5-1

Page Layout tab

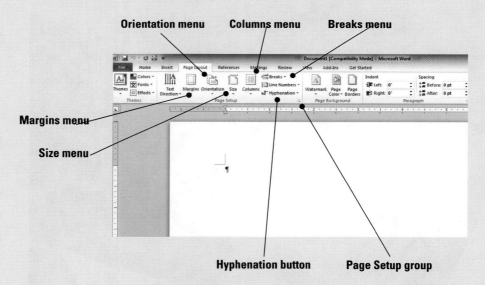

In the Paragraph group, Word contains features that control how a paragraphs breaks within the document and pages. You control the pagination in the document by preventing widows and orphans to break in the document, or keeping text together, lines together, and determining where page breaks will occur in the document.

You can manage the text flow in the document by creating multiple columns in a document, customize the column settings, and insert column breaks in the Page Setup group.

In the Insert tab, you can insert a blank page in the document to begin a new page.

SETTING PAGE LAYOUT

The Bottom Line

The layout of a page helps communicate your message. Although the content of your document is obviously very important, having appropriate margins, page orientation, and paper size all contribute to the document's readability and appearance.

Setting Margins

Margins are the blank borders that occupy the top, bottom, and sides of a document. You can change margins from Word's default size of one inch using commands in the Page Setup group in the Page Layout tab. You can choose from a gallery or set Customize Margins in the Page Setup dialog box. In the Page Setup group, click the Margins menu, and a set of predefined margin settings are available for selection. Click the setting of your choice and the whole document will reflect the changes. Click the Custom Margins command to display the Page Setup dialog box, where you can specify custom margin sizes. In this exercise, you customize a document's margins.

STEP BY STEP   **Set Margins**

GET READY. Before you begin these steps, be sure to launch Microsoft Word.

1. **OPEN** the *proposal* file for this lesson.
2. Delete the extra blank lines above *USA Health Resources*.
3. On the Page Layout tab, in the Page Setup group, click the drop-down arrow to display the Margins menu; then choose Narrow, as shown in Figure 5-2. The margins are set to 0.5" from top, bottom, left, and right.

@ The *proposal* file for this lesson is available on the book companion website or in WileyPLUS.

WileyPLUS Extra! features an online tutorial of this task.

Figure 5-2

Margins menu

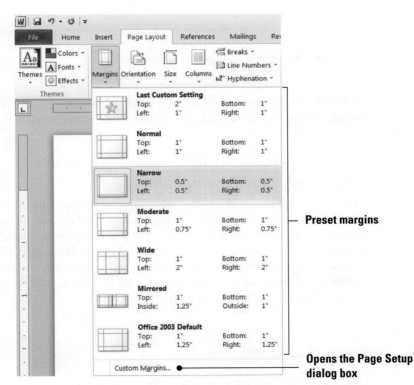

4. In the Page Setup group, click the drop-down arrow to display the Margins menu; then click Custom Margins to open the Page Setup dialog box shown in Figure 5-3. Change the bottom, left, and right margins to 1" and the top margin to 2". Changing the margins affects all pages within the document. Click OK.

Figure 5-3

Page Setup dialog box

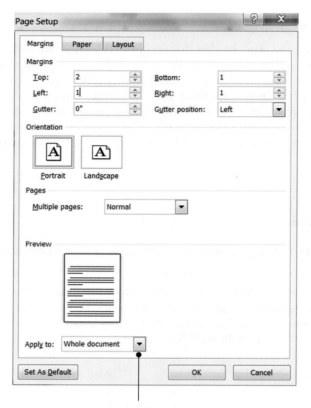

Select how margin settings are applied.

5. SAVE the document in the lesson folder of your USB flash drive as *draft_proposal*. PAUSE. LEAVE the document open to use in the next exercise.

Selecting a Page Orientation

A document's orientation determines what direction the text extends across the page. A document in portrait orientation is 8 ½″ × 11″, whereas a document in landscape orientation is 11″ × 8½″. As you plan and format a document, you must choose its page orientation. In this exercise, you change a document's orientation from portrait (the default) to landscape In **Portrait orientation**, a format commonly used for business documents, text extends across the shorter length of the document. **Landscape orientation**, commonly used for brochures, graphics, tables, and so on, orients text across the longer dimension of the page.

STEP BY STEP   **Select a Page Orientation**

USE the document that is open from the previous exercise.

1. In the Page Setup group of the Page Layout tab, click the drop-down arrow to display the Orientation menu, then select Landscape, as shown in Figure 5-4. The page orientation changes to Landscape.

2. Click the File tab, then Print, to preview the document in Backstage view. On the right side of the pane, the document displays in landscape.

Figure 5-4

Orientation menu

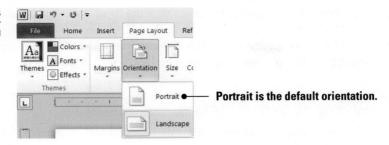

Portrait is the default orientation.

3. **SAVE** document as *draft1_proposal* in the lesson folder on your USB flash drive.

PAUSE. LEAVE the document open to use in the next exercise.

Choosing a Paper Size

While the standard paper size of 8½″ × 11″ is the default setting, Word provides several options for formatting documents for a variety of paper sizes. For instance, invitations, postcards, legal documents, or reports all require a different paper size. Many printers provide options for printing on different sizes of paper, and in some cases, you may need to change or customize the paper size in Word as you format your document. Legal documents, for example, must be formatted for 8½″ × 14″ paper. In this exercise, you will change the size of paper from the default.

STEP BY STEP   **Choose a Paper Size**

USE the document that is open from the previous exercise.

1. In the Page Setup group of the Page Layout tab, click the **drop-down arrow** to display the Orientation menu, then select **Portrait**. The orientation is changed back to portrait from the previous exercise.

2. From the Page Setup group of the Page Layout tab, click the **drop-down arrow** to display the Size menu, then select **Legal**, as shown in Figure 5-5. Word provides preset document sizes, or you can customize the paper size by clicking the **More Paper Sizes** button.

Figure 5-5

Size menu

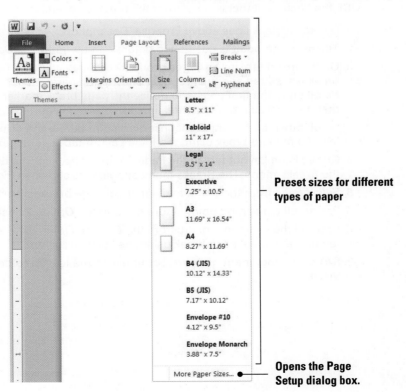

Preset sizes for different types of paper

Opens the Page Setup dialog box.

3. Click the Page Layout tab, then click the drop-down arrow to display the Size menu; next, select Letter.

4. **SAVE** document as *draft2_proposal* in the lesson folder on your USB flash drive.

PAUSE. LEAVE the document open to use in the next exercise.

WORKING WITH BREAKS

The Bottom Line

Word automatically inserts page breaks in multipage documents. There may be times, however, when you will be working with documents that contain various objects or special layouts that require you to control where a page or section breaks. You can insert and remove these manual page breaks and section breaks, and you can control word hyphenation or set nonbreaking spaces in Word.

Inserting and Removing a Manual Page Break

A **page break** is the location in a document where one page ends and a new page begins. You may also decide where to insert the manual page break or set specific options for those page breaks. Page breaks display as a single dotted line with the words Page Break in the center in the Print Layout view (as shown in Figure 5-6). In Print Layout view, Word displays a document page by page, one after the other, on a blue background. In this exercise, you learn to insert and remove a manual page break.

The Breaks menu contains options for inserting three types of breaks:

* **Page:** Inserts a manual page break where one page ends and a new page begins
* **Column:** Inserts a manual column break where text will begin in the next column after the column break
* **Text Wrapping:** Separates the text around objects on a web page, such as caption text from body text

STEP BY STEP **Insert and Remove a Manual Page Break**

USE the document that is open from the previous exercise.

1. Delete all blank lines above Proposal Description.

2. The insertion point is positioned before *P* in the *Proposal Description* heading.

3. On the Insert tab, in the Pages group, click the Page Break button. A manual page break is inserted and the Proposal Description paragraph is forced to the next page. Scroll up to the first page and notice the page break marker that has been inserted and that displays as a single dotted line, as shown in Figure 5-6.

4. Scroll down and position the insertion point before the *O* in the *Option 1* heading to insert a manual break using the Page Layout tab to force text to the next page.

5. On the Page Layout tab, in the Page Setup group, click the drop-down arrow to display the Breaks menu. The Breaks menu appears, as shown in Figure 5-7.

6. Select Page from the menu and a manual page break is inserted.

7. Position the insertion point before the *O* in the *Option 2* heading and repeat step 5.

8. Position the insertion point before the *O* in the *Option 3* heading and press Ctrl+Enter to enter a manual page break using the keyboard shortcut.

9. **SAVE** the document as *draft3_proposal* in the lesson folder on your USB flash drive.

Take Note   Click the Show/Hide **¶** button to view page breaks and section breaks for editing purposes.

Figure 5-6

Page Break in Print Layout View

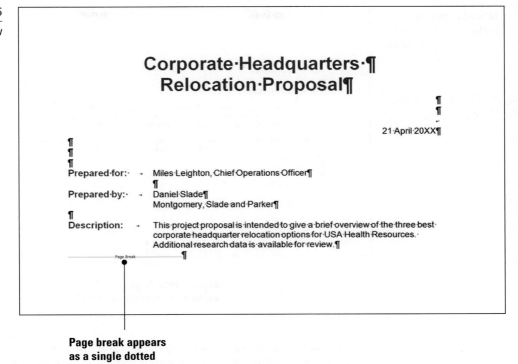

**Page break appears
as a single dotted**

Figure 5-7

Breaks menu

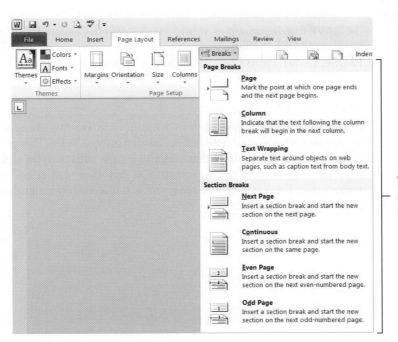

**The two types of break
are Page breaks and
Section Breaks.**

10. Scroll to the second page and notice the manual page break marker, shown in Figure 5-8.

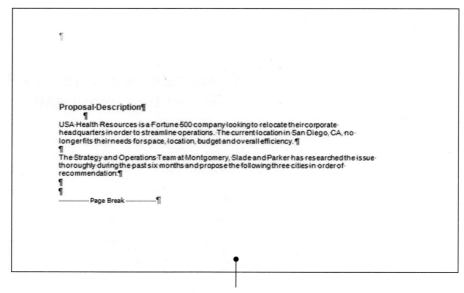

**Second page displays hidden
marks and manual page break.**

11. On page 2, select the Page Break marker and press the Backspace key. The page break is deleted, and text from the previous page is moved to page 2.

12. Scroll up to page 1, select the Page Break marker below the last paragraph in the Description, and press the Backspace key. The Proposal Description heading is moved to page 1.

13. Select the remaining Page Break markers and press Delete.

14. **SAVE** the document as *draft4_proposal* in the lesson folder on your USB flash drive, then **CLOSE** the file.

PAUSE. LEAVE Word open to use in the next exercise.

Another Way
You can also insert a manual page break by pressing Ctrl+Enter.

Inserting Section Breaks

A **section break** is used to create a layout or formatting changes in a portion of a document. It appears with a dotted double line, labeled *Section Break*. You can use section breaks to create a section in your document that contains a page with margins and orientation that is different from the remainder of the document. You can select and delete section breaks just as you can remove page breaks. In this exercise, you will insert a continuous section break and then change the margins for that section.

There are four available options for creating section breaks in Word, as shown in Table 5-1.

Type	Description
Next Page	Inserts a section break and starts the new section on the next page.
Continuous	Inserts a section break and starts the new section on the same page
Even Page	Inserts a section break and starts the new section on the next even-numbered page
Odd Page	Inserts a section break and starts the new section on the next odd-numbered page

Section breaks can be used to change types of formatting for:

- Columns
- Footnotes and endnotes
- Headers and footers
- Line numbering
- Margins
- Page borders
- Page numbering
- Paper size or orientation
- Paper source for a printer
- Vertical alignment of text on a page

Take Note   Remember that when you delete a section break, you remove the section formatting as well.

Using Hyphenation

Hyphens, shown as the punctuation mark -, are used to join words and separate syllables of a single word. By default, **hyphenation** is off in Word; all words appear on a single line, rather than hyphenated. As you format a document, however, you might need to determine when to apply a hyphen.

Note the differences here between a document with hyphenation and one without hyphenation.

Without hyphenation:

As a marketing associate for First Bank, you are involved in a wide variety of marketing and communications projects.

With hyphenation:

As a marketing associate for First Bank, you are involved in a wide variety of marketing and communications projects.

CONTROLLING PAGINATION

A well-organized and formatted document will capture and maintain the reader's attention.

Controlling Widows and Orphans

To maintain an appealing appearance and readable content, you may need to keep the first or last line of a paragraph from appearing alone on the page. Word provides options for keeping text lines together and avoiding single lines of text at the top or bottom of a page. In this exercise, you will manage Word's Widow/Orphan Control.

A **widow** is the last line of a paragraph that appears at the top of a page, as shown in Figure 5-9.

Figure 5-9

A widow at the top of a page

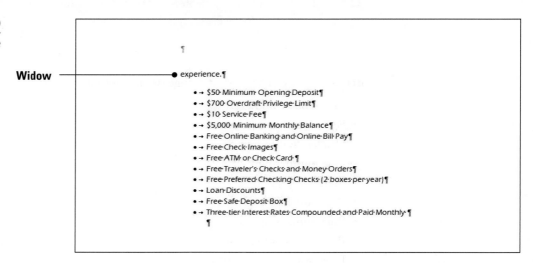

An **orphan** is the first line of a paragraph that appears alone at the bottom of a page, as shown in Figure 5-10.

Figure 5-10

An orphan at the bottom of a page

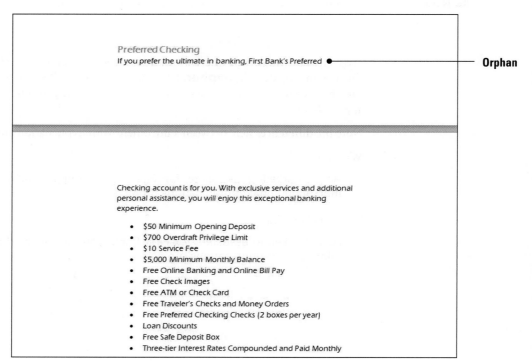

STEP BY STEP   **Turn on Widow/Orphan Control**

OPEN the *checking* document from the data files for this lesson.

@ The *checking* file for this lesson is available on the book companion website or in WileyPLUS.

1. Scroll to the top of page 2 and notice the widow *experience. . .* at the top of the page.
2. On page 1 of the document, select the **three-line paragraph** under Preferred Checking, including the widow.
3. On the Home tab, in the Paragraph group, click the **dialog box launcher**. The Paragraph dialog box appears.
4. Click the **Line and Page Breaks** tab, as shown in Figure 5-11.

Figure 5-11

Paragraph dialog box

By default, Widow/Orphan Control is on.

Paragraph

Indents and Spacing | Line and Page Breaks

Pagination
- [ ] Widow/Orphan control
- [ ] Keep with next
- [ ] Keep lines together
- [ ] Page break before

Formatting exceptions
- [ ] Suppress line numbers
- [ ] Don't hyphenate

Textbox options
Tight wrap:
None

Preview

Tabs...   Set As Default   OK   Cancel

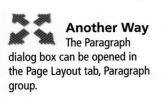

Another Way
The Paragraph dialog box can be opened in the Page Layout tab, Paragraph group.

5. Click the check box to select **Widow/Orphan Control**, then click **OK**. Notice that another line of the paragraph moves to the second page. By default, Widow/Orphan Control is on, and in this exercise, Widow/Orphan Control was off.
6. **SAVE** the document as *checking_choices* in the lesson folder on your USB flash drive.

PAUSE. LEAVE the document open to use in the next exercise.

Keeping a Paragraph's Lines on the Same Page

To keep all sentences of a paragraph on the same page, you can use Word's Keep Lines Together command. By default, the Keep Lines Together feature in Word is off. To keep the lines of a paragraph together, select the paragraph, then open the Paragraph dialog box in the Page Layout tab and click to select the Keep Lines Together check box from the Line and Page Breaks tab.

Keeping Two Paragraphs on the Same Page

Word considers any line of text followed by an Enter to be a paragraph. For instance, when you press Enter after keying a heading, the heading becomes a paragraph. To keep two paragraphs on the same page, you will select both paragraphs, then, in the Lines and Page Break tab of the Paragraph dialog box, click to select the Keep with Next check box. While working in your document, you realize that you need to keep two paragraphs together on the same page, such as the heading and text below it. In this situation, you would use Word's Keep with Next command.

SETTING UP COLUMNS

The Bottom Line

Columns are vertical blocks of text in which text flows from the bottom of one column to the top of the next. Newspapers, magazines, and newsletters are formatted in columns because of the large amounts of text. Text formatted into columns will produce shorter lines and a white space between columns. By default, Word documents are formatted as single column, but you can change that formatting to display multiple columns or columns of varying widths.

Creating Columns

In this exercise, you will practice creating columns within an existing Word document.

STEP BY STEP	**Create Columns**

OPEN the *checking_choices4* document from the data files for this lesson.

@ The *checking_choices4* file for this lesson is available on the book companion website or in WileyPlus.

1. Place the insertion point in front of *F* in Free Checking on page 1.
2. On the Page Layout tab, in the Page Setup group, click the **drop-down arrow** to display the Columns menu. The Columns menu appears, as shown in Figure 5-12.

Figure 5-12

Columns menu

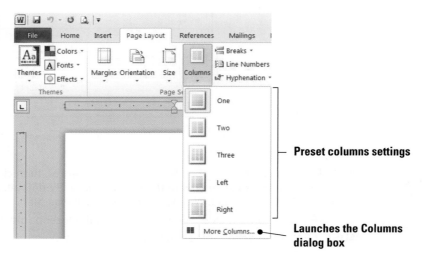

Preset columns settings

Launches the Columns dialog box

3. Select **Two**. The text in the document following the Personal Checking Choices heading is formatted into two columns.
4. **SAVE** the document as *checking_draft* in the lesson folder on your USB flash drive.

PAUSE. LEAVE the document open to use in the next exercise.

Troubleshooting When formatting existing text into columns, avoid selecting the document's title heading if you wish to keep it as a single column.

Formatting Columns

In addition to Word's common column formats, you can customize column formats to fit the text and the purpose of your document. By default, when you click the Columns button and select from the Column menu options, the whole document is formatted as columns. Using the Columns dialog box, you can apply column formatting to the whole document or a selected part of the document, only. You also can change a document formatted in multiple columns back to a single-column document. In this exercise, you learn to format columns in Word.

On the Page Layout tab, in the Page Setup group, the Columns menu lists these options for creating common column formats:

- **One:** Formats the text into a single column
- **Two:** Formats the text into two even columns
- **Three:** Formats the text into three even columns
- **Left:** Formats the text into two unequal columns—a narrow one on the left and a wide one on the right
- **Right:** Formats the text into two uneven columns—a narrow one on the right and a wide one on the left
- **More Columns:** Contains options for customizing columns

Click the Line Between box to insert a vertical line between columns.

STEP BY STEP   **Format Columns**

USE the document that is open from the previous exercise.

1. On the Page Layout tab, in the Page Setup group, click the drop-down arrow to display the Columns menu. The insertion point should be position in front of *Free Checking*.
2. Select More Columns. The Columns dialog box appears, as shown in Figure 5-13.

Figure 5-13

Columns dialog box

Change the number of columns.

Column width can be automatically set or adjusted manually.

Preset columns options

Insert Line between columns.

Spacing refers to space between columns.

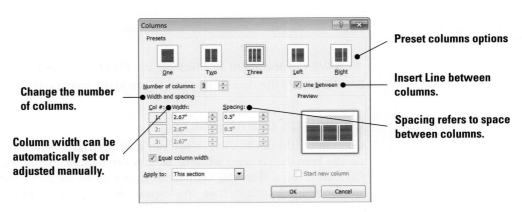

3. In the Number of columns box, key 3 or click the up arrow once.
4. Click the Line between check box.
5. Click OK.
6. Position the insertion point before the *S* in the Senior Preferred heading.
7. In the Page Layout tab, within the Paragraph group, click the dialog box launcher. In the Line and Page Breaks tab of the dialog box, click to deselect the Page Break Before box and click OK. The Page Break Before command is removed from the document and the text moves to the previous page. Click OK.
8. In the Page Layout tab, change the Orientation option to Landscape and click Margins, then Custom Margins to open the Page Setup dialog box. Change the Top and Bottom margin settings to 0.5", and in the Apply To selection box at the bottom of the Margins tab, notice that this will affect the Whole Document. Click OK.

9. Place the insertion point in front of the *V* in *Value Checking*. Click the drop-down arrow to display the Breaks menu, then select Columns to insert a column break. Value Checking and the text below move to the second column.

10. Place the insertion point in front of the *P* in Preferred Checking and click the drop-down arrow to display the Breaks menu, then select Column break. Preferred Checking and the text below move to the third column.

11. Place the insertion point in front of the *S* in Senior Preferred Checking and click the drop-down arrow to display the Breaks menu, then select Column. The text is moved to the top of the next page.

12. Select the two headings beginning with First Bank . . . Personal Checking Choices.

13. Click the drop-down arrow in Columns and select One. The first two headings are now single columns.

14. Press the Enter key after the *s* in Choices. Notice the Continuous Section Break separating the heading and the columns.

15. Select the two headings and on the Home tab, in the Paragraph group, click the Center button. Applying the Center feature does not affect the text in the columns as shown in Figure 5-14.

Figure 5-14

Formatted with columns

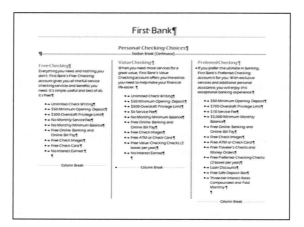

16. **SAVE** the document as *checking_draft1* in the lesson folder on your USB flash drive.

PAUSE. LEAVE the document open to use in the next exercise.

Changing Column Widths

Column widths can be even or you can specify varying column widths. Word provides an option to keep the columns with the same width by selecting the Equal Column Width option. Column width and spacing settings are displayed for the first column only and can be set to a specific width. In this exercise, you learn to change column widths in Word documents.

STEP BY STEP   Change Column Widths

USE the document that is open from the previous exercise.

1. Place your insertion point anywhere in the first column.

2. On the Page Layout tab, in the Page Setup group, click the drop-down arrow to display the Columns menu.

3. Select More Columns. The Columns dialog box appears.

4. Key 2 in the Number of Columns box or click the down arrow.

5. Select the text in the Width box and key 3.25. Press the Tab key to move to the Spacing box. Notice that the spacing adjusted automatically to 2.5. Click OK. The Apply to section will only affect the columns.

6. On the Page Layout tab, in the Page Setup group, click the drop-down arrow to display the Columns menu and select More Columns.

7. Click the Three columns button. Select the text in the Width box and key 2.3. Press the Tab key to move to the Spacing box. Notice that the spacing adjusted automatically to 1.05. Click OK.

8. **SAVE** the document as *checking_draft2* in the lesson folder on your USB flash drive, then **CLOSE** the file.

PAUSE. LEAVE the document open to use in the next exercise.

INSERTING A BLANK PAGE INTO A DOCUMENT

The Bottom Line

When creating or editing a document, you may need to insert a blank page to add more text, graphics, or a table. Rather than pressing the Enter key enough times to insert a blank page, Word provides a Blank Page command. You can insert a blank page at any point within a document—the beginning, middle, or end. To insert a blank page, position the insertion point and click the Blank Page command in the Pages group on the Insert tab. To delete a blank page, use the Show/Hide (¶) button to display hidden characters, then select and delete the page break.

SKILL SUMMARY

In This Lesson, You Learned How To:
Set page layout
Work with breaks
Control pagination
Set up columns
Insert a blank page into a document

Knowledge Assessment

True/False

Circle T if the statement is true or F if the statement is false.

T F 1. A page height that is larger than the page width is characteristic of portrait orientation.

T F 2. In Word, the default margin size is 1.5 inches for the top, bottom, left, and right margins.

T F 3. Columns are blank spaces on the sides, top, and bottom of a document.

T F 4. Paper size refers to landscape or portrait orientation.

T F 5. Widow/Orphan Control is on by default.

T F 6. A column break moves text from one column to the next.

T F 7. Use Widow/Orphan Control to keep all lines of a paragraph together on the same page.

T F 8. Word considers a heading a paragraph.

T F 9. A horizontal line can be placed between columns.

T F 10. A page break is the location in a document where one page ends and a new page begins.

Multiple Choice

Select the best response for the following statements.

1. What is the term for the last line of a paragraph when it is left alone at the top of a page?
   a. Orphan
   b. Widow
   c. Widow/Orphan Control
   d. Keep Lines Together

2. What is the first line of a paragraph that is left alone at the bottom of a page called?
   a. Widow
   b. Orphan
   c. Widow/Orphan Control
   d. Keep Paragraphs Together

3. Pressing **Ctrl+Enter** produces what?
   a. A section break
   b. A next page break
   c. A page break
   d. A continuous break

4. Using this type of break will determine where the page break begins and ends.
   a. Section break
   b. Page break
   c. Next Page break
   d. Text wrapping

5. Which would be used to move vertical blocks of text from the bottom of one block of text to the top of the next block of text (on the same page)?
   a. Column breaks
   b. Section breaks
   c. Two columns
   d. Three columns

6. Which of the following will also insert a blank page when pressed twice.
   a. **Shift+Enter**
   b. **Ctrl+Enter**
   c. **Alt+Enter**
   d. None of the above

7. Which of the following displays the Columns dialog box?
   a. Columns button
   b. More Columns command
   c. Right-click
   d. All of the above

8. A column heading should be formatted as:
   a. single column
   b. two columns
   c. left column
   d. right column

9. The distance between columns is called:
   a. Gap
   b. Spacing
   c. Opening
   d. Hole

10. To avoid a word or paragraph appearing at the top or bottom of a page, which control would need to be turned on?

   a. Keep paragraphs together

   b. Keep lines together

   c. Widow/Orphan control

   d. Keep with next

Competency Assessment

Project 5-1: YMCA Newsletter

Format some data for the YMCA into a two-column newsletter.

GET READY. LAUNCH Word if it is not already running.

@ The *ynews* file for this lesson is available on the book companion website or in WileyPLUS.

1. **OPEN** *ynews* from the data files for this lesson.
2. Click the Show/Hide ¶ ⟨¶⟩ button.
3. Position the insertion point before the *M* in the heading, Mother's Day Out. . . .
4. On the Page Layout tab, in the Page Setup group, click the Breaks button and select Continuous from the menu.
5. On the Page Layout tab, in the Page Setup group, click the Columns button and select Two.
6. Position the insertion point before the *F* in the Fall Soccer. . . heading.
7. On the Page Layout tab, in the Page Setup group, click the Breaks button and select Column.
8. On the Page Layout tab, in the Page Setup group, click the Columns button and click More Columns.
9. In the Columns dialog box, click the up arrow on the Width box to change to 2.8. The number in the Spacing box should adjust to .9".
10. Click the Line Between box and click OK.
11. Click the Show/Hide ¶ ⟨¶⟩ button.
12. **SAVE** the document as *ymca_newsletter* in the lesson folder on your USB flash drive, then **CLOSE** the file.

PAUSE. LEAVE Word open for the next project.

Project 5-2: Computer Use Policy

You are updating First Bank's computer use policy and you need to separate each section in the document by inserting a manual page break.

GET READY. LAUNCH Word if it is not already running.

@ The *computeruse-policy* file for this lesson is available on the book companion website or in WileyPLUS.

1. **OPEN** *computerusepolicy* from the data files for this lesson.
2. Position the insertion point before the *S* in the *Section Two* heading on page 1.
3. On the Insert tab, in the Pages group, click the Page Break button.
4. Scroll to the next heading and position the insertion point before the *S* in *Section Three*.
5. On the Insert tab, in the Pages group, click the Page Break button.

6. Scroll to the remaining headings and position the insertion point before the *S* in each of the headings for *Section Four, Section Five, Section Six, Section Seven, Section Eight, Section Nine,* and *Section Ten.*

7. On the Insert tab, in the Pages group, click the Page Break button.

8. **SAVE** the document as *new_computeruse_policy* in the lesson folder on your USB flash drive, then **CLOSE** the file.

PAUSE. LEAVE Word open for the next project.

Proficiency Assessment

Project 5-3: Coffee Shop Brochure

Your supervisor at the Grand Street Coffee Shop asks you to format the information in their coffee menu as a brochure.

GET READY. LAUNCH Word if it is not already running.

The *coffeemenu* file for this lesson is available on the book companion website or in WileyPLUS.

1. **OPEN** *coffeemenu* from the data files for this lesson.
2. Change the page orientation to Landscape.
3. Position the insertion point before the *C* in the Coffee heading.
4. Create an uneven, two-column format using the Left column setting. Position the insertion point in front of Coffee and select text to the end of the document.
5. Increase the amount of space between columns to .7″. The document should fit to one page.
6. **SAVE** the document as *coffee_shop_brochure* in the lesson folder on your USB flash drive, then **CLOSE** the file.

PAUSE. LEAVE Word open for the next project.

Project 5-4: Mom's Favorite Recipes

Your mom asks you to help her create a small cookbook filled with her favorite recipes that she can share with family and friends. She has emailed you a Word document containing a few recipes to help you get started with creating a format.

GET READY. LAUNCH Word if it is not already running.

The *recipes* file for this lesson is available on the book companion website or in WileyPLUS.

1. **OPEN** *recipes* from the data files for this lesson.
2. Select the heading, Main Dishes and make this a one column heading.
3. Position the insertion point after the *e* in the *Chicken Pot Pie* heading and create a *Two Column* document.
4. Position the insertion point anywhere within the *Chicken Pot Pie* recipe.
5. Format this and the remaining recipes in the *Main Dishes* section into two even columns with .9″ spacing between columns and a line between.
6. Position the insertion point before the *E* in the *Easy Pumpkin Bread/Muffins* heading and insert a column break.
7. Position the insertion point before the *R* in the *Ranch Chicken* heading and insert a column break.
8. Position the insertion point before the *C* in the *Chocolate Zucchini Bread* heading and insert a column break.
9. Click the Show/Hide ¶ button to hide formatting marks.
10. **SAVE** and the document as *favorite_recipes* in the lesson folder on your USB flash drive, then CLOSE the file.

PAUSE. LEAVE Word open for the next project.

Mastery Assessment

Project 5-5: Threefold Bank Brochure

The Checking Choices document needs to be formatted to accommodate the whole document on one page. Your task is to use the features learned in this lesson and apply them to this document as shown in Figure 5-15.

GET READY. LAUNCH Word if it is not already running.

1. **OPEN** *checkingacctchoices* from the data files for this lesson.
2. Reformat the document using a page size of 8½ x 14 with Landscape orientation. Create the brochure to look like the one shown in Figure 5-15.

Figure 5-15

Checking Brochure

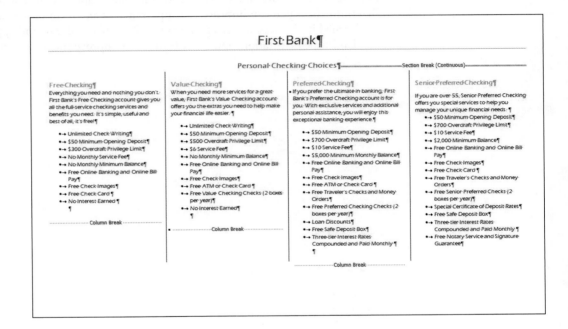

3. Remove the Next Page section break after the heading, *Personal Checking Choice*. Delete the blank line above *Free Checking*. Change the columns to **four** columns, and add column breaks before each column heading. After *Personal Checking Choices* apply a Spacing After to 18 pt.
4. **SAVE** the document as *checking_brochure* in the lesson folder on your USB flash drive, then **CLOSE** the file.

PAUSE. LEAVE Word open for the next project.

Project 5-6: Reformat the YMCA Newsletter

As an alternative to the layout you created earlier, reformat the YMCA newsletter with two uneven columns.

GET READY. LAUNCH Word if it is not already running.

1. **OPEN** *ynewsletter* from the data files for this lesson.
2. Reformat the newsletter with two uneven columns using the Right column setting.
3. Format the document on one page. (Hint: Delete the column break in the first column and add a column break in front of *Volunteer Coaches. . . .*)
4. **SAVE** the document as *right_ymca_newsletter* in the lesson folder on your USB flash drive, then **CLOSE** the file.

STOP. CLOSE Word.

INTERNET READY

Have you considered starting your own business someday? Use the Internet to research small business checking accounts from three different banks. What are the fees? What services are offered? What are the restrictions? Create a three-column document comparing the account features of each bank side by side.

Workplace *Ready*

CREATING COLUMNS

Visit the Student Government Association on your campus and review their marketing materials. Determine how you can improve the appearance of any form on file and incorporate the skills you learned in this lesson. Select a form that is a single column and apply three columns, letter size, landscape orientation, and other features to improve the document.

Creating Tables 6

LESSON SKILL MATRIX

In This Lesson, You Will Learn The Following Skills:

Creating a Table

Formatting a Table

Managing Tables

KEY TERMS

- **ascending**
- **cells**
- **descending**
- **header row**
- **merge cells**
- **sort**
- **split cells**
- **tables**

Karen Archer is an executive recruiter. Many large companies hire her to find professional talent to fill communications and marketing executive positions within their firms. You were recently hired as her assistant, and although the business is small, you are expected to display a high degree of professionalism, confidentiality, and integrity. Because it is a small business, you are asked to perform many different duties. One of your main duties is to assist Ms. Archer with the constant updating of tables that contain data related to current clients, potential clients, and potential candidates for placement. Microsoft Word's table tools can help you successfully manage this information. In this lesson, you will learn to format lists as well as create, format, and manage tables.

CREATING A TABLE

A **table**, such as the one shown in Figure 6-1, is an arrangement of data made up of horizontal rows and vertical columns. **Cells** are the rectangles that are formed when rows and columns intersect. Tables are ideal for organizing information in an orderly manner. Calendars, invoices, and contact lists are all examples of tables that you see and use every day. Word provides several options for creating tables, including the dragging method, the Insert Table dialog box, table drawing tools, and the Quick Table method.

Figure 6-1

A table created in Word

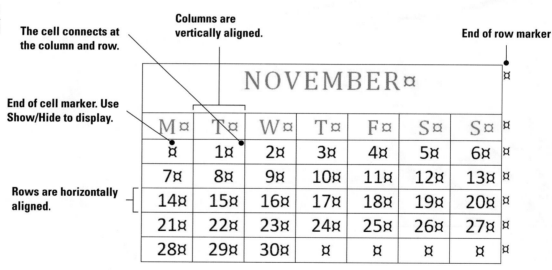

Inserting a Table by Dragging

In this exercise, you learn how easily and quickly you can create a table from the Table menu by dragging the mouse pointer to specify the number of rows and columns. Using this method, you can create a new empty table with up to eight rows and ten columns.

STEP BY STEP   **Insert a Table by Dragging**

GET READY. Before you begin these steps, **LAUNCH** Microsoft Word and **OPEN** a new blank Word document.

1. On the Insert tab, in the Tables group, click the Table button. The Insert Table menu appears.

2. Point to the cell in the fifth column, second row. The menu title should read *5×2 Table*, as shown in Figure 6-2. Click the mouse button to create the table.

Figure 6-2

Insert Table menu

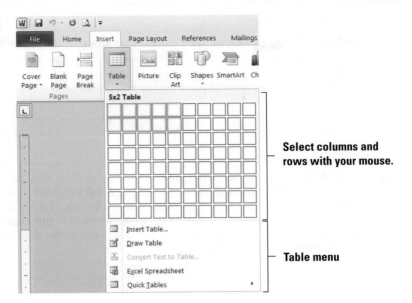

Select columns and
rows with your mouse.

Table menu

3. Click below the table and press **Enter** twice to insert a blank line.

4. **SAVE** the document as *tables* in the lesson folder on your USB flash drive.

PAUSE. LEAVE the document open to use in the next exercise.

Using the Insert Table Dialog Box

The Insert Table dialog box lets you create large tables by specifying up to 63 columns and thousands of rows. In this exercise, you use the Insert Table dialog box to insert a table with nine columns and three rows. Note that in the Insert Table dialog box, you can click the up and down arrows or key in the number of columns and rows needed in a table.

STEP BY STEP | **Use the Insert Table Dialog Box**

USE the document that is open from the previous exercise.

1. On the Insert tab, in the Tables group, click the **Table** button. Select **Insert Table** from the menu. The Insert Table dialog box appears.

2. In the Number of columns box, click the **up arrow** until **9** is displayed.

3. In the Number of rows box, click the **up arrow** until **3** is displayed, as shown in Figure 6-3.

Figure 6-3

Insert Table dialog box

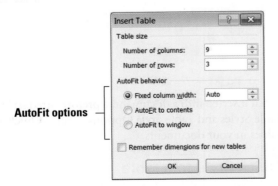

AutoFit options

4. Click **OK** to insert the table. You inserted a new table with 9 columns and 3 rows.

5. Click below the table and press **Enter** twice to insert a blank line.

6. **SAVE** the document in the lesson folder on your USB flash drive then **CLOSE** the file.

PAUSE. LEAVE Word open to use in the next exercise.

Drawing a Table

Word provides the option to draw complex tables using the Draw Table command, which lets you draw a table as you would with a pencil and piece of paper. The Draw Table command transforms the mouse pointer into a pencil tool, which you can use to draw the outline of the table, then draw rows and columns exactly where you need them.

Take Note   You have now seen two ways to insert a blank table. Text separated by commas, tabs, paragraphs, or another character can also be converted to a table with the Convert Text to Table command on the Table menu.

Troubleshooting   When drawing tables with the pencil tool, note that this tool will draw squares and rectangles as well as lines. If you are trying to draw a straight line and you move the pencil off your straight path, Word may think you are trying to draw a rectangle and insert one for you. If this happens, just click the Undo button on the Quick Access Toolbar and try again. It might take a bit of practice to master the difference between drawing straight lines and drawing rectangles.

Take Note   A table can be moved to a new page or a new document by clicking the move handle to select the table and then using the Cut and Paste commands. You can also use the Copy command to leave a copy of the table in the original location.

SOFTWARE ORIENTATION

Design Tab on the Table Tools Ribbon

After inserting a table, Word displays Table Tools in the Ribbon, as shown in Figure 6-4. It is important to become familiar with the commands available in the Design tab under Table Tools. Use this figure as a reference throughout this lesson as well as the rest of this book.

Table Tools are displayed on the Ribbon when a table is inserted.

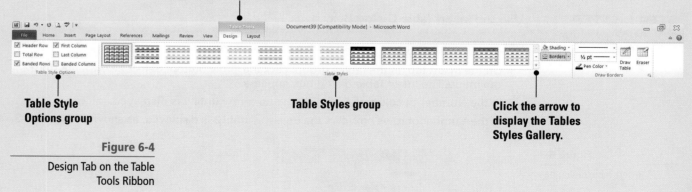

Table Style Options group

Table Styles group

Click the arrow to display the Tables Styles Gallery.

Figure 6-4

Design Tab on the Table Tools Ribbon

FORMATTING A TABLE

The Bottom Line   Once a table has been inserted into a document, a preformatted style can be applied using Quick Styles from the Table Styles and Table Style Options groups. Quick Styles add a professional appearance to the tables in your documents.

Applying a Quick Style to a Table

With Quick Styles, it easy to quickly change a table's formatting. You can apply styles to tables in much the same way you learned to apply styles to text in previous lessons, by positioning the insertion point in the table before selecting a style from the Quick Styles gallery. You can preview the style before applying it and change the style as many times as needed. You can modify an existing Table Style or create a New Table Style and add it to the gallery, then modify or delete it, as appropriate. In this exercise, you apply a Quick Style to a table in your Word document.

STEP BY STEP   **Apply a Quick Style to a Table**

OPEN *clients* from the data files for this lesson.

 The *clients* file for this lesson is available on the book companion website or in WileyPLUS.

1. The insertion point is positioned in the table.
2. On the Design tab, in the Table Styles group, click the **More** ⌄ button to view a gallery of Quick Styles.
3. Scroll through the available styles. Notice that as you point to a style, Word displays a live preview, showing you what your table will look like if you choose that style.
4. Scroll down to the fourth row under the Built-in section and select the fourth style over in the row, the **Medium List 2 – Accent 3** style, as shown in Figure 6-5.

Figure 6-5

Quick Style gallery

WILEY PLUS EXTRA

WileyPLUS Extra! features an online tutorial of this task.

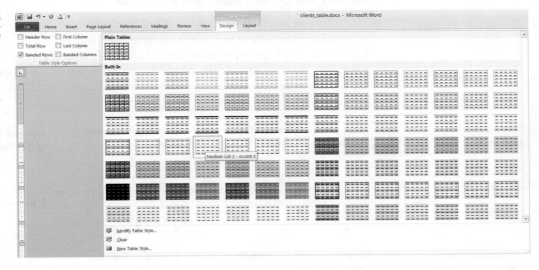

5. **SAVE** the document as *clients_table* in the lesson folder on your USB flash drive.

PAUSE. LEAVE the document open to use in the next exercise.

Turning Table Style Options On or Off

Table Style Options enable you to change the appearance of the Quick Styles you apply to your tables. Table Style Options, which are linked to the Table Style you have selected, apply globally throughout the table. For example, if you select the Banded Columns option, all even-numbered columns in the table will be formatted differently than the odd-numbered columns. In this exercise, you learn to turn Table Style Options on or off by clicking each option's check box.

Table Style Options include the following:

- **Header Row:** Formats the top row of the table
- **Total Row:** Formats the last row, which usually contains column totals
- **Banded Rows:** Formats even rows differently than odd rows
- **First Column:** Formats the first column of the table
- **Last Column:** Formats the last column of the table
- **Banded Columns:** Formats even columns differently than odd columns

STEP BY STEP   **Turn Table Style Options On or Off**

USE the document that is open from the previous exercise.

1. The insertion point should still be in the table. If you click outside the table, the Design and Layout tabs will not be available.

2. On the Design tab, in the Table Style Options group, click the **First Column** check box. Notice that the format of the first column of the table changes, as do the Table Styles in the Quick Style gallery.

3. Click the **Banded Rows** check box to turn the option off. Color is removed from the rows.

4. Click the **Banded Rows** check box to turn it on again. Color is reapplied to every other row.

5. **SAVE** the document in the lesson folder on your USB flash drive.

PAUSE. LEAVE the document open to use in the next exercise.

SOFTWARE ORIENTATION

Layout Tab on the Table Tools Ribbon

When you are working with tables, Word displays a new contextual Table Tools ribbon that is only visible when a table is in use. The Table Tools Ribbon has two tabs: the Design tab and the Layout tab. The Layout tab, as shown in Figure 6-6, includes commands for changing the entire format of a table as well as commands for changing the appearance of individual table components, such as cells, columns, and rows. Use this figure as a reference throughout this lesson as well as the rest of this book.

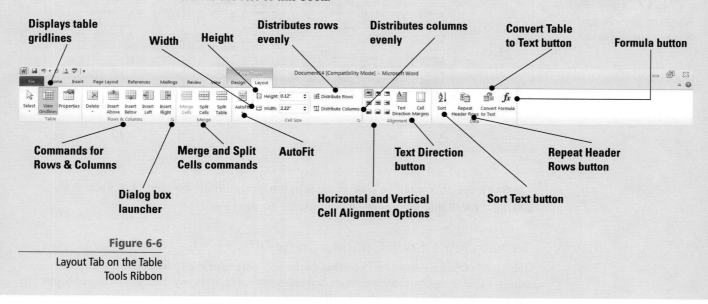

Figure 6-6

Layout Tab on the Table Tools Ribbon

MANAGING TABLES

The Bottom Line

As with any document that you edit, some adjustments are always necessary when you work with tables. After you create a table, you can resize and move its columns; insert columns and rows; change the alignment or direction of its text; set the header row to repeat on several pages; organize data through sorting by text, number, or date; convert text and tables; merge and split cells; and work with the table's properties. Word's gridlines make all such edits easier.

Resizing a Row or Column

Word offers a number of tools for resizing rows or columns. You can resize a column or row a couple of ways using the mouse. You can use commands in the Cell Size group on the Layout tab to adjust height and width, and Word's AutoFit command enables you to adjust column width to fit the size of table contents, the window, or to fit all content to a fixed column width. In addition, the Table Properties dialog box allows you to set the measurements at a precise height for rows or ideal width columns, cells, and tables. In this exercise, you practice using these techniques to resize rows and columns in a Word table.

STEP BY STEP   **Resize a Row or Column**

USE the document that is open from the previous exercise.

1. On the Layout tab, in the Table group, click the **View Gridlines** button to display gridlines and enable more precise editing.

2. Click in the first column and position the mouse pointer over the horizontal ruler on the first column marker. The pointer changes to a double-headed arrow along with the ScreenTip *Move Table Column*, as shown in Figure 6-7.

Figure 6-7

Horizontal Ruler on the first column marker

Column marker on ruler. Columns can be adjusted manually by dragging.

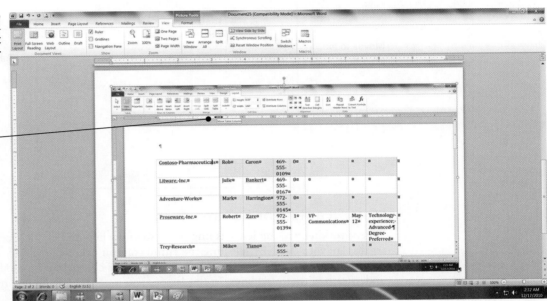

3. Click and drag the border to the right until the contents in the cell extend in a single line along the top of the cell.

4. On the Layout tab, in the Cell Size group, click the **AutoFit** button to open the drop-down menu, as shown in Figure 6-8. On the drop-down menu, click **AutoFit Contents**. Each column width changes to fit the data in the column.

Figure 6-8

AutoFit button and menu

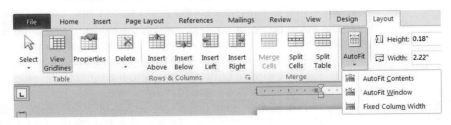

Another Way
Position the pointer outside the table, above the column containing the phone numbers. The pointer changes to a down selection arrow. Click to select the column.

Another Way
The Table Properties dialog box can be accessed from the shortcut menu by right-clicking anywhere in the table and selecting Table Properties.

5. Position the insertion point in the phone number column of the table. In the Table group, of the Layout tab, click the **Select** button and choose **Select Column** from the drop-down menu.

6. On the Layout tab, in the Cell Size group, click the **up arrow** in the Width box until it reads **1.1"** and the column width changes.

7. Place the insertion point anywhere in the first row. In the Table group, click the **Select** button, then **Select Row** from the drop-down menu. The first row is selected.

8. On the Layout tab, in the Cell Size group, click the **dialog box launcher**. The Table Properties dialog box appears.

9. Click the **Row** tab in the dialog box. Click the **Specify height** check box. In the Height box, click the **up arrow** until the box reads **0.5"**, as shown in Figure 6-9.

10. Click the **Next Row** button to apply your changes to the row that follows the selected row in the table. Notice the selection moves down one row. Click **OK**.

11. Click in any cell to remove the selection.

12. **SAVE** the document as *clients_table1* in the lesson folder on your USB flash drive.

PAUSE. LEAVE the document open to use in the next exercise.

Figure 6-9

Table Properties dialog box

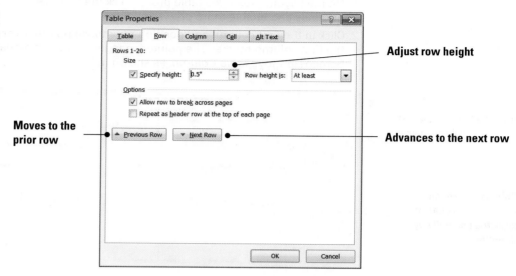

Moving a Row or Column

When working with tables, it is important to know how to rearrange columns and rows to better display your data. By selecting the entire column or row, drag and drop is used for moving data to a new area in the table. The mouse pointer changes and resembles an empty rectangle underneath with dotted lines. In this lesson, you practice moving text from rows and columns.

 Ref   The Cut and Paste commands were covered Lesson 2.

STEP BY STEP   **Move a Row or Column**

USE the document that is open from the previous exercise.

1. In the table, select the fourth row of data, which contains the information for Proseware, Inc. In the Table group, click the **Select** button, then **Select Row** from the drop-down menu.

2. The insertion point is positioned on the selected row, hold down the mouse button. Notice the mouse pointer changes to a move pointer with a dotted insertion point.

3. Drag the dotted insertion point down and position it before the *W* in *Wingtip Toys*. Release the mouse button and click in the table to deselect. The row is moved to the position above the Wingtip Toys row.

4. Place the insertion point in the second column of the table, which contains first names. Click the **Select** button, in the Table group, then **Select Column** from the drop-down menu.

5. Position the pointer inside the selected cells and right-click to display the shortcut menu. Select **Cut** to delete that column of text and move the remaining columns to the left.

6. Place the insertion point on the phone numbers column.

NEW to Office 2010

7. Right-click to display the shortcut menu, then under the Paste Options section, click **Insert as New Column**. A new Paste Options menu is displayed with the options Insert as New Column, Nest Table, Insert as New Row, and Keep Text Only. Selecting the first option to **Insert as New Column**; the first name column is pasted to the left of the phone number column. Click anywhere in the table to deselect.

8. **SAVE** the document as *clients_table2* in the lesson folder on your USB flash drive.

PAUSE. LEAVE the document open to use in the next exercise.

Take Note   Instead of using the shortcut menu, you can also use the Cut and Paste commands in the Clipboard group on the Home tab to cut and move rows and columns.

Setting a Table's Horizontal Alignment

The horizontal alignment for a table can be set to the left or right margins or centered. Tables inserted into a report should align with the document to maintain the flow of the report. In this exercise, you will practice using the Table Properties dialog box to set a table's horizontal alignment.

STEP BY STEP   **Set a Table's Horizontal Alignment**

USE the document that is open from the previous exercise.

1. Position the insertion point anywhere inside the table. On the Layout tab, in the Table group, click the Select button, then Select Table.
2. On the Layout tab, in the Table group, click the Properties button. The Table Properties dialog box appears.
3. Click the Table tab, if necessary. In the Alignment section, click Center, as shown in Figure 6-10.

Figure 6-10

Table Properties dialog box

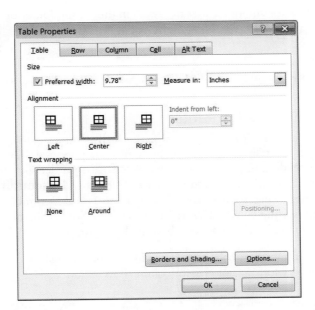

4. Click OK. The table is centered horizontally on the page. Click anywhere within the table to deselect.
5. **SAVE** the document on your USB flash drive in the lesson folder.

PAUSE. Leave the document open to use in the next exercise.

Creating a Header Row

A **header row** is the first row of the table that is formatted differently and should be repeated for tables that extend beyond one page. When you specify a header row in the Table Style Options group, the row is distinguished from the entire table. Column headings are usually placed in the header row. In this exercise, you will practice repeating heading rows for lengthy tables.

STEP BY STEP   **Create a Header Row**

USE the document that is open from the previous exercise.

1. Place the insertion point on the first row of the table.
2. On the Layout tab, in the Rows & Columns group, click Insert Above ⊞ . A new blank row is inserted.

3. On the Design tab, in the Table Style Options group, click the Header Row check box to apply a distinctive format to the header row.

4. Key headings in each cell within the first row of the table, as shown in Figure 6-11.

Figure 6-11

Header row

Company·Name¤	Contact·Person¤	¤	Phone·Number¤	Number·of·Current·Open·Positions¤	Position·Title¤	Date·Posted¤	Notes¤
Contoso·Pharmaceuticals¤	Caron¤	Rob¤	469-555-0109¤	0¤	¤	¤	¤
Litware,·Inc.¤	Bankert¤	Julie¤	469-555-0167¤	0¤	¤	¤	¤

5. Select the first row of the table. On the Table group of the Layout tab, click the Select button and Select Row.

6. On the Home tab, in the Font group, click the Bold **B** button. The header rows are bolded.

7. On the Layout tab, in the Data group, click the Repeat Header Rows button. Scroll down and view the headings on the second page. Click anywhere in the table to deselect.

8. **SAVE** the document as *clients_table3* in the lesson folder on your USB flash drive.

PAUSE. LEAVE the document open to use in the next exercise.

Take Note   Repeating rows are only visible in Print Layout view or on a printed document.

Sorting a Table's Contents

To **sort** data means to arrange it alphabetically, numerically, or chronologically. Sorting displays data in order so that it can be immediately located. Text, numbers, or dates can be sorted in ascending or descending order. **Ascending** order sorts text from beginning to end, such as from A to Z, 1 to 10, and January to December. **Descending** order sorts text from the end to the beginning, such as from Z to A, 10 to 1, and December to January. In this exercise, you practice sorting data in a Word table using the Sort dialog box, which you access through the Sort command on the Layout tab in the Data group.

Take Note   You can sort up to three columns of data in the Sort dialog box. Before beginning the sort process, you must select the column (or columns) to be sorted.

STEP BY STEP   **Sort a Table's Contents**

USE the document that is open from the previous exercise.

1. Place the insertion point on the first column to select the Company Name column. On the Table group of the Layout tab, click the Select button and Select Column.

2. On the Layout tab, in the Data group, click the Sort button. The Sort dialog box appears, as shown in Figure 6-12. The Company Name data is listed in the Sort By text box, with Ascending Order selected by default.

Figure 6-12

Sort dialog box

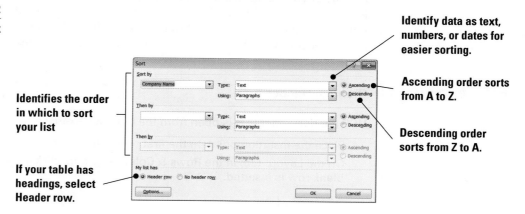

Identifies the order in which to sort your list

If your table has headings, select Header row.

Identify data as text, numbers, or dates for easier sorting.

Ascending order sorts from A to Z.

Descending order sorts from Z to A.

3. Click OK. Note that the table now appears sorted in ascending alphabetical order by company name.

4. **SAVE** the document as *clients_table4* in the lesson folder on your USB flash drive.

PAUSE. LEAVE the document open to use in the next exercise.

Merging Table Cells

The ability to merge and split table cells provides flexibility in customizing tables. To **merge cells** means to combine two or more cells into one. Merging cells is useful for headings that extend over several columns. To **split cells** means to divide one cell into two or more cells. Cells may be split when more than one type of data needs to be placed in one cell. The Split Cells dialog box enables you to split a cell into columns or rows. In this lesson, you practice using commands in the Merge group on the Layout tab to merge.

STEP BY STEP	**Merge and Split Table Cells**

USE the document that is open from the previous exercise.

1. Position the insertion point on the header row located on page 1. Select the cell that contains the Contact Person heading and the empty cell to the right of it.

2. On the Layout tab, in the Merge group, click the Merge Cells button. The selected columns merge into one cell.

3. **SAVE** the document as *clients_table5* in the lesson folder on your USB flash drive.

PAUSE. LEAVE the document open to use in the next exercise.

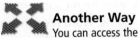

Another Way
You can access the Merge Cells command on the shortcut menu. The Merge Cells command is visible only when you have multiple cells selected in a table.

Changing the Position of Text in a Cell

Word provides you with nine options for aligning text in a cell. These options enable you to control the horizontal and vertical alignment of cell text, such as Top Left, Top Center, and Top Right. To change cell text alignment, select the cell or cells you want to align and click one of the nine alignment buttons in the Alignment group on the Layout tab. In this lesson, you practice changing the text alignment within a cell.

STEP BY STEP	**Change the Position of Text in a Cell**

USE the document that is open from the previous exercise.

1. Select the table's header's row, with the headings on page 1. On the Layout tab in the Table group, click the Select button, then click Select Row.

2. In the Alignment group, click the Align Center ☰ button. The header row is centered horizontally and vertically within the cell.

3. **SAVE** the document in the lesson folder on your USB flash drive.

PAUSE. LEAVE the document open to use in the next exercise.

Changing the Direction of Text in a Cell

Rotating text in a cell provides additional options for creating interesting and effective tables. Changing the direction of text in a heading can be especially helpful. To change the direction of text in a cell, click the button three times to cycle through the three available directions. After reviewing Project 6-3, this is needed to include the steps. I've already saved the changes but do not know how to remove the strike through markings.

STEP BY STEP **Change the Direction of Text in a Cell**

USE the document that is open from the previous exercise.

1. Select the cell that contains the Company Name heading.
2. On the Layout tab, in the Alignment group, click the Text Direction button three times to rotate the text direction to align to the right cell border, the left cell border, and then back to the top cell border. As you click the Text Direction button, the button face rotates to match the rotation of the text direction in the selected cell.
3. **SAVE** the document in the lesson folder on your USB flash drive.

PAUSE. LEAVE Word open to use in the next exercise.

Converting Text to Table or Table to Text

Text separated by a paragraph mark, tab, comma, or other character can be converted from text to a table or from a table to text. To convert text to a table, first select the text, then click the Insert tab button, then click the Table button, and finally select Convert Text to Table. The Convert Text to Table dialog box will appear, and Word will determine the number of columns needed. In this exercise, you practice using this technique to convert Word text into a table.

STEP BY STEP **Convert Text to Table or Table to Text**

OPEN the *part_numbers* document in your lesson folder.

1. Select the whole document.
2. On the Insert tab, on the Table group, click the Table button. The Table menu appears.
3. Click Convert Text to Table. The Convert Text to Table dialog box opens. Word recognizes the number columns and rows and places the number 10 in the Number of rows box—notice that it is shaded gray, making it unavailable to change. (See Figure 6-13.) Keep the default settings.
4. Click OK. The selected text was separated by paragraph marks and by selecting the default of one column, Word converts the text to a table, as shown in Figure 6-14.
5. **SAVE** the document as *part_numbers_table* in the lesson folder on your USB flash drive.
6. Position the insertion point anywhere in the table and click the Layout tab.
7. In the Table group, click the Select button, then click Select Table to select the entire table.

@ The *part_numbers* file for this lesson is available on the book companion website or in WileyPLUS.

Figure 6-13

Convert Text to Table dialog box

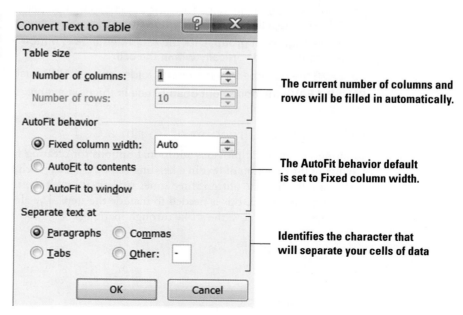

The current number of columns and rows will be filled in automatically.

The AutoFit behavior default is set to Fixed column width.

Identifies the character that will separate your cells of data

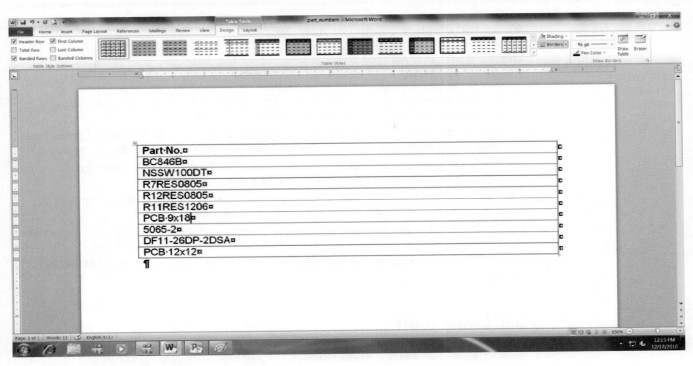

Figure 6-14

Document converted from text to a table

8. In the Data group, click the **Convert to Text** button. The Convert Table to Text dialog box opens. The default setting in the Convert Table to Text dialog box is Paragraph marks. A table can be converted to text and separated by paragraph marks, tabs, commas, and other characters (see Figure 6-15).

Figure 6-15

Convert Table to Text dialog box

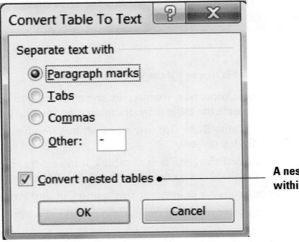

A nested table, which is a table within a table, can be converted.

9. Click **OK**. The document is converted to text separated by paragraph marks.

10. **SAVE** the document as *part_numbers_text* in the lesson folder on your USB flash drive, then **CLOSE** the file.

PAUSE. LEAVE Word open to use in the next exercise.

Inserting and Deleting a Column or Row

The Word Layout tab in the Rows and Columns group, makes it easy to insert a row above or below a column; to the left or right; and to delete cells, columns, rows, and table. In the exercise, you learn to insert a column and row and delete a row.

Insert and Delete a Column or Row

OPEN the *part_numbers_table* documents in your lesson folder.

1. Place the insertion point on the fourth row.

2. On the Layout tab, in the Rows & Columns group, click the Insert Above button; a blank row is inserted above the fourth row.

3. The blank row is selected. Click the Delete button in the Rows & Columns group, then click Delete Row from the drop-down menu. The blank row is deleted from the table.

4. In the Cell Size group, click the AutoFit button, then select AutoFit Contents. The data in the table automatically resizes to fit in the column width.

5. Place your insertion point anywhere in the table, and in the Row & Columns group, click Insert Right. A new column is inserted to the right.

6. On the Rows & Columns group, click the Delete button, then click Delete Column. The Delete button menu allows you to delete cells, rows, and the entire table.

7. **SAVE** the document in the lesson folder on your USB flash drive, then **CLOSE** the file.

CLOSE Word.

SKILL SUMMARY

In This Lesson, You Learned How To:
Create a table
Format a table
Manage tables

Knowledge Assessment

True/False

Circle T if the statement is true or F if the statement is false.

T   F   1. When you know how many rows and columns you need in a table, the quickest way to create the table is by dragging over the grid in the Table menu.

T   F   2. Turning Table Style Options on or off has no effect on the Quick Styles in the Table Styles gallery.

T   F   3. When Word converts text to tables, it uses paragraph marks, tabs, and commas to determine how to organize the data within the table.

T   F   4. You can move a column or row using Cut and Paste.

T   F   5. Sorting can only sort one column of data at a time.

T   F   6. If a hyphen exists within a section of text, and you are converting that text to a table, the hyphen will create a new column.

T   F   7. Text can be aligned both horizontally and vertically in a cell.

T   F   8. Word provides four options for changing the direction of text in a cell.

T   F   9. You can sort single-level lists, such as bulleted or numbered lists.

T   F   10. The Repeat Header Rows button is used for tables that extend to multiple pages.

Multiple Choice

Select the best response for the following statements.

1. Using the Sort feature in a table will sort selected content in what order?
   a. Ascending
   b. Descending

   c. Alphabetically order

   d. All of the above

2. An arrangement of data made up of horizontal rows and vertical columns is called a:

   a. Menu.

   b. Heading.

   c. Table.

   d. Merge.

3. Built-in preformatted tables that can be inserted and used in your documents are called:

   a. Table Styles Options.

   b. Tables.

   c. Quick Tables.

   d. Insert Tables.

4. The rectangles that are formed when rows and columns intersect are known as:

   a. cells.

   b. merged cells.

   c. split cells.

   d. tables.

5. Which sort order sorts text from the end to the beginning?

   a. Descending.

   b. Ascending.

   c. Plunging.

   d. Downward.

6. Sorted data can consist of:

   a. text.

   b. numbers.

   c. dates.

   d. All of the above

7. Which option would you choose to arrange data alphabetically, numerically, or chronologically?

   a. Filter

   b. Group

   c. Sort

   d. Category dialog box

8. When you create a table in Word, two new Ribbon tabs appear. Which of the following are in a new Table Tools tab?

   a. Page Layout

   b. Design

   c. Insert

   d. Merge Cells

9. The first row of a table that is formatted differently than the rest of the table is called a:

   a. total row.

   b. banded column.

   c. header column.

   d. header row.

10. Combining two or more cells into one uses a Word feature called:

   a. Split Cells.

   b. Merge Cells.

   c. Merge All Cells.

   d. Merge Selected Cells.

Competency Assessment

Project 6-1: Placements Table

Ms. Archer, the executive recruiter, asks you to start working on a placements table that will list the candidates that have been placed, the companies that hired them, and the date of hire.

GET READY. LAUNCH Word if it is not already running.

@ The *placements* file for this lesson is available on the book companion website or in WileyPLUS.

1. **OPEN** *placements* from the data files for this lesson.
2. Place the insertion point in the last column. Select the last column in the table. In the Layout tab, in the Table group, click the Select button and Select Columns.
3. On the Layout tab, in the Cell Size group, click the down arrow in the Width box until it reads .9".
4. Place the insertion point in the first column and select the first column in the table. In the Table group, click the Select button and Select Columns.
5. On the Layout tab, in the Cell Size group, click the down arrow in the Width box until it reads .9".
6. Select the Company column and change the width to 1.5".
7. Select the Date of Placement column and change the width to 1.3". Click in the table to deselect.
8. On the Design tab, in the Table Style Options group, click the Header Row check box and Banded Rows check box to turn on. Place your insertion point within the table.
9. On the Design tab, in the Table Styles group, select the Medium Shading 1 - Accent 1 style in the ninth column, second row in the Built-In gallery.
10. Select the Last column in the table.
11. On the Layout tab, in the Data group, click the Sort button. Under the *My list has* section, select Header Row. In the Sort dialog box, click OK. This will sort the column by date.
12. The table is selected. On the Layout tab, in the Table group, click the Properties button.
13. In the Table Properties dialog box, click Center alignment in the Table tab and click OK.
14. Select the header row.
15. On the Layout tab, in the Alignment group, click Align Center.
16. **SAVE** the document as *placements_table* in the lesson folder on your USB flash drive, then **CLOSE** the file.

LEAVE Word open for the next project.

Project 6-2: Quarterly Sales Data

Create a table showing the quarterly sales for Coho Vineyard.

GET READY. LAUNCH Word if it is not already running.

1. Create a new blank document.
2. On the Insert tab, in the Tables group, click the Table button. Drag to create a table that has 5 columns and 6 rows.
3. Enter the following data in the table as shown:

20XX				
	First Quarter	Second Quarter	Third Quarter	Fourth Quarter
Mark Hanson	19,098	25,890	39,088	28,789
Terry Adams	21,890	19,567	32,811	31,562
Max Benson	39,400	35,021	19,789	21,349
Cathan Cook	34,319	27,437	28,936	19,034

4. Select the first row. On the Layout tab, in the Merge group, click the Merge Cells button.

5. With the row still selected, center the title by clicking the Align Center button in the Alignment group on the Layout tab.

6. On the Design tab, in the Table Styles Options group, click the Banded Columns check box to turn on. The Header Row, First Column, and Banded Rows options should be turned on already.

7. On the Design tab, in the Table Styles gallery, click the More button to display the gallery. On the seventh column, choose the orange Dark List - Accent 6.

8. **SAVE** the document as *quarterly_sales* in the lesson folder on your USB flash drive.

9. On the Layout tab, click the Select button in the Table group, and then choose Select Table from the drop-down menu.

10. In the Data group, select Convert to Text, then select the Tabs section.

11. **SAVE** the document as *quarterly_sales2* in the lesson folder on your USB flash drive, then **CLOSE** the file.

LEAVE Word open for the next project.

Proficiency Assessment

Project 6-3: Sales Table

Ms. Archer asks you to create a sales table including data from the past two years. She can use this table to set goals and project future income.

GET READY. LAUNCH Word if it is not already running.

@ The *sales* file for this lesson is available on the book companion website or in WileyPLUS.

1. **OPEN** *sales* from the data files for this lesson.

2. Select the columns headings containing the months and change the text direction for all the months so that they begin at the bottom of the column and extend to the top.

3. Increase the row height of the row containing the months to 0.9 inches so that the text all fits on one line.

4. Use the AutoFit Contents for the selected months.

5. Select the last row and Delete.

6. Make sure the Header Row, Banded Columns, and First Column Table Style Options are the only ones turned on.

7. Merge all the cells in the first row and center the heading.

8. Merge all the cells in the second row and center the subheading.

9. Choose the Medium Shading 2 - Accent 2 Table Style format.

10. Center the table horizontally in the Tables Properties dialog box.

11. **SAVE** the document as *sales_table* in the lesson folder on your USB flash drive, then **CLOSE** the file. **Leave** Word open for the next project.

Project 6-4: Client Contact Table

Ms. Archer needs you to create a quick contact list.

GET READY. LAUNCH Word if it is not already running.

1. **OPEN** *client_table_2* from the data files for this lesson.

@ The *client_table_2* file for this lesson is available on the book companion website or in WileyPLUS.

2. Delete the last four columns: Number of Current Open Positions, Position Title, Date Posted, and Notes.

3. Change the page orientation to Portrait.

4. Change the width of the Company Name column to 1.9 inches.

5. Delete the Total row and turn off the Total Row option in Table Styles Options.

6. Change the style to the purple Light List –Accent 4 style.

7. Center the table horizontally on the page.

8. Change the alignment for the first row to Align Center.

9. Change the header row height to 0.4 inches.

10. **SAVE** the document as *new_client_table* in the lesson folder on your USB flash drive, then **CLOSE** the file.

LEAVE Word open for the next project.

Mastery Assessment

Project 6-5: Quarterly Sales Table Update

The Coho Winery's Quarterly Sales Table includes some formatting mistakes. Find and correct the four problems within this document.

GET READY. LAUNCH Word if it is not already running.

@ The *problem* file for this lesson is available on the book companion website or in WileyPLUS.

1. **OPEN** *problem* from the data files for this lesson.

2. Find and correct four errors in the table.

3. **SAVE** the document as *fixed_quarterly_sales* in the lesson folder on your USB flash drive, then **CLOSE** the file.

LEAVE Word open for the next project.

Project 6-6: Soccer Team Roster

As coach of your child's soccer team, you need to distribute a roster to all of your players with contact information, uniform numbers, and assigned snack responsibilities. You received a rough list from the league and you would like to convert it to table form. You haven't converted text to a table before, but you're confident you can do it.

GET READY. LAUNCH Word if it is not already running.

@ The *soccer_team* file for this lesson is available on the book companion website or in WileyPLUS.

1. **OPEN** *soccer_team* from the data files for this lesson.

2. Select all the text.

3. On the Insert tab, in the Tables group, click the Table button. Select Convert Text to Table from the menu.

4. In the Convert Text to Table dialog box, key 4 in the Number of columns box. Click the Commas button under the Separate Text At section and click OK.

5. Use what you learned in this lesson to format the table as shown in Figure 6-16. Start by removing extra spaces or words, adjusting column widths, and aligning text. Sort the table by snack date, insert a header row with the following headings for each column (Name, Uniform, Telephone Numbers, Snacks) and choose the Medium Grid 3 – Accent 2 Table Style.

Figure 6-16

Name¤	Uniform¤	Telephone·Number¤	Snacks¤	¤
Annette·Hill¤	#·4¤	806-555-0110¤	snack·responsibility· on·9/9¤	¤
Brian·Groth¤	#·3¤	806-555-0134¤	snacks·on·9/16¤	¤
Maria·Hammond¤	#2¤	806-555-0175¤	snacks·of·9/23¤	¤
Russell·King¤	#·7¤	806-555-0161¤	snacks·on·9/30¤	¤
Lee·Oliver¤	#8¤	806-555-0154¤	snacks·on·10/7¤	¤
Chris·Preston¤	#6¤	806-555-0182¤	snacks·on·10/14¤	¤
Garrett·Young¤	#9¤	806-555-0192¤	snacks·on·10/28¤	¤
Dylan·Miller¤	#1¤	806-555-0149¤	snacks·on·11/4¤	¤
Eric·Parkinson¤	#5¤	806-555-0170¤	snacks·on·11/11¤	¤

6. **SAVE** the document as *soccer_roster* in the lesson folder on your USB flash drive, then **CLOSE** the file.

STOP. **CLOSE** Word.

 INTERNET READY

Search the Internet for job openings that interest you. Create a table to record data about at least five positions. Include columns for the job title, salary, location, contact person, and any other information that would help you in a job search. Use what you have learned in this chapter to format the table in an attractive way that you could easily maintain.

Workplace *Ready*

CREATING TABLES

Most people working in business are familiar with the many advantages of using Excel for creating tables. What some people may not realize is that Word provides many of the same capabilities. By creating a table and performing basic calculations directly within a Word document, you can turn an ordinary word processing document into a comprehensive business illustration.

Having just completed your college education, you are excited to begin your new career with Woodgrove Bank. As a Banking Associate in the Mortgage Department, one of your main responsibilities is to produce a monthly Mortgage Status memo. This memo includes monthly information on the number of new mortgage applications, the dollar amount of each, and their current status.

Presenting this information in a table format will provide for the most appealing design. However, you also need to include a brief introductory paragraph recapping the monthly information, as well as calculations for the total dollar amount of new mortgage applications. This report should be sent out in a memo format. By using Word, you can easily meet all of your objectives in just one program.

A co-worker reminds you that Word provides several memo templates, and you decide to choose one when initially creating your document. Memo templates provide replaceable text for To, From, Subject, Date, and CC information. Below this, you can enter your monthly recap paragraph. Finally, you can use Word's Table options to create and format a table with the desired number of columns and rows.

Once the table has been created and the information has been entered into the appropriate cells, you can use Word's Table Layout and Design tools to enhance your table's appearance. Word provides many of the same capabilities you would find in Excel, such as merging cells, splitting cells, aligning text, auto-fitting text, sorting, and much more.

With so many possibilities, Word is a true all-in-one business tool.

7 Using Illustrations and Graphics

LESSON SKILL MATRIX

In This Lesson, You Will Learn The Following Skills:

Inserting and Formatting Pictures in a Document

Inserting and Formatting Shapes, WordArt, and SmartArt

Inserting and Formatting Clip Art

Compressing and Resetting Images

Making Text Graphically Appealing

KEY TERMS

- caption
- clip art
- Clip Organizer
- compress
- crop
- drop cap
- embedded object
- floating object
- inline object
- linked object
- pull quote
- resetting
- scale
- screen clippings
- screenshot
- shapes
- SmartArt graphics
- WordArt

Margie's Travel is a full-service travel agency that specializes in providing services associated with tours, cruises, adventure activities, group travel, and vacation packages all geared toward seniors. Agents at Margie's Travel frequently need to enhance a document with graphics, pictures, or drawings. Word provides eye-catching travel information, signs, brochures, and flyers using SmartArt, clip art, and shapes. In this lesson, you learn how to insert SmartArt graphics, clip art, pictures, screenshots, and shapes and apply artistic art in a document. You will work with pictures to resize; scale; crop; rotate; apply a Quick Style; adjust color, brightness, and contrast; compress a resetting; and work with text boxes.

SOFTWARE ORIENTATION

Insert Tab and Picture Tools

The Insert tab, shown in Figure 7-1, contains a group of features that you can use to add graphics to your document in Word 2010. Commands in the Illustrations group enable you to add several types of graphics to enhance your Word documents, including pictures, clip art, shapes, SmartArt, charts, and screenshots. The Text group contains options to improve the appearance of the document by adding a text box, WordArt, drop cap, or other text object.

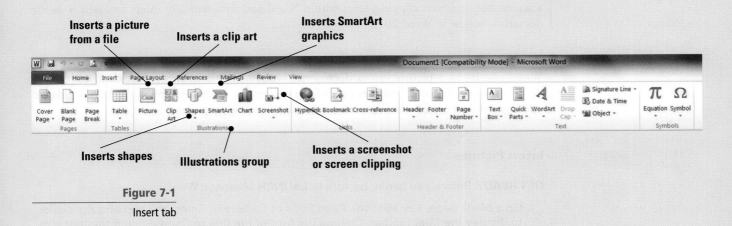

Figure 7-1

Insert tab

The Picture Tools tab, shown in Figure 7-2, is a contextual command tab that appears after you have added a picture to the Word document. Formatting options on the Picture Tools tab enable you to make changes to the graphic object, including removing its background; applying corrections to improve brightness, sharpness, and contrast to the picture; applying color; adding artistic effects; adding borders; enhancing the image with picture effects; cropping; and resizing.

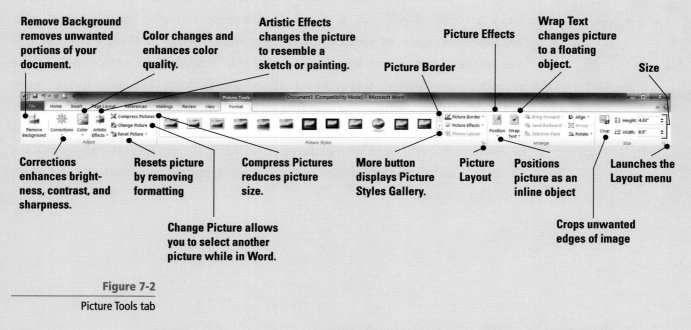

Remove Background removes unwanted portions of your document.

Color changes and enhances color quality.

Artistic Effects changes the picture to resemble a sketch or painting.

Picture Effects

Picture Border

Wrap Text changes picture to a floating object.

Size

Corrections enhances brightness, contrast, and sharpness.

Resets picture by removing formatting

Compress Pictures reduces picture size.

More button displays Picture Styles Gallery.

Picture Layout

Positions picture as an inline object

Launches the Layout menu

Change Picture allows you to select another picture while in Word.

Crops unwanted edges of image

Figure 7-2

Picture Tools tab

Use these figures as a reference throughout this lesson, as well as the rest of the book.

INSERTING AND FORMATTING PICTURES IN A DOCUMENT

The Bottom Line

Word offers a number of tools to help you capture your readers' attention with illustrations that include pictures, clip art, shapes, SmartArt, charts, and screenshots. You can format images in a number of ways, including converting them to SmartArt; adding captions; resizing, cropping, and rotating them; applying styles; adjusting color and tone; and applying Artistic Effects, which are new in Word 2010. Word also enables you to insert a screenshot and screen clipping and compress and reset the pictures that you've added to your documents. The ability to capture a screenshot or screen clipping from within Word and automatically insert and edit it in the document is new in Word 2010.

Inserting Pictures

When you insert a picture into a document, Word marks it as an **embedded object** by default—which means it becomes part of the document. Inserting a picture is very similar to opening a document file. In this exercise, you learn to insert a picture.

STEP BY STEP   **Insert Pictures**

GET READY. Before you begin, be sure to **LAUNCH** Microsoft Word.

1. On a blank page, key Visit the Palm Trees of California. Select the text and right-click to display the Mini toolbar. Change the font of the title to Cambria, and the font size to 28 pt., and then center on the page. Deselect the text.

 Ref

In Lesson 3, you learned to change fonts and font sizes, and alignments were covered in Lesson 4.

2. Press Enter.

3. Click the Insert tab, in the Illustrations group, then click the Picture button. The Insert Picture dialog box appears.

4. Click the dialog box's drop-down directory to navigate to your USB flash drive for the data files for this lesson and click to select the picture file named *palms* (see Figure 7-3).

Insert Picture dialog box drop-down directory

Change your view to display image.

@ The *palms* picture file for this lesson is available on the book companion website or in WileyPLUS.

USB flash drive

Preview area

5. Click Insert. The picture appears within your document at the cursor location, and the Format tab opens with the Picture Tool command groups.
6. **SAVE** the document as *palm_trees* in your USB flash drive in the lesson folder.

PAUSE. LEAVE the document open to use in the next exercise.

Take Note

Another option is to insert a picture as a **linked object**, which creates a connection between the document and picture, but doesn't combine them in the same file. Using linked objects can help minimize the file size of your final document, while still including pictures, photographs, and other objects that can eat up file space.

Formatting Pictures

The Formatting tab with Picture Tools appears whenever you insert a picture into a document or click on an existing picture within the document. The Picture Tools provide many options, such as cropping, resizing, scaling, and rotating. When you **crop** a picture, you trim the horizontal or vertical edges to get rid of unwanted areas. **Scale** increases or decreases the original picture's height and width by percentage. In this exercise, you will crop, resize, scale, and rotate a picture within a document.

STEP BY STEP **Crop, Resize, Scale, and Rotate a Picture**

USE the document you left open from the previous exercise.

1. The picture should be selected. In the Size group, click the Crop button. The mouse pointer becomes a cropping tool, and cropping handles appear on the edges of the picture, as shown in Figure 7-4.
2. Position the cropping tool over the top-right cropping handle. Then click and drag down and left until it is past the street sign in the picture. Release the mouse button and then click the Crop button again to remove the cropping handles. The image is trimmed to remove the unwanted area and displays only the cropped area. You can also use the Height and Width buttons in the Size group to crop by precise measurements. The picture height should be 4.33" and the picture width 2.86". If the measurements do not match, edit the settings in the Size group.

Figure 7-4

Cropping a picture

Visit·the·Palm·Trees·of·California¶

Green

Cropping handles appear on the edges of the picture.

3. In the Size group, launch the **dialog box launcher** to display the Layout dialog box, as shown in Figure 7-5. In the Layout dialog box, you can resize the picture by changing the exact measurements of the height and width or rescale it by changing the height and width percentages.

Figure 7-5

Layout dialog box

Another Way
You can also rotate a picture by selecting it and dragging the rotation handle—the round green arrow that appears at the top of a selected picture or shape—in the direction you want to rotate the picture.

4. Key **3.91"** in the Height Absolute text box. In the Rotate section, key **350** in the text box. The whole height of the picture will be slightly altered and the position of the picture will rotate 350 degrees.

5. In the Scale section, both the **Lock Aspect Ratio** and **Relative To Original Picture Size** check boxes should be selected. When the Lock Aspect Ratio box is selected, you will be able to scale the picture in proportion by height and width by the same percentage. When the Relative To Original Picture Size box is selected, the scaling is comparative to the original size. The original size of the picture is listed below the Layout dialog box under the Original Size section.

Take Note   In cropping, you remove unwanted portions of the picture, and in scaling, the original picture is increased or decreased in size to fit in the document.

6. Under the Scale section, click the **Height downward pointing arrow** until **62%** appears. The width of the active picture automatically changes to 62%. The Absolute Height dimension also changes to 3.71", to maintain the picture's original size.

7. Click **OK** to apply your changes and close the dialog box. Deselect the picture.

8. **SAVE** the document as *travel_palms* in your USB flash drive in the lesson folder.

PAUSE. LEAVE the document open to use in the next exercise.

Applying a Picture Style to a Picture

Applying a Picture Style to a picture allows you to select from various designs and give the picture an added appeal. Choosing from the available options and the More button provided in the gallery adds interest to your picture. **Captions** consist of few descriptive words and are used for figures, tables, and equations. Adding a caption to a picture provides readers with information regarding the image. Formatting a picture using the Picture Layout enables you to use one of the built-in SmartArt graphics with a caption placeholder. SmartArt graphics will be covered later in this lesson. In this exercise, you learn to apply a Quick Style, insert a border, add effects, and add a caption by applying a Picture Style to a picture.

STEP BY STEP   **Apply a Picture Style to a Picture**

USE the document that is open from the previous exercise.

1. To display the Picture Tools, select the picture.
2. Click the Format tab, and in the Picture Styles group, click the More ▼ button to display the Picture Style gallery, shown in Figure 7-6.

Figure 7-6
Picture Style gallery

More button displays the Picture Styles gallery.

3. Click Bevel Rectangle in the second row, ninth option to apply that style to the image.
4. In the Picture Styles group, click the Picture Border button to display the menu shown in Figure 7-7. Click the Weight submenu, then 2 ¼. The border weight is increased and is more noticeable. Click the Picture Border button again, and under the Theme Colors section, select Dark Blue Text 2. The picture is now surrounded by a colored border.

Figure 7-7
Picture Border menu

Picture Border displays the menu.

5. In the Picture Styles group, click the Picture Effects button to display the menu shown in Figure 7-8. Scroll through each Effects option to preview how it changes the appearance of your picture. Click the Shadow effect option, and in the Perspective section of the pop-up menu that appears, select Perspective Diagonal Lower Left (the first option in the second row of the section) to apply that shadow effect to your image. The picture displays with a shadow on the lower-left side.

Figure 7-8
Picture Effects menu

Picture Effects options

6. **SAVE** the document as *travel_palms1* in your USB flash drive in the lesson folder.
PAUSE. LEAVE the document open for the next exercise.

Converting a Picture to a SmartArt Graphic

SmartArt graphics have preformatted designs with placeholders that allow you to enter text as a caption. In this exercise, you learn to convert a picture to a SmartArt graphic with a caption.

STEP BY STEP	Convert a Picture to a SmartArt Graphic

NEW
to Office 2010

USE the document that is open from the previous exercise.

1. The picture should be selected to display the Picture Tools.

2. In the Pictures Styles group on the Format tab, click the **Picture Layout** button, and select the **Bending Picture Caption List** in the second row, fifth option (see Figure 7-9). The preset layout appears—each layout enables you to apply a picture with text. You can add a caption in the text area by adding a short description to your picture. The Picture Layout button automatically converts the picture to a SmartArt graphic and the picture is resized to accommodate a caption. The SmartArt Tools Design tab is activated.

Figure 7-9

Picture Layout gallery

Documents with pictures must be saved before converting them to a SmartArt graphics.

Take Note   The Picture Layout tab is inactive until the document is saved.

3. Key **Sunny California** in the placeholder [Text], shown in Figure 7-10. Text is automatically adjusted to fit in the placeholder, which is the caption for the picture. Click outside of the graphic to deselect.

Figure 7-10

SmartArt with caption

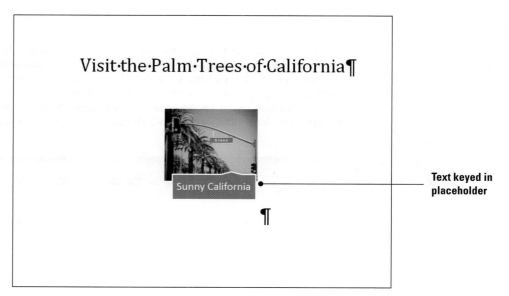

Text keyed in placeholder

4. **SAVE** the document as *travel_palms_caption* in your USB flash drive in the lesson folder and close the file.

PAUSE. LEAVE the document open to use in the next exercise.

Troubleshooting Before you can use the Picture Layout feature in a new document, you must save the file.

Adjusting a Picture's Brightness, Contrast, and Color and Adding Artistic Effects

Although Word does not have all the advanced features of a stand-alone photo-editing program, it does offer many ways for you to adjust pictures—including correcting a picture's brightness, contrast, and color and adding an artistic effect (see Table 7-1). The Artistic Effects feature can give the picture the appearance of a drawing, sketch, or painting. In this exercise, you will adjust the picture's brightness, contrast, and color and apply an artistic effect.

Table 7-1

Adjust Group—Provides Options to Enhance or Return Your Picture to Its Original Form

Type	Purpose
Remove Background	Removes unwanted portions of a background.
Corrections	Sharpen and Soften adjusts picture by highlighting the pixel colors. Brightness and Contrast alters the adjustment between the brightness and darkness of a picture.
Color	Color Saturation can be an intense deep color or a dim color. Color Tone adjusts the color cast of a picture that contains a dominance of one color by adjusting the color temperature to enhance the details. Recolor adjusts the image by changing the color to a gray scale or sepia tone for an added impact.
Artistic Effects	Applies distinct changes to an image to give it the appearance of a pencil drawing, line drawing, blur, watercolor sponge, film grains photocopy, texturizer, and more.
Compress Picture	Reduces the size of an object.
Change Picture	Changes the image while maintaining the size of the current image.
Reset Picture	Removes all formatting from the picture or resets picture and size back to its original size.

STEP BY STEP   **Adjust a Picture's Brightness, Contrast, and Color and Add Artistic Effects**

WileyPLUS Extra! features an online tutorial of this task.

OPEN the *travel_palms1* document completed earlier in the lesson.

1. To display the Picture Tools, select the picture.

2. Click the *Format tab*, and in the *Adjust group*, click the Corrections button to display the menu shown in Figure 7-11.

3. In Brightness and Contrast section, select the fourth option in the fourth row (Brightness: +20% and Contrast: +20%) to increase the brightness and contrast of your image by 20%. Notice the difference in the picture with an increased brightness and contrast.

Figure 7-11

Corrections gallery

Corrections gallery provides a preview of the corrected picture.

4. On the Format tab, in the Adjust group, click the **Color** button to display the menu shown in Figure 7-12.

Figure 7-12

Color gallery

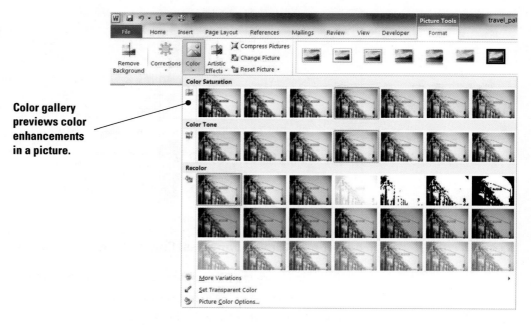

Color gallery previews color enhancements in a picture.

5. Scroll through the options and notice how your picture changes. In the Color Saturation section, select Saturation 200%. The higher the saturation percentage, the more vibrant the colors appear in the picture, consequently making the nature's color in the picture more noticeable. Click the Color button again to display the menu. In the ColorTone section, select Temperature 5300 K. The lower temperature tone creates a picture with a slight tint blue color, while the higher temperature makes the picture appear with an orange tint color. Under *Recolor*, No Recolor is selected by default.

6. **SAVE** the document as *travel_palms2* in your USB flash drive in the lesson folder.

7. On the Format tab, in the Adjust group, click the Artistic Effects button to display the menu shown in Figure 7-13.

Figure 7-13

Artistic Effects gallery

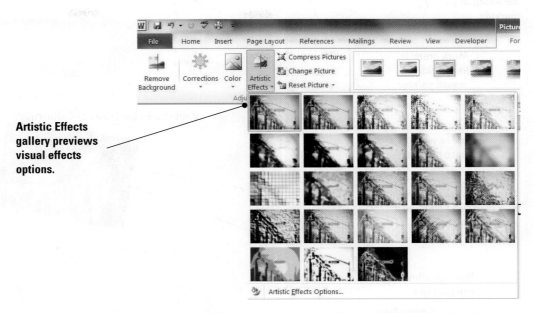

Artistic Effects gallery previews visual effects options.

8. Select the Crisscross Etching option from the Artistic Effects gallery; the effect is applied to the selected image in the fourth row, third option. The impression of the picture is now of an etching sketch. Deselect the picture.

9. SAVE the document as *travel_palms3* in your USB flash drive in the lesson folder.

PAUSE. LEAVE the Word document open to use in the next exercise.

Removing Backgrounds

NEW to Office 2010

Remove Background is a new feature in Word 2010 that removes portions of images you have inserted into documents. You can use the Remove Background options either to automatically remove the image background or to mark and remove specific portions of the image. In this exercise, you learn to use the Remove Background features.

STEP BY STEP   **Remove Background**

USE the document that is open from the previous exercise.

1. To display the Picture Tools, select the picture.

2. Click the Format tab, and in the Adjust group, click the Remove Background button. The Background Removal tab opens, as shown in Figure 7-14, and the picture is surrounded by a color selection marquee. A magenta color overlays the image, marking everything that is to be removed from the image.

3. To change the area of the picture that will be kept, resize the marquee by dragging the upper-left handle up until it meets the upper-left corner of the picture. Then drag the middle-bottom handle down to the bottom of the picture, and drag the right-middle handle to the left until it rests immediately beside the street light. Everything outside these boundaries will be removed from the image.

Take Note   Removing a background may take practice; therefore, you may need to use the Undo button to begin again.

Background Removal will remove unwanted portions of the document automatically or by marking.

Mark changes by drawing with the mouse pointer

Confirm changes and click Keep Changes

Mark areas to keep with the mouse pointer

Mark areas to remove with the mouse pointer

Document is surrounded by a marquee selection – magenta color marks everything to remove.

Handles allow you to resize

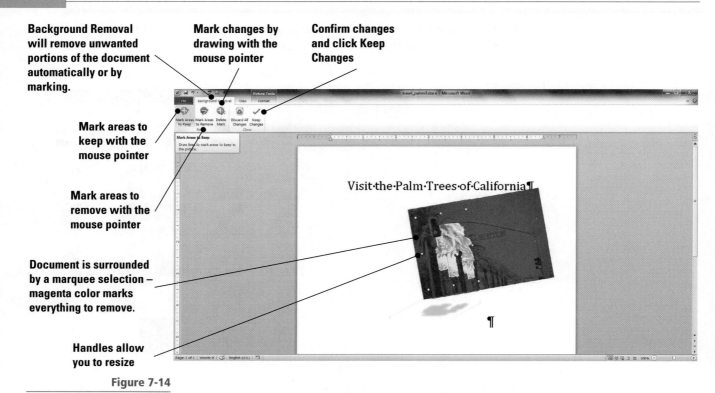

Figure 7-14

Background Removal

4. In the Close group, click Keep Changes to remove the designated area of the image, and then click outside the image to deselect. Your edited image should be similar to the one shown in Figure 7-15. Removing the background of a picture is similar to cropping except that the background removal focuses on the picture you wish to point out. In this exercise, the sky, palm trees, and light pole have been removed.

Figure 7-15

Document without background

5. **SAVE** the document as *palms_no_background* in your USB flash drive in the lesson folder.

6. The palm picture is still selected. To keep the top and bottom parts of the palm tree, click the Remove Background button in the Adjust group. In the Refine group, click the Mark Areas To Keep button, press and hold the left mouse button and draw around the palm tree to the right and below the street light. As you mark the area of keep, a circle with a plus symbol marks an area to keep.

7. Click the Mark Areas Remove button, press and hold the left mouse button and draw around the mark area to keep, and then continue marking the palm tree until it is completely marked. As you mark the area, the magenta color will appear and the smaller palm trees will be marked.

8. Click the Keep Changes button. Your document should match Figure 7-16.

Figure 7-16

Document with removal
of palm trees

Visit·the·Palm·Trees·of·California¶

¶

9. **SAVE** the document as *palms_removed* in your USB flash drive in the lesson folder and close the file.

PAUSE. LEAVE the Word document open to use in the next exercise.

Arranging Text around a Picture

Arranging pictures and text together on the page is simple using Word's Positioning and Text Wrap commands. The Positioning command automatically positions the object in the location you select on the page. The Wrap Text command determines the way text wraps around the picture or other objects on the page, depending on the option you select. To configure the picture as an **inline object** that moves along with the text that surrounds it, select the In Line with Text option. If you choose to format the picture as a **floating object**, Word positions the image precisely on the page, and allows the text to wrap around it in one of several available formats. In this exercise, you learn to position text around a picture.

STEP BY STEP | **Arrange Text around a Picture**

OPEN the *travel_palms2* document completed earlier in the lesson.

1. Place the insertion point on the line below the picture and press Enter. Key the following text:

Our charming desert cities, warm sun, and hot mineral springs make California the perfect vacation destination. So come visit the palm trees and experience this magical place.

2. Select the text; right-click to use the Mini toolbar to change the font size to 14 pt. Deselect the text.

3. To display the Picture Tools, select the picture.

4. On the Format tab, and in the Arrange group, click the Position button to display the menu shown in Figure 7-17.

Figure 7-17

Position menu

Position gallery previews several text and picture positioning options.

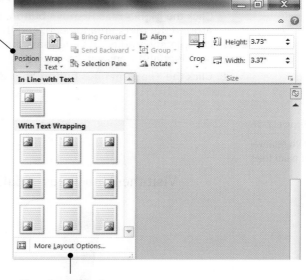

More Layout Options

**Another Way**
The Wrap Text feature in the Arrange group on the Format tab provides additional options for text wrapping.

5. Select Position in Middle Center with Square Text Wrapping. Delete the extra blank line below the heading. Place your insertion point anywhere in the paragraph you keyed in step 1, and press Ctrl+L to align text left. The text is now positioned at the top of the page and the picture is centered, as shown in Figure 7-18. If you were to add more text to this document, it would wrap around the image, which would remain centered in the middle of the page.

Figure 7-18

Image positioned around text

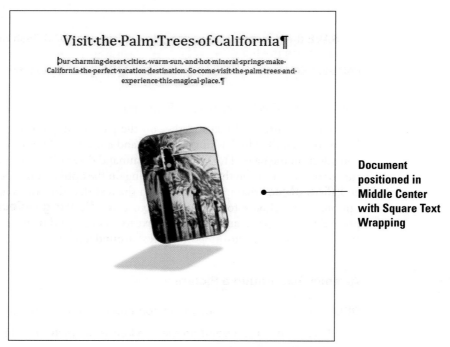

Document positioned in Middle Center with Square Text Wrapping

6. **SAVE** the document as *travel_palms5* in your USB flash drive in the lesson folder.

PAUSE. LEAVE the document open to use in the next exercise.

Inserting a Screenshot or Screen Clipping

Word 2010 has added new features to the Illustrations group. The new Screenshot feature will capture a picture of the whole screen or part of the screen and save it in the format of your choice. **Screenshots** are images of the entire current display on your computer screen. **Screen clippings**, however, are image captures of only the part of your screen that you have selected. In this exercise, you learn to insert a screenshot and a screen clipping.

STEP BY STEP   **Insert a Screenshot or Screen Clipping**

USE the document that is open from the previous exercise.

1. On the View tab, in the Zoom group, click the One Page button so that the entire page is displayed on your computer screen for the image capture. Do not minimize the display, or the screenshot will not capture the image of this document.

2. Press Ctrl+N to open a new blank document.

3. On the Insert tab, in the Illustrations group, click the Screenshot button; the Available Windows gallery opens, displaying the *travel_palms5* document, as shown in Figure 7-19. If you have more than one window open, you will see images from all open documents in the Screenshot Available Windows area. Minimize or close the other windows.

Figure 7-19

Screenshot displaying Available Windows

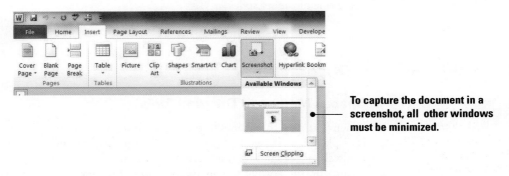

To capture the document in a screenshot, all other windows must be minimized.

4. Under the Available Windows area, click the travel_palms5 document to insert a screenshot of that document, as currently displayed, into the blank document.

5. **SAVE** the new document as *screenshot_palms* in your USB flash drive in the lesson folder (it remains the active document). Click below the image to deselect it, and then press the Enter key twice.

6. Click the Insert tab, in the Illustrations group, click the Screenshot button drop-down arrow, then select Screen Clipping from the menu that appears. The active document fades away, the *travel_palms5* document appears, and the mouse pointer changes to a crosshair (+).

7. Click and drag the mouse pointer over the heading, Visit the Palm Trees of California. When you release the mouse button, the heading is placed in the *screenshot_palms* document as shown in Figure 7-20. Click outside the heading to deselect it.

Figure 7-20

Document with screen clipping

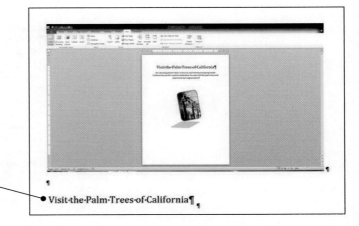

Screen clipping enables you to select portions of text or a picture.

Visit·the·Palm·Trees·of·California¶

8. **SAVE** the document as *screen_clipping* in your USB flash in the lesson folder and close the file.

9. **CLOSE** the *travel_palms5* document.

PAUSE. LEAVE the document open to use in the next exercise.

INSERTING AND FORMATTING SHAPES, WORDART AND SMARTART

The Bottom Line

Word provides illustrations to enhance your document with different preset shapes, SmartArt, and WordArt. **Shapes** are figures such as lines, rectangles, block arrows, equation shapes, flow-charts, stars and banners, and callouts. You may also insert a drawing canvas. The Drawing Tools make it possible for you to change the shape, add text, apply styles, fill with theme or standard colors, gradient, texture colors, and apply preset effects. **SmartArt graphics** are graphical illustrations available from a list of various categories, including List diagrams, Process diagrams, Cycle diagrams, Hierarchy diagrams, Relationship diagrams, Matrix diagrams, and Pyramid diagrams. The Smart Tools enable you to manipulate the shape by adding shapes, bullets, and text; changing the layout and colors; and applying special effects using styles. **WordArt** is a feature that creates decorative effects with text. The Drawing Tools allow you to format the WordArt by adding special effects to the text or outline, applying preset effects, and transforming the shape using one of the set styles.

SOFTWARE ORIENTATION

Shapes Menu and Drawing Tools

When you click the Shapes button in the Illustrations group of the Insert tab, the Shapes menu is displayed, as shown in Figure 7-21. The menu contains options for an assortment of ready-made shapes, including lines, arrows, stars, and banners. After you insert a shape into a Word document, the Format tab opens containing the Drawing Tools shown in Figure 7-22. You use these tools to format a shape's style, fill, color, outline, and many other attributes.

Figure 7-21

Shapes menu

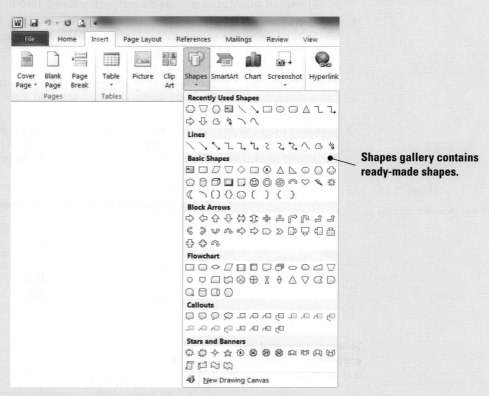

Shapes gallery contains ready-made shapes.

Edit Shape: Points in the shape can be reshaped or you can change the shape. Note, new document shapes must be saved before this feature is activated.

Adds text to shape

Adds color within shape

Adds color or changes the width of the outline

Height button

Launches the Layout dialog box

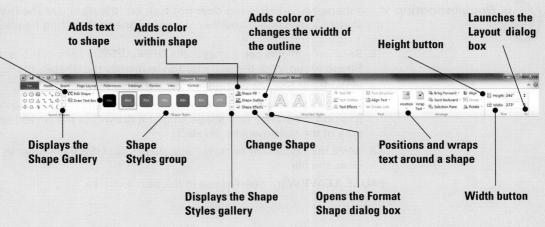

Displays the Shape Gallery

Shape Styles group

Change Shape

Positions and wraps text around a shape

Displays the Shape Styles gallery

Opens the Format Shape dialog box

Width button

Figure 7-22

Drawing Tools

Use these figures as a reference throughout this lesson, as well as the rest of the book.

Inserting Shapes

Word provides many different ready-made shapes to choose from such as lines, rectangles, arrows, equation shapes, callouts, stars, banners, and more. Inserting a shape in a document opens the Format tab containing Drawing Tools in several command groups. You can use these tools to insert shapes, apply shape styles, add a shadow or 3-D effect to inserted shapes, arrange the shape on the page, and size it. In this exercise, you learn to insert a shape, add a style from the gallery, and add a 3-D effect to the shape.

STEP BY STEP   **Insert Shapes**

OPEN *travel* from the data files for this lesson.

The *travel* document file for this lesson is available on the book companion website or in WileyPLUS.

WileyPLUS Extra! features an online tutorial of this task.

1. Click and drag to select the text **Picture Yourself Here** and the picture below it. On the Home tab, in the Paragraph group, click the **Align Text Right** button and deselect.
2. Click the **Insert** tab, in the Illustrations group, then click the **Shapes** button to display the Shapes menu.
3. In the Block Arrows section, click the **Curved Right Arrow** shape. The cursor turns into a crosshair (+).
4. Place the crosshair in front of the word Picture. Click and drag down toward the chairs on the left of the photograph to create the arrow shown in Figure 7-23.

Figure 7-23

Block arrow shape

Troubleshooting If the shape you are drawing does not turn out the right size the first time, you can adjust the shape by selecting it and then dragging one of the sizing handles.

5. Because you inserted a shape, the Drawing Tools Format tab is open. In the Insert Shape group, click the More button to display the Shapes menu.

6. In the Basic Shapes section, click the Smiley Face shape.

7. Place the crosshair (+) inside the curve of the arrow. Click and drag to insert and position the smiley face shape so that it fits within the curved space. Click in a blank area of the document to deselect.

8. **SAVE** the document as *travel_update* in your USB flash drive in the lesson folder and close the file.

PAUSE. LEAVE Word open to use in the next exercise.

Grouping Shapes into a Single Drawing

A drawing can be a single object or multiple objects grouped together, and it can include lines, rectangles, arrows, equation shapes, callouts, stars, banners, and more. The Shapes menu contains a number of shapes you can use to draw a flowchart—a type of drawing that presents a diagram of the tasks and timelines involved in completing a process, or that shows the hierarchy of personnel within an organization.

STEP BY STEP | **Create a Flowchart**

OPEN a new blank Word document.

Another Way
Click the File tab, then Options to open the Word Options dialog box. In the left side category, click Advanced, then under the Editing options section, click the check box at Automatically create drawing canvas when inserting AutoShapes to enable.

1. At the top of the document, key Margie's Travel. Select the text and use the Font command group tools on the Home tab to change the font to Cambria and font size to 24 pt. In the Paragraph group, click the Center button to center the text horizontally on the page. Deselect text and press Enter.

2. Key Organization Chart. Select the text and in the Home tab, change the font size to 20 pt. Deselect the text and press Enter. The text is centered and inserted in the document.

3. Click the Insert tab, and in the Illustrations group, click the Shapes button to display the Shapes menu.

4. At the bottom of the Shapes menu, click New Drawing Canvas. The drawing canvas frame appears on the document and the Drawing Tools Format tab (see Figure 7-24).

PAUSE. LEAVE Word open to use in the next exercise.

Figure 7-24

Drawing canvas

Margie's·Travel¶

Organization·Chart¶

Drawing canvas

Using SmartArt Graphics

SmartArt graphics are visual representations of information that can help communicate your message or ideas more effectively. SmartArt graphics and designer-quality illustrations can contribute to eye-catching documents that draw the attention of the target audience. Table 7-2 gives some examples of the type of information you can display with each category of SmartArt graphics. Earlier in this lesson, you learned to convert pictures to SmartArt with captions. In this exercise, you learn to insert SmartArt graphics into Word documents and add a caption to the graphics.

Table 7-2

SmartArt Graphic Categories

Type	Purpose
List	Show nonsequential or grouped blocks of information
Process	Show a progression of steps in a process, timeline, task, or workflow
Cycle	Show a continuing sequence of stages, tasks, or events in a circular flow
Hierarchy	Show a decision tree or create an organization chart
Relationship	Illustrate connections or interlocking ideas; show related or contrasting concepts
Matrix	Show how parts relate to a whole
Pyramid	Show proportional, foundation-based, containment, overlapping, or interconnected relationships

STEP BY STEP **Use SmartArt Graphics**

OPEN a new, blank document.

1. Click the **Insert** tab, in the Illustrations group, click the **SmartArt** button. The Choose a SmartArt Graphic dialog box appears.

2. Click the **Relationship** category and then select **Equation** as shown in Figure 7-25. Use the scroll bar to locate the equation graphic in the third column, sixth option.

Figure 7-25

Choose a SmartArt Graphic dialog box

Several categories of SmartArt are available with preview option.

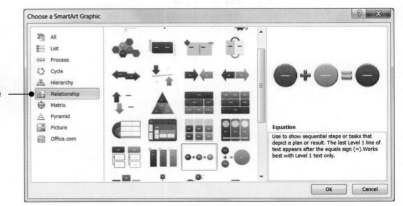

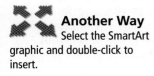
Another Way
Select the SmartArt graphic and double-click to insert.

3. Click **OK** to insert the Equation SmartArt graphic into your document. The placeholders are placed in the graphic and ready for you to key information. Text can be keyed in the placeholders or in the Text Pane.

4. On the Design tab, click the Text Pane button to enable—the text pane appears enabling you to key text in each element of the graphic equation. The first placeholder is selected by default and ready for you to key text, as shown in Figure 7-26.

Figure 7-26

The Text Pane

Enable or disable Text Pane button

The Text Pane makes entering text easy.

Description of SmartArt graphic

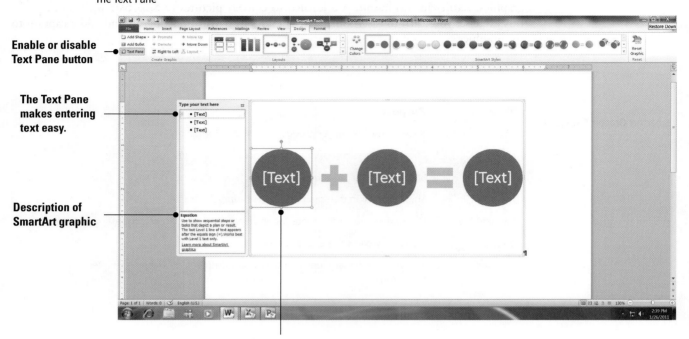

Placeholder for text

5. Key the information as displayed in Figure 7-27. Click to move to the next element and key the remaining text. As you key text, Word automatically adjusts the text to fit in the graphic. If you press the Enter key at the end, another element is added to the equation. Click the Close button in the Text Pane or in the Create Graphic group; click the Text Pane button to close.

Figure 7-27

Text added to SmartArt graphic

The Text Pane makes entering text easy.

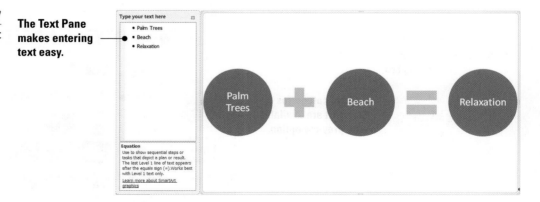

6. In the Design tab, in the Layouts group, click the drop-down arrow at the More arrow to produce the Layouts gallery, then select More Layouts. The Choose a SmartArt Graphic dialog box appears. Select Picture, then select Bubble Picture List (fourth column, seventh position) from the menu that appears. Click OK. The equation's graphic is replaced with the Bubble Picture List, and text is carried over to the new layout. The text you added in step 5 now appears as captions beside the bubbles in the SmartArt graphic. An image icon appears in the middle of each circle.

7. To add an image to a bubble, click the first image icon for the Palm Trees; the default Insert Pictures dialog box opens. Use the scroll bar to locate your USB flash drive and click the lesson folder. Click the image for the palms to select, then click **Open** or double-click on image. The image is inserted in the first bubble and is automatically resized and adjusted.

8. Click the image in the bubble for the second image by Beach. The Insert Picture dialog box opens. Select the beach picture, and click **Open** or double-click on the image. The beach image is inserted in the bubble by the caption, Beach.

9. For the Relaxation Bubble List, click the image in the bubble. The Insert Picture dialog box opens. Select the relaxing at the beach picture and click **Open** or double-click on the image. The relaxing at the beach image is inserted in the bubble by the caption, Relaxation. The document should resemble Figure 7-28.

Figure 7-28

SmartArt with captions and images

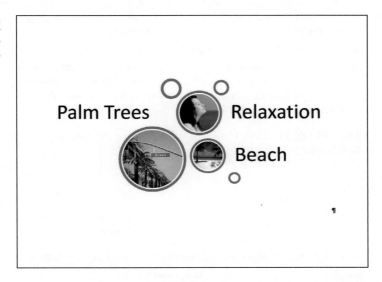

10. On the Design tab, in the SmartArt Styles group, click the **Change Colors** button. Then under the Primary Theme Colors section, click **Dark 2 Outline**. The Bubble graphic now has an outline style applied. Click outside the Bubble graphic layout to deselect.

11. **SAVE** the document as *travel_sign* in your USB flash drive in the lesson folder and close the file.

PAUSE. LEAVE Word open to use in the next exercise.

INSERTING AND FORMATTING CLIP ART

The Bottom Line

Clip art is a collection of media files available for you to insert in Microsoft Office documents that can include illustrations, photographs, video, or audio content. You can search the entire Microsoft Office Clip Art Gallery, or you can limit your search by using the Clip Organizer. The **Clip Organizer** collects and stores clip art, photos, animations, videos, and other types of media to use. You can categorize clips into a collection for easy access. After you insert a clip art object into your document, you can position it within text on the page, add a caption, resize the clip art, apply artistic effects, compress the clip art, and more.

Inserting, Resizing, and Adding a Caption to Clip Art

Clip art refers to picture files and are inserted in a document. The clip can be resized for better management within the document so that you can position it correctly. In this exercise, you learn how to insert a clip art graphic image file, resize the image, and add a caption to it.

STEP BY STEP   **Insert, Resize, and Add a Caption to a Clip Art**

OPEN a new, blank Word document.

1. Key **Explore the World** and select text. On the Home tab, Font group, change the font to **Cambria** and font size to **36 pt**. In the Paragraph group, click the **Center** button. Deselect the text.

2. Press **Enter**.

3. Click the **Insert** tab and, in the Illustrations group, click **Clip Art**. The Clip Art pane appears to the right of your document.

4. In the Search For box, key **travel**. Clip art appears in the results box.

5. In the Results Should Be box, click the **drop-down arrow** to view the four types of media searches. Maintain the default selection: All Media Types (if you wanted to limit your search, you could click to deselect this check box then click the check boxes beside the collections you wish to search).

6. Click **Go** to produce the search results.

7. In the Results pane, scroll down and in the first column sixth option click the **airliners, airplanes, concepts . . . option**. A ScreenTip will appear displaying the keywords for the clip art. Click the drop-down arrow by the clip art, and then click **Insert**. The image should match Figure 7-29.

 Ref   Earlier in this lesson, the Picture Tools were introduced for pictures. They are used the same way for clip art.

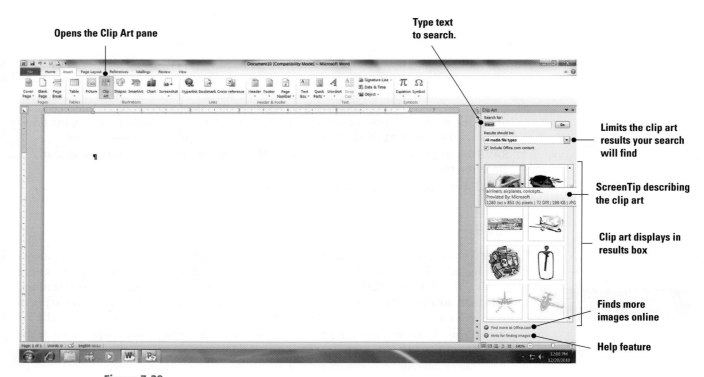

Figure 7-29

Clip Art pane with search results on travel

8. With the clip art selected, hold the **Shift** key (to maintain the proportions of the clip art picture) as you click and drag the bottom-right sizing handle of the clip art to make it smaller—2.11″ in height and 3.17″ wide. You can also use the Height and Width buttons in the Size group to crop by precise measurements.

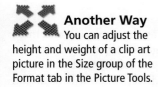

Another Way
You can adjust the height and weight of a clip art picture in the Size group of the Format tab in the Picture Tools.

9. Close the Clip Art pane.
10. **SAVE** the document as *travel_overseas* in your USB flash drive in the lesson folder.
11. Select the travel clip art image you have inserted in your document to display the Picture Tools Format tab.
12. In the Picture Styles group, click the Picture Layout button and, in the menu that appears, select Snapshot Picture List (first row, fourth option). The original image is carried over into the new layout with a [Text] placeholder.
13. The Snapshot Picture List contains a placeholder for text. In the *text* placeholder, key Traveling by Air. *Traveling by Air* is a caption describing the picture. Click outside the SmartArt graphic to deselect. Your document should match Figure 7-30.

Figure 7-30

Document with SmartArt and caption

14. **SAVE** the document with the same filename in your USB flash drive in the lesson folder.

PAUSE. LEAVE the document open to use in the next exercise.

Formatting Clip Art

As you've seen in earlier exercises, the Picture Tools Format tab provides a number of commands for enhancing your document's appearance. You can use these tools to apply Artistic Effects features to a clip art picture, and then position the clip art automatically around the text. Compressing reduces the file size of clip art.

Organizing Clip Art

The Microsoft Clip Organizer collects and stores clip art, photos animations, videos, and other types of media to use. You can use the organizer to add, delete, copy, and move clips, and to change keywords and captions. You also can take clips from a file, scanner, or camera, or online and place them in a personalized folder or in one of the existing folders in the organizer. These folders are categorized into collections for easy access. Table 7-3 displays the types of media files you can add to the Clip Organizer and their file extensions.

Table 7-3

Types of Media Files

File Type	Extension
Microsoft Windows Metafile	.emf, .wmf
Windows Bitmap	.bmp, .dib, .rle
Computer Graphics Metafile	.cgm
Graphics Interchange Format	.gif
Joint Photographic Experts Group	.jpg
Portable Network Graphics	.png
Macintosh PICT	.pct
Tagged Image File Format	.tif
Vector Markup Language	.vml
Microsoft Windows Media	.avi, .asf, .asx, .rmi, .wma, .wax, .wav

COMPRESSING AND RESETTING IMAGES

When you compress an image, it reduces the file size, thereby reducing the resolution and making the documents more manageable to share. You can compress images for clip art and pictures. Larger images may take up space on your USB flash drive. When you **compress** an image, you can make it occupy less space on your hard drive or USB flash drive, which will allow you to open and save your document more quickly and reduces the download time for file sharing. **Resetting** a picture will discard all formatting changes you made to the picture, including changes to contrast, color, brightness, and style.

Compressing Images

Compressing and resetting images will save space when sharing images by email. In this exercise, you learn to compress and reset an image in preparation for sharing by email.

STEP BY STEP   **Compress Images**

OPEN the *travel_palms2* document competed in an earlier exercise.

1. To display the Picture Tools, select the *travel_palms2* picture.
2. Click the Format tab, and in the Adjust group, and click the Compress Pictures button to display the *Compress Pictures* dialog box, shown in Figure 7-31.

Figure 7-31

Compress Pictures dialog box

Identify your target output for this document (print, web, etc.) and Word will recommend an ideal compression size.

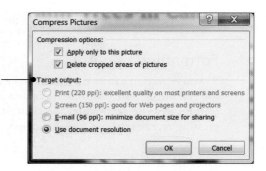

3. In the Compress Options section, check marks indicate which features are activated.
4. In the Target Output section, select the E-mail (96 ppi): minimize document size for sharing radio button. By selecting the radio button, the picture file size will be compressed to make the document ready for sharing via email. The other Target Outputs compress the picture to print correctly on printers and screens and to view on web pages and projectors.
5. Click OK to apply your choices.
6. **SAVE** the document as *travel_pic_compress* in your USB flash drive in the lesson folder.

PAUSE. LEAVE the document open to use in the next exercise.

 **Troubleshooting**   You will not see the compression take place. To verify that the file is smaller after compressing pictures, you can compare the document's properties before and after performing the command. Keep in mind that if your picture is already smaller than the compression option chosen, no compression will occur.

Resetting an Image

When resetting a picture's brightness and contrast, the color is reset using the Reset Picture command. You may also choose to Reset Picture and Size. In this exercise, you learn to reset an image.

STEP BY STEP   **Reset an Image**

USE the document that is open from the previous exercise.

1. To display the Picture Tools, select the travel palms picture.
2. Click the Format tab, and in the Adjust group, click the drop-down arrow to display the Reset Picture menu; then select Reset Picture. Formatting changes you made to the picture earlier are discarded.
3. **SAVE** the document as *travel_reset* to your USB flash drive in the lesson folder and close the file.

CLOSE Word.

MAKING TEXT GRAPHICALLY APPEALING

The Bottom Line

Word's Text Box command lets you insert professionally formatted text elements such as pull quotes and drop caps quickly.

Creating a Drop Cap

A **drop cap** is a large initial letter that drops down two or more lines at the beginning of a paragraph to indicate that a new block of information is beginning and to give interest to newsletters or magazine articles. A **pull quote** is a sentence or other text displayed within a box on the page for emphasis and for ease of movement, and they are often used along with drop caps in newsletters, advertisements, and magazines.

To insert a drop cap, select the first character at the beginning of the paragraph, then click the Insert tab. In the Text group, click the Drop Cap button, the Drop Cap menu appears as shown in Figure 7-32. The online WileyPlus tutorial will demonstrate how easy it is to insert a Drop Cap in a document.

Figure 7-32

Drop Cap menu

The default settings for Font, number of Lines to drop, and Distance from text are shown in Figure 7-33.

Figure 7-33

Drop Cap dialog box

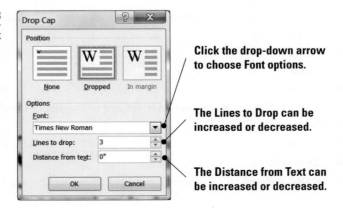

Click the drop-down arrow to choose Font options.

The Lines to Drop can be increased or decreased.

The Distance from Text can be increased or decreased.

SKILL SUMMARY

In This Lesson, You Learned How To:
Insert and format pictures in a document
Insert and format shapes, WordArt and SmartArt
Insert and format clip art
Compress and reset images
Make text graphically appealing

Knowledge Assessment

True/False

Circle T if the statement is true or F if the statement is false.

T F 1. Images shared by email should be compressed to avoid a long download time.

T F 2. In a new document, images can be converted to SmartArt with captions.

T F 3. You can use the Remove Background tool to select what areas of an inserted image to keep and what areas to discard.

T F 4. Resetting a picture will remove formatting that you have applied to it.

T F 5. Themes cannot be customized.

T F 6. Captions can be inserted using SmartArt graphics.

T F 7. A floating object does not wrap text around it.

T F 8. To capture a screenshot, all applications should be minimized.

T F 9. Screen clippings capture the entire display of your computer screen.

T F 10. Resetting an image does not remove all formatting changes.

Multiple Choice

Select the best response for the following statements.

1. In the Clip Art pane, you can search for which media type?
   a. Illustrations
   b. Photographs
   c. Videos
   d. Audio
   e. All of the above

2. Decreasing the size of a picture file by reducing the resolution is called _____.
   a. Compressing
   b. Rotating
   c. Cropping
   d. Resizing

3. Lines, block arrows, stars, and banners are examples of what?
   a. Diagrams
   b. Shapes
   c. Flowcharts
   d. Quick Styles

4. Which tools provide options for formatting shapes?

    a. Drawing

    b. Picture

    c. Text

    d. Effects

5. The _____ will capture a picture of the whole program window.

    a. Copy button

    b. Print Screen button

    c. Screenshot button

    d. None of the above

6. Which command enables you to remove unwanted parts from a picture?

    a. SmartArt

    b. Contrast

    c. Rotate

    d. Crop

7. The Artistic Effect is available on which tool?

    a. Picture

    b. Drawing

    c. Recolor

    d. Format

8. What element can you use to provide a short descriptive label for an image in a newsletter or magazine?

    a. Caption

    b. Text

    c. Drop cap

    d. All of the above

9. Which command allows you to change the appearance of an inserted image without the use of photo-editing programs?

    a. Artistic Effect

    b. Corrections

    c. Color

    d. None of the above

10. Which command would you use to discard all the formatting changes made to a picture?

    a. Original

    b. Undo

    c. Reset

    d. Discard

Competency Assessment

Project 7-1: House for Sale

In your position at Tech Terrace Real Estate, you are asked to add a photo to a flyer that is advertising a house for sale and format it attractively.

GET READY. LAUNCH Word if it is not already running.

1. **OPEN** *tech_house* from the data files for this lesson.

2. Place the insertion point on the first line of the document.

3. On the Insert tab, in the Illustrations group, click **Picture**.

4. Navigate to the data files for this lesson and select the **housephoto** file.

5. On the Format tab, in the Size group, click the **Crop** button.

@ The *tech_house* document file for this lesson is available on the book companion website or in WileyPLUS.

6. Click the bottom-right cropping handle and drag up until the sidewalk is outside the selection area and release the mouse button to crop out the sidewalk.

7. On the Format tab, in the Picture Styles group, click the More button.

8. Click Center Shadow Rectangle in the gallery.

9. On the Format menu, in the Adjust group, click the Color button.

10. In the Recolor section, click Sepia.

11. **SAVE** the document as *house_flyer* in your USB flash drive in the lesson folder and **CLOSE** the file.

PAUSE. LEAVE Word open for the next project.

Project 7-2: Student Leadership Association Fundraiser

The Student Leadership Association is having a garage sale to raise money for scholarships. Your task is to complete the flyer by inserting and resizing the clip art on items that will be sold.

GET READY. LAUNCH Word if not already running.

1. **OPEN** the *garage sale* file from the lesson folder.

2. Change the orientation to landscape.

3. Select *Garage Sale* and make the text **bold**, **center**, 72 pts. Change the font color to Red, Accent 2, Darker 50%.

4. Select 7 a.m. to 3 p.m., and make the text **bold**, **center**, 48 pts. Change the font color to Dark Blue, Text 2.

5. Select *11441 George Dieter St.*, and make the text **bold**, **center**, 48 pts. Change the font color to Orange, Accent 6, Darker 25%.

6. Select *Directions: Exit I-10 ....on the left side*, and make the text center, 28 pts. **Bold** only "Directions:".

7. Click the Insert tab and in the Illustrations group, click Clip Art.

8. In the Search For box, key garage sales.

9. Place the insertion point in front of *G* in *Garage*. In the second column, second row, select Household items in garage sale. Size the height of clip art to 1.89" and width to 2.11".

10. Place the insertion point after *e* in *Sale*. In the second column, fifth row, select *People standing in the yard at a garage sale*. Size the height of clip art to 1.89" and width to 2.11".

11. **SAVE** the document as *garage sale flyer* in your USB flash drive in the lesson folder.

LEAVE Word open for the next project.

@The *garage sale* document file for this lesson is available on the book companion website or in WileyPLUS.

Proficiency Assessment

Project 7-3: House for Sale Flyer

You need to make some additions and changes to the flyer completed in Project 7-1.

GET READY. LAUNCH Word if it is not already running.

1. **OPEN** the *house_flyer* you completed for Project 7-1.

2. Convert the picture to a SmartArt graphic and select Titled Picture Blocks. In the text placeholder, key House for Sale.

3. **SAVE** the document as *house_for_sale* in your USB flash drive in the lesson folder and close the file.

PAUSE. LEAVE Word open for the next project.

Project 7-4: Resetting an Image

For this project, you will reset an image to its original size.

GET READY. LAUNCH Word if not already running.

@ The *sitting at the beach* file for this lesson is available on the book companion website or in WileyPLUS.

1. **OPEN** the *sitting at the beach* file from the lesson folder.
2. Reset the picture and size.
3. **SAVE** the document as *sitting at the beach reset* in your USB flash drive in the lesson folder.

LEAVE Word open for the next project.

Mastery Assessment

Project 7-5: Formatting a Flyer

A coworker at Keyser Garden & Nursery tried to create a sales flyer about roses, but was not familiar with formatting tools and ran into trouble. She asks if you can open the file and try to correct the problems and help format it.

@ The *rose_bushes* document file for this lesson is available on the book companion website or in WileyPLUS.

GET READY. LAUNCH Word if it is not already running.

1. **OPEN** *rose_bushes* from the data files for this lesson.
2. Use the skills learned in this lesson to correct the problems and format the document to look like Figure 7-34.

Figure 7-34

Rose Bush document

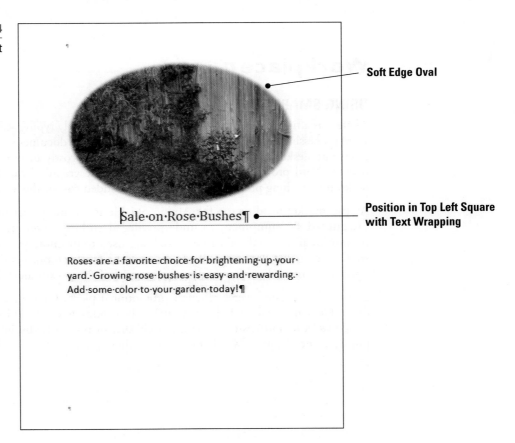

Soft Edge Oval

Position in Top Left Square with Text Wrapping

Sale·on·Rose·Bushes¶

Roses·are·a·favorite·choice·for·brightening·up·your· yard.·Growing·rose·bushes·is·easy·and·rewarding.· Add·some·color·to·your·garden·today!¶

3. **SAVE** the document as *rose_sale* in your USB flash drive in the lesson folder and close the file.

PAUSE. LEAVE Word open for the next project.

Project 7-6: Removing the Background Image

For this project you will remove the background in the image.

GET READY. LAUNCH Word if not already running.

 The *relaxing at the beach* file for this lesson is available on the book companion website or in WileyPLUS.

1. **OPEN** the *relaxing at the beach* file from the lesson folder.
2. Change the orientation to landscape and center.
3. Remove all of the blue background.
4. **SAVE** the document as *picture with no background* in your USB flash drive in the lesson folder.

LEAVE Word open for the next project.

INTERNET READY

When creating a document, you are not limited to inserting only the clip art and other media that comes installed with Word. A single click can open up a whole new world of options. At the bottom of the Clip Art pane, notice the Find more at Office.com link. You can click the link to browse dozens of categories and download clips. Next time you need to enhance your document with clip art or other media, expand your options by going online.

Search the Internet for tips on how to create reader-friendly, professional-looking newsletters, brochures, and other types of desktop publishing documents. Use the information you find to create a newsletter. Include a pull quote, drop cap, text box, and WordArt in your newsletter.

Workplace *Ready*

USING SMARTART

There was a time when doing anything other than simply typing sentences and paragraphs in a word processing document was unheard of. Enhancing a document with graphics used to require a separate desktop publishing programs, which were costly to purchase and often difficult to master. Word provides you with many of the same graphical capabilities you find in today's desktop publishing programs, but without the added cost or the learning curve.

As the marketing director for Alpine Ski House, a nonprofit organization that provides discounted ski equipment to underprivileged children, you are often called on to create promotional materials. These materials are used to promote your organization's mission, as well as to solicit donations. Being a nonprofit organization, your company tries to keep its operating costs as low as possible, so you work within an extremely tight budget.

You need to create several different promotional pieces for your upcoming annual donation drive. These materials include items such as brochures, flyers, and pledge cards. Outsourcing the design work to a professional desktop publisher or printer is absolutely out of the question, so put your knowledge of Word's many formatting options to use and design the items yourself.

Working with Themes, Quick Parts, Page Backgrounds, and Headers and Footers

8

LESSON SKILL MATRIX

In This Lesson, You Will Learn The Following Skills:

Formatting, Creating, and Customizing a Theme

Using Quick Parts in a Document

Formatting a Document's Background

Creating and Modifying Headers and Footers

KEY TERMS

- **building blocks**
- **content controls**
- **document theme**
- **fields**
- **footer**
- **header**
- **watermarks**

You are a content manager for Flatland Hosting Company, a position in which you are responsible for writing and editing all client material, such as hosting guidelines and agreements. When creating and revising documents, several Word commands can help you work more efficiently. In this lesson, you learn to apply a theme to a document, add content to a document using quick parts, and insert page numbers, headers, and footers.

FORMATTING, CREATING, AND CUSTOMIZING A THEME

The Bottom Line

Word provides features such as themes and Quick Parts to produce creative and professional documents. In this lesson, you learn to change the appearance of the document using the existing and customized themes and inserting building blocks in the document.

Formatting a Document with a Theme

Predefined formatting preferences allow you to change the overall appearance of the document by selecting and applying a theme. A **document theme** is a set of predefined formatting options that includes theme colors, fonts, and effects. You can apply one of the preexisting themes or create and customize a theme. Document themes contain the following elements: theme colors, theme fonts, and theme effects. In this exercise, you learn how to apply a document theme in Word.

Theme colors contain four text and background colors, six accent colors, and two hyperlink colors. Click the Theme Colors button to change the colors for the current theme, as shown in Figure 8-1.

Figure 8-1

Theme Colors menu

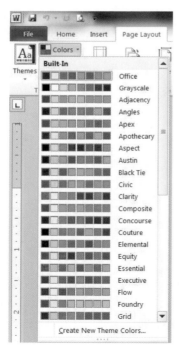

Theme fonts contain a heading font and a body text font. Click the Theme Fonts button to change the fonts for the current theme, as shown in Figure 8-2.

Figure 8-2

Theme Fonts menu

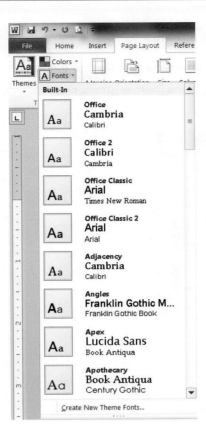

Theme effects are sets of lines and fill effects. Click the Theme Effects button to change the effects for the current theme, as shown in Figure 8-3.

Figure 8-3

Theme Effects menu

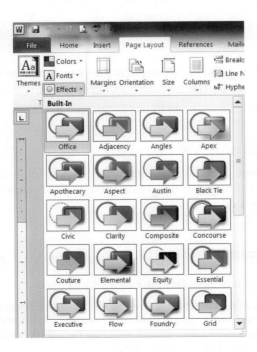

Format a Document with a Theme

OPEN the *hosting* document from the data files for this lesson.

1. On the Page Layout tab, in the Themes group, click Themes; the Themes menu opens, as shown in Figure 8-4.

Figure 8-4

Document Themes menu

The *hosting* document for this lesson is available on the book companion website or in WileyPLUS.

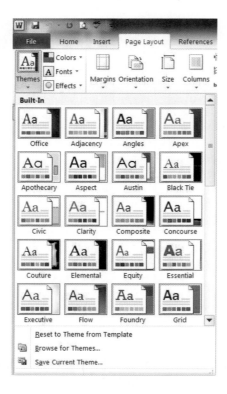

WileyPLUS Extra! features an online tutorial of this task.

2. Place your insertion point over any built-in theme and notice that the document changes to display a live preview of your document.

Take Note   Applying a theme changes the overall design of the entire document.

3. Click the Grid theme and the elements are applied to the document.
4. **SAVE** the document as *hosting_term* in your USB flash drive in the lesson folder.

PAUSE. LEAVE the document open to use in the next exercise.

Creating and Customizing a Theme

In a business environment, the company may want to show consistency by customizing a theme to be used for reports throughout the organization. In this exercise, you create, customize, and apply a new theme to a document.

Create and Customize a Theme

USE the document that is open from the previous exercise.

1. In the Themes group, click the Theme Colors button to open the Colors menu (refer to Figure 8-1). The Theme Colors contain predefined formatting colors with text and background colors, six accent colors, and two hyperlink colors. These colors can be customized and saved with a new name.
2. At the bottom of the Colors menu, click Create New Theme Colors; the Create New Theme Colors dialog box opens (see Figure 8-5).

Figure 8-5

Create New Theme Colors dialog box

There are 12 settings for each color set—the defaults are displayed.

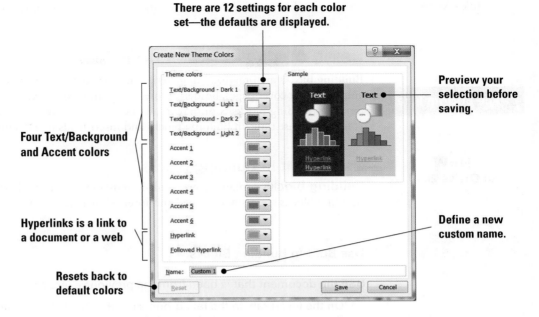

Four Text/Background and Accent colors

Hyperlinks is a link to a document or a web

Preview your selection before saving.

Define a new custom name.

Resets back to default colors

Take Note

Throughout this chapter you will see information that appears in black text within brackets, such as [Press **Enter**], or [your email address]. The information contained in the brackets is intended to be directions for you rather than something you actually type word-for-word. It will instruct you to perform an action or substitute text. Do not type the actual text that appears within brackets.

Another Way

You can edit the Colors and Fonts in the Styles group, under Change Styles.

3. In the *Name* text box, replace Custom 1 by keying **Corporate_[your initials]**. Click **Save**; the dialog box closes and you have defined a new custom theme color name based on default colors.

4. Click **Colors** and under the Custom section place your insertion point over Corporate_[your initials]. Right-click this theme name, then click **Edit** from the pop-up menu that appears. The Edit Theme Colors dialog box appears.

5. In the list of theme colors, click the **Accent 2 drop-down arrow** to produce a menu of colors for this element. In the fourth column of the menu's sixth row select **Tan, Text 2, Darker 50%**. Click **Save**. You changed the default color to a specific color and created your own custom theme colors for your document.

6. Click the **Fonts** button to produce the Theme Fonts menu (refer to Figure 7-2). In the menu, click **Create New Theme Fonts**; the Create New Theme Fonts dialog box opens. In the Name text box, replace Custom 1 by keying **CorporateFonts_[your initials]**.

7. Change the Heading Font and Body Font to **Arial**; notice the preview of your font choices that appears in the Sample pane of the dialog box. Click **Save** to close the dialog box and apply your font choices to the document.

Take Note

A quick way to change fonts is by keying the font name.

8. Click the **Effects** button and select **Concourse** from the menu that appears (refer to Figure 8-3). When applying shapes to your document, such as a bevel shape, the shape will display based on the effect you selected. Notice the change in the bevel shape on page one by the second paragraph under the heading *Introduction* (see Figure 8-6).

Figure 8-6

Sample Bevel Shape with Theme Effects

Applying one of the Theme Effects produces a different effect on the bevel shape.

arbiter as the interpretation of the following. By utilizing Flatland Hosting's services, you agree to be bound by the terms herein outlined.

Questions or comments regarding this document should be forwarded to Flatland Hosting at: info@flatlandhostingcompany.com

9. **SAVE** the document as *hosting_term1* in your USB flash drive in the lesson folder.

PAUSE. LEAVE the document open to use in the next exercise.

Take Note   Document themes are the same throughout all Office programs and can share the same appearance.

USING QUICK PARTS IN A DOCUMENT

Building blocks are organized in galleries and sorted by category. In the Building Block gallery, you can insert cover pages, headers, footers, page numbers, text boxes, and watermarks. Another term for building blocks is AutoText, and both features are used the same way. In this exercise, you learn to use built-in building blocks and insert fields in a document.

NEW to Office 2010

Using Built-In Building Blocks

Building blocks contain several built-in reusable content such as text, graphics, and objects. Building blocks are easily managed and inserted in a document for a quick format.

STEP BY STEP   **Use Built-In Building Blocks**

USE the document that is open from the previous exercise.

1. On the Insert tab, in the Text group, click the Quick Parts button to display the Quick Parts menu, as shown in Figure 8-7.

Figure 8-7

Quick Parts menu

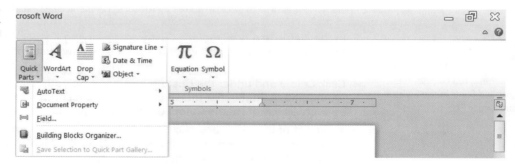

2. Click the Building Blocks Organizer menu option to display the Building Blocks Organizer dialog box, as shown in Figure 8-8. In the left pane of the dialog box, the preformatted elements or building blocks are listed by name; the Gallery column indicates the gallery that contains each building block, and the Category column indicates each element's general type, while the Template column indicates within which template the element is stored. You can use the buttons at the bottom of the dialog box to delete and edit selected building blocks. The right pane previews your selections.

3. Click the Name heading to sort the building blocks by name.

4. Scroll down the list and select Confidential 1 Watermark.

 Troubleshooting You can adjust the Name column by dragging the resize bar to the right to change the width.

5. Click the Insert button. The Confidential watermark appears behind the text on every page.

6. Display the Building Blocks Organizer dialog box. Click the Gallery heading to sort the building blocks by gallery.

7. Scroll down and select the Austin Pull Quote from the Text Box gallery. Click Insert and pull quote is inserted in the document as shown in Figure 8-9. You can key text in the placeholders or drag and drop text in the area.

Figure 8-8

Building Blocks Organizer

Easily sort list by column heading

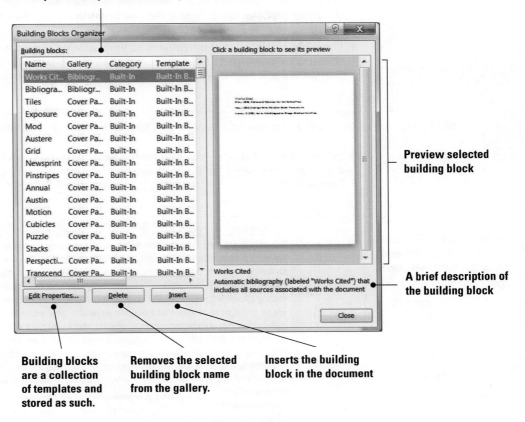

Preview selected building block

A brief description of the building block

Building blocks are a collection of templates and stored as such.

Removes the selected building block name from the gallery.

Inserts the building block in the document

Figure 8-9

Document with text box pull quote

Place pointer on hyphenated lines around text box to drag and drop to the end of first paragraph.

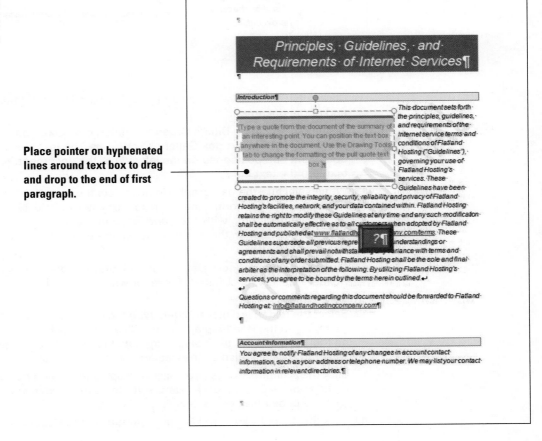

8. Under the heading, Introduction, select the second paragraph beginning with "Questions or comments. . . ." Move the selected text inside the quote area by dragging and dropping. Delete the line break and one paragraph mark after the first paragraph under *Introduction*.

9. Place your pointer on the hyphenated lines around the quote text box—the pointer changes to four arrows to allow you to drag and drop. Drag the quote to the end of the first paragraph until it wraps around the last seven lines of the paragraph.

Troubleshooting Deselect the text box and select again to see the hyphenated lines around the text box.

10. Select the Bevel shape—the pointer changes to four arrows to allow you to drag to a new location. Drag the Bevel shape by the quote text box on the right margin (see Figure 8-10).

Figure 8-10

Document with text box pull quote wrapped around paragraph with bevel shape

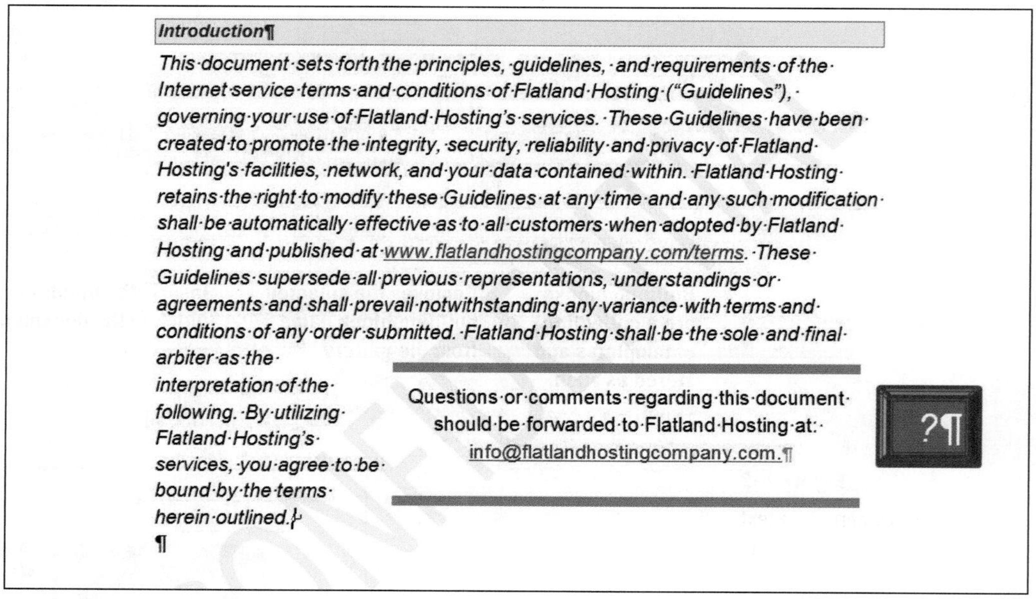

> **Introduction¶**
>
> This document sets forth the principles, guidelines, and requirements of the Internet service terms and conditions of Flatland Hosting ("Guidelines"), governing your use of Flatland Hosting's services. These Guidelines have been created to promote the integrity, security, reliability and privacy of Flatland Hosting's facilities, network, and your data contained within. Flatland Hosting retains the right to modify these Guidelines at any time and any such modification shall be automatically effective as to all customers when adopted by Flatland Hosting and published at www.flatlandhostingcompany.com/terms. These Guidelines supersede all previous representations, understandings or agreements and shall prevail notwithstanding any variance with terms and conditions of any order submitted. Flatland Hosting shall be the sole and final arbiter as the interpretation of the following. By utilizing Flatland Hosting's services, you agree to be bound by the terms herein outlined.
>
> Questions or comments regarding this document should be forwarded to Flatland Hosting at: info@flatlandhostingcompany.com.¶

11. Click outside the Bevel shape and press **Ctrl+End** to move the insertion point to the end of the document.

12. Display the Building Blocks Organizer dialog box. Scroll down and select **Alphabet Sidebar** from the Text Box Gallery. Click **Insert.** The text box is inserted at the end of the document and positioned on the left side of the document. Your next step is to insert text into the text box.

13. When selecting the paragraph, do not select the paragraph mark; this will avoid displaying the horizontal line in the Text Box twice. Select the paragraph above Refusal of Service beginning with "*You and Flatland Hosting further agree . . .*" and drag and drop the selection in the text box. Delete the two paragraph marks above the heading, Refusal of Service.

14. Click the **Building Blocks Organizer** to display the dialog box and select **Austin** in the Headers Gallery. Click **Insert.** A header with a border is inserted in every page of the document.

15. Select the text in the placeholder, *Type the document title* and key **Flatland Hosting Company** in the Header placeholder. Click the **Close Header and Footer** button located on the Header & Footer Tools Design tab. Inserting a header from the Building Block will automatically display the Header & Footer Tools tab.

16. Click the **Building Blocks Organizer** to display the dialog box and select **Conservative** in the Footers Gallery. Click **Insert.** A footer is inserted in every page of the document with the page number displayed.

17. Click the **Close Header and Footer** button from the Header & Footer Tools Design tab.

18. Click the **Building Blocks Organizer** to display the dialog box and select **Austin** in the Cover Page Gallery. Click **Insert**. The cover page is inserted as page 1.

19. Key the following information in the placeholders:

Abstract: Flatland Hosting Company will set guidelines and requirements for use of Flatland Hosting services.

Document Title: Flatland Hosting Company automatically appears

Subtitle: Guidelines & Agreements

Type the Author Name: A. Becker

20. **SAVE** the document as *hosting_term2* in your USB flash drive in the lesson folder and **CLOSE** the file.

PAUSE. LEAVE Word open to use in the next exercise.

Another Way
On the Insert tab, in the Pages group, click the Cover Page button to insert a cover page.

Troubleshooting If you experience problems in saving the author's name, complete one of the following actions: (1) Click the File tab, then Options. In the General category, under Personalize your copy of Microsoft Office section, key the author's name by the User name box and initials. (2) Click the File tab and in the section Prepare for Sharing, click the *Allow this information to be saved in your file link* and then save.

(X) Ref   Later in this lesson, you will learn to insert a watermark in the Page Background group.

Another Way
In the Header & Footer group, you can insert a header or footer or page number.

Inserting an Equation

Microsoft Word 2010 has built-in equations, which can be inserted from the Quick Parts gallery or using the Equations command. You can use the Equation Tool Design tab, which displays when an equation is inserted in a document, to edit or construct your own equation. In this exercise, you learn to insert equations in a document.

STEP BY STEP   **Insert an Equation**

OPEN a new blank Word document.

1. Click the **Insert** Tab and, in the Text group, click the **Quick Parts** button then click the **Building Blocks Organizer**.

2. In the Building Block Organizer dialog box, locate and click the **Expansion of a Sum** equation in the Equation Gallery. Click **Insert**. The Expansion of a Sum equation is inserted in the document. Position the insertion point after the equation placeholder and then press the **Enter** key twice to place a blank line below the placeholder.

3. In the Building Block Organizer dialog box, locate and click the **Area of Circle** equation, then click **Insert**. Position the insertion point after the equation placeholder and then press the **Enter** key twice to place a blank line below the placeholder.

4. In the Building Block Organizer dialog box, locate and click the **Binomial Theorem** equation. Click **Insert**. Click outside the equation placeholder, and press the **Enter** key twice.

5. **SAVE** the document as *equations* in your USB flash drive in the lesson folder and **CLOSE**.

Another Way
In the Insert tab, Symbols group, click the Equation button and select an equation from the built-in menu.

PAUSE. LEAVE Word open to use in the next exercise.

Inserting a Field from Quick Parts

A **field** is a placeholder where Word inserts content in a document. Word automatically uses fields when specific commands are activated, such as those for inserting dates, page numbers, and a table of contents. When you insert a date field in a document, the date will be updated automatically each time the document is opened. In this exercise, you learn to insert a field in a document.

Fields, also called field codes, appear between curly brackets ({ }) when displayed. Field codes are turned off by default. To display field codes in a document, press Alt+F9. To edit a field, place the insertion point within the field and right-click and then click Edit Field.

STEP BY STEP   **Insert a Field from Quick Parts**

The *hosting_term2* document file for this lesson is available on the book companion website or in WileyPLUS.

OPEN the *hosting_term2* document from the lesson folder.

1. Press **Ctrl+End** to move to the end of the document. The insertion point is positioned on the last paragraph mark.
2. Key **Last Updated:** in bold and press the spacebar once after the colon.
3. On the Insert tab, in the Text group, click the **Quick Parts** button.
4. Click **Field** on the menu. The Field dialog box is displayed (see Figure 8-11).

Figure 8-11

Field dialog box

Select category by
clicking drop-down arrow.

Available
Field options

Date formats

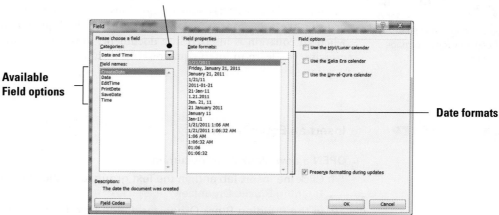

Another Way
On the Insert tab, in the Text group, click Date & Time to open the Date and Time dialog box.

5. From the Categories drop-down list, click **Date and Time**.
6. In the Field Names list, click **Date**.
7. In the Date Formats list, select the ninth option with the **Day Month Year** format and click **OK** to close the dialog box and insert the date and time field in your document. The document should look similar to the one shown in Figure 8-12, with the exception that the current date will appear.
8. **SAVE** document as *hosting_term3* in your USB flash drive in the lesson folder and **CLOSE**.

PAUSE. LEAVE Word open to use in the next exercise.

Figure 8-12

Document with Date field inserted

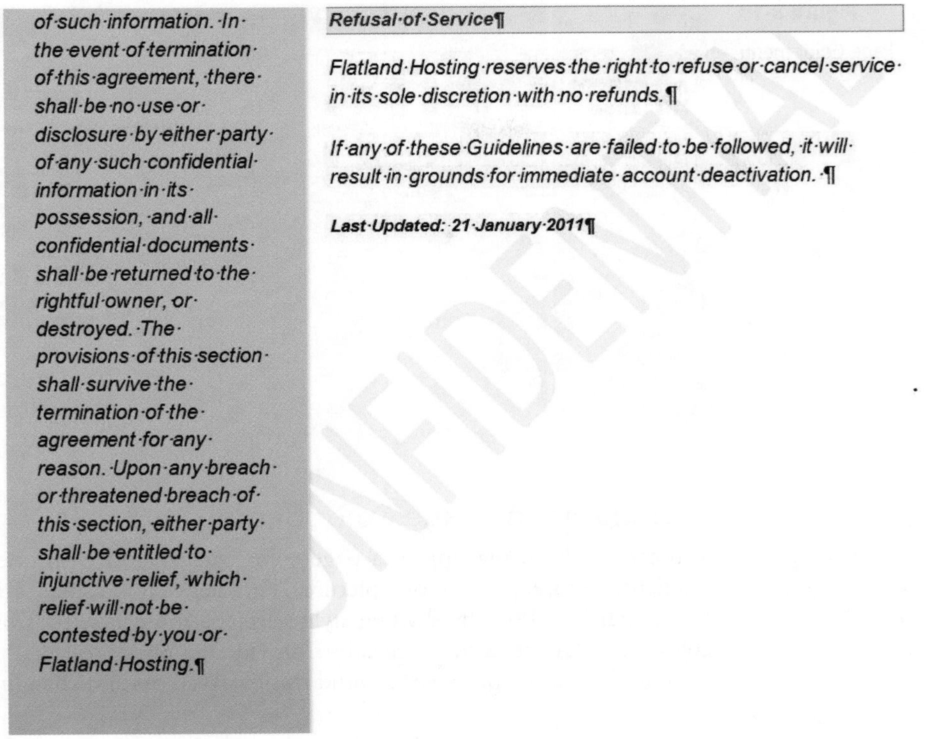

of·such·information.·In· the·event·of·termination· of·this·agreement,·there· shall·be·no·use·or· disclosure·by·either·party· of·any·such·confidential· information·in·its· possession,·and·all· confidential·documents· shall·be·returned·to·the· rightful·owner,·or· destroyed.·The· provisions·of·this·section· shall·survive·the· termination·of·the· agreement·for·any· reason.·Upon·any·breach· or·threatened·breach·of· this·section,·either·party· shall·be·entitled·to· injunctive·relief,·which· relief·will·not·be· contested·by·you·or· Flatland·Hosting.¶

Refusal·of·Service¶

Flatland·Hosting·reserves·the·right·to·refuse·or·cancel·service· in·its·sole·discretion·with·no·refunds.¶

If·any·of·these·Guidelines·are·failed·to·be·followed,·it·will· result·in·grounds·for·immediate·account·deactivation.·¶

Last·Updated:·21·January·2011¶

FORMATTING A DOCUMENT'S BACKGROUND

The Bottom Line

Word's enhanced features allow the user to produce a creatively formatted document by changing the background color, inserting a watermark, and adding a border to the document.

Inserting a Page Color

Adding a background color to the title page of a report conveys originality. You may want to distinguish your research paper from others, for example, by adding a background color to the first page. It is important to use background colors in moderation and to choose a page color that will not interfere with the text. If text is dark, for example, then the background color should be light, and if text is light, a dark background would improve the document's readability. In this exercise, you learn to insert a page color in a document.

WileyPLUS Extra! features an online tutorial of this task.

STEP BY STEP   **Insert a Page Color**

OPEN *hosting_term* from your USB flash drive for this lesson.

@ The *hosting_term* document file for this lesson is available on the book companion website or in WileyPLUS.

1. Click the **Page Layout** tab.
2. In the *Page Background* group, click the **Page Color** button to open the color menu and gallery, as shown in Figure 8-13. Click to select **White, Background 1, Darker 5%**; the page color is applied.
3. **SAVE** the document as *hosting_term4* in your USB flash drive in the lesson folder.

PAUSE. LEAVE the document open to use in the next exercise.

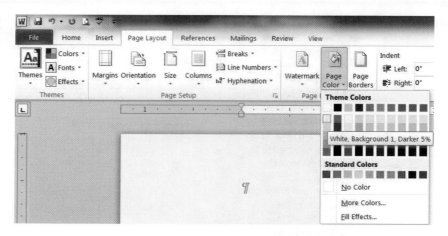

Figure 8-13

Page Color menu

Formatting the Page Color Background

You can apply formatting to a page color background with one color or fill effect, such as, gradient, texture, pattern, or a picture. A gradient fill is a shape fill that changes from one color to another based on the shading style selected. You can select from one color or two to preset colors. The layout of the page colors provides emphasis to the document. In this exercise, you learn to format the page background using two colors and changing the shading style.

STEP BY STEP   **Format the Page Color Background**

USE the document that is open from the previous exercise.

1. With the Page Layout tab active, click the **Page Color** button, and in the menu that appears, click **Fill Effects**. The Fill Effects dialog opens with the Gradient tab active.

2. Under the Colors section, select **Preset** and then click the **drop-down arrow** under the Preset colors section to view available background colors.

3. In the Gradient tab under the Colors section, select **Two colors**. Two options appear, Color 1 and Color 2. Under Color 2 click the **drop-down arrow** to produce the color palette. In the ninth column third row, select **Brown, Accent 5, Lighter 60%**. The selected color appears in the box under Color 2 (see Figure 8-14).

Figure 8-14

Fill Effects dialog box

Fill Effects	? X

Gradient | Texture | Pattern | Picture

Colors

○ O**n**e color   Color **1**:

● **T**wo colors

○ Pre**s**et   Color **2**:

Transparency

F**r**om: ◄   ►   0 %

T**o**:   ◄   ►   0 %

Shading styles   **Variants**

○ **H**orizontal

○ **V**ertical

○ Diagonal **u**p

○ Diagonal **d**own

○ **F**rom corner

● F**r**om center   Sample:

☐ Rotate fill effect with shape

OK   Cancel

4. Under the Variants section, samples of the two colors are displayed. Under the Shading Styles section, you have choices on how the style should appear in the document. Select **From Center**. Notice the lower-right corner produces Color 1 in the center and Color 2 outside. Click **OK**.

5. **SAVE** the document as *hosting_term5* in your USB flash drive in the lesson folder.

PAUSE. LEAVE the document open to use in the next exercise.

Adding a Watermark

In business, some documents may contain sensitive information, and the nature of a document's status should be clearly conveyed on its pages. Word provides built-in text, called **watermarks**, that display lightly behind text as words, such as, *confidential*, *draft*, or *urgent*. Watermarks can be customized to include text or images, including company logos. In this lesson, you learn to customize a watermark and insert it into a document.

STEP BY STEP   **Add a Watermark**

USE the document that is open from the previous exercise.

1. In the Page Background group of the Page Layout tab, click the **Watermark** menu and scroll down to select **Custom Watermark**. The Printed Watermark dialog box opens. Select the **Text watermark** radio button and then click the **drop-down arrow** next to Text and select **Draft**. You can customize text watermarks by keying content in the text box or you can select from the drop-down menu.

2. Click the **drop-down arrow** by Font and select **Calibri**. This will change the text watermark font.

3. In the Color text box click the **drop-down arrow** and select **Gray-50%, Accent 6** in the Theme Colors (see Figure 8-15).

Figure 8-15

Printed Watermark dialog box

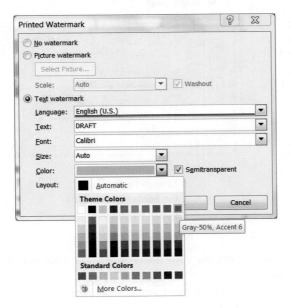

4. Click **OK**. The watermark is inserted on all pages. Note, if you click **Apply**, the dialog box remains open and you can view your watermark in the document. When you click **OK**, the dialog box closes and you're back in the document screen.

5. **SAVE** the document in your USB flash drive in the lesson folder.

PAUSE. LEAVE the document open to use in the next exercise.

 Ref   Earlier in this lesson, you learned to insert a watermark using the Building Blocks Organizer.

Adding a Page Border

The Page Borders command allows you to insert a border around a document's page. Adding a border adds to the page or frame of a page and improves the appearance of the document. Applying elements by changing the color, width, and style adds emphasis to the page. In this lesson, you learn to add elements to a page border and insert them into a document.

STEP BY STEP   **Add a Page Border**

USE the document that is open from the previous exercise.

1. In the Page Background group of the Page Layout tab, click the Page Borders button. The Borders and Shading dialog box appears.
2. In the Setting section, click the Shadow option. Notice the lower-right bottom has a shadow effect to the border.
3. Click the drop-down arrow on the Color menu and in the ninth column, first row choose Brown, Accent 5. You are applying a specific color to the border.
4. Click the drop-down arrow on the Width menu and choose 2 1/4 pt. The width of the border is increased to provide emphasis.
5. Click the drop-down arrow on the Apply To menu and click This section–First page only as shown in Figure 8-16. The page border is applied to the first page only.

Figure 8-16

Borders and Shading dialog box

Border lines styles can give a document a different appearance.

Allows you to preview before confirming your selection

Setting contains five options.

A specific color can be applied to borders.

Determine where the border will be applied in the document.

Change the weight of the border by selecting one of the options.

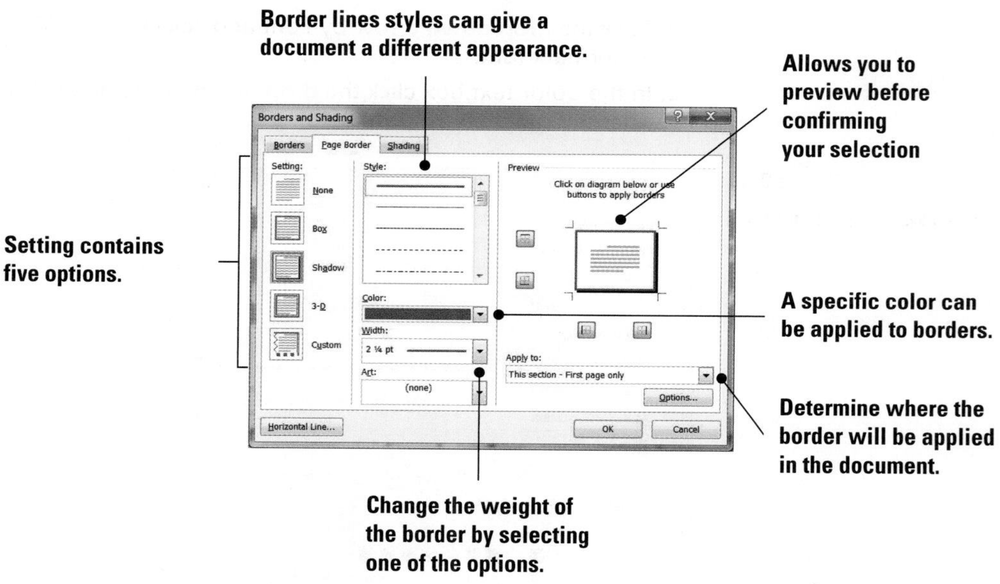

6. Click OK. Scroll and review your document and notice that the border does not appear on other pages.
7. Select the bevel shape on page 1 and press Delete.
8. **SAVE** the document as *hosting_term6* to your USB flash drive in the lesson folder.

PAUSE. LEAVE the document open to use in the next exercise.

CREATING AND MODIFYING HEADERS AND FOOTERS

The Bottom Line

A **header** appears on the top of a page and a **footer** appears at the bottom of the document's page. The Header & Footer group contains commands for inserting built-in headers, footers, and page numbers into a Word document.

The Page Number button in the Header & Footer group has commands for inserting page numbers at the top, bottom, or in the margin of a page using the built-in gallery. In this exercise, you learn to insert page numbers in a document.

Adding Page Numbers

STEP BY STEP   **Add Page Numbers**

USE the document that is open from the previous exercise.

1. Place the insertion point anywhere on the first page.
2. Click the Insert tab.
3. In the Header & Footer group, click the Page Number button, and in the menu that appears, point to Bottom of Page; in the pull-down menu, select Plain Number 2, as shown in Figure 8-17. Page numbers are inserted on all pages. Notice that the Headers & Footer Tools opens with the Design tab active.

Figure 8-17

Page Number menu

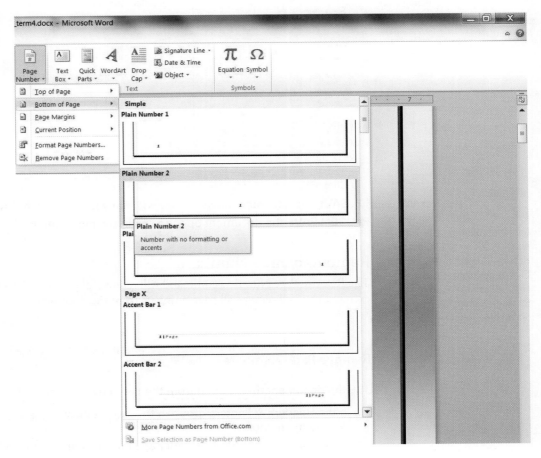

4. In the Design tab, in the Close group, click the Close Header and Footer button. The Header & Footer Tools closes.
5. SAVE the document in your USB flash drive in the lesson folder.

PAUSE. LEAVE the document open to use in the next exercise.

Formatting Page Numbers

Word provides various types of numbering formats to choose from, such as, *1, 2, 3 . . .; i, ii, iii . . .;* or *a, b, c. . . .* In addition to choosing a numbering style, Word's page number formatting commands enable you to decide where page numbering will begin, pause, and continue. In this exercise, you learn to change the page number format.

STEP BY STEP   **Format Page Numbers**

USE the document that is open from the previous exercise.

1. In the Headers & Footers group in the Insert tab, click the Page Number button to display the menu.
2. Click Format Page Numbers. The Page Number Format dialog box appears.
3. In the Number Format text box, click the drop-down arrow and select the lowercase roman numerals option (i, ii, iii, . . .) as shown in Figure 8-18. Selecting this option will change the number format to lowercase Roman numerals on all pages.

Figure 8-18

Page Number Format dialog box

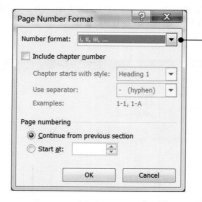

Click drop-down arrow to select format.

Another Way
Scroll down to the first footer on page 1 and double-click on the footer; the Header & Footer Tools display. Click Page Number and then Format Page Numbers to open the Page Number Format dialog box.

4. Click OK.
5. **SAVE** the document as *hosting_update* in your USB flash drive in the lesson folder.

PAUSE. LEAVE the document open to use in the next exercise.

Removing Page Numbers

The Remove Page Numbers command will remove all page numbering in the document. In this exercise, you will remove all page numbers from the document.

STEP BY STEP   **Remove Page Numbers**

USE the document that is open from the previous exercise.

1. In the Headers & Footers group in the Insert tab, click the Page Number button to display the menu.
2. Click Remove Page Numbers. All page numbers are removed from the document.
3. Click Undo to restore all page numbers.
4. **SAVE** the document in your USB flash drive in the lesson folder.

PAUSE. LEAVE the document open to use in the next exercise.

Inserting the Current Date and Time

Word's Insert tab contains a number of command groups that enable you to insert charts, graphs, images, and other elements into Word documents. In this exercise, you learn to use commands in the Insert tab to insert the date in a document.

STEP BY STEP   **Insert Current Date and Time**

USE the document that is open from the previous exercise.

1. Position the insertion point in the third line on page 1, under the heading. Key **Date Submitted:** and press the **spacebar** once after the colon.
2. In the Text group, in the Insert Tab, click **Date & Time**. The Date and Time dialog box opens, as shown in Figure 8-19.

Figure 8-19

Date and Time dialog box

Available format options →

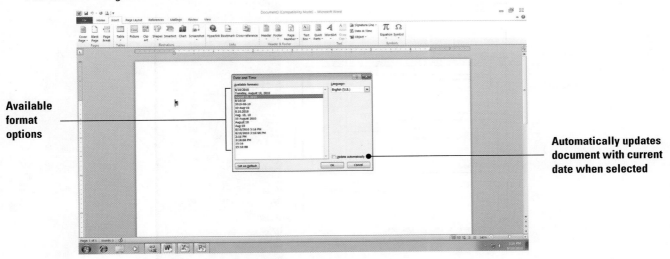

← **Automatically updates document with current date when selected**

3. In the Available Formats list, select the ninth option, which displays the Day Month Year date format. Click **OK**. The selected format with the current date is inserted in the document.
4. Press **Ctrl+End**. The insertion point is on the last paragraph mark. Key **Time Submitted:** and press the **spacebar** once after the colon.
5. Click the **Date & Time** command, and in the Date and Time menu that appears, select the fourth option from the bottom of the Available Formats list, which displays time in hours and minutes, using the 12-hour clock format.
6. **SAVE** the document in your USB flash drive in the lesson folder.

PAUSE. LEAVE the document open to use in the next exercise.

Inserting a Built-In Header or Footer

The Header and Footer commands provide options for inserting content at the top and bottom of pages and enable you to edit, remove, save, and view additional headers and footers online. You can choose to make the first page header and/or footer different from those on subsequent pages and place these elements on odd or even pages only using the Headers and Footers tools from the Design tab that appears when you insert one of these elements into your document. In this exercise, you learn to insert a built-in header and footer.

 Ref   Earlier in this lesson, you learned how to insert headers and footers using Quick Parts.

STEP BY STEP   **Insert a Built-In Header or Footer**

USE the document that is open from the previous exercise.

1. In the Header & Footer group in the *Insert* tab, click the Header button, and in the drop-down menu that appears, scroll down to select the Pinstripes option, as shown in Figure 8-20. The header is inserted on every page and the Header & Footer Design tab opens.

Figure 8-20

Header menu

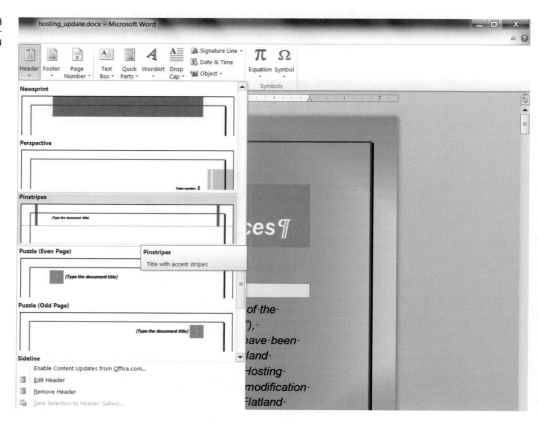

2. In the Options group of the Header & Footer Design tab, shown in Figure 8-21, click the Different First Page box. In the Navigation group, click Previous to go to the first page and notice the header is removed from the first page.

Figure 8-21

Header & Footer Tools

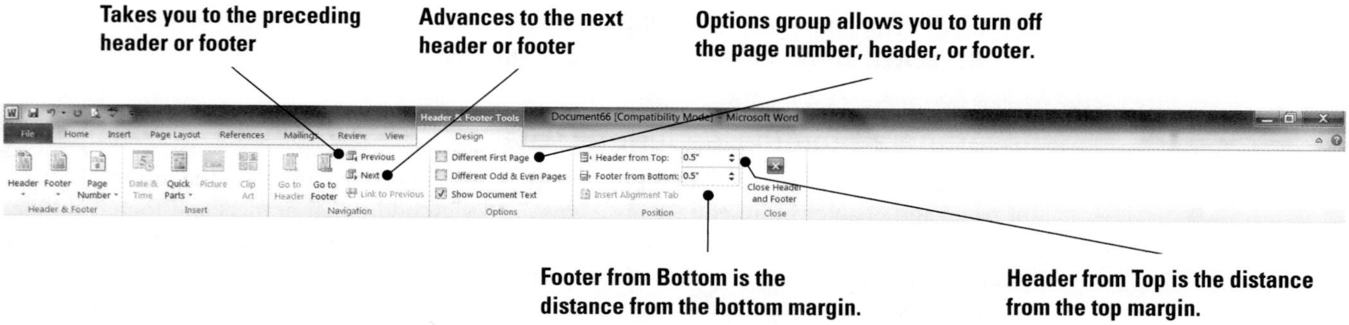

Takes you to the preceding header or footer

Advances to the next header or footer

Options group allows you to turn off the page number, header, or footer.

Footer from Bottom is the distance from the bottom margin.

Header from Top is the distance from the top margin.

3. In the Navigation group, click Next to go to the header area of page 2.

4. In the Header & Footer group, click the Footer button and scroll down to click Pinstripes from the menu that appears. Notice the new footer inserts the word Page by the formatted page number that you inserted in a previous exercise (see Figure 8-22).

Figure 8-22

Footer with formatted
page number

Formatted page
number

5. Click the Close Header and Footer button on the Design tab.

6. **SAVE** the document as *hosting_update1* in your USB flash drive in lesson folder.

PAUSE. LEAVE the document open to use in the next exercise.

Adding Content to a Header or Footer

Content controls are individual programs that allow you to add information in a document, such as a header or footer. Content controls are used for templates, forms, and documents and are identified by a border and temporary text. In this exercise, you learn to add content to a placeholder in a header and footer.

STEP BY STEP   **Add Content to a Header or Footer**

USE the document that is open from the previous exercise.

Another Way
Click the Insert tab and in the Header & Footer group, click Edit Header.

1. Position the insertion point on the second page of the document and double-click the header to activate.

2. The placeholder [Type the document title] is selected.

3. Key Guidelines and Requirements, as shown in Figure 8-23, to create the text that will appear in your document's header.

Figure 8-23

Title in header

Content added
to header

4. On the Navigation group on the Design tab, click Go to Footer; the insertion point moves to the page ii footer. Click [Type text] and key Flatland Hosting Company to replace the placeholder.

5. Select the text in the footer, including the page number. Display the Mini toolbar by right-clicking. Click the drop-down arrow at the Font box and change the Font to Arial.

6. Click the Grow Font button on the Mini toolbar to increase the font size to 12.

7. Click the Italic button to turn off.

8. Click the footer to deselect.

9. Click the Close Header and Footer button on the Design tab to close. The Header & Footers Tools Design tab closes.

10. **SAVE** the document in your USB flash drive in the lesson folder.

PAUSE. LEAVE the document open to use in the next exercise.

Changing the Position of a Header or Footer

The header and footer default location is .5" from the top and bottom margins. The Position commands option on the Header & Footer Tools enable you to change this default setting. In this exercise, you learn to modify the header and footer position.

Change the Position of a Header or Footer

USE the document that is open from the previous exercise.

1. Point to the header on the second page and double-click to activate the Header & Footer tools.
2. In the Position group, in the Header & Footer Design tab, click the Header from Top scroll arrow until the measurement in the selection box changes to .2″.
3. In the Position group, click the Footer from Bottom scroll arrow until the measurement in the selection box changes to .2″.
4. **SAVE** the document in your USB flash drive in the lesson folder.

PAUSE. LEAVE the document open to use in the next exercise.

Removing a Header or Footer

In this exercise, you learn to use the Remove Header or Footer command to remove all headers and footers from the document.

Remove a Header or Footer

Another Way
Double-click the Header or Footer and press Delete. This will remove all headers or footers.

USE the document that is open from the previous exercise.

1. In the Design tab, in the Header & Footer group, click the Header button and the menu appears.
2. Click Remove Header. The headers are removed from the document.
3. To remove all footers in the document, click the Footer button in the Header & Footer group. The menu appears.
4. Click Remove Footer and footers are removed from the document.
5. **SAVE** and **CLOSE** the document as *hosting_final* in your USB flash drive in the lesson folder.

CLOSE Word.

SKILL SUMMARY

In This Lesson, You Learned How To:
Format, create, and customize a theme
Use Quick Parts in a document
Format a document's background
Create and modify headers and footers

Knowledge Assessment

True/False

Circle T if the statement is true or F if the statement is false.

T   F   1. A watermark is a text or graphic printed behind text.

T   F   2. To edit a header or footer, you must triple-click to activate a header or footer.

T   F   3. The Header & Footer Tools display in the Ribbon after a header or footer is inserted.

T   F   4. Built-in headers and footers provide instant design.

T   F   5. If you make any changes to the colors, fonts, or effects of the current theme, you can save it as a custom version and apply it to future documents.

T   F   6. A picture can be inserted as a page background.

T   F   7. A header and footer cannot be used in the same document.

T   F   8. You can specify a different header for odd and even pages.

T   F   9. Page colors are the background color of a page.

T   F   10. A footer can contain text or graphics.

Multiple Choice

Select the best response for the following statements.

1. Building blocks can be sorted by all EXCEPT which of the following?
   a. Name
   b. Creator
   c. Gallery
   d. Category

2. _____ is a new option within the Quick Parts menu.
   a. AutoComplete
   b. Auto Organizer
   c. AutoText Insert
   d. AutoText

3. Identify the tiny program that includes a label for instructing you on the type of text to include and a placeholder that reserves a place for your new text.
   a. Placeholder
   b. Fields
   c. Content Control
   d. All of the above

4. A document theme includes sets of which of the following?
   a. Colors
   b. Fonts
   c. Effects
   d. All of the above
   e. None of the above

5. A line inserted around the page is called a _____.
   a. Document page border
   b. Border
   c. Page border
   d. None of the above

6. To preview a style or a theme, you must do which of the following?
   a. Place your pointer over the choice
   b. Print the document
   c. Set up the document properties
   d. It is not possible to preview a style or theme.

7. The _____ provides a way to manage building blocks by editing, deleting, and/or inserting them.
   a. Quick Organizer
   b. Cover Page
   c. Text box
   d. Organizer

8. A _____ is a placeholder that tells Word to insert changeable data into a document.
   a. Field name
   b. Field
   c. Data field
   d. Data source

9. Customized company logos applied to a page background is called a(n)_____.
   a. MarkArt
   b. Insert picture command
   c. Watermark
   d. SmartArt

10. In the _____ dialog box, you can specify to insert a page border on only the first page of a document.
    a. Page Border
    b. Borders and Shading
    c. Page Border tab
    d. Line Border

Competency Assessment

Project 8-1: Elevator Communications

Montgomery, Slade & Parker uses elevator communications for in-house announcements, invitations, and other employee relations documents. In each elevator, a durable 8½" × 14" clear plastic frame has been installed in which announcements can be inserted and changed on a regular basis. Create a document for approval that recognizes employee award winners and invites employees to a reception to honor these award winners.

GET READY. LAUNCH Word if it is not already running.

1. **OPEN** *congratulations* from the data files for this lesson and **SAVE AS** *elevator_com* in your USB flash drive in the lesson folder.

@ The *congratulations* document file for this lesson is available on the book companion website or in WileyPLUS.

2. In the Page Background group, in the Page Layout tab click the Page Color menu. In the Theme Colors section, select Olive Green, Accent 3, Lighter 60%.

3. Click the Page Borders button. In the Borders and Shading dialog box, click Shadow in the Setting section. Click the Width menu and choose 3 pt. In the Color section, select Olive Green, Accent 3, Darker 50%. Click OK.

4. In the Page Setup group in the Page Layout tab, click the Size menu and select Legal.

5. Launch the Page Setup dialog box and click the Layout tab. In the Page section, change the Vertical Alignment to Center.

6. **SAVE** the document in your USB flash drive in the lesson folder and then **CLOSE**.

LEAVE Word open for the next project.

Project 8-2: Reference Letter

A former employee at Flatland Hosting Company has asked for a reference letter.

GET READY. LAUNCH Word if it is not already running.

@ The *reference letter* document file for this lesson is available on the book companion website or in WileyPLUS.

1. **OPEN** *reference_letter* from the data files for this lesson and **SAVE AS** *jasmine_reference* in your USB flash drive in the lesson folder.

2. In the Page Layout tab, in the Themes group, click Themes and click Origin from the gallery menu.

3. **SAVE** the document in your USB flash drive in the lesson folder and then **CLOSE**.

LEAVE Word open for the next project.

Proficiency Assessment

Project 8-3: Letterhead

Create a new letterhead for the Flatland Hosting Company.

GET READY. LAUNCH Word if it is not already running.

1. **OPEN** a new blank document and **SAVE AS** *FHCletterhead* in your USB flash drive in the lesson folder.

2. In the Insert tab, in the Header & Footer group, insert the Tiles built-in header and key the document title as Flatland Hosting Company. Bold the text and change the size to 18 pt.

3. Right-click the Content Control, Year, and click Remove Content Control.

4. Insert the Tiles built-in footer and key the company address as 1234 Grand Street, Forest Grove, OR 97116. Select the page number and press the Delete key. Close the Header and Footer.

5. **SAVE** the document in your USB flash drive in the lesson folder and then **CLOSE**.

LEAVE Word open for the next project.

Project 8-4: Two-Page Resume

Your friend Mike has revised and added some information to his resume, and it is now two pages long. Update the formatting to include a header and footer.

GET READY. LAUNCH Word if it is not already running.

@ The *mzresume2* document file for this lesson is available on the book companion website or in WileyPLUS.

1. **OPEN** *mzresume2* from the data files for this lesson and **SAVE AS** *mzresume2updated* in your USB flash drive in the lesson folder.

2. In the Page Layout tab, click the Margins menu and select Custom Margins. In the Page Setup dialog box, change the top, bottom, left, and right margins to 1.25".

3. Click OK.

4. In the Insert tab, in the Header & Footer group, click the Header menu and select Stacks.

5. In the header document title, key Resume of Michael J. Zuberi.

6. In the Options group, click the Different First Page box.

7. In the Navigation group, click Next. In the Header & Footer group, click the Footer button and select Stacks.

8. Select the Content Control, [Type the Company Name], and right-click and Remove Content Control. Close the Header and Footer.

9. **SAVE** the document in your USB flash drive in the lesson folder and then **CLOSE**.

LEAVE Word open for the next project.

Mastery Assessment

Project 8-5: Postcard

It's soccer season again, and the YMCA is sending out postcards to all participants who played last season.

GET READY. LAUNCH Word if it is not already running.

The *soccer* document file for this lesson is available on the book companion website or in WileyPLUS.

1. **OPEN** *soccer* from the data files for this lesson and **SAVE AS** *postcard* in your USB flash drive in the lesson folder.
2. Customize the page size to **4" x 6"**, the orientation to Landscape, and the margins to Narrow.
3. Insert a page border and add a red double-line page border with a box setting and set the width to 3/4 pt.
4. In the Fill Effects dialog box select One Color in the Color 1 section and select Red, Accent 2, Lighter 80%. In the Shading styles section, select Diagonal up. Under Variants, click the sample horizontal pattern in the lower-right corner.
5. Add a Custom Watermark in the Text watermark section and replace ASAP with YMCA SOCCER. Click the Horizontal button and click OK.
6. **SAVE** the document in your USB flash drive in the lesson folder and then **CLOSE**.

LEAVE Word open for the next project.

Project 8-6: Thank-You Card

Create thank-you notes that match the style of Mike's new two-page resume.

GET READY. LAUNCH Word if it is not already running.

1. Create a new blank document and **SAVE AS** *thankyou* in your USB flash drive in the lesson folder.
2. Customize the page size to **5.5" x 8.5"**, leave the orientation at the default, and change the margins to narrow. The goal is to format the document appropriately and fold the document in the middle so that the text, *Thank You,* will be on the front of the note card.
3. Refer to the built-in footer used in the *mzresume2updated* document and insert that footer in your current document. In the *Content Controls* placeholder, key Thank You. For consistency, use the same font, size, and style as Michael J. Zuberi's name on the resume.
4. **SAVE** the document in your USB flash drive in the lesson folder and then **CLOSE**.

CLOSE Word.

 INTERNET READY

Studies have identified which cities are the "Best Places to Live." Choose one of the top ten and find out why it ranked high. Create a promotional document touting the positive ranking and listing reasons for the ranking. The document could be a flyer, postcard, or letter that city officials could mail to prospective businesses and families who request information about the city.

Workplace *Ready*

CREATING A FLYER AND APPLYING THEMES AND QUICK PARTS

You are the assistant to two managers at Flatland Hosting Company. They have decided to distribute monthly flyers to all employees on new happenings within the company.

They have asked you to format the monthly flyer using the new skills you have learned in Word. Create a flyer promoting Internet services to employees at a discounted rate and include security and privacy issues. Be innovative; incorporate features such as adding a customized theme, watermark, page color, and page border, and apply an appropriate building block to produce a flyer that will capture employees' attention. Insert the current date as a footer.

9 Applying References and Hyperlinks

LESSON SKILL MATRIX

In This Lesson, You Will Learn The Following Skills:

Understanding Hyperlinks

Creating Footnotes and Endnotes

Creating a Table of Contents

KEY TERMS

- bookmark
- endnote
- footnote
- hyperlink
- tab leader
- table of contents

You have just begun a new career as a project manager at Proseware, Inc., a web development company. One of the responsibilities of this position includes meeting with new clients who want to develop new websites or redesign existing sites. To help make this process easier, you decide to create a template that you can use to plan website development for each client. Although the template is only about seven pages long, you know it will get longer as the sections are filled in and completed for each client. In this lesson, you will apply a hyperlink to text and graphics, apply bookmarks in a document, link to an email address, create endnotes and footnotes, and create a table of contents so that all sections of the document can be referred to easily among client representatives and coworkers during the planning and development of websites.

UNDERSTANDING HYPERLINKS

The Bottom Line

A **hyperlink** is a location to an internal or external page that readers follow when opening a new page. To access the page, you would press the left mouse button on the hyperlink. Hyperlinks can be applied to text or graphics and these can be in the document where the link would jump from one page to the next. Hyperlinks can be external links to a web page on the Internet. The hyperlink follows a specific target location within the document as a bookmark, as an email address, or to an external location. Hyperlinks can be applied to text or graphics. In this exercise, you learn to apply a hyperlink to text and an image, remove a hyperlink and ScreenTip, add a bookmark, and add an email as a hyperlink.

Applying a Hyperlink

Working with hyperlinks quickly takes you to the location within the document, web page, bookmark, or email address. In this exercise, you learn to insert a hyperlink in text and an image, add a ScreenTip, and remove a hyperlink and ScreenTip.

STEP BY STEP   **Apply a Hyperlink**

The *proseware_weblayout* document file for this lesson is available on the book companion website or in WileyPLUS.

GET READY. Before you begin these steps, be sure to launch Microsoft Word.

1. **OPEN** the *proseware_weblayout* document from the lesson folder.
2. On the Home tab, in the Paragraph group, click the Show/Hide button to enable.
3. Select the company name, Proseware, Inc.
4. On the Insert tab, in the Links group, click the Hyperlink button to open the Insert Hyperlink dialog box as shown in Figure 9-1. The Insert Hyperlink dialog box opens.

Figure 9-1

Insert Hyperlink dialog box

WILEY PLUS EXTRA

WileyPLUS Extra! features an online tutorial of this task.

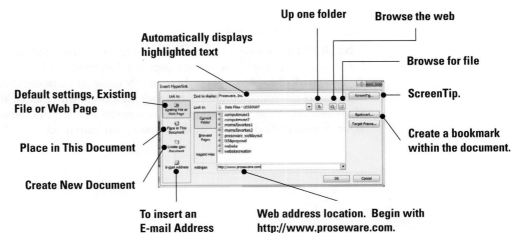

Up one folder   Browse the web

Automatically displays highlighted text

Default settings, Existing File or Web Page

Browse for file

ScreenTip.

Place in This Document

Create New Document

Create a bookmark within the document.

To insert an E-mail Address

Web address location. Begin with http://www.proseware.com.

5. In the Address box, key http://www.proseware.com/. Click OK. You have created a link for the company to link directly to the external website.

6. In text, the company name appears underlined in blue and is linked. Since this is a fictitious company, the link will direct you to the Microsoft official website. To check the link, press the Ctrl key and click to go directly to the website. Notice the ScreenTip appearing above the hyperlink. When you click on the link, the hyperlink changes to another color. Also, when you hover over the link, you will see the ScreenTip.

7. Select the first image to the top left. The next step is to link the graphic to the company website.

8. In the Links group, click the Hyperlink button. With the dialog box open, key http://www.proseware.com. As you begin keying, Autofill recognizes text and completes the entry for you.

9. Click the Screen Tip button. The Set Hyperlink ScreenTip dialog box appears. Key PWI. Click OK to close the Set Hyperlink Screen Tip dialog box. Click OK to close the Edit Hyperlink dialog box.

10. Place your insertion point over the first image and notice the ScreenTip PWI appears.

11. Repeat steps 6–8 for the second image and test your links.

12. **SAVE** the document as *proseware_weblayout_links* in your USB flash drive in the lesson folder.

PAUSE. LEAVE the document open to use in the next exercise.

Another Way
Using the shortcut Ctrl+K will open the Insert Hyperlink dialog box.

Removing a Hyperlink and ScreenTip

Once a hyperlink is removed, it will no longer be linked to a document or external web location. Hyperlinks are removed the same way for text and images. After a ScreenTip is deleted, it will not display in the hyperlink. In this exercise, you learn to remove a hyperlink and ScreenTip.

STEP BY STEP   **Remove a Hyperlink and ScreenTip**

USE the document open from the previous exercise.

1. Select the second image.

2. Use the shortcut keyboard command Ctrl+K to access the Insert Hyperlink dialog box.

3. Click Remove Link to remove the hyperlink.

4. Select the first image and on the Links group, click the Hyperlink button.

5. Click the Screen Tip button and delete PWI. Click OK.

6. Place your insertion point over the first image and notice the ScreenTip no longer appears.

7. **SAVE** the document as *proseware_weblayout_links1* in your USB flash drive in the lesson folder.

PAUSE. LEAVE the document open to use in the next exercise.

Adding a Bookmark

A **bookmark** is a location or a selection of text that you name and identify for future reference. For instance, you may like to revisit a page in a document and locate text; in this case, you could use the Bookmark dialog box and get there quickly using the name of the bookmark you created. Bookmark names can contain numbers, but they must begin with a letter. You cannot have any spaces in a bookmark name, so use an underscore to separate words or put the words together—for example, Trade_Secrets or TradeSecrets. In this exercise, you learn to add a bookmark inside a document.

STEP BY STEP   **Add Bookmark**

USE the document open from the previous exercise.

1. Select the Web Site Creation Strategy text.

2. On the Insert tab in the Links group, click the Hyperlink button. In the Insert Hyperlink dialog box, click the Bookmark button. The Select Place in Document dialog box opens.

3. Scroll up and select Top of the Document as shown in Figure 9-2. Click OK to close the Select Place in Document dialog box. Notice the Address bar in the Insert Hyperlink dialog box displays in the box #Top of the Document—this will link to the beginning of the document. Click OK to close the Insert Hyperlink dialog box.

Figure 9-2

Select Place in Document
dialog box

Bookmark is set to link
to top of document.

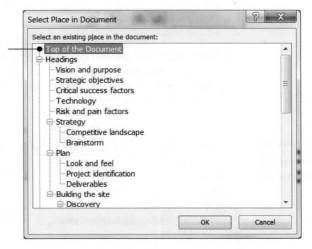

4. Press Ctrl+End to move to the end of the document.

5. Press Enter after the email image and key Back to Top.

6. Select Back to Top then press Ctrl+K to open the Insert Hyperlink dialog box.

7. Click the Bookmark button and scroll up and select Top of the Document. Click OK twice. The Back to Top link changes to a Bookmark link.

8. Test the Bookmark by pressing and holding the Ctrl key and clicking the Back to Top link. Notice that it automatically goes to the top of the document.

9. **SAVE** the document as *proseware_weblayout_links2* in your USB flash drive in the lesson folder.

10. The next step is to create bookmarks based on headings and use the Go To command to go directly to the bookmark.

11. On page 2, double-click to select the word Strategy. In the Links group, click the Bookmark button and key the word Strategy in the box. Click Add and the word Strategy is added, as shown in Figure 9-3. Complete step 11 again for the headings listed in the table below until the additional five text items are bookmarked. In the last item after clicking Add, click OK to close the Bookmark dialog box.

Figure 9-3

Bookmark dialog box

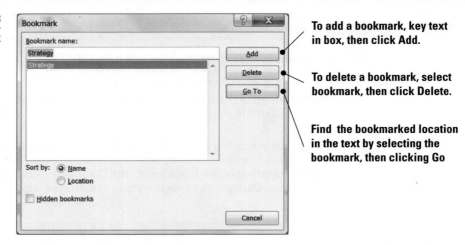

To add a bookmark, key text in box, then click Add.

To delete a bookmark, select bookmark, then click Delete.

Find the bookmarked location in the text by selecting the bookmark, then clicking Go

12. Bookmark names can contain up to 40 characters and spaces are not allowed when using Bookmarks; therefore, you would use an underscore to separate words. With Stabilization still highlighted, click **Bookmark** again. Your screen should match Figure 9-4. Click **Cancel**.

Figure 9-4

Bookmark dialog box with bookmarks added

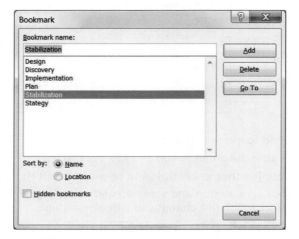

13. Position the insertion point at the beginning of the document by pressing **Ctrl+Home**. In the Links group click the **Bookmark** button. Test each link by selecting the bookmark name and then click the **Go To** button. Select **Design** and then click **Go To**, and the word is automatically highlighted in the document. After testing all bookmarks, click **Close**.

14. **SAVE** the document in your USB flash drive in the lesson folder.

PAUSE. LEAVE the document open to use in the next exercise.

 Ref

You can access the Go To command in one of the following ways: (1) use the Select Browse Object, (2) click the shortcut key F5, or (3) click the Edit group, and then click the Find Button. Using any one of these commands will open the Find and Replace dialog box, as you learned in Lesson 2.

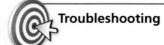 **Troubleshooting** If your bookmark does not run properly, delete the bookmark, select the text, key the same text, and then click Add.

Adding an Email as a Hyperlink

An email address link is used to provide contact information, elicit feedback, or request information. In this exercise, you learn to add an email as a hyperlink.

STEP BY STEP   **Add an Email as a Hyperlink**

USE the document open from the previous exercise.

1. Press **Ctrl+End** to move to the end of the document.
2. Click the email image to select it.

Take Note   Email links can be applied to text or images.

3. In the Links group of the Insert tab, click the **Hyperlink** button or press **Ctrl+K**. The Insert Hyperlink dialog box opens.
4. Under the Link to section, click **E-mail Address**. Notice the middle portion of the dialog box changes. In the E-mail address section, key **manager@proseware.com** in the box. Mail to automatically appears when you begin keying the email address. For the Subject box, key **Web Design** as displayed in Figure 9-5. Click the **ScreenTip** button to open the Set Hyperlink Screen Tip dialog box; then in the ScreenTip text box, key **Manager**. Click **OK** twice.

Key email address. Mailto: automatically displays.

To create a ScreenTip

Key a subject in the box.

Select E-mail Address to insert link.

Select image or text to create an e-mail link.

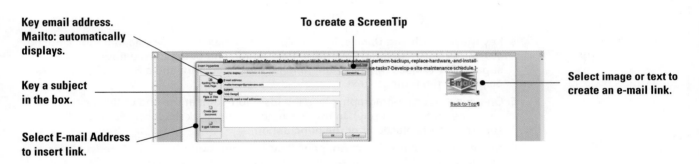

Figure 9-5

Insert Hyperlink dialog box
E-mail Address link

5. Hover your mouse over the E-mail image and the Screen Tip Manager appears. Test your email link by pressing the **Ctrl** key and clicking the left mouse button once. Outlook automatically opens with the email address and subject line inserted. This type of hyperlink is known as a mailto link.
6. **SAVE** the document in your USB flash drive in the lesson folder and close the file.

PAUSE. LEAVE Word open to use in the next exercise.

CREATING FOOTNOTES AND ENDNOTES

The Bottom Line

Both endnotes and footnotes are citations in a document. A **footnote** is placed at the bottom of the page in the document on which the citation is located, while an **endnote** is at the end of document. Footnotes and endnotes are automatically numbered. Edits to a footnote or endnote are made within the text. Deleting a footnote or endnote will automatically renumber the remaining footnotes or endnotes. As a student, you will use these in your research papers. In this lesson, you learn to insert a footnote and endnote into a document.

Creating Footnotes in a Document

STEP BY STEP	**Create Footnotes and Endnotes**

GET READY. Before you begin these steps, be sure to launch Microsoft Word.

The *firstladies* document file for this lesson is available on the book companion website or in WileyPLUS.

1. **OPEN** the *firstladies* document from the lesson folder.
2. Place the insertion point at the end of the third paragraph.
3. On the References tab, click the Insert Footnote button in the Footnotes group, as shown in Figure 9-6. A superscript 1 is placed after the paragraph and at the end of the document.

Figure 9-6

References tab

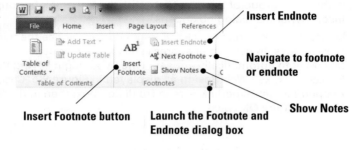

WileyPLUS Extra! features an online tutorial of this task.

4. Key Mayo, Edith and Denise, Meringolo. First Ladies: Political Role and Public Image. Washington: Smithsonian Institute, 1994. At the end of the third paragraph is a superscript 1, place the insertion point by the superscript and a ScreenTip appears displaying the footnote text.
5. On page 1, fourth paragraph, place the insertion point at the end of the second sentence (before Anthony). In the Footnotes group, click the Insert Footnote button. A superscript 2 is placed after the punctuation.
6. At the bottom of the document page, key Anthony, Carl Sferrazza. American's First Families: An Inside View of 200 Years of Private Life in the White House. New York: Simon & Schuster, Inc., 2000. The bottom of page 1 should resemble Figure 9-7.

Figure 9-7

Unformatted footnotes

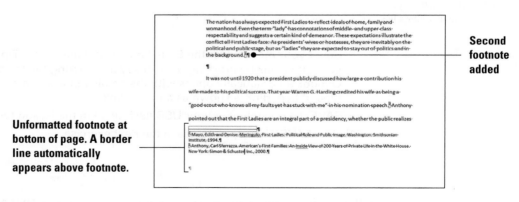

Unformatted footnote at bottom of page. A border line automatically appears above footnote.

Second footnote added

7. On page 2, fifth paragraph, end of third sentence, in the Footnotes group, click the Insert Footnote button. A superscript 3 is placed after the punctuation.
8. At the bottom of the document page, key Gutin, Mayra G. The President's Partner: The First Lady in the Twentieth Century. Westport: Greenwood Press, 1989.
9. **SAVE** the document as *firstladies_footnotes* in your USB flash drive in the lesson folder.

PAUSE. LEAVE the document open to use in the next exercise.

Formatting Footnotes and Endnotes

According to the Modern Language Association (MLA), a bottom-of-the-page footnote in MLA Style is single spaced with a hanging indent and double spacing between each footnote, whereas an endnote is double-spaced with no hanging indent. The dialog box contains additional options to change the numbering format and location for both footnotes and endnotes. In this lesson, you learn to format a footnote and endnote.

STEP BY STEP   **Format Footnotes**

USE the document open from the previous exercise.

1. Press and hold the left mouse button to select the first footnote beginning with Mayo. . . 1994.

2. On the Home tab, in the Paragraph group, launch the Paragraph dialog box and change the indent to a **hanging indent** and spacing after to **12**. Click **OK**.

3. Press and hold the **left mouse button** to select the second footnote and repeat step 2 to create a hanging indent.

4. For footnote number 3, repeat steps 1 to select and 2 to create a hanging indent. The footnotes have been formatted with a hanging indent and spaced appropriately.

5. Place your insertion point after the superscript 1 at the bottom of the document on page 1. On the References tab in the Footnotes group, click the **arrow** to launch the Footnote and Endnote dialog box. The Footnote and Endnote dialog box opens. In the Format section by Number format, click the **drop-down arrow** and select the uppercase Roman numerals, as shown in Figure 9-8. Click **Apply**. Notice the numbering format has changed.

Figure 9-8

Footnote and Endnote dialog box

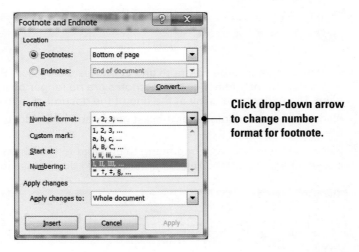

Click drop-down arrow to change number format for footnote.

6. In the third paragraph, place your insertion point before the first footnote superscript on page 1, press and hold the left mouse button to select the footnote. Launch the Footnote and Endnote dialog box. The Footnote and Endnote dialog box opens. In the Location section, by Footnotes, click the **drop-down arrow** and select **Below text**. Click **Apply**. The first footnote is moved below the third paragraph with a continuous section break.

7. Repeat the same steps for the second and third footnote to place them below text.

8. **SAVE** the document as *firstladies_footnotes1* in your USB flash drive in the lesson folder.

9. Place the insertion point behind the second footnote on the fourth paragraph, at the end of the second sentence. Delete the footnote. Notice the footnote number 3 is now 2. Footnotes are automatically renumbered and rearranged when one is deleted. Click **Undo** ↰.

10. **SAVE** the document in your USB flash drive in the lesson folder.

PAUSE. LEAVE the document open to use in the next exercise.

Converting Footnotes and Endnotes

It is easy to convert from a footnote to an endnote. The process is the same for both types of notes. In this exercise, you learn to convert from footnotes to endnotes and to format the endnote.

STEP BY STEP   **Convert Footnotes and Endnotes**

OPEN the *firstladies_footnotes* document completed earlier in this lesson.

1. The insertion point is at the beginning of the first footnote below the horizontal line.
2. On the References tab in the Footnotes group, click the **arrow** to launch the Footnote and Endnote dialog box. The Footnote and Endnote dialog box opens.
3. Click the **Convert** button. The Convert Notes dialog box opens. The first option *Convert all footnotes to endnotes* is selected, as shown in Figure 9-9. Click **OK** to convert the notes and close the Convert Notes dialog box.

Figure 9-9

Convert Notes dialog box

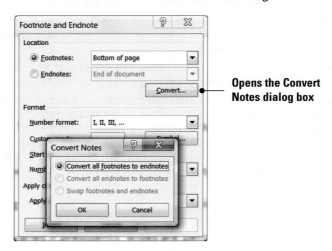

Opens the Convert Notes dialog box

4. Click **Insert** to close the Footnote and Endnotes dialog box. Scroll through to the end of the document and notice the footnotes are no longer positioned at the end of the page. The endnotes display at the end of the document in lowercase Roman numerals.
5. Place the insertion point after the last paragraph in the document and insert a page break.
6. Select the endnotes from beginning to end and format them by double spacing and create a hanging indent. The document should display as Figure 9-10.

Figure 9-10

Formatted endnote

Endnotes appear at the end of the document and are formatted with a hanging indent and double space.

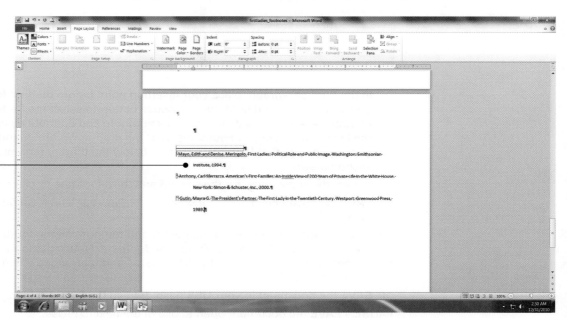

7. **SAVE** the document as *firstladies_endnotes* in your USB flash drive in the lesson folder and close the file.

PAUSE. LEAVE the document open to use in the next exercise.

CREATING A TABLE OF CONTENTS

The Bottom Line

A table of contents is usually found at the beginning of a long document to help readers quickly locate topics of interest. A **table of contents** is an ordered list of the topics in a document, along with the page numbers on which they are found. In this exercise, you learn to add a heading style and insert a table of contents.

Creating a Table of Contents from Heading Styles

Word makes inserting a table of contents easy using the built-in gallery of styles on the Table of Contents menu. The menu includes an automatic format and a manual format. Word automatically builds your table of contents using the Heading 1, Heading 2, and Heading 3 styles. In this exercise you will choose one of the automatic formats to create a table of contents (TOC).

STEP BY STEP   **Create a Table of Contents**

@ The *website*
document file for this
lesson is available on the
book companion website
or in WileyPLUS.

WileyPLUS Extra! features an
online tutorial of this task.

1. **OPEN** the *website* document from the data files for this lesson.
2. On the first page, fourth line, select **Planning the site**.
3. On the Home tab, in the Styles group, click the **Heading 1** style.
4. On the next line, select **Research**. Click the **Heading 2** style.
5. On the next line, select **Research and Scheduling**. On the Home tab, in the Styles group, click the **Heading 3** style.
6. Scroll through the document to verify that all the other headings have the correct styles applied to them. Before you can create a table of contents, heading styles must be applied to headings in the document as listed in Table 9-1.

Table 9-1

Headings and Styles Applied

Vision and Purpose	Heading 3	Risk Assessment	Heading 3
Strategic Objectives	Heading 3	Design	Heading 2
Critical Success Factors	Heading 3	Conceptual Design and Prototypes	Heading 3
Technology	Heading 3	Technology Architecture	Heading 3
Risk and Pain Factors	Heading 3	Quality Assurance	Heading 3
Strategy	Heading 2	Implementation	Heading 2
Competitive Landscape	Heading 3	Content Development	Heading 3
Brainstorm	Heading 3	Graphic Assets	Heading 3
Plan	Heading 2	Templates	Heading 3
Look and Feel	Heading 3	Functionality Testing	Heading 3
Project Identification	Heading 3	Updated Project Plan	Heading 3
Deliverables	Heading 3	Stabilization	Heading 2
Building the Site	Heading 1	Testing	Heading 3
Discovery	Heading 2	Bug Fixes	Heading 3
Team Structure	Heading 3	Deployment	Heading 3
Content	Heading 3	Maintenance Plan	Heading 3
Project Plan	Heading 3		

7. Return to page 1 by pressing **Ctrl+Home** and click on a blank line above the Web Site Creation Strategy title.

8. On the References tab, in the Table of Contents group, click the **Table of Contents** button. A gallery of built-in styles and a menu appears, as shown in Figure 9-11.

Figure 9-11

Table of Contents menu

9. Select the **Automatic Table 2** style. The table of contents is inserted in the document—scroll up to see the table of contents (see Figure 9-12). The table of contents is shaded in gray and each heading is linked to the document and follows the link.

10. Press the **Ctrl** key and click the mouse button to follow the link for Research.

11. **SAVE** your document as *website_template* in your USB flash drive in the lesson folder.

PAUSE. LEAVE the document open to use in the next exercise.

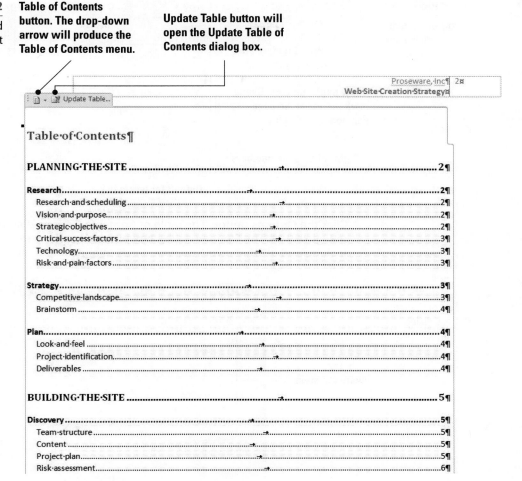

Formatting a Table of Contents

You can use styles other than Heading 1, Heading 2, and Heading 3 to create a table of contents. The Table of Contents Options dialog box provides options for choosing which styles you want to include and at what level you would like them to appear in the table of contents.

The Table of Contents dialog box has other options you can specify, including whether to show page numbers or right-align page numbers. You can also specify **tab leaders**, which are the symbols that appear between the table of contents topic and the tab set for the corresponding page number. In this lesson, you learn to format a table of contents by changing the alignment tab leaders and levels.

STEP BY STEP **Format a Table of Contents**

USE the document that is open from the previous exercise.

1. On the References tab, in the Table of Contents group, click the Table of Contents button.

2. Select Insert Table of Contents from the menu. The Table of Contents dialog box appears, as shown in Figure 9-13. The Print Preview box lists the styles used to create the table of contents. The Table of Contents dialog box offers options for you to specify whether to show page numbers and whether to right-align those page numbers. Tab leaders are symbols that serve as a visual guide from the headings to the page numbers. These can appear as periods, hyphens, lines, or none. The format for the Table of Contents can be changed to display different heading levels in the Table of Contents.

Figure 9-13

Table of Contents
dialog box

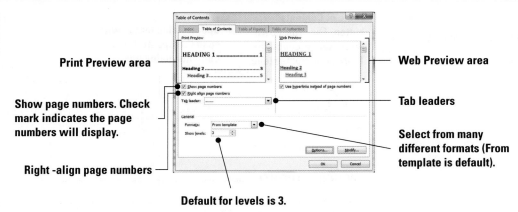

Print Preview area

Show page numbers. Check
mark indicates the page
numbers will display.

Right-align page numbers

Web Preview area

Tab leaders

Select from many
different formats (From
template is default).

Default for levels is 3.

3. Click the Options button. The Table of Contents Options dialog box appears, as shown in Figure 9-14. The Options dialog box provides options for choosing which styles to include and at what level you want them to appear in the table of contents.

Figure 9-14

Table of Contents
Options dialog box

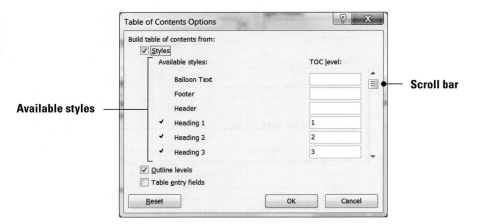

Available styles

Scroll bar

4. In the *Build table of contents from* section, scroll through the TOC level list. Notice the styles and their levels marked for inclusion in the table of contents.

5. Add a TOC level 4 by keying **4** in the box by Heading 4; a check mark is automatically placed by the heading. Click **OK** to close the Table of Contents Options dialog box, then click **OK** to close the Table of Contents dialog box.

6. If prompted to replace the selected table of contents, click **Yes**.

7. On the Home tab in the Styles group, notice that Heading 4 is now available. Scroll down to page 3 and select the RISK AND PAIN FACTORS heading. On the Styles group, select Heading 4—the format for the selected text automatically changes and the Heading 4 style is applied.

Take Note   To remove Heading 4, open the Table of Contents dialog box and delete 4.

8. Press **Ctrl+Home** to return to the beginning of the document. Click the References tab in the Table of Contents group, click the Table of Contents button, and then select Insert Table of Contents from the menu. The Table of Contents dialog box opens. Under the General section, click the drop-down arrow on the Formats menu and select Formal.

9. In the Print Preview section, click the drop-down arrow on the Tab leader drop-down menu and select hyphens. By default, the Tab leader uses periods.

10. In the General section, notice that under the Show levels option, 4 levels is displayed. Therefore the preview screen displays four levels.

11. Click **OK** to close the Table of Contents dialog box. Word displays a prompt asking you if you want to replace the selected table of contents. Click **Yes**.

12. The new format for the table of contents displays four levels. The Risk and pain factors heading is listed as a level four, so it now displays in the table of contents.

13. **SAVE** the document as *website_template1* in your USB flash drive in the lesson folder.

14. On the Table of Contents group, click the Table of Contents button, and then select Insert Table of Contents from the menu.

15. Click the check box for Right align page numbers to remove the check and turn off the right alignment. Notice that the Print Preview area displays no leaders. Click OK. A prompt box will appear asking if you want to replace the selected table of contents. Click Yes. The table of contents is updated with no alignment set.

16. **SAVE** the document as *website_template2* in your USB flash drive in the lesson folder.

PAUSE. LEAVE the document open to use in the next exercise.

Modifying a Table of Contents

Modifying a table of contents allows you to change the properties and formatting and to decide whether you want to apply the changes to the present document or the Quick Style list, or add to the template to reapply. Any changes made will allow you to automatically update the document. In this lesson, you learn to modify a table of contents by changing the formatting and turning off the Quick Style list.

STEP BY STEP   **Modify a Table of Contents**

USE the document that is open from the previous exercise.

1. Position the insertion point in the table of contents. On the References tab in the Table of Contents group, click the Table of Contents button, click Insert Table of Contents, and then click the Modify button in the lower right of the Table of Contents dialog box. The Style dialog box opens with TOC 1 selected, as shown in Figure 9-15.

Figure 9-15

Style dialog box

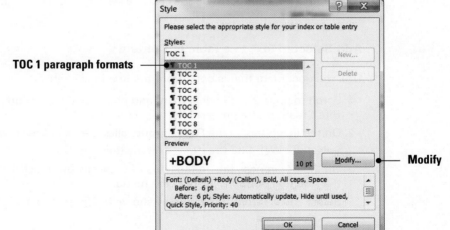

2. Click the Modify button from the Style dialog box. The Modify Style dialog box opens, as shown in Figure 9-16.

3. The alignment for TOC 1 is set to align text left; change this to center. Change the Font from Calibri to Arial and Size from 10 to 16. The commands shown in the Modify Style dialog box resemble the commands on the Home tab, in the Font and Paragraph groups.

4. At the bottom of the dialog box, click the Add to Quick Style list check box to remove the check and turn off. Modifications made to the style will apply only to this document and automatically update the table of contents.

5. Click OK to accept your changes and close the Modify Style dialog box. Click OK to close the Style dialog box. Click OK to close the Table of Contents dialog box.

6. A prompt will appear asking if you want to replace the selected table of contents. Click Yes. Notice the changes made to the Heading 1 style.

Figure 9-16

Modify Style dialog box

Font, font size, bold, italics, underline, and text color

Alignment settings

Preview area

Format button will display options to select.

Name of style

Type of style can be paragraph or character.

Style based on

Style for following paragraph

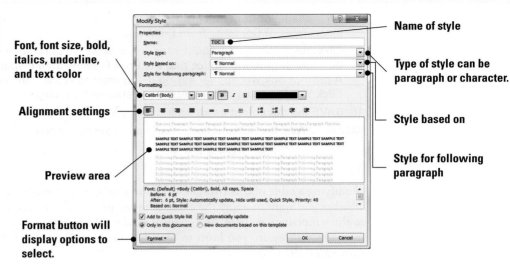

7. **SAVE** the document as *website_template3* in your USB flash drive in the lesson folder.

PAUSE. LEAVE the document open to use in the next exercise.

Adding Selected Text to a Table of Contents

Sometimes in a table of contents you might want to include text that has not been formatted with a heading style. The Add Text menu enables you to choose the level at which the new text will appear. The levels available in the previous exercise were Do Not Show in Table of Contents, Level 1, Level 2, and Level 3. When working with tables of contents in other documents that have more levels, additional options may be available on the menu.

STEP BY STEP **Add Selected Text to a Table of Contents**

USE the document that is open from the previous exercise.

1. Scroll to page 2 of the document and position the insertion point before the W in Web Site Creation Strategy.
2. On the Insert tab, in the Pages group, click the Page Break button.
3. Select the Web Site Creation Strategy text.
4. On the References tab, in the Table of Contents group, click the drop-down arrow by the Add Text button to display the menu.
5. Select Level 1 from the menu, as shown in Figure 9-17. Deselect the text.

Figure 9-17

Add Text button and menu

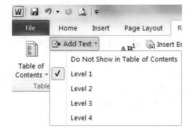

6. **SAVE** the document in your USB flash drive in the lesson folder.

PAUSE. LEAVE the document open to use in the next exercise.

Updating a Table of Contents

After adding new text, a new page, or modifying the table of contents, the next step is to update the table of contents. In this exercise, you learn to update the table of contents.

STEP BY STEP **Update a Table of Contents**

USE the document that is open from the previous exercise.

Another Way
You can also use the shortcut key F9 to open the Update the Table of Contents dialog box.

1. Scroll to the beginning of page 1 and click in the Table of Contents to select it. On the References tab, in the Table of Contents group, click the Update Table button.
2. The Update Table of Contents dialog box appears. The default, Update page numbers only, is selected, as shown in Figure 9-18; just click OK. Notice that the page numbers for the table of contents have been updated.

Figure 9-18

Update Table of Contents dialog box

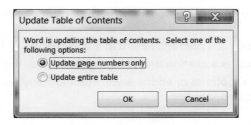

3. Click Update Table, and the Update Table of Contents dialog box appears. Click the Update entire table button, and click OK. Notice that *Web Site Creation Strategy 3* is added to the table of contents.
4. **SAVE** the document in your USB flash drive in the lesson folder.

PAUSE. LEAVE the document open to use in the next exercise.

Removing a Table of Contents

Remove a table of contents from the document.

STEP BY STEP **Remove a Table of Contents**

USE the document that is open from the previous exercise.

1. On the References tab, in the Table of Contents group, click Remove Table of Contents.
2. Delete the page break.
3. **SAVE** the document as *website_template_final* in your USB flash drive in the lesson folder.

Another Way
You can also update a table of contents using the shortcut key, F9.

CLOSE Word.

SKILL SUMMARY

In This Lesson, You Learned How To:
Understanding hyperlinks
Create footnotes and endnotes
Create a table of contents

Knowledge Assessment

True/False

Circle T if the statement is true or F if the statement is false.

T   F   1. A table of contents is usually found at the end of document.

T   F   2. The manual table of contents option allows you to create a table of contents on your own.

T   F   3. You can choose a hyphen as tab leaders for a table of contents.

T   F   4. Only text formatted with a heading style can be included in a table of contents.

T   F   5. You can choose to update only the page numbers in a table of contents.

T   F   6. Hyperlinks can be applied to text or graphics.

T   F   7. When you create an email link, the Outlook application will automatically open.

T   F   8. A bookmark is a reference point in a document.

T   F   9. An endnote is a citation and placed at the end of the document.

T   F   10. Deleting a footnote or endnote will automatically renumber the remaining footnotes or endnotes.

Multiple Choice

Select the best response for the following statements.

1. A table of contents is located at the _____ of the document.
   a. Middle
   b. End
   c. Beginning
   d. None of the above

2. Tab leaders can be changed into what types of symbols for use in a table of contents?
   a. Periods
   b. Hyphens
   c. Lines
   d. All of the above

3. Which menu will allow you to add content to the table of contents?
   a. Update Table
   b. Add Text
   c. Add Bookmark
   d. None of the above

4. When adding a page or text to a table of contents, it is recommended that you
   a. Click the Update Table button on the Ribbon
   b. Press F9
   c. Click the Update Table button above the table of contents
   d. All of the above

5. By default, a footnote is placed
   a. At the beginning of the document
   b. At the end of the document
   c. At the end of the page
   d. Below text

6. Formatting a footnote in a document, per MLA style, should be
    a. single spaced with a hanging indent and triple spaced
    b. single spaced with a hanging indent and doubled spaced between each footnote
    c. doubled spaced with a hanging indent and single spaced between each footnote
    d. No format is needed.

7. Hyperlinks can be linked
    a. From one page to another page
    b. As a website
    c. As email
    d. All of the above

8. Reference points in a document are created using which command?
    a. Bookmark
    b. Hyperlink
    c. Email
    d. All of the above

9. The Footnote and Endnote dialog box contains an option to change the page number format to
    a. Uppercase Roman numerals
    b. A1, A2, A3, etc.
    c. a and b
    d. It is not an option.

10. Endnotes can be converted to which of the following?
    a. Table of contents
    b. Footnote
    c. Hyperlink
    d. They cannot be converted.

Competency Assessment

Project 9-1: Mom's Favorite Recipes

You know that your mom will be sending you more recipes for her cookbook. You decide to create a table of contents using headings in the cookbook, making it easy to update as recipes are added.

GET READY. LAUNCH Word if it is not already running.

The *momsfavorites1* document file for this lesson is available on the book companion website or in WileyPLUS.

1. **OPEN** *momsfavorites1* from the data files for this lesson. On the Home tab, turn on your Show/Hide command.
2. Use the Go To command to go to page 3. Select the Breads heading and apply the Heading 1 style to it.
3. Select the Banana Nut Bread/Chocolate Chip Muffins heading and apply the Heading 2 style.
4. Apply the Heading 2 style to the remaining recipe headings.
5. On page 1, position the insertion point before the M in Main Dishes.
6. On the References tab, in the Table of Contents group, click the Table of Contents button. Select Automatic Table 1 from the menu.
7. Center Contents and apply the Title style.
8. Select the table and click the Update Table button. Update the page numbers only.
9. **SAVE** the worksheet as *moms_recipes_toc* in your USB flash drive and **CLOSE** the file.

PAUSE. LEAVE Word open for the next project.

Project 9-2: Margie's Travel

You will be updating the Explore the World flyer created in an earlier lesson. Since this flyer will be shared by email, you want to insert hyperlinks and Margie's email address.

GET READY. LAUNCH Word if it is not already running.

@ The *exploring_ world_flyer* document file for this lesson is available on the book companion website or in WileyPLUS.

1. **OPEN** the *exploring_world_flyer* document from the lesson folder.
2. Select the Explore the World text. On the Insert tab in the Links group, select Hyperlink.
3. In the address box, key http://www.margiestravel.com. Click OK.
4. Place the insertion point at the end of the paragraph, press Enter. Key Contact: Margie and align right.
5. Select Margie and in the Links group, click Hyperlink, then select E-mail address.
6. For the E-mail address, key Margie@margiestravel.com. Click OK.
7. **SAVE** the document as *world_flyer_update* in your USB flash drive and close the file.

LEAVE Word open for the next project.

Proficiency Assessment

Project 9-3: First Ladies

You will be modifying the First Ladies document by formatting the footnotes and changing the number format.

GET READY. LAUNCH Word if it is not already running.

@ The *firstladies4* document file for this lesson is available on the book companion website or in WileyPLUS.

1. **OPEN** the *firstladies4* document from the lesson folder.
2. At the end of page 1, select the first footnote and format the footnote with a hanging indent, single space and spacing after to 12 pts. between each footnote.
3. Complete the same process in step 2 for the second and third footnote.
4. Place the insertion point after the first footnote below the horizontal line. On the References tab in the Footnotes group, launch the Footnote and Endnote dialog box and change the number format to lowercase Roman numerals.
5. **SAVE** the worksheet as *firstladies4_update* in your USB flash drive in the lesson folder and **CLOSE** the file.

LEAVE Word open for the next project.

Project 9-4: Computer Use Policy Contents

Add a table of contents to the Computer Use Policy document.

GET READY. LAUNCH Word if it is not already running.

@ The *computeruse2* document file for this lesson is available on the book companion website or in WileyPLUS.

1. **OPEN** *computeruse2* from the data files for this lesson.
2. Select the title, Computer Use Policy, and apply the Title style.
3. Select Section One and apply the Heading 1 style.
4. Select Purpose and apply the Heading 2 style.
5. In the same manner, continue applying the Heading 1 and Heading 2 styles to the headings for the remainder of the document.
6. On page 1, position the insertion point before the C in Computer Use Policy and insert a built-in table of contents using the Automatic Table 1 style.
7. With the insertion point in front of the C in Computer Use Policy, insert a page break.
8. **SAVE** the document as *computer_use_toc* in your USB flash drive and **CLOSE** the file.

PAUSE. LEAVE Word open for the next project.

Mastery Assessment

Project 9-5: USA Proposal

You need to add a table of contents to the USA Proposal document. However, the document was created without using heading styles, and you cannot change the format of the document. Use the Add Text command to create a table of contents.

GET READY. LAUNCH Word if it is not already running.

The *USAproposal* document file for this lesson is available on the book companion website or in WileyPLUS.

1. **OPEN** *USAproposal* from the data files for this lesson.
2. Use the Add Text command to create a table of contents with three levels. Level 1 will be the Proposal Description, Level 2 will be the three Options, and Level 3 will be the cities listed under each option.
3. Add a page break at the beginning of the document and select the hidden mark and Clear Formatting and create a blank line.
4. Key Table of Contents. Change the font to Arial, font size to 20 pts, and spacing after to 12 pts and center.
5. Create a manual table of contents using the Formal format.
6. **SAVE** the document as *USA_proposal_toc* in your USB flash drive in the lesson folder and **CLOSE** the file.

PAUSE. LEAVE Word open for the next exercise.

Project 9-6: Computer Use Policy Contents Update

You will be using Project 9-4 to update a table of contents.

GET READY. LAUNCH Word if it is not already running.

1. **OPEN** the *computer_use_toc* completed in Project 9-4.
2. Delete all of Section Seven by selecting text beginning at Section Seven to the end of the paragraph under Encryption.
3. Renumber Section Eight to Section Seven, renumber Section Nine to Section Eight, and renumber Section Ten to Section Nine.
4. Return to the table of contents and update the entire table of contents.
5. **SAVE** the worksheet as *computer_toc_update* and **CLOSE** the file.

CLOSE Word.

INTERNET READY

The skills you are learning from this book are giving you a good foundation for using Word in the workplace. There may be times when you want to perform a task that goes beyond what you have already learned. The Internet can be a great resource for finding additional information. Use the Internet to search for information about one of the following bookmark topics and then write a brief paragraph answering the topic's question or explaining how to accomplish the task. Document your sources by including the URL in your answer.

- The Bookmark dialog box has a Hidden Bookmarks check box. What is the purpose of this check box? Is it possible to hide a bookmark? If so, how?

- It is easy to delete a bookmark using the Bookmark dialog box. Suppose you want to protect bookmarks from being deleted. Is this possible? If so, how? If not, why not?

- List the steps you would follow to create a hyperlink in an HTML page to a bookmark in a Word document.

- You want to highlight the bookmarks in your document by making them bold so you can see them better. Is this possible? If so, how?

10 Advanced Features

LESSON SKILL MATRIX

In This Lesson, You Will Learn The Following Skills:

Validating Content by Using Spelling and Grammar Checking Options

Sharing Documents

KEY TERMS

- **blog**
- **SkyDrive**

Blue Yonder Airlines is a large company with hundreds of employees. In your job as a human resources specialist, you are involved in hiring, employee benefit programs, and employee communications. Many of the documents you work with relate to employee issues, and you need to ensure that these documents are error free. In this lesson, you will learn to use the spelling and grammar feature. You will also learn how to share documents with other employees.

SOFTWARE ORIENTATION

The Proofing and Language Groups

The Proofing group contains commands for launching Word's spelling and grammar functions, searching through references, using the Thesaurus, and counting words by characters, paragraphs, and lines. The Language group contains commands for translating words or paragraphs and an option to select a language. These and other commands for reviewing and editing Word documents are located on the Review tab, shown in Figure 10-1.

Figure 10-1

Proofing and Language groups

Launches the Spelling & Grammar dialog box

Translates words or paragraphs into a different language

Language Options

Opens the Research Task Pane

Word count is located on status bar.

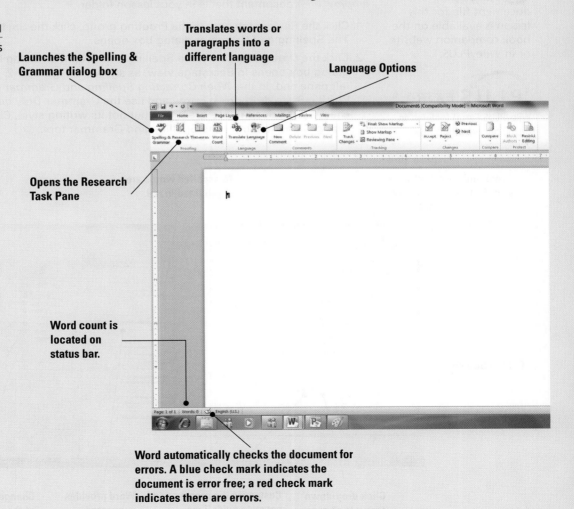

Word automatically checks the document for errors. A blue check mark indicates the document is error free; a red check mark indicates there are errors.

Use this figure as a reference throughout this lesson and the rest of this book.

VALIDATING CONTENT BY USING SPELLING AND GRAMMAR CHECKING OPTIONS

The Bottom Line

It is a good business practice to proof a document to ensure it is error free before sharing or printing it. Word provides proofing tools such as a Spelling and Grammar checking function, Thesaurus, Word Count tracker, and a Research tool that provides searchable access to reference books and online research and business sites. All of these tools and commands are located on the Ribbon on the Review tab. The status bar also contains Word Count and Proofing Error buttons that give you quick access to some proofing features. On the status bar, Word automatically displays the document's word count.

Using the Spelling and Grammar Feature

Word's Spelling and Grammar feature automatically checks the spelling and grammar in a document. Word underlines misspelled words with a wavy red line and underlines grammatical errors with a wavy green line. Word will also detect if words are used inappropriately and it underlines the word with a wavy blue line. In other words, the word is in the dictionary but not used correctly in the context. In this exercise, you learn to use Word's automatic Spelling and Grammar feature and its options to proof and correct your document.

STEP BY STEP   **Check Spelling and Grammar**

The *employ_offer* document file for this lesson is available on the book companion website or in WileyPLUS.

WILEY PLUS **EXTRA**

WileyPLUS Extra! features an online tutorial of this task.

GET READY. Before you begin these steps, **LAUNCH** Microsoft Word and **OPEN** the *employ_offer* document that is in your lesson folder.

1. Click the **Review** tab and, in the Proofing group, click the **Spelling & Grammar** button. The Spelling and Grammar dialog box opens.

2. Click the **Options** button in the Spelling and Grammar dialog box; the Word Options dialog box opens in Backstage view, as shown in Figure 10-2. Select **Proofing** in the left pane and, in the *When Correcting Spelling and Grammar in Word* section, click the **Writing Style drop-down arrow** and use the **Grammar Only** default to set the tool for checking the document's grammar, but not its writing style. Click **OK** to apply your changes and to launch the Spelling and Grammar tool.

Figure 10-2

Word Options in Backstage view Spelling and Grammar dialog box

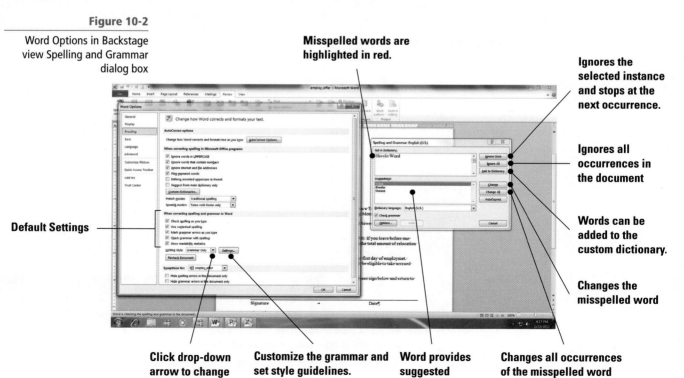

Misspelled words are highlighted in red.

Ignores the selected instance and stops at the next occurrence.

Ignores all occurrences in the document

Words can be added to the custom dictionary.

Changes the misspelled word

Default Settings

Click drop-down arrow to change Writing Style.

Customize the grammar and set style guidelines.

Word provides suggested corrections.

Changes all occurrences of the misspelled word throughout the document

3. The first word the tool highlights is Sheela, a proper noun not contained in the tool's dictionary. The Spelling and Grammar dialog box opens, with the potential error identified in the upper pane as Not in Dictionary (see Figure 10-3). With the correct spelling highlighted in the Suggestions pane, click the **Change All** button to correct all occurrences of the misspelling.

Figure 10-3

Spelling and Grammar dialog box

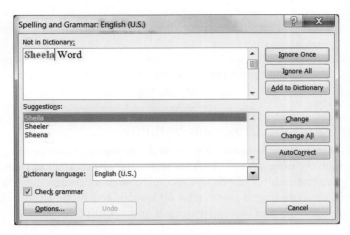

4. The word *confim* is misspelled; with the correct spelling highlighted in the Suggestions pane, click the **Change All** button.

5. The next misspelled word is *begining*. Click the **Change All** button.

6. The next misspelled word is *asistance*. Click the **Change All** button. A prompt will appear when the Spelling and Grammar check is complete. Click **OK**.

7. Word has the option for users to ignore misspelled words. In this case, the previous user ignored misspellings. You will be rechecking the document to ensure you have captured all errors. Click the **File** tab, then **Options** to open the Word Options dialog box in Backstage.

8. Select **Proofing** in the left pane and, in the *When Correcting Spelling and Grammar in Word* section, click the **Recheck Document** button. A prompt appears stating *This operation resets the spelling checker and the grammar checker so that Word will recheck words and grammar you previously checked and chose to ignore. Do you want to continue?* Click **Yes** (see Figure 10-4). The document flags misspellings.

Figure 10-4

Microsoft Word resets spelling and grammar checker

9. In the Proofing group, click the **Spelling and Grammar** button. The Spelling and Grammar dialog box opens.

10. The Spelling and Grammar tool next highlights **Suurs**. This spelling is correct, so click **Ignore All**. The tool now will ignore every occurrence of this spelling in the document.

Take Note   Ignore Once will ignore the occurrence once and will stop at the next occurrence.

11. The next misspelled work is *employmet*; again, click the **Change All** button to correct all occurrences. A prompt will appear when the Spelling and Grammar check is complete. Click **OK**.

Take Note

Another Way

Click the Proofing Error button on the status bar (or press the keyboard shortcut, F7). Word displays a shortcut menu with suggested words.

When Word detects a spelling error, you can choose to change one occurrence of the instance or change all instances. Click Change to change a single occurrence or click Change All to Change all occurrences in the document.

12. SAVE the document as *employment_offer* in your USB flash drive in the lesson folder.

PAUSE. LEAVE the document open to use in the next exercise.

Take Note

If you run the Spelling and Grammar command in the middle of the document, it will check from that point to the end of the document. A prompt will appear asking if you want to continue checking the document from the beginning.

Changing the Grammar Settings

Word's grammar settings enable you to determine the punctuation and other stylistic guidelines by which the program will check for and detect errors. You can change the writing style to check for grammar only or check stylistic rules, such as contractions, hyphenated and compound words, sentence length (more than 60 words), and more. In this exercise, you learn to change the style settings and customize them to meet your needs.

STEP BY STEP   **Change the Grammar Settings**

USE the document from the previous exercise.

1. Click the **File** tab and then **Options** to open the Word Options dialog box in Backstage.

2. Select **Proofing** in the left pane and in the *When Correcting Spelling and Grammar in Word* section, click the **Settings** button to open the Grammar Settings dialog box. This dialog box lists the writing style where you can customize the Grammar Only or Grammar & Style (see Figure 10-5).

Figure 10-5

Grammar Settings dialog box

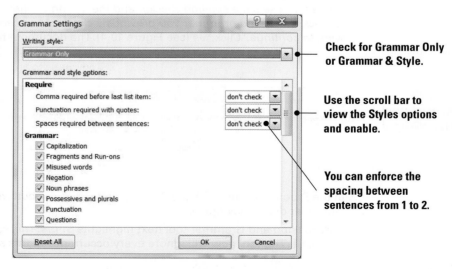

3. Click the **drop-down arrow** in the Writing Style section and select **Grammar & Style**.

4. Under the Require section, the *Spaces required between sentences* setting is set to **don't check**. Click the **drop-down arrow** and select **2**. You are changing the style to reflect two spaces after the punctuation between each sentence. Click **OK**.

5. In the Word Options dialog box, under *When Correcting Spelling and Grammar in Word* section, click the Recheck Document button, then click OK. A prompt appears stating that *This operation resets the spelling checker and the grammar checker so that Word will recheck words and grammar you previously checked and chose to ignore. Do you want to continue?* Click Yes. Click OK to close the Word Options dialog box. Word flags and marks the punctuation at the end of sentences with a green wavy line. Notice in the second paragraph, the document flags "are issued." Right-click on the phrase and a pop-up menu appears. It states "Passive Voice (consider revising)."

6. Repeat steps 1 and 2 to open the Grammar Settings dialog box.

7. Under the Require section, click the drop-down arrow to change the Spaces required between sentences setting to don't check.

8. Scroll down and disable all styles with the exception of Clichés, Colloquialisms, and Jargons. One style is kept active. Click OK.

9. In the Word Options dialog box, under the *When Correcting Spelling and Grammar in Word* section, click the Recheck Document button. A prompt appears stating that *This operation resets the spelling checker and the grammar checker so that Word will recheck words and grammar you previously checked and chose to ignore. Do you want to continue?* Click Yes. Click OK to close the Word Options dialog box. Notice "are issued" in the second paragraph is no longer flagged. In the third paragraph, the phrase "in the amount of" is flagged with a wavy line.

10. When you right-click on the phrase, the pop-up menu appears. Click About This Sentence. The Help menu appears, indicating this is a cliché and the marked word or phrase may be overused or unnecessary to the meaning of your sentence. To remove it, you would repeat steps 6–9 to disable Clichés, Colloquialisms, and Jargons.

11. Click the Options button in the Spelling and Grammar dialog box; the Word Options dialog box opens in Backstage view. Select Proofing in the left pane and, in the *When Correcting Spelling and Grammar in Word* section, click the Writing Style command box drop-down arrow and select Grammar Only to set the tool for checking the document's grammar. Click OK to apply your changes.

12. **SAVE** your document in your USB flash drive in the lesson folder then CLOSE the file.

PAUSE. LEAVE the document open to use in the next exercise.

SHARING DOCUMENTS

Word contains a feature that will remove unwanted information from your document. The Document Inspector is used to find and remove hidden data and personal information in Word 2010 documents as well as earlier versions. It is a good idea to practice inspecting the document before sharing an electronic copy such as an email attachment. In this exercise, you will inspect the document and remove personal information.

STEP BY STEP	Use the Document Inspector

@ The *emploffer* document file for this lesson is available on the book companion website or in WileyPLUS.

OPEN the *emploffer* document from your lesson folder.

1. Click the File tab and by Prepare for Sharing click the Check for Issues button, then click Inspect Document.

2. The Document Inspector dialog box appears. Click the Inspect button (see Figure 10-6).

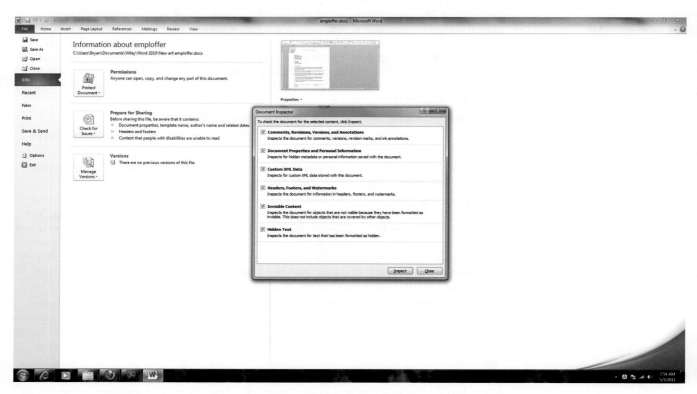

Figure 10-6

Document Inspector dialog box

3. In the *Document Properties and Personal Information* section, click Remove All. Personal information from the properties is removed and the document is ready to be shared. The items are removed and the dialog box is updated.

4. Leave the Headers, Footers, and Watermarks as is. Click Close.

5. In the Prepare for Sharing section, click the link to Allow this information to be saved in your file.

6. Click the Save As button to open the Save As dialog box. Save the document as *emploffer_1* in your USB flash drive in your lesson folder.

PAUSE. LEAVE the document open to use in the next exercise.

Checking Accessibility

The Accessibility Checker determines if there are potential errors in your document and will alert you that the content may be difficult for an individual with a disability to read. Accessibility is defined as being accessible to those with disabilities. Before sharing your document, it is important to inspect your document in case someone with a disability will be opening the document. In this exercise, you learn to check if there are errors in your document.

STEP BY STEP   **Check Accessibility**

USE the document that is open from the previous exercise.

1. Click the File tab and click the Check for Issues button, then click Check Accessibility.

2. The Accessibility Checker appears on the right pane, as shown in Figure 10-7. If there are errors in your document, the Accessibility Check will show errors, warnings, or tips.

Figure 10-7

Accessibility Checker Inspection Results

Errors ——

Warnings ——

Read more about making documents accessible link.

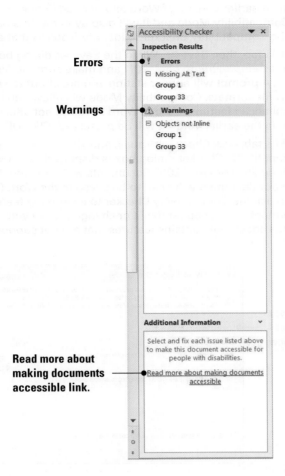

3. Click the **File** tab and notice that below Prepare for Sharing indicates that "Content that people with disabilities are unable to read." Word flags the document letting you know that there are problems in the document and not everyone will be able to read it.

4. **SAVE** the document with the same filename in your USB flash drive and **CLOSE** the file.

PAUSE. LEAVE Word open to use in the next exercise.

Checking Compatibility

Before sharing documents, it is good practice to check whether the document is error free and the formatting appears professional. Word's built-in Compatibility Check will ensure that a document's features are compatible with other versions of Word. The Compatibility Checker searches a document for features that are not supported by earlier versions of Word and lists a summary of these features. When documents are opened in an earlier version, they will open in Compatibility Mode and display in the Title bar. It is recommended that you run the Compatibility Checker to identify features that are supported. In this exercise, you learn to check for issues in a document.

Use the Compatibility Checker

1. **OPEN** the *employment_offer* document from the lesson folder. When documents are created in an earlier version of Word and opened in newer versions of Word, they will open in Compatibility Mode and it will display in the Title bar. It is recommended that you run the Compatibility Checker to identify features that are supported.

2. Click the File tab, then Save As. When the Save As dialog box opens, save the document as *employment_offer_2011* and make sure the file type displays as Word Document. A prompt will appear stating you are about to save your document to one of the new file formats. Compatibility Mode will allow you to edit your document, and the enhanced features used in Word 2010 will not affect your document—your document in the earlier version will be preserved. Click OK.

3. Click the File tab, click Check for Issues, and click Check Compatibility. The Microsoft Word Compatibility Checker dialog box is displayed as shown in Figure 10-8. When sharing Word 2010 or Word 2007 documents with individuals using earlier versions of Word, your document will need to be saved in the Word 97-2003 format. It is good practice to use the Compatibility Checker to ensure the features you have included in your document will not be removed or changed when you save it in the Word 97-2003 format. This document contains features that are not supported by earlier versions.

Figure 10-8

Microsoft Word Compatibility Checker dialog box

Click drop-down arrow to select versions to show.

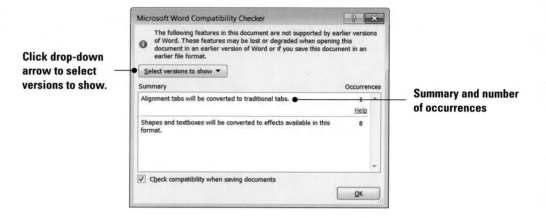

Summary and number of occurrences

4. Click OK.
5. **SAVE** the document with the same filename in your USB flash drive.
PAUSE. LEAVE the document open to use in the next exercise.

Sending Documents

Electronic documents are sent via email, web, and Internet fax. In Backstage view, you can save the document in a PDF and XPS format and attach it to email. You can also change and create a document in different file formats. In this exercise, you will send a document by email, SkyDrive, discuss how installation of drivers is used for the Internet fax, change files type, create PDF/XPS documents, and register and publish a blog.

Send Documents via Email Using Outlook

USE the document open from the previous exercise.

1. For this exercise, you must be using Microsoft Outlook. Check with your instructor to determine whether you have access to Outlook on your computer.

2. Click the File tab, then click Save & Send. Send using email is automatically selected.

3. Under Send Using E-mail, click Send as attachment. The open document is automatically attached to the email message and is ready to be sent.

4. Key the email address of a friend, classmate, or coworker in the *To* box and click the Send button.

PAUSE. LEAVE the document open to use in the next exercise.

STEP BY STEP   **Send Documents via SkyDrive**

Windows Live **SkyDrive** is an online service provided by Microsoft. SkyDrive is an online file storage location where you can store documents and pictures. Microsoft has provided 25GB of free online storage space, and SkyDrive is password protected—so you control who has access to your files.

You can share your documents in Word, Excel, PowerPoint, and OneNote; create your personal album; and share pictures with your contacts or on your social networking site; create and send emails, and manage your contacts; add events to your calendar and share; access Messenger with real-time chat; and stay updated and connected to your social networking sites, such as Facebook, MySpace, and LinkedIn.

USE the document open from the previous exercise.

1. For this exercise, you will need a .NET Passport account. The Windows Live Office is part of SkyDrive and if you have a Hotmail, Messenger, or Xbox Live account, you already have a Windows Live ID and may skip steps 2 and 3.

2. If you need a Windows Live account, complete steps 2 and 3. You must be connected to the Internet to complete the registration process. Click the File tab, then click the Save & Send button. Under the Save & Send section click the Save to Web button. On the right side of the screen under Sign In, click the link, Sign up for Windows Live SkyDrive (see Figure 10-9).

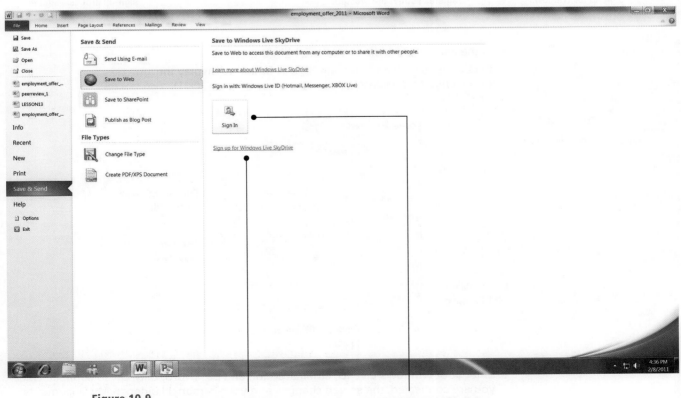

Figure 10-9

Backstage—Save & Send

Sign up for Windows Live SkyDrive.

Sign into Windows Live SkyDrive after you create an account.

Another Way
Launch the Internet, and key signup.live.com in the address bar.

3. The Internet opens at the Windows Live website, as shown in Figure 10-10. Click the **Sign up** button and follow the prompts on your screen to complete the registration for a Windows Live account. Once you complete the process, exit the Internet. You will be signing in to your account in the Word's Save and Send section of Backstage.

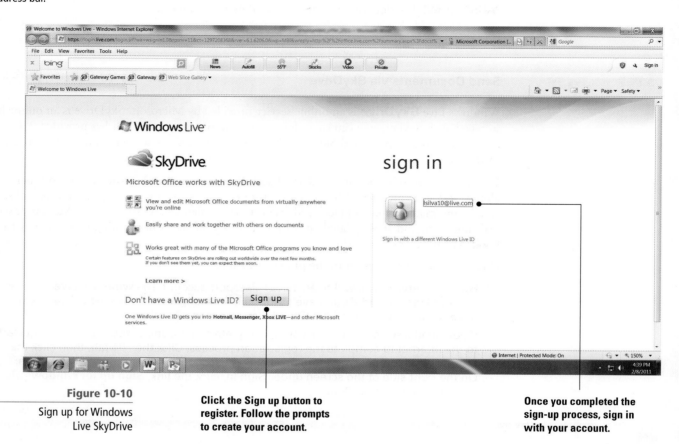

Figure 10-10

Sign up for Windows Live SkyDrive

Click the Sign up button to register. Follow the prompts to create your account.

Once you completed the sign-up process, sign in with your account.

4. In the **File** tab, click the **Save & Send** button.

5. Click **Save to Web** and click the **Sign In** button to display the *Connecting to docs.live.net* dialog box (see Figure 10-11).

Figure 10-11

Connecting to docs.live.net

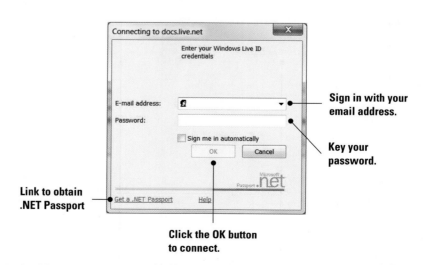

Sign in with your email address.

Key your password.

Link to obtain .NET Passport

Click the OK button to connect.

6. Enter your Windows Live ID, email account, and password. Click **OK** to connect. Once you are connected, the screen changes and your Personal Folders > My Documents folders will appear. You will be able to upload, create, edit, and share documents in a web browser (see Figure 10-12).

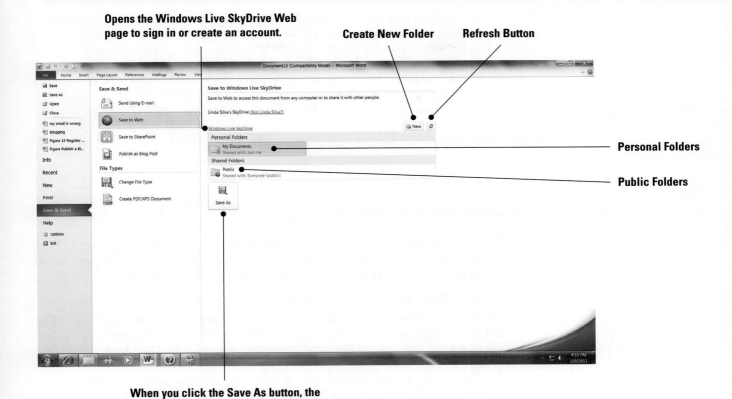

Opens the Windows Live SkyDrive Web page to sign in or create an account.

Create New Folder

Refresh Button

Personal Folders

Public Folders

When you click the Save As button, the Save As dialog box opens with a target location to save your document.

Figure 10-12

Backstage–Save to Windows Live SkyDrive

7. Select **My Documents** under Personal Folders. You have an option to share information in the Public folder and you can grant individuals permission to view and edit the contents in your folder. You can also create a new folder in which to place your documents.

8. Click the **Save As** button. The Save As dialog box appears and the address bar displays the location of your folder as well as the filename (see Figure 10-13). Click **Save**.

Figure 10-13

Save As dialog box

SkyDrive file location

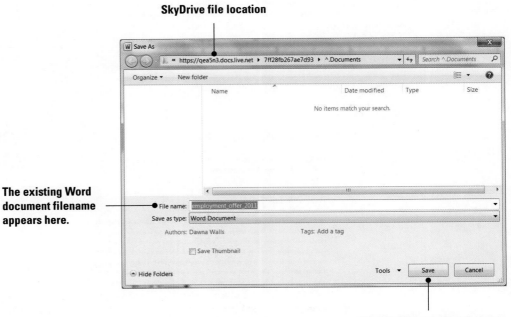

The existing Word document filename appears here.

Click the Save button to save in the docs.live.net account.

9. Launch the Internet and sign in to your Windows Live account to view your document.

10. At the top screen in your Windows Live Account, click the Office link, then Your Documents. Double-click the My Documents folder. You have an option to edit your document in the browser, open it in Word, or Share it (with an option to add permissions), and under More you can view the versions history, move, copy, rename, download, and view properties.

11. In step 9, you signed in to your email account. Keep your Windows Live email account open.

PAUSE. LEAVE the document open for the next exercise.

STEP BY STEP | **Send Documents via Internet Fax**

Word provides the Internet Fax feature without the use of a fax machine. You can send Office documents online as Internet faxes. To set up your computer to send Internet faxes, you would need to install the Windows Fax Printer Driver or rely on a Fax Service provider.

USE the document open from the previous exercise.

1. By default the Windows Fax feature is disabled and it must be installed before sending documents via Internet fax. A utility is built into Windows Vista and Windows 7 to use the Windows Fax and Scan utility. For Windows XP, you will need to add Microsoft Fax in the Add/Remove Programs in the Control Panel.

2. The Internet fax command is available in Backstage view. This feature has the capability to send Internet faxes without a fax machine.

3. On the File tab select Save & Send and then click Send as Internet Fax. A prompt will appear stating *To use Fax Services to send your fax, you must sign up with a fax service provider.* If you click OK, your web browser opens and you choose a provider. Your screen would resemble Figure 10-14. Each fax service provider charges a fee for their services. Check with your instructor to see if the services are available.

Figure 10-14

Available Fax Services

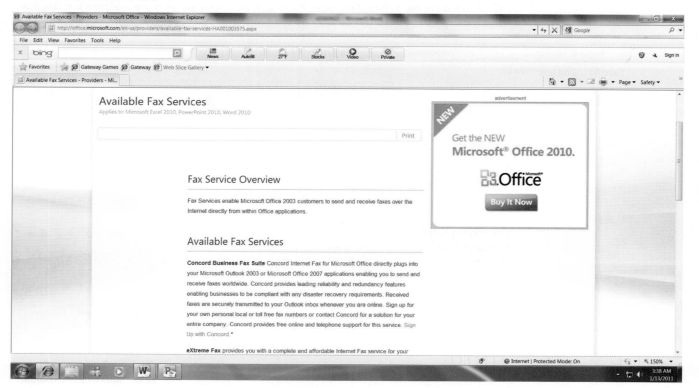

4. After a fax service provider is selected and an account is set up, a New Fax window opens with the current document attached. Complete the fax form, then click Send.

5. Exit the Internet.

PAUSE. LEAVE the document open for the next exercise.

STEP BY STEP **Change and Create File Types**

USE the document open from the previous exercise.

1. On the File tab, select Save & Send.

2. Under File Types, click Change File Type. You will be saving a Word document as another file type. The right side of the screen displays Document File Types and Other File Types. When you select one of the file types, it will automatically add the appropriate file extension to the document.

Take Note In Lesson 1, you learned to save a document and change file types.

3. Under Other File Types, select Single File Web Page as shown in Figure 10-15. A web page will be created for this Word document as a single file web page. The extension associated with the single file web page is .MHT. The file extension .MHT is reserved for web pages, and .MHT is commonly used for HTML (HyperText Markup Language).

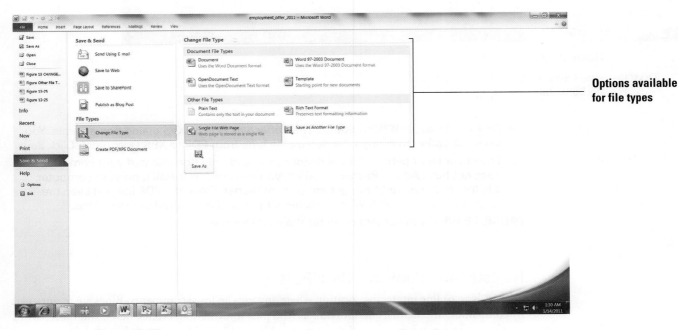

Options available for file types

Figure 10-15

Backstage view—Change File Type

4. Click the Save As button. After saving the document as a single file web page, it will open in Word. Notice that the elements applied in the document are gone. You can also view the document in a web browser.

5. **CLOSE** the single file web page.

6. **OPEN** the *employment_offer_2011* document from the lesson folder. You are opening the same document as a Word document with the extension .DOCX.

7. Click the File tab and select Save & Send.

8. Under File Types click the Create PDF/XPS Document. As you learned in Lesson 1, .PDF and .XPS are file formats that preserve document formatting. The PDF file will open in the Adobe Reader Viewer while the XPS file will open in the XPS Viewer. The right side of the Save & Send screen changes as shown in Figure 10-16.

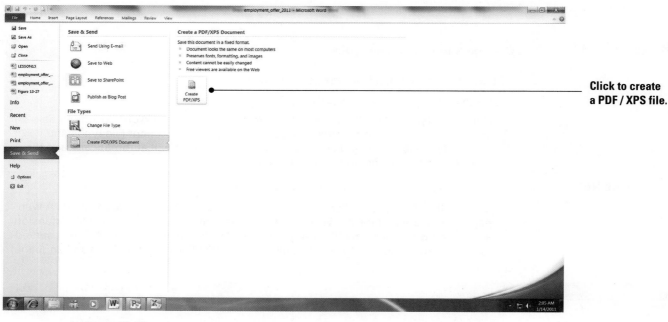

Figure 10-16

Backstage view—Create a PDF/XPS Document

9. Click the Create PDF/XPS button. The *Publish as PDF or XPS* dialog box appears. You have the option to change the default file type from PDF to XPS Document. Click Save.

10. The document opens in Adobe Reader as a read-only document. If your computer does not have Adobe Reader installed, you will need to install it on your computer. It is free to download from get.adobe.com/reader. Close the PDF file and keep the *employment_offer_2011* Word document open and minimized to the taskbar.

PAUSE. LEAVE the document open for the next exercise.

Register and Publish a Blog Post

A **blog** is an online interactive location where anyone can leave comments. Blogs are maintained by companies, instructors, and individuals who post information, events, news, and more. Word provides a feature where you can register your blog's URL, add a post, and publish it.

STEP BY STEP   **Register and Publish a Blog Post**

OPEN a blank document screen.

1. A Word document can be published as a blog post or you can create a new blog.

2. On the File tab select New.

3. Under the Available Templates section, select Blog post and then double-click or click the Create button.

4. The Register a Blog Account dialog box opens, as shown in Figure 10-17. Click the Register Now button, then click the drop-down arrow and select WordPress. Click the Next button. WordPress services are free.

Figure 10-17

Register a Blog Account dialog box

Register Now button links to an external website.

5. At the WordPress website, you will be required to enter a WordPress address or you can get your own URL with a custom domain name, for example, wordwise2010. As you enter a domain name, the screen will display whether the name is available. Enter any name you would like for your URL and, once it displays as being available, complete the registration process by entering your username and password. (It should be a strong password—the screen will indicate if it is weak or strong.) Enter your password again, then enter your email address. If you would like to subscribe to their blog and learn about new themes, features, and other news, click to add a check mark in the check box. Click the Sign Up button and check your email to activate your blog by clicking on the link in the email.

6. Click the link sent to your email account by WordPress.com. Your screen should resemble Figure 10-18 stating that *Your account is now active*. In the first paragraph, click your URL link to open your blog site. Your site should resemble Figure 10-19. You can customize the site by changing the theme and features.

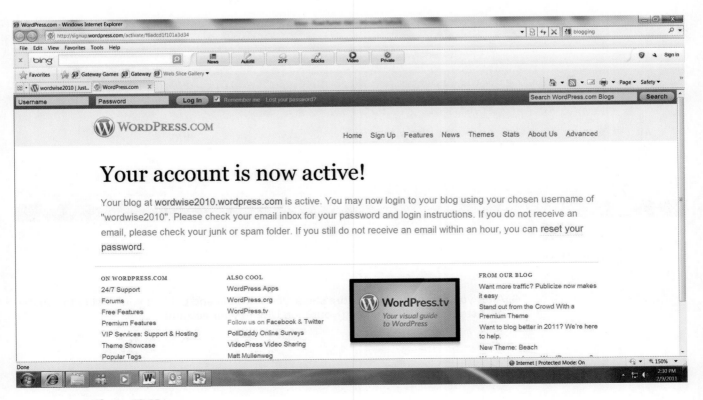

Figure 10-18

Your personalized URL—Your account is now active

Figure 10-19

Your personalized blog site

7. The Word screen displays [Enter Post Title Here]. Key, **What do you think about the NEW features in Word 2010?** In the Blog Post tab, in the Blog group, the Publish button contains two options, **Publish** and **Publish as Draft** (see Figure 10-20).

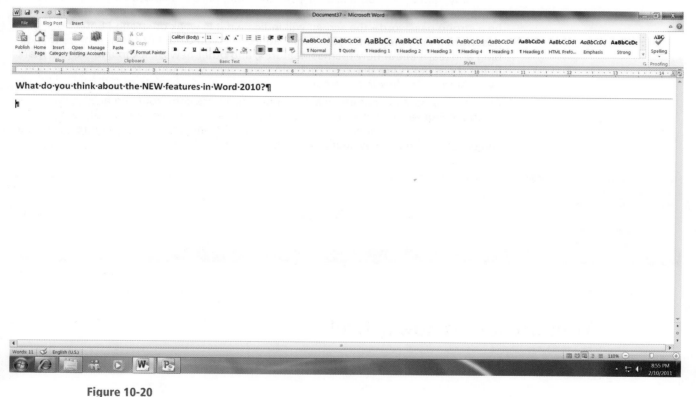

Figure 10-20

New post entered

8. After you complete a few more steps, you will post and publish your first blog. On the next step, you will be adding your blog URL to your account.

9. On the Blog group, click the **Manage Accounts** button to display the Blog Accounts dialog box, as shown in Figure 10-21.

Figure 10-21

Blog Accounts

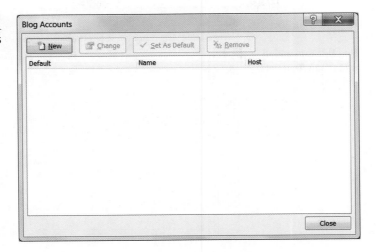

10. Click the **New** button. When the New Blog Account dialog box opens, click the drop-down arrow to display the menu. Select **WordPress**, and click **Next**. The New WordPress Account dialog box opens as shown in Figure 10-22. Enter your Blog Post URL, *<Enter your blog URL here>* for example, wordwise2010.wordpress.com, then enter your username and password. If you would like Word to remember your password, click the Remember Password box to add a check mark. Another option is Picture Options. When you publish your blog post, your picture needs to be uploaded to a picture provider on their storage location. Options to consider if you decide to upload a picture: you can upload to your my blog provider, My own server, and None—Don't upload pictures. For this exercise, do not use the Picture Options.

Figure 10-22

New WordPress Account
dialog box

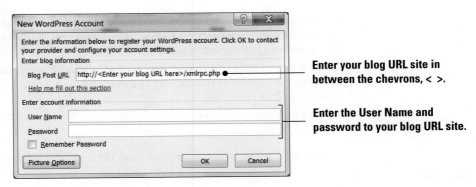

11. After entering your Blog Post URL, username, and password, a prompt will appear stating *When Word sends information to the blog service provider, it may be possible for other people to see that information. This includes your user name and password. Do you want to continue?* Click **Yes**.

12. Click the Manage Accounts button again in the Blog group to see your account, as shown in Figure 10-23. Click Close.

Figure 10-23

Blog Accounts Entry

Blog URL site added
to Manage Accounts
dialog box

13. Click the Publish button on Blog group to display the *Connect to [your Blog URL]* dialog box. Figure 10-24 displays *Connect to wordwise2010*. Key your username and password to post and publish.

Figure 10-24

Connect to wordwise2010

14. A yellow prompt will appear in your Word blog document screen stating, *This post was published to <your blog URL site>* followed by the time and date. For example, *This post was published to wordwise2010 at 10:41:40 AM 2/9/2011.*

15. Close the blog post. A prompt may appear stating *Do you want to save changes made to the document? If you click "Don't Save," a recent copy of this file will be temporarily available.* Click Don't Save.

16. When you click the Home Page 🏠 button on the Blog group, it will automatically

Home
Page

launch the Internet directly to your Blog URL website after you have logged in.

Take Note   You can blog and publish from your blog URL site.

17. The Insert Category button allows you to categorize postings on your blog. When you click this button, a drop-down menu appears below the blue horizontal line. When you categorize your blog post, you can select from the drop-down menu. In the meantime, you do not see any category. If you clicked the Insert Category button, click the Undo 🔙 button on the Quick Access Toolbar to remove. The Open Existing button opens a published blog.

PAUSE. LEAVE Word open for the next exercise.

STEP BY STEP	**Publish a Word Document as a Blog**

1. You are now ready to publish an existing Word document as a blog. Click the taskbar to display the *employment_offer_2011* Word document on your screen.

2. Click the File tab, then click Save & Send. The Save & Send command appears on your screen. Click Publish as Blog Post to display the options for different sites to publish your blog. Click the Blog Post button on the right side of the screen. The *employment_offer_2011* document is inserted in the Word Blog layout and appears below the horizontal line without any formatting or any of the Word elements applied.

3. Click the Publish button in the *Blog* group to display *Connect to <your Blog URL site>*. The example shown in Figure 10-24 displays *Connect to wordwise2010*. Enter your username and password, then click OK.

4. A prompt will appear stating, *When Word sends information to the blog service provider, it may be possible for other people to see that information. This includes your username and password. Do you want to continue?* Click Yes.

5. A yellow prompt will appear on the screen stating *This post was published to your <Blog URL site> at time is displayed and date.* For example, *This post was published to your wordwise2010 at 4:12:14 PM 2/9/2011* (see Figure 10-25).

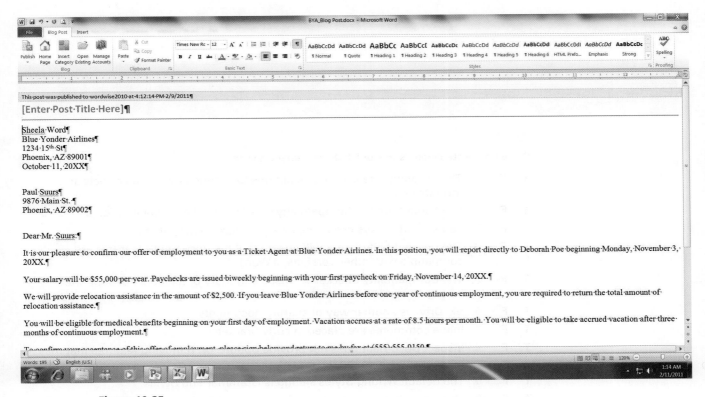

Figure 10-25

Post published

6. Close the blog post. A prompt may appear stating *Do you want to save changes made to the document? If you click "Don't Save," a recent copy of this file will be temporarily available.* Click Save.

7. Save the document as *BYA_Blog Post* in your USB flash drive in the lesson folder.

8. Close the *employment_offer_2011* Word document.

PAUSE. CLOSE Word.

Remove a Blog on Your Blog Site

1. **LAUNCH** the Internet and log in to your blog URL site. On the left side of the screen, click Post, and all posts will appear.
2. Add a check mark in the check box and hover your mouse pointer over the post to delete, then select Trash. Click Apply.
3. Log out of your blog URL site. Have fun blogging!

CLOSE the Internet.

SKILL SUMMARY

In This Lesson, You Learned How To:
Validate content by using spelling and grammar checking options
Share documents

Knowledge Assessment

True/False

Circle T if the statement is true or F if the statement is false.

T F   1. The proofing screen contains options to change how Word corrects and formats text.

T F   2. You should run the Compatibility Checker on all document files.

T F   3. You should always proof documents before sharing them.

T F   4. The Compatibility Check will ensure that the document's features are compatible with other versions of Word.

T F   5. The Compatibility Checker will list a summary of features not supported by earlier versions.

T F   6. SkyDrive is another way of sharing documents.

T F   7. Inline comments are placed in curly brackets.

T F   8. Inspect Document does not provide options on removing features that may have been used in the document.

T F   9. The default Writing Styles setting is Grammar and Styles.

T F   10. The status bar contains a proofing error button for quick access.

Multiple Choice

Select the best response for the following statements.

1. The proofing option, Two Initial Caps, is found in which option?
   a. CorrectCaps
   b. AutoCorrect
   c. Grammar Settings
   d. Exceptions

2. Which command(s) open the Spelling and Grammar feature?
   a. F7
   b. Shift+F7
   c. Spelling and Grammar button
   d. a and c

3. Internet faxing is available to users
   a. At no charge
   b. For a fee by service providers
   c. Only if you have access to a fax machine
   d. It is not available

4. Word provides blogging as an option, but as a user you must
   a. Registering a blog URL
   b. Post and publish
   c. Maintain your blog URL site
   d. All of the above

5. You must register a space name before
   a. Blogging
   b. Posting a blog
   c. Sharing
   d. Publishing

6. If your document contains potential problems where the content is difficult to read by an individual with a disability, you would be alerted under which command?
   a. Check Accessibility
   b. Check Compatibility
   c. Inspect Document
   d. No command is available

7. Before sharing a document, it is good practice to remove personal information using which command?
   a. Check Accessibility
   b. Check Compatibility
   c. Inspect Document
   d. No command is available

8. The Proofing Errors icon is located in the:
   a. Ribbon.
   b. Task Bar.
   c. Status bar.
   d. None of the above

9. After creating and formatting a document, you should perform this action before sharing?
   a. Saving
   b. Printing
   c. Spelling
   d. Faxing

10. To correct every occurrence of the misspelled word, you would select:
   a. Change.
   b. Correct.
   c. Correct All.
   d. Change All.

Competency Assessment

Project 10-1: Research Paper

You are writing a paper about the health benefits of wine and are ready to check the spelling in your document.

GET READY. LAUNCH Word if it is not already running.

1. **OPEN** the *benefits_of_wine* document from the lesson folder.
2. On the Review tab in the Proofing group, click the Spelling and Grammar button.
3. Click the Options button in the Spelling and Grammar dialog box to change the Writing Style. The Word Options screen opens in Backstage view. Select Proofing and under the section *When correcting spelling and grammar in Word*, click the drop-down arrow beside the Writing Style command box and select Grammar Only. Click OK.
4. The Spelling and Grammar check will stop on the words/phrases listed in the following table; for each misspelled word, take the action indicated in the table.

@ The *benefits_of_wine* document file for this lesson is available on the book companion website or in WileyPLUS.

Misspelled Word	Corrected Word	Action to Take
Choleterol	cholesterol	Change All
polyphenl	Polyphenol	Change All
But what about white wine?		Ignore Rule
Stuttaford		Ignore All
Healthspan		Ignore All
Teissedre		Ignore All
The USDA makes it clear...		Ignore All
cancers		Ignore All
Agatston		Ignore All

5. When the prompt appears stating that the spelling and grammar check is completed, click OK.
6. **SAVE** the document as *benefits_of_wine_final* in your USB flash drive in the lesson folder.

LEAVE Word open for the next project.

Project 10-2: Computer Use Policy

Your manager has asked you to format the computer use policy document appropriately and have it ready for a meeting in an hour.

GET READY. LAUNCH Word if not already running.

@ The *computeruse2* document file for this lesson is available on the book companion website or in WileyPLUS.

1. **OPEN** *computeruse2* from the lesson folder.
2. Change the default settings for the Save AutoRecover minutes. In the File tab, under *Help*, click Options, and then Save.
3. Under the *Save document* section, click the down arrow by Save AutoRecover information until it changes to 5 minutes.

4. On page 1, select the content within the border beginning with *Disclaimer . . . All rights reserved*. Add the Olive Green, Accent 3, Lighter 40% shading color. Add a page border with a shadow style with the border color of Olive Green, Accent 3, Darker 50%, 2¼" wide.

5. Select *COMPUTER USE POLICY*, bold, 18 pts.

6. Select *Section One* through *Sections Ten*, change the style to Intense Reference.

7. **CLOSE** the document without saving. A prompt should appear on your screen. *If you don't save, a recent copy of the document will be temporarily available*. If the prompt did not appear, check step 2. Click Don't Save. In the next exercise, you will be recovering your unsaved document.

LEAVE Word open for the next project.

Proficiency Assessment

Project 10-3: Proofing Your Document

@ The *job descripton* file for this lesson is available on the book companion website or in WileyPLUS.

Your manager, Sonny, is out-of-town and would like to review the changes you made to your job description. You will be sharing this document with him via email. Use the Spelling and Grammar to correct the misspellings.

GET READY. LAUNCH Word if it is not already running.

1. **OPEN** the *job description* document in the lesson folder.

2. Check the spelling in your document.

3. Send the document to your instructor.

4. **SAVE** the document as *job description first review* in your USB flash drive in the lesson folder and close the file.

LEAVE Word open for the next project.

Project 10-4: Prepare Scholarship Letter for Distribution

Your task is to remove all document properties in the scholarship letter before sharing via email with students.

GET READY. LAUNCH Word if it is not already running.

@ The *scholarship* document file for this lesson is available on the book companion website or in WileyPLUS.

1. **OPEN** *scholarship* from the lesson folder.

2. SAVE the document as *scholarship letter* in a PDF format in your USB flash drive in the lesson folder and close the file.

LEAVE Word open for the next project.

Mastery Assessment

Project 10-5: Blue Yonder Airlines Stock Agreements

Blue Yonder Airlines employs you, and one of your recent responsibilities is proofing all documents. The stockholders agreement document contains many misspelled words. Use the Spelling and Grammar check to correct the misspellings.

GET READY. LAUNCH Word if it is not already running.

@ The *stock_ agreement* document file for this lesson is available on the book companion website or in WileyPLUS.

1. **OPEN** the *stock_agreement* document from the lesson folder.
2. Locate all errors and correct them.
3. **SAVE** the document as *stock_agreement_final* in your USB flash drive in the lesson folder and close the file.

LEAVE Word open for the next project.

Project 10-6: Stock Agreement Finalized

You have finalized the stock agreement document and are ready to share it with employees. Your task is to save the document as a PDF file before sending it to eligible employees.

GET READY. LAUNCH Word if not already running.

@ The *stock_ agreement_2* document file for this lesson is available on the book companion website or in WileyPLUS.

1. **OPEN** the *stock_agreement_2* document from the lesson folder.
2. **SAVE** and **Publish** the document as *stock_agreement* in your USB flash drive in the lesson folder.

LEAVE Word open for the next project.

Microsoft® Excel® 2010

LESSON SKILL MATRIX

In This Lesson, You Will Learn The Following Skills:

Starting Excel

Working in the Excel Window

Changing Excel's View

Working with an Existing Workbook

Working with Excel's Help System

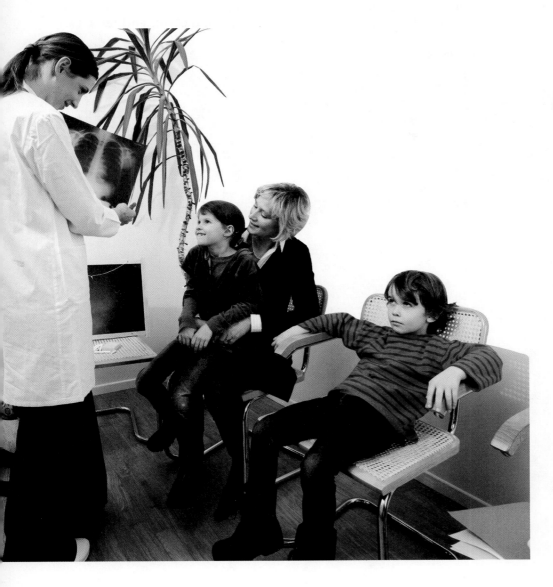

KEY TERMS

- active cell
- Backstage
- cell
- column
- command tab
- command group
- Dialog Box Launcher
- File tab
- Help system
- hotkey
- Keytip
- Name box
- Quick Access Toolbar
- Ribbon
- row
- ScreenTip
- workbook
- worksheet

Contoso, Ltd., provides specialty health care for the entire family—prenatal through geriatric care. The practice, owned by Dr. Stephanie Bourne, has an expanding patient list. It currently employs a staff of 36, which includes three additional family practice physicians. Each physician has unique patient contact hours; the office is open from 7 a.m. to 7 p.m. on Mondays and from 8 a.m. to 4 p.m. other weekdays. The office manager must track revenue and expenses for the practice and maintain a large volume of employee data. Microsoft Excel is an ideal tool for organizing and analyzing such data. In this lesson, you will learn how to enter text and numbers into an Excel worksheet to keep up-to-date employee records.

SOFTWARE ORIENTATION

Microsoft Excel's Opening Screen

NEW to Office 2010

Microsoft Office Excel 2010 provides powerful new and improved tools that enable users to organize, analyze, manage, and share information easily. When you open Excel, you immediately see some of its most important new features. A broad band, called the **Ribbon**, runs across the top of the window. The Ribbon is organized into task-oriented **command tabs**. Each

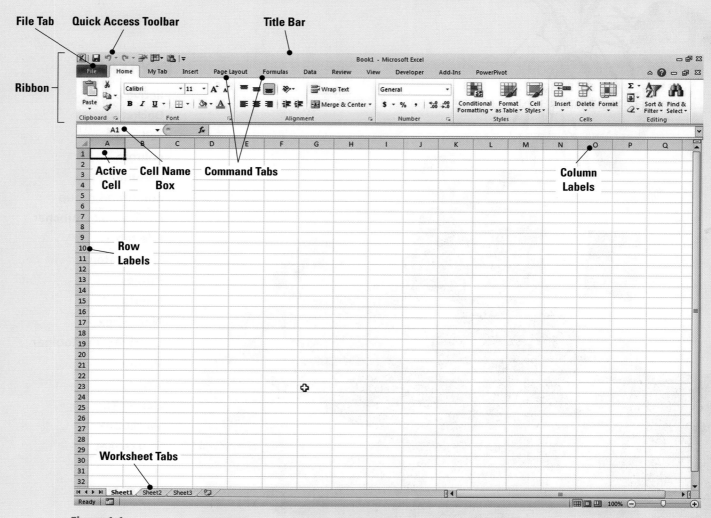

Figure 1-1

Excel's opening screen

tab is divided into task-specific **command groups** appropriate to the type of work the user is currently performing. The tabs and groups replace the menus and multiple toolbars that were present in Excel 2007. When you first launch Excel, you will see a screen similar to the one shown in Figure 1-1. (The Developer and Add-Ins tabs may not appear on your screen if the default settings have been changed or other preferences have been set.) Use Figure 1-1 as a reference throughout this lesson and the rest of this book.

STARTING EXCEL

The Bottom Line

To work efficiently in Microsoft Excel, you need to become familiar with its primary user interface. You can open Microsoft Office Excel 2010 by clicking the Start menu, All Programs, Microsoft Office, and then Office Excel 2010.

Excel opens with a blank **workbook**, or spreadsheet file, as shown in Figure 1-1. The filename (Book1) and the program name (Microsoft Excel) appear in the title bar at the top of the screen; the Book1 title remains until you save the workbook with a name of your choice. The new workbook contains three **worksheets**—similar to pages in a document or a book—where you can enter information. The sheet tabs are located just above the Status bar and are identified as Sheet1, Sheet2, and Sheet3. You can rename worksheets to identify their content and add additional worksheets as needed.

Starting Excel

In this exercise, you learn to use the Start menu to open Excel and view the new workbook's first blank worksheet.

STEP BY STEP | **Start Excel**

GET READY. To complete this exercise, make sure your computer is running and Microsoft Excel is installed. Then, follow these steps:

1. Click the Start menu, and then click All Programs.
2. On the list of programs, click Microsoft Office 2010.
3. Click Microsoft Office Excel 2010. A blank workbook will open, and the worksheet named Sheet1 will be displayed.

PAUSE. LEAVE the worksheet open to use in the next exercise.

WileyPLUS Extra! features an online tutorial of this task.

A worksheet is a grid composed of rows, columns, and cells. Worksheet **columns** go from top to bottom and are identified by letters; **rows** go from left to right and are identified by numbers. Each box on the grid is a **cell** and is identified by the intersection of a column and a row. Thus, the first cell in an open worksheet is A1. You enter information by keying it into the **active cell**, which is outlined by a bold black line; this is also called a highlighted cell.

WORKING IN THE EXCEL WINDOW

The Bottom Line

When you launched Excel in the previous exercise, the program opened a new workbook and displayed a blank worksheet. You just learned about some of the most important components of the Excel worksheet. In this lesson, you explore the Excel window and learn to identify and customize the Quick Access Toolbar, the Ribbon, and other important onscreen tools and components. You also learn to open and use Backstage view, Microsoft's replacement for the Office button and File tab commands found in previous versions of Office.

Using Onscreen Tools

The **Quick Access Toolbar** gives you fast and easy access to the tools you use most often in any given Excel session. It appears on the left side of the title bar, above the Ribbon (although you can move the toolbar below the Ribbon if you want it closer to your work area). You can add and remove commands to and from the toolbar so that it contains only those commands you use most frequently. In this lesson, you learn to move and customize the Quick Access Toolbar by adding and removing commands. You also learn how to use **ScreenTips**—small, onscreen windows that display descriptive text when you rest the pointer on a command or control.

STEP BY STEP	Use Onscreen Tools

GET READY. Use the workbook you opened in the previous exercise to perform these steps:

1. Place the cursor at the bottom of each command on the Quick Access Toolbar and read the description that appears as a ScreenTip.

Take Note

Use ScreenTips to remind you of a command's function. Enhanced ScreenTips display in a larger window that contains more descriptive text than a ScreenTip. Most Enhanced ScreenTips contain a link to a Help topic.

2. Click the drop-down arrow at the right side of the Quick Access Toolbar. From the drop-down list, select **Open**. The Open icon is added to the Quick Access Toolbar. Click the down arrow again and select **Quick Print** from the drop-down list (see Figure 1-2).

Figure 1-2

Customizing the Quick Access Toolbar

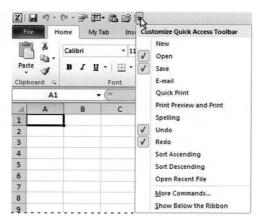

Another Way
To add a command to the Quick Access Toolbar, you can also right-click any icon on the Ribbon and then click Add to Quick Access Toolbar.

3. Next, right-click the toolbar, then select **Show Quick Access Toolbar Below the Ribbon**.
4. Right-click the **Home** tab and click **Minimize the Ribbon**; now, only the tabs remain on display, increasing your workspace.
5. Click the drop-down arrow on the right side of the Quick Access Toolbar to produce a menu of options, then select **Minimize the Ribbon** to turn off the option and make the Ribbon commands visible.
6. Right-click the **Quick Access Toolbar** again and choose **Show Quick Access Toolbar Above the Ribbon** from the pop-up menu.
7. Right-click the **Open** command, and select **Remove from Quick Access Toolbar**.

Take Note

If you want to add commands to the Quick Access Toolbar that do not appear in the drop-down list, click More Commands on the drop-down list. The Excel Options dialog box will open. You can also right-click the Quick Access Toolbar or any Ribbon tab and select Customize Quick Access Toolbar to open the Excel Options window.

PAUSE. LEAVE the workbook open to use in the next exercise.

By default, the Quick Access Toolbar contains the Save, Undo, and Redo commands. As you work in Excel, customize the Quick Access Toolbar so that it contains the commands you use most often. Do not, however, remove the Undo and Redo commands. These commands are not available on the command tabs.

Navigating the Ribbon

The Ribbon organizes tools from the Menu Toolbar into an easier, more useful user interface. Having commands visible on the work surface enables you to work more quickly and efficiently. As you've seen in earlier exercises, the Ribbon in Microsoft Office Excel 2010 is made up of a series of tabs, each related to specific kinds of tasks that users perform in Excel. By pressing and releasing the Alt key, you can reveal **Keytips**, or small "badges" displaying keyboard shortcuts for specific tabs and commands on the Ribbon and Quick Access Toolbar. In this exercise, you learn how to navigate between Excel tabs and use their commands and Keytips.

Take Note   Keytips are sometimes also referred to as **hotkeys** in Excel. Note, however, that when you use Microsoft Office 2010 Help, no reference is listed for hotkeys; only Keytips is referenced.

Within each tab on the Ribbon, commands are organized into related tasks called command groups, as shown in Figure 1-3. For example, consider the Home tab, which groups all the options that were part of the Standard and Formatting toolbars in previous Office versions. When the Home tab is displayed, you see the Clipboard group, which contains the command buttons to cut, copy, and paste data. These commands allow you to revise, move, and repeat data within a worksheet. Similarly, you can use commands in the Editing group to fill adjacent cells, sort and filter data, find specific data within a worksheet, and perform other tasks related to editing worksheet data.

Figure 1-3

Home tab command groups

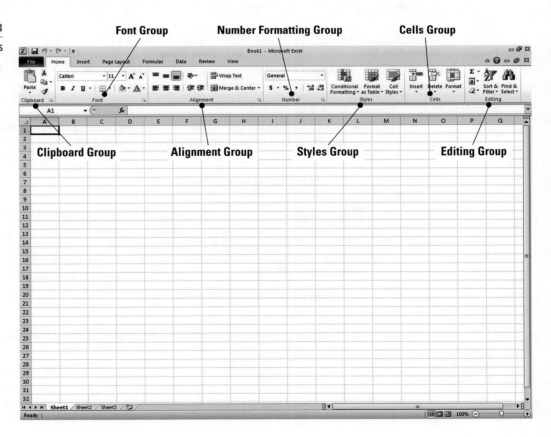

STEP BY STEP   **Navigate the Ribbon**

USE the previous worksheet for this exercise, making sure you complete the following steps:

1. With the Home tab active, click cell A1; your Ribbon should look similar to the one shown in Figure 1-4.

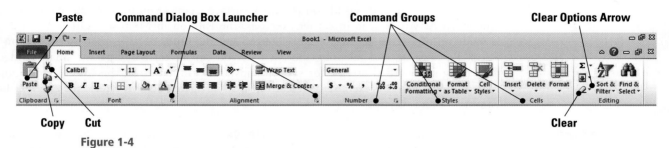

Paste   Command Dialog Box Launcher   Command Groups   Clear Options Arrow

Copy   Cut   Clear

Figure 1-4

Ribbon with Home tab active

2. Click the Insert tab; your screen should now look similar to the one shown in Figure 1-5. Commands on the Insert tab enable you to add charts and illustrations and to perform other functions that enhance your Excel spreadsheets.

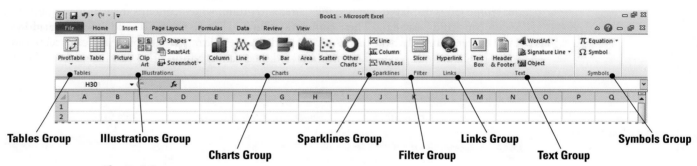

Tables Group   Illustrations Group   Sparklines Group   Links Group   Symbols Group

Charts Group   Filter Group   Text Group

Figure 1-5

Ribbon with the Insert tab active

3. Click the Home tab.

4. Press and release the Alt key to produce onscreen Keytips that show keyboard shortcuts for certain commands (see Figure 1-6).

Figure 1-6

Keytips on the Ribbon

Quick Access Toolbar shortcuts

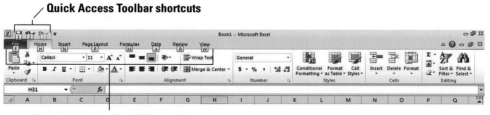

Alt Key shortcuts for Ribbon tabs

5. Press the Esc key or press the Alt key again to turn off the Keytips.

Take Note   Keyboard shortcuts enable you to issue commands in Excel without using the mouse (so you don't have to take your hands from the keyboard). You use keyboard shortcuts by pressing the key shown in the Keytip while also pressing and holding the Alt key. When you press and release the Alt key by itself, Excel displays the shortcuts for the Quick Access Toolbar.

PAUSE. CLOSE the workbook.

Introducing Backstage

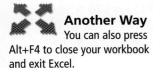

Another Way
You can also press Alt+F4 to close your workbook and exit Excel.

The most noticeable new feature in Microsoft Office 2010 is Backstage. The Backstage view enables you to easily navigate and customize the different features you most frequently use in Excel. Backstage will be covered in more depth in Lesson 2—but first, you need to know how to access it.

STEP BY STEP   **Access Backstage**

OPEN a new workbook for this exercise. Then, follow these steps:

1. Click the **File** tab. This opens Backstage view (see Figure 1-7).

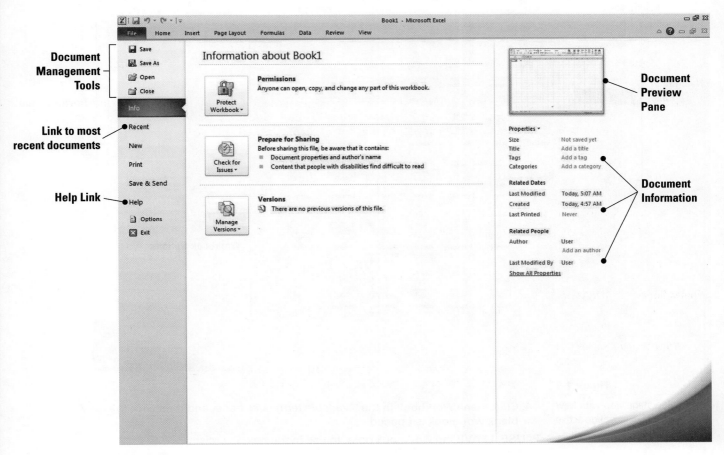

Figure 1-7
Backstage view

2. Notice that the Excel Backstage view is green. The Office suite has customized colors to designate which application you are using.

 Ref   The use and tools of Backstage are covered in depth in Lesson 2.

PAUSE. CLOSE the workbook and exit Excel.

Another Way
Pressing Alt+F also allows you to activate Backstage view.

NEW to Office 2010

Using the Microsoft Office File Tab and Backstage View

In Microsoft Office 2010, the Office button is replaced by the **File tab**. Clicking the File tab takes you to the Microsoft Office Backstage view, with its navigation bar of commands extending down the left side of the Excel window. **Backstage** view helps you access and use file management features, just as the Ribbon offers commands that control Excel's authoring features. In this exercise, you learn to use the File tab to open Backstage view. You also use Backstage commands to create a new, blank workbook.

STEP BY STEP   **Use the File Tab to Open Backstage View and Create a New Workbook**

GET READY. LAUNCH Excel to open a new, blank workbook. Then, follow these steps:

1. Click the **File** tab to open Backstage view.
2. Click **Close** in the navigation bar; your workbook disappears, but Excel remains open.
3. Click the **File** tab again, then click **New**; the *Available Templates* pane opens (see Figure 1-8).

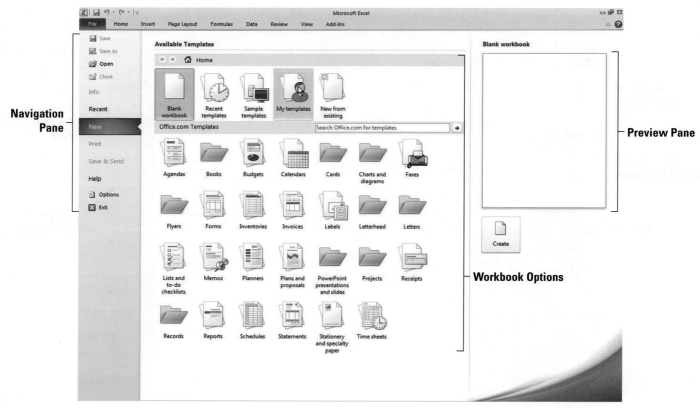

Figure 1-8

Backstage view with New option active

4. Click **Blank Workbook** in the *Available Templates* pane, and then click **Create**. A new blank workbook is opened.

PAUSE. LEAVE the workbook open to use in the next exercise.

As you have seen, a new blank workbook contains three worksheets. You can enter data in each of the worksheets, and Excel saves the worksheets as one workbook, rather than as separate documents.

CHANGING EXCEL'S VIEW

The Bottom Line

On the Ribbon, the View tab holds commands for controlling the appearance of the displayed document. You can also open and arrange new windows and split windows for side-by-side document views.

Changing Excel's View

Some command group headers in the Ribbon tabs have an arrow in their lower-right corner; this is called a **Dialog Box Launcher**. Clicking the arrow opens a dialog box, or a task pane containing more options for that particular group of commands. In this exercise, you learn how to use the View tab commands (including those you access through the Dialog Box Launcher) to change Excel's view within the open window.

STEP BY STEP	**Change Excel's View**

USE the open workbook from the previous exercise. Then, follow these steps:

1. The Home tab should be active. If it is not, click **Home** to activate it.

2. Select cell **A1** to make it active. Then type **456** and press **Tab**.

3. Click the **Dialog Box Launcher** arrow in the lower-right corner of the Font group of commands. The *Format Cells* dialog box, shown in Figure 1-9, opens. In most cases, your default font in Excel will be Calibri, point size 11, with no bolding or italics.

Figure 1-9

Format Cells dialog box

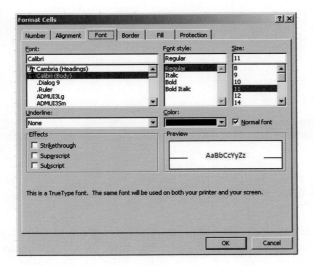

4. Notice that the Font tab of the dialog box is active. Change the font to **Arial**, then click **OK**.

5. Cell B1 should now be the active cell in your worksheet. Key **456** in this cell, then press **Tab**. Notice the difference in size and appearance between this number and the one you keyed in cell A1.

6. Click the **View** tab.

7. Click **Page Layout** view. Your workbook should look like Figure 1-10. In this view, you can see the margins, and you can add a header or footer.

Another Way
To change a font, you can type the first few letters of the name of the font you are searching for and Excel will locate it on the font list. You can also scroll through the list and choose your font type.

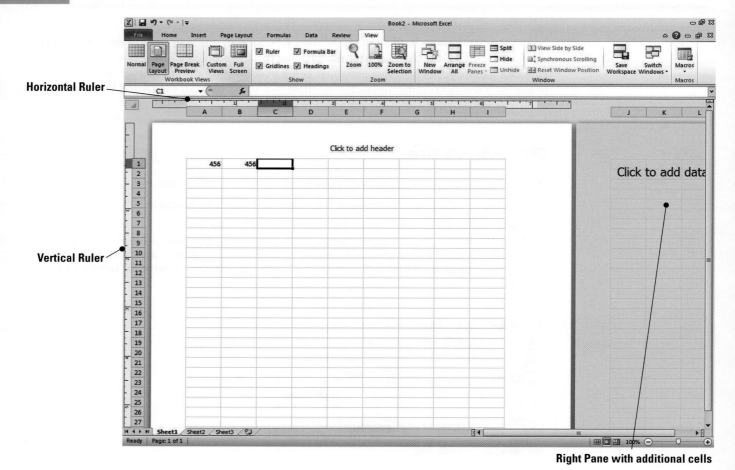

Horizontal Ruler

Vertical Ruler

Right Pane with additional cells

Figure 1-10

Page Layout view

PAUSE. LEAVE the workbook open to use in the next exercise.

As demonstrated in the exercise, you can preview your printed worksheet by clicking the Ribbon's View tab, then clicking Page Layout in the Workbook Views group (first section). This view enables you to fine-tune pages before printing. You can change your worksheet's layout and format in both this view and Normal view. You can also use the rulers to measure the width and height of your worksheet and determine whether you need to change its margins or print orientation.

 Ref   You will learn how to use additional commands in Lessons 2 and 3.

Splitting a Window

When a worksheet contains a great deal of data, you can see only a small portion of the worksheet in Excel's Normal and Page Layout views. The Split command enables you to overcome this limitation by viewing the worksheet in four quadrants. After issuing this command, you can use the scroll bars on the right and at the bottom of the window to display different sections of the worksheet at the same time so that you can more easily compare or contrast data. In this exercise, you learn to split the Excel window and use the scroll bars to view different sections of a worksheet. You also practice keying data into cells within the split windows, and you learn how to remove the split to return to single-window view.

STEP BY STEP   **Split a Window**

USE the worksheet you left open in the previous exercise. Then, follow these steps:

1. Press **Ctrl+Home** to make cell **A1** active.
2. With the **View** tab active, click the **Split** command in the Window group.
3. Choose the lower-right quadrant by clicking any cell in that area, then scroll down to Row 30.
4. Key **235** in cell H30 and press **Enter**. The data you entered in cells A1 and B1 should be visible along with what you just entered in cell H30, as shown in Figure 1-11.

Figure 1-11

Working in a split window

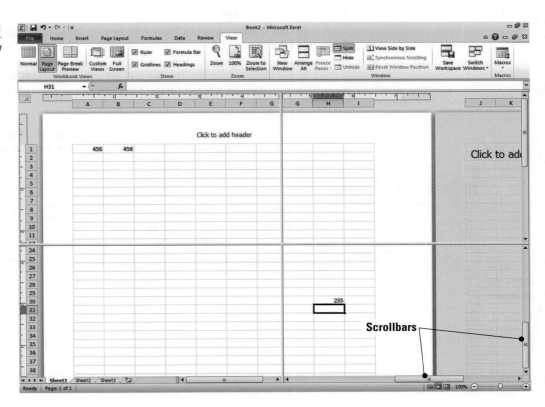

5. Click **Split** to remove the split. The data in cell H30 is no longer visible. However, if you click the **Split** command once more, you will again see all the data in this worksheet.

PAUSE. LEAVE the workbook open to use in the next exercise.

Take Note   The Split command is especially useful when you need to compare various portions of a long worksheet.

When you use a worksheet that contains a small amount of data, it is easy to scroll through the worksheet and focus on specific cells. As you become experienced in working with Excel, however, you may find yourself working on much larger worksheets. The ability to view more than one section of a worksheet at the same time by using split windows is especially useful when you need to compare different sections of data.

Opening a New Window

Splitting a window allows you to look at two sections of a worksheet side by side. You can also view two sections of a worksheet by using the New Window command. In this section, you learn to use the New Window command on the View tab to open a new window in Excel. You also learn to use the Switch Window command to change the active window, and you learn how to close multiple windows.

STEP BY STEP   **Open a New Window**

USE the open workbook from the previous exercise to complete these steps:

1. Make **A1** the active cell.
2. With the View tab active, click **New Window** in the Window group. A new window titled *Book2:2* opens.
3. Scroll down in the window until cell H30 is visible, as shown in Figure 1-12. Although cell A1 is not visible, it is still the active cell. It is important to note that you have opened a new view of the active worksheet—not a new worksheet.

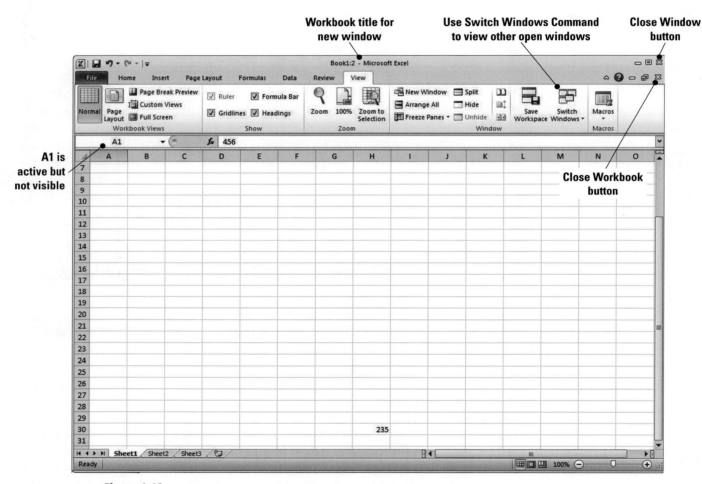

Figure 1-12

A new window

4. Click **Switch Windows**; a drop-down list of all open windows appears. *Book2:2* is checked, which indicates that it is the active window.
5. Click **Book2:1**. You will now see the original view of the worksheet with cell A1 active.
6. Click **Switch Windows** and make Book2:2 active.

7. Click the **Close Window** button (in the upper-right corner of the workbook window) to close Book2:2. The window closes, and the title Book2 tells you that you are now looking at the only open view of this workbook.

Clicking the Close Window button will close only the new window opened at the beginning of this exercise. If you use the Close command in the Microsoft File tab, you will close the entire workbook.

8. Click the **File** tab and then click **Close**.
9. When asked if you want to save the changes to Book2, click **No**.

PAUSE. LEAVE Excel open to use in the next exercise.

WORKING WITH AN EXISTING WORKBOOK

Many workbooks require frequent updating because existing data has changed or new data must be added. Workers frequently open an existing workbook, update information, and then save the workbook to be revised again at a later time. Often, files are created by one person, then used and/or updated by others. Filenames should reflect the type of data contained in the file. A descriptive filename enables workers to locate and retrieve files quickly. Filenames can be up to 255 characters long, including the filename extension. However, most workers use short, descriptive filenames that clearly identify the content of the workbook.

Opening an Existing Workbook

When you save an Excel 2010 file, the program automatically adds the .xlsx extension to the end of the file's name. This extension identifies the program in which the file can be opened. For example, .xlsx is the file extension used in Excel. To open a file, you must also identify the drive and folder that contain the file. In your local computer environment, generally by default, your local drive is designated as C:.

In this exercise, you will use commands from the File tab in Backstage view to find and open an existing workbook.

Open an Existing Workbook

BEFORE you begin this exercise, log in to the WileyPLUS website for your course and download the appropriate data files for this lesson. Then, perform these steps:

1. Within Excel, click the **File** tab. Documents you recently created or edited will appear on the right side in the Recent Documents area.
2. Click **Open**. The Open dialog box will appear.

Throughout this chapter you will see information that appears in black text within brackets, such as [Press **Enter**], or [your email address]. The information contained in the brackets is intended to be directions for you rather than something you actually type word for word. It will instruct you to perform an action or substitute text. Do **not** type the actual text that appears within brackets.

3. In the Recent Workbooks area, click [the name of the data files for this lesson]. (Again, lesson files can be downloaded from the companion website or accessed for download from WileyPLUS.)

By default, the Open dialog box lists only the files that were created in the program you are using—in this case, Excel. To see files created in other programs, you can select All Files in the Files of type box at the bottom of the Open dialog box.

4. Select *Contoso Employee Info* from the listed files, and then click **Open**. The file opens, as shown in Figure 1-13, with the workbook name displayed in the title bar.

Figure 1-13

Opening an existing worksheet

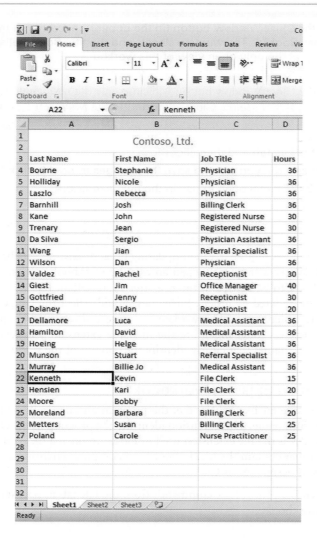

PAUSE. LEAVE the workbook open to use in the next exercise.

If you are familiar with Microsoft Word, you know that when you open a file, the program places your cursor and screen display at the beginning of the document. When you open an Excel workbook, however, the active cell is the same one that was active when you last saved the file. For example, when you open the Contoso Employee Info workbook, A22 is the active cell in Normal view, because A22 was the active cell displayed in Normal view when the file was last saved. This feature enables you to continue working in the same location when you return to the workbook.

Navigating a Worksheet

An Excel worksheet can contain more than one million rows and more than sixteen thousand columns. There are several ways to move through worksheets that contain numerous rows and columns. You can use the arrow keys, the scrollbars, or the mouse to navigate through a worksheet. In the following exercises, you will explore the different methods for moving through a worksheet.

| STEP BY STEP | **Navigate a Worksheet** |

USE the workbook you left open in the previous exercise to perform these steps:

1. Press **Ctrl+Home** to move to the beginning of the document (cell A1).
2. Press **Ctrl+End** to move to the end of the document (cell D27).
3. Click cell **A27** to make it the active cell, and press **Page Up**. The cursor moves to cell A1.
4. Click cell **A3** to make it active, then press **Ctrl+Page Down** to go to the last row of data (cell A27).
5. Press **Ctrl+Right Arrow**. The cursor moves to D27, the last column in the range of data. The unused cells below the data are considered a range.
6. Press **Ctrl+Down Arrow**. The cursor moves to the last possible row in the worksheet.

 Ref

Take Note

> You will learn about ranges in more depth in Lesson 3.

Ctrl+Arrow allows you to move to the start and end of ranges of data. The title, which spans all the columns, is not considered part of the worksheet's data range.

 Another Way
The cell **Name box** is located below the Ribbon at the left end of the formula bar. When you key a cell location in this box and press Enter, the cursor moves to that cell. This is another way to efficiently navigate your worksheet.

7. Press **Ctrl+Home**.
8. Press **Scroll Lock** while you press the **Right Arrow** key. This moves the active column one column to the right.
9. Use the vertical scrollbar (refer to Figure 1-11) to navigate from the beginning to the end of the data.
10. If your mouse has a wheel button, roll the wheel button forward and back to quickly scroll through the worksheet.

Take Note

When Scroll Lock is on, *scroll lock* is displayed on the left side of the Status bar. If you want to use the arrow keys to move between cells, you must turn off Scroll Lock. Some keyboards come equipped with an onboard scroll lock key, while others do not. This is an option not a necessity.

PAUSE. CLOSE the workbook before moving to the next exercise.

WORKING WITH EXCEL'S HELP SYSTEM

| The Bottom Line |

The **Help system** in Excel 2010 is rich in information, illustrations, and tips that can help you complete any task as you create worksheets and workbooks. When you install Excel, you automatically install hundreds of help topics on your computer. Excel can also access thousands of additional help topics online.

Using the Help System

Finding the right information in Excel's Help system is easy: You can pick a topic from the Help system's table of contents, browse a directory of Help topics, or perform keyword searches by entering terms that best describe the task you want to complete. In this exercise, you learn to open the Help dialog box and move between its online and offline topics.

Take Note

If you aren't sure what an onscreen tool does, just point to it. Once the mouse pointer rests on a tool, a box called a ScreenTip appears. A basic ScreenTip displays the tool's name and shortcut key (if a shortcut exists for that tool). Some of the Ribbon's tools have enhanced ScreenTips, which also provide a brief description of the tool.

STEP BY STEP   **Use the Help System**

OPEN a new worksheet for this exercise. Then, follow these steps:

1. Position your mouse pointer over the Help button, as shown in Figure 1-14, in the upper-right corner of your Excel screen. A ScreenTip appears, telling you that this button enables you to access Excel's Help features.

Figure 1-14

Help button

2. Click the Help button; the Help window opens, as shown in Figure 1-15.

Figure 1-15

Help window

Another Way
Even if Excel is set to work offline, you can still search for help online. To do so, instead of clicking the Search button, click the drop-down arrow next to it. When the menu appears, click the Content from Office Online link. The choice will affect only the current search, not Excel's overall settings.

3. In the Help window, click on the Getting started with Excel hyperlink. The next screen gives you additional hyperlinked subcategories.
4. Navigate through three of the subtopics in the Help window.
5. Click the Office Help Connection Status button in the bottom-right corner of the Help window. This produces the Connection Status dialog box shown in Figure 1-16. This feature enables you to choose whether the Help window displays online or offline Help content.

Figure 1-16

Connection Status dialog box

Another Way
You can access the Help Feature at any time by pressing the F1 key.

6. CLOSE the Help window.
CLOSE your workbook.

Excel's Help window gives you access to various help topics that offer information about specific Excel features or tools. Help topics can assist you with virtually any task, feature, or problem you encounter when working with Excel.

The Help window is set up like a browser, with links to specific categories and topics, and it features some of the same tools you will find in your web browser, including:

Back: Jumps to the previously opened Help topic

Forward: Jumps to the next opened Help topic

Stop: Stops any action in progress

Refresh: Reloads the current Help topic

Home: Returns to the initial Help Dialog Window

Print: Allows you to print the current Help topic

Take Note

Many Excel dialog boxes contain a Help button. When you click it, a Help window opens with information about that dialog box.

You can find help in several different ways. For example, you can open the table of contents and scan the list for help on a specific topic or feature. You can also enter a keyword or phrase in the Search box, then click the Search button. When you do this, related help topics appear in the Help window.

The Search button gives you additional options when looking for help. When you click the drop-down arrow next to the Search button, you have the option to search for help online or offline, look for Excel templates, find information about formulas and spreadsheet development, and more.

The Connection Status menu lets you use other help topics that are available online or just those topics installed on your computer (referred to as "offline help"). If your computer has an "always on" connection to the Internet, such as a cable modem or LAN connection, you may want to set the Connection Status to *Show content from Office Online*, which is Microsoft's online-based built-in help system. If your computer uses a dial-up modem, or if you simply choose not to use this feature, choose the *Show content only from this computer* option to work with the offline help feature and topics installed on your machine.

SKILL SUMMARY

In This Lesson, You Learned How To:
Start Excel
Work in the Excel window
Change Excel's view
Work with an existing workbook
Work with Excel's help system

Knowledge Assessment

Fill in the Blank

Complete the following sentences by writing the correct word or words in the blanks provided.

1. An arrow at the bottom of a group header on the Ribbon tells you that a(n) _____ is available that will offer additional options.
2. A selected cell is called the _____.
3. _____ view is a new feature in Office 2010 that enables you to easily navigate and customize different features in Excel.
4. After a file has been opened, the filename appears in the _____.
5. When you split a window, the window is divided into _____ panes.
6. When you click the Help button, the _____ opens.
7. A cell is formed by the intersection of _____.
8. The _____ can be customized and contains the commands you use most frequently.
9. A new Excel workbook opens with _____ worksheets.
10. An active cell is identified because it is the _____ cell.

True/False

Circle T if the statement is true or F if the statement is false.

T   F   1. Pressing the F1 key will activate Backstage.
T   F   2. Pressing the Alt key will activate ScreenTips that help you use the keyboard shortcuts.
T   F   3. Ctrl+O will open a new blank workbook.
T   F   4. The Quick Access Toolbar appears on the right side of the title bar, above the Ribbon.
T   F   5. Ctrl+F will activate Backstage.
T   F   6. Keytips can guide you to access the Backstage area.
T   F   7. Excel opens with a new blank workbook displayed.
T   F   8. The columns in a worksheet are identified by numbers.
T   F   9. The active cell in a worksheet is outlined by a bold black line.
T   F   10. Page Layout view is useful when preparing your data for printing.

Competency Assessment

Project 1-1: Utilizing Help

Use this lesson to better familiarize yourself with the Help System.

GET READY. LAUNCH Excel if it is not already running.

1. On the right side of the Ribbon, click the Help button.
2. When the Help window opens, key How to use Excel Help into the Search bar, and press Enter.
3. When the next screen appears, find the link to *What's New in Excel 2010* and click on it.
4. Choose three of the topics that interest you and examine them.
5. Click the Back button as needed to return to the previous topic searched. Click it again to go back to the Search results window.

6. Click on the article titled *Use Office Excel 2010 with earlier versions of Excel*. Examine and read the contents.

7. Close the **Help** window. The **Close** button is in the upper-right corner of the window.

CLOSE the workbook.

Project 1-2: Utilizing the Ribbon

GET READY. LAUNCH Excel if it is not already running.

1. Click the **File** tab. This is your instant access to Backstage. Click several of the commands in Backstage that are shown on the navigation bar on the left side of the Excel window. Get a feel for the environment.

2. Click the **Home** tab. Move your cursor over the **Ribbon**, reading the various ScreenTips that appear as your cursor rests over individual Ribbon elements.

3. In the **Font** command group area, click the **arrow** next to the font box. Note that the first font at the top of the font list is displayed. Click on the drop-down arrow again to hide the list.

4. In the font box, type a **T**. You will see the list change. Choose Times New Roman. Note the corresponding change in font.

5. Move your cursor up to the Quick Access Toolbar and click the **Undo** arrow. Note that your font returns to the default font face, either Times New Roman or Calibri.

6. Click the **Insert** tab. Move your cursor over the Ribbon and examine it while reading the **ScreenTips**.

7. Next click the **View** tab. Once again mouse over the Ribbon and examine its features.

8. Click the **File** tab again to display Backstage view.

Click the **Exit** command at the bottom of the navigation bar to close the application completely. If prompted to save the document, choose No.

Proficiency Assessment

Project 1-3: Organizing Data

You are consolidating your life and have items in storage you would like to sell. Because you are not yet sure about the value of these items, you need to gather research information (data) about them. Worksheets are excellent tools for organizing information so you can make easy comparisons between sets of data.

1. Identify a list of at least ten items that you have in storage that you would like to sell as quickly, efficiently, and inexpensively as possible. They can range from large items to small items.

2. **START** Excel and create a new workbook. Click the **File** tab and save this workbook as *Items for Sale_1*.

3. In cell **A1**, key **Item**. Press **Enter**.

4. In cell **B1**, type **Cost**.

5. In cell **C1**, key **Sell For**.

6. In cell **D1**, key **Sold**.

7. In cell **E1**, key **Donated**.

8. Beginning in cell **A2**, key the name of your first item. Repeat this step in cells **A3–A11** until you have 10 items listed.

9. Minimize Excel.

10. Open a web browser on your computer and navigate to your favorite search engine.

11. In the keywords box for your search, key **Price of [your item](Amount)**, then click **Enter**. View your results. Don't be discouraged—it might take a few tries to get some information.

12. When you have an estimated price for your first item, key it in cell B2.
13. Repeat steps 11 and 12 until you have keyed in the estimated values for all 10 items.
CLOSE Excel.

Project 1-4: Changing Data

In this exercise, you will use the previously created workbook to accommodate changes to your data.

LAUNCH Excel.

1. Click the File tab to engage Backstage.
2. Move your cursor to the Recent command; the command will highlight green.
3. Click the Recent command. The screen displays your most recent documents, including your workbook titled *Items for Sale_1*.
4. Click on this file to open it. **SAVE** the file as *Items for Sale_2*.
5. Make cell C2 active by clicking it, then key in the amount to sell that item at auction.
6. If you predict an item that you have might not sell, put an X in the appropriate box for donated in the cell created in column E.
7. Click the Close button in the upper-right corner of Excel. When prompted to save the worksheet, click OK.

PAUSE. CLOSE the workbook and **LEAVE** Excel open for the next exercise.

Mastery Assessment

Project 1-5: Altering a Workbook

In this exercise, you will use the Home and File tabs to open and edit your worksheet titled *Items for Sale_1*.

OPEN Excel.

1. Click the File tab, and then click the Recent button in the navigation pane.
2. Open the worksheet *Items for Sale_1*. Save the file as *Items for Sale_3*.
3. Click Ctrl+Home to go to the beginning of the worksheet.
4. Now that cell A1 is active, click on the View tab.
5. Click the Full screen button. You are now in full screen view. Notice the split screen view and no Ribbon. To exit full screen view, press Esc.
6. Click Page Break Preview. The Welcome to Page Break Preview dialog box will appear to tell you how to drag break lines; click OK to close the box. Note that your active data cells are highlighted in blue. Click the Normal view button to return to your original state. Note that now a dotted line denotes your page breaks.

PAUSE. CLOSE Excel. If prompted to save the file, do so.

Project 1-6: Altering Excel's View

In this project, you will continue to explore the Ribbon and its features.

START Excel.

1. **OPEN** *Items for Sale_1* from Backstage. **SAVE** the file as *Items for Sale*.
2. Click the View tab on the Ribbon.
3. Click the Page Layout button. Examine your data in this view.
4. On the Ribbon, in the Zoom command group, click the Zoom to Selection button. Notice that you now see all your data in extreme close-up view.
5. On the Quick Access Toolbar, click the Undo arrow.

6. Click the New Window button in the Window command group.

7. Click the Arrange All button in the same command group.

8. When the Arrange Windows dialog box appears, choose Horizontal. Click OK. Take note of the arrangement of Book 1:1 and Book 1:2.

9. Click the Arrange All button again and choose Tiled. Click OK. Your windows are now side by side.

10. On the left side, in Book 1:2, click the Close button in the upper-right corner.

11. Now that only Book 1 is remaining, click the Maximize button to return the worksheet to full screen.

12. Return to Normal view by clicking the Normal button in the Workbook Views command group on the Ribbon.

CLOSE and **SAVE** this worksheet.

INTERNET READY

In this lesson, you learned how to navigate the Ribbon, use Onscreen Tools, and begin to manipulate a worksheet. Use Excel's Help system to gain further knowledge of these topics.

1. Click the Help button on the right side of the Ribbon.

2. Key Ribbon in the Search box at the top of the Help window.

3. Click Search. From the search result, open a topic that will provide information about selecting cells.

4. Repeat Steps 2 and 3 for Onscreen Tools, Backstage, and Excel views.

5. Share your findings with your instructor and classmates.

2 Using Backstage

LESSON SKILL MATRIX

In This Lesson, You Will Learn The Following Skills:

Accessing and Using Backstage View

Printing with Backstage

Changing the Excel Environment in Backstage

Accessing and Using Excel Templates

KEY TERMS

- **default settings**
- **Definitive Command**
- **Document properties**
- **Fast Command**
- **Print options**
- **tab**
- **template**

Contoso, Ltd., employs hundreds of employees. The company likes to reward its employees by having monthly potluck dinners. They also like to share the homemade recipes within their company. These recipes are published for everyone on a quarterly basis. In particular, the recipes are housed and submitted for print in Excel worksheets. In this lesson, you will learn how to create the types of worksheets Contoso uses for this task. You will also learn how to share and send these worksheets to others.

SOFTWARE ORIENTATION

Microsoft 2010 Excel Backstage View

NEW to Office 2010

As you learned in Lesson 1, Backstage view enables you to use and master Excel's file management features—functions that aren't related to creating workbooks. (The commands you use when creating and editing workbooks are contained in the Ribbon and the Quick Access Toolbar.) Backstage view replaces the system of layered menus, toolbars, and panes used in previous versions of Excel.

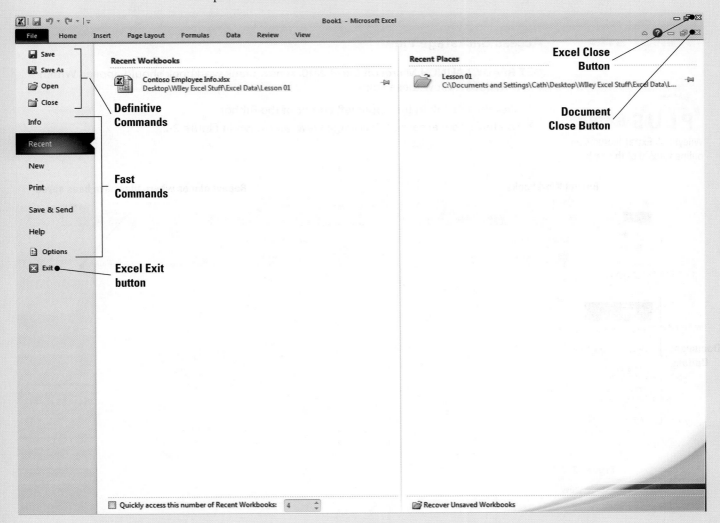

Figure 2-1

Backstage view

Backstage view's left-side navigation pane (Figure 2-1) gives you access to workbook and file-related commands, including Save, Save As, Open, and Close. The navigation pane also holds a series of **tabs**—Recent, Info, New, Print, Save & Send, Help, and Options—that you can click to access groups of related functions and commands. The Exit button on the navigation pane closes Excel.

ACCESSING AND USING BACKSTAGE VIEW

The Bottom Line

In the Excel 2010 window, you will see the green File tab in the upper-left corner. This is your access to Backstage view. When you click the File tab for Backstage, you will see a navigation pane containing many of the same commands that could be accessed through the Microsoft Office button in previous versions of Excel. In this section, you access Backstage view and use these commands to close a file.

By default, when you first enter Backstage view, the Info Fast Command is active. A **Fast Command** provides quick access to common functions and is located on the left navigation pane. Fast Commands include Print, Info, Recent, Save & Send, and New. Backstage view also contains Definitive Commands, such as Save, Save As, and Close. When you use **Definitive Commands**, these commands close Backstage view and return you to your workbook.

In this exercise, you revisit how to access Backstage view.

STEP BY STEP   **Access Backstage View**

GET READY. LAUNCH Microsoft Excel 2010. A new blank workbook should appear. Within the workbook, follow these steps:

WileyPLUS Extra! features an online tutorial of this task.

1. Click the File tab in the upper-left corner of the Ribbon.
2. You have now accessed Backstage view, as shown in Figure 2-2.

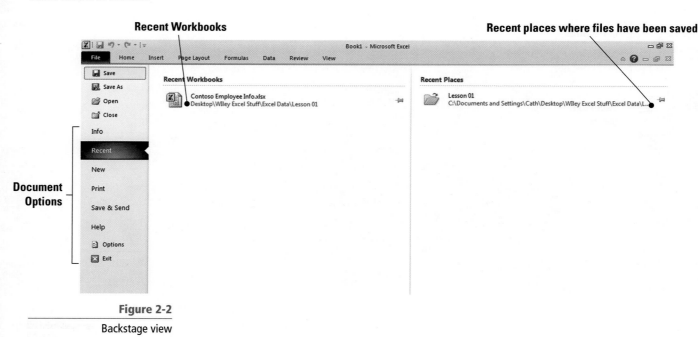

Figure 2-2

Backstage view

Another Way
If you use Print Preview quite often, you can save yourself time and steps by adding it to the Quick Access Toolbar in order to create a shortcut to Backstage view. This process will be explained in greater depth later in this lesson.

3. Take a few moments to familiarize yourself with this view and the tools in its navigation pane.

CLOSE Excel.

Saving a Document with Backstage

In Excel, you can use Backstage view to view, save, print, and organize workbooks or worksheets. In this exercise, you create a new workbook in Excel, edit its contents, and then save the workbook using Backstage view.

STEP BY STEP | **Save a Document with Backstage**

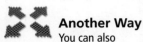

Another Way
You can also click Ctrl+N to open a new workbook and activate the Backstage area.

GET READY. LAUNCH Microsoft Excel 2010; a new blank workbook will open. Using this workbook, complete the following steps:

1. In the new workbook, cell A1 should be the active cell. Key **Recipe** in this cell, and notice that the text appears in both the cell and the Formula Bar as you type.

2. Press **Tab**; the text is entered into cell A1, and B1 becomes the active cell.

3. Now key **Recipe Description** and press **Tab**. The text is entered into B1, and C1 becomes the active cell. Note that the text from B1 is flowing over into cell C1.

4. Key **Cooking Directions** into C1 and press **Tab**. Note that the text in cell B1 has now been hidden behind cell C1, and the contents of cell C1 are seen flowing into cell D1. In order to view the data in the column, you must double-click the column divider. Place your cursor on the divider between column B and C and double click. Note that the column resizes to accommodate the data. Refer to Figure 2-3.

Figure 2-3

Adjusting a column to fit data

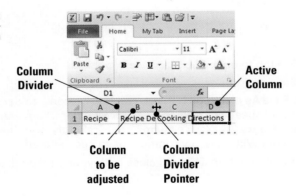

5. Key **Main Ingredients** into cell D1, then press **Tab**.

6. Key **Alternate Ingredients** into cell E1 and press **Tab**.

7. Key **Serving Size** into F1 and press **Tab**.

8. Repeat the process explained in step 4 to adjust all columns to fit the data. Refer to Figure 2-3 as needed.

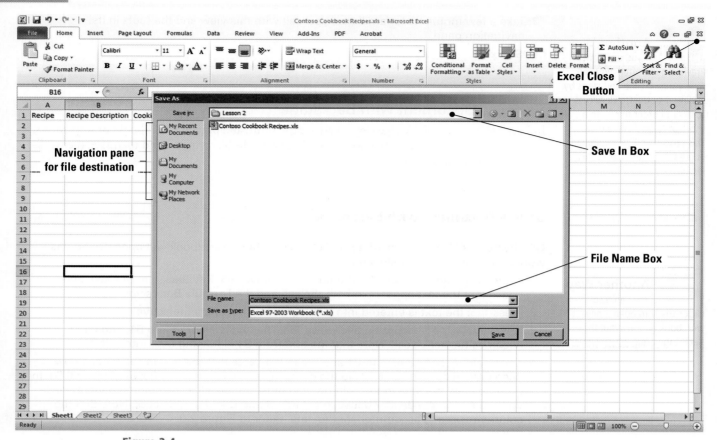

Figure 2-4

Save As dialog box

9. Click the **File** tab to open Backstage view.

10. Click the **Save** option.

11. When the **Save As** dialog box opens, create a Lesson 2 folder in My Documents and save your worksheet as *Contoso Cookbook Recipes*. Your window should appear as shown in Figure 2-4. Your view may differ slightly from the figure if the default settings in your Windows environment have been altered.

PAUSE. Click the **Exit** button. This will close both your workbook and Excel.

Another Way
In the Word section, you were asked to save files to a USB drive. In this lesson you will save files to the My Documents directory on your computer. Your instructor may ask you to save to a different location based on your school's policies.

To use the Save As feature, you would follow the steps in the previous lesson, but choose Save As and complete your task. You should choose the Save As option to save to a different destination, change a file's name, and/or change a file's format.

Take Note

In Excel, the AutoRecover feature is installed by default. It will automatically save your workbook every 10 minutes. This can be customized to suit your needs. You can review and change these features in Excel Options.

PRINTING WITH BACKSTAGE

The Bottom Line

The Backstage area contains Excel's Print commands and options. You can use the Print dialog box to manipulate workbook elements such as margins, orientation, paper size, and so on.

Printing and Previewing with Backstage

Backstage view includes a Print Preview pane in the Print dialog box so you can preview your workbook as you choose Print options. In this exercise, you learn to use the Print and Print Preview features in Excel.

STEP BY STEP   **Print and Print Preview with Backstage**

GET READY. LAUNCH Microsoft Excel 2010. Then, follow these steps:

1. Click the **File** tab in the upper-left corner of the Ribbon to access Backstage.

2. Click the **Recent** command in the Backstage view navigation pane.

3. You should now see your recently created and used workbooks. Click on *Contoso Cookbook Recipes* to open the file.

Another Way
You can also Click Ctrl+O to open a workbook on your computer. This keystroke activates the Open dialog box, which allows you to navigate to the file you want to open.

Print button in navigation pane

Print Options Area

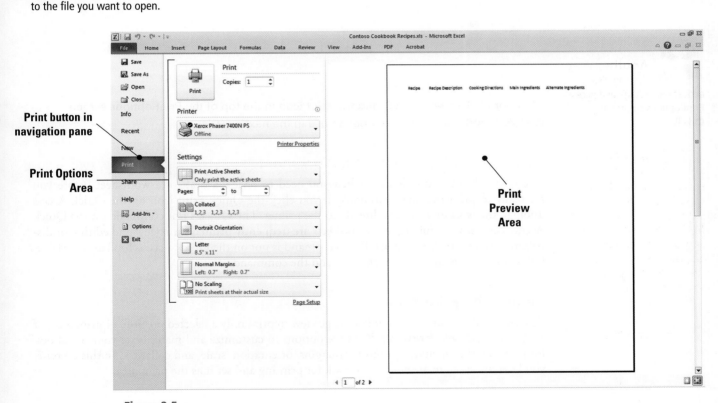

Figure 2-5

Document preview

4. Click the **File** tab to open Backstage. In the navigation pane, click **Print**. Note that this opens the Print options page of Backstage (see Figure 2-5). Take a moment to preview the workbook in the Print Preview section in the right pane and to read

through the Print options listed in the center section of the page. The printing options section of the window is shown in Figure 2-6.

Figure 2-6

Printing options

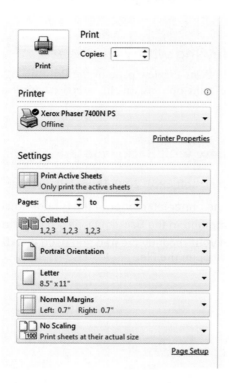

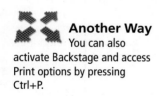
Another Way
You can also activate Backstage and access Print options by pressing Ctrl+P.

5. To print your worksheet, click the **Print** icon in the top of the Print options screen.
PAUSE. LEAVE the worksheet open to use in the next exercise.

Using Quick Print to Print a Worksheet

The Quick Print option is used when you need to review a draft of a worksheet before you are ready to print the final workbook. If you click the Quick Print icon on the Quick Access Toolbar, the worksheet is sent directly to the printer. The Quick Print command on the Quick Access Toolbar is useful because worksheets are frequently printed for review and editing or distribution to others. If the Quick Print command is not on the Quick Access Toolbar by default, follow the steps in an earlier exercise to add the command.

Setting the Print Area

You can use the Print options in Backstage view to print only a selected portion, or print area, of an Excel workbook. **Print options** are options to customize and manipulate your workbook for printing; they include options for margins, orientation, scale, and collation. In this exercise, you learn to select an area of a workbook for printing and set it as the print area.

STEP BY STEP   **Set a Print Area**

GET READY. With *Contoso Cookbook Recipes* already open, follow these steps:

1. Click the Page Layout tab on the Ribbon.

2. Mouse over the Print Area button on the Ribbon in the *Page Setup* area. Note the tool tip that pops up defining the task to be completed.

3. On the worksheet, click cell A1, hold the mouse button, and drag the cursor to cell F6. Your cells should highlight in blue, as shown in Figure 2-7.

Figure 2-7

Setting print area

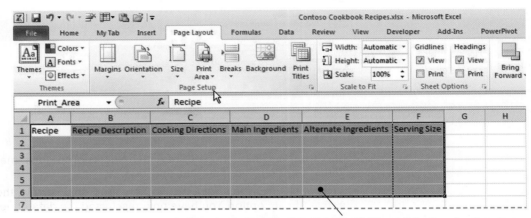

Highlighted Cells with dashed outline indicate Print Area has been set

4. With these cells highlighted, click the Print Area button drop-down arrow and choose Set Print Area from the menu that appears. You have now set the print area.

5. Click the File tab to access Backstage.

6. In the Print Preview pane on the right pane of the Print window, you should see the highlighted cells of your print area. You will not print at this time.

7. **PAUSE. SAVE** the workbook.

CLOSE Excel.

Printing Selected Worksheets with Backstage

In this exercise, you learn to access the options for printing individual worksheets within a workbook. You can use these options to print the current worksheet only or to print multiple worksheets that you have selected by page number.

STEP BY STEP   **Print Selected Worksheets with Backstage**

GET READY. LAUNCH Excel 2010. Then perform these steps:

1. Open Backstage view and click Recent in the navigation pane; in the list of Recent workbooks, click *Contoso Cookbook Recipes* to open the file.

2. Press Ctrl+P to activate Print options in the Backstage navigation pane.

3. In the *Settings* section of the center pane in Print options, click the Print Active Sheets drop-down arrow. In the drop-down menu that appears, as shown in Figure 2-8, you can choose several printing options for your workbook or worksheet.

Figure 2-8

Worksheet print options

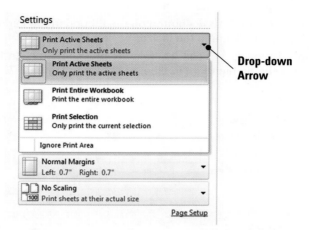

Drop-down Arrow

4. Click Print Selection in the Print Active Sheets drop-down menu; this option enables you to print *only* your current selection.

5. Once again click the Print Active Sheets drop-down arrow, then choose the Print Active Sheets option. You have now reselected the default option.

6. Click the Print icon at the top-left corner of the Print window.

CLOSE the workbook. **LEAVE** Excel open for the next exercise.

CHANGING THE EXCEL ENVIRONMENT IN BACKSTAGE

The Bottom Line

Backstage view also offers a number of commands and options for changing the Excel work environment. In this section, you learn to manipulate various elements of the Excel environment, such as the Ribbon, Quick Access Toolbar, Excel Default Settings, and Workbook Properties.

Customizing the Quick Access Toolbar with Backstage

You can't change the size of the Quick Access Toolbar, but you can customize it by adding and subtracting command buttons. In this exercise, you customize the Quick Access Toolbar by adding commands for functions you use most frequently in Excel, and by organizing the command buttons on the toolbar to best suit your working needs and style.

STEP BY STEP **Customize the Quick Access Toolbar with Backstage**

GET READY. LAUNCH Excel 2010. Then, take these actions:

1. Click the File tab to access Backstage view.

2. Locate and click the Options button in the navigation pane. The *Excel Options* window opens (see Figure 2-9).

Figure 2-9

Customizing the Quick Access
Toolbar options

Commands List   **Default Commands Group**   **Moved Command**

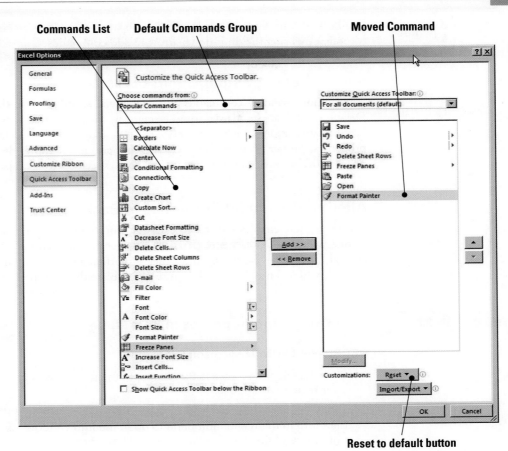

Figure 2-9

Customizing the Quick Access
Toolbar options

Reset to default button

3. In the left pane of the window, click Quick Access Toolbar item to open the *Quick Access Toolbar Options* dialog box. Refer to Figure 2-9. The left pane of this dialog box lists the commands that you could possibly add to the toolbar and the right pane shows the commands that are currently included on the toolbar.

4. In the left pane, click Format Painter, then Click the Add button in the center of the pane to move Format Painter to the Quick Access Toolbar.

5. Using the same process, move five more commands of your choice to the Quick Access Toolbar. When done, click OK to apply your changes (the changes don't take effect until you click OK).

6. Your Quick Access Toolbar should now include additional command buttons, much like the example shown in Figure 2-10. Similarly, you can remove any command that you add to the toolbar. Note that default commands cannot be removed. At any time you can reset the toolbar to its default settings. (See Figure 2-9.) Because your document was not affected by the toolbar changes, you will not be prompted to save any workbook changes.

Figure 2-10

Customized Quick Access
Toolbar

New Quick Access Toolbar Icons

CLOSE Excel.

Ref   In Lesson 1, in Using Onscreen Tools, you were shown how to customize the Quick Access Toolbar by using the drop-down arrow to add commands.

Excel's Default Settings with Backstage

The Options window commands also enable you to modify the **default settings** in Excel. Default settings are standard settings installed by the application as presets so that the application has the same settings each and every time it is accessed. These defaults can include worksheet properties, printer settings, font style and size, and much more. By default, for example, Excel opens with three worksheets in a new workbook, specific settings, a particular font size, and so on.

Altering Document Properties in Backstage

Backstage view enables you to access your workbook properties more easily and view them in one window. **Document properties** identify who created the document, when it was created, how large the file is, and other important information about the workbook. In this exercise, you will use this next lesson to manipulate those properties.

STEP BY STEP   **Alter Document Properties in Backstage**

GET READY. LAUNCH Microsoft Excel 2010.

1. Click the **File** tab to access Backstage; in the navigation pane, click **Recent**, to view your recent workbooks.
2. Open *Contoso Cookbook Recipes* from the list of recently opened workbooks.
3. Click **Info** in the navigation pane to open the Info window, as shown in Figure 2-11. The right pane of the window lists the workbook properties of the currently opened file.

Figure 2-11

Document properties

Info button in navigation pane   **Document Properties**

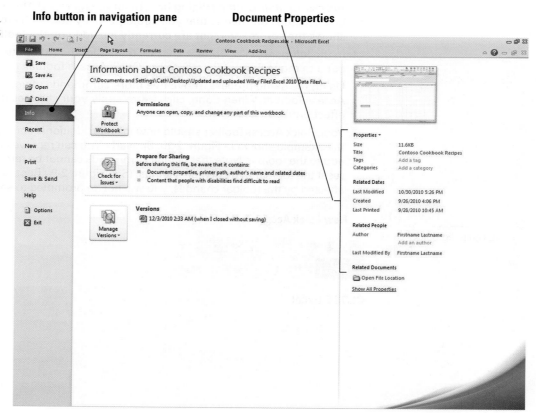

4. Click the **Properties** drop-down arrow to produce the drop-down menu shown in Figure 2-12. Click **Show Document Panel** to open the document panel.

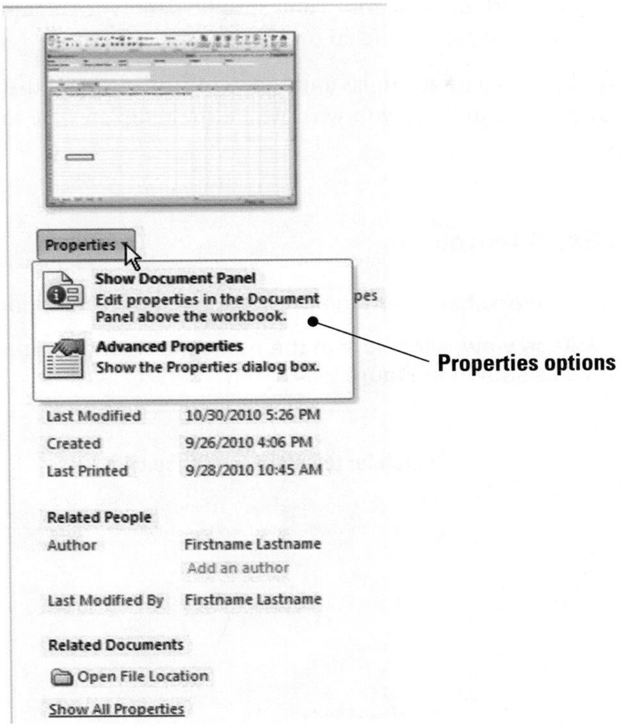

Figure 2-12

Properties drop-down menu

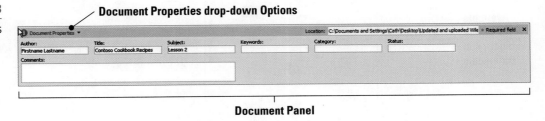

Properties options

5. In the document panel's Author text box, key **[your name]**. Key **Contoso Cookbook Recipes** in the *Title* text box, and **Lesson 2** in the *Subject* text box. The document panel should resemble the one shown in Figure 2-13.

Figure 2-13

Changing document properties

Document Properties drop-down Options

Document Panel

6. Click the **X** button in the upper right-hand corner of the document panel to close and save your changes.
7. Click the **File** tab to access Backstage, then click **Info** in the navigation pane. The workbook changes have been made.

PAUSE. LEAVE Excel open for the next exercise.

You will now be able to change and manipulate other document properties by accessing this feature in Backstage.

 Ref   We will address more advanced document properties in later lessons.

ACCESSING AND USING EXCEL TEMPLATES

Excel has numerous **templates** that are included in the application, and many more templates are available online at Office.com. Templates are files that already include formatting and formulas complete with designs, tools, and specific data types. Examples of these are budgets, loan models, invoices, calendars, and so on.

Many templates contain formulas and functions to help you customize them for your purposes. The exercise will familiarize you with where the templates are located and how to choose and use them.

STEP BY STEP   Access Excel Templates

USE the open worksheet from the previous exercise. Then, perform these steps:

1. In Backstage view, click **New** in the navigation pane to open the *Available Templates* window, as shown in Figure 2-14.

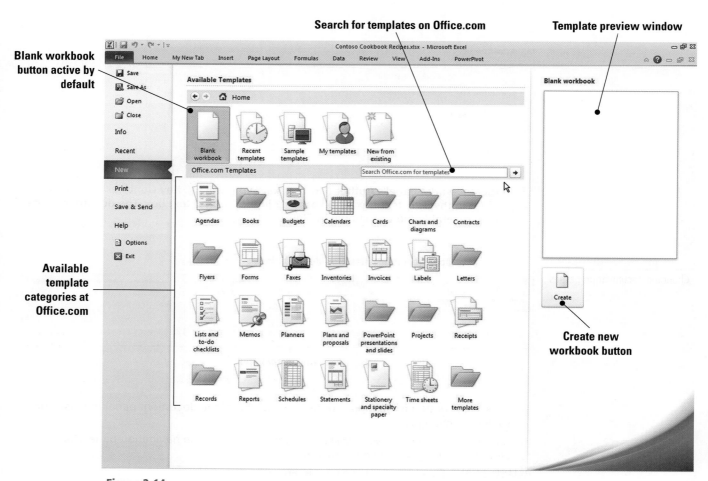

Figure 2-14

New File Options

2. Click the **Sample Templates** icon in the top-row gallery. The collection of sample templates included in Excel 2010 appears in the window.

3. Click the **Personal Monthly Budget** template listing; a preview of the template appears in the Preview pane. Your view should resemble Figure 2-15.

Figure 2-15

Templates

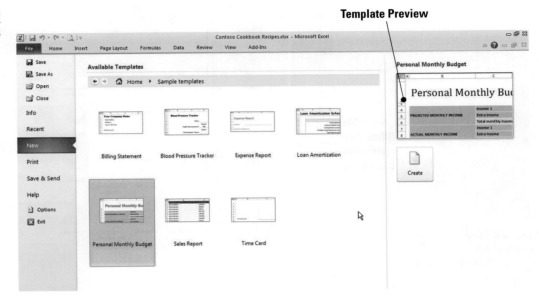

4. Click the **Create** button. The document properties panel opens, giving you the option to edit the properties before you begin working in the template.

5. In the document panel's Author text box, key **[your name]**. Key **Using Templates** in the *Title* text box and **Lesson 2** in the *Subject* text box. Close the document properties pane.

6. **CLOSE** the worksheet. When prompted to save changes, save the worksheet as *First Template*.

PAUSE. LEAVE Excel open for the next exercise. **CLOSE** Excel.

Accessing Excel Templates Online

Excel only comes with certain templates installed in the application itself. If you have an Internet connection, you have a direct link to templates at Office.com. You can search the Office archives for a template that suits your needs. Once found, the template can be instantly downloaded into the application and used. Once edited to your satisfaction, you can save it to your local environment to be used again and again. Figure 2-16 gives you an overview of the available templates categories offered in Office.com.

Figure 2-16

Template categories

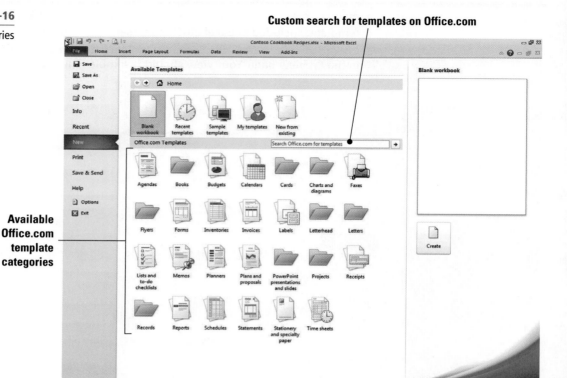

Custom search for templates on Office.com

Available Office.com template categories

SKILL SUMMARY

In This Lesson, You Learned How To:
Access and use Backstage view
Print with Backstage
Change the Excel environment in Backstage
Access and use Excel templates

Knowledge Assessment

Fill in the Blank

Complete the following sentences by writing the correct word or words in the blanks provided.

1. The area where you can save, choose a template, change document properties, and close or exit Excel is the _____.

2. To change a printer or margin settings, you click the File tab and use the _____ options.

3. You can customize the _____ for quicker access to the most commonly used commands.

4. By default the Quick Access toolbar is positioned _____ the Ribbon.

5. The _____ command in the Backstage navigation pane enables you to view and open your most recently used workbooks.

6. To view and alter your workbook's properties, you would access the _____ window in Backstage.

7. _____ are standard settings installed by the application.

8. To open Backstage, you click on the _____.

9. The Advanced Properties can also be accessed when the _____ is displayed in the worksheet.

10. The _____ contain vital information about your workbook such as file size, author, and date created.

True/False

Circle T if the statement is true or F if the statement is false.

T F 1. You cannot preview a worksheet in Backstage.

T F 2. Backstage view enables you to access the Microsoft website for custom templates.

T F 3. Use Ctrl+N to create a new workbook.

T F 4. When you want to access an Excel template, you click on the Template command in the Theme group on the Page Layout tab.

T F 5. A definitive command is located on the right navigation pane.

T F 6. You can view templates in the Recent section of Backstage view.

T F 7. You can access Backstage view by pressing Ctrl+N.

T F 8. By default, Excel starts a new workbook with four worksheets.

T F 9. In Excel, you can add your most commonly used commands to the Quick Access Toolbar.

T F 10. Backstage view has replaced the Microsoft Office button.

Competency Assessment

Project 2-1: Setting Print Area

Create a worksheet listing several different movies and their genre, then set a specific print area within the worksheet.

GET READY. LAUNCH Excel if it is not already running.

1. From Backstage, Click New and then click the Create button in the right pane of the Available Templates window to create a new worksheet.

2. Select cell A1, key Movie, and press Tab.

3. With B1 already active, key Genre.

4. Beginning in cell A2, key the data shown below. Ignore AutoComplete if prompted to use. You will learn more about this in future lessons.

Movie	Genre
Gone with the Wind	Drama
The Untouchables	Action
Frankenstein	Horror
Forrest Gump	Drama
Toy Story	Children's Animation

5. Double-click the column divider between columns A and B to adjust the column A width to display all of the text.

6. Double-click the label divider between columns B and C to adjust the column B width to display all of the text.

7. Click, hold, and drag the mouse from cell **A1** to **F3** to highlight. Click the Page Layout tab; in the Page Setup command group, click the Print Area drop-down arrow, and choose Set Print Area.

8. **SAVE** the worksheet as *Movies 2_1* and then close the file.

CLOSE Excel.

Project 2-2: Printing a Specific Area or Worksheet

You will print an active area and a specific worksheet.

GET READY. OPEN the file from the Lesson 2 folder titled *Movies 2_1*.

1. Open Backstage view.

2. Click Print in the Backstage navigation pane.

3. In the Settings section of the Print window, click the Print Active Sheets drop-down arrow, and click the Print Selection option in the drop-down menu.

4. Click the Print button in the upper section of the Print Settings to print the selected area of the worksheet.

5. Again in the Settings options, open the Print Active Sheets drop-down menu, and choose Print Active Sheets.

6. Click the Print button in the upper section of the Print Settings to print the active worksheet.

7. **PAUSE. SAVE** the workbook as *Movies 2_2*.

CLOSE Excel.

Proficiency Assessment

Project 2-3: Managing Document Properties

You are setting up a home office with new computer and communications equipment. Because you are not yet sure of your budget, you need several price options for each piece of equipment. Worksheets are excellent tools for organizing information so you can make easy comparisons between sets to data such as wholesale versus over the counter.

GET READY. LAUNCH Excel if it is not already running.

1. Identify a list of at least 12 pieces of equipment that a state-of-the-art home office needs. Some of these may include a desktop or laptop computer; a combination scanner, printer, and fax; a cordless phone; a cell phone; and so on.

2. **OPEN** Excel and **CREATE** a worksheet to store the list of equipment you have gathered. In Row 1, create column headings for your data. Beginning in cell A1, key Low End, Moderate, and High End so that you can enter three prices (amounts) for each equipment item.

3. Using advertisements from office supply stores and other retailers (or Internet resources, if available), find low-end, moderate, and high-end options for each equipment item you have listed. These options can be sale prices from ads, or just everyday prices for the items you've found.

4. Key your amounts of the items into the worksheet.

5. Adjust column and cell width so that you can clearly see all of the data you have entered.

6. Access Backstage, and click on Info.

7. You will modify the following elements in document properties:

Author:	Your First and Last Name
Title:	Project 2-3
Subject:	Lesson 2 Project
Tags:	Equipment
Categories:	Excel Lesson 2

8. Close the Document Properties window. You have now saved your settings.

9. Access Backstage and click on Info in the navigation pane to view your changes to your workbook properties. You will be able to view some of your changes. In order to see more, click the Show All Properties link at the bottom of the workbook properties.

10. **SAVE** your document as *Equipment 2_3*.

PAUSE. LEAVE Excel open for the next project.

Project 2-4: Changing the Quick Access Toolbar

You will customize the Quick Access Toolbar to accommodate commands for users who are not familiar with Excel and the Ribbon.

GET READY. LAUNCH Excel if it is not already running.

1. With the Home tab active, on the Ribbon, in the Alignment group, right-click on Center and choose Add to the Quick Access Toolbar.

2. Repeating these steps as necessary, using the appropriate tabs and groups, add the following commands to the toolbar: Borders, Increase Indent, Copy, Cut, and Paste. Note the changes to the toolbar in the upper-left portion of the screen.

3. To remove the new icons from the Quick Access Toolbar, right-click an icon in the Quick Access Toolbar and select Remove from Quick Access Toolbar. Repeat the process to remove the other icons you added.

EXIT Excel.

Mastery Assessment

Project 2-5: Customizing the Quick Access Toolbar

In class, you learned how to customize the Quick Access Toolbar. Your instructor has instructed you to select the following commands: Freeze Panes, Insert Functions, Name Manager, and Refresh All.

GET READY. LAUNCH Excel if not already running.

1. Click the File tab to access Backstage view.

2. Click the Options button in the navigation pane.

3. In the Excel Options window, click Quick Access Toolbar.

4. Add each of the commands to the Quick Access Toolbar.

5. Click OK.

LEAVE Excel open for the next project.

Project 2-6: Resetting the Quick Access Toolbar

In this exercise, you will be resetting the Quick Access Toolbar back to its default.

GET READY. LAUNCH Excel if not already running.

6. Click the File tab to access Backstage view.

7. Click the Options button in the navigation pane.

8. In the Excel Options window, click Quick Access Toolbar.

9. Reset to default.

10. Click OK.

LEAVE Excel open for the next project.

INTERNET READY

As was mentioned at the beginning of this lesson, Contoso, Ltd., is dedicated to treating its employees well. Use web search tools to locate five additional recipes to add to the cookbook spreadsheet. Use family and friends for research in this venture if possible. I am sure there is a favorite, mouth-watering recipe that will come to mind that you would love to include and share with others. Include two main courses, two side dishes, and one dessert. Find out as much information about the recipe as you can and include this in the worksheet. If you are able, add a new column to your spreadsheet to include a history of the recipe and ethnic origin.

Workplace *Ready*

MANAGING THE ENVIRONMENT IN EXCEL

Many Excel users don't realize that they can arrange and manage the Excel environment to suit their individual needs.

With the ability in Excel to customize by adding and managing toolbars, changing default settings, managing the Quick Access Toolbar and Ribbon, you can give the end user a more manageable and workable environment.

Your accounting department in your firm needs both the Quick Access Toolbar and the Ribbon customized to accommodate frequently used commands for accounting. Take time to create three new Ribbon tabs that will organize commonly used commands from the following tab groups:

Home:	Number, Cells
Formulas:	Function Library, Formula Auditing
Insert:	Charts

You can also take time to add common commands not already on the Quick Access Toolbar that would be more convenient there than clicking through tabs to use them.

This will give you practice and offer you and the end user a way to organize and use Excel to its greatest potential.

LESSON SKILL MATRIX

In This Lesson, You Will Learn The Following Skills:

Creating Workbooks

Entering and Editing Basic Data in a Worksheet

Using Data Types to Populate a Worksheet

Cutting, Copying, and Pasting Data

Editing a Workbook's Keywords

Saving the Workbook

KEY TERMS

- auto fill
- AutoComplete
- copy
- copy pointer
- cut
- fill handle
- formula bar
- keywords
- label
- move pointer
- natural series
- Office Clipboard
- paste
- range
- selecting text

Purchasing a home is usually the biggest financial investment most people make in a lifetime. Real estate agents advise and assist those who want to buy a new home or sell their present home. Agents must be licensed by their state. Many licensed agents also become Realtors®. This is a trademarked name that an agent can use only when he or she joins the local, state, and national associations of Realtors®. Fabrikam, Inc., located in Columbus, Ohio, is a real estate firm owned by Richard Carey and David Ortiz. Fabrikam has five full-time sales agents. Fabrikam uses an Excel workbook to track each agent's sales data by date of last sale. In this lesson, you will continue to view, add, and manipulate data in an Excel 2010 spreadsheet similar to that used by the Contoso, Ltd.

SOFTWARE ORIENTATION

Excel's Home Tab

The Ribbon in Microsoft Office Excel 2010 is made up of a series of tabs, each related to specific kinds of tasks that workers do in Excel. The Home tab, shown in Figure 3-1, contains the commands that people use the most when creating Excel documents. Having commands visible on the work surface enables you to work quickly and efficiently. Each tab contains groups of commands related to specific tasks or functions.

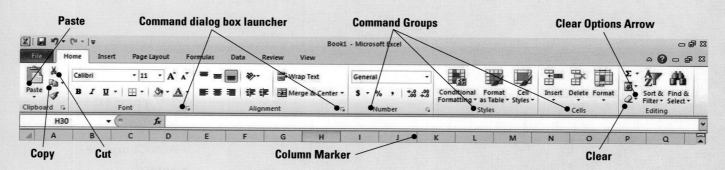

Figure 3-1

Worksheet/Workbook view

Below, in Figure 3-2, you see the Home tab, its command groups, and other Ribbon tools. Your screen may vary if default settings have been changed or if other preferences have been set. Use this figure as a reference throughout this lesson as well as the rest of this book.

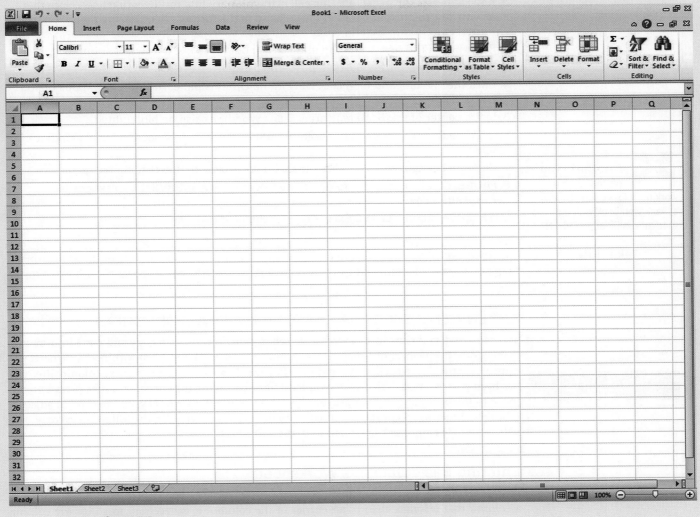

Figure 3-2

Home tab

CREATING WORKBOOKS

There are three ways to create a new Microsoft Excel workbook. You can open a new, blank workbook using the File tab to access Backstage. You can open an existing Excel workbook, enter new or additional data, and save the file with a new name, thus creating a new workbook. You can also use a template to create a new workbook. A template is a model that has already been set up to track certain kinds of data, such as sales reports, invoices, etc.

Starting a Workbook from Scratch

When you want to create a new workbook, launch Excel and a blank workbook is ready for you to begin working. If you have already been working in Excel and want to begin a new workbook, click the File tab, click New, and then click Create to create a blank workbook. Worksheets usually begin with a title that sets the stage for the reader's interpretation of the data contained in a worksheet. In this exercise, you will create a new Excel workbook to be used as a sales report.

Start a Workbook from Scratch

GET READY. LAUNCH Excel. A blank workbook opens with A1 as the active cell.

1. Key Fabrikam, Inc in cell A1. This cell is the primary title for the worksheet. Note that as you key, the text appears in the cell and in the formula bar. See the definition of formula bar in the "Editing a Cell's Contents" exercise on page 347.
2. Press Enter. The text is entered into cell A1, but looks like it flows over into B1.
3. **In cell** A2, key Monthly Sales Report. Press Enter.
4. **Click the** File tab, and then click New in the Options pane. The *New Workbook* dialog box will open.
5. In the center of the *Backstage* area, Blank Workbook will be highlighted.
6. Click the Create button on the bottom right of the screen. A second Excel workbook is opened.
7. Click the File tab, and then click Close. Book2 is closed. Book1 remains open.
8. **PAUSE.** Create a Lesson 3 folder in My Documents and **SAVE** the workbook as *Fabrikam Sales_3*.

CLOSE the workbook. **LEAVE** Excel open for the next exercise.

Another Way
When you are working in Excel, you can open a blank workbook with the shortcut combination Ctrl+N.

Take Note   Text is stored in only one cell even when it appears to extend into adjacent cells. If an entry is longer than the cell width and the next cell contains data, the entry appears in truncated form.

ENTERING AND EDITING BASIC DATA IN A WORKSHEET

The Bottom Line

You can key data directly into a worksheet cell or cells. You also can copy and paste information from another worksheet or from other programs. To enter data in a cell within a worksheet, you must make the desired cell active and then key the data. To move to the next column after text has been entered, press Tab. When you have finished keying the entries in a row, press Enter to move to the beginning of the next row. You also can use the arrow keys to move to an adjacent cell. Press Enter to accept the proposed entry or continue keying. In the following exercise, you will add a new employee's information to the worksheet.

Entering Basic Data in a Worksheet

In Excel, column width is established based on the existing data. When you add an entry in a column that is longer than other entries in the column, it is necessary to adjust the column width to accommodate the entry.

Enter Basic Data in a Worksheet

GET READY. OPEN the workbook titled *Contoso Employee Info*.

1. Move to cell A28.
2. **Key** Simon and press Tab.
3. **Key** Britta and press Tab.
4. Key Administrative Assistant and press Tab.
5. **Key** 36 and press Enter.
6. **Double-click the** column marker (line between two columns, refer to Figure 3-1) between columns C and D to so that the entire text is visible in column C.

PAUSE. LEAVE the workbook open to use in the next exercise.

The *Contoso Employee Info* file for this lesson is available on the book companion website or in WileyPLUS.

Take Note   When you key text that is longer than the cell, the text extends into the next cell. However, when you press Tab and move to the next cell, the overflow text is not displayed. The text is still there. You will learn more about adjusting the column width later in this lesson.

Editing a Cell's Contents

One advantage of electronic records versus manual ones is that changes can be made quickly and easily. To edit information in a worksheet, you can make changes directly in the cell or edit the contents of a cell in the **formula bar**, located between the Ribbon and the worksheet. When you enter data in a cell, the text or numbers appear in the cell and in the formula bar. You can also enter or edit data directly in the formula bar. Before changes can be made, however, you must select the information that is to be changed. **Selecting text** means that you highlight the text that is to be changed. You can select a single cell, a row, a column, a range of cells, or an entire workbook. A range of cells is simply a group of more than one cell. They can be adjacent or nonadjacent.

STEP BY STEP	Select, Edit, and Delete Cell Contents

USE the workbook from the previous exercise.

1. Select cell **A22** as shown in Figure 3-3.

Figure 3-3

Editing a selected cell

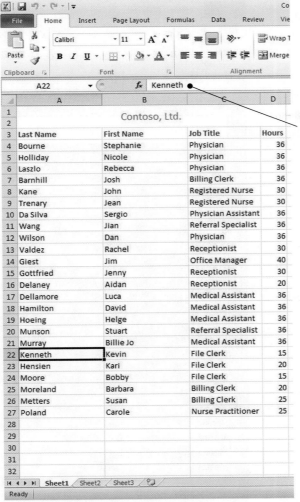

Formula bar reflects what is typed or present in a cell

2. Select the existing text in cell **A22**. Key **Kennedy** and press **Enter**.

3. **Click cell A15** and, while holding down the left mouse button, drag the cursor to select all cells in that row through cell **D15**. You have selected the entire record for **Jenny Gottfried**.

4. **Press** Delete. The information is deleted and row 15 is now blank.

5. **With cells A15 to D15 still selected, right-click to display the shortcut menu.**

6. **Press** Delete. The *Delete* dialog box will be displayed.

7. Click the Shift cells up option as shown in Figure 3-4, and then click OK.

Figure 3-4

Delete a row

8. Click the Select All button, shown in Figure 3-5, to select all cells in the worksheet.

Figure 3-5

Select all cells

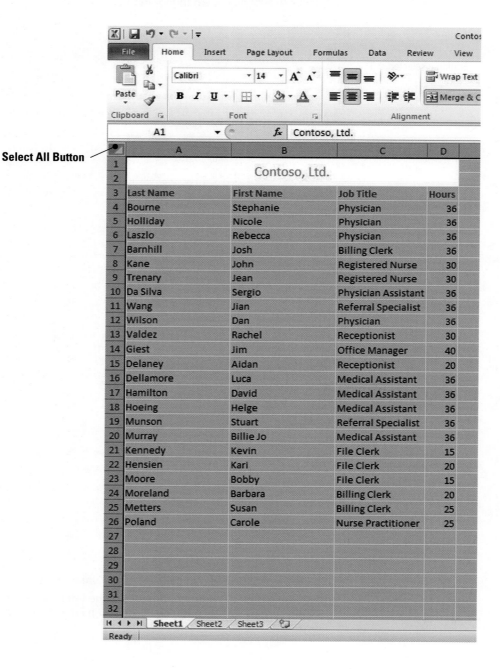

9. Click **any worksheet cell** to deselect the worksheet.

10. **To select all cells containing data, select** A1 and press **Ctrl+A**. Click **any worksheet cell** to deselect the cells.

PAUSE. SAVE the workbook and **LEAVE** Excel open to use in the next exercise.

Take Note   If you edit a cell's contents and change your mind before you press Enter, press Esc and the original text will be restored. If you change the content of a cell and then do not want the change, Click the undo button  on the Quick Access Toolbar. The deleted text will be restored.

You can begin editing by double-clicking the cell to be edited and then keying the replacement text in the cell. Or you can click the cell and then click in the formula bar.

When you are in Edit mode:

- The insertion point appears as a vertical bar and other commands are inactive.
- You can move the insertion point by using the direction keys.

Use the Home key on your keyboard to move the insertion point to the beginning of the cell, and use End key to move the insertion point to the end. You can add new characters at the location of the insertion point.

To select multiple characters, press Shift while you press the arrow keys. You also can use the mouse to select characters while you are editing a cell. Just click and drag the mouse pointer over the characters that you want to select.

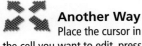

Another Way
You can right-click a cell or a selected range of cells and choose Delete from the menu that appears.

Another Way
Place the cursor in the cell you want to edit, press F2, and edit directly in the cell.

As you have seen in the preceding exercises, there are several ways to modify the values or text you have entered into a cell:

- Erase the cell's contents.
- Replace the cell's contents with something else.
- Edit the cell's contents.

To erase the contents of a cell, double-click the cell and press Delete. To erase more than one cell, select all the cells that you want to erase and then press Delete. Pressing Delete removes the cell's contents, but does not remove any formatting (such as bold, italic, or a different number format) that you may have applied to the cell.

USING DATA TYPES TO POPULATE A WORKSHEET

The Bottom Line

You can enter three types of data into Excel: text, numbers, and formulas. In the following exercises, you will enter text (labels) and numbers (values). You will learn to enter formulas in Lesson 8. Text entries contain alphabetic characters and any other character that does not have a purely numeric value. The real strength of Excel is its ability to calculate and to analyze numbers based on the numeric values you enter. For that reason, accurate data entry is crucial.

Entering Labels and Using AutoComplete

Labels are used to identify numeric data and are the most common type of text entered in a worksheet. Labels are also used to sort and group data. If the first few characters that you type in a column match an existing entry in that column, Excel automatically enters the remaining characters. This **AutoComplete** feature works only for entries that contain text or a combination of text and numbers.

STEP BY STEP   **Enter Labels and Use AutoComplete**

OPEN *Fabrikam Sales_3* from the Lesson 3 folder.

Troubleshooting   To verify that AutoComplete is enabled, click the File tab accessing Backstage, click Options, and then click Advanced in the navigation pane. In the Editing options section, click the *Enable AutoComplete for cell values* check box if it is not already checked. Click OK.

1. Click cell **A4** to enter the first column label. Key **Agent** and press **Tab**.
2. **Key** **Last Closing** and press **Tab**.
3. **In cell** C4, key **January** and press **Enter**.

WileyPLUS Extra! features an online tutorial of this task.

Take Note   When you press Tab to enter data in several cells in a row and then press Enter at the end of the row, the selection moves to the beginning of the next row.

4. Select **A5** to enter the first-row label and key **Richard Carey**.
5. **Select** A6 and key **David Ortiz**.
6. **Select** A7 and key **Kim Akers**.
7. Select **A8** and key **Nicole Caron**.
8. **Select** A9 and key **R**. As shown in Figure 3-6, AutoComplete is activated when you key the *R* because it matches the beginning of a previous entry in this column. AutoComplete displays the entry for **Richard Carey**.

Figure 3-6

AutoComplete

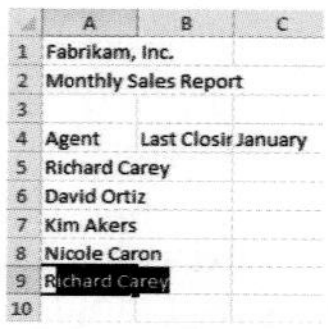

9. **Key a** Y. The AutoComplete entry disappears. Finish keying an entry for **Ryan Calafato**.
10. **Double-click the** marker between columns A and B. This resizes the columns to accommodate the data entered.
11. Double-click the marker between columns B and C. All worksheet data should be visible.

Take Note   Excel bases the list of potential AutoComplete entries on the active cell column. Entries that are repeated within a row are not automatically completed.

PAUSE. LEAVE the workbook open to use in the next exercise.

To accept an AutoComplete entry, press Enter or Tab. When you accept AutoComplete, the completed entry will exactly match the pattern of uppercase and lowercase letters of the existing entry. To delete the automatically entered characters, press backspace. Entries that contain only numbers, dates, or times are not automatically completed. If you do not want to use the AutoComplete option, the feature can be turned off.

Entering Dates

Dates are often used in worksheets to track data over a specified period of time. Like text, dates can be used as row and column headings. However, dates are considered serial numbers, which means that they are sequential and can be added, subtracted, and used in calculations. Dates can also be used in formulas and in developing graphs and charts. The way a date is initially displayed in a worksheet cell depends on the format in which you enter it. In Excel 2010, the default date format uses four digits for the year. Also by default, dates are right-justified in the cells.

Enter Dates

USE the workbook from the previous exercise.

1. Click cell **B5**, key **1/4/20XX** (with XX representing the current year), and press **Enter**. The number is entered in B5, and B6 becomes the active cell.

2. **Key 1/25/XX** and press **Enter**. The number is entered in B6, and B7 becomes the active cell.

3. Key **1/17** and press **Enter**. *17-Jan* is entered in the cell, and if you were to go back and click on B7, then *1/17/20XX* appears in the formula bar.

4. Key **1/28** in B8 and press **Enter**.

5. **Key January 21, 2008** and press **Enter**. *21-Jan-08* will appear in the cell. (If you enter a date in a different format than specified, your worksheet may not reflect the results described.) The date formats in column B are not consistent. You will apply a consistent date format in the next lesson.

Another Way
Ctrl+; (semicolon) will enter the current date into a worksheet cell; Ctrl+: (colon) will enter the current time.

PAUSE. LEAVE the workbook open to use in the next exercise.

Excel interprets two-digit years from 00 to 29 as the years 2000 to 2029; two-digit years from 30 to 99 are interpreted as 1930 to 1999. If you enter 1/28/08, the date will be displayed as 1/28/2008 in the cell. If you enter 1/28/37, the cell will display 1/28/1937.

If you key January 28, 2008, the date will display as 28-Jan-08, as shown in Figure 3-7. If you key 1/28 without a year, Excel interprets the date to be the current year. 28-Jan will display in the cell, and the formula bar will display 1/28/ followed by the current year. In the next lesson, you will learn to apply a consistent format to series of dates.

Figure 3-7

Date formats

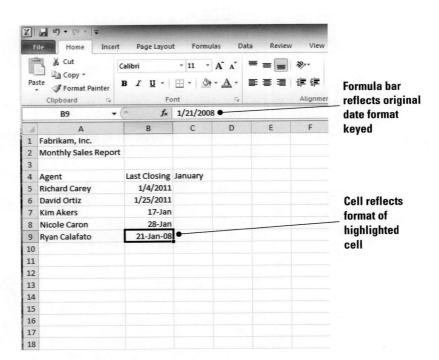

When you enter a date into a cell in a particular format, the cell is automatically formatted. Subsequent numbers entered in that cell will be converted to the date format of the original entry.

Take Note

Regardless of the date format displayed in the cell, the formula bar displays the date in month/day/four-digit-year format because that is the format required for calculations and analyses.

Entering Values

Numeric values are the foundation for Excel's calculations, analyses, charts, and graphs. Numbers can be formatted as currency, percentages, decimals, and fractions. By default, numeric entries are right-justified in a cell. Applying formatting to numbers changes their appearance but does not affect the cell value that Excel uses to perform calculations. The value is not affected by formatting or special characters (such as dollar signs) that are entered with a number. The true value is always displayed in the formula bar.

STEP BY STEP   **Enter Values**

USE the workbook from the previous exercise.

1. Click cell **C5**, key **$275,000**, and press **Enter**. Be sure to include the $ and the comma in your entry. The number is entered in C5, and C6 becomes the active cell. The number is displayed in the cell with a dollar sign and comma; however, the formula bar displays the true value and disregards the special characters.

2. **Key 125000** and press **Enter**.

3. **Key 209,000** and press **Enter**. The number is entered in the cell with a comma separating the digits; the comma does not appear in the formula bar.

4. Key **258,000** and press **Enter**.

5. **Key 145700** and press **Enter**. Figure 3-8 illustrates how your spreadsheet should look with the values you have just keyed.

Figure 3-8

Value unaffected by formatting

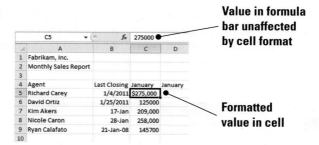

Value in formula bar unaffected by cell format

Formatted value in cell

PAUSE. LEAVE the workbook open to use in the next exercise.

Special characters that indicate the type of value can also be included in the entry. The following chart illustrates special characters that can be entered with numbers.

Character	Used To
+	Indicate a positive value
– or ( )	Indicate a negative value
$	Indicate a currency value
%	Indicate a percentage
/	Indicate a fraction
.	Indicate a decimal
,	Separate the digits of an entry

Filling a Series with Auto Fill

Excel provides **auto fill** options that will automatically fill cells with data and/or formatting. To populate a new cell with data that exists in an adjacent cell, use the Fill command. The **fill handle** is a small black square in the lower-right corner of the selected cell. To display the fill handle, hover the cursor over the lower-right corner of the cell until it turns into a +. Click and drag the handle from cells that contain data to the cells you want to fill with that data, or have Excel automatically continue a series of numbers, numbers and text combinations, dates, or time periods, based on an established pattern. In this exercise, you use the auto fill option to populate cells with data.

STEP BY STEP   **Fill a Series with Auto Fill**

USE the workbook from the previous exercise.

1. Select **D4** and click the Fill button in the Editing command group in the Home tab on the Ribbon; the Fill options menu appears, as shown in Figure 3-9.

Figure 3-9

Fill Command drop-down menu

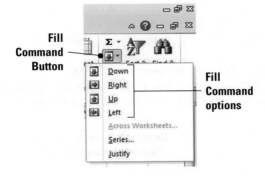

Another Way
To quickly fill a cell with the contents of the cell above, press Ctrl+D; press Ctrl+R to fill the cell to the right.

2. From the menu, click **Right**. The contents of C4 (January) is filled into cell **D4**.

3. **Select** C10 and click the Fill button. Choose **Down**. The content of C9 is copied into C10.

4. Click the Fill handle in cell C5, as shown in Figure 3-10, and drag to F5 and release. The *Auto Fill Options* button appears in **G6**.

Figure 3-10

Fill handle

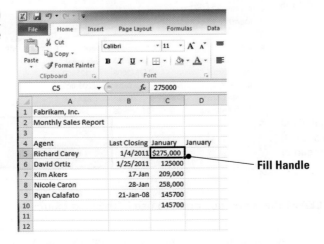

Take Note   A **range** is a group of adjacent cells that you select to perform operations on all of the selected cells. When you refer to a range of cells, the first cell and last cell are separated by a colon (e.g., D5:F5).

5. Click the **Auto Fill Options** drop-down arrow, and choose *Fill Formatting Only* from the options list that appears.

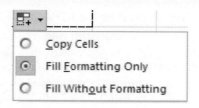

6. Click the Fill handle in C4 and drag to H4 and release. Excel recognizes January as the beginning of a natural series and completes the series as far as you take the fill handle. By definition, a **natural series** is a formatted series of text or numbers. For example, a natural series of numbers could be 1, 2, 3, or 100, 200, 300, or a natural series of text could be Monday, Tuesday, Wednesday, or January, February, March.

7. Select C13, key 2007, and press Enter.

8. **Click the** Fill handle in C13 and drag to D13 and release. The contents of C13 are copied.

9. In D13, key 2008 and press Enter. You have created a natural series of years.

10. Select C13 and D13. Click the Fill handle in D13 and drag to G13 and release. The cells are filled with consecutive years.

Take Note   When Excel recognizes a series, the default fill option is to complete the series. When you use the fill handle and a series is not present, the default is to copy the cell contents. The Fill Options button also allows you to fill formatting only or to fill without formatting.

11. Select cells F4:H4. With the range selected, press Delete.

12. **Select** C10:G13. Press Delete. You have cleared your Sales Report worksheet of unneeded data. Your worksheet should look like Figure 3-11.

Figure 3-11

Fabrikam worksheet

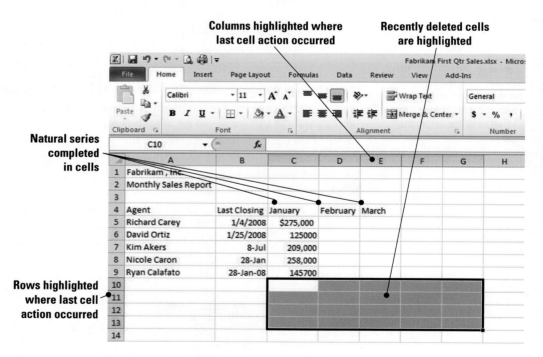

PAUSE. LEAVE the workbook open to use in the next exercise.

After you fill cells using the fill handle, the Auto Fill Options button appears so that you can choose how the selection is filled. In Excel, the default option is to copy the original content and formatting. With auto fill you can select how the content of the original cell appears in each cell in the filled range.

If you choose to fill formatting only, the contents are not copied, but any number that you key into a cell in the selected range will be formatted like the original cell. If you click Fill Series, the copied cells will read $275,001, $275,002, and so on. The Auto Fill Options button remains until you perform another function.

Take Note   When you key sufficient data for Excel to recognize a series, the fill handle will do the rest. For example, to record daily sales, you might want to have consecutive columns labeled with the days of the week. If you key Monday in the first cell, you can fill in the rest of the days by dragging the fill handle from the Monday cell to complete the series.

CUTTING, COPYING, AND PASTING DATA

The Bottom Line

After you have entered data into a worksheet, you frequently need to rearrange or reorganize some of it to make the worksheet easier to understand and analyze. You can use Excel's cut, copy, and paste commands to copy or move entire cells with their contents, formats, and formulas. These processes will be defined and covered as the exercises in this section continue. You can also copy specific contents or attributes from the cells. For example, you can copy the format only without copying the cell value or copy the resulting value of a formula without copying the formula itself. You can also copy the value from the original cell but retain the formatting of the destination cell.

Cut, copy, and paste functions can be performed in a variety of ways by using:

- The mouse
- Ribbon commands
- Shortcut commands
- The Office Clipboard task pane

Copying a Data Series with the Mouse

By default, drag-and-drop editing is turned on so that you can use the mouse to **copy** (duplicate) or move cells. Just select the cells or range of cells you want to copy and hold down Ctrl while you point to the border of the selection. When the pointer becomes a **copy pointer**, you can drag the cell or range of cells to the new location. As you drag, a scrolling ScreenTip identifies where the selection will be copied if you released the mouse button. In this exercise, you practice copying data with the mouse.

STEP BY STEP   **Copy a Data Series with the Mouse**

USE the workbook from the previous exercise.

1. Select the range A4:A9.
2. **Press Ctrl** and hold the button down as you point the cursor at the bottom border of the selected range. The copy pointer is displayed.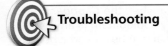

 Troubleshooting Be sure to hold down the Ctrl key the entire time you are selecting a data series for copying with the mouse, or you will move the series instead of copying it.

3. With the copy pointer displayed, hold down the left mouse button and drag the selection down until A12:A17 is displayed in the scrolling ScreenTip below the copy box.
4. Release the mouse button. The data in A4:A9 appears in A12:A17.

PAUSE. LEAVE the workbook open to use in the next exercise.

Moving a Data Series with the Mouse

Data can be moved from one location to another within a workbook in much the same way as copying. To move a data series, select the cell or range of cells and point to the border of the selection. When the pointer becomes a **move pointer**, you can drag the cell or range of cells to a new location. When data is moved, it replaces any existing data in the destination cells. In this exercise, you practice moving a data series from one range of cells to another.

STEP BY STEP   **Move a Data Series with the Mouse**

USE the workbook from the previous exercise.

1. Select **B4:B9**.
2. Point the cursor at the bottom border of the selected range. The move pointer is displayed.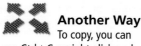
3. With the move pointer displayed, hold down the left mouse button and drag the selection down until B12:B17 is displayed in the scrolling ScreenTip below the box.
4. Release the mouse button. In your worksheet, the destination cells are empty; therefore, you are not concerned with replacing existing data. The data previously in B4:B9 is now in B12:B17.
5. Select the range of cells from C4:E9.
6. Point the cursor at the left border of the selection to display the move arrows.
7. Drag left and drop the range of cells in the same rows in column B (B12:B17). Note that a dialog box will warn you about replacing the contents of the destination cells.
8. Click **Cancel**. Double-click on any empty cell to cancel your actions.

PAUSE. LEAVE the workbook open to use in the next exercise.

Take Note   When you attempt to move a selection to a location that contains data, a caution dialog box opens. "Do you want to replace the contents of the destination cells?" is a reminder that moving data to a new location replaces the existing data. You can click OK or cancel the event.

Copying and Pasting Data

The **Office Clipboard** collects and stores up to 24 copied or cut items that are then available to be used in the active workbook, in other workbooks, and in other Microsoft Office programs. You can **paste** (insert) selected items from the Clipboard to a new location in the worksheet. **Cut** (moved) data is removed from the worksheet but is still available for you to use in multiple locations. If you copy multiple items and then click Paste, only the last item copied will be pasted. To access multiple items, you must open the Clipboard task pane. In this exercise, you use commands in the Clipboard group and the Clipboard task pane to copy and paste cell data.

STEP BY STEP   **Copy and Paste Data**

USE the workbook from the previous exercise.

Another Way
To copy, you can use Ctrl+C or right-click and then click Copy on the shortcut menu. You can use Ctrl+V to paste the last cut or copied data.

1. On the *Home* tab ribbon, click the Clipboard Dialog Box Launcher; the *Clipboard task pane* opens on the side of the worksheet. The most recently copied item is always added at the top of the list in this pane, and it is the item that will be copied when you click Paste or use a shortcut command.
2. Select **C5** and key **305000**. Press **Enter**.
3. **Select** C5 and click the Copy command button in the Clipboard group; the border around C5 becomes a flashing marquee. A check mark will also appear next to the copy button in the Clipboard group on the Ribbon.
4. Select **C8**; the flashing marquee (dotted flashing line around the highlighted cells) identifies the item that will be copied. Click the Paste button in the Clipboard group. The *Paste Options* menu appears.
5. Select **D5**. Right-click and then click Paste on the shortcut menu. The flashing border remains active on cell C8. A copied cell will not deactivate until the data is pasted or another cell is double-clicked.

Take Note

With the new feature, Paste with Live Preview, if you mouse over the Paste options in either the right-click menu, or the paste menu in the Clipboard group, you will be able to view your changes before actually implementing them.

6. With D5 selected as the active cell, press **Delete** to remove the data from D5. When you perform any function other than Paste, the flashing border disappears from C5. You can no longer paste the item unless you use the Clipboard pane.

7. Select **C6**, key **185000**, and press **Enter**.

8. **You can copy data from one worksheet or workbook and paste it to another worksheet or workbook. Select** A1:A9 and click **Copy** in the Clipboard command group.

9. Click the **Sheet2** tab to open the worksheet.

10. Cell **A1** will be highlighted as active. Click the **Paste** drop-down arrow in the Clipboard group. In the menu that appears, click **Keep Source Column Widths**. This will make sure that your column formatting does not change when you paste your copied selection (Figure 3-12).

Figure 3-12

Paste options

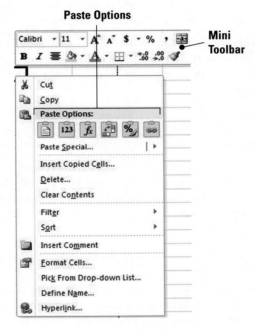

Take Note

If Collect Without Showing Office Clipboard is selected in Clipboard Options, cut or copied items will be stored on the Clipboard, but you must display the task pane to paste any item except the last one.

11. Click the **Sheet1** tab to return to that worksheet. With cell C9 active, click the **$305,000** item in the task pane to paste the item into cell C9. Refer to Figure 3-12. Click **Undo** to clear cell C9.

12. Close the Clipboard task pane.

PAUSE. LEAVE the workbook open to use in the next exercise.

Ref   In Lesson 5, you will use some of the Paste Special options.

Take Note

When you cut or copy data and then paste it into a new location, by default, Excel pastes the original cell contents and formatting. Additional options are available when you click the arrow below the Paste command. You can copy a range of data in a column and click Transpose to paste the data into columns. Other options allow you to copy formulas, to copy values instead of formulas, and to copy cells containing borders and paste the data without the border.

As illustrated in Figure 3-13, the Clipboard stores items copied from other programs as well as those from Excel. The program icon and the beginning of the copied text are displayed.

Figure 3-13

Office Clipboard task pane

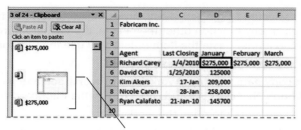

Items copied to clipboard

When you copy or cut data from a worksheet, a flashing border appears around the item and remains visible after you paste the data to one or more new locations. It will continue to flash until you perform another action or press Esc. As long as the marquee flashes, you can paste that item to multiple locations without the Clipboard being open.

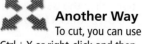

Another Way

Press Ctrl+C twice to display the Office Clipboard task pane. If this shortcut does not open the Clipboard, open the Clipboard with the Dialog Box Launcher, click Clipboard Options, and enable this shortcut. You can also press Alt+H then F and O to perform the same function. Repeat the last keystroke to close the Clipboard task pane.

When you move the cursor over a Clipboard item, an arrow appears on the right side that allows you to paste the item or delete it. You can delete individual items, or click Clear All to delete all Clipboard items. When the task pane is open, you can still use the command buttons or shortcuts to paste the last copied item.

Clipboard Options allow you to display the Clipboard automatically. If you do not have the Clipboard automatically displayed, it is a good idea to check Collect Without Showing Office Clipboard so that you can access items you cut or copied when you open the Clipboard.

To close the Clipboard task pane, click the Dialog Box Launcher or the Close button at the top of the pane. Clipboard items remain, however, until you exit all Microsoft Office programs. If you want the Clipboard task pane to be displayed when Excel opens, click the Options button at the bottom of the Clipboard task pane and check the Show Office Clipboard Automatically option.

Cutting and Pasting Data

Most of the options for copying and pasting data also apply to cutting and pasting. The major difference is that data copied and pasted remains in the original location as well as in the destination cell or range. Cut and pasted data appears only in the destination cell or range. In this exercise, you will cut and paste cell contents.

STEP BY STEP | **Cut and Paste Data**

Another Way

To cut, you can use Ctrl+X or right-click and then click Cut on the shortcut menu.

USE the workbook from the previous exercise.

1. Click **Sheet2** to make it the active worksheet.
2. **Select** **A8** and click **Cut** in the Clipboard group; the contents of cell A8 are cut from that cell and moved to the clipboard.
3. Select **A9** and click **Paste** to add the former contents of cell A8 to A9.

Take Note

When you delete text, it is not stored on the Clipboard. If you want to remove data but think that you might use the text later, use Cut rather than Delete. By using the Cut feature, you will be able to access the data or information from the clipboard if needed. Deleted text can be restored only with Undo.

4. Click **Undo**. The data is restored to A8.

PAUSE. LEAVE the workbook open to use in the next exercise.

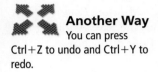

Another Way
You can press Ctrl+Z to undo and Ctrl+Y to redo.

You can undo and repeat up to 100 actions in Excel. You can undo one or more actions by clicking Undo on the Quick Access Toolbar. To undo several actions at once, click the arrow next to Undo and select the actions that you want to reverse. Click the list and Excel will reverse the selected actions.

To redo an action that you undid, click Redo on the Quick Access Toolbar. When all actions have been undone, the Redo command changes to Repeat.

In the preceding exercises, you learned that Excel provides a number of options for populating a worksheet with data. There are also several ways you can accomplish each of the tasks. To cut, copy, and paste, you can use Ribbon commands, shortcut key combinations, or right-click and use a shortcut menu. As you become more proficient in working with Excel, you will decide which method is most efficient for you.

EDITING A WORKBOOK'S KEYWORDS

The Bottom Line

Assigning **keywords** to the document properties makes it easier to organize and find documents. You can assign your own text values in the Keywords field of the Document Properties panel.

Assigning Keywords

For example, if you work for Fabrikam, Inc., you might assign the keyword *seller* to worksheets that contain data about clients whose homes the company has listed for sale. You could then search for and locate all files containing information about the owners of homes your company has listed. You can assign more than one keyword to a document.

STEP BY STEP   **Assign Keywords**

USE the workbook from the previous exercise.

1. In the Document Properties panel, click the Keywords field and key Agent, Closing.
2. Click the Document Properties drop-down arrow in the panel's title bar, and then click Advanced Properties in the drop-down menu (see Figure 3-14); the *Properties* dialog box opens.

Figure 3-14

Properties drop-down menu

Document Properties drop-down menu

     Ref

As covered in Lesson 2, altering the document properties by adding and modifying keywords makes changes to the document properties.

3. Click the Summary tab in the dialog box to see the properties you entered.
4. Click the Statistics tab to see the date you created the file (today).
5. Click OK to close the Properties dialog box.
6. Click the Close button (X) at the top of the Document Information panel.

PAUSE. LEAVE the workbook open to use in the next exercise.

After a file has been saved, the Statistics tab will record when the file was accessed and when it was modified. It also identifies the person who last saved the file. After a workbook has been saved, the Properties dialog box title bar will display the workbook name. Because you have not yet saved the workbook you have been using, the dialog box title bar said *Book1 Properties*. You can view a document's properties from the Open dialog box or from the Save As dialog box when the workbook is closed. You can also view properties from the Print dialog box.

SAVING THE WORKBOOK

The Bottom Line

When you save a file, you can save it to a folder on your computer's hard drive, a network drive, a disk, CD, or any other storage location. You must first identify where the document is to be saved. The remainder of the Save process is the same, regardless of the location or storage device.

Naming and Saving a Workbook Location

When you save a file for the first time, you will be asked two important questions: Where do you want to save the file? What name will you give to the file? In this lesson, you practice answering these questions in the Save As dialog box. By default in all Office applications, documents are saved to the My Documents folder.

STEP BY STEP   **Name and Save a Workbook Location**

USE the workbook from the previous exercise.

1. Click the **File** tab to open Backstage view. Click the **Save As** button in the navigation bar to open the Save As dialog box.
2. **In the** *Save As Type* text box at the bottom of the dialog box, choose **Excel Workbook** from the drop-down arrow (.xlsx extension if it is not already chosen as the default).
3. **In the** *Save As* dialog box, click the **Create New Folder** button ⬜ to open the *New Folder* dialog box. The New Folder dialog box pops up to allow you to name the new folder you are about to create. Refer to Figure 3-15.

Figure 3-15

New Folder dialog box

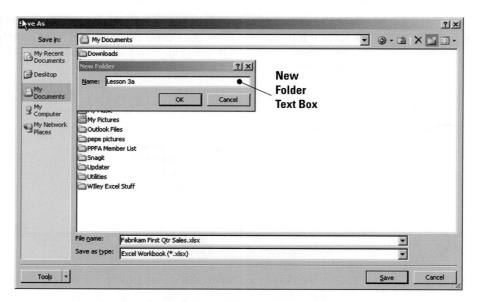

New Folder Text Box

4. In the *New Folder* dialog box, key **Excel Lesson 3a** and click **OK**. The New Folder dialog box closes and the Save As name box shows that the file will be saved in the Excel Lesson 3 folder.
5. **Click in the** **File Name** box and key *Fabrikam First Qtr Sales*.
6. Click the **Save** button.

PAUSE. LEAVE the workbook open to use in the next exercise.

Saving a Workbook under a Different Name

You can save an existing workbook with a new name to create a new workbook. For example, the sales report you created in the preceding exercises is for the first quarter. When all first-quarter data has been entered, you can save the file with a new name and use it to enter second-quarter data. You can also use an existing workbook as a template to create new workbooks. When saving an existing workbook, the Save As dialog box can be accessed in the Backstage navigation bar. Then i the File name box, key the file name then Save.

Saving a Workbook in a Previous Excel Format

Files created in earlier versions can be opened and revised in Excel 2010. You can save a copy of an Excel 2010 workbook (with the .xlsx file extension) that is fully compatible with Excel 97 through Excel 2010 (with the .xls file extension) versions. The program symbol displayed with the filenames will be different, but it is a good idea to give the earlier edition file a different name.

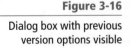

STEP BY STEP   **Save a Workbook for Use in a Previous Excel Version**

USE the workbook from the previous exercise.

1. Click the File tab and then click Save As.
2. **In the** *Save A Copy Of The Document* pane, click Excel 97–2003 Workbook.
3. In the *Save As* dialog box, in the *File Name* box, key Fabrikam First Qtr Sales 97-03. Click the *Save as type* dropdown box and select Excel 97–2003 Workbook (*.xls). (See Figure 3-16.) Click Save. Close the workbook.
4. **Press** Ctrl+O to display the Open dialog box. Select Fabrikam First Qtr Sales 97-03. Scroll to the right to view the file type and see that it is saved to be compatible with earlier Excel editions.

Figure 3-16

Dialog box with previous version options visible

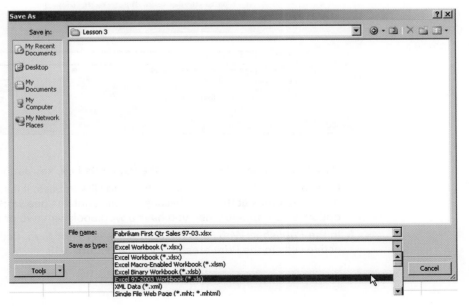

5. Click (but do not open) *Fabrikam First Qtr Sales*.
6. Click the Views drop-down arrow. Click Properties on the list. The properties you entered earlier are displayed. Click Open.

PAUSE. LEAVE the workbook open to use in the next exercise.

Saving in Different File Formats

You can save an Excel 2010 file in a format other than .xlsx or .xls. The file formats that are listed as options in the Save As dialog box depend on what type of file format the application supports. When you save a file in another file format, some of the formatting, data, and/or features may be lost.

STEP BY STEP	**Choose and Save a Different File Format**

USE the workbook from the previous exercise.

1. Click the File tab and click Save As. When the *Save As* dialog box opens, click the Save as Type box.
2. Choose Single File Web Page from the drop-down menu, as shown in Figure 3-17.

Take Note   The screen shots in this book were taken using the Windows XP operating system. If your computer is running a different version of the Windows operating system (such as Windows 7 or Windows Vista), your screen may look slightly different than the images in this book.

Figure 3-17

Other file format options

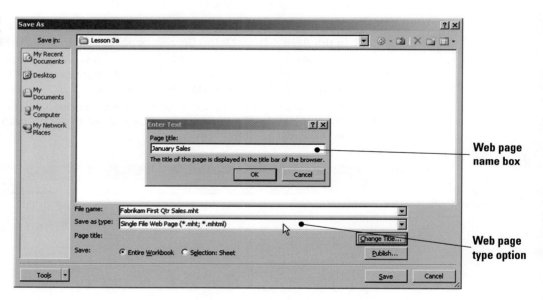

3. Click the Change Title button. In the Page title box, key January Sales. Click OK.
4. Click the Selection: Sheet radio button and click Publish. It is not necessary to publish the entire workbook at this time because it only contains one worksheet. The entire workbook option is appropriate when you have a workbook with two or more worksheets.
5. In the *Publish as Web Page* dialog box, select Print Area. Cells $A$1:$B$9 will be the active cells in the Print area as shown in Figure 3-18.

Figure 3-18

Publish a worksheet as a
web page

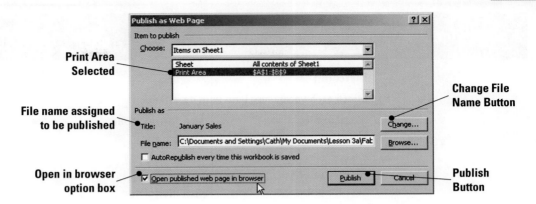

6. Click the check box in front of the *Open published web page in browser* option.

7. Click the Publish button. Refer to Figure 3-18. The default browser assigned to your Windows environment opens with the January Sales web page displayed.

8. Close the browser window.

9. Click the File tab and click Close in the Backstage view navigation bar.

10. **If prompted to save changes, click** Yes. The workbook is closed but Excel remains open.

CLOSE Excel.

Take Note   Excel 2010 also allows you to save your workbooks in PDF (Portable Documents Format) and XPS (XML Paper Specification) formats. Adobe PDF format ensures your printed or viewed file retains the formatting that you intended, and that data in the file cannot easily be changed. The Microsoft XPS format also ensures that when the file is viewed online or printed, it retains exactly the format that you intended, and that data in the file cannot be easily changed. Both of these options are available from the Save As Type drop-down menu.

SKILL SUMMARY

In This Lesson, You Learned How To:
Create workbooks
Enter and edit basic data in a worksheet
Use data types to populate a worksheet
Cut, copy, and paste data
Edit a workbook's keywords
Save the workbook

Knowledge Assessment

Matching

Match each vocabulary term with its definition.

a. auto fill

b. AutoComplete

c. copy

d. document properties

e. fill handle

f. formula bar

g. label

h. paste

i. range

j. file format

_____ 1. A command used to insert a cut or copied selection to a cell or range of cells.

_____ 2. To use a worksheet or workbook outside Excel, you have the option to save as a different _____.

_____ 3. A small black square in the lower-right corner of selected cells that you can use to copy one cell to adjacent cells or to create a series.

_____ 4. A bar at the top of the Excel window where you can enter or edit cell entries or formulas.

_____ 5. A group of adjacent cells that you select to perform operations on all of the selected cells.

_____ 6. To place a duplicate of a selection on the Office Clipboard.

_____ 7. An Excel feature that helps you quickly enter data into cells.

_____ 8. An Excel feature that automatically fills cells with data from another cell or range or completes a data series.

_____ 9. Entries that identify the numeric data in a worksheet.

_____ 10. Details about a file that describe or identify it and include details such as the author.

True/False

Circle T if the statement is true or F if the statement is false.

T   F   1. You can accept an AutoComplete entry by pressing Tab or Enter.

T   F   2. If you key June 5, 2010 in a cell, the formula bar will display June 5, 2010 as well.

T   F   3. Use Ctrl+: to enter the current date in a worksheet cell.

T   F   4. When you paste data into a cell or range of cells that contain data, the data that is replaced is copied to the Office Clipboard.

T   F   5. You can assign keywords so that others can search for your documents online.

T   F   6. Use the fill handle to create a natural series such as the months of the year.

T   F   7. When you open Excel, the application opens by default to the Backstage area.

T   F   8. The Office Clipboard collects items cut or copied from Excel worksheets only.

T   F   9. An existing workbook can be opened by pressing the Ctrl+N keys.

T   F   10. Workbooks can be saved as web pages, PDF files, and for use in previous versions of Excel.

Competency Assessment

Project 3-1: Advertising Budget

Create a new workbook for Fabrikam, Inc., that can be used to compare actual expenses with budgeted amounts.

GET READY. LAUNCH Excel if it is not already running.

1. Click the File tab and click New.
2. **Blank Workbook will be highlighted, then click the** Create button below the Preview pane.
3. Select A1 and key Fabrikam, Inc.
4. **Select** A2 and key Advertising Budget.
5. **Beginning in A4, key the following labels and values; press** Tab between each to move to a new cell:

Media	Vendor	Budgeted
Print	Lucerne Publishing	2000
Radio	Northwind Traders	$1,500
Door-to-Door	Consolidated Messenger	1200
Print	Graphic Design Institute	500
Television	Southridge Video	3000

6. If necessary, double-click the column marker between columns to adjust the column width to display all of the text in the column.
7. **SAVE** the workbook in the Lesson 3 folder you created in an exercise. Save the workbook as *Advertising Budget 3-1*.
8. **CLOSE** the file.

LEAVE Excel open for the next project.

Project 3-2: Set Document Properties and Assign Keywords

Use the Document Properties panel to assign document properties to an existing workbook.

@ The *Employees* file for this lesson is available on the book companion website or in WileyPLUS.

OPEN the *Employees* file.

1. Click the File tab.
2. **Point to** Info in the left-hand panel and select Show Documents Panel from the Properties pull-down menu.
3. **In the Author field, key** [your name]. Press Tab.
4. **In the Title field, key** Employees and press Tab.
5. **In the Subject field, key** Hours Worked and press Tab.
6. **In the Keywords field, key** Job Title, Hours.
7. Click the Close (X) button at the top of the Document Information Panel.
8. **SAVE** the workbook as *Employees 3-2* and **CLOSE** the file.

LEAVE Excel open for the next project.

Proficiency Assessment

Project 3-3: Monthly Advertising Expense

Use an existing workbook to create a new workbook that will track monthly advertising costs.

@ The *Advertising Expense* file for this lesson is available on the book companion website or in WileyPLUS.

OPEN the *Advertising Expense* file.

1. Select D4 and key January.
2. **Select** D4. Use the fill handle to enter the months of the year.
3. Select A10. Click Fill in the Editing group on the Home tab.
4. Choose Down and press Enter.
5. **Select** B10, key Trey Research, and press Enter.
6. Select C10, key 2500, and press Enter.
7. Open the Document Information Panel and key [your name] in the author, Advertising Expense in the title and Monthly Expenses in the subject text boxes.
8. Close the Document Information Panel.
9. SAVE the workbook in your Lesson 3 folder as *Advertising Expense 3-3*.
10. CLOSE the workbook.

LEAVE Excel open for the next project.

Project 3-4: Advertising Expenditures

Fourth Coffee specializes in unique coffee and tea blends. Create a workbook to track and classify expenditures for January.

GET READY. LAUNCH Excel if it is not already running.

1. Click the File tab. Open a new blank workbook.
2. In A1 key Fourth Coffee.
3. **In A2 key** January Expenditures.
4. Enter the following column headings in row 4. Date, Check No., Paid to, Category, and Amount.
5. Enter the following expenditures:
   - January 3, paid $3000 to Wide World Importers for coffee, Check No. 4076.
   - January 20, paid $600 to Northwind Traders for tea, Check 4077.
   - January 22, paid $300 to City Power and Light for utilities.
   - January 28, paid $200 to A. Datum Corporation for advertising.
6. Checks are written sequentially. Use the fill handle to enter the missing check numbers.
7. Adjust column headings as needed.
8. SAVE the workbook as *Expenses 3-4*. CLOSE the workbook.

LEAVE Excel open for the next project.

Mastery Assessment

Project 3-5: Home Sales Data

The *Sales Research* file for this lesson is available on the book companion website or in WileyPLUS.

Fabrikam receives sales research data from the local association of Realtors, which it uses as a benchmark for evaluating its sales performance.

OPEN the *Sales Research* file.

1. **OPEN** the Office Clipboard. If it contains items, click Clear All so that only data for this project will be on the Clipboard.
2. Use AutoFill to add the remaining months in column A.
3. **The data for March and April are reversed. Use the** Copy **command to place the data for March (B6:G6) on the Clipboard. Copy the data as one item.**
4. **Use the mouse to move B7:G7 to B6:G6. Paste the April data from the Clipboard to B7:G7.**
5. Beginning with A1, set the Print Area to include all data for January through June. Print the selected area.
6. Click the Select All button in the upper-left corner of the worksheet. Copy the entire worksheet to the Clipboard.
7. Paste the data to Sheet2. Adjust column widths if necessary.
8. **SAVE** the workbook as *Sales Research 3-5*. **CLOSE** the workbook.

LEAVE Excel open for the next project.

Project 3-6: Fourth Coffee

An employee has begun an inventory worksheet for Fourth Coffee. You want to use the company name and logo from the inventory sheet to create a banner for a website.

The *FC Inventory* file for this lesson is available on the book companion website or in WileyPLUS.

OPEN the *FC Inventory* file.

1. **SAVE** the workbook as a Single File Web Page.
2. **In** Print Area, in the publish web page dialog box, choose Selection A1:E1.
3. **Click** Publish. You have just created the banner for the company's new web page.
4. **CLOSE** the browser and all other open files.

LEAVE Excel open for the next project.

INTERNET READY

More than fifteen shortcut combinations were given in the first two lessons. Create a worksheet to list at least fifteen shortcut combinations. Decide how many columns you will need.

Each column must have a label that identifies its contents. Use the Excel Help on your computer and Microsoft Help online. Save your file as *Excel Shortcuts*.

When you have finished, close Excel.

4 Formatting Cells and Ranges

LESSON SKILL MATRIX

In This Lesson, You Will Learn How To:
Inserting and Deleting Cells
Manually Formatting Cell Contents
Copying Cell Formatting with the Format Painter
Formatting Cells with Styles
Working with Hyperlinked Data
Applying Conditional Formatting to Cells
Clearing a Cell's Formatting

KEY TERMS

- attribute
- character
- conditional formatting
- default
- font
- Format Painter
- hyperlink
- merged cells
- Mini toolbar
- point
- select
- style

Contoso Ltd.'s income is generated by four physicians and the physician's assistant (PA). Ideally, physicians are scheduled to see no more than 35 patients per day, but every effort is made to accommodate patients who need immediate medical attention. Working in collaboration with the physicians, the PA sees patients who need an appointment when all the physicians' schedules are full. Many chronically ill patients whose conditions require frequent monitoring are scheduled with the PA. By law, a PA can treat no more than 25 patients a day. The firm is considering adding a nurse practitioner (NP) to balance the patient load. An NP is a registered nurse who provides some of the same care as a physician. For instance, in most states, an NP can prescribe medications. In this lesson, you will use Excel to manage and sort the relevant data associated with Contoso's physicians and their assistants.

SOFTWARE ORIENTATION

Formatting Excel Worksheets

The Home tab displayed in Figure 4-1 contains the formatting commands that you will use to enhance the appearance of the worksheets you create. You will use commands from every group on this tab as you learn to insert and delete cells, apply basic formatting to text, copy formatting, and apply styles and conditional formatting.

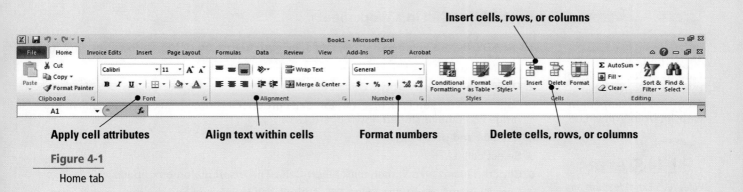

Figure 4-1

Home tab

The elements and features of the Home tab are those that are most often used to edit and develop workbooks and worksheets in Microsoft Excel. Your screen may vary if your default settings have been changed or if other preferences have been set. If so, use Figure 4-1 as a reference as needed throughout this lesson and the rest of the book.

INSERTING AND DELETING CELLS

As shown in Figure 4-2, when you click the arrow below the Insert command in the Cells group on the Ribbon, you can insert cells, worksheet rows, worksheet columns, or even a new worksheet into a workbook. Similar options apply to the Delete command—here, you can delete a cell, a worksheet row, a worksheet column, or an entire worksheet. Inserting and deleting items requires that you first select these items in your worksheet and workbook. To **select** means to click in an area to make it active. You can also select multiple areas by clicking, holding, and dragging to highlight a group of cells, rows, or columns. In the exercises that follow, you will explore the process of adding and deleting cells.

Figure 4-2

Insert options

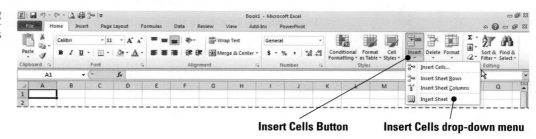

Insert Cells Button   **Insert Cells drop-down menu**

Inserting a New Cell in a Worksheet

After creating a worksheet, you may decide that you need to add additional data or delete unnecessary data. To enter additional text or values within the existing data, you need to insert cells in your worksheet. You can either insert a cell or cells and shift down the other cells in the same column, or you can shift other cells in the same row to the right.

STEP BY STEP   **Insert a New Cell in a Worksheet**

 The *Contoso Patient Visits* Info file for this lesson is available on the book companion website or in WileyPLUS.

 EXTRA

WileyPLUS Extra! features an online tutorial of this task.

 Another Way
You can also select a cell or range, right-click on the selection, and then click Insert to open the Insert dialog box. In that dialog box, you can click the direction in which you want to shift the cells.

Another Way
You can repeat the action of inserting a cell by clicking Redo on the Quick Access Toolbar.

GET READY. Before you begin these steps, be sure to turn on or log on to your computer:

1. **LAUNCH** Excel. The Home tab will be active on the Ribbon.
2. **OPEN** the *Contoso Patient Visits* data file.
3. Select cell F5, then click Insert in the Cells group. F5 is now blank and the cells in the range F5:F8 have shifted down one row.
4. Key **604** and press Enter.
5. Select cell J4.
6. Click the Insert arrow, then click Insert Cells. The *Insert* dialog box opens.
7. Click Shift cells right, then click OK. A blank cell is inserted and the data is shifted to the right.
8. With cell J4 still active, key **580** and press Enter.
9. Select K7:L7 and click the Insert arrow.
10. Click Insert Cells.
11. Click Shift cells right and click OK. The data has shifted two cells to the right.
12. Select cell K7, key **475**, and press Tab.
13. Key **611** and press Enter.
14. Select N3:N9. Click the Insert arrow and click Insert Cells.
15. The Shift cells right option is already selected; click OK. Cells are inserted so that November's data can be entered later. See Figure 4-3.
16. **PAUSE. SAVE** the workbook as *Contoso Patient 1*.

LEAVE the workbook open to use in the next exercise.

Figure 4-3

Group of cells moved and aligned

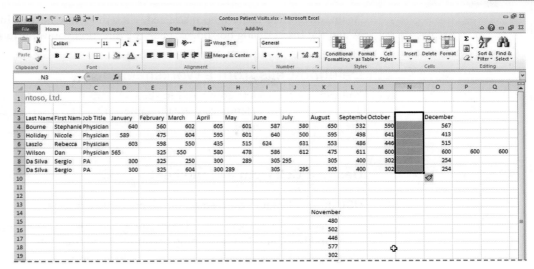

Additions and changes are common activities in Microsoft Office Excel 2010 workbooks. In the previous exercise, Contoso created an Excel workbook to track the number of patients treated during a month to determine whether to hire a nurse practitioner. After creating and saving the workbook, the administrative assistant discovered that corrections were needed and additional data must be added to the workbook.

As demonstrated in the exercise, if you click Insert in the Cells group, a blank cell is inserted and, by default, the existing cells move down in the column. If, however, you click the arrow next to Insert and select Insert Cells, the Insert dialog box shown in Figure 4-4 opens, and you can choose to shift cells to the right. By default, the option box has the shift cells down option selected. The dialog box also allows you to insert a row or a column in a worksheet. Note that when working with active cells that have been inserted, when you continue to use these cells, the last action performed will be the selected option in the dialog box when you reuse the tool.

Figure 4-4

Insert dialog box

To insert blank cells in a worksheet, select the cell or the range of cells where you want to insert the new blank cells. The number of cells you select must match the number of cells that you want to insert. Thus, as Figure 4-5 illustrates, if you want to insert two cells, you must select two cells.

Figure 4-5

Your selection must match the number of cells to be inserted

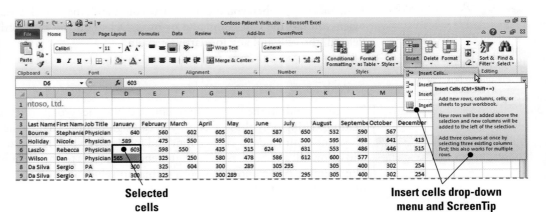

Selected cells

Insert cells drop-down menu and ScreenTip

Again, once the cells have been selected, click the arrow next to Insert, then click Insert Cells. When the Insert dialog box opens, click the direction you want to shift the cells.

Deleting Cells from a Worksheet

You can use the Delete command in the Cells group to delete cells, ranges, rows, or columns. The principles for deleting cells are the same as those for inserting cells except that the direction the cells shift is reversed.

STEP BY STEP | **Delete a Cell from a Worksheet**

USE the worksheet you created in the previous exercise.

1. Select **C3:C9**. Click **Delete** in the Cells group. The *Job Title* data is removed from the worksheet, and the remaining columns are shifted left.
2. Select **A9:N9** and click **Delete**. The duplicate entry of data is removed.
3. Select **K13:K18** and click **Cut** in the Clipboard group.
4. Select **M3** and click **Paste**. The November data is now pasted into the space you made when you shifted cells in the previous exercise. Your worksheet should now resemble the one shown in Figure 4-6.

Figure 4-6

Completed paste of cell group

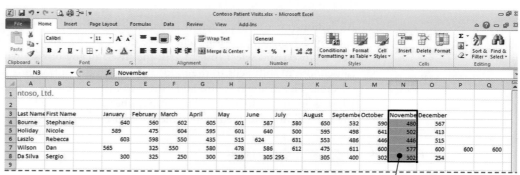

Moved Cells

5. **SAVE** your workbook.

PAUSE. LEAVE the workbook open to use in the next exercise.

As shown, you can click Delete in the Cells group to eliminate cells from a worksheet. Any data to the right of the deleted cell or cells will automatically shift left. If you want to shift cells up rather than left, click the arrow next to Delete, then click Delete Cells to open the Delete dialog box.

Another Way
You can also right-click your selected cells and then choose Delete on the shortcut menu to open the Delete dialog box.

Remember that when you use the Delete command, the cells themselves are deleted. In contrast, when you use the Cut command or press Delete on the keyboard, only the cell contents are deleted; the cells and any formatting remain.

MANUALLY FORMATTING CELL CONTENTS

The Bottom Line

The commands in the Font, Alignment, and Number groups (Figure 4-7) are used for basic formatting. Using only those groups, you can significantly change the appearance of a worksheet. Use Font commands to change font and font size; to bold, italicize, and underline data; and to add color, fill, and borders. Use Alignment commands to choose how data is aligned within cells. Use Number commands to apply a format to values and to increase or decrease the number of digits after a decimal.

Figure 4-7

Basic formatting command groups

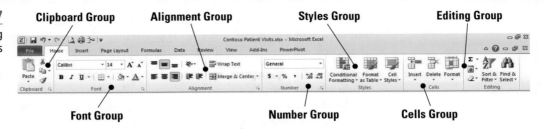

Selecting Cells and Ranges

To apply formatting to text and values in an existing worksheet, you must first select the data. When you select data, you identify the cell or range of cells in which you want to enter data or apply formatting. You can select cells, ranges, rows, columns, or the complete worksheet. The cells in a range can be adjacent or nonadjacent. You can also place a cell in editing mode and select all or part of its contents Table 4-1 offers information about making selections.

STEP BY STEP   **Select Cells and Ranges**

USE the workbook from the previous exercise to complete these steps:

1. Select cell **A3**. Hold down the left mouse button and drag to **B8** to select the range, then release the mouse button.
2. Click the **Row 3 heading** to select the entire row.
3. Click the **column C header**, press and hold **Ctrl**, and click **E**, **G**, and **I** to select nonadjacent columns.
4. Click the **File** tab, then click **Save As**.
5. When the Save As dialog box opens, create a **Lesson 4** folder.
6. **SAVE** your workbook in the folder and name it *Patient Visits*.

PAUSE. LEAVE the workbook open to use in the next exercise.

Table 4-1

Making selections in Excel

To Select	Do This
A single cell	Click the cell or press the arrow keys to move the cell.
A range of cells	Click the first cell in the range and drag your cursor to the last cell, or hold down Shift while you press the arrow keys to extend the selection.
A large range of cells	Click the first cell in the range and hold down Shift while you click the last cell.
All cells in a worksheet	Click the Select All button (intersection of the column and row headings), or press Ctrl+A.
Nonadjacent cells or cell ranges	Select the first cell or range and hold down Ctrl while you select the other cells or ranges.
An entire row or column	Click the row or column heading.
Adjacent rows or columns	Drag your cursor across the row or column headings.
Nonadjacent rows or columns	Click the column or row heading of the first row or column of the selection. Hold down Ctrl while you click the column or row headings of other rows or columns you want to add to the selection.
The contents of a cell	Double-click the cell, then drag across the contents that you want to select.

When you make a selection, the cell or range is highlighted on the screen. These highlights do not appear in a printout, however. If you want cells to be highlighted when you print a worksheet, you must use formatting features to apply shading.

Excel provides many ways to format labels and values in a worksheet. In the business world, worksheets are usually printed or shared with others electronically. Therefore, you want your worksheet or workbook to be as eye-catching and understandable as possible. You can improve the design of a worksheet in several ways. For instance, you can:

- Change the alignment
- Change the font style and enlarge the text for titles
- Format titles and labels in bold and/or italics
- Apply special formatting attributes

Each of these formatting options is described in the following sections.

Aligning Cell Contents

Text and numbers in a worksheet can be aligned to the left, to the right, or at the center. By default, when you enter alphabetic characters or alphabetic characters combined with numbers or symbols, the cell content is left-aligned, but when you enter numbers, the content is right-aligned. You can use Alignment commands to change this default alignment or to override previous alignment formatting.

STEP BY STEP   **Align Cell Contents**

USE the worksheet you created in the previous exercise. Then, do the following:

1. Select **A3:N3**.
2. In the Alignment group, click **Center**. The column labels are now horizontally centered.
3. Click **C4**, press **Shift**, and click **N8**. The cell range containing the values is selected. Release the **Shift** key and click **Align Text Right**. All cells containing values are now right-aligned.

PAUSE. LEAVE the workbook open to use in the next exercise.

As illustrated in Figure 4-8, the alignment that has been applied to the active cell is shown by the highlighted commands in the Alignment group. Proper alignment and spacing greatly improve the readability of worksheet data.

Figure 4-8

Active cell alignment is highlighted

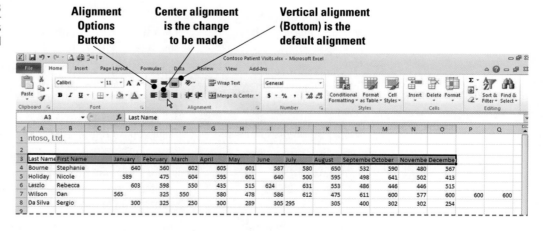

Choosing Fonts and Font Sizes

A **font** is a set of text characteristics designed to appear a certain way. The font determines the appearance of the cell contents. The **default**, or predefined, font for Excel 2010 is 11-point Calibri. This is an easy-to-read font that takes up less space than Arial, which was the default in earlier Excel versions.

STEP BY STEP   **Choose Fonts and Font Sizes**

USE the workbook from the previous exercise.

1. Select the column labels in row 3.
2. Click the Font arrow. Scroll up the list of font names and click Arial. Notice that the font size is unchanged (still 11 point), but Arial is larger than the default Calibri font. (See Figure 4-9.)

Figure 4-9

Changing fonts

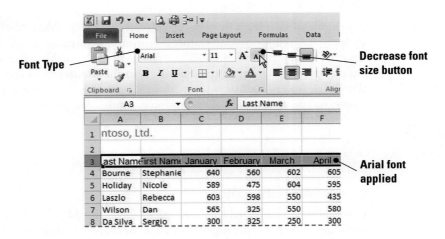

3. With row 3 still selected, click Decrease Font Size. The number 10 appears in the Font Size box, and the labels now fit within the column width.
4. **SAVE** the workbook.

PAUSE. LEAVE the workbook open to use in the next exercise.

On Excel's Options page, you can change the default font used in all new workbooks. If you chose a different default font and/or font size, that font is used only in workbooks that you create *after* you change the default and restart Excel. Existing workbooks are not affected.

Of course, you can also change the font for only a selected cell, a range of cells, or for characters within text. To change the font, select the font that you want in the Font box. You can then change the size in the Font Size box or click Increase Font Size or Decrease Font Size until the size you want is displayed in the Font Size box. To improve the overall design of a worksheet, the font size is usually enlarged for titles and labels.

Font size is measured in points. Each time you click Decrease Font Size or Increase Font Size, the size changes by a set amount that matches the size options on the Font Size list. **Points** refer to the measurement of the height of the characters in a cell. One point is equal to 1/72 inch.

Applying Special Character Attributes

In addition to changing font and font size, you can apply special **attributes** to a font that add visual appeal. An attribute is a formatting characteristic, such as bold, italic, or underlined text. Applying special characteristics to specific text or values adds interest to a worksheet and calls attention to specific data.

STEP BY STEP   **Apply Special Character Attributes**

USE the workbook from the previous exercise to carry out these steps:

1. Select **A4**. Hold down the left mouse button and drag to B8. Click Bold **B** in the Font group.
2. Click cell **A3**. Press **Shift** and click **N3** to select the column labels. Click Italic in the Font group, then click Bold.
3. **SAVE** the workbook.

PAUSE. LEAVE the workbook open to use in the next exercise.

Although you are adding multiple instances of special formatting to the worksheets in these exercises to improve your skills, in real-life situations, it is wise to have a clear, logical design plan that presents data in an easy-to-understand format. To this end, it is best not to overuse special character attributes. Keep in mind that the focus of your worksheet should be on the data and the information it conveys.

When you select text for formatting, you can also use the **Mini toolbar**, shown in Figure 4-10, to apply selected formatting features. This unique formatting tool was new in Excel 2007 and has carried over to Excel 2010. When you right-click, the Mini toolbar displays above the short-cut menu. Just click any of the toolbar's available features to apply them to selected text. Unlike the Quick Access Toolbar, which can be customized, you cannot customize the Mini toolbar. However, you can turn off the Mini toolbar in Excel Options.

Figure 4-10

Mini toolbar

Changing Font Color

Color enhances the visual appeal of a worksheet. To add color to the text in your worksheet, you must first select the cell, range of cells, text, or characters that you want to format with a different color. A **character** can be a letter, number, punctuation mark, or symbol.

STEP BY STEP   **Change Font Color**

USE the workbook from the previous exercise.

1. Select the column labels if they are not already selected. Click the Font Color arrow.
2. Click Blue in the list of standard colors. (See Figure 4-11.)

Figure 4-11

Font color options

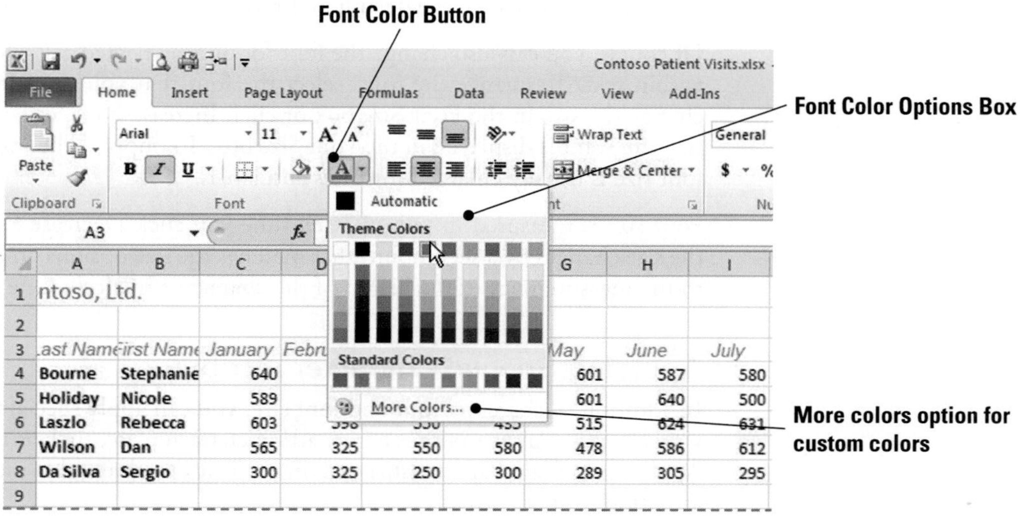

3. Select **A4:B8**. Click the **Font Color** arrow, then click **Red** in the standard colors.

4. **SAVE** the workbook.

PAUSE. LEAVE the workbook open to use in the next exercise.

Take Note   If you choose a color and change your mind, click Undo on the Quick Access Toolbar or press Ctrl+Z.

Black is the default, or automatic, font color in Excel, but you can easily change text color. The most recently applied color appears on the Font Color button. To apply that color, make a selection and click Font Color. To apply a different text color, click the arrow next to Font Color. You can choose a theme color or a standard color. You can also click More Colors to open the Colors dialog box, in which you can choose from additional standard colors or create colors to your own specifications.

 Ref   You will learn about Document Themes in Lesson 5. The default Office theme is the basis for the colors that appear under Theme Colors and Standard Colors on the Font Color menu.

Filling Cells with Color

You can also call attention to cells by adding a background color and/or pattern. You can use a solid color or apply special effects, such as gradients, textures, and pictures. Use the Fill Color command in the Font group to change the background color of a cell. The most recently used fill color appears on the Fill Color button.

STEP BY STEP   **Fill Cells with Color**

USE the workbook from the previous exercise and follow these steps:

1. Select **A3:N3**.
2. Click the **Font Dialog Box Launcher**.
3. Click the **Fill** tab.
4. In the Background Color section, click the light blue color (second box) in column 5, as shown in Figure 4-12.

Figure 4-12

New fill color

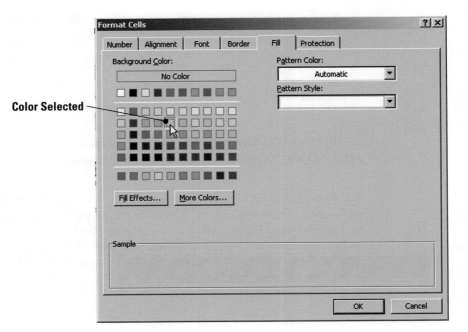

5. Add a second color in the Pattern Color box. Click the arrow and click the third box in column 5.

6. Click the Pattern Style arrow and click the pattern at the end of the first row. At the bottom of the dialog box, you can see a sample of how the pattern and color will look in the selected cells. Adjust any column widths to the appropriate size to accommodate the data. (See Figure 4-13.)

Figure 4-13

New pattern color and pattern style

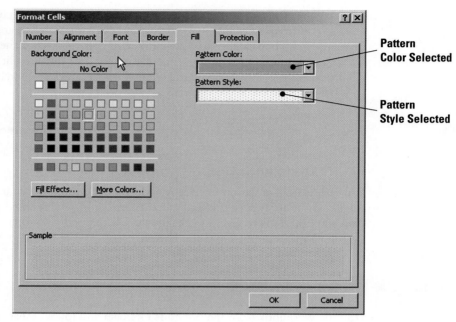

7. Click OK to apply the color and the fill pattern. Click in any empty cell to deselect your heading row. Your headings should resemble Figure 4-14.

Figure 4-14

Background changes in pattern and color

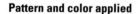

Pattern and color applied

	Last Name	First Name	January	February	March	April	May	June
4	Bourne	Stephanie	640	560	602	605	601	587
5	Holiday	Nicole	589	475	604	595	601	640
6	Laszlo	Rebecca	603	598	550	435	515	624
7	Wilson	Dan	565	325	550	580	478	586
8	Da Silva	Sergio	300	325	250	300	289	305
9								

8. **SAVE** and **CLOSE** the *Patient Visits* workbook.

PAUSE. LEAVE Excel open to use in the next exercise.

No color (clear) is the default background. To add color and shading, select the cells to which you want to add special effects. The color palette you used to apply font color is also used for background color. To apply the color shown on the Fill Color button, simply make a selection and click the button. To apply a different fill color, click the arrow next to Fill Color and apply either a theme color or a standard color. You can also click More Colors to open the Colors dialog box and custom blend colors.

As demonstrated, you can also apply a background color and add a pattern effect. To do so, first select the range of cells to which you want to apply a background color with fill effects, then click the Font group's Dialog Box Launcher. The Format Cells dialog box opens. Click the Fill tab. As shown in Figure 4-15, make a selection in the Pattern Style box to add a pattern to the background color.

Figure 4-15

Add a pattern to a cell's background color

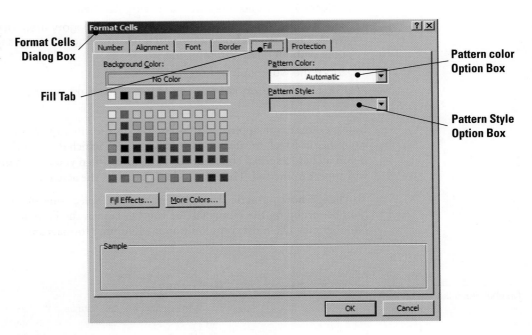

Applying Number Formats

Most of the data that you use in Excel is numeric. Applying accurate formatting to numeric data makes this information easier to interpret—and therefore more useful. Number formatting can be applied to cells before data is entered, or data can be selected and formatted after it has been entered. Formatting changes the appearance of numbers; it does not change their value. The actual value is always displayed in the formula bar.

STEP BY STEP **Apply Number Formats**

GET READY. With Excel running, perform these actions:

The *Contoso Revenue* file for this lesson is available on the book companion website or in WileyPLUS.

WileyPLUS Extra! features an online tutorial of this task.

1. **OPEN** *Contoso Revenue*. Click the Sheet1 tab if necessary to make it the active worksheet.
2. Select **B4:D10** and click the Accounting Number Format ($) button in the Number group. The selected data is reformatted to monetary values, the decimal points are aligned, and the column width is increased to accommodate the selected number format.
3. With the text still selected, click the Decrease Decimal button in the Number group twice. The data is rounded to whole dollars.
4. Select **B10:D10**. Click Comma Style (,) then click Decrease Decimal twice to show whole numbers. Row 10 data relates to the number of patients, not monetary values. Accounting style was inappropriately applied to this data.

5. Click the Sheet2 tab.

6. Select B7:B11. Click the Number Dialog Box Launcher.

7. Click Number in the Category area. Key 0 in the *Decimal places* box and place a check mark in the *Use 1000 Separator* box. Click OK.

8. Format B6 with Accounting and zero decimals.

9. Select C7:C11. Click the Number Dialog Box Launcher.

10. The Number tab is active. Click Date in the Category area. Then click the 03/14/01 date style. Click OK. By doing this, you are formatting blank cells to accept data at a later date without having to reformat.

11. **SAVE** the workbook as *Revenue*.

PAUSE. LEAVE the workbook open to use in the next exercise.

In this exercise, you applied formatting to Contoso's first-quarter revenue data. When you enter a number in Excel, the default format is General, which displays the data exactly as you enter it. If you include a special character such as $ or % when you enter a number, the special character will appear in the cell. The format does not affect the actual cell value.

To change how numeric data appears, you can select one of the formatting options in the Number group on the Home tab, or you can launch the Format Cells dialog box and click the Number tab. The most commonly applied number formats are summarized in Table 4-2.

Table 4-2

Number group buttons on the Home tab

Format Category	Description
General	This is the default number format that Excel applies when you key a number. Numbers are displayed just the way you key them. If a cell is not wide enough to show the entire number, a number with decimal places will be rounded.
Number	This format is used for the general display of numbers. You can specify the number of decimal places that you want to use, whether you want to use a thousands separator, and how you want to display negative numbers.
Currency	This format is used for general monetary values and displays the default currency symbol with numbers. You can specify the number of decimal places that you want to use, whether you want to use a thousands separator, and how you want to display negative numbers.
Accounting	This format is also used for monetary values. Currency symbols and decimal points are aligned in this format.
Date	This format displays days, months, and years in various styles, such as January 7, 2011, 7-Jan, and 1/7/2011.

If pound symbols (###) appear in a cell, it means that the numeric value entered is wider than the cell. If you plan to apply a number format to this data, it is not necessary to adjust column width first because the column width will be adjusted automatically when you apply a number format.

After you choose a number format, you will need to further specify how you want the numbers to appear. You can use the commands in the Number group to apply formats and to increase or decrease the number of decimal places displayed in worksheet data. When you decrease the number of decimal places, the data becomes less precise because the numbers following the decimal point are rounded. This lack of preciseness is insignificant, however, when you are dealing with large numbers.

Wrapping Text in a Cell

When a cell is formatted to wrap text, any data in the cell automatically breaks to fit the column width. If you later change the column width, the text wrapping adjusts automatically. When text is wrapped, row height is also adjusted to accommodate the wrap.

STEP BY STEP   **Wrap Text in a Cell**

USE the workbook from the previous exercise to perform these steps:

1. Select **Sheet1**. Select cell **A7** and click **Wrap Text** in the Alignment group. The row height is adjusted and the cell's full text is displayed on two lines. (See Figure 4-16.)

Figure 4-16

Wrap Text button

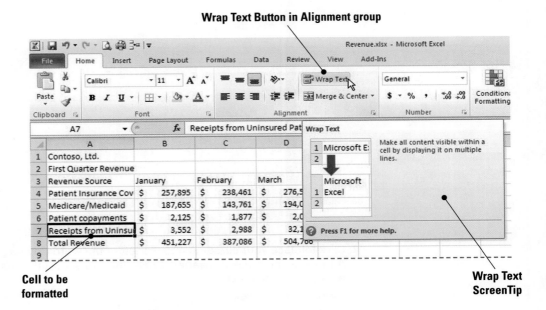

Take Note   If you format a cell for text wrapping and all wrapped text is not visible, it may be because the row is set to a specific height. You will learn to modify row height in Lesson 5.

2. Double-click cell **A4**. The Status bar displays Edit, indicating that the cell is in edit mode. (See Figure 4-17.)

Figure 4-17

Cell in Edit mode

Cell to be formatted

Edit mode on status

3. Click to place your cursor just to the left of the word Coverage and press **Alt+Enter**. A manual line break is inserted. Press **Enter** to accept the change. You have manually wrapped the cell text.

4. **SAVE** the workbook.

PAUSE. LEAVE the workbook open to use in the next exercise.

Take Note   Remember that you can edit a cell in the formula bar as well as in the cell itself.

As demonstrated in this exercise, if you want the text in a cell to appear on multiple lines, you can format the cell so that the text wraps automatically, or you can enter a manual line break. To wrap text automatically, select the text you want to format and click Wrap Text in the Alignment group. To start a new line of text at a specific point in a cell, double-click the cell to place it in Edit mode, then click the location where you want to break the line and press Alt+Enter.

Merging and Splitting Merged Cells

You can use the Merge & Center command in the Alignment group to merge cells. A **merged cell** is created by combining two or more horizontally or vertically adjacent cells. When you merge cells, the selected cells become one large cell that spans multiple columns or rows. You can split cells that have been merged into separate cells again, but you cannot split a single worksheet cell that has not been merged. Merging is a useful tool when combining data from other sources.

STEP BY STEP   **Merge and Split Merged Cells**

USE the workbook from the previous exercise.

1. Select **A1:D1**. Click **Merge & Center** in the Alignment group. The content previously in cell A1 is now centered across columns A, B, C, and D. (See Figure 4-18.)

Figure 4-18

Merging and centering cells

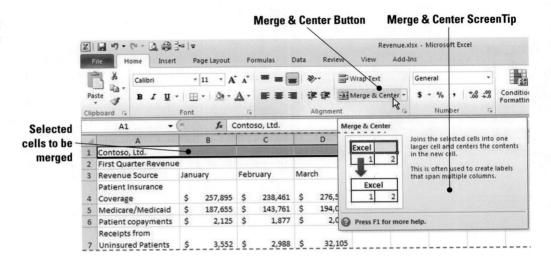

2. Select **A2:D2**. Click **Merge & Center**.

3. Select **A4:A5** and click **Merge & Center**. A dialog box opens to remind you that the data in A5 will be deleted in the merge. (See Figure 4-19.)

Figure 4-19

Merge warning dialog box

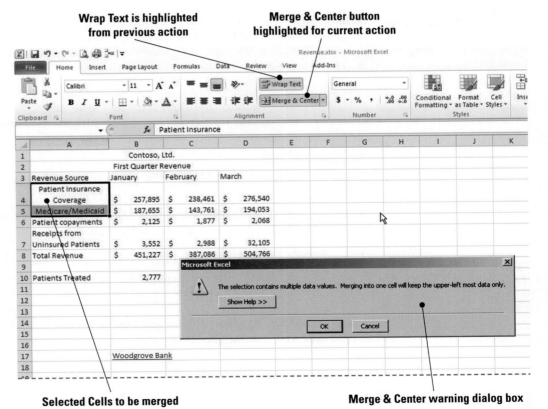

4. Click **OK**. Cells A4 and A5 are merged, and the data originally in A4 is centered in the merged cell.

5. Click the arrow next to **Merge & Center** and click **Unmerge Cells**. The cells are unmerged, but note that the data from cell A5 has been deleted.

6. Select **A5**, key **Medicare/Medicaid**, and press **Enter**. (See Figure 4-20.)

Figure 4-20

Unmerge cells option

Another Way
Whereas Merge & Center combines cells and centers the content, the Merge Across button in the Alignment group will merge cells and align the text flush left.

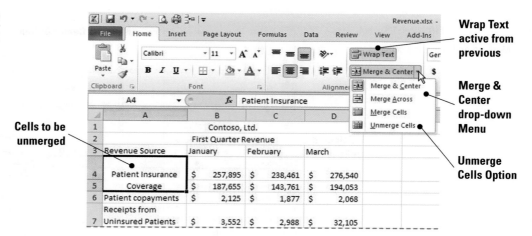

7. Select **A4:A5** and click **Align Text Left** in the Alignment group.
8. **SAVE** the workbook.

PAUSE. LEAVE the workbook open to use in the next exercise.

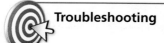

Another Way
With a merged cell active, you can click Merge & Center to unmerge the cells.

As shown in the previous exercise, when you merge cells, the data that you want to appear in the merged cells will be the content from the upper-left cell of the selected range. Only the data in the upper-left cell will remain in the newly merged cell; data in the other cells included in the merge will be deleted.

Cells can be merged in a row or a column—but in either situation, the content of the upper-left cell will be centered in the merged cell. If the cells to be merged contain information that will be deleted in the merge, the Excel dialog box shown in Figure 4-19 opens to caution you that only the content of the upper-left cell will remain after the merge.

To merge cells without centering the contents of the upper-left cell, click the arrow next to Merge & Center, then click Merge Cells. Any text you enter in such a merged cell will be left aligned.

With a merged cell active, click Merge & Center to split the merged cell. You can also click the arrow next to Merge & Center and choose Unmerge Cells.

Troubleshooting   If the Merge & Center button is unavailable, the selected cells may be in editing mode. To cancel this mode, press Enter or Escape (Esc).

A merged cell takes the name of the original upper-left cell. As shown in Figure 4-21, when you merged cells A1:D1 in the previous exercise, the merged cell is named A1.

Figure 4-21

Merged cells have one name

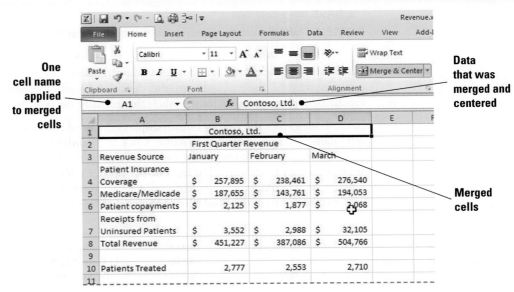

Placing Borders around Cells

You can use borders to enhance a worksheet's visual interest and to make it easier to read. You can either apply Excel's predefined border styles, or you can customize borders by specifying a line style and color of your choice. Borders are often used to set off headings, labels, or totals.

STEP BY STEP   **Place Borders around Cells**

USE the workbook from the previous exercise to complete these actions:

1. Select cell **A1** and click the arrow next to Bottom Border [icon] ▾ in the Font group on the Ribbon.
2. Click **More Borders**. The *Format Cells* dialog box opens with the Border tab displayed.
3. Under Line, click the **Style** displayed in the **lower-right corner**.
4. Click the **Color arrow**, then click **Red**.
5. Under Presets, click **Outline**. The red border is previewed in the Border box.
6. Click **OK**. The dialog box closes and the border is applied to **A1**.
7. With **A1** selected, click **Increase Font Size** until the value in the Font Size box is 20 points. Click on cell A11. Your border should resemble Figure 4-22.

Figure 4-22

Formatted border

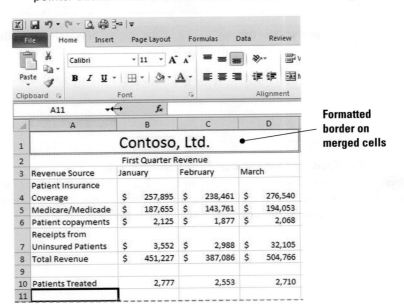

8. **SAVE** the workbook.

PAUSE. LEAVE the workbook open to use in the next exercise.

To add a border, select the cell or range of cells to which you want to call attention. For example, you may want to place a border around the titles, around the cells displaying the total revenue for the first quarter, or around the labels that identify the months.

In the Font group, the Border button displays the most recently used border style, and the button's name changes to that style name. Click the Border button (not the arrow) to apply that style, or you can click the arrow and choose a different border style. Click More Borders to apply a custom or diagonal border. On the Border tab of the Format Cells dialog box, click a line style and a color. You can select a border style from the presets or create a style with the line-placement options in the Border area. Notice that Figure 4-23 displays the two diagonal borders.

Figure 4-23

Borders options

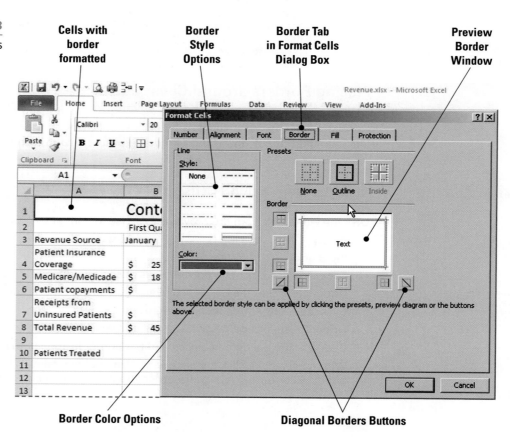

Take Note

If you apply two different types of borders to a shared cell boundary, the most recently applied border will be displayed.

COPYING CELL FORMATTING WITH THE FORMAT PAINTER

The Bottom Line

The **Format Painter** is an Excel feature that allows you to copy formatting from a cell or range of cells to another cell or range of cells. Located in the Clipboard group on the Home tab, it is one of Excel's most useful tools. It allows you to quickly copy attributes that you have already applied and "paint" those attributes onto other data.

Copy Cell Formatting with the Format Painter

USE the workbook from the previous exercise.

1. With **A1** active, click **Format Painter**. [icon] A flashing border appears around A1, indicating this is the formatting to be copied.

2. Click cell **A2**.

3. With A2 selected, right-click to display the Mini toolbar. Click the **Font Size** arrow and choose **14**. The font size of the subtitle is reduced.

4. Select **A1:A2** and click **Format Painter**.

5. Click the **Sheet2** tab and select **A1:A2**. The formatting from the Sheet1 titles have been applied to the Sheet2 titles.

6. Click the **Sheet1** tab.

7. **SAVE** the workbook.

PAUSE. LEAVE the workbook open to use in the next exercise.

Another Way
The Format Painter is available on the Mini toolbar as well as in the Clipboard group.

You can use the Format Painter to copy formats, including font, font size, font style, font color, alignment, indentation, number formats, and borders and shading. To copy formatting from one location to another, select the cell or range that has the formatting you want to copy, then click Format Painter in the Clipboard group. The mouse pointer turns into a white plus sign with the paint brush beside it. Drag the mouse pointer across the cell or range of cells that you want to format.

To copy the formatting to several cells or ranges of cells, double-click Format Painter, and then drag the mouse pointer across each cell or range of cells that you want to format. When you're done, click Format Painter again or press Esc to turn off the Format Painter.

FORMATTING CELLS WITH STYLES

The Bottom Line

A **style** is a set of formatting attributes that you can apply to a cell or range of cells more easily than by setting each attribute individually. Style attributes include fonts and font sizes, number formats, and borders and shading. Excel has several predefined styles that you can apply; you can also modify or duplicate a cell style to create a custom cell style.

Applying a Cell Style

To apply a cell style to an active cell or range, click Cell Styles in the Styles group on the Home tab, then choose the cell style that you want to apply. You can apply more than one style to a cell or range.

STEP BY STEP   **Apply a Cell Style**

USE the workbook from the previous exercise.

1. With cells A1:A2 already selected, click **Cell Styles** in the Styles group. The Cell Styles gallery opens. (See Figure 4-24.)

Figure 4-24

Cell Styles gallery

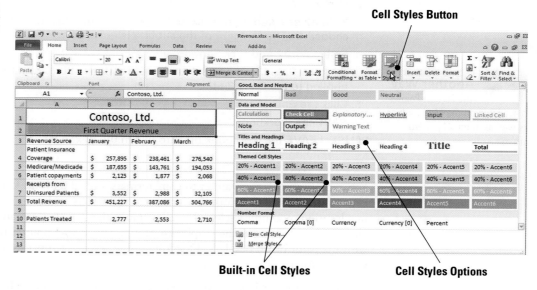

2. Click **20%—Accent4** under *Themed Cell Styles*. The themed shading is applied to A1 and A2. The style changes the font size as well as the cell shading.
3. Select **A1** and click **Cell Styles**.
4. Click **Heading 1** under *Titles and Headings*. This heading style is now applied to the cell.
5. Select **A2** and click **Cell Styles**. The cell style has just been applied to the cell.
6. Click **Heading 2** under *Titles and Headings*. This heading style is now applied to the cell.
7. Select **A8:D8** and click **Cell Styles**.
8. Click **Total** under *Titles and Headings*. This heading style is now applied to the range of cells. Then click cell A12. Your worksheet should resemble Figure 4-25.

Figure 4-25

Worksheet with styles applied

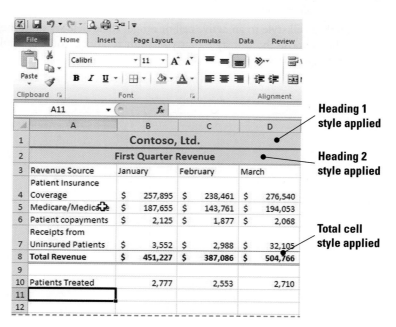

9. **SAVE** the workbook.

PAUSE. LEAVE the workbook open to use in the next exercise.

When you view defined styles in the Cell Styles gallery, you can see the formatting that will be used when you apply each style. This feature allows you to assess the formatting without actually applying it.

Experiment with combining styles to achieve your desired effect. For example, you can click a themed cell style, which will apply shading to the cell. Then, you can click Cell Styles again and click Heading 1, which applies font face, font size, and special formatting effects such as bold or italics.

If you are not pleased with a style you apply, you can Undo the style or apply another style to the cell or range. To remove a cell style from selected cells without deleting the cell style, select the cells that are formatted with that cell style. Click Cell Styles and click Normal. To delete the cell style and remove it from all cells formatted with that style, right-click the cell with the cell style, then click Delete.

Take Note   You cannot delete the Normal cell style.

Modifying a Cell Style

You can also modify or duplicate a cell style to create your own custom style. When doing so, you can either add or delete style attributes.

STEP BY STEP   **Modify a Cell Style**

USE the workbook from the previous exercise.

1. With A12 active, click **Cell Styles** in the *Styles* group. The *Cell Styles* gallery opens.

2. Right-click **20%—Accent6** under *Themed Cell Styles*. Click **Duplicate**. See Figure 4-26. The Style dialog box opens.

Figure 4-26

Right-click option on a style

Cell Styles Option Box   Cell Styles Button

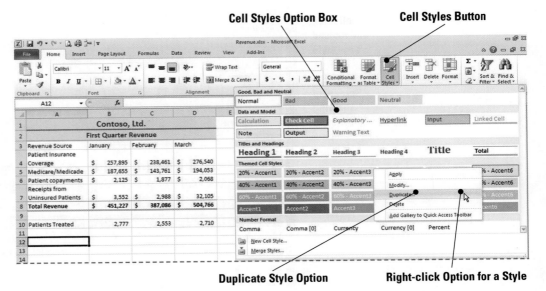

Duplicate Style Option   Right-click Option for a Style

3. Key **Accent Revised** in the Style name box.

4. Click **Format**. Click the Font tab.

5. Click **Italic** in the Font style box.

6. Click 12 in the Size box.

7. Click the Border tab and click your choice of a broken line in the Line Style box.

8. Click the two diagonal borders below the Border box. Click OK. Your formatting modifications will be shown in the Style dialog box. (See Figure 4-27.)

Figure 4-27

Formatting options changed in the Style dialog box

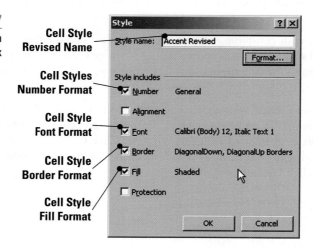

9. Click OK to close the dialog box.

10. Click Cell Styles in the Styles group. Your Accent Revised cell style should be the first style in the *Custom* section. Click Accent Revised to apply the style to A12.

11. Use the Format Painter to apply your style to B12:D12. Double-click on cell A15. Your changes should resemble Figure 4-28.

Figure 4-28

New style in styles option box

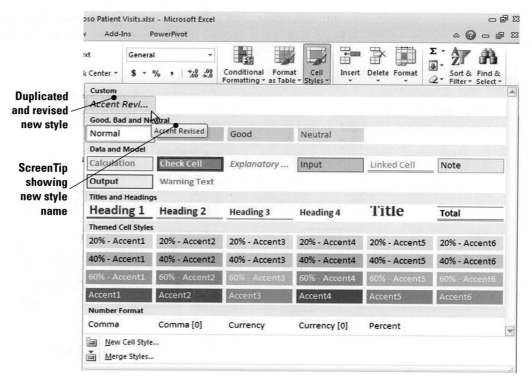

12. **SAVE** the workbook.

PAUSE. LEAVE the workbook open to use in the next exercise.

In this exercise, you duplicated a cell style and then modified the style to create your own custom style. Your custom style was added to the styles gallery. If you had used the Modify command, the existing style would have reflected the formatting changes you made.

Duplicating an existing style and then modifying it is preferable. To modify an existing style, click Cell Styles in the Styles group. When the styles gallery is displayed, right-click the cell style that you want to change, then click Modify. The Style dialog box shown in Figure 4-29 will open with the current style name displayed but not accessible. This tells you that any changes you make to the style will be made to the existing style rather than a customized style.

Figure 4-29

Style dialog box

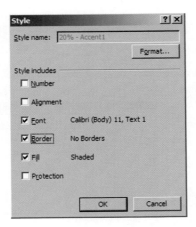

If you'd rather create a new customized style, right-click a style, then click Duplicate. Key an appropriate name for the new cell style you want to create. Then, to change the cell style, click Format. The Format Cells dialog box opens. On the various tabs in the dialog box, select the formatting that you want for the new style. Click OK when you have completed your changes. The changes will be reflected on the Style dialog box. When you are satisfied with the style attributes, click OK. The new cell style is added to the styles gallery and identified as a custom style.

WORKING WITH HYPERLINKED DATA

The Bottom Line

For quick access to related information in another file or on a web page, you can insert a hyperlink in a worksheet cell. Hyperlinks enable you to supplement worksheet data with additional information and resources.

A **hyperlink** is an image or a sequence of characters that opens another file or web page when you click it. The target file or web page can be on the World Wide Web, on an intranet, or on your personal computer. In a workbook containing your personal banking records, for example, you might insert a hyperlink to jump to your bank's online bill-paying service.

Placing a Hyperlink in a Cell

It is easy to embed a hyperlink in a workbook cell. Just click the cell where you want to create the hyperlink and identify the source to which you want to connect. The resulting hyperlink appears in the cell as blue underlined text. When you point to the hyperlink, a ScreenTip describing the link or giving the location of the file appears.

STEP BY STEP   **Place a Hyperlink in a Cell**

USE the workbook from the previous exercise. Verify that you can access the Internet, then perform these steps:

1. With cell A15 active, click the Ribbon's Insert tab.
2. Click Insert Hyperlink in the Links group. The Insert Hyperlink dialog box opens, as shown in Figure 4-30.

Figure 4-30

Insert Hyperlink dialog box

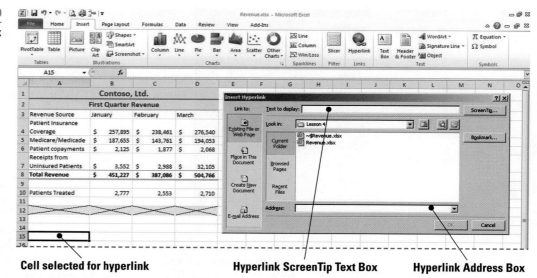

Cell selected for hyperlink   Hyperlink ScreenTip Text Box   Hyperlink Address Box

Another Way

Ctrl+K will open the Insert Hyperlink dialog box, or you can right-click and then select Hyperlink on the shortcut menu.

Take Note   When you key www, Excel recognizes it as the beginning of a web address and *http://* is supplied automatically.

3. In the *Text to display* box, key Microsoft. This is the blue, underlined text that will appear in A15.
4. Click ScreenTip. The *Set Hyperlink ScreenTip* dialog box opens.
5. Key Go to Microsoft's Help and Support Center. Click OK. The text you keyed will replace the default ScreenTip.
6. In the Address box, key www.support.microsoft.com and click OK. The hyperlink text appears in A15. Click on cell B15.

7. Point to the cell containing the hyperlink. Notice the customized ScreenTip displays. The newly inserted hyperlink and ScreenTip are shown in Figure 4-31.

Figure 4-31

Hyperlink inserted in cell

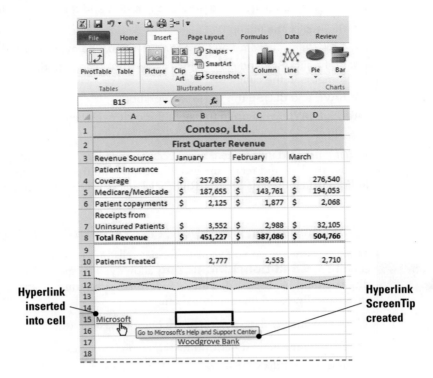

Hyperlink inserted into cell

Hyperlink ScreenTip created

8. Click the left mouse button to open the hyperlink. The web browser opens and connects to Microsoft's Help and Support.

9. Click the **Excel** button on the taskbar to return to your workbook.

10. Key **[your email address]** in A17 and press **Enter.** If you do not have an email address, key *someone@example.com*.

11. **SAVE** the workbook.

PAUSE. LEAVE the workbook open to use in the next exercise.

In this exercise, you created a hyperlink using the Hyperlink command on the Insert tab. You can also create a hyperlink to an email address or an Internet address by typing the address directly in the cell. For example, if you key someone@example.com or www.microsoft.com in a worksheet cell, an automatic hyperlink is created.

The default ScreenTip identifies the full address of the hyperlink and provides instructions for following the link. You can specify the information you want in the tip when you create the link or you can edit it later, as shown in Figure 4-31.

To edit a hyperlink, click and hold to select the cell containing the hyperlink. Right-click and then click Edit Hyperlink to open the Edit Hyperlink dialog box. You can edit the text that displays in the link, the ScreenTip text, or the address where the link will take you. You also can cut or copy a hyperlink and paste it into another cell in the worksheet or another worksheet altogether.

Removing a Hyperlink from a Cell

Within Excel, you can delete a hyperlink and the text that represents it, turn off a single hyperlink, or turn off several hyperlinks at once.

Remove a Hyperlink from a Cell

USE the workbook from the previous exercise and do the following:

1. Right-click the link in D17.
2. Click Clear Contents on the shortcut menu. The hyperlink and text are removed.
3. Right-click B17 and click Remove Hyperlink. The hyperlink is removed and the text remains in the cell.
4. **SAVE** and **CLOSE** the *Revenue* workbook.

PAUSE. LEAVE Excel open to use in the next exercise.

As demonstrated in this exercise, you can remove a hyperlink and the associated text, or you can remove the link and retain the text. To remove multiple links, press Shift and select the hyperlinks to be removed or deleted. Right-click and click the appropriate action.

APPLYING CONDITIONAL FORMATTING TO CELLS

The Bottom Line

There are times when you want to format cells in a particular way only if they meet a specific condition. **Conditional formatting** allows you to specify how cells that meet a given condition should be displayed. Thus, conditional formatting means that Excel applies formatting automatically, based on established criteria.

When you analyze data, you often ask questions, such as:

- Who are the highest performing sales representatives?
- In what months were revenues highest or lowest?
- What are the trends in profits over a specified time period?

Conditional formatting helps answer such questions by highlighting interesting cells or ranges of cells. With conditional formatting, fonts become visual guides that help the reader understand data distribution and variation.

Using the Rule Manager to Apply Conditional Formats

On what conditions or criteria do you want to analyze the data contained in a worksheet? The answer to this question provides the basis for establishing conditional formats. Once data is selected, you can choose one of five preset specific conditional formats that provide a visual analysis of a worksheet or selected range of data. For example, you can specify that when the value in a cell is greater than a given number, the value will be displayed with a particular font or background color. You can even establish multiple conditional formatting rules for a data range.

Use the Rule Manager to Apply Conditional Formats

@ The *Patient Visit Data* file for this lesson is available on the book companion website or in WileyPLUS.

WileyPLUS Extra! features an online tutorial of this task.

GET READY. OPEN the *Patient Visit Data* file. Then, do the following:

1. Click the Home tab if it is not active. Select A1:N1. Merge and center the range and apply the Heading 1 style. (Refer to the "Merge & Split Cells" and the "Apply a Cell Style" exercises as a reference if needed.)
2. Select A2:N2. Merge and center the range and apply the Heading 2 style.
3. Select C4:N8 and click Conditional Formatting in the Styles group.
4. Click Highlight Cells Rules and click Greater Than.
5. In the *Greater Than* dialog box, key 600 and click OK. The highlighted data represents the months in which the doctors were seeing more than the ideal number of patients.
6. With the range still selected, click Conditional Formatting.

7. Mouse over **Highlight Cells Rules** and click **Less Than**.

8. In the *Less Than* dialog box, key **560**. In the *With* box, select **Green Fill with Dark Green Text** and click **OK**. The highlight now contrasts the months in which the patient load was less than expected. Refer to the *Conditional Formatting* dialog box in Figure 4-32.

Figure 4-32

Conditional formatting Less Than box

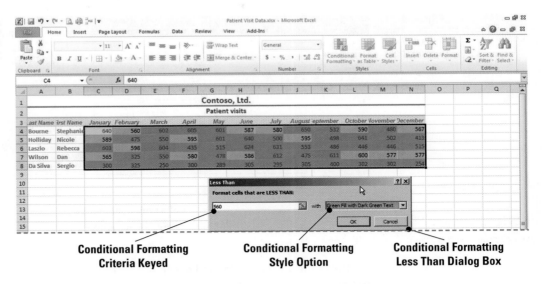

Conditional Formatting Criteria Keyed   **Conditional Formatting Style Option**   **Conditional Formatting Less Than Dialog Box**

9. Click **Conditional Formatting** and mouse over **Top/Bottom Rules**.

10. Click **Top 10%**. In the dialog box, accept **10%** and click **Yellow Fill with Dark Yellow Text**. Click **OK**.

11. Click **Conditional Formatting** and click **Manage Rules** at the bottom of the list.

12. In the *Show formatting rules for* box, click **This Worksheet**. The three conditional formatting rules you have applied are displayed. Position the Conditional Formatting Rules Manager dialog box below the worksheet data so you can view the data and the conditional formatting rules. Notice that the first and third rules apply to overlapping data. Therefore, if a cell value exceeds 600 and that value also falls within the top 10%, the 10% formatting will be applied. See Figure 4-33.

Figure 4-33

Conditional Formatting Rules Manager dialog box

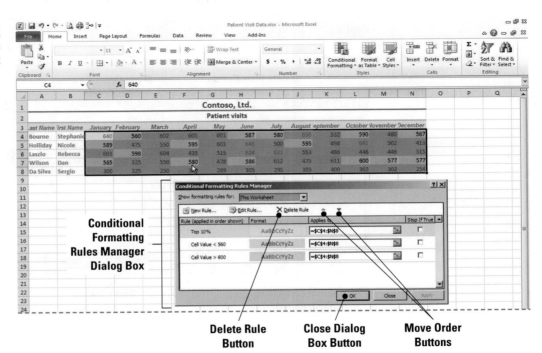

Conditional Formatting Rules Manager Dialog Box

Delete Rule Button   **Close Dialog Box Button**   **Move Order Buttons**

13. Click the Cell Value > 600 rule and click the up arrow twice to move the rule to the top of the list. Click **Apply** and then click **OK**. Click the **Close** button to close the *Conditional Formatting* dialog box. Click on any empty cell to deselect the range. All values greater than 600 are now formatted with the dark red font. Click in any empty cell. Your worksheet should resemble Figure 4-34.

Figure 4-34

Conditional formatting applied to worksheet

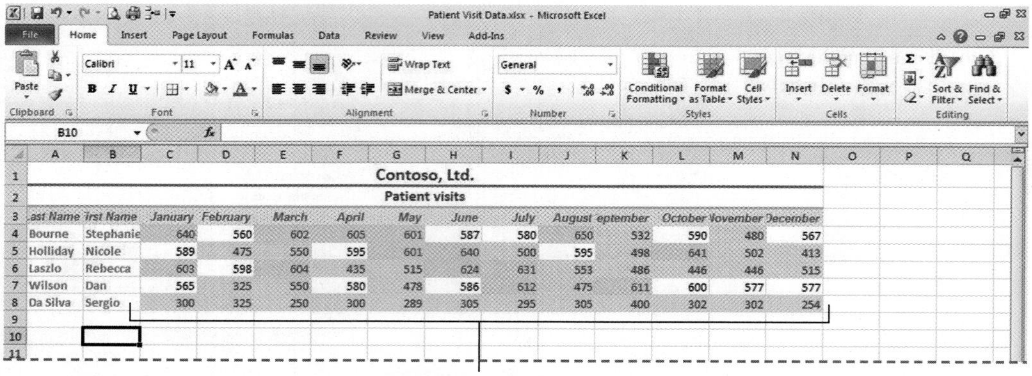

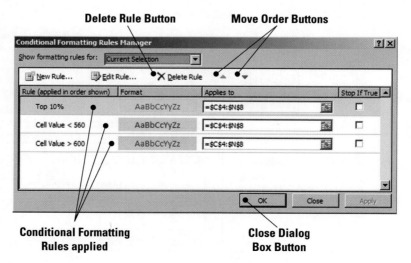

Cells with Conditional Formatting Applied

14. **SAVE** the workbook in the Lesson 4 folder.

PAUSE. LEAVE the workbook open to use in the next exercise.

In this lesson's exercises, you have worked with data related to the number of patients treated each month at Contoso, Ltd. You can use Excel's Rule Manager to apply conditional formatting to provide visual analyses of the data in the *Patient Visit Data* workbook.

In addition, you can display the Conditional Rules Manager to see what rules are in effect for the worksheet and apply those rules at an appropriate time. From the Conditional Formatting Rules Manager, you can add new rules, edit existing rules, or delete one or all of the rules. The rules are applied in the order in which they are listed in the Conditional Formatting Rules Manager. You can apply all the rules, or you can apply specific rules to analyze the data. As you can see in Figure 4-35, formatting is visible when the Conditional Formatting Rules Manager is open. Thus, you can experiment with the formats you want to apply and the order in which they are applied.

Figure 4-35

Conditional Formatting Rules Manager

Applying Multiple Conditional Formatting Rules

Multiple conditional formatting rules can be true. By default, new rules are always added to the top of the list and therefore have a higher precedence. Conditional formatting takes precedence over manual formatting that has been applied to the worksheet or any given cell or range, as shown in the following exercise.

STEP BY STEP   **Applying Multiple Conditional Formatting Rules**

USE the workbook from the previous exercise.

1. Click on the Column C header to highlight the entire column. Click on the arrow below the Insert Rows button then click Insert Sheet Columns. A new column is inserted. The Format Painter button emerges with your new column. Click on it and accept the first option (default) of *Format Same as Left*.

2. Click on C3 and key Job Title, then press Enter.

3. In cell C4, key Physician, then press Enter. Click C4 again to activate it, then click and hold and drag the contents to C7.

4. Click C8 and key PA. You have now reentered the data that was removed in a previous exercise.

5. Select D8:N8. Click Conditional Formatting and click Highlight Cells Rules.

6. Click Less Than. Key 300 in the value box and click Red Text. Click OK.

7. Click Conditional Formatting, then click Manage Rules. In the *Show formatting rules for* box, click This Worksheet. Although the last rule has the highest precedence, it applies only to the PA's schedule and therefore does not conflict with any of the rules that apply to the physicians' schedules.

8. Click the Close button to close the dialog box. You will not apply any changes in the *Conditional Formatting Manager* dialog box. Click on any empty cell to view your changes.

9. **SAVE** the workbook.

PAUSE. LEAVE the workbook open to use in the next exercise.

Applying Specific Conditional Formats

Excel has three preset conditional formats that use color and symbols to provide visual guides to help you understand data distribution and variation: color scales, icon sets, and data bars.

STEP BY STEP   **Apply Specific Conditional Formats**

USE the workbook from the previous exercise. Then, do the following:

1. Click Conditional Formatting.

2. Mouse over Clear Rules and then click Clear Rules from Entire Sheet. All conditional formatting is cleared from the data.

3. Select D4:O8. Click Conditional Formatting.

4. Mouse over Data Bars and click Blue Data Bar in the *Gradient Fill* section (first choice). Data bars show that the longer the dark blue portion of the bar is, the higher the value is in relation to other cells in the data range.

5. Repeat Steps 1 and 2 to clear the Data Bars. (See Figure 4-36.) The data range will still be selected.

Figure 4-36

Clear data bars or conditional formatting

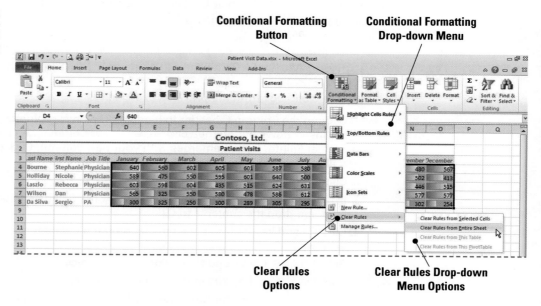

6. Click **Conditional Formatting**. Mouse over Color Scales and click the **Red-Yellow-Green Color Scale** (first option in the second column). The darker colors indicate the lower values.

7. Once again refer to Steps 1 and 2 to clear the Formatting Rules. Refer to Figure 4-36 if necessary. Click **Conditional Formatting**. Mouse over Icon Sets then click the **3 Flags set** in the Indicators group.

8. **SAVE** the workbook as *Patient Visits with Icons*.

PAUSE. LEAVE the workbook open to use in the next exercise.

A two-color scale helps you compare a range of cells by using a gradation of two colors. The shade of the color represents higher or lower values. The shade of the color in a three-color scale represents higher, middle, and lower values.

You can use an icon set to interpret and classify data into three to five categories. Each icon represents a range of values. For example, in the three-flag icon set, the green flag represents higher values, the yellow represents middle values, and the red represents lower values.

A data bar helps you see the value of a cell relative to other cells in the data range. The length of the data bar represents the value in the cell. A longer bar represents a higher value, and a shorter bar represents a lower value. Data bars are useful in spotting higher and lower numbers, especially with large amounts such as those in a retailer's after-Thanksgiving sales report.

CLEARING A CELL'S FORMATTING

The Bottom Line

The Clear command in the Editing group on the Home tab lets you clear contents and formatting or allows you to selectively remove contents or formatting. When you want to redesign the appearance of an existing worksheet, click Clear and then click Clear Formats. The content will remain, and you then can choose to apply manual formatting, styles, or conditional formatting. Clearing all formatting ensures that you are starting with a clean formatting slate.

STEP BY STEP | **Clear a Cell's Formatting**

USE the workbook from previous exercise.

1. Press Ctrl+A to select the entire worksheet.
2. Click the Clear button in the *Editing* group. (See Figure 4-37.)
3. Click Clear Formats. All formatting is cleared from the data. If you selected Clear All, the data would be removed as well as the formatting.

Figure 4-37

Clear button and options in the Editing group

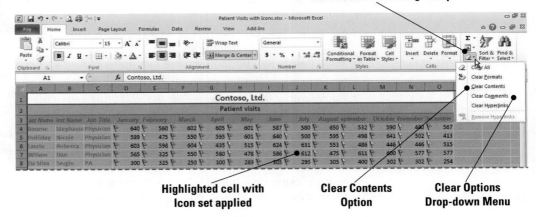

Clear Button in Editing Group

Highlighted cell with Icon set applied　**Clear Contents Option**　**Clear Options Drop-down Menu**

4. **CLOSE** the file without saving.
CLOSE Excel.

Take Note　If you select Clear All, contents and formatting are removed. Selecting Clear Contents will remove the data within the selected range, but the formatting will remain.

SKILL SUMMARY

In This Lesson, You Learned How To:
Insert and delete cells
Manually format cell contents
Copying cell formatting with the format painter
Formatting cells with styles
Working with hyperlinked data
Applying conditional formatting to cells
Clearing a cell's formatting

Knowledge Assessment

Fill in the Blank

Complete the following sentences by writing the correct word or words in the blanks provided.

1. When a single cell is created by combining two or more selected cells, the new cell is referred to as a(n) _____.

2. A(n) _____ is a set of formatting attributes that you can apply as a group to a selected cell or range of cells.

3. A shortcut or link that opens a stored document or connects with the Internet is called a(n) _____.

4. When formatting is applied to data based on established criteria, it is said to be _____ formatting.

5. Bold, italics, and underlining are examples of formatting _____.

6. You can apply formatting to multiple cells with the _____.

7. By default, a feature introduced in Excel 2007 called the _____ displays above the right-click shortcut menu.

8. Font sizes can be changed by clicking the _____ button on the Ribbon.

9. The _____ option allows you to change the font color, font type, and heading styles for a cell's content.

10. Right-clicking on a built-in Cell Style and selecting any option from the drop-down menu opens the _____ dialog box.

True/False

Circle T if the statement is true or F if the statement is false.

T F 1. When you insert a cell into a row, all data in that row is shifted down.

T F 2. When you shift cells down and data in another cell is replaced, that data is copied to the Office Clipboard.

T F 3. You can select a large range of cells by selecting the first cell in the range, pressing Shift, and selecting the last cell in the range.

T F 4. You can merge cells horizontally, but not vertically.

T F 5. If you want the dollar sign and decimals to align in a column, apply the Accounting format.

T F 6. When you wrap text in a cell, the row height is automatically adjusted to accommodate the multiple-line text.

T F 7. Any cell in a worksheet can be split.

T F 8. When you apply a style to text, any conflicting formatting in the cell or range is replaced by the style format.

T F 9. When you choose the Remove a hyperlink option, the link and the text are removed.

T F 10. If you select an entire worksheet and click Clear and Clear All, then the worksheet will be blank.

Competency Assessment

Project 4-1: Apply Basic Formatting

In this project, you will apply formatting attributes to a workbook used to track annual utilities expenses.

GET READY. LAUNCH Excel if it is not already running. Then, do the following:

@ The *Utilities* file for this lesson is available on the book companion website or in WileyPLUS.

1. Click the File tab and click Open.
2. **OPEN** the *Utilities* file from the data files for this lesson.
3. Select A8:G8. Click the Insert arrow in the Cells group and click Insert Cells.
4. Click OK on the Insert dialog box to shift the cells down.
5. Select A27:G27 and click Cut in the Clipboard group.
6. Select A8 and click Paste in the Clipboard group.
7. Select A2:G2. Click Bold in the Font group.
8. Select the column labels and click Center in the Alignment group.
9. With the column labels still selected, click the Font Color arrow and click Red.
10. Click Quick Print on the Quick Access Toolbar.
11. Click the File tab. Click Save As.
12. **SAVE** the workbook as *Utilities 4-1* in your Lesson 4 folder.

LEAVE the workbook open for the next project.

Project 4-2: Enhance a Worksheet Appearance

In this exercise, you will apply additional formatting attributes to an existing workbook.

USE the workbook from Project 4-1. Then, perform these steps:

1. Select A1. Click the arrow in the Font box and click Cambria.
2. With A1 still selected, click Increase Font Size until the Font Size box shows 16 point.
3. Apply the Green font color to the title.
4. Select A1:G1 and click Merge & Center in the Alignment group.
5. With only the merged A1 cell still selected, click Middle Align in the Alignment group.
6. Select F2 and click Wrap Text in the Alignment group.
7. With F2 selected, click the Format Painter in the Clipboard group. Drag the Format Painter across all column labels.
8. Adjust column width if necessary so that all column labels are completely visible.
9. Select the labels and click Middle Align.
10. Click B3, press Shift, and click G15 to select the range that contains values. Apply the Number format to the range.
11. Print the worksheet.
12. **SAVE** the workbook as *Utilities 4-2* in the Lesson 4 folder.

CLOSE the workbook. **LEAVE** Excel open for the next project.

Proficiency Assessment

Project 4-3: Format Training Budget

Graphic Design Institute's Training Department provides in-house technical and soft-skills training for the firm's 1,200 employees. Apply the formatting skills you learned in Lesson 4 to give the Training Budget worksheet a professional finish.

@ The *Training Budget* file for this lesson is available on the book companion website or in WileyPLUS.

GET READY. OPEN *Training Budget* from the data files for this lesson. Then, do the following:

1. Merge and center cells A1:E1.
2. Key Graphic Design Institute as the worksheet title.
3. Click Cell Styles in the Styles group and apply the 40%—Accent1 style to the title.
4. Click Cell Styles and apply the Heading 1 style.
5. Merge and center cells A2:E2. Key the subtitle Training Department Budget.
6. Apply the 20%—Accent1 fill to the subtitle. Apply the Heading 2 style.
7. Merge and center the blank row above the column labels.
8. Select the column labels and apply the Note style.
9. Key TOTAL in A18 and apply the Total style to row 18.
10. Select D6:E17. Click the Number group Dialog Box Launcher. Click the Number category, set decimal places to 0, and check Use 1000 separator.
11. Select the nonadjacent cells D5:E5, E18. Apply the Currency format and reduce decimals to 0.
12. Print the worksheet.
13. **SAVE** the workbook as *Training Budget 4-3*.

LEAVE the workbook open for the next project.

Project 4-4: Hyperlinks

In this project, you will create and edit hyperlinks that connect a worksheet with selected web pages. You'll then insert links to send email messages to selected recipients.

USE the *Training Budget 4-3* workbook from Project 4-3.

1. Label cell B4 Contact.
2. Click the Insert tab.
3. Select B5 and click Hyperlink.
4. Key A. Datum Corporation as the text to display.
5. Key www.adatum.com in the address box. Click OK.
6. In B11, create a hyperlink that displays as Lucerne Publishing at www.lucernepublishing.com.
7. In B16, create a hyperlink for Margie's Travel. The address is www.margiestravel.com.
8. Select B16 and click Hyperlink to open the Edit Hyperlink dialog box. Edit the ScreenTip to read Corporate contract for all travel.
9. Select B13 and create an email link for the consultant: someone@example.com.
10. **PRINT** the worksheet. **SAVE** the workbook as *Training Budget 4-4*. **CLOSE** the workbook.

LEAVE Excel open for the next project.

Project 4-5: Format Sales Report

Litware, Inc., wants to apply Font and Alignment group formatting to enhance its sales report's appearance and readability. You are responsible for making this change.

GET READY. OPEN *Litware Sales* from the data files for this lesson. Then take the following actions:

@ The *Litware Sales* file for this lesson is available on the book companion website or in WileyPLUS.

1. Merge and center the title and apply the Heading 1 style.
2. Merge and center the subtitle and apply the Heading 2 style.
3. Select A1:G2 Click the Border arrow to open the Format Cells dialog box.
4. Under Line Style, select the last line style in column 2.
5. Click the Color arrow and click Red.
6. Click Outline and Inside in Presets. Click OK.
7. Select B4 and use the fill handle to extend the months across the remaining columns of data.
8. Select the labels in row 4. Center the labels and apply the Red font color. Add a Thick Box border.
9. Apply the Accounting format to the values in row 5. Reduce decimals to 0.
10. Select B6:G12 and apply the Number format with comma separator and 0 decimals.
11. Apply the Total style to row 13.
12. **PRINT** the workbook. **SAVE** the workbook as *Litware Sales 4-5*.

LEAVE the workbook open for the next project.

Project 4-6: Apply Conditional Formatting to the Sales Report

Next, you will apply conditional formatting to the Litware, Inc., sales report to highlight the top performing sales representatives.

USE the workbook from Project 4-5.

1. Select B13:G13.
2. Click Conditional Formatting and click Highlight Cells Rules.
3. Click Greater Than. In the Greater Than dialog box, key 140,000 and click OK. Total sales exceed $140,000 for February and May.
4. Select B5:G12. Click Conditional Formatting, click Top/Bottom Rules, and then click Top 10%. When the dialog box opens, four cells are highlighted.
5. Drag the dialog box below the data range. Change the Top percentage number to 1. Format cells that rank in the Top 1% with a red border and click OK. Deborah Poe was the top sales performer with $25,874 for the month of May.
6. Click Conditional Formatting and click Icon Sets. Click 3 Flags. Colored flags are applied to the sales data. Green flags mark the top 10%; red flags mark the bottom 10%; and yellow flags mark the middle range.
7. Print the worksheet.
8. Click Conditional Formatting and click Manage Rules.
9. In the dialog box, show the formatting for This Worksheet. The formatting rules are listed in the order you created them.
10. Delete the Icon Set rule.
11. **PRINT** the worksheet. **SAVE** the workbook as *Litware Sales 4-6*. **CLOSE** the workbook.

LEAVE Excel open for the next project.

INTERNET READY

In this lesson, you applied formatting styles that are preset in Excel. You also created a custom style. Open Excel Help and key create style in the Excel Help Search box. Open the Apply, create, or remove a cell style link. Click Create a custom cell style.

Merge four cells in an open worksheet and key your name in the cell. Follow the steps provided to create a custom style. Use your first name as the style name. Include the following formats in the style:

- **Alignment:** Horizontal Center Vertical Center
- **Font:** CG Omega, 16 point, Italic
- **Border:** Style: Broken line (your choice)
  Color: Green
  Presets: Outline
- **Fill:** Pattern Color: Yellow
  Pattern Style: Thin Vertical Stripe Pattern Style

Key your name in cell A1 of a new blank workbook. Apply the style to your name. Save the workbook as *My Style*.

Formatting Worksheets 5

LESSON SKILL MATRIX

In This Lesson, You Will Learn How To:

Working with Rows and Columns

Using Themes

Modifying a Worksheet's Onscreen and Printed Appearance

Inserting Headers and Footers

Preparing a Document for Printing

KEY TERMS

- boundary
- column heading
- column width
- document theme
- footer
- gridlines
- header
- orientation
- page break
- Page Break Preview
- Paste Special
- Print Preview
- row heading
- row height
- scaling

Margie's Travel is an agency that sells travel-related products and services to clients on behalf of third parties such as airlines, hotels, and cruise lines. The company also custom designs corporate and leisure travel packages for its clients. The agency's owner, Margie Shoop, specializes in creative, detailed, and personalized service to assure clients they will have an enjoyable and trouble-free travel experience. She employs experienced and knowledgeable travel consultants whose goal is to save clients time, effort, and money. The company maintains a 24/7 emergency service hotline and nationwide toll-free accessibility for business travelers and tourists. The company manages various aspects of its business, including travel itineraries, tour packages, vendor lists, frequent traveler lists, and customer requests, using the Excel workbook format.

SOFTWARE ORIENTATION

Page Layout Commands

One of the easiest ways to share information in a worksheet or workbook is to print copies for others to review. To prepare worksheets for printing and distribution, you will continue to use some of the Home tab command groups, but you will primarily use the Page Layout command groups shown in Figure 5-1. Applying formatting options from these command groups will ensure that your printed worksheets are more useful, more readable, and more attractive.

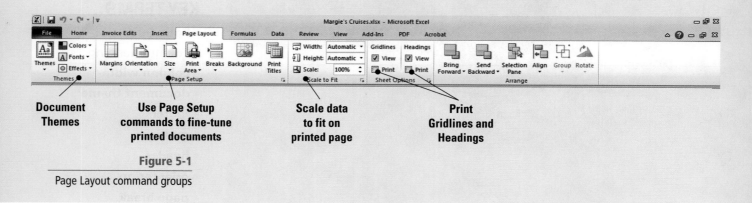

Figure 5-1

Page Layout command groups

WORKING WITH ROWS AND COLUMNS

The Bottom Line

When you open a new worksheet, the columns and rows in that worksheet are uniform. However, uniformity rarely fits the data you want to include in a worksheet or workbook. For some columns, you might need only two or three characters; for others, you will need to increase the **column width** to accommodate more data than will fit in the default column width of 8.43 characters.

Inserting or Deleting a Row or Column

Many times, after you've already entered data in a worksheet, you will need to insert additional rows or columns. To insert a row, select the row or a cell in the row *below* which you want the new row to appear. The new row will then be inserted *above* the selected cell or row. For example, to insert a row above row 10, click any cell in row 10. To insert multiple rows, select the same number of rows as you want to insert.

Inserting columns works the same way. If you want to insert a column to the left of column D, click any cell in column D. Columns are inserted to the left of the selected cell, and by default, the inserted column is formatted the same as the column to the left.

The same principles apply when you need to delete a row or column. In the following exercise, you will delete an entire row from a worksheet.

Take Note   It does not matter which column you use to select cells when you want to insert rows or which row you select when you want to insert columns.

STEP BY STEP   **Insert or Delete a Row or Column**

The *Margie's Cruises* file for this lesson is available on the book companion website or in WileyPLUS.

WileyPLUS Extra! features an online tutorial of this task.

Another Way   After you insert a row or column, you can select the location where you want to insert another row or column and press Ctrl+Y.

GET READY. Locate the Lesson 5 folder to access the exercise files. Then, follow these steps:

1. **OPEN** the *Margie's Cruises* data file. The Home tab will be active.
2. Select any cell in row 12; then press **Ctrl** and select a cell in row 17. Click the arrow next to Insert in the Cells group and click **Insert Sheet Rows**.
3. Select any cell in column A. Click the arrow under the **Insert cells** button in the Cells group, then click **Insert Sheet Columns**.
4. In A5, key **Destination**.
5. Select **A6:A11**. Click **Merge & Center** in the Alignment group.
6. Select **A13:17**. Click **Merge & Center**.
7. Select **A19:23**. Click **Merge & Center**.
8. Label the merged cells **Mexico** (A6), **Hawaii** (A13), and **Alaska** (A19).
9. Select **A6:A23**. Click the **Middle Align** button in the Alignment group and **Bold** in the Font group.
10. Select any cell in row 2. Click the arrow under the Delete button in the Cells group and click **Delete Sheet Rows**.
11. Click the row header for the new row 2. Right-click the highlighted row and click **Delete**.

PAUSE. LEAVE the workbook open to use in the next exercise.

Modifying Row Height and Column Width

By default, all columns in a new worksheet are the same width and all rows are the same height. In most worksheets, you will want to change some column or row defaults to accommodate more or less data. Changes can be made using the Format commands in the Cells group on the Home tab.

Modifying row height and column width can make a worksheet's contents easier to read and increase its visual appeal. You can set a row or column to a specific height or width, change the height or width to fit the contents, or change the height or width by dragging the **boundary**, or the line between rows or columns.

STEP BY STEP   **Modify Row Height and Column Width**

USE the workbook from the previous exercise to perform these steps:

1. Click the heading for column D. Press and hold the mouse button and drag to select column E. Release the mouse button.
2. Click **Format** in the Cells group.
3. Under *Cell Size*, click **Column Width** on the options list, as shown in Figure 5-2.

Figure 5-2

Cell Size options

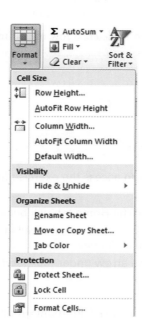

4. In the Column Width dialog box (shown in Figure 5-3), key **15**. Click **OK**. You have adjusted the column width to the specific size of 15.

Figure 5-3

Column Width dialog box

5. Select column **C**. Click **Format**, then click **AutoFit Column Width**. This command adjusts the column width to fit the longest entry in the column.
6. Click the right boundary of column G and drag to the right until the **ScreenTip** says **Width: 17.00**.
7. Click any cell in column A. Click **Format** in the Cells group.
8. Under Cell Size, click **Column Width**.
9. In the *Column Width* dialog box, key **16**. Click **OK**.
10. Set the width for column B to **30** characters.
11. Select row **3** and click **Format**. Click **Row Height** and key **25** in the Row Height dialog box. Click **OK**.

12. **CREATE** a Lesson 5 folder and **SAVE** the workbook, as shown in Figure 5-4.

Figure 5-4

Save the worksheet with
changes applied.

Adjusted Row Height   **Adjusted Column Widths**   **Format Cells, Rows and Columns button**

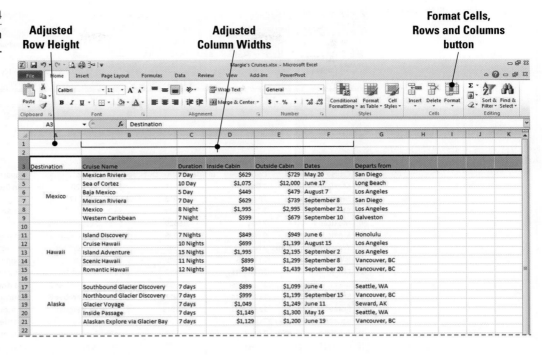

Another Way
When formatting
rows and columns, you can
press Enter instead of clicking
the OK button in the dialog
box.

PAUSE. LEAVE the workbook open to use in the next exercise.

Take Note
In previous lessons, when you double-clicked the right column boundary, you were utilizing the AutoFit Column Width option.

Row height, or the top-to-bottom height of a row, is measured in points; one point is equal to 1/72 inch. The default row height is 15 points, but you can specify a row height of 0 to 409 points. Although you can specify a column width of 0 to 255 characters, the default column width is 8.43 characters (based on the default font and font size). If a column width or row height is set to 0, then the corresponding column or row is hidden.

As you learned in Lesson 2, when the text you enter exceeds the column width, the text overflows to the next column, or it is truncated when the next cell contains data. Similarly, if the value entered in a column exceeds the column width, the #### symbols, shown in Figure 5-5, indicate the number is larger than the column width.

Figure 5-5

Symbols indicating a number is larger than the column width

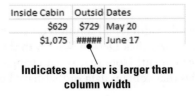

Indicates number is larger than column width

Another Way
To quickly autofit
the entries in all rows on a
worksheet, click Select All, then
double-click one of the column
boundaries.

Depending on the alignment of the data in your columns, worksheet data may appear crowded when you use the AutoFit Column Width option because this option adjusts column width to the exact width of the longest entry in the column. Therefore, after using this option, you may want to use the mouse to drag the right column boundary when a column with right-aligned data is adjacent to one with left-aligned data, as shown in Figure 5-6.

Figure 5-6

Separate right-aligned and
left-aligned columns

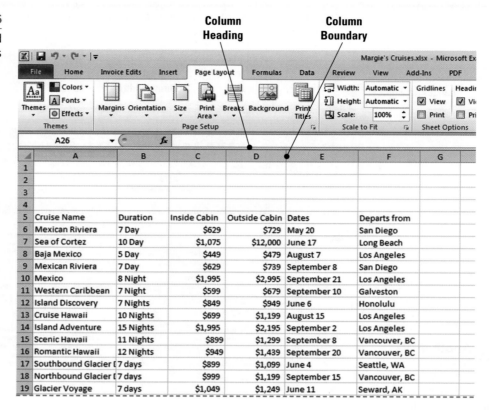

When you drag the boundary, the width of the column in characters and pixels appears in a
ScreenTip above the column headings. See Figure 5-7 for an example.

Figure 5-7

Column width is shown

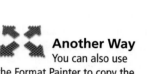

Another Way
You can also use
the Format Painter to copy the
width of one column to other
columns. To do so, select the
heading of the first column,
click the Format Painter, and
then click the heading of the
column or columns to which
you want to apply the column
width.

In Excel, you can change the default width for all columns on a worksheet or a workbook. To do
so, click Format; then, under Cell Size, click Default Width. In the Standard Width dialog box,
key a new default column measurement. Note that when changing the default column width
or row height, columns and rows that contain data or that have been previously formatted will
retain their formatting.

Take Note   When you are more familiar with the ways to modify rows and columns, you will likely use one
method consistently.

Formatting an Entire Row or Column

To save time, achieve a consistent appearance, and align cell contents in a consistent manner, you often want to apply the same format to an entire row or column. To apply formatting to a row or column, click the **row heading** or **column heading** (its identifying letter or number) to select it, then apply the appropriate format or style.

STEP BY STEP   **Format an Entire Row or Column**

USE the workbook from the previous exercise to carry out the following steps:

1. Select **A1:G1**, then click **Merge & Center**. With A1 selected, click **Cell Styles** in the Styles group and click **Heading 1** under *Titles and Headings*.
2. Key **Margie's Travel** and press **Enter**.
3. With A1 selected, click **Increase Font Size** until the font size is 20 points. Notice that the height of row 1 increased to accommodate the larger font size. (See Figure 5-8.)

Figure 5-8

Font size applied

Merge & Center button

Merge Cells with increased font size applied

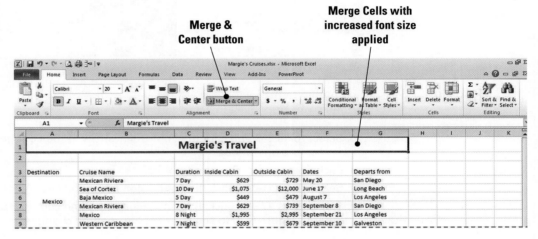

Troubleshooting If you select row 1 rather than the data range and apply the style, the bottom border style effect will extend to the end of the row (cell XFD1).

4. Merge and center A2:G2. Apply the **Heading 2** style.
5. Key **Cruise Options, Prepared for Fabrikam, Inc.**, and press **Enter**.
6. Click on the newly merged **A2** and increase the font size to **16 points**. Note that the period after Inc. is highlighted in light blue. Please include this when you key the heading.
7. Select **A3:G3** and apply **Heading 3** style to the column labels. Increase the font size to **12 points**.
8. Select row **3**. Click **Middle Align and Center** in the Alignment group.
9. Select columns **D** and **E**. Click the **Number Format** box and click **Accounting**. Refer to Figure 5-9 to view the formatting changes in your worksheet.

Figure 5-9

Heading, alignment, and font size applied

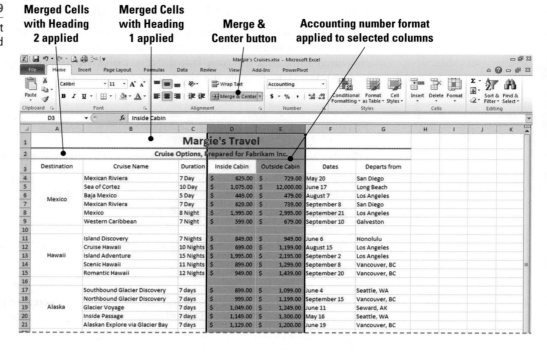

Take Note   Accounting format will be applied to any number you enter in column C or D, even if, for example, you enter the number as currency.

10. Select rows **5–9** and click the **Font Color** arrow in the Font group. This activates the font colors option box.

11. Click **Green** under Standard Colors.

12. Select rows **11–15**. Click the **Font Color** arrow and click **Purple** under Standard Colors.

13. Select rows **17–21**. Click the **Font Color** arrow and click **Red** under Standard Colors. Refer to Figure 5-10 to see your final formatting changes.

Figure 5-10

Formatting applied

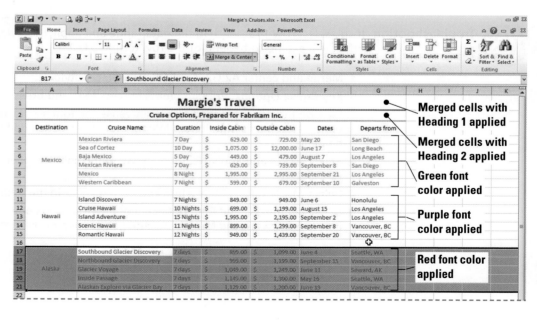

14. **SAVE** the workbook.

PAUSE. LEAVE the workbook open to use in the next exercise.

Formatting rows and columns rather than applying formatting to the range of cells that contain data has an advantage: Later, when you insert rows or columns or add additional data to a worksheet, it will be formatted correctly.

Hiding or Unhiding a Row or Column

You may not want or need all rows and columns in a worksheet to be visible all the time, particularly if the worksheet contains a large number of rows or columns. You can hide a row or a column by using the Hide command or by setting the row height or column width to zero. When rows are hidden, they do not appear onscreen or in printouts.

STEP BY STEP   **Hide or Unhide a Row or Column**

USE the workbook from the previous exercise. Then, do the following:

1. Click the column **D** header to select the entire column. Click **Format** in the Cells group.
2. Mouse over Hide & Unhide and click **Hide Columns** in the Visibility group. This process will hide column D from view. A thick line appears when you have hidden the column.
3. Click the row **11** header, press **Shift**, and click the row **15** heading. Click **Format** in the Cells group. This has selected all five rows.
4. Mouse over Hide & Unhide and click **Hide Rows** in the Visibility group. A thick line has once again appeared to show your action of hiding the rows.
5. Click **Quick Print** 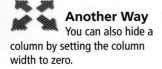 on the Quick Access Toolbar. As shown in Figure 5-11, you can recognize when rows or columns are hidden because numbers are skipped in the row headings or letters are skipped in the column headings. When you view your printed worksheet, note that it does not show the hidden rows or column.

Another Way
You can also hide a column by setting the column width to zero.

Figure 5-11

Hidden column and rows

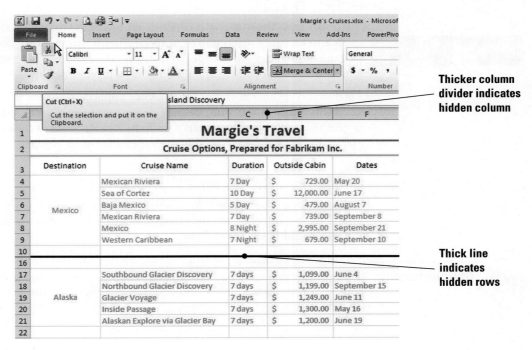

6. Select columns **C** and **E** (which are columns on each side of the hidden column).
7. Click **Format**, mouse over Hide & Unhide, and click **Unhide Columns** in the Visibility group. Column D is again visible.

Take Note   You must click the row or column heading to select the entire row or column when you want to display a hidden row or column. Selecting the data in the rows or columns will not release the hidden rows or columns.

8. Select row **10**, press **Shift**, and select row **16**. Click **Format**. Point to Hide & Unhide and click **Unhide Rows** in the Visibility group. As a result of this action, your worksheet returns to its original state from before beginning the exercise.

9. **SAVE** the workbook.

PAUSE. LEAVE the workbook open to use in the next exercise.

A worksheet may contain rows or columns of sensitive data that you are not using or do not want to be visible while you are working in other areas of the worksheet. For example, if a person who is working with the Margie's Cruises worksheet wants to focus on or print the cruises to only one destination, the rows containing the data for the other destinations can be hidden.

To make hidden rows visible, select the row above and the row below the hidden row or rows and use the Format commands to Unhide Rows. If the first row is hidden, use the Go To feature to make the row visible. To display hidden columns, select the adjacent columns and follow the same steps used for displaying hidden rows.

You can also hide or unhide multiple rows or columns using this same method.

 Troubleshooting When you select rows 10 and 16 to unhide the hidden rows, you must select them in a way that includes the hidden rows. Press Shift when you select row 16 or select row 10 and drag to include row 16. If you select row 10, press Ctrl, and click row 16, the rows will not unhide.

 Ref   You will learn more about the Go To feature in Lesson 6.

USING THEMES

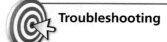
The Bottom Line

A **document theme** is a predefined set of colors, fonts, lines, and fill effects that can be applied to an entire workbook or to specific items within a workbook, such as charts or tables. Document themes were introduced in Excel 2007, and you can use them to quickly and easily format an entire document and give it a fresh, professional look.

Themes can be shared across other Office applications, such as Microsoft Office Word and Microsoft Office PowerPoint. Because document themes can be shared, this feature enables you to give all your Office documents a uniform look in terms of colors, fonts, and effects. (Effects, such as shadows or bevels, modify the appearance of an object.)

Choosing a Theme for a Worksheet

Excel has several predefined document themes. When you apply a theme to a worksheet or workbook, the colors, fonts, and effects contained within that theme replace any styles that were already applied to cells or ranges.

 Troubleshooting If you or another user has customized one or more document themes, those themes will appear at the top of the list, and you may have to scroll down to see all of Excel's built-in themes.

STEP BY STEP   **Choose a Theme for a Worksheet**

USE the workbook from the previous exercise.

1. Click the Page Layout tab to make it active.
2. Click Themes. The first 20 built-in themes are displayed in a preview window (see Figure 5-12). Mouse over each theme and observe the changes in the title lines of your worksheet.

Figure 5-12

Built-in document themes

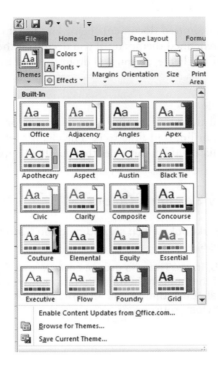

3. Scroll down and click Verve to apply that style to your worksheet.
4. Click the File tab to access Backstage. Click Save As and save the workbook in the Lesson 5 folder as *Verve Theme*. Here, you changed the default document theme by selecting another predefined document theme. As you can see, document themes that you apply immediately affect the styles that have already been applied in your document.

Take Note   Because you increased the font size after you applied Heading 1 to the title, the font size remains at 20 points. If you had changed the font size before applying the heading style, the title would be displayed in 14 points, because that is the default font size for themes.

5. Click Themes and click Opulent. The appearance of your document is significantly changed.
6. Click Save As and save the workbook in the Lesson 5 folder. Name your workbook *Opulent Theme*.

PAUSE. LEAVE the workbook open to use in the next exercise.

Figure 5-12 shows 20 built-in themes for Excel 2010, but when you scroll down, you can see all the built-in themes. The styles that you applied in the previous exercises were the styles associated with the default Office theme. When you opened the styles gallery, the colors, fonts, and effects that were displayed were those that make up the Office theme.

Remember that styles are used to format specific cells or ranges within a worksheet; document themes are used to apply sets of styles (colors, fonts, lines, and fill effects) to an entire document. All of the default Office theme styles you applied to the titles in a previous exercise were changed when you applied a different theme.

In this exercise, you applied two document themes so that the owner of Margie's Travel can select the one that will be used on all company documents. By saving both themes, the owner can compare the differences between the two and then choose which theme to use. Because themes are consistent in all Microsoft Office 2010 programs, all of the company documents for Margie's Travel can have a uniform appearance.

Many companies create a customized document theme and use it consistently. You can experiment by applying various predefined themes until you decide on the "look" that appeals to you, or you can design a customized theme, as you will do in the next exercise.

Customizing a Theme

You can create a customized theme by making changes to one or more of an existing theme's components—colors, fonts, or line and fill effects. The changes you make to one or more of a theme's components immediately affect the styles that you have applied in the active document.

STEP BY STEP   **Customize a Theme by Selecting Colors**

USE the *Opulent Theme* workbook, which should be open from the previous exercise, to complete the following steps:

1. On the **Page Layout** tab, in the Themes group, click **Colors**. Figure 5-13 illustrates the color array for some of the built-in themes. Remember, you have to scroll through the entire list to see them all. Each theme has an array of accent colors that are the same as the accents in the Styles group.

Figure 5-13

Theme colors

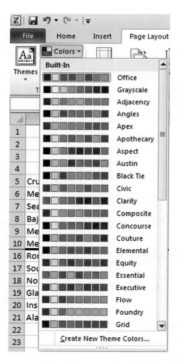

2. Click **Create New Theme Colors**. The *Create New Theme Colors* dialog box opens (see Figure 5-14), showing the colors used in the Opulent theme that is currently applied to the worksheet. Move the dialog box so that you can see the worksheet titles and column labels.

Figure 5-14

Create New Theme Colors dialog box

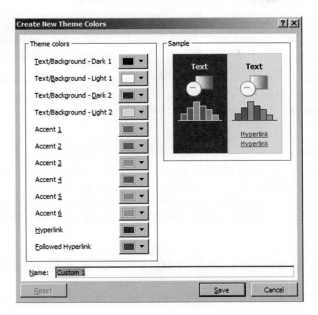

3. Click the **Text/Background—Dark 2** arrow. The current color is highlighted under *Theme Colors*. Click **Accent 6** to change the color to orange.

4. Click the arrow next to **Accent 1** in the dialog box and click **Accent 6** under *Theme Colors*. In the *Name* box, key **My Colors**. Click **Save**. The font and line color in the worksheet titles reflect the customized theme colors. Refer to Figure 5-15 to see the worksheet with custom theme colors.

Figure 5-15

Modified theme applied

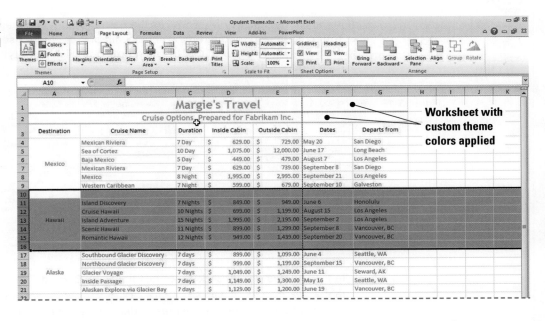

PAUSE. LEAVE the workbook open to use in the next exercise.

Take Note   To return all theme color elements to their original colors, click the Reset button in the Custom Colors dialog box before you click Save.

In the Create New Theme Colors dialog box, click the button next to the theme color element that you want to change. The theme colors are presented in every color gallery with a set of lines and shades based on those colors. By selecting colors from this expanded matched set, you can make formatting choices for individual pieces of content that will still follow the themes. When the theme colors change, the gallery of colors changes and so does all document content using them.

It is easy to create your own theme that can be applied to all of your Excel workbooks and other Office 2010 documents. You can choose any of the color combinations shown in Figure 5-13, which represent the built-in themes, or you can create your own combination of colors.

When you clicked Create New Theme Colors, the dialog box shown in Figure 5-14 opened. Theme colors contain four text and background colors, six accent colors, and two hyperlink colors. You can change any or all of these when you customize a theme.

Customizing a Theme by Selecting Fonts and Effects

Now that you have customized the color of your themes, you are ready to choose the font for your theme. Use fonts and effects that create a unique image for your documents. Themes contain a heading font and a body font. When you click the Theme Fonts button, you see the name of the heading font and the body text font that is used for each theme.

STEP BY STEP   **Customize a Theme by Selecting Fonts and Effects**

USE the workbook from the previous exercise. Then, do the following:

1. On the Page Layout tab, click **Fonts** in the Themes group.
2. Click **Create New Theme Fonts**. In the Heading font box, click **Bookman Old Style**.
3. In the Body font box, click **Poor Richard**. The sample is updated with the fonts that you selected.

 Troubleshooting If your customized theme font is not automatically applied, click Cell Styles and click the customized heading font to apply it.

4. In the Name box, key **My Fonts** as the name for the new theme fonts. Click **Save**. Your customized theme fonts will be available for you to use to customize any of the built-in themes or to use the next time you click Cell Styles on the Home tab. (See Figure 5-16.)

Figure 5-16

Customized font theme

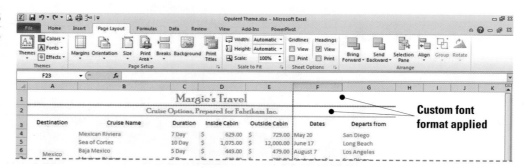

5. In the Themes group, click **Themes**. Click **Save Current Theme**.
6. In the *File name* box, key **My Theme**. Click **Save**. Your customized document theme is saved in the Document Themes folder, and it is automatically added to the list of custom themes that now appears at the top of the themes preview window.
7. Click on **Themes**. Your theme is now viewable in *Custom* themes.
8. On the Page Layout tab, in the Themes group, click **Effects**. Theme effects are sets of lines and fill effects. Mousing over the effects will show subtle changes in the cells. (See Figure 5-17).

Figure 5-17

Figure 5-17

Custom theme and effects

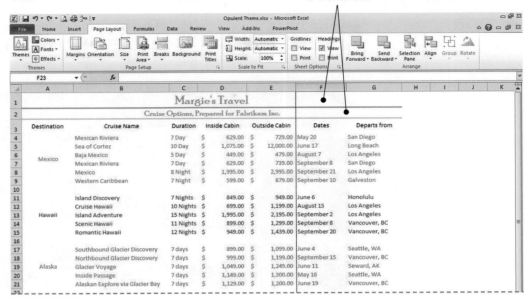

Custom theme applied
to worksheet

9. Click the **Aspect** effect to apply it to the workbook. Click **Undo** in the Quick Access Toolbar to undo the theme effect. Do not save the workbook.

PAUSE. LEAVE the workbook open to use in the next exercise.

You can customize any of the built-in themes by changing the attributes of the theme. For example, say you like the colors in the Verve theme but you want to use a different font. In this situation, first apply the Verve theme, then click Theme Fonts and apply the font of your choice.

You can then save the resulting theme and apply it to other documents. You cannot change the built-in theme effects, but you can apply a different built-in effect to modify the appearance of the theme you are editing, which can include changing the shading, beveling, or other effects.

MODIFYING A WORKSHEET'S ONSCREEN AND PRINTED APPEARANCE

The Bottom Line

You can draw attention to a worksheet's onscreen appearance by displaying a background picture. You can also add color to worksheet tabs. **Gridlines** (the lines that display around worksheet cells), row headings, and column headings also enhance a worksheet's appearance. Onscreen, these elements are displayed by default, but they are not printed automatically.

Formatting a Worksheet Background

You can use a picture as a sheet background for display purposes only. A sheet background is saved with your worksheet, but it is not printed and it is not retained in a worksheet or as an item that you save as a web page. Because a sheet background is not printed, it cannot be used as a watermark.

STEP BY STEP   **Format a Worksheet Background**

@ The *Sunset* image and the *Open Sea* image are available on the book companion website or in WileyPLUS.

USE the workbook from the previous exercise. Then, perform these steps:

1. On the Page Layout tab, in the Page Setup group, click **Background**.

2. Click the *Sunset* image from the student data files and then click **Insert**. The selected picture is displayed behind the text and fills the sheet. (See Figure 5-18.)

Figure 5-18

Sunset background

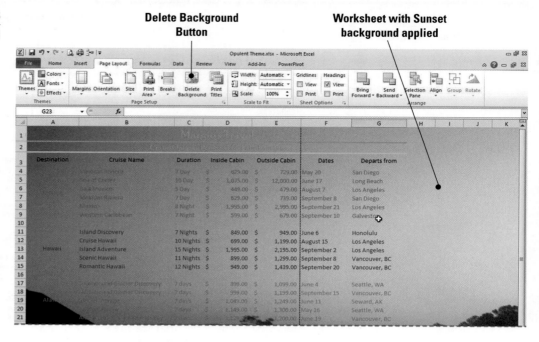

3. In the Sheet Options group, click **View** to remove the gridlines.

4. Select **A1:G21**, click the **Home** tab, and click the **Fill Color arrow**. To improve readability, click **Lavender Background 2, Darker 25%** to add solid color shading to cells that contain data. The higher the percentage of the fill color, the darker the fill that will be applied. Before you apply fill colors, you can mouse over them and their effect will preview in the worksheet.

5. Click anywhere in the worksheet. Click the **Page Layout** tab. In the Page Setup group, click **Delete Background**. The background is removed, but the shading applied to the data range remains.

6. On the Page Layout tab, in the Page Setup group, click **Background** and select the *Open Sea* image from the student data files. Click **Insert**. (See Figure 5-19.)

Figure 5-19

Open Sea background

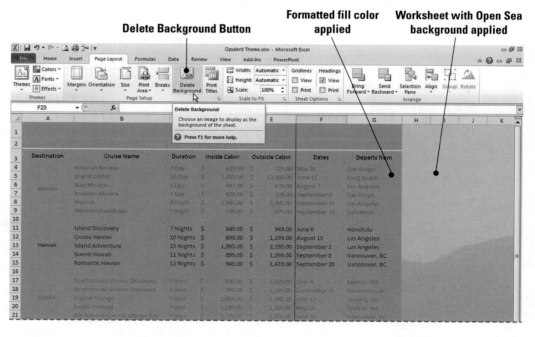

7. **SAVE** the file in the Lesson 5 folder as *Background*. The background will be saved with the worksheet.

8. Click **Delete Background** in preparation for the next exercise.

9. Select A1:G21. Right-click the selected cells, click the arrow on the fill button in the Mini-toolbar, and select No fill.

PAUSE. LEAVE the workbook open to use in the next exercise.

Say that the owner of Margie's Travel often uses worksheets in presentations to clients and also provides clients with printed copies. You can increase the effectiveness of these worksheet presentations by adding an appropriate background picture and adding color to worksheet tabs. It is best to remove gridlines when a sheet background is used, but printing gridlines makes printed worksheets easier to read. Printing column and row headings can also help identify the location of data during discussions.

Changing the Color of a Worksheet Tab

By default, a new workbook contains three blank worksheets identified as Sheet1, Sheet2, and Sheet3. You often use more than one worksheet to enter related data because it is easier to move between sheets than to scroll up and down through large amounts of data. Adding color to the worksheet tabs makes it easier to locate needed information.

STEP BY STEP **Change the Color of a Worksheet Tab**

USE the workbook from the previous exercise.

1. Right-click the Sheet1 tab and mouse over Tab Color. Under *Standard Colors*, click Green.
2. Right-click the Sheet2 tab and mouse over Tab Color. Click Purple.
3. Right-click the Sheet3 tab and mouse over Tab Color. Click Red.
4. Click the Sheet1 tab. Select A1:A3. Click Copy.
5. Click Sheet2. Select A1 and click Paste.
6. Click the Paste Options button and click Keep Source Column Widths. (See Figure 5-20.)

Figure 5-20

Keep Source Column Widths

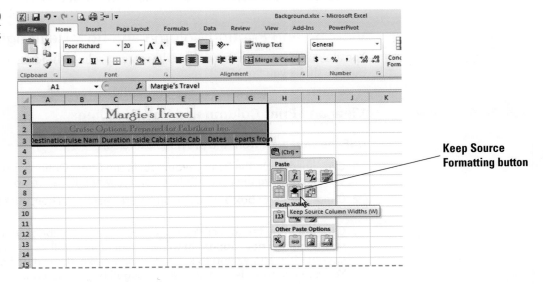

Keep Source Formatting button

7. Click Sheet3. Select A1 and click Paste.
8. Click the Paste Options button and click Keep Source Column Widths.
9. On the Sheet1 worksheet, select A11:G15 and click Cut.
10. On the Sheet2 worksheet, select A4 and click Paste.
11. Cut the Alaska data from Sheet1 and paste it to A4 on Sheet3. Note that each worksheet tab is color coded to match the font format in that worksheet.

PAUSE. LEAVE the workbook open to use in the next exercise.

The original workbook contained data about cruises to three destinations all in a single worksheet. In this exercise, you separated the data so that data related to each destination is now on a separate worksheet in the workbook.

Viewing and Printing a Worksheet's Gridlines

You can have gridlines visible on your work surface or work without them. By default, gridlines are present when you open a worksheet. You can also choose whether gridlines are printed. A printed worksheet is easier to read when gridlines are included.

Take Note   Worksheets print faster if you print without gridlines.

STEP BY STEP   **View and Print a Worksheet's Gridlines**

USE the workbook from the previous exercise.

1. Click the Sheet1 tab. On the Page Layout tab, in the Sheet Options group, remove the check mark from the View option in the Gridlines section.
2. In the Page Setup group, click Orientation, then click Landscape. In the Scale to Fit group, click 1 page in the Width box.
3. Click Quick Print on the Quick Access Toolbar. Gridlines should not be present on the work surface or in the printout.
4. Click the Sheet2 tab to make it the active worksheet. Click the Print check box under Gridlines. Click Orientation, then click Landscape. Each worksheet has its own properties. When you access orientation for Sheet2, you will notice that Portrait is the default.
5. In the Scale to Fit group, click 1 page in the Width box. Click Quick Print. Although gridlines are not present on the work surface, they are included on the printout.
6. With Sheet3 as the active worksheet, check View and Print under Gridlines. Click Orientation and Landscape.
7. Click Quick Print. Gridlines are present on both the work surface and the printout.

PAUSE. LEAVE the workbook open to use in the next exercise.

Viewing and Printing Column and Row Headings

You also can choose whether to have the row and column headings of your worksheet print. This exercise shows you how.

STEP BY STEP   **View and Print Column and Row Headings**

USE the workbook from the previous exercise.

1. Click Sheet1. On the Page Layout tab, in the Sheet Options group under Headings, click View to remove the check. Column and row headings are now removed from the display.
2. Check the View box again. Headings are restored. Then, click the Print check box under Headings.
3. Click the View tab and click Page Layout in the Workbook Views group. Column and row headings now appear in the worksheet as it will be printed. Remember, Page Layout view allows you to see a worksheet exactly as it will appear on a printed page. You can use this view to see where pages begin and end.

PAUSE. LEAVE the workbook open to use in the next exercise.

INSERTING HEADERS AND FOOTERS

The Bottom Line   You can add headers or footers to your worksheets to provide useful information about the worksheet, such as who prepared it, the date it was created or last modified, the page number, and so on. Headers and footers are visible in Page Layout view and appear on printouts.

A **header** is a line of text that appears at the top of each page of a printed worksheet. **Footers** are lines of text that appear at the bottom of each page. You can add predefined header or footer information to a worksheet; insert elements such as page numbers, date and time, and filename; or add your own content to a header or footer.

Adding Page Numbers to a Worksheet

To add or change a header or footer, click the Insert tab, then click Header & Footer in the Text group. The worksheet displays in Page Layout view, a Design tab (as shown in Figure 5-21) is added to the Ribbon, and the Header & Footer Tools command groups are displayed.

Figure 5-21

Design tab for Headers and Footers

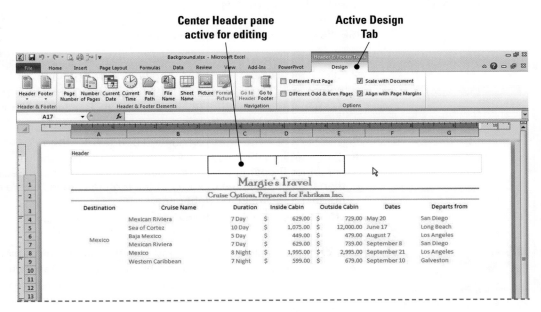

Take Note The addition of the Design tab illustrates one advantage of Excel's Ribbon interface. With the Ribbon, instead of every command being available all the time, some commands appear only in response to specific user actions.

STEP BY STEP **Add Page Numbers to a Worksheet**

USE the workbook from the previous exercise to perform these steps:

1. With Sheet1 active, click the **Insert** tab, then click the **Header & Footer** button in the Text group. The worksheet is now displayed in Page Layout view. Note that the center Header text box is active and the Design tab is added to the Ribbon. The Header & Footer Design tab command groups are thus available for you to use in the worksheet.

2. By default, your cursor will appear in the center Header section. Press **Tab** to move to the right pane in the Header section of the worksheet.

3. Click **Page Number** in the Header & Footer Elements group. The code **&[Page]** appears in the text box. This symbol (&) indicates that the appropriate page number will be added to each page of the printed worksheet.

4. Click the **Go to Footer** button in the Navigation group.

5. Click the **left text box** in the footer and click **Sheet Name** in the Header & Footer Elements group. Press **Tab** twice to go to the right footer pane.

6. Click **Current Date** in the Header & Footer Elements group. Then click anywhere in the worksheet outside the header and footer to close the Design tab.

7. **SAVE** the workbook in the Lesson 5 folder as *Cruises*.

PAUSE. LEAVE the workbook open to use in the next exercise.

You can create headers and footers by keying the text that you want to appear, or, as you practiced in this exercise, you can click one of the predefined elements to insert codes for headers or footers that Excel provides. When your workbook is printed, Excel replaces these codes with the current date, current time, and so on.

Inserting a Predefined Header or Footer

On the Design tab, the Header & Footer group contains predefined headers and footers that allow you to automatically add text to the header or footer, such as the date, page number, number of pages, name of the sheet, and so on.

STEP BY STEP **Insert a Predefined Header or Footer**

USE the workbook from the previous exercise.

1. Click the Sheet3 worksheet. Click the View tab.
2. Click Page Layout view in the Workbook Views group.
3. Click the center Header pane. Click on the Header & Footer Tools Design tab now that it has become active. Click Sheet Name in the Header and Footer Elements group. &Tab appears in the pane.
4. Click Go to Footer in the Navigation group. Click the left footer pane.
5. Click Footer in the Header & Footer group and click the last option in the list, which combines Prepared by, Current Date, and Page Number. Because the footer is wider than the left pane, the majority of the footer is moved to the center pane, and the page number appears in the right pane.

PAUSE. LEAVE the workbook open to use in the next exercise.

Another Way
You can access the Header and Footer text boxes by clicking Page Layout view on the right side of the status bar.

Many of Excel's predefined headers and footers combine one or more elements. In the previous exercise, you inserted a combined entry by clicking it. You can then customize the appearance of your header or footer in Page Layout view. Within this view, once you have the header or footer selected, you can edit the text it contains using the Font group on the Home tab. In this way, you can change font type or size, add special effects, or add other options to your text.

Adding Content to a Header or Footer

Excel's predefined headers and footers will not always meet your needs. When this happens, you can simply key text into any of the header or footer text boxes.

Text isn't the only type of content you can add to a header or footer, though. For instance, you may be familiar with the watermark functionality that is available in Microsoft Word. You cannot insert a watermark in Excel, but you can mimic one by displaying a graphic in a header or footer. This graphic will appear behind the text, and it will display and print in the style of a watermark.

STEP BY STEP **Insert Text and Graphics into a Header or Footer**

USE the workbook from the previous exercise.

1. With Sheet3 still active, click the center Header pane and delete the existing header.
2. Key For Presentation to Client in the center pane. Then press Tab to move to the right Header pane.
3. Click the Design tab if it is not already active. Click Picture in the Header and Footer Elements group. Select the *Sailing* image from student data files for Lesson 5 and click Insert.
4. Click Format Picture on the ribbon.
5. In the *Format Picture* dialog box, under *Size and rotate*, set the height to 8.5" and press Tab. Notice the width changes automatically. This happens because *Lock aspect ratio* is checked. Press OK.
6. Click anywhere on the worksheet to deselect Headers & Footers editing. The image now appears behind the header and footer text.

The *Sailing* image is available on the book companion website or in WileyPLUS.

7. **SAVE** and **CLOSE** the workbook.

LEAVE the workbook open for the next exercise.

Using Headers to Print Titles

Using the headers in Excel will allow you to customize the title printing options and how they appear on the printed page. You can use these options to skip printing first page titles and print to odd pages only. In this next section you will apply these printing options to your worksheet.

STEP BY STEP | **Use a Header to Print Titles on Specific Pages**

USE the workbook from the previous exercise.

1. Click the **Insert** tab on the Ribbon. In the Text group, click **Header & Footer**. By default Excel will open the Header in the Center pane for editing.

2. Key **Margie's Client List for Printing**.

3. On the Headers & Footers Design tab, in the Options group, select the **Different Odd & Even Pages** check box. This will allow you to specify that the headers and footers on odd-numbered pages should be different from those on even-numbered pages.

4. Again on the Design tab, in the Options group, select the **Different First Page** check box. This option allows you to ignore the header title on the first page. You will not have a title because you will be leaving the center Header text box blank.

5. Click on the **File** tab to enter Backstage. Click on **Print**. You will now be able to view the title printing options that you selected for both the first page and odd and even pages.

6. Do not save the worksheet.

CLOSE Excel.

PREPARING A DOCUMENT FOR PRINTING

The Bottom Line

When worksheet data prints on more than one page, you can use the Page Break Preview command on the View tab to control where page breaks occur. This allows you to break data where it is most logical, so that printed documents are well-organized and easy to read.

In the next set of exercises, you will use Page Layout view on the View tab to view headers and footers, change page breaks, and change page margins at the top, sides, and bottom of a worksheet (see Figure 5-22).

Figure 5-22

Page Layout view

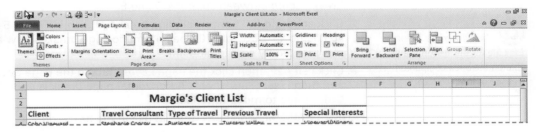

Adding and Moving a Page Break

The **Print Preview** window displays a full-page view of a worksheet just as it will be printed. With Print Preview, you can check the format and overall layout of a worksheet before actually printing it. You cannot make changes to the document in Print Preview, however.

A **page break** is a divider that breaks a worksheet into separate pages for printing. Excel inserts automatic vertical page breaks (shown as a broken line) based on paper size, margin settings, scaling options, and the positions of any manual page breaks (shown as a solid line) that you insert. In the **Page Break Preview** window, shown in Figure 5-23, you can quickly adjust automatic page breaks to achieve a more desirable printed document.

As you learned in Lesson 2, all printing options in Excel 2010 are now organized in Backstage view.

Figure 5-23

Page Break Preview window

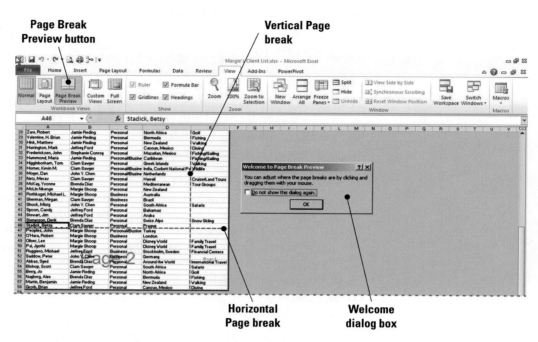

Page Break Preview button — Vertical Page break — Horizontal Page break — Welcome dialog box

---

STEP BY STEP   **Add and Move a Page Break**

OPEN the *Margie's Client List* workbook from the student data files in the Lesson 5 folder. Then, follow these steps:

1. On the View tab, click **Page Break Preview** if necessary. If a dialog box welcoming you to the view is displayed, read its contents and click **OK** to continue. (See Figure 5-23.) Note that an automatic page break occurs after row 46, and another automatic page break occurs between columns D and E.

2. Click and hold the horizontal page break (as seen in Figure 5-23) and drag it upward so it is now below row 40. The automatic page break is now a manual page break represented by a solid blue line.

3. Click cell **A22**, then click the **Page Layout** tab. In the Page Setup group, click **Breaks** and then **Insert Page Break**. A horizontal page break is added above row 22. Press **Ctrl+Home** to move to cell A1.

PAUSE. LEAVE the workbook open to use in the next exercise.

@ The *Margie's Client List* file for this lesson is available on the book companion website or in WileyPLUS.

Take Note   When you move an automatic page break, it becomes a manual page break.

Use manual page breaks to control page break locations. You can drag an automatic page break to a new location to convert it to a manual page break.

Setting Margins

Margins are an effective way to manage and optimize the white space on a printed work-sheet. Achieving balance between data and white space adds significantly to the readability and appearance of a worksheet. In Excel, you can choose one of three built-in margin sets (shown in Figure 5-24), or you can create customized margins using the Page Setup dialog box.

Figure 5-24

Built-in margin options

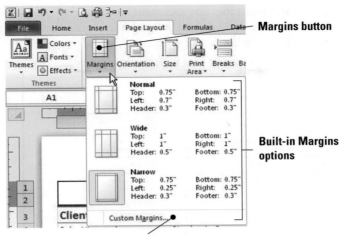

Margins button

Built-in Margins options

Custom Margins option

STEP BY STEP | **Set Margins**

USE the workbook from the previous exercise.

1. Click the View tab on the Ribbon. In the Workbook Views group, click the Page Layout button.
2. Click the Page Layout tab. In the Page Setup group, click the arrow on the Margins button, then click Narrow.
3. Mouse over the Zoom slider on the right corner of the status bar and increase the zoom to 100% if necessary. Depending on whether this feature has been previously used, the zoom might be set to a different value. The Zoom slider allows you to zoom out or in, depending on how you need to view a worksheet's contents.
4. Click Page Break Preview on the Status bar. The margin adjustment has moved the vertical page break to between columns E and F. Again the Page Break welcome dialog box appears. Click OK to continue.
5. Click Margins, then click Custom Margins. In the Page Setup dialog box, change the left and right margins to 0.5. Click OK.
6. Click cell A22, click Breaks in the Page Setup group, then click Remove Page Break.
7. Click the vertical page break line and drag it to the right of column E.
8. Click the File tab. Click Print and Print Preview. The worksheet will now print on two pages, with all columns fitting to one page wide.
9. Print the worksheet or click on the Home tab to leave Backstage and Print Preview without printing.

PAUSE. CLOSE the workbook without saving any changes.

The Normal margin setting is the default for a new workbook. You can also set custom margins in Excel. Narrower margins, for example, allow more area for data when you print a workbook. When you click Custom Margins at the bottom of the Margins list, the Page Setup dialog box will open with the settings that have been applied to the open worksheet. You can change any of the settings to create a custom margin setting. Header and footer margins automatically adjust when you change the page margins.

Worksheets that do not fill an entire page can be centered vertically and horizontally, thereby evenly distributing the page's white space. Use the Margins tab of the Page Setup dialog box for this function.

Setting a Worksheet's Orientation

Printed worksheets are easiest to read and analyze when all of the data appears on one piece of paper. Excel's orientation and scaling features give you control over the number of printed pages of worksheet data. You can change the **orientation** of a worksheet so that it prints either vertically or horizontally on a page. A worksheet that is printed vertically uses the Portrait

Another Way
You can also alter the margins in Page Layout view by clicking the top or bottom border on the margin area in the ruler. When a vertical two-headed arrow appears, drag the margin to the size you want.

orientation and looks like the document shown on top in Figure 5-25. Portrait orientation is the default setting. A worksheet printed horizontally uses the Landscape orientation, shown in Figure 5-25 at the bottom of the page.

Figure 5-25

Portrait and landscape orientation

Margie's Client List

Client	Travel Consultant	Type of Travel	Previous Travel
Coho Vineyard	Stephanie Conroy	Business	Tuscany Valley
Coho Winery	Stephanie Conroy	Business	France
Contoso Pharmaceuticals	Margie Shoop	Business	Vienna, Austria
Trey Research	John Y. Chen	Business	Copenhagen, Denmark
Fabrikam, Inc.	Brenda Diaz	Business	Lisbon, Portugal
Ashton, Chris	Jeffrey Ford	Personal	Brussels, Belgium
Bolender, Corinna	Jamie Reding	Personal	Oslo, Norway
Caro, Fernando	Ciam Sawyer	Personal	Stockholm, Sweden
Ihrig, Ryan	Margie Shoop	Personal	Barcelona, Spain
Ingle, Marc J.	Margie Shoop	Personal	Naples, Italy
Keil, Kendall	Stephanie Conroy	Personal	Athens, Greece
Kim, Jim	Brenda Diaz	Personal	Athens, Greece
Li, Yale	John Y. Chen	Personal	Naples, Italy
McAskill-White, Katie	Jeffrey Ford	Personal	Rome, Italy
McGuel, Alejandro	Jeffrey Ford	Personal	Israel
Myer, Ken	Ciam Sawyer	Personal	Latin America
Nash, Mike	Margie Shoop	Personal	Mexico
Seidl, Birgit	Margie Shoop	Personal	Bahamas
Sutton, Brad	John Y. Chen	Personal	Australia
Teal, Andy	Ciam Sawyer	Personal	Hawaii
Tiano, Mike	Jeffrey Ford	Personal	Mediterranean
Vargas, Garrett R.	Stephanie Conroy	Personal	Alaska
Waldal, Deb	Brenda Diaz	Personal	Around the World
Walton, Bryan	Brenda Diaz	Personal	South Africa
Zare, Robert	Jamie Reding	Personal	North Africa
Valentine, H. Brian	Jamie Reding	Personal	Bermuda
Hink, Matthew	Jamie Reding	Personal	New Zealand
Harrington, Mark	Jeffrey Ford	Personal	Cancun, Mexico
Fredericksen, John	Stephanie Conroy	Personal	Mazatlan, Mexico
Hammond, Maria	Jamie Reding	Personal/Business	Caribbean
Higginbotham, Tom	Ciam Sawyer	Personal	Greek Islands
Homer, Kevin M.	Ciam Sawyer	Personal/Business	India, Corbett National Park
Moyer, Dan	John Y. Chen	Personal/Business	Netherlands
Netz, Merav	Ciam Sawyer	Personal	Hawaii
McKay, Wonne	Brenda Diaz	Personal	Mediterranean
McLin Nkenge	Margie Shoop	Personal	New Zealand
Rothkugel, Michael L.	Margie Shoop	Business	Australia

Portrait Orientation

Margie's Client List

Client	Travel Consultant	Type of Travel	Previous Travel	Special Interests
Coho Vineyard	Stephanie Conroy	Business	Tuscany Valley	Vineyard/Winery
Coho Winery	Stephanie Conroy	Business	France	Vineyard/Winery
Contoso Pharmaceuticals	Margie Shoop	Business	Vienna, Austria	Medical Research
Trey Research	John Y. Chen	Business	Copenhagen, Denmark	Medical Research
Fabrikam, Inc.	Brenda Diaz	Business	Lisbon, Portugal	
Ashton, Chris	Jeffrey Ford	Personal	Brussels, Belgium	History
Bolender, Corinna	Jamie Reding	Personal	Oslo, Norway	
Caro, Fernando	Ciam Sawyer	Personal	Stockholm, Sweden	
Ihrig, Ryan	Margie Shoop	Personal	Barcelona, Spain	
Ingle, Marc J.	Margie Shoop	Personal	Naples, Italy	
Keil, Kendall	Stephanie Conroy	Personal	Athens, Greece	Cruise/Land Tours
Kim, Jim	Brenda Diaz	Personal	Athens, Greece	Cruise/Land Tours
Li, Yale	John Y. Chen	Personal	Naples, Italy	Museums, Art History
McAskill-White, Katie	Jeffrey Ford	Personal	Rome, Italy	Religion
McGuel, Alejandro	Jeffrey Ford	Personal	Israel	Religion
Myer, Ken	Ciam Sawyer	Personal	Latin America	
Nash, Mike	Margie Shoop	Personal	Mexico	Diving
Seidl, Birgit	Margie Shoop	Personal	Bahamas	
Sutton, Brad	John Y. Chen	Personal	Australia	
Teal, Andy	Ciam Sawyer	Personal	Hawaii	Sailing
Tiano, Mike	Jeffrey Ford	Personal	Mediterranean	
Vargas, Garrett R.	Stephanie Conroy	Personal	Alaska	Cruise/Land Tours
Waldal, Deb	Brenda Diaz	Personal	Around the World	International Travel
Walton, Bryan	Brenda Diaz	Personal	South Africa	Safaris
Zare, Robert	Jamie Reding	Personal	North Africa	Golf
Valentine, H. Brian	Jamie Reding	Personal	Bermuda	Fishing
Hink, Matthew	Jamie Reding	Personal	New Zealand	Walking
Harrington, Mark	Jeffrey Ford	Personal	Cancun, Mexico	Diving
Fredericksen, John	Stephanie Conroy	Personal	Mazatlan, Mexico	Fishing/Sailing
Hammond, Maria	Jamie Reding	Personal/Business	Caribbean	Fishing/Sailing

Landscape Orientation

STEP BY STEP   **Set a Worksheet's Orientation**

The *Margie's Client List* document file for this lesson is available on the book companion website or in WileyPLUS.

WileyPLUS Extra! features an online tutorial of this task.

OPEN *Margie's Client List* again from the student data files. Then, do the following:

1. Click the Page Layout tab.

2. Click Orientation in the Page Setup group and click Landscape. Scroll through the document to see that it will now print on two pages with each page containing all columns.

3. In the Page Setup group, click Print Titles. The *Page Setup* dialog box opens. Click the Collapse dialog box icon next to *Rows to repeat at top*.

4. Click row 3 (the column labels). Row 3 data is identified in the dialog box. Press Enter. Click OK to accept the changes and close the dialog box.

5. Click the File tab, click Print, and view the Print Preview. Click the Next Page arrow at the bottom of the Print Options window to advance to page 2 in the Print Preview. Notice that the column labels appear on page 2 of the document.

6. Click on the Home tab.

PAUSE. LEAVE the workbook open to use in the next exercise.

Orientation is the way your workbook or worksheet appears on the printed page. There are two settings: Portrait and Landscape. Portrait is a vertical printing of the workbook, and Landscape is the horizontal aspect. By default, all workbooks and worksheets are printed in Portrait. Use the Landscape orientation when the width of the area you want to print is greater than the height. Data is easier to read when all the columns fit on one page. This can often be accomplished by changing a worksheet's orientation to Landscape. When you can't fit all of the data on one printed page by changing the orientation, you can shrink or reduce it using Excel's scaling options, as described in the next exercise.

Scaling a Worksheet to Fit on a Printed Page

Scaling refers to shrinking or stretching printed output to a percentage of its actual size. One use for scaling is to resize a document so that it fits on a single page. Before attempting to change the scaling for a worksheet's output, the maximum width and height must be set to "Automatic" (see Figure 5-26).

Figure 5-26

Scaling a worksheet to fit on one page

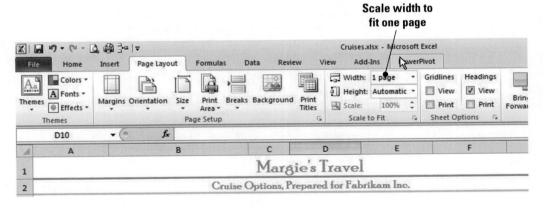

STEP BY STEP   **Scale a Worksheet to Fit on a Printed Page**

USE the workbook from the previous exercise.

1. On the Page Layout tab, click Orientation, then click Portrait. Notice that column E no longer fits on the same page with columns A–D.

2. In the Scale to Fit group, click the Width arrow and click 1 page. Then click the Height arrow and select 1 page. The scale of the worksheet is reduced so that all columns and rows fit on the same page.

3. Click the **File** tab, then click **Print**. View the Print Preview pane to the right. Notice that all columns appear on the page, and the height is one page as well. When output is reduced, it shrinks the height and width proportionally.

4. **SAVE** the workbook as *Client List* and **CLOSE** the workbook.

CLOSE Excel.

The most common reason for scaling a worksheet is to shrink it so that you can print it on one page. You can also enlarge the sheet so that data appears bigger and fills up more of the printed page. When the Width and Height boxes are set to automatic, you can click the arrows in the Scale box to increase or decrease scaling of the printout. Each time you click the arrow, the scaling changes by 5%.

Take Note

Remember that width and height must be set to automatic if you want to specify a scale, such as 75%.

Using Paste Special to Copy Special Data

You may not always want to copy everything from source cells to your destination cells. For example, you may want to copy only the current values of formulas rather than the formulas themselves. In such cases, you can use **Paste Special** to perform irregular cell copying.

When you paste data, Excel normally copies all the information in the range of cells you selected. However, there are times when you only need to paste formula results or the formatting of a cell rather than all of the cell's content. This is where Excel's Paste Special command comes into play. You can use this command to specify a number of options, such as pasting only cell contents without formatting or only formatting without cell contents.

To paste particular parts of a cell selection, on the Home tab, click the arrow below the Paste button. Then, click Paste Special on the drop-down menu to open the Paste Special dialog box, which is shown in Figure 5-27.

Figure 5-27

Paste Special dialog box

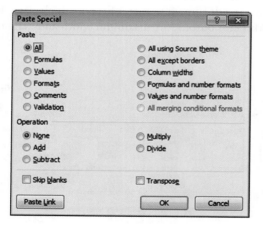

The Paste Special dialog box has many different paste options. Table 5-1 describes each option in the Paste group of the Paste Special dialog box.

Table 5-1

Paste group options

Option	Resulting Action
All	Pastes your cell selection, including all formatting, formulas, content, etc. This is also the default Paste.
Formulas	Pastes the formulas, text, and numbers in your cell selection without the formatting.
Values	Pastes the calculated value of formulas in the current cell selection.
Formats	Pastes only the formatting from the cell selection—and none of the content.
Comments	Pastes only the Comments or notes attached to the current cell selection.
Validation	Pastes only the data validation rules that you set up with the Data Validation command.
All using Source theme	Pastes all the content and information in the cell selection plus the cell styles.
All except borders	Pastes all the content and information in the cell selection without copying any borders.
Column widths	Applies the column widths of the cells copied to the Clipboard to the columns where the cells are pasted.
Formulas and number formats	Pastes all the cell content, including formulas, and retains any formatting applied to the numbers and formulas.
Values and number formats	Pastes all cell content, converting formulas to their calculated values, and applies any number or formula formatting from the original cells.
All merging conditional formats	Pastes any conditional formatting that was applied to the original cell content.

You can also perform an arithmetic operation on values in the destination range. Table 5-2 explains the options in the Operation group of the Paste Special dialog box.

Table 5-2

Operation group options in the
Paste Special dialog box

Option	Resulting Action
None	Performs no mathematical operation between the original data in the Clipboard and your selected destination cell range.
Add	Adds the values you cut or copy to the Clipboard to the values in the cell range where you paste.
Subtract	Subtracts the values you cut or copy to the Clipboard from the values in the cell range where you paste.
Multiply	Multiplies the values you cut or copy to the Clipboard with the values in the cell range where you paste.
Divide	Divides the values you cut or copy to the Clipboard by the values in the cell range where you paste.

Take Note   The new Paste with Live Preview feature is also available with Paste Special. If you mouse over the Paste options in either the right-click menu, or the paste menu in the Clipboard group, you will be able to view your changes before actually implementing them.

Finally, there are a few more options available at the bottom of the Paste Special dialog box, shown in Table 5-3.

Table 5-3

Additional Paste Special options

Option	Resulting Action
Skip blanks	Selecting this check box will paste only from the cells in your copied selection that aren't empty.
Transpose	Selecting this check box will cause your cell data to change orientation. Row data will become column data, and column data will become row data.
Paste Link	Click this button when you want to establish a link between the copies you're pasting and the original entries. This ensures that any changes to the original cells will be automatically updated in the pasted copies.

SKILL SUMMARY

In This Lesson, You Learned How To:

Work with rows and columns

Use themes

Modify a worksheet's onscreen and printed appearance

Insert headers and footers

Prepare a document for printing

Knowledge Assessment

Fill in the Blank

Complete the following sentences by writing the correct word or words in the blanks provided.

1. The _____ option allows you to enlarge or shrink worksheet data to achieve a more logical fit on the printed page.

2. There are _____ header and footer text boxes on a workbook page where you can enter information.

3. You can manually adjust page breaks in the _____ view.

4. You can mimic a watermark on printouts by adding a(n) _____ to a header or footer.

5. Applying a(n) _____ will override any formatting styles that have been applied to a data range.

6. To format an entire row or column, you must select its _____.

7. A(n) _____ is a block of text that appears at the top of each printed page.

8. Row _____ will automatically expand to accommodate increased font size.

9. Document themes are used to apply sets of styles, including colors, fonts, and _____.

10. _____ is a setting that specifies the direction a worksheet appears on the printed page.

True/False

Circle T if the statement is true or F if the statement is false.

T F   1. You can insert a graphic in the header or footer of a worksheet.

T F   2. Column width and row height can be changed.

T F   3. After you enter a manual page break, you cannot remove it.

T F   4. You can center a worksheet's data horizontally, but not vertically.

T F   5. You can hide a column by setting its width to zero.

T F   6. Hidden rows are not displayed onscreen, but they will appear when the page is printed.

T F   7. You can change page endings in Page Break Preview view.

T F   8. You can use one of Excel's predefined Header & Footer elements to enter the name of a worksheet's author.

T F   9. You cannot make changes to a worksheet in the Print Preview window.

T F 10. By default, gridlines will print in an Excel worksheet.

Competency Assessment

Project 5-1: Working with Rows and Columns

The School of Fine Arts has developed a workbook to track enrollment for the academic year. Enrollments for courses in two departments have been entered. In the following exercise, you will apply the formatting techniques you learned in this lesson to enhance the appearance of the two worksheets in the workbook.

@ The *SFA Enrollment* file for this lesson is available on the book companion website or in WileyPLUS.

GET READY. LAUNCH Excel if it is not already running. Then, do the following:

1. **OPEN** the *SFA Enrollment* data file. Sheet1 should be active and the Home tab should be displayed.

2. Click A1, click the Insert arrow in the Cells group, then click Insert Sheet Rows.

3. Select A1:C1 and click Merge & Center in the Alignment group.

4. With A1 selected, key **School of Fine Arts**.

5. Select A2:C2 and click Merge & Center. To overwrite the exiting text, key **Fine Arts Department**.

6. Merge and center A3:C3 and key **Enrollment**, replacing the existing text.

7. Select row **4**, click the Insert arrow, then click Insert Sheet Rows.

8. In A5, key **Call No.**. Please include the period to abbreviate "number."

9. In B5, key **Course**.

10. In C5, key **Fall**, replacing the existing text.

11. Select row **5**. Click Bold and Italic in the Font group. Click the Center button in the Alignment group.

12. Select row **1**. Click Format in the Cells group and click Row Height under Cell Size.

13. Key **20** in the Row Height dialog box and click OK.

14. Click the bottom boundary for row **2** and drag down until the ScreenTip says the height is **18.00 points (24 pixels)**.

15. Click the Sheet2 tab and repeat steps 2–14. If necessary, double-click the boundary between columns to adjust the column width to display all of the text.

16. In A2, key **Media Studies Department**.

17. **SAVE** the workbook in your Lesson 5 folder. Name the workbook *SFA Enrollment 5-1*.

CLOSE the workbook. **LEAVE** Excel open for the next project.

Project 5-2: Working with Rows and Columns

In this exercise, you will insert columns and rows to add additional data to the client list for Margie's Travel. You'll also apply styles and a document theme to add visual appeal.

@ The *Client Update* file for this lesson is available on the book companion website or in WileyPLUS.

OPEN the *Client Update* file for this lesson, then perform these steps:

1. With column E selected, click the Insert arrow in the Cells group and click Insert Sheet Columns.
2. In E3, key Anticipated Travel.
3. Insert a row above row 3.
4. Select columns C and D. Click Format in the Cells group. Under Visibility, point to Hide & Unhide and click Hide Columns.
5. Click the Page Layout tab, then click Themes in the Themes group. Click Metro.
6. Select cell A1. Open the Home tab and click Middle Align in the Alignment group.
7. Select A4:F4. Click Cell Styles. Apply Heading 3 to the column labels.
8. Enter the following anticipated travel for the listed clients:

   Keil, Kendall   Romantic Hawaii Cruise
   Nash, Mike   Aruba
   Li, Yale   Paris

9. **SAVE** the workbook as *Client Update 5-2*.

LEAVE the workbook open for the next project.

Proficiency Assessment

Project 5-3: Modifying a Worksheet's Onscreen Appearance

In this project, you will create a customized theme for Margie's Travel and prepare the document for printing on two pages.

USE the workbook from Project 5-2.

1. With the Home tab active, select A1. Increase the font size to 20.
2. Select row 4. Increase the font size to 14.
3. Click the Page Layout tab.
4. In the Themes group, click the Colors button, then click Create New Theme Colors.
5. Change the third Text/Background to Purple.
6. Key your name in the Name box. Click Save.
7. Set gridlines to print.
8. Insert a footer that prints the file name in the left Footer pane.
9. Insert a footer that prints the page number in the right Footer pane.
10. On the Page Layout tab, click the Print check box under Headings. Set the column headings to print on the second page. Click Page Break Preview. Move the horizontal automatic page break to the bottom of row 40 and move the vertical page break to the right of column F.
11. Print the worksheet.
12. **SAVE** the workbook in your Lesson 5 folder as *Client Update 5-3*.

CLOSE the workbook. **LEAVE** Excel open for the next project.

Project 5-4: Preparing a Worksheet for Printing

In this project, you will apply styles and a theme to a School of Fine Arts worksheet. You will also create and apply a custom margin setting and print the worksheet with gridlines and headings.

@ The *SFA Enrollment Update* file for this lesson is available on the book companion website or in WileyPLUS.

OPEN the *SFA Enrollment Update* data file for this lesson.

1. The workbook should open to Sheet1. Apply Heading 1 to cell A1.
2. Apply Heading 2 to A2.
3. Apply Heading 3 to A3.
4. Apply the Oriel theme to the worksheets.
5. Click Margins and Custom Margins to open the Page Setup dialog box.
6. For Sheet1, set the top, bottom, left, and right margins to 1.5.
7. Center the data horizontally and vertically.
8. Print Sheet2 with gridlines.
9. Print Sheet1 with headings.
10. Add blue color to the Sheet1 tab and green to the Sheet2 tab.
11. **SAVE** the workbook as *SFA Enrollment 5-4*.

LEAVE the workbook open for the next project.

Mastery Assessment

Project 5-5: Updating and Printing a Workbook

In this project, you will add additional data to an existing workbook and prepare the workbook for printing.

USE the workbook from Project 5-4.

1. On Sheet1, select A1:C5. Copy the heading to Sheet3.
2. Click the Paste Options button. Click Keep Source Column Widths.
3. On Sheet3, enter the following data for the Biomedical Art Department enrollments:

MED114	Principles of Biology	463
MED115	Human Forms	236
MED116	Biomedical Art Methods	365
MED351	Traditional and Digital Color	446
MED352	3D Modeling	234
MED353	Advanced Problem in Biomedical Art	778
MED354	3D Texture	567
ILL302	Digital Imaging and Illustration	643
ILL303	Storyboarding	234
ILL304	Drawing Beyond Observation	123
DRG333	Visual Editor	434

4. Color the Sheet3 tab orange.
5. Insert a footer in the center text box that reads Academic Year 20XX (with XX being the current year).
6. In the left Footer text box, key Current as of and click Current Date.
7. Center Sheet3 vertically and horizontally.
8. Access Backstage. Print the sheet with gridlines.
9. **SAVE** the workbook as *SFA Enrollment 5-5*.

CLOSE the workbook; **LEAVE** Excel open for the next project.

Project 5-6: Fixing the Fitness Classes Worksheet

The owner of Margie's Travel plans to meet with each travel consultant to discuss his or her client list. For this project, you will insert manual page breaks in a worksheet so that each consultant's data prints on a separate page.

@ The *Anticipated Travel* worksheet and *Lighthouse* image file for this lesson are available on the book companion website or in WileyPLUS.

OPEN the *Anticipated Travel* file from the student data files for this lesson.

1. Check the worksheet for existing headers and footers.

2. In the right Header box, insert the *Lighthouse* image from the student data files for this lesson. Click Format Picture. Set the scale to 10% of its original size, so that the image appears only in the header.

3. In the center Footer box, click Footer and click the last option in the predefined footers.

4. Unhide columns C and D.

5. Set the orientation to Landscape.

6. Open the Page Break Preview and move and add page breaks so that each consultant's client list appears on a different page.

7. Titles and column labels should print on each page.

8. Scale the data so that it is only one page wide.

9. Print the complete worksheet with gridlines. You should have a page for each consultant.

10. **SAVE** the workbook as *Anticipated Travel 5-6*. **CLOSE** the workbook.

LEAVE Excel open for the next project.

INTERNET READY

Use the *Anticipated Travel 5-6* workbook from the previous project.

You and two friends from class have an appointment with Stephanie Conroy, a travel consultant with Margie's Travel, to plan your next vacation.

Add your name and your friends' names to the client list. Identify Stephanie as your consultant.

List at least one special interest for each of you.

Go online and find an ideal vacation spot that will fulfill the special interests for all of you. For example, if the three interests were golfing, theater, and swimming, where could you vacation that would satisfy the three interests?

Save the revised workbook as *My Vacation*. When you have finished, close Excel.

LESSON SKILL MATRIX

In This Lesson, You Will Learn The Following Skills:

Organizing Worksheets

Working with Multiple Worksheets

Using Zoom and Freeze to Change the Onscreen View

Finding and Replacing Data

KEY TERMS
- freeze
- group worksheets
- hide
- string
- unhide
- zoom

The School of Fine Arts (SFA) is a private college that is recognized as a leader in art education. More than 2,500 students are enrolled in its four-year programs of study. Admission requires an audition and/or portfolio presentation. Students pursue a BA degree in one of six majors: Fine Arts, Media Studies, Biomedical Arts, Dramatic Arts, Interior Design, Advertising, and Graphic Arts. The school also offers a degree program for students who wish to combine major areas of concentration. In addition to its degree programs, SFA offers continuing education courses and Saturday and summer courses for children, teens, and adults who hope to pursue a career in the creative arts or who have exceptional artistic talent.

SOFTWARE ORIENTATION

Worksheet Management

An Excel workbook should contain information about a unique subject. For example, SFA might have one workbook for enrollment data, one for faculty course assignments, and one for summer workshop course offerings. Each worksheet within a workbook should contain a subset of information about that workbook. The number of worksheets that a workbook can contain is limited only by the available memory of your computer.

Figure 6-1

Commands to organize worksheets

In this lesson, you will learn to copy worksheets between workbooks, manage and reorganize sheets by hiding and unhiding worksheets, and use Excel's search tools to find and replace information in a worksheet or workbook. To accomplish these tasks, you will use commands in the Home tab's Cells and Editing groups. (See Figure 6-1.)

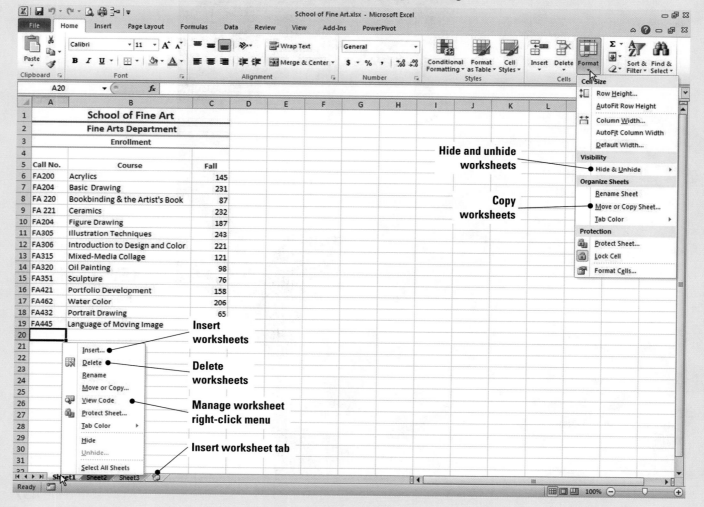

ORGANIZING WORKSHEETS

A new, blank Excel workbook has three worksheets. You can add to, delete from, and move and copy these worksheets as desired. You can also rename worksheets and hide and unhide worksheets when you need to do so. The flexibility to organize worksheets with similar subject matter together in one file enables you to effectively and efficiently manage related data.

Copying a Worksheet

Just as you can copy data from one cell or range in a worksheet to another cell or range, you can copy data from one worksheet to another within a workbook. For example, when a new worksheet will contain information similar to that contained in an existing worksheet, you can copy the worksheet and delete cell contents or overwrite existing data with new data. When you copy a worksheet, you retain the structure and formatting of the original worksheet so that you don't need to rebuild it from scratch. You can copy a worksheet using the Home tab's Format commands, the mouse, or the shortcut menu.

STEP BY STEP   **Copy a Worksheet**

@ The *School of Fine Arts* file for this lesson is available on the book companion website or the WileyPLUS website.

GET READY. Before you begin these steps, **LAUNCH** Microsoft Excel 2010.

1. **OPEN** the *School of Fine Arts* data file for this lesson.
2. With the Sheet1 tab active, click Format in the Cells group on the Home tab.
3. Click Move or Copy Sheet. The dialog box shown in Figure 6-2 opens.

Figure 6-2

Move or Copy dialog box

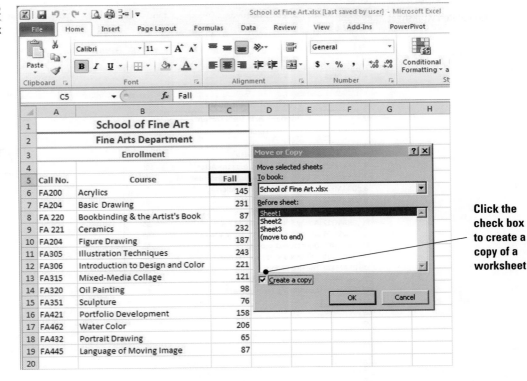

Click the check box to create a copy of a worksheet

WILEY PLUS *EXTRA*

WileyPLUS Extra! features an online tutorial of this task.

4. Sheet1 is selected by default. Select the Create a copy box as shown in Figure 6-2 and click OK. A copy of Sheet1 is inserted to the left of Sheet1 and is named Sheet1 (2).
5. Click the Sheet3 tab and hold down the left mouse button. A down arrow appears at the boundary between Sheet2 and Sheet3, and the cursor becomes an arrow pointing to the left of a blank document symbol.
6. Press and hold Ctrl. A plus sign appears in the cursor document. Move the cursor to the right until the down arrow appears on the right side of Sheet3. Release the mouse button and Ctrl key. The new sheet is named Sheet3 (2).

Another Way
You can also right-click a sheet tab to display the shortcut menu, then click Move or Copy to display the corresponding dialog box.

7. With Sheet3 (2) active, select cell **A2** and key **Dramatic Arts Department**.

When you use the Format command or the shortcut menu to copy a worksheet, the Move or Copy dialog box shown in Figure 6-2 lets you identify the worksheet you want to copy. By default, the copied worksheet is inserted before the sheet you select in the dialog box. You can, however, place the worksheet in other locations by choosing the destination in the Move or Copy dialog box.

8. Select **A6:C18** and press **Delete**.

9. Enter the following data for the Dramatic Arts Department, beginning in cell A6:

Another Way
Rather than delete the existing data, you can overwrite it. Select A6 and begin keying new data. Press Tab and key the data for B6. Press Tab and key the data for C6 and press Enter, etc. As you move to the next cell, the existing text is selected and it will be deleted when you enter new text.

DRAM321	Acting Studio I: Discover the Actor	106
DRAM322	Naturalism and Realism Techniques	95
DRAM326	Acting Studio: Improvisation	87
DRAM302	Acting Studio: Comedy	69
DRAM301	Fundamentals of Dance	110
DRAM312	Acting Studio: Shakespeare	95
DRAM315	Acting Studio: Iconoclastic Voices	95
DRAM400	Dialects and Accents	95
DRAM401	Advanced Voice and Diction	75
DRAM420	Theatre History	125
DRAM435	Acting for Film and TV	76
DRAM460	Auditioning Techniques	95

10. Adjust all column widths to display all data. (See Figure 6-3.)

Figure 6-3

Completed worksheet

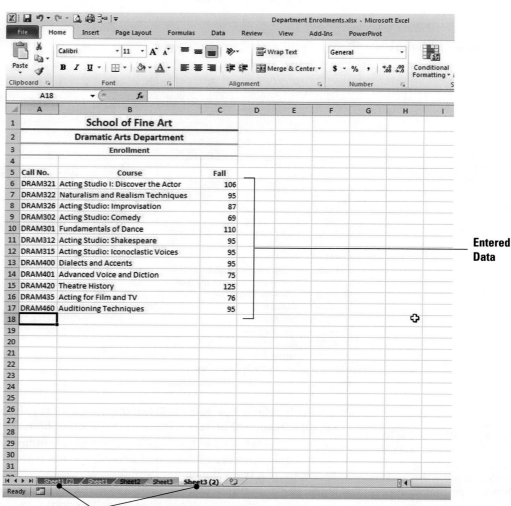

Entered Data

Copied Worksheets

11. Click the **File** tab and select Save As. Create a Lesson 6 folder. **SAVE** the workbook in the folder as *Department Enrollments*.

PAUSE. LEAVE the workbook open to use in the next exercise.

When an existing worksheet contains formatting that you want to use in a new worksheet, it is more efficient to copy the existing worksheet than to start the new worksheet from scratch. You can then delete or overwrite the existing data with new data. You will not need to format the new worksheet—the formatting is copied with the data. By copying worksheets, you can be assured that formatting is consistent among all the worksheets in a workbook.

In the preceding exercise, you used two methods to copy a worksheet, resulting in a workbook that has five worksheets. Notice that when you copy a worksheet, the new sheet is identified as a copy by a number in parentheses following the worksheet name. When you click and hold the left mouse button on the worksheet tab, the cursor becomes a new worksheet icon and an arrow appears next to the active worksheet tab, as shown in Figure 6-4.

Figure 6-4

Copying a worksheet using the mouse

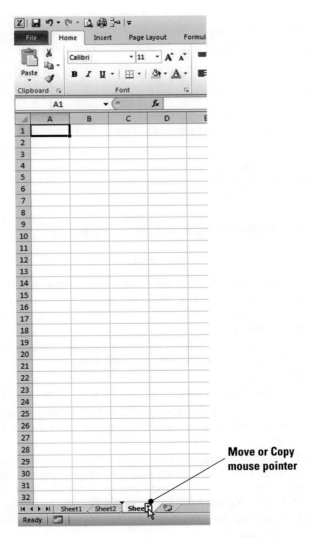

Move or Copy mouse pointer

Take Note   Notice that when a worksheet is copied, the tab color is copied as well as the worksheet, contents, and formatting.

Renaming a Worksheet

When a workbook contains multiple worksheets with data, it is helpful to replace the generic names Sheet1, Sheet2, and so on with names that identify the data contained in each sheet. In our example, each of the worksheets contains information about one department in the School of Fine Arts. Renaming the tabs with department names will allow you to quickly locate enrollment data.

STEP BY STEP   **Rename a Worksheet**

Another Way
You can also right-click the sheet tab to activate the sheet tab drop-down menu.

USE the workbook you saved in the previous exercise to carry out these steps:

1. Double-click the Sheet1 (2) tab to select the tab name.
2. Key Interior Design and press Enter. The new name appears on the worksheet tab.
3. Key Interior Design Department in A2 of the sheet. Select A6:C19 and press Delete. You will enter data for this department in a later exercise.
4. Click the Sheet1 tab. Click Format and click Rename Sheet. Key Fine Arts and press Enter.
5. Click the Sheet2 tab. Rename the sheet Media Studies and press Enter.
6. Click the Sheet3 tab. Rename the sheet Biomedical Arts and press Enter.
7. Click Sheet3 (2). Rename the sheet Dramatic Arts and press Enter.
8. Check each worksheet to ensure that the shortened name on the sheet tab matches the department name in A2.

PAUSE. LEAVE the workbook open to use in the next exercise.

By naming the worksheets, you make it much easier to locate enrollment data for any course in a department. Each worksheet name indicates the type of data contained in the sheet.

Repositioning the Worksheets in a Workbook

Now that the worksheets in the Department Enrollments workbook are appropriately named, you can rearrange them in any way you wish. An alphabetical arrangement is a logical way to organize the worksheets in this workbook.

STEP BY STEP   **Reposition the Worksheets in a Workbook**

USE the workbook from the previous exercise.

1. Click the Biomedical Arts tab. Click Format in the Cells group.
2. Click Move or Copy Sheet. The *Move or Copy* dialog box opens. You want this sheet to be the first sheet listed in the *Before sheet* box, so click OK to move Biomedical Arts before Interior Design.
3. Click the Dramatic Arts tab. Hold down the mouse button and move the worksheet to the left. Release the mouse when the down arrow is on the right side of the Biomedical Arts tab.
4. Click the Fine Arts tab. Click Format, then click Move or Copy Sheet.
5. Click Interior Design in the dialog box. Click OK to move Fine Arts before Interior Design. The Fine Arts sheet is moved to the third position and the sheets are now in alphabetic order.
6. Click the Dramatic Arts tab. Click Format and then Tab Color. Click Red under Standard Colors. As noted previously, when you copied worksheets, the tab color was copied as well as the contents and formatting. Changing the tab color for the copied worksheets ensures that each tab has a different color.
7. Right-click the Interior Design tab, click Tab Color, and click Purple under Standard Colors.
8. **SAVE** the workbook with the same name.

PAUSE. LEAVE the workbook open to use in the next exercise.

Hiding and Unhiding a Worksheet

You may hide columns and rows when you want to exclude particular columns or rows from a printout or when you want to hide sensitive or confidential information while you are working with other data in a worksheet. You can apply the same procedure to **hide** (make a worksheet invisible) and **unhide** (make visible again) worksheets. To hide a worksheet using the shortcut menu, right-click the worksheet tab, then Hide. If a worksheet is hidden, the Unhide option will be active on the shortcut menu.

You can hide several worksheets at the same time. To do so, hold down Ctrl and click the tab(s) of the sheet(s) you want to hide. You cannot, however, select multiple worksheets in the Unhide dialog box; you must unhide worksheets individually.

Inserting a New Worksheet into a Workbook

You can insert one or multiple worksheets into an existing workbook. The Insert Worksheet tab (Figure 6-5) at the bottom of a worksheet was introduced in Excel 2007 as a new feature that allows you to quickly insert a new worksheet at the end of the existing worksheets. To insert a new worksheet before an existing worksheet, select the worksheet tab before the place where you want to insert the new sheet and use the Insert command in the Cells group.

Figure 6-5

Insert Worksheet tab

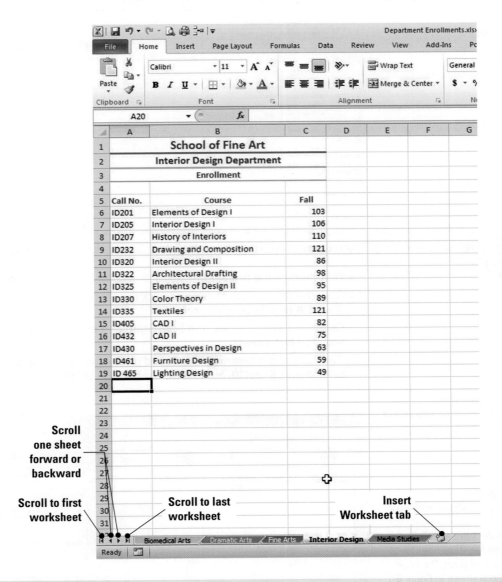

Insert a New Worksheet into a Workbook

USE the workbook from the previous exercise.

1. Click the **Insert Worksheet** tab next to the Media Studies tab. A new worksheet (Sheet6) is inserted. When you insert a new worksheet, it is blank and has the generic Sheet1 title. When you inserted a worksheet before the existing sheets were named, the new sheet was given the next consecutive number, such as Sheet6.

2. Click the Biomedical Arts tab and click the Insert arrow in the Cells group to display the options shown in Figure 6-6. Click Insert Sheet. A blank sheet (Sheet7) is inserted before the Biomedical Arts worksheet. As more worksheets are added to a workbook, you may not be able to see all worksheet tabs. When this happens, use the scroll arrows, shown in Figure 6-5, to move through all worksheets.

Figure 6-6

Insert options menu

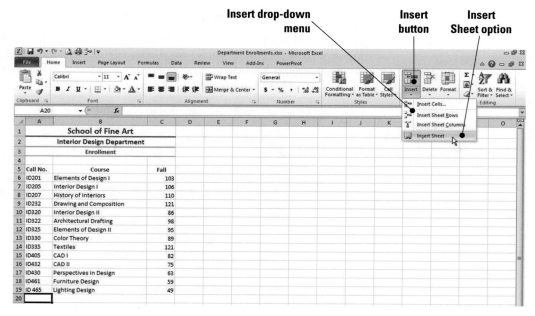

 Troubleshooting If the Biomedical Arts tab is not visible, use the scroll arrow to move to the first worksheet.

3. Double-click the Sheet7 tab, key Advertising, and press Enter.

4. Click the Dramatic Arts tab and click the Insert arrow in the Cells group. Click Insert Sheet. A new Sheet8 is inserted.

5. Click Advertising, press and hold Shift, and click Biomedical Arts. You have now selected two sheets.

6. Click Insert and Insert Sheet. Based on the previous step's selection, two worksheets, Sheet9 and Sheet10, are inserted before the Biomedical Arts worksheet.

Figure 6-7

Insert dialog box

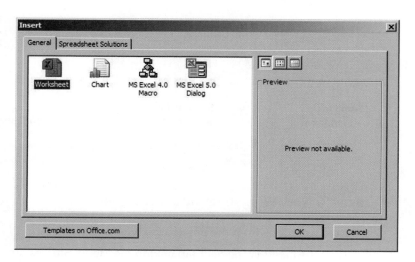

 Another Way
You can right-click a worksheet tab and click Insert on the shortcut menu to insert a worksheet. The Insert dialog box shown in Figure 6-7 will open, and you can insert a blank worksheet from the General tab, insert a worksheet based on a template from the Spreadsheet Solutions tab, or insert an online template if you are connected to the Internet.

PAUSE. LEAVE the workbook open to use in the next exercise.

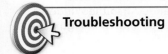

Troubleshooting When you open the Insert dialog box, multiple Excel files may be shown on the General tab. The listed files represent templates that have been downloaded, created by you, or created by another user.

Take Note When inserting multiple worksheets at the same time, press and hold Shift, then select the same number of worksheet tabs that you want to insert in the open workbook. Recall that in the exercise, when you selected the tabs of two existing worksheets, clicked Insert, and clicked Insert Sheet, two new worksheets were inserted.

Deleting a Worksheet from a Workbook

If a workbook contains blank worksheets or worksheets that hold data that is no longer needed, you can delete the unnecessary sheets. You can delete a worksheet by locating the worksheet then click the Delete arrow in the Cells group then Delete Sheet. In the next exercise, you will learn how to delete worksheets.

Take Note You can delete more than one worksheet at a time. To select adjacent sheets, click the first sheet tab, press and hold the Shift key, and then click the second sheet tab. To select nonadjacent sheets, click the first sheet tab, click and hold the Ctrl key, and then click all the sheet tabs you want to include.

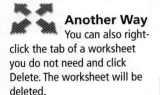

Another Way
You can also right-click the tab of a worksheet you do not need and click Delete. The worksheet will be deleted.

Bottom Line

WORKING WITH MULTIPLE WORKSHEETS

In Excel, you can **group worksheets**, a feature that allows you to enter and edit data on several worksheets at the same time or apply formatting to multiple worksheets. When sheets are grouped, you can enter data in one worksheet and have it appear in multiple worksheets in a workbook. When multiple worksheets are selected, [*Group*] appears in the title bar at the top of the worksheet. Be cautious. When you change data in grouped sheets, you may accidentally replace data on other sheets.

Working with Multiple Worksheets in a Workbook

Working with a group of worksheets is a time-saving technique. You can view several worksheets within a workbook at the same time. This feature allows you to make quick visual comparisons and ensures that changes made to grouped sheets will not overwrite existing data. You can group worksheets and enter data on all worksheets within the group at the same time. In the next exercise, you will learn to work with multiple worksheets by grouping and ungrouping and arranging them.

STEP BY STEP **Work with Multiple Worksheets in a Workbook**

USE the workbook from the previous exercise.

1. Right-click any worksheet tab and click Select All Sheets. The title bar now reads Department Enrollments.xlsx [Group].
2. In cell B20, key Total Enrollment and press Enter. You have just added the contents of cell B20 in all the selected sheets.

Take Note If you copy a data range from a worksheet to grouped worksheets, the Paste Options button does not appear. Some formatting, such as column width, is not copied.

Another Way
If you want to group some but not all worksheets within a workbook, press Ctrl and click the tab of each worksheet you want to include in the group.

3. Right-click any worksheet tab and click Ungroup Sheets.
4. Click the View tab and then the Biomedical Arts tab. Next, click New Window in the Windows group.
5. Click the Dramatic Arts tab and click New Window.

6. Click the **Fine Arts** tab to make the sheet active and click **Arrange All** in the Windows group. The *Arrange Windows* dialog box opens. Click **Vertical**, as shown in Figure 6-8. Click on **Windows of active workbook**.

Figure 6-8

Arrange Windows dialog box

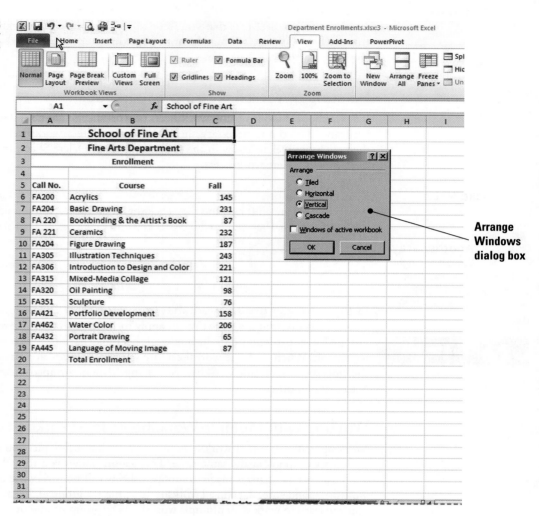

Arrange Windows dialog box

Take Note   Data that you copy or cut in grouped sheets cannot be pasted on another sheet because the size of the copy area includes all layers of the selected sheets and is different from the paste area in a single sheet. Therefore, make sure that only one sheet is selected before you attempt to copy or move data from a grouped sheet to another worksheet.

7. Click **OK**. Your screen should look like Figure 6-9, with the three worksheets displayed side by side.

Figure 6-9

Vertically tiled worksheets

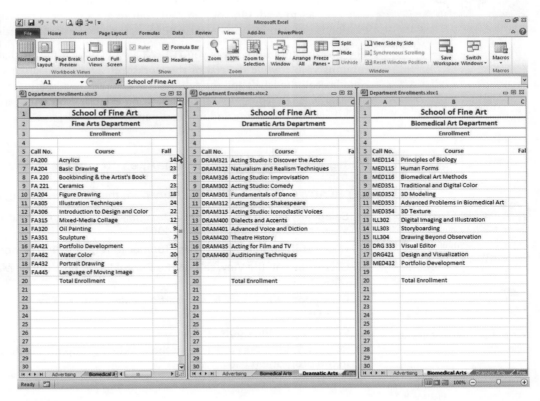

PAUSE. LEAVE the workbook open to use in the next exercise.

Take Note

The New Window and Arrange All options enable you to display worksheets side by side for a quick visual comparison. You can enter and edit data, scroll, and move around in the individual windows just as you would in a "normal" view window. You can also click a cell in any of the displayed worksheets to make changes or to select cells or ranges.

Hiding and Unhiding Worksheet Windows in a Workbook

Any worksheet can be used and viewed in a separate window in the workbook view by applying it to a new window. These new windows can be arranged so that you can work in them without having to click back and forth on the worksheet tabs. This is an important feature to use when comparing like sheets and data. To hide a worksheet window, click the View tab and in the Window group, click the Hide button. To unhide, click the Unhide button, then select the worksheet to unhide.

If you click Hide in the Window group with one worksheet window open, the entire workbook is hidden. Excel remains open, but the taskbar no long displays the worksheet name. This feature allows you to quickly mask confidential data from view.

Take Note

Do not confuse the Hide and Unhide commands you used in this lesson with those you may have learned in an earlier lesson. The View tab commands in this exercise are used to hide and unhide active windows and window views in a workbook. The Hide and Unhide commands in the Format options, as described in previous exercises, are used to hide and unhide rows, columns, and worksheets. When you hide a sheet with the Format command, other worksheets in the workbook remain visible and accessible. When you use the Hide Window command, you must use the Unhide command to access any worksheet hidden in the workbook.

USING ZOOM AND FREEZE TO CHANGE THE ONSCREEN VIEW

The Bottom Line

Excel's **Zoom** feature allows you to make a worksheet appear bigger or smaller on your screen. You can use this feature to zoom in on a portion of a worksheet so that it appears larger and the data is easier to read. Or, you can zoom out to get a better perspective of the entire worksheet, making it easier to identify formatting inconsistencies or problematic spacing or alignment.

The Freeze Panes feature lets you **freeze** a pane, which means that you keep certain rows or columns visible while the rest of the worksheet scrolls. You often want to freeze the row that contains column labels and the column that contains row headings so that it is always clear what the data you see represents. In the following exercise, you will learn to zoom in and out of a worksheet and also freeze and unfreeze panes.

Using Zoom and Freeze to Change the Onscreen View

 The *SFA Staff Directory* file for this lesson is available on the book companion website or in WileyPLUS.

 **WILEY PLUS EXTRA**

WileyPLUS Extra! features an online tutorial of this task.

GET READY. OPEN *SFA Staff Directory* from the data files for this lesson.

1. Select any cell in the *SFA Staff Directory* worksheet. Click Zoom to Selection on the View tab. Zoom is increased to 400%.
2. Click Undo on the Quick Access Toolbar to return to 100% zoom.
3. Click Zoom on the View tab. In the *Zoom* dialog box, under *Magnification*, click 200%. Click OK.
4. Click Zoom and under *Magnification*, click Custom. Key 150 in the percentage box and click OK.
5. Click 100% in the Zoom group.
6. Select A5. Click Freeze Panes in the Window group on the View tab. Click Freeze Panes in the drop-down list.

Figure 6-10

Freeze Panes options

Another Way
The Freeze First Column and Freeze Top Row commands shown in Figure 6-10 are quick and easy to use if your worksheet begins with column and row headings, but when the data is preceded by a title and subtitle, you must tell Excel where you want the "freeze" to be located. That is why you need to select the cell below the line that you want to be visible as you move through the worksheet.

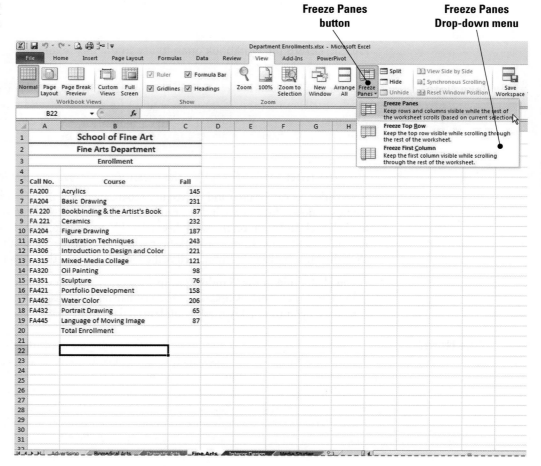

7. Press **Ctrl+End**. Row 4 with the column labels appears at the top of the screen to let you know what each column represents, even when the active cell is the last cell in the data range.

8. Press **Ctrl+Home** to return to the top of the data. Click **Freeze Panes** and select **Unfreeze panes**.

PAUSE. LEAVE the workbook open to use in the next exercise.

You can also use the Zoom scale on the Status bar to customize magnification. To zoom in (magnify), select a size greater than 100%; to zoom out (shrink), select a size less than 100%.

Some mouse devices have built-in zooming capabilities. If your mouse has a wheel, hold down Ctrl while you rotate the wheel forward or backward to increase and decrease zoom.

Take Note

The Freeze Top Row and Freeze First Column commands do not work together. When you want to freeze the first row and first column at the same time, locate the "freeze point" and use the Freeze Panes command.

FINDING AND REPLACING DATA

The Bottom Line

The Find and Replace options let you locate specific data quickly and, if necessary, replace it with new data. These features are most effective in large worksheets in which all of the data is not visible on the screen, thus saving you the time of scanning through vast amounts of data to find the information you need.

Locating Data with the Find Command

If you want to locate a particular item of data that isn't immediately visible, you can scan the worksheet visually to look for the needed data. A much easier and quicker way is to use the Find & Select commands shown in Figure 6-11.

STEP BY STEP   **Locate Data with the Find Command**

USE the workbook from the previous exercise.

1. Click **Find & Select** in the Editing group on the Home tab. (See Figure 6-11.)

Figure 6-11

Find & Select commands

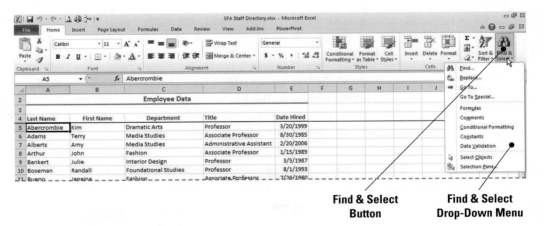

Find & Select Button   Find & Select Drop-Down Menu

2. Click **Find**. The *Find and Replace* dialog box opens with the Find tab displayed.

3. Key **tutor** in the *Find what* box. It does not matter whether you key the text in uppercase or lowercase; Excel will find each instance of the word.

Troubleshooting If you had selected the Match case check box when you searched for *tutor,* the search would not have found any data because the word *tutor* is capitalized each time it occurs in the worksheet. Therefore, a data match would not be found if you searched for a lowercase word. When the search was completed, a dialog box would have informed you that Excel could not find the data you requested.

Take Note   It does not matter which cell is currently the active cell when you enter a search string. If you do not select a range of cells, Excel will search the entire worksheet.

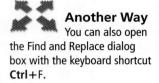

Another Way
You can also open the Find and Replace dialog box with the keyboard shortcut **Ctrl+**F.

4. Click **Find All**. The box is expanded to list all occurrences of "tutor" in the worksheet. You see that the search results lists both academic and writing tutors, so you need to refine the search criteria. If you click **Find Next** after you key the search string, Excel selects the cell in which the first occurrence of the string is found. You can edit the cell or click Find Next and continue to browse through the worksheet. The cursor will stop at each cell where the search string is located.

5. Key **writing tutor** in the *Find what* box and click **Find All**. The worksheet contains data for two individuals whose title is Writing Tutor.

6. Click **Options** on the dialog box to view the default settings for the Find feature.

7. **CLOSE** the dialog box.

PAUSE. LEAVE the workbook open to use in the next exercise.

When you enter the text or number that you want to find and click Find All, Excel locates all occurrences of the search string and lists them at the bottom of the dialog box, as shown in Figure 6-12. A **string** is any sequence of letters or numbers in a field.

Figure 6-12

Find All search results

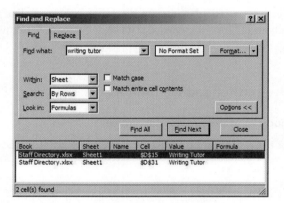

The Options button on the Find tab allows you to set additional parameters for the search. As shown in Figure 6-13, the default is to search the active worksheet, but you can also search an entire workbook. You can locate instances in which only the case (capitals or lowercase) matches the search string you key or the entire cell contents match the search string—more precise search strings create more concise search results.

Figure 6-13

Set search parameters

Find and Replace

Replacing Data with the Replace Command

To look for specific data and replace it with other data, you can use the Replace tab on the Find and Replace dialog box. You can quickly find and replace all or some occurrences of a character string in a worksheet. Replacing data with the click of a button can save you the time of finding occurrences of the data and repeatedly keying replacement data.

STEP BY STEP   **Replace Data with the Replace Command**

Another Way
To display the Replace dialog box without using the Find & Replace feature, press Ctrl+H.

USE the workbook from the previous exercise.

1. Click **Find & Select** in the Editing group.
2. Click **Replace**. The Find and Replace dialog box opens with the Replace tab displayed.
3. In the *Find what* box, key **Johnson**.
4. In the *Replace with* box, key **Johnston**, as shown in Figure 6-14.

Figure 6-14

Replace tab of the Find and Replace dialog box

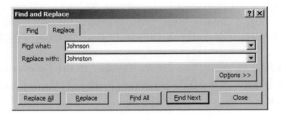

5. In the *Search* box, click **By Columns**, then click **Find Next**. The first occurrence of Johnson is not the one you are looking for, so click **Find Next** until you locate the entry for Tamara Johnson.

 Troubleshooting   If the Find and Replace dialog box obstructs your view of column A where the search data will be located, click the dialog box title bar and drag the box to the right so that you have a clear view of columns A and B.

6. Click **Replace** and click **Close**.
7. Click **Find & Select** and then click **Replace**. Key **Advertising** in the *Find what* field and key **Advertising and Graphic Arts** in the *Replace with* field.
8. Click **Replace All**. A dialog box tells you that Excel made nine replacements. Click **OK**, then click **Close** to close the dialog box.

 **Troubleshooting**   Use discretion when deciding whether to use Replace All or Find Next when looking for specific data. For instance, when you needed to correct the spelling of the last name of a specific individual, you did not know whether there were other entries with the last name Johnson. Therefore, as a precaution, you needed to find each entry and decide whether to replace it with the corrected spelling. If you had chosen Replace All, you would have incorrectly changed two other last names in the directory.

9. **SAVE** your workbook in the Lesson 6 folder. Name the file *Staff Directory*.

PAUSE. LEAVE the workbook open to use in the next exercise.

As you have seen in this exercise, the Replace All command allows you to quickly change the contents of multiple cells. When the staff directory was created, it was easier to key *Advertising* rather than the complete name, *Advertising and Graphic Arts*. You corrected all nine occurrences of the department name, however, by clicking Replace All.

Navigating Data with the Go To Command

As you learned in an earlier lesson, you can key a cell location in the Name box, press Enter, and Excel makes the designated cell active. Another method of moving to a specific cell is to use the

Go To feature. In the following exercise, you will use the Go To feature to navigate the worksheet and enter new data and to unhide the first worksheet row.

STEP BY STEP   **Navigate Data with the Go To Command**

USE the workbook you saved in the previous exercise.

1. On the View tab, click **Freeze Panes** and select **Unfreeze Panes**. This removes the freeze so you can display all rows.
2. Click **Ctrl+A**. On the Home tab, click **Format**, mouse over **Hide & Unhide**, and click on **Unhide** rows. This will make the hidden row 1 visible.
3. Click **Find & Select**, then click **Go To**. The Go To dialog box is displayed.
4. Key **A1** in the *Reference* box and click **OK**. Column headers A through E become highlighted. A1 is still hidden.

Take Note   The Reference box is not case sensitive. Entering A1 or a1 will have the same effect.

5. In the Cells group, click **Format**, click **Hide & Unhide**, and click **Unhide Rows**. Row 1 is displayed.
6. Click **Find & Select**, then click **Go To**. Key **E67** in the Reference box and click **OK**.
7. Key **5/15/06** in E67 as the date on which Professor Young was hired. Press **Enter**.
8. Click **Find & Select** and click **Go To Special**.
9. In the *Go To Special* dialog box, click **Blanks** and select **OK**, as shown in Figure 6-15. The blank cells within the data range are highlighted.

Figure 6-15

Go To Special dialog box

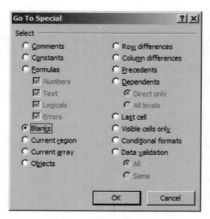

10. Press **Tab** three times until E13, the first blank cell in the Date Hired column, is the active cell. Enter **6/8/87** and press **Tab** to move to the next blank cell. Enter the following dates. Press **Tab** after each entry:

Gronchi	12/8/05
Hasselberg	10/20/00
Kahn	11/2/03
Liu	6/5/07
Male	7/10/00
Vande Velde	3/1/01
Wadia	6/1/02
Yang	6/1/02

Another Way
Ctrl+G is the keyboard command to display the Go To dialog box.

11. **SAVE** the *Staff Directory* workbook and **CLOSE** the workbook.

CLOSE Excel.

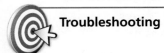

Troubleshooting The reason you needed to tab three times to reach E13 is the blank cells in the heading rows. Remember that when cells are merged, entries in the merged cells are considered to be in the upper-left cell. Therefore, Excel considers the remaining cells in the merge to be blank.

Take Note As you experienced in the preceding exercises, the Find & Select features allow you to find and, if necessary, quickly replace existing data. The Go To feature is a fast way to move to specific cell references, especially in a large worksheet.

In the exercises you completed in this lesson, you worked with relatively small amounts of data. In the business world, however, people often work with worksheets that contain massive amounts of data. The Find & Select and Go To features are most effective in large worksheets where it can take a significant amount of time to scan numerous rows and/or columns to find the data you need.

SKILL SUMMARY

In This Lesson, You Learned How To:
Organize worksheets
Work with multiple worksheets
Use zoom and freeze to change the onscreen view
Find and replace data

Knowledge Assessment

Matching

Match each vocabulary term with its definition.

a. Hide command   f. Find & Select

b. freeze   g. zoom in

c. group worksheets   h. zoom out

d. string   i. Go To Special

e. search and replace   j. Arrange All command

_____ 1. To find and quickly replace existing data.

_____ 2. To make certain rows or columns remain visible on your screen even when you scroll your worksheet.

_____ 3. To make a worksheet appear larger on the screen.

_____ 4. To make a workbook or worksheet invisible.

_____ 5. Any sequence of letters or numbers that you type.

_____ 6. To make a worksheet appear smaller on the screen.

_____ 7. Selecting multiple worksheets in which you enter and edit data.

_____ 8. A command you can use to locate blank cells in a worksheet.

_____ 9. A feature you can use to locate and replace specific data in a worksheet.

_____ 10. A feature that allows you to visually compare worksheets.

Multiple Choice

Circle the choice that best completes or responds to the following statements.

1. To find data using the Find and Replace dialog box, you must enter a sequence of characters called a:

    a. range.

    b. string.

    c. cell address.

    d. menu.

2. You can tell that worksheets are grouped by:

    a. a bracket around the grouped sheets.

    b. the word *group* on the sheet tabs.

    c. the word *group* in the title bar.

    d. the words *grouped sheets* on the Status bar.

3. When Sheet1 has been copied, the new worksheet tab is named:

    a. copy of Sheet1.

    b. Sheet1 (2).

    c. Sheet1 Copy.

    d. Sheet2.

4. Which of the following is **not** a way to insert a new worksheet into a workbook?

    a. On the Home tab, click Insert and click Insert Sheet.

    b. Right-click a sheet tab, click Insert, and then click Insert Worksheet.

    c. On the Insert tab, click New Sheet.

    d. On the Home tab, click Format, click Move or Copy Sheet, and click Create a Copy.

5. To insert multiple worksheets at one time, what action is needed in addition to selecting the same number of tabs as the number of sheets to insert?

    a. Press and hold Shift as you select the tabs.

    b. Press and hold Ctrl as you select the tabs.

    c. Press Shift after you select the tabs.

    d. Press Ctrl after you select the tabs.

6. To enter data in multiple worksheets at one time, you must:

    a. use the Arrange command in the Window group on the View tab.

    b. use the Freeze command in the Window group on the View tab.

    c. use the Format command in the Cells group on the Home tab.

    d. group all worksheets and enter data in the open worksheet.

7. If you want to magnify the data on the screen:

    a. decrease zoom to less than 100%.

    b. increase zoom to 100%.

    c. increase zoom to more than 100%.

    d. increase the font size in the data range.

    e. both b & c.

    f. both b & d.

8. To move or copy a sheet, you would:

    a. right-click the sheet tab, then select Move or Copy Sheet.

    b. click the Format arrow then Move or Copy Sheet.

    c. use the cut and paste command.

    d. a and b.

9. To rename a worksheet, you would perform which action.

    a. worksheets cannot be renamed.

    b. right-click on sheet tab, then rename.

    c. click the Format arrow in the Cells group, then Rename Sheet.

    d. b & c

10. When you use the Freeze command,

    a. data cannot be entered in the worksheet.

    b. you cannot scroll through the worksheet.

    c. you cannot change the worksheet view.

    d. the column and/or row headings remain visible as you scroll through the worksheet card.

Competency Assessment

Project 6-1: School of Fine Arts Enrollments

In this exercise, you will move and copy worksheets, rename worksheets, change the tab color, and rearrange worksheets within a workbook.

GET READY. LAUNCH Excel if it is not already running.

@ The *SFA Enrollments* file for this lesson is available on the book companion website or in WileyPLUS.

1. **OPEN** the *SFA Enrollments* data file for this lesson.
2. With the Advertising tab active, click Ctrl+A. This selects the entire worksheet.
3. Click Format in the Cells group on the Home tab. Click Move or Copy Sheet.
4. In the Move or Copy dialog box, click the Create a copy box and click OK.
5. On the Advertising (2) worksheet, select A2 and key Foundational Studies. Press Enter.
6. Select A6:C20 and press Delete.
7. Click Format, click Rename Sheet, and key Foundations. Press Enter.
8. Click Format, click Tab Color, and click Dark Red.
9. Click Format and click Move or Copy Sheet. In the Before sheet box, click (move to end) and click OK.
10. **SAVE** the workbook as *SFA Enrollments 6-1* and then **CLOSE** the file.

LEAVE Excel open for the next project.

Project 6-2: Renaming and Repositioning Worksheets

For this project, you will rename worksheets, reposition worksheets, and insert and delete worksheets from a workbook.

GET READY. LAUNCH Excel if not already running.

@ The *Training Expenditures* document file for this lesson is available on the book companion website or in WileyPLUS.

1. **OPEN** the *Training Expenditures* data file for this lesson.
2. Right-click Sheet1. Click Rename and key Budget. Press Enter.
3. Double-click the Sheet2 tab. Key January. Press Enter.
4. Rename Sheet3 March and press Enter.
5. Rename Sheet4 Previous Qtr. and press Enter.
6. Click the Insert Worksheet tab. Rename the new sheet Summary
7. Click the March tab and click the Insert arrow in the Cells group on the Home tab. Click Insert Sheet.
8. Name the new worksheet February.
9. Click the Previous Qtr. Tab. Click the Delete arrow in the Cells group on the Home tab. Click Delete Sheet.
10. Reposition the Summary sheet tab in front of Budget.

11. SAVE the workbook as *Training Expenditures 6-2*.

LEAVE Excel open for next project.

Proficiency Assessment

Project 6-3: Graphic Design Institute, Part 2

In this project, you will move between worksheets, change the workbook view, and group worksheets to enter data on multiple sheets.

USE the workbook from the previous project.

1. Click the View tab to make it active.
2. On the Budget worksheet, select E18 and click Zoom to Selection in the Zoom group.
3. Click 100% in the Zoom group.
4. Click Zoom In on the Status bar and increase magnification to 150%.
5. Click the January tab and click Select All. Click Copy.
6. Click the Summary sheet tab, select A1, and click Paste.
7. On the February worksheet, select A1, right-click, and click Paste. Click the Paste Options button and select Keep Source Formatting.

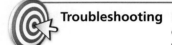 **Troubleshooting** If the formatting is not copied, make the January worksheet active and select the text containing the formatting. Double-click the Format Painter and apply the formatting to the necessary cells.

8. Double-click A2 to put it in Edit mode (noted on Status bar). Select January, key February, and press Enter.
9. Select C4 and key February.
10. Delete the January expenditures from C5:C17. Then enter the February expenditures for the items listed next. (Not all items have February expenditures; leave those cells blank.)

Courseware development	$2,500
Courseware purchase	400
Certification	250
Train-the-trainer	1,200
Hardware purchases	10,500
Consulting fees	150
Instructor fees	4,000
Travel	600
Per diem	400

11. Select A2 on the Summary worksheet and key Quarterly Expenditures.
12. Copy C4:C18 from the February worksheet to the Summary sheet. Paste the data next to the January data.
13. Copy C4:C18 from the March worksheet to the Summary sheet. Paste the data next to the February data.
14. Select A1:E1 and click Merge & Center two times.
15. Click Merge & Center two times for cells A2:E2.
16. SAVE the workbook as *Training Expenditures 6-3*. CLOSE the workbook.

LEAVE Excel open for the next project.

Project 6-4: School of Fine Arts Directory

For this project, you will update the school's staff directory.

GET READY. LAUNCH Excel if it is not already running.

@ The *Updated Directory* file for this lesson is available on the book companion website or in WileyPLUS.

1. **OPEN** the *Updated Directory* data file for this lesson.
2. At the bottom of the worksheet, add information for three new staff members:

DeGrasse, Kirk	Media Studies	Associate Professor	2/15/07
Sheperdidian, Janet	Student Services	Academic Advisor	3/1/07
Playstead, Craig	Administration	Associate Dean	4/1/07

3. Gail Erickson has been promoted to Professor. Click **Find & Select**. Change her title.
4. Use the Find & Select feature to replace BioMedical with Biomedical Art.
5. Use Find & Select to go to A33. Sidney Higa's title should be Vice President.
6. Click **Format** and change the name of Sheet1 to **Directory**.
7. Click **Sheet2**. Press **Ctrl** and click Sheet3. Click **Format** and hide the blank worksheets.
8. Name the workbook *Staff Directory 6-4*.
9. **SAVE** and **CLOSE** the workbook.

LEAVE Excel open for the next project.

Mastery Assessment

Project 6-5: School of Fine Arts Course Recommendations

Debra Core, an academic advisor, has asked you to search the enrollment data and highlight courses for some of the continuing education students with whom she is working.

GET READY. LAUNCH Excel if it is not already running.

@ The *Advisor Recommendations* file for this lesson is available on the book companion website or in WileyPLUS.

1. **OPEN** the *Advisor Recommendations* data file for this lesson.
2. Identify the courses that investigate various aspects of color.
   a. Use the Find & Select options to search the entire workbook.
   b. Use *color* as the search string.
   c. In the Within field, click **Workbook**.
   d. Find all courses that have color as part of the course name.
3. Your search should return a list of six courses. Add yellow fill color to highlight each course.
   a. Click the **first course** (Biomedical Arts). Click **Fill Color**.
   b. Click the **second course** and click **Fill Color** in the Fonts group.
   c. Continue until the six courses have been highlighted.
4. Identify the available painting courses.
   a. Use *painting* as the search string.
   b. Search the workbook and mark painting courses with a light blue fill.
5. Mark photography courses with a light green fill.
6. **SAVE** the workbook as *Advisor Recommendations 6-5*. **CLOSE** the file.

LEAVE Excel open for the next project.

Project 6-6: Contoso, Ltd.

This exercise has you use the Find & Select command to locate specific information and fill blank spaces in a worksheet. Be sure to freeze the column headings so they remain visible as you scroll through the list of Contoso employees.

GET READY. LAUNCH Excel if it is not already running.

1. **OPEN** the *Contoso Employees* data file for this lesson.
2. Use the Freeze Panes command so that the column headings in row 4 remain visible as you scroll to the end the data range.
3. Find and Replace all occurrences of Billing Clerk with Accounts Receivable Clerk.
4. Use Find and Replace options to find all blank cells on the worksheet. Key Records Management in each blank in column C.
5. **SAVE** the workbook as *Contoso Employees 6-6*.

LEAVE Excel open for the next project

INTERNET READY

In this lesson, you worked with data files for the School of Fine Arts. Open *College Comparisons* in the data files for this lesson. Go online and investigate colleges that offer degrees in your career interest area. Use the College Comparisons worksheet to record information about three colleges that offer a degree program in your area of interest. Fill in as much information as you can locate about each college. Based on your limited research, indicate which college would be your choice to pursue the degree you investigated. Save the file and exit Excel.

LESSON SKILL MATRIX

In This Lesson, You Will Learn The Following Skills:

Ensuring Your Data's Integrity

Sorting Data

Filtering Data

KEY TERMS

- **ascending order**
- **AutoFilter**
- **comparison operator**
- **criteria**
- **descending order**
- **duplicate value**
- **filter**

An employee's name is added to the list of Contoso, Ltd.'s employees whenever a person joins the company. However, viewing the employee list according to the employees' positions would be more useful to the office manager when he develops the work schedule. Reorganizing the data enables the office manager to ensure that the office is fully staffed when it is open. The office manager also needs to update employee data files with additional data. Because other employees often need to access the files, he plans to restrict the data that can be entered in some files to ensure that valid results are obtained when data entry is complete and the data is analyzed for decision making. Excel is primarily a tool for organizing, analyzing, and presenting numerical information. Sorting data from highest to lowest or smallest to largest, for example, lets you quickly and easily identify trends and generate forecasts or probabilities. In this lesson, you will learn to use commands on Excel's Data tab to sort, filter, and display data needed for specific purposes.

SOFTWARE ORIENTATION

Excel's Data Tab

The command groups on Excel's Data tab, shown in Figure 7-1, enable you to sort and filter data, convert text to columns, ensure valid data entry, conduct what-if analyses, and outline data. You can also get external data into Excel by using Data commands.

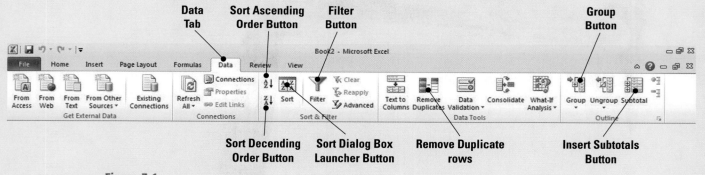

Figure 7-1

Data tab

In this lesson, you will learn many ways to use the command groups on Excel's Data tab to manage spreadsheet data. Use Figure 7-1 throughout this lesson as a guide to these powerful commands.

ENSURING YOUR DATA'S INTEGRITY

The Bottom Line

Ensuring valid data entry is an important task for Excel users. In many worksheets that you create, other users may enter data to get desired calculations and results. Restricting the type of data that can be entered in a cell is one way to ensure data integrity. You may want to restrict data entry to a certain range of dates, limit choices by using a drop-down list, or make sure that only positive whole numbers are entered. And, because it's not uncommon for users to inadvertently enter duplicate rows of information in lengthy spreadsheets, you need to have a mechanism for finding and eliminating duplicate information.

Restricting Cell Entries to Certain Data Types

When you decide what data type you want to use in a cell or range of cells and how you want it used, formatted, or displayed, you are ready to set up the validation **criteria** for that data. Data Validation is the feature in Excel that will manage data that is to be entered or displayed based on your specified criteria. When you restrict (validate) data entry, it is necessary to provide immediate feedback to instruct users about the data that is permitted in a cell. This feedback is on the form of alerts and error messages that you create. You can provide an input message when a restricted cell is selected or provide an instructive message when an invalid entry is made. In this exercise, you learn how to validate data and restrict data entry while supplying clear feedback to users to assure a smooth, trouble-free data entry experience. This is vital to worksheet performance because it restricts errors in data entry.

STEP BY STEP | **Restrict Cell Entries to Certain Data Types**

 The *Employee Data* data file for this lesson is available on the book companion website or in WileyPLUS.

WILEY PLUS *EXTRA*

WileyPLUS Extra! features an online tutorial of this task.

GET READY. Before you begin these steps, be sure to **LAUNCH** Microsoft Excel.

1. **OPEN** the *Employee Data* data file for this lesson.

2. Select the cell range D3:D50.

3. On the Data tab, in the Data Tools group, click **Data Validation**. You will now begin to set your validation criteria.

4. On the Settings tab of the Data Validation dialog box, select **Whole number** in the Allow box. This sets the number format for your validation.

5. Key 15 in the Minimum box and 40 in the Maximum box. You have now set your whole number range. The *Data Validation* dialog box should look like Figure 7-2.

Figure 7-2

Restrict data entry using the Data Validation dialog box

6. Click the **Error Alert** tab in the dialog box. Be sure the Show error alert after invalid data is entered check box is selected. Key **Invalid Entry** in the Title box. This will display an alert when an invalid entry has been made to the cell.

7. Key **Only whole numbers can be entered** in the error message box as shown in Figure 7-3. This will display the error message that you want the user to see.

Figure 7-3

Error alert message

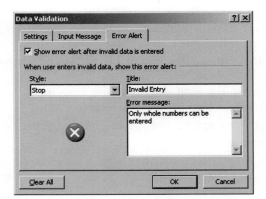

8. Click the Input Message tab and in the Input Message box, key Enter a whole number between 15 and 40. Click OK. This will create the message for the user to follow to correct their error.

9. Select cell D6, key 35.5, and press Enter. The Invalid Entry dialog box (Figure 7-4) opens, displaying the error message you created.

Figure 7-4

Invalid entry message

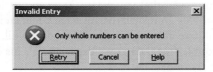

10. Click Retry to close the error message; key 36, and press Enter.

11. Use the following employee information to key values in row 29. Patricia Doyle was hired today as a receptionist. She will work 20 hours each week.

12. Create a Lesson 7 folder and **SAVE** the file as *Contoso Data*.

PAUSE. LEAVE the workbook open to use in the next exercise.

You have just taken the first step toward ensuring the integrity of data entered in the *Contoso Data* workbook. An employee cannot inadvertently enter text or values that are outside the parameters you set in the validation criteria. By extending the range beyond the current data, when new employee data is entered, the validation criteria will be applied.

You can specify how you want Excel to respond when invalid data is entered. In the preceding exercise, you accepted the default value, Stop, in the Style box on the Error Alert tab (Figure 7-3). If you select Warning in the Style box, you will be warned that you have made an entry that is not in the defined range, but you can choose to ignore the warning and enter the invalid data.

Take Note   If you do not enter an Error Alert title or text, the Excel default message will be displayed: *The value you entered is not valid. A user has restricted values that can be entered in this cell.*

Allowing Only Specific Values to Be Entered in Cells

To make data entry easier, or to limit entries to predefined items, you can create a drop-down list of valid entries. The entries on the list can be forced-choice (i.e., yes, no) or can be compiled from cells elsewhere in the workbook. A drop-down list displays as an arrow in the cell. To enter information in the restricted cell, click the arrow and then click the entry you want.

STEP BY STEP   **Allow Only Specific Values to Be Entered in Cells**

USE the workbook from the previous exercise.

1. Select E3:E29. Click Data Validation in the Data Tools group on the Data tab.

2. Click the Settings tab, in the Allow box, select List. The In-cell drop-down check box is selected by default.

3. In the Source box, key Yes, No. Click OK to accept the settings. An arrow now appears to the right of the cell range.

4. Click E3. Click the arrow to the right of the cell. You now see the list options you created in the previous step.

5. If the value in column D is 30 or more hours, from the newly created drop-down list, choose Yes. If it is less than 30 hours, select No.

6. Continue to apply the appropriate response from the list for each cell in E4:E29.

7. **SAVE** the workbook.

PAUSE. LEAVE the workbook open to use in the next exercise.

In the previous exercise, Contoso, Ltd. provided health insurance benefits to those employees who work 30 or more hours each week. By applying a Yes, No list validation, the office manager can quickly identify employees who are entitled to insurance benefits. You restricted the input for column E to two choices, but a list can include multiple choices. As you did in the exercise, the choices can be defined in the Source box on the Settings tab.

Use a comma to separate choices. For example, if you wanted to rate a vendor's performance, you might have three choices: Low, Average, and High.

There are a variety of other ways to limit data that can be entered into a cell range. You can base a list on criteria contained in the active worksheet, within the active workbook, or in another workbook. Enter the range of cells in the Source box on the Settings tab or key the cell range for the criteria. You can calculate what will be allowed based on the content of another cell. For example, you can create a data validation formula that enters yes or no in column E based on the value in column D. You will learn to create formulas in the next lesson.

Data validation can be based on a decimal with limits, a date within a timeframe, or a time within a timeframe. You can also specify the length of the text that can be entered within a cell.

 **Troubleshooting** Always test the data validation to make sure that it works correctly. Try entering both valid and invalid data in the cells to make sure that your settings work as you intend and that the expected message appears when invalid data is entered.

Removing Duplicate Cells, Rows, or Columns from a Worksheet

A **duplicate value** occurs when all values in the row are an exact match of all the values in another row. In a very large worksheet, data may be inadvertently entered more than once. This is even more likely to happen when more than one individual enters data in a worksheet. Duplicate rows or duplicate columns need to be removed before data is analyzed. When you remove duplicate values, only the values in the selection are affected. Values outside the range of cells are not altered or removed. In the next exercise, you will learn how to remove duplicate cells, rows, or columns from a worksheet.

STEP BY STEP **Remove Duplicate Cells, Rows, or Columns from a Worksheet**

USE the workbook from the previous exercise.

1. Select **A3:E29**. In the Data Tools group, click **Remove Duplicates**. The Remove Duplicates dialog box shown in Figure 7-5 opens.

Figure 7-5

Identify duplicate values to be removed

Data selections to search for duplicate values —

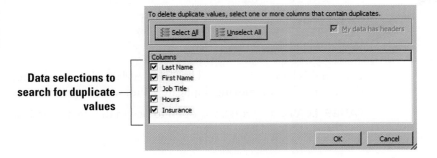

2. Remove the check from Hours and Insurance. You will identify duplicate employee data based on last name, first name, and job title.

3. My data has headers is selected by default. Click OK. Duplicate rows are removed and the confirmation box shown in Figure 7-6 appears informing you that two duplicate values were found and removed.

Figure 7-6

Duplicate values removed

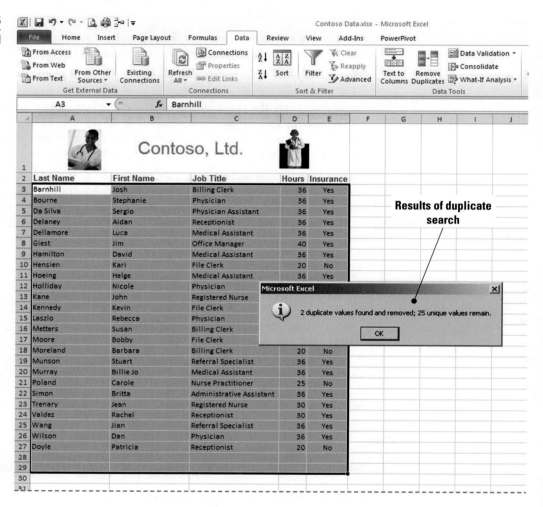

Results of duplicate search

2 duplicate values found and removed; 25 unique values remain.

4. Click OK. SAVE the workbook.

Take Note   Because you are permanently deleting data, it is a good idea to copy the original range of cells to another worksheet or workbook before removing duplicate values. You saved the file at the end of the previous exercise; therefore, you have a backup if you inadvertently remove data that you do not intend to remove.

Later in this lesson you will to learn to filter data. You can filter for unique values first to confirm that the results of removing duplicate values will return the result you want.

PAUSE. LEAVE the workbook open to use in the next exercise.

Take Note You are working with a relatively small amount of data in the practice exercises, and it would not take a great deal of time to review the data and identify duplicate entries. However, if a company has hundreds of employees, you can see the benefit of this Excel feature.

You can specify which columns should be checked for duplicates. When the Remove Duplicates dialog box (Figure 7-5) opens, all columns are selected by default. If the range of cells contains many columns and you want to select only a few columns, you can quickly clear all columns by clicking Unselect All and then selecting the columns you want to check for duplicates. In the data used for this exercise, it is possible that an employee had been entered twice, but the number of hours was different. If you accepted the default and left all columns selected, that employee would not have been removed.

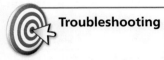 **Troubleshooting** Regardless of the format applied to and displayed in a cell, the cell's true value is displayed in the Formula bar. Duplicate values are determined by the value displayed in the cell and not necessarily the true value stored in the cell. This is an important distinction when dates are entered in different formats. For example, if Aug 5, 2008 is entered in one row and 08/05/2008 is entered in another row, the values are considered unique—not duplicate. It is a good idea to check formatting before removing duplicate values.

SORTING DATA

The Bottom Line

Excel's database functions allow you to sort by text, numbers, dates, and times in one or more columns, that is, on a single criterion or on multiple criteria. Sorting data enables you to quickly visualize and understand the data better. You can rearrange and locate the data that you need to make more effective decisions.

Sorting Data on a Single Criterion

Data can be sorted on a single criterion (one column) in ascending or descending order. In **ascending order**, alphabetic data appears A to Z, numeric data appears from lowest to highest or smallest to largest, and dates appear from oldest to most recent. In **descending order**, the opposite is true—alphabetic data appears Z to A, numeric data appears from highest to lowest or largest to smallest, and dates appear from most recent to oldest. In this exercise you will sort data.

STEP BY STEP **Sort Data on a Single Criterion**

USE the workbook from the previous exercise.

1. Before you begin, Delete the contents of row 1 from your worksheet.
2. Select **D2:D29** (column heading and data in column D).
3. On the Data tab, click the **Sort** button.

4. A Sort Warning message appears and by default prompts you to expand the data selection. Click **Continue with current selection** option and click the **Sort** button. The *Sort* dialog box opens. Excel will automatically organize your column information. It recognizes the header, understands the numeric values, and gives you the sort options. You will accept what Excel has selected. See Figure 7-7. Click **OK** to accept the first single sort criteria.

Figure 7-7

Sort dialog box

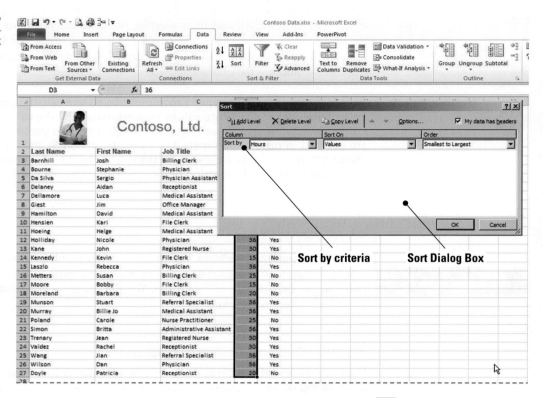

5. Select any cell in column A and click the **Sort A to Z** button. Data is sorted by last name. You have chosen your second single criteria of sorting alphabetically from A–Z.

6. Select **A2:E29** and click the **Sort** button to launch the Sort dialog box shown in Figure 7-8.

Figure 7-8

Single sort criterion

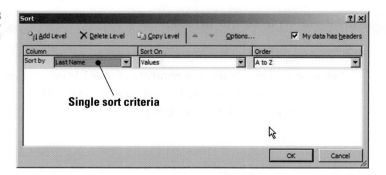

7. In the Column section's Sort by box, click the **arrow** to activate the drop-down list and select **Job Title**. Click **OK**. You have selected the third single sort criteria. Note that your worksheet is now sorted by Job Title.

8. Click the **Sort** button in the Sort & Filter group; the data range is automatically selected and the Sort dialog box opens. Select **Hours** in the Column section's Sort by box. Excel will automatically change the Order options to Largest to Smallest. Click **OK**. You have now selected you last single sort criteria. Note that your worksheet is once again sorted by the data in the Hours column.

PAUSE. LEAVE the workbook open to use in the next exercise.

Take Note	Sort and Filter commands are in the Editing group on the Home tab as well as the Sort & Filter group on the Data tab.

In this exercise, you sorted data on one criterion. Unless the worksheet contains multiple merged cells, you do not need to select data to use the Sort commands. The Sort A to Z and Sort Z to A commands automatically sort the data range on the column that contains the active cell.

It is best to have column headings that have a different format than the data when you sort a data range. By default, the heading is not included in the sort operation. In your worksheet, a heading style was applied to the column headings. Therefore, Excel recognized the header row and *My data has headers* was selected by default on the Sort dialog box.

Sorting Data on Multiple Criteria

When working with large files, you often need to perform a multiple-criteria sort, for example, sorting data by more than one column. Using Excel's Sort dialog box, you can identify each criterion by which you want to sort. In this exercise, you will sort the Contoso employee data by job title and then sort the names alphabetically within each job category.

STEP BY STEP	**Sort Data on Multiple Criteria**

USE the workbook from the previous exercise.

1. Select the range A2:E27, if it isn't already selected.
2. Click **Sort** in the Sort & Filter group on the Data tab to open the dialog box.
3. Select **Job Title** in the Column section's Sort by box and **A to Z** in the Order box.
4. Click the **Add Level** button in the dialog box to identify the second sort criteria. A new criterion line is added to the dialog box.
5. In the Then by box in the Column section select **Last Name** as the second criterion. **A to Z** should be the default in the Order box as shown in Figure 7-9. Click **OK**. You have now sorted using multiple criteria; first by job title and then alphabetically by last name.

Figure 7-9	
Multiple-criteria sort	

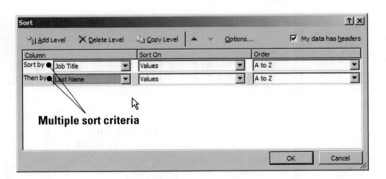

6. **SAVE** the workbook.

Take Note	In Excel, you can sort by up to 64 columns. For best results, the range of cells that you sort should have column headings.

PAUSE. LEAVE the workbook open to use in the next exercise.

You can continue to add levels in the Sort dialog box to expand your sort criteria, and you can delete or copy a criterion level. To change the sort order, select the criterion and click the up or down arrow. Entries higher in the list are sorted before entries lower in the list. To sort by case sensitivity, so that Excel sorts lowercase entries before uppercase entries, click the Options button in the Sort dialog box to open the Sort Options dialog box shown in Figure 7-10.

Figure 7-10

Case sensitive sort criteria

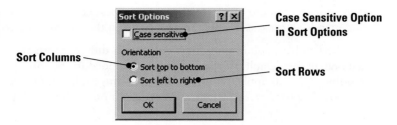

Sorting Data Using Conditional Formatting

If you have conditionally formatted a range of cells with an icon set, you can sort by the icon. Recall that an icon set can be used to annotate and classify data into categories. Each icon represents a range of values. For example, in a three-color arrow set, the green up arrow represents the highest values, the yellow sideways arrow represents the middle values, and the red down arrow represents the lower values.

STEP BY STEP | **Sort Data Using Conditional Formatting**

USE the workbook from the previous exercise.

1. On the Home tab, click **Find & Select** in the Editing command group, and click **Conditional Formatting** in the drop-down menu. A message is returned that no cells in the worksheet contain conditional formatting. Click **OK** to close the message box. This step is to make sure there are no conditional formatting rules in place.

 Ref | You learned about applying conditional formatting in Lesson 4, Formatting Cells and Ranges.

2. Select **D3:D29**. Click **Conditional Formatting** in the Styles group, and then open the **Icon Set** gallery. See Figure 7-11.

Figure 7-11

Icon Set styles gallery

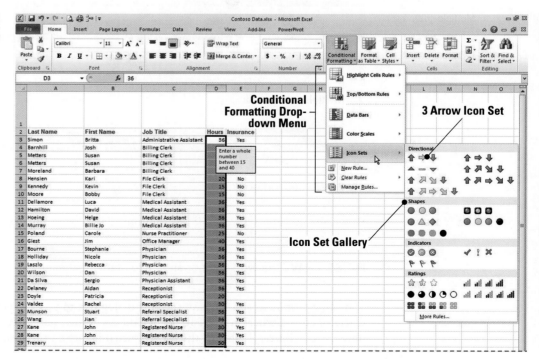

3. Click the **3 Arrows icon set**. Each value in the selected column now has an arrow that represents whether the value falls within the high, middle, or low range of your data.

4. Select **A3:E29**. On the Home tab, click **Sort & Filter** and then click **Custom Sort** (see Figure 7-12); the Sort dialog box opens.

Figure 7-12

Sort and Filter drop-down menu

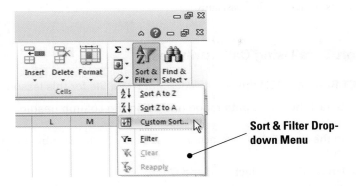

Sort & Filter Drop-down Menu

5. Select **Hours** in the Sort by box. Select **Cell Icon** in the Sort On section's drop-down list. Click the **green arrow** under *Order* (see Figure 7-13).

Figure 7-13

Sort dialog box

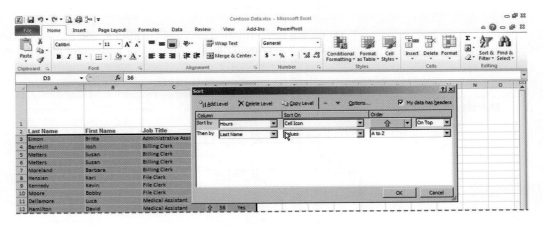

**Troubleshooting** This sort will result in the green arrows (highest values) on top. However, the medium and low range values are not sorted. You need to implement a multiple-criteria sort.

6. Select **Hours** in the Then by box. Select **Cell Icon** under Sort On and accept the yellow arrow and **On top** in the Order field. Click **OK**. Data is sorted by icon set. Your criteria caused your data to sort first by the Green arrow Icon and then by the Yellow.

7. **SAVE** your workbook as *Contoso Icons*. **CLOSE** the workbook.

PAUSE. LEAVE Excel open to use in the next exercise.

The first time you perform a sort, you must select the entire range of cells, including the column header row. When you want to sort the data using different criteria, select any cell within the data range and the entire range will be selected for the sort. You need to select the data only if you want to use a different range for a sort.

Sorting Data Using Cell Attributes

If you have formatted a range of cells by cell color or by font color, you can create a custom sort to sort by colors. In this exercise, you learn to sort by cell attribute (in this case, color) using the Sort dialog box to select the order in which you want the colors sorted.

At Contoso, Ltd., each medical assistant is assigned to work with a specific physician. To assist with scheduling, the office manager created the *MA Assignments* worksheet with color-coded assignments for the physician/medical assistant. The color coding serves as a reminder that the two must be scheduled for the same days and hours when the weekly schedule is created. Color coding enables you to sort the data so that the work assignments are grouped for the physician and his or her medical assistant.

STEP BY STEP   **Sort Data Using Cell Attributes**

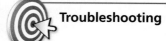 The *MA Assignment* file for this lesson is available on the book companion website or in WileyPLUS.

GET READY. OPEN the *MA Assignments* data file for this lesson.

1. Select the entire data range (including the column headings). On the Data tab, click Sort.
2. In the Sort dialog box, accept Last Name in the Sort by box. Under Sort On, select Cell Color.
3. Under Order, select Pink and On Top.
4. Click the Add Level button in the dialog box and select Last Name in the Sort By box. In the Sort On section, select Cell Color. Select Yellow and On Top in the Order section.

Take Note   Excel also allows you to sort by font color. To do this, in the Sort On section, you would select Font Color instead of Cell Color.

5. Using the same method you used in step 4, add a level for Green and then add a level for Blue. You should have a criterion for each color as illustrated in Figure 7-14. Click OK.

Figure 7-14

Multiple cell attribute sort

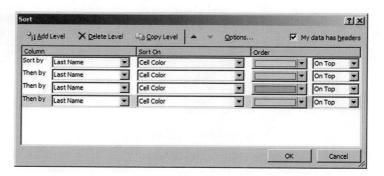

6. **SAVE** the workbook in your Lesson 7 folder as *MA Assignments*.

PAUSE. LEAVE the workbook open to use in the next exercise.

Troubleshooting When a worksheet contains unevenly sized merged cells, if you do not select data before you open the Sort dialog box, you will receive an error message that tells you a sort requires merged cells to be identically sized. The *MA Assignments* worksheet contained two rows with merged cells. Therefore, you had to select the data range (including column labels) the first time you sorted the worksheet. If you performed additional sorts, Excel would remember the data range and you would not need to select it again.

Most sort operations are by columns, but you can custom sort by rows. Create a custom sort by clicking Options on the Sort dialog box. You can then choose *Sort left to right* under Orientation (refer to Figure 7-10).

Sort criteria are saved with the workbook so that you can reapply the sort each time the workbook is opened. Table 7-1 summarizes Excel's default ascending sort orders. The order is reversed for a descending sort.

Table 7-1

Default ascending sort order

Value	Ascending Sort Order
Numbers	Smallest negative number to largest positive number.
Dates	Earliest date to most recent date.
Text	Alphanumeric data is sorted left to right, character by character. For example, A5, A501, A51 are correctly sorted. Numbers and symbols are sorted before text. If the Case sensitive option is active, lowercase text is sorted before uppercase text.
Logical values	False is placed before true.
Blank cells	In both ascending and descending sorts, blank cells are placed last.

FILTERING DATA

The Bottom Line

Worksheets can hold as much data as you need, but you may not want to work with all of the data at the same time. You can temporarily isolate specific data in a worksheet by placing a restriction, called a **filter**, on the worksheet. Filtering data enables you to focus on the data pertinent to a particular analysis by displaying only the rows that meet specified criteria and hiding rows you do not want to see. You can use Excel's AutoFilter feature to filter data, and you can filter data using conditional formatting or cell attributes.

Using AutoFilter

AutoFilter is a built-in set of filtering capabilities. Using AutoFilter to isolate data is a quick and easy way to find and work with a subset of data in a specified range of cells or table columns. You can use AutoFilter to create three types of filters: list value, format, or criteria. Each filter type is mutually exclusive. For example, you can filter by list value or format, but not both. In the next exercise, you will use AutoFilter to organize your data.

STEP BY STEP   **Use AutoFilter**

USE the workbook from the previous exercise.

1. Select **A3:E28**. Click **Filter** on the Data tab in the Sort & Filter group; a filter arrow is added to each column heading.

2. Click the filter arrow in the JobTitle column. The AutoFilter menu shown in Figure 7-15 is displayed.

Figure 7-15

Text values to filter

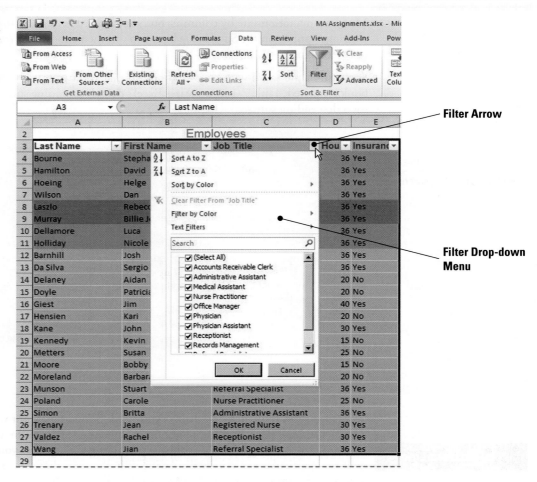

Troubleshooting To make the AutoFilter menu wider or longer, click and drag the grip handle at the bottom

3. Currently the data is not filtered, so all job titles are selected. Click Select All to deselect all titles.

4. Click Accounts Receivable Clerk and Receptionist. Click OK. Data for six employees who hold these titles is displayed. All other employees are filtered out. See Figure 7-16.

Figure 7-16

Filtered data

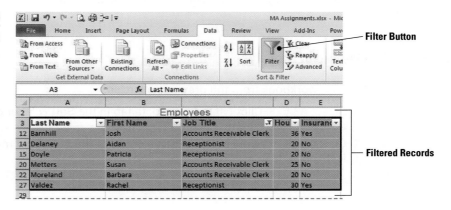

PAUSE. LEAVE the workbook open with the filtered data displayed to use in the next exercise.

In this exercise, you used two text filters to display only the receptionists and accounts receivables clerks. This information is especially useful when the office manager is creating a work schedule. This feature allows him or her to isolate relevant data quickly.

Creating a Custom AutoFilter

You can create a custom AutoFilter to further filter data by two comparison operators. A **comparison operator** is a sign, such as *greater than* or *less than*, that is used in criteria to compare two values. For example, you might create a filter to identify values *greater than* 50 but *less than* 100. Such a filter would display values from 51 to 99.

STEP BY STEP   **Create a Custom AutoFilter**

USE the workbook from the previous exercise.

1. With the filtered list displayed, click the **filter arrow** in column D. In the AutoFilter menu, point to Number Filters. As shown in Figure 7-17, the menu expands to allow you to customize the filter.

Figure 7-17

Numeric comparison criteria

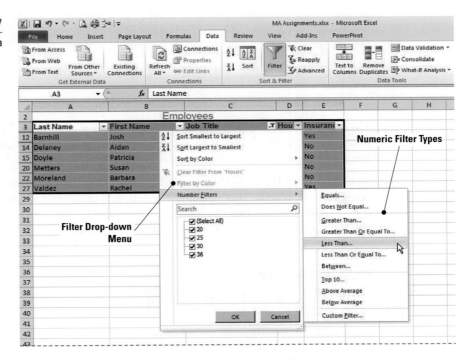

2. Select **Less Than** on the expanded menu and key **30** in the amount box. Click **OK**. The AutoFilter menu closes and the filtered list is reduced to four employees who work fewer than 30 hours per week.

3. Click the **Filter** button in the Sort & Filter group on the Data tab to display all data. With the data range still selected, click **Filter** again.

4. Click the **filter arrow** in column D to open the AutoFilter menu. Point to Number Filters and select **Greater Than**. Key **15** and press **Tab** twice to move to the second comparison operator criteria box.

5. Click the arrow for the comparison operator drop-down list and select is less than as the second comparison operator and press Tab. Key 30 and click OK. The list should be filtered to six employees.

6. Click the Filter button to once again display all data.

Take Note   To remove a filter from a set of data (and see all the data in the worksheet again), you click on the Filter button again. This will make all the data visible again.

7. SAVE and **CLOSE** the workbook.

PAUSE. LEAVE Excel open to use in the next exercise.

Comparison operators are used to create a formula that Excel uses to filter numeric data. The operators are identified in Table 7-2.

Table 7-2

Comparison operators

Button Name	Formatting Applied
=	Equal to
>	Greater than
<	Less than
>=	Greater than or equal to
<=	Less than or equal to
<>	Not equal to

Equal to and *Less than* are options for creating custom text filters. Text Filter options also allow you to filter text that begins with a specific letter (Begins With option) or text that has a specific letter anywhere in the text (Contains option).

As illustrated in Figure 7-18, you can design a two-criterion custom filter that selects data that contains both criteria (*And* option) or selects data that contains one or the other of the criteria (*Or* option). If you select *Or*, less data will be filtered out, giving a much wider filter. When choosing the *And* option, it narrows your filtered data.

Figure 7-18

Two-criterion custom AutoFilter

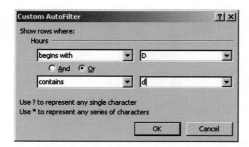

Creating a filter is also known as "defining" a filter.

Filtering Data Using Conditional Formatting

If you have conditionally formatted a range of cells, you can filter the data by that format. A conditional format is a visual guide that helps you quickly understand variation in a worksheet's data. By using conditional formatting as a filter, you can easily organize and highlight cells or ranges in order to emphasize the values based on one or more criteria. In the following exercise, you learn to use icon sets to identify the number of hours employees work each week.

STEP BY STEP | **Filter Data Using Conditional Formatting**

OPEN *Conditional Format* from the data files for this lesson.

1. Select A3:E32. On the *Data* tab, click Filter.
2. Click the filter arrow in column D. Point to Filter by Color in the *AutoFilter* menu that appears. Click the green flag under the *Filter by Cell* icon. Data formatted with a green flag (highest number of work hours) is displayed.
3. Click the filter arrow in column D. Point to Filter by Color. Click the red flag under the *Filter by Cell* icon. The data formatted by a green flag is replaced in the worksheet by data formatted with a red flag (lowest number of work hours).
4. Click Filter to remove the filter arrows.

PAUSE. LEAVE the workbook open to use in the next exercise.

Filtering Data Using Cell Attributes

If you have formatted a range of cells with fill color or font color, you can filter on those attributes. It is not necessary to select the data range to filter using cell attributes. Excel will search for any cell that contains either background or font color. In the following exercise, icon sets are used to identify the number of hours employees work each week, and font color has been used to identify the medical assistant assigned to each physician. In the next exercise, you will use font attributes as your filter criteria.

STEP BY STEP | **Filter Data Using Cell Attributes**

USE the workbook from the previous exercise.

1. Select any cell in the data range and click the Filter button in the Sort & Filter group on the Data tab.
2. Click the arrow next to the Title header (Contoso, Ltd.) and point to Filter by Color. Click More Font Colors. A dialog box opens that displays the font colors used in the worksheet.
3. As in Figure 7-19, the first color appears in the Selected field. Click OK. The heading rows are displayed. These are the colors in the Oriel theme that was applied to this worksheet.

Figure 7-19

Available font colors

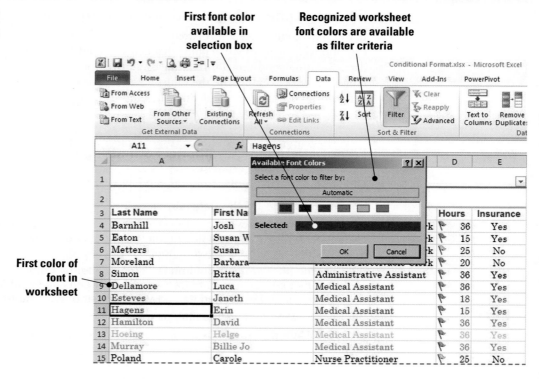

First font color available in selection box

Recognized worksheet font colors are available as filter criteria

First color of font in worksheet

4. Click the **filter arrow** next to the Title header again and click **Clear Filter From "Contoso, Ltd."**

5. Click the **Title header filter arrow** again and point to Filter by Color. Select **Purple** in the *Filter by Font Color* drop-down menu (3rd selection). Data for Dr. Blythe (new physician) and his two medical assistants is displayed because you chose the Purple font in your sort criteria.

6. Click the **Filter** button to clear the filter arrows.

7. **CLOSE** the file. You have not made changes to the data, so it is not necessary to save the file.

In the preceding exercises, you used Excel's Sort and Filter features to organize data using a variety of criteria. Both Sort and Filter allow you to select and analyze specific data. The two functions have a great deal in common. In both instances, you can focus on data that meets specific criteria. Unrelated data is displayed when you sort; it is hidden when you use the filter command.

SKILL SUMMARY

In This Lesson, You Learned How To:
Ensure your data's integrity
Sort data
Filter data

Knowledge Assessment

Fill in the Blank

Complete the following sentences by writing the correct word or words in the blanks provided.

1. Enables you to remove duplicate values is called _____.
2. Values in the row that are an exact match of all the values in another row are referred to as _____.
3. Excel uses _____ rules to determine which worksheet rows to display.
4. In _____, sorted values appear Z to A or highest to lowest.
5. The _____ are conditions specified to limit which records to include in the result of a sort or filter.
6. A sign used in criteria to compare two values is a(n) _____.
7. Using a(n) _____ allows you to apply a built-in set of filtering capabilities.
8. In _____ sort order, values appear A to Z or smallest to largest.
9. You can also sort by the icon when applying _____.
10. You can quickly rearrange the data sequence when you use Excel's _____ feature.

True/False

Circle T if the statement is true or F if the statement is false.

T F 1. You can sort a data range using conditional formatting.

T F 2. When numbers are sorted in ascending order, the largest number is on top.

T F 3. You can create a custom AutoFilter that will isolate data that falls between a high and low number.

T F 4. You can filter data to display all cells with a specific background color and cells that contain specific text.

T F 5. In a case-sensitive sort, lowercase letters will be sorted before uppercase letters.

T F 6. To temporarily isolate a specific list of rows in a worksheet containing data, use the Sort feature.

T F 7. The Data Validation command enables you to locate and remove duplicate values in a worksheet.

T F 8. You cannot sort a range by cell icon.

T F 9. When filtering data, Excel does not provide an option to reapply.

T F 10. Data validation enables you to allow only specific values to be entered in cells.

Competency Assessment

Project 7-1: Analyze Semiannual Sales Data

Litware, Inc., has divided its sales representatives into two teams that are in competition for sales rewards. The sales report worksheet has been color coded to identify team members. In this exercise, you will sort the team data.

GET READY. LAUNCH Excel if it is not already running.

@ The *Semi Annual Sales* file for this lesson is available on the book companion website or in WileyPLUS.

1. **OPEN** the *Semi Annual Sales* data file for Lesson 7.
2. Click the Data tab to make it active.
3. Select A4:H12. The data range should include the column headings but not the monthly totals.
4. Click Sort in the Sort & Filter group. My Data Has Headers should be selected by default. If not, select it.
5. In the Sort dialog box, select Total (or Column H) in the Sort by field. In the Sort On field, select Values. Select Largest to Smallest (descending) in the Order field. Click OK. The sales representative with the highest total sales is listed first. The rest are listed in descending order.
6. With the data still selected, click Sort. Sort by Sales Representative. Sort on Font Color. In the Order fields, select Red and On Top. Click OK. The red team is listed first. Within the red team, representatives are listed in descending order in terms of sales.
7. **SAVE** the workbook as *Semi Annual Sales 7-1*. **CLOSE** the file.

LEAVE Excel open for the next project.

Project 7-2: Ensuring Data Integrity

Create a workbook that you will use to collect survey responses from a random sample of students at your college. Your survey will consist of ten questions, and you will survey ten students.

GET READY. LAUNCH Excel if it is not already running.

1. Click the File tab and open a new blank workbook.
2. Select A2, key Survey Questions, and press Tab.
3. Key Student 1 and press Tab. Key Student 2 and press Tab.
4. Select B2:C2. Use the fill handle to complete the series to Student 10 (cell K2).
5. Select A3 and key In what year did you begin college? Press Enter.
6. Key Have you met with an advisor this year? Press Enter.
7. Key How many hours per week do you study? Press Enter.
8. Select B3:K3. On the Data tab, click Data Validation.
9. On the Settings tab, in the Allow box, select Whole number. In the Data box, select less than or equal to. In the Maximum field, enter the current year in 20XX format.
10. Click the Input Message tab. In the Input message box, key Enter year in 20XX format. Click OK. The input message should be displayed when you close the dialog box.
11. Select B4:K4. Click Data Validation.
12. Click the Settings tab if necessary. In the Allow box, select List. In the Source box, key Yes, No. Click OK. A drop-down arrow should be displayed next to the active cell.
13. Resize the columns if necessary.
14. **SAVE** the workbook as *Survey 7-2* and then **CLOSE** the file.

LEAVE Excel open for the next project.

Project 7-3: Filter Data on Multiple Criteria

The Litware sales manager needs to filter the sales report data in a variety of ways so that he can use it in team meetings to acknowledge those who have achieved sales objectives and to motivate the teams. Create the filters for the sales manager.

GET READY. LAUNCH Excel if it is not already running.

@ The *Sales Teams* file for this lesson is available on the book companion website or in WileyPLUS.

1. **OPEN** *Sales Teams* from the data files for this lesson.
2. Select A4:H12. Click **Filter**. Click the arrow in the Total column.
3. Click **Number Filters** and then click **Greater Than**. Key **100,000** in the dialog box. Click **OK**. Four sales representatives are displayed.
4. Click **Filter** to display all data. Select any cell that contains data and create a filter to display the Red Team's statistics. (Hint: Because entire rows are color coded, you do not have to select the data. Data does not have to be sorted when you filter for color.)
5. **SAVE** the workbook as *Red Team*.
6. Click **Filter** to display all data. Click **Filter** again to display the filter arrows.
7. Click a **filter arrow** and display the Blue Team's statistics.
8. **SAVE** the workbook as *Blue Team*. **CLOSE** the workbook.

LEAVE Excel open for the next project.

Project 7-4: Sort and Filter Using Conditional Formatting

Each year *Fortune Magazine* surveys employees and publishes a list of the ten best employers based on employee ranking. The Top Ten worksheet contains additional information about the top ten companies in terms of their size (number of employees), percentage of minorities, and percentage of women. In this exercise, you will sort using conditional formatting to determine how many women in the workforce are employed by Top Ten companies.

GET READY. LAUNCH Excel if it is not already running.

@ The *Top Ten* file for this lesson is available on the book companion website or in WileyPLUS.

1. **OPEN** the *Top Ten* data file for this lesson.
2. Select the data range, including the column headings. Click **Sort** on the Data tab.
3. Sort the data by % Minorities. Click **Cell Icon** in the Sort On field.
4. Under Order, place the green flagged data (highest) on top. Click **OK**. Because you sorted by one criterion, the highest is on top, but the red and yellow are intermixed.
5. Click **Sort** to add a second criterion to sort on yellow flags, which represent the middle range.
6. With the data range selected, click **Filter**. Arrows are added to the column headings.
7. Click the **filter arrow** in the % Women column. Choose to **filter by color**.
8. Select the **green arrow**. Women comprise more than 60 percent of the workforce in two of the top ten companies.
9. **SAVE** the workbook as *Top Ten 7-4*. **CLOSE** the workbook.

LEAVE Excel open for the next project.

Mastery Assessment

Project 7-5: Semiannual Sales Data

Litware, Inc. has divided its sales representatives into two teams that are in competition for sales rewards. The sales report worksheet has been color coded to identify team members In this exercise, you will sort the team by color and in ascending order.

GET READY. LAUNCH Excel if not already running.

@ The *Semi Annual Sales* document file for this lesson is available on the book companion website or in WileyPLUS.

1. **OPEN** the *Semi Annual Sales* data file for lesson 7.
2. Select the data range and sort by font color with the Blue Team on top followed by the red team.
3. **SAVE** the workbook as *Semi Annual 7-5*.

LEAVE Excel open for the next project.

Project 7-6: Sorting

The Records Management Director at Contoso has asked you to sort the data in a specific order..

GET READY. LAUNCH Excel if not already running.

@ The *Salary* document file for this lesson is available on the book companion website or in WileyPLUS.

4. **OPEN** the *Salary* data file for this lesson 7.
5. Select the data range and sort in ascending order by job title, job category then by salary (smallest to largest).
6. **SAVE** the workbook as *Salary 7-6*.

LEAVE Excel open for the next project.

INTERNET READY

In this lesson, you worked with salary data for a medical facility. The salary figures were based on average earnings for employees in medical care facilities in the Midwest. Go online and research salary data for your chosen profession. Identify three positions in which you might like to work. Conduct research into the average salary in those professions in three different cities in different parts of the country. For example, you might find earnings information for accountants in New York City, New York; St. Louis, Missouri; and Seattle, Washington. Create a worksheet to report your research findings. Format all data appropriately. Save your worksheet as *Salary Research* and exit Excel.

Workplace*Ready*_____

MANAGING LISTS IN EXCEL

Microsoft Excel provides numerous templates that can be downloaded and used to start new worksheets. Templates are time-saving tools that eliminate the need for you to spend time setting up the structure of a worksheet and applying complex formatting and formulas.

All you need to do is enter the raw data, because the template has built-in formatting and formulas.

When you click the File tab and click New in Backstage view's navigation bar, the New Workbook window opens, as shown in the Figure 7-20. There are buttons to Recent templates and Sample templates in the top section to the right of the Blank workbook button. The Office.com Available Templates are organized into categories of templates that can be downloaded from Microsoft Office Online. Although some are personal-use templates, the majority are business templates. You can browse templates by category and select and download a template of your choice. You can then use it as the basis for a new workbook.

Figure 7-20

Available templates

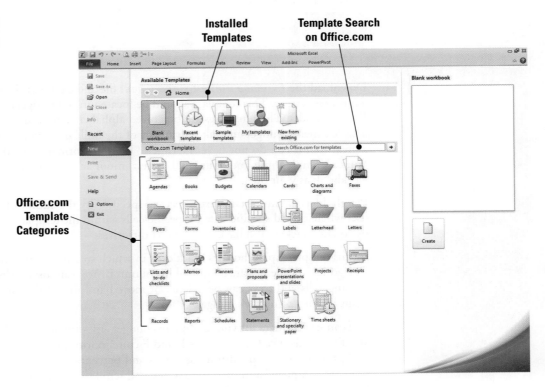

The Expense Budget template (Figure 7-21) can be downloaded from Microsoft Office Online.

Figure 7-21

Expense budget template

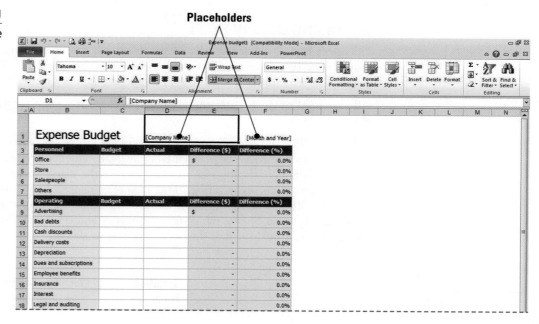

Download the *Expense Budget spreadsheet* file and explore this template that can be used in a business setting. This template should be located in the Budgets category and in the Business Budgets folder. The templates are organized alphabetically. You can use this template to create a basic expense budget and take advantage of the built-in formulas and structure. Templates are a great tool if you do not have the time to design a formatted workbook from the ground up. You can simply input your data, make a few minor adjustments as needed, and save and use the workbook as your own.

Placeholders are important text directives specified by the author of the template that direct the user where to add specific data in specific cells within the template. They are always surrounded by square brackets and have specific text directives.

In this template, placeholders mark cells in which to enter your company's name and the date. Categories of expenses are identified in column B. You can insert cells and rows if necessary. The existing cells and rows can be deleted or moved and the labels can be edited to reflect the line items in your company's budget.

You can key the data for your company's budget amounts and actual expenditures in columns C and D. The data cells in columns E and F contain formulas to calculate the difference between budget and actual expenditures as values and percentages. When you enter data, both calculations are completed automatically. When you scroll to the bottom of the worksheet, you see that formulas have been created to total each column.

You can easily see that using this template to create a company expense budget would take far less time than creating the worksheet from scratch. With a template you just enter the data—Excel provides the formulas and performs all the calculations.

LESSON SKILL MATRIX

In This Lesson, You Will Learn The Following Skills:

Building Basic Formulas

Using Cell References in Formulas

Using Cell Ranges in Formulas

Summarizing Data with Functions

Using Formulas to Create Subtotals

Controlling the Appearance of Formulas

KEY TERMS

- absolute cell reference
- arguments
- constant
- external reference
- formula
- function
- mathematical operator
- mixed reference
- name
- operand
- reference
- relative cell reference
- scope

Most people agree that it is vitally important for a business to have a realistic budget. It is equally important for an individual to have a personal budget—a plan for managing income and expenses.

Katie Jordan has been managing, or more accurately, spending her money without a formal budget. In fact, the only budget she prepared was one she scribbled on the back of her résumé immediately after being offered what she considered to be her dream job. Since that time, Katie has changed jobs several times. Now, she wants to purchase a condominium, and she realizes that she needs to create a comprehensive personal budget that will enable her to realize her goal of home ownership.

Katie uses Excel in her job as a marketing analyst at Tailspin Toys. She plans to use Excel to track her expenditures and to develop a realistic budget. She has conducted online research and developed a preliminary budget. This is her first step toward financial independence. Formulas make Excel a powerful tool. In this lesson, you will learn to write simple formulas and use many of Excel's functions with built-in formulas that enable you to perform many types of calculations.

SOFTWARE ORIENTATION

Formulas Tab

In this Lesson, you'll use command groups on the Formulas tab, as shown in Figure 8-1. These commands are your tools for building formulas and using functions in Excel.

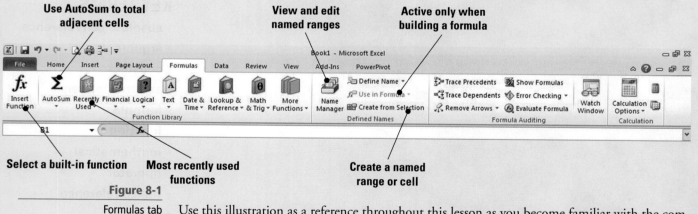

Use AutoSum to total adjacent cells

View and edit named ranges

Active only when building a formula

Select a built-in function   **Most recently used functions**

Create a named range or cell

Figure 8-1

Formulas tab

Use this illustration as a reference throughout this lesson as you become familiar with the command groups on the Formulas tab and use them to create formulas.

BUILDING BASIC FORMULAS

The Bottom Line

The real strength of Excel is its ability to perform common and complex calculations. A **formula** is an equation that performs calculations, such as addition, subtraction, multiplication, and division, on values in a worksheet. When you enter a formula in a cell, the formula is stored internally and the results are displayed in the cell. Formulas give results and solutions that help you assess and analyze data.

Creating a Formula that Performs Addition

A formula consists of two elements: operands and mathematical operators. **Operands** identify the values to be used in the calculation. An operand can be a constant value, a cell reference, a range of cells, or another formula. A **constant** is a number or text value that is entered directly into a formula. **Mathematical operators** specify the calculations to be performed. To allow Excel to distinguish formulas from data, all formulas begin with an equal sign (=).

In this exercise, you will learn how to create basic formulas that perform mathematical computations and apply the formulas using various methods.

Take Note   You can begin a formula with a + or − as the beginning mathematical operator, but Excel changes it to = when you press Enter.

When you build a formula, it appears in the formula bar and in the cell itself. When you complete the formula and press Enter, the value displays in the cell and the formula displays in the formula bar. You can edit a formula in the cell or in the formula bar the same way you can edit any data entry.

STEP BY STEP   **Create a Formula that Performs Addition**

GET READY. Before you begin these steps, **LAUNCH** Microsoft Excel and **OPEN** a blank workbook.

1. Select **A1** and key =25+15. Press **Tab**. Excel calculates the value in A1, and displays the sum of *40* in the cell.
2. In B1, key +18=35. Press **Tab**. The sum of the two numbers, *53*, appears in the cell.

Take Note   Formulas should be keyed without spaces, but if you key spaces, Excel eliminates them when you press Enter.

3. Select **B1** to display the formula for that cell in the formula bar. As illustrated in Figure 8-2, although you entered + to begin the formula, when you pressed Enter, Excel replaced the + with = as the beginning mathematical operator. This is the Excel formula auto correct feature.

Figure 8-2

Formula begins with equal sign

Cell containing formula

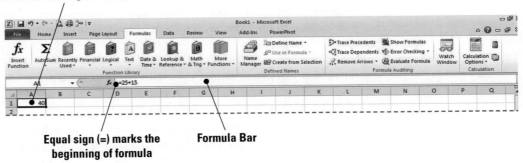

Equal sign (=) marks the beginning of formula   **Formula Bar**

4. Select **A3**. Click the formula bar and key =94+89+35. Press **Enter**. The sum of the three numbers, *218*, appears in the cell.
5. Select **A3** and click the formula bar. Select 89 and key 98. Press **Enter**. Notice that your sum changes to *227*.

PAUSE. LEAVE the workbook open to use in the next exercise.

Creating a Formula that Performs Subtraction

The same methods you used to create a formula to perform addition can be used to create a formula to perform subtraction. When you create a subtraction formula, enter = followed by the positive number and then enter a minus sign to indicate subtraction. When you create a subtraction formula, the minus sign *must* precede the number to be subtracted. In this exercise, you practice creating a formula that performs subtraction.

STEP BY STEP   **Create a Formula that Performs Subtraction**

USE the workbook from the previous exercise.

1. Select **A5**. Key **=456−98**. Press **Enter**. The value in A5, *358*, appears in the cell.
2. Select **A6** and key **545−13−8**. Press **Enter**. The value in A6 should be *524*.
3. In A8, create a formula to subtract 125 from 189. The value in A8 should be *64*.

 Troubleshooting   If your formula returned a negative value (i.e., −64), you reversed the order in which the numbers should have been entered.

PAUSE. LEAVE the workbook open to use in the next exercise.

When you entered a formula to subtract 125 from 189, you could have entered =189−125 or = −125+189. Either formula would yield a positive 64. If the positive number is entered first, it is not necessary to enter a plus sign.

If you find that you've made a mistake in your formula (such as returning the negative number mentioned earlier), you can select the cell with the erroneous function, press F2 to take you to the formula bar, and edit your function. Once you've made your corrections, press Enter to revise.

Take Note   When you have a cell selected, pressing F2 will always activate the formula bar for that cell.

Creating a Formula that Performs Multiplication

The formula to multiply 33 by 6 is =33*6. If a formula contains two or more operators, operations are not necessarily performed in the order in which you read the formula. The order is determined by the rules of mathematics, but you can override standard operator priorities by using parentheses. Operations contained in parentheses are completed before those outside parentheses. In this exercise, you learn to create formulas that perform multiplication.

STEP BY STEP   **Create a Formula that Performs Multiplication**

USE the workbook from the previous exercise.

1. Select **D1**. Key **=125*4** and press **Enter**. The value that appears in D1 is *500*.
2. Select **D3** and key **=2*7.50*2**. Press **Enter**. The value in D3 is *30*.
3. Select **D5** and key **=5*3**. Press **Enter**. The value in D5 is *15*.
4. Select **D7** and key **=5+2*8**. The value in D7 is *21*.
5. Select **D9** and key **=(5+2)*8**. The value in D9 is *56*.

PAUSE. LEAVE the workbook open to use in the next exercise.

When you added parentheses to the last formula you entered in this exercise, you changed the order of the calculations. When you entered the formula without parentheses, Excel multiplied 2 by 8 and added 5 for a value of 21. When you entered (5+2)*8, Excel performed the addition first and returned a value of 56. The order of calculations will be further illustrated in the next exercise.

Creating a Formula that Performs Division

The forward slash is the mathematical operator for division. When a calculation includes multiple values, you must use parentheses to indicate the part of the calculation that should be performed first.

STEP BY STEP	**Create a Formula that Performs Division**

USE the workbook from the previous exercise.

1. Select **D7** and create the formula =**795/45**. Press **Enter**. Excel returns a value of *17.66667* in D7.

Take Note   The results of the formula calculation rounded the value 17.66667 after the seventh digit (eighth character) because the standard column width is 8.43. In other words, the value was rounded at that number of places only because of the column width.

2. Select **D7**. Excel applied the number format to this cell when it returned the value in step 1. Click the **Accounting Number Format ($)** button, on the Home tab in the Numbers group, to apply the accounting format to cell D7. The number is rounded to *$17.67* because two decimal places is the default setting for the accounting format.
3. Select **D9** and create the formula =**65−29*8+97/5**. Press **Enter**. The value in D9 is *−147.6*.
4. Select **D9**. Click in the formula bar and place parentheses around 65−29. Press **Enter**. The value in D9 is *307.4*.
5. **CLOSE** but do not save the workbook.

PAUSE. LEAVE Excel open to use in the next exercise.

Excel does not necessarily perform the operations in the same order that you enter or read them in a formula, which is left to right. Excel uses the rules of mathematics to determine which operations to perform first when a formula contains multiple operators. This is also known as the order of evaluation in Excel.

The order is:

- negative number (−)
- percent (%)
- exponentiation (^)
- multiplication (*) and division (/)
- addition (+) and subtraction (−)

For example, consider the following equation:

$$5 + 6 * 15 / 3 - 1 = 34$$

Following mathematical operator priorities, the first operation would be 6 multiplied by 15 and that result would be divided by 3. Then 5 would be added and finally, 1 would be subtracted, giving you 34. Figure 8-3 illustrates the formula entered into Excel.

Figure 8-3

Structure of a formula

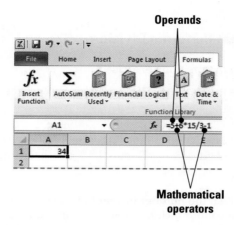

When you use parentheses in a formula, you indicate which calculation to perform first, which overrides the standard operator priorities. Therefore, the result of the following equation would be significantly different from the previous one. Figure 8-4 illustrates the Excel formula. Here is the mathematical formula:

$$(5 + 6) * 15 / (3 - 1) = 82.5$$

Figure 8-4

Parentheses control the order of operations

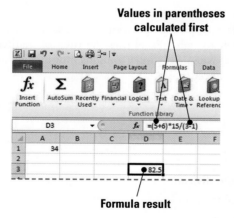

USING CELL REFERENCES IN FORMULAS

The Bottom Line

A cell **reference** in a formula identifies a cell or a range of cells on a worksheet and tells Excel where to look for the values you want it to calculate in the formula. Using cell references (cell names; A1, B1, and so on) enables you to re-use the formulas you write, by updating the data in the formulas, rather than rewriting the formulas themselves. With references, you can use values contained in different parts of a worksheet in one formula or use the value from one cell in several formulas. You can also refer to cells on another worksheet in the same workbook, as well as to other workbooks. Excel recognizes two types of cell references—relative and absolute.

Using Relative Cell References in a Formula

A cell reference identifies a cell's location in the worksheet, based on its row number and column letter. When you include a **relative cell reference** in a formula and copy that formula, Excel changes the reference to match the column or row to which the formula is copied. A relative cell reference is, therefore, one whose references change "relative" to the location where it is copied or moved. You use relative cell references when you want the reference to automatically adjust when you copy or fill the formula across rows or down columns in ranges of cells. By default, new formulas use relative references. In this exercise, you practice creating and using relative cell references in formulas.

You are about to learn two methods for creating formulas using relative references:
- By keying in an equal sign to mark the entry as a formula and then keying the formula directly into the cell; and
- By keying an equal sign and then clicking a cell or cell range included in the formula (rather than keying cell references).

The second method is usually quicker and eliminates the possibility of typing an incorrect cell or range reference. When you complete the formula and press Enter, the value displays in the cell and the formula displays in the formula bar.

STEP BY STEP   **Use Relative Cell References in a Formula**

GET READY. LAUNCH Microsoft Excel if it is not already open.

 The *Personal Budget* file for this lesson is available on the book companion website or in WileyPLUS.

1. **OPEN** the *Personal Budget* data file for this lesson.
2. Select **B7** and key =sum(B4: (colon). As shown in Figure 8-5, cell B4 is outlined in blue, and the reference to B4 in the formula is also blue. The ScreenTip below the formula identifies B4 as the first number in the formula. The reference to B4 is based on its relative position to B7, the cell that contains the formula.

WILEY PLUS *EXTRA*

WileyPLUS Extra! features an online tutorial of this task.

Figure 8-5

Color-coordinated cell references

Cell reference in formula and outline around referenced cells are color coordinated

Formula as it is being keyed in B7

Formula ScreenTip

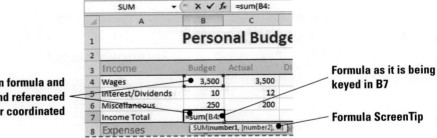

3. Key **B6** and press **Enter**. The total of the cells, *3,760*, appears in B7.
4. Select **B15**. Key =sum(and click **B10**. As shown in Figure 8-6, B10 appears in the formula bar and a flashing marquee appears around B10. Excel now knows that you are selecting this cell to be used in the formula.

Figure 8-6

Including a cell in a formula

Select first cell to include formula

8	Expenses	Budget	Actual	Difference
9	Home			
10	Mortgage/Rent	950	950	
11	Utilities	236	230	
12	Telephone	56	67	
13	Home Repairs	100	75	
14	Home Security	35	35	
15	Home Total	=sum(b10:		
16	Daily Living	SUM(number1, [number2], ...)		

5. Click and drag the flashing marquee to B14. As shown in Figure 8-7, the formula bar reveals that values within the B10:B14 range will be summed (added). Note, this step allows you to input a range of cells in the formula by highlighting instead of typing the formula in the cell.

Take Note
You can use either uppercase or lowercase when you key a cell reference in a formula. For example, it would not matter whether you keyed B4 or b4 in the formula you entered.

Figure 8-7

Extend the cell range for a formula

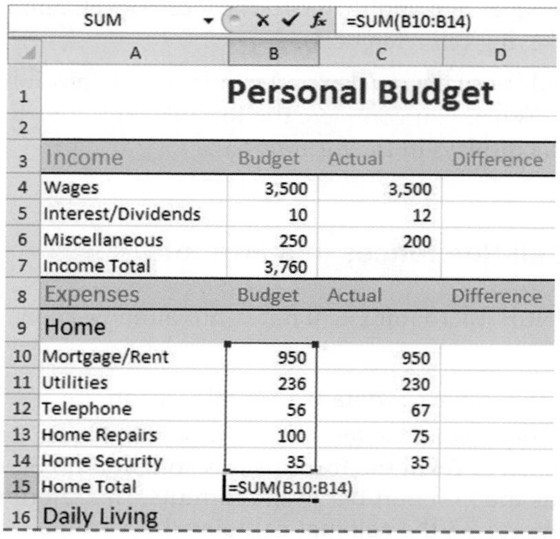

6. Press Enter to accept the formula. Select B15. As illustrated in Figure 8-8, the value is displayed in B15 and when you click on the cell the formula is displayed in the formula bar. Take note that each cell reference is the cell's unique name. No matter what numeric value is assigned in the cell, the cell reference (B1, C10, etc.) never changes.

Figure 8-8

A formula displayed in the formula bar

Formula tells Excel to add the information of the cell range

Value returned by formula

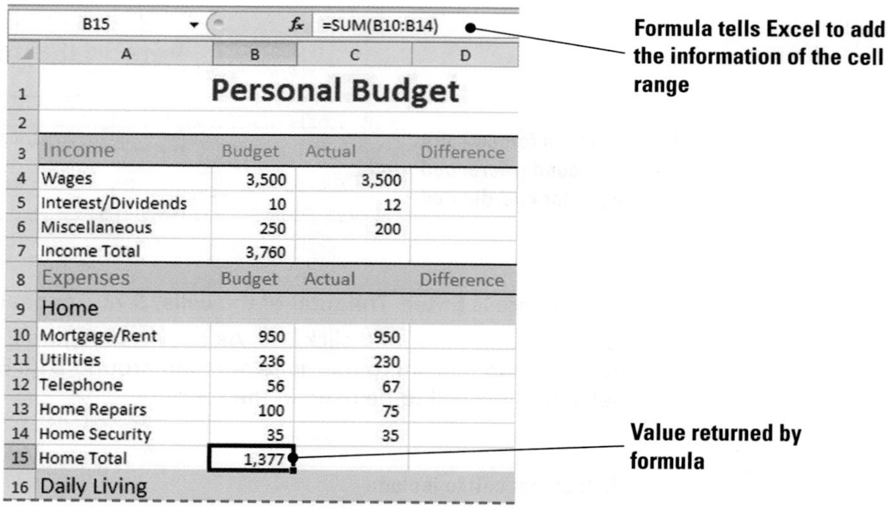

7. Once again, the goal of this step is to create a simple formula. Select D4 and key =. Click B4 and key −. Click C4 and press Enter. By default, when a subtraction formula yields no difference (a zero answer), Excel enters a hyphen.

Take Note Open the Format Cells dialog box to change the way Excel displays "no difference" results. On the Numbers tab, you can choose to display 0, for example.

8. Select **D4** again. Click and drag the fill handle to D7 to select this range of cells. You are now copying the formula from the previous step into a new range of cells.

9. Use the fill handle to copy the formula in B7 to C7. Notice that the amount in D7 changes when the formula is copied. When you copied the formula to C7, the position of the cell containing the formula changed, so the reference in the formula changed to C7 instead of B7.

10. Select **D7** and click **Copy**. Select **D10:D15** and click **Paste**. Your formula has now been copied to the range of cells and Excel has automatically adjusted the cell references accordingly. Note that D7 is still highlighted by the flashing marquee.

11. Select **D17:D21** and click **Paste**. Your formula from D7 is now copied to the second range of cells and the references are adjusted. Note that the flashing marquee is still surrounding D7. You have the ability to copy one formula into multiple locations without having to recopy it.

12. Create a Lesson 8 folder and **SAVE** your worksheet as *Budget*.

PAUSE. LEAVE the workbook open to use in the next exercise.

Another Way
You can select a cell and click the formula bar to key a formula.

Using Absolute Cell References in a Formula

Sometimes you do not want a cell reference to change when you move or copy it. For example, when you review your personal budget, you might want to know what percentage of your income is budgeted for each category of expenses. Each formula you create to calculate those percentages will refer to the cell that contains the total income amount. The reference to the total income cell is an **absolute cell reference**—a reference that does not change when the formula is copied or moved.

Absolute cell references include two dollar signs in the formula. The absolute cell reference $B$7 in this exercise, for example, will always refer to cell B7 because dollar signs precede both the column (B) and row (7). When you copy or fill the formula across rows or down columns, the absolute reference will not adjust to the destination cells. By default, new formulas use relative references, and you must edit them if you want them to be absolute references.

STEP BY STEP   **Use Absolute Cell References in a Formula**

USE the workbook from the previous exercise.

1. Select **B15**. Use the fill handle to the right to copy the formula to C15. You have just extended the formula to cell C7 to calculate the information in the range of cells above C7.

2. Select **B21**. Key =sum(and select **B17:B20**. Press **Enter**. You have just created a formula to calculate the range of cells selected as illustrated in Figure 8-9. Note that the formula you copied and applied to D21 was automatically calculated when you pressed **Enter**.

Figure 8-9

Formulas copied and entered are applied to cell ranges

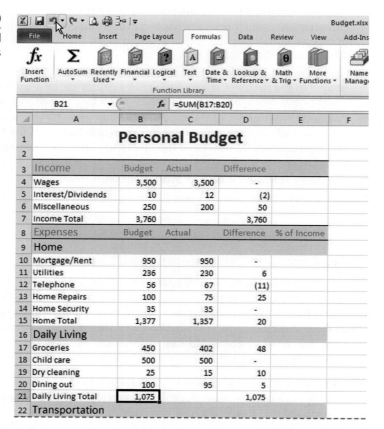

Take Note

It is not necessary to key the closing parenthesis when you complete the selection for a formula. Excel supplies it when you press Enter.

3. Select **B21** and drag the fill handle to C21. You have copied the formula to the adjacent cell.

4. Select **E10**. Key = and click **B10**. Key / and click **B7**. Press **Enter**. You now have a decimal value of .253 as your formula result.

5. Select **E10** again. On the formula bar, click in front of B7 to edit the formula; change B7 (relative cell reference) to $B$7 (absolute cell reference). The edited formula should read =B10/$B$7 as illustrated in Figure 8-10. Press **Enter**. An absolute reference should be understood to be a value that you never want to change in your formula. By default, Excel will copy a formula into selected ranges as a relative cell reference unless you instruct it to do otherwise. Once you apply the absolute reference, Excel recognizes it and the program will not try to modify it to a relative reference again.

Figure 8-10

Adding an absolute reference
to a formula

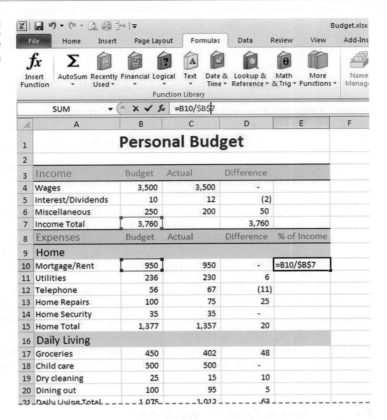

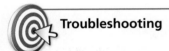
Troubleshooting When you enter a formula that will yield a result less than a whole number, be sure the cell is formatted for decimals. If the cell is formatted for whole numbers, the cell will display 0 or 1 rather than the expected value.

6. Select **E10** and drag the fill handle to E15. You have now applied the formula with the absolute reference $B$7 to each of the cells in the range.

7. With E10:E15 still selected, click the **Percent Style** button (%) in the Number group on the Home tab. Click **Increase Decimal**. The values should display with one decimal place and a % as illustrated in Figure 8-11.

Figure 8-11

Applying percent format to the
formula results

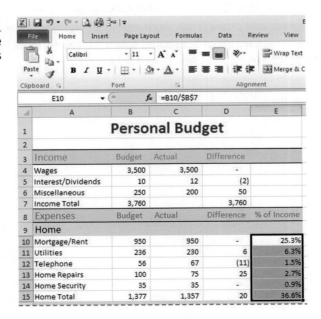

8. **SAVE** your workbook.

PAUSE. LEAVE the workbook open to use in the next exercise.

You can also create a mixed reference in which either a column, or a row, is absolute or the other is relative. For example, if the cell reference in a formula were $B7 or B$7, you would have a **mixed reference** in which one component is absolute and one is relative. The column is absolute and would remain unchanged in the formula, and the row is relative if the reference is $B7, changing as the mixed reference is copied to $B7, $B8, and so on.

If you copy or fill a formula across rows or down columns, the relative reference automatically adjusts, and the absolute reference does not adjust. For example, if you copied or filled a formula containing the mixed reference $B7 to a cell in column C, the formula in the destination cell would be =$B8. The column reference would be the same because that portion of the formula is absolute. The row reference would adjust because it is relative.

Referring to Data in Another Worksheet

As mentioned earlier, cell references can link to the contents of cells in another worksheet within the same workbook. You might need to use this strategy, for example, to create a summary of data contained in several worksheets. The principles for building these formulas are the same as those for building formulas referencing data within a worksheet. In this exercise, you practice building and using formulas that contain references to data in other worksheets. You will also learn how to refer to cells and ranges of cells outside of your active worksheet.

STEP BY STEP **Refer to Data in Another Worksheet**

USE the workbook you saved in the previous exercise.

1. Click Sheet2 to make it the active sheet.
2. Select B4. Key = to indicate the beginning of a formula. Click Sheet1 and select B7. Press Enter. The value of cell B7 on Sheet1 is displayed in cell B4 of Sheet2. The formula bar displays =Sheet1!B7.
3. With Sheet2 still the active sheet, select B4 and drag the fill handle to D4. The values from Sheet1 row 4 are copied to Sheet2 row 4.
4. On the Home tab, click Format and click Rename Sheet. As you recall, you renamed worksheet tabs in previous exercises.
5. Key Summary and press Enter.
6. Make Sheet1 active. Click Format and click Rename Sheet.
7. Key Expenses and press Enter. Both worksheet tabs are now renamed.
8. Make the Summary sheet active and select B4. The formula bar now shows the formula as =Expenses!B7. See Figure 8-12.

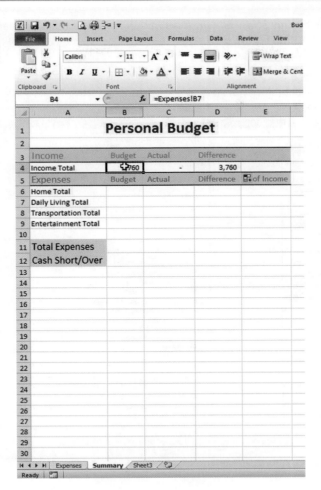

Figure 8-12

Referred cell reference in another worksheet

9. **SAVE** your workbook.

PAUSE. LEAVE the workbook open to use in the next exercise.

In this exercise, you referenced data in another worksheet within the Budget workbook. In the next exercise, you will reference data in another workbook. By renaming the worksheets within this workbook, you have prepared it for the next exercise.

Referencing Data in Another Workbook

An **external reference** refers to a cell or range on a worksheet in another Excel workbook, or to a defined name in another workbook. Although external references are similar to cell references, there are important differences. You normally use external references when working with large amounts of data and complex formulas that encompass several workbooks. In this exercise, you will learn how to refer to data in another workbook.

USE the workbook you saved in the previous exercise.

1. Click the **File** tab and click **Options**.

2. On the Options window, click **Advanced**.

3. Scroll to find *Show all windows in the Taskbar*, if it isn't already selected, select it and click **OK**. See Figure 8-13.

Figure 8-13

Advanced options in Excel options

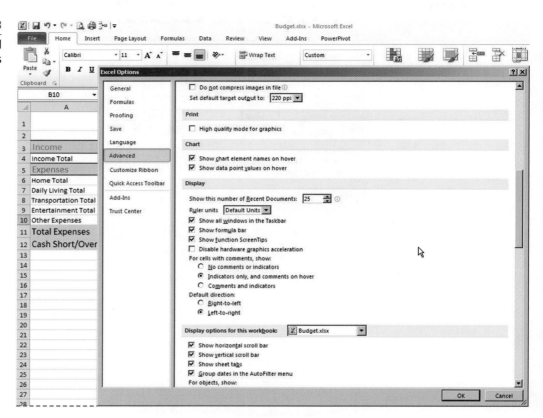

Troubleshooting If your system administrator has disabled the *Show all windows in the Taskbar* option, you will need to use the Switch Windows command in the Windows group on the View tab to move between the two workbooks.

 The *Financial Obligations* file for this lesson is available on the book companion website or in WileyPLUS.

4. You are still in the Summary worksheet. In A10, key **Other Expenses** and press **Tab**.

5. **OPEN** the *Financial Obligations* data file for this lesson. This is the source workbook. The Budget workbook is the destination workbook.

6. Switch to the Budget workbook, and with B10 still active, key = to indicate the beginning of a formula. Change to the Financial Obligations workbook and select **B8**. A flashing marquee will identify this cell reference.

7. Press **Enter** to complete the external reference formula. Select **B10**. Your external reference has now been copied to this cell as illustrated in Figure 8-14. The formula bar displays square brackets around the name of the source workbook, indicating that the workbook is open. When the source is open, the external reference encloses the workbook name in square brackets, followed by the worksheet name, an exclamation point (!), and the cell range on which the formula depends.

Figure 8-14

External reference copied

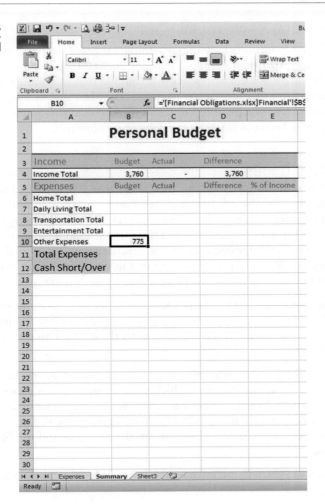

8. **CLOSE** the Financial Obligations workbook. When the source workbook is closed, the brackets are removed and the entire file path is shown in the formula. The formula bar in the Budget worksheet now displays the entire path for the source workbook as illustrated in Figure 8-15 because the source file is now closed.

Figure 8-15

File path to external reference

Entire file path to closed file

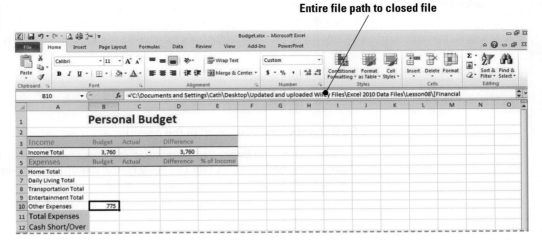

9. **SAVE** the destination workbook.

PAUSE. LEAVE the workbook open to use in the next exercise.

USING CELL RANGES IN FORMULAS

You can simplify formula building by naming ranges of data and using that name in selections and formulas rather than keying or selecting the cell range each time. In the business environment, you will often use a worksheet that contains data in hundreds of rows and columns. After you name a range, you can select it from the Name box and then perform a variety of functions, such as cutting and pasting it to a different workbook as well as using it in a formula. By default, a named range becomes an absolute reference in a formula.

Naming a Range

A **name** is a meaningful and logical identifier that you apply in Excel to make it easier to reference the purpose of a cell reference, cell range, constant, formula, or table. Naming a range clarifies the purpose of the data within the range of cells. Naming ranges or an individual cell according to the data they contain is a time-saving technique, even though it may not seem so when you work with limited data files in practice exercises. A good example could be to name a range such as B7:B17 as *Total Items* so that in future formula construction and reference, you only need to key Total Items and Excel will recognize the range to which you are referring.

You must select the range of cells you want to name before you use the Name box to create a named range. When you create a name using the Define Name command, you have the opportunity to select the range after you enter the name. This option is not available when you use the Name box.

All names have a scope, either to a specific worksheet or to the entire workbook. The **scope** of a name is the location within which Excel recognizes the name without qualification. For example, in step 1 in the next exercise, when you create the name Income_Total for cell B7, the New Name box, shown in Figure 8-16, identifies the scope as part of the workbook. This means the named cell can be used in formulas on the Expenses and the Summary worksheets in this workbook.

In this exercise, you will use three methods to name cells and ranges of cells. You will create the names by:

- Clicking Define Name on the Formulas tab and selecting the cell or range to be included in the name.
- Selecting a cell or range and entering a name in the Name box next to the formula bar.
- Selecting a cell or range that includes a label and clicking the Create from Selection button on the Formulas tab.

Take Note   There are several syntax rules for creating names. For example, the first character must be a letter, an underscore character (_), or a backslash (\). You cannot use a C, c, R, or r as a defined name, and you must use the underscore or period as word separators rather than spaces.

STEP BY STEP   **Name a Range**

USE the workbook you saved in the previous exercise.

1. Select **B7** on the Expenses worksheet and click **Define Name** in the Name Manager group on the Formulas tab. The New Name dialog box shown in Figure 8-16 opens with Excel's suggested name for the range.

Figure 8-16

New name dialog box

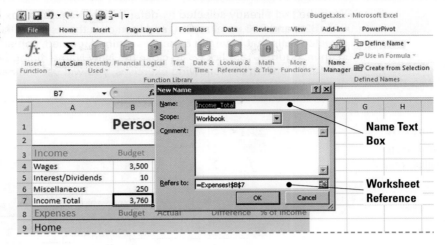

2. Click **OK** to accept Income_Total as the name for B7. Note that the Income_Total name now appears in the name box instead of the default cell reference of B7. See Figure 8-17.

Figure 8-17

Applying a defined name

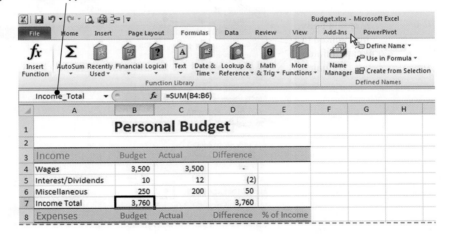

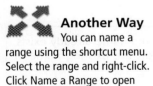

Another Way

You can name a range using the shortcut menu. Select the range and right-click. Click Name a Range to open the New Name dialog box.

3. Select **B36**. Click **Define Name**. In the New Name dialog box, with the Name box highlighted for entry, key **Expenses**. Accept the default in the *Scope* box.

4. Click the **Collapse Dialog** button and proceed to select the range that makes up total expenses.

5. With the text already selected by default in the *Refers to* box, press **Ctrl** and click **B15**, **B21**, **B28**, and **B33**, release Ctrl, and then click the **Expand Dialog** button. You have just selected cells that have the Expenses defined, named, copied, and applied to them as seen in Figure 8-18. Click **OK** to close the New Name dialog box. Some of the selected cells are blank. In the following exercises, you will use the names you just created to fill them.

Figure 8-18

Applying defined names to multiple cells

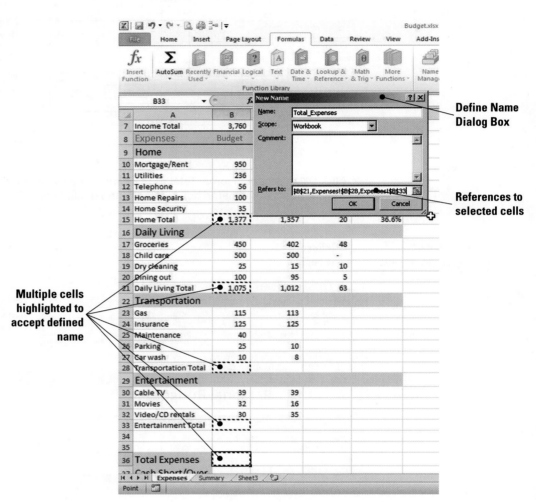

Define Name Dialog Box

References to selected cells

Multiple cells highlighted to accept defined name

Troubleshooting   If, in the process of naming a range, you receive a message that the name already exists, display the Name Manager (discussed later in this lesson) and edit the existing name or delete it and begin again.

6. Select **B23:B27** and click in the Name box to the left of the formula bar. Key **Transportation** and press **Enter**.

7. Select **B30:B32** and click **Define Name**. Key **Entertainment** in the Name box on the dialog box. Click **OK**.

8. Select **A15:B15**. Click **Create from Selection**. The left column will be selected as in Figure 8-19. Click **OK**. The dialog box closes. While naming this range doesn't change the current worksheet, you will use the range you just named in a later exercise.

Figure 8-19

Create names from selection

PAUSE. LEAVE the workbook open to use in the next exercise.

Changing the Size of a Range

If you need to change the parameters of a named range, you can easily redefine the range by using the Name Manager on the Formulas tab. The Name Manager contains all the information about named ranges. It allows you to view summaries of the names you have applied in the worksheet. In the following exercise, you will edit the range for Home_Total.

STEP BY STEP   **Change the Size of a Range**

USE the workbook from the previous exercise.

1. Click **Name Manager** on the Formulas tab. From the Name Manager window (see Figure 8-20), click to select **Home_Total** and click **Edit**. The Edit Name dialog box opens. You are going to change the scope (size) of the range rather than the name.

Figure 8-20

Name manager dialog box

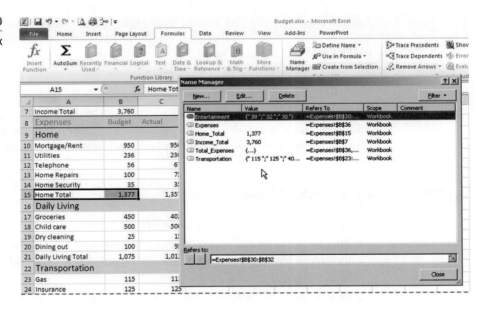

Take Note   Home_Total is the range you named in the Name a Range exercise earlier in this lesson, using the Create from Selection command.

2. The Home_Total range is identified in the Refers To box at the bottom of the Edit Name dialog box. Click the **Collapse Dialog** button and select **B10:B14**.

3. Click **Expand Dialog** to view the dialog box as shown in Figure 8-21. Click **OK** to accept your changes and close the dialog box.

Figure 8-21

Editing a previously named range

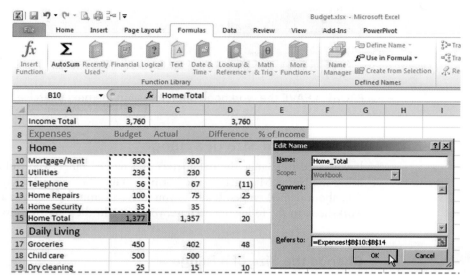

4. Click **Close** to close the Name Manager dialog box. **SAVE** the workbook.

PAUSE. LEAVE the workbook open to use in the next exercise.

In the previous exercise, you used the Name Manager dialog box to extend the reference for a named range. You can also rename a range, or use the Names in combination with the Filter function to display names that meet specific criteria that you are filtering, such as names scoped to the worksheet or names scoped to the workbook.

Keeping Track of Ranges

Use the Name Manager dialog box to work with all of the defined names in the workbook. From this dialog box you can also add, change, or delete names. You can use the Name Manager as a convenient way to confirm the value and reference of a named reference or to determine its scope.

STEP BY STEP **Keep Track of Ranges**

USE the workbook from the previous exercise.

1. Click **Name Manager** on the Defined Names group on the Formulas tab. You will use the Name Manager to modify previously created names and create new ones.

2. Select **Income_Total** and click **Edit**.

3. Select **_Total** in the Name field and press **Delete**. Click **OK** to accept your changes and close the dialog box.

4. Click **New**. Key **Short\Over** in the Name box. Be sure to use the backslash. You are specifying the name of a new range you will create in the next step. If you accidently key a forward slash, you will get an error dialog box. Click **OK** and return to the name and fix the error.

 **Troubleshooting** You will receive an error message if you use the forward slash in a name. Although the forward slash is used in the Short/Over label on the worksheets, you can use only the underscore or the backslash as a word divider in a named range.

5. In the *Refers To* box, key **=Income–Expenses**. Click **OK**. You have now used names to create a formula.

6. Click **Close** to close the Name Manager dialog box. **SAVE** the workbook.

PAUSE. LEAVE the workbook open to use in the next exercise.

If you defined a named reference after you entered a cell reference in a formula, you may want to update the existing cell reference to the defined name. Select an empty cell, click the arrow next to Define Name, and click Apply Names. On the Apply Names dialog box, click one or more names, and click OK.

You can create a list of defined names in a workbook to make it simpler to keep track of your data. It is easier to remember names than to memorize cells and cell ranges. Just select an area of a worksheet with two empty columns, one for the name and one for a description. Select the upper-left cell of the list. Click Use in Formula and click Paste Names. Click Paste List.

Creating a Formula that Operates on a Named Range

You have created several named ranges in the previous exercises, which you will use in the next exercise to fill cells on the worksheets in your Budget workbook.

STEP BY STEP   **Create a Formula that Operates on a Named Range**

USE the workbook from the previous exercise.

1. On the Expenses worksheet, select **B28**. Key **=sum(**. Click **Use in Formula** in the Defined Names group on the Formulas tab. The Use in Formula drop-down list appears. It contains all the Defined names that you created as seen in Figure 8-22.

Figure 8-22

Use in Formula drop-down list

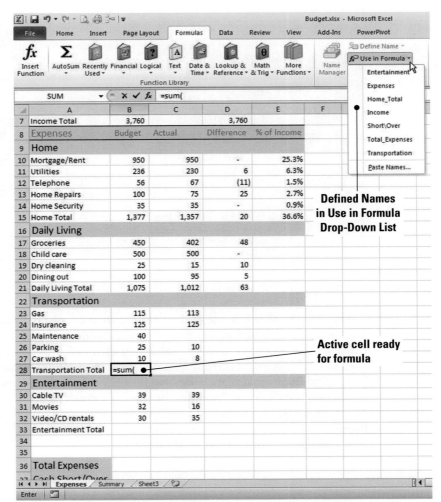

2. Click **Transportation** on the drop-down list. Key the closing parenthesis in the formula and press **Enter**. You have now defined the Transportation name for use in formulas for the selected range.

3. Select **B33**. Click the formula bar and key the following formula **=sum(Entertainment)**, and press **Enter**.

4. On the Summary worksheet, select **B11**. Key the formula **=sum(** and click **Use in Formula**. Select **Expenses** from the list of named cells and ranges. Press **Enter**. **SAVE** the workbook.

PAUSE. LEAVE the workbook open to use in the next exercise.

SUMMARIZING DATA WITH FUNCTIONS

The Bottom Line

A **function** is a predefined formula that performs a calculation. Excel's built-in functions are designed to perform all sorts of calculations—from simple to complex. When you apply a function to specific data, you eliminate the time involved in manually constructing a formula. Using functions ensures the accuracy of the formula's results.

A function consists of a function name and function arguments and specified syntax. See Table 8-1 for a list of the most commonly used Excel functions. The arguments are enclosed in parentheses in the formula. This lets Excel know where the formula begins and where it ends. The arguments are in logical format from the left of the formula to the right in the parenthesis; (argument1, argument2, ...) and are performed in that order, from left to right. Depending on the function, an **argument** can be a constant value, a single-cell reference, a range of cells, or even another function. If a function contains multiple arguments, the arguments are separated by commas.

Table 8-1

Most commonly used Excel functions

Function	Description	Formula Syntax
SUM	Takes all of the values in each of the specified cells and totals their values.	=SUM(first value, second value,...)
AVERAGE	Calculates the arithmetic mean, or average, for the values in a range of cells.	=AVERAGE(first value, second value,...)
MIN	Determines the smallest value of a given list of numbers or arguments.	=MIN(first value, second value,...)
MAX	Analyzes an argument list to determine the highest value (the opposite of the MIN function).	=MAX(first value, second value,...)

Using SUM

Adding a range of cells is one of the most common calculations performed on worksheet data. You can use the SUM function to easily and accurately select the cells to be included in a calculation. The AutoSum function makes that even easier, by calculating (by default) the total from the active cell to the first nonnumeric cell. In previous exercises, you created a formula to perform addition by keying or selecting the cells to include and connected them with the plus sign. Using the SUM or AutoSum function is a much easier way to achieve the same result. AutoSum is a built-in feature of Excel that recognizes adjacent cells in rows and columns as the logical selection to perform the AutoSum. In this exercise, you will use the most commonly used functions, beginning with the SUM function.

STEP BY STEP   Use SUM

USE the workbook from the previous exercise.

1. On the Expenses worksheet, select **C28**. Click **Insert Function** in the Function Library group on the Formulas tab. The Insert Function dialog box shown in Figure 8-23 opens.

Figure 8-23

Accept default name or create a name

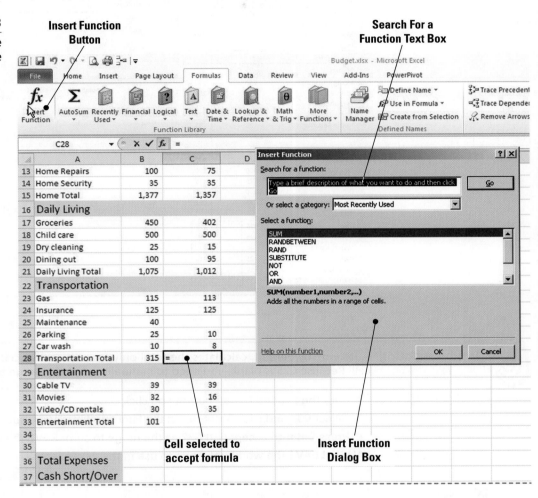

2. SUM is selected by default. Click **OK**. The Functions Arguments box for SUM opens.

3. In the Function Arguments box, the default range shown is C26:C27. Click the **Collapse Dialog** button in the Number1 field and select the cell range **C23:C27**. This has now applied the SUM function and its arguments to the selected cell range as illustrated in Figure 8-24.

Take Note   The Insert Function dialog box will select the most recently used function by default; in this case that is SUM. If you have used another function more recently, that function will be selected.

Figure 8-24

Change default range of cells

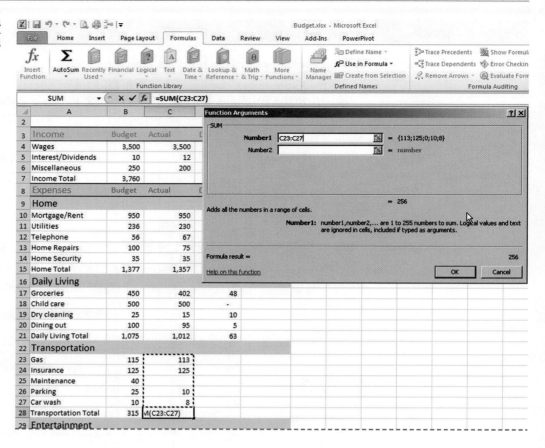

 **Troubleshooting** AutoSum, by default, calculates the total only from the active cell to the first nonnumeric cell. Because C25 is blank, you need to manually select the range to be calculated.

4. Click the Expand Dialog button and click OK.

5. Select C33 and click AutoSum in the Function Library group.

6. Press Enter to accept C30:C32 as the range to sum. **SAVE** the workbook.

PAUSE. LEAVE the workbook open to use in the next exercise.

Take Note   Because it is used so frequently, AutoSum is available on the Formulas tab in the Function Library group and on the Home tab in the Editing group.

Using COUNT

Statistical functions, such as SUM and COUNT, are used to compile and classify data to present significant information. Use the COUNT function to count the number of numeric entries in a range. For example, in a worksheet used to calculate wages, you can apply the COUNT function to determine how many of the employees have worked over 40 hours in a work week. You will apply the COUNT function in the following exercise.

STEP BY STEP **Use COUNT**

USE the workbook from the previous exercise.

1. On the Expenses worksheet, select **A39** and key **Expense Categories**. Press **Tab**.

2. Click **Insert Function** in the Function Library group on the Formulas tab. The Insert Function dialog box opens.

3. On the Insert Function dialog box, key **COUNT** in the *Search for a Function* text box and click **Go**. The function will appear at the top of the function list and be selected by default in the Select a function window. Click on **COUNT** and click **OK**. You want to count only the expenses in each category and not include the category totals.

4. Click the **Collapse Dialog** button for Value1.

5. Select **B10:B14** and press **Enter**. You have selected the range of cells for Value1 and Home_Total is now entered in the Value1 text box instead of the cell range.

6. Click the **Collapse Dialog** button for Value2 and select **B17:20**. Press **Enter**. B17:B20 now appears in the Value2 text box. You have selected the range of cells for Value2.

Take Note As you add arguments, the Value fields on the Function Arguments dialog box expand to allow you to enter multiple arguments.

7. Collapse the dialog box for Value3. Select **B23:B27** and press **Enter**. The identified range is one you named in a previous exercise. That name (Transportation) appears in the Value3 box rather than the cell range, and the values of the cells in the Transportation and Entertainment named ranges appear to the right of the value boxes.

8. In the Value4 box, key **Entertainment**. You have now manually applied the name Entertainment for Value4. Your entries in the Function Arguments dialog box should look similar to those shown in Figure 8-25.

Figure 8-25

Assign named ranges in function

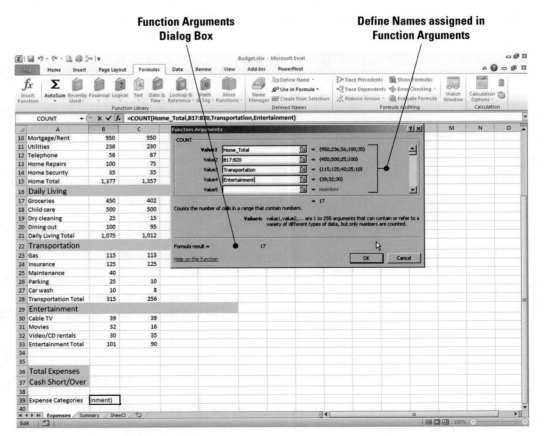

9. Click **OK** to accept the function arguments. Excel returns a value of 17 in B39. **SAVE** the workbook.

PAUSE. LEAVE the workbook open to use in the next exercise.

Take Note   Text or blank cells are ignored in a COUNT formula. If a cell contains a value of 0 (zero), the COUNT function will recognize it and count it as a cell with a number.

Using COUNTA

Use the COUNTA function to count the number of cells in a range that are not empty. COUNTA counts both text and values in a selected data range. You can use this formula to count the number of entries in a particular worksheet or range of cells. You will use this formula in the next exercise.

STEP BY STEP   **Use COUNTA**

USE the workbook from the previous exercise.

1. On the Expenses worksheet, select **A40** and key **Cells Containing Data**. Press **Tab**.
2. Click **Insert Function** in the Function Library group on the Formulas tab. The Insert Function dialog box opens.

 Another Way
By default the most recently used functions are displayed when the Insert Function dialog box opens. You can click the arrow in the category field and select All to display a list of all functions.

3. On the Insert Function dialog box, select **COUNTA**. If COUNTA does not appear in your list, key COUNTA in the *Search for a function* box and click **Go**. The function will appear at the top of the function list and be selected by default. Click **OK**.
4. Select **B4:B33** in the Value1 box. Click **OK**. The formula is applied and Excel returns a value of 26.

PAUSE. LEAVE the worksheet open to use in the next exercise.

COUNTA returns a value that indicates the number of cells that contain data. Empty cells within the data ranges are ignored.

Using AVERAGE

The AVERAGE function adds a range of cells and then divides by the number of cell entries. It might be interesting to know the average difference between what you budgeted for expenses and the amount you actually spent during the month. Before you can calculate the average, however, you will need to finish calculating the differences.

STEP BY STEP   **Use AVERAGE**

USE the worksheet from the previous exercise.

1. Select **D21** and right-click. Click **Copy**. You are copying the formula in D21 for the next step.
2. Select **D23**, right-click and click **Paste**. You have just pasted the formula into cell D23.
3. Use the fill handle in cell D23 to copy the formula to the range D24:D28.
4. Copy the formula in D28 and paste it to D30.
5. Use the fill handle in cell D30 to copy the formula to D31:D33.
6. In A41, key **Average Difference** and press **Tab**.
7. Click **Recently Used** in the Function Library group and click **AVERAGE**. If AVERAGE does not appear in your recently used function list, key AVERAGE in the *Search for a function* box and click **Go**. The function will appear at the top of the function list and be selected by default. Click **OK**. You are applying the AVERAGE formula to cell A42.

8. Click the **Collapse Dialog** button in Value1. Press **Ctrl** and select the category totals (D15, D21, D28, and D33). Notice that the arguments are separated by a comma.

9. Click **Expand Dialog**. Click **OK**. Your screen should resemble the screenshot in Figure 8-26. There is a $38 average difference between the amount budgeted and the amount you spent in each category.

Figure 8-26

AVERAGE formula applied to worksheet

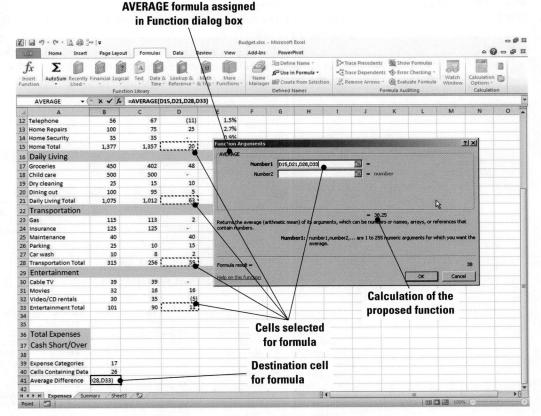

Take Note   The exact value returned for the AVERAGE formula was 38.25. Because column B is formatted for zero decimals, the value returned by the formula is 38.

10. **SAVE** and **CLOSE** the *Budget* workbook.

PAUSE. LEAVE Excel open to use in the next exercise.

Although you entered the numbers (cell references) as one number, if you open the Function Arguments dialog box after the formula has been entered, each cell reference is in a separate Number box.

Using MIN

The MIN formula returns the smallest number in a set of values. For example, a professor would use the MIN function to determine the lowest test score; a sales organization would determine which sales representative earned the lowest commission or which employee earns the lowest salary. Maximum values are usually calculated for the same set of data. You will learn to apply the MIN function in the next exercise.

STEP BY STEP   **Use MIN**

 The *Personnel* file for this lesson is available on the book companion website or in WileyPLUS.

Another Way
You can display the Insert Function dialog box by clicking the Insert Function button on the Formula bar.

GET READY. OPEN the *Personnel* data file for Lesson 8.

1. Select **A22** and key **Minimum Salary**. Press **Tab**.
2. Click the **Recently Used** button in the Function Library group on the Formulas tab. The MIN function is not listed. Key **=min** in cell B22 and double-click on **MIN** when it appears on the drop-down list below cell B22. Excel inputs the MIN command and an opening parenthesis is added to your formula.
3. Select **E6:E19** and press **Enter**. You have now finished creating the formula arguments and applied the MIN function. Excel returns a value of $25,000 as the minimum salary for the personnel. See Figure 8-27.

Figure 8-27

MIN function applied to worksheet

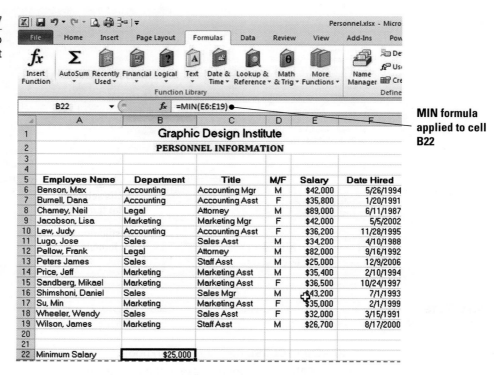

MIN formula applied to cell B22

4. **SAVE** the workbook as *Analysis*.

PAUSE. LEAVE the workbook open to use in the next exercise.

Using MAX

The MAX function returns the largest value in a set of values. Minimum values are usually calculated for the same set of data.

STEP BY STEP   **Use MAX**

USE the worksheet from the previous exercise.

1. In A23, key **Maximum Salary** and press **Tab**.
2. Click **Insert Function** in the Function Library group and key **MAX** in the *Search for a function* box and click **Go**. When the MAX function appears, it will be selected by default, click **OK**.
3. Click the **Collapse Dialog** button in Number1 text box and select **E6:E19**.

4. Click the Expand Dialog button and click OK. Excel applies and calculates the function on the range and returns the maximum salary value of $89,000 in cell A24.

5. **SAVE** and **CLOSE** the workbook.

PAUSE. LEAVE Excel open to use in the next exercise.

USING FORMULAS TO CREATE SUBTOTALS

The Bottom Line

You can calculate subtotals using the SUBTOTAL function, but it is generally easier to create a list by using the Subtotal command in the Outline group on the Data tab. After the subtotal list has been created, you can edit it using the SUBTOTAL function.

Selecting Ranges for Subtotaling

Groups are created for subtotaling by sorting the data. Data must be sorted by groups to insert a SUBTOTAL function. Subtotals are calculated with a summary function, and you can use the SUBTOTAL function to display more than one type of summary function for each column.

STEP BY STEP   **Select Ranges for Subtotaling**

1. **OPEN** the *Personnel* data file for this lesson.

2. Select **A5:F19** (the data range and the column labels). Click **Sort** in the Sort & Filter group on the Data tab.

Troubleshooting If you do not include the labels in the data selection, Excel will prompt you to include the labels so that you can sort by label rather than the column heading.

@ The *Personnel* file for this lesson is available on the book companion website or in WileyPLUS.

3. On the Sort dialog box, select **Department** as the sort by criterion. Select the My data has headers check box if it is not selected. Click **OK**. The list is sorted by department.

4. With the data range still selected, click **Subtotal** in the Outline group on the Data tab. The Subtotal dialog box opens.

5. Select **Department** in the *At each change in* box. Sum is the default in the *Use function* box.

WILEY **PLUS** *EXTRA*

WileyPLUS Extra! features an online tutorial of this task.

6. Select **Salary** in the *Add subtotal to* box. Deselect any other column labels. Select **Summary below data** if it is not selected. Click **OK**. Subtotals are inserted below each department with a grand total at the bottom.

7. With the data selected, click **Subtotal**. On the dialog box, click **Average** in the *Use function* box.

8. Click **Replace current subtotals** to deselect it. Click **OK**.

9. **SAVE** the workbook as *Dept Subtotals*.

PAUSE. LEAVE Excel open to use in the next exercise.

Take Note   Subtotals are calculated with a summary function, such as SUM, COUNT, or AVERAGE. You can display more than one type of summary function for each column. Grand totals, on the other hand, are derived from the detail data, not from the values in the subtotals. Therefore, when you used the AVERAGE summary function, the grand total row displayed an average of all detail rows in the list, not an average of the values in the subtotal rows.

Modifying a Range in a Subtotal

You can change the way data is grouped and subtotaled by modifying the subtotal range using the SUBTOTAL function. This option is not available when you create subtotals from the Data tab commands.

STEP BY STEP   **Modify a Range in a Subtotal**

USE the worksheet you saved in the previous exercise.

1. Insert a row above the Grand Total row.
2. Key Sales/Marketing Total in B29.
3. Copy the subtotal formula from E47 to E49.
4. In the Formula bar, change the function 9 (which includes hidden values) to 109 (which ignores hidden values) to exclude the sum and average subtotals for the individual departments within the data range. Otherwise, the formula result will include the average salary and the total salaries as well as the actual salaries for individual employees.
5. Replace the range in the Formula bar with E21:E45 and press Enter. The salaries for the sales and marketing departments combined are $310,000, which are now entered into the cell.
6. **SAVE** the workbook as *Dept Subtotals Revised*. **CLOSE** the workbook.

PAUSE. LEAVE Excel open to use in the next exercise.

Building Formulas to Subtotal and Total

In the previous exercise, you copied and modified a formula to create a subtotal for a combined group. You can accomplish the same result by using the SUBTOTAL function to build a formula and add subtotals to data that you cannot or do not want to sort into one category in order to use the built-in function in the Data tab's subtotal function.

STEP BY STEP   **Build Formulas to Subtotal and Total**

@ The *Personnel* file for this lesson is available on the book companion website or in WileyPLUS.

1. **OPEN** the *Personnel* data file for this lesson.
2. Insert a row above row 11.
3. Select E11 and click Recently Used in the Formula Library group on the Formulas tab. The Recently Used formula drop-down list appears. Note that the SUBTOTAL function is not there. Click on the Insert Function option. Key SUBTOTAL in the *Search for a function* box and click Go. When the SUBTOTAL function appears, it will be selected by default, click OK.
4. Key 9 in the *Function_num* box on the Function Arguments dialog box.
5. Click the Collapse Dialog button in Ref1 and select E6:E10. You are inputting your first reference.
6. Click Expand Dialog and click OK to accept your changes and close the dialog box.
7. Select B11 and key Support Staff Total.
8. Select B21 and key Sales and Marketing Total.
9. Select E21 and click Recently Used. Click SUBTOTAL. Use the same procedure in step 4 to create a subtotal for the values in E12:E20. You are creating another subtotal formula. Format the subtotal for currency and expand the column to accommodate the data.

10. Press **Ctrl** and select row **11** and row **21**. Click **Bold** on the Home tab to emphasize the subtotals. Compare your worksheet to Figure 8-28.

Figure 8-28

SUBTOTAL applied in worksheet

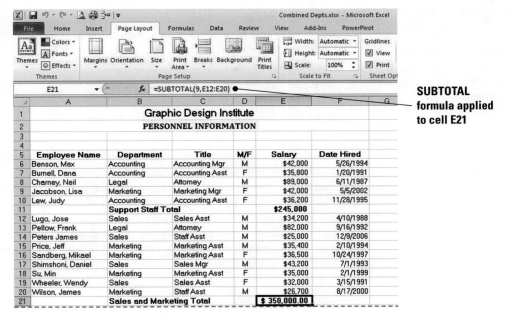

SUBTOTAL formula applied to cell E21

11. **SAVE** the workbook as *Combined Depts*.

PAUSE. LEAVE the workbook open to use in the next exercise.

When you use the Subtotal command on the Data tab, subtotal entries have a predefined format, and you can create multiple subtotals, as you did in a previous exercise. When you use the SUBTOTAL function, you must build the formula and label and format the subtotal entries manually.

Take Note   If the workbook is set to automatically calculate formulas, the Subtotal command recalculates subtotal and grand total values automatically when you edit the detail data.

CONTROLLING THE APPEARANCE OF FORMULAS

The Bottom Line   When you work with extremely large worksheets that contain numerous formulas, you sometimes need to see all formulas to audit the calculations in the worksheet. You can display and print the worksheet with all formulas visible.

Displaying Formulas on the Screen

When you create a formula, the result of the calculation is displayed in the cell and the formula is displayed in the Formula bar. You may need to see all formulas on the screen in order to audit them. As you learn in this lesson, you can click the Show Formulas command to display the formula in each cell instead of the resulting value.

Display Formulas on the Screen

 **Another Way**
You can also press Ctrl+` (grave accent) to switch between formulas and their values. The accent is located to the left of the number 1 key on most keyboards.

GET READY. With the workbook *Combined Depts* already open, perform the following steps:

1. Click Show Formulas in the Formula Auditing group on the Formulas tab. All worksheet formulas are displayed.
2. Click Show Formulas. Values are displayed.
3. **SAVE** and **CLOSE** the workbook. When you open the workbook again, it will open with values displayed.

PAUSE. LEAVE Excel open to use in the next exercise.

If you work with dates and times, you will find it useful to understand Excel's date and time system. Although you normally do not have to be concerned with serial numbers, when you displayed the worksheet formulas in the preceding exercise, you probably wondered what happened to the numbers in your worksheet. Excel stores dates as sequential serial numbers. By default, January 1, 1900 is serial number 1, and January 2, 1900 is serial number 2, and so on. This serial number date system allows you to use dates in formulas. For example, you can enter a formula to calculate the number of days you have lived by creating a formula to subtract your birth date from today's date.

Printing Formulas

When you audit the formulas in a large worksheet, you may find it useful to print the worksheet with the formulas displayed. To gain maximum benefit from the printed copy, print gridlines and row and column headers. In this exercise, you will display formulas for printing and adjust the print settings.

Print Formulas

1. **OPEN** *Budget* from your Lesson 8 folder. This is the exercise you saved earlier.
2. Click Show Formulas in the Formula Auditing group on the Formulas tab. The formulas appear in the spreadsheet.
3. Click the Page Layout tab and click Print in Gridlines and Print in Headings in the Sheet Options group.
4. Click Orientation in the Page Setup group and click Landscape.
5. Click the File tab. Click on Print and view the Print Preview.
6. Click the Page Setup link at the bottom of the print settings to open the Page Setup dialog box.
7. On the Page tab of the dialog box, click Fit to: and leave the defaults as 1 page wide by 1 tall.
8. Click the Header/Footer tab. Click Custom Header and key your name in the left section. Refer to Figure 8-29. Click OK to accept your changes and close the Page Setup dialog box.

Figure 8-29

Custom print settings applied

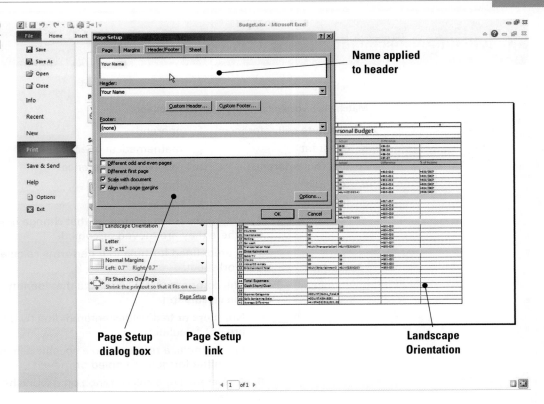

Name applied to header

Page Setup dialog box

Page Setup link

Landscape Orientation

9. Click the **Print** button at the top-left corner of the Backstage view window. When prompted, click **OK** to print the document.

10. **SAVE** the workbook with the same name. **CLOSE** the workbook.

CLOSE Excel.

SKILL SUMMARY

In This Lesson, You Learned How To:
Build basic formulas
Use cell references in formulas
Use cell ranges in formulas
Summarize data with functions
Use formulas to create subtotals
Control the appearance of formulas

Knowledge Assessment

Matching

Match each vocabulary term with its definition.

a. absolute cell reference   f. operand

b. constant   g. mathematical operator

c. external reference   h. relative cell reference

d. formula   i. mixed reference

e. function   j. scope

_____ 1. In formulas, cell references that change in relation to the location where they are moved or copied.

_____ 2. A predefined formula that performs calculations on values in a worksheet.

_____ 3. The components of a formula that identify the values to be used in the calculation.

_____ 4. Numbers or text values entered directly into a formula. These values are not calculated.

_____ 5. In a formula, a reference to a specific cell that does not change when the formula is copied or moved.

_____ 6. A reference to a cell or range on a worksheet in another Excel workbook.

_____ 7. An equation that performs calculations on values in a worksheet.

_____ 8. The formula component that specifies what calculations are to be performed.

_____ 9. A cell reference in which the column is absolute and the row is relative or vice versa.

_____ 10. The location within which a name is recognized without qualification.

Multiple Choice

Select the best response for the following statements.

1. Which of the following is not a mathematical operator?

   a. ×

   b. +

   c. −

   d. *

2. Which function automatically totals cells directly above or to the left of the cell containing the formula?

   a. COUNT

   b. AutoFill

   c. AutoSum

   d. SUM

3. Which of the following shows a formula for an external reference?

   a. =Sum(Expenses)

   b. =Sum(B6:b10)

   c. =Expenses!B7

   d. ='[Financial Obligations.xlsx]Sheet1'!$B$2

4. Which of the following shows a formula for a reference to another worksheet in the same workbook?

   a. =Sum(Expenses)

   b. =Sum(B6:b10)

   c. =Expenses!B7

   d. ='[Financial Obligations.xlsx]Sheet1'!$B$2

5. Which of the following shows a formula that references a named range?

   a. =Sum(Expenses)

   b. =Sum(B6:b10)

   c. =Expenses!B7

   d. ='[Financial Obligations.xlsx]Sheet1'!$B$2

6. Which character designates a cell reference as absolute?

   a. ^

   b. @

   c. $

   d. #

7. The COUNTA function

   a. counts the number of cells in a range that contain values.

   b. counts all cells in the range.

   c. counts the number of cells that are not empty.

   d. counts the text entries in the range.

8. The COUNT function is an example of a _____ function.

   a. logical

   b. financial

   c. statistical

   d. text

9. Which of the following is an acceptable name for a named range?

   a. C

   b. C_Contracts

   c. C/Contracts

   d. C Contracts

10. Which of the following statements accurately describes the default selection for AutoSum?

   a. By default, AutoSum totals all entries above the cell in which the formula is located.

   b. By default, AutoSum calculates the total from the active cell to the first nonnumeric cell.

   c. AutoSum does not have a default selection.

   d. You must make the selection before clicking AutoSum.

Competency Assessment

Project 8-1: Create Formulas to Calculate Income and Expenses

An employee at Tailspin Toys has entered second quarter income and expense data into a worksheet. You will enter formulas to calculate monthly and quarterly totals.

GET READY. LAUNCH Excel if it is not already running.

@ The *Tailspin Toys* file for this lesson is available on the book companion website or in WileyPLUS.

1. **OPEN** *Tailspin Toys* from the data files for this lesson.

2. Select **E4** and key =B4+C4+D4 and press **Enter**.

3. Select **B6**. On the Formulas tab, in the Function Library group, click **Insert Function**.

4. In the Insert Function dialog box, select SUM and click OK.

5. In the Function Arguments dialog box, click the Collapse Dialog button and click B4. Key - and click B5.

6. Click the Expand Dialog button and click OK to close the dialog box.

7. Select B6 and use the fill handle to copy the formula to C6:D6.

8. Click B11 and click AutoSum in the Function Library group. Press Enter to accept B8:B10 as the cells to total.

9. Select B11 and use the fill handle to copy the formula to C11:D11.

10. Select B13 and click Insert Function in the Function Library group. On the Insert Function dialog box, SUM will be the default. Click OK.

11. Click the Collapse Dialog button for Number1 and click B6. Key - and click B11. Press Enter and click OK to close the dialog box.

12. Select B13 and use the fill handle to copy the formula to C13:D13.

13. Select E4. Click AutoSum in the Function Library group. Press Enter to accept the range as B4:D4. Copy the formula to E5:E14. Then delete the data in cells E7 and E12.

14. Select B15, key =B13-B14, and press Enter. Copy the formula to C15:E15.

15. **SAVE** the workbook as *Tailspin Toys 8-1* and then **CLOSE** the file.

LEAVE Excel open to use in the next project.

Project 8-2: Use AutoSum to Total Sales; Calculate Percentage of Increase

Blue Yonder Airlines has created a workbook to analyze sales for its first four years of operation. Enter formulas to determine the total sales for each division and the percentage increase/decrease each year.

GET READY. LAUNCH Excel if it is not already running.

@ The *Blue Yonder* file for this lesson is available on the book companion website or in WileyPLUS.

1. **OPEN** the *Blue Yonder* data file for this lesson.

2. Select F4 and click AutoSum in the Function Library group on the Formulas tab.

3. Press Enter to accept B4:E4 as the range to add.

4. Use the fill handle to copy the formula in F4 to F5:F8.

5. Select B12 and key =(C4-B4)/C4. Press Enter. This formula calculates the percentage increase in sales from 2005 to 2006. The numbers in parentheses yield the amount of the increase. The increase is then divided by the 2006 sales.

6. Select B12. Use the fill handle to copy the formula to B13:B15.

7. With the cell range B12:B15 still selected, use the fill handle to copy the formulas in the selected range to C12:D15.

8. Select F12. Key =(E4-B4)/E4 and press Enter. This enters a formula to calculate the percentage increase from the first year (2005) to the most recent (2008).

9. Copy the formula in F12 to F13:F15.

10. **SAVE** the workbook as *Blue Yonder 8-2* and then **CLOSE** the file.

LEAVE Excel open for the next project.

Proficiency Assessment

Project 8-3: Calculate Totals and Percentages

In the previous project, you calculated total sales for Blue Yonder's first four years of operation. You also calculated the percentage of increase or decrease in sales for each year. In this project, you will calculate expense totals and percentage increase or decrease.

GET READY. LAUNCH Excel if it is not already running.

@ The *Blue Yonder Expenses* file for this lesson is available on the book companion website or in WileyPLUS.

1. **OPEN** the *Blue Yonder Expenses* data file for this lesson. Expense History worksheet should be the active worksheet.

2. Select B8 and click AutoSum to total the 2005 expenses.

3. Copy the formula in **B8** to **C8:F8**.

4. Select **F4** and click **AutoSum** to total Corporate Contracts expenses for the four-year period.

5. Copy the formula in F4 to F5:F7.

6. In B12, create a formula to calculate the percentage increase in Corporate Contracts expenses from 2005 to 2006. Begin with 2006 expenses minus 2005 expenses, divided by 2006. Use parentheses to instruct Excel which function to perform first.

7. Copy the formula from B12 to B13:B15 and to C12:D15.

8. In F12, create a formula to calculate the percentage increase in expenses from 2005 to 2008. Remember to construct the formula to subtract and then divide.

9. Click **Percentage Style (%)** in the Number group. If necessary, click **Increase Decimal** to display one position after the decimal point.

10. Copy the formula in F12 to F13:F15.

11. **SAVE** the workbook as *Blue Yonder Expenses 8-3* and then **CLOSE** the file.

LEAVE Excel open for the next project.

Project 8-4: Create Formulas in a Template Worksheet

Tailspin Toys wants to project income and expenses for the third quarter based on its performance in the second quarter. A template has been created for the projections. In this project, you will create formulas for the calculations that affect only this worksheet. In the next exercise, you will create formulas that refer to data in another worksheet in this workbook. You are creating a template, so the values returned by your formulas will be $0 until you use the template in the next exercise.

GET READY. LAUNCH Excel if it is not already running.

@ The *Tailspin Projections* file for this lesson is available on the book companion website or in WileyPLUS.

1. **OPEN** the *Tailspin Projections* data file for this lesson.

2. In the Third Qtr worksheet, key **0** (zero) as a placeholder in B4 and in B5.

3. Select **B6** and enter a formula to subtract the cost of goods sold from sales. The value returned will be $0.

4. Key **0** as a placeholder in B8:B10.

5. Select **B11** and click **AutoSum** to calculate total expenses.

6. Select **B13** and enter a formula to subtract total expenses from the gross margin.

7. Federal taxes are estimated to be 34% net income. Select **B14** and enter a formula to multiply net income before taxes by 34%.

8. In B15, enter a formula to calculate net income after taxes.

9. **SAVE** the workbook as *Tailspin Projections 8-4*.

LEAVE the workbook open for the next project.

Mastery Assessment

Project 8-5: Refer to Data in Another Worksheet

Tailspin Toys wants to set goals for the third quarter based on its performance in the second quarter. Its goal is to increase sales by 10% while keeping costs and expenses to 5%. You will create formulas to calculate the projections.

USE the workbook you saved in Project 8-4.

1. Make Third Qtr the active sheet and display the Formulas. The formula to establish the sales goal for third quarter will be second quarter total sales + (second quarter total sales *10%).

2. Select **B4**, click **Recently Used** in the Function Library group, and click **SUM** in the *Select a function* box. Select **Second Qtr E4** as the Number1 function argument.

3. In the *Number2 argument* box, key +(and click **Second Qtr**. Select **E4**.

4. Continuing in the *Number2 argument* box, key *10%) and press **Enter**. Your completed formula should read =SUM('SecondQtr'!E4,+('Second Qtr'!E4*10%)).

5. On the Third Quarter worksheet, select **B5**. Click **Recently Used** in the Function Library group and click **SUM**. Select **Second Qtr E5** as the Number1 function argument.

6. In the *Number2 argument* box, key +(and click **Second Qtr**. Select **E5**.

7. Continuing in the Number2 argument box, key *5%) and press **Enter**.

8. Copy the formula in B5 to B8:B10.

9. **SAVE** the workbook as *Tailspin Projections 8-5* and then **CLOSE** the file.

LEAVE Excel open for the next project.

Project 8-6: Name a Range and Use the Range in a Formula

Blue Yonder Airlines wants to analyze the sales and expense data from its four-year history.

GET READY. LAUNCH Excel if it is not already running.

@ The *Income Analysis* file for this lesson is available on the book companion website or in WileyPLUS.

1. **OPEN** the *Income Analysis* data file for this lesson.

2. Select **B4:E4** and click **Define Name** on the Formulas tab. Accept the defaults in the dialog box and click **OK**.

3. Repeat Step 2 and name the other three income sources.

4. On the Analysis worksheet, select **B5** and create a formula to calculate the four-year average for corporate contract sales. Use the Corporate Contracts named range in the formula.

5. Create a formula using the appropriately named range in B6, B7, and B8.

6. In column C, create a formula to calculate the maximum sales for each division.

7. Show the formulas on the screen. Adjust column width, if necessary, to display the entire formulas.

8. Print the Analysis worksheet in landscape orientation with gridlines and column headings included.

9. **SAVE** the workbook as *Income Analysis 8-6* and then **CLOSE** the file.

LEAVE Excel open for the next project.

INTERNET READY

As mentioned at the beginning of this lesson, a personal budget helps you make sound financial decisions and enables you to reach financial goals. Various governmental organizations and private financial counselors recommend percentages of your income to allocate for housing, transportation, etc. Use web search tools to find recommended guidelines for the percentage of income you should allocate in various spending categories. Be sure to use "personal budget guidelines" to avoid business and government budget sites.

From your research, create a worksheet that lists the categories and percentages that you think are reasonable for your personal or family budget. Save the workbook as *My Budget*. close Excel.

Using Advanced Formulas and Securing Workbooks 9

LESSON SKILL MATRIX

In This Lesson, You Will Learn The Following Skills:

Using Formulas to Conditionally Summarize Data

Using Formulas to Look Up Data in a Workbook

Adding Conditional Logic Functions to Formulas

KEY TERMS

- arguments
- array
- conditional formula
- lookup functions
- table

Fabrikam, Inc., uses several of Excel's analytical tools to review sales data during strategic planning activities. Fabrikam's owners have created a standard bonus program as a part of the company's employee-retention efforts, as well as a performance bonus program to recognize sales agents who have been instrumental in achieving the company's strategic goals. The standard bonus is based on years of service to Fabrikam, and the performance bonus is awarded when an agent reaches his or her sales goal for the year. To determine which agents will receive the performance bonus, Fabrikam's accountants must create formulas to analyze the company's sales data. Excel's built-in formulas are the perfect solution to compute and display all the calculations the accountants need. You will learn to apply these formulas in the exercises in this lesson.

SOFTWARE ORIENTATION

The Formulas Tab

In this lesson, you will use commands on the Formulas tab to create formulas to conditionally summarize data, look up data, apply conditional logic, and format and modify text. The Formulas tab is shown in Figure 9-1.

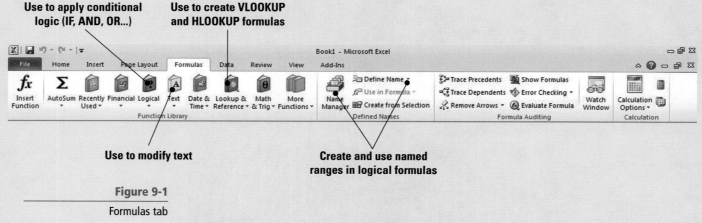

Use to apply conditional logic (IF, AND, OR...)

Use to create VLOOKUP and HLOOKUP formulas

Use to modify text

Create and use named ranges in logical formulas

Figure 9-1

Formulas tab

The formulas tab contains the command groups you will use to create and apply advanced formulas in Excel. Use this illustration as a reference throughout the lesson.

USING FORMULAS TO CONDITIONALLY SUMMARIZE DATA

The Bottom Line

As you learned in Lesson 8, a formula is an equation that performs calculations, such as addition, subtraction, multiplication, and division, on values in a worksheet. When you enter a formula in a cell, the formula is stored internally and the results are displayed in the cell. Formulas give results and solutions that help you assess and analyze data. As you also learned, you can use a conditional format, which changes the appearance of a cell range based on a criterion, to help you analyze data, detect critical issues, identify patterns, and visually explore trends.

Conditional formulas add yet another dimension to data analysis by summarizing data that meets one or more criteria. A **conditional formula** is one in which the result is determined by the presence or absence of a particular condition. Conditional formulas used in Excel include the functions SUMIF, COUNTIF, and AVERAGEIF.

Using SUMIF

The SUMIF function calculates the total of only those cells that meet a given criterion or condition. The syntax for the SUMIF function is SUMIF(range, criteria, sum_range). The values that a function uses to perform operations or calculations in a formula are called **arguments**. Thus, the arguments of the SUMIF function are range, criteria, and sum range, which, when used together, create a conditional formula in which only those cells that meet a stated criterion are added. Cells within the range that do not meet the criterion are not included in the total.

STEP BY STEP   **Use SUMIF**

@ The *Fabrikam Sales* file for this lesson is available on the book companion website or in WileyPLUS.

GET READY. Before you begin these steps, **LAUNCH** Microsoft Excel. Then, do the following:

1. **OPEN** the *Fabrikam Sales* file for this lesson.

2. Select cell **A20** and key **Sum of sales over $200,000**. Press **Enter**. If necessary, select **A20** and click **Wrap Text** in the Alignment group on the Home tab. You have now formatted the cell to wrap the text that will be keyed.

3. Select **C20**. Click the **Formulas** tab and in the Function Library group, click **Insert Function**. The Insert Function dialog box opens. Within the dialog box, key **SUMIF** in the *Search for function* text box and click **Go**. The SUMIF function will appear at the top of the function list and will be selected by default in the *Select a Function* window.

4. Click **OK** to close the Insert Function dialog box; the Function Arguments dialog box now opens automatically because you selected a formula. This dialog box allows you to edit the formula you selected.

5. In the Function Arguments dialog box, click the **Collapse Dialog** button and select the cell range **C5:C16**. Press **Enter**. By doing this, you are applying the cell range that the formula will use in the calculation.

6. In the Criteria box, key **>200000**, as shown in Figure 9-2. You do not have to enter the range in the Sum_range box. If you leave the range blank, Excel sums the cells you enter in the Range box. You have now applied your criteria to sum all values greater than $200,000.

Figure 9-2

The function arguments dialog box guides you in building SUMIF formulas

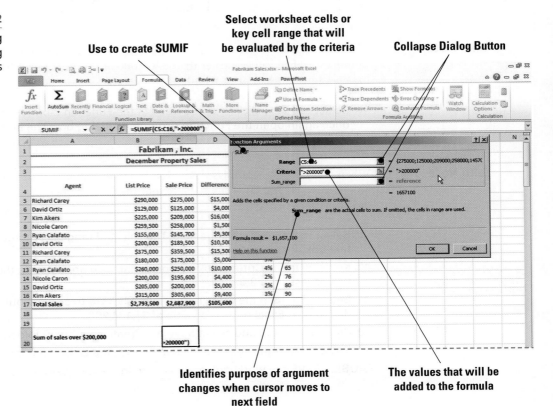

Select worksheet cells or key cell range that will be evaluated by the criteria

Use to create SUMIF

Collapse Dialog Button

Identifies purpose of argument changes when cursor moves to next field

The values that will be added to the formula

Troubleshooting It is not necessary to key dollar signs or commas when entering dollar amounts in the Function Arguments dialog box. If you key them, Excel removes them from the formula and returns an accurate value.

7. Click **OK** to accept the changes and close the dialog box. You see that $1,657,100 of Fabrikam's December revenue came from properties valued in excess of $200,000. (See Figure 9-3.)

Figure 9-3

Function arguments being applied

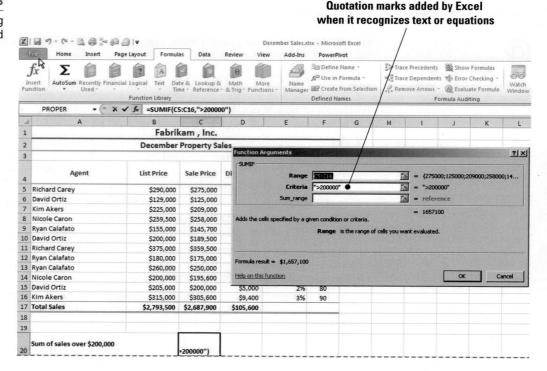

Take Note   The result of the SUMIF formula in C20 does *not* include the property value in C15 because the formula specified values greater than $200,000. To include this value, the criterion would have to be >= (greater than or equal to).

8. Select cell **C21**, click **Recently Used** in the Function Library group, and click **SUMIF** to once again open the Function Arguments dialog box. The insertion point should be in the Range box.

Take Note   When you click Recently Used, the last function that you used appears at the top of the list. Similarly, when you click Insert Function, the Insert Function dialog box opens with the last-used function highlighted.

9. Select **E5:E16** in the Range field. The selected range is automatically entered into the text box. Press **Tab**.

10. Key **<3%** in the Criteria box and press **Tab**. You are entering the criteria to calculate all values less than 3%.

11. Select **C5:C16** in the Sum_range field. Click **OK** to accept your changes and close the dialog box. Excel returns a value of $1,134,200.

12. Click the **File** tab and select **Save As**. Create a Lesson 9 folder.

13. **SAVE** the workbook as *December Sales* in the Lesson 9 folder.

PAUSE. LEAVE the workbook open for use in the next exercise.

Table 9-1 explains the meaning of each argument in the SUMIF syntax. Note that if you omit Sum_range from the formula, as you did in the first calculation in the preceding exercise, Excel evaluates and adds the cells in the range if they match the criterion.

Table 9-1

Arguments in the SUMIF syntax

Argument	Explanation
Range	The range of cells that you want the function to evaluate. Blank and text values are ignored.
Criteria	The condition or criterion in the form of a number, expression, or text entry that defines which cells will be added.
Sum_range	The actual cells to add if the corresponding cells in the range match the criteria.

Using SUMIFS

The SUMIFS function adds cells in a range that meet multiple criteria. It is important to note that the order of arguments in this function is different from the order used with SUMIF. In a SUMIF formula, the Sum_range argument is the third argument; in SUMIFS, however, it is the first argument. In this exercise, you will create and use two SUMIFS formulas, each of which analyzes data based on two criteria. The first SUMIFS formula will add the selling price of the properties that Fabrikam sold for more than $200,000 and that were on the market 60 days or less. The second formula adds the properties that sold at 98% (<3%) of their listed price within 60 days.

STEP BY STEP   **Use SUMIFS**

USE the workbook from the previous exercise to perform the following actions:

1. Select C22. Click **Insert Function** in the Function Library group on the Formulas tab.
2. Key SUMIFS in the *Search for a Function* box and click **Go**. SUMIFS will be highlighted in the Function box.
3. Click **OK** to accept the function.
4. In the Function Arguments dialog box, select C5:C16 in the Sum_range box. This adds your cell range to the argument of the formula.
5. In the Criteria_range1 box, select F5:F16. In the Criteria1 box, key <=60. This specifies that you want to calculate only those values that are less than or equal to 60. When you move to the next text box, notice that Excel places quotation marks around your criteria. It applies these marks to let itself know that this is a criterion and not a calculated value.
6. In the Criteria_range2 box, select C5:C16. You are now choosing your second cell range.
7. In the Criteria2 box, key >200000. Click **OK**. You have now applied a second criterion that will calculate values greater than 200,000. Excel calculates your formula, returning a value of $742,000.
8. Select C23 and click **Recently Used** in the Function Library group.
9. Select SUMIFS. In the Sum_range box, select C5:C16.
10. In the Criteria_range1 box, select F5:F16. Key <60 in the Criteria1 box.
11. In the Criteria_range2 box, select E5:E16. Key <3% in the Criteria2 box. Your Function Arguments dialog box should look like Figure 9-4. Click **OK**. After applying this formula, Excel returns a value of $433,000. (See Figure 9-4.)

Figure 9-4

SUMIFS formula applies two or
more criteria

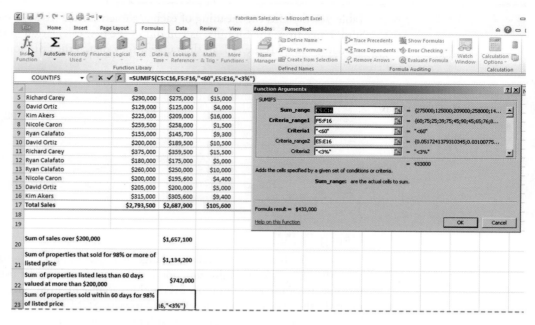

12. SAVE the workbook.

PAUSE. LEAVE the workbook open to use in the next exercise.

The formulas you used in this exercise analyzed the data on two criteria. You can continue to add up to 127 criteria on which data can be evaluated.

Because the order of arguments is different in SUMIF and SUMIFS, if you want to copy and edit these similar functions, be sure to put the arguments in the correct order (first, second, third, and so on).

Using COUNTIF

When used in a conditional formula, the COUNTIF function counts the number of cells in a given range that meet a specific condition. The syntax for the COUNTIF function is COUNTIF(range, criteria); the range is the range of cells to be counted by the formula, and the criteria are the conditions that must be met in order for the cells to be counted. The condition can be a number, expression, or text entry. In this exercise, you practice using the COUNTIF function to calculate values >=200,000. The range you will specify in this COUNTIF formula is the selling price of homes sold during the specified period. The criterion selects only those homes that sold for $200,000 or more.

STEP BY STEP   **Use COUNTIF**

USE the workbook from the previous exercise.

1. Select **C24**. Click **Insert Function** in the Function Library group.
2. Key **COUNTIF** in the *Search for a Function* box and click **Go**. COUNTIF will be highlighted in the Function dialog box.
3. Click **OK** to accept the function and close the dialog box. This opens the Function Arguments dialog box.
4. In the Function Arguments dialog box, select **B5:B16** in the Range box. You have now selected your range for calculation.
5. In the Criteria box, key **>=200000**. Click **OK**. You have set your criteria of values greater than or equal to $200,000. Excel returns a value of 8.
6. Select **C25** and click **Recently Used** in the Function Library group.
7. Select **COUNTIF**. In the Functions Arguments box, in the Range box, select **C5:C16**.

8. In the Criteria box, key **>=200000**. Click **OK**. Excel returns a value of 6 when the formula is applied to the cell.

9. **SAVE** the workbook.

PAUSE. LEAVE the workbook open to use in the next exercise.

Using COUNTIFS

The COUNTIFS formula counts the number of cells within a range that meet multiple criteria. The syntax is COUNTIFS(range1, criteria1, range2, criteria2, and so on). You can create up to 127 ranges and criteria. In this exercise, you will perform calculations based on multiple criteria for the COUNTIFS formula.

STEP BY STEP   **Use COUNTIFS**

USE the workbook from the previous exercise.

1. Select **C26**. Click **Insert Function** in the Function Library group.

2. Key **COUNTIFS** in the *Search for a function* box and click **Go**. COUNTIFS will be highlighted in the Function box.

3. Click **OK** to accept the function and close the dialog box.

4. In the Function Arguments dialog box, select **F5:F16** in the Criteria_range1 box. You have selected your first range for calculation.

5. In the Criteria1 box, key **>=60**. The descriptions and tips for each argument box in the Function Arguments dialog box are replaced with the value when you navigate to the next argument box, as illustrated in Figure 9-5. The formula result is also displayed, enabling you to review and make corrections if an error message occurs or an unexpected result is returned. You have now set your first criterion. Excel shows the calculation up to this step as a value of 8.

Figure 9-5

Arguments and results for COUNTIFS formula

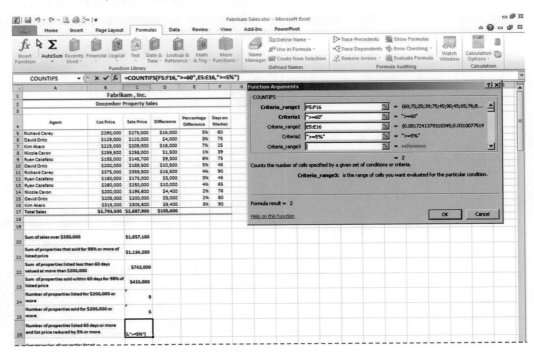

6. In the Criteria_range2 box, select **E5:E16**. You have selected your second range to be calculated.

7. In the Criteria2 box, key **>=5%**. Click **OK**. You have set your second criterion. When you click **OK**, Excel returns a value of 2.

8. **SAVE** the workbook.

PAUSE. LEAVE the workbook open to use in the next exercise.

A cell in the range you identify in the Function Arguments box is counted only if *all* of the corresponding criteria you specified are true for that cell. If a criterion refers to an empty cell, COUNTIFS treats it as a 0 value.

Take Note

When you create formulas, you can use the wildcard characters question mark (?) and asterisk (*) in your criteria. A question mark matches any single character; an asterisk matches any sequence of characters. If you want to find an actual question mark or asterisk, type a grave accent (`) preceding the character. You will apply this technique later in the lesson.

Using AVERAGEIF

The AVERAGEIF formula returns the arithmetic mean of all the cells in a range that meet a given criteria. The syntax is AVERAGEIF(range, criteria, average_range). In the AVERAGEIF syntax, *range* is the set of cells you want to average. For example, in this exercise, you use the AVERAGEIF function to calculate the average number of days properties valued at $200,000 or more were on the market before they were sold. The range in this formula is B5:B16 (cells that contain the listed value of the homes that were sold). The criterion is the condition against which you want the cells to be evaluated, that is, >=200000. Average_range is the actual set of cells to average—the number of days each home was on the market before it was sold.

STEP BY STEP **Use AVERAGEIF**

USE the workbook from the previous exercise.

1. Select **C27** and click **Recently Used** in the Function Library group.
2. Click **AVERAGE**. Key **B5:B16** in the Number1 box and click **OK**. A mathematical average for this range is returned.
3. Select **C28** and click **Insert Function** in the Function Library group.
4. Select **AVERAGEIF** from the function list or use the function search box to locate and accept the AVERAGEIF function; the Function Arguments dialog box now opens.
5. In the Function Arguments dialog box, select **B5:B16** in the Range box.
6. In the Criteria box, key **>=200000**.
7. In the Average_range box, select **F5:F16**. Click **OK** to close the dialog box. Excel returns a value of 63.33, as illustrated in Figure 9-6.

Figure 9-6

Results for AVERAGEIF formula

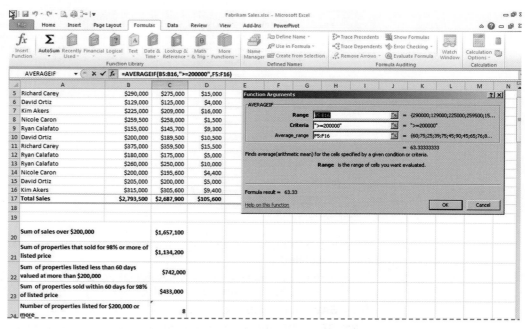

8. **SAVE** the workbook.

PAUSE. LEAVE the workbook open to use in the next exercise.

Using AVERAGEIFS

An AVERAGEIFS formula returns the average (arithmetic mean) of all cells that meet multiple criteria. The syntax is AVERAGEIFS(average_range, criteria_range1, criteria1, criteria_range2, criteria2, and so on). You will learn to apply the AVERAGEIFS formula in the following exercise.

STEP BY STEP   **Use AVERAGEIFS**

USE the workbook from the previous exercise.

1. Select **C29**. Click **Insert Function** in the Function Library group.
2. Key **AVERAGEIFS** in the *Search for a function* box and click **Go**. AVERAGEIFS will be highlighted in the Function box.
3. Click **OK** to accept the function and close the dialog box.
4. In the Function Arguments dialog box, select **F5:F16** in the Average_range box. Press **Tab**.
5. In the Criteria_range1 box, select **B5:B16** and press **Tab**. You have selected your first criteria range.
6. In the Criteria1 box, key **<200000**. You have set your first criteria.
7. In the Criteria_range2 box, select **E5:E16** and press **Tab**. You have now selected your second criteria range.
8. In the Criteria2 box, key **<=5%**. Click **OK**. Excel returns a value of 60.
9. **SAVE** and **CLOSE** the workbook.

PAUSE. LEAVE Excel open to use in the next exercise.

You entered only two criteria for the SUMIFS, COUNTIFS, and AVERAGEIFS formulas you created in the previous exercises. However, in very large worksheets, you often need to use multiple criteria in order for the formula to return a value that is meaningful for your analysis. You can enter up to 127 conditions that data must match in order for a cell to be included in the conditional summary that results from a SUMIFS, COUNTIFS, or AVERAGEIFS formula.

The following statements summarize how values are treated when you enter an AVERAGEIF or AVERAGEIFS formula:

- If Average_range is omitted from the function arguments, the range is used.
- If a cell in Average_range is an empty cell, AVERAGEIF ignores it.
- If a range is blank or contains a text value, AVERAGEIF returns the #DIV0! error value.
- If a cell in a criterion is empty, AVERAGEIF treats it as a 0 value.
- If no cells in the range meet the criteria, AVERAGEIF returns the #DIV/0! error value.

Take Note   You can reference another worksheet in the same workbook in a conditional formula, but you cannot use references to another workbook.

USING FORMULAS TO LOOK UP DATA IN A WORKBOOK

The Bottom Line

When worksheets contain long and sometimes cumbersome lists of data, you need a way to quickly find specific information within these lists. This is where Excel's **lookup functions** come in handy. Lookup functions are an efficient way to search for and insert a value in a cell when the desired value is stored elsewhere in the worksheet or even in a different workbook. VLOOKUP and HLOOKUP are the two lookup formulas that you will be using in this section. These functions can return cell references identifying where certain information is found, or they can return the actual contents of the found cell. As you work through the following exercises, note that the term **table** refers to a range of cells in a worksheet that can be used by a lookup function.

Using VLOOKUP

The V in VLOOKUP stands for *vertical*. This formula is used when the comparison values are located in a column to the left of the data that you want to find. The VLOOKUP function syntax is LOOKUP(lookup_value, table_array, col_index_num).

An **array** is used to build single formulas that produce multiple results or that operate on a group of arguments. You create and use array constants whenever you need to add sets of values that don't change (such as month names or pi) to your array formulas. Constants in your formulas process faster because they reside in memory and not in the workbook. The data in a table array must be arranged in rows and columns. It can be a constant or a formula. The VLOOKUP function searches for a value in the first column of a table array on the worksheet and then returns a value from a specific column, in the same row as the value it found, into a different location in the worksheet. In the next exercise, you will apply this formula to calculate employee bonuses.

When working with VLOOKUP and HLOOKUP functions and arguments, there are several key points to keep in mind:

- If lookup_value is smaller than the smallest value in the first column of table_array, VLOOKUP returns the #N/A error value.
- Table_array values can be text, numbers, or logical values. Uppercase and lowercase text is equivalent.
- The values in the first column of the table_array selection must be placed in ascending sort order, otherwise VLOOKUP may not give the correct value. The lookup table you use in this exercise lists years of service in ascending order.
- If the Range_lookup argument is True or omitted, an exact or approximate match is returned. If VLOOKUP cannot find an exact match, it returns the next largest value that is less than the value you have specified in lookup_value.
- If Range_lookup is False, VLOOKUP will find only an exact match. If an exact match is not found, the error value #N/A is returned.

STEP BY STEP   **Use VLOOKUP**

GET READY. LAUNCH Microsoft Excel if it is not already open.

1. **OPEN** the *Fabrikam Bonus* data file for this lesson.
2. With the Bonus sheet active, select **C15:F24** in the worksheet. Click the Formulas tab, and then click **Define Name** in the Defined Names group. The New Name dialog box opens.
3. Key **Bonus** in the Name box on the New Name dialog box. Click **OK** to close the dialog box. You have defined the range name.

Take Note   Arguments used in VLOOKUP or HLOOKUP are not case sensitive, so you can key them in uppercase, lowercase, or any combination of uppercase and lowercase characters. Also, the VLOOKUP and HLOOKUP function names are not case sensitive.

4. Select **E5** and click **Insert Function**.
5. In the *Search for a Function* box, key **VLOOKUP** and click **OK**. The Function Arguments dialog box opens with the cursor in the Lookup_value box.
6. Key **D5** and press **Tab**. The insertion point moves to the Table_array box.
7. In the Table_array box, click the **Collapse Dialog box** button. In the Defined Names group, click **Use in Formula** and select **Bonus**. Press **Tab**. The insertion point moves to the next text box.
8. In the Col_index_num box, key **2**, which is the column containing the standard bonus amounts. Press **Tab**.

9. In the Range_lookup box, key **True**; the same bonus is paid for a range of years, so you enter True in the Range_lookup box so that a value will be returned for all agents who have been with the company more than one year. Your Function Arguments dialog box should look similar to the one shown in Figure 9-7. Click **OK**. Excel returns a value of $750.

Figure 9-7

VLOOKUP in function arguments dialog box

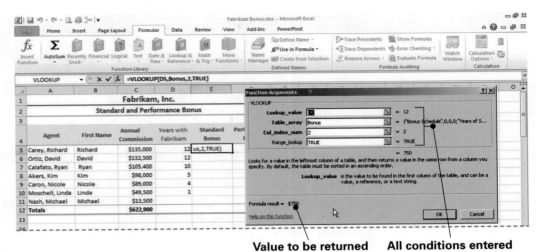

Value to be returned   **All conditions entered**

10. Using the fill handle in E5, copy the formula to the range E6:E11. This will calculate bonuses for the other sales agents. The N/A error message appears in E11 because a value is not available for agents who have been employed for less than one year. (Agents become eligible for a bonus only after a full year of service.) You will change this error message in another exercise.

11. **SAVE** the workbook as *Employee Bonus*.

PAUSE. LEAVE the workbook open to use in the next exercise.

Take Note   True in the Range_lookup box will return the closest value. False returns only an exact value. If you leave the Range_lookup box empty, Excel will enter True when you click OK.

Table 9-2 shows the argument components used in the VLOOKUP and HLOOKUP formulas. Refer also to Figure 9-8 and Figure 9-9.

Table 9-2

Function syntax for VLOOKUP

Key Combination	Formatting Applied
Lookup_value	The value to be found in the column or row; this can be a constant value, a text value enclosed in quotation marks, or the address or name of a cell that contains a numeric or text constant.
Table_array	Two or more columns of data. Use a reference to a range or a range name. The values in the first column of Table_array are the values searched by Lookup_value.
Row_index_num	The numeric position of the row that is to be searched for by HLOOKUP.
Col_index_num	The numeric position of the column that is to be searched for by VLOOKUP. The column number in Table_array from which the matching value must be returned. A Col_index_num of 1 returns the value in the first column in Table_array; a Col_index_num of 2 returns the value in the second column in Table_array, and so on.
Range_lookup	A logical value that specifies whether you want VLOOKUP to find an exact match or an approximate match. If the function is to return the nearest value, even when there is no match, this value should be set to True; if an exact match is required, this value should be set to False; if this argument is not included, the function assumes the value to be True.

Figure 9-8

VLOOKUP in the function
arguments dialog box

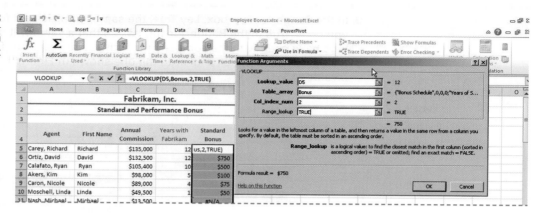

Figure 9-9

HLOOKUP in the function
arguments dialog box

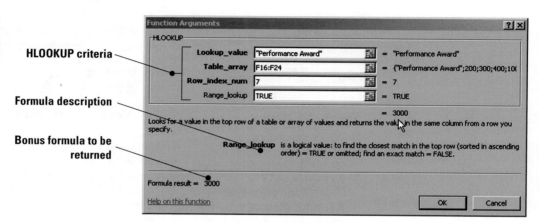

Using HLOOKUP

HLOOKUP searches for a value in the top row of a table or an array and then returns a value in the same column from a row you specify in the table or array. Use HLOOKUP when the comparison values are located in a row across the top of a table of data and you want to look down a specified number of rows. In the following exercise, you will use an HLOOKUP formula to determine who is eligible for the performance bonus.

STEP BY STEP   **Use HLOOKUP**

USE the workbook from the previous exercise.

1. Select **F5** and click **Insert Function** in the Function Library group.
2. In the *Search for a Function* box, key **HLOOKUP** and click **OK**. The *Function Arguments* dialog box opens with the cursor in the Lookup_value box.
3. Enter the HLOOKUP formula **=HLOOKUP("performance award",F16:F24,7,true)** in the argument boxes, as shown in Figure 9-9. Click **OK**. The performance bonus of 3000 is entered into the cell.
4. **SAVE** the workbook.

PAUSE. LEAVE the workbook open to use in the next exercise.

It may be difficult to remember the syntax for an HLOOKUP or VLOOKUP function. Remember, you can always use the Function Arguments dialog box to help you remember the order of the arguments for any and all formulas. When you click in each field, review the tips that appear on the right side of each box, as well as the explanation below the argument boxes that tells the purpose of each argument in the formula.

ADDING CONDITIONAL LOGIC FUNCTIONS TO FORMULAS

The Bottom Line

You can use the AND, OR, and NOT functions to create conditional formulas that result in a logical value, that is, True or False. Such formulas test whether conditions are true or false and make logical comparisons. In addition, you can use the IF, AND, and OR functions to create a conditional formula that results in another calculation or in values other than True or False.

Using IF

The result of a conditional formula is determined by the state of a specific condition or the answer to a logical question. An IF function sets up a conditional statement to test data. An IF formula returns one value if the condition you specify is true and another value if it is false. The IF function requires the following syntax: IF(logical_test, value_if_true, value if false). In this exercise, you will use an IF function to determine who is eligible for the performance bonus.

STEP BY STEP   **Use IF**

USE the workbook you saved in the previous exercise.

1. Click the Performance worksheet tab to make it the active worksheet.
2. Select **D5**. Click **Logical** in the Function Library group and click **IF**. The Function Arguments dialog box opens.
3. Key **C5>=B5** in the Logical_test box. This component of the formula determines whether the agent has met his or her sales goal.
4. Key **Yes** in the Value_if_true box. This is the value returned if the agent met his or her goal. Keep in mind as you enter these values that they aren't case sensitive. Keying **yes** will therefore yield the same results in the formula. The output text in the cell will directly reflect what you have keyed.
5. Key **No** in the Value_if_false box and click **OK**.
6. With D5 still selected, use the fill handle to copy the formula to D6:D11. Excel returns the result that four agents have earned the performance award by displaying Yes in the cells. (See Figure 9-10.)

Figure 9-10

Using the IF function

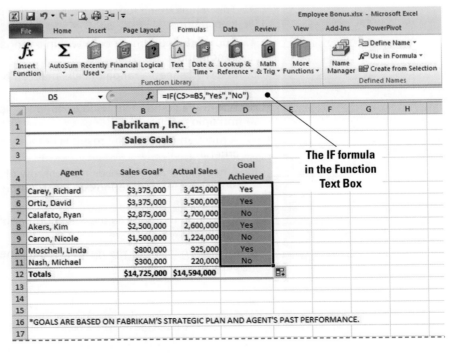

7. **SAVE** the workbook.

PAUSE. LEAVE the workbook open to use in the next exercise **CLOSE** Excel.

SKILL SUMMARY

In This Lesson You Learned How To:
Use formulas to conditionally summarize data
Use formulas to look up data in a workbook
Add conditional logic functions to formulas

Knowledge Assessment

Matching

Match each vocabulary term with its definition.

a. IF
b. arguments
c. array
d. conditional formula
e. HLOOKUP

f. CountIF
g. SUMIF
h. SUMIFS
i. Table
j. VLOOKUP

_____ 1. A function used to look up information stored in the first column of an Excel table in the worksheet.

_____ 2. Checks if a condition is met and returns one value if True, and another value if False.

_____ 3. The values that a function uses to perform operations or calculations.

_____ 4. Counts the number of cells within a range that meet the given condition.

_____ 5. In a worksheet, a range of cells that can be used by a lookup formula.

_____ 6. A formula component used to build single formulas that produce multiple results.

_____ 7. A function in which the result is determined by the state of multiple criteria.

_____ 8. A function that references the first row of an Excel table in the worksheet in order to look up information stored in the same column.

_____ 9. A function that returns the total number of cells that meet one condition.

_____ 10. A function in which the result is determined by the state of a particular condition.

Multiple Choice

Select the best response for the following statements.

1. Which function is used to sum values in a range?
   a. SUMIFS
   b. COUNTIF
   c. SUMIF
   d. AVERAGEIFS

2. Which function automatically counts cells that meet multiple conditions?
   a. COUNTIF
   b. COUNT
   c. COUNTIFS
   d. SUMIFS

3. Which function automatically counts cells that meet a specific condition?
   a. COUNTIF
   b. COUNT
   c. COUNTIFS
   d. SUMIFS

4. In the formula =SUMIFS(C5:C16,F5:F16,"<=60","B5:B16,">200000"), the range of cells to be added is:
   a. =C5:C16.
   b. =F5:F16.
   c. =B5:B16.
   d. =C5:F16.

5. In the formula =SUMIFS(C5:C16,F5:F16,"<=60","B5:B16,">200000"), <=60 means:
   a. if the value in C5:C16 is greater than or equal to 60, the value in C5:16 will be included in the total.
   b. if the value in F5:F16 is greater than or equal to 60, the value in C5:16 will be included in the total.
   c. if the value in B5:BF16 is less than or equal to 60, the value in C5:16 will be included in the total.
   d. if the value in F5:F16 is less than or equal to 60, the value in C5:16 will be included in the total.

6. *Criteria range* in a formula refers to:
   a. the worksheet data to be included in the formula's results.
   b. the range containing a condition that must be met in order for data to be included in the result.
   c. the type of formula being used for the calculation.
   d. the type of data contained in the cells to be included in the formula.

7. Which function returns one value if a condition is true and a different value when the condition is *not* true?
   a. AND
   b. OR
   c. IF
   d. IFERROR

8. Which function is used to count values in a range if a criteria is met?
   a. COUNTIF
   b. COUNTIFS
   c. COUNT
   d. all of the above

9. An argument is surrounded by:
   a. ( )
   b. { }
   c. [ ]
   d. < >
10. A function used to look up information stored in the top row of an Excel table.
   a. VLOOKUP
   b. HLOOKUP
   c. LOOKUP
   d. LOOKUP FUNCTIONS

Competency Assessment

Project 9-1: Creating SUMIF and SUMIFS Formulas to Conditionally Summarize Data

Salary information for Contoso, Ltd., has been entered in a workbook so the office manager can analyze and summarize the data. In the following exercise, you will calculate sums with conditions.

GET READY. LAUNCH Excel.

@ The *Salaries* file for this lesson is available on the book companion website or in WileyPLUS.

1. **OPEN** the *Salaries* data file for this lesson.
2. Select **F4** and click **Insert Function** in the Function Library group.
3. If the SUMIF function is not visible, key **SUMIF** in the *Search for a function* box and click **Go**. Select **SUMIF** from the *Select a function* list. Click **OK**.
4. In the Function Arguments dialog box, select **C4:C33** in the Range field.
5. In the Criteria box, key **>100000**.
6. Click **OK**. Because the range and sum range are the same, it is not necessary to enter a sum range.
7. Select **F5** and click **Insert Function**. Select **SUMIFS** and click **OK**.
8. In the Function Arguments dialog box, select **C4:C33** as the sum range.
9. Select **D4:D33** as the first criteria range.
10. Key **>=10** as the first criterion.
11. Select **C4:C33** as the second criteria range.
12. Key **>60000** as the second criterion. Click **OK** to finish the formula.
13. **SAVE** the workbook as *Salaries 9-1*. **CLOSE** the file.

LEAVE Excel open to use in the next project.

Project 9-2: Creating COUNTIF and AVERAGEIF Formulas

In this exercise, you will enter COUNTIF and AVERAGEIF formulas to analyze and summarize grades for a course at the School of Fine Arts.

GET READY. LAUNCH Excel if it is not already running.

@ The *SFA Grades* file for this lesson is available on the book companion website or in WileyPLUS.

1. **OPEN** the *SFA Grades* data file for this lesson.
2. Select **N4** and click **Insert Function** in the Function Library group on the Formulas tab.
3. If the COUNT function is not visible, key **COUNT** in the *Search for a function* box and click **Go**. Select **COUNT** from the *Select a function* list. Click **OK**.
4. Select **L4:L41** in the Value1 field. Click **OK**.
5. Select **N5** and click **Insert Function**.

6. Select COUNTIF and click OK.
7. In the Range field, key $M$4:$M$41. This is an absolute reference.
8. Key A in the Criteria field and click OK.
9. Copy the formula in N5 to N6:N8.
10. Select N6. In the formula bar, select A (the criterion) and key B. Press Enter.
11. Select N7. In the formula bar, select A (the criterion) and key C. Press Enter.
12. Select N8. In the formula bar, select A (the criterion) and key D. Press Enter.
13. Select N10, click Insert Function, and select AVERAGEIF.
14. Select M4:M41 as the range to evaluate.
15. Key A as the criterion. Select L4:L41 in the Average_range field. Click OK.
16. **SAVE** the workbook as *SFA Grades 9-2* and then **CLOSE** the file.

LEAVE Excel open for the next project.

Proficiency Assessment

Project 9-3: Creating LOOKUP Formulas

In this project, you will use a lookup table to determine an employee's end-of-year bonus.

GET READY. LAUNCH Excel if it is not already running.

@ The *Contoso Bonus* file for this lesson is available on the book companion website or in WileyPLUS.

1. **OPEN** the *Contoso Bonus* data file for this lesson.
2. Select B36:C44 and on the Formulas tab, click Define Name.
3. Key Bonus in the Name box and click OK.
4. Select E4 and click Lookup & Reference in the Function Library group. Click VLOOKUP.
5. Select D4 in the Lookup_value field. Press Tab.
6. Key Bonus in the Table_array field. Press Tab.
7. Key 2 in the Col_index_num field. Press Tab.
8. Key True in the Range_lookup field. Click OK.
9. Use the fill handle to copy the formula from E4 to E5:E33.
10. **SAVE** the workbook as *Contoso Bonus 9-3*, and then **CLOSE** the file.

LEAVE Excel open for the next project.

Project 9-4: Using the HLookup Function

You are working as a teaching assistant and the professor has asked you to post the letter grade for each student.

GET READY. LAUNCH Excel if not already running.

@ The *Grade Book* file for this lesson is available on the book companion website or in WileyPLUS.

1. **OPEN** the *Grade Book* data file for this lesson.
2. Select M4 and click Formula tab then click the Lookup Reference in the Function Library group. Click HLOOKUP.
3. Select L4 in the Lookup_value field. Press Tab.
4. Select P7:T8 in the Table_array field then press F4. Press Tab.
5. Key 2 in the Row_index_num field. Click OK.
6. Use the fill handle to copy the formula from M4 to M5:M41.
7. **SAVE** the workbook as *Grade Book 9-4*.

LEAVE Excel open for the next project.

Project 9-5: Creating Conditional Logic Formulas

Professor Garrett Young has asked you to create formulas to identify the highest and lowest achieving students in one of his classes.

@ The *Grades* file for this lesson is available on the book companion website or in WileyPLUS.

GET READY. LAUNCH Excel if it is not already running.

1. **OPEN** the *Grades* file for this lesson.
2. Select **M4** and click **Logical** in the Function Library group.
3. Select **IF** on the function list.
4. Key **L4>=90%**.
5. In the Value_if_true box, key **High**.
6. In the Value_if_false box, press **Spacebar**. (Pressing the spacebar will insert a space so that the cells that do not meet the criterion will be blank.) Click **OK**.
7. Using the fill handle, copy the formula in M4 to M5:M27.
8. Select **N4**, click **Logical**, and click **IF**.
9. Key **L4<70%**.
10. In the Value_if_true box, key **Low**.
11. In the Value_if_false box, press **Spacebar**. Click **OK**.
12. Copy the formula in N4 to N5:N27.
13. **SAVE** the workbook as *Grades 9-5* and then **CLOSE** the file.

LEAVE Excel open for the next project.

Project 9-6: Using the IF Function and Conditional Formatting

You are working as a teaching assistant and the professor has asked you to use a logical function to determine who has passed or failed the course. In this project, you will use the IF function to determine if the student has passed the course and apply a conditional formatting to highlight those students who have failed.

GET READY. LAUNCH Excel if not already running.

1. **OPEN** the *Grade Book 9-4* that you completed in an earlier exercise.
2. Select **G25** and change the grade to zero.
3. Select **N3** and key **Pass / Fail**.
4. Select **N4** and click **Logical** in the Function Library group.
5. Select **IF** on the function list.
6. Key **L4>=70**.
7. In the Value_if_true, key **Pass**.
8. In the Value_if_false, key **Fail**. Click **OK**.
9. Copy the formula in N4 to N5:N41.
10. **SAVE** the workbook as *Grade Book 9-6*.

LEAVE Excel open for the next project.

INTERNET READY

If you are employed, does your employer provide a seniority-based bonus similar to the one offered by Fabrikam in the practice exercises? If your employer offers a bonus program, create a lookup table similar to the ones you used in this chapter that could be used to assign bonus amounts to employees.

Go online and research a company where you would like to seek employment when you complete your coursework. What salary and benefits are provided? If you can locate data related to a bonus or profit-sharing program, create a lookup table with the information. Create only the lookup table that could be added to a salary worksheet. For example, Payscale .com, a private research group, reported that in 2006, the average annual bonus for an administrative assistant was $800. Such a bonus might be tied to years of service or to an employee's performance ranking.

Create a worksheet to report your research findings. Format all data appropriately. Save your worksheet as *Bonus and Incentives*. Close Excel.

10 Creating and Modifying Charts

LESSON SKILL MATRIX

In This Lesson, You Will Learn The Following Skills:

Building Charts

Formatting a Chart with a Quick Style

Formatting the Parts of a Chart Manually

Modifying a Chart

KEY TERMS

- **axis**
- **chart**
- **chart area**
- **chart sheet**
- **data labels**
- **data marker**
- **data series**
- **embedded chart**
- **legend**
- **legend keys**
- **plot area**
- **title**

Fourth Coffee owns espresso cafes in 15 major markets. Its primary income is generated from the sale of trademarked, freshly brewed coffee and espresso drinks. The cafes also sell a variety of pastries, packaged coffees and teas, deli-style sandwiches, and coffee-related accessories and gift items. In preparation for an upcoming budget meeting, the corporate manager wants to create charts to show trends in each of the five revenue categories for a five-year period and to project those trends to future sales. Because Excel allows you to track and work with substantial amounts of data, it is sometimes difficult to see the big picture by looking at the details in a worksheet. With Excel's charting capabilities, you can summarize and highlight data, reveal trends, and make comparisons that might not be obvious when looking at the raw data. You will use charts, PivotTables and several other useful tools to filter and present the data for Fourth Coffee.

SOFTWARE ORIENTATION

The Insert Tab

The Insert tab contains the command groups you'll use to create charts in Excel (see Figure 10-1). To create a basic chart in Excel that you can modify and format later, start by entering the data for the chart on a worksheet. Then, you can select that data and choose a chart type to graphically display the data. Simply by choosing a chart type, a chart layout, and a chart style—all of which are within easy reach on the Insert tab's ribbon—you will have instant professional results every time you create a chart.

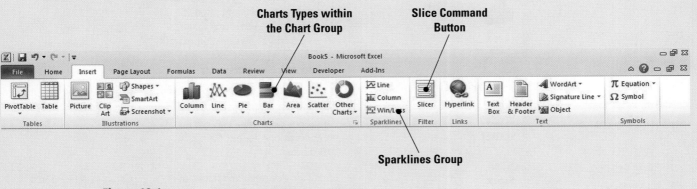

Figure 10-1

Insert tab

Use this illustration as a reference throughout this lesson as you become familiar with and use Excel's charting capabilities to create attention-getting illustrations that communicate an analysis of your data.

BUILDING CHARTS

The Bottom Line

A **chart** is a graphical representation of numeric data in a worksheet. Creating a chart is quick and easy in Excel, and the program provides a variety of chart types from which to choose. To build a chart in Excel, you must first select the data that will be included in the chart, then choose the type of chart in which you want to display the data.

When you want to create a chart or change an existing chart, you can choose from 11 chart types and numerous subtypes. Table 10-1 gives a brief description of each Excel chart type.

Table 10-1

Chart types

Icon	Chart Name	Function	Data Arrangement
Column	Column	Useful for showing data changes over a period of time or illustrating comparisons among data.	Columns or rows
Line	Line	Useful for showing trends in data at equal intervals. Displays continuous data over time set against a common scale. Values are represented as points along a line.	Columns or rows
Pie	Pie	Useful for showing the size of items in one data series, proportional to the sum of the items. Data points are displayed as a percentage of a circular pie.	One column or row
Bar	Bar	Useful for illustrating comparisons among individual items. Useful when axis labels are long or values are durations. Values are represented as horizontal rectangles.	Columns or rows
Area	Area	Useful for emphasizing magnitude of change over time; can be used to draw attention to the total value across a trend. Shows relationship of parts to the whole. Values represented as shaded areas.	Columns or rows
Scatter	Scatter	Useful for showing relationships among the numeric values in several data series or plotting two groups of numbers as one series of XY coordinates.	Columns or rows
Stock	Stock	Useful for illustrating the fluctuation of stock prices or scientific data.	Columns or rows in a specific order
Surface	Surface	Useful for finding optimum combinations between two sets of data. Use this chart when categories and data series are numeric values.	Columns or rows

Doughnut	Doughnut	Useful for displaying the relationship of parts to a whole; can contain more than one data series. Values are represented as sections of a circular band.	Columns or rows
Bubble	Bubble	Useful for comparing three sets of values. The third value determines the size of the bubble marker.	Columns with x values in first column and y values in adjacent columns
Radar	Radar	Useful for showing the trends of values relative to a center point; represents values as points that radiate from the center. Lines connect values in the series.	Columns or rows

Selecting Data to Include in a Chart

Excel's Ribbon interface makes it incredibly simple to create a chart. As you will see in the following exercise, you can create one of the common chart types by clicking its image on the Insert tab. More important than the chart type, however, is the selection of the data you want to display graphically. What aspects of the data do you want viewers to notice? The answer to that question is a major factor in selecting an appropriate chart type. In this exercise, you will learn to select data for use in an Excel chart that returns your calculations and data in a color-coded pie chart with sections identified by numbers, legends, titles, and other various data information.

STEP BY STEP   **Select Data to Include in a Chart**

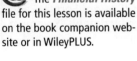

The *Financial History* file for this lesson is available on the book companion website or in WileyPLUS.

WileyPLUS Extra! features an online tutorial of this task.

GET READY. Before you begin these steps, **LAUNCH** Microsoft Excel.

1. **OPEN** the *Financial History* file for this lesson.
2. Select B4:B10 (the 2004 data) on the Sales History worksheet.
3. On the **Insert** tab, in the Charts group, click the **Pie** button. Click the **first** 2-D Pie chart. A color-coded pie chart with sections identified by number is displayed and the Chart Tools tabs (Design, Layout, and Format) become available, with the Design tab active. This chart, however, doesn't work: It includes the column label (2004) and total sales amount as its two largest portions, and these amounts should not be included in an analysis of sales for 2004.
4. Click in the chart's white space and press Delete. The chart is now deleted and the Chart Tools tab disappears.

5. Select **B5:B9**, click the **Insert** tab, click **Pie** in the Charts group, and click the **first** 2-D Pie chart. The correct data is displayed, but the chart is difficult to interpret with only numbers to identify the parts of the pie as illustrated in Figure 10-2.

Figure 10-2

Pie chart before formatting

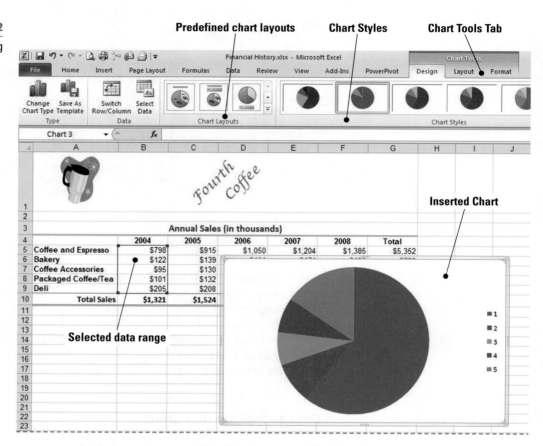

6. Click in the chart's white space and press **Delete**.

7. Select **A4:B9**, click the **Insert** tab, and click **Pie** in the Charts group. Click the **first** 2-D Pie chart. As illustrated in Figure 10-3, the data is clearly identified with a title and a label for each pie section.

Troubleshooting When you insert a chart into your worksheet, the Chart Tools tabs (Design, Format, and Layout) become available in Excel's Ribbon with the Design tab active by default. You must select the Insert tab on the Ribbon each time you want to insert a chart.

Figure 10-3

Formatted pie chart

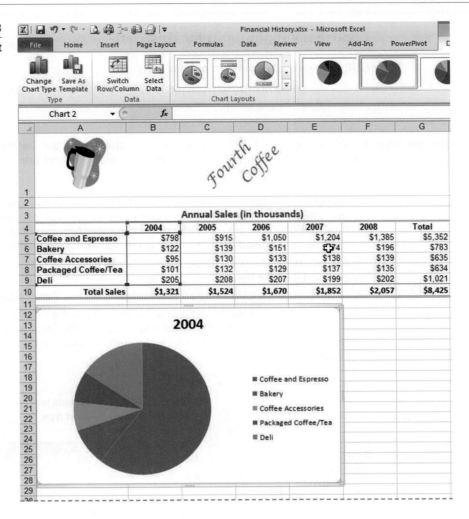

8. **CREATE** a Lesson 10 folder and **SAVE** the workbook as *Building Charts*.

PAUSE. LEAVE the workbook open to use in the next exercise.

This exercise illustrates that the chart's data selection must contain sufficient information to interpret the data at a glance. You will improve the display in subsequent exercises when you apply predefined layouts and styles. Excel did not distinguish between the column B label and its data when you selected only the data in column B. Although the label is formatted as text, because the column label was numeric, it was interpreted as data to be included in the graph. When you expanded the selection to include the row labels, 2004 was correctly recognized as a label and displayed as the title for the pie chart.

When you selected data and created a pie chart, the chart was placed on the worksheet. This is referred to as an **embedded chart**, meaning it is placed on the worksheet rather than on a separate **chart sheet**, a sheet that contains only a chart.

Choosing the Right Chart for Your Data

You can create most charts, such as column and bar charts, from data that you have arranged in rows or columns in a worksheet. Some charts, such as pie and bubble charts, require a specific data arrangement. The pie chart cannot be used for comparisons across periods of time or for analyzing trends. The column chart works well for comparisons. In a 2-D or 3-D column chart, each data marker is represented by a column. In a stacked column, data markers are stacked so that a column represents a data series. In this exercise, you learn how to create a column chart to illustrate the significant increase in coffee and espresso sales at Fourth Coffee during a five-year period.

STEP BY STEP   **Choose the Right Chart for Your Data**

USE the workbook from the previous exercise.

1. On the Sales History worksheet, click on the pie chart's white space and press Delete to delete the pie chart.

> **Troubleshooting**   To delete a chart, click in the white space then press the Delete key on your keyboard. If you click on the graphic or another chart element and press Delete, only the selected element will be deleted.

2. Select A4:F9, click the Insert tab, and click Column in the Charts group on the Insert tab. Click 3-D Clustered Column on the drop-down list (first subtype under 3-D Column). The column chart illustrates the sales for each of the revenue categories for the five-year period. The Chart Tools tab appears with the Design tab active.

3. Anywhere on the chart, click, hold and drag the chart below the worksheet data and position it at the far left.

4. Click outside the column chart to deselect it. Notice that the Chart Tools tab disappears.

5. Select A4:F9, click the Insert tab, and click Line in the Charts group. Click 2-D Line with Markers (first chart in the second row). Position the line chart next to the column chart. Note that the Chart Tools tab is on the Ribbon with the Design tab active. Refer to Figure 10-4.

Figure 10-4

Bar chart and line chart

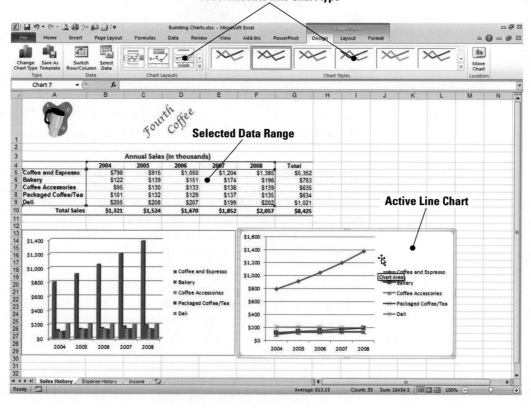

6. **SAVE** the workbook with the same name, *Building Charts*.

PAUSE. LEAVE the workbook open to use in the next exercise.

The column and line charts provide two views of the same data, illustrating that the chart type you choose depends on the analysis you want the chart to portray. The pie chart, which shows values as part of the whole, accurately displayed the distribution of sales for one year. Column and line charts allow you to make comparisons over a period of time as well as comparisons among items.

The line chart you created in this exercise is shown in Figure 10-5. The chart includes data markers to indicate each year's sales. A **data marker** is a bar, area, dot, slice, or other symbol in a chart that represents a single data point or value that originates from a worksheet cell. Related data markers in a chart constitute a **data series**. The line chart is a good analysis tool. The chart you created illustrates not only the growth in coffee and espresso sales, but reveals a modest increase in bakery sales and static activity in the sale of packaged products.

Figure 10-5

Line chart with data markers

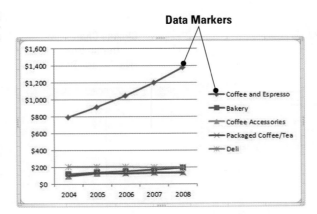

Creating a Bar Chart

Bar charts are similar to column charts and can be used to illustrate comparisons among individual items. Data that is arranged in columns or rows on a worksheet can be plotted in a bar chart. Clustered bar charts compare values across categories. Stacked bar charts show the relationship of individual items to the whole of that item. The side-by-side bar charts you create in this exercise illustrate two views of the same data. You can experiment with chart types and select the one that best portrays the message you want to convey to your target audience.

STEP BY STEP   **Create a Bar Chart**

USE the workbook from the previous exercise.

1. Click the Expense History workbook tab.
2. Select A4:F9. Click the Bar icon in the Charts Group on the Insert tab.

Take Note   A ScreenTip displays the chart type name when you rest the mouse pointer over a chart type or chart subtype.

3. Click the Clustered Bar in 3-D subtype. The data is displayed in a clustered bar chart and the Design tab is active on the Chart Tools tab.
4. Position the clustered bar chart on the left below the worksheet data.
5. Deselect the chart by clicking anywhere on the worksheet; select A4:F9. On the Insert tab, click the Bar icon in the Charts group.
6. Click Stacked Bar in 3-D.
7. Position the stacked bar graph next to the 3-D bar graph.
8. **SAVE** and **CLOSE** the workbook.

PAUSE. LEAVE Excel open to use in the next exercise.

The Charts group on the Insert tab contains six of the eleven chart types. To create one of these charts, select the worksheet data and click the icon. You can insert one of the other five chart types by clicking the Charts Dialog Box Launcher to open the Change Chart Type dialog box shown in Figure 10-6.

Figure 10-6

Change chart type dialog box

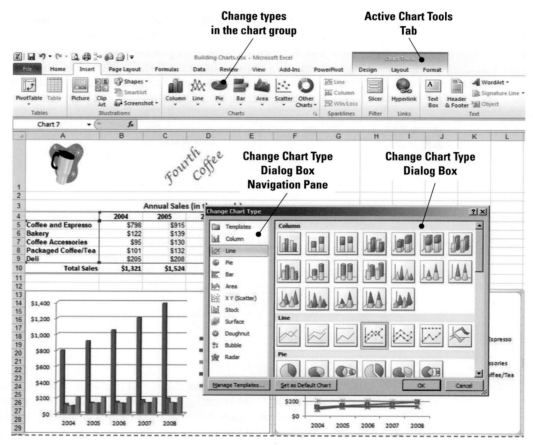

Another Way
You can open the Insert Chart dialog box by clicking Other Charts and then clicking All Chart Types at the bottom of the drop-down list.

When you click a chart type in the left pane of the dialog box, the first chart of that type is selected in the right pane. You can also scroll through the right pane and select any chart subtype.

When you apply a predefined chart style, the chart is formatted based on the document theme that you have applied. The Metro theme was applied to the Financial History workbook. The Metro theme colors were therefore applied to the charts you created in the preceding exercises.

FORMATTING A CHART WITH A QUICK STYLE

The Bottom Line

After you create a chart, you can instantly change its appearance by applying a predefined layout or style. Excel provides a variety of useful quick layouts and quick styles from which you can choose. As shown in Figure 10-7, when you create a chart, the chart tools become available and the Design, Layout, and Format tabs are added to the Ribbon.

Figure 10-7

Chart tools tab activates when a chart is inserted

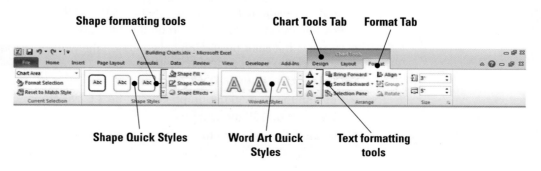

Formatting a Chart with a Quick Style

Predefined layouts and styles are timesaving features that you can use to enhance the appearance of your charts. Quick styles, as defined by Microsoft, are the Chart Styles available on the Chart Style group of the Design Tab in the Chart Tools tab. They are Quick Styles because you can click them in an instant instead of searching through the Chart Styles Gallery. In this exercise, you will apply a Quick Style to your chart.

STEP BY STEP   **Format a Chart with a Quick Style**

GET READY. LAUNCH Microsoft Excel if it is not already open.

1. **OPEN** the *Financial History* file for this lesson.

2. On the Expense History worksheet tab, select **A4:A9**. Press **Ctrl** and select **F4:F9**. You have selected two nonadjacent ranges to use for your chart.

3. On the **Insert** tab, click **Pie** in the Charts group and click **Pie** (the first option on the left) under 2-D. The 2008 data is displayed on the chart and the Design tab is active (see Figure 10-8).

Figure 10-8

Quick Style applied to chart

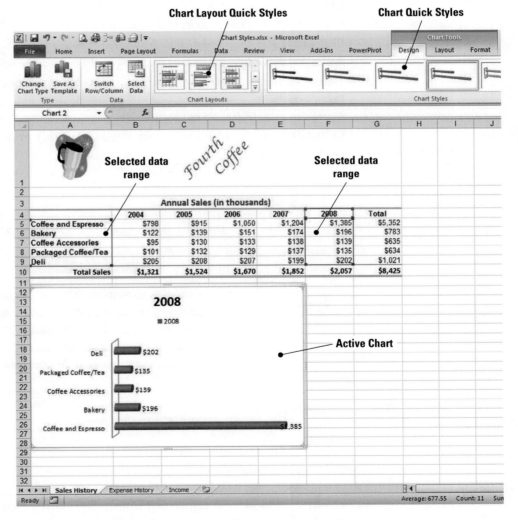

4. In the Chart Layouts group on the Design tab, click **Layout 1**. The pie chart now displays the percentage that each sales category contributes to total sales. When you apply Layout 1 and Style 4 to the expense chart, additional information is added to the chart and the appearance changes.

5. In the Chart Styles group, click **Style 4**. The chart's color scheme is changed. Position the chart below the data. You have just applied a Quick Style.

6. On the Sales History worksheet, select **A4:A9**. Press **Ctrl** and select **F4:F9**. You have again selected nonadjacent cell ranges to use in the next chart.

7. Click **Bar** in the Charts group and click **Clustered Horizontal Cylinder** (third row). The clustered bar chart appears on the worksheet.

8. Drag the chart below the worksheet data.

9. Click **Layout 2** in the Chart Layouts group on the Design tab. Click **Style 4** in the Chart Styles group. You have applied your second Quick Style.

10. **SAVE** the workbook as *Chart Styles*.

PAUSE. LEAVE the workbook open to use in the next exercise.

Take Note   To see all predefined styles, click the More arrow in the Chart Styles Group.

FORMATTING THE PARTS OF A CHART MANUALLY

The Bottom Line   The Format tab provides a variety of ways to format chart elements. To format a chart element, click the chart element that you want to change, then use the appropriate commands from the Format tab.

The following list defines some of the chart elements you can manually format in Excel. These elements are illustrated in Figure 10-9:

- **Chart area:** The entire chart and all its elements.
- **Plot area:** The area bounded by the axes.
- **Axis:** A line bordering the chart plot area used as a frame of reference for measurement.
- **Title:** Descriptive text that is automatically aligned to an axis or centered at the top of a chart.
- **Data labels:** Text that provides additional information about a data marker, which represents a single data point or value that originates from a worksheet cell.
- **Legend:** A box that identifies the patterns or colors that are assigned to the data series or categories in a chart.

Figure 10-9

Chart elements

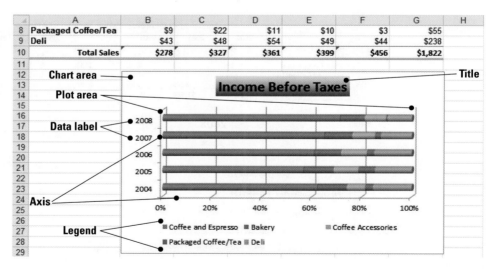

Changing a Chart's Fill Color or Pattern

Use commands on the Format tab to add or change fill colors or patterns applied to chart elements. Select the element to format and launch the Format dialog box or use the commands in the Shape Styles group on the Format tab to add fill color or a pattern to the selected chart element. When you select any chart element and click Format Selection, an element-specific dialog box opens. For example, if you click the data series, the Format Data Series dialog box opens. The Shape Fill color choices are those associated with the theme applied to the worksheet. You can use the Shape Fill command to fill any shape with color, gradient, or texture. In this exercise, you will customize the look of your chart by modifying the fill colors and patterns.

STEP BY STEP **Change the Chart's Fill Color or Pattern**

USE the workbook from the previous exercise.

1. Click in the chart area of the Clustered Horizontal Cylinder chart on the Sales History worksheet to display the Chart Tools on the Ribbon.

2. Click the **Format** tab and click **Format Selection** in the Current Selection group. The Format Chart Area dialog box opens. See Figure 10-10.

Figure 10-10

Format chart area dialog box

Format Selection Button	Format Chart Area Navigation Pane	Format Chart Area Dialog Box	Format Chart Area Options Pane

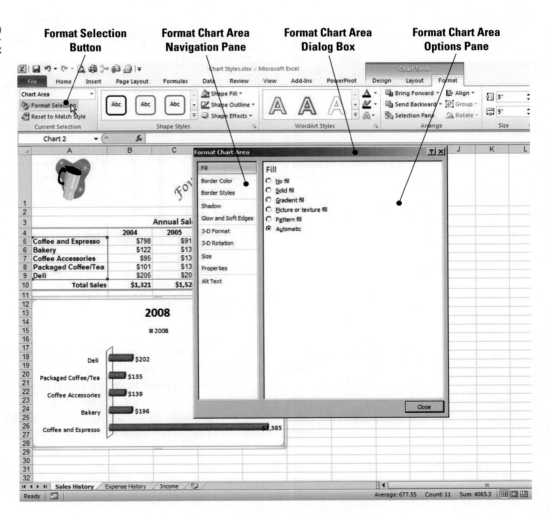

Take Note   To display the Chart Tools, you must select the chart. If a worksheet cell is active, the Design, Layout, and Format tabs are not available.

3. Select **Solid fill**. Click the **Color** arrow and click **Olive Green, Accent 3, Lighter 40%**. A light green fill has been added to the entire background chart area.

4. Select **Picture or texture fill**. Click the **Texture** arrow and click **Newsprint** (center of selection options). The textured format replaces the color fill as the background in the chart area.

5. Click **Close** to close the dialog box.

6. In the Current Selection group, click the **arrow** in the Chart Elements selection box and click **Plot Area**. The plot area in the chart becomes active as illustrated in Figure 10-11.

Figure 10-11

Chart elements area

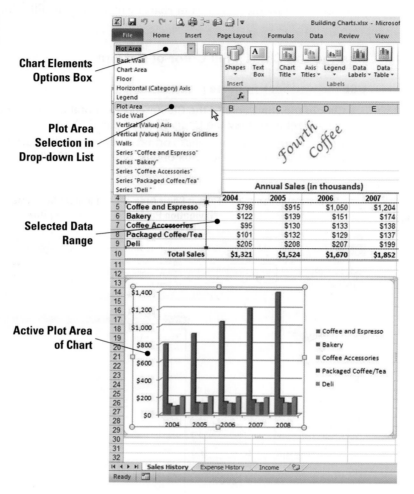

7. Click the **More** arrow next to the colored outlines window in the Shape Styles group. The Outline Colors Style Gallery opens.

8. Mouse over the Outline Style gallery to locate and click **Subtle Effect – Blue, Accent 1**. This applies a light blue gradient style to the plot area.

9. In the Current Selection group, click the arrow in the Chart Elements selection box and click **Legend**. This action makes the legend inside the chart active. Press **Delete**.

Take Note

Legend Keys appear to the left of legend entries and identify the color-coded data series. Because this chart contains only one data series, the legend is unnecessary.

10. **SAVE** your workbook.

PAUSE. LEAVE the workbook open to use in the next exercise.

When you use the mouse to point to an element in the chart, the element name appears in a ScreenTip. You can select the element you want to format by clicking the arrow next to the Chart Elements box in the Current Selection group on the Format tab. Figure 10-11 shows the list of chart elements in the bar chart on the Sales History worksheet. This list is chart specific. Legend is not listed because you deleted that element from the chart. When you click the arrow, the list will include all elements that you have included in the displayed chart.

Changing the Chart's Border Line

You can outline any or all chart elements. Just select the element and apply one of the predefined outlines or click Shape Outline to format the shape of a selected chart element. You can apply a border around any chart element as well as around the entire chart. Select an element or the chart and use the colored outlines in the Shape Styles group on the Format tab, or click Shape Outlines and choose a Theme or Standard color for the border.

STEP BY STEP | **Change the Chart's Border Line**

USE the workbook you saved in the previous exercise.

1. In the Current Selection group, click the arrow in the Chart Elements selection box and click Chart Area. The chart area section on the chart becomes active.

2. Click the more arrow next to the colored outlines window in the Shape Styles group. The Outline Colors Style Gallery opens.

3. Scroll through the outline styles to locate and click Colored Outline – Blue, Accent 1. The chart is outlined with a light blue border.

4. In the Current Selection group, click the arrow in the Chart Elements selection box and click Plot Area.

5. Mouse over the Outline Style gallery to locate and click Colored Outline – Red, Accent 2. A red border is placed around the plot area.

6. In the Current Selection group, click the arrow in the Chart Elements selection box and click Walls. This activates the walls inside your chart. Mouse over the Outline Style gallery to locate and click Colored Outline – Black, Dark 1. Your chart will resemble Figure 10-12.

Figure 10-12

Formatted chart elements

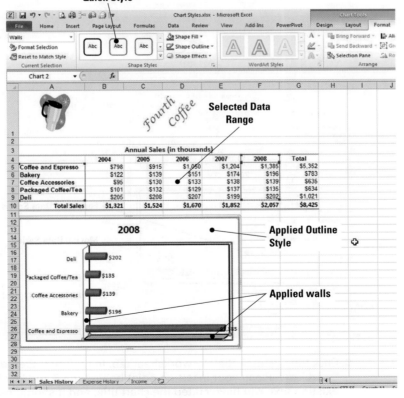

7. SAVE your workbook.

PAUSE. LEAVE the workbook open to use in the next exercise.

Formatting the Data Series

The chart is a communication tool, and you use formatting to call attention to significant data. When you clarified the chart title in the pie chart, you clarified the chart's contents. In this exercise, you make the bar chart's content easier to understand when you add a data series and format the series to call attention to the figures. You can apply fill color to the data series; outline the series with a border; change the shape; or add special effects to the columns, bars, and so on, that represent the data series.

STEP BY STEP **Format the Data Series**

USE the workbook you saved in the previous exercise.

1. Select the chart on the Sales History worksheet. Click the arrow in the Chart Elements selection box and select Series "2008". This makes the cylinders in the chart active.
2. In the Shape Styles group, click Shape Fill. The color gallery opens.
3. Point to Texture. Click Denim. Your chart cylinders have now had the Denim texture applied.
4. Click the arrow in the Chart Elements selection box and click Series "2008" Data Labels. The data labels in your chart are now active.
5. Click Shape Outline in the Shape Styles group. This opens the color gallery.
6. Click Blue under Standard Colors.
7. Mouse over the data series for coffee and espresso on the bottom cylinder to activate the crosshair cursor. Click and hold the left mouse button to drag the data series above the bar so that the label is completely visible. See Figure 10-13.

Figure 10-13

Move a formatted data series

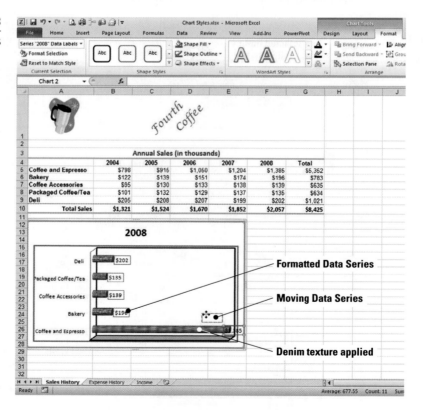

8. Click the Expense History worksheet tab. In the Chart Elements selection box click Chart Title. Place your insertion point behind the 8 and key Expenses at the end of the existing text. You have edited the chart title, and it should read 2008 Expenses.
9. **SAVE** the workbook. **CLOSE** the workbook.

PAUSE. LEAVE Excel open to use in the next exercise.

Take Note   The data series is the most important element of the chart. Use formatting tools to call attention to the graphic and the label.

Modifying a Chart's Legend

You can modify the content of the legend, expand or collapse the legend box, edit the text that is displayed, and change character attributes. A finished chart should stand alone—that is, the chart should contain sufficient data to convey the intended data analysis. In the chart you modify in this exercise, changing the font colors in the legend to match the blocks in the columns provides an additional visual aid that enables the viewer to quickly see the income contribution for each category. In the next exercise, you will learn to modify a chart's legend.

STEP BY STEP   **Modify a Chart's Legend**

 The *Financial History* file for this lesson is available on the book companion website or in WileyPLUS.

OPEN the *Financial History* file for this lesson.

1. On the Sales History worksheet, select the cell range A4:F9.
2. Click **Column** in the Charts group on the Insert tab; the Column chart options menu appears.
3. Select **Stacked Column in 3D** from the Column chart menu; the chart is inserted and the *Chart Tools* tabs become available.
4. Click the **more** arrow at the bottom right of the Chart Layouts group When the Layout gallery opens, click **Layout 4**. The legend has moved and appears below the plot area.

Take Note   When you applied Layout 4 to the column chart, the legend was placed at the bottom of the chart. You can click the legend border and move it to any location on the chart. All other elements of the quick layout will remain the same.

WILEY **PLUS** *EXTRA*

WileyPLUS Extra! features an online tutorial of this task.

5. Click to select the chart's **legend** and in the Outline styles, click the **Colored Outline – Blue, Accent 1** style. This will enclose the legend in a light blue border as illustrated in Figure 10-14.

Figure 10-14

Formatted legend

Formatted Selection Button

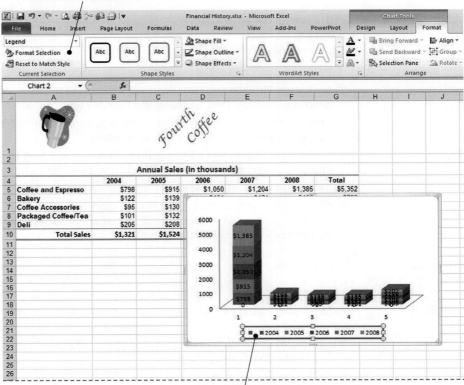

Formatted Legend

6. With the legend still selected right-click to display the shortcut menu. Click **Font**; the Font dialog box appears.

7. In the Font dialog box, select **Small Caps** in the Effects option area and click **OK**. This applies the small capital letter format to the text in the legend.

8. Place your mouse cursor directly on the text for Coffee and Espresso in the legend; right-click to display the shortcut menu and click **Font**. The *Font* dialog box opens.

9. In the Font dialog box, click the **Font color** button, and then click **Green** from the drop-down color palette. Click **OK** to apply the color to the Coffee and Espresso legend text and close the dialog box.

10. Repeat step 9 for each legend item and apply the following font colors:

    Bakery: **Red**

    Coffee Accessories: **Orange**

    Packaged Coffee/Tea: **Light Blue**

    Deli: **Blue**

11. **SAVE** the file as *Chart 1*.

PAUSE. LEAVE the workbook open to use in the next exercise.

MODIFYING A CHART

The Bottom Line

You can modify a chart by adding or deleting elements or by moving or resizing the chart. You can also change the chart type without having to delete the existing chart and create a new one. Adding elements to a chart can provide additional information that was not available in the data you selected to create the chart. For example, the stacked column chart you worked with in the preceding exercise does not have a title and it does not indicate that the sales amounts are in thousands. That kind of information can be displayed in labels. Labels make it easy to understand chart data. You can display series names, category names, and percentages in data labels. To prevent data labels from overlapping, and to make them easier to read, you can adjust their positions on the chart. In this exercise, you learn to use the Layout tab commands to add chart labels.

STEP BY STEP **Add Elements to a Chart**

USE the workbook from the previous exercise.

1. With the chart still active click the **Layout** tab.

2. Click **Axis Titles** in the Labels group, then point to the Primary Vertical Axis Title in the drop-down menu that appears; the Primary Vertical Axis Title options list is displayed.

3. Click **Vertical Title**. An Axis title text box appears in the chart. Select the Axis Title text, and key **(In Thousands)** in the title text box.

4. Click **Chart Title** in the Labels group. Click **Above Chart** in the drop-down menu that appears. A text box displaying Chart Title is inserted above the columns.

5. Select the text and replace it with **Sales History**.

6. Click **Data Labels** in the Labels group. Click **None**. The Labels are removed from each column in the chart. Click on **Data Labels** again to restore the labels showing the dollar amount of sales in each category.

Take Note

Because of the chart size, the data labels are difficult to read. You will correct this in a subsequent exercise.

7. Click **Gridlines** in the Axes group. Point to Primary Vertical Gridlines and click **Major Gridlines**.

8. In the Labels group, click **Axis Titles** then and point to **Primary Horizontal Axis Title**. The drop-down menu appears.

9. Click **Title Below Axis**.

10. Key **Annual Sales** in the Axis Title text box as illustrated in Figure 10-15.

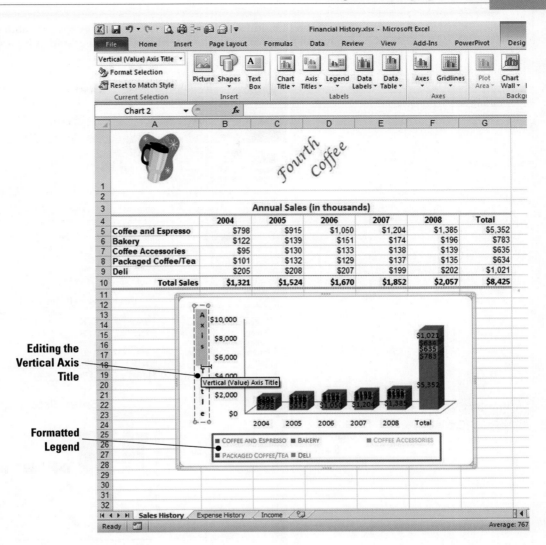

**Another Way**
Rather than select
and replace the text in the text
boxes, you can key the new
text in the formula bar. When
you press Enter, the new text
replaces the generic text in the
title boxes.

11. **SAVE** the workbook with the same name.

PAUSE. LEAVE the workbook open to use in the next exercise.

Deleting Elements from a Chart

When a chart becomes too cluttered, you may need to delete nonessential elements. You can use the Layout tab commands to delete chart elements, or you can select an element on the chart and press the Delete key. You can also select an element in the Current Selection group and press Delete. You will use this next exercise to delete elements from the chart.

STEP BY STEP   **Delete Elements from a Chart**

USE the workbook from the previous exercise.

1. On the Layout tab in Chart Design tools, click Axis Titles and point to Primary Horizontal Axis Title. Click None. There is now no horizontal axis in the chart.

2. Click Gridlines in the Axes group, point to Primary Vertical Gridlines. Click None. There are now no gridlines in the chart.

3. Click the **Design** tab and click **Switch Row/Column**. The data display is changed to have all sales for one category stacked as illustrated in Figure 10-16.

Figure 10-16

Using switch row/column

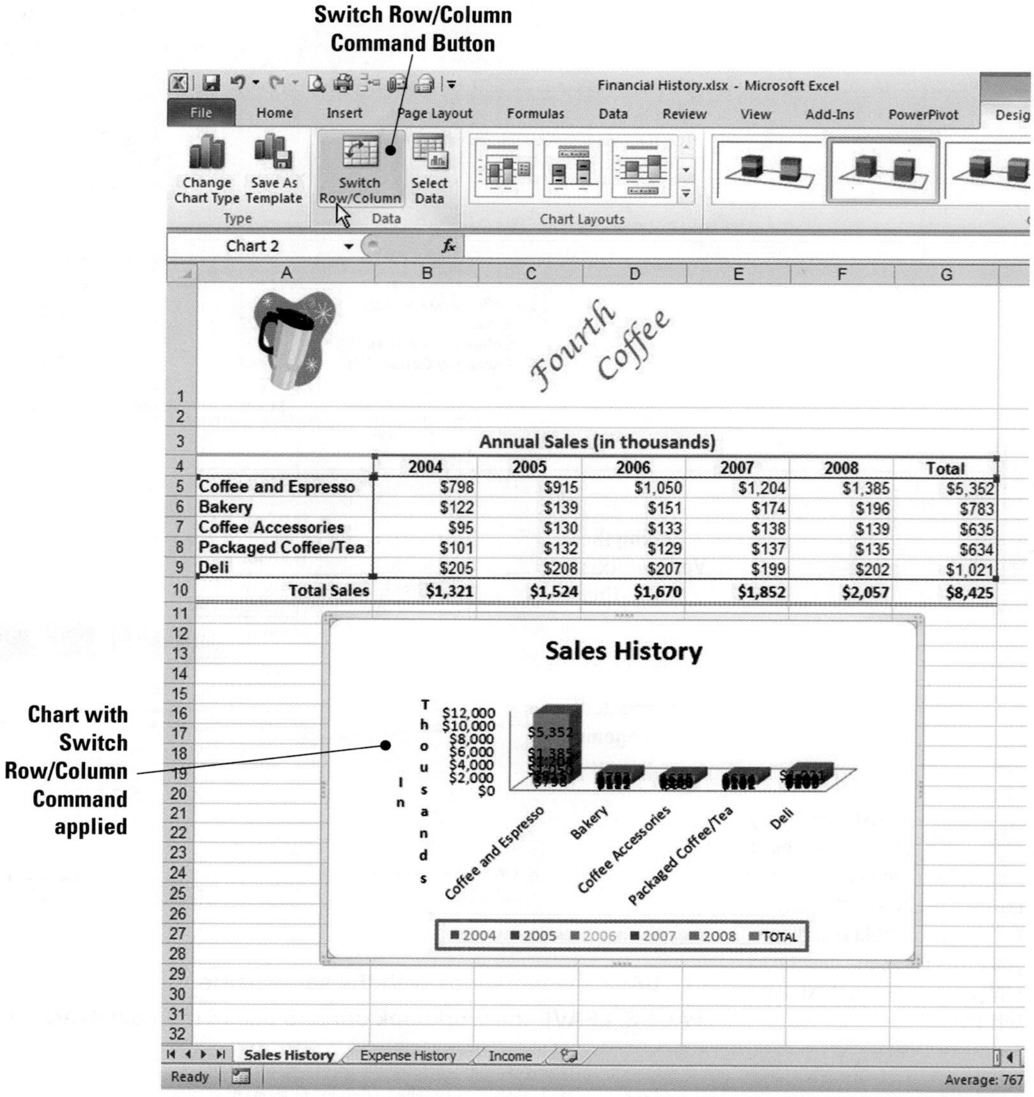

Switch Row/Column Command Button

Chart with Switch Row/Column Command applied

Another Way
You can also delete a chart element by right-clicking on the element and pressing Delete.

4. Click **Switch Row/Column** to Undo.

5. **SAVE** the workbook.

PAUSE. LEAVE the workbook open to use in the next exercise.

Take Note

It is important to remember that whether the chart is embedded in the worksheet or located on a chart sheet, the chart is linked to the worksheet data. Any changes in the worksheet data will be reflected in the chart. Likewise, if the worksheet data is deleted, the chart will be deleted as well.

Moving a Chart

When you insert a chart, by default, it is embedded in the worksheet. You can click a corner of a chart or the midpoint of any side to display move handles (four-sided arrow). You can use the move handles to drag the chart to any location on the worksheet. Sometimes you want a chart to be on a chart sheet so that it can be reviewed without the worksheet data. In this exercise, you will move charts in the workbook.

STEP BY STEP **Move a Chart**

USE the workbook from the previous exercise.

1. Click a blank area in the Sales History chart to deselect any previous actions.
2. Mouse over the chart to activate the move pointer (crosshairs). Click, hold and drag the chart so that it is centered in columns B to G.
3. The chart remains selected. Click the Design tab.
4. Click Move Chart Location. The *Move Chart* dialog box shown in Figure 10-17 opens, with the default setting—New Sheet—selected. This setting places the chart as an object in a new worksheet.

Figure 10-17

Move chart dialog box

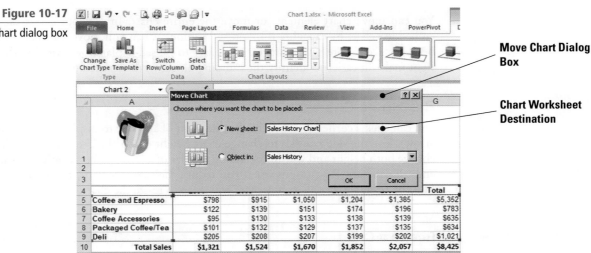

5. The New Sheet selection option is selected in the dialog box, key Sales History Chart in the text box. Click OK. A chart sheet is inserted before the Sales History sheet. The chart sheet becomes the active sheet, and the Chart Tools tabs are displayed as illustrated in Figure 10-18.

Figure 10-18

Chart sheet created

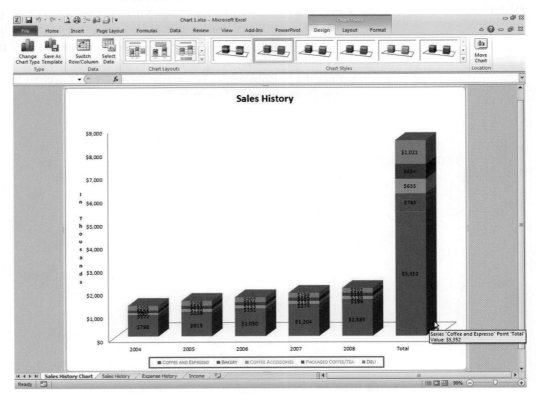

6. On the Layout tab, in the Labels group, click Legend. Click Show Legend at Right; the legend moves to the right side of the chart in the chart sheet, which makes the elements in the chart easier to read.

Take Note   The Chart Tools that you used on the Design, Layout, and Format tabs can be applied to the chart sheet. The data series amounts were difficult to read when you applied them to the embedded chart. They are easy to read and can be used for analysis when the chart is moved to a chart sheet.

7. **SAVE** and **CLOSE** the workbook.

PAUSE. LEAVE Excel open to use in the next exercise.

You can move chart elements or move the entire chart. In previous exercises, you moved an embedded chart by dragging it to a new location. When you move the chart to a new sheet, it becomes even more important for the chart to be self-explanatory. Moving the legend to the right makes it easier to identify the building blocks in the stacked columns.

Resizing a Chart

You can click a corner of a chart or the midpoint of any side to display sizing handles (two-sided arrow). Use the side handles to change chart height or width. Use the corner sizing handles to change both height and width. Increasing the size of a chart makes it easier to read, especially an embedded chart. Be cautious when you reduce the size of a chart, however. Titles and legends must be readable. In this exercise you will learn to resize the chart.

STEP BY STEP   **Resize a Chart**

GET READY. LAUNCH Microsoft Excel if it is not already open.

@ The *Financial History 2* file for this lesson is available on the book companion website or in WileyPLUS.

1. **OPEN** the *Financial History 2* file for this lesson.
2. Click a blank area in the chart on the Expense History worksheet to make the chart active and display the Chart Tools tabs.
3. Click the top-left sizing handle and drag the left edge of the chart to the bottom of row 9 at the left edge of the worksheet. You are using the sizing handles to resize the chart.
4. Click the top-right sizing handle and align the right edge of the chart with the column G right boundary.
5. Click the bottom-center sizing handle and drag the chart boundary to the bottom of row 35 as shown in Figure 10-19.

Figure 10-19

Resizing chart with sizing handles

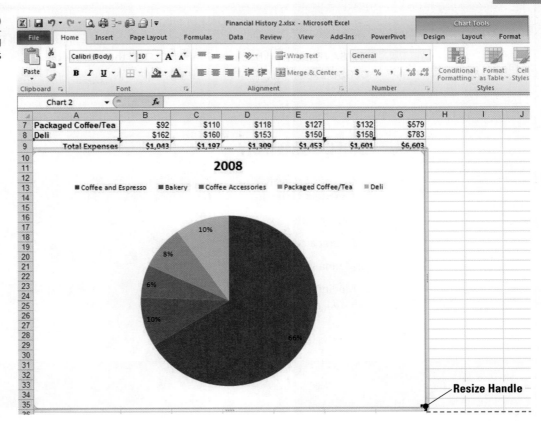

6. Click the **Sales History** worksheet tab to make the Sales History worksheet active. Click a blank area in the chart. Click the **Format** tab.

7. In the Size group, click the Shape Height **up arrow** until the height is 3.5.

8. In the Size group, click the Shape Width **down arrow** until the width is 4.0.

9. **SAVE** the workbook as *Chart 2*. **CLOSE** the workbook.

PAUSE. LEAVE Excel open to use in the next exercise.

Choosing a Different Chart Type

For most 2-D charts, you can change the chart type and give it a completely different look. If a chart contains multiple data series, you can also select a different chart type for any single data series, creating a combined chart. You cannot combine a 2-D and a 3-D chart, however.

STEP BY STEP   **Choose a Different Chart Type**

GET READY. LAUNCH Microsoft Excel if it is not already open.

@ The *Financial History* file for this lesson is available on the book companion website or in WileyPLUS.

1. **OPEN** the *Financial History* file for this lesson.

2. On the Expense History worksheet, select **A4:F9**.

3. On the Insert tab, click **Bar** and click **Stacked Bar in 3-D**. This inserts the stacked bar in a 3-D chart into your worksheet. The Design tab becomes active as soon as the chart is inserted into the worksheet.

4. Click **Layout 2** in the Charts Layout group.

5. Select the chart title text box and key **Expense History**.

6. On the *Design* tab, click **Change Chart Type**.

7. Click **Stacked Horizontal Cylinder**, in the second row, second option in the Change Chart type dialog box. Click **OK**.

8. On the Sales History worksheet, select **A4:B9**. On the Insert tab, click **Pie**. Click **Pie 2D**.

9. Click **Layout 1** on the Design tab.
10. Click **Change Chart Type** and click **Exploded Pie in 3-D**. Click **OK**.
11. **SAVE** the workbook as *Chart 3*. **CLOSE** the workbook.
CLOSE Excel.

SKILL SUMMARY

In This Lesson You Learned How To:
Build charts
Format a chart with a Quick Style
Manually format the parts of a chart
Modify a chart

Knowledge Assessment

Matching

Match each vocabulary term with its definition.

a. axis
b. chart
c. chart area
d. chart sheet
e. data labels

f. data marker
g. data series
h. embedded chart
i. legend
j. title

_____ 1. A box that identifies the patterns or colors that are assigned to a data series or categories in a chart.

_____ 2. A graphical representation of numeric data in a worksheet.

_____ 3. A bar, area, dot, slice, or other symbol in a chart that represents a single data point or value that originates from a worksheet cell.

_____ 4. A chart that is placed on a worksheet rather than on a separate sheet.

_____ 5. A sheet in a workbook that contains only a chart.

_____ 6. The entire chart and all its elements.

_____ 7. Related data points that are plotted in a chart.

_____ 8. A line bordering the chart plot area used as a frame of reference for measurement.

_____ 9. Descriptive text that is automatically aligned to an axis or centered at the top of a chart.

_____ 10. A label that provides additional information about a data marker, which represents a single data point or value that originates from a worksheet cell.

Multiple Choice

Select the best response for the following statements.

1. Which chart type shows values as parts of a whole?
   a. Column
   b. Bar
   c. Area
   d. Pie

2. What type of chart appears on a worksheet with other data?
   a. Chart sheet
   b. Embedded
   c. PivotChart
   d. Mixed

3. What part of a chart do you click when you want to select the entire chart?
   a. Chart area
   b. Plot area
   c. Chart title
   d. Legend

4. What happens to a chart if the source data is deleted?
   a. Nothing.
   b. The chart will move to the area where the data was located.
   c. The data in the chart is deleted.
   d. You will be asked if you want the chart deleted.

5. What is the first step that should be taken when creating a chart?
   a. Providing a name for the chart
   b. Selecting the chart type
   c. Selecting the range of cells that contain the data the chart will use
   d. Choosing the data labels that will be used in the chart

6. If you want to print only the chart in a worksheet, what should you do before printing?
   a. Click the chart to select it and then print.
   b. Select the *Print chart only* option in the Page Setup dialog box.
   c. Move the chart to a new sheet by itself and then print that sheet.
   d. You cannot print only the chart if it is part of a larger worksheet.

7. To change the location of a legend on a chart, use the Legend command on which Ribbon tab?
   a. Insert
   b. Format
   c. Layout
   d. Design

8. A column chart represents values as
   a. Horizontal bars
   b. Vertical bars
   c. Horizontal lines
   d. Vertical lines

9. To move a chart from a worksheet to a chart sheet
   a. Use the move handles and drag it to the new location.
   b. Use the Move Chart Location command on the Design tab.
   c. Cut the chart from the worksheet and paste it to a new workbook sheet.
   d. You cannot move the chart after it has been created.

10. Which of the following statements is **not** true?

   a. You can change both the height and width of a chart with commands on the Format tab.

   b. You can use the sizing handles to change the height and width of a chart.

   c. You must delete an existing chart in order to have the data displayed in a different chart type.

   d. When a chart sheet is created, it no longer appears on the worksheet containing the data series.

Competency Assessment

Project 10-1: Create a Pie Chart

Blue Yonder Airlines has created a workbook to analyze sales for its first four years of operation. The manager wants to create charts that reflect an analysis of the data.

GET READY. LAUNCH Excel.

@ The *BY Financials* file for this lesson is available on the book companion website or in WileyPLUS.

1. **OPEN** the *BY Financials* file for this lesson.
2. On the Income worksheet, select **A3:A7**. Press **Ctrl** and select **E3:E7**.
3. Click the **Insert** tab. Click **Pie** and click **Pie in 3-D**.
4. Click **Layout 1** in the Chart Layouts group on the Design tab.
5. Click **Move Chart Location**.
6. Select **New Sheet** and click **OK**.
7. Right-click the **Chart1** tab and click **Rename**.
8. Key **2008 Income Chart** and press **Enter**.
9. **SAVE** the workbook as *BY Financials 10-1*.
10. **CLOSE** the workbook.

LEAVE Excel open for the next project.

Project 10-2: Create a Bar Chart

Create a bar chart to analyze trends in Fourth Coffee's income before taxes.

@ The *Financial History* file for this lesson is available on the book companion website or in WileyPLUS.

1. **OPEN** the *Financial History* file for this lesson.
2. Make the Income worksheet active. Select **A4:F9** and click the **Insert** tab.
3. Click **Bar** in the Charts group, and click **100% Stacked Horizontal Cylinder**.
4. Click in the **Chart Area** and click the **Layout** tab.
5. Click **Legend** and click **Show Legend at Bottom**.
6. Click the **Chart Area** to display the move handles. Move the chart so that the top-left corner is aligned with B12.
7. Click the **bottom-right sizing handle** and increase the size of the chart so that it fills B12:G29.
8. **SAVE** the workbook as *Financial History 10-2*.

LEAVE the workbook open to use in the next project.

Project 10-3: Modify a Bar Chart

In the previous project, you created a bar chart to analyze trends in Fourth Coffee's income before taxes. Modify the chart by adding additional chart elements.

USE the workbook from the previous project.

1. Select the chart area and click Chart Title in the Labels group on the Layout tab.
2. Click More Title Options and click Gradient fill.
3. In the Preset colors box, click Moss (first option in the third row) and click Close. The Chart Title text box is selected.
4. In the Chart Title text box, key Income Before Taxes and press Enter.
5. Click Axis Titles and click Primary Vertical Axis Title.
6. Click Rotated Title. The Axis Title text box is selected.
7. In the Axis Title text box, key in thousands and press Enter.
8. Right-click the Axis Title text box and click Font.
9. Click Font color and click Green. Click OK.
10. **SAVE** the workbook as *Financial History 10-3*.
11. **CLOSE** the file.

LEAVE Excel open for the next project.

Project 10-4: Create a Line Chart

In this exercise, you will build Line charts to view the results of the data calculations with data markers.

GET READY. LAUNCH Excel if it is not already running.

@ The *BY Financials* file for this lesson is available on the book companion website or in WileyPLUS.

1. **OPEN** the *BY Financials* file for this lesson.
2. On the Annual Sales worksheet, select A3:E7. Click Line on the Insert tab and then click Line.
3. Click Stacked line with Markers.
4. Apply Layout 3.
5. Click Chart Title and key Blue Yonder Airlines in the formula bar.
6. Click Plot Area and click Format Selection.
7. Click Border Color and click Gradient line.
8. Click Preset Colors and click Daybreak (first row, fourth option from left).
9. Click Direction and click Linear Diagonal. Click Close.
10. Click Chart Area, click Format Selection, and click Solid fill.
11. In the Fill Color area, click Color and click Blue, Accent 1, Lighter 80%.
12. Click Close.
13. **SAVE** the workbook as *BY Financials 10-4*.

LEAVE the workbook open for the next project.

Mastery Assessment

Project 10-5: Create a Doughnut Chart

In this exercise, you will apply data results in a doughnut chart.

GET READY. LAUNCH Excel if it is not already running.

1. **USE** the workbook from the previous project.
2. Click the Annual Expenses tab. Select A3:E7 and click Other Charts on the Insert tab.
3. Click Doughnut.
4. Click Layout 2.
5. On the Format tab, click the Size dialog box launcher. Set both height and width to 5 inches.
6. Key Annual Expenses as the chart title.
7. Print the chart only.
8. **SAVE** the workbook as *BY Financials 10-5*. **CLOSE** the workbook.

LEAVE Excel open for the next project.

Project 10-6: Fixing the Fitness Classes Worksheet

Fourth Coffee's corporate manager wants to change the chart type and some of the formatting in the chart prepared in a previous exercise.

GET READY. LAUNCH Excel if it is not already running.

@ The *Income Chart* file for this lesson is available on the book companion website or in WileyPLUS.

1. **OPEN** the *Income Chart* file for this lesson.
2. Select the chart. Click the Design tab.
3. Click Layout 3.
4. On the Layout tab, click Axis Titles, click Primary Horizontal Axis Title, choose Title Below Axis, and then key Percentage of Income below the axis.
5. Click Data Labels and add data labels to the bars.
6. Right-click the chart title and click Font. Click Font color and click Red – Accent 2 under Theme Colors.
7. Click Small Caps and click OK.
8. On the Layout tab, in the Current Selection group, click the down arrow next to Chart Title and choose Legend.
9. Click Colored Outline – Red Accent 2 on the Format tab.
10. On the Design tab, click Move Chart Location. Click New Sheet and click OK.
11. **SAVE** the workbook as *Income Chart 10-6* and then **CLOSE** the file.

LEAVE Excel open for the next project.

Microsoft® PowerPoint® 2010

LESSON SKILL MATRIX

In This Lesson, You Will Learn The Following Skills:

Working in the PowerPoint Window

Working with an Existing Presentation

KEY TERMS

- Backstage view
- command
- current slide
- dialog box launcher
- dialog box
- drop-down arrow
- drop-down list
- File tab
- group
- I-beam pointer
- KeyTip
- Mini toolbar
- Normal view
- Notes Page view
- placeholder
- Quick Access Toolbar
- Reading View
- Ribbon
- ScreenTip
- shortcut menu
- Slide Show view
- Slide Sorter view
- tab
- text box
- views
- zoom

Blue Yonder Airlines is a small but rapidly growing company that offers charter flights to adventurous or exotic locations. The service is designed for small groups, such as corporate management teams or directors who want to mix business and pleasure in a packaged getaway. As an enterprise account manager, your job is to introduce Blue Yonder Airlines to executives in mid-sized and large companies. Your goal is to convince these managers to use your charter service when arranging off-site gatherings that require group travel. Microsoft PowerPoint 2010 provides the perfect set of tools for presenting this information to your potential customers. In this lesson, you will start PowerPoint and open an introductory presentation about Blue Yonder Airlines. You will learn to navigate, edit, save, print, and close a presentation.

SOFTWARE ORIENTATION

Microsoft PowerPoint's Opening Screen

Before you begin working in Microsoft PowerPoint, you should be familiar with the primary user interface. When you first start Microsoft PowerPoint, you will see a screen similar to the one shown in Figure 1-1. However, if your copy of PowerPoint has been customized, what you see may be slightly different from what is shown. You can use this figure as a reference throughout this lesson and the rest of this book.

Figure 1-1

The PowerPoint window

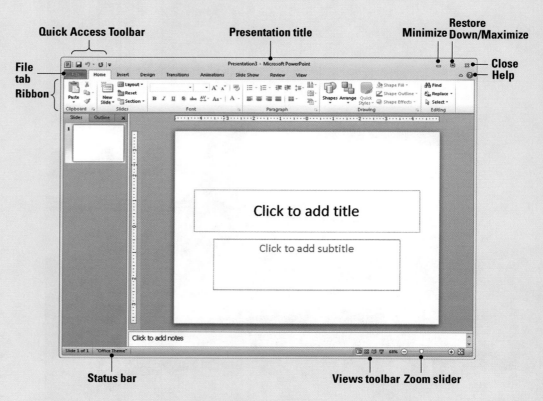

The Ribbon across the top of the window contains a set of tabs; each tab has a different collection of buttons and tools on it. Additional tabs appear when you select certain types of content, such as graphics or tables.

WORKING IN THE POWERPOINT WINDOW

The Bottom Line

To use PowerPoint 2010 efficiently, you need to learn how to navigate in the PowerPoint application window.

Starting PowerPoint

Before you can use PowerPoint, you need to start the program. In this exercise, you learn to start PowerPoint using the Start button and the Microsoft Office menu.

Start PowerPoint

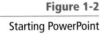

WileyPLUS Extra! features an online tutorial on this task.

GET READY. Before you begin these steps, make sure that your computer is on. Log on, if necessary.

1. On the Windows taskbar at the bottom of your screen, click the Start button, and then click All Programs. A menu of installed programs appears.
2. Click Microsoft Office. A submenu opens, listing the available programs in your installation of Microsoft Office.
3. Click Microsoft PowerPoint 2010, as shown in Figure 1-2. PowerPoint starts and a new, blank presentation appears in the PowerPoint window.

Figure 1-2

Starting PowerPoint

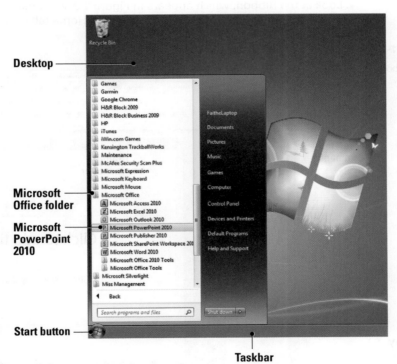

Another Way

If PowerPoint has recently been used on your computer, it may appear on the top level of the Start menu, when you first click the Start button. If it appears there, you can click that shortcut to start the program, rather than clicking All Programs and Microsoft Office to find it.

Another Way

You can also click the Start button and then begin typing PowerPoint; after you have typed the first few letters, PowerPoint should appear above the Start button; click on it there to start the program.

PAUSE. LEAVE the blank presentation open to use in the next exercise.

Selecting Tools and Commands

A **command** is a tool (such as an icon, a button, or a list) that tells PowerPoint to perform a specific task. Each tab provides commands that are relevant to the kind of task you are performing—whether you are formatting a slide, adding animations to a presentation, or setting up a slide show for display. Most of the tools and commands for working with PowerPoint are accessible through PowerPoint's Ribbon. In addition to the Ribbon, PowerPoint also offers tools and commands on the File menu (also known as **Backstage view**), a Quick Access toolbar, a floating mini-toolbar, and a status bar.

Using the Ribbon

In this exercise, you learn how to select commands from the **Ribbon**, which is the tabbed toolbar at the top of the window. The Ribbon is divided into **tabs**, and each tab contains several **groups** of related commands.

On the Ribbon, some command groups feature a tool called a **dialog box launcher**—a small arrow in the group's lower-right corner. You can click the arrow to open a **dialog box**, which provides tools and options related to a specific task. To close a dialog box without accepting any changes you may have made to it, click the Cancel button.

Some of the Ribbon's tools have small, downward-pointing arrows next to them. These arrows are called **drop-down arrows**; when you click one, a **drop-down list** opens, displaying options you can choose (such as a list of fonts). You can choose the option you want by clicking it.

If you need more space on your screen, you can minimize (hide) the Ribbon by double-clicking the active tab. To restore the Ribbon, double-click the active tab again.

STEP BY STEP   **Use the Ribbon**

USE the new, blank presentation that is still open from the previous exercise.

1. Look at the Ribbon, which appears in Figure 1-3. Note that each tab contains several groups of related commands. By default, the Home tab is active.

Figure 1-3

The Ribbon

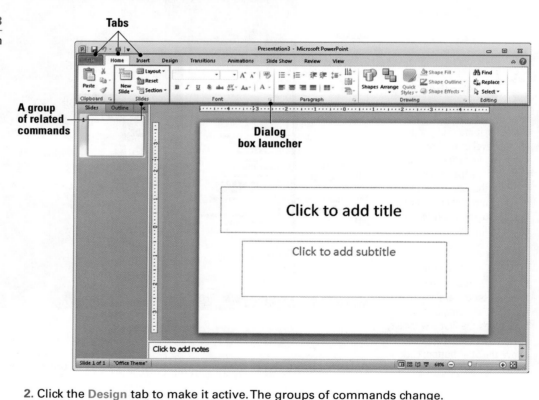

Another Way
You can also open the Font dialog box by pressing Ctrl+Shift+F. Many common commands have keyboard shortcuts; the PowerPoint Help system (covered later in this lesson) can help you identify them.

2. Click the Design tab to make it active. The groups of commands change.
3. Click the Home tab.
4. On the slide, click anywhere in the text Click to add title. The text disappears and a blinking insertion point appears.

          Ref   You will learn about adding and editing text later in this lesson.

5. In the lower-right corner of the Font group, click the dialog box launcher (the small box with a diagonal, downward-pointing arrow, as shown in Figure 1-3). Clicking this button opens PowerPoint's Font dialog box. Click Cancel to close the dialog box.

6. In the Font group, click the Font list drop-down arrow. A drop-down list appears, as shown in Figure 1-4. This list shows all the fonts that are currently available for use. The default font for titles is Calibri.

Figure 1-4

The Font list

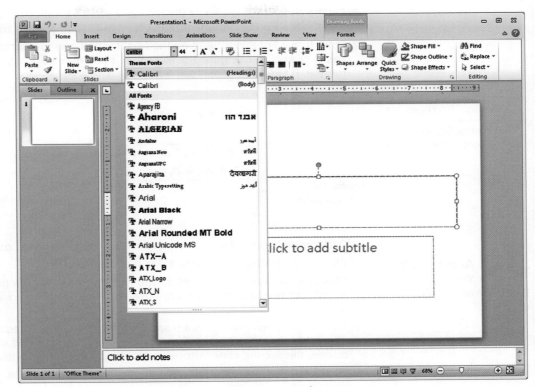

Another Way
You can also minimize the Ribbon by right-clicking one of its tabs and clicking Minimize the Ribbon. Repeat that procedure to redisplay the Ribbon. You can also use the arrow to the left of the Help button that appears as a question mark in a blue circle in the upper-right corner of the PowerPoint window to minimize or restore the Ribbon.

7. Click the drop-down arrow again to close the list.

8. Double-click the Home tab. This action minimizes the Ribbon, hiding the groups of commands but leaving the tabs' names visible on the screen.

9. Double-click the Home tab again to redisplay the groups.

PAUSE. LEAVE the presentation open to use in the next exercise.

Take Note

If you aren't sure what a command does, just point to it. When the mouse pointer rests on a tool, a ScreenTip appears. A basic **ScreenTip** displays the tool's name and shortcut key (if a shortcut exists for that tool). Some of the Ribbon's tools have enhanced ScreenTips that also provide a brief description of the tool.

Using the Mini Toolbar

In this exercise, you practice using the **Mini toolbar**, a small toolbar that appears when you point to text that has been selected (highlighted). The Mini toolbar displays tools for formatting text appearance and alignment. The Mini toolbar is faint and semi-transparent until you point to it; then it becomes bright and opaque, indicating that the toolbar is active. If you right-click selected text, PowerPoint displays both the Mini toolbar and a **shortcut menu**, which displays additional commands.

Use the Mini Toolbar

USE the presentation that is still on the screen from the preceding exercise.

1. On the slide, double-click at the insertion point's location. Because you double-clicked, the insertion point is highlighted. A faint Mini toolbar appears.

2. Point to the Font command on the Mini toolbar; the toolbar becomes brighter and easier to see, as in Figure 1-5. Note that if you move the mouse pointer away from the toolbar, it fades.

Figure 1-5

The Mini toolbar appears by the highlighted insertion point

Mini toolbar

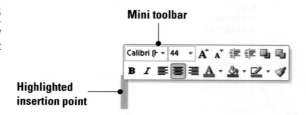

Highlighted insertion point

3. Click the Font drop-down arrow in the Mini toolbar. The list of available fonts opens.

4. Click the Font drop-down arrow again to close the list.

Another Way
You can also press Esc to close an open drop-down list.

5. Move the mouse pointer back to the highlighted insertion point, then right-click. A shortcut menu with commonly used commands appears along with the Mini toolbar.

6. Move the mouse pointer to a blank area of the slide (such as the upper-left corner), then click twice. The first click removes the Mini toolbar and shortcut menu from the screen; the second click restores the slide to its original state.

PAUSE. LEAVE the presentation open to use in the next exercise.

Using the Quick Access Toolbar

The **Quick Access Toolbar** displays commands that you use frequently. By default, the Save, Undo, and Redo commands appear on the toolbar. You can add any commands to the Quick Access Toolbar for easy access to the commands you use most frequently. You can also choose where the Quick Access Toolbar appears via the Customize Quick Access Toolbar button's menu. In this exercise, you learn to use and customize the Quick Access Toolbar.

The Save command quickly saves an existing presentation while you are working on it or when you are done with it. If you have not yet given the presentation a file name, PowerPoint will prompt you for a name by launching the Save As dialog box, as happened in the preceding exercise. If you have previously saved the file, the dialog box does not reopen.

The Undo command lets you reverse ("undo") the action of your last command. The Redo button lets you reverse an undo action. If either the Undo or Redo command is gray, then you cannot undo or redo.

Use the Quick Access Toolbar

USE the presentation that is still open from the previous exercise.

1. Look for the Quick Access Toolbar in the upper-left corner of the PowerPoint window. The Quick Access Toolbar appears in Figure 1-6, with its tools labeled. Yours may look different if it has been customized.

Figure 1-6

The Quick Access Toolbar

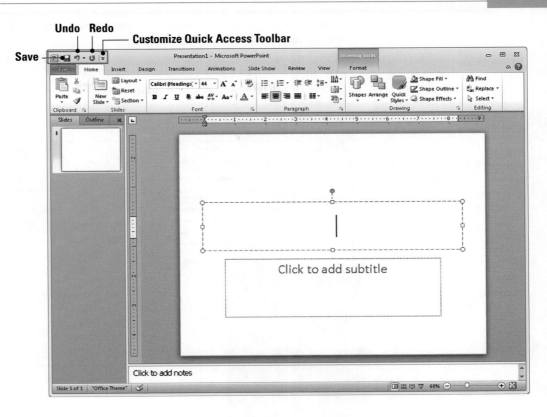

2. Click the Save button on the Quick Access Toolbar. The Save As dialog box appears.

3. Click Cancel to close the dialog box.

Another Way
You can also press Esc to close a dialog box.

4. Click the Customize Quick Access Toolbar button. A menu appears, as shown in Figure 1-7. This menu lets you choose the tools you want to appear on the Quick Access Toolbar.

Figure 1-7

Customizing the Quick Access Toolbar

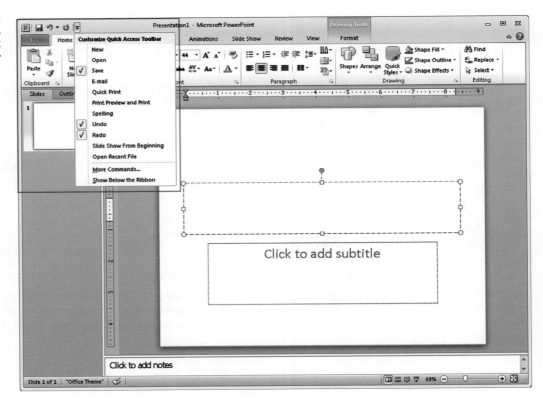

5. Click Show Below the Ribbon. The toolbar moves down and appears directly beneath the Ribbon.

6. Click the Customize Quick Access Toolbar button again. Click Show Above the Ribbon. The toolbar moves back to its original location.

7. On the Home tab, right-click the Bold button. A shortcut menu appears, as in Figure 1-8.

Figure 1-8

Adding a button to the Quick Access Toolbar

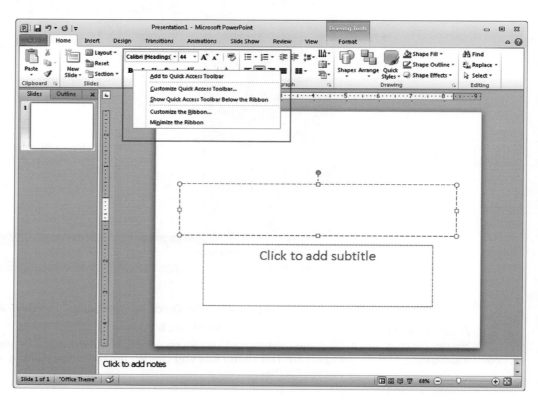

8. Click Add to Quick Access Toolbar. A copy of the Bold button appears on the toolbar.

9. On the Quick Access Toolbar, right-click the Bold button. A shortcut menu appears.

10. Click Remove from Quick Access Toolbar. The copy of the Bold button is removed.

PAUSE. LEAVE the presentation open to use in the next exercise.

Using KeyTips

When you press the Alt key, small letters and numbers—called **KeyTips**—appear on the Ribbon. To issue a command by using its KeyTip, press the Alt key, and then press the key or keys that correspond to the command you want to use. Every command on the Ribbon has a KeyTip.

STEP BY STEP   **Use KeyTips**

USE the presentation that is still open from the previous exercise.

1. Press Alt. Letters and numbers appear on the Ribbon and the Quick Access Toolbar, as shown in Figure 1-9. These characters show you which keyboard keys you can press to access the tabs or the items on the Quick Access Toolbar.

Figure 1-9

KeyTips

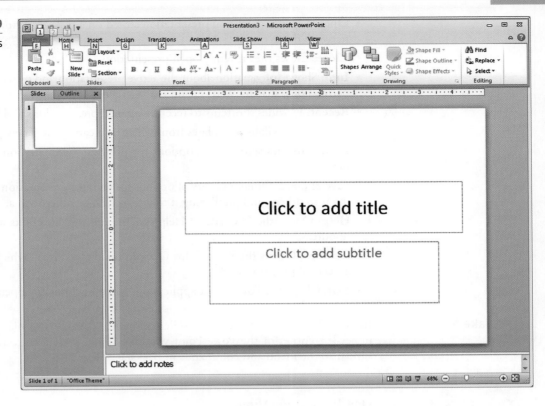

2. Press **N** to activate the Insert tab. When the Insert tab opens, notice that a new set of letters appears. These characters show you which keys to use to insert different kinds of objects in the current slide.

Another Way
If you accidentally press Alt, you can clear KeyTips from the screen by pressing Esc.

3. Press **P** to open the Insert Picture dialog box.

4. Click **Cancel** to close the dialog box and remove KeyTips from the display.

PAUSE. LEAVE the presentation open to use in the next exercise.

KeyTips are one type of *keyboard shortcut*. In addition to the KeyTips, there are also many other key combinations you can press to issue common commands that open dialog boxes, select and manipulate text, save, print, and much more. For example, Ctrl+S saves the current presentation, and Ctrl+Z reverses the last action taken. The PowerPoint Help system, covered later in this lesson, provides a complete list of keyboard shortcuts available.

Keyboard shortcuts let you issue commands without using the mouse. This is handy for experienced typists who prefer to keep their hands on the keyboard as much as possible. In fact, if you master keyboard shortcuts, you may find that you use the mouse less often over time.

Take Note

You must press Alt each time you want to see a tab's KeyTips. If you issue one command by keyboard shortcut, you have to press Alt again to redisplay the tab's KeyTips before you can issue another one.

Using Backstage View

NEW to Office 2010

The **File tab** is not a regular tab; instead of displaying Ribbon commands, it displays a full-screen menu called Backstage view. Each command you select along the left side of the Backstage view screen displays a different dialog box or page of options and commands in the right panel.

Commands on the menu in Backstage view include the following:

- **Save:** Saves the current presentation using PowerPoint's default file format.
- **Save as:** Lets you save a presentation in PowerPoint's default format or in several other file formats.

- **Open:** Opens an existing presentation stored on a disk, either on your computer's disk or a network drive.
- **Close:** Closes the currently open presentation.
- **Info:** Shows information about the active presentation and provides commands that control permissions, sharing, and version management.
- **Recent:** Provides shortcuts to recently opened presentations and file locations.
- **New:** Lists available templates from which you can create a new presentation.
- **Print:** Provides settings and options for printing a presentation in any of a variety of formats.
- **Save & Send:** Offers a variety of options for saving a presentation in different formats, sending it to others, and publishing it to video, CD, or other media.
- **Help:** Opens the PowerPoint Help system, and provides links for other help and support resources.
- **Options:** Opens the PowerPoint Options dialog box, from which you can configure many aspects of program operation.
- **Exit:** Closes the PowerPoint application, and also closes any open files.

Take Note   In PowerPoint 2007, instead of a File command, there was a Microsoft Office button in the upper-left corner of the PowerPoint window. Clicking that button opened a menu that was similar to the menu and commands in Backstage view.

STEP BY STEP   Use Backstage View

USE the presentation you used in the previous exercise.

1. Click the **File** tab on the Ribbon. Backstage view opens, as shown in Figure 1-10.

Figure 1-10

Backstage view

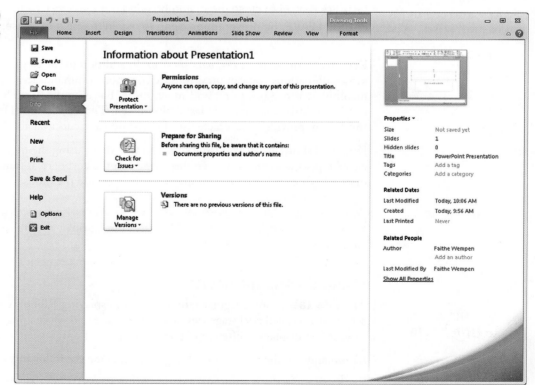

2. Click **Save & Send**. A page of commands and subcommands appears, as in Figure 1-11. Send Using E-mail is selected by default, and the right side of the window lists commands for sending your work to others.

Figure 1-11

The Save & Send commands in Backstage view

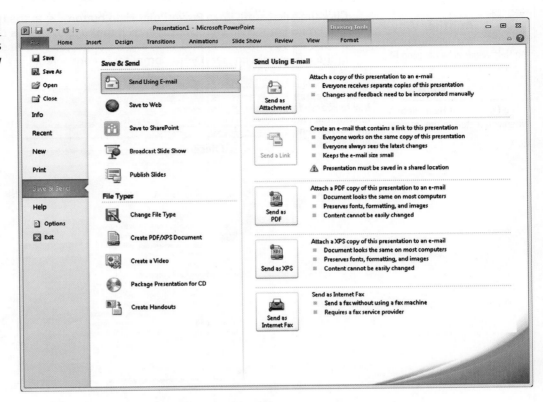

3. Click **Create a Video**. Options and commands for doing that activity appear at the right.
4. Click **Recent**. A list of recently opened files appears.
5. Click **New**. A list of templates appears.
6. Click **Open**. The Open dialog box appears.
7. Click **Cancel** to close the dialog box without making a selection.
8. Click the **File** tab again to redisplay Backstage view.
9. Click the **Home** tab to leave Backstage view.

PAUSE. LEAVE the presentation open to use in the next exercise.

Another Way
You can also press Esc to close Backstage view.

Another Way
To open the File menu by using KeyTips, press Alt, and then press F.

Working with PowerPoint's Help System

PowerPoint's Help system is rich in information, illustrations, and tips that can help you complete any task as you create a presentation. Some of PowerPoint's help information is stored on your computer, and much more is available via the Internet. Finding the right information is easy: you can pick a topic from the Help system's table of contents, browse a directory of help topics, or perform keyword searches by entering terms that best describe the task you want to complete. In this exercise, you learn to access and use PowerPoint's Help system.

STEP BY STEP   Use the Help System

USE the presentation that is open from the previous exercise.

Another Way
You can also open the Help window by pressing F1.

1. Click the Microsoft Office PowerPoint Help button ❓ at the right end of the Ribbon. The PowerPoint Help window appears. If the Help system is connected to the Internet, it appears as shown in Figure 1-12, and a Connected to Office.com indicator appears in the lower-right corner if your computer is connected.

Figure 1-12

The PowerPoint Help window when connected to the Internet

Use this Search box to search for information within the PowerPoint help system.

When connected to Internet, online Help search is also available.

Indicator shows connection status.

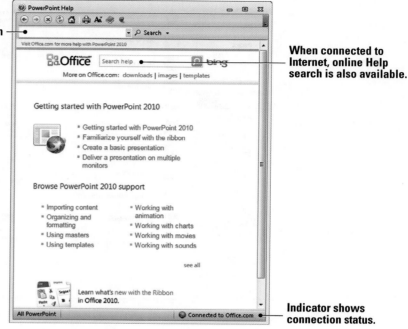

2. Click the Connected to Office.com button. The Connection Status menu appears.

3. Click Show content only from this computer. Notice that the Connected to Office.com button now appears as Offline, and the Help window changes as in Figure 1-13.

Figure 1-13

The PowerPoint Help window when offline

When not connected to Internet, only local search is available.

Connection indicator shows Offline.

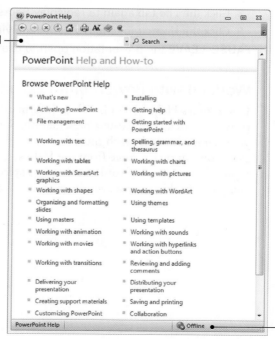

Take Note   Even if Office is set to work offline, you can still search for help online. Instead of clicking the Search button, click the drop-down arrow button to its right. When the menu opens, click Content from Office Online. The choice will affect only the current search.

> **4.** Click the Search box, type **Ribbon**, and then click the Search button or press **Enter**. A list of help topics appears, as shown in Figure 1-14.

Figure 1-14

Searching for help articles about the Ribbon

Change Font Size button

Type search word here.

Read this article.

Show Table of Contents button

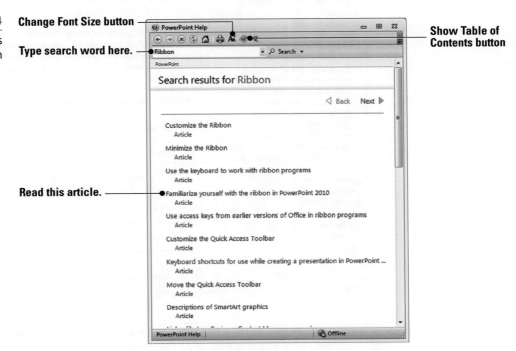

> **5.** Click the **Familiarize yourself with the Ribbon in PowerPoint 2010** hyperlink. The corresponding article appears. Read the article if you wish.
>
> **6.** Click the **Show Table of Contents** button. The Table of Contents opens in a pane on the left side of the Help window. The article about the Ribbon continues to appear at the right side.
>
> **7.** Scroll up to the top of the Table of Contents pane and click the **What's New?** link.
>
> **8.** Click **What's New in PowerPoint 2010?**. The help topic appears in the window, as shown in Figure 1-15.

Figure 1-15

Article explaining the new
features in PowerPoint 2010

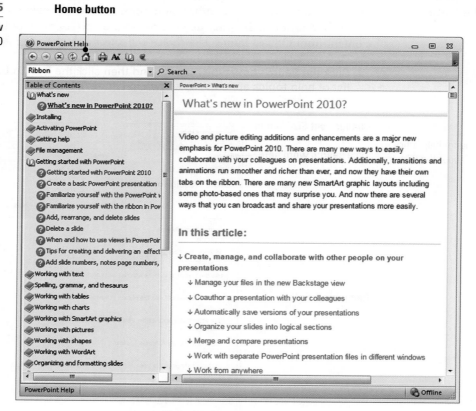

9. Click the Home button. The top-level topic list appears in the right pane. The left pane continues to show the Table of Contents.

10. Click the Close button to close the Help window.

PAUSE. LEAVE the presentation open to use in the next exercise.

PowerPoint's Help window gives you access to many different help topics. A help topic is an article about a specific PowerPoint feature. Help topics can assist you with virtually any task or problem you encounter while working with PowerPoint.

The Help window is set up like a browser window and features some of the same tools you will find in your Web browser, including:

- **Back:** Jumps to the previously opened Help topic.
- **Forward:** Jumps to the next opened Help topic.
- **Stop:** Stops any action in progress.
- **Refresh:** Reloads the current Help topic.
- **Home:** Returns to the initial Help window.
- **Print:** Prints the currently open Help topic.

Take Note   Many PowerPoint dialog boxes contain a Help button. When you click it, a Help window opens with information about the dialog box.

You can find help in several ways. For example, you can open the Table of Contents and scan the list for help on a specific topic. You can also type a word or phrase into the Search box, and then click the Search button. A list of related help topics appears in the Help window.

The Search button gives you more options when looking for help. If you click the drop-down arrow next to the Search button, you can search for help online or offline, look for PowerPoint templates, find information for developers, and more.

The Connection Status menu lets you decide whether to access the help topics that are available online, or just those topics that are installed on your computer (called "offline help"). If your computer has an "always on" connection to the Internet—such as a cable modem or a LAN connection—you will probably want to access online content. If your computer has a dial-up connection, or if you simply do not want to download help topics every time you click the Help button, you can choose *Show content only from this computer* to work with only locally stored help topics.

Closing a Presentation

When you close a presentation, PowerPoint removes it from the screen. PowerPoint continues running so you can work with other files. You should always save and close any open presentations before you exit PowerPoint or shut down your computer. In this exercise, you will practice closing an open presentation.

STEP BY STEP | **Close a Presentation**

USE the presentation that is open from the previous exercise.

1. Click the **File** tab; Backstage view appears.
2. Click **Close**. PowerPoint clears the presentation from the screen.

PAUSE. LEAVE PowerPoint open to use in the next exercise.

WORKING WITH AN EXISTING PRESENTATION

The Bottom Line

If you want to work with an existing presentation, you need to open it. After opening a presentation, you can use PowerPoint's View commands to change the way the presentation is displayed onscreen; different views are suitable for different types of presentation editing and management tasks. You can also use PowerPoint's Zoom tools to make slides look larger or smaller on the screen. The following exercises show you how to view your slides in different ways, and how to add, edit, and delete text on your slides. You will then learn how to print a presentation and to save it to a disk.

Opening an Existing Presentation

PowerPoint makes it easy to work on a presentation over time. If you can't finish a slide show today, you can reopen it later and resume working on it. The Open dialog box lets you open a presentation that has already been saved on a disk. Presentations can be stored on any disk on your PC or network or on removable media (such as a CD). You can use the Look In box to navigate to the file's location, and then click the file to select it. This exercise shows you how to use the Open button to open an existing presentation—one that has already been created and saved as a file on a disk.

STEP BY STEP | **Open an Existing Presentation**

WileyPLUS Extra! features an online tutorial of this task.

GET READY. To open an existing presentation, do the following.

1. Click the **File** tab to open Backstage view.
2. Click **Open**. The Open dialog box appears, as shown in Figure 1-16.

Figure 1-16

The Open dialog box

Another Way
You can also open the Open dialog box by pressing Ctrl+O.

 The *Blue Yonder Overview* file is available on the book companion website or in WileyPLUS.

Another Way
Instead of clicking the file's name in the Open dialog box and then clicking the Open button, you can double-click the file's name to open the presentation.

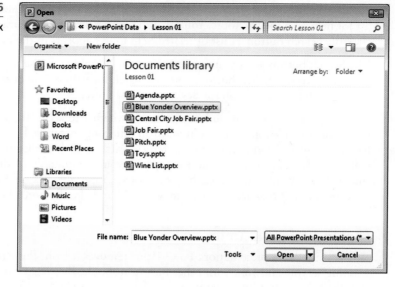

3. Locate and select *Blue Yonder Overview*, then click Open. The presentation appears on your screen, as shown in Figure 1-17.

Figure 1-17

The *Blue Yonder Overview* presentation

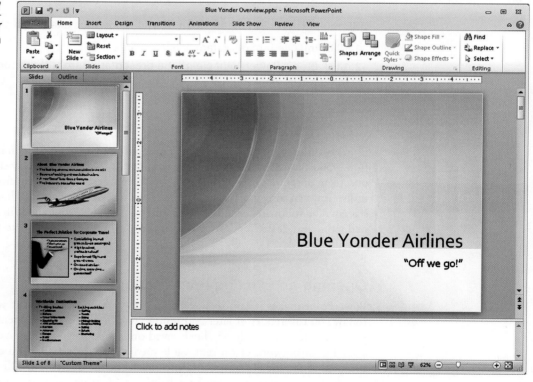

Another Way
If a presentation has been opened recently, its name should appear on the Recent Documents list. After opening Backstage view, click Recent, and then click the presentation's name to open it.

PAUSE. LEAVE the presentation open to use in the next exercise.

Viewing a Presentation in Different Ways

PowerPoint's various **views** enable you to see your presentation in a variety of ways. For example, in Normal view, you can work with just one slide at a time, which is helpful when you are adding text or graphics to a slide. Alternately, in Slide Sorter view, you can view all the slides in a presentation at the same time, which makes it easy to rearrange the slides. The following exercise shows you how to change PowerPoint's views.

STEP BY STEP   **Change PowerPoint's Views**

USE the presentation that you opened during the previous exercise.

1. Click the View tab, as shown in Figure 1-18. Notice that the Normal button is highlighted on both the Ribbon and the Views toolbar in the bottom-right corner of the PowerPoint window.

Figure 1-18

Normal view, with the View tab selected

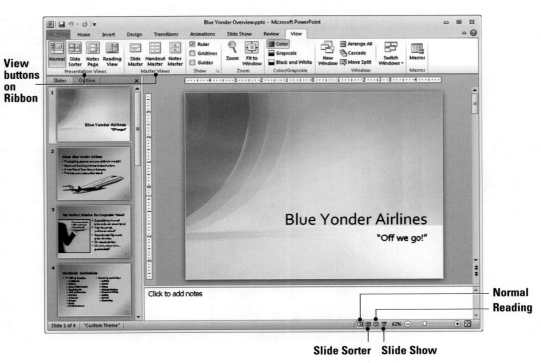

2. Click the Slide Sorter View button to change to Slide Sorter view, as shown in Figure 1-19.

Figure 1-19

Slide Sorter view

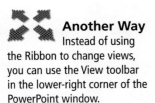

Another Way
Instead of using the Ribbon to change views, you can use the View toolbar in the lower-right corner of the PowerPoint window.

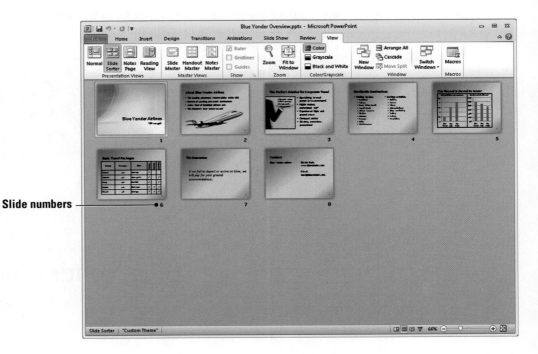

Take Note   If formatted slides are hard to read in Slide Sorter view, press Alt and click a slide to see its heading clearly.

3. Click **slide 2**, and then click the **Notes Page View** button. PowerPoint switches to Notes Page view, as shown in Figure 1-20.

Figure 1-20

Notes Page view

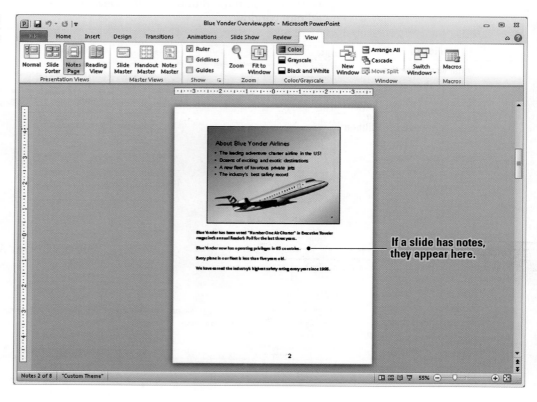

Take Note   There is no button for Notes Page view on the Views toolbar at the bottom of the PowerPoint window; you must access it via the Ribbon.

4. Click the **Slide Show** tab, and click **From Beginning**. The first slide of the presentation fills the screen, as shown in Figure 1-21.

Figure 1-21

Slide Show view

Another Way
You can also switch to Slide Show view by pressing F5.

5. Press **Esc** to exit Slide Show view and return to Notes Page view.

6. Click the **View** tab, and click the **Reading View** button. The first slide appears in a reading window. It looks just like Figure 1-21 except it does not fill the screen.

7. Close the reading window by pressing Esc.

8. On the View toolbar, click the **Normal View** button. PowerPoint switches back to Normal view.

PAUSE. LEAVE the presentation open to use in the next exercise.

PowerPoint provides these views:

- **Normal view** is the default view that lets you focus on an individual slide. The slide you are currently editing is called the **current slide**. The current slide appears in the Slide pane, which is the largest of the view's three panes. Below the Slide pane is the Notes pane, where you can add and edit notes you want to associate with the current slide. In the left pane—called the Slides/Outline pane—you can use the Slides tab to jump from one slide to another, as you will see later in this lesson. On the Outline tab, you can add text to a slide or copy or move text from one slide to another.

- **Slide Sorter view** displays all the slides in a presentation on a single screen. (If there are more slides than can fit in one screen, you can use scroll bars to move slides in and out of view.) In Slide Show view, you can reorganize a slide show by dragging slides to different positions. You can also duplicate and delete slides in this view.

- **Notes Page view** shows one slide at a time, along with any notes that are associated with the slide. This view lets you create and edit notes. You may find it easier to work with notes in this view than in Normal view. You can also print notes pages for your presentation; they are printed as they appear in Notes Page view.

- **Slide Show view** lets you preview your presentation on the screen, so you can see it the way your audience will see it.

- **Reading view** is like Slide Show view except it's in a window rather than filling the entire screen. Displaying the presentation in a window enables you to also work in other windows at the same time.

(X) **Ref**

You will work with PowerPoint's printing options and practice previewing a presentation later in this lesson.

Using Zoom

PowerPoint's **zoom** tools let you change the magnification of slides on the screen. By zooming out, you can see an entire slide; by zooming in, you can inspect one area of the slide. Both views have advantages: higher magnifications make it easier to position objects on the slide, and lower magnifications enable you to see how all the parts of a slide look as a whole. In this exercise, you practice using the zoom tool.

STEP BY STEP **Use Zoom**

Another Way
You can click the Zoom level indicator at the far left of the Zoom control (located on the right end of the Status Bar) to display the Zoom dialog box.

USE the presentation that is open from the previous exercise.

1. Click the **slide** in the Slide pane, to ensure that the Slide pane is active. As a reminder, the Slide pane is the large pane on the right side of Normal view, in which one slide appears at a time.

2. On the View tab, click the **Zoom** button. The Zoom dialog box appears, as shown in Figure 1-22.

Figure 1-22

The Zoom dialog box

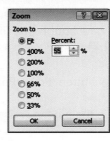

 Another Way
You can drag the Zoom control's slider bar to the right or left to change the zoom level. However, in Normal view, the slider controls only the Slides pane, regardless of what pane is selected. If you want to change the zoom for the Slides/Outline pane, you must use the dialog box.

3. Click the **200%** option button, then click **OK**. In the Slide pane, the slide is magnified by 200%. Notice that you can no longer see the entire slide.

4. Click the **Zoom Out** button at the left end of the Zoom control, at the lower-right of the screen, as shown in Figure 1-23. Continue clicking the button until the zoom level drops to 100%. Notice that, even at 100% magnification, the slide is too large for the Slide pane.

Figure 1-23

Using the Zoom controls

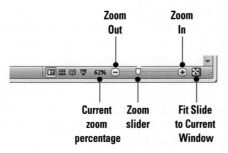

Take Note

You can resize the Slide pane by dragging its bottom border up or down, or by dragging its left-hand border to the right or left. The Slides/Outline pane and Notes pane also change size when you drag the borders.

5. Click the **Fit slide to current window** button at the far right end of the Zoom control. PowerPoint zooms out to fit the entire slide in the Slide pane.

PAUSE. LEAVE the presentation open to use in the next exercise.

You can use either the Zoom dialog box or the Zoom control to change magnification levels. In the Zoom dialog box, you can zoom in or out by choosing one of seven preset magnification levels, or you can use the Percent spin control to set the zoom level precisely. All zoom options are available in Normal view. In Slide Sorter view, some zoom options are available, but the Fit slide to current window tool is not.

Viewing Multiple Presentations at Once

You can have multiple presentations open at the same time in PowerPoint, and you can arrange their windows so that they are all visible at once. This makes it easy to drag-and-drop content between windows, and also to compare different versions of a presentation. In the following exercise you will open two presentations and arrange them.

STEP BY STEP | **Arrange Multiple Presentation Windows**

@ The *Job Fair 1* file is available on the book companion website or in WileyPLUS.

USE the presentation that is open from the previous exercise.

1. Click the **File** tab.

2. Click **Open**. The Open dialog box appears.

3. Locate and open *Job Fair 1*. The presentation appears on your screen.

4. Click the **View** tab.

5. Click **Arrange All** in the Window command group. The presentations appear side-by-side, as in Figure 1-24.

Figure 1-24

Two presentations open
side-by-side

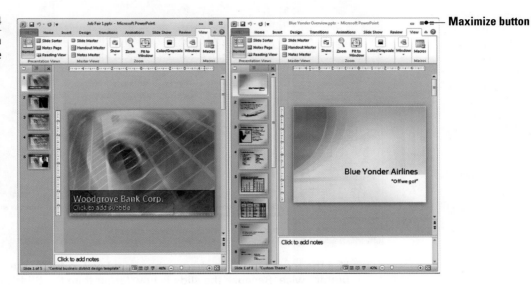

Maximize button

6. Use the Close button to close the Job Fair presentation, as you learned in "Closing a Presentation" earlier in this lesson.

7. In the Blue Yonder Overview window, click the **Maximize** button 🔲 in the upper-right corner. The PowerPoint window once again fills the screen.

PAUSE. LEAVE the presentation open for the next exercise.

Moving Between Slides

PowerPoint provides a number of methods for moving through a presentation in different views. You can move from one slide to another with either the mouse or the keyboard. You can specify that a certain slide should be displayed, or you can browse the available slides to identify the one you want based on its content.

Using the Mouse to Scroll Through a Presentation

PowerPoint's scroll bars let you move up and down through your presentation. When you drag the scroll box in the Slide pane, PowerPoint displays a ScreenTip with the slide number and slide title to show which slide will appear on screen when you release the mouse button. Click the scroll buttons to move up or down one line or one slide at a time, depending on the current zoom level. Click and hold a scroll button to move more quickly or drag a scroll box to move even more quickly. In this exercise, you use the mouse to scroll through a PowerPoint presentation.

STEP BY STEP   **Scroll Through a Presentation Using the Mouse**

USE the presentation that is open and maximized from the previous exercise.

1. Click the **scroll down** button on the right side of the Slide pane, as shown in Figure 1-25. Because the zoom level is set at Fit Slide to Current Window, slide 2 appears on the screen.

Figure 1-25

Scroll tools

Separate scroll bar for Slides/Outline pane

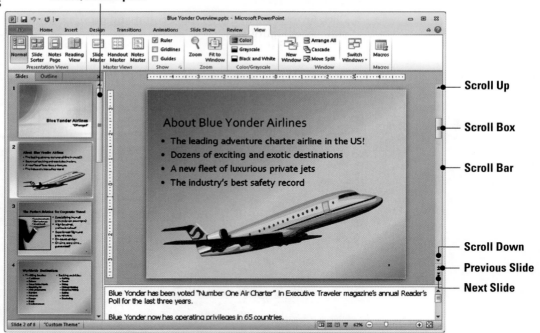

- Scroll Up
- Scroll Box
- Scroll Bar
- Scroll Down
- Previous Slide
- Next Slide

2. Use the zoom control to change the zoom level to 100%, then click the scroll down button twice. Because the slide is now larger than the Slide pane, the scroll button scrolls the slide down in small increments instead of jumping to the next slide.

3. Click the **Fit to Window** button in the Zoom command group on the View tab Ribbon.

4. At the bottom of the scroll bar, click the Next Slide button twice. Slide 3 appears, and then slide 4 appears.

5. In the Slides tab of the Slides/Outline pane, scroll down to locate slide 5, and click it. The selected slide appears in the Slide pane, as shown in Figure 1-26.

Figure 1-26

Click a slide's thumbnail image on the Slides tab to jump to that slide

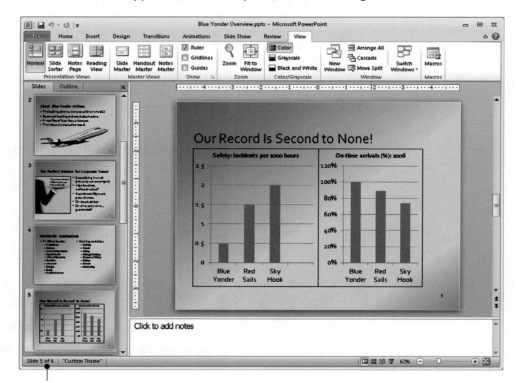

The current slide's number appears on the status bar

Take Note	The current slide's number always appears in the lower-left corner of the status bar.

6. Point to the scroll box that appears to the right of the Slides/Outline pane, and then drag the scroll box all the way down to the bottom of the scroll bar. The last slide (slide 8) appears on the Slides tab, but slide 5 remains visible in the Slide pane.

7. Click the Previous Slide button (at the bottom right of the Slide pane, as shown earlier in Figure 1-25). Slide 4 appears in the Slide pane; notice that the slide also appears highlighted on the Slides tab.

8. Click the scroll box that appears to the right of the Slide pane, and then drag the scroll box all the way up to the top of the scroll bar. You return to the beginning of the presentation.

PAUSE. LEAVE the presentation open for the next exercise.

In Normal view, both the Slide pane and the Slides/Outline pane have scroll bars, buttons, and boxes. If there is text in the Notes pane, scroll tools will appear there to let you move up and down through the text, if necessary. In Slide Sorter view and Notes Page view, scroll tools will appear on the right side of the window if they are needed.

In Normal view, you can click the Previous Slide button to move up to the previous slide and click the Next Slide button to move to the following slide.

Using the Keyboard to Move Through a Presentation

Your keyboard's cursor control keys let you jump from one slide to another, as long as no text or object is selected on a slide. If text is selected, the arrow keys move the insertion point within the text; however, the Page Up, Page Down, Home, and End keys will still let you move from slide to slide. In this exercise, you practice using the keyboard to navigate through presentations.

STEP BY STEP   **Move Through a Presentation Using the Keyboard**

USE the presentation that is open from the previous exercise.

1. With slide 1 visible in Normal view in the Slide pane, press Page Down on your keyboard. Slide 2 appears.

2. Press Page Down to jump to slide 3.

3. Press Page Down to jump to slide 4.

4. Press Page Up to go back to slide 3.

5. Press Page Up to move up to slide 2.

6. Press Page Up to view slide 1.

7. Press End to jump to slide 8, the last slide in the presentation.

8. Press Home to return to slide 1.

PAUSE. LEAVE the presentation open to use in the next exercise.

Working with Text

Text is not typed directly onto a slide in PowerPoint, but instead is placed in **text boxes**. A text box is, as the name implies, a box that holds text that you type into it. Most of the available slide layouts have one or more placeholders that become text boxes when you type text into them, and you can also add more text boxes manually to slides, as you will learn in Lesson 3. Text can be placed on a slide either by typing it directly into a text box or placeholder, or by typing in the Outline pane in Normal view. In the following exercises, you will practice adding text to a placeholder; adding text to the Outline tab; selecting, replacing, and deleting text on a slide; and copying and moving text from one slide to another.

Adding Text to a Placeholder

In this exercise, you practice entering text in a **placeholder**, which is a box that can hold either text or a graphic object. The placeholders available depend on the slide layout. In the Blue Yonder presentation, slide 1 is an example of a Title Slide layout; it contains two placeholders—one for the title and one for the subtitle. Placeholders make it easy to add text—just click in the placeholder, and then type the text.

STEP BY STEP　　**Add Text to a Text Placeholder**

USE the presentation that is open from the previous exercise.

1. Click the Home tab. On slide 1, click at the beginning of the slide's title (Blue Yonder Airlines). The borders of the title's placeholder appear, as shown in Figure 1-27, and a blinking insertion point appears before the word *Blue*.

Figure 1-27

The title placeholder and insertion point

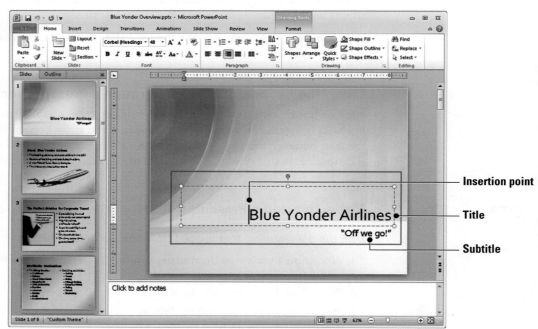

2. Click the slide's subtitle, which is the second line of text. The subtitle's placeholder appears, as does the insertion point.
3. Go to slide 4 by clicking the slide in the Slides/Outline pane, or by pressing Page Down until it appears.
4. Click after the word *Snorkeling* in the second column. The insertion point appears.
5. Press Enter to start a new line, and type Scuba.
6. Press Enter, and then type Sightseeing. Your slide should look like the one shown in Figure 1-28.

Figure 1-28

Slide 4 with added text

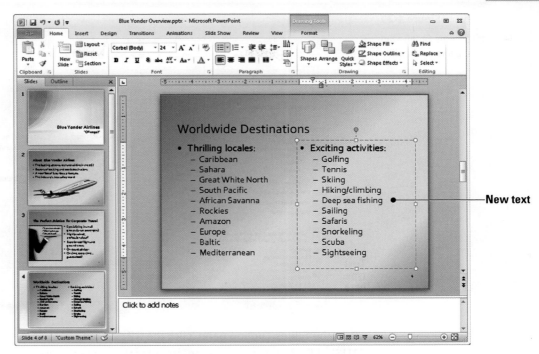

PAUSE. LEAVE the presentation open for the next exercise.

Adding Text on the Outline Tab

Working on the Outline tab is like working in a word processor. PowerPoint displays the text from each slide on the Outline tab, without any backgrounds, placeholders, or anything else that might distract you from your writing. You can navigate a presentation on the Outline tab the same way you use the Slides tab—scroll to the desired slide's outline, and then click it. Here, you practice adding text on the Outline tab.

STEP BY STEP	Add Text on the Outline Tab

USE the presentation that is open from the previous exercise.

1. Go to slide 8. This slide is supposed to contain contact information, but the mailing address and telephone number are missing.

2. In the Slides/Outline pane, click the Outline tab. Because slide 8 is the current slide, its text is highlighted on the tab.

Take Note   Remember that you can adjust the Zoom level for the Outline tab, or any other pane, as needed if the content is not shown at a convenient size for working with it.

3. On the Outline tab, click after the word *Airlines* to place the insertion point there.
4. Press Enter to start a new line.
5. On the new line, type 12 Ferris St., and then press Enter. As you type the new text on the Outline tab, notice that it appears on the slide.
6. Type Diehard, TN 34567, and then press Enter.
7. Type (707) 555-AWAY. Your slide should look like the one shown in Figure 1-29.

Figure 1-29

Text added to the Outline tab
appears on the slide

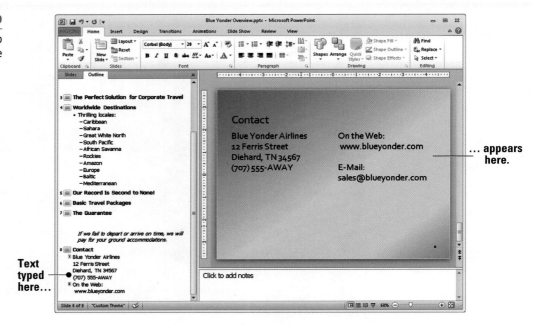

8. In the Slides/Outline pane, click the **Slides** tab.

PAUSE. LEAVE the presentation open for the next exercise.

Selecting, Replacing, and Deleting Text

You can edit, replace, and delete text directly on a slide. First, you must select the text to let PowerPoint know you want to edit it. You can select any amount of text by dragging the mouse pointer across it. When you move the mouse pointer over text, it changes to an **I-beam pointer**, a vertically oriented pointer that resembles the letter I. This pointer makes it easy to select text precisely. In this exercise, you practice editing text in PowerPoint.

STEP BY STEP   **Select, Replace, and Delete Text**

USE the presentation that is open from the previous exercise.

1. Go to slide 3, and in the fourth item of the bulleted list on the right, double-click the word **advisor** to select it, as shown in Figure 1-30.

Figure 1-30

Selected text

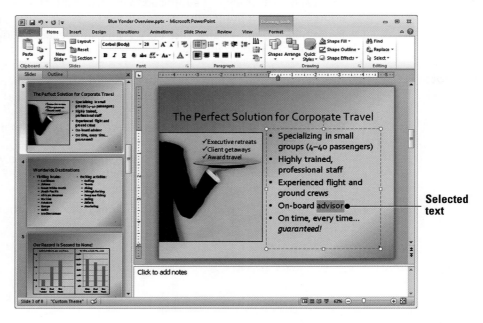

2. While the text is selected, type concierge. The new text replaces the selected text.

3. Go to slide 7, and select the word ground by dragging the mouse pointer over it. (The mouse pointer changes from an arrow to an I-beam whenever it is in a text placeholder, as shown in Figure 1-31.)

Figure 1-31

Selecting text and the I-beam pointer

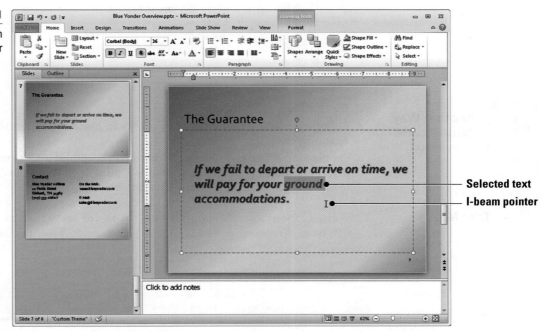

4. Press Delete to delete the word from the slide.

PAUSE. LEAVE the presentation open for the next exercise.

Whenever you select text in PowerPoint—whether it is a single character or all the text on a slide—it is highlighted with a colored background. Once the text is selected, you can type new text in its place or delete it.

Take Note   Only text from text-based placeholders appears in the Outline pane; text from manually created text boxes (see Lesson 2) and from graphics and charts does not appear.

Copying and Moving Text from One Slide to Another

In this exercise, you practice copying and moving text from one slide to another, using the Copy, Cut, and Paste commands. You can use these commands on many kinds of objects in PowerPoint, including pictures, charts, and placeholders. Don't be surprised if these commands become your most frequently used tools, because they can save you a great deal of typing.

STEP BY STEP   **Copy and Move Text from One Slide to Another**

USE the presentation that is open from the previous exercise.

1. Go to slide 2, and in the slide's title placeholder, select Blue Yonder Airlines by dragging the mouse pointer across the text.

2. On the Home tab, click the Copy button, as shown in Figure 1-32.

Figure 1-32

Clipboard tools

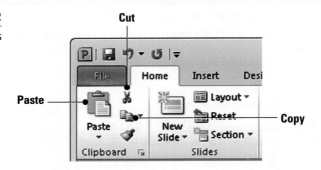

Another Way
You can issue the Copy command by pressing Ctrl+C.

3. Go to slide 7.
4. Click **between the two words of the title** to place the insertion point before the word *Guarantee.*
5. On the Home tab, click the **Paste** button. PowerPoint inserts the copied text at the insertion point's position, as shown in Figure 1-33. Press the **Spacebar** if necessary to insert a space before the word *Guarantee.*

Take Note   The Paste Options icon that appears near the pasted text in Figure 1-33 opens a menu when clicked; from that menu you can choose pasting options. In this case you will ignore the icon, accepting the default pasting options.

Figure 1-33

Selected text has been copied to slide 7

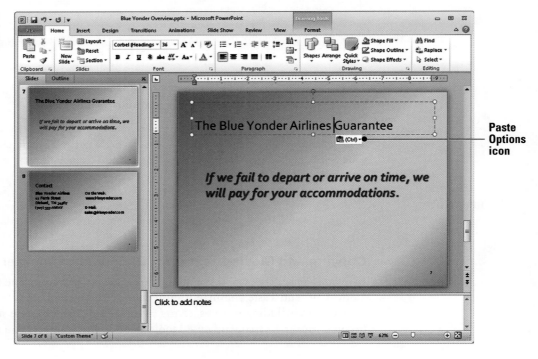

Paste Options icon

Another Way
You can issue the Paste command by pressing Ctrl+V.

Another Way
You can issue the Cut command by pressing Ctrl+X.

6. Go to slide 3.
7. Select the last item of the bulleted list on the right side of the slide.
8. On the Home tab, click the **Cut** button. The selected item is removed from the list.
9. Go to slide 2.
10. Click below the last item of the bulleted list, just above the airplane's tail.
11. On the Home tab, click the **Paste** button. The item appears at the bottom of the list.
12. Click anywhere in the blank area around the slide to clear the placeholder's border from the screen. Your slide should look like the one shown in Figure 1-34.

Figure 1-34

Selected text has been
moved to slide 2

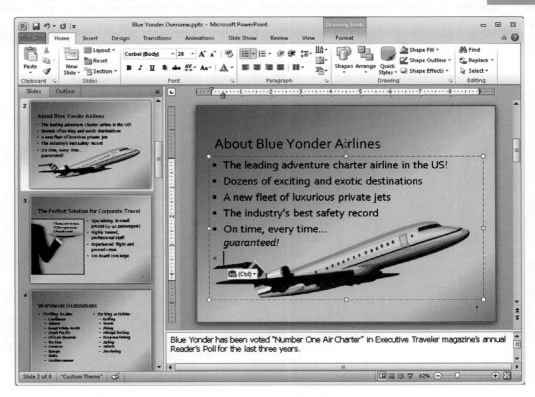

Figure 1-34

Selected text has been
moved to slide 2

PAUSE. LEAVE the presentation open for the next exercise.

Printing a Presentation

PowerPoint's Print command sends the currently open presentation to the printer. The default
settings produce a printout of the entire presentation, one slide per page, on whatever printer is
set up in Windows as the default.

STEP BY STEP   **Print a Presentation with the Default Settings**

USE the presentation that is open from the previous exercise.

Another Way
You can press
Ctrl+P instead of steps 1 and 2.

1. Click the **File** tab.
2. Click **Print**. Print options appear. You will learn about them in Lesson 2; leave the
   defaults set for now.
3. Click the **Print** button. PowerPoint prints the entire presentation, using the default print
   settings, assuming your PC has at least one printer set up.

Ⓧ Ref   Printing options are discussed in Lesson 2.

PAUSE. LEAVE the document open to use in the next exercise.

Saving an Edited Presentation

Whenever you work on a presentation, you should save it to a disk—especially if you have made
changes that you want to keep. In this exercise, you will practice saving a presentation with a
different file name, in native PowerPoint 2010 format.

STEP BY STEP   **Save an Edited Presentation**

> **USE** the presentation that is open from the previous exercise.
>
> 1. Click the **File** tab to open Backstage view.
> 2. Click **Save As**. The Save As dialog box appears, as shown in Figure 1-35. The file location defaults to whatever location was most recently accessed.

Figure 1-35

Save As dialog box

> 3. Select the location where you want to save your files (ask your instructor for guidance), and then type *Blue Yonder Introduction* in the File name box.

Take Note   Ask your instructor if you should append your initials to the end of each file name for the exercises in this book, to keep your files separate from those of other students.

> 4. Click **Save**.
> 5. Click the **Close** button to close the presentation.
>
> **PAUSE. LEAVE** PowerPoint open to use in the next exercise.

 Ref

> Presentations created in PowerPoint 2007 and 2010 are incompatible with earlier versions of PowerPoint. However, you can save in an earlier format for backward compatibility; that skill is covered in Lesson 2.

When you need to save an existing presentation in a new location or with a different file name, use the Save As command. In the Save As dialog box, you can specify a different disk drive and folder to store the file; you can also give the file a different name in the File name box. After the presentation is saved in the new location and with its new file name, you can click the Save button on the Quick Access Toolbar when you need to resave the file.

Take Note   You can also download a free conversion utility for earlier versions of PowerPoint that will allow them to open files in PowerPoint 2007/2010 format. See http://office.microsoft.com/en-us/office-2003-resource-kit/office-converter-pack-HA001151358.aspx?redir=0 for details.

Exiting PowerPoint

When you exit PowerPoint, the program closes and is removed from your computer's memory. In this exercise, you will practice exiting PowerPoint.

STEP BY STEP   **Exit PowerPoint**

GET READY. In order to exit PowerPoint, do the following.

1. Click the File tab.
2. Click Exit. PowerPoint closes.

SKILL SUMMARY

In This Lesson, You Learned How To:
Work in the PowerPoint window
Work with an existing presentation

Knowledge Assessment

Matching

Match the term in Column 1 to its description in Column 2.

Column 1	Column 2
1. Tab	a. Includes the Slide, Notes, and Slide/Outline panes
2. Ribbon	b. A small toolbar that appears when you point to selected text
3. Normal view	c. Shows the keyboard key that will issue a command
4. Current slide	d. To highlight text for editing
5. Backstage view	e. A set of related tools on the Ribbon
6. Mini toolbar	f. Displays commands for managing files
7. Placeholder	g. The slide you are editing
8. KeyTip	h. A Ribbon tool that opens a dialog box
9. Dialog box launcher	i. A large toolbar that presents tools in related groups
10. Select	j. A box, built into many slides, that holds text or an object

True/False

Circle T if the statement is true or F if the statement is false.

T F 1. If you need more room on the screen, you can hide the Ribbon.

T F 2. When you start PowerPoint, the last presentation you worked on appears on the screen.

T F 3. When you save a presentation that has been previously saved, clicking the Save button on the Quick Access Toolbar reopens the Save As dialog box.

T F 4. The Quick Access Toolbar appears faint, but turns brighter as the mouse pointer gets closer.

T F 5. To close a dialog box without accepting any changes you may have made to it, click the Cancel button.

T F 6. You can use the Undo command to reverse the last action you took.

T F 7. To print a presentation, open Backstage view and click Print.

T F 8. Backstage view gives you access to all of PowerPoint's design tools.

T   F   9. You can use the Cut and Paste commands to move text from one slide to another slide.

T   F   10. In Normal view, PowerPoint displays five different panes for viewing different aspects of your slides.

Competency Assessment

Project 1-1: The Central City Job Fair

As personnel manager for Woodgrove Bank, you have accepted an invitation to give a presentation at a local job fair. Your goal is to recruit applicants for positions as bank tellers. You have created the presentation but need to finish it.

GET READY. LAUNCH PowerPoint if it is not already running.

@ The *Job Fair 1* file is available on the companion website or in WileyPLUS.

1. Click the File tab and open the presentation named *Job Fair 1* from the data files for this lesson.

2. Save the presentation as *Central City Job Fair*.

3. On slide 1, click in the subtitle box to place the insertion point there, and then type Central City Job Fair. Go to slide 2.

4. In the title of slide 2, select the words Woodgrove Bank by dragging the mouse pointer over them, and then replace the selected text by typing Us.

5. In the bulleted list, click after the word *assets* to place the insertion point there.

6. Press Enter to move the insertion point down to a new, blank line.

7. Type Voted "Best Local Bank" by City Magazine, 2010. The new text will wrap to fit in the box.

8. Click the Next Slide button to go to slide 3. In the slide's outline, select the words *Help Wanted* (do not select the colon), and then press Delete to delete the text.

9. Type Now Hiring.

10. Click at the end of the first item in the bulleted list, and then press Enter to create a new line in the list.

11. Type Responsible for cash drawer and station bookkeeping.

12. Click the Slides tab, and then press Page Down to go to slide 4.

13. Select the last item in the bulleted list by dragging the mouse pointer across it.

14. On the Ribbon, click the Home tab, if necessary, and then click the Cut button. On the Slides tab, click slide 5.

15. Click at the end of the last item in the bulleted list to place the insertion point there, and then press Enter.

16. On the Ribbon, click the Paste button. The item you cut from slide 4 is pasted into slide 5.

17. **SAVE** the presentation and **CLOSE** the file.

LEAVE PowerPoint open for the next project.

Project 1-2: Messenger Service

Consolidated Messenger is a new company offering in-town courier service to corporate and private customers. As the company's owner, you want to tell as many people as possible about your new service, and a presentation can help you do it. You need to review your presentation, make some minor changes, and print it.

GET READY. LAUNCH PowerPoint if it is not already running.

@ The *Pitch* file is available on the companion website or in WileyPLUS.

1. Click the File tab and open the presentation named *Pitch* from the data files for this lesson, and save it as *Messenger Pitch*.
2. Read slide 1. On the Slides tab, click slide 2 and read it.
3. Click the scroll down box to go to slide 3, and then read it.
4. Click the Next Slide button to go to slide 4, and then read it.
5. Press Page Down to go to slide 5, and then read it.
6. Press Enter to go to slide 6, and then read it.
7. Press Home to return to the beginning of the presentation.
8. On slide 1, select the words and Delivery by dragging the mouse pointer over them.
9. Press Delete to delete the selected text from the subtitle. Go to slide 2.
10. On slide 2, select the word delayed and type scheduled in its place.
11. Select the third item in the bulleted list (24-hour emergency service) by dragging the mouse pointer over it.
12. On the Home tab of the Ribbon, click the Copy button. Go to slide 5.
13. On slide 5, click at the end of the last item in the bulleted list to place the insertion point there.
14. Press Enter to move the insertion point down to a new, blank line. On the Ribbon, click the Paste button.
15. Click at the end of the newly pasted line to move the insertion point there, and then type $250. Go to slide 6.
16. On slide 6, click at the end of the last line of text in the left-hand column, and then press Enter.
17. Type 555-1087 (daytime), and then press Enter.
18. Type 555-1088 (emergency), and then press Enter.
19. Type 555-1089 (fax).
20. Go to slide 1. Click the File tab.
21. When Backstage view opens, click Print. Then click the Print button to print with the default settings.
22. **SAVE** the presentation and **CLOSE** the file.

LEAVE PowerPoint open for the next project.

Proficiency Assessment

Project 1-3: The Big Meeting

You are the director of documentation at Litware, Inc., which develops software for use in elementary schools. You have scheduled a conference with the writing staff and are working on an agenda for the meeting. Because the agenda is a single PowerPoint slide, you can display it on a projection screen for reference during the meeting.

@ The *Agenda* file is available on the companion website or in WileyPLUS.

1. **OPEN** the *Agenda* file from the data files for this lesson and save it as *Final Agenda*.
2. Copy the second line of the bulleted list and paste the copy below the original as a new bullet point.
3. In the newly pasted line, replace the word *Upcoming* with Revised.
4. On the Outline tab, add a new line to the end of the agenda. On the new line, type Adjourn.

5. Print the presentation.

6. **SAVE** the presentation, then **CLOSE** the file.

LEAVE PowerPoint open for the next project.

Project 1-4: Job Fair, Part 2

You have decided to make some last-minute changes to your presentation before going to the job fair.

@ The *Job Fair 2* file is available on the companion website or in WileyPLUS.

1. **OPEN** *Job Fair 2* from the data files for this lesson and save it as *Final Job Fair*.

2. Copy the word *Woodgrove* on slide 1. In the title of slide 2, delete the word *Us* and paste the copied word in its place.

3. On slide 2, change the word *owned* to managed.

4. On slide 4, add the line References a must to the bottom of the bulleted list.

5. Print the presentation.

6. **SAVE** the presentation, then **CLOSE** the file.

LEAVE PowerPoint open for the next project.

Mastery Assessment

Project 1-5: Price Fixing

You are the general manager of the restaurant at Coho Winery. It's time to update the staff on the restaurant's new wine selections and prices, and a slide show is a good way to give everyone the details. An easy way to handle this job is to open last season's presentation and update it with new wines and prices.

@ The *Wine List* file is available on the companion website or in WileyPLUS.

1. **OPEN** *Wine List* from the data files for this lesson and save it as *New Wine List*.

2. Move *Coho Premium Chardonnay—$29.99* from slide 2 to the bottom of slide 4.

3. On slide 3, increase the price of every wine by one dollar.

4. Print the presentation.

5. **SAVE** the presentation, then **CLOSE** the file.

LEAVE PowerPoint open for the next project.

Project 1-6: A Trip to Toyland

As a product manager for Tailspin Toys, you introduce new products to many other people in the company, such as the marketing and sales staff. You need to finalize a presentation about several new toys.

@ The *Toys* file is available on the companion website or in WileyPLUS.

1. **OPEN** *Toys* from the data files for this lesson and save it as *New Toys*.

2. Copy *List Price: $14.99* on slide 2 and paste it at the bottom of the bulleted lists on slides 3 and 4.

3. Change the teddy bear's name from *Rory* to George.

4. Change the top's speed from *800* to 1,200.

5. Print the presentation.

6. **SAVE** the presentation and **CLOSE** the file.

EXIT PowerPoint.

INTERNET READY

Use PowerPoint Help to access online information about the new features in PowerPoint 2010. *Up to Speed with PowerPoint 2010* provides a short online course or demo explaining the new features. Browse these or other topics in PowerPoint's Help online.

Presentation Basics 2

LESSON SKILL MATRIX

In This Lesson, You Will Learn The Following Skills:

Creating a New Blank Presentation

Saving a Presentation

Creating a Presentation from a Template

Adding, Deleting, and Organizing Slides

Creating a Presentation from Existing Content

Adding Notes to Your Slides

Printing a Presentation

KEY TERMS

- **contiguous**
- **handout**
- **indent level**
- **layout**
- **non-contiguous**
- **note**
- **Presenter view**
- **slide library**
- **template**
- **themes**
- **thumbnails**

Northwind Traders is a retailer of high-quality outdoor apparel and accessories for men, women, and children. The company has six stores in the Minneapolis–St. Paul area and a thriving online presence. As an assistant general manager, you help oversee the company's daily operations, hire and train new employees, and develop strategic plans. You also perform day-to-day functions assigned by the general manager. Your job frequently requires you to present information to an audience—for example, when training new workers on company policies or when providing executives with information about revenue or expenses. These duties often require you to create presentations from scratch, and PowerPoint 2007 lets you do that in several ways. In this lesson, you will learn different methods for creating presentations. You will also learn how to organize the slides in a presentation, add notes to your slides, select printing options, preview a slide show, and save a presentation for the first time.

SOFTWARE ORIENTATION

Microsoft PowerPoint's New Presentation Dialog Box

PowerPoint's New Presentation window gives you many choices for creating a new presentation. Figure 2-1 shows the New Presentation window. It is accessed by clicking the File tab to enter Backstage view, then clicking New.

Figure 2-1

New Presentation window

Click here to start with a blank presentation.

Select one of these categories.

The templates or themes in the chosen category appear here.

The Preview pane shows what your selected theme or template looks like.

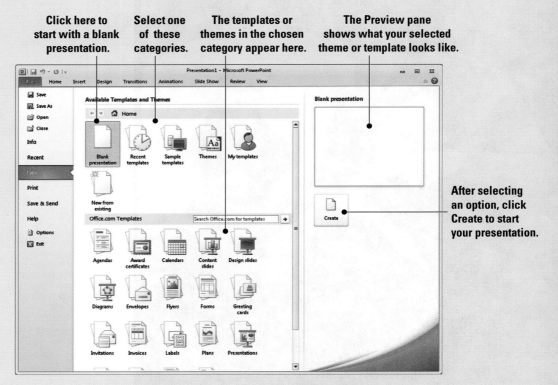

After selecting an option, click Create to start your presentation.

This window enables you to create a new, blank presentation; work from a template or theme stored on your computer; search for templates online; or create a new presentation from an existing one.

CREATING A NEW BLANK PRESENTATION

When you start PowerPoint, a new, blank presentation appears, containing a single slide. The fastest and simplest way to create a new presentation is to start with a blank presentation. You can add text to the presentation, and then format the slides later.

Creating a Blank Presentation

You can use the single slide that opens with a new, blank presentation to begin creating your new presentation. In this exercise, you will learn how to open a blank presentation.

STEP BY STEP   **Create a Blank Presentation**

GET READY. Before you begin these steps, make sure that your computer is on. Log on, if necessary.

1. **START** PowerPoint, if the program is not already running.
2. Click the File tab. Backstage view opens.
3. Click New. The New Presentation window opens, as shown previously in Figure 2-1.

Take Note   You need to use the New Presentation window only when another presentation is open, when no presentation is open, or when you want to create a new presentation based on a template or theme.

4. In the Available Templates and Themes pane, click the Blank Presentation icon, then click the Create button in the lower-right corner of the New Presentation window. A new, blank presentation appears in Normal view, as shown in Figure 2-2.

Figure 2-2

A blank presentation begins with a title slide

The thumbnail of the slide appears blank because the empty text placeholders do not appear on it.

The default slide uses the Title Slide layout.

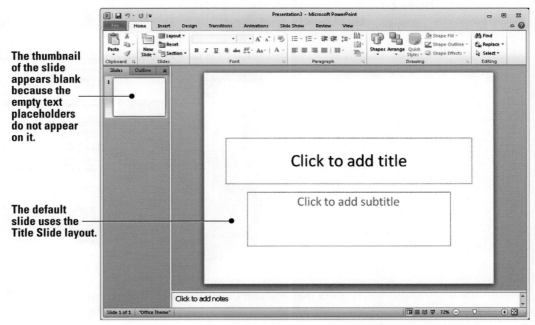

Another Way
Press Ctrl+N to open a new, blank presentation without using the New Presentation window. If another presentation is already open, the blank presentation opens in a separate window.

PAUSE. LEAVE the blank presentation open to use in the next exercise.

There are two advantages to using a blank presentation to start a slide show. First, PowerPoint displays a blank presentation every time the program starts, so you always have immediate access to the first slide of a new presentation. Second, because the presentation is not formatted (meaning there are no backgrounds, colors, or pictures), you can focus on writing your text. Many experienced PowerPoint users prefer to start with a blank presentation because they know they can format their slides after the text is finished.

Changing a Slide's Layout

Most slides have a **layout**—a predefined arrangement of placeholders for text or objects (such as charts or pictures). PowerPoint has a variety of built-in layouts that you can use at any time. Layouts are shown in the Layout gallery as **thumbnails**—small pictures showing each available layout. Choose the layout that is best suited to display the text or objects you want to place on the slide. You can change a slide's layout at any time to arrange text or objects on the slide exactly the way you want. The following exercise shows you how to apply a different layout to the current slide.

STEP BY STEP   **Choose a Different Layout**

WileyPLUS Extra! features an online tutorial of this task.

USE the new, blank presentation that is still open from the previous exercise.

1. Click the **Home** tab to make it active, if necessary, then click **Layout**. A drop-down menu (called a *gallery*) appears, displaying PowerPoint's default layouts, as shown in Figure 2-3. The title of the gallery is Office Theme, indicating that all these layouts come from the default theme (named Office).

Figure 2-3

Choosing a new layout

Click Layout to open a gallery of available layouts.

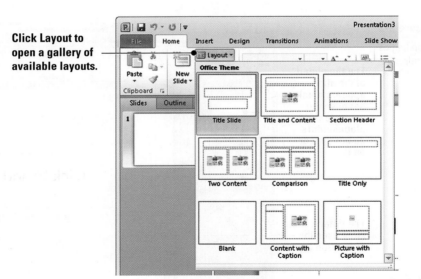

2. Click the **Title and Content** thumbnail in the gallery. The gallery closes and PowerPoint applies the chosen layout to the current slide, as shown in Figure 2-4.

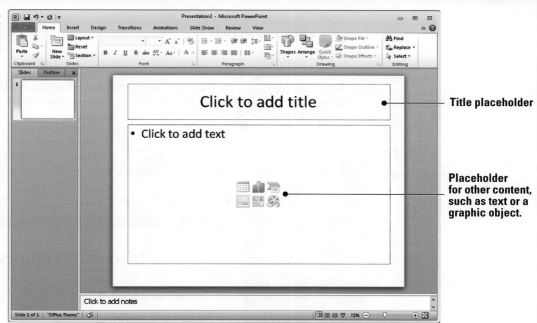

Figure 2-4

The new layout applied
to the current slide

Title placeholder

Placeholder
for other content,
such as text or a
graphic object.

Another Way
To change a slide's
layout, right-click a blank
area of the slide outside a
placeholder. When the shortcut
menu opens, point to Layout,
and then click a layout.

PAUSE. LEAVE the presentation open to use in the next exercise.

In this exercise, you chose the Title and Content layout, which contains a placeholder for the slide's title and a second placeholder that can display text, a picture, a table, or some other kind of object.

Ⓧ   Ref   You will work with other slide layouts in Lesson 4.

You can change a slide's layout whether the slide is blank or contains text. If the slide already has text, PowerPoint will fit the text into the new layout's placeholders. If the new layout does not have an appropriate placeholder for the existing content, the existing content remains on the slide, but is not part of the layout.

Adding Text to a Blank Slide

If a blank slide has one or more text placeholders, you can easily add text to the slide. To enter text, just click the sample text in the placeholder, and then type your text. In this exercise, you will enter text into a blank slide's placeholders to create a set of discussion points for a meeting of store managers. The slide you work with in this exercise has a title placeholder and a content placeholder that can hold text and other types of content.

STEP BY STEP   **Add Text to a Blank Slide**

USE the slide that is still on the screen from the preceding exercise.

1. Click the title placeholder at the top of the slide. The text *Click to add title* disappears and a blinking insertion point appears in the placeholder.
2. Type **Discussion Points**.
3. Click the text at the top of the lower placeholder. The words *Click to add text* disappear and the insertion point appears.
4. Type **Customer surveys**, then press **Enter** to move the insertion point down to a new line.
5. Type **Inventory tracking** and press **Enter**.

6. Type **Absenteeism policy** and press **Enter**.

7. Type **Break** and press **Enter**.

8. Type **Store security** and press **Enter**.

9. Type **Store closing procedures** and press **Enter**.

10. Type **Cash drawer management**, then click anywhere in the blank area outside the placeholder to clear its borders from the screen. Your slide should look like the one shown in Figure 2-5.

Figure 2-5

The completed slide

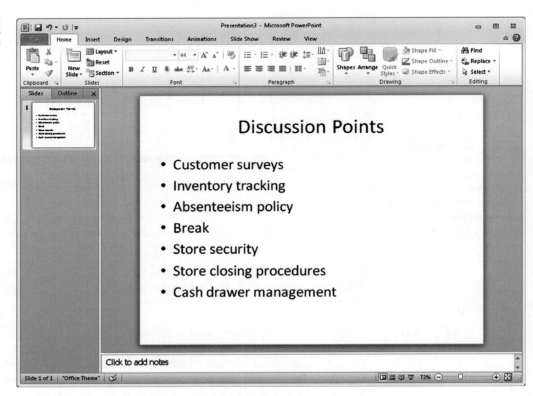

PAUSE. LEAVE the presentation open to use in the next exercise.

Take Note

If you click any of the icons in the lower placeholder, PowerPoint will display tools for adding non-text content, such as a table or chart. These types of content are covered in later lessons.

Even when a multiple-slide presentation is not needed at a meeting, displaying an agenda, a list of discussion points, or a list of breakout rooms can be helpful for the group.

SAVING A PRESENTATION

The Bottom Line

When you create a new presentation, it exists only in your computer's memory. If you want to keep the presentation, you must save it on a disk or to a network location or flash drive. After you save a file, you can close it, then reopen it again later and resume working on it. The following exercises show you how to save a new presentation to a disk, how to save the presentation in a different file format, and how to work with PowerPoint's Save options.

Saving a New Presentation for the First Time

When you save a presentation for the first time, PowerPoint displays the Save As dialog box so you can give the presentation a name before saving it. In this exercise, you will name and save the presentation you created earlier.

STEP BY STEP Save a New Presentation

Another Way
When saving a presentation for the first time, you can open the Save As dialog box by pressing Ctrl+S.

USE the presentation that is still on the screen from the preceding exercise.

1. On the Quick Access Toolbar, click Save. The Save As dialog box appears.
2. Navigate to the folder where you want to save your files.
3. Select the text in the File name box by dragging the mouse pointer over it, and then press Delete to delete it.
4. Type Managers Meeting, as shown in Figure 2-6.

Figure 2-6

Saving the presentation for the first time

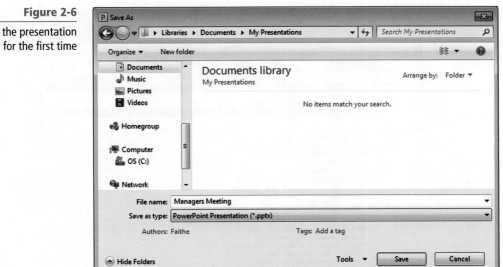

5. Click Save. PowerPoint saves the presentation in the folder you chose, under the name you have given it.

PAUSE. LEAVE the presentation open to use in the next exercise.

When you save a presentation (or any type of document), be sure to give it a name that describes its contents. This will help you identify your presentations more easily when you are trying to find the right one.

Choosing a Different File Format

PowerPoint can save presentations in several different file formats. In this exercise, you will save your presentation in a format that is compatible with earlier versions of PowerPoint.

STEP BY STEP Choose a Different File Format

USE the *Managers Meeting* presentation that is still open from the previous exercise.

1. Click the File tab, then click the Save As command. The Save As dialog box reappears.
2. Next to Save as Type, click the current type: PowerPoint Presentation. A menu of file types opens.

3. Click **PowerPoint 97-2003 Presentation.** The file type changes. See Figure 2-7.

Figure 2-7

Saving with a different file format

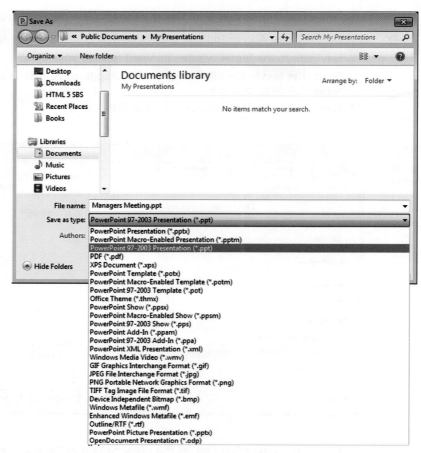

4. Navigate to the folder where you want to save your files. (This step is not necessary if you want to save the file in the same folder you used in the previous exercise.)

Take Note Because you are saving the presentation in a different file format, it is not necessary to give it a new name. Files of different formats can have the same file name. This exercise renames it anyway.

5. Select the file's name in the File name box, delete the name, and then type **Old Format Discussion Points**.

6. Click **Save**, and then close the presentation.

PAUSE. LEAVE PowerPoint open to use in the next exercise.

By default, PowerPoint 2010 saves presentations in a type of XML format, which is not compatible with earlier versions of PowerPoint. If you want to be able to use a presentation with an older version of PowerPoint, you can save it by using the PowerPoint 97-2003 Presentation file format. (PowerPoint 2007 uses the same XML-based format as PowerPoint 2010, so no special version is necessary to share with users of PowerPoint 2007.)

You can save a presentation in other formats as well. For example, if you select the PowerPoint Show format, the presentation will always open in Slide Show view, rather than in Normal view. You can also save a presentation as a template, or as a series of graphics, or in a macro-enabled format.

Working with Save Options

PowerPoint has settings that control the default file location, the default file format, and more. If you find yourself frequently changing the file location or file type when you save a presentation, it may be worth your time to change the settings in PowerPoint that specify the defaults. In the following exercise, you learn how to modify the application's save settings.

STEP BY STEP	Set the Save Options

Take Note   No presentation is open as you begin this exercise, but that's not important. These steps can be completed without having a presentation open.

GET READY. To set the save options, do the following:

1. Click the **File** tab and then click **Options**. The PowerPoint Options dialog box opens.
2. Click the **Save** category in the left panel of the dialog box. The Save Options appear in the right panel.
3. Click on the **Save Files In This Format drop-down list** and examine the available file types. See Figure 2-8. Do not change the current setting (PowerPoint Presentation).

Figure 2-8

Choices available for the default file format in which to save

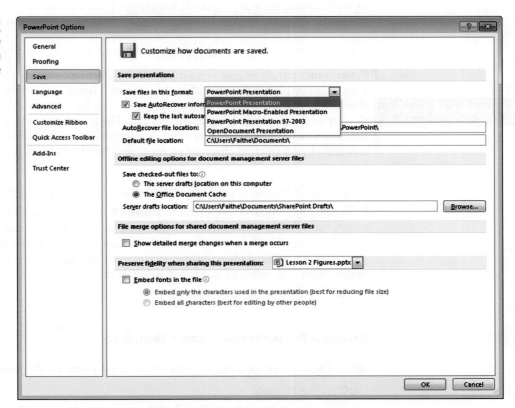

4. In the Default file location text box, take note of the location referenced.

Take Note   By default, files are stored in the Documents (or My Documents) folder for the current user. In Windows Vista and Windows 7, this is the C:\Users*username*\Documents folder, where username is the current user. That's what appears as the default in Figure 2-8, for example.

5. (Optional) Change the location in the Default file location text box to the location where you are storing your completed work for this course. If you do this, you will not have to change the location for saving and opening files every time you want to save or open files for class exercises and projects.

6. Click **OK** to close the dialog box.

7. Click **Save**, then close the presentation.

PAUSE. LEAVE PowerPoint open to use in the next exercise.

You can choose to create regular PowerPoint 2010 presentations, PowerPoint 97-2003 presentations, macro-enabled presentations, or OpenDocument presentations by default. OpenDocument is a widely accepted generic format for presentation files, useful for sharing files with people who use OpenOffice and other freeware office suites.

You can set a default save location of any accessible drive, including not only folders on your hard disk, but also network locations and removable drives. (It is not usually a good idea to set the default location to a drive that is not always available, however.) The location you specify will appear in both the Save As and Open dialog boxes by default.

Also in the save options, you can set an interval at which PowerPoint autosaves your work. Autosaving helps PowerPoint recover any work that would otherwise be lost if your PC shuts off or crashes while there are unsaved changes to a presentation. The default interval is 10 minutes.

CREATING A PRESENTATION FROM A TEMPLATE

The Bottom Line

PowerPoint's templates give you a jump start in creating complete presentations. A **template** is a reusable sample file that includes a background, layouts, coordinating fonts, and other design elements that work together to create an attractive, finished slide show. Templates may (but are not required to) contain sample content, too. The templates in the Themes category in the New Presentation window contain no sample content—only formatting. You can insert your own text and objects (such as charts or pictures) and build a finished presentation very quickly.

Using a Template as the Basis for a Presentation

Each template employs one or more **themes**. A theme is a collection of settings including colors, fonts, background graphics, bullet graphics, and margin and placement settings. Power-Point has several built-in templates, and you can create your own templates or download new ones from Microsoft Office Online. In this exercise, you will use a built-in template to start a presentation that, when finished, will help you show pictures and descriptions of new products to a group of store managers.

STEP BY STEP **Create a Presentation from a Template**

GET READY. To create a presentation from a template, do the following:

1. Click the **File** tab.

2. Click **New** in the left panel of Backstage view to open the New Presentation window.

3. Under Available Templates and Themes, click **Sample Templates**. Thumbnail images of the templates stored on your PC appear, as shown in Figure 2-9. A preview of the selected template appears in the Preview pane on the right side of the New Presentation window.

Figure 2-9

Selecting a sample template

Sample of template appears here.

Click Back to
return to previous
screen.

Select a template.

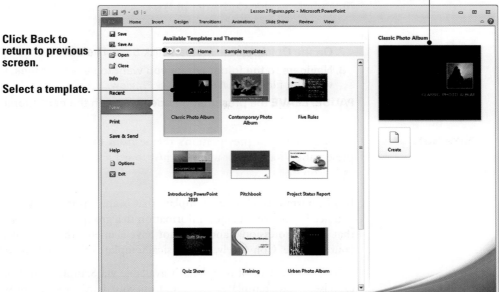

4. Click the Classic Photo Album thumbnail, then click Create in the Preview pane.
   PowerPoint opens a new presentation based on the selected template. It contains
   several sample slides with text and graphics.

5. On slide 1, select CLASSIC PHOTO ALBUM and type NORTHWIND TRADERS
   to replace it.

6. Click the text in the subtitle placeholder to place the insertion point there, and then
   type New Product Preview. See Figure 2-10.

Figure 2-10

Customizing the text on the
first slide

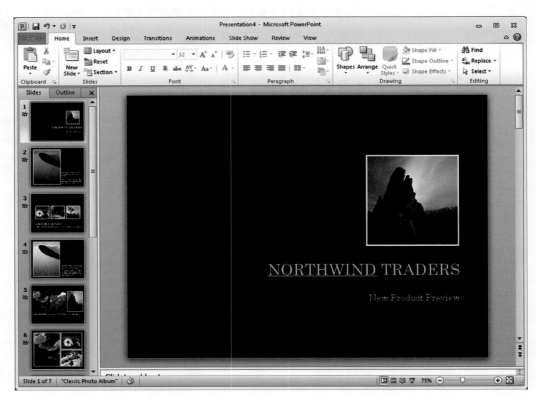

Take Note   In Figure 2-10, and perhaps on your screen too, NORTHWIND has a wavy red underline, indicating that the word is not in PowerPoint's dictionary. You can ignore that for now. Lesson 3 covers using the spell-check feature.

  7. On the Quick Access Toolbar, click **Save**. The Save As dialog box appears.
  8. Navigate to the folder where you want to save your files, then save the presentation with the file name *New Product Preview*.

PAUSE. LEAVE the presentation open to use in the next exercise.

Take Note   You can change a presentation's theme from the Design tab; you don't have to create a new presentation based on a template just to get a new look. You will learn how to change themes in Lesson 4.

It is important to choose a template that is appropriate for your audience and your message. If you need to deliver business information to a group of managers, for example, choose a template that looks professional and does not have elements that will distract the audience from getting your message. Conversely, a whimsical template might work better for a group of young people.

A basic assortment of templates is available via Sample Templates, as you saw in the preceding exercise. These templates are stored on your hard disk, along with PowerPoint itself, and are always available. You can also access other templates online by selecting from the Office.com Templates section of the New Presentation window.

ADDING, DELETING, AND ORGANIZING SLIDES

The Bottom Line   A template's sample slides can provide a basic structure as a starting point, but you will probably want to make some changes. In PowerPoint it is easy to add, delete, and reorder the slides in a presentation to suit your unique needs.

Adding a New Slide to a Presentation

You can add as many new slides as you want to a presentation. The following exercise shows you how to insert a new slide into the current presentation in two different ways: using the New Slide command, and using the Slides/Outline pane.

STEP BY STEP   **Add a New Slide**

USE the *New Product Preview* presentation that is still open from the previous exercise.

  1. On the Home tab, click the **New Slide button drop-down arrow**. A gallery opens, showing thumbnail images of the slide layouts that are available for this template, as shown in Figure 2-11.

Figure 2-11

New Slide gallery

Click the desired layout.

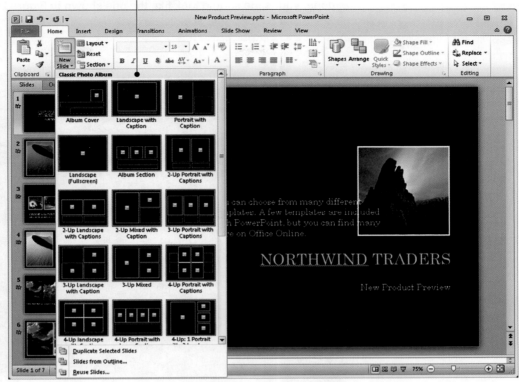

2. Scroll down to the bottom of the gallery, then click **Title and Content**.

Take Note   To view the New Slide gallery, you must click the New Slide button's drop-down arrow. If you click the face of the New Slide button, PowerPoint will insert the default new slide for the current template.

3. On the new slide, click the **title placeholder** and type **THIS YEAR'S NEW PRODUCTS**.

4. Click the sample text at the top of the second placeholder, and then type the following items, placing each item on its own line:

   Women's jackets

   Men's jackets

   Boots

   Backpacks

   Flannel shirts

   Fleece

   Turtlenecks

   Underwear

   Socks

5. Click in the area surrounding the slide to clear the placeholder's border. When you are done, your slide should look like the one shown in Figure 2-12.

Figure 2-12

The inserted slide

6. On the View tab, click the **Normal** button to switch to Normal view, and in the Slides/Outline pane, click the **Outline** tab.

Take Note   Some of the slides in the Outline tab show no text in their Title placeholder; that's because this presentation is based on a photo album template.

7. Click to place the text insertion point after the word *Socks* in slide 2 and press **Enter**, creating a new paragraph. At this point the new paragraph is a bullet on slide 2.

8. Press **Shift+Tab**. The new paragraph is promoted into a new slide title.

9. Type **Clearance Items** and press **Enter**. A new paragraph appears. Because the previous paragraph was a slide title, the new one is too.

10. Press **Tab**. The new paragraph is indented so that it is a bullet on the Clearance Items slide.

11. Type the following items, pressing **Enter** after each one to place it in its own paragraph:

    Biking accessories

    Camping supplies

    Spelunking gear

12. After all the text is typed in for the new slide, it appears in the Outline as shown in Figure 2-13.

Figure 2-13

A slide added via the Outline

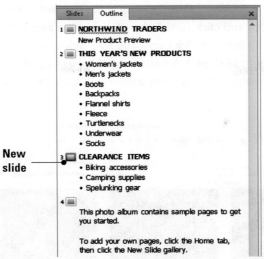

Another Way
With the Slides tab selected in the Slides/Outline pane, you can click to place a flashing horizontal line after an existing slide, and then press Enter to create a new blank slide that uses the same layout as the one before it.

New slide

PAUSE. LEAVE the presentation open to use in the next exercise.

Duplicating Selected Slides

If you want several similar slides in a presentation, you may be able to save some time by duplicating some of the slides and then modifying the copies. The following exercise shows how to select the slides you want to duplicate, even when they are non-contiguous, and make copies of them. You will also learn how to use the Duplicate Selected Slides command to make duplicates of slides.

STEP BY STEP   **Duplicate Non-Contiguous Slides**

USE the *New Product Preview* presentation that is still open from the previous exercise.

1. Click the Slide Sorter button on the View tab to switch to Slide Sorter view. The presentation's slides appear together in a single pane.
2. Change the Zoom level to 90% for the Slide Sorter pane by clicking the **minus sign** button at the left end of the Zoom slider. See Figure 2-14.

Figure 2-14

Slide Sorter view at 90% Zoom

Choose Slide Sorter view.

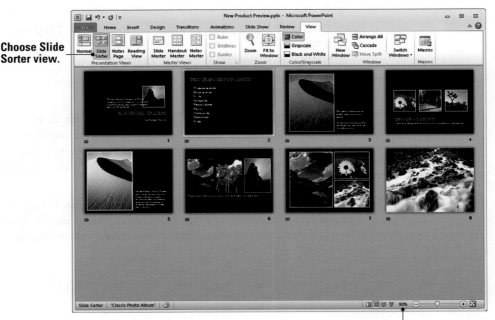

Set Zoom level to 90%.

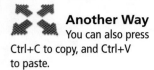

Another Way
You can also press Ctrl+C to copy, and Ctrl+V to paste.

3. Click slide 4. A yellow outline appears around it, indicating that it is selected.
4. Hold down Ctrl and click slide 7. A yellow outline appears around it too.
5. Click the Home tab and click Copy. The two slides are copied to the Clipboard.
6. Click to the right of slide 9. A flashing vertical line appears there.
7. On the Home tab, click Paste. The copied slides are pasted after slide 9, as in Figure 2-15.

Figure 2-15

Copied slides are pasted

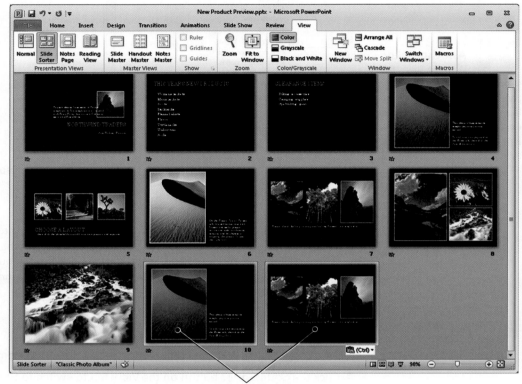

Pasted copies

8. Click slide 2 to select it.
9. On the Home tab, open the New Slide button's drop-down list.
10. Click Duplicate Selected Slides. A copy of slide 2 is pasted directly following the original slide 2.
11. **SAVE** the presentation file and **CLOSE** it.

PAUSE. LEAVE PowerPoint open for the next exercise.

Contiguous means "together." **Non-contiguous** slides are not adjacent to one another in the presentation. As you just learned, to select non-contiguous slides, hold down Ctrl as you click each one you want. To select contiguous slides, you can use the Shift type. Click the first slide in the group, and then hold down Shift as you click the last slide in the group. All the intervening slides are selected also.

You can also select slides from the Slides/Outline pane. On the Slides tab, select slide thumbnails just as in Slide Sorter view. On the Outline tab, click the small rounded rectangle (the Slide icon) to the left of the slide title to select everything on that slide. See Figure 2-16.

Figure 2-16

To select a slide on the Outline tab, click its Slide icon

Slide icon ——

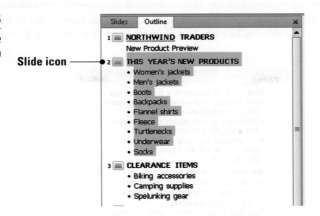

Rearranging the Slides in a Presentation

It is important to organize your slides so they best support your message. In PowerPoint, reorganizing slides is a simple drag-and-drop procedure. In Slide Sorter view (or on the Slides tab in Normal view), you can click a slide and drag it to a new location in the presentation. A line shows you where the slide will be placed when you drop it. Moving a slide is a simple procedure, as you will learn in the following exercise.

STEP BY STEP | **Rearrange the Slides in a Presentation**

GET READY. To rearrange the slides in a presentation, do the following:

@ The *Management Values* file is available on the book companion website or in WileyPLUS.

1. **OPEN** the *Management Values* presentation and save it as *Management Values Final*.
2. Click the View tab, then click the Slide Sorter button to switch to Slide Sorter view. The presentation's slides appear together in a single window.
3. Use the Zoom control in the Status Bar to set the Zoom to 70%.
4. Click slide 5 and begin dragging it toward the space between slides 3 and 4. When a vertical line appears between slides 3 and 4 (as shown in Figure 2-17), release the mouse button. The moved slide is now slide 4.

Figure 2-17

Moving a slide in Slide Sorter view

Drag the slide from here...

...to here.

5. Switch to Normal view, and display the Outline tab in the Slides/Outline pane.
6. On the Outline tab, click the icon to the left of slide 7's title. All the text from slide 7 is selected.

7. Drag slide 7's icon downward. When a vertical line appears between slides 8 and 9, release the mouse button. The moved slide is now slide 8. See Figure 2-18.

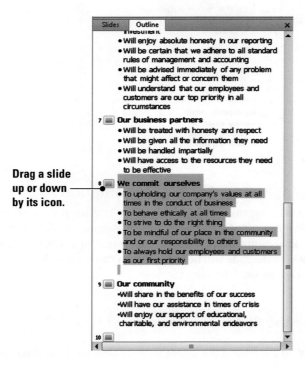

Drag a slide up or down by its icon.

8. In the Slides/Outline pane, display the Slides tab, and select slide 8.

9. Drag slide 8 downward. When a vertical line appears between slides 9 and 10, as in Figure 2-19, release the mouse button. The moved slide is now slide 9.

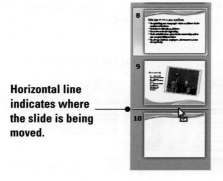

Horizontal line indicates where the slide is being moved.

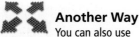

Another Way
You can also use the Clipboard to move slides: select a slide and use the Cut command (Ctrl+X) to move it to the Clipboard, and then position the insertion point and use the Paste command (Ctrl+V) to paste it from the Clipboard.

10. **SAVE** the presentation.

PAUSE. LEAVE the presentation open to use in the next exercise.

Deleting a Slide

When you don't want to keep a slide in a presentation, you can delete it. The following exercise shows you how.

STEP BY STEP **Delete a Slide**

USE the *Management Values Final* presentation that is still open from the previous exercise.

Another Way
You can also delete a selected slide by clicking the Delete button on the Home tab.

1. In Slide Sorter view, click slide 10.
2. Press the Delete key. The slide is removed from the presentation.
3. **SAVE** the presentation.

CLOSE the presentation file. **LEAVE** PowerPoint open for the next exercise.

To select more than one slide at a time for deletion, hold down the Ctrl key and click each slide you want to delete. (If you change your mind, you can deselect the selected slides by clicking in a blank area of the PowerPoint window.) You can then delete all the selected slides at the same time.

PowerPoint does not ask whether you are sure if you want to delete a slide, so it's important to be careful before deleting. If you accidentally delete a slide, click the Undo button on the Quick Access Toolbar right away to bring the slide back. See Figure 2-20.

Figure 2-20

Undo an accidental deletion

CREATING A PRESENTATION FROM EXISTING CONTENT

The Bottom Line

If the content you want to present already exists in another form, it makes sense to reuse it rather than starting from scratch. PowerPoint imports content easily from a variety of formats, including Word outlines, other PowerPoint presentations, and slide libraries.

Using Content from Word

Microsoft Word's Outline view enables you to create a well-structured hierarchical outline consisting of multiple heading levels. You can then open such outlines in PowerPoint, where each of the major headings becomes a slide title and each of the minor headings becomes a bullet of body text.

STEP BY STEP **Start a Presentation from a Word Outline**

GET READY. To start a presentation from a Word outline, do the following:

1. Click the File tab.
2. Click Open to display the Open dialog box.
3. If needed, navigate to the folder that contains the data files for this lesson. The Open dialog box might have opened to that location automatically.
4. Open the File type drop-down list by clicking the All PowerPoint Presentations button.
5. In the File type list, click All Outlines. The file listing in the dialog box changes to show outlines (including Word documents). The file location is the same; the only thing that's changed is the filter that determines which file types are displayed. See Figure 2-21.

Figure 2-21

Open a Word outline file

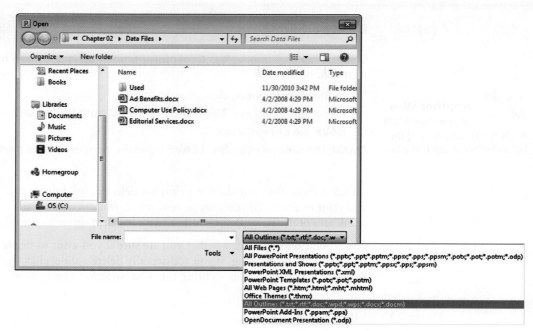

 The *Computer Use Policy* file is available on the book companion website or in WileyPLUS.

Take Note

6. Click *Computer Use Policy.docx*.
7. Click the **Open** button. The outline opens as a new presentation.
8. **SAVE** the new presentation as *Computer Use Policy Final.pptx*.

Even though you used the Open command and not the New command, PowerPoint still started a new presentation. Look at the file name in the title bar of the application; it is a generic name such as Presentation5, not the name of the original Word document. That's why you have to save it in step 8.

PAUSE. LEAVE the presentation open to use in the next exercise.

If you create an outline in Microsoft Word, you can import it into PowerPoint and generate slides from it. Before you can create slides from a Word outline, the outline must be formatted correctly. Paragraphs formatted with Word's Heading 1 style become slide titles. Paragraphs formatted with subheading styles (such as Heading 2 or Heading 3) are converted into bulleted lists in the slides' subtitle placeholders. Any Word document may be opened in PowerPoint and converted to a presentation, but documents that are not structured as outlines may require quite a bit of cleanup in PowerPoint after importing.

Promoting or Demoting Outline Content

After importing data from a Word outline or other external source, you may find that the outline levels are not set as you would like them for some text. You can promote a paragraph to make it a higher level in the outline, or demote it to make it a lower level.

STEP BY STEP **Promote and Demote Content**

USE the *Computer Use Policy Final* presentation that is still open from the previous exercise.

1. Select **slide 2**, and click at the beginning of the second line of the bulleted list (*Desktops, laptops and handheld systems*).
2. Press **Tab**. The second bulleted list item is demoted, making it subordinate to the preceding item in the list (*Computers:*).

3. Click at the beginning of the third line of the bulleted list (*Network servers and hardware*) and press Tab. The item is demoted.

4. Select the last two bullets on the slide and press Tab. They are both demoted to a lower outline level. Figure 2-22 shows the completed slide.

Ownership

- **Computers:**
  - **Desktops, laptops and handheld systems**
  - **Network servers and hardware**
- **Software:**
  - **Operating systems, network operating systems, applications and e-mail programs**
  - **Data, including e-mail messages**

5. In the Slides/Outline pane, click the Outline tab.

6. On the Outline tab, select the last three paragraphs on slide 2 (The *Software* heading and both of its subordinate bullet points).

7. Press Shift+Tab. The Software heading is promoted to its own slide, and the two bullet points beneath it are promoted to first-level bullet points.

8. Delete the colon (:) following *Software* on the slide title. See Figure 2-23.

Software

- **Operating systems, network operating systems, applications and e-mail programs**
- **Data, including e-mail messages**

9. Select the slide 2 title (Ownership) and press Delete to remove it. The bullets that were subordinate to it move to slide 1.

10. On slide 1, select the bullets that were previously subordinate to Ownership (Computers: and the two bullet points subordinate to it) and press Shift+Tab. The selected text is promoted to its own slide.

11. Select the Computers: title on the slide layout and type Hardware to replace it. Figure 2-24 shows the completed slide.

Hardware

- **Desktops, laptops and handheld systems**
- **Network servers and hardware**

12. **SAVE** the presentation and then close the file.

PAUSE. LEAVE PowerPoint open to use in the next exercise.

Just like the headings in a book's outline, some of the items in a list are superior while others are subordinate. In a PowerPoint slide, the relationship between items in a list is shown by indent level. An item's **indent level** is the distance it is indented from the placeholder's left border. Superior items are indented less than subordinate ones. You can change the indent level of an item in a list by using the Decrease List Level and Increase List Level buttons on the Home tab of the Ribbon. Promoting a paragraph to the top level makes it into the title of its own slide, and everything subordinate to it becomes the slide's content.

Reusing Slides from Presentations and Libraries

It is easy to reuse a slide from one presentation in another. This technique frees you from creating the same slide from scratch more than once. In addition, some companies store frequently used slides in Slide Libraries on their file servers, so multiple users can draw from a common pool of premade slides. The following exercise shows you how to locate a slide from a different presentation or from a slide library and insert it into the current presentation.

STEP BY STEP	Reuse a Slide from a Presentation

REOPEN the *New Product Preview* presentation that you created earlier in this lesson.

1. On the Home tab, click the New Slide button drop-down arrow. At the bottom of the gallery that appears, click Reuse Slides. The Reuse Slides task pane opens on the right side of the PowerPoint window, as shown in Figure 2-25.

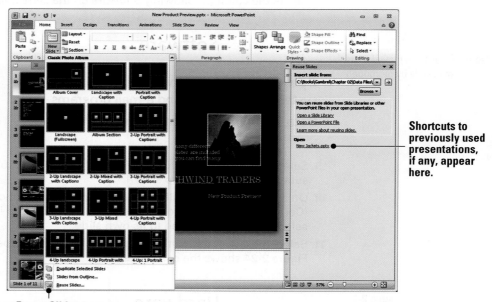

Choose Reuse Slides to open the Reuse Slides task pane.

Shortcuts to previously used presentations, if any, appear here.

Figure 2-25

Reuse Slides task pane provides access to existing content

@ The *New Jackets* file is available on the book companion website or in WileyPLUS.

2. In the task pane, click the Browse button. A drop-down list opens. Click Browse File. The Browse dialog box opens.

3. Locate and open *New Jackets*. The presentation's slides appear in the task pane, as shown in Figure 2-26.

Figure 2-26

New Jackets presentation
open in the Reuse Slides
task pane

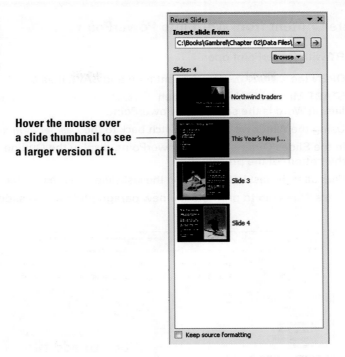

**Hover the mouse over
a slide thumbnail to see
a larger version of it.**

4. In the task pane, hover the mouse over slide 2. A larger version of the slide appears.

5. In the Slides/Outline pane, on the Slides tab, click slide 2 to select it.

6. In the task pane, click slide 2 of the *New Jackets* presentation. The slide is inserted into the *New Product Preview* presentation as the new slide 3.

7. Click the Close button in the upper-right corner of the task pane.

8. **SAVE** and **CLOSE** the *New Product Preview* presentation.

PAUSE. LEAVE PowerPoint open to use in the next exercise.

Over time, you will probably create many presentations, and some of them may share common information. The Reuse Slide command lets you copy slides from one presentation to another. By copying finished slides in this manner, you can avoid recreating similar slides over and over again.

You can import slides from other presentations, as you just practiced, or you can import them from slide libraries. A **slide library** is a feature on a SharePoint server that enables people to publish presentations with each slide saved as an individual file, so that others can reuse slides on an individual basis without having to think about which presentation they originally came from. Because using a slide library requires access to a SharePoint server that has special software installed on it for slide libraries, this book does not practice using one. However, the steps for selecting a slide from a slide library are very similar to those for selecting from a presentation. Follow the preceding steps, but in step 2, instead of choosing Browse File, choose Browse Slide Library.

Pasting Content from Other Sources

PowerPoint readily accepts content from almost any Windows application. One way to import content is to use the Clipboard, because nearly all Windows applications support Clipboard use. You can use the Paste Options icon after pasting content to choose how it will be pasted, or use Paste Special to select special pasting methods. In this exercise, you learn how to paste content from a Word document into PowerPoint, and you practice using the Paste Special command to maintain the content's original formatting.

STEP BY STEP **Paste Content from Word into PowerPoint**

START with PowerPoint open.

@ The *Cashier Training* and *Other Resources* files are available on the book companion website or in WileyPLUS.

1. **OPEN** the *Cashier Training* presentation and **SAVE** it as *Cashier Training Final*.
2. **START** Microsoft Word, and open *Other Resources.docx* in it. The procedure for opening files in Word is the same as in PowerPoint.
3. Using the Windows taskbar, switch back to the *Cashier Training Final* file in PowerPoint.
4. In the Slides/Outline pane in PowerPoint, display the Outline tab, and scroll down to the bottom of the presentation.
5. Click after the last bullet point on the last slide and press Enter, creating a new paragraph.
6. Press Shift+Tab to promote the new paragraph to a new slide. See Figure 2-27.

Figure 2-27

Create a new slide at the end of the presentation to hold the imported content

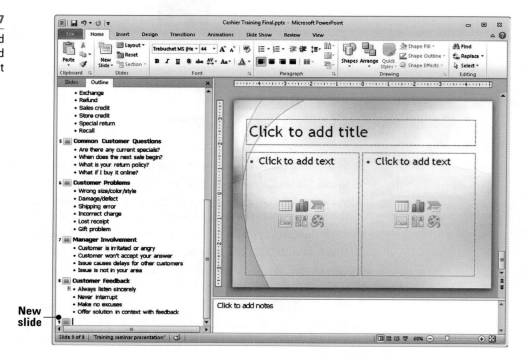

7. Using the Windows taskbar, switch to the *Other Resources* file in Word. Select the heading (Other Resources) and press Ctrl+C to copy it to the Clipboard.
8. Switch back to PowerPoint. If the insertion point is not already on the Outline tab next to the slide 9 icon, click to place it there.
9. Press Ctrl+V to paste the text. The text appears as the slide's title, and a Paste Options icon 📋 **(Ctrl)** ▾ appears below the text. If you don't see the icon, move the mouse pointer over slide 9's icon to the left of the pasted text.
10. Click the Paste Options icon to open its menu. Its menu contains three icons, shown in Figure 2-28.

Figure 2-28

Use the icons on the Paste options menu to specify how pasted content should be pasted

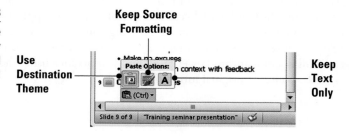

11. Click Keep Source Formatting (the middle icon). The pasted text's font changes to the original font it had in the Word document.

12. Switch to the *Other Resources* file in Word, and select the bulleted list. Press Ctrl+C to copy it to the Clipboard.

13. Switch to PowerPoint, and click the Click To Add Text placeholder on the left side of the slide (in the Slide pane) to move the insertion point into that text box.

14. On the Home tab, click the Paste button drop-down arrow. A menu opens, containing the same types of icons as found on the Paste Options icon's menu (step 6), and also containing a Paste Special command. See Figure 2-29.

Figure 2-29

Use the Paste button's menu to select special types of pasting

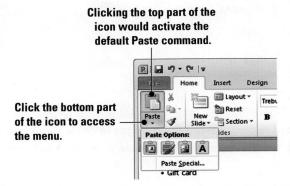

15. Click Paste Special. The Paste Special dialog box opens.

16. Verify that the Paste option button is selected.

17. On the As list, click Formatted Text (RTF). See Figure 2-30.

Figure 2-30

Paste Special dialog box

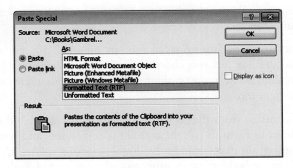

18. Click OK. The text is pasted into the slide keeping the text's original formatting. The text overflows the placeholder's borders. That is normal at this point.

19. Triple-click the last bullet on the slide (Special training) to select it, and press Ctrl+X to cut it to the Clipboard.

20. Click in the Click To Add Text placeholder on the right side of the slide, and press Ctrl+V to paste the bullet into that placeholder box. The finished slide should resemble Figure 2-31.

Figure 2-31

The completed imported content

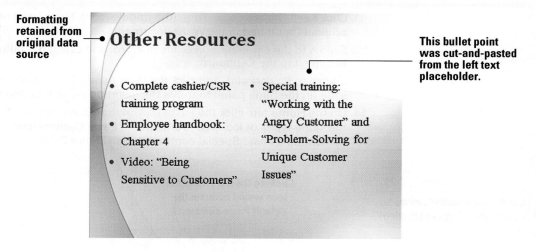

Formatting retained from original data source

This bullet point was cut-and-pasted from the left text placeholder.

21. **SAVE** the *Cashier Training Final* presentation.
22. **CLOSE** Word without saving the changes to *Other Resources.docx*.
PAUSE. LEAVE the presentation open to use in the next exercise.

Pasting from one application to another using the Clipboard works for almost all Windows-based applications, because they support the Clipboard. You can also drag-and-drop content from the other application's window into PowerPoint, but that works only if the source application supports drag-and-drop (not all applications do).

When you paste content into PowerPoint from other applications via the Clipboard, by default the pasted content takes on the formatting of the PowerPoint slide on which you place it. Using the Paste Options, or Paste Special, you can force the content to keep the formatting it had in its original source file.

There are other uses for Paste Special too. In Figure 2-30, for example, you saw that the Paste Special dialog box lets you choose to either Paste or Paste Link. Pasting a link creates a dynamic connection between the original and the copy, so that if the original changes, the copy in PowerPoint changes too.

If you choose a format from the As list that includes the word "Object," as in Microsoft Word Document Object in Figure 2-30, the content is embedded, and you will be able to reopen it in the original application that created it by double-clicking it later. In the preceding exercise, you neither pasted nor embedded; you simply pasted using non-default formatting.

ADDING NOTES TO YOUR SLIDES

The Bottom Line

A **note** is a piece of additional information you associate with a slide. Notes might not fit on a slide, but might contain information which the presenter wants to tell the audience as they view the slide. Suppose, for example, you are using a chart to show financial data to the audience but do not have room on the slide for a lot of details. You can add those details as notes, and they will remind you to share the details with your audience during your presentation. Notes do not appear on the screen when you show your presentation to an audience, but you can view notes in a couple of ways. The following exercises show you how to add notes to your slides.

Adding Notes in the Notes Pane

When you have just a few lines of notes to type, you may find it easier to work in the Notes pane in Normal view than to switch to Notes Page view. Just click in the Notes pane and start typing. Notes you enter here will not be displayed to the audience during the slide show; they are for your own reference only.

STEP BY STEP **Add Notes in the Notes Pane**

USE the *Cashier Training Final* presentation that is still open from the previous exercise.

1. Display slide 2 in Normal view.
2. Click in the Notes pane (below the Slide pane) to place the insertion point there.
3. In the Notes pane, type Emphasize the importance of building customer goodwill as a cashier. Your screen should look like the one shown in Figure 2-32.

Figure 2-32

Type notes in the Notes pane below the slide in Normal view

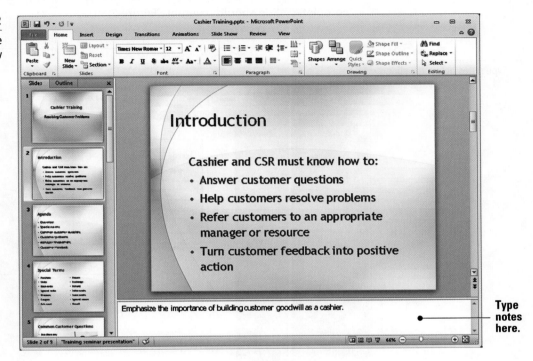

4. **SAVE** the presentation.

PAUSE. LEAVE the presentation open to use in the next exercise.

Take Note   You can edit and delete text in the Notes pane just as you can in the Slide pane or on the Outline tab. Select text with the mouse pointer; use the Delete and Backspace keys to delete text.

Notes do not appear on the screen in Slide Show view, so the audience does not see them. You can see your notes by printing them or by using PowerPoint's **Presenter view**. Presenter view lets you use two monitors when delivering your presentation to an audience. One monitor displays your slides in Slide Show view. You can use the second monitor to view your notes, among other things.

Adding Notes in Notes Pages View

Notes Page view is a special view that displays each slide along with its associated notes. Each slide and its notes appear on a white background; the content is sized as it would be when printed on a standard sheet of paper. You can view and edit notes directly in the note placeholder, which is located below the slide. In this exercise, you learn how to add notes in Notes Pages View.

STEP BY STEP   **Add Notes in Notes Page View**

USE the *Cashier Training Final* presentation that is still open from the previous exercise.

1. Display slide 2 if it is not already displayed.
2. On the View tab, click the **Notes Pages** button to switch to Notes Page view.
3. On the vertical scroll bar, click below the scroll box once to move to slide 3.
4. Click in the **Click To Add Text box** below the slide, and type **Welcome employees to the training session and introduce yourself. Briefly go through the agenda points.** The completed slide should resemble Figure 2-33.

Figure 2-33

Type notes below the slide in Notes Page view

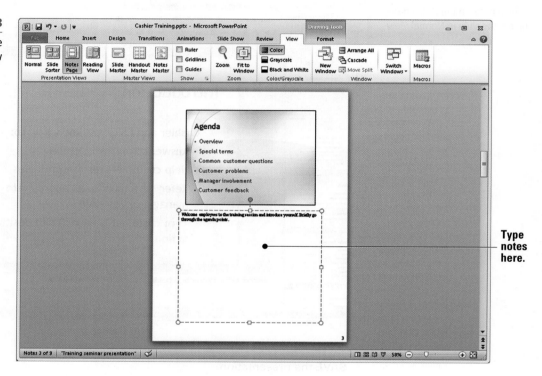

5. **SAVE** the presentation.

PAUSE. LEAVE the presentation open to use in the next exercise.

Take Note   If you have difficulty seeing what you are typing, use the Zoom control to zoom in.

PRINTING A PRESENTATION

The Bottom Line

PowerPoint gives you many options for printing your slides. In the following exercises, you learn how to preview a presentation before printing it, how to choose a printer, how to set print options, and how to print a presentation in both color and grayscale mode.

Using Print Preview and Changing the Print Layout

PowerPoint's Print Preview feature shows you how your slides will look on paper before you print them. When you change to a different print layout, Print Preview reflects the change, so you can try out different potential layouts for your presentation printouts before committing one to paper. This exercise shows you how to use Print Preview.

STEP BY STEP **Use Print Preview and Change the Print Layout**

USE the *Cashier Training Final* presentation that is still open from the previous exercise.

1. Switch to Normal view, and display slide 1.
2. Click the **File** tab, and click **Print**. A preview of the print job appears on the right side of the window. The default print layout is Full Page Slides, as in Figure 2-34.

Figure 2-34

Print Preview appears to the right of the print options in Backstage view.

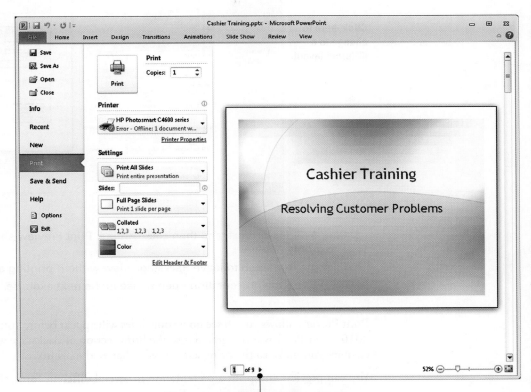

Click arrow to advance to the next page.

Take Note   If the printer selected under the Printer heading prints only in black and white, Print Preview will display your slides in grayscale. The default printer is set within Windows, not within PowerPoint; open the Printers folder in the Control Panel in Windows to change the default printer.

3. Click the right-pointing arrow at the bottom of the window. A preview of slide 2 appears.
4. To the left of the preview, under the Settings heading, click **Full Page Slides** to open a menu of layouts.
5. Click **6 Slides Vertical** on the menu of layouts. Print Preview changes to show a page containing six small slides, as in Figure 2-35.

Figure 2-35

Print Preview shows how the page will print with the chosen layout

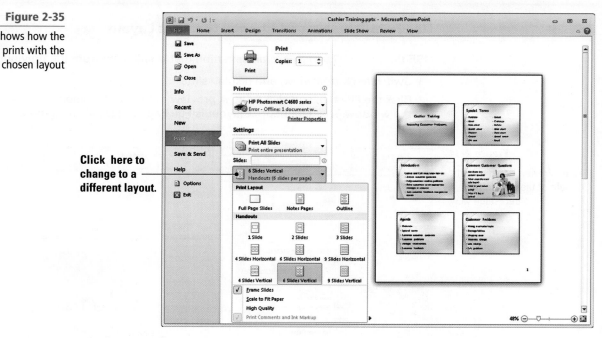

Click here to change to a different layout.

6. Click **6 Slides Vertical**, and then click **Outline**. Print Preview shows the presentation as a text-only outline.

7. Click the **Home** tab to leave Backstage view without printing anything.

PAUSE. LEAVE the presentation open to use in the next exercise.

Print Preview allows you to see how your slides will appear before you print them. In PowerPoint 2010, Print Preview is integrated into the Print section of Backstage view, so you can see how the changes you make to the print settings will change the printout.

You can preview and print a presentation in several different formats:

- **Full Page Slides:** One slide prints per page as large as possible.
- **Notes Pages:** One slide prints per page with any notes below it.
- **Outline:** The text of the presentation prints in outline form; graphics do not print.
- **Handouts:** Multiple slides print per page, designed for distribution to an audience. The exact number depends on the setting you choose (between two and nine).

Setting Print Options

In addition to choosing a layout, PowerPoint lets you set a number of other attributes before printing a presentation. The following exercise shows you how to set some of these printing options. One of these options is grayscale mode, in which there are no colors; each color appears as a shade of gray. Grayscale mode is often used for draft copies because it minimizes the use of expensive colored ink or toner.

STEP BY STEP   **Set Print Options**

Another Way
You can also press Ctrl+P to open the Print section of Backstage view.

USE the *Cashier Training Final* presentation that is still open from the previous exercise.

1. Click the **File** tab, and click **Print**. The printing options and Print Preview appear in Backstage view.

2. In the Copies box at the top of the window, type **2** to print two copies.

3. Click the name of the printer under the Printer heading. A menu appears of other available printers (if any). See Figure 2-36.

Figure 2-36

Other available printers appear on the Printer list

4. Click away from the open menu to close it without making a change.

5. In the Slides text box (under Print All Slides), type **1-3**. This sets only the first three slides to be printed, and Print All Slides changes to Custom Range.

6. Click the **Custom Range** button, and note the command at the bottom of its menu: Print Hidden Slides. That option is not currently available because there are no hidden slides in this presentation.

7. Click away from the menu to close it without making a change.

8. Click the **Collated** button to open a menu of collation options. When you are printing multiple copies, you can choose to have the copies collated or not.

9. Click away from the Collated button's menu to close it without making a change.

10. Click the **Color** button to open a menu of color options.

Take Note   If a black and white printer is selected, the Color button will appear as a Grayscale button instead.

11. Click **Pure Black and White** from the Color button's menu. Print Preview changes to show how the setting will affect the printouts.

Take Note   In some presentations, there is a difference between Grayscale and Pure Black and White modes. In this particular presentation, there is not, because there are no non-background graphics to convert to grayscale images. Figure 2-37 shows the preview of slide 1 in Pure Black and White mode.

Figure 2-37

A preview of slide 1 in Pure
Black and White mode

Printout will omit background and will show text in black.

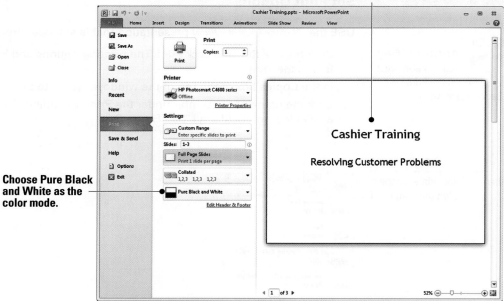

**Choose Pure Black
and White as the
color mode.**

12. Click the Full Page Slides button to open its menu.

13. At the bottom of the menu, click Frame Slides. A border is added to each slide.

14. If you want to print now, click the Print button. Otherwise click the Home tab or press
Esc to leave Backstage view without printing.

PAUSE. LEAVE the presentation open to use in the next exercise.

The Print section of Backstage view provides an array of options that help you print your
presentations exactly the way you want. You can select a printer and enter a number of copies, a
page range, and a color mode, as you saw in the preceding exercise. You can also choose a print
layout, and specify whether a multi-copy print job should be collated or not.

At the bottom of the Full Page Slides button's menu are some extra commands. One of these,
Frame Slides, you saw in the preceding exercise. Here's a complete list of the commands:

- **Frame slides:** This option prints a fine black border around each slide.

- **Scale to fit paper:** If your printer uses unusual-size sheets, this option tells PowerPoint
to scale the slides to fit on the paper.

- **High quality:** If your slides are formatted with shadows under text or graphics, choose
this option to print the shadows.

- **Print comments and ink markup:** This option lets you print any comments and handwritten notes that have been added to the presentation. The option is not available
if the presentation does not include comments or markups.

Previewing a Presentation on the Screen

Before you show your presentation to an audience, you should preview it in Slide Show view. In
Slide Show view, PowerPoint displays every slide in the presentation, in order from beginning to
end. To advance to the next slide, you can click the left mouse button. To move to other slides
besides the next one, you can right-click and select other options from the menu that appears.
This exercise shows you how to use PowerPoint's tools for running a slide show on your own
computer's screen.

Preview a Presentation

USE the *Cashier Training Final* presentation that is still open from the previous exercise.

1. On the Slide Show tab, click **From Beginning**. PowerPoint changes to Slide Show view and the first slide appears in full-screen mode.

Take Note   You can also switch to Slide Show view by pressing F5 or by clicking the Slide Show View icon in the lower-right corner of the PowerPoint window.

2. Click the left mouse button to move to the next slide. Keep clicking the mouse until all of the slides have been viewed. When you click the mouse on the last slide, PowerPoint displays a black screen.

Take Note   You can exit from Slide Show view at any time by pressing Esc. You do not have to go through every slide.

3. Click the left mouse button once more to return to Normal view.
4. **SAVE** and **CLOSE** the *Cashier Training Final* presentation.

EXIT PowerPoint.

SKILL SUMMARY

In This Lesson, You Learned How To:
Create a new blank presentation
Save a presentation
Create a presentation from a template
Add, delete, and organize slides
Create a presentation from existing content
Add notes to your slides
Print a presentation

Knowledge Assessment

Matching

Match the term in Column 1 to its description in Column 2.

Column 1

1. Note
2. Template
3. Handout
4. Print Preview
5. Presenter view
6. Demote
7. Layout
8. Thumbnail
9. Grayscale
10. Indent level

Column 2

a. Shows how a presentation will appear on paper
b. A black-and-white printing mode that saves colored ink or toner
c. Additional information associated with a slide that the audience will not see
d. A predefined arrangement of placeholders
e. To decrease the outline level of a paragraph on a slide
f. A small picture of a slide
g. The distance from a placeholder's left border
h. A predesigned presentation
i. A printed copy of a presentation for audience use
j. Lets you see notes on one screen while the audience sees slides on another

True/False

Circle T if the statement is true or F if the statement is false.

T   F   1. A new, blank presentation appears on your screen when you launch PowerPoint.

T   F   2. Once a layout has been applied to a slide, it cannot be changed.

T   F   3. When you save a presentation for the first time, the Save As dialog box appears.

T   F   4. If you want to be able to use a presentation with an older version of PowerPoint, you can save it by using the PowerPoint 97-2003 Presentation file format.

T   F   5. Many PowerPoint templates feature a set of complementing colors, fonts, and effects called a layout.

T   F   6. You can copy and paste content from most Windows applications into PowerPoint.

T   F   7. One way to copy a slide is to right-click its thumbnail and then click Copy.

T   F   8. Notes appear on the screen with the slides in Slide Show view.

T   F   9. PowerPoint can print just the text of your slide without printing any graphics via an Outline layout.

T   F   10. If you use a printer that does not print in color, your slides will appear in grayscale when viewed in Print Preview.

Competency Assessment

Project 2-1: Tonight's Guest Speaker

As director of the Citywide Business Alliance, one of your jobs is to introduce the guest speaker at the organization's monthly meeting. To do this, you will create a new presentation from a theme template, and then reuse a slide with information about the speaker from a different presentation.

GET READY. LAUNCH PowerPoint if it is not already running.

1. Click the File tab, and then click New to open the New Presentation window.
2. Click Themes. Click Apex and then click Create.

3. In the Click to Add Title placeholder box, type Citywide Business Alliance.

4. In the Click to Add Subtitle placeholder box, type Guest Speaker: Stephanie Bourne.

5. On the Home tab, click the arrow below the New Slide button to open its menu, and then click Reuse Slides.

6. In the Reuse Slides task pane, click the Browse button, and then click Browse File.

7. Navigate to the location where the sample files for this lesson are stored and open the *Bourne.pptx* presentation file.

@ The *Bourne* file is available on the book companion website or in WileyPLUS.

8. In the Reuse Slides task pane, click slide 1. The slide is added to your new presentation. Close the task pane.

9. Click the File, and then click Print. The Print controls appear in Backstage view.

10. Click the Color button, and on the menu that appears, click Grayscale.

11. Click the Full Page Slides button, and on the menu that appears, click 2 Slides.

12. Click Print to print the handout in grayscale mode.

13. Click the File tab and click Save As.

14. Open the Save as type drop-down list and click PowerPoint 97-2003 Presentation.

15. Navigate to the folder where you want to save the presentation.

16. Select the text in the File name box, press Delete, and then type Speaker.

17. Click Save. If the Compatibility Checker task pane appears, click Continue.

18. **CLOSE** the file.

LEAVE PowerPoint open for use in the next project.

Project 2-2: Advertise with Us

As an account manager for The Phone Company, you are always trying to convince potential customers of the benefits of advertising in the local phone directory. A PowerPoint presentation can help you make your case. You need to create a presentation from a Word document that lists some reasons why businesses should purchase ad space in your directory.

GET READY. LAUNCH PowerPoint if it is not already running.

1. If you start PowerPoint, a new blank presentation appears automatically. If PowerPoint was already running and there is not a new blank presentation open, press Ctrl+N to start a new blank presentation.

2. Click in the slide's title placeholder, and then type Why Advertise with Us?.

3. Click in the subtitle placeholder, and then type The Phone Company.

4. Click outside the text placeholder to clear its border.

5. On the Ribbon's Home tab, click the New Slide drop-down arrow. At the bottom of the gallery of slide layouts, click Slides from Outline.

6. In the Insert Outline dialog box, locate and select the Microsoft Word document named *Ad Benefits*. Click Insert. PowerPoint inserts five new slides using content from the outline.

@ The *Ad Benefits* file is available on the book companion website or in WileyPLUS.

7. Switch to Slide Sorter view. Drag slide 5 to a new position between slides 1 and 2.

8. Click slide 6, and then press Delete to remove the slide from the presentation.

9. Switch to Notes Page view, and then go to slide 1.

10. Click in the text box below the slide, and then type Give the client a copy of the directory.

11. Switch to Normal view.

12. On the Quick Access Toolbar, click Save. The Save As dialog box opens.

13. Navigate to the folder where you want to save the presentation.

14. Replace the default name in the File name box with Benefits.

15. Click Save. **CLOSE** the file.

LEAVE PowerPoint open for use in the next project.

Proficiency Assessment

Project 2-3: Send People to Their Rooms

You are an assistant marketing manager at Shelbourne, Ltd., which develops process control software for use in manufacturing. You are coordinating a set of panel discussions at the company's annual sales and marketing meeting. At the start of the afternoon session, you must tell the groups which conference rooms to use for their discussions. To help deliver your message, you need to create a single-slide presentation that lists the panels' room assignments. You can display the slide on a projection screen for reference while you announce the room assignments.

1. **CREATE** a new, blank presentation.
2. Change the blank slide's layout to Title and Content. In the slide's title placeholder, type Panel Discussions.
3. In the second placeholder, type the following items, placing each item on its own line:

    Aligning with Partners, Room 104

    Building Incentives, Room 101

    Creating New Value, Room 102

    Managing Expenses, Room 108

    Opening New Markets, Room 112

    Recapturing Lost Accounts, Room 107

    Strengthening Client Relationships, Room 110

4. In the Notes pane, type Refreshments will be delivered to each room during the 3:00 pm break.
5. Print one copy of the presentation.
6. **SAVE** the presentation as *Room Assignments*, then **CLOSE** the file.

LEAVE PowerPoint open for use in the next project.

Project 2-4: Editorial Services

You are the editorial director for Lucerne Publishing, a small publishing house that provides editorial services to other businesses. Your sales manager has asked you to prepare a simple presentation that lists the services offered by your editorial staff. You can create this presentation from an outline that was created earlier.

@ The *Editorial Services* file is available on the book companion website or in WileyPLUS.

@ The *About Lucerne* file is available on the book companion website or in WileyPLUS.

1. **CREATE** a new, blank presentation.
2. Type Lucerne Publishing in the title placeholder.
3. Type Editorial Services in the subtitle placeholder, and then click outside the placeholder.
4. Use the Slides from Outline command to locate the Microsoft Word document named *Editorial Services*, and then click Insert.
5. In the Slides/Outline pane, click slide 6.
6. Use the Reuse Slides command to locate and open the *About Lucerne* presentation, and then add slide 3 from that presentation to the end of your new presentation as the final slide.
7. Print one copy of the presentation in a layout that shows nine slides per page.
8. **SAVE** the presentation as *Lucerne Editorial Services*, and then **CLOSE** the file.

LEAVE PowerPoint open for use in the next project.

Project 2-5: The Final Gallery Crawl

As director of the Graphic Design Institute, you have volunteered to coordinate your city's last-ever gallery crawl—an annual charity event that enables the public to visit several art galleries for one price. Fortunately, this year's crawl is almost identical to last year's event, so when you create a presentation for the local arts council, you can use last year's presentation as the basis for a new one.

 The *Gallery Crawl* file is available on the book companion website or in WileyPLUS.

1. **OPEN** the New Presentation window, and start a new presentation using the existing file *Gallery Crawl*.
2. In Slide Sorter view, switch the positions of slides 6 and 7.
3. In Normal view, reword the subtitle of slide 1 to read Our last ever!
4. Print the presentation in grayscale.
5. View the presentation from beginning to end in Slide Show view.
6. **SAVE** the presentation as *Final Gallery Crawl*, and then **CLOSE** the file.

LEAVE PowerPoint open for use in the next project.

Project 2-6: The Final, Final Gallery Crawl

Having just finished your presentation for the last-ever gallery crawl, you realize that one of the museum curators uses an older version of PowerPoint. You need to save a copy of the presentation so he can use it on his computer.

The *Final Gallery Crawl* file is available on the book companion website or in WileyPLUS.

1. **OPEN** *Final Gallery Crawl* from the data files for this lesson, or open the version you created in Project 2-5.
2. **SAVE** the presentation with the file name *Compatible Gallery Crawl* in PowerPoint 97-2003 format. **CLOSE** the file without making any other changes.

EXIT PowerPoint.

INTERNET READY

Use PowerPoint Help to access online information about presentation templates. Learn how to download new templates from Office Online, and then download at least one new template to your computer.

Workplace *Ready*

PRESENTING WITH A PURPOSE

Many professionals have experienced "death by PowerPoint." They can tell you what it's like to sit through a presentation that is boring or too long and will usually tell you that the presenter did not understand how to use slides effectively. But an ineffective presentation can be worse than dull; it can actually prevent your audience from getting your message.

The following guidelines will help you (and your audience) get the most from a slide show:

- **Be brief:** Make only one major point per slide, using only a few bullets to support that point. A presentation should include only enough slides to support its major points.
- **Write concisely:** Keep your text short; sentence fragments work well on slides.
- **Focus on content:** Formatting is nice, but too much formatting can overwhelm the text and obscure your message.
- **Keep graphics relevant:** A nice picture can enhance a slide's meaning; a chart or table may support your point better than words alone. But use graphics only where they are needed.
- **Be consistent:** Use the same fonts, background, and colors throughout the presentation. If you use different design elements on each slide, your audience will become distracted (and maybe irritated).
- **Make sure slides are readable:** Ask someone else to review your slides before you show them to your audience. Make sure the reviewer can read all the text and see the graphics clearly.
- **Practice, practice, practice:** Never deliver a presentation "cold." Practice running the slide show and delivering your comments along with it. Practice your spoken parts out loud. Be sure to work on your timing, so you know just how long to keep each slide on the screen before going to the next one. Ask someone to watch you practice and offer feedback.

LESSON SKILL MATRIX

In This Lesson, You Will Learn The Following Skills:

Formatting Characters

Formatting Paragraphs

Working with Lists

Inserting and Formatting WordArt

Creating and Formatting Text Boxes

Using Proofing Tools

KEY TERMS

- bulleted list
- fonts
- Format Painter
- formatting
- line spacing
- numbered list
- Quick Style
- text boxes
- texture
- WordArt

Fourth Coffee is a "boutique" company devoted to producing and distributing fine coffees and teas. As the sales manager for Fourth Coffee, you often produce and deliver presentations to your staff and managers on topics such as realizing the full profit potential of your delivery systems. Whenever you create a presentation, consider how the information appears to your viewers. If the text in your slides is difficult to read or haphazardly formatted, or if you cram too much text into your slides, your presentations will not be professional looking. In this lesson, you learn some basics of text formatting, including formatting characters and paragraphs, creating and formatting lists, using WordArt to "jazz up" your text, and creating and modifying text boxes.

SOFTWARE ORIENTATION

Microsoft PowerPoint's Basic Text Formatting Tools

Most of PowerPoint's basic text formatting tools are found on the Home tab of the Ribbon, as shown in Figure 3-1. These are the tools you will use most often when working with text.

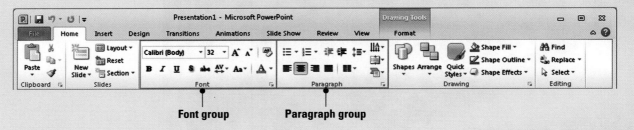

Font group   **Paragraph group**

Figure 3-1

Basic text formatting tools

There are two groups of text formatting tools on the Ribbon: the Font group and the Paragraph group. They allow you to fine-tune the text on your slides, right down to an individual character. These groups also provide access to the Font and Paragraph dialog boxes, which give you even more control over your text's appearance.

FORMATTING CHARACTERS

The Bottom Line

The term **formatting** refers to the appearance of text or objects on a slide. Most of PowerPoint's tools are devoted to formatting the various parts of your slides. All PowerPoint presentations are formatted with specific fonts, font sizes, and font attributes such as style and color. You can change the way characters look on a slide by using commands in the Font group on the Home tab or the Mini toolbar. The Format Painter can save you time by allowing you to copy formats from selected text to other text items.

Choosing Fonts and Font Sizes

Fonts (sometimes called typefaces) are sets of characters, numbers, and symbols in a specific style or design. You can change the font and font size at any time on your slides. The following exercise shows you how to do this both with the Mini toolbar and with the Ribbon.

Choose Fonts and Font Sizes

@ The *Sales Pipeline* file is available on the book companion website or in WileyPLUS.

WILEY
PLUS *EXTRA*

WileyPLUS Extra! features an online tutorial of this task.

GET READY. Before you begin these steps, make sure that your computer is on. Log on, if necessary.

1. Start PowerPoint, if the program is not already running.
2. Locate and open *Sales Pipeline* and save it as *Sales Pipeline Formats*.
3. Go to slide 2. In the first row of the table, double-click **Timing**. The Mini toolbar appears above the selected text (Figure 3-2). It appears semi-transparent until you point at it, and then it appears more brightly.

Figure 3-2

The Mini toolbar

Font size

Font —

4. Click the **Font drop-down arrow**. A list of fonts appears.
5. Click **Berlin Sans FB Demi**. PowerPoint applies the chosen font to the selected text.
6. Click the **Font Size drop-down arrow**. A list of font sizes appears. See Figure 3-3.

Figure 3-3

Choosing a new font size from the Mini toolbar

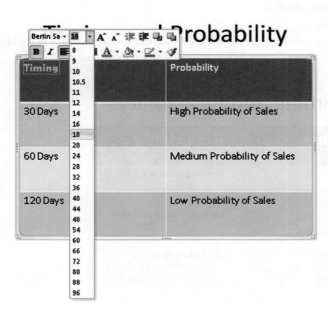

7. Click **32**. PowerPoint applies the chosen font size to the selected text.
8. Double-click **Probability** in the top right cell of the table.

9. On the Home tab of the Ribbon, click the **Font drop-down arrow**. A list of fonts appears. See Figure 3-4.

Figure 3-4

Choosing a new font from the Ribbon

Theme fonts are the default fonts, used for any text that does not have some other font applied.
Select a font.
Selected text
Sales Pipeline.pptx - Microsoft PowerPoint
Theme Fonts
Calibri (Headings)
Calibri (Body)
Recently Used Fonts
Berlin Sans FB Demi
All Fonts
and Probability
Probability
High Probability of Sales
Medium Probability of Sales
Low Probability of Sales
Click to add notes

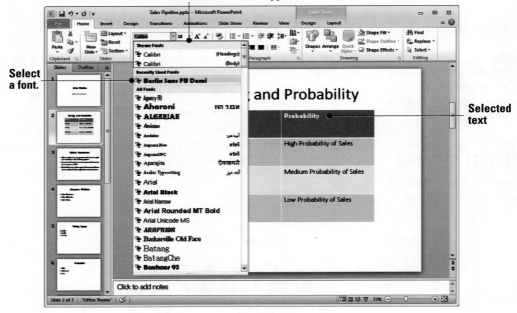

10. Select the **Berlin Sans FB Demi** font.
11. On the Home tab of the Ribbon, click the **Font Size drop-down arrow**. A list of font sizes appears.
12. Click **32**.
13. Click away from the selected text to deselect it. Your slide should look like the one shown in Figure 3-5.

Figure 3-5

The new font and font size applied to the table headings

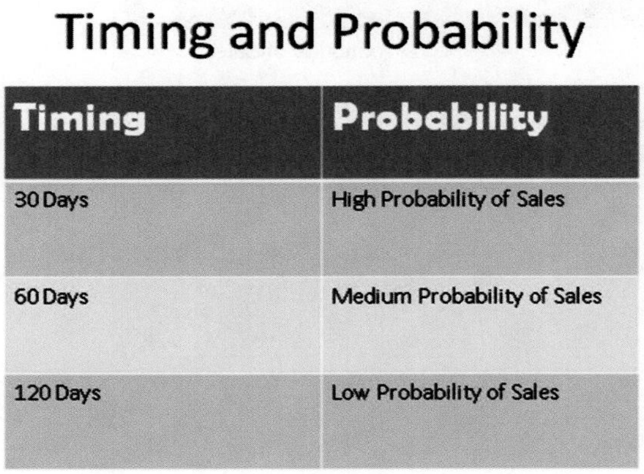

Timing and Probability
Timing
Probability
30 Days
High Probability of Sales
60 Days
Medium Probability of Sales
120 Days
Low Probability of Sales

14. **SAVE** the presentation.

PAUSE. LEAVE the presentation open to use in the next exercise.

Take Note

To maintain formatting consistency between slides in a presentation, you might prefer to change the font and font size on the Slide Master, which flows down the change to all slides automatically. Lesson 4 covers Slide Masters.

By default, PowerPoint presentations have two fonts: one font for the headings and one for the body text. (The same font can be used for both.) These font choices are a result of the theme. A theme is a set of formatting specifications, including the colors, fonts, graphic effects, and slide layouts available. All presentations have a theme, even blank ones.

To return to the default fonts provided by the theme, select a font from the Theme Fonts section of the Font drop-down list, as shown in Figure 3-4. If you choose anything other than a theme font, as in the preceding exercise, applying a different theme will have no effect on that text, because manually applied fonts take precedence over theme fonts.

Using AutoFit to Change Text Size

By default, text in the placeholder boxes on a slide layout are set to AutoFit, so that if you type more text into them than will fit, the text automatically gets smaller so that it will fit into the placeholder box. If you then delete some of the text so that there is more room available, the text once again enlarges, up to its default size. You can change the AutoFit setting for a text box or placeholder as needed.

STEP BY STEP	Change AutoFit Behavior

USE the *Sales Pipeline Formats* presentation that is still open from the preceding exercise.

1. On slide 3, type the following additional bullet points at the bottom of the slide:

   • Helps Engineering staff do long-range planning for future product enhancements

   • Provides Marketing staff with critical data about customer needs and preferences

   As you begin to type the second bullet point, AutoFit engages, and makes the text in the text box smaller so that it will all continue to fit.

2. Click the AutoFit icon in the lower-left corner of the text box. A menu appears. See Figure 3-6.

Figure 3-6

Set AutoFit behavior

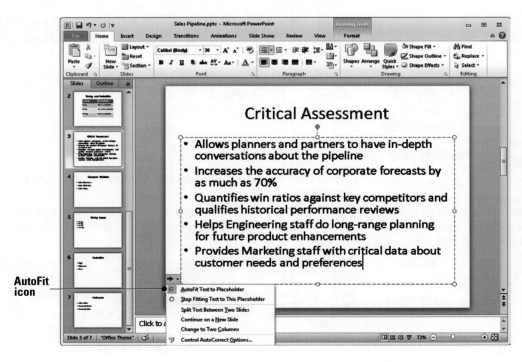

AutoFit icon

3. Click **Stop Fitting Text to This Placeholder**. The text returns to its default size and overflows the bottom of the text box.

Take Note   Notice the other choices in Figure 3-6. You can choose to split text between two slides, continue on a new slide, or change to a two-column layout.

4. Click the **AutoFit** icon again, and click **AutoFit Text to Placeholder**.

5. **SAVE** the presentation.

PAUSE. LEAVE the presentation open to use in the next exercise.

AutoFit is enabled by default because it is a useful feature that most users appreciate in most situations. Rather than finding the maximum font size by trial and error that will allow the text to fit in the allotted space, you can rely on AutoFit to figure that out for you. There are some situations, though, where AutoFit may not be appropriate. For example, you might want the slide titles to always appear in the same size font.

Take Note   In manually created text boxes (covered later in this lesson), AutoFit is not enabled by default; instead, the text box itself resizes as needed to hold the text.

Applying Font Styles and Effects

Text on a PowerPoint slide can be boldfaced or italicized (called *font styles*), underlined, or formatted with other attributes such as strikethrough or shadow (called *effects*). In the following exercise, you will apply a font style and an effect to text on a slide, as well as adjust character spacing.

STEP BY STEP   **Apply Font Styles and Effects**

USE the *Sales Pipeline Formats* presentation that is still open from the previous exercise.

1. On slide 2, double-click **Timing** in the top left cell of the table. The Mini toolbar appears above the selected text. Point to the Mini toolbar so you can see it better.

2. Click the **Italic** button on the Mini toolbar, shown in Figure 3-7. PowerPoint formats the selected text in italic.

Figure 3-7

Italicize selected text from the Mini toolbar

Italics button

Another Way
To apply italic formatting to a selection, you can also press Ctrl+I or click the Italic button in the Font group of the Ribbon. You can also right-click and choose Font.

3. Double-click **Probability** in the top right cell of the table and italicize it using any method.

4. Double-click **Timing** in the top left cell of the table, and then click the **Font dialog box launcher** on the Ribbon, shown in Figure 3-8, to produce the Font dialog box.

Figure 3-8

Click the dialog box launcher in the Font group

Dialog box launcher

5. In the Font dialog box, on the Font tab, click to mark the Small Caps check box.

6. Click the Character Spacing tab.

7. Click the Spacing drop-down arrow, then click Expanded in the list, as shown in Figure 3-9.

Figure 3-9

Character Spacing tab of the Font dialog box

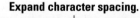

Expand character spacing.

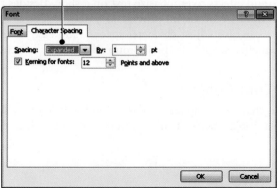

8. Click OK. PowerPoint places 1 point of spacing between the letters and applies the Small Caps effect.

9. Double-click Probability in the top right cell of the table.

10. On the Quick Access Toolbar, click the Repeat button. PowerPoint repeats the last command you issued, applying the new character spacing to the selected text. Your slide should look like the one shown in Figure 3-10.

Figure 3-10

Completed text formatting

Repeat button

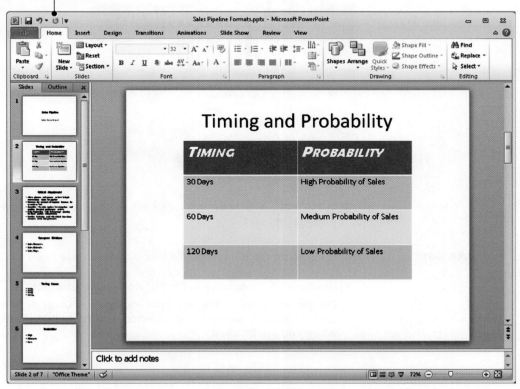

11. **SAVE** the presentation.

PAUSE. LEAVE the presentation open to use in the next exercise.

 Ref   WordArt styles can also be used to format text and apply effects. They are covered later in this lesson.

Use font styles and effects to emphasize text on a slide. Besides the standard font styles—bold, italic, and underline—PowerPoint provides a variety of special effects such as strikethrough and small caps. You can also adjust character spacing and case to give your text a special look. To access more font effects, click the Font group's dialog box launcher to open the Font dialog box.

Changing Font Color

An easy way to change text appearance is to modify its color. Use the Font Color button in the Font group to access a palette of colors you can apply to selected text.

STEP BY STEP   **Change Font Color**

USE the *Sales Pipeline Formats* presentation that is still open from the previous exercise.

1. On slide 2, double-click **Timing** in the top left cell of the table. The Mini toolbar appears above the selected text.

2. Click the **Font Color drop-down arrow** on the Mini toolbar. A palette of colors appears, as shown in Figure 3-11.

Figure 3-11

Choosing a different font color from the Mini toolbar

Click the arrow to open the Font Color button's palette.

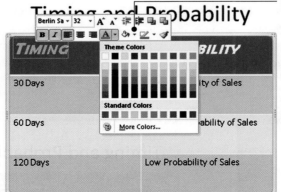

3. In the first row of theme colors, click **Orange, Accent 6**. PowerPoint applies the color to the selected text.

Take Note   When you hold the mouse pointer over a color box, the color's name appears in a ScreenTip.

4. Double-click **Probability** in the top right cell of the table.

5. On the Home tab on the Ribbon, click the **Font Color drop-down arrow** and apply the color **Orange, Accent 6** to the selected text. Your slide should resemble Figure 3-12 when you are finished.

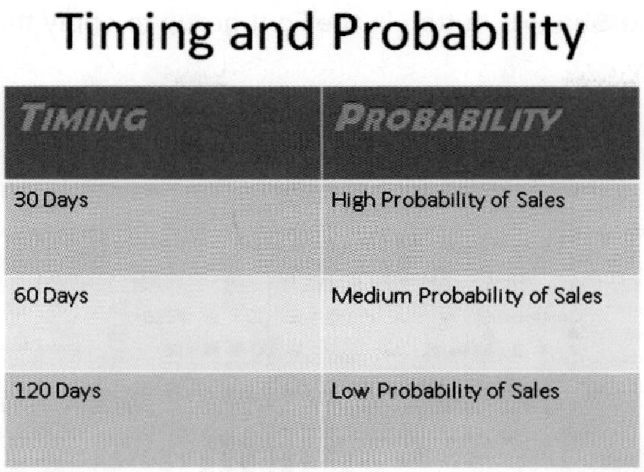

Figure 3-12

Color has been applied to the
table headings

Timing and Probability

TIMING	PROBABILITY
30 Days	High Probability of Sales
60 Days	Medium Probability of Sales
120 Days	Low Probability of Sales

    6. SAVE the presentation.

PAUSE. LEAVE the presentation open to use in the next exercise.

PowerPoint provides an almost limitless selection of colors that can be applied to fonts. You can select any color for your text, but it is usually best to use one of the colors provided by the presentation's theme, as you did in the preceding exercise. Each PowerPoint theme includes a set of coordinating colors, which appear in the color palette when you click the Font Color button. By selecting one of the theme's colors, you can be sure that all the font colors in your slides will look well together on the screen, making them easier to read.

If you want to use a color that is not included in the theme, select one of the Standard Colors at the bottom of the color palette (see Figure 3-11) or click More Colors to open the Colors dialog box. In the Colors dialog box, you can choose from dozens of standard colors or create a custom color.

The difference between a theme color and a standard color is apparent when you switch to a different theme or color scheme, as you will learn to do in Lesson 4. A theme color will change to match the new colors for the presentation, but a standard color will remain fixed.

Copying Character Formats with the Format Painter

As you format text in your presentations, you will want to keep similar types of text formatted the same way. **Format Painter** is a tool that copies formatting from one block of text to another. In this exercise you will use Format Painter to copy some formatting.

STEP BY STEP   **Copy Character Formats with the Format Painter**

USE the *Sales Pipeline Formats* presentation that is still open from the previous exercise.

    1. On slide 2, select the text in the title placeholder.

    2. Change the font color to **Blue, Accent 1, Darker 25%**.

Take Note   To find that color, point to the Blue Accent 1 color in the palette (fifth from the left) and then slide the mouse down over the various tints and shades of that color until you find the one for which the ScreenTip shows *Darker 25%*.

    3. Click the **Bold** button in the Ribbon's Font group to apply the bold font style.

4. Click the **Text Shadow** button in the Font group to apply the shadow font style. See Figure 3-13.

Figure 3-13

Format the title text

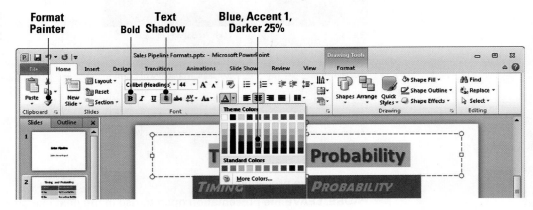

5. With the text still selected, click the **Format Painter** button in the Clipboard group.

6. Go to slide 3 and click the word **Assessment**. The formatting is painted onto that word.

7. Click the **Format Painter** button again to copy the formatting that is now applied to Assessment.

8. Drag across the word *Critical*, releasing the mouse button when the word is selected. The formatting is painted onto that word.

9. Double-click the **Format Painter** button. Double-clicking it makes the feature stay on until you turn it off.

10. Go to each of the remaining slides in the presentation and drag across all the text in the title of each slide, then use Format Painter to apply the new formatting to the text.

11. If you accidentally click anywhere that does not contain editable text, the Format Painter feature turns off. If that happens, select some of the already formatted text and then click the Format Painter button to turn the feature back on.

12. When you are finished painting formatting, press **Esc** or click the **Format Painter** button again to turn the feature off.

13. **SAVE** the presentation.

PAUSE. LEAVE the presentation open to use in the next exercise.

Format Painter makes it easy to apply the same formatting to multiple blocks of text, no matter where they are in the presentation. If you want to copy a format only once, simply click the button. To copy a format multiple times, double-click the button, and the feature will stay on until you turn it off. Not only does this tool reduce your workload, but it also ensures consistency throughout a presentation. (Another way to achieve consistency is to make changes to the Slide Master rather than to individual slides; you'll learn about that in Lesson 4.)

The Format Painter can copy not only character formats but paragraph formats such as alignments and line spacing. You learn about paragraph formats in the next section.

FORMATTING PARAGRAPHS

The Bottom Line

You can change the look of paragraph text by modifying alignment or line spacing. When you apply formatting to a paragraph, all the text within that paragraph receives the same formatting.

Aligning Paragraphs

By default, PowerPoint aligns text along the left margin. In this exercise, you change the alignment of items in a bulleted list to customize a slide's appearance.

STEP BY STEP   **Align Paragraphs**

USE the *Sales Pipeline Format* presentation that is still open from the previous exercise.

1. On slide 4, click in the second bulleted item (*Sales Districts*).

2. On the Home tab, click the **Center** button in the Ribbon's Paragraph group. PowerPoint aligns the paragraph in the center of the text box.

3. Click in the third bulleted item (*Sales Reps*).

4. Click the **Align Text Right** button in the Paragraph group. PowerPoint aligns the paragraph to the right side of the text placeholder. Your slide should look like the one shown in Figure 3-14.

Figure 3-14

Aligning paragraphs to the left, center, and right

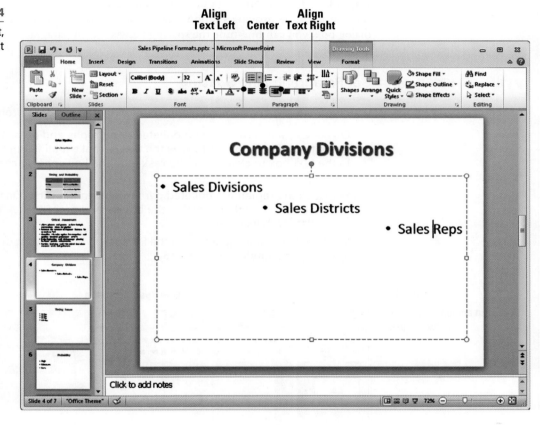

5. **SAVE** the presentation.

PAUSE. LEAVE the presentation open to use in the next exercise.

Another Way
The paragraph alignment tools also appear on the Mini toolbar when you right-click within a paragraph.

When you apply paragraph formats such as alignment, you do not have to select the entire paragraph of text. Just click anywhere in the paragraph and apply the format. The formatting applies to the entire paragraph, even if the paragraph is several lines or sentences long.

When you begin a new paragraph by pressing Enter after an existing paragraph, the new paragraph keeps the same alignment and formatting as the paragraph above it. For example, if you start a new paragraph after a paragraph aligned to the right, the new paragraph aligns to the right as well.

PowerPoint provides four paragraph alignment options:

Another Way
To left-align text, press Ctrl+L. To center text, press Ctrl+E. To right-align text, press Ctrl+R. You can also right-click and choose Paragraph and set alignment in the Paragraph dialog box.

- **Align Text Left** aligns the paragraph at the left edge of the object in which the text resides, whether the object containing the text is a placeholder, a table cell, or a text box.
- **Center** aligns the paragraph in the center of the object.

- **Align Text Right:** Aligns the paragraph at the right edge of the object.
- **Justify:** Aligns text to both the left and right margins to distribute the paragraph of text evenly across the width of the object, if possible. PowerPoint justifies text by adding spaces between words and characters. The final line of a justified paragraph is left-aligned, so if the paragraph occupies only one line, it will appear left-aligned.

Setting Line Spacing

In this exercise, you learn how to adjust **line spacing** to allow more or less room between lines of a paragraph, and also between paragraphs. Line spacing changes can help you display text more attractively or fit more text on a slide. By default, PowerPoint formats your paragraphs so that one line of blank space lies between each paragraph and between the lines within a paragraph. Use the Line Spacing button to adjust the spacing to 1.0, 1.5, 2.0, 2.5, or 3.0. You also can use the Line Spacing Options command to display the Paragraph dialog box. With this dialog box, you can fine-tune the spacing between each paragraph.

STEP BY STEP	Set Paragraph Line Spacing

USE the *Sales Pipeline Formats* presentation that is still open from the previous exercise.

1. On slide 3, select the last two bulleted paragraphs and press Delete. You are doing this so that AutoFit no longer resizes the text to make it all fit, and so there is enough room in the text box to clearly see the results of the line spacing change you are going to be making.

2. Select all the remaining bulleted paragraphs on the slide. One way to do this is to click inside the text box that contains the bullets and press Ctrl+A. You can also drag across the bullets to select them.

3. Click the Line Spacing button in the Paragraph group. A list of line spacing options appears, as shown in Figure 3-15.

Figure 3-15

Set an amount of spacing between lines

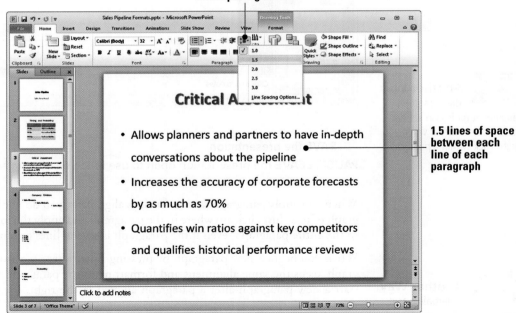

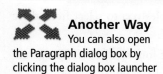

Another Way
You can also open the Paragraph dialog box by clicking the dialog box launcher in the Paragraph group.

4. Select 1.5. PowerPoint formats the paragraphs so each line is separated by 1.5 lines of blank space.

5. Click the Line Spacing button again, and click Line Spacing Options at the bottom of the menu. The Paragraph dialog box opens.

6. In the Spacing section of the dialog box, set the following values:

   Before: 0 pt

   After: 9 pt

7. Open the Line Spacing drop-down list and click Exactly. Then in the text box to its right, type 38. The dialog box settings should look like Figure 3-16.

Figure 3-16

In the Paragraph dialog box, you can set spacing both between lines within a paragraph and before/after each paragraph

Space before the paragraph

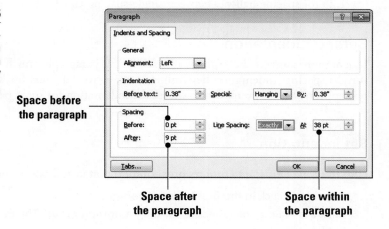

Space after the paragraph

Space within the paragraph

8. Click OK. The settings are applied to all the bullets on the slide.

9. Click away from the bullets to deselect them. The slide should resemble Figure 3-17.

Figure 3-17

The slide with line spacing applied

Critical Assessment

- Allows planners and partners to have in-depth conversations about the pipeline

- Increases the accuracy of corporate forecasts by as much as 70%

- Quantifies win ratios against key competitors and qualifies historical performance reviews

10. **SAVE** the presentation.

PAUSE. LEAVE the presentation open to use in the next exercise.

The Line Spacing drop-down list in the Paragraph dialog box enables you to select from these settings:

- **Single:** Sets the spacing to what single spacing would be for the font size in use. The actual amount changes depending on the largest font size used in that paragraph.
- **1.5 Lines:** Sets the spacing halfway between single spacing and double spacing.
- **Double:** Sets the spacing to what double spacing would be for the font size in use.
- **Exactly:** Sets the spacing to a precise number of points. If you change the font size(s) in use, this value does not change automatically.
- **Multiple:** Enables you to specify a multiplier for spacing. For example, you might enter 1.25 for spacing halfway between single-spacing and 1.5 Lines spacing.

Setting Indentation

Indentation controls the horizontal spacing of a paragraph, much as line spacing controls its vertical spacing. Indentation determines how far from the text box's left and right margins the text appears. In this exercise you will set the indentation for some paragraphs.

STEP BY STEP   **Set Indentation**

USE the *Sales Pipeline Formats* presentation that is still open from the previous exercise.

Another Way
Instead of clicking the dialog box launcher, you can right-click and choose Paragraph.

1. On slide 3, click in the first bulleted paragraph.
2. Click the **dialog box launcher** for the Paragraph group. The Paragraph dialog box opens.
3. In the Indentation section of the dialog box, set the **Before Text** value to **0.7"**. See Figure 3-18.

Figure 3-18

Change the indentation in the Paragraph dialog box

The Before Text indent applies to all lines of the paragraph.

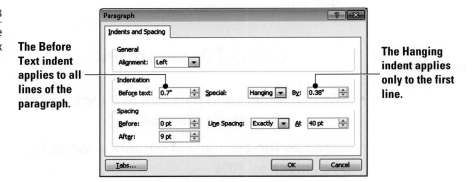

The Hanging indent applies only to the first line.

Take Note   The Before Text setting refers to the paragraph as a whole. A hanging indent is a reverse indent, and applies only to the first line.

4. Click **OK**. The new setting is applied. Both lines of the first bullet are indented more than the other bullets, as in Figure 3-19. The placement of the bullet in relation to the rest of the text has not changed.

Figure 3-19

The result of a change to the
Before Text indentation setting
for the first paragraph

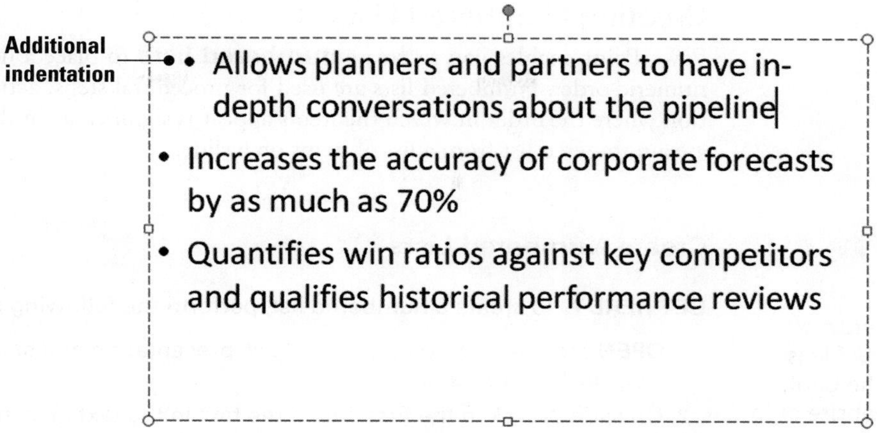

Additional
indentation

- Allows planners and partners to have in-depth conversations about the pipeline
- Increases the accuracy of corporate forecasts by as much as 70%
- Quantifies win ratios against key competitors and qualifies historical performance reviews

5. Use **Format Painter** to copy the first paragraph's formatting to the other two paragraphs, or select those paragraphs and repeat steps 3-4.

6. Click in the first paragraph again.

7. Click the **dialog box launcher** for the Paragraph group. The Paragraph dialog box opens.

8. Set the Hanging indent to **0.6"** and click **OK** to apply the new setting.

Take Note   The bullet character has moved to the left in relation to the paragraph; the paragraph text has not moved.

9. Use **Format Painter** to copy the first paragraph's formatting to the other two paragraphs, or select those paragraphs and repeat steps 6-7 for them.

10. **SAVE** the *Sales Pipeline Formats* presentation and close it.

PAUSE. LEAVE PowerPoint open to use in the next exercise.

By promoting and demoting bulleted paragraphs in the outline level, as you learned to do in Lesson 2, you can indirectly control their indentation. However, you can also directly change paragraphs' indentations via the Paragraph dialog box without altering their outline level. This is useful when you want to change how a paragraph is formatted without changing its meaning or importance in the presentation's message.

There are two indentation settings. The first one, Before Text, applies to all lines in the paragraph. The second one is a specialty setting that varies according to the paragraph type:

- **Hanging:** A reverse indent. The first line (which usually contains a bullet character when Hanging is used) is reverse-indented by the specified amount. In other words, the first line has a lesser indent than the other lines, so it hangs off into the left margin. In the preceding steps, the hanging indent was 0.6".

- **First Line:** A standard first-line indent. The first line is indented an extra amount on top of what is specified for the Before Text indentation setting.

- **(None):** This setting removes any special indents for the first line.

Indents can be set for any paragraph, but are often the most useful for bulleted and numbered lists. You will learn more about creating and formatting lists in the next section.

WORKING WITH LISTS

The Bottom Line   Lists make the information on slides easy to read and remember. PowerPoint provides for several levels of bulleted lists that you can modify for special effects. You can also create numbered lists when your slide text implies a specific order.

Creating Numbered Lists

PowerPoint enables you to create **numbered lists** to place a list of itemized information in numeric order. Numbered lists are used for procedural steps, action items, and other information where the order in which the items appear is significant. In the following exercise, you create a numbered list from a list of items on a slide.

 **STEP BY STEP**   **Create Numbered Lists**

 The *Leveraging Corporate Cash* file is available on the book companion website or in WileyPLUS.

WILEY PLUS EXTRA

WileyPLUS Extra! features an online tutorial of this task.

GET READY. To create a numbered list, perform the following steps:

1. **OPEN** the *Leveraging Corporate Cash* presentation and save it as *Leveraging Corporate Cash Lists*.
2. On slide 2, click in the first line of the text in the text placeholder (*Determine inventory turnover*).
3. Click the **Numbering** button in the Paragraph group. PowerPoint formats the sentence with a number 1.
4. Select the last three lines in the text placeholder.
5. Click the **Numbering** button. PowerPoint applies numbers 2 through 4.
6. Click outside the text placeholder to clear any text selection. Your slide should look like the one shown in Figure 3-20.

Figure 3-20

A numbered list

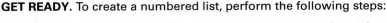 **Numbering button**

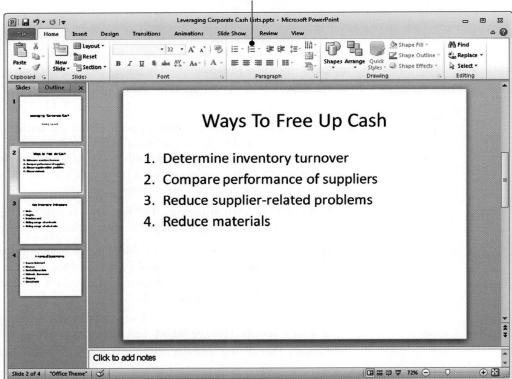

 **Another Way**
To number a paragraph, right-click the paragraph, and then click Numbering on the shortcut menu.

7. Click in the text box containing the numbered list and press **Ctrl+A** to select the entire list.

Another Way
You can also drag across the list to select it.

8. Click the **down arrow** to the right of the Numbering button, opening a gallery of numbering styles.
9. Click the uppercase Roman numeral style as in Figure 3-21.

Figure 3-21

Changing the numbered list's numbering style

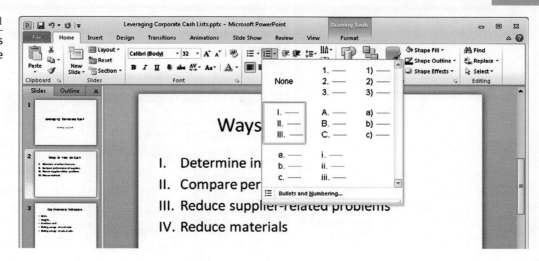

10. **SAVE** the presentation.

PAUSE. LEAVE the presentation open to use in the next exercise.

When you create a numbered list on a slide, you can continue it automatically after the last item by pressing Enter. PowerPoint automatically numbers the new paragraph with the next number in the sequence of numbers so you can continue the list uninterrupted. To turn off numbering, press Enter twice or click the Numbering button on the Home tab.

By default, PowerPoint numbers items using numerals followed by periods. You can, however, change the numbering format to numerals followed by parentheses, upper- or lowercase Roman numerals, or upper- or lowercase letters. To change the numbering format, click the Numbering button's drop-down arrow and select a new format from the gallery.

For even more control over the numbering format, click Bullets and Numbering on the gallery to display the Bullets and Numbering dialog box. You can use this dialog box to choose what number to start the list with, change the size of the numbers, or change their color. You will work with that dialog box in the next exercise.

Working with Bulleted Lists

Bullets are small dots, arrows, circles, diamonds, or other graphics that appear before a short phrase or word. A **bulleted list** is a set of paragraphs (two or more) that each start with a bullet symbol. Bulleted lists are the most popular way to present items on PowerPoint presentations. In fact, most of PowerPoint's text placeholders automatically format text as a bulleted list. In the following exercise, you will change the formats of a bulleted list.

STEP BY STEP	**Work with Bulleted Lists**

USE the *Leveraging Corporate Cash Lists* presentation that is still open from the previous exercise.

1. On slide 3, select all of the bulleted list items in the text box. To do this, you can either drag across them or press **Ctrl+A**.

2. Click the drop-down arrow to the right of the Bullets button in the Paragraph group. PowerPoint displays a gallery of bullet styles.

Take Note   If a series of paragraphs does not have bullets, you can add them by selecting the paragraphs, and then clicking the Bullets button in the Paragraph group.

3. Click **Check mark bullet**, as shown in Figure 3-22. PowerPoint applies the bullet style to the selected paragraphs.

Figure 3-22

Select a different bullet character

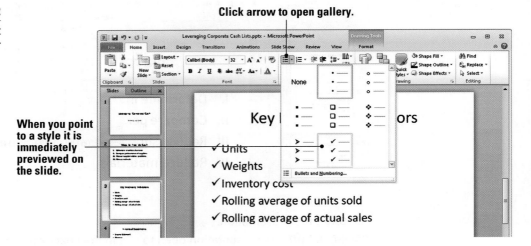

4. With the text still selected, click the **Bullets drop-down arrow** again, and then click **Bullets and Numbering**. The Bullets and Numbering dialog box appears, as shown in Figure 3-23.

Figure 3-23

The Bullets and Numbering dialog box

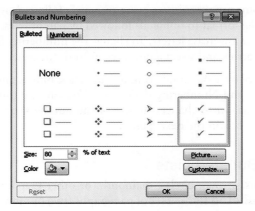

5. In the Size box, type **80**. This reduces the bullets' size to 80% of the text's size.

6. Click the **Color drop-down arrow**, and then click **Blue, Accent 1**. (It's the fifth color from the right on the first line.) This changes the color of the bullets.

7. Click **OK**. PowerPoint applies the selections.

8. **SAVE** the *Leveraging Corporate Cash Lists* presentation and close it.

PAUSE. LEAVE PowerPoint open to use in the next exercise.

Each PowerPoint theme supplies bullet characters for up to nine levels of bullets, and these characters differ according to theme. When you create a bulleted list on your slide, you can continue it automatically after the last item by pressing Enter. PowerPoint automatically adds the new paragraph with a bullet.

INSERTING AND FORMATTING WORDART

The Bottom Line

The **WordArt** feature allows you to use text to create a graphic object. PowerPoint's WordArt feature can change standard text into flashy, eye-catching graphics. Use WordArt's formatting options to change the WordArt fill or outline color or apply special effects. You can also apply WordArt styles to any slide text to give it special emphasis.

Inserting a WordArt Graphic

In this exercise, you enhance the appearance of slide titles by converting them to WordArt.

STEP BY STEP **Insert a WordArt Graphic**

The *Full Profit Potential* file is available on the book companion website or in WileyPLUS.

GET READY. To insert a WordArt graphic, perform the following steps:

1. **OPEN** the *Full Profit Potential* presentation, and save it as *Full Profit*. Notice that the first slide has a subtitle, but no title placeholder.
2. Click the Insert tab on the Ribbon, and click the WordArt button to display a gallery of WordArt styles, as shown in Figure 3-24.

Figure 3-24

Gallery of WordArt styles

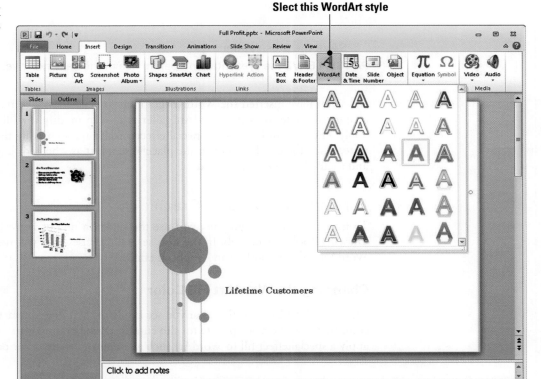

3. Click the Gradient Fill – Orange Accent 1 WordArt style. PowerPoint displays the WordArt graphic with the sample text *Your Text Here*.

4. Type **Full Profit** to replace the sample text. Your slide should resemble Figure 3-25.

Figure 3-25

A new WordArt graphic
on a slide

5. **SAVE** the presentation.

PAUSE. LEAVE the presentation open to use in the next exercise.

After you have inserted the WordArt graphic, you can format it in a number of ways. You can change the style from the WordArt gallery, you can modify the fill or the outline, or you can apply a number of interesting special effects. You can also modify the text of the graphic at any time. Click the graphic to open the placeholder, just as when editing a slide's title or body text, and then edit the text as desired.

Formatting a WordArt Graphic

To format a WordArt graphic, you use the tools on one of PowerPoint's contextual tabs, the Drawing Tools Format tab. In the next several exercises, you will use these tools to modify the WordArt's fill and outline and apply an effect.

Changing the WordArt Fill Color

The WordArt *fill color* is the color you see inside the WordArt characters. You can change the fill color by using the color palette for the current theme or any other available color. You can also apply a special effect fill to WordArt such as a texture, gradient, or pattern.

STEP BY STEP   **Apply a Solid Fill Color to WordArt**

USE the *Full Profit* presentation that is still open from the previous exercise.

1. Select the **WordArt graphic** on slide 1. Note that the Drawing Tools Format tab becomes active on the Ribbon.

2. Click the **Drawing Tools Format** tab and locate the WordArt Styles group.

3. Click the **Text Fill drop-down arrow**. PowerPoint displays the Theme Colors palette.

4. Click the **Blue, Accent 2, Darker 25%** theme color as the fill color, as shown in Figure 3-26. PowerPoint changes the fill of the graphic.

Figure 3-26

Filling a WordArt object with a solid color

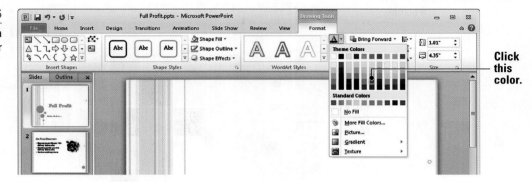

5. **SAVE** the presentation.

PAUSE. LEAVE the presentation open to use in the next exercise.

One way to fine-tune the graphic you have inserted is to change the fill color of the WordArt object. You can use any of the colors on the Theme Colors palette to make sure the object coordinates with other items in the presentation.

You can also choose from the Standard Colors palette or select another color from the Colors dialog box. To access these colors, click More Fill Colors on the palette (Figure 3-26) to open the Colors dialog box. You can "mix" your own colors on the Custom tab or click the Standard tab to choose from a palette of premixed colors.

Applying a Texture Fill to WordArt

Textures are graphics that repeat to fill an object with a surface that resembles a familiar material, such as straw, marble, paper, or wood. The texture graphics are specially designed so that the left edge blends in with the right edge (and the top edge with the bottom edge), so that when you place copies side by side, it looks like one seamless surface. In this exercise, you practice applying a texture fill to WordArt.

STEP BY STEP **Apply a Texture Fill to WordArt**

USE the *Full Profit* presentation that is still open from the previous exercise.

1. Select the WordArt graphic on slide 1 if it is not already selected.

2. On the Drawing Tools Format tab, click the **Text Fill drop-down arrow**. PowerPoint displays the Theme Colors palette.

3. Point to Texture, and then click the Green Marble texture. See Figure 3-27. PowerPoint changes the fill of the graphic.

Figure 3-27

Filling a WordArt object with a texture

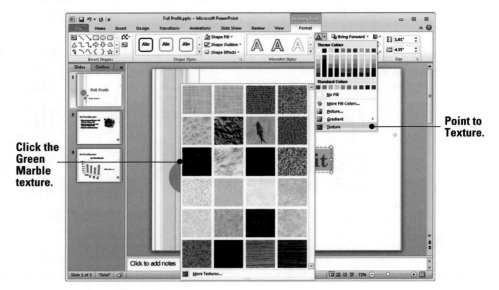

4. **SAVE** the presentation.

PAUSE. LEAVE the presentation open to use in the next exercise.

Changing the WordArt Outline Color

Most WordArt styles include a colored outline around the edges of the WordArt characters. Just as with a WordArt object's fill color, you can fine-tune the outline color of the object. You have the same color options as for changing a fill color. The Text Outline Theme Colors palette also allows you to remove the outline, change its weight, or apply a dash style to the outline. In this exercise, you learn how to change the outline color to fine-tune a WordArt graphic.

STEP BY STEP **Change the WordArt Outline Color**

USE the *Full Profit* presentation that is still open from the previous exercise.

1. Select the WordArt graphic on slide 1 if necessary.
2. Click the Text Outline drop-down arrow. PowerPoint displays the Theme Colors palette. See Figure 3-28.

Figure 3-28

Changing the border color of a WordArt object

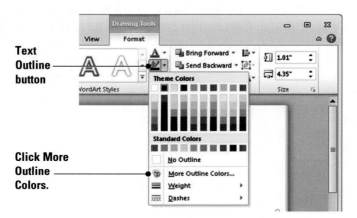

3. Click **More Outline Colors**. The Colors dialog box opens.

4. On the standard tab, click a **dark green hexagon**. See Figure 3-29.

Figure 3-29

Choose a color from the Colors dialog box

Select a dark green hexagon.

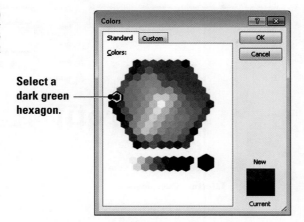

5. Click **OK**. The dark green background blends in with the green texture fill, so it is not obvious to see.

6. Zoom in on the object to 200% to see it more clearly. Zoom out to 100% when you are finished looking at the border.

7. With the WordArt still selected, click the **Text Outline drop-down arrow** again, point to Weight, and click **3 pt**. The outline becomes more dramatic and easier to see.

8. Click the **Text Outline drop-down arrow** again, and click **No Outline**. The outline disappears.

PAUSE. LEAVE the presentation open to use in the next exercise.

Applying Special Effects to WordArt

You can apply special effects to your WordArt objects, such as shadows, reflections, glows, transformations, and more. These effects can also be applied to the other object types that you will learn about in later lessons, such as drawn lines and shapes.

STEP BY STEP | **Apply Special Effects to WordArt**

USE the *Full Profit* presentation that is still open from the previous exercise.

1. Select the WordArt graphic on slide 1, if necessary.

2. Click the **Text Effects drop-down arrow**. PowerPoint displays the Text Effects menu.

3. Click **Reflection**. PowerPoint displays the reflection special effects, as shown in Figure 3-30.

Figure 3-30

A reflection special effect added to the WordArt object

4. Click **Tight Reflection, touching**. PowerPoint adds the reflection special effect to the WordArt object.

5. Click the WordArt graphic and drag it close to the subtitle, as shown in Figure 3-31.

Figure 3-31

The WordArt text repositioned above the subtitle

6. **SAVE** the presentation.

PAUSE. LEAVE the presentation open to use in the next exercise.

WordArt special effects provide a way to spice up an ordinary slide. Although you should not use WordArt special effects on all your slides, you may want to look for spots in your presentations where a little artistic punch will liven up your slide show. Always consider your audience and your topic when adding special effects. For example, a presentation discussing plant closings and layoffs would not be an appropriate place for a cheerful-looking WordArt graphic.

Formatting Text with WordArt Styles

You do not have to insert a WordArt graphic to use the WordArt styles. You can apply WordArt styles to any text in a slide. Applying WordArt styles to regular text in a presentation is an additional way to format the text to customize the presentation. You can use the same features you used to format the WordArt graphic to format a title or bulleted text: Text Fill, Text Outline, and Text Effects. In this exercise, you practice applying WordArt styles to text.

STEP BY STEP   **Format Text with WordArt Styles**

USE the *Full Profit* presentation that is still open from the previous exercise.

1. Go to slide 2.
2. Select the slide title, On-Time Delivery.
3. On the Drawing Tools Format tab, click the More button, as shown in Figure 3-32, to produce the WordArt Styles gallery.

Figure 3-32

The More button opens the WordArt Styles gallery

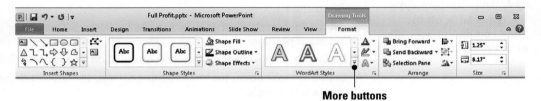

More buttons

4. Click the Fill – Accent 2, Warm Matte Bevel WordArt style. See Figure 3-33. The style is applied to the selected text.

Figure 3-33

Select a WordArt style

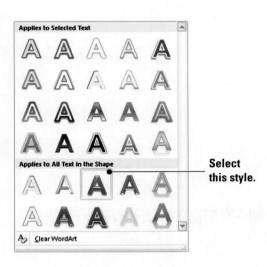

Select this style.

5. Click outside the text placeholder to clear its border. The title should look like the one shown in Figure 3-34.

Figure 3-34

The title with WordArt applied

On-Time Delivery

6. **SAVE** and close the *Full Profit* presentation.

PAUSE. LEAVE PowerPoint open to use in the next exercise.

CREATING AND FORMATTING TEXT BOXES

The Bottom Line

Although PowerPoint layouts are very flexible and provide a number of ways to insert text, you may occasionally need to insert text in a location for which there is no default placeholder. **Text boxes** are the answer in this circumstance. A text box is a free-floating box into which you can type text. You can use text boxes as containers for extra text that is not part of a placeholder. A text box can hold a few words, an entire paragraph of text, or even several paragraphs of text. Text boxes make it easy to position content anywhere on a slide.

Adding a Text Box to a Slide

Text boxes can be used to place text on a slide anyplace you want it. In this exercise, you add a text box to a slide and then insert text into the text box.

STEP BY STEP

Add a Text Box to a Slide

@ The *Profit Analysis* file is available on the book companion website or in WileyPLUS.

1. **OPEN** the *Profit Analysis* presentation and save it as *Profit Analysis Boxes*.
2. Go to slide 1.
3. On the Insert tab, click Text Box in the Text group. The cursor changes to a text insertion pointer.
4. Move the pointer to the right side of the slide about two-thirds of the way up.
5. Click and hold down the mouse button. Drag the mouse down and to the right to create a rectangle.
6. Release the mouse button. The rectangle changes to a text box, as shown in Figure 3-35.

Figure 3-35

Inserting a text box

Take Note

When you release the mouse button after creating a text box, the Ribbon automatically displays the Home tab.

7. Type Fourth Coffee in the text box.
8. Click outside the text box to clear its border. Your slide should look like the one shown in Figure 3-35.
9. **SAVE** the presentation.

PAUSE. LEAVE the presentation open to use in the next exercise.

You have two options when creating a text box. If you simply click the slide with the text box pointer, you create a text box in which text will not wrap. As you enter text, the text box expands horizontally to accommodate the text. If you want to create a text box that will contain the text in a specific area, with text wrapping from line to line, you draw a desired width with the text box pointer, as you did in the preceding steps. When text reaches that border, it wraps to the next line.

Take Note   You can change a text box's wrap setting. Right-click its border and click Format Shape. On the Text Box tab of the Format Shape dialog box, mark or clear the Wrap Text in Shape check box.

Resizing a Text Box

Text boxes can be resized to make room for the addition of other text boxes or objects or to rearrange a text box's contents. In this exercise, you practice resizing text boxes on a PowerPoint slide.

STEP BY STEP	Resize a Text Box

USE the *Profit Analysis Boxes* presentation that is still open from the previous exercise.

1. On the View tab, click to mark the **Ruler** check box so that rulers appear around the slide.
2. Display slide 2.
3. On the Insert tab, click **Text Box** in the Text group.
4. Drag to draw a text box under the Divisional Breakdown title. Make the text box approximately 4" wide.

Take Note   The height you draw the text box does not matter because the height automatically fits the content. When blank, the text box is one line high. It expands as you type more lines.

5. Type the following items into the text box, pressing **Enter** after each item to start a new paragraph, as shown in Figure 3-36.

    Sales

    Marketing

    Purchasing

    Production

    Distribution

    Customer Service

    Human Resources

    Product Development

    Information Technology

    Administration

Figure 3-36

Type text into the text box

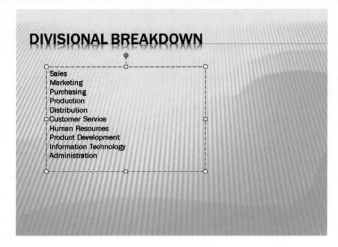

6. Move the mouse pointer to the white square in the middle of the text box's right border. This is a resizing handle, or selection handle. The pointer changes to a double-headed arrow, as shown in Figure 3-37.

Figure 3-37

Position the mouse pointer over the right-side handle on the text box frame

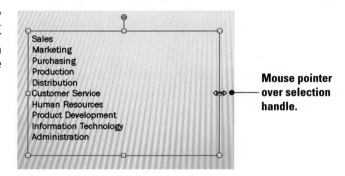

7. Click and hold down the mouse button.

Take Note   A text box has eight resizing handles: one in each corner and one in the middle of each side.

8. Drag the mouse pointer to the left until the text box's right border is close to the text (all entries should still be on a single line).

9. Release the mouse button. The text box resizes to a smaller size. Your slide should look like the one in Figure 3-38.

Figure 3-38

The resized text box

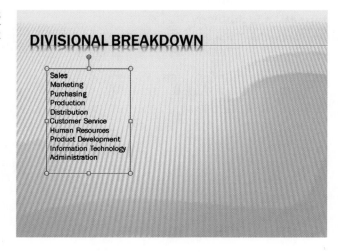

10. Click outside the text box to clear its border.

11. **SAVE** the presentation.

PAUSE. LEAVE the presentation open to use in the next exercise.

Formatting a Text Box

You can apply many different types of formatting to text boxes to make them more eye-catching and graphical. You can apply a Quick Style, add a border, or apply a solid, gradient, texture, or pattern fill to its background.

Applying a Quick Style to a Text Box

PowerPoint's **Quick Styles** allow you to quickly format any text box or placeholder with a combination of fill, border, and effect formats to make the object stand out on the slide. In this exercise, you apply a Quick Style to a text box, but PowerPoint also provides Quick Styles for other features such as tables, SmartArt graphics, charts, and pictures.

STEP BY STEP | **Apply a Quick Style to a Text Box**

USE the *Profit Analysis Boxes* presentation that is still open from the previous exercise.

1. Go to slide 1.

2. Click the Fourth Coffee text box to select it.

3. On the Home tab, click the Quick Styles button to display a gallery of Quick Styles.

4. Select the Intense Effect—Accent 6 Quick Style, the last thumbnail in the last row. See Figure 3-39. The Quick Style formatting is applied to the text box.

Figure 3-39

A Quick Style applied to a text box

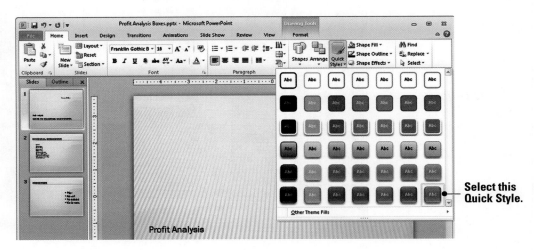

Select this Quick Style.

5. **SAVE** the presentation.

PAUSE. LEAVE the presentation open to use in the next exercise.

There are several advantages to using Quick Styles to format an object. Each Quick Style provides a number of formatting options that would take more time to apply separately. Quick Styles give a professional appearance to slides. Using Quick Styles can also make it easy to format consistently throughout a presentation.

Applying Fill and Border Formatting to a Text Box

If you want more control over formatting applied to a text box, you can use the Shape Fill and Shape Outline tools to set the formatting for a text box on your own. In this exercise, you apply fill and border formatting to a text box.

STEP BY STEP   **Apply Fill and Border Formatting to a Text Box**

USE the *Profit Analysis Boxes* presentation that is still open from the previous exercise.

1. Go to slide 2.
2. Click inside the text box list. PowerPoint displays the text box border and sizing handles.
3. On the Drawing Tools Format tab, click the **Shape Fill drop-down arrow** in the Drawing group. The Theme Colors palette for the text box fill color appears.
4. Click the **Light Yellow, Background 2, Darker 25%** theme color. PowerPoint formats the text box fill with this color. See Figure 3-40.

Figure 3-40

Select a shape fill

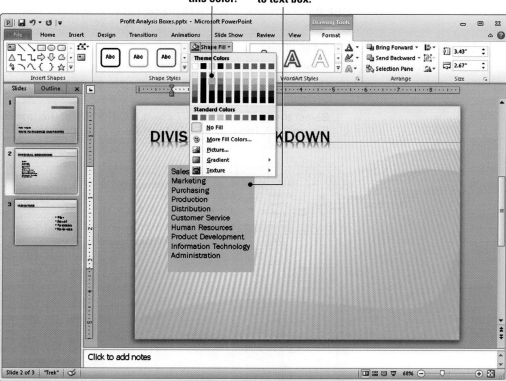

5. Click the **Shape Outline drop-down arrow**. The Theme Colors palette for the text box border color appears.
6. Click the **Orange, Accent 1, Darker 25%** theme color. PowerPoint formats the text box border with this color.
7. Click the **Shape Outline drop-down arrow** again.
8. Click **Weight**. A menu with line weights appears.
9. Click **3 pt**. PowerPoint resizes the text box border to a 3-point border size. See Figure 3-41.

Figure 3-41

A 3-pt shape outline
has been applied

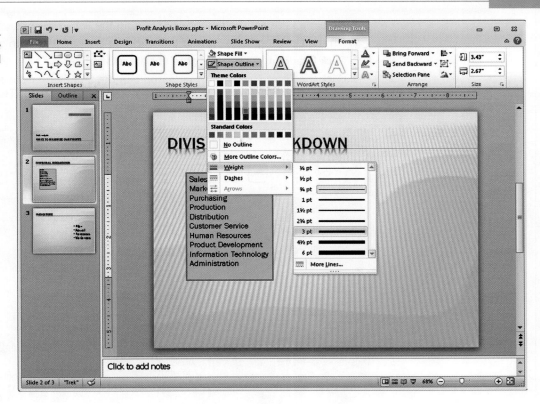

Take Note You can change the style of a text box's outline from solid to dashed or dotted by selecting the Dashes option from the Shape Outline drop-down menu.

10. **SAVE** the presentation.

PAUSE. LEAVE the presentation open to use in the next exercise.

Applying Special Fills to a Text Box

You are not limited to plain solid colors for text box fills. You can fill using gradients, patterns, textures, and pictures to create interesting special effects. In this exercise, you insert a picture and apply a gradient color to a text box.

STEP BY STEP **Apply Picture and Gradient Fills to a Text Box**

USE the *Profit Analysis Boxes* presentation that is still open from the previous exercise.

1. On slide 1, select the Fourth Coffee text box.
2. On the Drawing Tools Format tab, click the Shape Fill button. A menu opens.
3. In the menu, click Picture. The Insert Picture dialog box opens.
4. Navigate to the location of the data files for this lesson and click Coffee.jpg.
5. Click Insert. The Insert Picture dialog box closes and the picture is inserted as a background in the text box, as in Figure 3-42.

Figure 3-42

A picture applied as a text box
background

6. On slide 2, select the text box containing the list.

7. On the Drawing Tools Format tab, click the Shape Fill button. A menu appears.

8. Click Gradient. A menu of gradient presets appears.

9. Click the From Top Left Corner sample in the Light Variations section. See Figure 3-43. To determine the name of a sample, point at it so a ScreenTip appears with its name.

Figure 3-43

Select a gradient preset

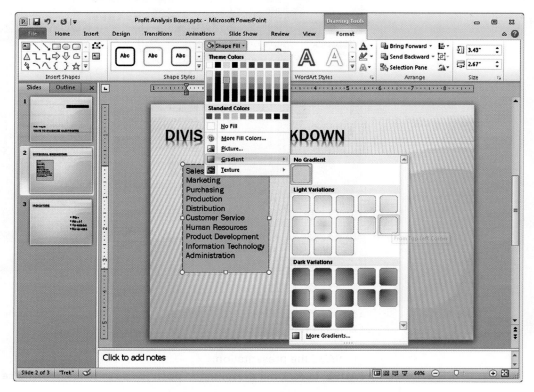

10. On the Drawing Tools Format tab, click Shape Fill, click Gradient, and click More Gradients. The Format Shape dialog box opens.

11. Click the Color button, and click Orange, Accent 2 (see Figure 3-44). The new gradient color is immediately applied to the text box.

Figure 3-44

Select a different color for the gradient

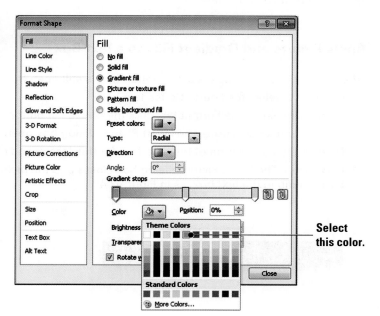

Select this color.

12. Click **Close** to close the dialog box.

13. **SAVE** the presentation.

PAUSE. LEAVE the presentation open to use in the next exercise.

Gradient fills can be much more complex than the simple ones you applied in the preceding exercise. You can choose from several preset color combinations in the Format Shape dialog box (Figure 3-44), or create your own color combinations. The slider in the dialog box can be adjusted to create multipoint gradient effects in which you choose exactly which colors appear and in what proportions. You can also adjust the brightness and transparency of the gradient at various points in the fill.

Applying Texture and Pattern Fills

Texture and pattern fills are alternatives to plain colored fills. As you learned earlier in the lesson, a texture fill repeats a small graphic to fill the area; texture graphics are specially designed so that the edges blend together and it looks like a single graphic. Texture graphics usually simulate some type of textured material like wood, marble, or fabric. A pattern fill is a repeating pattern that consists of a background color and a foreground color, like the pattern on a checked table cloth or a pinstripe suit. In the following exercise you apply texture and pattern fills to a text box.

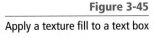

STEP BY STEP   Apply Texture and Pattern Fills to a Text Box

USE the *Profit Analysis Boxes* presentation that is still open from the previous exercise.

1. On slide 2, click and drag to draw a new text box to the right of the existing one, approximately 4.5" in width.

2. In the new text box, type the following: Each division makes a unique and valuable contribution to the organization.

3. Select the new text box, and on the Drawing Tools Format tab, click Shape Fill, and point to Texture in the menu that appears.

4. Click the Papyrus texture (see Figure 3-45). It is applied to the text box.

Figure 3-45

Apply a texture fill to a text box

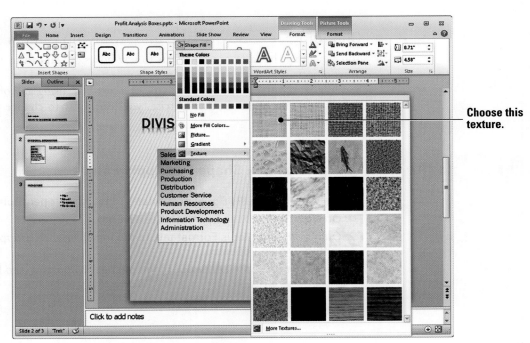

Choose this texture.

5. On slide 3, select the text box containing the bulleted list.

6. Right-click the text box's border and click **Format Shape**. The Format Shape dialog box opens.

7. Click **Fill**, and then click **Pattern Fill**. A selection of patterns appears.

8. Click the **Light Downward Diagonal** pattern (third pattern in first row).

9. Click the **Foreground Color** button to browse for a color.

10. Click **Light Yellow Background 2, Darker 25%**. See Figure 3-46.

Figure 3-46

Apply a pattern fill to a text box

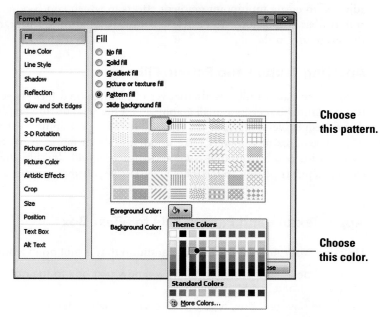

11. Click **Close** to close the dialog box. The new background appears in the text box.

12. **SAVE** the presentation.

PAUSE. LEAVE the presentation open to use in the next exercise.

Changing Text Box Shape and Applying Effects

You can apply the same special effects to text boxes as you can to WordArt, drawn shapes, and other objects. These special effects include reflection, glow, 3-D effects, shadows, soft edges, and beveling. You can also modify the shape of a text box, using any of the dozens of preset shapes that PowerPoint offers. In this exercise, you learn how to change the shape of a text box and apply shape effects.

STEP BY STEP   **Change Text Box Shape and Apply Effects**

USE the *Profit Analysis Boxes* presentation that is still open from the previous exercise.

1. On slide 1, select the Fourth Coffee text box.

2. On the Drawing Tools Format tab, in the Insert Shapes group, click the **Edit Shape** button. A menu opens.

3. Click **Change Shape**. A fly-out menu of shapes appears (see Figur 3-47).

Figure 3-47

Choose a different shape for the text box

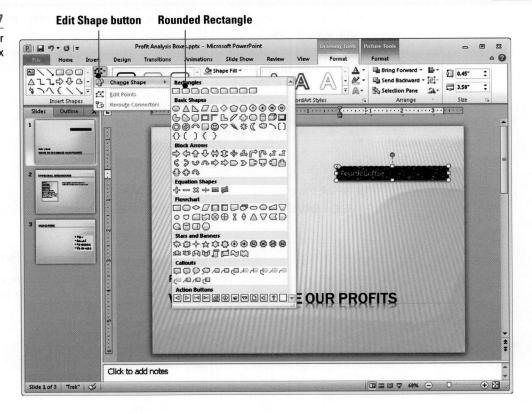

Edit Shape button **Rounded Rectangle**

4. In the first row, click the **Rounded Rectangle**; the new shape is applied to the text box.

5. Click away from the shape so that you can see it better. The corners of the text box are now rounded.

6. On slide 2, select the Each Division text box on the right.

7. On the Drawing Tools Format tab, click the **Shape Effects** button. A menu of effects appears.

8. Point to Bevel to produce the Bevel options menu.

9. Click the **Circle bevel** effect (first effect in the first row of the Bevel section), as shown in Figure 3-48. The bevel effect is applied to the text box.

Figure 3-48

Select a bevel effect

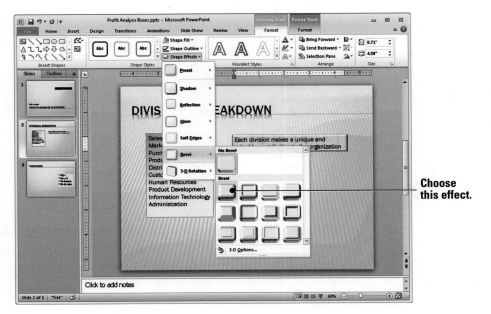

Choose this effect.

10. Click the Shape Effects button again, and point to Shadow to produce the shadow options menu.

11. Click the Offset Diagonal Bottom Right shadow (the first shadow in the Outer section).

12. Click away from the text box to see the changes better. It should resemble Figure 3-49.

Figure 3-49

The text box with bevel and shadow effects applied

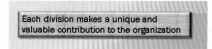

13. **SAVE** the presentation.

PAUSE. LEAVE the presentation open to use in the next exercise.

Changing the Default Formatting for New Text Boxes

If you are going to create lots of text boxes in a presentation, there are ways you can save time in formatting them. One way is to redefine the default for new text boxes to match your desired settings, as you learn to do in this exercise.

STEP BY STEP   **Change the Default Formatting for New Text Boxes**

USE the *Profit Analysis Boxes* presentation that is still open from the previous exercise.

1. On slide 2, select the text box on the right.

Take Note   Make sure you select its outer border rather than clicking inside it. (For this activity, it makes a difference.) The outer border should appear solid, not dashed, when selected.

2. Right-click the text box's outer border. A menu appears, as shown in Figure 3-50.

Figure 3-50

Make the current text box's formatting the default for new text boxes

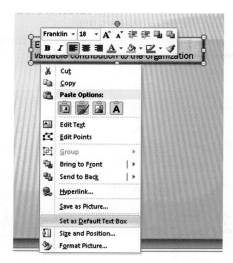

3. Click Set as Default Text Box.

4. On the Insert tab, click Text Box, and drag to draw another text box on slide 2. Notice that it is formatted the same as the other one.

5. Delete the new text box without typing anything in it. To delete a text box, click its border to select it, and then press Delete on the keyboard.

6. **SAVE** the presentation.

PAUSE. LEAVE the presentation open to use in the next exercise.

Working with Text in a Text Box

You can format the text within a text box in a number of ways: adjust alignment, change text orientation, set text margins, modify the text wrap settings, and even set the text in multiple columns.

Aligning Text in a Text Box

You use the same alignment options in a text box that are available for a text placeholder: left, center, right, and justify. By default, PowerPoint aligns text in new text boxes to the left. If you align text to a different position, such as right, and then add a new paragraph by pressing Enter from that text, the new paragraph keeps the right-aligned formatting. In the following exercise, you align text to the center of the text box.

STEP BY STEP	**Align Text in a Text Box**

USE the *Profit Analysis Boxes* presentation that is still open from the previous exercise.

1. On slide 1, click anywhere in the first line in the Profit Analysis text box.
2. Click the **Center** button. PowerPoint aligns the text so that it is centered between the left and right border of the text box.
3. Repeat this process for the Ways to Maximize Our Profits text box.
4. Click outside the text box to clear its border. Your slide should look like the one in Figure 3-51.

Figure 3-51

Center the text in the title and subtitle boxes on the first slide

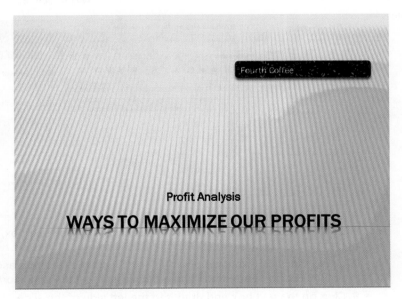

5. **SAVE** the presentation.

PAUSE. LEAVE the presentation open to use in the next exercise.

Take Note   If you resize a text box that has centered text, the text re-centers automatically based on the final size of the text box.

The Justify alignment option keeps long passages of text even on the left and right margins of a text box, similar to the way newspapers and many books align text. PowerPoint adds extra space between words if necessary to stretch a line to meet the right margin. This can result in a very "gappy" look that you can improve by adjusting font size and/or the width of the text box. The last line of each paragraph is not affected, since Justify does not work on single-line paragraphs.

Orienting Text in a Text Box

You can change the text direction in a text box so that text runs from bottom to top or stacks one letter atop the other. This can make text in the text box more visually interesting. You can also change orientation by rotating the text box itself. The following exercise shows how to rotate the text in a text box in two different ways.

STEP BY STEP   **Orient Text in a Text Box**

USE the *Profit Analysis Boxes* presentation that is still open from the previous exercise.

1. Go to slide 1.
2. Select the Fourth Coffee text box.
3. On the Home tab, click the Text Alignment drop-down arrow in the Paragraph group. Ensure that the text is formatted to appear at the top of the text box.
4. On the Home tab, click the Text Direction drop-down arrow in the Paragraph group. A menu of text direction choices displays.
5. Click Rotate all text 270°, as shown in Figure 3-52. PowerPoint changes the orientation of the text in the text box to run from the bottom of the text box to the top.

Figure 3-52

Rotate the text 270 degrees

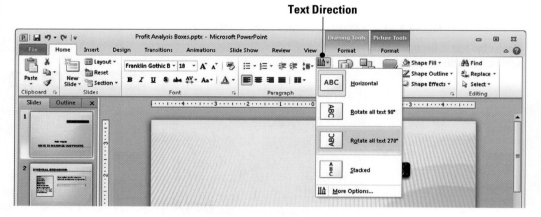

6. Drag the bottom selection handle downward on the text box, increasing the height of the text box so the text appears in a single vertical column.
7. Using the Font Size drop-down list on the Home tab, increase the text size to 32 points. Resize the text box again if necessary so the text is on a single line.
8. Click on the text box and drag it to the left side of the slide.

9. Click outside the text box to clear its border. Your slide should look like the one in Figure 3-53.

Figure 3-53

The rotated, resized, and moved text box

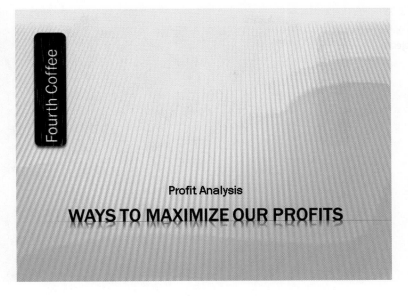

Take Note The coffee bean graphic in the text box was distorted when the text box was resized. It is still usable, though, because now it looks like a stylized texture. If you wanted to maintain the coffee bean graphic while rotating the text, you could use the method shown in the following steps instead to rotate the entire text box.

10. Draw another text box on slide 1 and type **Sales Department** in the text box.
11. Move the mouse to the round, green rotation handle at the top center of the text box. The mouse pointer changes to an open-ended circle with an arrow point.
12. Click and hold down the mouse button.
13. Move the mouse to the right so that the outline of the text box starts to rotate around its center, as shown in Figure 3-54.

Figure 3-54

Manually rotating a text box

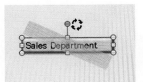

14. Rotate the text box to about a 30-degree angle, and then release the mouse button.
15. Move the rotated text box into the upper-right corner of the slide.

16. Click outside the text box to clear its sizing handles. Your slide should look like the one in Figure 3-55.

Figure 3-55

The completed slide with rotated objects

17. **SAVE** the presentation.

PAUSE. LEAVE the presentation open to use in the next exercise.

Orienting text boxes can be a design enhancement for your slides. For example, you might create a text box that includes your company name in it. Instead of drawing the text box horizontally on the slide, draw it so it is taller than wide and then choose one of the Text Direction button options to change text orientation. You can also rotate a text box or any placeholder for a special effect.

Setting the Margins in a Text Box

PowerPoint enables you to set the margins in a text box. Margins control the distance between the text and the outer border of the text box. In this exercise you will change the right and left margins on a text box.

STEP BY STEP   **Set the Margins in a Text Box**

USE the *Profit Analysis Boxes* presentation that is still open from the previous exercise.

1. Go to slide 3.
2. Select the text box on the right side of the slide, and drag it to the left side of the slide, under the Indicators title.
3. Right-click inside the text box and click Format Shape on the shortcut menu. The Format Shape dialog box opens.
4. Click Text Box in the left pane of the Format Shape dialog box. Text box layout options appear, as shown in Figure 3-56.

Figure 3-56

Set the margins in the Format Shape dialog box

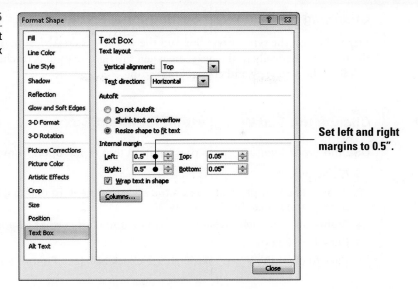

Set left and right margins to 0.5".

5. Click the Left spin button (up arrow) to set the left margin at 0.5".
6. Click the Right spin button to set the right margin at 0.5". Figure 3-56 shows the correct settings.
7. Click Close. PowerPoint applies the margin changes to the text box.
8. Widen the text box to 4" so that each bullet point appears on a single line. Your slide should look like the one shown in Figure 3-57.

Figure 3-57

Text box with new margins

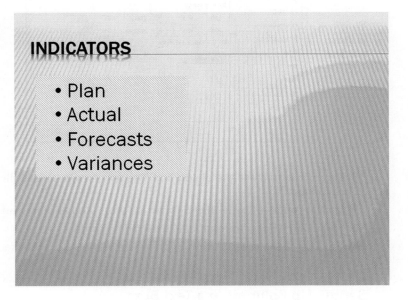

9. **SAVE** the presentation.

PAUSE. LEAVE the presentation open to use in the next exercise.

Resizing text box margins enables you to fine-tune text placement within a text box. For example, if you want text to appear 1 inch away from the left side of the text box, change the Left box to 1.0. You might want to do this if your slide design needs to have text align with other items placed on the slide. If you have chosen to format a text box or placeholder with a fill, increasing margins can also prevent the text from appearing to crowd the edges of the text box.

Changing the Text Wrap Setting for a Text Box

Depending on the type of text box and the way it was created, it may or may not be set to wrap the text automatically to the next line when the right margin is reached. In the next exercise you will learn how to view and change this setting.

STEP BY STEP	Change the Text Wrap Setting for a Text Box

USE the *Profit Analysis Boxes* presentation that is still open from the previous exercise.

1. Go to slide 2.
2. If there is an empty text box on the slide, delete it. To delete a text box, select its outer border and press the Delete key.
3. Right-click the Each division… text box and click Format Shape.
4. Click Text Box on the left.
5. Click to clear the Wrap text in shape check box (see Figure 3-58).

Figure 3-58

The Wrap Text in Shape check box controls text wrap

Wrap text in shape text box

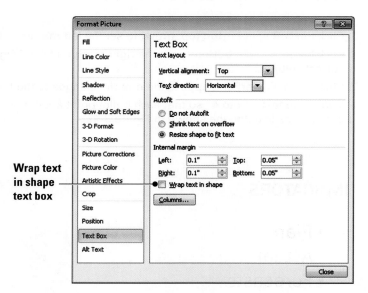

6. Click Close to close the dialog box. The text now overruns the slide because it is on a single line.
7. Click in the text box, and click after the word *and* to place the insertion point there.
8. Press Shift+Enter to manually insert a line break.

PAUSE. LEAVE the presentation open to use in the next exercise.

Setting Up Columns in a Text Box

PowerPoint enables you to create columns in text boxes to present information you want to set up in lists across the slide but do not want to place in PowerPoint tables. As you enter text or other items into a column, PowerPoint fills up the first column and then wraps text to the next column. Viewers of your presentation may have an easier time reading and remembering lists formatted into multiple columns. You can create columns in any text box, placeholder, or shape. In the following exercise you will change a text box so that it uses two columns.

| STEP BY STEP | **Set Up Columns in a Text Box** |

USE the *Profit Analysis Boxes* presentation that is still open from the previous exercise.

1. On slide 2, drag the *Each division...* text box to the bottom of the slide.
2. Click in the text box that contains the list of divisions.
3. On the Home tab, click the Columns button. A menu appears, as shown in Figure 3-59.

Figure 3-59

Set the text box in two columns

4. Click Two Columns. PowerPoint formats the list of items into two columns. The columns are truncated at this point because the text box is not wide enough.
5. Drag the right border of the text box to the right to widen it enough that two columns can appear side by side with neither one truncated.
6. On the Drawing Tools Format tab, click the Shape Height button's down-pointing spin arrow, decreasing the shape height, until each column contains five lines of text, as shown in Figure 3-60.

Figure 3-60

Decrease the shape height and increase its width to accommodate the multicolumn list

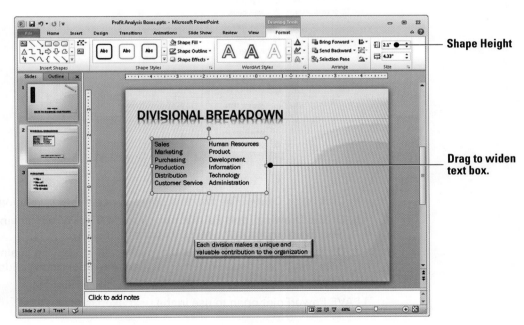

 **Another Way**
If you need two lists on a slide but do not want to use columns, create two text boxes and position them side by side, or switch to a slide layout that contains two side-by-side placeholder boxes.

7. **SAVE** the *Profit Analysis Boxes* presentation.

PAUSE. LEAVE the presentation open to use in the next exercise.

Take Note   If the column choices in the Column drop-down menu do not meet your needs, click the More Columns option to display the Columns dialog box. Here you can set any number of columns and adjust the spacing between columns.

Aligning Text Boxes on a Slide

In addition to aligning the text within a text box, you can align the text box itself with other objects on the slide, including other text boxes. Doing so ensures that the items on a slide align precisely and neatly with one another when it is appropriate for them to do so. For example, you might have two text boxes side by side, and top-aligning them with one another ensures that the slide's overall appearance is balanced.

STEP BY STEP   **Align Text Boxes**

USE the *Profit Analysis Boxes* presentation that is still open from the previous exercise.

1. On slide 2, click the text box that contains the bulleted list, to select the text box. Click the border, not inside the box.
2. Hold down the Shift key and click the text box at the bottom of the slide. It is also selected.
3. On the Drawing Tools Format tab, click the **Align** button. A menu appears, as shown in Figure 3-61.

Figure 3-61

Choose how text boxes should align

4. Click **Align Center**. The two text boxes are centered in relation to one another.
5. On the Drawing Tools Format tab, click the **Align** button again, and click **Align to Slide**. Nothing changes in the text box placement yet.
6. On the Drawing Tools Format tab, click the **Align** button again, and click **Align Center**. Both text boxes become center-aligned in relation to the slide itself.
7. **SAVE** and close the *Profit Analysis Boxes* presentation.

LEAVE PowerPoint open to use in the next exercise.

Take Note   The Left, Right, and Center commands on the Align menu refer to horizontal alignment, either in relation to the slide or to other selected content. The Top, Middle, and Bottom commands refer to vertical alignment.

USING PROOFING TOOLS

The Bottom Line   The Spelling and Thesaurus features in PowerPoint help you ensure your presentation's text is professionally written and edited, free from spelling errors.

Checking Spelling

The Spelling feature in PowerPoint compares each word in the presentation to its built-in and custom dictionaries, and flags any words that it does not find, plus any instances of repeated words, such as *the the*. You can then evaluate the found words and decide how to proceed with each one. Misspelled words appear with a wavy red underline in the presentation, and you can deal with each one individually by right-clicking it. Alternately you can open the Spelling dialog box and work through all the possible misspellings at once. In this exercise, you practice using PowerPoint's Spelling feature using both of those methods.

STEP BY STEP	Check Spelling

@ The *TV Options* file is available on the book companion website or in WileyPLUS.

GET READY. To check spelling, perform the following tasks:

1. **OPEN** the *TV Options* presentation and save it as *TV Options Corrected*.
2. On slide 1, notice that the word *Satelite* is misspelled, and that it has a wavy red underline.
3. Right-click the word *Satelite*. A list of possible spelling corrections appears.
4. In the list, click **Satellite**. The correction is made (See Figure 3-62).

Figure 3-62

Correct a single misspelled word from the shortcut menu

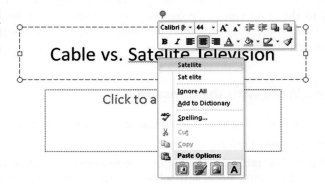

5. On the Review tab, click **Spelling** in the Proofing group. The Spelling dialog box opens, and the Spelling feature finds and flags the next misspelled word, as shown in Figure 3-63. The Change to Suggestions list contains only one possible correction.

Figure 3-63

Correct multiple spelling errors quickly with the Spelling dialog box

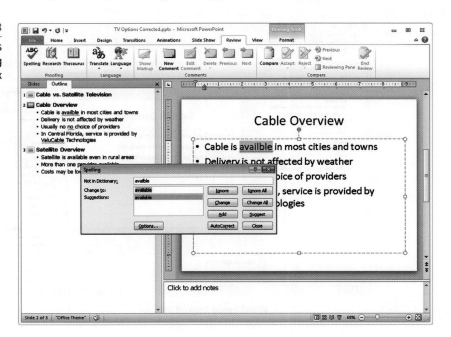

6. Click **Change** to change to the correct spelling of *available.* The next problem identified is a repeated word, *no.*

7. Click **Delete** to delete one of the words *no.* The next problem that appears is a proper name, *ValuCable*, which is actually a correct spelling.

8. Click **Ignore** to ignore the potential misspelling. You could have also clicked Add to add it to the dictionary, but because it is a made-up word for this exercise, Ignore is more appropriate.

9. Click **Change** to change to the correct spelling of *cable.* A message appears that the spelling check is complete.

10. Click **OK** to close the dialog box.

11. **SAVE** the presentation.

PAUSE. LEAVE the presentation open for the next exercise.

Use caution with the Change All button, because it may make changes you do not intend. For example, if you correct all instances at once where you have typed *pian* instead of *pain*, it will also change all instances of *piano* to *paino*.

Using the Thesaurus

A thesaurus is a reference book or utility that offers suggestions for words that are similar in meaning to the word you are looking up (synonyms) or that are opposite in meaning (antonyms). PowerPoint includes a built-in thesaurus. In the following exercise you will use it to find an alternate word.

STEP BY STEP | **Change a Word with the Thesaurus**

USE the *TV Options Corrected* presentation that is still open from the previous exercise.

1. On slide 3, select the word **Costs**.

2. On the Review tab, click **Thesaurus**. The Research task pane opens with the Thesaurus controls displayed, along with a list of terms related to the word you have selected.

3. In the Research task pane, hover the mouse pointer over the word Charges. Click the **down arrow** that appears to the right of Charges, then click **Insert** from the menu that appears, as shown in Figure 3-64. The word *Costs* changes to *Charges* on the slide.

Figure 3-64

Find word alternatives with Thesaurus

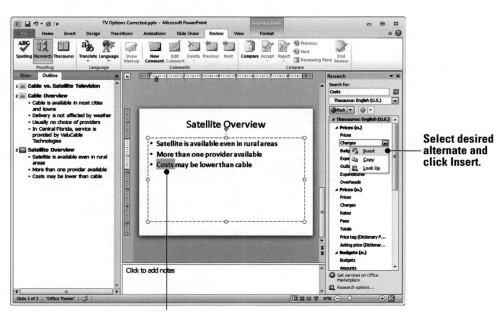

Select desired alternate and click Insert.

Word being looked up

4. In the task pane, click the word **Prices**. The display changes to show synonyms of that word.

5. Click the **Back** button in the task pane to return to the list of synonyms for Costs.

SAVE the presentation and **EXIT** PowerPoint.

SKILL SUMMARY

In This Lesson, You Learned How To:
Format characters
Format paragraphs
Work with lists
Insert and format WordArt
Create and format text boxes
Use proofing tools

Knowledge Assessment

Fill in the Blank

Fill in each blank with the term or phrase that best completes the statement.

1. A(n) _____ is a container for text on a slide.

2. A(n) _____ is a set of characters, numbers, and symbols in a specific style or design.

3. The _____ feature, when needed, shrinks the size of the text in a text box in order to fit it in the box.

4. A(n) _____ is a symbol that appears to the left of each paragraph in a list.

5. The _____ feature enables you to copy formatting from one block of text to another.

6. _____ text is aligned to both the left and right margins of a text box.

7. A(n) _____ indent is a reverse indent for the first line of a paragraph, where the first line is indented less than the other lines.

8. A(n) _____ object is text in the form of a graphic.

9. The _____ in PowerPoint can be used to look up synonyms.

10. To _____ a text box, drag one of its selection handles.

Multiple Choice

Circle the correct answer.

1. You can select a different font from the _____ tab on the Ribbon.
   a. Home
   b. Font
   c. Layout
   d. Review

2. You can select fonts and font sizes either from the Ribbon or the _____.
    a. Status bar
    b. Scroll bar
    c. Mini toolbar
    d. File menu

3. Which of the following is not a paragraph alignment type?
    a. All
    b. Center
    c. Justify
    d. Right

4. When selecting a color, such as from the Font Color button's palette, the colors on the top row are:
    a. standard colors
    b. tints
    c. shades
    d. theme colors

5. Most of PowerPoint's text placeholders automatically format text as a(n) _____ list.
    a. numbered
    b. bulleted
    c. sorted
    d. itemized

6. Reflection is one type of _____ you can apply to WordArt.
    a. effect
    b. font
    c. alignment
    d. spacing

7. A text box's _____ determine(s) how close the text comes to the sides, top, and bottom border of the box.
    a. orientation
    b. margins
    c. padding
    d. alignment

8. To apply a WordArt style to existing text on a slide, you must first:
    a. format the text with a Quick Style
    b. insert a text box
    c. select the text
    d. change the text's alignment

9. What does it mean when a word has a wavy red underline?
    a. The word is inconsistently formatted compared to the surrounding text.
    b. There is a grammar error.
    c. The word is not in the dictionary.
    d. The capitalization does not match that of the surrounding text.

10. A thesaurus enables you to look up synonyms and _____.
    a. alternate spellings
    b. antonyms
    c. translations
    d. pronunciations

Competency Assessment

Project 3-1: Blended Coffees

As director of marketing for Fourth Coffee, you have prepared a product brochure for new company employees. This year's brochure includes a new page of refreshments that you need to format. You will use Quick Styles to format the title and text placeholders. You will also correct a spelling error.

GET READY. LAUNCH PowerPoint if it is not already running.

@ The *Coffee Products* file is available on the book companion website or in WileyPLUS.

1. **OPEN** the *Coffee Products* presentation and save it as *Coffee Products Brochure*.
2. Go to slide 2 and click anywhere in the slide title.
3. Click the Quick Styles button to display the Quick Styles gallery.
4. Click the Moderate Effect – Orange, Accent 1 style.
5. Click in any of the bulleted product items.
6. Click the Quick Styles button.
7. Click the Subtle Effect – Orange, Accent 1 style.
8. Right-click the red-underlined word and select *caffeine* as the correct spelling.
9. **SAVE** the presentation and **CLOSE** the file.

LEAVE PowerPoint open for the next project.

Project 3-2: Typecasting with Typefaces

As an account representative for the Graphic Design Institute, you are responsible for securing sales leads for your company's print and poster division. One way to do this is to send out a promotional flyer using a slide from a company PowerPoint presentation. As you select the slide, you notice that the fonts are not appropriate for your flyer. You need to modify both the font and size of the slide's text.

@ The *Graphic Designs* file is available on the book companion website or in WileyPLUS.

1. **OPEN** the *Graphic Designs* presentation.
2. On slide 1, select all the text under the three photographs.
3. Click the Font drop-down arrow.
4. Click Brush Script MT.
5. Click the Font Size drop-down arrow.
6. Click 32.
7. Click anywhere in the second paragraph (*Graphic Design Institute*).
8. Click the Center button in the Paragraph group.
9. Select the first paragraph of text, and then click the Format Painter in the Clipboard group.
10. Go to slide 2, and then drag the Format Painter pointer over the text on the right side of the slide.
11. **SAVE** the presentation as *Graphic Designs Final* and **CLOSE** the file.

LEAVE PowerPoint open for the next project.

Project 3-3: Destinations

@ The *New Destinations* file is available on the book companion website or in WileyPLUS.

As the owner and operator of Margie's Travel, you are involved with many aspects of sales, marketing, customer service, and new products and services. Today you want to format the text in a slide presentation that includes new European destinations.

1. **OPEN** the *New Destinations* presentation.
2. Go to slide 2 and select the slide's title text. Click the Bold button to make the title boldface.
3. Select all the text in the bulleted list. Click the Align Text Left button to align the list along the left side of the text placeholder.
4. With the list still selected, open the Bullets and Numbering dialog box. Change the bullets' color to Orange, Accent 2, and then resize the bullets so they are 90% of the text's size.
5. Click the Font Color drop-down arrow, and then change the list's font color to Dark Green, Background 2, Lighter 80%.
6. Click Text Box on the Insert tab, and then click below the picture on the slide to create a nonwrapping text box.
7. In the text box, type Companion Flies Free until Jan. 1!.
8. On the Home tab, click the Quick Styles button and apply the Colored Outline – Olive Green, Accent 1 Quick Style to the text box.
9. **SAVE** the presentation as *New Destinations Final* and **CLOSE** the file.

LEAVE PowerPoint open for the next project.

Project 3-4: Business To Business Imports

@ The *World Wide Importers* file is available on the book companion website or in WileyPLUS.

You are the lone marketing research person in your company, World Wide Importers. You often find exciting and potentially highly profitable new products that go overlooked by some of the senior staff. You need to draw attention to these products, and PowerPoint can help. Create a short presentation that uses WordArt to jazz up your presentation. This presentation will focus on precision equipment your company can start importing.

1. **OPEN** the *World Wide Importers* presentation.
2. With slide 1 on the screen, on the Home tab, open the WordArt gallery and select Gradient Fill – Aqua Accent 1, Outline – White, Glow – Accent 2. (It's the first style in the fourth row.)
3. In the WordArt text box that appears, type World Wide Importers. Reposition the text box so it is just above the subtitle and centered between the left and right edges of the slide.
4. On the Drawing Tools Format tab, in the WordArt Styles group, open the Text Fill color palette and click Aqua, Accent 1, Darker 25%.
5. Open the Text Effects menu and select the Cool Slant bevel effect. (It's the rightmost style in the first row of the Bevel section.)
6. Go to slide 2 and select all the text in the bulleted list.
7. Change the font size to 24, and then change the line spacing to 1.5.
8. Click the Numbering button to convert the list into a numbered list.
9. Go to slide 3. Insert a text box under the slide's title. Type the following items into the text box, putting each item on its own line:
   Digital controls
   Heat sensors
   Laser guides
   Light sensors
   Motion detectors
   Pressure monitors
   Regulators
   Timing systems

10. Select all the text in the text box and change the font size to 24.

11. On the Home tab, open the Quick Styles gallery and click Colored Fill – Gray 50%, Accent 4.

12. Click the Columns button, and then click Two Columns.

13. Resize the text box as needed, so that four items appear in each column within the text box.

14. **SAVE** the presentation as *World Wide Importers Final* and **CLOSE** the file.

LEAVE PowerPoint open for the next project.

Mastery Assessment

Project 3-5: Pop Quiz

As an instructor at the School of Fine Art, you decide to use a slide show to give beginning students the first pop quiz on art history. You need to finish the presentation by formatting the text and removing some unneeded text boxes.

1. **OPEN** the *Art History* presentation.

2. On slides 2, 3, and 4, do each of the following:

   a. Format the slide's title with the Intense Effect – Dark Blue, Dark 1 Quick Style.

   b. Convert the bulleted list of answers into a numbered list.

   c. Delete the text box (containing the correct answer) at the bottom of the slide.

3. **SAVE** the presentation as *Art History Final* and **CLOSE** the file.

LEAVE PowerPoint open for the next project.

@ The *Art History* file is available on the book companion website or in WileyPLUS.

Project 3-6: Graphic Design Drafts

As the manager of the account representative that prepared the Graphic Designs slide, you want to put a few finishing touches on the slide before it is published. To protect against someone inadvertently printing the slide, you need to add a text box across the entire slide that labels the slide as a "Draft."

1. **OPEN** the *Graphic Designs Final* presentation you completed in Project 3-2.

2. **SAVE** the presentation as *Graphic Designs Draft*.

3. Add a text box at the top of slide 1, and type DRAFT into the text box.

4. Rotate the text box at a 45-degree angle across the center photo on the slide.

5. Enlarge the text to 88 points. Resize the text box as needed by dragging its sizing handles so the text fits properly inside the box.

6. Using Text Effects on the Drawing Tools Format tab, apply the Aqua, 18 point glow, Accent Color 1 glow effect to the text.

7. **SAVE** and **CLOSE** the presentation.

CLOSE PowerPoint.

INTERNET READY

Launch your browser and visit the Microsoft website at http://www.microsoft.com. On the Microsoft home page, click in the Search box, type the word *fonts*, and then click the Search button. Look for pages on the Microsoft site that offer information about fonts; read the information to learn about how fonts are created and to find tips for using fonts wisely in your documents and presentations.

4 Designing a Presentation

LESSON SKILL MATRIX

In This Lesson, You Will Learn The Following Skills:

Formatting Presentations with Themes

Changing Slide Backgrounds

Working with Different Layouts

Inserting a Date, Footer, and Slide Numbers

Linking to Web Pages and Other Programs

Working with Sections

Customizing Slide Masters

KEY TERMS

- action
- action button
- font theme
- footer
- header
- hyperlink
- layout
- layout master
- section
- slide master
- theme

Southridge Video is a small company that offers video services to the community, such as videography for special events, video editing services, and duplication and conversion services. As a sales representative for Southridge Video, you often present information on the company to those who are considering the use of professional-level video services. In this lesson, you will add design elements to a simple presentation to polish and improve its appearance. You will also learn how to break down a presentation into sections and to customize slide masters to make global changes to a presentation.

SOFTWARE ORIENTATION

Microsoft PowerPoint's Themes Gallery

PowerPoint's Themes gallery offers 40 unique designs you can apply to presentations to format the slides with colors, fonts, effects, and backgrounds. Figure 4-1 shows the Themes gallery.

Figure 4-1

The Themes gallery

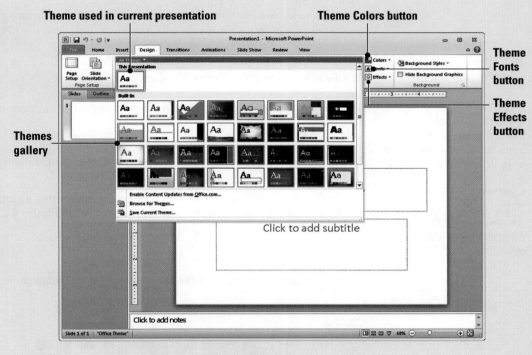

Use PowerPoint's built-in themes to give your presentation a polished, professional look without a lot of trial and error. You can preview a theme by pointing at it in the Themes gallery, and then apply it to the presentation by clicking it.

FORMATTING PRESENTATIONS WITH THEMES

A PowerPoint **theme** includes a set of colors designed to work well together, a set of fonts (one for headings and one for body text), special effects that can be applied to objects such as pictures or shapes, and often a graphic background. The theme also controls the layout of placeholders on each slide. Use a theme to quickly apply a unified look to one or more slides in a presentation (or to the entire presentation). You can also modify a theme and save your changes as a new custom theme.

PowerPoint makes it easy to see how a theme will look on your slides by offering a *live preview*: As you move the mouse pointer over each theme in the gallery, that theme's formats display on the current slide. This formatting feature takes a great deal of guesswork out of the design process—if you don't like a theme's appearance, just move the pointer to a different theme or click outside the gallery to restore the previous appearance.

Clicking a theme applies it to all slides in a presentation. You can also apply a theme to a single slide or a selection of slides by making the selection, right-clicking the theme, and choosing Apply to Selected Slides.

A theme differs from a template in that it contains no sample content—only formatting specifications.

Applying a Theme to a Presentation

In this exercise, you learn how to select a theme from the Themes gallery to replace the default blank design and create a more visually appealing design for your PowerPoint presentations.

Apply a Theme to a Presentation

The *Special Events* file is available on the book companion website or in WileyPLUS.

WILEY
PLUS *EXTRA*

WileyPLUS Extra! features an online tutorial of this task.

GET READY. Before you begin these steps, make sure that your computer is on. Log on, if necessary.

1. **START** PowerPoint, if the program is not already running.
2. Locate and open the *Special Events* presentation and save it as *Special Events Final*.
3. Make sure slide 1 is selected.
4. On the Design tab, click the More button in the Themes group. PowerPoint's available themes display in the Themes gallery, as shown in Figure 4-2.

Figure 4-2

The Themes gallery

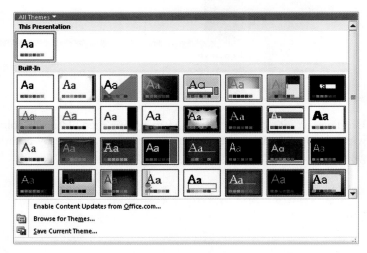

5. Point to any of the themes in the gallery. Notice that a ScreenTip displays the theme's name and the theme formats are instantly applied to the slide behind the gallery.

6. Right-click the Clarity theme (second theme in the second row); a pop-up menu appears. In the menu, click **Apply to Selected Slides.** The Clarity theme is applied only to slide 1.

Take Note
The theme names are in alphabetical order in the gallery. The Clarity theme might be located on a different row depending upon the size of your monitor.

7. Click the More button again in the Themes group to reopen the Themes gallery.

8. Right-click the Origin theme, and click **Apply to All Slides** to apply it to all slides.

9. Scroll through the slides to see how the theme has supplied new colors, fonts, bullet symbols, and layouts. Slide 1 should resemble Figure 4-3.

Figure 4-3

Origin theme applied to all slides in the presentation

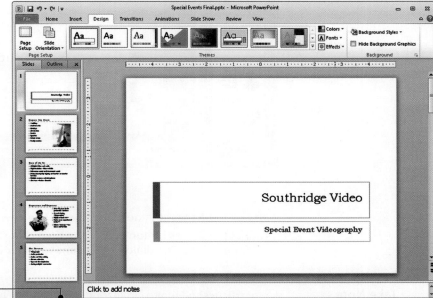

Current theme name appears on the status bar.

10. SAVE the presentation.

PAUSE. LEAVE the presentation open to use in the next exercise.

Take Note
The name of the current theme is displayed on the status bar to the right of the slide number information.

Changing Theme Colors

If you don't like the colors used in the theme you've chosen, you can change them. You can select the colors from some other theme, or you can create your own color theme. When you apply the colors from another theme, your current theme fonts, background graphics, and effects remain the same—only the colors change. In this exercise, you choose a different color theme for a presentation.

STEP BY STEP **Change Theme Colors**

USE the *Special Events Final* presentation that is still open from the previous exercise.

1. Click the Colors button in the Themes group. A gallery displays showing color palettes for all available themes.

2. Move the pointer over some of the color palettes to see the live preview of those colors on the current slide (see Figure 4-4).

Figure 4-4

Apply a different color theme to the presentation

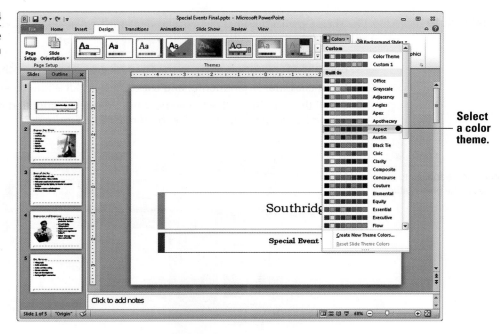

Select a color theme.

3. Click the **Aspect** theme color palette. The new colors are applied to the presentation.
4. Click the **Colors** button again, and then click **Create New Theme Colors** at the bottom of the gallery. The dialog box opens to allow you to replace colors in the current color palette.

Take Note   Color palettes and font combinations are identified by theme name to make it easy to select them.

5. Click the drop-down arrow next to the light green color designated for Hyperlinks.
6. Click **Gray 80% Background 2, Lighter 25%** on the Theme Colors palette to change the color for hyperlinks to a medium gray (see Figure 4-5).

Figure 4-5

The Create New Theme Colors dialog box

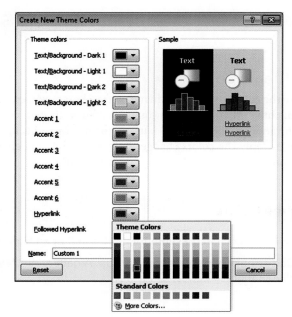

7. Select the text in the Name box and type Southridge in its place.

8. Click Save to save the new color palette.

9. **SAVE** the presentation.

PAUSE. LEAVE the presentation open to use in the next exercise.

To create a unique appearance, you can choose new colors for theme elements in the Create New Theme Colors dialog box. This dialog box displays the theme's color palette and shows you what element each color applies to. A preview area shows the colors in use; as you change colors, the preview changes to show how the new colors work together. If you don't like the choices you have made, use the Reset button to restore the default colors.

You can save a new color theme to make it available for use with any theme. Saved color themes display at the top of the Theme Colors gallery in the Custom section. To save a color theme, on the Design tab, click Colors, and click Create New Theme Colors.

Changing Theme Fonts

Each theme supplies a combination of two fonts to be applied to headings and text. Collectively these two fonts are called a **font theme**. Each font theme's name is the same as the theme from which it came. For example, there is an overall theme called Origin, and also a font theme called Origin that consists of its fonts. That's useful because you can pick and choose elements of different themes to use in your presentation—the layouts of one theme, the colors of another, and the fonts of yet another. In the following exercise, you choose a different font theme for a presentation.

STEP BY STEP **Change Theme Fonts**

USE the *Special Events Final* presentation that is still open from the previous exercise.

1. Click the Fonts button in the Themes group. A gallery displays showing font combinations for all available themes.

2. Move the pointer over some of the font combinations to see the live preview of those fonts on the current slide.

3. Click the Trek font combination, as shown in Figure 4-6. The new fonts are applied to the presentation.

Figure 4-6

Choose a new theme font

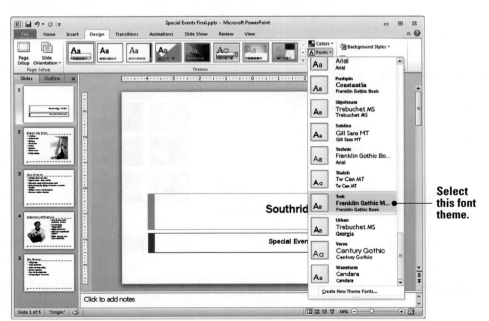

4. SAVE the presentation.

PAUSE. LEAVE the presentation open to use in the next exercise.

PowerPoint supplies a wide variety of font combinations to allow you to choose among traditional *serif fonts* and contemporary *sans serif* fonts. A serif is a "tail" or flourish on the edges of each letter, such as the tiny vertical lines hanging off the top edges of a capital T. The body text in this book uses a serif font; the headings use a sans-serif font. The choice you make depends a great deal on the subject of your presentation and the impression you are trying to convey with your slides.

As with theme colors, you can select your own theme fonts and save them to be available to apply to any theme. Click Create New Theme Fonts at the bottom of the Theme Fonts gallery, select a heading font and body font, and then save the combination with a new name.

CHANGING SLIDE BACKGROUNDS

The Bottom Line

Themes provide a default background for all slides formatted with that theme. To customize a theme or draw attention to one or more slides, you can apply a different background.

Selecting a Theme Background

The Background Styles gallery allows you to choose from plain, light, or dark backgrounds and gradient backgrounds that gradually change from light to dark. Background colors are determined by the theme. Some background styles include graphic effects such as fine lines or textures over the entire background. Use the Background Styles gallery to quickly apply a different solid-color or gradient background based on theme colors. You can apply a background to one or more selected slides or to all slides in the presentation. In this exercise, you will select a background style from the preset backgrounds provided by the theme.

STEP BY STEP   **Select a Theme Background**

USE the *Special Events Final* presentation that is still open from the previous exercise.

1. Go to slide 1.
2. On the Design tab, click the Background Styles button in the Background group. A gallery displays as shown in Figure 4-7, showing some background styles created using the theme's designated background colors.

Figure 4-7

Background Styles gallery

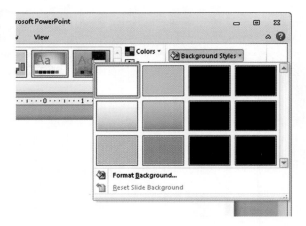

Take Note   Hover the pointer on a background style to see its name and preview it on the current slide.

3. Right-click **Style 6**, then click **Apply to Selected Slides**. The background style is applied to slide 1 only.

4. **SAVE** the presentation.

PAUSE. LEAVE the presentation open to use in the next exercise.

The area of the slide that is considered to be "background" can change depending on the theme. For example, some themes have graphics overlaid on a colored background, so that your choice of background color peeks through in only a few spots.

Applying a Custom Background

The same background options that you learned about in Lesson 3 for text boxes also apply to slide backgrounds. Use the Format Background dialog box to create and modify any background, even a default theme background. You can apply a solid color or gradient fill, or select a picture or texture for the background. Options for each of these fill types allow you to modify the fill to suit your needs. In this exercise, you will create your own custom background.

STEP BY STEP **Apply a Custom Background**

USE the *Special Events Final* presentation that is still open from the previous exercise.

1. With slide 1 still active, click the **Background Styles** button, then click **Format Background** at the bottom of the gallery. The Format Background dialog box opens. It shows a gradient because the style you selected in the previous exercise was a gradient.

Take Note If you wished to apply a solid color background to the slide, you would select the Solid Fill option from the Format Background dialog box.

Another Way
Display the Format Background dialog box by right-clicking any blank area of the slide background and then clicking Format Background from the shortcut menu. Or, click the Background group's dialog box launcher.

2. Click the **Preset Colors drop-down arrow** and in the drop-down list, click the **Gold** preset. The slide background changes behind the dialog box.

3. Click the **Type drop-down arrow** and click **Rectangular** in the drop-down list (see Figure 4-8). The pattern of the gradient changes.

Figure 4-8

Format Background dialog box with gradient controls

Select Gradient fill if it is not already selected.

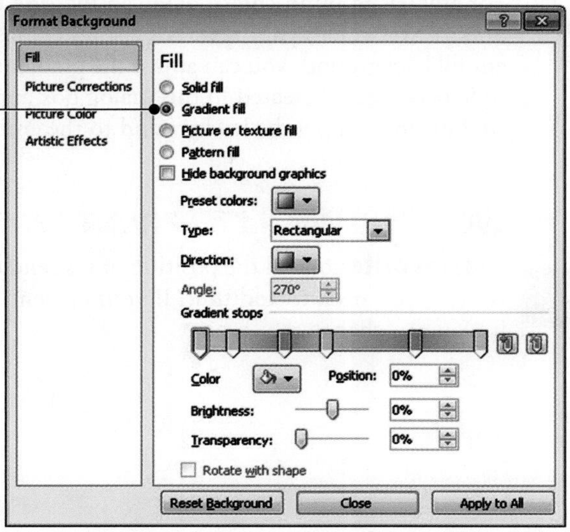

4. Click the Solid Fill option button. The controls change to those for solid colors.

5. Click the Color drop-down arrow and in the gallery that appears, click Tan, Accent 6 (the last color in the color theme gallery).

6. Drag the Transparency slider to 35%. The fill lightens because it is now partly transparent. See Figure 4-9.

Figure 4-9

Options for solid-color background fills

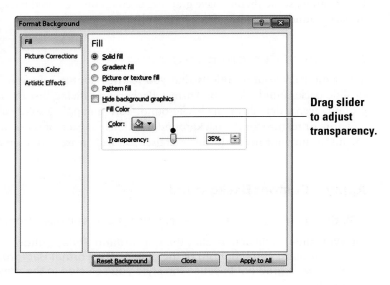

7. Click Picture or texture fill. The controls change to those for pictures and textures.

8. Click the Texture button, and then click the Sand texture (third texture in second row).

9. Click Pattern. The controls change to those for patterns.

10. Click the 10% pattern (first pattern in second row).

11. Open the Foreground Color drop-down list and click Orange, Accent 1.

12. Click Close. The pattern background is applied to only the current slide (slide 1).

13. **SAVE** the presentation.

PAUSE. LEAVE the presentation open to use in the next exercise.

Another Way
If you had wanted to apply the new background to all the slides, you could have clicked Apply to All before clicking Close in step 12.

For any background choice, you can increase transparency to "wash out" the background so it doesn't overwhelm your text. For a solid color, you might increase its transparency. For a gradient fill background, you can adjust the gradient by adding or removing colors. By default, a new slide background created in this dialog box applies only to the current slide. Click the Apply to All button to apply the background to the entire presentation.

WORKING WITH DIFFERENT LAYOUTS

The Bottom Line

Slide **layouts** control the position of text and objects on a slide. Select a layout according to the content you need to add to it. If your current layout does not present information as you want it, you can change the layout.

Working with a Different Slide Layout

If you have applied a theme, the slide layout gallery shows available layouts with theme formatting. If more than one theme is in use in the presentation (for example, if you applied a different theme to only selected slides), the slide layout gallery shows available layouts from all themes so you can pick and choose among a greater variety of layout options. In this exercise, you learn to apply a different slide layout to a PowerPoint slide. In this exercise, you will choose a different layout for a slide.

STEP BY STEP   **Work with a Different Slide Layout**

USE the *Special Events Final* presentation that is still open from the previous exercise.

1. Click the Home tab on the Ribbon.
2. Go to slide 5 and click New Slide in the Slides group. PowerPoint adds a new slide with the same layout as slide 5, Title and Content.
3. Type the title Contact Information.
4. Type the following information as the first bullet point in the text placeholder:

   457 Gray Road

   North Hills, OH 45678

Take Note   Use Shift+Enter after typing *Road* to start a new line without starting a new paragraph.

5. Type these additional bullet points:

   Phone: (513) 555-6543

   Fax: (513) 555-5432

6. Select the entire bulleted list and click the Bullets button on the Home tab to turn off the bullets. Your slide should look like Figure 4-10.

Figure 4-10

Add contact information to the slide

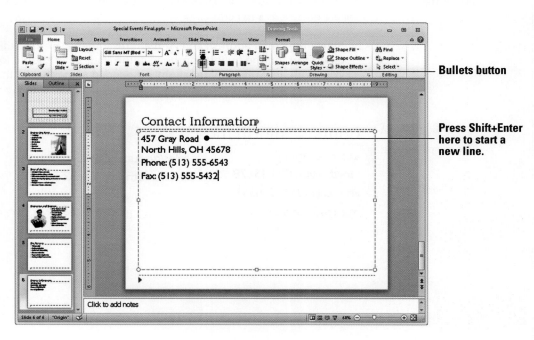

7. On the Home tab, click the **Layout** button to display the slide layout gallery shown in Figure 4-11.

Figure 4-11

Slide layout gallery

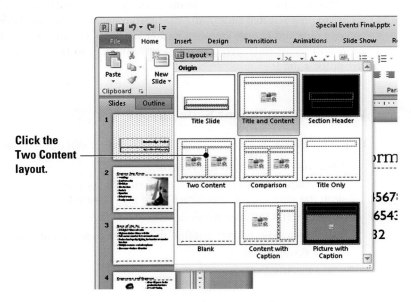

Click the
Two Content
layout.

8. Click **Two Content** to change the layout to two side-by-side content placeholders.

9. In the second placeholder, type the following bullet points:

sales@southridgevideo.com

www.southridgevideo.com

Take Note   If you press the spacebar after typing an email or Web address, PowerPoint automatically formats the text as a hyperlink.

10. Select the email address and Web address, then click the **Bullets** button on the Home tab to turn off the bullets for those items. Your slide should look similar to Figure 4-12. Widen the text placeholder slightly if needed so neither of the addresses wrap to two lines.

Figure 4-12

The completed slide

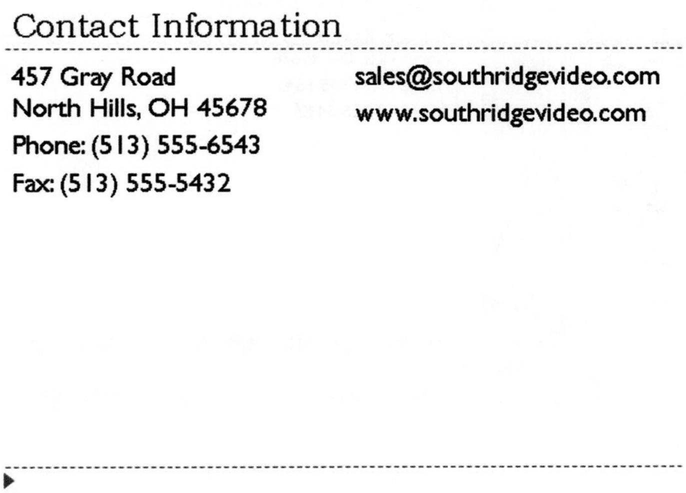

Contact Information

----

457 Gray Road   sales@southridgevideo.com
North Hills, OH 45678   www.southridgevideo.com
Phone: (513) 555-6543
Fax: (513) 555-5432

11. SAVE the presentation.

PAUSE. LEAVE the presentation open to use in the next exercise.

The layouts that appear in the slide layout gallery depend on the layouts stored in the Slide Master, which you will learn about later in this lesson.

INSERTING A DATE, FOOTER, AND SLIDE NUMBERS

Adding a date, footer, and slide numbers to a presentation can help you identify and organize slides. In this exercise, you learn how to apply these useful elements to one or more slides.

Inserting a Date, Footer, and Slide Numbers

A **footer** is text that repeats at the bottom of each slide in a presentation. Use a footer to record the slide title, company name, or other important information that you want the audience to keep in mind as they view the slides. In this exercise, you apply a footer, a date, and slide numbers to a PowerPoint presentation.

STEP BY STEP   **Insert a Date, Footer, and Slide Numbers**

USE the *Special Events Final* presentation that is still open from the previous exercise.

1. Click the **Insert** tab, and then click the **Header & Footer** button. The Header and Footer dialog box opens.
2. Click the **Date and time** check box, and then click **Update automatically** if it isn't already selected.
3. Click to select the **Slide number** check box.
4. Click the **Footer** check box and then type **Special Events** in the text box below the check box.
5. Click the **Don't show on title slide** check box. The dialog box should resemble Figure 4-13 at this point. The date will be today's date rather than the date shown in Figure 4-13.

Figure 4-13

Header and Footer dialog box

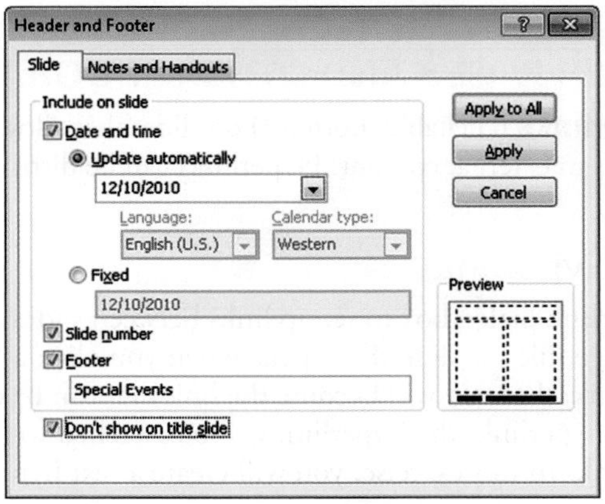

6. Click **Apply to All** to apply the date, footer, and slide number to all slides except the title slide. Slide 6 should look similar to Figure 4-14.

Figure 4-14

A slide number, footer, and date on a slide

Contact Information

457 Gray Road
North Hills, OH 45678
Phone: (513) 555-6543
Fax: (513) 555-5432

sales@southridgevideo.com
www.southridgevideo.com

Slide
number   Special Events   12/10/2010   Footer
    ▶ 6   Date

Another Way
You can also open the Header & Footer dialog box by clicking the Date & Time button or the Slide Number button.

7. **SAVE** the presentation.

PAUSE. LEAVE the presentation open to use in the next exercise.

You have two choices when inserting a date: a date that automatically updates by changing to the current date each time the presentation is opened or a fixed date, which stays the same until you decide to change it. If it is important to indicate when slides were created or presented, use a fixed date.

You may have noticed that the Header and Footer dialog box has another tab, the Header tab. When you create notes pages and handouts, you can specify a **header** to appear at the top of every page. A header is repeated text, much like a footer, except it appears at the top of each page. Headers do not appear onscreen in Slide Show view—only on printouts. You can also create footers for notes pages and handouts.

The Bottom Line

LINKING TO WEB PAGES AND OTHER PROGRAMS

You can set up **hyperlinks** (clickable shortcuts) on slides that allow you to jump to a specific slide in the presentation or to external content. Hyperlinks can be displayed as either text or a graphic.

Adding a Text Hyperlink

Use the Insert Hyperlink dialog box to set up links between slides or from slides to other targets. (The *target* is the page, file, or slide that opens when you click a link.) If you select text before inserting the hyperlink, that text will become the link that can be clicked. If you select a graphic before inserting the hyperlink, the hyperlink will be attached to the graphic, so that clicking it activates the hyperlink. In this exercise, you will create a text hyperlink.

STEP BY STEP   **Add a Text Hyperlink**

USE the *Special Events Final* presentation that is still open from the previous exercise.

1. Go to slide 6, and select the website address (www.southridgevideo.com).
2. Click the **Hyperlink** button on the Insert tab. The Insert Hyperlink dialog box opens.

Take Note

Depending on how you typed the address in the previous exercise, PowerPoint may have already turned www.southridgevideo.com into a hyperlink. If so, the Edit Hyperlink dialog box opens instead.

3. Click in the Address box and type http://www.southridgevideo.com as the target of the link text (see Figure 4-15).

Figure 4-15

The Insert Hyperlink dialog box

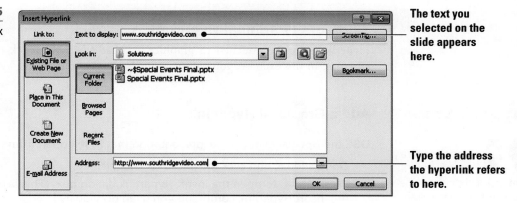

4. Click OK. The website address is formatted with the theme's hyperlink color and an underline.

5. Go to slide 1, and select Southridge Video.

6. Click the Hyperlink button on the Insert tab. The Insert Hyperlink dialog box opens.

7. In the Link To list on the left side of the dialog box click Place in This Document. A list of slides from the current presentation appears.

8. Click 6. Contact Information, as shown in Figure 4-16.

Figure 4-16

Creating a hyperlink to another slide

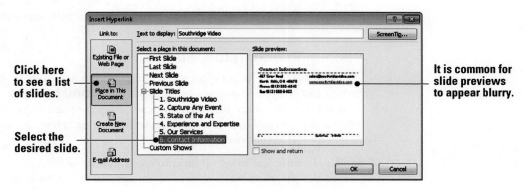

9. Click OK; PowerPoint identifies slide 6 as the target for this hyperlink.

10. **SAVE** the presentation.

PAUSE. LEAVE the presentation open to use in the next exercise.

You can create links to a number of different types of targets using the Insert Hyperlink dialog box.

- Choose **Existing File or Web Page** to link to any web page or any file on your system or network. Use the Look in box, the Browse the Web button, or the Browse File button to locate the desired page or file, or type the URL or path in the Address box.

- Choose **Place in This Document** to display a list of the current presentation's slides and custom shows. Click the slide or custom show that you want to display when the link is clicked.

- Choose **Create New Document** to create a link to a new document. You supply the path and the name for the new document and then choose whether to add content to the document now or later.
- Choose **E-mail Address** to type an email address to which you want to link.

You can add hyperlinks to a slide in Normal view, but the links will work only in Slide Show view.

Adding a Graphical Hyperlink

Hyperlinks can be attached to graphics, so that when you click the graphic, the hyperlink executes. In this exercise, you will make an existing graphic into a hyperlink.

STEP BY STEP	**Add a Graphical Hyperlink**

Another Way You can also right-click and choose Hyperlink to open the Insert Hyperlink dialog box.

USE the *Special Events Final* presentation that is still open from the previous exercise.

1. Go to slide 4, and click the photo to select it.
2. Press **Ctrl+K** to open the Insert Hyperlink dialog box. (This is a keyboard shortcut for the Insert Hyperlink command you used previously.)
3. Click **Place in This Document**. A list of slides from the current presentation appears.
4. Click **6. Contact Information**.
5. Click **OK**.
6. **SAVE** the presentation.

PAUSE. LEAVE the presentation open to use in the next exercise.

If you need to change a link's target, click anywhere in the link and then click the Hyperlink button, or right-click it and click Edit Hyperlink. The Edit Hyperlink dialog box opens, offering the same functionality as the Insert Hyperlink dialog box. You can remove a link by right-clicking the link and selecting Remove Hyperlink from the shortcut menu.

Adding an Action to a Slide

Use **actions** to perform tasks such as jumping to a new slide or starting a different program. Actions can be applied to text or shapes such as **action buttons**. An action button is a shape from the Shapes gallery to which you can assign a hyperlink or some other action. (You can assign actions to any object, not just an action button. However, action buttons are specifically designed for that purpose.)

Besides allowing you to set up links to specific slides or files, you can use action settings to run a particular program, run a macro, or perform an action with an object such as an embedded Excel worksheet. You can also play a sound from a list of default sounds or any sound file on your system.

STEP BY STEP	**Add an Action to a Slide**

USE the *Special Events Final* presentation that is still open from the previous exercise.

1. Go to slide 5.
2. Click the **Shapes** button on the Insert tab to display a gallery of drawing shapes.
3. Click the **Action Button: Information** shape in the middle of the last row of shapes, as shown in Figure 4-17.

Figure 4-17

Create an information
action button

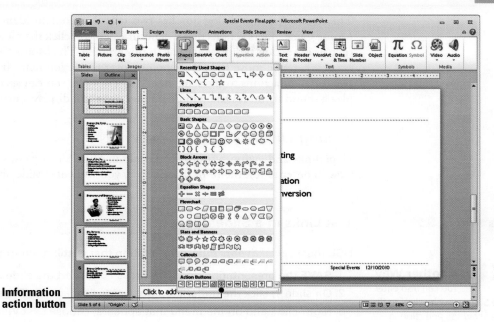

**Imformation
action button**

Another Way
The Shapes button
is also available on the
Home tab.

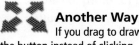

Another Way
If you drag to draw
the button instead of clicking,
you can make it any size
you like.

4. The pointer changes to a crosshair. Click near the bottom of the slide to draw the button there at its default size. As soon as you release the mouse button, the Action Settings dialog box opens.

5. Click **Hyperlink to** and then click the **drop-down arrow** of the text box below it.

6. Scroll to the bottom of the list of possible link targets and click **Other File**, as shown in Figure 4-18. The Hyperlink to Other File dialog box opens.

Figure 4-18

Choose to hyperlink
to another file

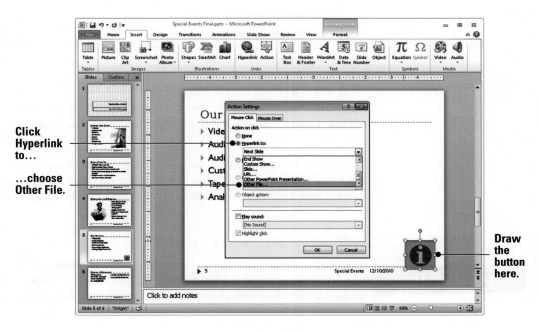

**Click
Hyperlink
to…**

**…choose
Other File.**

**Draw
the
button
here.**

@ The *Service Fees*
file is available on the
book companion website
or in WileyPLUS.

7. Navigate to the data files for this lesson, click the *Service Fees* file, and then click **OK** to apply your selection and return to the Action Settings dialog box.

8. Click **OK** again to close the Action Settings dialog box.

9. **SAVE** the presentation.

PAUSE. LEAVE the presentation open to use in the next exercise.

The Action Settings dialog box has two tabs that contain identical options. The default tab, Mouse Click, offers actions that will occur when you click the mouse pointer on the action item, such as the action button you drew in this exercise. The Mouse Over tab offers actions that will occur when you move the mouse pointer over the action item. It is therefore possible to attach two different actions to the same item. For example, you can specify that an action button will play a sound if you rest the mouse pointer on it and display a new slide if you click it.

Testing Links in a Slide Show

Hyperlinks and action buttons work only in Slide Show view, so you must enter Slide Show view in order to test them. In this exercise, you will enter Slide Show view and test hyperlinks.

STEP BY STEP   **Test Links in a Slide Show**

Another Way
You can also enter Slide Show view by clicking the Slide Show tab and clicking From Beginning.

USE the *Special Events Final* presentation that is still open from the previous exercise.

1. **SAVE** the presentation and then press F5 to start the slide show from slide 1.
2. On slide 1, click the underlined Southridge Video text. The show jumps to slide 6.
3. Right-click, and on the menu that appears, choose Last Viewed to return to slide 1.
4. Click the mouse button three times to advance to slide 4, and then click the photo. The show jumps to slide 6.
5. Right-click, and on the menu that appears, choose Last Viewed to return to slide 4.
6. Click the mouse button to advance to slide 5, and then click the Information button. A spreadsheet opens in Excel.
7. Close Excel without making or saving any changes.
8. On the Windows taskbar, switch back to the running presentation show.
9. Click the mouse button to advance to slide 6.
10. Click the underlined hyperlink.

Take Note   The website address you entered is a dummy address supported by Microsoft to allow you to practice creating links. It redirects you to a Microsoft site.

11. Close the web browser and end the slide show.
12. Close the presentation, saving your changes to it.

PAUSE. LEAVE PowerPoint open to use in the next exercise.

When you activate links or actions during a slide show, the target of the link or action is displayed in the full screen, like the slides in the slide show. After working with the external content, you can return to the slide show by selecting it from the taskbar in Windows.

WORKING WITH SECTIONS

The Bottom Line

To organize a long presentation, you can create **sections**, which are dividers that group slides into logical clusters, as folders organize groups of related papers. You can then work with the sections rather than with individual slides, moving or deleting an entire section as a group.

Creating Sections

You can create sections that organize the slides for easier management. This is especially useful in a lengthy presentation that covers multiple topics; each topic can be a section. In this exercise, you create some sections and then use them to manipulate content.

STEP BY STEP   **Create Sections**

USE the *Blue Yonder Introduction* presentation.

The *Blue Yonder Introduction* file is available on the book companion website or in WileyPLUS.

1. Locate and open the *Blue Yonder Introduction* presentation and save it as *Blue Yonder Sections*.

2. Go to slide 2. In the Slides tab of the Slides/Outline pane on the left of the PowerPoint screen, right-click slide 2 and click Add Section from the menu that appears (see Figure 4-19). A new section bar labeled Untitled Section appears in the Slides/Outline pane above slide 2, indicating that the new section begins with that slide.

Figure 4-19

Add a section

Right-click the slide the section should begin with.

Click Add Section.

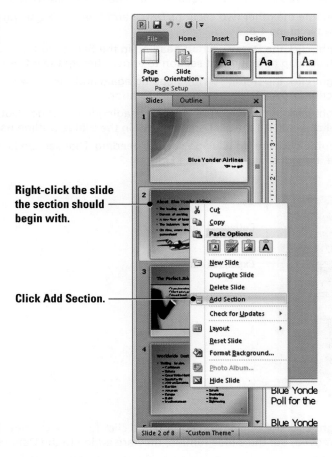

3. Go to slide 5. In the Slides/Outline pane, right-click slide 5 and click Add Section. Another new section (also labeled Untitled) appears above slide 5 in the Slides/Outline pane. Repeat these actions to create another new section above slide 7.

4. Click the Untitled Section bar above slide 2. Slides 2, 3, and 4 become selected.

5. Right-click the Untitled Section bar you just clicked and choose Rename Section from the menu that appears. The Rename Section dialog box opens, as shown in Figure 4-20.

Figure 4-20

Rename a section

6. Type Introduction in the Section Name box and click Rename.
7. Rename the other two sections Detail and Conclusion, using the same actions you used in steps 4-6.
8. Right-click the Detail section heading in the Slides/Outline pane and click Move Section Up to move that section to appear before the Introduction section.
9. Right-click the Detail section heading again and click Move Section Down. The Detail section moves back to its original location.
10. Right-click the Introduction section heading in the Slides/Outline pane and click Collapse All. All the sections collapse in the Slides/Outline pane.
11. Double-click the Conclusion section heading. That section is expanded so you can see the individual slides in it. See Figure 4-21.

Figure 4-21

Collapse and expand sections

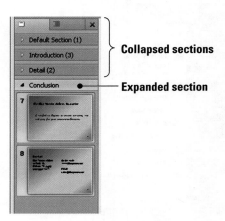

12. Right-click the Conclusion section and click Remove Section. The section heading is removed, but the slides remain; they are added to the Detail section.
13. Click the Introduction section heading to select it, and then on the Design tab, click Background Styles. On the background styles palette that appears, right-click Style 1 (the white background) and click Apply to Selected Styles. Only the slides in the selected section change their background color.
14. **SAVE** the presentation and **CLOSE** it.

PAUSE. LEAVE PowerPoint open to use in the next exercise.

Sections offer an easy way of selecting groups of slides together, so you can move them, format them, or even delete them. To delete an entire section, right-click the section header and click Remove Section & Slides. In the preceding exercise, you removed a section but kept the slides. Sections also enable you to rearrange groups of slides easily, by moving a section up or down in order.

Sections are invisible to the audience when you present a slide show. If you want to make it more obvious that you have organized the presentation into sections, you may wish to insert summary slides at the beginning or end of each section.

SOFTWARE ORIENTATION

PowerPoint's Slide Master View

Slide Master view, shown in Figure 4-22, provides tools for modifying the master slides on which all of the current presentation's layouts and formats are based. You can modify the slide master itself, or any of the individual layout masters subordinate to it.

Figure 4-22

Slide Master view

Modify the slide master to change all layouts.

Modify any of the layout masters to affect only slides that use that layout.

Format the sample here.

Use the tools on the Slide Master tab and the slide in the Slide pane to customize formats that will apply to all slides in a presentation. If you make changes to the topmost slide in the left pane, the changes apply to all layouts. If you click a specific layout below it to change, the changes apply to all slides that use that layout.

CUSTOMIZING SLIDE MASTERS

The Bottom Line

The **slide master** for a presentation stores information on the current theme, layout of place-holders, bullet characters, and other formats that affect all slides in a presentation. If you want to make design changes that will apply to many or all slides in a presentation, you can save a great deal of time by modifying the slide master rather than applying changes on each slide. Slide Master view makes it easy to change formats globally for a presentation by displaying the slide master and all layouts available in the current presentation. Customizing a slide master makes it easy to apply changes consistently throughout a presentation.

Applying a Theme to a Slide Master

To customize a slide master, you use Slide Master view. Slide Master view has its own tab on the Ribbon to provide tools you can use to change the masters. In this exercise, you apply a theme to a slide master to change its look.

STEP BY STEP   Apply a Theme to a Slide Master

 The *Rates* file is available on the book companion website or in WileyPLUS.

GET READY. To apply a theme to a slide master, perform the following steps:

1. Locate and open the *Rates* presentation and save it as *Rates Masters*.
2. With slide 1 active, click the View tab.
3. Click the Slide Master button in the Presentation Views group. Slide Master view opens with the Title Slide Layout selected in the left pane, as shown in Figure 4-23.

Figure 4-23

Slide Master view with the Title Slide layout selected

WILEY PLUS *EXTRA*

WileyPLUS Extra! features an online tutorial of this task.

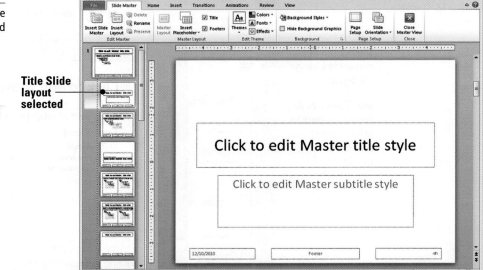

4. Click the first slide in the left pane, the slide master for the current theme. (It's the top slide in the left pane, the one that is slightly larger than the others.)
5. Click the Themes button in the Slide Master tab to produce the Themes gallery; click the Solstice theme in the gallery. The theme is applied to the slide master as well as all slide layouts in the left pane, as shown in Figure 4-24

Figure 4-24

A new theme applied to the slide master and its layouts

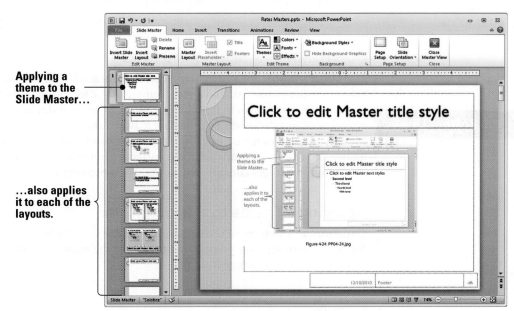

Take Note   Remember, you can find a theme's name by hovering the mouse over it. The themes appear in alphabetical order.

> 6. **SAVE** the presentation.
>
> **PAUSE. LEAVE** the presentation open in Slide Master view to use in the next exercise.

The slide master, displayed at the top of the left pane, looks like a blank Title and Content slide. To make a change to the master, edit it just the way you would edit any slide using tools on any of the Ribbon's tabs. For example, to change the font of the slide title, click the title, display the Home tab, and use the Font list to select a new font. Change bullet characters by clicking in any of the nine levels of bullets and then selecting a new bullet character from the Bullets and Numbering dialog box.

Some changes you make to the slide master display on the masters for other slide layouts. You can also click any of these layouts to display it in the Slide pane so you can make changes to that layout. Any changes you make to these layouts will display on slides that use those layouts. Your changed masters display in the slide layout gallery to be available when you create new slides.

Moving and Resizing Placeholders on a Slide Master

You may have noticed that some designs place slide content in different locations from others. This is because the placeholders on the slide master are positioned differently. You can move and resize the placeholders on the slide master to create different effects yourself. Each slide master has a set of **layout masters** that determine the number, type, and position of the placeholders on a particular type of slide. In Slide Master view, the layout masters are beneath the Slide Master, and slightly indented in the left pane to show that they are subordinate to it. Any changes you make to the placeholders on the Slide Master itself flow down to the layout masters. In this exercise, you change the layout for a particular layout master.

STEP BY STEP   **Move and Resize Placeholders**

USE the *Rates Masters* presentation that is still open from the previous exercise.

1. In Slide Master view, click to select the layout master for the Title Slide Layout in the left pane (hover your cursor over the slide to see a KeyTip indicating the layout master's name). The Title Slide layout master appears in the right pane.

2. In the Title Slide layout master, click the outer border of the subtitle placeholder (click to edit Master subtitle style) to select that text box.

3. Drag the bottom selection handle upward to decrease the height of the subtitle placeholder to 1″ (see Figure 4-25).

Figure 4-25

Resizing a placeholder

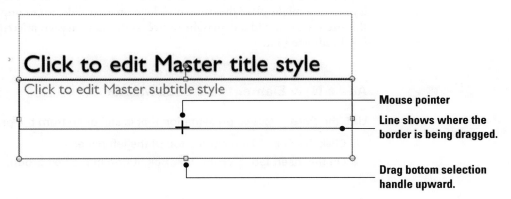

Click to edit Master title style

Click to edit Master subtitle style

Mouse pointer

Line shows where the border is being dragged.

Drag bottom selection handle upward.

4. Position the mouse pointer over the border of the subtitle placeholder, but not over a selection handle, so that the mouse pointer becomes a four-headed arrow (see Figure 4-26). Click and drag the box to the bottom of the slide.

Figure 4-26

Moving a placeholder

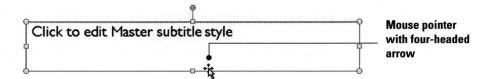

Mouse pointer with four-headed arrow

5. Using the same process as in step 4, move the title placeholder immediately above the subtitle, as shown in Figure 4-27.

Figure 4-27

The completed slide layout master

6. **SAVE** the presentation.

PAUSE. LEAVE the presentation open in Slide Master view to use in the next exercise.

Adding New Elements to a Slide Master

If you add a picture or text to a slide master layout, it will display on all slides that use that layout. You might place the company's logo on each slide, for example, or a copyright notice. In this exercise, you add a copyright notice to the slide master, affecting every layout master that is subordinate to it.

STEP BY STEP   **Add a New Element to a Slide Master**

USE the *Rates Masters* presentation that is still open from the previous exercise.

1. Click the Slide Master at the top of the left pane.
2. On the Insert tab, click the Text Box button in the Text group.

3. In the bottom left corner of the slide master, click to place a new text box, and type **Copyright 2012 Southridge Video**. See Figure 4-28.

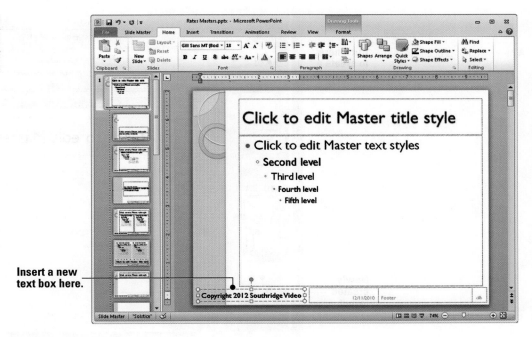

4. Select all the text in the copyright notice and change its color to **Tan, Background 2, Darker 25%**.

5. Click the **Slide Master** tab, and then click the **Close Master View** button to return to Normal view.

6. View each slide to confirm that the copyright text appears on each one.

PAUSE. LEAVE the presentation open in Slide Master view to use in the next exercise.

Creating a Custom Layout Master

If you need to create a number of slides with a layout different from any of the default layouts, you can create a new custom layout to your own specifications. Or, if you want some slides to use a modified version of one of the default layouts, but you also want to retain that original layout, you may want to create your own slide layout. In this exercise you create a custom layout.

STEP BY STEP   **Create a Custom Layout Master**

USE the *Rates Masters* presentation that is still open from the previous exercise.

1. On the View tab, click **Slide Master** to return to Slide Master view.

2. Click the **Slide Master** at the top of the left pane.

3. On the Slide Master tab, click Insert Layout. A new blank layout appears at the bottom of the left pane. It is blank except for a title placeholder and the copyright information, as shown in Figure 4-29.

Figure 4-29

A new layout has been created

Click here to create a new layout.

Newly created layout

4. On the Slide Master tab, click the Insert Placeholder button's drop-down arrow. A menu opens, as in Figure 4-30.

Figure 4-30

Select a type of placeholder

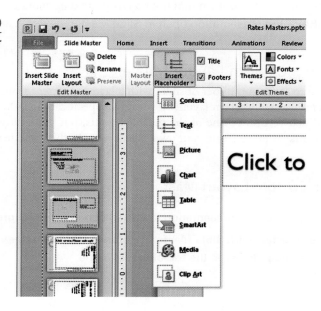

5. In the menu, click Text. The mouse pointer turns into a crosshair.

6. Draw a new text placeholder on the slide in the position shown in Figure 4-31.

Figure 4-31

Draw a text placeholder as shown here

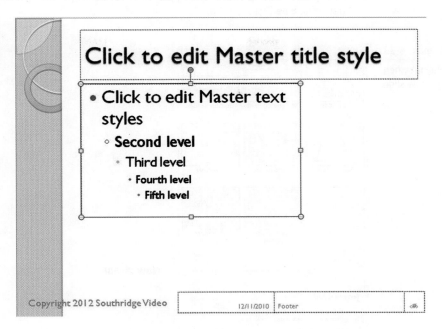

7. Click the Insert Placeholder drop-down arrow again, and click Picture in the menu that appears. Draw a placeholder box to the right of the text placeholder, as shown in Figure 4-32.

Figure 4-32

Draw a picture placeholder as shown here

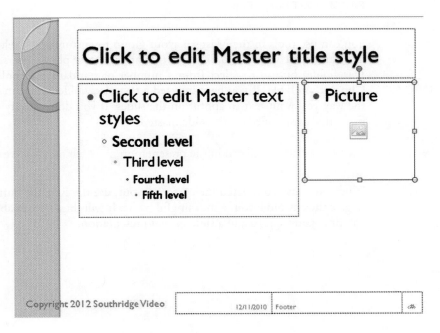

8. Right-click the new layout master in the left pane and click Rename Layout in the menu that appears.

9. In the Rename Layout dialog box, type Text and Picture and click OK.

10. On the Slide Master tab, click Close Master View.

11. On the Home tab, click the New Slide button's drop-down arrow. On the gallery of layouts that appears, click your new layout, Text and Picture, to create a new slide using it. See Figure 4-33.

Figure 4-33

Use the new layout when creating a new slide

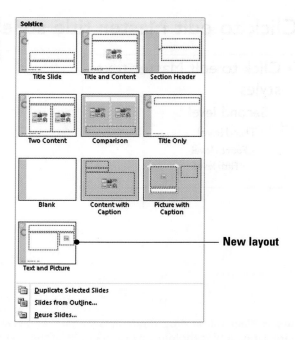

New layout

12. **SAVE** the presentation.

PAUSE. EXIT PowerPoint.

You can use tools in the Master Layout group to customize placeholders for your new layout. You can decide whether to display a title or the footer placeholders, and you can use the Insert Placeholder button to select from a number of standard placeholders, such as Text, Picture, Clip Art, or Table. If you have inserted a text placeholder, you can format the placeholder text the way you want text to appear on the slides. If you don't specify formatting, the text will be formatted as specified on the slide master.

Take Note   Custom layouts are stored in the presentation in which they are created.

When you have completed the custom layout, use the Rename button on the Slide Master tab to give the custom layout a meaningful name. It will then be available in the slide layout gallery any time you want to add a slide in that presentation.

SKILL SUMMARY

In This Lesson, You Learned How To:
Format presentations with themes
Change slide backgrounds
Work with different layouts
Insert a date, footer, and slide numbers
Link to web pages and other programs
Work with sections
Customize slide masters

Knowledge Assessment

Fill in the Blank

Fill in each blank with the term or phrase that best completes the statement.

1. A(n) _____ is a file containing color, font, layout, and effect settings that you can apply to a presentation to change its appearance.

2. A slide's _____ determines the positioning and types of placeholders on it.

3. Text that repeats at the bottom of each slide is a(n) _____.

4. Underlined text on a slide usually means that the text is a(n) _____ and opens a web page or another slide when clicked.

5. A(n) _____ button can be placed on a slide to perform a certain activity or jump to a certain slide when clicked.

6. You can organize slides into _____, which group slides together for easier handling.

7. To ensure consistency, make formatting changes to the _____ rather than individual slides.

8. The individual layouts associated with a particular slide master are called _____ masters.

9. To create your own layout, start a new layout and then add one or more _____.

10. Hyperlinks must be tested in _____ view.

Multiple Choice

Circle the correct answer.

1. Which of these does a theme *not* include?
   a. A color palette
   b. Fonts
   c. Graphic effects
   d. Sample content

2. Themes are applied from which tab?

   a. Home

   b. Insert

   c. Design

   d. Transitions

3. How are PowerPoint's built-in font themes named?

   a. They use the same names as the themes from which they come.

   b. They are numbered from 1 to 255.

   c. They are lettered from A to Z.

   d. They are named according to the first font in the font theme.

4. From which tab do you apply a different layout to a slide?

   a. Home

   b. Insert

   c. Design

   d. Transitions

5. Which of these is *not* a type of fill you can use for a slide background?

   a. Solid color

   b. SmartArt

   c. Texture

   d. Gradient

6. To link to a slide in the current presentation, choose _____ in the Insert Hyperlink dialog box.

   a. Existing File or Web Page

   b. Place in This Document

   c. Create New Document

   d. Show Current Slides

7. Where do slide headers appear, if used?

   a. Onscreen during Slide Show view

   b. On printouts of handouts and notes pages

   c. Neither place

   d. Both places

8. After assigning a hyperlink to a graphic, you can test it in _____ view.

   a. Normal

   b. Slide Show

   c. Slide Sorter

   d. Notes Pages

9. Action buttons are selected and inserted from the _____ button's menu on the Insert tab.

   a. Clip Art

   b. SmartArt

   c. Shapes

   d. WordArt

10. What happens when you move a section header?

    a. All the slides in the section move along with it.

    b. The header moves but not the slides in its section.

Competency Assessment

Project 4-1: Service with a Smile

You're the sales manager for a large chain of auto dealerships that prides itself on service and warranty packages that give customers a sense of security. The company, Car King, is rolling out a new line of extended warranties to offer its customers. You have created a presentation that details three levels of warranties. Now you need to improve the look of the slides to make customers take notice.

GET READY. LAUNCH PowerPoint if it is not already running.

The Warranty Plans file is available on the book companion website or in WileyPLUS.

1. **OPEN** the *Warranty Plans* presentation and save it as *Warranty Plans Final*.
2. With slide 1 active, click the New Slide button to insert a new Title and Content slide.
3. Click the Layout button, and then click Title Slide.
4. Type the title Car King and the subtitle Extended Warranty Plans.
5. Drag the slide above slide 1 in the Slides tab so the title slide becomes the first slide.
6. Click the Design tab, and then click the More button to display the Themes gallery.
7. Click Foundry to apply this theme to all slides.
8. Click the Fonts button on the Design tab, and then scroll down to locate and click the Metro theme font combination.
9. Click the Colors button on the Design tab, and then click Create New Theme Colors.
10. Click the Accent 1 drop-down arrow, then click the Tan, Text 2, Darker 25% color.
11. Click the Accent 2 drop-down arrow, then click the Tan, Text 2, Darker 50% color.
12. Type CarKing as the color scheme name, and then click Save.
13. Go to slide 1, if necessary.
14. Click the Background Styles button, and then click Style 7.
15. **SAVE** the presentation and **CLOSE** the file.

LEAVE PowerPoint open for use in the next project.

Project 4-2: Special Delivery

As a marketing manager for Consolidated Delivery, you have been asked to prepare and present information on the company's services to a prospective corporate client. You need to add some interactive features to a standard presentation to make your delivery especially interesting.

The Messenger Service file is available on the book companion website or in WileyPLUS.

1. **OPEN** the *Messenger Service* presentation and save it as *Messenger Service Links*.
2. Go to slide 2 and select the text Contact Consolidated in the text box at the bottom of the slide.
3. Open the Insert Hyperlink dialog box (Ctrl+K is one way), click Place in This Document, and then click 6. Our Numbers in the list of slide titles. Click OK.
4. Go to slide 5 and use the Shapes gallery on the Insert tab to select the Information action button.

The Contract Plans file is available on the book companion website or in WileyPLUS.

5. Draw a button near the bottom of the slide and set the action to Hyperlink to: Other File. Select the file *Contract Plans*.
6. Go to slide 6, select the website address, and use the Insert Hyperlink dialog box to create a link to http://www.consolidatedmessenger.com.
7. Insert an automatically updating date, slide numbers, and the footer Consolidated Messenger on all slides except the title slide. (You may need to adjust the location of your action button on slide 5 after you add slide numbers and the footer.)
8. Press F5 to run the slide show from slide 1. Advance to slide 2 and test the link at the bottom of the slide. Slide 6 displays.
9. Right-click slide 6, point to Go to Slide, and then click 2. Our Services to return to slide 2.
10. Advance to slide 4, and then to slide 5.

11. On slide 5, click the action button to open the *Contract Plans* file. Close Microsoft Word to return to the slide show.

12. Advance to slide 6 and click the website link. Close the browser and end the slide show.

13. **SAVE** the presentation and **CLOSE** the file.

LEAVE PowerPoint open for use in the next project.

Proficiency Assessment

Project 4-3: Travel Tips

You are an assistant at Sunny Day Travel and your boss has created the beginnings of a presentation containing travel tips for various destination types. Because there will eventually be many slides per destination, you will organize the slides into sections for the destination types and make some changes to the slide master that will improve the slides' look.

@ The *Travel Tips* file is available on the book companion website or in WileyPLUS.

1. **OPEN** the *Travel Tips* presentation and save it as *Travel Tips Sections*.

2. Go to slide 2. Notice that the title is obscured by the graphic.

3. Switch to Slide Master view, and select the slide master (the topmost slide in the left pane).

4. Drag the bottom border of the title placeholder upward so its bottom aligns with the 2" mark on the vertical ruler.

5. Close Slide Master view, and confirm on slide 2 that the title no longer overlaps the graphic.

6. Create a section that starts with slide 3. Name it Sand and Sun.

7. Create a section that starts with slide 6. Name it Adventure.

8. Create a section that starts with slide 9. Name it Cruise.

9. Create a section that starts with slide 12. Name it City.

10. Create a section that starts with slide 15. Name it Summary.

11. Move the City section before the Cruise section.

12. On slide 2, select the graphic for Sand and Sun, and create a hyperlink that jumps to slide 3.

13. Create additional hyperlinks for the other three graphics, jumping to the first slide in their respective sections.

14. **SAVE** the presentation and **CLOSE** the file.

LEAVE PowerPoint open for use in the next project.

Project 4-4: Senior Meals

As the activities director for Senior Meal Services, you are responsible for educating your staff about the dietary recommendations for senior citizens. You have created a presentation, and now you will modify its slide master, theme, and colors to make it more appealing.

@ The *Meals* file is available on the book companion website or in WileyPLUS.

1. **OPEN** the *Meals* presentation and save it as *Senior Meals*.

2. Apply the Pushpin theme.

3. Change the font theme to Newsprint.

4. Display the slide master, and change the background on the slide master to Style 2.

5. Close Slide Master view, and go to slide 1.

6. Select the website address on slide 1, and make it into a live hyperlink.

7. Set the current date to appear at the bottom of each slide, and for it to *not* be automatically updated.

8. **SAVE** the presentation and **CLOSE** the file.

LEAVE PowerPoint open for use in the next project.

Mastery Assessment

Project 4-5: The Art of the Biography

You work for the editorial director of Lucerne Publishing. She has asked you to fine-tune a presentation on new biographies she plans to deliver to the sales force. You want to make some global changes to the presentation by customizing the presentation's slide masters, and you need to create a new layout that you will use to introduce sections of biographies.

@ The *Biographies* file is available on the book companion website or in WileyPLUS.

1. **OPEN** the *Biographies* presentation and save it as *Biographies Masters*.
2. Switch to Slide Master view and apply a new theme of your choice to the slide master.
3. In the left pane, click the Title and Content layout and then click the Insert Layout button in the Edit Master group to insert a new layout.
4. Deselect Title in the Master Layout group to remove the title placeholder from the new layout.
5. Insert a text placeholder in the center of the slide. Delete the sample bulleted text, remove bullet formatting, and change font size to 40 point. Center the text in the placeholder.
6. Apply a new background style to this new layout.
7. Click the Rename button in the Edit Master group and type Introduction as the new layout name.
8. Close Slide Master view.
9. Insert a new slide after slide 1 using the Introduction layout. Type American History in the placeholder.
10. **SAVE** the presentation and **CLOSE** the file.

LEAVE PowerPoint open for use in the next project.

Project 4-6: Adventure Works

You are a coordinator for Adventure Works, a company that manages outdoor adventures for children and teenagers. To introduce your programs, you have created a presentation to show at local schools and recreation centers. Finalize the presentation with design elements and effects that will catch the eye.

@ The *Adventures* file is available on the book companion website or in WileyPLUS.

1. **OPEN** the *Adventures* presentation.
2. Apply a suitable theme to the presentation. Customize theme colors or fonts if desired.
3. Make the email address and website address on slide 5 active hyperlinks.
4. Change the layout to slide 1 to Title Slide.
5. Add a footer that contains the text Adventure Works to all slides, including the title slide.
6. **SAVE** the presentation as *Adventures Final* and **CLOSE** the file.

EXIT PowerPoint.

INTERNET READY

Have you ever wanted to create your own digital movies? Use an Internet search tool to locate information on digital video cameras. Select two that seem to offer quality for a reasonable price and make a list of their features. Create a new presentation with a theme of your choice, insert a title, and add a Comparison slide. List the two cameras you have researched in the subheading placeholders and key features for each camera in the text placeholders. Save the presentation with an appropriate name.

5 Adding Tables, Charts, and SmartArt Graphics to Slides

LESSON SKILL MATRIX

In This Lesson, You Will Learn The Following Skills:

Creating Tables

Formatting Tables

Building Charts

Formatting Charts with Quick Styles

Adding SmartArt to a Slide

Modifying SmartArt

KEY TERMS

- **assistant**
- **charts**
- **cells**
- **data marker**
- **data series**
- **legend**
- **organization chart**
- **SmartArt diagrams**
- **SmartArt layout**
- **subordinates**
- **table**
- **text pane**
- **top-level shape**

You are an assistant director of ATM operations at Woodgrove Bank. Your job is to help oversee the placement and use of ATMs in your bank's branches and other locations. You often deliver presentations to bank officers to keep them up to date on ATM activities. The best way to organize information that has several related components is to use a table. Distributing information in rows and columns makes the data easy to read and understand. Use the table features of Microsoft Office PowerPoint 2010 to modify the structure and appearance of a table to improve readability and visual interest.

SOFTWARE ORIENTATION

A PowerPoint Table

Tables are designed to organize data in columns and rows, as shown in Figure 5-1.

Figure 5-1

A PowerPoint table and the table tools on the Ribbon

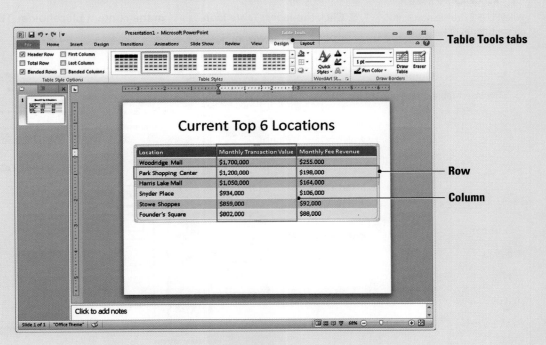

The Table Tools Design tab, shown above, and the Table Tools Layout tab provide tools for modifying and formatting a table. These tabs become active only when a table is selected.

CREATING TABLES

The Bottom Line

When you want to organize complex data on a slide, use a **table**. A table is a grid into which you can type text in the individual **cells** at the intersection of each column and row. A table's column and row structure makes data easy to understand. If you need to organize numerical data that may be used in calculations, you can insert an Excel worksheet right on a slide and use Excel's tools to work with the data.

Inserting a Table

PowerPoint has automated the process of creating a table so that you can simply specify the number of columns and rows and then type data to achieve a professionally formatted result. PowerPoint offers several ways to insert a table. The simplest is to click the Insert Table icon in any content placeholder. You can also insert a table with the Insert Table dialog box. In this exercise, you create tables using both methods.

STEP BY STEP	Insert a Table

 The *ATMs* file is available on the book companion website or in WileyPLUS.

WILEY PLUS *EXTRA*

WileyPLUS Extra! features an online tutorial of this task.

GET READY. Before you begin these steps, make sure that your computer is on. Log on, if necessary.

1. **START** PowerPoint, if the program is not already running.
2. Locate and open the *ATMs* presentation and save it as *ATMs Final*.
3. Click below slide 4 in the Slides/Outline pane and press Enter to insert a new slide with the Title and Content layout after slide 4.
4. On the new slide, click in the title placeholder and type the slide title Proposed ATM Locations.
5. Click the Insert Table icon in the content placeholder. The Insert Table dialog box opens, as shown in Figure 5-2.

Figure 5-2

The Insert Table dialog box

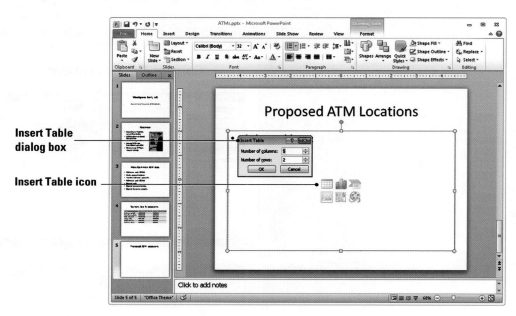

Insert Table dialog box

Insert Table icon

6. In the Number of Columns text box, type 3 to specify three columns, press Tab to move to the Number of Rows text box, and then type 6 to specify six rows. Click OK. PowerPoint creates the table in the content area, as shown in Figure 5-3. Notice that formats specified by the current theme have already been applied to the table.

Figure 5-3

The new table

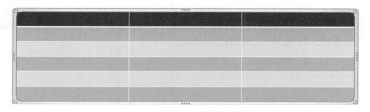

Proposed ATM Locations

Another Way
You can open the Insert Table dialog box by clicking the Table drop-down arrow on the Insert tab and then clicking Insert Table.

7. Click in the first table cell in the top row and type **Location**. Press **Tab** to move to the next cell and type **Site Study Complete**. Press **Tab** to move to the third cell in the row and type **Nearest Competing ATM**.

8. Type the following information in the table cells, pressing **Tab** to move from cell to cell. Your table should look like Figure 5-4 when you complete it.

1. Springdale Cineplex	Yes	More than 2 miles
2. Glen Avenue BIG Foods	No	Three blocks
3. Findlay Market Square	Yes	One block
4. Center City Arena	Yes	One block
5. Williams State College	No	Half a mile

Figure 5-4

The table with data typed in it

Proposed ATM Locations

Location	Site Study Complete	Nearest Competing ATM
1. Springdale Cineplex	Yes	More than 2 miles
2. Glen Avenue BIG Foods	No	Three blocks
3. Findlay Market Square	Yes	One block
4. Center City Arena	Yes	One block
5. Williams State College	No	Half a mile

9. Insert a new slide with the Title and Content layout at the end of the presentation, and click to display the new slide.

10. On the Insert tab, click **Table** to produce the Table menu and grid.

11. Drag across the grid to select a 5 × 5 block, as in Figure 5-5, and then release the mouse button to create the table.

Figure 5-5

Use the Table button to select a 5×5 block.

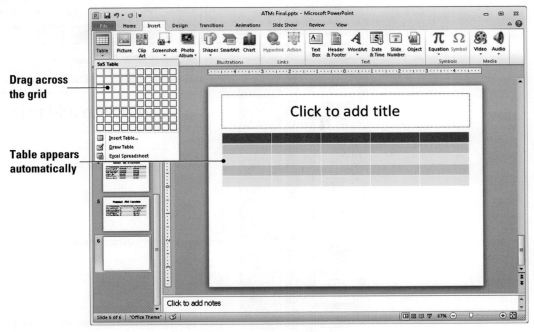

12. Delete the new slide on which you just created the table.

13. **SAVE** the presentation.

PAUSE. LEAVE the presentation open to use in the next exercise.

By default, PowerPoint sizes a new table to fill the width of the content placeholder. If you have only a few columns, you may find the table a little too spacious. You will learn later in this lesson how to adjust column widths and row heights to more closely fit the data you have entered.

If you need to reposition a table on a slide, you can do so by simply dragging its outer frame, as with any other object on a slide. You can resize a table overall by positioning the mouse pointer over one of the corners of its frame, so the mouse pointer becomes a double-headed arrow, and then dragging in or out; this changes the sizes of all rows and columns proportionally.

Drawing a Table

Drawing a table enables you to create a table with different row and column sizes, and with different numbers of rows per column (or columns per row). In this exercise, you will draw a table.

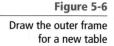 **Draw a Table**

USE the *ATMs Final* presentation that is still open from the previous exercise.

1. Insert a new slide at the end of the presentation with the Title Only layout.
2. On the Insert tab, click Table to open the Table menu, and click Draw Table. The mouse pointer changes to a pencil.
3. Click and drag the mouse pointer to draw a frame approximately 3" high and the same width as the slide's title placeholder box.

   When you release the mouse button, the new table appears (which has only one big cell), and the Table Tools Design tab is displayed. See Figure 5-6.

Figure 5-6

Draw the outer frame for a new table

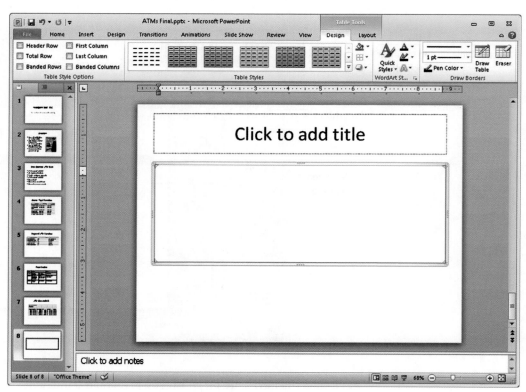

4. On the Table Tools Design tab, click **Draw Table** in the Draw Borders command group. The mouse pointer becomes a pencil again.

5. Click and drag to draw a horizontal line that divides the table in half horizontally. A dotted horizontal line appears. Release the mouse button to accept it.

Take Note   Drag to draw the lines starting slightly inside the border, rather than on the border's edge. If you start dragging too close to the border, PowerPoint creates a new table frame rather than adding to the existing table.

The drawing pencil mouse pointer should stay on; if it turns itself off, click the Draw Table button again to re-enable it.

6. Drag a vertical line through the middle of the table to divide it in half vertically.

7. Drag another vertical line that divides only the lower-right cell of the table vertically.

8. Drag another horizontal line that divides only the lower-right cells of the table horizontally. Figure 5-7 shows the completed table.

Figure 5-7

A drawn table

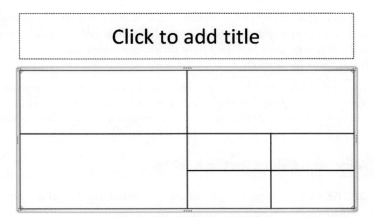

9. Press **Esc** to turn off the pencil cursor on the mouse pointer.

10. Type the text shown in Figure 5-8 into the slide's title placeholder and into the table. You will format this table later in the lesson.

Figure 5-8

The table with text added

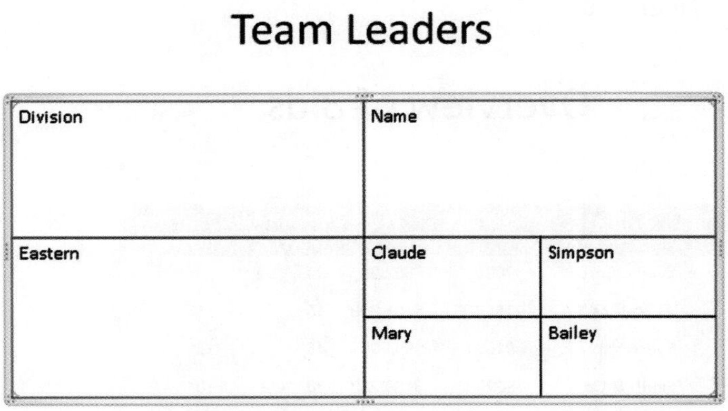

Team Leaders

Division	Name	
Eastern	Claude	Simpson
	Mary	Bailey

11. **SAVE** the presentation.

PAUSE. LEAVE the presentation open to use in the next exercise.

Drawing a table is useful when you need a table that has different numbers of rows or columns in different spots, as you saw in the preceding exercise. You can also draw a table to create rows and columns of different heights and widths.

FORMATTING TABLES

PowerPoint provides default formats to all new tables so that they have an appealing aesthetic. You may want to modify formatting, however, because you do not like the default colors or you want a different look. Use the tools on the Table Tools Design and Table Tools Layout tabs to apply new formatting options.

Changing Table Text Alignment and Orientation

Text can be aligned both vertically and horizontally within a cell. You can also change the text's orientation (rotation) to create visual interest. Use the same tools to align content horizontally in a table cell that you use to align text in a text placeholder. Changing alignment in table cells can improve readability as well as make a table more attractive.

Vertical alignment options control how content appears from top to bottom of a cell. The default option is top alignment, but column heads often look better centered vertically in table cells. When column headings have differing numbers of lines, standard procedure is to align all headings at the bottom.

Use options on the Text Direction menu to change the orientation of text for a special effect. Vertical text or text that reads from bottom to top makes a unique row header, for example. In this exercise, you will change the text direction and alignment in table cells.

STEP BY STEP   **Align and Orient Text in a Table**

GET READY. To align and orient text in a table, do the following:

1. **OPEN** the *Bids* presentation and save it as *Final Bids*.
2. Go to slide 2, and click in the merged cell at the far left of the table.
3. Click the Table Tools Layout tab, and then click the Text Direction button to display a menu of orientation options.
4. Click Stacked. This option will stack text with each letter below the previous one.
5. Type Vendor in the merged cell. The text stacks in the merged cell as shown in Figure 5-9.

@ The *Bids* file is available on the book companion website or in WileyPLUS.

Figure 5-9

Stacked text orientation

Overview of Bids

		Model	Price	Price Holds (days)	Warranty (years)
V e n d o r	Datum Corp.	2001	$98,500	30	10
	AT Metrics	1515TG	$101,800	45	15
	Touch-Val	P1004	$99,000	45	12
	Smith & Co.	SC2008	$100,250	30	10
	True-Touch	TT7809	$95,700	30	10

6. Select the text you just typed. Click the Home tab, and then click the Character Spacing button. Click Very Tight (see Figure 5-10).

Figure 5-10

Set the character spacing

Character Spacing button

Horizontal alignment buttons

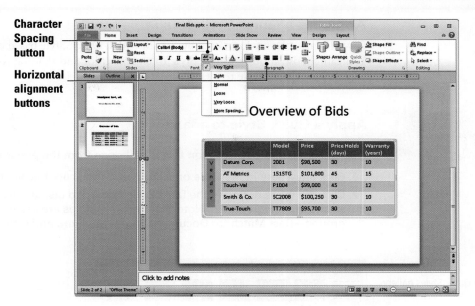

Take Note   When you move the I-beam pointer over rotated or stacked text, its orientation changes to match the text orientation.

7. With text still selected, click the **Bold** button in the Font group on the Home tab.
8. Select the cells with numbers in the Price column. Click the **Align Text Right** button in the **Paragraph** group to align all text in that column along the right side of the cells.
9. Select the cells with numbers in the last two columns. Click the **Center** button to center the contents of those cells.
10. Select the cells in the column header row. Because they are already blue, you won't be able to see that they are selected.
11. Click the **Table Tools Layout** tab, and click the **Align Bottom** button in the Alignment group. All column headings now align at the bottom of the cells, as shown in Figure 5-11.

Figure 5-11

Set vertical alignment

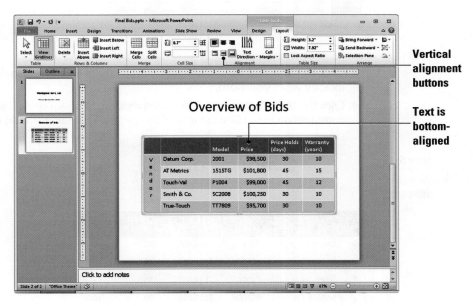

Vertical alignment buttons

Text is bottom-aligned

Another Way
Horizontal alignment buttons also appear on the Table Tools Layout tab.

12. **SAVE** the presentation.
PAUSE. LEAVE the presentation open to use in the next exercise.

Applying a Quick Style to a Table

PowerPoint tables are formatted by default with a Quick Style based on the current theme colors. You can choose another Quick Style to change color and shading formats. In this exercise, you will apply a Quick Style to a table.

STEP BY STEP | **Apply a Quick Style to a Table**

USE the *Final Bids* presentation that is still open from the previous exercise.

1. Click anywhere in the table on slide 2, and then click the Table Tools Design tab.
2. Click the More button in the Table Styles group to display the Quick Styles gallery, as shown in Figure 5-12. Note that the table styles are organized into several groups—Best Match for Document, Light, Medium, and Dark.

Figure 5-12

Table Quick Styles gallery

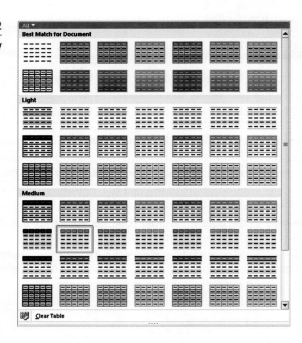

3. Click the Themed Style 2–Accent 6 table style. This is a colorful alternative, but not exactly what you want.
4. Click the More button again, and then click the Medium Style 3 style, a black and gray combination in the first column of the gallery. Your table should look similar to Figure 5-13.

Figure 5-13

New Quick Style applied to entire table

Overview of Bids

		Model	Price	Price Holds (days)	Warranty (years)
V e n d o r	Datum Corp.	2001	$98,500	30	10
	AT Metrics	1515TG	$101,800	45	15
	Touch-Val	P1004	$99,000	45	12
	Smith & Co.	SC2008	$100,250	30	10
	True-Touch	TT7809	$95,700	30	10

PAUSE. LEAVE the presentation open to use in the next exercise.

Colors available for Quick Style formats are controlled by theme. If you apply a Quick Style and then change the theme, the Quick Style colors will adjust to those of the new theme.

You may on occasion want to remove all table formatting to present data in a simple grid without shading or border colors. You can remove formatting by clicking Clear Table at the bottom of the Quick Styles gallery. Once you have cleared formats, you can reapply them by selecting any table style.

SOFTWARE ORIENTATION

A PowerPoint Chart

Charts can help your audience understand relationships among numerical values. Figure 5-14 shows a sample PowerPoint chart with some standard chart features labeled.

Figure 5-14

Components of a chart

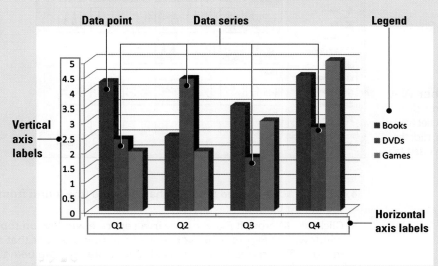

A chart can compare multiple data series, as in Figure 5-14, with each series represented by a different color or pattern. A **legend** explains what each color represents. Category axis labels explain what the groupings of bars represent (on the horizontal axis) and vertical axis labels explain the meaning of the numeric values (on the vertical axis). Optional elements such as gridlines behind the chart help make the chart more readable.

BUILDING CHARTS

The Bottom Line

Charts are visual representations of numerical data. Chart features such as columns, bars, lines, or pie slices make it easy to understand trends or compare values. Once you have created a chart in PowerPoint, you can easily modify the data on which the chart is based, choose a different type of chart to display the data, change the layout of the chart, and modify its formats.

Inserting a Chart from a Content Placeholder

Excel opens when you create a chart in PowerPoint, and you enter the data in Excel that you want to plot on the chart. Then when you return to PowerPoint, the chart appears with the data presented. As with tables and other objects such as diagrams and pictures, the easiest way to insert a chart is to click the Insert Chart icon in any content placeholder. PowerPoint guides you the rest of the way to complete the chart. In the following exercise, you place a chart on a slide using a content placeholder.

STEP BY STEP   Insert a Chart

GET READY. Before you begin these steps, make sure that your computer is on. Log on, if necessary.

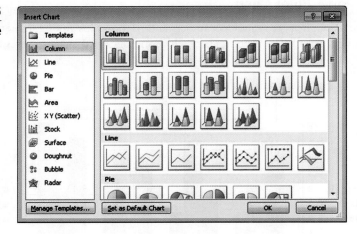

The *Revenues* file is available on the book companion website or in WileyPLUS.

1. **START** PowerPoint, if the program is not already running.
2. Locate and open the *Revenues* presentation and save it as *Revenues Final*.
3. Go to slide 3. Click the Insert Chart icon in the center of the content placeholder. The Insert Chart dialog box opens, as shown in Figure 5-15, showing chart types and subtypes.

Figure 5-15

Select a chart type and subtype

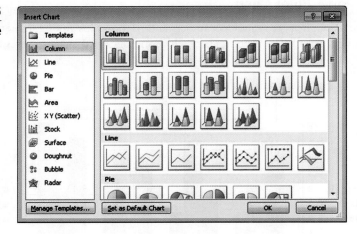

Another Way
To insert a chart on a slide that does not have a content placeholder, click the Chart button on the Insert tab.

4. Click the 3D Clustered Column chart subtype (the fourth from the left in the top row of the dialog box).
5. Click OK. Microsoft Excel opens in a separate window on top of the PowerPoint window. See Figure 5-16. Notice the bright-blue border that surrounds the data range in Excel. This *range border* is used to indicate the data being charted.

Figure 5-16

An Excel sheet opens for entering the data for the chart

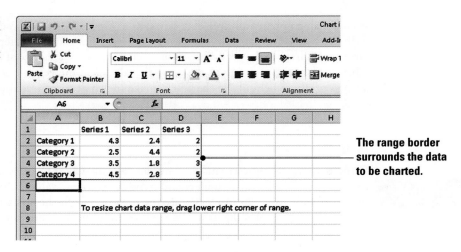

The range border surrounds the data to be charted.

6. Drag the marker in the bottom right corner of the range border so that the range includes only cells A1:C5.
7. Select Column D, and then press Delete to clear the selected cells.
8. Click cell B1 and type 2010, replacing the current entry. Then press Tab to move to cell C1. Type 2011, and press Enter.

9. Beginning in cell A2, type the following data in Excel to complete the chart:

Spring	$89,000	$102,000
Summer	$54,000	$62,000
Fall	$102,000	$118,000
Winter	$233,000	$267,000

10. Close Excel and return to PowerPoint. The chart appears with the data you entered, as in Figure 5-17.

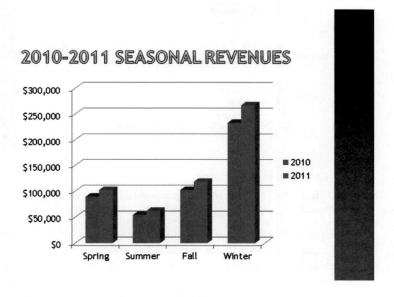

11. **SAVE** the presentation.

PAUSE. LEAVE the presentation open to use in the next exercise.

Choosing a Different Chart Type

After creating a chart, you may choose to change its type and/or its layout. If you decide that the chart type you have chosen does not display the data the way you want, you can choose a different chart type or subtype.

Different chart types display the data series differently. A **data series** consists of all the data points for a particular category, such as all the columns for Quarter 1 values. A data point, sometimes called a **data marker**, is one column or point in a series. The default chart type is a Column chart. In this exercise, you change a chart's type.

STEP BY STEP   **Choose a Different Chart Type**

USE the *Revenues Final* presentation that is still open from the previous exercise.

1. In PowerPoint, click the Change Chart Type button on the Chart Tools Design tab. The Change Chart Type dialog box opens, showing the same options that appeared when you first created the chart.

2. On the list of chart types at the left, click Bar.

3. Click the Clustered Horizontal Cylinder subtype, and then click OK. The rectangular columns change to 3-D cylinders, as shown in Figure 5-18. Don't worry if the text is not readable; you will learn to fix that later in this lesson.

Another Way
You also can use a shortcut to change the chart's type. Right-click almost anywhere in the chart and then click Change Chart Type on the shortcut menu.

Figure 5-18

A new chart type applied

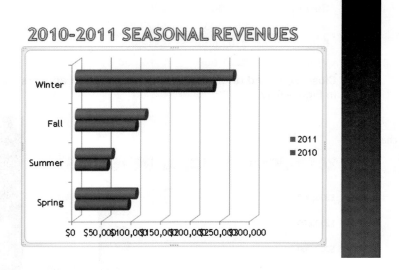

4. **SAVE** the presentation.

PAUSE. LEAVE the presentation open to use in the next exercise.

You can change any chart type to any other type, but the result may not always be what you expect, and you may lose some data. For example, when you change from any multiseries chart (such as a clustered bar or line) to a pie chart, only the first data series appears on the chart. In addition, when you change from a vertical to a horizontal chart, as in the preceding exercise, some of the axis labels may need adjustment, as in Figure 5-18.

If you apply a chart type that does not display your data as you want, use Undo to reverse the change and then try another type.

Troubleshooting Changing from a 2-D chart type to a 3-D type can yield unexpected results. For some chart types, PowerPoint may display the new chart type in a rotated perspective view that you might not like. It is best to decide when you create the original chart whether you want it to use 2- or 3-D, and then stick with those dimensions when making any change to the chart type.

Applying a Different Chart Layout

PowerPoint supplies several preformatted chart layouts that you can apply quickly to modify the default layout. These layouts may adjust the position of features, such as the legend, or add chart components such as titles and data labels. In this exercise, you choose a different chart layout.

Apply a Different Chart Layout

USE the *Revenues Final* presentation that is still open from the previous exercise.

1. With the chart on slide 3 selected, click the **More** button in the Chart Layouts group on the Chart Tools Design tab. The Chart Layout gallery displays, as shown in Figure 5-19.

Figure 5-19

The Chart Layout gallery

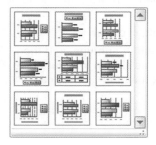

Take Note   The thumbnails in the Chart Layout gallery show in miniature the new layout and elements of the chart.

2. Click **Layout 2** in the gallery. The layout is modified to place the legend above the chart and add data labels to each of the bars. See Figure 5-20.

Figure 5-20

The chart with Layout 2 applied to it

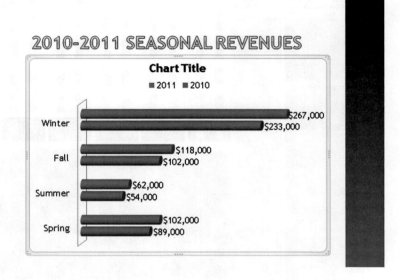

3. Switch to the **Chart Tools Layout** tab.
4. Click the **Chart Title** button to open a menu, and click **None**. The chart title is removed. (It's not necessary because the slide itself provides a title.)
5. **SAVE** the presentation and then **CLOSE** the file.

PAUSE. LEAVE PowerPoint open to use in the next exercise.

PowerPoint charts can be customized in a very wide variety of ways by adding and removing chart elements such as titles, labels, and gridlines. If you do not want to take the time to add elements, PowerPoint's chart layouts can provide you with some standard appearance options to choose from.

FORMATTING CHARTS WITH QUICK STYLES

The Bottom Line   Chart Quick Styles provide instant formatting to change the look of a chart. A Quick Style can change colors and borders of data markers, apply effects to the data markers, and apply color to the chart or plot area.

Applying a Quick Style

You can use a Quick Style to format a chart if you do not have time to adjust formatting of chart elements such as data series or the individual data points in a series. In this exercise, you apply a Quick Style to a chart.

STEP BY STEP   **Apply a Quick Style to a Chart**

@ The *Conditions* file is available on the book companion website or in WileyPLUS.

GET READY. To apply a quick style to a chart, perform the following steps:

1. **OPEN** the *Conditions* presentation and save it as *Conditions Final*.
2. Go to slide 2 and click the chart to select it.

3. On the Chart Tools Design tab, click the **More** button in the Chart Styles group. The Quick Styles gallery appears, as shown in Figure 5-21.

Figure 5-21

The Chart Quick Styles gallery

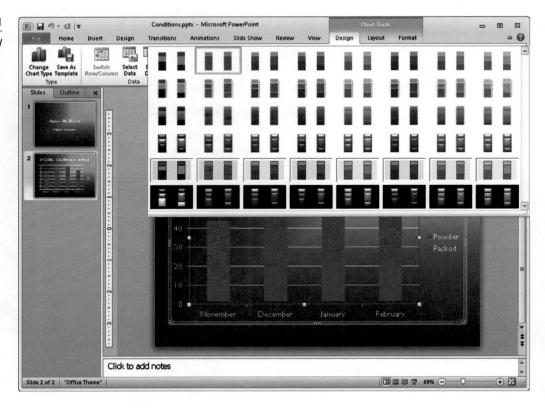

4. Click **Style 7**. The data series' colors change to variations of another theme color. This is not quite dramatic enough for your purpose.

5. Click the **More** button again, and then click **Style 43**. This style applies new theme color, bevel effects, and different chart background colors, as shown in Figure 5-22.

Figure 5-22

The chart is more interesting with the new Quick Style applied

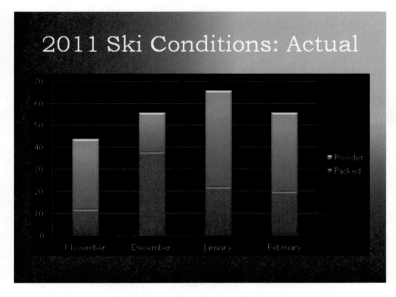

6. **SAVE** the presentation and then **CLOSE** the file.

PAUSE. LEAVE PowerPoint open to use in the next exercise.

SOFTWARE ORIENTATION

Choosing a SmartArt Graphic

PowerPoint 2010 offers eight different types of SmartArt diagrams, with many layouts for each type. Figure 5-23 shows the dialog box that appears when you choose to insert a SmartArt diagram.

Figure 5-23

Choose a SmartArt Graphic dialog box

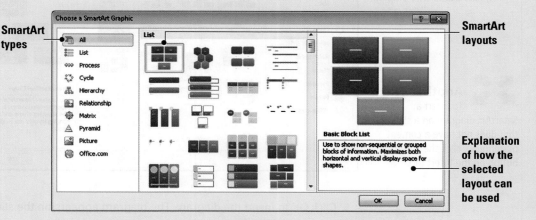

When you click a layout, the right pane of the dialog box shows you a close-up view of the selected layout and provides information on how to use the layout. This description can help you decide whether the layout will be appropriate for your information.

ADDING SMARTART TO A SLIDE

The Bottom Line

Use the Insert SmartArt Graphic icon in any content placeholder to start a new diagram. After you have selected a type and a layout, you can add text to the diagram. PowerPoint also lets you use existing bullet items to create a SmartArt diagram.

Inserting a SmartArt Graphic

SmartArt diagrams (also called SmartArt graphics) are visual representations of information you want to communicate. SmartArt diagrams show items of related information in a graphical way that makes their relationships easy to understand. You can use SmartArt diagrams to present text information in a more visually interesting way than the usual bulleted or numbered formats. An **organization chart** is a type of diagram that shows the relationships among personnel or departments in an organization. Organization charts are included in the Hierarchy type SmartArt layouts. In this exercise, you insert a SmartArt graphic diagram.

STEP BY STEP | **Insert an Organization Chart SmartArt Graphic**

GET READY. Before you begin these steps, make sure that your computer is on. Log on, if necessary.

1. **START** PowerPoint, if the program is not already running.
2. Locate and open the *Litware* presentation and save it as *Litware Final*.
3. Go to slide 3, and click the Insert SmartArt Graphic icon in the center of the content placeholder. The Choose a SmartArt Graphic dialog box opens.

@ The *Litware* file is available on the book companion website or in WileyPLUS.

WileyPLUS Extra! features an online tutorial of this task.

4. Click **Hierarchy** in the type list in the left side of the dialog box. The layouts for the Hierarchy type are displayed.

5. Click the first layout in the first row, the Organization Chart. Read the description of the Organization Chart layout in the right pane of the dialog box. See Figure 5-24.

Figure 5-24

The Hierarchy layouts in the Choose a SmartArt Graphic dialog box

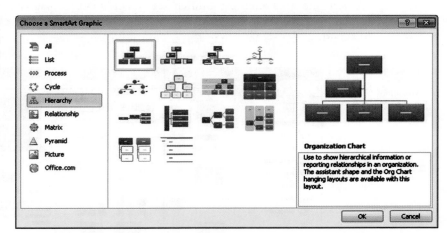

Another Way
To insert a SmartArt diagram on a slide that does not have a content placeholder, click the SmartArt button on the Insert tab.

6. Click **OK** to insert the diagram. The diagram appears on the slide, as shown in Figure 5-25.

Figure 5-25

A new, blank organization chart diagram

Text Pane button

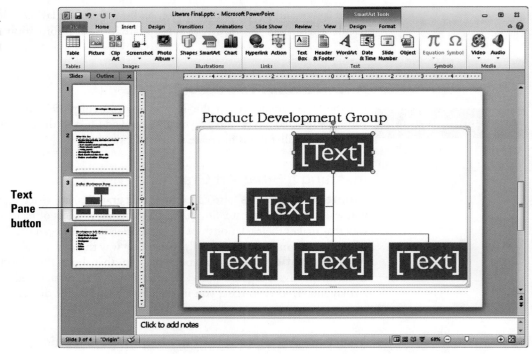

7. **SAVE** the presentation.

PAUSE. LEAVE the presentation open to use in the next exercise.

The Choose a SmartArt Graphic dialog box sorts its many layouts by types such as List, Process, Hierarchy, and so on. A **SmartArt layout** is a particular arrangement of shapes that a diagram can have. The following general descriptions of SmartArt types can help you choose a type and a specific layout within that type:

- **List** layouts display information that does not have to be in a particular order, such as a list of items to purchase.
- **Process** layouts show the steps in a process or timeline, such as the steps in a manufacturing process.
- **Cycle** layouts are useful for showing a repeating process, such as a teaching cycle of preparing for a semester, teaching a class, and submitting grades.
- **Hierarchy** layouts show levels of subordination, such as in an organization chart or a tournament bracket.
- **Relationship** layouts show connections among items, such as the relationship between supply and demand.
- **Matrix** layouts show how parts relate to a whole, similar to a pie chart.
- **Pyramid** layouts display relationships in terms of proportion, from largest at the bottom to smallest at the top.
- **Picture** layouts include placeholders for one or more graphics in addition to the text placeholders.

More layouts can also be found at Office.com. Click the Office.com category to see what's available.

Some layouts appear in more than one type's listing. For example, most of the Picture layouts are also categorized as other types.

Adding Text to a SmartArt Diagram

A new SmartArt diagram appears on the slide with empty shapes to which you add text (and in some cases, pictures) to create the final diagram. The appearance and position of these shapes are guided by the layout you chose, and shape color is controlled by the current theme. As you enter text in the diagram, PowerPoint resizes the shapes to accommodate the longest line of text in the diagram. Font size is also adjusted for the best fit, and PowerPoint keeps the font size the same for all shapes. In this exercise, you learn how to add text to the SmartArt diagram organizational chart you have inserted in your PowerPoint slide.

An organization chart, such as the one you create in this section, has some special terminology and layout requirements. In an organization chart, there can be only one **top-level shape**, which is typically occupied by the name of the person or department at the head of the organization. Persons or departments who report to the top-level entity are **subordinates**. An **assistant** is a person who reports directly to a staff member and usually appears on a separate level.

STEP BY STEP   **Add Text to a SmartArt Diagram**

USE the *Litware Final* presentation that is still open from the previous exercise.

1. If the text pane is not already open, click the Text Pane arrows on the left side of the SmartArt object frame (refer to Figure 5-25). This opens the Text pane.
2. Click next to the bullet at the top of the Text pane to place the insertion point there. Type Ted Hicks to enter the name in the top-level shape of the diagram. Notice that as you type the text in the Text pane, it appears in the top shape of the diagram, as shown in Figure 5-26, and that the text automatically resizes to fit in the shape.

Figure 5-26

Typing a name in the top-level shape

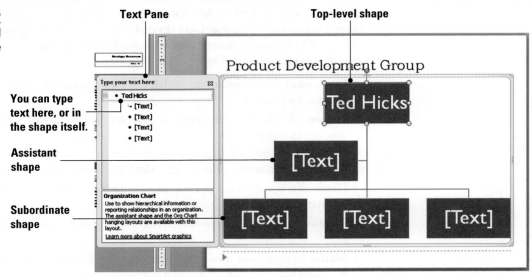

3. Click in the bullet item below Ted Hicks in the Text pane, then type Rose Lang. Rose Lang is an assistant to Ted Hicks, and as such, she has an assistant shape on a level between the top-level shape and the subordinate shapes.

4. Click in the next bullet item in the Text pane and type Marcus Short. Marcus Short is a subordinate to Ted Hicks.

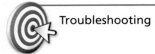 Troubleshooting   Do not press Enter after typing the names because that inserts a new shape. If you accidentally do so, click the Undo button on the Quick Access Toolbar to undo the addition.

5. Click in the next bullet item and type Ellen Camp.

6. Click in the last bullet item and type Pat Cramer.

7. Click the Close button (X) in the Text pane to hide it. You will complete the text entry by typing directly in the diagram's shapes.

8. Click just to the right of the name Hicks in the top-level shape, press Enter, and type Director. Notice that the text size adjusts in all the shapes to account for the additional entry in the top-level shape.

9. Click after the name Lang in the assistant shape, press Enter, and type Assistant Director.

10. Use the same process to type the title Reading Products for Marcus Short, Linguistics Products for Ellen Camp, and Writing Products for Pat Cramer.

11. Click away from the SmartArt to deselect it. Your slide should look similar to Figure 5-27.

Figure 5-27

The completed organization chart

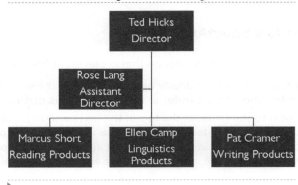

12. **SAVE** the presentation.

PAUSE. LEAVE the presentation open to use in the next exercise.

Text in a diagram appears either within a shape or as a bulleted list, depending on the diagram type and layout option. In the previous exercise, you inserted text only in shapes because an organization chart does not offer the option of bulleted text. Figure 5-28 shows a list type diagram that contains both shape text and bulleted text.

Figure 5-28

Shape text and bulleted text in a diagram

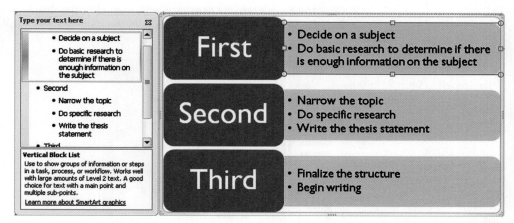

You can display or hide the **Text pane**, which is the panel to the left of a new diagram in which you can type diagram text. In the Text pane, shape text (that is, text that appears in shapes) appears as the top-level bullet items and text that appears on the diagram in bulleted text format is indented below the shape text, similar to the way several levels of bulleted text appear in a content placeholder.

You can use the Text pane to enter text, or you can enter text directly in each shape. Click next to a bullet in the Text pane or click any [Text] placeholder and begin typing text. If you need more bullet items than are supplied in the default layout, press Enter at the end of the current bullet item to add a new one, or click the Add Bullet button in the Create Graphic group on the SmartArt Tools Design tab.

If you don't want to use the Text pane, you can close it to get it out of the way. To redisplay it, click the Text Pane button on the left border of the SmartArt container, or click the Text Pane button in the Create Graphic group on the SmartArt Tools Design tab. You can also right-click anywhere in the diagram and then click Show Text Pane on the shortcut menu.

Take Note   If you need to edit text you have entered in a diagram, you can click the text to activate it and then edit the text as necessary. You can also right-click a shape, click Edit Text on the shortcut menu, and make the necessary changes.

Converting Text or WordArt to a SmartArt Diagram

As you work with slide text, you may realize that the information would work well as a SmartArt diagram. In this situation, you do not have to retype the text in the SmartArt diagram shapes. Simply convert the bulleted list to a diagram. You can create a diagram from any bulleted list on a slide or any WordArt object. You can choose one of the common diagrams in the Convert to SmartArt gallery, or you can access the Choose a SmartArt Diagram dialog box to choose any diagram type or layout. In this exercise, you learn how to convert a list into a SmartArt Cycle diagram, and you convert WordArt text into a single SmartArt object.

STEP BY STEP   Convert Text or WordArt to a SmartArt Diagram

> **USE** the *Litware Final* presentation that is still open from the previous exercise.

1. Go to slide 4 and select the bulleted list.
2. Click the Home tab, if necessary, and then click the Convert to SmartArt button in the Paragraph group. PowerPoint displays the gallery shown in Figure 5-29.

Figure 5-29

The Convert to SmartArt Gallery

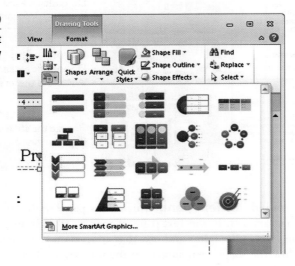

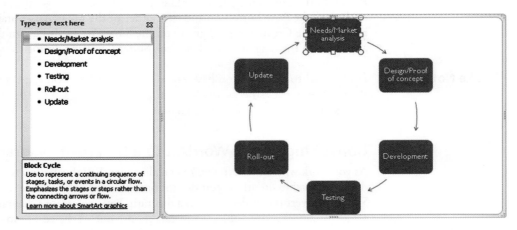

Another Way
Right-click in a bulleted list, and then click Convert to SmartArt on the shortcut menu.

3. Click More SmartArt Graphics at the bottom of the gallery. The Choose a SmartArt Graphic dialog box opens.
4. Click Cycle, then click the Block Cycle layout. Read the description of how best to use the Block Cycle layout.
5. Click OK. The bulleted list is converted to a cycle diagram, as shown in Figure 5-30.

Figure 5-30

Bulleted list converted to a SmartArt diagram

Take Note   The Text pane might appear automatically, as shown in Figure 5-30; if it does not, you can leave it hidden for now, or you can display it by clicking the Show Text Pane arrows on the left side of the SmartArt frame.

Take Note   You may notice that the text in the shapes is quite small. You will learn how to modify shape and text size later in the lesson.

6. Go to slide 1, and triple-click the Developer Orientation WordArt object to select it.

7. On the Home tab, click **Convert to SmartArt**, then click **Vertical Bullet List** (the first layout in the first row). The WordArt text is converted to a single-item SmartArt object. See Figure 5-31.

Figure 5-31

WordArt converted to a SmartArt diagram

8. **SAVE** the presentation.

PAUSE. LEAVE the presentation open to use in the next exercise.

MODIFYING SMARTART

The Bottom Line

Although a new SmartArt graphic makes an interesting visual statement on a slide in its default state, you will probably want to make some changes to the graphic to customize it for your use. You can apply a wide variety of formatting changes to modify appearance, and you can also change layout or orientation and add or remove shapes. You can even change the diagram type to another that better fits your data.

Applying a Style to a SmartArt Diagram

Like other graphic objects, SmartArt diagrams can be quickly and easily formatted by applying a SmartArt style. Styles apply fills, borders, and effects to improve the appearance of the diagram's shapes. In this exercise, you will apply a style to a diagram.

STEP BY STEP **Apply a Style to a SmartArt Diagram**

USE the *Litware Final* presentation that is still open from the previous exercise.

1. Go to slide 3 and click once on the diagram to select it. Take care to select the diagram itself, and not a particular shape within it.

2. Click the SmartArt Tools Design tab to activate it.

3. Click the More button in the SmartArt Styles group. The SmartArt Style gallery appears, as shown in Figure 5-32.

Figure 5-32

The SmartArt Style gallery

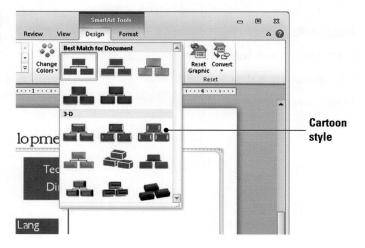

4. Click the **Cartoon** style. PowerPoint applies the style, as shown in Figure 5-33.

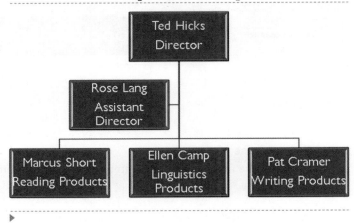

Product Development Group

5. Go to slide 1, click the **SmartArt** object, and repeat steps 2-4 to apply the same style.

6. Go to slide 4, click the **SmartArt** object, and repeat steps 2-4 to apply the same style.

7. SAVE the presentation and **CLOSE** it.

PAUSE. LEAVE the presentation open to use in the next exercise.

SmartArt styles can instantly improve a new diagram by applying visual effects to the shapes. Review the results carefully, however, after applying a SmartArt style. If your shapes contain several lines of text, some of the 3-D styles may obscure the text or cause it to run over on the edges—not a very attractive presentation.

If you do not like the formatting you have applied, you can easily revert to the original appearance of the diagram. Click the Reset Graphic button on the SmartArt Tools Design tab to restore the diagram to its default appearance.

SKILL SUMMARY

In This Lesson, You Learned How To:
Create tables
Format Tables
Build charts
Format charts with Quick Styles
Add SmartArt to a slide
Modify SmartArt

Knowledge Assessment

Matching

Match the term in Column 1 to its description in Column 2.

Column 1	Column 2
1. Table Source	a. Diagram type that shows relationships among departments or personnel
2. Draw Table	b. Diagram type that can show steps in a timeline
3. SmartArt	c. Holds the name of the person or department at the head of the organization
4. Organization chart	d. An arrangement of columns and rows used to organize data
5. Process	e. Panel in which you can type diagram text
6. Top-level shape	f. Option you can use to create a table frame and insert columns and rows where you want them
7. Matrix	g. Tab that allows you to apply a Quick Style to a table
8. Text pane	h. Visual representation of information
9. Table Tools Design	i. A set of preset formatting that can be applied to a table
10. Quick Style	j. Diagram type that shows how parts relate to a whole

Ture/False

Circle T if the statement is true or F if the statement is false.

T F 1. To create a new table, click the Insert Object button and then select the type of table to create.

T F 2. By default, a new table is sized to fit the content placeholder in which it was created.

T F 3. Use the Blank Table option to quickly remove all formatting from a table.

T F 4. If you do not specify that a picture should be tiled over selected cells, it will display in each table cell.

T F 5 List type diagrams show information that has to be in a particular order.

T F 6. Text in a SmartArt diagram can appear either in a shape or in a bulleted list.

T F 7. Use a Cycle type diagram if you want to show a repeating process.

T F 8. You can apply a style to a SmartArt diagram from the SmartArt Tools Layout tab.

T F 9. SmartArt can be converted to a bulleted list or to shapes.

T F 10. The default PowerPoint chart type is a pie chart.

Competency Assessment

Project 5-1: Job Fair

You work for Lucerne Executive Recruiters, a company that specializes in finding employees for a variety of clients. You are planning to give a brief presentation at a local job fair and need to prepare a slide that lists some currently available jobs for which you are recruiting candidates. You can use a table to display this information.

@ The *Jobs* file is available on the book companion website or in WileyPLUS.

GET READY. LAUNCH PowerPoint if it is not already running.

1. **OPEN** the *Jobs* presentation and save it as *Jobs Final*.
2. Go to slide 2, and click the Insert Table icon in the content placeholder.

3. Create a table with four columns and seven rows.

4. Type the following information in the table:

Title	Company	Salary Range*	Posted
Senior Editor	Litware, Inc.	$30K–$42K	5/01
Sales Associate	Contoso Pharmaceuticals	$55K–$70K	5/10
District Manager	Tailspin Toys	$65K–$80K	4/30
Accountant	Fourth Coffee	$53K–$60K	4/27
Production Assistant	Fabrikam, Inc.	$38K–$45K	5/07
Loan Officer	Woodgrove Bank	$42K–$54K	5/12

*Starting salary based on experience

5. Format the table as follows:

   a. Select the Salary Range and Posted columns, and then click the Center button on the Home tab.

   b. Click in the last row of the table, and then click the Align Text Right button.

6. **SAVE** the presentation and then **CLOSE** the file.

LEAVE PowerPoint open for use in the next project.

Project 5-2: Voter Turnout

You are a member of the Center City Board of Elections. You have been asked to create a presentation to deliver to the Board showing how turnout has varied in the city over the past four presidential elections. You can create a line chart to display this data clearly.

GET READY. LAUNCH PowerPoint if it is not already running.

@ The *Turnout* file is available on the book companion website or in WileyPLUS.

1. **OPEN** the *Turnout* presentation.

2. Go to slide 2, click the Insert Chart icon in the content placeholder, and then click Line. Click OK to accept the default subtype.

3. Starting in cell A1, type the following data in the Excel worksheet:

Year	Turnout
1996	0.62
2000	0.74
2004	0.49
2008	0.40

4. Adjust the range border to include only the data you typed and then delete all extra data on the sheet.

5. Close the Excel worksheet.

6. Click Layout 12 in the Chart Layout gallery.

7. Click Style 36 in the Quick Style gallery.

8. Click the legend to select it, then press Delete.

9. Select one of the data points, then click Data Labels on the Chart Tools Layout tab. Click Above.

10. Right-click one of the data labels, then click Format Data Labels. Change the number format to Percentage with 0 decimal places.

11. **SAVE** the presentation as *Turnout Final* and **CLOSE** the file.

LEAVE PowerPoint open for use in the next project.

Project 5-3: Power Up

You are an operations manager for City Power & Light. You have been asked to give a presentation to department heads about scheduled maintenance of power substations around the city. Use a table to present the maintenance schedule.

@ The *Power* file is available on the book companion website or in WileyPLUS.

1. **OPEN** the *Power* presentation and save it as *Power Final*.
2. Go to slide 3. On the Insert tab, click Table and drag over the grid to create a table with two columns and seven rows.
3. Type the following information in the table:

Substation	Week of
Eastland	July 13
Morehead	October 1
Huntington	June 6
Parkland	May 21
Midtown	July 28
Elmwood	December 11

4. Apply a Quick Style of your choice to the table.
5. Turn on the First Column table style, and change any other table style option that improves the look of the table. For example, you might change the font color.
6. Delete the last row of the table.
7. Rearrange the rows so that the dates in the second column are in chronological order.
   Tip: Create a new blank row, and use it as a temporary holding area when moving rows.
8. Click the outside border of the table, hold down the mouse button, and drag straight down to move the table down about half an inch.
9. **SAVE** the presentation and **CLOSE** the file.

LEAVE PowerPoint open for use in the next project.

Project 5-4: Visitors Welcome

You work in the Tourist Bureau for the town of Lucerne. As part of your regular duties, you compile a presentation that shows information on visitors. You have created a slide that shows visitors by age. The chart needs some modification and formatting.

@ The *Tourists* file is available on the book companion website or in WileyPLUS.

1. **OPEN** the *Tourists* presentation.
2. Go to slide 2 and view the chart. The line chart type does not seem appropriate for the data.
3. With the chart selected, click the Change Chart Type button and select the first chart in the Pie category.
4. Apply Layout 6 and Quick Style 10.
5. **SAVE** the presentation as *Tourists Final* and **CLOSE** the file.

LEAVE PowerPoint open for use in the next project.

Mastery Assessment

Project 5-5: More Power

You are a financial analyst for City Power & Light. Senior managers have asked you to determine how much power sales increased from 2010 to 2011, based on customer types. You can compare rates of power sales using a bar chart.

1. **OPEN** a new blank presentation and apply a theme of your choice.
2. Change the layout of the first slide to Title and Content, and type the slide title 2010–2011 Sales.
3. Create a Clustered Bar chart, and type the following chart data:

	Industrial	Commercial	Residential
2010	$3,010	$4,273	$5,777
2011	$2,588	$3,876	$4,578

4. Apply Layout 3 to the chart, and change the chart title to Sales by Customer Type.
5. Apply a Quick Style of your choice to the chart.
6. **SAVE** the presentation as *Power Sales* and **CLOSE** the file.

LEAVE PowerPoint open for use in the next project.

Project 5-6: Patient Visits

You are a veterinarian hoping to attract investors to your clinic. You have created a chart to be used in a presentation for prospective investors. You want to show investors the reasons for patient visits during a given month, by percentage. You are not satisfied with your chart, however, so you want to improve it before the investor meeting.

@ The *Patients* file is available on the book companion website or in WileyPLUS.

1. **OPEN** the *Patients* presentation.
2. In the chart worksheet, edit the values to become percentages (for example, change 38 to 0.38 and apply the Percent style).
3. Change the chart type from Bar to a 3D Pie Chart.
4. Apply a chart layout to add a legend and data labels. Delete the chart title if your layout added one.
5. Apply a Quick Style, or change the fill of some or all of the pie slices.
6. **SAVE** the presentation as *Patients Final* and **CLOSE** the file.

EXIT PowerPoint.

INTERNET READY

You want to take a vacation over the winter holidays next year, but you have not yet decided whether to go skiing, enjoy the sun on a Caribbean island, or venture down under to Australia. Using Internet search tools, find several interesting ski packages in Canada and Europe, resort packages in the Caribbean, and lodgings in Sydney, Australia.

Determine the local price for all these excursions. Create a PowerPoint presentation with a table that lists your possible destinations and dates of travel. Add a new slide and insert a worksheet. Enter the destinations and their costs and the conversion rate to convert local costs to dollars. Create formulas to convert costs so you can compare all package costs in U.S. dollars.

Workplace *Ready*

CHOOSING THE RIGHT TYPE OF CHART

Each PowerPoint chart type is designed to present a specific type of data. When you create a chart, you should select the chart type that will best display your data. Some of the most commonly used chart types are described below:

- **Column charts:** Column charts are generally used for showing data changes over a period of time or for comparing items. Categories (such as Quarter 1 or 2012) display on the horizontal axis (the X axis), and values display on the vertical axis (the Y axis).

- **Bar charts:** Bar charts are often used to compare individual items. They are especially useful when values are durations. Categories display on the vertical axis and values display on the horizontal axis.

- **Line charts:** Line charts are best used to display values over time or trends in data. Categories are usually evenly spaced items, such as months or years, and display on the horizontal axis.

- **Pie charts:** Pie charts are used to show the relationship of an individual category to the sum of all categories. Data for a pie chart consists of only a single column or row of data in the worksheet.

- **Area charts:** Area charts are used to show the amount of change over time as well as total value across a trend. Like a pie chart, an area chart can show the relationship of an individual category to the sum of all values.

You can learn more about chart types and subtypes and how they are designed to be used by consulting PowerPoint's Help files.

6 Adding Graphics and Multimedia to a Presentation

LESSON SKILL MATRIX

In This Lesson, You Will Learn The Following Skills:

Adding a Picture to a Slide

Formatting Graphical Elements

Adding Shapes to Slides

Organizing Objects on a Slide

Adding Media Clips to a Presentation

KEY TERMS

- **aspect ratio**
- **audio**
- **clip art**
- **constrain**
- **crop**
- **gridlines**
- **guides**
- **keyword**
- **lassoing**
- **order**
- **poster frame**
- **reset**
- **rulers**
- **scaling**
- **video**

You are the director of promotions for the Baldwin Museum of Science. The museum is especially interested in attracting teachers and students to their permanent exhibits, so you have scheduled appearances at a number of high schools in your area, where you plan to present PowerPoint slide shows about the museum and various aspects of science. PowerPoint's graphics capabilities allow you to include and customize pictures, shapes, and movies to enliven your presentations. You can also add sounds to provide the finishing touch to a presentation.

SOFTWARE ORIENTATION

Microsoft PowerPoint's Clip Art Task Pane

The Clip Art task pane, shown in Figure 6-1, allows you to search for graphic and multi-media content you can use to embellish and illustrate your slides. The gallery format of the task pane makes it easy to review content and choose a file to insert.

Figure 6-1

The Clip Art task pane

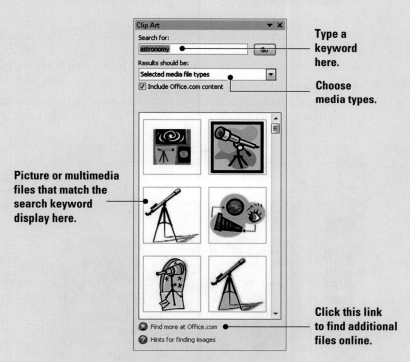

You can use the Clip Art task pane to locate and insert line drawings, photographs, animated graphics, and sound files. If you have a live Internet connection, you have access to thousands of files on the Office Online website.

ADDING A PICTURE TO A SLIDE

The Bottom Line

Pictures can be used to illustrate a slide's content or provide visual interest to help hold the audience's attention. You can insert clip art files that are installed with or accessed through Microsoft Office, or you can insert any picture with a compatible file format.

Inserting a Clip Art Picture

Clip art is predrawn artwork in a wide variety of styles relating to a wide variety of topics. Microsoft Office supplies access to thousands of clip art graphics that you can insert in documents, worksheets, and databases as well as in PowerPoint presentations. Microsoft Office clip art files include not only drawn graphics but photos and other multimedia objects. Use the Clip Art icon in any content placeholder to open the Clip Art task pane and search for clip art pictures. To locate clips, conduct a search through the Clip Art task pane, using a **keyword**—a descriptive word or phrase that relates to the topic you want to illustrate. In this exercise, you learn how to insert a Clip Art picture into a PowerPoint slide.

STEP BY STEP	Insert a Clip Art Picture

@ The *Exhibits* file for this lesson is available on the book companion website or in WileyPLUS.

GET READY. Before you begin these steps, make sure that your computer is on. Log on, if necessary.

1. **START** PowerPoint, if the program is not already running.
2. Locate and **OPEN** the *Exhibits* presentation and save it as *Exhibits Final*.
3. Go to slide 4 and click the **Clip Art** icon in the empty content placeholder. The Clip Art task pane opens.

Take Note   The Clip Art task pane may show the keyword(s) used in the most recent search for clip art.

WileyPLUS Extra! features an online tutorial of this task.

4. Select any existing text in the Search for box and press Delete to remove it.
5. Type **gears** in the Search For box.
6. Click the **Results should be drop-down arrow**, and remove check marks from all options *except* Photographs, as shown in Figure 6-2.

Figure 6-2

Choose to search for Photographs only

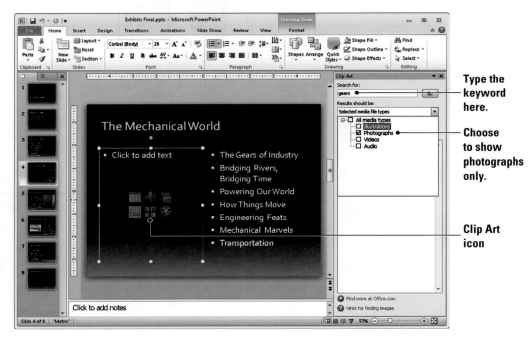

Type the keyword here.

Choose to show photographs only.

Clip Art icon

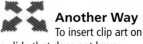
Another Way
To insert clip art on a slide that does not have a content placeholder, click the Clip Art button on the Insert tab.

7. Click the **Go** button near the top of the task pane. PowerPoint searches for clip art photographs that match the keyword and displays them in the task pane.
8. Click the picture of gears shown in Figure 6-3, or one similar to it. The picture is inserted in the content placeholder. (The picture may not take up the entire placeholder.)

Figure 6-3

Select a photograph of gears

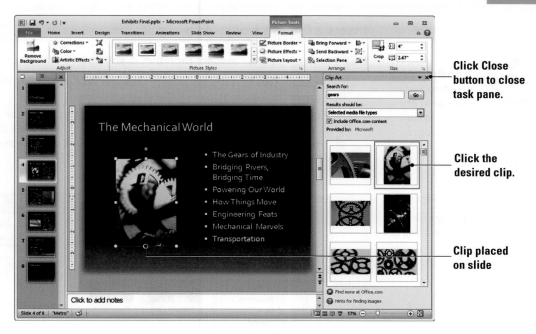

9. Click the **Close** button in the **Clip Art** task pane to close the pane.

10. **SAVE** the presentation.

PAUSE. LEAVE the presentation open to use in the next exercise.

If you have a live Internet connection, PowerPoint will search online graphic files (via Office.com) and display them in the task pane. You can also go directly to the Office Online clip art website by clicking the *Find more at Office.com* link at the bottom of the Clip Art task pane.

Take Note   If you find a clip you like on Office Online, you can download it to your computer by right-clicking it and choosing Make Available Offline. Office will store the clip on your hard disk for future use.

Many clip art graphics are humorous in appearance and may not be suitable for corporate communications or presentations on serious topics. You can use the Clip Art task pane to search for photographs as well as clip art graphics. Photographs provide a more sophisticated and professional look for a presentation. The Clip Art task pane also allows you to search for movies and sound files.

When you insert clip art by using the Clip Art icon in a content placeholder to open the Clip Art task pane, PowerPoint will try to fit the graphic you select into the content placeholder. The graphic may not use up the entire placeholder area, depending on its size and shape. If you insert a graphic on a slide that doesn't have a placeholder, it will generally appear in the center of the slide. You can adjust the graphic's size and position by dragging it, as you will learn later in this lesson.

If you decide you don't like a picture you have inserted, you can easily delete it. Click the picture to select it and then press Delete to remove it from the slide.

Inserting a Picture from a File

You do not have to rely on PowerPoint's clip art files to illustrate your presentation. You can download many pictures for free on the Internet or create your own picture files using a digital camera. In this exercise, you will insert a picture from a file that has already been created.

STEP BY STEP   Insert a Picture from a File

Another Way
Click the Insert Picture from File icon in any content placeholder to open the Insert Picture dialog box.

USE the *Exhibits Final* presentation that is still open from the previous exercise.

1. Go to slide 3 and on the Insert tab, click the Picture button. The Insert Picture dialog box opens.
2. Navigate to the location of the data files for this lesson, click *Astronomy.jpg*, as shown in Figure 6-4, and then click Insert. The dialog box may look different from the one shown in Figure 6-4, depending on your Windows version and the other files in the folder. The picture appears on the slide.

Figure 6-4

Locate a picture file in the Insert Picture dialog box

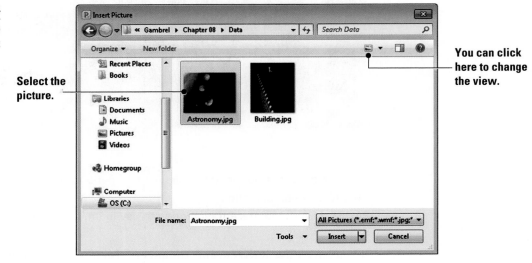

@ The *Astronomy.jpg* file is available on the book companion website or in WileyPLUS.

3. **SAVE** the presentation.

PAUSE. LEAVE the presentation open to use in the next exercise.

PowerPoint supports a variety of picture file formats, including GIF, JPEG, PNG, TIFF, BMP, and WMF. Be aware that graphic formats differ in how they store graphic information, so some formats create larger files than others.

If you take your own pictures using a digital camera, you do not have to worry about copyright issues, but you should pay attention to copyright permissions for pictures you locate from other sources. It is extremely easy to save any picture from a web page to your system. If you are going to use the picture commercially, you need to contact the copyright holder, if there is one, and ask for specific permission to reuse the picture.

Take Note   U.S. government sites such as NASA, the source of the picture you inserted in the previous exercise, make images available without requiring copyright permission.

FORMATTING GRAPHICAL ELEMENTS

The Bottom Line

PowerPoint provides many options for improving the appearance of pictures. You can reposition and resize them, rotate them, apply special effects such as Quick Styles, adjust brightness and contrast, and even recolor a picture for a special effect. If you do not like formatting changes you have made, you can reset a picture to its original appearance.

Using the Ruler, Gridlines, and Guides

In Normal view and Notes Page view, you can turn on PowerPoint's horizontal and vertical **rulers**, which help you measure the size of an object on the slide, as well as the amount of space between objects. PowerPoint's drawing **guides** line up with measurements on the ruler to provide nonprinting guidelines you can use when positioning objects on a slide. PowerPoint also provides **gridlines**, a set of dotted horizontal and vertical lines that overlay the entire slide. In this exercise, you learn how to use the ruler, guides, and gridlines to position objects so that they align with other objects on a slide and appear consistently throughout a presentation. You can move or copy guides to position them where you need them.

As you move the pointer on a slide, short dotted lines show the pointer position on both the horizontal and vertical rulers. This allows you to be fairly precise when undertaking tasks such as resizing or cropping. You can move guides anywhere on the slide and copy them to create additional guides. To remove a guide, drag it off the slide. Turn on gridlines when you want to arrange a number of objects on the slide or draw shapes to specific sizes.

Take Note   You can adjust the spacing of the dots in the gridlines in the Grid and Guides dialog box.

STEP BY STEP   **Use the Ruler, Gridlines, and Guides**

USE the *Exhibits Final* presentation that is still open from the previous exercise.

1. Go to slide 3. On the View tab, click **Ruler** in the Show/Hide group if this option is not already selected. The vertical and horizontal rulers appear in the Slide pane.

2. Click to mark the **Gridlines** check box. A grid of regularly spaced dots overlays the slide, as shown in Figure 6-5.

Figure 6-5

Rulers and gridlines

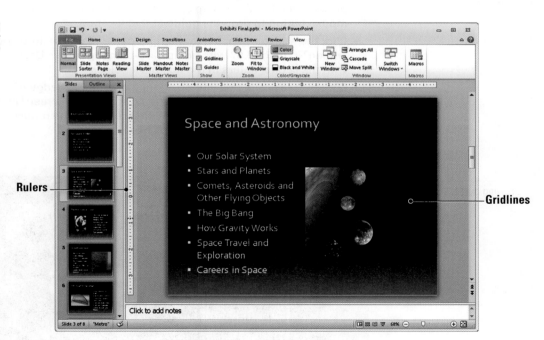

Another Way
Right-click a slide outside of any placeholder, and then click Ruler.

3. Right-click the current slide near the bottom of the slide (outside any placeholder), and then click **Grid and Guides**. The Grid and Guides dialog box opens, as shown in Figure 6-6.

Figure 6-6

Grid and Guides dialog box

Another Way
Press Alt+F9 to show or hide the guides.

4. In the Guide Settings area of the dialog box, click to mark the **Display drawing guides on screen** check box, then click **OK**. The default vertical and horizontal drawing guides display, intersecting at the center of the slide.

5. The guides will be more useful for positioning pictures in this presentation, so you can turn off the gridlines: click the **View** tab, and click **Gridlines** in the Show/Hide group to remove the check mark and hide the gridlines.

6. Click the **text placeholder** on slide 3 to activate it. You will use the placeholder's selection border to help you position guides.

7. Click the **vertical guide** above the slide title. You should see a ScreenTip that shows the current position of the guide—0.0, indicating the guide is at the 0 inch mark on the horizontal ruler.

8. Click and drag the guide to the left until it aligns on the left border of the text placeholder. The ScreenTip should read 4.50 with a left-pointing arrow. Release the mouse button to drop the guide at that location.

9. Click the **horizontal guide** to the right of the planet picture and drag upward until the ScreenTip reads 1.67 with an upward-pointing arrow. Drop the guide. It should align with the capital letters in the text placeholder.

10. Click the **vertical guide** you positioned near the left edge of the slide, hold down **Ctrl**, and drag a copy of the guide to the right until the ScreenTip reads 4.50 with a right-pointing arrow. Drop the guide by first releasing the mouse button and then releasing the Ctrl key. Your slide should look like Figure 6-7.

Figure 6-7

Drawing guides positioned on the slide

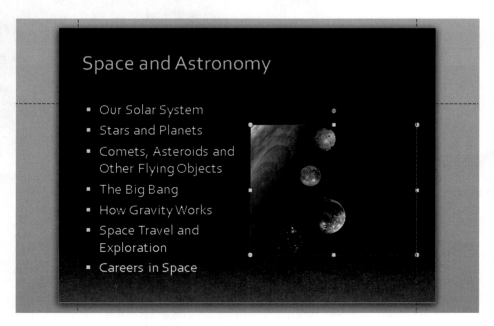

11. Go to slide 4, click the gear picture, and drag it until the upper-left corner of the picture snaps to the intersection of the vertical and horizontal guides. Your slide should look like Figure 6-8.

Figure 6-8

Picture repositioned using the guides

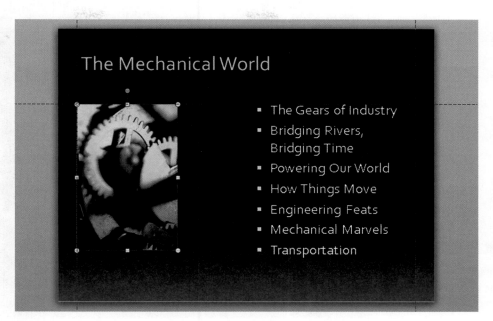

12. Go to slide 5 and drag the picture down and to the left so its upper-right corner snaps to the intersection of the guides.

13. Go to slide 6 and drag the picture up and to the left to snap to the intersection of the two guides.

14. On the View tab, clear the **Guides** check box to turn off the guides.

15. **SAVE** the presentation.

PAUSE. LEAVE the presentation open to use in the next exercise.

By default, objects "snap"—automatically align—to the gridlines even if the gridlines are not currently displayed. This feature can be helpful when you are positioning objects, but you may sometimes find that it hinders precise positioning. You can temporarily override the "snapping" by holding down Alt as you drag an object. Or, you can display the Grid and Guides dialog box and deselect the *Snap objects to grid* check box.

Rotating or Flipping an Object

You can rotate or flip pictures to change their orientation on a slide. Rotating spins the picture around its center; flipping creates a mirror image of it. Rotating and flipping can provide additional visual interest for a graphic or fit it more attractively on a slide.

STEP BY STEP   **Rotate an Object**

USE the *Exhibits Final* presentation that is still open from the previous exercise.

1. Go to slide 3, and click the picture to select it.

2. Click the **Picture Tools Format** tab, click **Rotate** in the Arrange group, and then click **Flip Horizontal** in the drop-down menu that appears. The picture reverses its orientation so the planet is on the right and its moons are on the left, as shown in Figure 6-9.

Figure 6-9

The picture has been flipped horizontally

Figure 6-9

The picture has been flipped horizontally

Another Way
Click the Arrange button on the Home tab, click Rotate, and choose a rotation option.

3. Drag the picture up into the upper-right corner of the slide, so that the top and right edges of the picture align with the top and right edges of the slide, as in Figure 6-10.

Figure 6-10

Drag the picture to the upper-right corner of the slide

4. Go to slide 5 and click the picture to select it.

5. Click the **Picture Tools Format** tab, click **Rotate**, and then click **Rotate Right 90°**. Then repeat that command to rotate the picture another 90 degrees.

6. **SAVE** the presentation.

PAUSE. LEAVE the presentation open to use in the next exercise.

PowerPoint offers some set rotation options, such as rotating right or left 90 degrees. For more control over the rotation, you can drag the green rotation handle above the selected object, or click More Rotation Options on the Rotate button's menu to open the Size and Position dialog box, where you can type a specific rotation amount.

Cropping Objects

You have several options for adjusting the size of a picture or other graphic object. You can crop an object to remove part of the object, drag a side or corner, specify exact measurements for an object, or scale it to a percentage of its original size. When you **crop** a picture, you remove a portion of the graphic that you think is unnecessary in order to focus attention on the most important part of a picture. The portion of the picture you cropped is not deleted. You can restore the cropped material by using the crop pointer to drag outward to reveal the material that was previously hidden.

STEP BY STEP   **Crop a Picture**

USE the *Exhibits Final* presentation that is still open from the previous exercise.

1. Go to slide 4 and click the picture to select it.
2. Click the **Picture Tools Format** tab.
3. Click the **Crop** button in the **Size** group. (Click the upper part of the button, not the arrow below it.) The pointer changes to a crop pointer and crop handles appear around the edges of the picture.
4. Click to position the pointer on the top center crop handle and drag downward until the short dotted line on the vertical ruler is on the 1.5-inch mark, as shown in Figure 6-11.

Figure 6-11

Drag the crop handle down to remove a portion of the picture

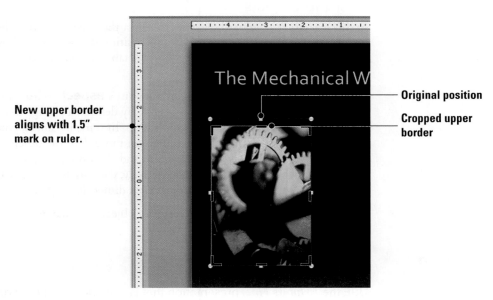

New upper border aligns with 1.5" mark on ruler.

Original position

Cropped upper border

5. Release the mouse button, and then click the **Crop** button again to complete the crop.
6. On the View tab, mark the **Guides** check box to turn the guides back on.

7. Click and drag the cropped picture back up to the intersection of the two guides. Your slide should look similar to Figure 6-12.

Figure 6-12

The picture has been cropped and repositioned

Drag the picture up to realign with guides.

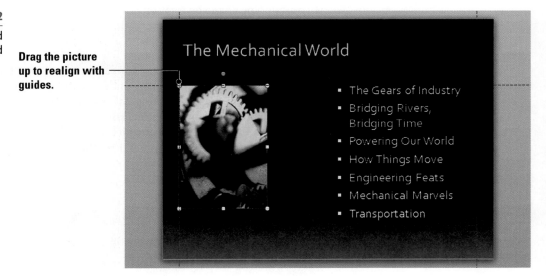

8. On the View tab, clear the Guides check box to turn the guides off.
9. **SAVE** the presentation.

PAUSE. LEAVE the presentation open to use in the next exercise.

Resizing Objects

In this exercise, you learn three ways to adjust the size of a picture: by simply dragging a corner, by setting measurements in the Size and Position dialog box, and by setting a measurement in the Size group on the Picture Tools Format tab. You can use these options to resize any object on a slide.

Generally, you will want to maintain a picture's **aspect ratio** when you resize it. The aspect ratio is the relationship of width to height. By default, a change to the width of a picture is also applied to the height to maintain aspect ratio. In some instances, you may want to distort a picture on purpose by changing one dimension more than the other. To do so, you must deselect the *Lock aspect ratio* check box in the Size and Position dialog box. You are then free to change width and height independently. Alternatively, you can drag a side selection handle on the object (not a corner); this allows you to adjust each dimension separately.

In the following exercise, you will resize an object and change its aspect ratio.

STEP BY STEP   **Size or Scale an Object**

USE the *Exhibits Final* presentation that is still open from the previous exercise.

1. Go to slide 3 and click the picture to select it.
2. Click and drag the lower-left corner of the picture diagonally until the short dotted line on the horizontal ruler is at 0 inches, as shown in Figure 6-13. (Don't worry that the slide title is partially covered; you'll fix this problem in a later exercise.)

Figure 6-13

Resize a picture by dragging a corner

Align left edge of picture with 0 on ruler.

3. Go to slide 4 and click the picture to select it.

4. Right-click the picture, then click **Size and Position** from the shortcut menu. The Format Picture dialog box opens.

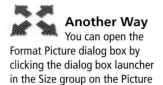**Another Way**
You can open the Format Picture dialog box by clicking the dialog box launcher in the Size group on the Picture Tools Format tab.

5. Click the **Lock aspect ratio** check box to deselect this option. You can now specify the height and width independently.

6. In the Size and Rotate area of the dialog box, click the **Height up arrow** until the height is 4.1 inches. Click the **Width up arrow** until the width is 4.2 inches. See Figure 6-14.

Figure 6-14

Format Picture dialog box

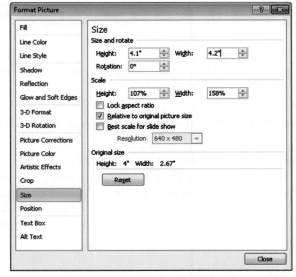

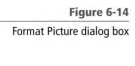**Another Way**
You can also specify a percentage of the original dimensions, instead of an exact size. This is called **scaling**.

7. Click **Close** to close the dialog box. Your slide should look similar to Figure 6-15.

Figure 6-15

The picture has been resized

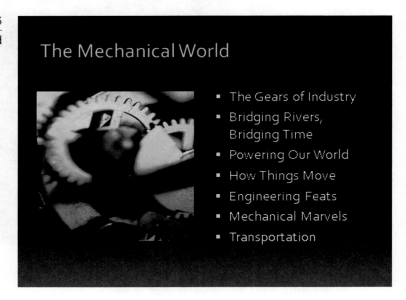

8. Go to slide 5 and click the picture to select it.
9. Click the **Picture Tools Format** tab, then click the **Width down arrow** in the Size group until the picture's width is 4.2 inches. See Figure 6-16.

Figure 6-16

The Width and Height settings on the Ribbon

10. Drag the picture to align its upper-right corner with the intersection of the two guides near the right edge of the slide.
11. **SAVE** the presentation.
PAUSE. LEAVE the presentation open to use in the next exercise.

You can **reset** a picture to its original appearance to remove any sizing or format changes you have made to it. To do this, open the Format Picture dialog box and click the Reset button on the page containing the setting to reset. For example, to reset the size, click Size at the left side of the dialog box and then click Reset. Refer to Figure 6-14. You can also restore a picture's original appearance by clicking the Reset Picture button in the Adjust group on the Picture Tools Format tab.

Applying a Style to a Picture

PowerPoint provides a number of styles you can use to apply borders and other effects to pictures. You can easily apply styles with heavy borders, shadow and reflection effects, and different shapes such as ovals and rounded corners. Use styles to dress up your pictures or format them consistently throughout a presentation.

STEP BY STEP	Apply a Style to a Picture

USE the *Exhibits Final* presentation that is still open from the previous exercise.

1. Go to slide 5 and click the picture to select it if necessary.
2. On the Picture Tools Format tab, click the **More** button in the Picture Styles group. The Picture Styles gallery appears, as shown in Figure 6-17.

Figure 6-17

The Picture Styles gallery

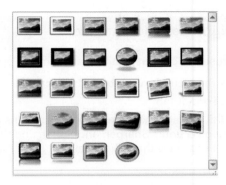

3. Click the **Soft Edge Oval** style. Your picture should look like the one in Figure 6-18.

Figure 6-18

The style gives the picture a different look

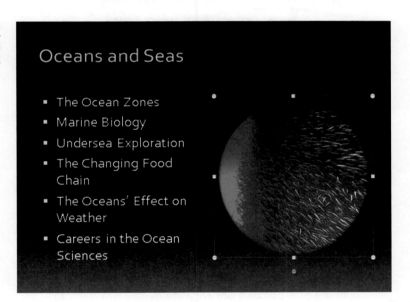

4. **SAVE** the presentation.

PAUSE. LEAVE the presentation open to use in the next exercise.

Take Note   The style's picture borders are black or white by default, but you can apply any color to the border using the Picture Border button.

If you have a number of pictures in a presentation, be careful not to apply too many different styles to the pictures. Using just one or two styles throughout a presentation makes it seem more unified and consistent.

Correcting Brightness and Sharpness

You may need to modify a picture's appearance to make it show up well on a slide. This can be particularly important with pictures you insert from files, which may not have been photographed using the optimal settings. In PowerPoint 2010, Brightness, Contrast, and Sharpness/Softness are all controlled from the same menu and the same tab of the Format Picture dialog box. For presets, you can select from the Corrections button's menu. For precise amounts, you can use the dialog box.

STEP BY STEP   **Adjust a Picture's Brightness and Sharpness**

USE the *Exhibits Final* presentation that is still open from the previous exercise.

1. Go to slide 6 and click the picture to select it. This picture is a bit dark.
2. Click the Picture Tools Format tab.
3. In the Adjust group, click Corrections. A palette of corrections appears, as in Figure 6-19. Notice that there are two sections: Sharpen and Soften and Brightness and Contrast. The center selection in each section is the current setting.

Figure 6-19

Select from the Corrections button's palette

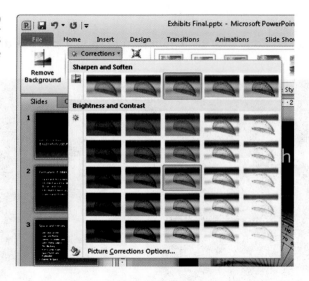

4. In the Brightness and Contrast section, click the Brightness +20% Contrast; 0% (Normal) setting.
5. Click the Corrections button again, reopening the menu.
6. In the Sharpen and Soften section, click Sharpen: 25%.
7. Click the Corrections button again, and click Picture Corrections Options. The Format Picture dialog box opens.
8. Drag the Soften/Sharpen slider to 30% and drag the Contrast slider to 10%, as shown in Figure 6-20.

Another Way
You can use the increment arrow buttons to set the values instead of dragging if you find that easier.

Figure 6-20

Correct a picture from the
Format Picture dialog box

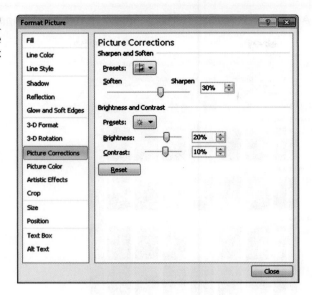

9. Click **Close** to close the dialog box.

10. **SAVE** the presentation.

PAUSE. LEAVE the presentation open to use in the next exercise.

Applying Color Adjustments

Color adjustments enable you to correct minor exposure or color problems in an image without having to open it in a third-party photo editing program. You can improve the look of a picture by making subtle adjustments, or apply dramatic adjustments that distort the image for a special effect.

Each of the three sections on the Color button's palette controls a different aspect of the color. Color *Saturation* determines the intensity of the color, ranging from 0% (grayscale, no color) to 400% (extremely vivid color). Color *Tone* refers to the subtle tint of the image's color, ranging from warmer shades (more red) to cooler shades (more blue). *Recolor* enables you to select color wash to place over the image or to set it to grayscale, black and white, or washout. In this exercise, you will make some color corrections on a photo.

STEP BY STEP   **Apply Color Adjustments**

USE the *Exhibits Final* presentation that is still open from the previous exercise.

1. Go to slide 5 and click the picture to select it.

2. Click the **Picture Tools Format** tab.

3. In the Adjust group, click **Color**. A palette of color choices appears, as in Figure 6-21.

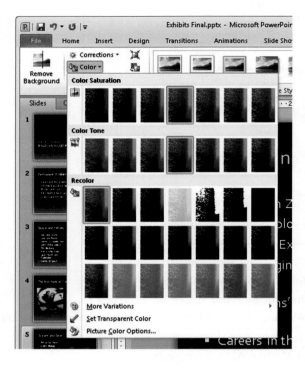

Figure 6-21

Select color correction presets
for the picture

4. In the Color Saturation section, click **Saturation 66%**.

5. Click **Color** again to reopen the palette, point at **More Variations**, and in the Standard Colors group, click **Light Green**.

6. Click **Color** again to reopen the palette, and click Picture **Color Options**. The Format Picture dialog box opens.

7. In the Color Tone section, set the **Temperature** slider to **10,000**. See Figure 6-22.

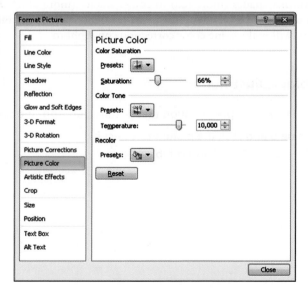

Figure 6-22

Fine-tune color corrections
from the Format Picture
dialog box

8. Click **Close** to close the dialog box.

9. **SAVE** the presentation.

PAUSE. **LEAVE** the presentation open to use in the next exercise.

Adding Effects to a Picture

There are two types of effects that you can apply to a picture: picture effects (such as Glow, Shadow, and Bevel), which affect the outer edges of the picture, and artistic effects (such as Chalk Sketch or Line Drawing), which affect the picture itself.

Adding Picture Effects

Picture effects apply to the edges of a picture, and not to the picture itself. For example, you can apply a beveled frame to a picture, or make its edges fuzzy. In the following exercise, you will apply a bevel and a glow effect.

STEP BY STEP | **Add Picture Effects to a Picture**

USE the *Exhibits Final* presentation that is still open from the previous exercise.

1. Go to slide 4 and click the picture to select it.
2. Click the **Picture Tools Format** tab.
3. Click the **Picture Effects** button, point to **Presets** in the drop-down menu that appears, and click **Preset 5**. A preset formatting effect is applied.
4. Click the **Picture Effects** button, point to **Bevel**, and click **Relaxed Inset**. A different bevel is applied.
5. Click the **Picture Effects** button, point to **Glow**, and click **Periwinkle, 8 point glow, Accent color 5**. An 8-point periwinkle blue glow is placed around the picture.
6. Click away from the picture to deselect it so you can see it more clearly. The slide should look like Figure 6-23.

Figure 6-23

The slide after picture effects have been applied to the picture

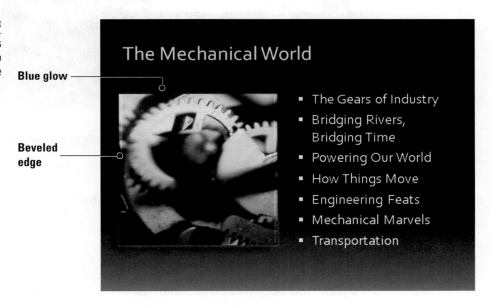

7. **SAVE** the presentation.

PAUSE. LEAVE the presentation open to use in the next exercise.

Adding Artistic Effects

Artistic effects are new in PowerPoint 2010. They enable you to transform the picture itself, not just the outer edges. Some of the effects, such as the Pencil Sketch effect you apply in this exercise, can even make the picture look less like a photograph and more like a hand-drawn work of art.

Add Artistic Effects to a Picture

USE the *Exhibits Final* presentation that is still open from the previous exercise.

1. Go to slide 7 and click the picture to select it.
2. Click the **Picture Tools Format** tab.
3. Click **Artistic Effects** in the Picture Styles group to open the Artistic Effects gallery, and point to several different settings in the gallery. Observe their effect on the image behind the open palette.
4. Click **Paint Strokes**. Your slide should look similar to Figure 6-24.

Figure 6-24

Apply artistic effects to an image

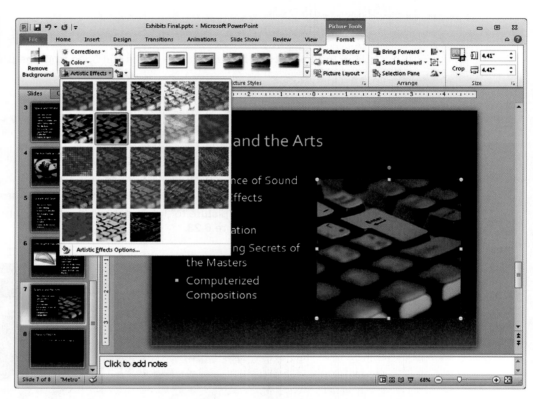

5. **SAVE** the presentation.

PAUSE. LEAVE the presentation open to use in the next exercise.

Removing an Image's Background

Some graphic file formats allow a photo to have a transparent background, but most photos don't use transparency. If you want to make areas of a certain color transparent in the copy of the photo you use in your presentation, you can do so with the Remove Background command. You learn how to use the Remove Background command in this exercise.

Remove an Image Background

USE the *Exhibits Final* presentation that is still open from the previous exercise.

1. Go to slide 3 and click the picture to select it.
2. On the Picture Tools Format tab, click **Remove Background**. The Background Removal tab appears on the Ribbon, and the picture turns purple except for one planet, as shown in Figure 6-25. The purple areas are the parts that will be removed.

Figure 6-25

Tools for removing a photo's background

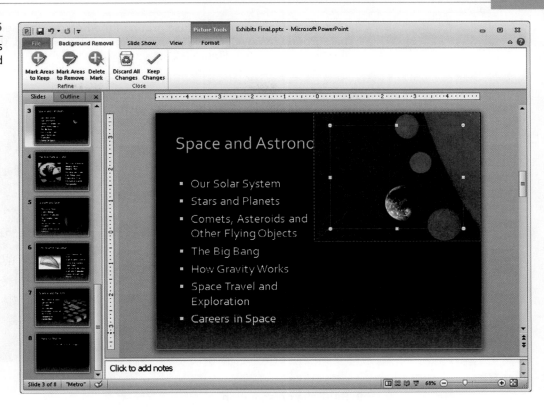

3. Zoom in to **100%** zoom using the Zoom slider in the bottom right corner of the PowerPoint window, and adjust the display so you can see the photo clearly.

4. Notice that inside the picture is a rectangular border with selection handles. Only content within this rectangle will be kept. Drag the corner selection handles of that rectangle so that the entire picture is inside that area.

5. On the Background Removal tab, click **Mark Areas to Keep**.

6. Click one of the planets. If the entire planet does not turn back to its original color with a single click, continue clicking different parts of it until the entire planet appears in its original colors (See Figure 6-26). Zoom in further if needed to see what you are doing.

Figure 6-26

Adjust the areas to keep

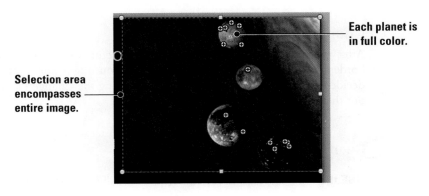

Each planet is
in full color.

Selection area
encompasses
entire image.

 **Troubleshooting** If you make a mistake and click too much, and the whole background turns black, press Ctrl+Z to undo your last action and try again.

7. Repeat step 6 until only the background is purple, and all planets appear in their original colors. You may need to click and drag the pencil mouse pointer to remove the purple from some areas of the planets.

8. Click **Keep Changes** in the Close group of the Background Removal tab to finalize the background removal. Now that the background is removed, the slide title is no longer partly obscured. See Figure 6-27.

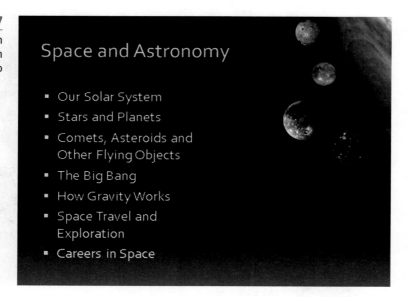

9. SAVE the presentation.

PAUSE. LEAVE the presentation open to use in the next exercise.

The amount of effort required to remove a photo's background accurately depends on the individual photo and on the amount of contrast between the background and the foreground image. You may need to click several times on different parts of the image to mark them to keep. Other photos may be almost perfectly done with the default setting.

It's easy to make a mistake when marking areas for background removal. The Undo command (Ctrl+Z) easily reverses your last action and can be used when a particular marked area doesn't turn out as you expect. You can also use the Mark Areas to Remove command on the Background Removal tab to mark areas that have erroneously been marked for keeping.

Changing a Picture

After you have made multiple changes to a picture's settings in PowerPoint, such as applying borders, specifying an exact size, and so on, you might not want to lose those settings if you decide to use a different picture instead. By using the Change Picture command, you can swap out the image while retaining the settings.

STEP BY STEP   **Change a Picture**

USE the *Exhibits Final* presentation that is still open from the previous exercise.

@ The *Gears.jpg* file is available on the book companion website or in WileyPLUS.

1. Go to slide 4.

2. Right-click the picture and click **Change Picture**. The Insert Picture dialog box opens.

3. Navigate to the folder containing the data files for this lesson and click *Gears.jpg*.

4. Click **Insert**. The picture is replaced, but the previously applied formatting (such as the glow effect) remains.

5. If the picture is not aligned attractively, drag it to move it as needed.

6. SAVE the presentation.

PAUSE. LEAVE the presentation open to use in the next exercise.

Compressing the Images in a Presentation

When adding pictures to a presentation, you may need to consider the ultimate size of the presentation. Pictures will add considerably to the presentation's file size. This can make a large presentation difficult to store or work with. Compressing images reduces the file size of a presentation by reducing its resolution (dots per inch). This can make the presentation easier to store and to email to others, and it speeds up display if you have to work on a slow projector or computer system.

STEP BY STEP   **Compress the Images in a Presentation**

USE the *Exhibits Final* presentation that is still open from the previous exercise.

1. In Windows, navigate to the folder containing *Exhibits Final.pptx* that you created earlier in this lesson.

2. To check the size of the file, right-click the file and click Properties to produce the file's Properties dialog box. The file Size is listed on the General tab of the dialog box.

3. In PowerPoint, click any picture in the presentation to select it, and then click the Picture Tools Format tab.

4. Click Compress Pictures in the Adjust group. The Compress Pictures dialog box opens.

5. Click the Email (96 ppi) option button.

6. Clear the Apply only to this picture check box. See Figure 6-28. If you wanted to compress only the selected picture, you would leave this option checked.

Figure 6-28

Compress the pictures in the presentation

7. Click OK.

8. **SAVE** the presentation. PowerPoint applies the compression settings you selected.

9. In Windows, repeat step 1 to recheck the presentation's file size.

PAUSE. LEAVE the presentation open to use in the next exercise.

The compression utility allows you to choose several options that can reduce file size. You can choose to delete the hidden portions of cropped pictures, for example. You can also choose a target output setting. If you know your slides will be presented on the web or projected on a monitor, you can choose the lowest dpi (dots per inch) setting. Presentations to be shown on a screen do not have to have the same quality as materials that might be printed because the monitor screen itself is limited in the quality it can display. You can compress pictures individually, or apply the same setting to all pictures in the presentation.

ADDING SHAPES TO SLIDES

The Bottom Line

PowerPoint offers drawing tools that enable you to create both basic and complex drawings. Use line tools and shapes to construct the drawing. You can easily add text to shapes to identify them and format the drawing using familiar fill, outline, and effects options.

Drawing Lines

PowerPoint supplies a number of different line tools so you can draw horizontal, vertical, diagonal, or free-form lines.

To draw a line, you select the Line tool, click where you want to begin the line, hold down the mouse button, and drag to make the shape the desired size.

You can use the Shift key to **constrain** some shapes to a specific appearance. For example, you can hold down Shift while drawing a line to constrain it to a vertical, horizontal, or 45-degree diagonal orientation.

STEP BY STEP **Draw Lines**

USE the *Exhibits Final* presentation that is still open from the previous exercise.

1. Go to slide 8. You will create a map on this slide to show potential visitors how to get to the museum. As you work, refer to Figure 6-29 for position of objects.

Figure 6-29

The streets and street names have been added

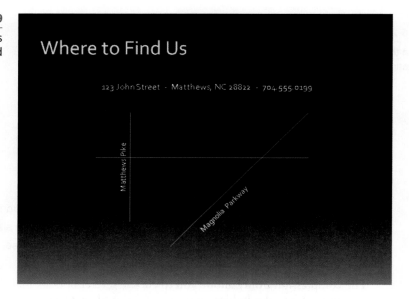

2. Click the **View** tab, and then click **Gridlines** to turn gridlines on.
3. Create the first street for the map as follows:
   a. Click the **Home** tab (or **Insert** tab), then click the **Shapes** button to display the gallery of drawing shapes.
   b. Click **Line** in the Line group. The pointer takes the shape of a crosshair.
   c. Locate the intersection of vertical and horizontal gridlines below the letter *n* in *John*, click at the intersection, and drag downward to create a vertical line three "blocks" long.

Take Note You can also access the Shapes gallery on the Drawing Tools Format tab.

4. Add the street name as follows:

    a. Click **Text Box** on the Insert tab, click anywhere on the slide, and type the text **Matthews Pike**.

    b. Click the outer border of the text box to select all content within the text box, and change the font size to **16**.

    c. On the Drawing Tools Format tab, click **Rotate**, and click **Rotate Left 90°**.

    d. Move the rotated street name just to the left of the vertical line, as shown in Figure 6-29.

5. Select the **Line** tool again, hold down **Shift**, and draw the diagonal line shown in Figure 6-29.

Take Note   Holding down the Shift key constrains the line to be exactly 45 degrees or exactly vertical or horizontal as you drag.

6. Select the **Line** tool again and draw the horizontal line shown in Figure 6-29.

7. Add the street name for the diagonal street as follows:

    a. Insert a text box anywhere on the slide, and type **Magnolia Parkway**.

    b. Change the font size to **16**.

    c. With the text box still selected, click **Arrange**, point to **Rotate**, and click **More Rotation Options**. The Size and Position dialog box opens.

    d. Type **–45** in the Rotation box, and then click **Close**.

    e. Move the rotated text box to the right of the diagonal line, as shown in Figure 6-29.

8. On the View tab, clear the **Gridlines** check box to turn off gridlines again.

9. **SAVE** the presentation.

PAUSE. LEAVE the presentation open to use in the next exercise.

Selected shapes have selection handles (also called sizing handles) that you can use to adjust the size of the object. Some complex shapes have yellow diamond adjustment handles that allow you to modify the shape. Drag a selected shape anywhere on a slide to reposition it.

Lines and other shapes take their color from the current theme. You can change color, as well as change outline and other effects, at any time while creating a drawing.

Drawing Basic Shapes

PowerPoint's many shape tools allow you to create multisided, elliptical, and even freeform shapes. The Shapes gallery contains well over 100 different shapes. Just select a shape and then drag on the slide to draw it there, or click on the slide to create a shape with a default size and orientation.

When creating shapes, you can simply "eyeball" the size, use the rulers or gridlines to help you size, or use the Height and Width settings in the Size group on the Drawing Tools Format tab to scale the objects. Setting precise measurements can help you maintain the same proportions when creating objects of different shapes, for example, when creating circles and triangles that have to be the same height and width. You can also constrain a shape while drawing it by holding down the Shift key to maintain its aspect ratio. In the following exercise, you will draw some basic shapes.

STEP BY STEP   Draw Basic Shapes

USE the *Exhibits Final* presentation that is still open from the previous exercise. As you work, refer to Figure 6-30 to help you position and size objects.

1. On the Home tab, click **Shapes**, and then click the **Rectangle** tool. Hold down the mouse button, and drag to create the tall shape above the horizontal line shown in Figure 6-30.

Figure 6-30

Basic shapes have been added to the map

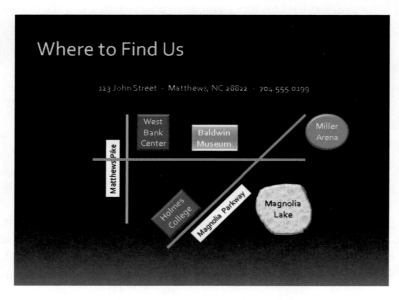

2. With the shape still selected, click the **Drawing Tools Format** tab. Note the measurements in the Size group. If necessary, adjust the size so the shape is 1 inch high by 0.9 inches wide.
3. Select the **Rectangle** tool again and use it to create the wider rectangle shown in Figure 6-30. This shape should be 0.7 inch high by 1.2 inches wide.
4. Select the **Oval** tool, hold down **Shift**, and draw the circle shown in Figure 6-30. This shape should be 1 inch high and wide.
5. Click the **Rectangle** tool and create a rectangle 0.7 inches high by 1 inch wide near the lower end of the diagonal street.
6. Click the shape's green rotation handle and drag to the right to rotate the shape so its right side is parallel to the diagonal road, as shown in Figure 6-30.
7. Click the **Freeform** tool in the Lines group in the Shapes gallery. Near the bottom of the slide (so you can easily see the line you are drawing), draw an irregular oval shape to represent a lake. The shape should be about 1.4 inches high and 1.5 inches wide.

 Troubleshooting When using the Freeform tool, if you return to the exact point at which you started drawing, PowerPoint will automatically close and fill the shape with color. If your shape does not fill, double-click to end it, click Undo, and start again.

8. Drag the lake shape to the right of the diagonal line, as shown in Figure 6-30.
9. **SAVE** the presentation.

PAUSE. LEAVE the presentation open to use in the next exercise.

You can save yourself some time when drawing similar or identical shapes by copying shapes. Copy a selected shape, use Paste to paste a copy on the slide, then move or modify the copy as necessary. You can also select a shape, hold down the Ctrl key, and drag a copy of the shape to a new location.

If you are creating a drawing in which you want to show connections between objects, you can use connectors from the Lines group of the Shapes gallery. Connectors automatically snap to points on shape sides, so you can easily draw an arrow, for instance, from one shape to another. As you reposition objects, the connectors remain attached and adjust as necessary to maintain the links between shapes.

Adding Text to Shapes

You can often improve a drawing by labeling the shapes to state what they represent. In Power-Point, you can add text by simply clicking and typing the text. When you add text to a shape, the shape takes the function of a text box. PowerPoint automatically wraps text in the shape as in a text box; if the shape is not large enough to display the text, words will break up or the text will extend above and below the shape. You can solve this problem by resizing the shape or changing the text's size. You can use any text formatting options you like when adding text to shapes, just as when inserting text into a placeholder or text box. To select text in a shape to edit it, drag over it with the I-beam pointer. In the following exercise, you will add some text to shapes.

STEP BY STEP	Add Text to Shapes

USE the *Exhibits Final* presentation that is still open from the previous exercise.

1. Click in the tall rectangle above the horizontal street, and then type **West Bank Center**.
2. Click in the wide rectangle shape, and then type **Baldwin Museum**.
3. Click in the circle shape, and then type **Miller Arena**.
4. Drag the right border of the circle slightly to the right to increase the shape's size so that the text fits.
5. Click in the rotated rectangle, and then type **Holmes College**. Note that the text is rotated as well.
6. Drag the right border of the rotated rectangle slightly up and to the right to increase the shape's size so that the text fits.
7. Click in the freeform lake object, and then type **Magnolia Lake**.
8. Drag over the *Baldwin Museum* text to select it, and then click the **Bold** button to boldface the text. Your map should look similar to Figure 6-31.

Figure 6-31

The map with text added to the shapes

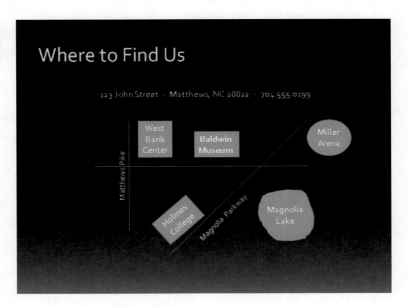

9. **SAVE** the presentation.

PAUSE. LEAVE the presentation open to use in the next exercise.

Take Note   To adjust the way text appears in a shape, right-click the shape, click Format Shape, and access the Text Box settings. For example, you can align the text vertically and horizontally within the shape.

Formatting Shapes

You can apply many of the same formatting effects to drawn lines and shapes that you apply to other objects in PowerPoint. For example, you can change the fill color or texture, add borders, and use effects such as shadows and bevels. You can also save the formatting of a shape as the new default for future shapes you draw. In the following exercise, you will modify a shape by changing its border, fill, and effects.

STEP BY STEP   **Change a Shape's Border, Fill, and Effects**

USE the *Exhibits Final* presentation that is still open from the previous exercise.

1. On the drawing on slide 8, format the *Matthews Pike* line and label as follows:
   a. Click the vertical line that represents Matthews Pike.
   b. On the Drawing Tools Format tab, click the **Shape Outline** button, and then click the **Gold, Accent 3** theme color.

Take Note   You can use the Shape Outline button in the Drawing group on the Home tab or in the Shape Styles group on the Drawing Tools Format tab.

   c. Click the **Shape Outline** button again, point to Weight, and click **6 pt**.
   d. Click the outside border of the Matthews Pike text box to select all content in the text box, and on the Home tab, click **Font Color**, and click **Black, Background 1**.
   e. With the text box still selected, click the **Shape Fill** button, and then click **White, Text 1**.
2. Click the horizontal line and repeat steps 1a-1c to format the line with the **White, Text 1, darker 35%** theme color and **6 pt**. weight. (Don't worry about the street crossing over the *Matthews Pike* text box. You will fix this problem in a later exercise.)
3. Click the diagonal Magnolia Parkway line, click the **Shape Outline** button, point to Weight, and click **6 pt**.
4. Format the *Magnolia Parkway* text box following steps 1d and 1e to change text to black and the fill to white.
5. Format the other shapes as follows:
   a. Click the **West Bank Center shape** above the horizontal street, hold down **Shift**, and click each additional filled shape until all are selected. (Do *not* click any of the lines or the street name text boxes.)
   b. Click **Shape Outline**, and then click **No Outline**. You have removed outlines from the selected shapes.
   c. Click anywhere on the slide to deselect the selected shapes.
   d. Click the **West Bank Center shape**, click **Shape Fill**, and click **Periwinkle, Accent 5, Darker 25%**.
   e. Click the **Miller Arena shape** and fill with **Gold, Accent 3, Darker 25%**.
   f. Click the **Holmes College shape** and fill with **Pink, Accent 2, Darker 25%**.
6. Apply a texture to the Magnolia Lake shape by doing the following:
   a. Click the **Magnolia Lake shape**.
   b. On the Home tab, click **Shape Fill**, point to Texture, and click the **Water Droplets** texture.
   c. Click the **Font Color** button's arrow to open its palette and click **Black, Background 1**.
7. Click the **Baldwin Museum shape**, and on the Drawing Tools Format tab, open the Shapes Styles gallery and click **Periwinkle, Intense Effect, Accent 5**.
8. Select all the filled shapes except the Baldwin Museum shape and the street name text boxes, click **Shape Effects**, point to **Bevel**, and click **Circle**. Your map should look similar to Figure 6-32.

Figure 6-32

The map has been formatted

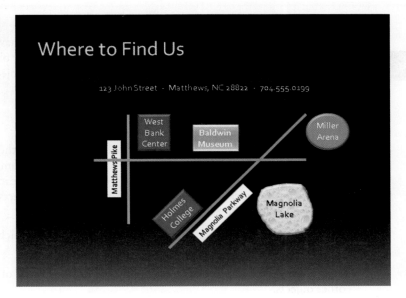

9. **SAVE** the presentation.

PAUSE. LEAVE the presentation open to use in the next exercise.

By now, you should be familiar with applying fills, outlines, and effects. You can format shapes using these options just as you formatted table cells, chart data markers, and SmartArt shapes in previous lessons.

Note that you can access fill, outline, and effect options from either the Home tab or the Drawing Tools Format tab. PowerPoint makes these options available on both tabs to minimize the amount of switching you have to do if you are also formatting text.

Save time when applying the same kinds of formats to a number of objects by selecting all the objects that need the same formatting. You can then apply the format only once to modify all the selected objects. To select several objects, you use the Shift-click method: click the first object you want to select, hold down the Shift key, and then click additional objects. If you select an object for your group by mistake, click it again to exclude it from the selection group.

Setting a New Default Format

Changing the default settings for drawn shapes enables you to create drawings more easily, without having to reformat every shape you draw. Define the settings you use most often as the default, and then you need to change only the shapes that are exceptions to your general rule. In this exercise, you will set a shape's formatting to be the default for new shapes.

STEP BY STEP   **Set the Formatting for the Current Shape as the Default**

USE the *Exhibits Final* presentation that is still open from the previous exercise.

1. On the drawing on slide 8, select the West Bank Center shape.
2. Right-click the shape and click Set as Default Shape.
3. **SAVE** the presentation.
4. Draw another rectangle anywhere on the slide. The new rectangle is formatted the same way as the *West Bank Center* shape.
5. Delete the rectangle you just drew.
6. **SAVE** the presentation.

PAUSE. LEAVE the presentation open to use in the next exercise.

ORGANIZING OBJECTS ON A SLIDE

It is not uncommon to have to adjust the layout of objects you have added to slides. You may find that objects need to be reordered so they do not obscure other objects, or need to be aligned on the slide to present a neater appearance. You can also group objects together to make it easy to move or resize them all at once.

Setting the Order of Objects

Objects stack up on a slide in the **order** in which you created them, from bottom to top. If you insert a slide title on a slide, it will be the object at the bottom of the stack. The last item you create or add to the slide will be at the top of the stack. You can envision each object as an invisible layer in the stack. You can adjust the order in which objects stack on the slide by using Arrange commands or the Selection and Visibility pane.

Some objects can obscure other objects because of the order in which you add them to the slide. You use the Order options to reposition objects in the stack:

- **Bring to Front:** Moves the selected object to the front or top of the stack, on top of all other objects.
- **Bring Forward:** Moves an object one layer toward the front or top of the stack. Use this option if you need to position an object above some objects but below others.
- **Send to Back:** Moves an object all the way to the back or bottom of the stack, below all other objects.
- **Send Backward:** Moves an object one layer toward the back or bottom of the stack.

In this exercise, you will arrange some objects by changing their stacking order.

STEP BY STEP   **Set the Order of Objects**

USE the *Exhibits Final* presentation that is still open from the previous exercise.

1. Go to slide 3, and click the picture to select it.
2. Cancel the background removal you did earlier by doing the following:
   a. On the Picture Tools Format tab, click the Remove Background button. The Background Removal tab appears.
   b. Click Discard All Changes. The picture is restored to its default solid background, and the slide title is once again obscured.
3. With the picture still selected, click the Send Backward button's down arrow and on the menu that appears, click Send to Back. The picture moves behind the slide title placeholder, as shown in Figure 6-33.

Figure 6-33

The picture moves behind the text

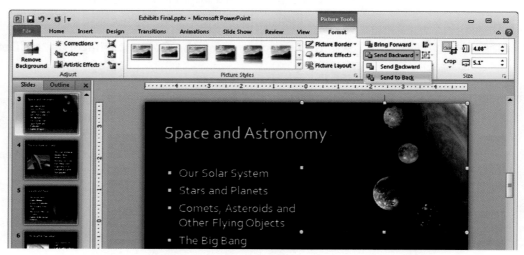

4. Go to slide 8. Click the **Arrange** button, and then click **Selection Pane**. The Selection and Visibility pane opens, as shown in Figure 6-34, showing the current slide content in the order in which it was created, from bottom to top. This order is determined by the order in which the objects were added to the slide.

Figure 6-34

The Selection and Visibility pane shows the current slide content

 **Another Way**
You can also display the Selection and Visibility pane by clicking Select on the Home tab, then clicking Selection Pane.

Take Note The Arrange tools are available on both the Home tab and the Picture Tools Format tab.

 **Troubleshooting** Don't be concerned if the list in your Selection and Visibility pane doesn't exactly match the one shown in Figure 6-34. The order and numbering of objects in the pane can be affected by many actions.

5. Click the gold **Matthews Pike street line** in the map to see how it is identified in the Selection and Visibility pane—it will have a name such as *Straight Connector 4* and should be near the bottom of the list of objects. Then click the **horizontal street line** to see its name.

6. Click the **Matthew Pike street line** again to select it. Click the **Re-order up arrow** until the selected Straight Connector is above the horizontal Straight Connector in the Selection and Visibility pane. Notice that the gold line is now on top of the light gray line in the map.

7. Click the **Matthews Pike text box** and click the **Re-order up arrow** until the text box is on top of the horizontal gray line in the map.

8. Click the **Magnolia Parkway street line** and click the **Re-order up arrow** until the diagonal street is above the horizontal street in the map.

9. You have one more shape to add to the map: an arrow that labels the horizontal street as John Street and indicates that the street is one way. Click **Shapes** on the Home tab, click **Right Arrow** in the Block Arrows group, and draw a block arrow as shown in Figure 6-35. The arrow should be about 0.7 inches high and 5.2 inches wide.

Take Note Notice that the shape's formatting matches that of the West Bank Center shape, because of the default you set earlier in the lesson.

Figure 6-35

Draw a block arrow

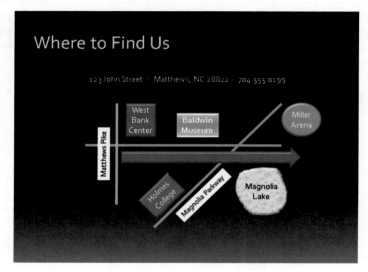

10. In the arrow, key **John Street**, press **Tab** twice, and type **ONE WAY**.

Take Note   Note that the Right Arrow object has been added at the top of the Selection and Visibility pane.

11. Using the Shape Fill button, apply the **Green, Accent 1, Darker 50%** color to the arrow.

12. Right-click a blank area of the block arrow (to the left of the words *John Street*, for example), point to **Send to Back**, and click **Send to Back**. The arrow moves behind all lines and shapes, as shown in Figure 6-36. Note the position of the Right Arrow object in the Selection and Visibility pane.

Figure 6-36

The completed map

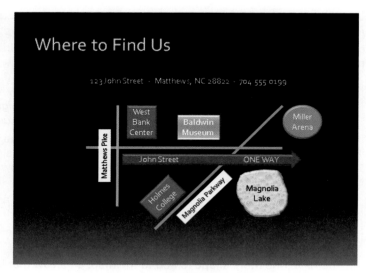

13. Close the **Selection and Visibility** pane.

14. If any of your shapes obscures the text on the block right arrow, adjust their positions as necessary.

15. **SAVE** the presentation.

PAUSE. LEAVE the presentation open to use in the next exercise.

You can clearly see the stacking order of objects on a slide using the Selection and Visibility pane. This pane is similar to the Layers palette in a program such as Illustrator or Photoshop. It allows you to easily move objects up or down in the stacking order. You can click the visibility "eye" to hide objects that might be in your way as you work on another object—a handy feature when creating a complex drawing.

If you do not want to use the Selection and Visibility pane, you can use options on the Home tab's Arrange button menu to reorder objects, or you can use buttons in the Drawing Tools Format tab in the Arrange group. You can also access these options readily by right-clicking an object and selecting the appropriate command from the shortcut menu.

Take Note

Arrange options also display on other Format tabs, such as the Picture Tools Format and SmartArt Tools Format tabs.

Aligning Objects with Each Other

Your drawings will present a more pleasing appearance if similar items are aligned with each other or to the slide. Use PowerPoint's alignment options to position objects neatly.

PowerPoint's alignment options allow you to line up objects on a slide both horizontally and vertically:

- Use **Align Left**, **Align Center**, or **Align Right** to align objects horizontally so that their left edges, vertical centers, or right edges are lined up with each other.
- Use **Align Top**, **Align Middle**, or **Align Bottom** to align objects vertically so that their top edges, horizontal centers, or bottom edges are lined up with each other.

You can also use distribute options to space objects evenly, either vertically or horizontally. This feature can be a great time-saver when you have a number of objects that you want to spread out evenly across a slide.

PowerPoint allows you to align (or distribute) objects either to each other or to the slide. If you select Align Selected Objects on the Align menu, PowerPoint will adjust only the selected objects. If you select Align to Slide, PowerPoint will rearrange objects using the entire slide area.

STEP BY STEP   **Align Objects with Each Other**

USE the *Exhibits Final* presentation that is still open from the previous exercise.

1. On slide 8, click the **West Bank Center shape**, hold down **Shift**, and click the **Baldwin Museum** shape and the **Miller Arena** shape. These landmarks are all different distances from the *John Street* horizontal line but can be aligned for a neater appearance.
2. Click the **Drawing Tools Format** tab if necessary, click **Align**, and click **Align Bottom**. The shapes are now aligned at the bottom so they are the same distance from the horizontal line, as shown in Figure 6-37.
3. **SAVE** the presentation.

PAUSE. LEAVE the presentation open to use in the next exercise.

Figure 6-37

Align the selected shapes
at their bottoms

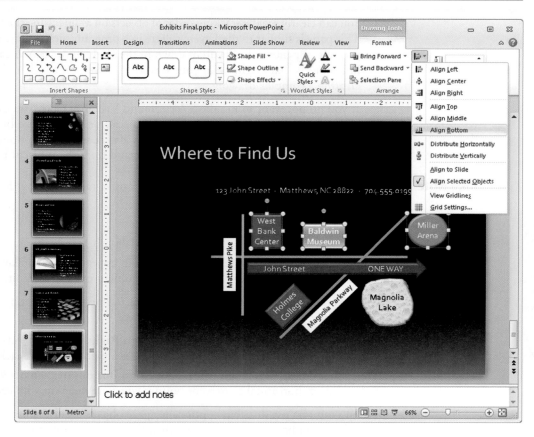

Grouping Objects Together

When a drawing consists of a number of objects, it can be tedious to move each one if you need to reposition the drawing. Grouping objects allows you to work with a number of objects as one unit. In the following exercise, you group objects into a single unit.

STEP BY STEP   **Group Objects Together**

USE the *Exhibits Final* presentation that is still open from the previous exercise.

1. Click above and to the left of the map, and then hold down the left mouse button and drag downward and to the right until you have included the entire map in the selected area. See Figure 6-38. This is called **lassoing** the shapes.

Figure 6-38

To lasso a group of shapes, use
the mouse pointer to draw a
box around them

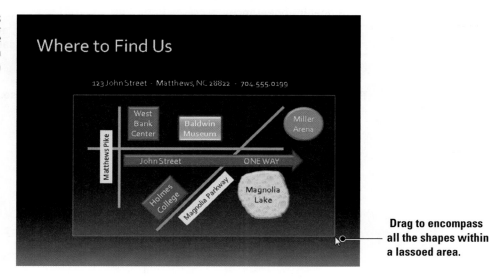

Drag to encompass
all the shapes within
a lassoed area.

2. Release the mouse button. All the shapes within the selection lasso are selected.

3. Click the **Drawing Tools Format** tab, click the **Group** button, and then click **Group**, as in Figure 6-39. All objects are surrounded by a single selection border.

Figure 6-39

Use the Group command to group the selected shapes

4. **SAVE** the presentation and **CLOSE** the file.

PAUSE. LEAVE PowerPoint open to use in the next exercise.

If a drawing contains a number of objects, it makes sense to group the objects when you are finished with the drawing. You can more easily reposition a grouped object, and you can also apply formatting changes to all objects in a group much more quickly than by applying formats to each individual object. To select a group, click any object in the group.

If you find that you need to work further with one object in a group, you can simply click it to activate it. It remains part of the group while you modify it. Most modifications are possible without ungrouping. (Exception: you cannot move the object separately from its group.) If you need to remove objects or make sweeping changes to a group, you can use the Ungroup option to release the group into its component parts. PowerPoint remembers the objects that are in the group so you can use Regroup if desired to restore the group.

If you are creating a very complex drawing, you can group portions of the drawing, then group those groups. This makes it easy to reuse portions of a drawing—simply ungroup the entire drawing, copy the group you need elsewhere, and regroup the whole.

Take Note

It is easy to miss an object when selecting parts of a complex drawing to create a group. To check that you have all objects selected, move the group. You will easily see if one or more objects do not move with the group. Undo the move, click the group, click any other objects that need to belong to the group, and issue the Group command again.

ADDING MEDIA CLIPS TO A PRESENTATION

The Bottom Line

Audio (sound) and **video** (moving picture) clips can add interest to a presentation by drawing the audience's attention more than a static show. You can include your own audio and video clips that you have recorded or acquired on disk, or select from clips provided by Microsoft via the Clip Art task pane. You can also apply formatting styles to audio and video content, as you do for images.

Adding an Audio File to a Slide

You can add audio from files or from the Clip Organizer. You can specify when the sound will play, how loud it will be (in comparison to the overall sound level), and which user controls will be available onscreen.

You have a number of options for adding audio to a presentation:

- Use **Audio from File** if you have an audio file in a supported format that you want to insert. PowerPoint can handle AIFF, AU, MIDI, MP3, WAV, and WMA files.

- Use **Clip Art Audio** to open the Clip Art task pane and search for an audio file in the same way you searched for clip art. PowerPoint automatically selects Audio in the Results should be list and displays sounds on your system. You can use a keyword search to find specific sounds.

• Use **Record Audio** if you want to record your own audio to play on the slide. You must have a microphone to record audio.

The Audio Tools playback tab provides a number of tools for working with an audio file. You can preview the audio, set its volume for the slide show, hide the sound icon during the slide show (don't use this option if you want to be able to play the audio by clicking on it during the presentation), loop the audio so it repeats until you stop it, adjust whether the audio plays automatically or when you click it, and adjust the maximum audio file size.

In this exercise, you will add audio clips to slides using the Clip Art task pane and using an audio clip from a file.

STEP BY STEP   **Add an Audio Clip to a Slide**

@ The *Lobby* file is available on the book companion website or in WileyPLUS. WileyPLUS.

OPEN the *Lobby Final* presentation.

1. Go to slide 1, and on the Insert tab, click the arrow under the Audio button. On the menu that appears, click Clip Art Audio. The Clip Art task pane opens, showing audio clips available.

2. Click any of the clips that appear in the results. A sound icon appears in the center of the slide. See Figure 6-40.

Figure 6-40

An audio clip inserted on a slide

Audio clip ——

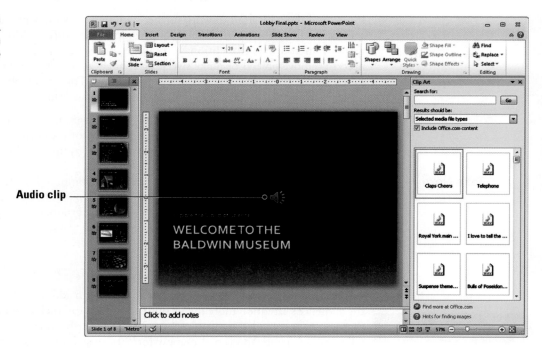

3. Press F5 to switch to Slide Show view, and click the sound icon on the slide. The sound plays.

4. Press Esc to return to Normal view, and close the Clip Art task pane.

5. Select the sound icon on the slide and press Delete on the keyboard to remove it.

6. With slide 1 still displayed, on the Insert tab, click the arrow under the Audio button and click Audio from File. The Insert Audio dialog box opens.

@ The *Beethoven's Ninth.wma* file is available on the book companion website or in WileyPLUS.

7. Navigate to the data files for this lesson, click *Beethoven's Ninth*, and click Insert. An icon appears in the center of the slide.

8. Open the Start drop-down list and click Automatically.

9. Mark the Hide During Show check box.

10. On the Audio Tools Playback tab, click the Volume button, and then click Medium. Figure 6-41 shows the settings on the Audio Tools Playback tab.

Figure 6-41

Adjust the sound clip's volume, start setting, and visibility

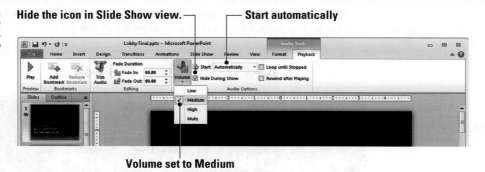

Hide the icon in Slide Show view. ⌐ ⌐ Start automatically

Volume set to Medium

11. View the first two slides in Slide Show view, and notice that the sound quits after the first slide. Press **Esc** to return to Normal view.

12. Select the sound icon on slide 1.

13. On the Audio Tools Playback tab, open the **Start drop-down list** and click **Play Across Slides**.

14. Watch the first several slides in Slide Show view. This time notice that the sound continues as you move from slide 1 to slide 2. Then press **Esc** to return to Normal view.

15. **SAVE** the presentation.

PAUSE. LEAVE the presentation open to use in the next exercise.

Adding a Video to a Slide

You can insert videos from files or from the Clip Art task pane to add visual interest or information to a presentation. PowerPoint 2010 has greatly improved its video support from previous versions, and it now accepts Flash videos as well as many standard formats such as Windows Media, QuickTime, and MP4.

You have three options for inserting a video on a slide:

- Use **Video from File** if you have a video file in a supported format that you want to insert. PowerPoint can handle ASF, AVI, MPEG, or WMV files.
- Use **Video from Web Site** to link to a video clip from a website, such as YouTube.
- Use **Video from Clip Organizer** to open the Clip Art task pane and search for a video file the same way you searched for clip art. PowerPoint automatically selects Videos in the Results should be list and displays videos on your system. You can use a keyword search to find specific videos and search Office.com for more files.

In this exercise, you insert a video clip from a file and set it to play automatically.

STEP BY STEP   **Add a Video to a Slide**

USE the *Lobby Final* presentation that is still open from the previous exercise.

1. Go to slide 8 and click the **Insert Media Clip** icon in the empty placeholder box. See Figure 6-42. The Insert Video dialog box opens.

Figure 6-42

Click the Insert Media Clip icon in the placeholder

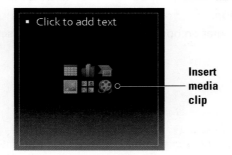

Insert media clip

@ The *Sunspot.mpeg* file is available on the book companion website or in WileyPLUS.

2. Navigate to the folder containing the data files for this lesson and select *Sunspot. mpeg*. Then, click Insert. The clip appears in the placeholder, with playback controls beneath it. See Figure 6-43.

Figure 6-43

The video clip appears on the slide

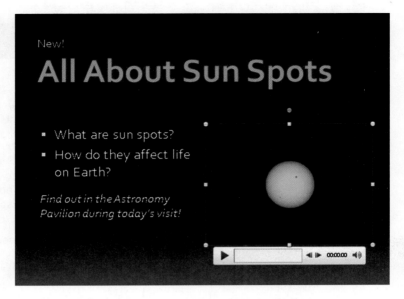

3. On the Animations tab, click Animation Pane. The Animation Pane opens. Notice that there is an animation event for the video clip already there, as shown in Figure 6-44.

Figure 6-44

The video clip is part of the slide's animation sequence

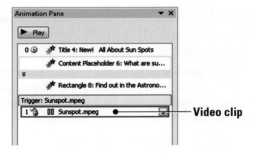

4. On the Video Tools Playback tab, open the Start drop-down list and click Automatically.

Take Note

Notice that a second event is added in the Animation Pane, for pausing the video clip on mouse click.

5. Close the Animation Pane.
6. On the Slide Show tab, click From Current Slide to watch this slide in Slide Show view.
7. **SAVE** the presentation.

PAUSE. LEAVE the presentation open to use in the next exercise.

Take Note   Files identified as videos in the Clip Organizer are actually more like animated clip art graphics. They tend to be relatively small and cannot be significantly enlarged without a corresponding loss of quality. But they can still provide multimedia interest on a slide.

The Video Tools Options tab provides some of the same options you find on the Audio Tools Options tab. In addition, you can choose to play the video in the full screen during the slide show and rewind it back to the first frame after it finishes playing.

Formatting Video or Audio Content

Any video clip on a slide and any audio clip that has a visible icon on a slide can be formatted with PowerPoint's built-in styles. This works just like the style-based formatting for graphic objects: You select a style from a gallery. You can then customize it as desired by applying formatting. You can also choose a frame of the video clip that will appear on the slide whenever the video clip is not playing.

Choosing a Poster Frame

A **poster frame** is an image that displays on the slide when the video clip is not actively playing. You can use an outside image, but it is often easier to select a frame from the video clip itself. Poster frames are useful because often the first frame of the video clip is not an image that is meaningful or recognizable. Instead of choosing Current Frame from the menu, as you will do in this exercise, you can choose Image from File to select your own image. To remove any poster frame so that the first frame of the video clip is once again the default image for the clip, choose Reset from the menu. In this exercise, you choose a poster frame to display for a video clip.

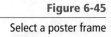   **Choose a Poster Frame**

USE the *Lobby Final* presentation that is still open from the previous exercise.

1. On slide 8, click the video clip.
2. Click the **Play** button (the right-pointing triangle) below the video clip to begin its playback. When you see the image onscreen that you want to use as the poster frame, click the clip to pause it.
3. On the Video Tools Format tab, click **Poster Frame** and click **Use Current Frame**. See Figure 6-45.

Figure 6-45

Select a poster frame

4. **SAVE** the presentation.

PAUSE. LEAVE the presentation open to use in the next exercise.

Applying a Video Style and Formatting

Whereas the tools on the Video Tools Playback tab control the clip's motion effects, the tools on the Video Tools Format tab control its static appearance, including its borders, effects, and any color or contrast corrections. The tools here are very similar to those for graphic images, which you learned about earlier in this lesson. In this exercise, you will apply a video style and some picture corrections.

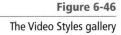 **STEP BY STEP** **Apply a Video Style and Formatting**

USE the *Lobby Final* presentation that is still open from the previous exercise.

1. On slide 8, click the video clip.

2. On the Video Tools Format tab, click the More button in the Video Styles group, opening the Video Styles gallery, as shown in Figure 6-46.

Figure 6-46

The Video Styles gallery

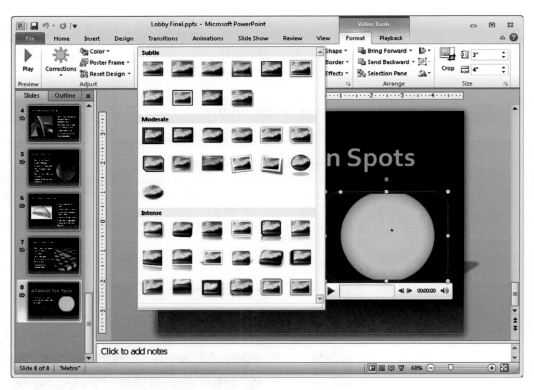

3. In the Subtle section, click the Simple Frame, White style. The frame of the video clip changes.

4. Click the Video Shape button, and on the Shapes palette that appears, click the Rounded Rectangle. The shape of the video clip's frame changes.

5. Click the Video Border button, and on the palette of colors that appears, click Periwinkle, Accent 5, Darker 50%.

6. Click the Video Effects button, point to Glow, and click Periwinkle, 5 pt glow, Accent Color 5.

7. Click the Video Effects button, point to Shadow, and in the Perspective section, click Perspective Diagonal Upper Right. Figure 6-47 shows the completed formatting. Yours may look different, depending on the image you chose for the poster frame.

Figure 6-47

The formatted clip

8. On the Video Tools Format tab, click the Corrections button, and click Brightness: 0% (Normal), Contrast +20%.

9. On the Slide Show tab, clear the Show Media Controls check box. This prevents the media controls under the video clip from appearing in Slide Show view.

10. SAVE the presentation.

PAUSE. LEAVE the presentation open to use in the next exercise.

Take Note   Part of the clip's appearance is the media control bar, or the thick gray bar that appears beneath the clip. If the presentation is self-running, you might prefer to hide that from the audience. To do so, clear the Show Media Controls check box on the Slide Show tab.

Sizing and Arranging Video or Audio Content

Video clips (and audio clips that have a visible icon) can be sized and arranged like any other content on a slide. You can drag them to move or resize them or specify exact measurements. You can also align them with other content using the Align tools, which you learned earlier when working with drawn shapes. In this exercise, you change the size of a video clip and align it on the slide using guides.

STEP BY STEP   **Size and Arrange a Video Clip**

USE the *Lobby Final* presentation that is still open from the previous exercise.

1. On slide 8, select the video clip.

2. On the Video Tools Format tab, type 3 in the Height box and then click away from it. The value in the Width box changes proportionally.

3. Click the video clip again to select it, if necessary.

4. On the View tab, click the Guides check box to turn on the guides. Drag the horizontal guide down so it aligns with the 1" mark on the vertical ruler.

5. Move the text box containing the bullets up so its upper-left corner aligns with the intersection of the guides at the left side of the slide.

6. Move the video clip so its upper-right corner aligns with the intersection of the guides at the right side of the slide. See Figure 6-48.

Figure 6-48

Use the guides to arrange the
slide content

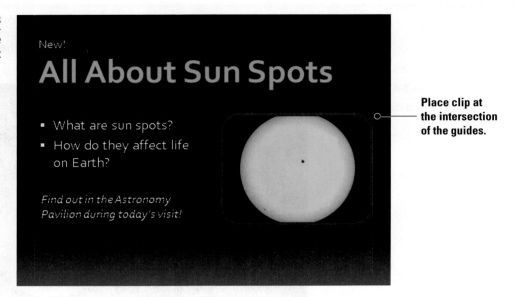

**Place clip at
the intersection
of the guides.**

Take Note   Because there is a glow around the clip's border, it may not appear to align precisely with the guides. The glow may hang slightly over the lines.

> 7. **SAVE** the presentation.
> **PAUSE. LEAVE** the presentation open to use in the next exercise.

There are many ways to size and arrange audio and video clips in PowerPoint. To size a clip, you can drag one of its selection handles, enter precise measurements in the Height and Width boxes on the Video Tools Format tab, or right-click the clip and choose Size and Position to open the size controls in the Format Video dialog box.

To move (arrange) a clip, you can drag it where you want it, with or without the Guides and/or Gridlines to help you. You can also specify a precise position on the Position tab of the Format Video dialog box, or use the Align command on the Video Tools Format tab to align the clip with other clips or with the slide itself.

Take Note   The Align command works only if you are aligning similar objects. In the preceding exercise, you could not have aligned the text box and the video clip with one another using the Align command because when you select both objects, the Video Tools Format tab is no longer available, and that's where the Align command resides.

Compressing Media

If you plan on sharing a presentation that contains audio and video clips, you may want to compress the media in the presentation to make the overall file size smaller. This is similar to the Compress Pictures command for graphics, but it works with video and audio files. You can choose high, medium, or low quality, depending on how you plan to use the presentation file. In the following exercise, you will compress media in a presentation.

STEP BY STEP   **Compress Media**

USE the *Lobby Final* presentation that is still open from the previous exercise.

> 1. Click the **File** tab.
> 2. Under the Media Size and Performance heading, click **Compress Media**. A menu opens showing three choices for media quality. See Figure 6-49.

Figure 6-49

Compress media according to the usage you intend

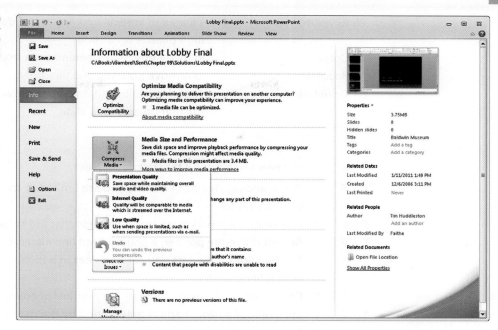

3. Click Internet Quality. The Compress Media dialog box opens, showing the progress of compressing each clip.

4. When each clip shows Compressed, click Close.

EXIT PowerPoint.

SKILL SUMMARY

In This Lesson, You Learned How To:
Add a picture to a slide
Format graphical elements
Add shapes to slides
Organize objects on a slide
Add media clips to a presentation

Knowledge Assessment

Matching

Match the term in Column 1 to its description in Column 2.

Column 1	Column 2
1. Order	a. Predrawn graphics you can use to illustrate a slide
2. Clip art	b. The relationship of width to height for a picture
3. Guides	c. A descriptive word or phrase you can use to search for specific types of objects
4. Constrain	d. Sizing to a percentage of the original size
5. Aspect ratio	e. Color wash to place over the image.
6. Scaling	f. To force a drawing tool to create a shape such as a perfect square or circle

7. Keyword	g. A series of vertical and horizontal dotted lines that help you align objects on a slide
8. Crop	h. To move one object behind or in front of another
9. Recolor	i. To remove portions of a picture you don't need
10. Gridlines	j. Nonprinting lines that you can move or copy to help you position objects on a slide

True/False

Circle T if the statement is true or F if the statement is false.

T F   1. When adding clip art to a slide, you are limited to the pictures stored on your computer.

T F   2. PowerPoint allows you to insert pictures that are stored in BMP format.

T F   3. As you move the pointer, a short dotted line also moves on both rulers.

T F   4. The Recolor option lets you select colors in a picture and replace them with other colors.

T F   5. Compressing an image reduces the number of colors used.

T F   6. The color of a new shape is determined by the default shape formatting.

T F   7. To add text to a shape, select the shape and begin typing.

T F   8. If you want an object to be at the bottom of a stack of objects, you would use Send to Back.

T F   9. You can format a single object in a group without having to ungroup all objects.

T F   10. PowerPoint does not have a feature to insert different shapes into a slide.

Competency Assessment

Project 6-1: Get the Picture

You are a recruiter for Woodgrove Bank, and you have prepared a presentation to be delivered at a local job fair. You need to locate a picture to illustrate one of the presentation's slides. You can use Microsoft Office clip art files to find a suitable picture.

GET READY. LAUNCH PowerPoint if it is not already running.

@ The *Job Fair* file is available on the book companion website or in WileyPLUS.

1. **OPEN** the *Job Fair* presentation and save it as *Job Fair Final*.

2. Go to slide 5 and click the Clip Art icon in the right-hand content placeholder.

3. Type **business** as the keyword, click the **Results should be drop-down arrow**, and select only **Photographs**.

4. Review the results to find a photograph of a professionally dressed business person and then click a picture you like to insert it into the placeholder.

5. Use the Size options on the Picture Tools Format tab to resize the picture to be as wide as the text in the left-hand placeholder, if necessary.

6. Click the View tab, and then click Gridlines. Use the gridlines to align the top of the picture with the top of the text in the left-hand placeholder.

7. Click the picture to select it, click Picture Effects on the Picture Tools Format tab, point to Shadow, and click any shadow effect.

8. Hide the gridlines.

9. **SAVE** the presentation.

LEAVE the presentation open for use in the next project.

Project 6-2: Final Touches

You have decided you need another picture in the Job Fair Final presentation. You have a picture file you think will work.

1. Go to slide 2 of *Job Fair Final* and click the Insert Picture from File icon in the right-hand content placeholder.

2. Navigate to the data files for this lesson, locate *Building.jpg*, click the file, and click Insert.

3. Right-click the picture and click Size and Position. In the Format Picture dialog box, scale the picture to 90% of its current height and width.

4. Press Alt + F9 to display drawing guides. Click the slide title placeholder to display its border, and then drag the vertical guide to the right to align with the right border of the slide title placeholder.

5. Drag the horizontal placeholder up to align with the top of the capital letter *E* in the first bulleted item in the left-hand placeholder.

6. Reposition the picture so that its upper-right corner snaps to the intersection of the two guides. Press Alt + F9 to hide the guides.

7. Click the More button in the Picture Styles group on the Picture Tools Format tab, and then click the Drop Shadow Rectangle Quick Style.

8. Right-click the picture, click Format Picture, and change Brightness to 5% and Contrast to 10%.

9. Click Compress Pictures in the Adjust group on the Picture Tools Format tab, and then click E-mail (96 ppi) and click OK.

10. **SAVE** the presentation and then **CLOSE** the file.

LEAVE PowerPoint open for use in the next project.

@ The *Building.jpg* file is available on the book companion website or in WileyPLUS.

Proficiency Assessment

Project 6-3: Go with the Flow

You are a professional trainer teaching a class on basic computer skills. For your class today, you need to explain the systems development life cycle (SDLC) to a group of students. You can use PowerPoint's drawing tools to create a flow chart that shows the process.

1. Create a new, blank presentation, and apply the Median theme. (Remember, the themes are in alphabetical order.)

2. Change the title slide to a Title Only slide, and type the slide title Systems Development Life Cycle (SDLC).

3. Draw five rectangles stacked vertically on the slide (or draw one and then copy it four times). You do not have to worry about alignment or distribution at this point.

4. Type Phase 1: Needs Analysis in the top rectangle.

5. Add text to the remaining rectangles as follows:

> Phase 2: System Design
>
> Phase 3: Development
>
> Phase 4: Implementation
>
> Phase 5: Maintenance

6. Resize the shapes as necessary so that text fits on a single line and all five rectangles fit on the slide with a small amount of space between each shape, as in Figure 6-50.

Figure 6-50

Draw these five rectangles and add text to them

7. Set the width and height of all five rectangles to be identical if they are not already.

8. With all five rectangles selected, use the Align Left command to align them with one another.

9. Use the Distribute Vertically command to equalize the spacing between the rectangles.

10. Apply a different Shape Styles color to each rectangle. (Use the same effect for all rectangles, but vary the colors for each.)

11. Group all drawing objects.

12. Use the Align Center command to align the object horizontally in the center of the slide.

13. **SAVE** the presentation as *SDLC Final.pptx* and then **CLOSE** the file.

LEAVE PowerPoint open for the next project.

Project 6-4: Enhancing Video

You have been asked by the K-9 Agility Network to add a video clip of a dog agility performance to their marketing presentation. The video provided is not the best quality, but you can do some things in PowerPoint to make it better.

1. **OPEN** the *Agility* presentation and save it as *Agility Final*.

2. Go to slide 8, and click the Insert Media Clip icon in the placeholder.

3. In the Insert Video dialog box, navigate to the location of the data files for this lesson, select *AgilityRun.wmv*, and click Insert.

4. On the Video Tools Format tab, click Crop, and then drag the top and bottom selection handles on the clip to crop out the black bars at the top and bottom. Click away from the video to finalize the cropping when finished.

5. Click in the Height box on the Video Tools Format tab and set the height to 4.5". Let the Width setting adjust itself automatically.

6. Drag the video clip up or down on the slide to center it vertically between the slide title and the bottom of the slide.

7. Click the Align button, and click Align Center to center the video clip on the slide.

8. Click the More button in the Video Styles group and click Beveled Rounded Rectangle in the Moderate section.

9. Click the Corrections button, and click Brightness: +20% Contrast: +40%.

10. On the Slide Show tab, clear the Show Media Controls check box.

11. Click From Current Slide, and then click the clip to start it playing. Watch the clip, and then press Esc to return to Normal view.

12. **SAVE** the presentation and then **CLOSE** the file.

LEAVE PowerPoint open for the next project.

Mastery Assessment

Project 6-5: Photo Flair

You are finalizing a presentation to introduce a speaker and want to do some work on the photo of the speaker you have included on a slide. You can use PowerPoint's picture tools to finalize the photo.

1. **OPEN** the *Speaker* presentation and save it as *Speaker Final*.
2. Go to slide 2 and select the picture.
3. Crop the picture to remove the coffee cup and newspaper at the right side of the picture.
4. Resize the photo so it is 4 inches high and align it with the top of the vertical line at the center of the slide.
5. Increase the contrast in the picture by 10%.
6. Draw a rectangle that exactly covers the picture. Remove the outline from the rectangle.
7. Click the down arrow key twice and the right arrow key twice to slightly offset the shape from the picture, and then send the shape behind the picture to act as a drop shadow.
8. Choose a new theme color for the rectangle shape that contrasts well with the picture but does not overwhelm it.
9. **SAVE** the presentation and then **CLOSE** the file.

LEAVE PowerPoint open for use in the next project.

Project 6-6: Logo Creation

Your Consolidated Courier presentation needs a new logo. You can create one using the Drawing tools in PowerPoint.

1. Create a new blank presentation.
2. Change the layout of the slide to Blank.
3. Draw the three shapes shown in Figure 6-51

Figure 6-51

Draw these three shapes

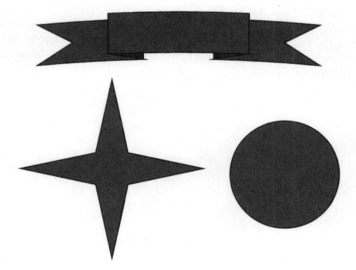

4. Select the banner shape, and fill it with the Dark Red standard color. Change its outline to the Orange standard color and set its Width to 0.25 pt.

5. In the banner shape, type **Consolidated Courier**, pressing **Enter** between the words so each appears on its own line. Set the font to Arial Black.

6. Select the star shape, and fill it with the Dark Red standard color. Remove its outline.

7. Select the circle, and fill it with the Fire preset gradient. Remove its outline.

8. Arrange, align, and size the three shapes into the logo shown in Figure 6-52.

Figure 6-52

Create this logo

9. **SAVE** the presentation as *Logo Final* and then **CLOSE** the file.

EXIT PowerPoint.

INTERNET READY

An organization that you belong to (such as a church or club) would like to be able to use PowerPoint to show the lyrics to a song that the group sings, so people who don't know the words can sing along. Use the Internet to find the lyrics to a song that a group sings. (If you don't belong to any group that sings songs, ask a friend to suggest one.) Then create a presentation that shows the lyrics for the first verse of the song. Break up the lyrics into multiple slides, so each slide shows the text large enough for the audience to easily see from a distance.

Find an audio clip of the song being sung and place it on the first slide. Set the audio clip to play across all slides in the presentation. Manually set the timing for each slide's transition to an appropriate amount so that the lyrics appear on-screen as the audio clip is singing them. If you like, instead of manually setting the timings, you can experiment with the Rehearse Timings feature found on the Slide show tab. For an extra challenge, use emphasis animations to dim each line of the song after it has been sung.

LESSON SKILL MATRIX

In This Lesson, You Will Learn The Following Skills:

Adjusting Slide Orientation and Size

Customizing Audience Handouts

Choosing Slides to Display

Rehearsing Your Delivery

Setting Up a Slide Show

Working with Presentation Tools

Broadcasting a Presentation

Recording a Presentation

Packaging a Presentation for CD Delivery

KEY TERMS

- annotate
- broadcast
- custom shows
- Handout Master
- ink
- landscape orientation
- orientation
- portrait orientation
- presentation tools
- timings

You are an engineer for A. Datum Corporation, a contractor specializing in pile-driving and heavy concrete construction. Your team has put together a bid on a large bridge construction project for the town of Center City, and you must present the bid package to the client. You will present a slide show for the client before reviewing the bid in detail. Your presentation will introduce your company and provide an overview of the bid itself. PowerPoint provides a number of tools that can help you set up your presentation, rehearse it, and then package it to use in the final presentation.

ADJUSTING SLIDE ORIENTATION AND SIZE

The Bottom Line

Orientation refers to the direction material appears on a page when printed. A page printed in **landscape orientation** is wider than it is tall, like a landscape picture that shows a broad panoramic view. A page printed in **portrait orientation** is taller than it is wide, like a portrait picture that focuses on a single upright figure. Slides are generally displayed at a standard size and orientation. You can adjust orientation and size for special impact or to meet the requirements of a specific projection device or output option.

Selecting Slide Orientation

By default, slides are displayed so they are wider than they are tall (landscape orientation). You may want to change the orientation of a presentation for a special case, such as to accommodate large graphics that have a portrait orientation or to print slides at the same orientation as other materials. You can easily change this orientation by using the Page Setup dialog box or a Ribbon command. In this exercise, you will practice changing slide orientation.

You cannot mix landscape and portrait orientations in a single presentation the way you can in a word processing document. All slides in a presentation must have the same orientation. However, if you need to display one or more slides in a different orientation, you can create a secondary presentation with the different orientation and then provide links between the main presentation and the secondary one. You can easily click the link during the slide show to jump to the secondary presentation and then click another link to return to your main presentation.

Presentation materials such as notes pages and handouts print in portrait orientation by default because this orientation allows the most efficient placement of slide images and text on the page. Adjusting orientation for these materials allows you to fit more information across the longest axis of the page—a plus if you have a great many notes for each slide.

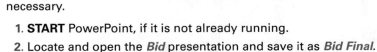

STEP BY STEP **Select Slide Orientation**

GET READY. Before you begin these steps, make sure that your computer is on. Log on, if necessary.

1. **START** PowerPoint, if it is not already running.
2. Locate and open the *Bid* presentation and save it as *Bid Final*.
3. Click the Design tab, and then click the Page Setup button. The Page Setup dialog box opens, as shown in Figure 7-1. Note the current width and height measurements at the left side of the dialog box.

Figure 7-1

Page Setup dialog box

4. Click **Portrait** in the Slides area of the dialog box. Note that the width and height measurements reverse.

5. Click **Landscape** in the Notes, Handouts & Outline area.

6. Click **OK**. The slides are now taller than they are wide, as shown in Figure 7-2.

Figure 7-2

The slides display in portrait orientation

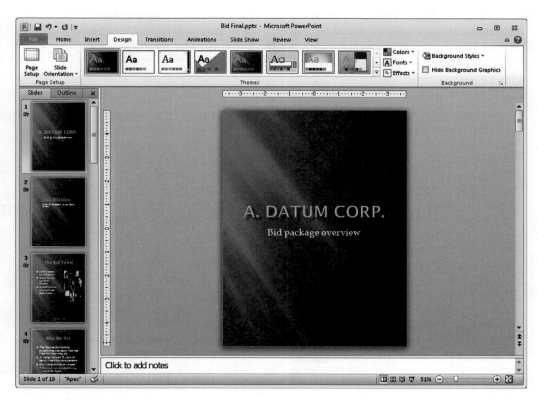

Take Note   You will see the result of this change to handout orientation later in this lesson.

7. Click the **Slide Orientation** button in the Page Setup group, and then click **Landscape**. The slides return to their default landscape orientation.

8. **SAVE** the presentation.

PAUSE. LEAVE the presentation open to use in the next exercise.

Setting Slide Size

Slides have a default size that you can change if you need to accommodate a particular kind of projection system or output. Use the Page Setup dialog box to adjust slide size. In this exercise, you try out several different slide sizes.

Slides are sized by default at a 4:3 aspect ratio that allows them to be shown on a standard monitor without distortion. The Slides sized for drop-down list lets you choose from a number of other standard size options, including different screen aspect ratios, standard U.S. and European letter paper sizes, 35 mm slides, overheads, and banners. For a wide-screen monitor, use a 16:9 aspect ratio. Slide sizes apply to all slides in a presentation, not just the currently selected slide.

STEP BY STEP   **Set Slide Sizes**

USE the *Bid Final* presentation that is still open from the previous exercise.

1. On the Design tab, click the **Page Setup** button. The Page Setup dialog box opens. Note the width and height measurements for the default slide size.
2. Click the **Slides sized for drop-down arrow**, then click **On-screen Show (16:9)**. The width and height measurements change to reflect the new slide size.
3. Click **OK**. The slides are now much wider than they are tall, as shown in Figure 7-3.

Figure 7-3

Slides display at their new size

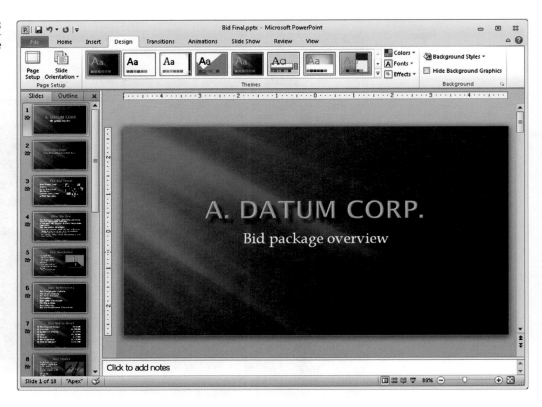

Take Note   The 16:9 option is an aspect ratio that is used for wide-screen monitors.

4. Click the **Page Setup** button again, click the **Slides sized for drop-down arrow**, then click **35mm Slides**.
5. Click **OK**. The slides are now the proper size to create slides that could be used in an old-style slide projector.
6. Click the **Page Setup** button again, click the **Slides sized for drop-down arrow**, and then click **On-screen Show (4:3)**.
7. Click **OK**. The slides are now the default size again.
8. **SAVE** the presentation.

PAUSE. LEAVE the presentation open to use in the next exercise.

If you do not find a suitable size for a specific need, you can create a custom slide size. Adjust the width and height as desired in the Page Setup dialog box to create the custom slide size.

Besides allowing you to set slide size and orientation, the Page Setup dialog box lets you choose the starting number for slides in a presentation. This is useful if you are combining several separate presentations into one comprehensive slide show.

CUSTOMIZING AUDIENCE HANDOUTS

You can help your audience follow a presentation by giving them handouts, which show small versions of the slides arranged in various ways on a page. Handout layouts are controlled by a **Handout Master**, as slide appearance is controlled by the Slide Master. You can customize the Handout Master to create your own handout layout. You can also export handouts to Microsoft Word, where you can customize them further.

Customizing the Handout Master

You can customize the layout of the Handout Master, which controls how handouts are formatted in PowerPoint. You can add text boxes to it, enable or disable certain placeholders, and format those placeholders. In this exercise, you customize the Handout Master in several ways.

You can create handouts that show one, two, three, four, six, or nine slides on a page. If you make changes to any of these layouts, the changes are reflected on all other layouts.

You cannot adjust the position or size of the slide placeholders in the Handout Master. (You can do that in Word, though, which you'll learn about in the next exercise.) You can, however, adjust both size and position of the Header, Date, Footer, and Page Number placeholders. You can also choose to hide some or all of these placeholders by deselecting their check boxes in the Placeholders group on the Handout Master tab.

The Handout Master tab allows you to change both slide orientation and handout orientation, using buttons in the Page Setup group. To further modify the appearance of handouts, you can change theme colors and fonts (but not the current theme) and apply a different background style. You can format the Header, Date, Footer, and Page Number placeholders like any text box or placeholder using Quick Styles, fills, or outlines.

Note that you can also customize the Notes Master in many of the same ways that you customize the Handout Master. Click the Notes Master button on the View tab to display the Notes Master tab. The Notes Master allows you to adjust the size and position of the slide image as well as other placeholders on the page.

STEP BY STEP   **Customize the Handout Master**

USE the *Bid Final* presentation that is still open from the previous exercise.

1. Click the Insert tab, click Header & Footer, and click the Notes and Handouts tab.
2. Set up headers and footers as follows:
   a. Click to mark the Date and time check box, and make sure the *Update automatically* option is selected.
   b. Click to mark the Header check box, and type the header A. Datum Corporation.
   c. Click to mark the Footer check box, and type the footer No Job Is Too Big for A. Datum.
   d. Click Apply to All.
3. Click the View tab, and then click the Handout Master button in the Presentation Views group. The Handout Master view opens as shown in Figure 7-4, with the header and footer you supplied in step 2.

Figure 7-4

Handout Master view

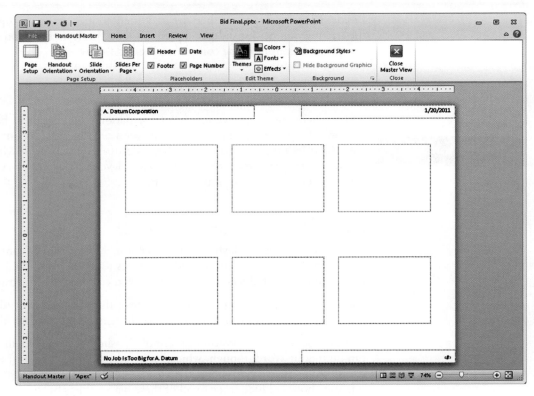

Take Note The master displays in landscape orientation because you changed the orientation in a previous exercise.

4. Click the Slides Per Page button in the Page Setup group, then click 3 Slides. The Handout Master displays the layout used to show three slides across the width of the page.

5. Click the Insert tab, click Text Box, and draw a text box above the center slide placeholder of the same width as the placeholder, as shown in Figure 7-5.

Figure 7-5

Add a text box to the Handout Master

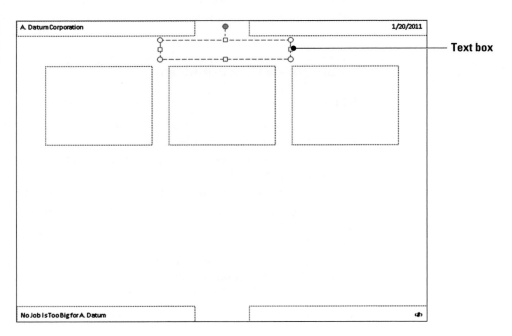

Text box

6. Type **Center City Bridge Project** in the text box.

7. Change the font size of the text box text to **18** if necessary, apply bold formatting, change the color to **Dark Blue, Text 2**, and **center** the text. Adjust the size of the text box as necessary to display the text on one line.

8. Click the outside border of the header placeholder in the upper-left corner of the master, hold down **Shift**, and click the date, footer, and page number placeholders.

9. Change the font size to **14 pt**, apply bold formatting, and change the color to **Dark Blue, Text 2**.

10. Click the **Handout Master** tab, and then click the **Close Master View** button to exit Handout Master view.

11. Click the **File** tab and click **Print**. Open the **Print All Slides** button's list and click **Handouts (3 Slides Per Page)**. Your customized handout master should resemble the one previewed in Figure 7-6.

Figure 7-6

Preview of the customized handout

Select the 3 Slides handout here.

Next Page

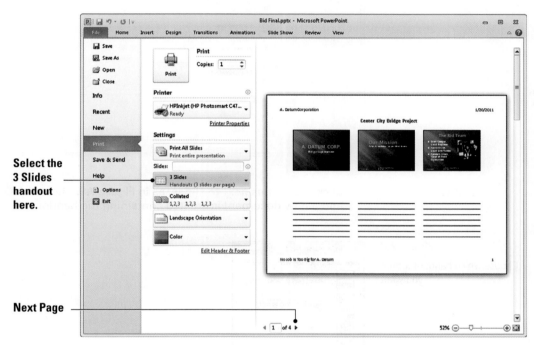

12. Click the **Next Page** arrow to see that the text box you added displays on each page of the handouts.

13. Click the **Print** button to print the handouts.

14. Click the **Close Print Preview** button to return to Normal view.

15. **SAVE** the presentation.

PAUSE. LEAVE the presentation open to use in the next exercise.

Exporting Handouts to Word

As you saw in the preceding exercise, there's a limit to what you can do with handout layouts in PowerPoint. For maximum control over handouts, including the ability to resize the slide images, you must export handouts to Word. In this exercise, you export handouts to Word.

STEP BY STEP | **Export Handouts to Word**

USE the *Bid Final* presentation that is still open from the previous exercise.

1. Click the **File** tab, click **Save & Send**, click **Create Handouts**, and then click the **Create Handouts** button (see Figure 7-7). The Send to Microsoft Word dialog box opens.

Figure 7-7

Choose to create handouts
from Backstage view

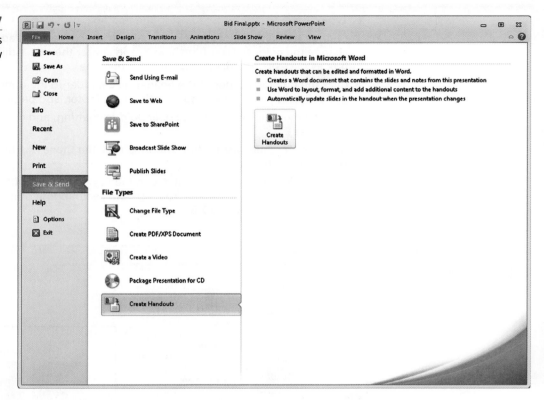

2. Click **Blank lines next to slides**, as in Figure 7-8. Then click **OK**. Microsoft Word opens and a new document is created containing the handouts.

Figure 7-8

Choose which handout format
you want

3. Click the first slide's image, and drag its lower-right corner selection handle to increase the image's size by about 0.25".

4. Drag across the horizontal lines in the first row to select them.

5. On the Home tab, click the **Line and Paragraph Spacing** button, and click **Remove Space After Paragraph**. The spacing between lines tightens up, as in Figure 7-9.

Figure 7-9

Change graphic size and spacing between lines

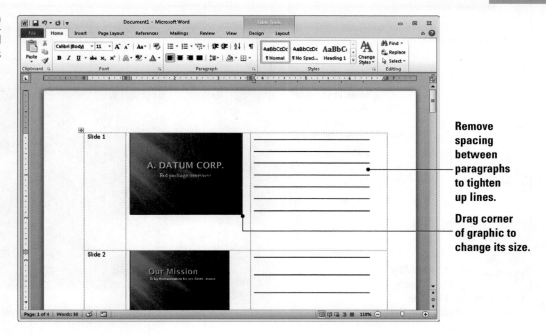

Remove spacing between paragraphs to tighten up lines.

Drag corner of graphic to change its size.

6. Repeat the changes from steps 3-5 for each slide.
7. **SAVE** the Word document as *Handouts.docx* and **EXIT** Word.

PAUSE. LEAVE the *Bid Final* presentation open to use in the next exercise.

CHOOSING SLIDES TO DISPLAY

The Bottom Line

You may want to present only a portion of the slides you have prepared on a specific subject. You can select the slides to display by hiding slides or by creating a custom slide show.

Omitting Selected Slides from a Presentation

You can omit slides from a presentation by hiding them. Use the Hide Slide button or command to hide a slide so it won't appear during the presentation. In this exercise, you hide a slide.

STEP BY STEP   **Hide a Slide**

USE the presentation that is still open from the previous exercise.

1. Go to slide 2, and then click the Slide Show tab.
2. Click the Hide Slide button in the Set Up group. The slide is shaded on the Slides tab, as shown in Figure 7-10, and the slide number is surrounded by a box with a diagonal bar across it.

Figure 7-10

A hidden slide is shaded in the Slides tab

The hidden slide is shaded and its number is crossed out on the Slides/Outline pane.

Another Way
Right-click a slide in the Slides tab or in Slide Sorter view, and click Hide Slide on the shortcut menu.

Another Way
Set a range of slides to show in the Set Up Show dialog box, covered later in this lesson.

3. Press **F5** to start the presentation from slide 1.
4. Click the mouse button and notice that slide 2, *Our Mission*, does not display—you go directly to slide 3, *The Bid Team*.
5. Press **Esc** to stop the slide show.

PAUSE. LEAVE the presentation open to use in the next exercise.

When you hide a slide, you can still see it in Normal view and Slide Sorter view. It is hidden only in Slide Show view, when you present the slides. You can unhide a slide using the same procedure you used to hide it.

If you find that you want to display a hidden slide during the presentation, you can show it using PowerPoint's presentation tools. You will learn more about controlling a presentation with these tools later in this lesson.

Creating a Custom Show

Here we look at how to create **custom shows** to customize presentations for different groups using slides from a single presentation. A comprehensive year-end corporate review presentation, for example, might include information on the company as a whole as well as on the operations of each department. You could show all of the slides to the board of directors and use custom shows to present to each department the general company statistics and the information specific to that department. Custom shows allow you to focus attention on the material most relevant to a specific audience. In this exercise, you will create a custom show that contains a subset of the slides in the main presentation.

You can create any number of custom shows in a presentation. When you set up a presentation for showing, you can specify that only the custom show slides will be presented. You can also choose to run the show while you are in Slide Show view.

You select the slides for a custom show in the Define Custom Show dialog box. Add slide titles from the main presentation to the custom presentation. You can adjust the order in which the slides display in the custom show: Use the up and down arrows to the right of the Slides in custom show list to move a selected title up or down in the list.

STEP BY STEP	**Create a Custom Show**

USE the *Bid Final* presentation that is still open from the previous exercise.

1. Click the **Slide Show** tab, if necessary, and then click the **Custom Slide Show** button in the Start Slide Show group.
2. Click **Custom Shows**. The Custom Shows dialog box opens.
3. Click the **New** button. The Define Custom Show dialog box opens.
4. In the Slide Show Name box, type **Corporate Information**.
5. Click **slide 2** in the *Slides in presentation* list, then click the **Add** button to place this slide in the *Slides in custom show* list.
6. Add slides 4, 5, and 6 to the custom show list. Your dialog box should look like Figure 7-11.

> ✕✕ **Another Way**
> You can quickly select more than one contiguous slide to add by clicking a slide in the list, holding down Shift, and then clicking additional slides. Hold down Ctrl to select non-contiguous slides.

Figure 7-11

Four slides have been added to the custom show

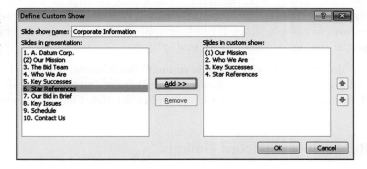

Take Note   The parentheses around slide 2's number indicate it is a hidden slide.

7. Click **OK**, and then click **Show**. The custom show starts with the second slide you added (the first slide, slide 2, is still hidden).
8. Click the mouse button to proceed through the slides of the custom show until the show ends.
9. **SAVE** the presentation.

PAUSE. LEAVE the presentation open to use in the next exercise.

Take Note   When you add slides to the Slides in custom show list, they are renumbered in the list, but the slide numbers on the slides do not change.

After you create a custom show, its name appears in the Custom Slide Show drop-down list, as well as in the Custom Shows dialog box. You can run the custom show from either list. You can also select the custom show in the Custom Shows dialog box and choose to edit the show, remove it, or copy it.

REHEARSING YOUR DELIVERY

> **The Bottom Line**

To make sure that your audience will have enough time to read and absorb the content on your slides, you can rehearse your delivery. When you rehearse a presentation, you read it just as if you were a member of the audience viewing the slides for the first time. Look at pictures, charts, and diagrams to read any information they supply. After you rehearse, you have the option of saving your timings to use during your presentation.

Rehearsing Timings

Rehearsing a presentation can help you set the **timings** for it. Slide timings are particularly important if you intend to show the slides as a self-running presentation that viewers cannot control. You should allow plenty of time for viewers to read and understand the content on each slide. (You will learn more about self-running presentations in the next section.) When you rehearse, you read the text on the slide out loud (or silently to yourself) to see how long each slide should appear onscreen. You can then choose to keep those timings after the rehearsal or discard them. In this exercise, you will rehearse timings for a presentation and record the timings for later use.

The Rehearsal toolbar that displays when you rehearse slides shows you how much time you have spent reading the current slide as well as the elapsed time for the entire presentation. You can pause the rehearsal if necessary, then resume it when you are ready to continue. You can also choose to start the time again for a particular slide.

Note that saving your rehearsed times applies timings to the slide that allow PowerPoint to control the slides for you. The presentation can run automatically without your having to click buttons to advance slides. If you have applied animations to slide objects, rehearsing will set the proper timing for those objects to display.

You do not have to save the slide timings after rehearsal if you do not want PowerPoint to control the slides for you. You can tell PowerPoint not to save the timings, or you can deselect Use Rehearsed Timings in the Set Up group on the Slide Show tab to remove slide timings.

STEP BY STEP   **Rehearse and Record Timings**

USE the *Bid Final* presentation that is still open from the previous exercise.

1. On the Slide Show tab, click the Rehearse Timings button. The slide show starts from slide 1 and the Rehearsal toolbar appears in the upper-left corner of the screen, as shown in Figure 7-12.

Figure 7-12

The Rehearsal toolbar appears in Slide Show view

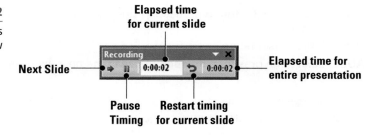

2. Read all the content on each slide, clicking the mouse button to display bullet items and advance slides. As you read, the timer is recording the time you spend. If you get interrupted, you can click the Pause button on the toolbar to pause.

3. When asked if you want to save the slide timings, click Yes. The presentation appears in Slide Sorter view, with the timing for each slide displayed below it, as shown in Figure 7-13.

Figure 7-13

Slide timings appear beneath each slide

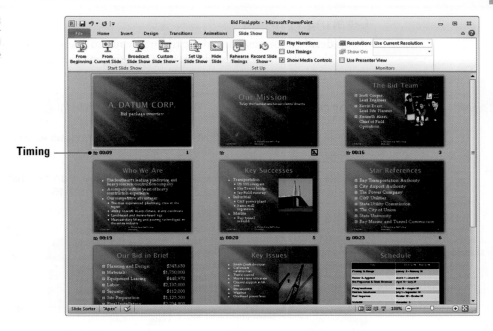

Timing

4. Press **F5** to start the slide show again from slide 1. This time, let PowerPoint control the slides according to the rehearsal times you set.

5. After three or four slides have displayed, press **Esc** to end the slide show. Switch to Normal view.

6. **SAVE** the presentation.

PAUSE. LEAVE the presentation open to use in the next exercise.

Adjusting Timing

After recording the timings for a presentation, you may decide that you need more or less time for a particular slide. You can change the timing on the Transitions tab. In the following exercise, you change the timing for an individual slide.

STEP BY STEP **Adjust a Slide's Timing**

USE the presentation that is still open from the previous exercise.

1. Click the **Transitions** tab.

2. Select the slide for which you want to change the timing.

3. Click the up or down arrows in the After box in the Timing group, to incrementally adjust the number of seconds up or down (see Figure 7-14).

Figure 7-14

Change the timing for a slide on the Transitions tab

Adjust the timing

Select the slide

PAUSE. LEAVE the presentation open to use in the next exercise.

Clearing Timings

If you decide not to use automatic timings, you can easily clear all the timings from all slides at once. The following exercise shows how to clear the timings for all slides.

Clear Slide Timings

USE the presentation that is still open from the previous exercise.

1. Click the Slide Show tab.
2. Click the arrow below the Record Slide Show button to open a menu, point to Clear, and click Clear Timings on All Slides. See Figure 7-15.

Figure 7-15

Clear all slide timings from the Slide Show tab

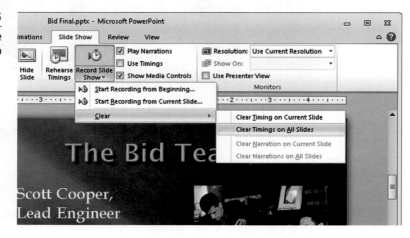

Another Way

You can also turn off all the automatic transitions by clearing the After check box on the Transitions tab and then clicking Apply to All. However, this does not remove the timings; it just disables their ability to execute automatically. You could later re-enable timings for all slides and have your previously set timings back.

3. **SAVE** the presentation.

PAUSE. LEAVE the presentation open to use in the next exercise.

SETTING UP A SLIDE SHOW

The Bottom Line

The Set Up Show dialog box allows you to make a number of decisions about how slides display during a presentation.

Setting Up a Slide Show

The following exercise walks you through the settings in the Set Up Show dialog box. Not all of these settings are applicable to the presentation being used for the example, but all are useful to know about because of the variety of presentations you may create in the future. In this exercise, you configure various settings that govern how a slide show runs in Slide Show view.

When setting up a slide show, you have the option of choosing a Show Type. The choices are:

- **Presented by a speaker (full screen)** is the option to choose if the slides will be presented by a moderator (you or some other person) to a live audience. The slides will display at full screen size.
- **Browsed by an individual (window)** is the option to choose if you are preparing the presentation for a viewer to review on his or her own computer. The slides display within a window that contains a title bar with size/close controls. You can also choose to display a scrollbar to make it easy for the individual to scroll through the slides.
- **Browsed at a kiosk (full screen)** is the option to choose if you intend to have the presentation run unattended, with no moderator. This option is a standard choice for trade shows or other venues where the slides can loop indefinitely for viewers to watch as long as they desire.

STEP BY STEP   **Set Up a Slide Show**

USE the *Bid Final* presentation that is still open from the previous exercise.

1. **SAVE** the presentation as *Bid Kiosk*.
2. On the Slide Show tab, click Set Up Slide Show. The Set Up Show dialog box opens.
3. Examine the settings in the Show Type section, but do not make a change yet.
4. In the Show Options section, mark the Loop continuously until 'Esc' check box.

Take Note   This setting is turned on automatically if you choose Browsed at a kiosk (full screen) as the show type.

5. Click to mark the Show without narration check box.

 Ref   Narrations are recorded when you record a presentation, which is covered later in this lesson.

6. Click to mark the Show without animation check box.
7. Click the Pen Color button, and click the purple square.

Take Note   The pen color is not important for this presentation because it will be self-running, but it's useful for future reference to know how to change it.

8. In the Show Type section, click Browsed at a kiosk.

   Several settings become unavailable when you choose this option, including Loop Continuously Until 'Esc' (which becomes permanently on) and Pen Color. That's why this exercise does not change the show type until after you have tried out those settings.
9. In the Show Slides section, click the Custom Show option button.

Take Note   The Corporate Information custom show is automatically selected because it is the only custom show in the presentation.

10. In the Advance Slides section, click the Use timings, if present option button. The dialog box should look like Figure 7-16 at this point.

Figure 7-16

The Set Up Show dialog box with custom settings applied

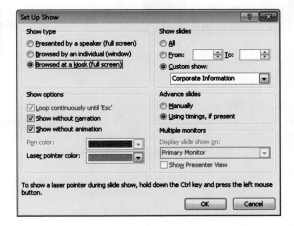

Take Note   If you have multiple monitors, the controls in the Multiple Monitors section will be available. (They are not available in Figure 7-17.) With multiple monitors, you can mark the Show Presenter View check box, so that one monitor displays presenter controls (including speaker notes) and the other monitor displays the slides in full-screen mode.

11. Click OK. The dialog box closes.

12. Examine the check boxes in the Set Up group on the Slide Show tab.

    Notice that the Play Narrations check box is cleared because of the check box you marked in step 3.

    Notice that the Timings check box is marked because of the option button you chose in step 8.

13. Clear the Show Media Controls check box.

    This setting is not directly applicable to this presentation because it has no video or audio clips in it. However, knowing how to turn on/off the onscreen controls for such clips is useful for future reference.

14. **SAVE** the presentation.

PAUSE. LEAVE the presentation file open to use in the next exercise.

SOFTWARE ORIENTATION

Presentation Tools in Slide Show View

When in Slide Show view, presentation tools appear in the bottom left corner of the screen. They are faint until you point at them; then they become bright icons that you can click to open menus. In Figure 7-17 the Menu button is active and its menu is open.

Figure 7-17

The presentation tools

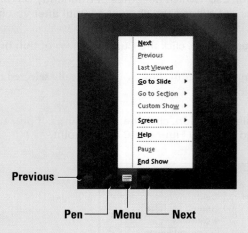

You can also display a navigation menu by right-clicking anywhere on the slide. The right-click menu contains an additional command, Pointer Options, which opens the same menu as the Pen button in the presentation tools.

WORKING WITH PRESENTATION TOOLS

The Bottom Line

PowerPoint offers a number of **presentation tools** you can use during a presentation to control the display of slides and mark directly on the slides if desired. You can use keyboard commands, mouse clicks, presentation tools, or menu commands to control the presentation. You can select from several marking options and colors to annotate your slides during the presentation.

Moving Through a Presentation

There are many ways to move through a presentation's slides. You can simply click to move from start to finish, ignoring any hidden slides. If you want to jump around to other slides that are not in the default sequence, you can use the navigation menu, keyboard shortcuts, or other techniques. In this exercise, you will practice moving through a presentation.

PowerPoint provides many methods so that you can use the tools that are most comfortable for you to go forward, backward, or to a specific slide. Table 7-1 summarizes the most popular navigation options in Slide Show view.

Table 7-1

Navigation Options in Slide Show View

Action	Keyboard	Mouse	Shortcut menu
Show the next slide or animation	N Enter Spacebar Page down Right arrow	Left mouse button	Next
Show the previous slide or animation	P Page up Backspace Left arrow		Previous
Go to the last slide viewed			Last Viewed
Go to a specific slide	Type slide number and press Enter		Go to Slide, then click slide title
End show	Esc		End Show

If you have chosen the *Browsed by an individual (window)* show type in the Set Up Show dialog box (Figure 7-16), the presentation tools at the lower-left corner of the screen do not display and you cannot use the mouse button to go to the next slide. You can use the keyboard options to go to the next or previous slide, or you can use the Next Slide and Previous Slide buttons on the scrollbar if you have chosen to display it. You can also right-click the slide and select Advance to move forward or Reverse to move backward through slides.

STEP BY STEP | **Move through a Presentation**

1. **REOPEN** the *Bid Final* presentation you worked with earlier in this lesson.

Take Note

An easy way to reopen Bid Final is: click the File tab, click Recent, and click the *Bid Final* file at the top of the list of recent files.

Another Way
You can also start the presentation from the beginning by pressing F5.

2. To confirm that all rehearsed timings are removed, click the Slide Show tab, click Record Slide Show, and, if it is available, click Clear. If the Clear command is unavailable, the timings have already been removed.

3. Click the From Beginning button to start the presentation from slide 1.

4. Move the pointer on the slide until you can see the presentation tools in the lower-left corner of the screen, as shown in Figure 7-17.

Another Way
To go to the next slide if it is hidden, you can press H.

5. Click the Next button (the right-pointing arrow at the far right of the tools). The next slide displays.

6. Click the Previous button (the left-pointing arrow at the far left of the tools). Slide 1 redisplays.

7. Right-click anywhere on the slide to display the presentation shortcut menu, point to **Go to Slide**, and then click the hidden slide, **(2) Our Mission**, as shown in Figure 7-18. The hidden slide displays.

Figure 7-18

Right-click the slide to display the menu, and then point at Go to Slide and click the desired slide

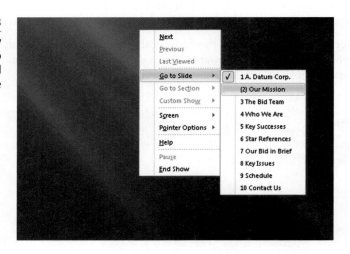

8. Press **Page Down** to display the next slide.

Another Way
You can also end the show by pressing Esc.

9. Click the **Menu** button in the presentation tools (the third button from the left) to display a menu similar to the presentation shortcut menu, and then click **Last Viewed**. The slide you previously viewed (slide 2) displays.

10. Right-click the screen again, then click **End Show** on the presentation shortcut menu to end the presentation.

PAUSE. LEAVE the presentation open to use in the next exercise.

As you work with PowerPoint, you will find that you develop a feel for the navigation tools that you find easiest to use. It is often more efficient, for example, to use keyboard options because they can be quicker than right-clicking and selecting options from shortcut menus.

Annotating Slides with the Pen or Highlighter

As you proceed through a presentation, you may want to pause to emphasize certain points. You can **annotate** (write) directly on a slide with the annotation tools in PowerPoint. You can control these tools, including setting the color and width of the onscreen pen, via the Pen menu in the presentation tools (refer back to Figure 7-16). Various pen types, thicknesses, and colors are available. In the following exercise, you create ink annotations during a slide show.

PowerPoint offers three different annotation pen options: Ball Point Pen, Felt Tip Pen, and Highlighter. These pen options have pointer sizes that roughly correspond to the actual writing instruments. You can change the ink color for any of the pen options.

The Black Screen and White Screen options allow you to replace the current slide with a black or white screen that you can use for annotations or to cover the current material if you want to keep it under wraps while you are discussing some other issue.

STEP BY STEP   **Annotate Slides**

USE the *Bid Final* presentation that is still open from the previous exercise.

Another Way
You can also right-click, point to Go to Slide, and select slide 7.

1. Press **F5** to start the presentation from slide 1, type **7**, and press **Enter**. Slide 7 appears.
2. Click the mouse button until all seven bullet items display on the slide.
3. Right-click the slide, point to **Pointer Options**, and click **Felt Tip Pen**. The pointer changes to a small, round, red pen pointer.
4. Right-click the slide, point to **Pointer Options**, and click **Ink Color**. Then click **Orange** in the Standard Colors palette.
5. Use the pen pointer to circle the value for site preparation, $1,125,500, as shown in Figure 7-19.

Figure 7-19

Make an annotation on a slide

Another Way
You can also use any other method of advancing the presentation to display all bullet points, such as pressing Enter, spacebar, or the right arrow key. This exercise uses a variety of navigation methods for practice.

Troubleshooting If you click too many times and advance to slide 8, press Backspace, Page Up, or the left arrow key to return to slide 7.

6. Press the **B** key on the keyboard. The screen is blacked out so you can annotate without the distraction of the slide material.
7. Use the pen pointer to draw a large U.S. currency symbol ($) in the middle of the slide.

Take Note   While a pen pointer is active, you cannot use the mouse button to advance slides.

8. Right-click the slide, point to **Screen**, and click **Unblack Screen**. The slide background is restored and the annotation disappears.
9. Click the **Pointer Options** button in the presentation tools (the second tool from the left) and click **Arrow**. The arrow pointer is restored.

Another Way
Press Esc to restore the arrow pointer.

10. Click or press **Enter** to go to slide 8.
11. Click or press **Enter** eight times to display all eight bullet items.

12. Click the **Pointer Options** button in the presentation tools, and then click **Highlighter**. Drag the highlighter pointer across the *Weather* bullet item to highlight it, as shown in Figure 7-20.

Figure 7-20

Highlighting text on a slide

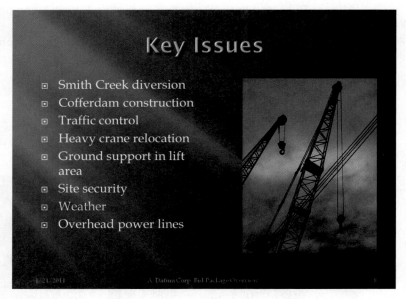

Another Way
Press E to remove all annotations on a slide.

13. Click the **Pointer Options** button, and then click **Erase All Ink on Slide**. The highlight you added is removed.

14. End the slide show. When asked if you want to keep your annotations, click **Keep**.

15. **SAVE** the presentation.

PAUSE. LEAVE the presentation open to use in the next exercise.

When you reach the end of the presentation (or end it early), if you have created any annotations, you are prompted to either save or discard them. If you save them, they are saved on the slide as **ink**, which is similar to a drawing you might do with the Shapes tool.

Editing Ink Annotations

You can move and delete individual annotations on slides as you would any other graphics, and you can also manage ink with the Ink Tools Pens tab. In the following exercise, you edit an ink annotation in Normal view and add a new annotation there.

STEP BY STEP   **Edit Ink Annotations**

USE the *Bid Final* presentation that is still open from the previous exercise.

1. In Normal view, display slide 7 and click the orange circle you drew as an annotation. Notice that both the Drawing Tools and Ink Tools contextual tabs appear on the Ribbon.

2. Click the **Ink Tools Pens** tab to examine the options available (see Figure 7-21).

Figure 7-21

Ink Tools Pens tab on the Ribbon

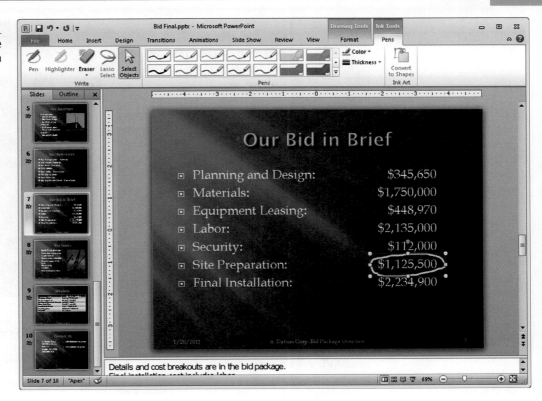

3. Click the **Color** button to open its palette, and click **Light Green**. The selected annotation changes color.

4. Click the **Thickness** button to open its menu, and click 3 pt. The selected annotation increases in thickness.

5. Click the **More** button in the Pens group to open a gallery of pen styles. See Figure 7-22.

Figure 7-22

Gallery of pen styles

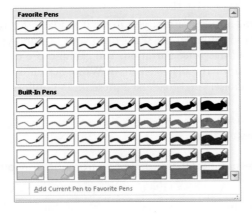

6. In the Built-In Pens section, click **Red Pen (1.0 mm)**.

Notice that the selected annotation does not change. These pen styles are for creating new annotations, not editing existing ones.

7. Drag to draw an underline beneath Site Preparation. See Figure 7-23.

Figure 7-23

Draw an additional annotation

8. On the Ink Tools Pens tab, click the Select Objects button to return to using the arrow pointer again.

9. **SAVE** the presentation.

PAUSE. LEAVE the presentation open to use in the next exercise.

BROADCASTING A PRESENTATION

The Bottom Line

Broadcasting a presentation over the Internet makes it possible for people to see the presentation who may not be able to attend in person. A broadcast is still a live show with a live speaker, but is delivered remotely.

Broadcasting a Presentation

When you **broadcast** a presentation, you make it available for people to watch online. You control the sequence and timing of the slides from your PC, and you can optionally speak into your microphone to add live voice narration. You can also use the ink annotation tools, pause or resume the show, and use the Black Screen or White Screen options or any other Slide Show view feature. In this exercise, you broadcast a presentation online.

STEP BY STEP | **Broadcast a Presentation**

USE the *Bid Final* presentation that is still open from the previous exercise.

1. If you do not have a Windows Live user ID, go to http://www.live.com and get one.

2. In PowerPoint, on the Slide Show tab, click Broadcast Slide Show. The Broadcast Slide Show dialog box opens.

Take Note

You must have a Windows Live ID to broadcast a presentation using the PowerPoint Broadcast Service. If you want to use some other service to broadcast your presentation, you can click Change Broadcast Service and specify one. Some large companies may have their own broadcast service.

3. Click **Start Broadcast**. A dialog box appears to log into Windows Live. See Figure 7-24.

Figure 7-24

Log into Windows Live

4. Enter your Windows Live login information and click **OK**. You are logged into the broadcast server. After a short wait, a link appears that you can share with audience members, as shown in Figure 7-25. The link you receive will be different from the one shown.

Figure 7-25

Share the link with audience members

5. (Optional) If you know people who want to see your broadcast, give them the link.

You can do this by clicking Send in Email and emailing them the link, or by distributing the link in some other method, such as manually writing it down on paper. You do not have to have any audience members in order to practice broadcasting, however.

Take Note

To see how a broadcast presentation looks when viewed remotely, team up with a classmate and take turns watching each other's shows.

6. Click **Start Slide Show**. The slide show opens in Slide Show view. You are now broadcasting.

7. Move through the presentation as you normally would. You can optionally use your microphone to comment on the slide content or read it aloud as you go. Figure 7-26 shows how a presentation broadcast looks to someone using Internet Explorer to view the link you provided to them.

Figure 7-26

A PowerPoint broadcast viewed
in Internet Explorer

User can click
here to watch
in full-screen
mode.

8. When you reach the last slide, click one more time to exit, returning to Normal view.
PAUSE. LEAVE the presentation open to use in the next exercise.

RECORDING A PRESENTATION

The Bottom Line

If you can't reach an audience in real time with your presentation, recording the presentation for later playback is an attractive option. You can record a presentation with or without narration (recorded audio commentary), annotations, and other features. You can also record the presentation from start to finish or re-record individual slides.

Recording an Entire Presentation

Recording a presentation, like broadcasting, helps you share your work remotely. The difference is that, with a recording, the audience does not need to be watching it live. They can view your presentation at their convenience. Recording a presentation saves narration, annotations, and timings. It does not create a separate file as a recording; all those settings are saved in the regular PowerPoint file. In the following exercise, you record a presentation from start to finish.

Take Note

In order to record narration, you will need a computer that has sound support and a microphone. You should set up and test the microphone ahead of time in Windows. In Windows 7, click Start, type microphone, and then click the Set Up a Microphone link at the top of the Start menu. Follow the prompts to prepare the microphone for recording.

STEP BY STEP   **Record a Presentation from the Beginning**

USE the *Bid Final* presentation that is still open from the previous exercise.

1. On the Slide Show tab, click the Record Slide Show button. The Record Slide Show dialog box opens, as shown in Figure 7-27.

Figure 7-27

The Record Slide Show dialog box

2. Make sure your microphone is ready.

3. Click **OK** to begin the recording.

4. Click through the presentation, reading the text of the slides into the microphone at a moderate pace. The Rehearsal toolbar appears as you work through the presentation, the same as when rehearsing timings.

Take Note   If you flub the narration when recording, keep going. You can re-record individual slides after you are finished.

5. When you reach the end of the presentation, click one more time to return to Normal view.

PAUSE. LEAVE the presentation open to use in the next exercise.

Recording the Current Slide

If you make a mistake in recording a certain slide, you can re-record it. In the following exercise, you re-record a single slide.

STEP BY STEP   **Record a Presentation from the Current Slide**

USE the *Bid Final* presentation that is still open from the previous exercise.

1. Display slide 8.

2. On the Slide Show tab, click the arrow under the Record Slide Show button and click **Start Recording from Current Slide**. The Record Slide Show dialog box opens.

3. Click **Start Recording**.

4. Click to advance the bullet points on slide 8 at a moderate speed, while reading the text for slide 8 into the microphone.

5. Instead of advancing to the next slide, press **Esc** to quit recording. PowerPoint returns to Normal view.

PAUSE. LEAVE the presentation open to use in the next exercise.

PACKAGING A PRESENTATION FOR CD DELIVERY

The Bottom Line   You may need to transport your presentation materials to another computer to run your slide show. The Package for CD feature streamlines the process of packing all the materials you need to show the presentation even if PowerPoint is not installed on the other computer.

Packaging a Presentation for CD

The Package for CD feature makes short work of packing all the files you need to show your slides, no matter what kind of system you have to use to run the show. It also provides a Web page interface that users can employ to watch the show via Web browser if they do not have PowerPoint. In this exercise, you create a version of your presentation on a CD that you can distribute to others.

Take Note   Previous versions of PowerPoint packaged presentations to CD along with a PowerPoint Viewer utility. PowerPoint 2010, however, takes a different approach; it packages presentations with a Web page on the CD. On this Web page is a link for downloading the PowerPoint viewer if it is needed. If you plan on showing the presentation somewhere that does not have Internet access, make sure you download the PowerPoint viewer ahead of time on the computer you will be working with if it does not have a full version of PowerPoint on it.

STEP BY STEP	Package a Presentation for CD

Take Note   You must have a writeable CD drive inserted in your system to complete this exercise. If you do not, or if you do not have a blank writeable CD disc available, skip this exercise.

USE the *Bid Final* presentation that is still open from the previous exercise.

1. Insert a blank writeable CD disc in your writeable CD drive. If an **AutoPlay** box pops up, close it.
2. Click the **File** tab, click **Save & Send**, click **Package Presentation for CD**, and click **Package for CD**. The Package for CD dialog box opens.
3. In the Name the CD box, type **Bid**, replacing the default name. See Figure 7-28.

Figure 7-28

Package for CD dialog box

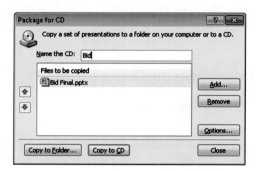

Take Note   You can optionally add other presentations onto the same CD to avoid using a separate CD for each presentation. To add other presentations, you would click Add and select the presentations to include. You could then reorder them with the up and down arrow buttons in the dialog box. This exercise packages only one presentation on CD, so it does not include these actions.

4. Click the **Options** button. The Options dialog box opens. Note that linked files are marked to be included, and TrueType fonts will be embedded. Note that you can also optionally specify passwords to control access to the presentation(s). See Figure 7-29.

Figure 7-29

The Options dialog box for packaging a presentation

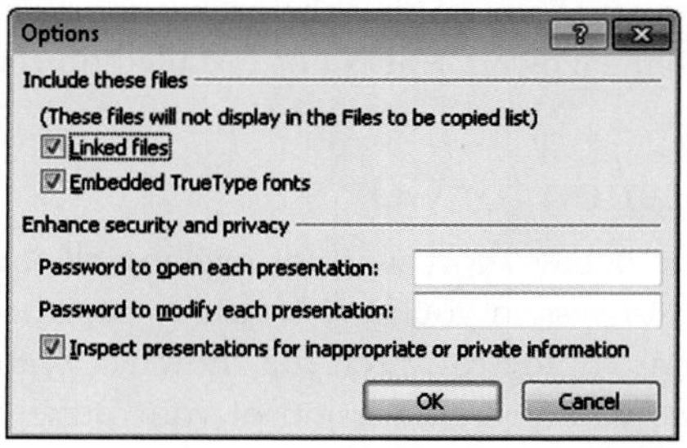

5. Click **OK** to accept the default settings and close the Options dialog box.
6. In the Package for CD dialog box, click **Copy to CD**.
7. A dialog box asks if you want to include linked files in your package. Click **Yes**.

8. A message appears that the presentation contains comments or annotations, stating that these will not be included. Click **Continue**.

9. Wait for the presentation to be written to the CD. It may take several minutes. The CD ejects when finished.

10. In PowerPoint, a message appears stating that the files were successfully copied to CD and offering to copy the same files to another CD. Click **No**.

11. Click **Close** to close the Package for CD dialog box.

12. To test your new CD, reinsert the CD into your computer. If an Auto Play box opens, click **Run PresentationPackage.html**. If no box opens, click the **Start** button, click **Computer**, and double-click the CD drive.

13. A Web page displays, showing a page that lists the presentations on the CD. (There is only one in this case.) A link also appears in the upper-right corner for downloading the PowerPoint Viewer (see Figure 7-30). You do not need it on your PC since you have the full version of PowerPoint.

Figure 7-30

The Web interface for a presentation CD

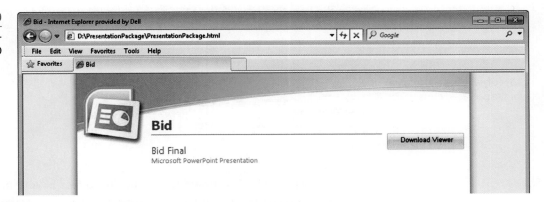

14. Click the name of the presentation (**Bid Final**). Respond to any security warnings you might see in your Web browser. The presentation opens in PowerPoint, in Protected View.

15. Click the **File** tab and click **Close** to close the copy of the presentation that originated from the CD. (The original *Bid Final* presentation is still open.)

PAUSE. LEAVE the presentation open to use in the next exercise.

To make the process of storing files on a CD more efficient, you can choose to copy more than one presentation to the same CD. Click the Add Files button to open additional presentations. This feature can reduce the amount of wasted space that results if you copy a single presentation to a CD.

The Options dialog box that you can access from the Package for CD dialog box gives you additional choices for the packaging process:

- Linked files, such as large movie and sound files, are included automatically, and you will normally want to retain this setting. You can, however, save the package without linked files if desired by deselecting this option.

- Embedding TrueType fonts is a good idea if you are not sure what fonts you might have access to on the system where you will run the presentation. Embedding fonts will add to file size but ensure the quality of your presentation's font appearance.

- You can specify a password to open or modify the presentation, and you can prompt PowerPoint to inspect the presentation for hidden or personal data you do not want to share.

Take Note

Package for CD works only with CD formats. If you want to store a presentation on a DVD, you can save materials in a folder as in step 8 of the previous exercise, and then use your system's DVD burning tools to copy the files to the DVD.

Packaging a Presentation to a Folder

In addition to using Package for CD to create materials to transport a presentation, you can use this feature to archive presentations onto a CD or into folders for storage. The packaging process pulls together all the files you need for a presentation, so your stored presentation provides an excellent long-term backup for your work. In this exercise, you package a presentation to a folder.

STEP BY STEP   **Package a Presentation to a Folder**

USE the *Bid Final* presentation that is still open from the previous exercise.

1. Click the File tab, click Save & Send, click Package Presentation for CD, and click Package for CD. The Package for CD dialog box opens.
2. Click Copy to Folder. The Copy to Folder dialog box opens.
3. In the Folder name box, change the default name to *Bid Proposal*.
4. In the Location box, change the path to the location where you store files for this lesson (see Figure 7-31).

Figure 7-31

Specify a folder and location for the packaged presentation

5. Click OK.
6. A dialog box asks if you want to include linked files in your package. Click Yes.
7. A message appears that the presentation contains comments or annotations, and that these will not be included. Click Continue.
8. Wait for the presentation to be written to the new folder. It should occur almost instantaneously (unlike when making a CD). The folder opens in Windows when it is finished. See Figure 7-32.

Figure 7-32

The packaged presentation in a folder

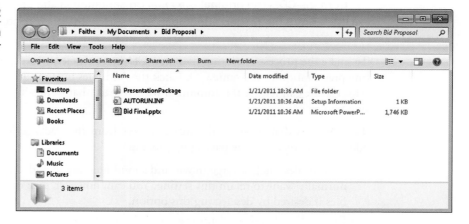

9. In the folder window, double-click the PresentationPackage folder to see what's inside it. The folder contains some graphics and support files that are needed to show the Web page (shown in Figure 7-30).
10. Close the folder window and return to PowerPoint. The Package for CD dialog box is still open.
11. Click Close to close the dialog box.
12. **SAVE** the presentation and then **CLOSE** the file.

EXIT PowerPoint.

SKILL SUMMARY

In This Lesson, You Learned How To:
Adjust slide orientation and size
Customize audience handouts
Choose slides to display
Rehearse your delivery
Set up a slide show
Work with presentation tools
Broadcast a presentation
Record a presentation
Package a presentation for CD delivery

Knowledge Assessment

Fill in the Blank

Fill in each blank with the term or phrase that best completes the statement.

1. Use the _____ dialog box to adjust slide size.

2. You can set up a presentation to loop continuously until you press the _____ key.

3. Use the _____ toolbar to view timings as you rehearse a presentation.

4. For more control over handouts, you can export them to _____ .

5. To display a hidden slide during a presentation, click _____ on the shortcut menu and then click the hidden slide.

6. If the computer on which you will present your slides does not have PowerPoint, you can use the _____ to show the presentation.

7. Customize the _____ to create your own handout layouts.

8. If you want to show your presentation on a projection screen, you can use a(n) _____ that accepts input from your computer.

9. When you _____ slides, you use the pointer to draw or write.

10. _____ a presentation to deliver it in real time over the Internet.

Multiple Choice

Circle the correct answer.

1. A slide that is wider than it is tall is displayed in:
   a. portrait orientation.
   b. column orientation.
   c. picture orientation.
   d. landscape orientation.

2. If you need to show slides on a wide-screen monitor, you might change their size to:
   a. Onscreen Show (16:9).
   b. Onscreen Show (3:4).
   c. 35 mm Slides.
   d. Ledger Paper (11×17 in).

3. Which of these is not one of the standard placeholders on the Handout Master?
   a. Date
   b. Header
   c. Page Number
   d. Author

4. To prevent a slide from displaying during a presentation, select it and then choose:
   a. Delete Slide.
   b. Hide Slide.
   c. Show/Hide Slide.
   d. Conceal Slide.

5. If you want to show only a selected series of slides from a presentation, the most efficient option is to:
   a. hide each slide you do not want to use.
   b. create an entirely new presentation and copy into it the slides you want to use.
   c. create a custom show of the slides you want to show.
   d. copy the presentation and then delete the slides you do not want to use.

6. When you rehearse timings, you should:
   a. skim over the content of each slide.
   b. read the entire content of each slide and look carefully at pictures and diagrams.
   c. allow yourself a set amount of time to view each slide regardless of its content.
   d. look only at the slide titles.

7. If you set up a slide show to be browsed by an individual, the slides display:
   a. using the full screen.
   b. in a virtual kiosk.
   c. in a window with a title bar.
   d. within the PowerPoint window.

8. Which of the following is *not* a way to advance to the next slide during a presentation?
   a. Press Home
   b. Press the spacebar
   c. Click the left mouse button
   d. Press Page Down

9. A quick way to restore the arrow pointer after you have used it for drawing is to:
   a. press End.
   b. double-click the screen.
   c. click the arrow pointer tool in the navigation tools.
   d. press Esc.

10. Package for CD can also package a presentation to
   a. a Web address.
   b. a printer.
   c. a folder on your hard disk.
   d. None of the above

Competency Assessment

Project 7-1: Preparing to Fly

You are nearly ready to present the slide show for Blue Yonder Airlines. Use the tools you have learned about in this lesson to finalize the presentation and create handouts.

GET READY. Launch PowerPoint if it is not already running.

 The *Airline* file is available on the book companion website or in WileyPLUS.

1. **OPEN** the *Airline* presentation and save it as *Airline Final.*
2. Click the Design tab, click the Slide Orientation button, and click Landscape.
3. Click the Page Setup button, click the Slides sized for drop-down arrow, and click On-screen Show (4:3). Click OK to close the dialog box.
4. Click the Slide Show tab, and then click the Set Up Slide Show button.
5. Choose the *Presented by a speaker* show type, clear the *Loop continuously until 'Esc'* check box, and choose to have slides advance Manually. Click OK to accept the new settings.
6. Click the Insert tab, click Header & Footer, and for Notes and Handouts, choose to display the date (update automatically), the header *Blue Yonder Airlines*, and page numbers. Click Apply to All to apply the setting to all slides.
7. Click the View tab, and then click Handout Master to open Handout Master view.
8. Center the header text and date in their placeholders, and right-align the page number in its placeholder. Close Handout Master view.
9. Hide the last slide in the presentation.
10. Click the File tab, click Print, and set the following print options:
    a. Choose to print handouts with four slides per page, in vertical order.
    b. In the Slides settings, deselect the *Frame* option.
    c. In the Print All Slides settings, deselect the *Print hidden slides* option.
11. Print the handouts.
12. **SAVE** the presentation and **CLOSE** the file.

LEAVE PowerPoint open for use in the next project.

Project 7-2: Twin Cities Crawl

You are ready to finalize the presentation you created to publicize the Twin Cities Gallery Crawl. You need to rehearse and set up the show and then package the presentation for delivery.

 The *Galleries* file is available on the book companion website or in WileyPLUS.

1. **OPEN** the *Galleries* presentation and save it as *Galleries Final.*
2. Click the Slide Show tab, and then click the Rehearse Timings button.
3. Read each slide. When the slide show ends, choose to save the rehearsed timings.
4. Click the Set Up Slide Show button, and set up the show to be browsed at a kiosk using the timings you saved to advance slides. Click OK to close the dialog box.
5. Click the File tab, click Save & Send, click Package Presentation for CD, and click Package for CD.
6. Type the package name Galleries. If you can copy to a CD, click Copy to CD and complete the packaging process. If you cannot copy to a CD, click Copy to Folder, select the folder in which you are storing solutions for Lesson 11, and complete the packaging process.
7. Close the Package for CD dialog box.
8. **SAVE** the presentation and then **CLOSE** the file.

LEAVE PowerPoint open for the next project.

Project 7-3: Final Airline Check

You want to run through the Airline Final presentation before delivering it to make sure you are familiar with content and how to display it during the slide show.

1. **OPEN** the *Airline Final* presentation you created in Project 7-1.
2. Hide slide 7.
3. Press F5 to view the presentation from slide 1.
4. Use the Next button in the presentation tools to move to slide 3.
5. Use the Previous button in the presentation tools to go backward to slide 1.
6. Right-click the slide to display the shortcut menu, and use Go to Slide to jump to slide 4.
7. Right-click the slide, click Pointer Options, and select the highlighter.
8. Highlight the bullet items *Caribbean* and *Scuba*.
9. Restore the arrow pointer and press Esc to end the show. Choose to save your annotations.
10. Rehearse timings for the presentation. When the presentation ends, save the slide timings.
11. Set up the slide show to use the slide timings you saved.
12. **SAVE** the presentation as *Airline Final Check* and then **CLOSE** the file.

LEAVE PowerPoint open for use in the next project.

Project 7-4: Year-End Review

You are ready to do the final tweaking of the year-end review for Contoso's Human Resources department. You will create a custom show to send to Contoso's president and CEO, customize handouts for the year-end review meeting, and adjust slide size for printing.

@ The *Review* file is available on the book companion website or in WileyPLUS.

1. **OPEN** the *Review* presentation and save it as *Review Custom*.
2. Create a custom show named Review Summary. Include in the custom show slides 1, 3, 4, 6, 7, 9, 10, and 12.
3. Change the slide size to Letter Paper (8.5 × 11 in).
4. Display a date that updates, the header *Contoso HR Year in Review*, and page numbers for all handouts and notes pages.
5. Display the handout master, and show the 3 Slides layout.
6. Select the Header and Date placeholders, center the text in these placeholders, and adjust the vertical alignment in these placeholders to Middle. (Hint: Use Align Text on the Home tab to set Middle alignment.)
7. Reduce the width of each placeholder (both at the top and the bottom of the handout layout) to 2.5 inches wide. (Hint: Use the Width box on the Drawing Tools Format tab.)
8. Move the Header and Date placeholders down about a quarter of an inch from the top of the page.
9. Center the Header placeholder over the slide image column, and center the Date placeholder over the empty column where the lines will appear to the right of the slide images. (You can check placement by displaying the handouts in Print Preview.)
10. Apply the Colored Outline, Red, Accent 2 shape style (from the Drawing Tools Format tab) to the Header and Date placeholders. Figure 7-33 shows the completed layout.

Figure 7-33

The modified handout layout

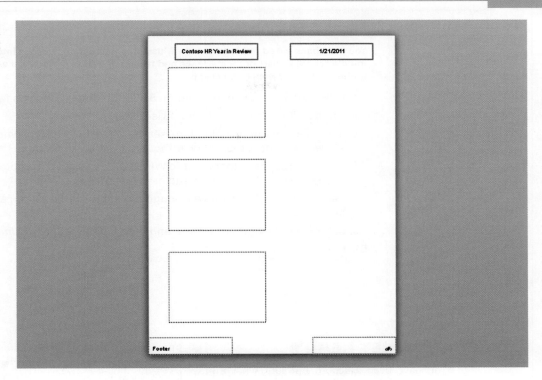

11. Print handouts with three slides per page.

12. **SAVE** the presentation.

LEAVE the presentation open for use the next project.

Mastery Assessment

Project 7-5: Review Final

You need to complete your preparation of the Review Custom presentation and test it before you send it to the HR executive staff.

1. **USE** the file from the previous exercise, and **SAVE** the presentation as *Review Final*.

2. Set the slides for normal screen 4:3 screen display.

3. Set up the slide show to display only the Review Summary custom show for an individual. Turn on the Show Without Animation option, and choose to advance slides manually.

4. Start the slide show from slide 1 and view the slides in the custom show, using keyboard options to advance slides.

5. **SAVE** the presentation and then **CLOSE** the file.

LEAVE PowerPoint open for use in the next project.

Project 7-6: Museum Broadcast

You have been asked to broadcast the Museum presentation over the Internet to some students at a middle school as part of their science and technology class project. You will prepare the presentation for broadcast and then broadcast it.

The *Museum* file is available on the book companion website or in WileyPLUS.

1. **OPEN** the *Museum* presentation. **SAVE** the presentation as *Museum Final*.
2. On the Slide Show tab, turn off Use Timings.
3. In the Set Up Show dialog box, set the Show Type to *Presented by a speaker (full screen)* and mark the **Show without animation** check box.
4. Begin a broadcast, logging into Windows Live when prompted. When the link appears to share, send it to your instructor in an email message.
5. Begin the broadcast. Move through the entire presentation, and then end the broadcast.
6. **CLOSE** the PowerPoint Viewer, and then **CLOSE** *Museum Final*.

EXIT PowerPoint.

INTERNET READY

You have been asked to find out what kind of equipment you would need to project presentations in a medium-sized conference room using a computer to control the show. Using the Internet, research what type of digital projector and pull-down screen you would need to purchase. Read reviews if possible to locate several options for good-quality components that are neither the most nor least expensive on the market. Create a presentation with your suggestions in a table or diagram. You may also want to research interactive whiteboards as an alternative to the projector-and-screen combination.

Workplace *Ready*

WAY TO PRESENT SLIDES

You have a number of options for projecting your slides when you are ready to give a presentation. The most popular options include projecting slides on a screen and displaying the slides on a computer monitor. You can also use new technology such as interactive whiteboards.

- **Projection options:** Slide projectors used to be noisy machines that shone bright light through 35-mm slides to project the image on a screen. These projectors are still available, as is the technology to create 35-mm slides from your PowerPoint files, but the most current projectors are digital devices that accept input from a computer. You can control the slide show from your computer monitor. When you use a digital projector, you project slides onto a screen.

- **Displaying slides on a computer monitor:** You do not need a projection device to present slides. You can display your presentation on a computer monitor, just as you do when using Slide Show view in PowerPoint. The computer monitor should be large enough for your audience to see the slide material clearly. Many computers allow you to connect more than one monitor to the video card, allowing you to use PowerPoint's Presenter view to control the slide show: the audience views the presentation on one monitor, while you use the other monitor to control the show.

- **Self-running or individual presentations:** You can also set up a presentation to run by itself on a monitor (see the *Setting Up a Slide Show* section earlier in this lesson), allow individuals to view a presentation on their own computers, or broadcast a presentation to viewers over the Internet.

- **Using an interactive whiteboard:** Interactive whiteboards allow you to project or display a presentation (or any other computer application) on a large white surface. The moderator can control slide display by simply touching the screen.

For best results in presenting slide shows from your computer, you should have a high-quality video card, sound card, and speakers. Quality sound and video components will make the most of multimedia files such as sounds and movies and allow transitions and animations to run smoothly.

If you do not have access to current technology, you can fall back on more traditional methods of presenting slides: you can submit PowerPoint files to photographic sources to prepare 35-mm slides that can be used in standard slide projectors. You can also print slides onto clear film to create transparencies that can be used with overhead projectors.

Microsoft® Outlook® 2010

LESSON SKILL MATRIX

In This Lesson, You Will Learn The Following Skills:

Starting Outlook

Working in the Outlook Window

Using Backstage View

Personalizing Outlook

KEY TERMS

- **Backstage view**
- **desktop shortcut**
- **feature**
- **fields**
- **fly-out**
- **folders**
- **gallery**
- **group**
- **item**
- **Navigation Pane**
- **People Pane**
- **Quick Access Toolbar (QAT)**
- **Reading Pane**
- **Ribbon**
- **Screen Tip**
- **Status bar**
- **Title bar**
- **To-Do Bar**

Resort Adventures is a luxury resort. During the summer, activities such as kayaking, canoeing, hiking, and horseback riding are available. In the winter months, visitors enjoy skiing, snowshoeing, and sleigh rides. Partners Mindy Martin and Jon Morris own and operate Resort Adventures. They work hard to ensure that guests enjoy their stay. Employees are well-trained and well-treated professionals. For one week every year, Mindy and Jon close the resort to guests and open the facilities to employees and their families.

Microsoft Outlook is an ideal tool for managing communication with their clients and their staff. Whether you need to send a message to a vendor making a late delivery, look up an old friend's phone number, or schedule a staff meeting, Outlook provides the tools that will save time and make your job easier. In this lesson, you will learn how to customize the Microsoft Outlook environment to suit your needs.

SOFTWARE ORIENTATION

Microsoft Outlook's Opening Screen

Before you begin working in Microsoft Outlook, you need to be familiar with the primary user interface. When you first launch Microsoft Outlook, you will see a screen similar to that in Figure 1-1.

Figure 1-1

The Inbox—Outlook 2010's opening screen

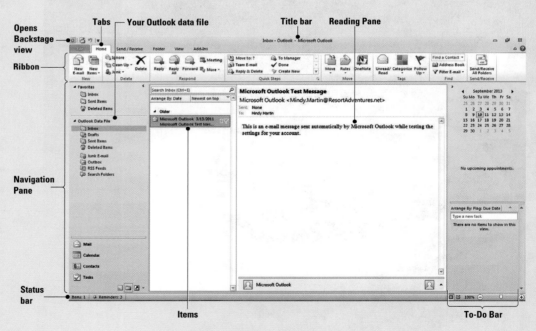

The elements and features of this screen are typical for Microsoft Outlook. Your screen may vary if default settings have been changed or if other preferences have been set. Use this figure as a reference throughout this lesson as well as the rest of this book.

STARTING OUTLOOK

Microsoft Outlook 2010 can be launched in two different ways. You can launch Outlook from the Start button on the Windows taskbar at the bottom of your screen. You can also launch Outlook by double-clicking a shortcut created on the Windows desktop.

Launching Outlook from the Start Menu

As in all Microsoft Office applications, using the Start button may be the most common method of launching Outlook. After Outlook is installed, click the Start button on the Windows taskbar, point to All Programs, point to Microsoft Office, and click Microsoft Office Outlook 2010. In this exercise, you will learn how to launch Outlook from the Start menu and familiarize yourself with the locations of many of Outlook's features.

STEP BY STEP   **Launch Outlook from the Start Menu**

Another Way
You can also locate the Microsoft Outlook link by typing the word Outlook in the Search programs and files box at the bottom of the Start menu.

GET READY. Before you begin these steps, be sure to turn on or log on to your computer.

1. Click the Start button.
2. Click All Programs, then click Microsoft Office. Click Microsoft Outlook 2010. Microsoft Outlook 2010 is launched.
3. Compare your screen to Figure 1-1 and locate each of the labeled elements.
4. Click the Close button in the upper-right corner.

PAUSE. You will launch Outlook again in the next exercise.

Launching Outlook from a Desktop Shortcut

As you saw in the previous exercise, you can launch Outlook from the Start menu. However, if you find that you open Outlook frequently, you might find it easier to create a desktop shortcut. A **desktop shortcut** is an icon placed on the Windows desktop that launches an application, opens a folder, or opens a file. Simply double-click the desktop shortcut to perform the specified action. In the next exercise, you will create an Outlook shortcut and use it to launch Outlook.

STEP BY STEP   **Launch Outlook from a Desktop Shortcut**

GET READY. Before you begin these steps, be sure that Microsoft Outlook is not running.

1. Click the Start button.
2. Click All Programs, then click Microsoft Office. Right-click Microsoft Outlook 2010. Point to Send To. Click the Desktop (create shortcut) option. The desktop shortcut shown in Figure 1-2 is created and appears on your desktop.

Figure 1-2

Desktop shortcut for Microsoft Outlook 2010

3. Minimize any applications so you can see the desktop.
4. Double-click the Microsoft Outlook 2010 desktop shortcut. Microsoft Outlook 2010 is launched.

PAUSE. LEAVE Outlook open to use in the next exercise.

As you have just seen, Outlook can be launched in two different ways. Use the method you prefer.

- Click the Start button on the Windows taskbar, point to All Programs, point to Microsoft Office, and click Microsoft Outlook 2010.
- Double-click the desktop shortcut.

Take Note   Once you've created a desktop shortcut for Outlook, you can right-click the shortcut and pin it to the taskbar for even more convenience, or click the shortcut and drag it down to your taskbar. Just click once on your new Outlook taskbar icon to launch Outlook and get to work.

In the previous exercise, you launched Microsoft Outlook. Outlook opens to your mailbox when launched, as shown in Figure 1-1. By default, the Outlook mailbox is divided into five main sections: the Ribbon, the Navigation Pane, the message list, the Reading Pane, and the To-Do Bar. You can use Outlook's onscreen tools to control the Outlook environment and access Outlook's features.

WORKING IN THE OUTLOOK WINDOW

The Bottom Line

Outlook has a variety of tools that help you organize your communication and manage your time. The Outlook 2010 window was designed to help you get your work done as quickly and efficiently as possible. In this section, you'll explore the Ribbon, which displays common commands in groups arranged by tabs. You will also learn about other onscreen tools to help you get your work done faster, such as the To-Do Bar and the Navigation Pane.

Using the Onscreen Tools

Outlook's onscreen tools enable you to access and control all of Outlook's features. To get the most out of Outlook, you'll want to familiarize yourself with each of the onscreen tools. The two tools that you'll be using most frequently are the Navigation Pane and the Ribbon. The **Navigation Pane** includes tools that help you navigate through Outlook's features, such as your mailbox, Calendar, notes, etc. When you hover your cursor over any command, a **ScreenTip** appears providing a brief description of the command's purpose in a small, pop-up text box. As you click buttons or select menu commands, the Outlook window changes to display the information you requested or to provide space to enter new information. The **Ribbon** contains the most commonly used commands and buttons you need for each of Outlook's features. These commands are sorted into **groups** of related commands. In this exercise, you'll use Outlook's onscreen tools to take a quick look at the Outlook features.

STEP BY STEP   **Use the Onscreen Tools**

GET READY. LAUNCH Outlook if it is not already running.

Take Note   We've added some content to the screens in this section so that you can see how your content will appear. Your screen will look different if default settings have been changed or other content has been added to your PC. Use these figures as a reference.

1. Locate the Navigation Pane. The Navigation Pane is located on the far left of the screen. The bottom third of this pane contains tools that help you access each of Outlook's primary functions, such as the Calendar and the Contacts list.
2. Click the Calendar button in the Navigation Pane. The Calendar is displayed showing today's date, as shown in Figure 1-3.

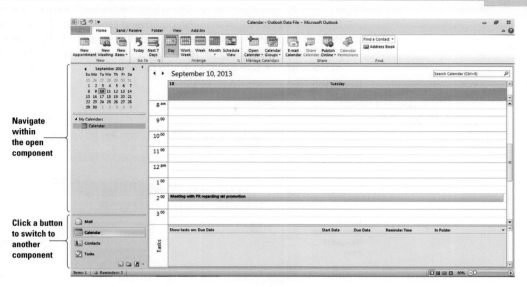

Figure 1-3

Outlook 2010 Calendar

Take Note

Notice that the top two-thirds of the Navigation Pane have changed. This section updates automatically to provide you with tools for navigating with the selected Outlook component, which in this case is the Calendar.

Another Way
You can also access Outlook Calendar by using the keyboard shortcut Ctrl+2.

3. Point to the small left-facing arrow at the top of the Navigation Pane. A ScreenTip appears identifying the arrow as the Minimize the Navigation Pane button (Figure 1-4). These minimize buttons are often referred to as collapse buttons.

Figure 1-4

Using ScreenTips

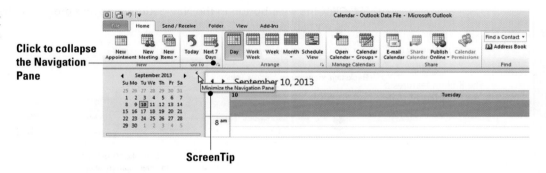

4. Click the Minimize the Navigation button in the Navigation Pane. The Navigation Pane collapses to show more of the Calendar, as shown in Figure 1-5.

Figure 1-5

Collapsed navigation

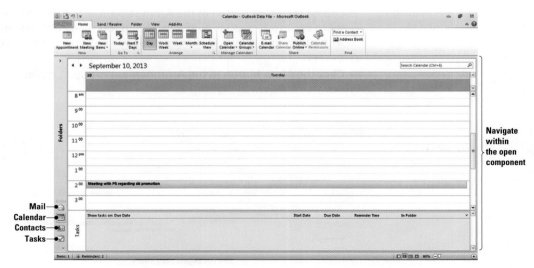

5. Click the word Folders on the collapsed Navigation Pane. A fly-out of the Navigation Pane is displayed showing you all the information in the Pane, as shown in Figure 1-6. A **fly-out** is a menu or pane that opens floating above the main window, instead of docked to a fixed place on the screen, which changes the way every other pane appears.

Figure 1-6

Fly-out Navigation Pane

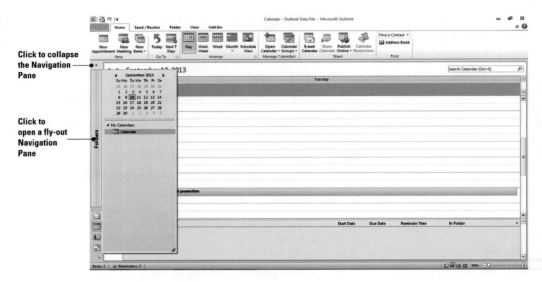

6. Click Folders again to remove the fly-out. Click the expand arrow on the Navigation Pane. The full Navigation Pane is restored.

7. Click the Mail button in the Navigation Pane and then click the View tab on the Ribbon, as shown in Figure 1-7.

Figure 1-7

The Ribbon features a variety of tools

Another Way
You can also access Outlook Mail by using the keyboard shortcut Ctrl+1.

8. Click the collapse arrow on the Ribbon. The Ribbon collapses into a single bar showing only the tab names. Click the expand arrow to restore the Ribbon.

9. Locate the More button in the Arrangement group. The More button tells you that there are more options available. When too many options are available to store neatly as buttons in a group, Outlook places the buttons in a dropdown window called a **gallery**.

10. Click the More button in the Arrangement group. A gallery of available views drops down, as shown in Figure 1-8.

Figure 1-8

The Arrangement gallery displayed

11. Click the **Home** tab. Click the **New E-mail** button in the New group. A window is displayed, as shown in Figure 1-9. Notice that it has its own Ribbon. The Ribbon is divided into tabs based on the type of options available. The options on each tab are organized into groups of similar commands.

Figure 1-9

The Untitled-Message window

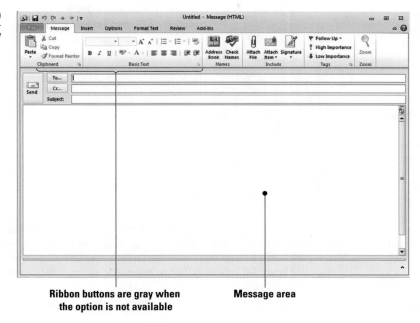

Ribbon buttons are gray when   Message area
the option is not available

12. Notice that most of the buttons in the Clipboard and Basic Text groups are gray. When buttons on the Ribbon are gray, it means that the option is not available. Since this message window contains no text, the options for formatting and working with text are not available.

 Ref   You'll learn more about working with e-mail messages in Lesson 2.

13. Click in the message area. Most of the buttons on the Ribbon are now available in preparation for entering text.

14. In the message area, key **Hello World**. The Ribbon fills with color as options become available. The Undo button also appears on the Quick Access Toolbar, as shown in Figure 1-10.

15. Click the **Undo** button. The last letter you typed is erased and the Redo button appears in the Quick Access Toolbar.

16. Click the **Redo** button to restore the *d*. The Redo button grays out again to let you know that there are no more actions that can be redone, as shown in Figure 1-10.

Figure 1-10

Accessing the Quick
Access Toolbar

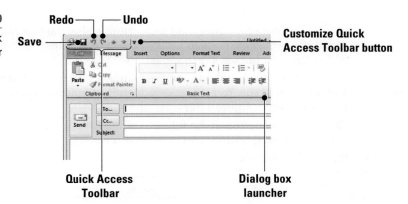

Redo —   — Undo

Save —   Customize Quick
                          Access Toolbar button

Quick Access   Dialog box
Toolbar   launcher

17. Click the Customize Quick Access Toolbar button. A list of available buttons is displayed, as shown in Figure 1-11. To add or remove buttons from the Quick Access Toolbar simply select or deselect a function from the list.

Figure 1-11

Customizing the Quick Access Toolbar

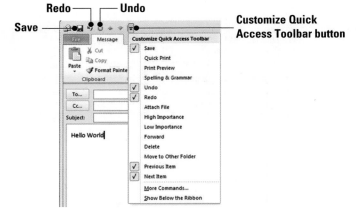

Redo **Undo**
Save **Customize Quick Access Toolbar button**

Another Way
The Customize Quick Access Toolbar offers a selection of commonly used buttons. If you want add a particular command that is not in the list, you can click More Commands to open the Customize Quick Access Toolbar window, where you can choose from every command in Outlook.

18. Drag the mouse over the word *Hello* in the message area to select it. In the Basic Text group on the Ribbon, click the dialog box launcher shown in Figure 1-10. A traditional Microsoft dialog box is displayed containing additional options for this command group, as shown in Figure 1-12. Notice that many of the same options are available in both locations.

Figure 1-12

Font dialog box

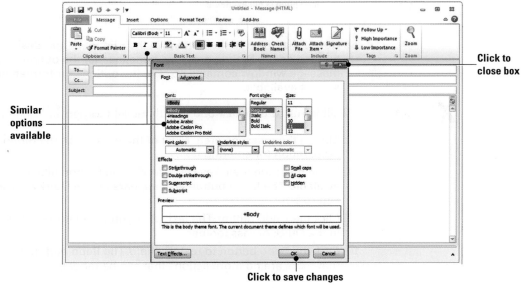

Similar options available

Click to close box

Click to save changes

Another Way
You can also close any window or dialog box by clicking the Close button in the top-right corner.

19. In the Font Style box, click Bold Italic. Notice how the text *Hello* in the Preview area of the dialog box changes to reflect your choice. Click the Cancel button to close the dialog box without saving changes.

20. Locate the Title bar at the top of the window. It tells you that this window is named Untitled—Message. You can always identify windows and dialog boxes using the Title bar, as shown in Figure 1-12.

21. Click the Close button at the far right of the Title bar to close the message window. If Outlook prompts you to save your work, click No.

PAUSE. LEAVE Outlook open to use in the next exercise.

Table 1-1 describes the basic functions of onscreen tools used to access Outlook's features. More detailed information about using each of the features is available in the following sections of this lesson and the remaining lessons.

Onscreen Tool	Description
Backstage	The Backstage view is new in Outlook 2010. Backstage can be accessed by clicking on the File tab in the Outlook Ribbon. The commands in Outlook's Backstage can be used to customize most Outlook features.
Groups	The Outlook 2010 Ribbon is divided into groups that contain buttons for frequently used commands.
Item	An **item** is a record stored in Outlook. A message, appointment, contact, task, or note is an item in Outlook.
Navigation Pane	The Navigation Pane provides access to each of Outlook's features, such as the Calendar and To-Do List. The Navigation Pane can be minimized to enlarge the Reading Pane.
Reading Pane	The **Reading Pane** displays information about the selected Outlook item. For example, in the mailbox, it displays the text of a selected e-mail message.
Ribbon	The Ribbon contains the menus and commands available in Outlook 2010. The Ribbon contains tabs that replace the menus in the old Menu bar. Each tab is divided into groups of commands that replace the old toolbar options.
Status bar	The **Status bar** identifies the number of items in the active feature. For example, when the Contacts tool is active, the number of contacts stored is displayed in the Status bar.
Title bar	The **Title bar** identifies the application and the active feature. For example, when the Calendar is active, the Title bar says "Calendar—Microsoft Outlook."
To-Do Bar	The To-Do Bar summarizes information about appointments and tasks.
Quick Access Toolbar	The **Quick Access Toolbar (QAT)** appears on the left side of the Title bar, above the Ribbon. If you want the toolbar closer to your work area, you can move it to below the Ribbon. This toolbar should contain the commands you use most frequently.

Outlook stores and organizes many of the little pieces of information that form the core of your daily activities. In a single day, you might use Outlook's Calendar, Mail, and Contacts features to schedule the meetings, look up the phone numbers, send e-mail messages, and set up reminders that help you arrive on time for every meeting.

In the previous exercise, you took a quick look at the different Outlook onscreen tools. In this exercise, you will look at some of the ways you can change the viewing options available in Outlook. The features you use most frequently are covered in more detail in the following lessons.

Changing Outlook's View

Every Outlook **feature** stores specific information and offers you several options for viewing that information. For example, the Contacts feature provides the names, addresses, and phone numbers for the individuals and companies you contact. The Calendar tracks your appointments and meetings. Mail enables you to send and receive e-mail messages. You can use Ribbon commands to change the way that information is shown to suit your needs. In this exercise, you'll use the View tab and other Ribbon commands to explore some of Outlook's different views.

STEP BY STEP   Change Outlook's View

GET READY. LAUNCH Outlook if it is not already running and ensure that the Home tab is active.

1. If necessary, click the Mail button in the Navigation Pane and then click the Inbox folder to display your mailbox.

2. Click the View tab to display more options.

3. Click Change View in the Current View group to see the basic viewing options for the Mail feature. The currently selected view is highlighted.

4. Three views are available for the Mail window. The default view is Compact, which shows the items in your mailbox as simple two-line items containing the sender, the date, and the subject.

5. Click Single. The Single view flattens the mailbox items into a single line with all the e-mail information spread out in columns.

6. Click Preview. Notice how the screen changes to provide a single compressed line for each item similar to Single view, except that Preview view does not have the Reading Pane.

Take Note   We've added some content to the screens in this section so that you can see how your content will appear. Your screen will look different if default settings have been changed or other content has been added to your PC. Use these figures as a reference.

7. Click Change View in the Current View group, as shown in Figure 1-13.

Figure 1-13

The Outlook Mailbox in Preview view

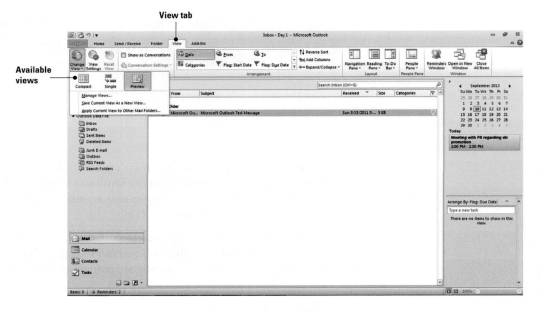

8. Select Compact to return to the default Mail view.

9. Click the Calendar button in the Navigation Pane to display the Calendar feature, and click the View tab to see the different Calendar viewing options.

10. You can change the arrangement of the onscreen Calendar in each view. Day is the default option. On the Home tab, click the Week button to show an entire week's schedule. Click the Month button to view an entire month. Click Work Week options. The Calendar view now displays the current workweek, as shown in Figure 1-14.

Figure 1-14

The Outlook Calendar in Work
Week arrangement

**Reset the default
settings for a view**   **View
tab**   **Change the arrangement
within a view**

**Available
views**

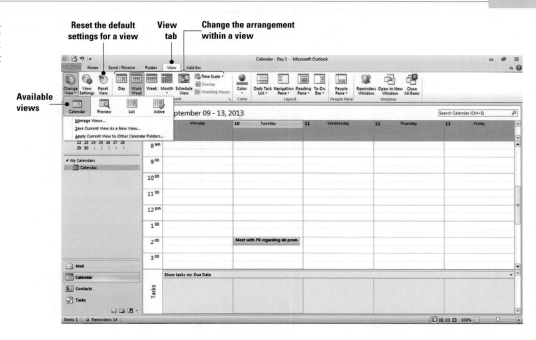

Take Note	The Work Week arrangement shows the workweek as Monday through Friday, by default. However, you can change the workweek to reflect your personal work schedule.

11. Click the View tab. Click Change View in the Current View group to see the available views. Make sure that the default Calendar is selected.

12. Click List. The Calendar changes to provide a simple list of calendar items. The Active view is similar, but only shows those events that have not already occurred.

13. Click Change View in the Current View group. Select Calendar. Click Reset View in the Current View group to change to the default Calendar view.

Take Note	Throughout this chapter you will see information that appears in black text within brackets, such as [Press **Enter**], or [your e-mail address]. The information contained in the brackets is intended to be directions for you rather than something you actually type word for word. It will instruct you to perform an action or substitute text. Do **not** type the actual text that appears within brackets.

Another Way
You can also access
Outlook Tasks by using the
keyboard shortcut Ctrl+4.

14. Click the Tasks button in the Navigation Pane. Your To-Do List is displayed. Click the *Type a new task* field and key Sample. [Press Enter.] The new task drops to the Task List and a flag appears indicating that the task is for today.

15. Click the Sample task. The Ribbon fills with color as options become available, as shown in Figure 1-15.

16. On the Home tab, click Change View in the Current View group to see the viewing options, as shown in Figure 1-15.

Figure 1-15

Available views in the Outlook To-Do List

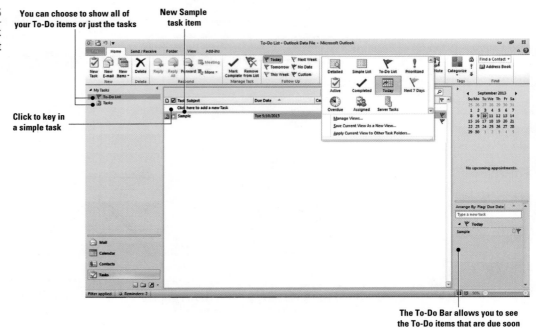

You can choose to show all of your To-Do items or just the tasks

New Sample task item

Click to key in a simple task

The To-Do Bar allows you to see the To-Do items that are due soon

17. Click on each option in the Change View gallery to see how the screen layout changes. You can choose from a number of different options—views that show all the details about a task item (Detailed) or views that let you filter your Task List to contain only items that fit the criteria you choose (Prioritized, Active, Completed, Today, Next 7 days, Overdue, Assigned).

18. On the View tab, click Change View and select Today. Select the Sample task and click Delete in the Delete group to remove your sample task.

19. Click the Folder List button in the Navigation Pane to display the Folder List in the upper area of the Navigation Pane, as shown in Figure 1-16.

Figure 1-16

The Folder List

Your Outlook data file

All Outlook items are stored in these folders

Folder List button

20. Click the Inbox in the Folder List to return to the Inbox.

PAUSE. LEAVE Outlook open to use in the next exercise.

In the previous exercise, you changed the view displayed in each of the commonly used Outlook features (Calendar, Contacts, Mail, Tasks, Notes). When you display Outlook's Folder List, you can see that each Outlook feature has its own folder, as shown in Figure 1-16. Every Outlook item (message, meeting, task, etc.) is stored in one of the folders in the Folder List.

Take Note   Because each Outlook feature is stored in a folder, the features themselves are sometimes referred to as **folders**.

If you create folders to help organize your Outlook items, those folders will typically appear as subfolders. For example, if you create a folder to store e-mails relating to a specific project you are working on, the Project folder will appear in the Folder List under the Inbox folder by default.

Table 1-2 briefly describes how these Outlook features are typically used.

Table 1-2

Descriptions of Outlook Features

Feature	Description
Mail	The Mail feature contains your e-mail messages. The Mail feature includes the following folders: Inbox (messages received), Sent Items (messages sent), Outbox (messages waiting to be sent), and Junk E-mail (unwanted messages you received that were not directed to another folder).
Calendar	The Calendar feature contains a calendar and appointment book to help you keep track of your schedule.
Contacts	The Contacts feature stores contact information about individuals, groups, and companies.
Tasks	The Tasks feature displays tasks and To-Do items.
Notes	The Notes feature stores small pieces of information on electronic sticky notes. Notes can be forwarded as e-mail messages.
Journal	The Journal feature automatically tracks communications and attachments as they are sent back and forth to contacts. The Journal is a great tool for keeping you organized and seeing how the Outlook items in different folders relate to one another.
Folder List	The Folder List identifies all of your Outlook folders. If your company or organization uses Microsoft Exchange Server, public folders you can access are also listed.

USING BACKSTAGE VIEW

The Bottom Line

Microsoft Outlook 2010 is designed to adapt to you. Outlook now places all of the settings and controls in one easy-to-navigate place called Backstage. You can use the **Backstage view** options to control the way Outlook acts and looks. You can use Backstage to create and modify accounts and to clean up your Outlook file. You can also use the *Options* area of Backstage to change all the settings used for mail, calendars, tasks, journals, and contacts, or use the Advanced options to access settings that control the way Outlook handles your information.

Using the File Tab to Open Backstage View

The File tab in Microsoft Office 2010 has replaced the Office button. Clicking the File tab opens the Microsoft Office Backstage view. You'll notice a menu-like list running down the left side of the window; this list is called a navigation pane. You can click any of the commands in the navigation pane to open a new Backstage page that contains the options and settings that were scattered among many different dialog boxes in Outlook 2007. In this exercise, you learn to use the File tab to open Backstage view and look over the options available through some of its commands.

STEP BY STEP   **Use the File Tab to Open Backstage View**

GET READY. LAUNCH Outlook if it is not already running.

1. In the Outlook window, click the Microsoft Outlook Test Message and then click the File tab. This opens the Backstage view with the Info page active, as shown in Figure 1-17. The Info page includes information about your account and tools for maintaining your mailbox.

WileyPLUS Extra! features an online tutorial of this task.

Troubleshooting If you no longer have the Microsoft Outlook Test Message, you can still complete the remaining steps in this exercise. However, the preview images in Backstage view will be different from those shown here.

Figure 1-17

Microsoft Office Backstage view for Outlook

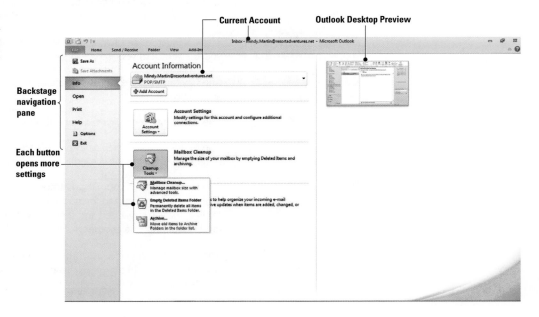

2. The right pane of the Backstage view window is the Preview pane. On the Info page, the preview simply shows you the current state of your main Outlook window. The Preview pane also appears on the Backstage view's Print page. Click the Print in the left navigation pane. The Print page opens and a preview appears in the right Preview pane.

3. Click the Table Style command in the Settings area and then the Memo Style. Notice how the preview changes.

PAUSE. LEAVE Outlook open to use in the next exercise.

Setting General Options

You can use the Microsoft Office Backstage to control many of the settings and options that used to be located on the Tools menu. When you click the Options command in Outlook's Backstage navigation pane, the Outlook Options dialog box opens. This one dialog box contains all of the options that you can use to customize the Outlook environment to suit your personal needs. These options are grouped according to type. The Outlook Options dialog box opens to the General

Options page. You can use the general options to set your user name, the color scheme, and the style of ScreenTip you want. You can also use these options to turn the Live Preview and the Mini Toolbar on or off. In this exercise, you'll set your user name and try modifying some of the options.

STEP BY STEP   **Set General Options**

GET READY. LAUNCH Outlook if it is not already running.

1. In the Outlook window, click the **Microsoft Office Test Message** and then click the **File** tab. This opens the Backstage view, with the Info page active (refer to Figure 1-17).

2. Click **Options** in the Navigation Pane. The Outlook Options dialog box opens to the General Options page.

3. Personalize Outlook by typing your name in the User Name box and your initials in the Initials box, as shown in Figure 1-18. When you personalize Outlook in Backstage view, your name will automatically be added to every Outlook item you create.

Figure 1-18

General Options page of the Outlook Options dialog box

Hover over the information circle for more information

Each item in the Navigation Pane opens an entire page of associated settings you can customize

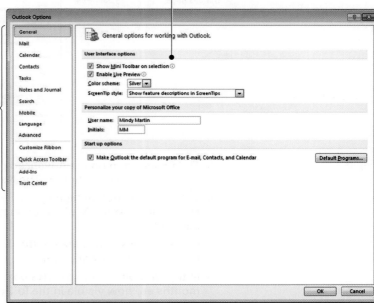

4. In the *User Interface options* area, click the color scheme dropdown box and select **Blue**. Click **OK**. Outlook applies the color to the Outlook window.

5. Click the **File** tab. This opens the Microsoft Office Backstage again.

6. Click **Options** in the navigation pane. The Outlook Options dialog box opens to the General Options page.

7. In the *User Interface options* area, click the color scheme dropdown box again and select **Silver**. Click **OK**. This will restore the default color to the Outlook window.

PAUSE. LEAVE the Outlook Options dialog box open to use in the next exercise.

Setting Advanced Options

Outlook 2010 gives you more control than ever when it comes to personalizing Outlook. You can use the Advanced options page of the Outlook Options dialog box to customize how the various panes of the Outlook window appear. You can also control specific aspects of the program to suit your needs, such as determining which folder appears when Outlook opens, or how Outlook should handle dial-up connections and international e-mails. You can also determine how often Outlook performs tasks like sending and receiving messages, AutoArchiving, and receiving RSS feeds. In this exercise, you'll change some of these settings to familiarize yourself with the process.

STEP BY STEP   **Set Advanced Options**

GET READY. LAUNCH Outlook if it is not already running.

1. Click the File tab again and select Options and then Advanced. The Advanced options page of the Outlook Options dialog box appears.

2. Click the top of the Outlook Options dialog box and drag it to the middle of your Outlook window. The Navigation Pane and To-Do Bar should be visible on either side of the Outlook Options dialog box, as shown in Figure 1-19.

Figure 1-19

Advanced Options page of the Outlook Options dialog box

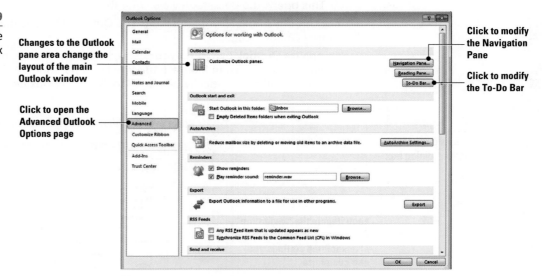

3. The first section on the Advanced page is the Outlook panes area. In this section, click the Navigation Pane button. The Navigation Pane Options dialog box appears.

4. With the Mail option highlighted, click the Move Down button two times, then click OK. Notice that the Mail button in the bottom of the Navigation Pane is now the third item in the list.

5. In the Outlook panes area of the dialog box, click the To-Do Bar button. The To-Do Bar Options dialog box appears.

6. In the *Number of month rows* box, type 3 and click OK. Notice that three calendar months are now visible in the To-Do Bar.

7. Scroll down, reading each of the available options. When you get to the *Send and receive* area, deselect the *Send immediately when connected* option. This change means that you need to manually tell Outlook when you're ready to send and receive messages.

8. Click Cancel. This will restore the default layout and settings.

PAUSE. LEAVE Outlook open to use in the next exercise.

Setting Language Options

Outlook 2010 also allows you to select your default language. You can choose to match the rest of Office or choose a different language as your default. If you prefer to use English as your default language but correspond with non-English speaking friends or coworkers on a regular basis, you can add the languages you need to the Editing Languages. When your create e-mails in another language, Outlook will look up your editing languages and offer you all the same spell-check and grammar tools that you're used to in Office. In this exercise, you'll set English as your default language and add Spanish to your Editing Languages.

STEP BY STEP **Set Language Options**

GET READY. LAUNCH Outlook if it is not already running.

1. Click the **File** tab again and select **Options** and then **Language**. The Language options page of the Outlook Options dialog box appears.

2. Click the **[Add additional editing languages]** box in the Choose Editing Languages area of the dialog box. A long list of available languages appears.

3. Scroll down the list and select **Spanish (United States)**. Click **Add**. Outlook adds the language to the Editing Languages list, which turns on all of its proofing tools for that language.

4. You can use the *Choose Display and Help Languages* area to change the language that appears onscreen, in ScreenTips and in the Help window. In the Display Language window, select **English**, if necessary. Your screen should look like Figure 1-20.

Figure 1-20

Language Options page of the Outlook Options dialog box

Changing the Editing Language changes the proofing tools that Outlook uses to check your writing

Changing the Display Language changes the language of menus and onscreen text

Changes the Screen-Tip Language

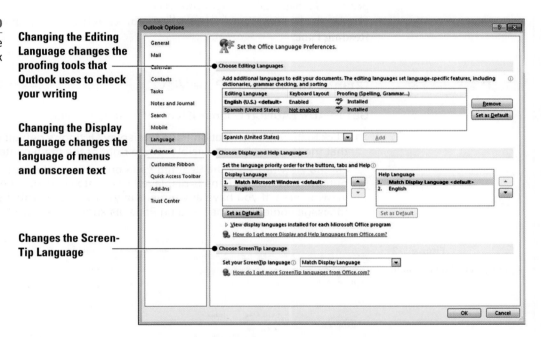

5. Click **Cancel**. Outlook will restore the default language options and return you to the main window.

PAUSE. LEAVE Outlook open to use in the next exercise.

As you've seen, you can use Outlook's Backstage view to access a wide variety of settings to help you customize the way Outlook looks and works to suit your needs (see Table 1-3).

Table 1-3

Options within Outlook's Backstage view

General	Personalize Outlook with your user name, turn on and off Live Preview, and change the color scheme.
Advanced	Customize the Outlook window's Navigation Pane, Reading Pane, and To-Do Bar. You can also AutoArchive your mailbox, set reminders, export Outlook information, synchronize RSS feeds, and set rules for international correspondence.
Language	You can add proofing tools for additional languages and set your own default language.

PERSONALIZING OUTLOOK

You can arrange the elements in the Outlook window to fit your needs. You have a great deal of control over the Outlook environment. In the previous exercise, you learned how to change the views for each Outlook feature, but you can go even further. You can resize, rearrange, hide, or display Outlook features to create an environment that meets your requirements. In this section, you'll learn how to rearrange your Outlook window by moving the Reading Pane and the To-Do Bar; add or delete columns in a List view; and add and remove elements from the To-Do Bar. In addition, you'll learn how to use the new People Pane to better connect to your contacts.

Changing the Reading Pane View

You can show, hide, or move the Reading Pane to fit your needs. Do you get a lot of long e-mail messages? Display the Reading Pane vertically on the right to display as much text as possible. Perhaps the messages you receive contain a lot of information in the item listing area. Display the Reading Pane horizontally. In this exercise, you'll learn to show, hide, and move the Reading Pane.

STEP BY STEP **Change the Reading Pane View**

GET READY. LAUNCH Outlook if it is not already running.

1. Click **Mail** in the Navigation Pane to display Outlook's default opening screen. Notice that the Reading Pane is visible on the right of the main content pane.

2. On the View tab, click the **Reading Pane** button in the Layout group. Select the **Bottom** option. The Reading Pane is displayed horizontally, across the bottom of the message viewing area. If you have any e-mails in your mailbox, you'll see a preview of the message contents in the Reading Pane, as shown in Figure 1-21.

Figure 1-21

Reading Pane displayed in the bottom position

Reading Pane

3. On the View tab, click the Reading Pane button in the Layout group. Select the Off option. The Reading Pane is hidden, as shown in Figure 1-22.

Figure 1-22

The Reading Pane is hidden.

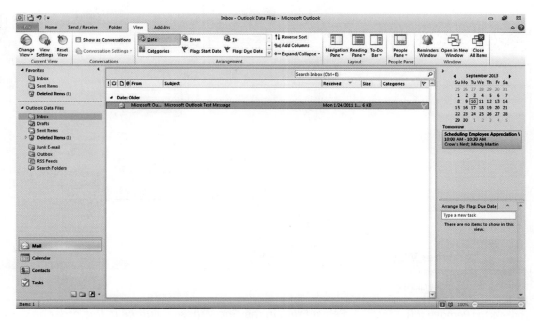

4. On the View tab, click the Reading Pane button again and select Right to restore the default view.

PAUSE. LEAVE Outlook open to use in the next exercise.

Showing or Hiding Fields in a List View

Another way you can personalize your Outlook window is by deciding which fields you want to see in a list view. In Outlook, **fields** are specific bits of information about an item. For example, an incoming e-mail message might contain fields of information, such *From, Subject, To, Received, Flag Status, Attachments*, and so on. You can click the View Settings button on the View tab to access the Advanced View Settings dialog box to add and remove fields that appear as columns in a List view. In this exercise, you'll add and remove a field from a List view.

STEP BY STEP	Show or Hide Fields in a List View

GET READY. LAUNCH Outlook if it is not already running and ensure that it shows the mailbox with the Reading Pane hidden.

1. Click the View tab and then click the Change View. Select Preview from the Change Views gallery.

2. Click View Settings to open the Advanced View Settings: Preview dialog box.

3. Click Columns. The Show Columns dialog box opens listing all of the available columns, as shown in Figure 1-23.

Figure 1-23

The Show Columns dialog box

Click to access the Advanced
View Settings dialog box

Click to add
selected column

Columns currently
showing in List view

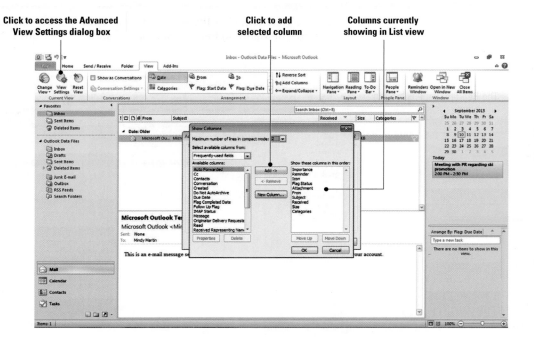

Another Way

You can also
remove a field by right-clicking
the field header in the List view
and selecting *Remove this
column* from the content menu.

4. Select **From** in the *Show these columns in this order* box, and then click the **Remove** button. Click **OK** twice to apply your changes and close the dialog boxes. The column changes have been applied to the mailbox, as shown in Figure 1-24.

Figure 1-24

The mailbox with modified columns

Click to revert back to the
defaults for the selected view

Click to access
the Advanced
View Settings
dialog box

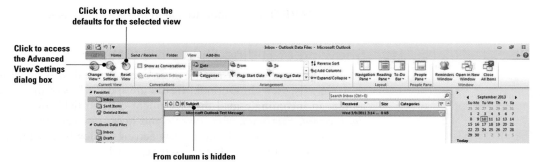

From column is hidden

Another Way

You can also change
the column order by selecting
the field name in either the Show
Columns dialog box or in the List
view itself and dragging the field
to the desired location.

5. Click the **View Settings** button, then click **Columns** in the Advanced View Settings: Preview dialog box.

6. Select **From** in the Available Columns box on the left of the dialog box and click the **Add** button. Notice that the From column is at the bottom of the *Show these columns in this order* list, meaning that it will appear at the far right column in Preview view list.

7. Click the **Move Up** button below the list repeatedly until the From column appears at the top of the list. Click **OK** twice to apply your changes and close the dialog boxes. The From column is visible again, but is located at the far left of the column headers.

8. Click **Reset View** in the Current View group on the View tab. Click **Yes** at the prompt to restore the mailbox to the default view.

PAUSE. LEAVE Outlook open to use in the next exercise.

Viewing, Hiding, and Minimizing the To-Do Bar

You can show, hide, or minimize the To-Do Bar in the same way that you worked with the Reading Pane. The **To-Do Bar** summarizes the current items that need your attention. In this exercise, you'll learn to show, hide, and minimize the To-Do Bar.

| STEP BY STEP | **View, Hide, and Minimize the To-Do Bar** |

GET READY. LAUNCH Outlook if it is not already running.

1. If necessary, click the Mail button in the Navigation Pane to display the mailbox.
2. Click the View tab and click the To-Do-Bar button in the Layout group. Select the Minimized option. The To-Do Bar is minimized to a slim pane on the right side of the Outlook window, as shown in Figure 1-25.

Figure 1-25

Minimized To-Do Bar

Click to change the To-Do Bar view

Click to expand the To-Do Bar

Another Way
You can also minimize the To-Do Bar simply by clicking the minimize button at the top left of the To-Do Bar.

3. Click the To-Do Bar button and select the Off option. The To-Do Bar is hidden.
4. Click the To-Do Bar button and select the Normal option. The To-Do Bar is restored to its original size and position.

PAUSE. LEAVE Outlook open to use in the next exercise.

Customizing the To-Do Bar

You can select the elements to include on the new To-Do Bar. The To-Do Bar summarizes the current Outlook items that need some follow-up. With a single glance, you can see your appointments, tasks, and e-mail messages that require some action. You can customize the To-Do Bar by changing which elements are visible and by rearranging its elements. In this exercise, you'll work with the To-Do Bar Options and the To-Do Bar button on the View tab to remove and add elements to the To-Do Bar.

| STEP BY STEP | **Customize the To-Do Bar** |

GET READY. LAUNCH Outlook if it is not already running.

1. If necessary, click the Mail button in the Navigation Pane to display the default mailbox view and verify that the To-Do Bar is displayed.
2. Click the View tab, click the To-Do Bar button, and select Options. The To-Do Bar Options dialog box is displayed, as shown in Figure 1-26.

Click to open the To-Do Bar Options dialog box

Figure 1-26

To-Do Bar Options dialog box

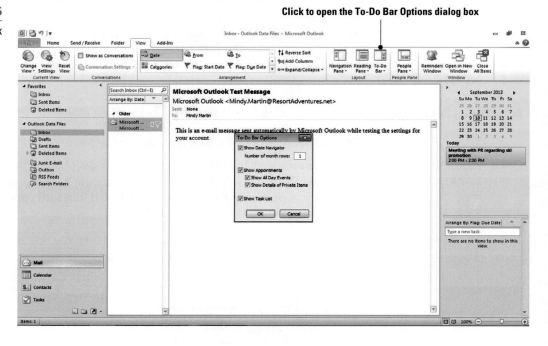

 Ref

This is the same dialog box that you accessed earlier in the lesson using the Advanced page of the Outlook Options dialog box.

3. Examine the options. The checkmark indicates that the element is currently displayed. The numbers indicate the number of months you want to display in the Date Navigator.

Another Way
You can also show or hide each of the other To-Do Bar elements by opening the View tab and selecting the To-Do Bar button.

4. Click the Show Task List checkbox and click the OK button. The dialog box closes and the Task List is removed from the To-Do Bar.

5. Click the View tab, click the To-Do Bar, and select the Task List option. Click OK. The Task List is again displayed on the To-Do Bar.

PAUSE. LEAVE Outlook open to use in the next exercise.

The To-Do Bar contains many different elements that can be added, removed, or modified using either the To-Do Bar Options dialog box or the Advanced page of the Outlook Options dialog box (see Table 1-4).

Table 1-4

To-Do Bar Element Descriptions

To-Do Bar Element	Description
Appointments	The Appointments element displays appointments scheduled in Outlook. You can select the number of appointments to be displayed.
Date Navigator	The Date Navigator displays a small calendar. You can select the number of months to be displayed.
Task Input Panel	Key new tasks into the Task Input Panel.
Task List	The Task List displays the tasks that have been assigned to you.

Using the People Pane

NEW
to Office 2010

The People Pane is a new feature in Outlook 2010. When you select an e-mail item, the **People Pane** shows you thumbnail images for the sender and all recipients. When you click on a person's thumbnail in the People Pane, the pane expands to show you all the e-mails, meetings, and attachments related to the selected person. This new shortcut lets you see at a glance every contact you've had with that person without having to open different windows. You can also use the People Pane to sync your Contacts list with your friends and contacts on social networking sites like Facebook and LinkedIn. In this exercise, you'll learn to show, hide, and minimize the People Pane and familiarize yourself with some of the People Pane's features.

STEP BY STEP   **Use the People Pane**

WileyPLUS Extra! features an online tutorial of this task.

Another Way
You can also find the People Pane at the bottom of each Contact window. Just double-click on a name in the Contacts list to view all their information and see their People Pane.

Take Note

GET READY. LAUNCH Outlook if it is not already running and ensure that it is open, in the default Mail view.

1. Click Mail in the Navigation Pane to display your mailbox. Select the Microsoft Outlook Test Message or another e-mail in your Inbox. If you don't have this message, you can click any message in the Inbox for the exercise.

2. On the View tab, click the People Pane button. When Outlook initially opens, the People Pane is turned off.

Your screen will look different if default settings have been changed or other content has been added to your PC. Use these figures as a reference.

3. Select the Normal option. The People Pane appears at the bottom of the Reading Pane, as shown in Figure 1-27. The People Pane appears in the bottom third of the Reading Pane. You'll notice a large picture placeholder and beside it is a box with a row of icons. At the top-right corner of the People Pane is a smaller thumbnail image.

Figure 1-27

The People Pane's default view

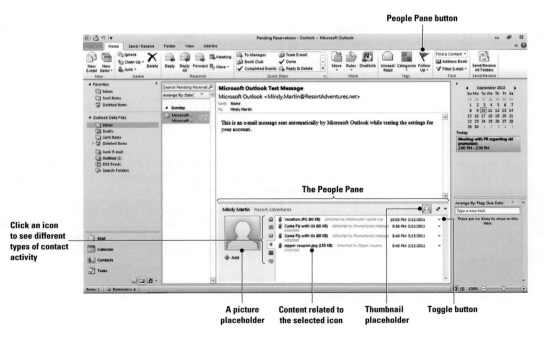

Click an icon to see different types of contact activity

A picture placeholder   Content related to the selected icon   Thumbnail placeholder   Toggle button

Take Note

Because the Test Message is from Outlook to you using your e-mail address as the sender, you see only one picture placeholder, which represents you. However, in most cases, you'll see multiple picture placeholders in the People Pane because most messages are conversations between two or more people.

4. In the People Pane, point to each of the icons next to the picture placeholder. The ScreenTips tell you what kind of information is available about this person. For example, in Figure 1-27, we've clicked the paperclip icon, which opens a list of every attachment that you've received from this person. In this case, there have been four attachments received. From here you could click the name of the attachment to open it or click the down arrow to the right of the attachment to open the original message.

5. Click the toggle button shown in Figure 1-28 to change People Pane views. The tabs and the content box are hidden so that the People Pane now shows a larger picture placeholder for you.

Take Note

If you click on a message to or from another person, you'll see picture placeholders for the sender and each recipient. This is the default People Pane view for messages with multiple people listed.

Figure 1-28

The People Pane in large thumbnail view

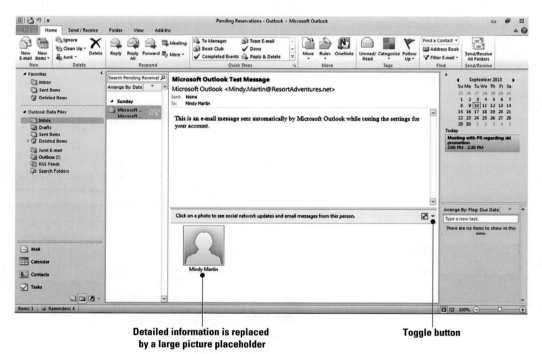

Detailed information is replaced by a large picture placeholder   Toggle button

6. If you have other messages in your Inbox, click on another message. The People Pane will change to show a picture placeholder for the sender and every recipient. If you don't have another message, use the following figures as a reference.

7. Click one of the picture placeholders to change back to the default view. In the top bar of the People Pane, you'll see multiple small thumbnail placeholders, as shown in Figure 1-29. Outlook highlights the thumbnail for the person currently displayed in the bottom part of the People Pane.

Figure 1-29

The People Pane with multiple contacts

Thumbnail placeholders represent
the sender and recipients

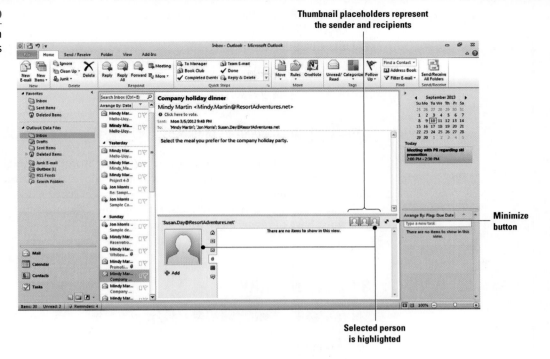

Minimize
button

Selected person
is highlighted

Take Note   As you build your Contacts list, you'll notice that each contact record includes a similar picture placeholder. You can replace the placeholders with actual photos of your contacts. When you click on a message to or from a contact for whom you've added a photo, you'll see their actual photo in the People Pane instead of the silhouette.

8. Click one of the non-highlighted placeholders. The People Pane changes to reflect the items related to the selected person.

9. Click the **minimize** button in the top-right corner of the People Pane to minimize it. The pane becomes a small bar at the bottom of the Reading Pane that shows only the thumbnail picture placeholder for the sender and each recipient, as shown in Figure 1-30.

Figure 1-30

The minimized People Pane

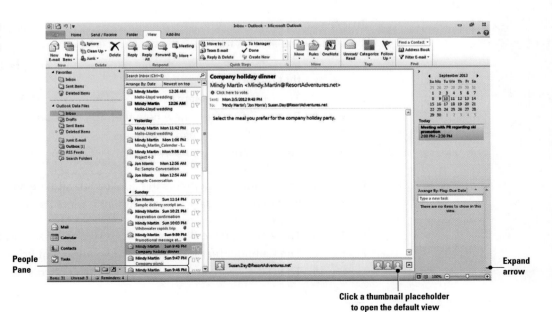

People
Pane

Expand
arrow

Click a thumbnail placeholder
to open the default view

10. Click the People Pane button again on the View tab, and select Off to turn off the People Pane.

PAUSE. CLOSE Outlook.

 Ref

You'll learn more about working with the People Pane in Lesson 2.

You can also use Outlook to sync contacts with a SharePoint MySite account. SharePoint is a cloud computing system set up by Microsoft. It allows you to store documents, contacts, and links in a convenient Internet server so that you can access it anywhere. If you are using a Share-Point account to store your contacts, syncing your My Site and Outlook together means that you won't have to retype all of your contacts.

SKILL SUMMARY

In This Lesson, You Learned How To:
Start Outlook
Work in the Outlook window
Use Backstage view to manage Outlook
Personalize Outlook

Knowledge Assessment

True/False

Circle T if the statement is true or F if the statement is false.

T F 1. In the To-Do Bar, you can see your appointments, tasks, and e-mail messages that require some action.

T F 2. The Outlook Contacts list is stored in the People Pane.

T F 3. Backstage view is a new help feature in Outlook.

T F 4. The Reading Pane can be hidden.

T F 5. You can hide columns from a list by selecting the field and pressing the Delete key.

T F 6. The Status bar identifies the application and the active feature.

T F 7. In Outlook, messages, appointments, contacts, tasks, and notes are called items.

T F 8. The Viewing Pane displays the text of a selected e-mail message.

T F 9. The Calendar feature contains an appointment book.

T F 10. The Date Navigator in the To-Do Bar can only display one month.

Multiple Choice

Select the letter of the term that best responds to or completes the following statements and questions.

1. A(n) _____ is a record stored in Outlook.
   - **a.** message
   - **b.** item
   - **c.** object
   - **d.** note

2. You can _____ a pane to save room in the Outlook window.
   - **a.** compress
   - **b.** minimize
   - **c.** rotate
   - **d.** shrink

3. You can use the _____ to control almost every aspect of the Outlook environment.
   - **a.** Options menu
   - **b.** Options tab
   - **c.** Backstage view
   - **d.** Preferences tab

4. What new feature groups all of your messages from a person in one place?
   - **a.** Reading Pane
   - **b.** Contact Pane
   - **c.** Filter Pane
   - **d.** People Pane

5. Click the _____ button to access the Show Columns dialog box where you can add and remove fields from a List view.
   - **a.** View Settings
   - **b.** Show Columns
   - **c.** View Options
   - **d.** Custom Views

6. How many views are available for the To-Do List feature?
   - **a.** 3
   - **b.** 11
   - **c.** 6
   - **d.** 7

7. Which pane provides access to the Outlook features, such as the Contacts and Calendar?
   - **a.** Navigation Pane
   - **b.** Navigation menu
   - **c.** Home menu
   - **d.** File tab

8. What pane displays the text of a selected e-mail message?
   - **a.** Preview Pane
   - **b.** Viewing Pane
   - **c.** Message Pane
   - **d.** Reading Pane

9. The _____ contains menus and commands available in Outlook 2010.
   - **a.** Toolbar
   - **b.** Options menu
   - **c.** Ribbon
   - **d.** Banner

10. The _____ button is the first feature listed in the Navigation Pane.
    a. Tasks
    b. Contacts
    c. Calendar
    d. Mail

Competency Assessment

Project 1-1: View the Outlook Ribbon

Become familiar with the Outlook Ribbon.

GET READY. LAUNCH Outlook if it is not already running.

1. If necessary, click the **Mail** button in the Navigation Pane to display the mailbox and verify that the To-Do Bar is displayed.
2. Click the **Home** tab. Click each of the dropdown buttons to see what options are available.
3. Click the **Send/Receive** tab. Click each of the dropdown buttons to see what options are available.
4. Click the **Folder** tab. Click each of the dropdown buttons to see what options are available.
5. Click the **View** tab. Click each of the dropdown buttons to see what options are available.
6. Click the **Add-Ins** tab, if you have one. Click each of the dropdown buttons to see what options are available.

LEAVE Outlook open for the next project.

Project 1-2: Use the Folder List

Use the Folder List to display the Outlook folders.

GET READY. LAUNCH Outlook if it is not already running.

1. Click the **Folder List** button in the Navigation Pane. The Folder List is displayed in the upper area of the Navigation Pane.
2. Click the **Calendar** folder in the Folder List. The Calendar is displayed.
3. Click the **Contacts** folder in the Folder List. The Contacts folder is displayed.
4. Click the **Folder List** button again. Click the **Deleted Items** folder in the Folder List. The Deleted Items folder is displayed. Any deleted Outlook items are stored here until this folder is emptied.
5. Right-click the **Deleted Items** folder in the Folder List. Note the Empty "Deleted Items" Folder option. Selecting this option permanently deletes these items.
6. Click the **Inbox** folder in the Folder List. By default, the Inbox folder contains any e-mail messages you have received.
7. Click the **Notes** folder in the Folder List. The Notes folder is displayed.
8. Click the **Tasks** folder in the Folder List. The Tasks folder is displayed.
9. Click the **Mail** button in the Navigation Pane to return to Outlook's default view.

LEAVE Outlook open for the next project.

Project 1-3: Use Keyboard Shortcuts to View Outlook Features

The main Outlook features can be accessed by keyboard shortcuts. Use the shortcuts to display the folders data.

GET READY. LAUNCH Outlook if it is not already running.

1. Identify the keyboard shortcuts used to display the Mail, Calendar, Contacts, Tasks, Notes, and Folder List tools.
2. Use the keyboard shortcuts to display the Outlook features.

LEAVE Outlook open for the next project.

Project 1-4: Customize the To-Do Bar

Change the number of months and appointments displayed in the To-Do Bar.

GET READY. LAUNCH Outlook if it is not already running.

1. If necessary, click the Mail button in the Navigation Pane to display the mailbox and verify that the To-Do Bar is displayed.
2. Display the options for Outlook's To-Do Bar.
3. Change the options to display two months and five appointments.
4. Return to the main Outlook window to see the changes in the To-Do Bar.
5. Display the options for Outlook's To-Do Bar again.
6. Change the options to the default values to display one month and three appointments.
7. Return to the main Outlook window to see the changes in the To-Do Bar.

LEAVE Outlook open for the next project.

Project 1-5: Identify the New Features in Outlook 2010

The People Pane discussed in this lesson is only one of many new features in Outlook 2010. Use Microsoft Office Help to locate information about the various new features in Outlook 2010.

GET READY. LAUNCH Outlook if it is not already running.

1. Use Backstage view to access Microsoft Office Help.
2. Do a help search. Key What's new in Microsoft Outlook 2010.
3. Read through the article to identify the new features that could affect how you use Outlook 2010.

LEAVE Outlook open for the next project.

Project 1-6: Customize a List View

The columns in a list view can be added, deleted, and rearranged.

GET READY. LAUNCH Outlook if it is not already running.

1. Click the Tasks button in the Navigation Pane to display the To-Do List and verify that the To-Do Bar is displayed.
2. Change to the Active view so that the tasks are shown as a list.

3. Remove the Due Date and Folder columns.

4. Using the Show Columns dialog box, add the Sensitivity and Company columns to the far left of the list.

5. Add the Reading Pane in the bottom position.

6. Collapse the Navigation Pane.

7. Remove the To-Do Bar.

8. Close Outlook. Start Outlook and use the Tasks keyboard shortcut to open the Task List. The customized view should be displayed.

9. Reset the Active view to the default columns and restore the Navigation Pane and the To-Do Bar.

CLOSE Outlook.

INTERNET READY

Unfortunately, you might not be the only user on your computer. You might share your computer with a coworker at the office or a family member at home. How can you keep your e-mail private without requiring passwords or a series of arcane gestures and dance steps? Use the Internet or Microsoft Office Outlook Help to investigate the different options you can use to secure your Outlook communications.

LESSON SKILL MATRIX

In This Lesson, You Will Learn The Following Skills:

Creating Messages

Sending Messages

Reading and Responding to Messages

Formatting Messages

Personalizing Messages

Creating and Formatting Graphic Message Content

Working with Attachments

Using Advanced Message Options

Locating Messages

KEY TERMS

- attachment
- attribute
- AutoComplete
- AutoPreview
- character
- clip art
- font
- Format Painter
- formatting attributes
- hyperlink
- Hypertext Markup Language (HTML)
- InfoBar
- Instant Search
- plain text

- **Quick Access Toolbar**
- **Quick Styles**
- **Rich Text Format (RTF)**
- **sensitivity**
- **signature**
- **SmartArt graphics**
- **style**
- **subject**
- **theme**

Mindy Martin and Jon Morris own and operate Resort Adventures, a luxury resort. They stay busy throughout the day, and frequently work different shifts to stay on top of the activities going on at different times. Sometimes, they rely on e-mail to keep each other informed. Outlook is the perfect tool for this task. Mindy and Jon also use Outlook to contact clients and create press releases. Outlook 2010's new ability to format and enhance messages makes it a great way to send professional and polished messages. In this lesson, you'll learn how to create, save, format, and print messages.

SOFTWARE ORIENTATION

Microsoft Outlook's Message Window

E-mail is the most frequently used Outlook component. The Message window, shown in Figure 2-1, should be familiar to every Outlook user.

Figure 2-1

Outlook Message window

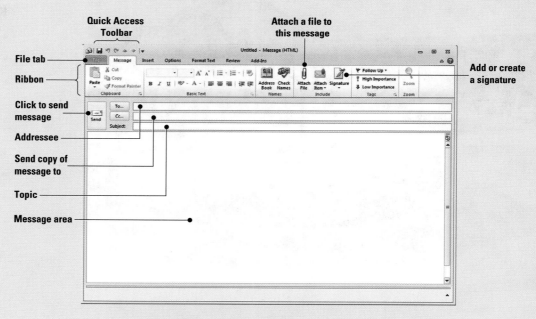

Many of the elements in the Message window are familiar to you if you use Microsoft Word 2010. The editor used to create messages in Outlook is based on Microsoft Word 2010. Your screen may vary if default settings have been changed or if other preferences have been set. Use this figure as a reference throughout this lesson as well as the rest of this book.

CREATING MESSAGES

Creating e-mail messages is probably the most common user activity in Outlook. Creating a simple e-mail message is not much harder than jotting a note on a Post-It®. In this section, you'll create a basic e-mail message and specify its format.

Composing a Message

Microsoft Outlook's e-mail component is a full-featured composition tool that provides many of the same functions found in Microsoft Word. Keying, copying, cutting, and deleting text in an Outlook message are identical to the same functions in Microsoft Word 2010. The **AutoComplete** function is another Word feature available in Outlook. It helps you quickly enter the names of the months and days of the week. AutoComplete cannot be turned off in Outlook 2010. In this exercise, you create a new e-mail message.

STEP BY STEP   Compose a Message

GET READY. LAUNCH Outlook if it is not already running.

1. If necessary, click the Mail button in the Navigation Pane to display the Mail folder, as shown in Figure 2-2.

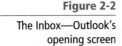

WileyPLUS Extra! features an online tutorial of this task.

Figure 2-2

The Inbox—Outlook's opening screen

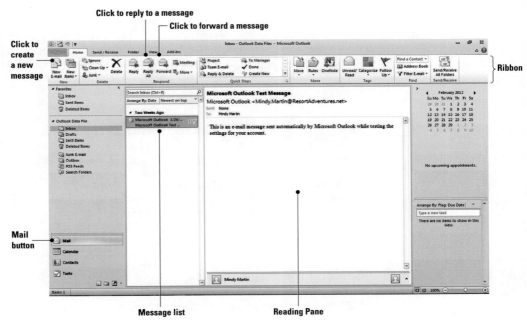

2. Click the New E-mail button on the Home tab. The Message window is displayed, as shown in Figure 2-1.

Take Note   Throughout this chapter you will see information that appears in text within brackets, such as [Press **Enter**] or [your e-mail address]. The information contained in the brackets is intended to be directions for you rather than something you actually type word for word. It will instruct you to perform an action or substitute text. Do not type the actual text that appears within brackets.

3. Click the message area.
4. Press **Enter** twice to add a blank line.
5. Key **Hi Jon,** [press **Enter** twice].

6. Key **Blue Yonder Airlines is running a contest in January. The winner gets free round-trip airfare to Cincinnati. Terry Crayton, a marketing assistant at Blue Yonder, asked if we would be interested in offering a free weekend at Resort Adventures as part of the prize. What do you think?** [Press **Enter** twice.]

7. Key **Let me know.** [Press **Enter** twice.]

8. Key **[your name].** [Press **Enter.**]

PAUSE. LEAVE the Outlook Message window open to use in the next exercise.

Regardless of the tool you use, the task of writing a message is the same. In normal business correspondence, you would be more formal in addressing the correspondence. However, this example is just a quick note between the partners at Resort Adventures.

Specifying Message Content Format

The most attractive e-mail messages contain formatted text. Formatting, including bullets, font sizes, font colors, and bold text, can convey just the right impression. Microsoft Outlook can send messages in Hypertext Markup Language (HTML), Rich Text Format (RTF), and plain text—formats described in Table 2-1. Because of its flexibility and the formatting options it provides, HTML is the default format for the message you compose and send. However, not all e-mail applications can display these effects. In this exercise, you will change the format for a message to plain text.

Table 2-1

Message Formats

Format	Description
HTML	**Hypertext Markup Language (HTML)** is used by web browsers to display information. HTML enables you to format text and insert items such as horizontal lines, pictures, and animated graphics. Older and less robust e-mail programs may not be able to display HTML.
RTF	**Rich Text Format (RTF)** uses tags to format text. It can be read by most word processors and newer e-mail programs, but it can't display animated graphics and some web page formatting.
Plain text	**Plain text** does not use any formatting. It can be read by all e-mail programs. Without formatting, though, the impression you can convey in your message is limited.

STEP BY STEP   **Select a Message Format**

USE the message you created in the previous exercise.

1. **OPEN** *Picture Signature* in the data files for this lesson. Select the table containing the picture and Mindy Martin's contact information. Right-click the table and click Copy on the shortcut menu. Close the *Picture Signature* document.

@ The *Picture Signature* file is available on the book companion website or in WileyPLUS.

2. Select the text Mindy Martin in the message window that you opened in the previous exercise and right-click.

3. Click Paste on the shortcut menu. Mindy's signature, including the picture of the stained-glass window, is pasted into the message.

4. In the Subject field, key Plain Text Message.

5. Click the Format Text tab, as shown in Figure 2-3.

6. In the Format group, click Plain Text. The Microsoft Outlook Compatibility Checker dialog box shown in Figure 2-3 is displayed. The items listed in the dialog box identify the changes that will occur in this particular message.

Figure 2-3

Formatted message and
Microsoft Outlook Compatibility
Checker dialog box

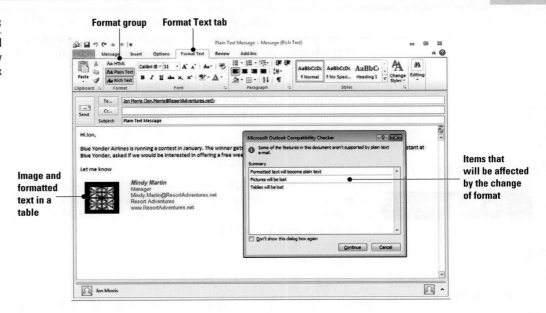

7. Click the **Continue** button. The picture and formatting are removed from the message, as shown in Figure 2-4.

Figure 2-4

Message converted to plain
text format

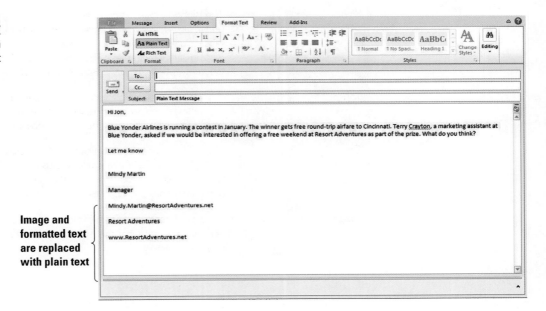

PAUSE. LEAVE the Plain Text Message—Message window open to use in the next exercise.

Take Note   When you reply to a message, Outlook automatically uses the format of the received message as the format for your reply. Thus if you receive a message in plain text, your reply will automatically be sent in plain text.

In the previous exercise, you saw how you can choose to use RTF or plain text for an individual message. If you find that most of the people you need to send messages to can't read messages in HTML format, you can change the default message format for all your outgoing messages. To change the default format, click the File tab to open Backstage view and select Options from the navigation pane. In the left navigation pane of the Outlook Options dialog box, select Mail. In the Compose messages area, click the *Compose messages in the format* dropdown arrow and select either Plain Text or RTF. Click OK to save your changes.

SENDING MESSAGES

The Bottom Line

Sending an e-mail message is easier than addressing and mailing a letter. An e-mail message can be sent to one or more recipients, resent if necessary, and saved for future reference. Table 2-2 describes the function of each element in the Message window. In this section, you'll address a message and send it. You'll then reopen the message, change the recipient, and resend it.

Table 2-2

Message Window Elements

NEW
to Office 2010

Element	Description
File tab	Use the File tab to access common Outlook settings and options.
Quick Access Toolbar	Use the **Quick Access Toolbar** to save, print, or undo your recent actions and redo your recent actions. The position and content of the Quick Access Toolbar can be customized.
Ribbon	The Ribbon organizes commands into logical groups. The groups are placed under tabs that focus on a particular activity. In the Message window, the tabs include Message, Insert, Options, and Format Text. The content of the Ribbon varies by the task. The Ribbon in the Message window contains different options from the Ribbon in the Contact window.
To	Key the name or e-mail address of the person or people who will receive the message you are sending. To send the message to several addressees, key a semicolon after a name before adding the next addressee.
Cc	The *Cc* field is optional. You can send a message without entering anything in the *Cc* field. Generally, you would use this to send a copy of the message to individuals who you think should be informed about the message content but from whom you don't expect any action.
Subject	Key a brief description of the information in the message. The **Subject** tells the recipient what the message is about and makes it easier to find the message later.

Showing and Hiding the *From* and *Bcc* Fields

The Outlook message window contains four standard fields that you can use to create and address your messages. However, there are two additional fields that you can use or hide as needed: *From* and *Bcc*. These fields are hidden by default, but you can use the Options tab to display them in the Message window.

Using the From field can be quite convenient when you use more than one e-mail account. For example, you might use one account for work and a different one for personal messages.

The Bcc field enables you to send a blind copy to someone. You would use this to send a copy of the message to an individual who should be informed about the message's content without notifying the recipient(s) listed in the *To* and *Cc* fields. The *Bcc* field is different from the *Cc* field in that no one else who receives the e-mail message knows that someone else received a blind copy. In this exercise, you'll turn on and off the From and Bcc fields.

STEP BY STEP   **Show or Hide the *From* and *Bcc* Fields**

USE the message you created in the previous exercise.

1. Click the Options tab. The Option tab displays the sending and delivery options as well as many options you can use to customize the message.

2. In the Show Fields group, click Bcc. The *Bcc* field appears in the Message window, as shown in Figure 2-5.

3. In the Show Fields group, click From. The *From* field appears in the Message window, as shown in Figure 2-5.

Figure 2-5

Displaying the *From* and *Bcc* fields

Click to toggle on and off the From and Bcc fields

Click the From button to select an alternate email address

The Bcc field

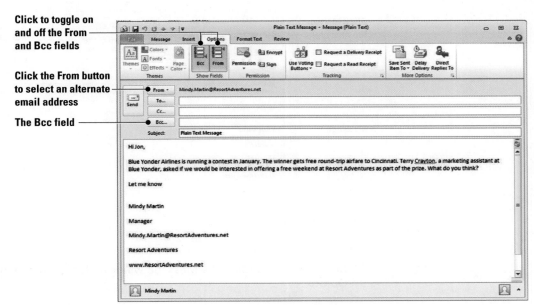

4. In the *Bcc* field, key [your e-mail address].

Take Note   Displaying and hiding the *From* and *Bcc* fields affects only the current Message window.

5. In the Show Fields group, click From. The *From* field is once again hidden from view.
PAUSE. LEAVE Outlook open to use in the next exercise.

Sending a Message

Addressing an e-mail message is similar to addressing a letter. In seconds, you can send an e-mail message to one or more recipients. In this exercise, you'll address an e-mail message and send it to the recipient.

STEP BY STEP   **Send a Message**

USE the message you worked on in the previous exercise.

1. Click the *To* field. Key someone@example.com or key [the e-mail address of a friend or coworker]. To send the message to more than one recipient, key a semicolon (;), and then key another e-mail address.

2. Select the text in the *Subject* field. Key Blue Yonder Airlines contest and press Enter. The message is now ready to send, as shown in Figure 2-6.

Troubleshooting The e-mail addresses used in this book are owned by Microsoft Corporation. Because they are not real e-mail addresses, you will receive either an error message or a message thanking you for using Microsoft products.

Figure 2-6

Message ready to be sent

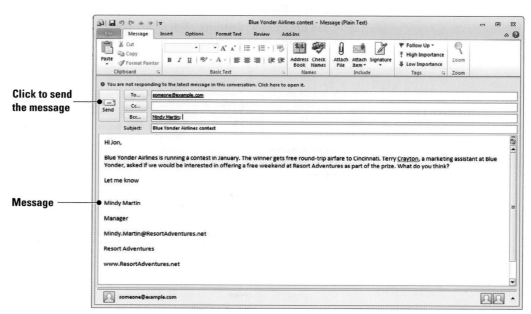

3. Click the Send button. The Message window closes, and the message is moved to the Outbox.

Take Note   If your computer is connected to the Internet, the message is sent to the addressee as soon as you click the Send button. If your computer is not connected to the Internet, the message will remain in the Outbox until you connect to the Internet and the message can be sent.

PAUSE. LEAVE Outlook open to use in the next exercise.

In the previous exercises, you used the Message window to compose and send an e-mail message. If your computer has not been connected to the Internet since you started this lesson, the message you sent will still be in the Outbox. Outgoing messages are moved to the Outbox when you click the Send button. They are moved to the Sent Items folder when you connect to the Internet and the messages are sent.

Resending a Message

Occasionally, you may want to resend a message. This commonly occurs when you want to send the same message to additional recipients or the recipient has accidentally deleted the message and needs another copy. In this exercise, you'll resend the message that you just sent.

STEP BY STEP   **Resend a Message**

USE the message you created in the previous exercise.

1. In the Navigation Pane, click the Sent Items folder. The e-mail messages you sent will be listed as items in the Sent Items folder, as shown in Figure 2-7.

Figure 2-7

Sent Items folder

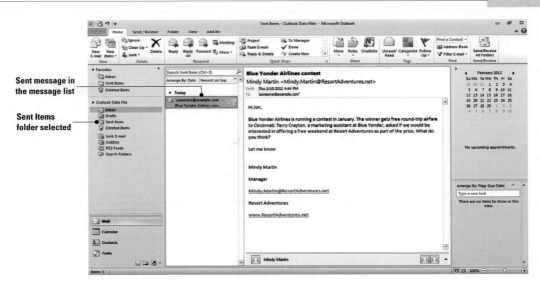

Sent message in the message list

Sent Items folder selected

 **Troubleshooting** If you haven't been connected to the Internet and your message is still sitting in the Outbox, click the Outbox folder instead of the Sent Items folder. Then continue with step 2.

2. In the list of items that have been sent, double-click the message you sent in the last exercise. The message is displayed in a new window, as shown in Figure 2-8. The title bar of the new window is the subject of the message.

Figure 2-8

Sent message

Title bar matches the subject

Actions button

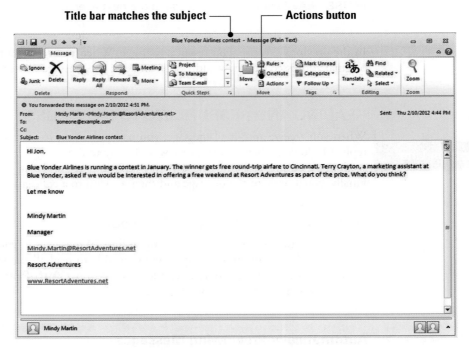

3. Click the Actions button in the Move group on the Home tab. Select the Resend This Message option from the menu that appears. This opens the message in a new window, which enables you to make modifications to the original message.

4. Click after the addressee in the To field. Key a semicolon (;) and an additional e-mail address, as shown in Figure 2-9. For this exercise, use your e-mail address as the addressee. By default in Outlook, someone who is listed as both a recipient in the *To* field and the *Bcc* field will only receive the message once.

Figure 2-9

Message ready to be resent

Addressee added before
resending the message   Original message window

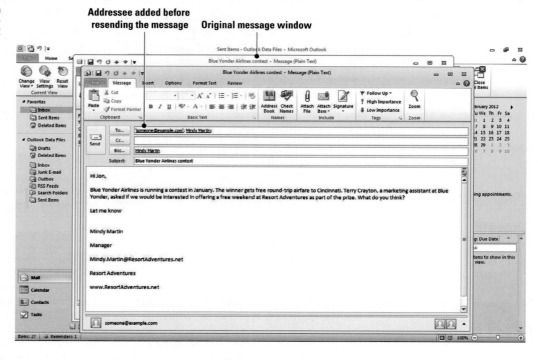

Figure 2-9

Message ready to be resent

5. Click the **Send** button. The Message window closes, and the message is moved to the Outbox. The message is sent when your computer is connected to the Internet.

6. Close the original Message window.

PAUSE. LEAVE Outlook open to use in the next exercise.

In the previous exercise, you resent a message. When you resend a message, you can delete the original addressee, add new addressees, and edit the message content.

READING AND RESPONDING TO MESSAGES

The Bottom Line

When you receive an e-mail message, you naturally want to read it and, in many cases, send a reply. Outlook enables you to preview and reply to a message with a few mouse clicks. In this section, you'll preview and read a new e-mail message and flag it as a reminder for yourself. Finally, you'll reply to the message and then forward to a colleague.

Automatically Previewing Messages

If you return to your desk after a meeting to find 20 messages in your Inbox and another meeting to attend in 5 minutes, it might be impossible to read all the messages and still get to the meeting on time. In this exercise, you learn how to use **AutoPreview** to view the first three lines of every message in the message list.

STEP BY STEP   **Automatically Previewing Messages**

USE the message you created in the previous exercise.

1. In the Navigation Pane, click the **Inbox** folder. The Inbox is displayed.

2. On the View tab, click the **Change View** button. The available views for this folder appear below the Current View group.

3. Select the **Preview** option. The Inbox folder's layout changes: The Reading Pane disappears, and the messages appear in a list format. Notice that the first three lines of text in each unread message is displayed, as shown in Figure 2-10.

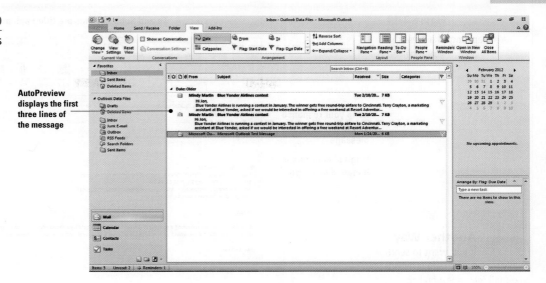

Figure 2-10

AutoPreview messages

AutoPreview displays the first three lines of the message

Take Note   By default, AutoPreview only displays a preview of the unread messages. If you want to view all messages this way, click the View Settings button and select Other Settings. In the AutoPreview area of the Other Settings dialog box, select the Preview All Items option and then click OK twice to close the dialog boxes.

4. On the View tab, click the **Change View** button. Select **Compact** from the available views. This turns off the AutoPreview function and returns to the default view.

PAUSE. LEAVE Outlook open to use in the next exercise.

AutoPreview requires more space in the message list. Therefore, you probably want to turn off the feature most of the time.

Sending a Reply to a Message

Not every message is going to require a reply, but many messages do need a response of some type. When you use the Reply function, your response is automatically addressed to the person who sent the message to you. In this exercise, you'll send a reply to a message.

STEP BY STEP   **Send a Reply to a Message**

USE the message you received when you sent a message to yourself in a previous exercise.

1. In the Inbox, click the message with the subject **Blue Yonder Airlines contest**. The message is selected and a preview appears in the Reading Pane.

2. Click the **Reply** button on the Home tab. The message is displayed in a new window, as shown in Figure 2-11. Note that the *To* and *Subject* fields are already filled and the contents of the original message are included at the bottom of the window. They are sent as part of the reply.

Take Note   In the *Subject* field, the text "RE:" was inserted before the original subject line. "RE:", which stands for "regarding," tells the recipient that the message is a reply about the Blue Yonder Airlines contest topic.

Figure 2-11

Replying to a message
you received

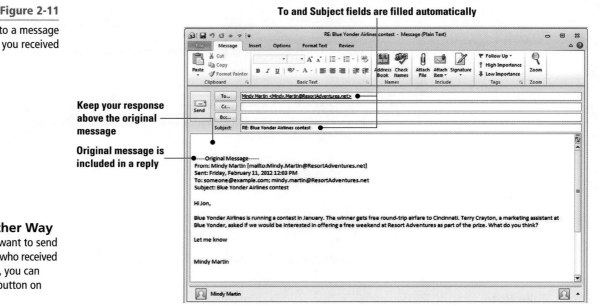

To and Subject fields are filled automatically

Keep your response above the original message

Original message is included in a reply

Another Way

If you want to send a reply to everyone who received an e-mail message, you can click the Reply All button on the Home tab.

Take Note

Before responding to a message, check the *To* line to ensure that you did not reply to all message recipients if you intended to reply to the sender only.

3. Key **The contest could be a good idea. Let's set up a meeting.**

4. Click the **Send** button. The Message window closes, and the reply is moved to the Outbox. The message is sent when your computer is connected to the Internet.

PAUSE. LEAVE Outlook open to use in the next exercise.

When a reply has been sent, the icon next to the original message is changed. An arrow pointing left, as shown in Figure 2-12, indicates that you replied to the message. When you view the main Outlook window, this icon tells you which messages you have answered.

Figure 2-12

Icon indicating that a reply
was sent

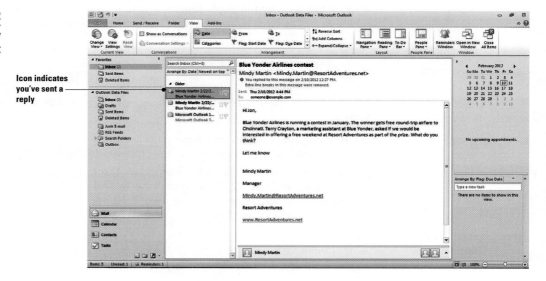

Icon indicates you've sent a reply

Forwarding a Message

Occasionally, you receive a message that should be sent to additional people. Outlook's Forward function is a quick method of sending the message to additional people without re-creating the original message. In this exercise, you'll forward a message to a colleague.

STEP BY STEP | **Forwarding a Message**

USE the message you received when you sent a message to yourself in a previous exercise.

1. In the Inbox, click the message with the subject Blue Yonder Airlines contest. The message is selected.
2. Click the Forward button on the Home tab. The message is displayed in a new window, as shown in Figure 2-13. The original message is included at the bottom of the window.

Take Note | Note that the *Subject* field is already filled. In the *Subject* field, the text "FW:" has been inserted before the original subject line. "FW:" tells the recipient that the message has been forwarded by the sender.

3. In the *To* field, key someone@example.com.
4. Click the message area above the original message. Key What is the value of the airfare and weekend at Resort Adventures?
5. [Press Enter.] Key [your name].

Figure 2-13

Forwarding a message you received

Subject field filled automatically

Key text above the original message

Original message is included

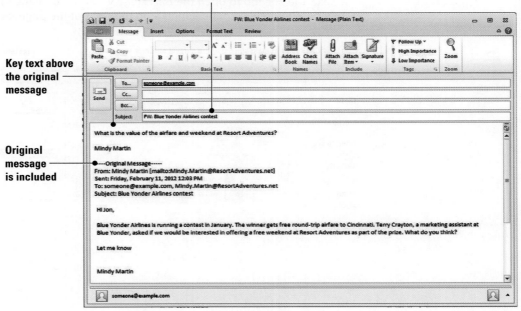

6. Click the Send button. The Message window closes, and the message is moved to the Outbox. The message is sent when your computer is connected to the Internet.

PAUSE. LEAVE Outlook open to use in the next exercise.

When a message has been forwarded, the icon next to the original message is changed. An arrow pointing right, as shown in Figure 2-14, indicates that you forwarded the message.

Figure 2-14

Icon indicating the message was forwarded

Forwarded message

Printing an E-mail Message

In Outlook 2010, each message is actually a document. As with any other documents you create or receive, you might want to have a hard copy of the information. You can use the tools on the Print page in Backstage view to preview and print the selected message. The Print page includes a preview pane that shows you how the message will look when printed so that you can make any necessary changes before sending it to the printer. The Print page also contains the various printing options you can select, such as the number of copies and the range of pages to print. You can choose printing options each time or simply print using the default options. In this exercise, you'll print a message.

STEP BY STEP **Print an E-mail Message**

 Troubleshooting Before printing your document, you will need to make sure you have selected a printer. If your computer is already set up to print, you will not need to complete step 5 of this exercise.

USE the message you created in the previous exercises.

1. In the Inbox, click the message with the subject Blue Yonder Airlines contest. The message is selected.

2. Click the **File** tab to open the Backstage view and click the **Print** option in the navigation pane. The preview pane appears on the right of the page, as shown in Figure 2-15.

Figure 2-15

Printing a message

Click to print message using the current settings

Preview of the selected message

Click to select a printer

Click to see additional settings

Message printing styles

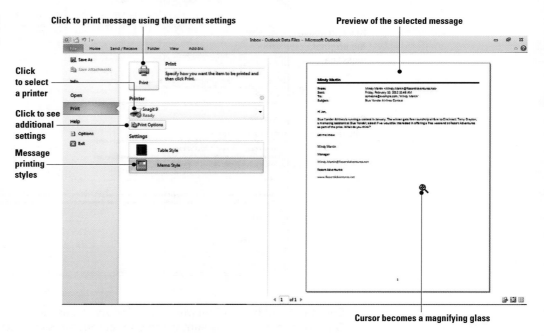

Cursor becomes a magnifying glass

Take Note Memo Style is the default style for printing messages. If you want to print the message list for the current folder, you can click Table Style.

3. Move the pointer over the document preview and notice that it changes to a magnifying glass, as shown in Figure 2-15.

4. Click the document to zoom in to 100% and again to zoom out to 50%.

5. Click the **Printer** button to display a list of available printers. Select the printer you want to use from the list.

 Troubleshooting You may need to set up a new printer before you can proceed.

6. Click the **Print Options** button to display the Print dialog box, as shown in Figure 2-16. Notice the available printing options.

Figure 2-16

Print dialog box

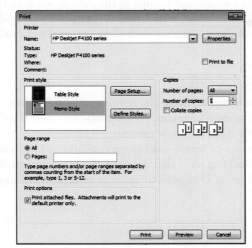

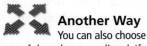
Another Way
If you already have a printer selected, you can simply click the large Print button to print the message using the default settings.

7. In the copies area, click the **upward-pointing arrow** next to the *Number of copies* box to change it to 2.

8. Click **Print** to print two copies of the letter.

PAUSE. LEAVE Outlook open to use in the next exercise.

You chose to print two copies of the message in this activity. If the message were longer, you could have chosen other options, such as printing a range of pages, collating the pages, or printing multiple pages per sheet.

Saving a Message in an External Format

Outlook stores a copy of every message you write or receive in one of its folders until you delete it. Saving messages in Outlook's folder structure in Outlook Message Format is often all you need. However, if you need a message available in a different format, you can choose to save it as a .txt file or as a fully formatted .html file. In this exercise, you'll save a copy of a message as a text file.

STEP BY STEP | **Save a Message in an External Format**

USE the message you created in the previous exercises.

1. Click the **File** tab to open the Backstage view and then click **Save As**. The Save As dialog box is displayed, showing the Documents folder.

2. Navigate to the **Outlook Lesson 2** folder. You can also choose a folder in which to store the file from the folder list.

Take Note

To create a new folder in the folder list to store your message, click the New Folder button in the menu bar.

Another Way
You can also choose any of the other types listed. If the message is in the default HTML format, saving it as an HTML document will also be a choice.

3. In the *Save As type* box, click the **downward-pointing arrow** and choose **Text Only**.

4. In the File Name box, key **Sample Saved Message**.

5. Click **Save** to close the dialog box and save the document.

6. Close the message window.

PAUSE. LEAVE Outlook open to use in the next exercise.

You can save a message as a file to a folder on your hard drive, a network location, a CD, the desktop, or another storage location. You just saved the message letter you created as a .txt file.

If you had chosen Outlook Message Format in the *Save as type* box, the message would be stored as a functioning Outlook message, which means that when you open the file it opens as a fully functioning message window, complete with all the normal options.

FORMATTING MESSAGES

The Bottom Line

Your e-mail messages convey an image about you and your business. In order to present the best image to clients and business contacts, the best business communications are as eye-catching and polished as possible. Outlook provides many ways to format the text in your message so as to improve the appearance of your e-mail communications. Outlook includes most of the same formatting and spellchecking tools that are available in Microsoft Word 2010. In this section, you'll format messages using Outlook's formatting tools, themes, and styles.

SOFTWARE ORIENTATION

Formatting Outlook Messages

As you learn to format messages, it is important to become familiar with the tools you will use. The Format Text tab displayed in Figure 2-17 contains the formatting commands that you will use to enhance the appearance of the messages you create.

Figure 2-17

Message window's Format Text tab

You will use commands from every group on the Format Text tab as you learn to apply formatting to text, copy formatting, and apply styles and themes.

Using Formatting Tools

Microsoft has a variety of fonts and font sizes to help you communicate your intended message, whether it is casual for your personal life or formal for the workplace. In addition to changing the font and font size, you can apply special **formatting attributes**, such as bold or italic, to characters within your text to give them special emphasis. A **character** can be a letter, number, punctuation mark, or symbol. In this exercise, you'll use Outlook's formatting tools to enhance the appearance of a message.

You can use the **Format Painter** to copy formats, including font, font size, font style, font color, alignment, indentation, number formats, borders, and shading. To copy formatting from one location to another, select the text that has the formatting you want to copy. Click Format Painter in the Clipboard group. The mouse pointer turns into a white plus sign with the paintbrush beside it. Drag the mouse pointer across the text you want to format.

To copy formatting to several locations, double-click the Format Painter button, and then drag the mouse pointer across each text item you want to format. When you're done, click the Format Painter again or press Esc to turn off the Format Painter.

STEP BY STEP   **Use Formatting Tools**

GET READY. LAUNCH Outlook if it is not already running.

1. If necessary, click the Mail button in the Navigation Pane to display the Mail folder.
2. Click the New E-mail button on the Home tab. The Message window is displayed, as shown in Figure 2-1.
3. Open the *Promotional Flyer* document in the data files for this lesson and select the text. Right-click and click Copy on the shortcut menu.
4. Back in Outlook, right-click the message area.
5. Click Paste on the shortcut menu. The text of the Promotional Flyer is pasted into the message.
6. Select all the text in the message area.
7. Click the Format Text tab to display the Font group, as shown in Figure 2-18.

@ The *Promotional Flyer* file is available on the book companion website or in WileyPLUS.

Figure 2-18

The Font group

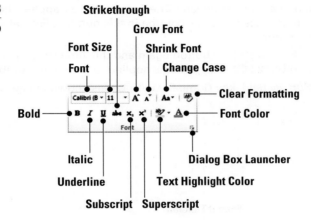

8. In the Font group click the dialog box launcher. The Font dialog box appears.
9. Click ++Body in the selection pane under the Font box. Press the down arrow to scroll through the list to select Verdana, as shown in Figure 2-19. Notice that the Preview area displays how your selected text will look with each font selected.

Another Way
You can also access the Font dialog box from the Basic Text group on the Home tab.

Figure 2-19

The Font dialog box

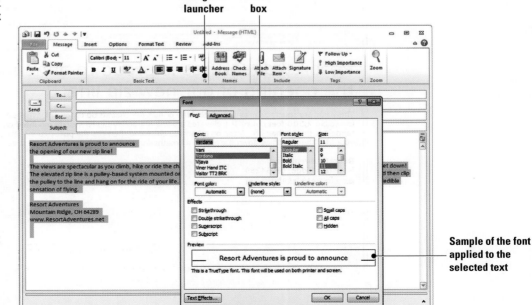

Another Way
You can also click the Font arrow button on the ribbon to open a menu that you can use to change the font of the selected text.

Another Way
You could also key the name of the font in the Font box.

10. Click OK to close the dialog box.

Another Way
You can also use the keyboard to apply bold. Select text and press Ctrl+B.

Another Way
You can also use the keyboard to apply Underline. Select text and press Ctrl+U.

Another Way
You can also use the keyboard to apply italics. Select text and press Ctrl+I.

Another Way
The Format Painter is available on the Mini toolbar as well as in the Clipboard group.

Another Way
You can use the Format Painter to change multiple selections. With the source formatting selected, double-click the Format Painter button. You can click any text to change it. Double-click to turn off the Format Painter.

11. Select the first sentence in the message area (be sure to select both lines). Click the **Font Size arrow** in the Font group and select **36**. The text size changes to 36.

12. With the text still selected, click the **Font Size** box and key **22** and press **Enter**. The text size shrinks considerably.

13. With the text still selected, click the **Grow Font** button three times and then the **Shrink Font** button one time. The text is now resized to 26.

14. With the text still selected, click the **Font Color arrow** and select **Blue, Accent 1, Darker 25%** from the gallery that appears. The text changes to medium blue color.

15. Select the text **Resort Adventures** near the bottom of the message and click **Bold**. The text is made bold to draw more attention to it.

16. Select the web address at the bottom of the message and click **Underline**.

17. Select the text **The Zipper** and click **Italic**.

18. Select the text **Resort** and click the **Format Painter** button in the Clipboard group. The formatting details are stored in the clipboard.

19. Click one of the zeros in 2,500 in the main paragraph. The text 500 becomes bold, but the rest of the number doesn't. The Format Painter applies the format to the entire word, but because there is a comma in this number, Format Painter interprets it as two different words.

20. Click the **Format Painter** button again and this time click and drag the cursor across the entire number 2,500. The format is applied to the entire number.

21. In the *Subject* field, key **Come Fly with Us**, as shown in Figure 2-20.

Figure 2-20

A formatted message

PAUSE. LEAVE the Outlook Message window open to use in the next exercise.

The font group in the Format Text tab contains the Font menu for changing the font, and the Font Size menu for changing its size. You can also access these commands on the Mini toolbar. Table 2-3 provides extra information about each character formatting tool.

Table 2-3

Formatting Tools

Button	Example	Description
Bold	**Sample bold text**	Emphasis formatting attribute that makes the selected text look darker and thicker.
Change Capitalization	Hello world hello world HELLO WORLD Hello World hELLO wORLD	The Change Case menu in the Font group has five options for changing the capitalization of text.
Font	Calibri **Times New Roman** Comic Sans	A **font** is a set of characters that have the same design. Each font has a unique name.
Font Color	Sample font color	Changes the color of the selected text. Click the down arrow next to the button to select a different font color.
Font Size	Size 8 Size 10 Size 12	Font sizes are measured in points. Point sizes refer to the height of text characters, with one point equaling approx. 1/72 of an inch.
Grow Font	Grow Grow Grow	Click the Grow Font button to increase the size of the selected text by one increment.
Italic	*Sample italic text*	Emphasis formatting attribute the makes the selected text look lighter and tilted to the right.
Shrink Font	Shrink Shrink Shrink	Click the Shrink Font button to decrease the size of the selected text by one increment.
Strikethrough	~~Sample strikethrough text~~	Emphasis formatting attribute that places a line through the center of the selected text.
Subscript	Sample $_{1\ subscript}$	Emphasis formatting attribute that places the selected text just below the line of the surrounding text.
Superscript	Sample $^{2\ superscript}$	Emphasis formatting attribute that places the selected text just above the line of the surrounding text.
Text Highlight	Sample highlight	Use the Text Highlight Color button in the Font group to highlight text, making it look as if it was marked with a highlighting pen. Click the down arrow next to the button to select a different highlight color. To remove highlighting select the highlighted text and choose No Color from the menu.
Underline	<u>Sample underlined text</u>	Emphasis formatting attribute that places an underline beneath the selected text. You can select the style and thickness of the line by click the Underline button arrow.
Clear Formatting	Sample unformatted text	Removes all formatting from the selected text.

Formatting Paragraphs

Depending on the type of information you want to convey in your message, you might want to apply paragraph formatting to make your message more understandable. Outlook contains a number of tools that you can use to change the appearance of paragraphs. You can change alignment and line spacing, create numbered and bulleted lists, sort paragraphs, and use shading and borders. To apply paragraph formatting, place the insertion point anywhere in a paragraph. Outlook will apply the formatting you chose to the entire paragraph. In this exercise, you will try out the different paragraph formatting options.

STEP BY STEP   **Format Paragraphs**

USE the message you created in the previous exercise.

1. If necessary, open the Come Fly with Us message that you worked on in the previous exercise and click the Format Text tab to display the Paragraph group, as shown in Figure 2-21.

Figure 2-21

The Paragraph group

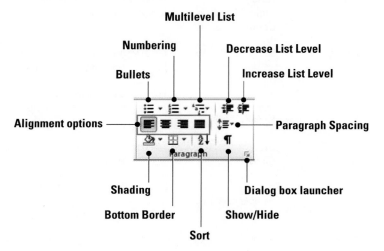

2. Click the Show/Hide button in the Paragraph group of the Format Text tab. The paragraph symbol (¶) appears at the end of each paragraph.
3. Select the paragraph symbol (¶) at the end of the first line and press Delete. Press Spacebar. The first sentence becomes one paragraph.
4. Click anywhere in the first paragraph and click the Paragraph group dialog box launcher. The Paragraph dialog box is displayed, as shown in Figure 2-22.

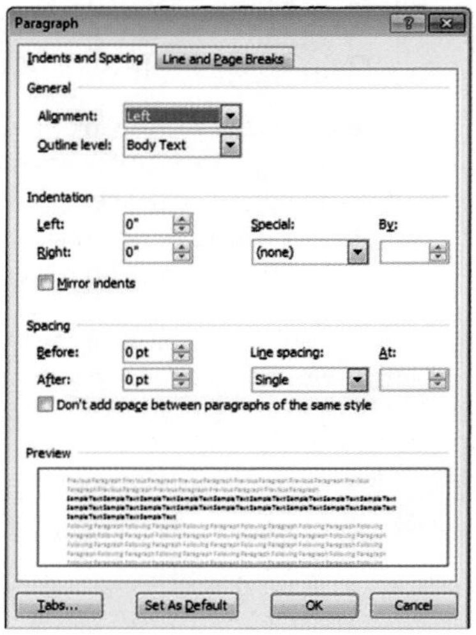

Figure 2-22

The Paragraph dialog box

5. In the After box in the Spacing area, key **18**. Click **OK** to close the dialog box. The spacing between the first paragraph and the second paragraph is increased.

6. Click the **Align Center** button in the Paragraph group of the Format Text tab. The paragraph where the insertion point is located is centered at the top of the message.

7. Click the **Shading button arrow** and select **Dark Blue**. Dark blue shading appears behind the main paragraph. Notice that the font color automatically changes to white to make text more readable.

8. Click the **Shading button arrow** again and select **Olive Green, Accent 3, Lighter 40%**. Since you've applied a lighter shading option, the font color automatically changes back to black to make text more readable.

9. Select the last three rows of text and click **Align Right**.

10. Click anywhere in the text Resort Adventures and click the **Borders button arrow**. A menu of border styles is displayed.

11. Click the **Top Border** button in the menu. A thin line appears above the text. Your message should look like the one in Figure 2-23.

Figure 2-23

Shading and aligning paragraphs

PAUSE. **LEAVE** the Outlook Message window open to use in the next exercise.

Applying Styles to a Message

Although formatting your messages makes them more appealing, it can also be time consuming. You can save time by selecting a style from Outlook's Quick Style gallery. A **style** is a set of formatting attributes that you can apply to text more easily than setting each formatting attribute individually. **Quick Styles** are predefined formats that you can apply to your document to instantly change its look and feel. Outlook eliminates the guesswork by allowing you to preview the formatting changes in your message before you commit to a style. In this exercise, you will apply Quick Styles to a message.

STEP BY STEP   **Apply Styles to a Message**

USE the message you created in the previous exercise.

1. If necessary, open the **Come Fly with Us** message that you worked on in the previous exercise and click the **Format Text** tab to display the Styles group, as shown in Figure 2-17.

2. Click anywhere in the first sentence and click the **More** button in the Styles group to display the Quick Styles gallery, as shown in Figure 2-24.

Figure 2-24

Quick Styles gallery

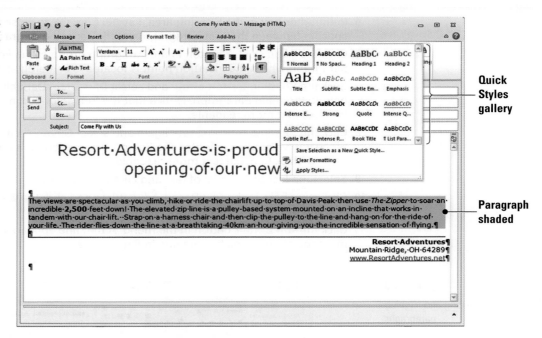

3. Place your pointer over any choice on the Styles Set menu and notice that your document changes to show you a preview of that style.

4. Click **Title**. The text changes font, color, and alignment to reflect the Title style.

5. Select the body paragraph that begins "*The views are spectacular...*" Click the **More** button to open the Quick Styles gallery again.

6. Place your pointer over any thumbnail in the gallery and notice that the paragraph changes to show you a preview of that style.

Take Note   You will notice that some of the thumbnails remove the background formatting and some do not. When you select a paragraph style, all the previous formatting for the paragraph is replaced with the new style.

7. Click the **Quote** thumbnail. Notice that style is applied to the paragraph you selected. Your message should look similar to Figure 2-25.

Figure 2-25

Message formatted with Quick Styles

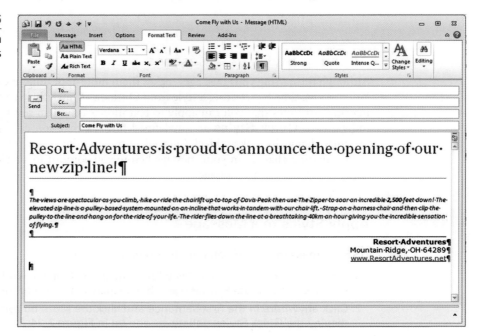

8. Click the Change Styles button in the Styles group. Point to Style Set and point to each of the Style Sets listed. Notice that the formatting of the entire message changes to reflect the style set.

9. Click on Traditional. The message changes to reflect the Traditional styles, as shown in Figure 2-26.

Figure 2-26

Message formatted with a Style Set

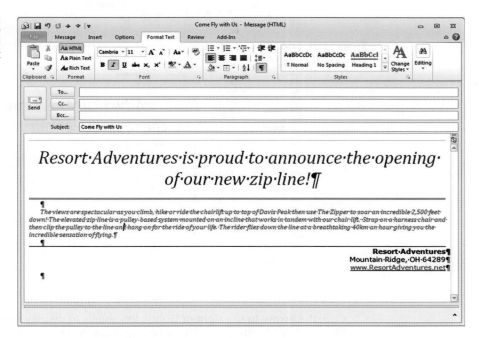

PAUSE. LEAVE the Outlook Message window open to use in the next exercise.

There are two kinds of Quick Styles—paragraph styles and character styles. A paragraph mark to the right of the style's name denotes a style created for paragraphs. When you choose paragraph styles, the formats are applied to all the text in the paragraph in which your insertion point is located, whether or not you have it all selected.

Character styles have the lowercase letter a beside them. Character styles are applied to individual characters you have selected within a paragraph rather than affecting the entire paragraph.

Style Sets are collections of Quick Style formats that go well together. When you select a Style Set from the Change Styles button, the entire message is changed to reflect the combination of styles in the set.

Creating Styles

Outlook allows you to create custom styles that you can save to the Styles list. You can then apply the custom style to future messages. You can also modify Quick Styles to suit your needs. In this exercise, you'll create a custom style.

STEP BY STEP   **Create Styles**

USE the message you created in the previous exercise.

1. If necessary, open the Come Fly with Us message that you worked on in the previous exercise and click the Format Text tab to display the Styles group (refer to Figure 2-17).

2. Select the text Mountain Ridge, OH 64289. Click the dialog box launcher for the Styles group. The Styles list is displayed as a floating box in the Message window.

3. Click the top of the Styles list and drag it to the left edge of the message window. The Styles list is docked to the side of the message, as shown in Figure 2-27.

Figure 2-27

Docked Styles list

Styles list

4. Click the Subtle Emphasis style. The style is applied to the selected text.

5. Click the arrow to the right of Subtle Emphasis to display the shortcut menu. Click Modify. The Modify Style dialog box appears, as shown in Figure 2-28.

Figure 2-28

Modify Style dialog box

6. Click the Bold button in the dialog box. Click the Font Color down arrow and click Dark Blue, Text 2, Lighter 60% in the standard colors section. Notice that the preview in the dialog box changes.

7. Click OK to apply your changes and close the dialog box. The appearance of the selected text changes.

8. Select the text Resort Adventures. Click the Italic button in the Font group.

9. Click the Font down arrow and select Cooper Std Black. Click the Font Color down arrow and select Dark Blue.

10. Click the Increase Font button twice to change the font size to 14.

11. Click the More button is the Styles group. Select Save Selection as a new Quick Style. The Create New Style from Formatting dialog box opens, as shown in Figure 2-29.

Figure 2-29

Create New Style from
Formatting dialog box

Figure 2-29

Create New Style from
Formatting dialog box

12. Key **Resort Adventures** in the Name box and click **OK**. The Resort Adventures style is
    displayed in the Styles list, as shown in Figure 2-30.

Figure 2-30

Creating a custom style

New style
added to
the list

13. Close the Come Fly with Us message window. Be sure to allow Outlook to save a copy
    of the message.
    PAUSE. LEAVE Outlook open to use in the next exercise.

You just learned that the Modify Style dialog box has basic formatting commands like the Font
menu; Font Size menu; Bold, Italic, and Underline buttons; and Font Color menu. When you
modify paragraph fonts you can also change alignment indents and spacing.

Applying a Message Theme

Message themes are another way to quickly change the overall design of your document using
formatting choices that are predefined in Outlook. A **theme** is a predefined set of colors, fonts,
and lines that can be applied to an entire message. Outlook contains the same collection of
themes that are available in the rest of Microsoft Office. You can apply an entire theme to your
message or choose from a variety of theme fonts, colors, and effects. In this exercise, you'll use a
theme to format an e-mail message.

STEP BY STEP   **Apply a Message Theme**

USE the message you created in the previous exercise.

1. Click **Drafts** in the Navigation Pane. Double-click the **Come Fly with Us** message that you worked on in the previous exercise and click the **Options** tab to display the Themes group, as shown in Figure 2-31.

Figure 2-31

The Themes group

2. In the Themes group, click **Page Color**. The Page Color gallery is displayed.
3. Select the **Tan, Accent 2** color from the Theme colors area.
4. In the Themes group, click **Themes** as shown in Figure 2-32.

Figure 2-32

The Themes gallery

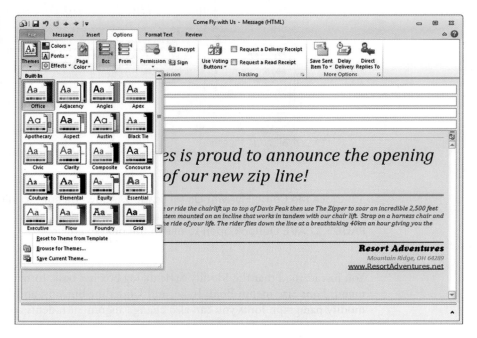

5. Place your pointer over any built-in theme and notice that the document changes to show you a preview of that theme.
6. Click **Executive**. The colors, fonts, and effects for that theme are applied to your message. Notice that the text *Resort Adventures* does not change because it uses a custom style.

PAUSE. LEAVE the Outlook Message window open to use in the next exercise.

Creating a New Theme

Although you used a theme to change the overall design of the entire message, you can also change individual elements by using the Theme Colors, Theme Fonts, and Theme Effects buttons. If you make any changes to the colors, fonts, or effects of the current theme, you can save it as a custom message theme and then apply it to other messages.

Create a New Theme

USE the message you created in the previous exercise.

1. If necessary, open the Come Fly with Us message that you worked on in the previous exercise and click the Options tab to display the Themes group.
2. In the Themes group, click Theme Fonts as shown in Figure 2-33.

Figure 2-33

The Theme Fonts gallery

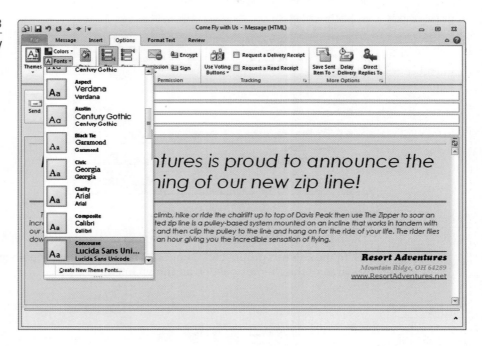

3. Place your pointer over any of the theme fonts and notice that the document changes to show you a preview of that theme.
4. Click the Concourse theme font. The fonts for that theme are applied to your message.
5. In the Themes group, click Theme Colors as shown in Figure 2-34.

Figure 2-34

The Theme Colors gallery

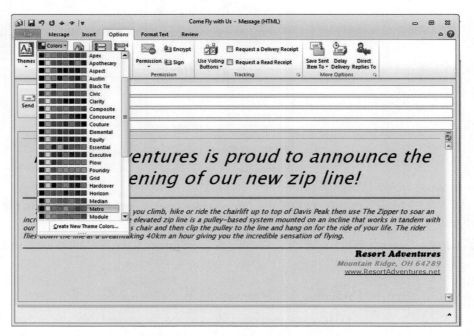

6. Click the Metro theme color. The colors for that theme are applied to your message.

7. In the Themes group, click Themes. Click the Save Current Theme option at the bottom of the Themes gallery. The Save Current Theme window is displayed with the text Theme1 already displayed in the *File name* box, as shown in Figure 2-35.

Figure 2-35

The Save Current Theme window

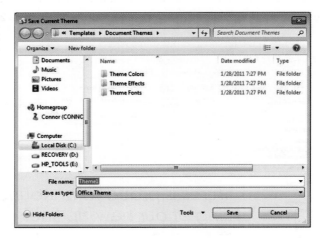

8. In the *File name* box, select the existing text and key Resort Adventures. Click Save.

9. In the Themes group, click Themes. The new custom theme appears in the Custom area of the Themes gallery, as shown in Figure 2-36.

Figure 2-36

The Resort Adventures theme displayed in the Themes gallery

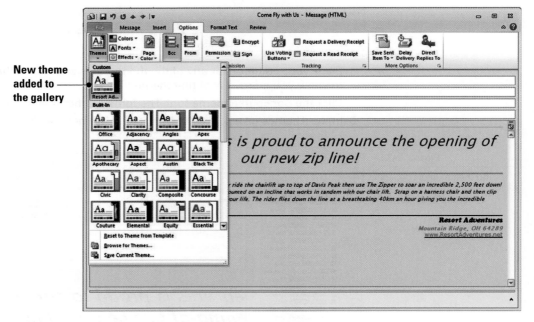

PAUSE. LEAVE the Outlook Message window open to use in the next exercise.

Take Note   You can share your custom theme throughout all Office programs, so all of your Office documents can have the same look and feel.

Document themes can contain the following elements:

• Theme colors contain four text and background colors, six accent colors, and two hyperlink colors. Click the Theme Colors button to change the colors for the current theme (refer to Figure 2-34).

- Theme fonts contain a heading font and a body text font. Click the Theme Fonts button to change the fonts for the current theme (refer to Figure 2-33).
- Theme effects are sets of lines and fill effects. Click the Theme Effects button to change the effects for the current theme (refer to Figure 2-37).

Figure 2-37

The Theme Effects gallery

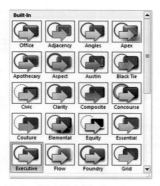

Using Paste Special

When you copy something from one source and paste it into an Outlook message, Outlook assumes you want to keep the source formatting. Sometimes this formatting works with your existing formatting, but often the pasted text clashes with the existing message. You can use the Paste Special feature to have more control over how the text appears. In this exercise, you'll use the Paste Special feature to copy and paste text into your message.

STEP BY STEP **Use Paste Special**

USE the message you created in the previous exercise.

1. If necessary, open the Come Fly with Us message that you worked on in the previous exercise and click the Home tab to display the Clipboard group.
2. Place the insertion point at the end of the main paragraph in the message. Press Enter twice to add some space between the paragraph and the horizontal line.
3. In your Internet browser, open the *Zipper Rates* web page document in the data files for this lesson.
4. Scroll down the web page. Select the text Some Highlights You Could Experience: and the bulleted list that follows. Press Ctrl+C, which is the keyboard shortcut for the Copy command.

The *Zipper Rates* file is available on the book companion website or in WileyPLUS.

Take Note   The Ctrl+C keyboard shortcut is a powerful tool. Using the shortcut allows you to copy text in almost any application and then paste it (by using the Paste button or the keyboard shortcut Ctrl+V) into Outlook.

5. Back in Outlook, click the message area one line below the main paragraph.
6. In the Clipboard group, click the Paste button. The copied text is pasted into the message using the original formatting from the web page and the Paste Options button appears at the end of the text. In this case, the new text does not match the text in the original message, as shown in Figure 2-38.

Figure 2-38

Pasting into a message

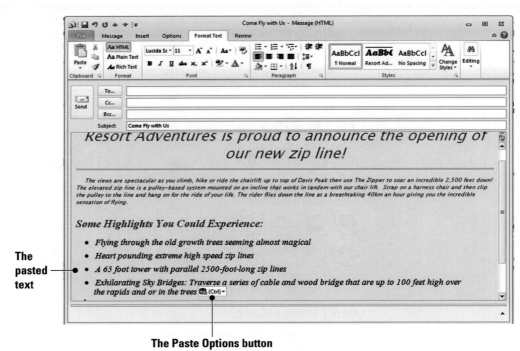

The pasted text

The Paste Options button

7. Click the Undo button. In the Clipboard group, click the Paste down arrow. The Paste Options are listed beneath the Paste button, as shown in Figure 2-39.

Figure 2-39

The Paste Options

Click to keep the text only

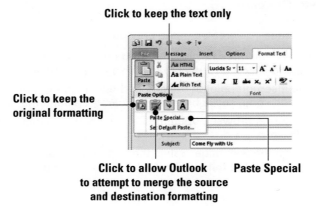

Click to keep the original formatting

Click to allow Outlook to attempt to merge the source and destination formatting

Paste Special

8. Select Paste Special. The Paste Special dialog box is displayed, as shown in Figure 2-40.

Figure 2-40

Paste Special dialog box

Inserts only the unformatted text

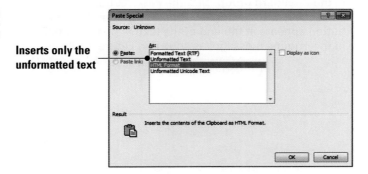

Another Way
You can also paste unformatted text by clicking the Paste Options button and selecting the Keep Text Only option.

9. Select **Unformatted Text** and click **OK**. The dialog box closes and the text is pasted into the message without any formatting. Click the **Format Text** tab.

10. Select the text **Some Highlights You Could Experience:** and select **Heading 1** from the Style gallery in the Styles group to apply the Heading 1 Quick Style to just this text selection.

11. Select the pasted list under the heading. Click the **Bullets** button in the Paragraph group. The new text is bulleted as it was in the browser window.

12. Click the **More** button to open the Style gallery. Select **Emphasis** from the Style gallery to give the bulleted items a style that blends well with the rest of the message.

13. Click the **Bullets down arrow** and select the **large circle** from the Bullet Library to change the bullets in the list, as shown in Figure 2-41.

Figure 2-41

Formatting the pasted text

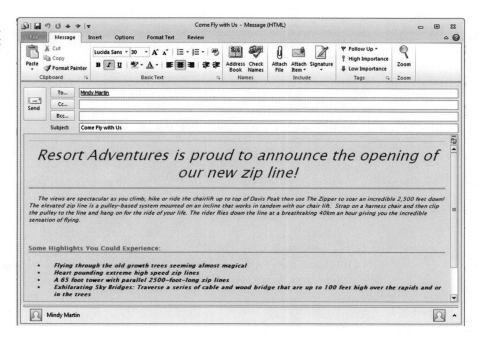

14. In the *To* field, key [your e-mail address].

15. Close the Come Fly with Us – Message window. Be sure to allow Outlook to save a copy of the message.

PAUSE. LEAVE Outlook open to use in the next exercise.

PERSONALIZING MESSAGES

The Bottom Line

You can personalize your messages in many ways. Formatting, colors, and images probably come to mind first. However, the signature is one of the most useful places to personalize your messages. In this section, you'll create a personal signature and attach it to a message. You'll also look into attaching your personal signature to all outgoing messages.

Creating a Personal Signature

A **signature** is text or images that Outlook automatically places at the end of your outgoing messages. A signature can be as fancy or as plain as you like. In this exercise, you'll create a personal signature.

STEP BY STEP   **Create a Personal Signature**

GET READY. LAUNCH Outlook if it is not already running.

1. If necessary, click the Mail button in the Navigation Pane to display the Mail folder.
2. Click the New E-mail button on the Home tab. The Message window is displayed.
3. Click the Signature button in the Include group on the Ribbon. In the dropdown list, click Signatures. The Signatures and Stationery dialog box is displayed, as shown in Figure 2-42.

Take Note   If you share your e-mail account with other users or if additional Outlook profiles have been created, signatures created by other users may be listed in the Signatures and Stationery dialog box.

Figure 2-42

Signatures and Stationery dialog box

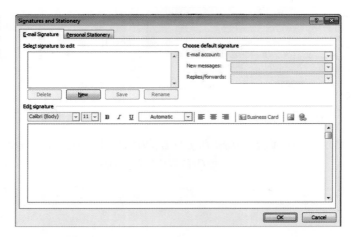

4. Click the New button to create a new signature. The New Signature dialog box is displayed, as shown in Figure 2-43.

Figure 2-43

New Signature dialog box

5. To name the new signature, key Lesson 2 into the *Type a name for this signature* field. Click OK. The New Signature dialog box is closed, and Lesson 2 is highlighted in the *Select Signature To Edit* list box.
6. Click in the empty Edit signature box. Any changes you make here are applied to the selected Lesson 2 signature. If additional signatures were listed, you could select a different signature and make changes to it.
7. Key [your name]. [Press Enter.]
   Key [your title]. [Press Enter.]
   Key [your e-mail address]. [Press Enter twice.]
   Key [the name of your company]. [Press Enter.]
   Key [the web address of your company]. [Press Enter.]

   If you do not have a title, company, or company website, key the information that applies to you.
8. Select all the text in the signature. In the toolbar above the *Edit Signature* box, click the Font dropdown box arrow and select Arial from the list.
9. In the Font Size box on the toolbar, key 10. Click the Font Color dropdown box arrow (the current selection is Automatic) to open a palette of Font colors, as shown in Figure 2-44.

Figure 2-44

Editing a signature

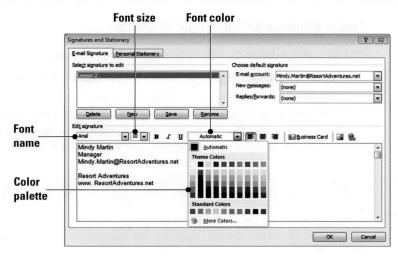

Font size Font color

Font name

Color palette

10. Select the color Blue.
11. Click in the *Edit Signature* box to deselect the text. Now select just your name in the Edit Signature box. Click **Bold** and **Italic** to apply those formatting attributes to the selected text. Change the font size to 12, as shown in Figure 2-45.

Figure 2-45

New signature

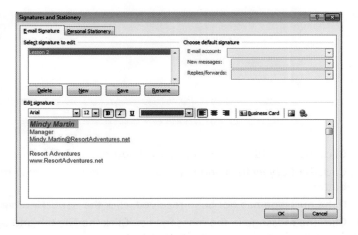

12. Verify that (none) is still selected in the *New Messages* and *Replies/Forwards* fields. Click **OK**. The dialog box is closed, and the signature is saved. Close the Message window.

PAUSE. LEAVE Outlook open to use in the next exercise.

Although you can include images and more complicated formatting, the formatting you can do in the Signatures and Stationery dialog box is limited. For example, you can't resize an image in the Signatures and Stationery dialog box. However, you can open a new message, use the formatting tools in the new Message window to create a signature you like, cut the signature, and paste it into the Signatures and Stationery dialog box as a new signature.

Adding a Signature to a Single Message

You can choose to add a signature to an individual message. This enables you to create and use more than one signature.

STEP BY STEP   **Add a Signature to a Single Message**

GET READY. LAUNCH Outlook if it is not already running.

1. If necessary, click the Mail button in the Navigation Pane to display the Mail folder.
2. Click the New E-mail button on the Home tab. The Message window is displayed.
3. In the message area, key I'm testing my new signature. Press Enter twice.
4. In the Include group on the Ribbon, click Signature. In the dropdown list, select Lesson 2. The signature is inserted into the message, as shown in Figure 2-46.

Figure 2-46

Message using the new signature

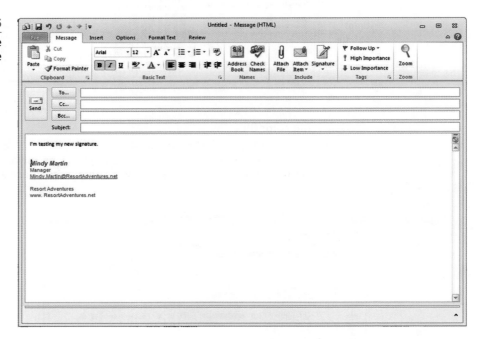

5. Click the *To* field and key your e-mail address.
6. Click the *Subject* field and key Testing signature in a single message. Click the Send button.
7. If the message has not been received, click the Send/Receive All Folders button.
8. Click the message in the message list. Click the File tab and select the Save As option. The Save As dialog box is displayed.
9. Navigate to folder where you want to save the file and click the Save button. The message is saved as Testing signature in a single message.htm.

PAUSE. LEAVE Outlook open to use in the next exercise.

 **Troubleshooting** If formatting has been applied to your e-mail messages or other signatures, the same formatting may be applied to the signature as you key the text. You can change the formatting after you key the signature.

You might want to create several signatures. This enables you to select the signature to match the message. When you send a personal message, use a signature that includes a picture from your favorite sport or a photo of your new puppy. When you send a business message, use a signature that includes your business information.

Adding a Signature to All Outgoing Messages

If you primarily use your e-mail account for the same type of e-mail (business or personal), you can select a signature that is automatically inserted into every outgoing message. This gives you a quick, consistent way to insert your signature.

STEP BY STEP **Add a Signature to All Outgoing Messages**

GET READY. LAUNCH Outlook if it is not already running.

1. If necessary, click the Mail button in the Navigation Pane to display the Mail folder.
2. Click the New E-mail button on the Home tab. The Message window is displayed.
3. Click the Signature button in the Include group on the Ribbon. In the dropdown list, click Signatures. The Signatures and Stationery window is displayed.
4. In the *New Messages* field, select Lesson 2, if necessary. Click OK. The Lesson 2 signature will automatically be added to every outgoing message. Close the message window.

PAUSE. LEAVE Outlook open to use in the next exercise.

Even if you use your e-mail account to send business and personal messages, you can save time by automatically adding a signature. When the automatic signature isn't appropriate, delete it from the message and insert the correct signature.

CREATING AND FORMATTING GRAPHIC MESSAGE CONTENT

The Bottom Line
Adding a chart, picture, or other illustration to a message captures attention and immediately portrays an idea of what the message is all about. In this section, you'll add hyperlinks and graphics to a message.

SOFTWARE ORIENTATION

The Insert Tab

Microsoft Office includes a gallery of media images you can insert into messages such as pictures, clip art, shapes, and SmartArt graphics. You can also insert external picture files. The insert tab, shown in Figure 2-47, contains a group of features that you can use to add graphics to your document. The Illustrations group has options for several types of graphics you can use to enhance your messages.

Figure 2-47

The Insert tab

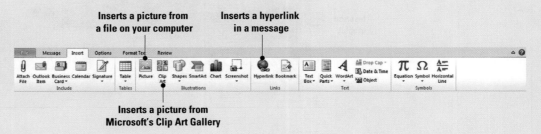

Inserts a picture from a file on your computer

Inserts a hyperlink in a message

Inserts a picture from Microsoft's Clip Art Gallery

Use this figure as a reference through this section as you become skilled in inserting and formatting illustrations within a message.

Inserting a Graphical Element

While the old adage "A picture is worth a thousand words" is perhaps an exaggeration, a visual element adds interest and calls attention to your messages. Unlike a message background that is displayed but does not print, pictures and other graphic objects are included in message printouts.

Graphics can be an integral part of creating a compelling message. You can insert or copy pictures into a message from image providers, Microsoft's clip art organizer (Microsoft Clip Organizer), or files on your computer. A well-chosen picture can portray a powerful message. In this exercise, you will insert a graphic element into a message.

STEP BY STEP   **Insert a Graphical Element**

USE the Come Fly with Us message you created in a previous exercise.

1. If necessary, click the Drafts button in the Navigation Pane to display the Mail folder. In the last exercise, you saved and closed the message window. Outlook automatically places messages that you've worked on but haven't sent in the Drafts folder.

2. Open the Come Fly with Us message that you worked on in the previous exercise and click the Insert tab to display the Illustrations group, as shown in Figure 2-47.

3. Place the insertion point at the end of the main paragraph in the message. Press Enter twice to add two lines of blank space.

4. In the Illustrations group, click Picture. The Insert Picture dialog box is displayed.

5. Select the *Vista.jpg* file in the data files for this lesson.

6. Click Insert. A large picture of a landscape near the resort is displayed in the message and the Picture Tools Format tab is displayed in the Ribbon, as shown in Figure 2-48.

7. Maximize the message window to see more of the image.

@ The *Vista* file is available on the book companion website or in WileyPLUS.

Figure 2-48

Inserting a graphic in a message window

PAUSE. LEAVE the Outlook Message window open to use in the next exercise.

The Insert Picture technique enables you to customize a message with selected photographs. The pictures you inserted in this exercise are digital photographs.

You can also insert clip art images in your messages. **Clip art** refers to picture files from the Clip Art task pane that can be inserted into a document. In the Clip Art task pane, you can also search for photographs, movies, and sounds. To include any of those media types, select the check box next to each in the *Result Should Be* box in the Clip Art task pane.

You can also insert SmartArt graphics. **SmartArt graphics** are visual representations of information that can help communicate your message or ideas more effectively.

Formatting Graphical Elements

Once you've inserted a graphic, you can alter it using the Picture Tools Formatting tab. There are many options for changing the graphic. For example, you can add shapes to the graphic, alter its direction, change the layout, and change the colors. In this exercise you make multiple formatting changes to the picture in an e-mail message. The same formatting options are available when you work with clip art, SmartArt, and shapes. You can quickly make adjustments to a picture or graphic that has been inserted into a message by using the tools in Table 2-4.

Table 2-4

Formatting Tools for Graphics

Tool	Description
Crop	When you crop a picture, you trim the horizontal or vertical edges to get rid of unwanted areas.
Resize	Change the size or scale of a graphic using the Shape Height and Shape Width tools in the Size group.
Picture Style	You can use Picture styles to change the shape of the image or add borders or 3D effects.
Corrections	You can make an image brighter or darker and improve the sharpness and contrast of the image.
Color	You can turn the picture into a grayscale, sepia-toned, washed-out, or black-and-white version.
Wrap Text	You can use text wrapping to change the way text wraps around the picture or drawing object.

STEP BY STEP   **Format Graphical Elements**

USE the Come Fly with Us message you created in a previous exercise.

1. If you closed the message window, click the **Drafts** button in the Navigation Pane to display the Mail folder. Double-click on the **Come Fly with Us** message that you worked on in the previous exercise. Click the **image** to display the Picture Tools Format tab, as shown in Figure 2-49.

Figure 2-49

The Picture Tools Format tab

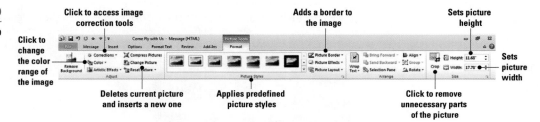

2. Click the **Height** box in the Size group and key **6.5** and press **Enter**. The image height changes to **6.5"** and the image width changes as needed to avoid warping the image.
3. In the Size group, click **Crop**. Crop handles appear at each corner and side of the image, as shown in Figure 2-50. Drag each of the crop handles toward the center of the image, as shown in Figure 2-50.

Figure 2-50

Cropping an image

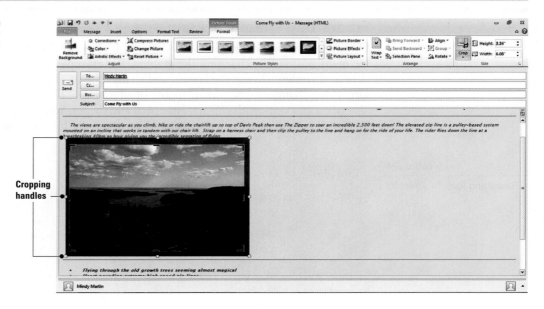

Cropping handles

4. Click the **Crop** button again to save your changes.

5. In the Picture Styles group, select the **Drop Shadow Rectangle** style. The image changes to match the style.

6. Click the **Picture Border** button in the Picture Styles group. Select **Dark Blue** from the color palette that appears. A thin blue-gray border is displayed around the image, as shown in Figure 2-51.

Figure 2-51

Applying Picture Styles to the image

Drop Shadow Rectangle   Click to add a picture border

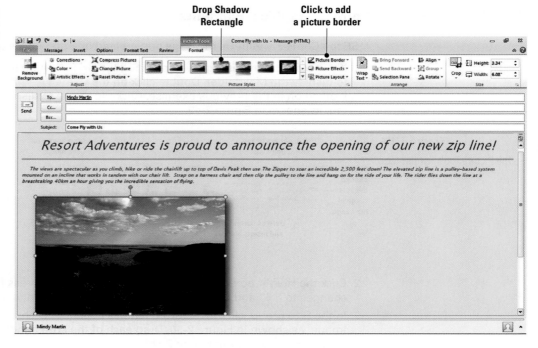

7. In the Adjust group, click **Color** and select **Saturation: 200%** in the Color Saturation area. The image is now brighter than the original.

8. Click the **Corrections** button and select **Brightness: 0%, Contrast: +20%** in the Brightness and Contrast area. The image is now brighter and warmer than the original.

9. Click **Wrap Text** in the Arrange group. Select **Square** from the list. The remaining text for the message moves up next to the image, as shown in Figure 2-52.

Figure 2-52

Adjusting an image

10. Click the Save button on the Quick Access Toolbar.

PAUSE. LEAVE the Outlook message window open to use in the next exercise.

Take Note

If at any time you want to revert back to the original graphic, click the Reset Picture button in the Adjust group to discard the formatting changes you have made.

Inserting a Hyperlink

For quick access to related information in another file or on a web page, you can insert a hyperlink in a message. A **hyperlink** is an image or sequence of characters that opens another file or Web page when you click it. The target file or web page can be on the World Wide Web, on the Internet, or on your personal computer. Hyperlinks enable you to supplement message information with additional materials and resources. It is easy to embed a hyperlink in a message. Just click where you want to create a hyperlink, or select the text or object you want to become a hyperlink, and click the Hyperlink button on the Insert tab. In this exercise, you'll insert a hyperlink into a message.

STEP BY STEP   **Insert a Hyperlink**

USE the Come Fly with Us message you created in a previous exercise.

1. If necessary, click the Drafts button in the Navigation Pane to display the Mail folder. Open the Come Fly with Us message that you worked on in the previous exercise.

2. If necessary, click the image in the message and click the Insert tab.

3. Click Insert Hyperlink in the links group. The Insert Hyperlink dialog box opens, as shown in Figure 2-53.

Figure 2-53

Insert Hyperlinks
dialog box

Figure 2-53

Insert Hyperlinks
dialog box

 The *Zipper Rates*
file is available on the
book companion website
or in WileyPLUS.

4. In the Address box, enter the URL of the *Zipper Rates.htm* file in your data files.

5. Click **ScreenTip** in the upper-right corner of the Insert Hyperlinks dialog box. The Set Hyperlink ScreenTip dialog box is displayed, as shown in Figure 2-54.

Figure 2-54

Set Hyperlink ScreenTip
dialog box

6. Key **For more information click here** in the ScreenTip Text textbox. Click **OK** twice to apply your changes and close the dialog boxes.

7. Click the message window's **Send** button to send the message to yourself.

8. If the message has not been received, click the **Send/Receive All Folders** button.

9. Click the message in the message list. Click the **File** tab and select the **Save As** option. The Save As dialog box is displayed.

10. In the *File name* box, key **Come Fly with Us**.

11. Navigate to the folder where you save your solution files and click the **Save** button. The message is saved as Come Fly with Us.msg.

PAUSE. LEAVE Outlook open to use in the next exercise.

WORKING WITH ATTACHMENTS

Attachments are files sent as part of an e-mail message. An attachment is a convenient way to send pictures, spreadsheets, and other types of files to e-mail recipient. In this section, you'll attach files and items to e-mail messages. You'll then preview, save, and print an attachment.

SOFTWARE ORIENTATION

The Attachment Tools Tab

Outlook's new Attachment Tools tab contains all of the tools you need to work with e-mail attachments.

Figure 2-55

The Attachment Tools tab

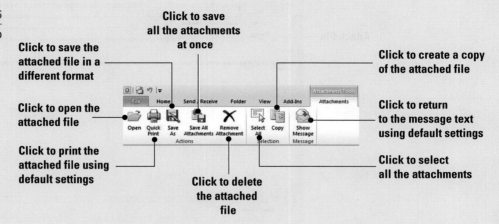

Click to save the attached file in a different format

Click to save all the attachments at once

Click to create a copy of the attached file

Click to open the attached file

Click to return to the message text using default settings

Click to print the attached file using default settings

Click to delete the attached file

Click to select all the attachments

The tools on the Attachment Tools tab are the same tools available when you right-click on an attachment icon.

Attaching an External File to a Message

Do you need to submit a five-page report to your supervisor at the home office? Perhaps you have a new product brochure to distribute to all the sales representatives, or you want to share a picture of your new puppy with a friend. Attach the file to an e-mail message and send it. When you attach a file to a message, the filename, size, and an icon representing the file are displayed in the *Attached* field. If you attach more than one file, the files are listed separately in the *Attached* field. In this exercise, you'll attach a file to a message.

STEP BY STEP   **Attach an External File to a Message**

GET READY. LAUNCH Outlook if it is not already running.

1. If necessary, click the Mail button in the Navigation Pane to display the Mail folder.
2. Click the New E-mail button on the Home tab. The Message window is displayed.
3. In the *To* field, key your e-mail address. You will send this message to yourself so you can use the attachment in the following exercises.
4. In the *Subject* field, key Zipper coupon attached.
5. Click the message area. Key Hi Jon, [Press Enter twice].
6. Key the following note: I attached a copy of the coupon for the new Zipper attraction. I'd like to get your opinion of it before sending it out with the Come Fly with Us promotional message we discussed earlier. [Press Enter twice.]
7. Key Thanks, [press Enter].
8. Key [your name].
9. Click the Attach File button in the Include group on the Ribbon. The Insert File dialog box is displayed.
10. Navigate to the data files for this lesson. Click the *Zipper Coupon* file and click Insert. The Insert File dialog box is closed, and the file is listed in the *Attached* field, as shown in Figure 2-56.

@ The *Zipper Coupon* file is available on the book companion website or in WileyPLUS.

Figure 2-56

Sending an attachment

Attach File button

Attach file —

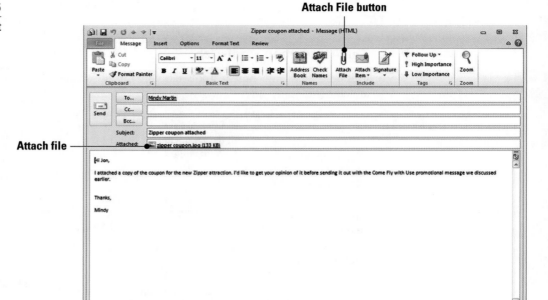

11. Click the Send button. The Message window closes, and the message is moved to the Outbox. The message is sent when your computer is connected to the Internet.

PAUSE. LEAVE Outlook open to use in the next exercise.

In the previous exercise, you attached an external file to an Outlook message window using the Attach Items button. You can also open a Windows Explorer window containing the file you want to attach and simply click and drag it to the message window. It will attach itself to the message and you're ready to share.

Attaching an Outlook Item to a Message

An attachment can also be an Outlook item, such as a contact, a note, or a task. In this exercise, you'll attach an Outlook message to another message.

STEP BY STEP   **Attach an Outlook item to a Message**

GET READY. LAUNCH Outlook if it is not already running.

1. If necessary, click Mail button in the Navigation Pane to display the Mail folder.
2. Click the New E-mail button on the Home tab. The Message window is displayed.
3. In the *To* field, key [your e-mail address].
4. In the *Subject* field, key Promotional message attached.
5. Click the message area. Key Hi Jon, [Press Enter twice].
6. Key the following note: I attached a copy of the Come Fly with Us promotional message we discussed. [Press Enter twice.]
7. Key Let me know what you think. [Press Enter.]
8. Key [your name].
9. Click the Attach Item button in the Include group on the Ribbon. Select Outlook Item. The Insert Item dialog box is displayed, as shown in Figure 2-57.

Figure 2-57

Attaching an Outlook item
to a message

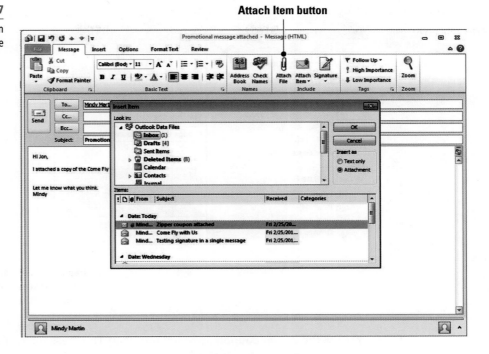

Attach Item button

10. If necessary, click **Inbox** in the *Look in* window. In the Items window, select **Come Fly with Us**.

11. Make sure that Attachment is selected in the *Insert As* area. Click **OK**. The Insert Item dialog box is closed, and the file is listed in the *Attached* field.

12. Click the **Send** button. The Message window closes, and the message is moved to the Outbox. The message is sent when your computer is connected to the Internet.

PAUSE. LEAVE Outlook open to use in the next exercise.

Previewing an Attachment in Outlook

Outlook's Attachment Previewer enables you to view attachments in the Reading Pane. Without needing to save and open an attachment, you can make critical decisions quickly and efficiently. In this exercise, you'll preview an attachment in Outlook.

STEP BY STEP   **Preview an Attachment in Outlook**

USE the Zipper coupon attached message with the attachment you sent a message to yourself in an earlier exercise.

1. If the message with the coupon attachment has not arrived yet, click the **Send/ Receive All Folders** button on the Home tab to check for new messages. The paper clip icon with the message, as shown in Figure 2-58, indicates that the message has an attachment.

Figure 2-58

Message with attachment received

Figure 2-58

Message with attachment received

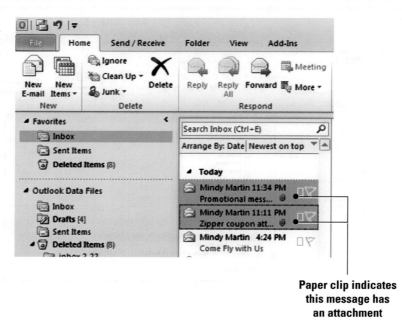

Paper clip indicates this message has an attachment

2. Click the Zipper coupon attached message. The message is displayed in the Reading Pane, as shown in Figure 2-59.

Figure 2-59

Reading Pane containing the message with attachment

Click to view the attached file

3. In the Reading Pane, click the attachment's filename. The attachment is displayed in the Reading Pane, as shown in Figure 2-60.

Take Note　　For some types of files, you may be asked if you want to preview the file before the attachment is displayed.

Figure 2-60

Attachment displayed in the
Reading Pane

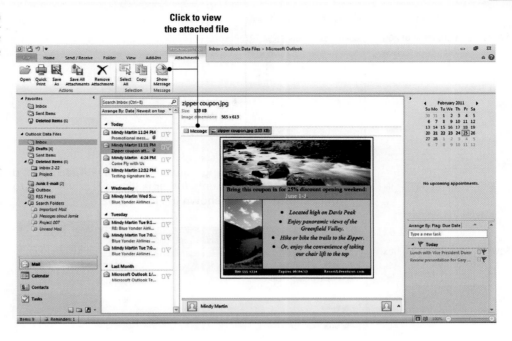

Click to view
the attached file

**Troubleshooting** For your protection, all scripts, macros, and ActiveX controls are disabled in a previewed document.

4. In the Reading Pane, click the Show Message icon to close the preview and display the message.

PAUSE. LEAVE Outlook open to use in the next exercise.

Saving an Attachment from the Message List

Attachments in the message list can be saved without having to preview the attachment. In the following exercise, you will save an attachment from the message list.

STEP BY STEP **Save an Attachment from the Message List**

USE the Zipper coupon attached message with the attachment you sent a message to yourself in an earlier exercise.

1. Click the Zipper coupon attached message in the message list.
2. Click the File tab to open Backstage view.
3. Click Save Attachments in the navigation pane. The Save All Attachments dialog box is displayed, as shown in Figure 2-61.

Figure 2-61

Save All Attachments dialog
box

4. Select Zipper Coupon.jpg. Click OK. The Save Attachment dialog box is displayed. By default, the My Documents folder is displayed. Navigate to the folder where you save your solution files, as shown in Figure 2-62.

Figure 2-62

Save Attachment dialog box

5. In the *File name* field, key Zipper Coupon from message list.

6. Click the Save button. A copy of the attachment is stored in your solutions folder.

PAUSE. LEAVE Outlook open to use in the next exercise.

Saving an Attachment from the Reading Pane

When you preview an attachment in the Reading Pane, you can use the new Attachment Tools tab to quickly save the attachment. In the following exercise, you will save an attachment from the Reading Pane.

STEP BY STEP **Save an Attachment from the Reading Pane**

USE the Zipper coupon attached message with the attachment you sent a message to yourself in an earlier exercise.

1. Click the Zipper coupon attached message in the message list.

2. In the Reading Pane, click the Zipper Coupon.jpg attachment. The Attachment Tools tab is displayed, as shown in Figure 2-63.

Figure 2-63

Saving an attachment using the
Attachment Tools tab

Click to save the attached file

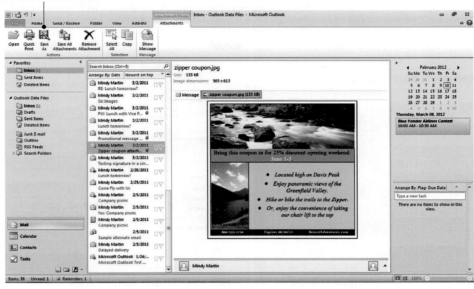

Another Way

If the message
contains multiple attachments,
click Save All Attachments to
save them all in one step.

3. Click the Save As button on the Attachment Tools tab. The Save Attachment dialog box is displayed, as shown in Figure 2-62.

4. If necessary, navigate to the folder where you save your solution files. In the *File name* field, change the name of the file to Zipper Coupon from Reading Pane. Click the Save button.

PAUSE. LEAVE Outlook open to use in the next exercise.

Saving an Attachment from an Open Message

It is easy to save an attachment from an open message window. You can use the Save Attachments option on the File tab, but you can also save the attachment from the attachment's shortcut menu. In the following exercise, you will save an attachment from an open message window.

STEP BY STEP   **Save an Attachment from an Open Message**

USE the Zipper coupon attached message with the attachment you sent a message to yourself in an earlier exercise.

1. Double-click the Zipper coupon attached message in the message list. The message is opened in a new window.

2. In the new window, right-click the Zipper Coupon.jpg attachment. The attachment's shortcut menu is displayed, as shown in Figure 2-64.

Figure 2-64

Attachment's shortcut menu

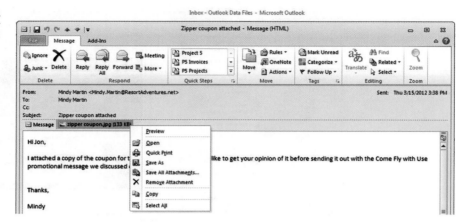

Figure 2-64

Attachment's shortcut menu

3. Select Save As on the shortcut menu. The Save Attachment dialog box is displayed.

4. If necessary, navigate to the folder where you save your solution files. In the *File name* field, change the name of the file to Zipper Coupon from message window. Click the Save button.

PAUSE. LEAVE Outlook open to use in the next exercise.

Opening an E-mail Attachment

You can open an attachment from the Reading Pane or from an open message. In the following exercise, you will open an attachment from each location.

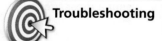

STEP BY STEP   Open an E-mail Attachment

USE the Promotional Message message with the attachment that you sent to yourself in an earlier exercise.

1. Click the Promotional Message message in the message list.

2. In the Reading Pane, double-click the attachment icon. The Come Fly with Us message window is displayed. Close the message window.

Troubleshooting It is safer to save an attachment and scan the file with an antivirus software program before opening an attachment. Do not open attachments from unknown sources.

3. Back in the Reading Pane, click the attachment icon once and click Open on the Attachments tab. The zipper coupon.jpg file opens in the default image viewing program, as shown in Figure 2-65.

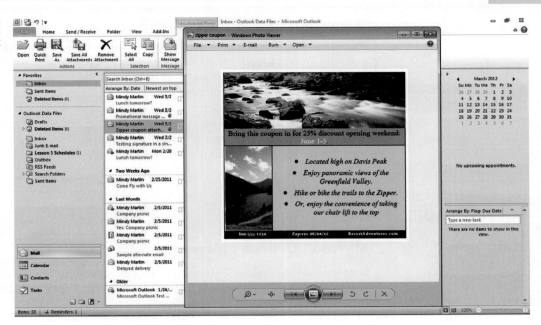

Figure 2-65

Opening an attachment

4. Close the message window. In the message list, double-click the Promotional Message message in the message list. The Promotional Message message window is displayed.

5. Double-click the Come Fly with Us attachment. The Come Fly with Us - Message window is displayed.

6. **CLOSE** both message windows.

PAUSE. LEAVE Outlook open to use in the next exercise.

Printing an Attachment

Printing an attachment is simple once you've set up your default printer in Outlook. Just use the Quick Print tool on the Attachments tab. In this exercise, you'll print an attachment from a message you received.

STEP BY STEP   **Printing an Attachment**

USE the Zipper coupon attached message with the attachment you sent a message to yourself in an earlier exercise. You need to have set up the printer in a previous exercise to complete this exercise.

1. Click the Zipper coupon attached message in the message list.

2. In the Reading Pane, click the zipper coupon.jpg attachment to display it in the Reading Pane.

3. Click the Quick Print button on the Attachments tab.

PAUSE. LEAVE Outlook open to use in the next exercise.

If you have not set up a printer previously, you can still print an attachment. Just click the attachment icon in the Reading Pane and click the Open button on the Attachments tab to open the attachment in a new window. From there, click the File tab and click the Print button in the Navigation Pane. In the Printer area, click the Printer dropdown arrow and select the printer you would like to use.

USING ADVANCED MESSAGE OPTIONS

Advanced message options enable you to specify settings that attract attention to the messages you send. You can use these advanced options to alert message recipients to the sensitive nature or importance of a message's contents, to remind the recipient that a reply is expected, and to trigger notification when a message you've sent has been delivered and/or read. You also can use these settings to direct message replies to a specific e-mail address, to configure message delivery options, to specify where Outlook will save sent items, or to send messages from multiple e-mail accounts. Many of these options are set in the Properties dialog box shown in Figure 3-1 or on the Options tab of the message window.

SOFTWARE ORIENTATION

Microsoft Outlook's Message Options

Some Microsoft Outlook 2010 options require more detail than is available on the Options tab. You can access the Properties window, shown in Figure 2-66, by clicking on the More Options dialog box launcher.

Figure 2-66

The Properties dialog box

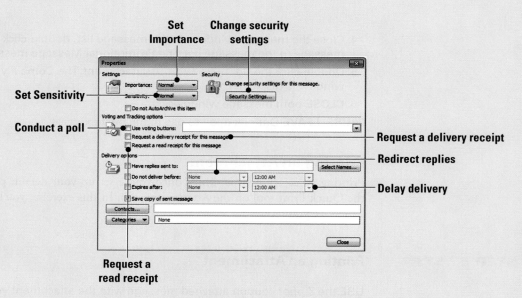

In the Message Properties dialog box, you can make decisions about these options for the message you are creating. These changes affect only the current message; they do not affect all messages you send.

Setting the Sensitivity Level

The **sensitivity** level of a message is an indicator of how secret the message's contents are. Although sensitivity does not affect how the message is sent or received, it does suggest how the recipient should treat the message and the type of information in the message. You set Outlook's Sensitivity settings—Normal, Personal, Private, and Confidential—in the Properties dialog box. In this exercise, you'll create a message and set the sensitivity level.

STEP BY STEP   **Set the Sensitivity Level**

GET READY. LAUNCH Outlook if it is not already running.

1. If necessary, click the Mail button in the Navigation Pane to display the Mail folder.

2. Click the New E-mail button on the Home tab. The Untitled—Message window is displayed. By default, the Message tab is selected.

3. Click the More Options dialog box launcher on the Options tab. The message Properties dialog box is displayed, as shown in Figure 2-67.

Figure 2-67

Setting the Sensitivity level of a message

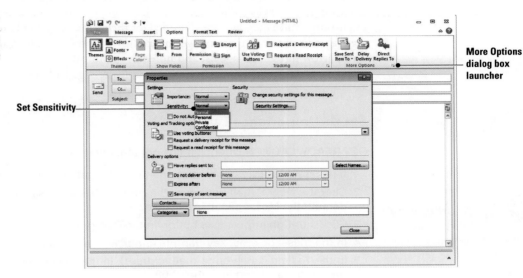

4. In the Settings area, click the Sensitivity setting dropdown arrow, as shown in Figure 3-9. Then select Confidential from the dropdown list.

5. Click the Close button to accept the Confidential setting and return to the message window.

6. In the message area, key Sample confidential message.

7. In the *To* field, key [your e-mail address]. In the *Subject* field, key Sample confidential message.

8. Click the Send button. The message is moved to the Outbox and it is sent when your computer is connected to the Internet.

9. When your computer is connected to the Internet, click the Send/Receive All Folders button on the Home tab if the message has not arrived yet.

10. When the new message appears in your Inbox, click the received message to select it. The message has the text *Please treat this as Confidential* in the InfoBar at the top of the message, as shown in Figure 2-68.

Figure 2-68

Confidential message received

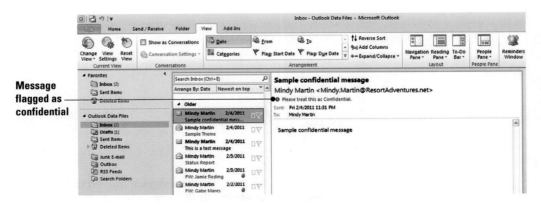

PAUSE. LEAVE Outlook open to use in the next exercise.

In this exercise, you saw that an InfoBar was added to the recipient's confidential message. An **InfoBar** is a banner containing information added automatically at the top of a message. An InfoBar is added for personal, private, and confidential messages. The messages are handled the same as any other message you send—the text in the InfoBar is the only difference.

The default sensitivity is normal. The InfoBar is not added to messages with a normal sensitivity.

Setting the Importance Level

Some e-mail messages are more important than others. Use the Importance setting to draw attention to a message. The importance level of a message can be set to High, Low, or Normal. High-importance messages are identified for the recipient by a red exclamation point in the message list and noted in the message InfoBar. Low-importance messages are marked with a blue down arrow in the message list and noted in the InfoBar. Normal-importance messages are not marked. In this exercise, you'll create a sample message with a high importance level.

STEP BY STEP	**Set the Importance Level**

GET READY. LAUNCH Outlook if it is not already running.

1. If necessary, click the **Mail** button in the Navigation Pane to display the Mail folder.
2. Click the **New E-mail** button on the Home tab. The Message window is displayed. By default, the Message tab is selected.
3. Click the **High Importance** button in the Tags group.
4. In the message area, key **Sample important message**.
5. In the *To* field, key [your e-mail address]. In the *Subject* field, key **Sample important message**, as shown in Figure 2-69.

Another Way
Select the importance in the message Properties dialog box.

Figure 2-69

Creating an important message

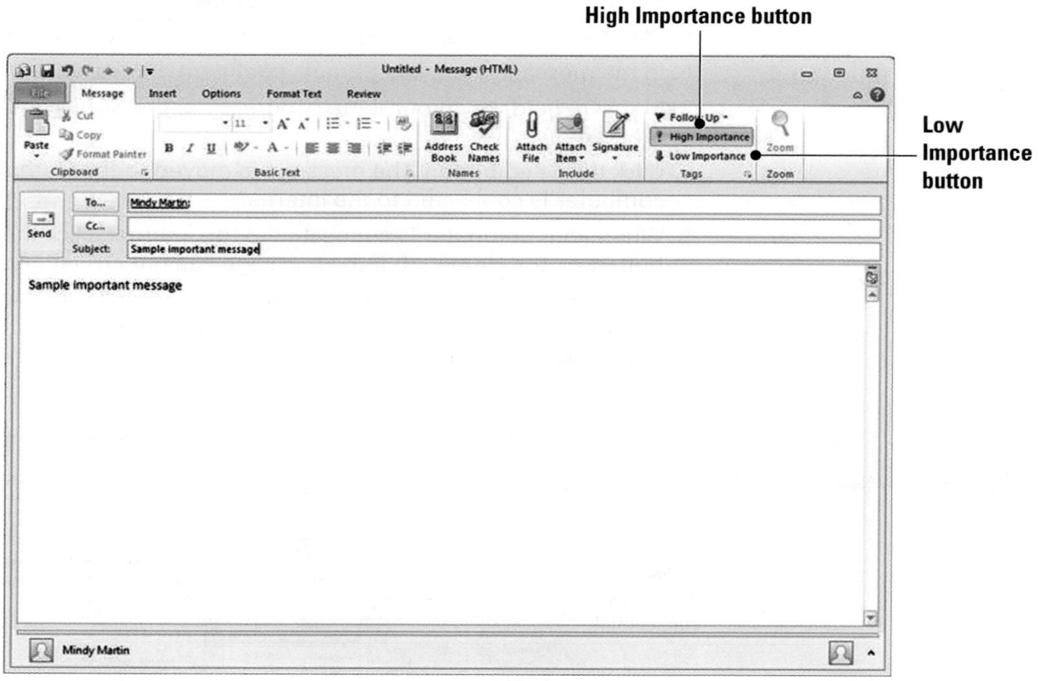

6. Click the **Send** button. The message is moved to the Outbox and it is sent when your computer is connected to the Internet.
7. Return to your Inbox, and click the **Send/Receive All Folders** button if the message has not arrived yet.

8. Select the new message, which is flagged with a red exclamation mark in your Inbox list. The text *This message was sent with High importance* appears in the InfoBar at the top of the message, as shown in Figure 2-70.

Figure 2-70

Important message received

High Importance message in the message lists

High Importance message in the Reading Pane

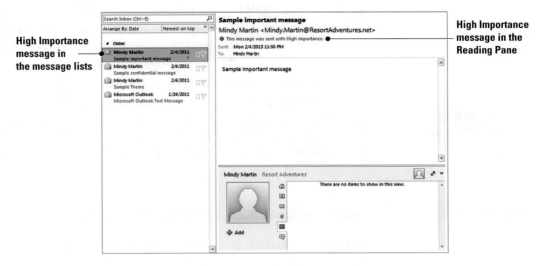

PAUSE. LEAVE Outlook open to use in the next exercise.

If you set the importance level of a message too high or low, you can reset the importance level to normal before you send it. Simply click the High Importance button or the Low Importance button that is currently selected.

LOCATING MESSAGES

The Bottom Line

What was the cost of that item? When is the project deadline? Important information is often exchanged through e-mail messages and finding that information can be critical. Outlook 2010 has several powerful tools that make it easy to locate the right message when you need it.

You can easily locate all messages and attachments from a specific contact using the People Pane. You can sort any Mail folder by any attribute. You can filter search results using Instant Search with its companion Search Contextual tab and Search Suggestions list. If you find that you need to perform the same search on a regular basis, you can create a custom search folder that will always contain your filtered items.

Sorting Messages by Attributes

In the message list, e-mail messages are usually listed by date. The newest messages are displayed at the top of the message list. One of the easiest ways to locate messages is by sorting the message list by another **attribute** such as size, subject, or sender. In this exercise, you'll sort the message list by different file attributes.

STEP BY STEP

Sort Messages by Attributes

GET READY. LAUNCH Outlook if it is not already running.

1. If necessary, click the **Mail** button in the Navigation Pane of the main Outlook window.

Another Way
To sort messages, click the View menu, click the Arrange By, and select an attribute.

2. Click **Arranged By** above the message list. Select the **Attachment** option. Messages are grouped by whether they include an attachment or not.

3. Click **Arranged By** above the message list. Select the **Subject** option. Messages are grouped by sender. Groups are listed in alphabetic order.

4. Click **Arranged By** above the message list. Select the **Date** option. Messages are grouped by date. Groups are listed in chronological order.

PAUSE. Leave Outlook open to use in the next exercise.

By default, messages are sorted by the date they are received. Sometimes, you can get a better picture of a situation by viewing all the messages from a particular sender or subject. Another way to see all the messages from a particular sender is by using the People Pane.

Using the People Pane to Find a Message

Outlook 2010's People Pane is a convenient way to locate messages and attachments based on the sender information. The Show e-mail messages page and Show attachments page in the People Pane (visible in both the Mail folder and individual contact records) collect everything from each contact in one convenient place. In this exercise, you'll locate an attachment using the People Pane.

STEP BY STEP   **Use the People Pane to Find an Attachment**

GET READY. LAUNCH Outlook if it is not already running.

Instant Search must be enabled.

1. If necessary, click the **Mail** button in the Navigation Pane of the main Outlook window.

2. In the Inbox, select a message you sent to yourself.

3. If the People Pane is not visible, click the **People Pane** button on the View tab and select **Normal**. The home page of the People Pane displays a list of messages that you've sent to yourself.

4. Click the **attachment icon** to open the *Show Attachments That You Have Received From This Person* list. A list of only those messages that included an attachment is displayed. The list is sorted by message date, as shown in Figure 2-71.

Figure 2-71

Locating an attachment in the People Pane

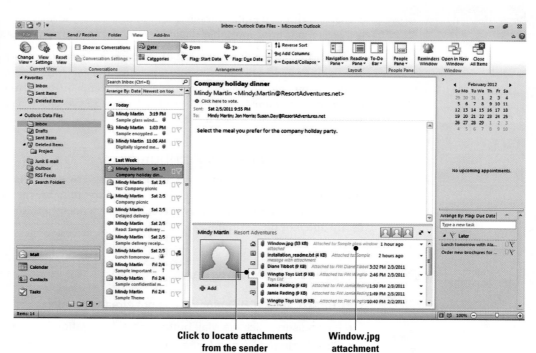

Click to locate attachments from the sender

Window.jpg attachment

5. Click on the message you sent to yourself that had an attachment called Window.jpg. The message window opens, showing the message that contained the Window.jpg attachment.

6. Close the message window.

PAUSE. Leave Outlook open to use in the next exercise.

You can use the People Pane to show all the messages from a particular sender stored anywhere within your mailbox. This can be the simplest way to find more messages from a contact. However, if you've received several messages from the same person, you might find that the list is too long to be convenient. As an alternative, you can use Instant Search to search for a specific message that contains specific attributes.

Using Instant Search

One of the biggest problems with searching through e-mail messages over time is that the searches usually produce far too many results. **Instant Search** now includes two features that you can use to filter through the results: Search Suggestions List and the Search Contextual tab. As you begin typing a keyword in the Instant Search box, results are immediately displayed in the mail list rather than waiting to complete the search to display the results. In this exercise, you'll locate an Outlook item using Instant Search to filter your results.

STEP BY STEP | **Use Instant Search**

GET READY. LAUNCH Outlook if it is not already running.

1. Click the **Mail** button in the Navigation Pane of the main Outlook window.

2. If necessary, click the **Inbox** folder in the Navigation Pane. The Instant Search box is displayed at the top of the Inbox, as shown in Figure 2-72.

Take Note   The Instant Search feature works in every Outlook folder.

3. In the Instant Search box, key **Sample**. As you key the search text; three things happen. Outlook displays the messages that match the text; the Search Suggestions list appears, allowing you to choose which part of the message includes the keyword; and the Search Tools tab appears, as shown in Figure 2-72.

Figure 2-72

Instant Search features

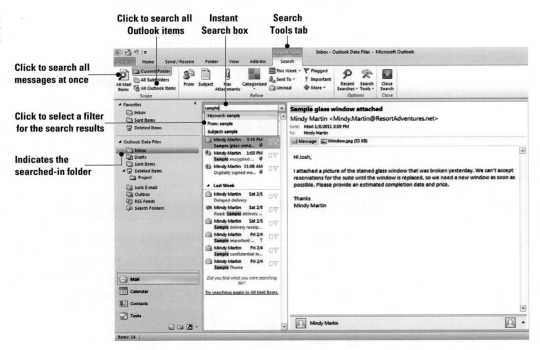

Take Note

Instant Search searches only the specific Outlook folder you're currently viewing—in this case, the Inbox. You can search any mail folder or search everywhere in Outlook at the same time by clicking the All Outlook Items link in the Search Tools tab.

4. Click the Subject: Sample from the Search Suggestions list. Only messages that include the word Sample in the subject line are displayed.

5. Click the Attachments button in the Search Tools tab. Only messages that include the word *Sample* in the subject line and have attachments are displayed, as shown in Figure 2-73.

Figure 2-73

Filtered search list

Using filters reduced the search results to a more manageable list

6. Click Inbox in the Navigation Pane to clear the search.

PAUSE. LEAVE Outlook open to use in the next exercise.

As you begin typing a search parameter in the Instant Search box, Outlook begins populating the mail list with items that contain your keyword, and the Search Suggestions list appears below the Instant Search box. By selecting one of the options in this list, you can filter the results based on where the keyword appears in the message.

Using Built-in Search Folders

If you find that you need to perform the same kind of search on a regular basis, you can save time by creating a custom search folder. Search folders are virtual folders stored in the Folder List in the Navigation Pane. A virtual folder looks and acts like a normal folder, but a virtual folder is really just a collection of links to messages that are stored in other folders. This allows you to maintain your folder organization while still offering you easy access to messages that fit your search needs. For example, you can access every unread e-mail message from every folder using the Unread Mail search folder.

STEP BY STEP   **Use Built-in Search Folders**

GET READY. LAUNCH Outlook if it is not already running.

1. If necessary, click the Mail button in the Navigation Pane.

2. On the Folder tab, click New Search Folder in the New group. The New Search Folder dialog box is displayed, as shown in Figure 2-74.

Figure 2-74

New Search Folder dialog box

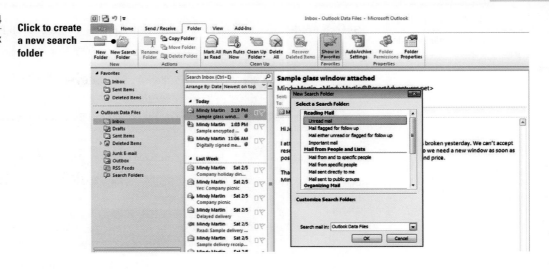

Click to create a new search folder

3. In the *Select a Search Folder* section of the dialog box, select **Important Mail** in the *Reading mail* portion of the list. Click **OK** to close the dialog box. Outlook displays a new folder at the bottom of the folder list in the Navigation Pane called Search Folders. The Important Mail folder appears within Search Folders, as shown in Figure 2-75.

Figure 2-75

Important Mail search folder

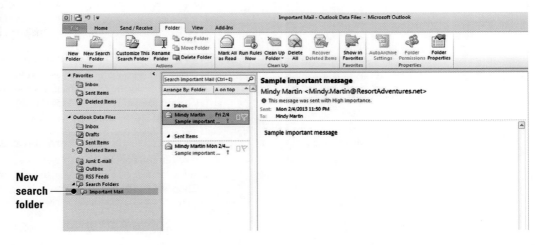

New search folder

PAUSE. LEAVE Outlook open to use in the next exercise.

Outlook provides a number of built-in search folders (see Table 2-5) for everything from unread mail to mail flagged for follow-up to mail containing specific keywords. You can also create a custom search folder containing any criteria you want.

Table 2-5

Built-in Search Folders

Search Folder	What Items Will Appear in the Search Folder
Unread mail	Holds any message from any folder that is marked as unread.
Mail flagged for follow up	Holds any message from any folder that has been flagged.
Mail either unread or flagged for follow-up	Holds any message from any folder that is marked as unread or flagged.
Important mail	Holds any message from any folder that is marked as important.
Mail from and to specific people	Holds any message from any folder that is either from or to contact(s) you choose. When selected, a new box is displayed in the lower portion of the New Search Folder dialog box. Click Choose to open your address book and select the names of people you want included in the search.
Mail from specific people	Holds any message from any folder that is from contact(s) you choose. When selected, a new box is displayed in the lower portion of the New Search Folder dialog box. Click Choose to open your address book and select the names of people you want included in the search.
Mail sent directly to me	Holds any message from any folder that specifically lists you in the *To* field.
Mail sent to public groups	Holds any message from any folder that is addressed to a contact group or distribution list chosen by you. When selected, a new box is displayed in the lower portion of the New Search Folder dialog box. Click Choose to open your address book and select the contact group(s) you want included in the search.
Categorized mail	Holds any message from any folder that you've organized using categories. When selected, a new box is displayed in the lower portion of the New Search Folder dialog box. By default, any category is included, but you can click Choose to open a new window in which you can specify the words you want included in your search.
Large mail	Holds any message from any folder that is at least a specified size. When selected, a new box is displayed in the lower portion of the New Search Folder dialog box. By default, the size limit is 100 KB, but you can click Choose to open a new window in which you can specify the size limit you want.
Old mail	Holds any message from any folder that is older than a specific date. When selected, a new box is displayed in the lower portion of the New Search Folder dialog box. By default, anything older than 1 week is included, but you can click Choose to open a new window in which you can specify the number of days, weeks, or months you want included.
Mail with attachments	Holds any message from any folder that has an attachment.
Mail with specific words	Holds any message from any folder that contains words that you specify. When selected, a new box is displayed in the lower portion of the New Search Folder dialog box. Click Choose to open a new window in which you can specify the words you want included in your search.
Create a custom Search Folder	Holds any message from any folder that meets the specified criteria. When selected, a new box is displayed in the lower portion of the New Search Folder dialog box. Click Choose to open a new window in which you can specify the name for the folder and the specific criterion you want to use.

SKILL SUMMARY

In This Lesson, You Learned How To:
Create messages
Send messages
Read and respond to messages
Format messages
Personalize messages
Create and format graphic message content
Work with attachments
Use advanced message options
Locate messages

Knowledge Assessment

Multiple Choice

Select the letter of the text that best completes the following statements.

1. The _____ feature automatically completes the names of the months and days of the week.
   a. Live Preview
   b. AutoComplete
   c. AutoDate
   d. AutoPreview

2. Text or images that are automatically placed at the end of your outgoing messages are called _____.
   a. stationery
   b. templates
   c. closing
   d. signatures

3. A file sent as part of an e-mail message is called a(n) _____.
   a. enclosure
   b. add on
   c. attachment
   d. supplement

4. To preview a style or theme _____.
   a. place your pointer over the choice
   b. print the document
   c. use Print Preview
   d. It is not possible to preview a style or theme

5. Choosing the number of copies or range of pages are options that are available when performing what process on a message?

   a. Previewing

   b. Assigning properties

   c. Printing

   d. Saving in a different format

6. The _____ indicates the topic of a message.

   a. Reference

   b. Topic

   c. RE:

   d. Subject

7. Use the _____ tab to alter the look of a graphic.

   a. Format

   b. Format Graphics tab

   c. Graphic Tools Format tab

   d. Picture Tools Format tab

8. The _____ contains all the messages for a given contact.

   a. message header

   b. contact record

   c. People Pane

   d. Received folder

9. What is the name of the banner containing information added automatically at the top of a message?

   a. Context bar

   b. InfoBar

   c. ScreenTip

   d. Trust Center

10. Which of the following allows you to filter search results?

    a. Arrange by field

    b. Search Context

    c. Search Suggestions List

    d. All of the above

True/False

Circle T if the statement is true or F if the statement is false.

T   F   1. Use the Message window to compose and send an e-mail message.

T   F   2. To send a message to several recipients, key a colon (:) after a name before adding the next addressee.

T   F   3. The Drawing Tools Format tab only appears when a picture is selected.

T   F   4. A message is moved to the Sent Items folder when you click the Send button.

T   F   5. When you send a reply, the text "RE:" is inserted before the original subject line.

T   F   6. When you make changes to the colors, fonts, or effects of the current theme, you permanently change the original theme.

T   F   7. Use the AutoComplete function to insert your signature before you send a message.

T   F   8. A red exclamation point is the icon used in the message list to indicate that a message is confidential.

T   F   9. The Instant Search feature displays items matching the search criterion before the search is complete.

T   F   10. An InfoBar is a banner containing information added automatically at the top of a message.

Project 2-1: Create an E-mail Message

Send an e-mail message to a friend inviting him to lunch tomorrow.

GET READY. LAUNCH Outlook if it is not already running.

1. On the Standard toolbar, click the New E-mail button to open a new Message window.
2. Key [a friend's e-mail address] in the *To* field. If you are not completing these exercises with a friend or coworker, key [your e-mail address] in the *To* field. This will give you a message to reply to in the next exercise.
3. In the Subject field, key Lunch tomorrow?
4. Click in the message area. Key Hi, [press Enter twice].
5. Key How about lunch tomorrow? [press Enter twice]. Key [your name].
6. Click the Send button.

LEAVE Outlook open for the next project.

Project 2-2: Reply to a Friend's E-mail Message

Reply to a friend's lunch request.

USE the e-mail you received at the end of Project 2-1 before starting this project.

1. If the message sent in Project 2-1 has not arrived, click the Send/Receive All Folders button on the Home tab.
2. In the message list, click the message sent in Project 2-1.
3. Click the Reply button on the Home tab.
4. Key I'll pick you up at 1:00 PM. Don't be late! [press Enter twice]. Key [your name].
5. Click the Send button.
6. Click the Send/Receive All Folders button on the Home tab.
7. In the message list, click the reply message.
8. Click the File tab and select the Save As option. The Save As dialog box is displayed.
9. Navigate to your solutions folder for Lesson 02. Save the message as RE Lunch tomorrow.htm.

LEAVE Outlook open for the next project.

Project 2-3: Send an Attachment

The last guest in the best suite at Resort Adventures accidentally broke the stained-glass window in the suite. You must replace the window before you can accept any reservations for the suite.

GET READY. LAUNCH Outlook if it is not already running.

 **Troubleshooting** The e-mail addresses provided in these projects belong to unused domains owned by Microsoft. When you send a message to these addresses, you will receive an error message stating that the message could not be delivered. Delete the error messages when they arrive.

@ The *Window.jpg* file is available on the book companion website or in WileyPLUS.

1. Create a new e-mail message to Nancy Anderson at the Graphic Design Institute. Nancy's e-mail address is Nancy@graphicdesigninstitute.com. Ask Nancy if she can design a window similar to the stained-glass window that was broken. Ask Nancy how long the project will take and how much it will cost.

2. Attach the *Window.jpg* file located in the data files for this lesson.

3. Be sure to include the signature you created in this lesson.

4. Send the message.

LEAVE Outlook open for the next project.

Project 2-4: Insert Pictures and Clip Art

Resort Adventures is in the progress of putting together a new brochure to publicize the resort's ski facilities. Put together a new e-mail message to a colleague containing two pictures and two clip art images.

GET READY. LAUNCH Outlook if it is not already running.

1. Create a new e-mail message and address it to yourself.

2. In the Subject field, key Ski Images.

3. In the Insert tab, click Pictures.

@ The *Ski 1.jpg* file is available on the book companion website or in WileyPLUS.

4. Navigate to the Data Files for Lesson 2 and insert *Ski 1.jpg*. Press Enter twice.

5. Repeat the process to insert the file *Ski 2.jpg* from your data files. [Press Enter twice.]

6. On the Insert tab, click Clip Art. The Clip Art task pane opens.

7. In the *Results should be* field, select Illustrations. All other media types should be deselected.

@ The *Ski 2.jpg* file is available on the book companion website or in WileyPLUS.

8. Key ski in the *Search for* field and click Go.

9. Scroll through the search results and double-click an image you like that represents skiing.

10. Close the Clip Art task pane.

11. Save the message to your Drafts folder in Outlook.

LEAVE Outlook open for the next project.

Mastery Assessment

Project 2-5: Format and Reset a Picture to Its Original State

Apply formatting to the images in your Ski Images message. You'll then reset one of the images back to its original state.

USE the e-mail you created at the end of Project 2-4 in this lesson.

1. Open Ski Images message in the Drafts folder.

2. Click the first picture. Increase the width to 6".

3. Click Corrections and select Sharpen: +50% and Brightness: +20% Contrast: +20%.

4. In the Picture Styles group, click Soft Edge Oval.

5. Click Color and click Grayscale.

6. Click the second picture. In the Picture Styles group, click Simple Frame, Black.

7. Click Picture Border and select Red in the Standard Colors.

8. In the Picture Border menu, select Weight and click 2 1/4 pt.

9. In the Picture Effects menu, select Perspective Diagonal Upper Right.

10. Select the second picture. Click Crop and crop excess from each side of the image. Change the height to 4". Place the crop tool at the lower-right corner and drag up to the desktop in the picture. Click Crop to complete the crop.

11. Select the third picture. In the Picture Styles group, select Drop Shadow Rectangle.

12. Click **Corrections** and select **Brightness: 0% (Normal)**, **Contrast: -40%**.

13. Click **Color** and select **Aqua, Accent color 5, Light**.

14. Save the message as **Ski Images.htm**.

15. Select the first picture and click **Reset Picture**.

16. Send the message.

LEAVE Outlook open for the next project.

Project 2-6: Create a Custom Theme

Blue Yonder Airlines has decided to give all their documents a branded look by creating a new custom theme to be used for all client-facing business documents.

GET READY. LAUNCH Outlook if it is not already running.

1. Open a new e-mail message and address it to someone@example.com.

2. In the *Subject* field, key **Custom Theme for Blue Yonder Airlines**.

3. Use the Outlook Help button to get more information about creating a custom theme.

4. Choose a custom set of colors, fonts, and/or effects that you feel would be a good choice for Blue Yonder Airlines.

5. Save the theme as **Custom_xxx** (where xxx are your initials).

6. Key a short paragraph explaining that you are creating a custom theme. Include a bulleted list outlining which colors, fonts, or effects you used. Format the paragraph with your custom theme.

7. SAVE the message in Outlook Message Format as **Custom Theme** and save the message then click **Send**.

CLOSE Outlook.

INTERNET READY

When creating a message, you are not limited to inserting only the clip art and other media that come installed with Outlook. A single click can open up a whole new world of options. At the bottom of the Clip Art task pane, notice the More at Office.com link. Click the link to connect to the clip art and media home page, as shown in Figure 2-76. You can browse dozens of categories, download the clip of the day, view featured collections, and more. Next time you need to enhance your messages with clip art or other media, expand your options by going online.

Figure 2-76

Office.com's Images and More page

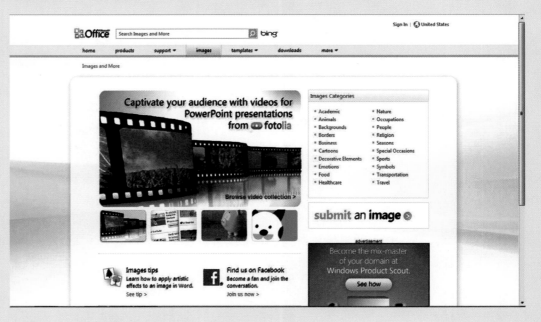

Workplace *Ready*

SENDING A WEEKLY CUSTOMER NEWSLETTER

Although sending unsolicited e-mail ads to people is frowned upon, sending newsletters and promotions to your customers is more popular than ever. The more professional these materials look, the more likely customers are to respond and to share them with others.

Steven Jacobs is the owner of a growing business that delivers locally grown fruits and vegetables. He has worked hard to develop a co-op of local farmers who supply him with produce for his expanding client list. Each week he sends his clients an e-mail newsletter containing information about the types of produce that are going to be included in their weekly deliveries, as well as information about how to prepare and cook the different food items.

Recently he has started including articles that spotlight the different farms and orchards in his co-op group. He has found that the customers have really responded to this information and feel a stronger connection to the farmer as well as the community. In fact, since he expanded the newsletter, he has been getting more and more calls from people who found out about his service because a friend or family worker had forwarded the newsletter to them.

Steven can't wait to introduce the next expansion to his newsletter. He is going to start offering boutique gourmet food products. He is putting together profiles of a wide variety of interesting food producers. He knows this type of content will appeal to the foodies in the community.

LESSON SKILL MATRIX

In This Lesson, You Will Learn The Following Skills:

Working with Folders

Managing Junk Mail

Creating and Running Rules

Managing Rules

KEY TERMS

- action
- condition
- Deleted Items folder
- Drafts folder
- exception
- Inbox folder
- Junk E-mail folder
- Outbox
- restore
- Really Simple Syndication (RSS)
- rule
- Sent Items folder
- spam
- template
- wizard

Mindy Martin, Adventure Works' co-owner, started using Outlook a couple of months ago. She was amazed to see that her Inbox currently contains 180 messages. Clearly, she needs some way to organize them. After a bit of thought, she decides to mimic the organization she uses with her paper documents. She begins creating folders for the main categories of vendors, events, and guests. If you don't take the time to organize and maintain your mailbox, things can quickly get out of hand. In this lesson, you'll learn how to manage your mailbox to organize and maintain your information.

SOFTWARE ORIENTATION

Microsoft Outlook's Folder List

The Folder List, shown in Figure 3-1, provides a complete list of Outlook's initial folders. It includes a folder for each Outlook component, such as the Calendar and Notes.

Figure 3-1

Outlook's Folder List

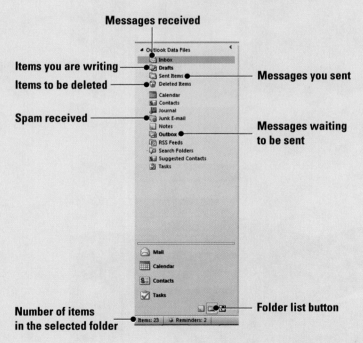

Although the Folder List includes every component, you will normally work only with the mail folders identified in Figure 3-1. The status bar at the bottom of the Outlook window displays the number of items in the selected folder. Create new folders to organize Outlook items by projects or individuals.

WORKING WITH FOLDERS

How often do you wander around your house looking for your car keys? If your answer is "rarely," you are already in the habit of putting things away so you know where to find them later. Organize your Outlook items in folders for the same reason. Items are easier to find when you put them away. In this section, you'll work with Outlook folders by creating, moving, deleting, and restoring them. You'll also move mail items from folder to folder.

Creating and Moving a Mail Folder

In your office, new documents arrive in your Inbox regularly. You look at the document, perform the associated tasks, and file the paper in a folder you labeled for that type of item. You don't place it back in your Inbox. If you piled up all your documents in your Inbox, in a few weeks or months you would have a stack of paper that was several inches tall. In the same way, you don't want to keep all your messages in your Inbox in Microsoft Outlook. In this exercise, you'll create and move Outlook folders.

STEP BY STEP   **Create and Move a Mail Folder**

GET READY. LAUNCH Outlook if it is not already running.

1. Click the Folder List button in the bottom of the Navigation Pane to display the Folder List shown in Figure 3-1. The four main Outlook folders (Inbox, Drafts, Sent Items, and Deleted Items) appear at the top of the list with the remaining Outlook folders in alphabetical order beneath them.

2. Click the Inbox folder and click the Folder tab to display Outlook's folder tools.

3. Click the New Folder button in the New group. The Create New Folder dialog box is displayed, as shown in Figure 3-2. Since you selected the Inbox in step 2, the Inbox is currently selected in the dialog box

Figure 3-2

Create New Folder dialog box

Key a name for the new folder

Select the location for the new folder

Another Way
To create a new folder, right-click any folder in the folder list and select New Folder.

4. In the *Name* field, key Lesson 4 to label the new folder. When creating a folder, use a name that identifies its contents. Don't use abbreviations that you won't remember next week or six months from now.

5. Click Outlook Data Files in the Select Where to Place the Folder list. This determines the location where the new folder will be placed when it is created. If you do not have the correct location selected, you can move the new folder later.

Troubleshooting For this exercise, you want to select the top-level folder. It's the folder that holds your Inbox, Sent Items folder, and so on. Depending on the settings on your computer and the type of e-mail account you have, this might be called Outlook Data Files, Personal Folders, or simply your e-mail address.

6. Click the OK button to close the dialog box and create the folder. The new folder is added to the Folder List.

7. In the Folder List, click the Lesson 4 folder to select it and then drag the folder down to the Notes folder. When the Notes folder is highlighted, drop the folder. An expand arrow is displayed next to the Notes folder, indicating that it contains a folder, as shown in Figure 3-3.

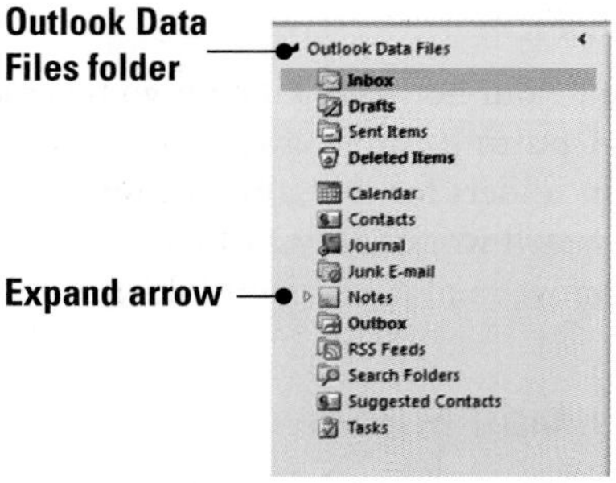

Figure 3-3

New folder created and moved
into the Notes folder

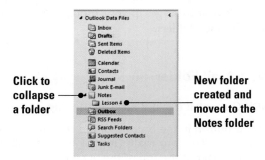

**Outlook Data
Files folder**

Expand arrow

8. Click the **expand arrow** next to the Notes folder. The Folder List expands to display the Lesson 4 folder, as shown in Figure 3-4.

Figure 3-4

Expanded Notes folder

**Click to
collapse
a folder**

**New folder
created and
moved to the
Notes folder**

9. Drag the Lesson 4 folder and drop it on the Outlook Data Files icon in the Folder List. The Lesson 4 folder is placed alphabetically in the Folders List, and the expand arrow is removed from the Notes folder.

PAUSE. LEAVE Outlook open to use in the next exercise.

Outlook provides several default mail folders that meet your most basic organizational needs. Table 3-1 identifies the default mail folders and describes their content.

Table 3-1

Default Mail Folders

Folder	Description
Deleted Items	The **Deleted Items folder** holds your deleted messages. Items in the Deleted Items folder can be restored to full use. However, if the item is deleted while in the Deleted Items folder, it will be permanently deleted from your computer. Emptying the Deleted Items folder permanently removes every item in the folder.
Drafts	The **Drafts folder** holds Outlook messages you write but haven't sent. You can return to a draft later to complete and send the message. If you close a message without sending it, a dialog box will ask if you want to save the draft. Click Yes to save the draft. Click No to discard the draft.
Inbox	By default, new messages to you are placed in this **Inbox folder** when they arrive.
Junk E-mail	The **Junk E-mail folder** contains messages identified as spam when they arrive.
Outbox	The **Outbox** holds outgoing messages in this folder until you are connected to the Internet. When an Internet connection is detected, the message is sent.
RSS Feeds	**Really Simple Syndication (RSS)** allows you to subscribe to content from a variety of websites offering the service. RSS is not covered in this book. Use Outlook's Help feature to find more information on RSS.
Sent Items	Items are automatically moved to the **Sent Items folder** after they have been sent.

Deleting and Restoring a Folder

You can delete an Outlook folder you no longer need. When you delete a folder, it is moved to Outlook's Deleted Items folder. Items in the Deleted Items folder are still on your computer. You can **restore** these items, that is, make them available for use again, by moving them out of the Deleted Items folder. In this exercise, you'll delete the Lesson 4 folder and restore it.

Troubleshooting Use caution. If you *delete* an item that is stored in the Deleted Items folder instead of moving the item to another folder, such as the Outlook Data File, the item is permanently removed from your computer and can no longer be restored.

STEP BY STEP **Delete and Restore a Folder**

GET READY. USE the folder you created in the previous exercises.

1. If necessary, click the Folder List button in the Navigation Pane to display the complete list of Outlook folders.

2. Right-click the Lesson 4 folder created in the previous exercise. Click Delete Folder from the shortcut menu. A warning dialog box is displayed, as shown in Figure 3-5.

Figure 3-5

Deleting a folder

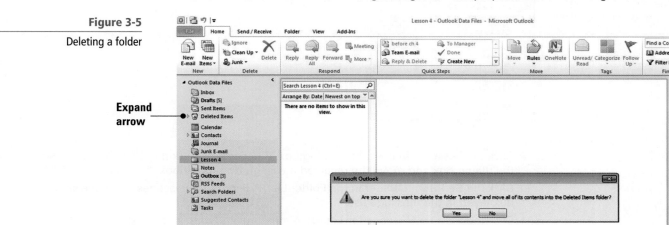

3. Click Yes to close the warning dialog box. The Lesson 4 folder is moved to the Deleted Items folder. It will not be removed from your computer until you empty the Deleted Items folder.

4. In the Folder List, click the expand arrow next to the Deleted Items folder. The Lesson 4 folder is displayed in the Deleted Items folder.

5. Drag the Lesson 4 folder and drop it on the Outlook Data Files icon in the Folder List. The Lesson 4 folder is placed in the Outlook Data Files, and the expand arrow is removed from the Deleted Items folder. The Lesson 4 folder has been restored, and it is now available for use.

PAUSE. LEAVE Outlook open to use in the next exercise.

Moving Messages to a Different Folder

Outlook uses folders to organize Outlook items. Messages arrive in the Inbox. Messages you send are stored in the Sent Items folder. To effectively organize your messages, create new folders for projects or individuals, and move the related messages into the new folders. In this exercise, you'll start organizing your mailbox by moving messages to different folders.

STEP BY STEP **Move Messages to a Different Folder**

GET READY. LAUNCH Outlook if it is not already running, and complete the previous exercises.

1. If necessary, click the Mail button in the Navigation Pane to display the Inbox.

2. Click the New E-mail button on the Home tab. The Message window is displayed. By default, the Message tab is selected.

3. In the *To* field, key [your e-mail address]. In the *Subject* field, key Sample Message for Lesson 4.

4. In the message area, key Sample Message for Lesson 4.

5. Click the Send button. The message is moved to the Outbox, and it is sent when your computer is connected to the Internet.

6. Return to your Inbox. Click the Send/Receive All Folders button if the message has not arrived yet. Because the message was sent to your e-mail address, the message is moved to the Sent Items folder and it arrives in your Inbox. You will move both copies of the message into the Lesson 4 folder.

Another Way
You can also open the Move Items dialog box by selecting the message and pressing Ctrl+Shift+V.

7. Right-click the Sample Message for Lesson 4 message that just arrived in your Inbox. Click Move on the shortcut menu. A list of potential folders is displayed.

8. Click Other Folder at the bottom of the list. The Move Items dialog box is displayed, as shown in Figure 3-6.

Figure 3-6

Move Items dialog box

9. Click the Lesson 4 folder in the dialog box, if necessary. Click the OK button to close the dialog box and move the received message from the Inbox to the Lesson 4 folder.

10. Click the Sent Items folder in the Folder List. A list of the messages you have sent is displayed in the message list.

11. Click the Sample Message for Lesson 4 message and drag it to the Lesson 4 folder. The message is moved from the Sent Items folder to the Lesson 4 folder.

12. Click the Lesson 4 folder in the Folder List. The two messages you moved are displayed in the message list, as shown in Figure 3-7.

Figure 3-7

Messages moved to the Lesson 4 folder

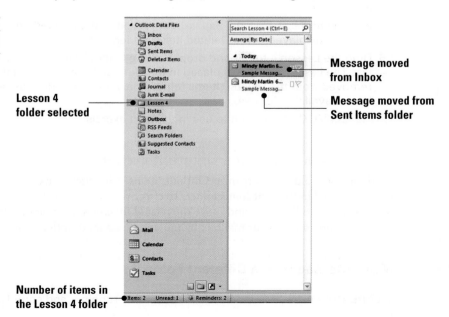

Lesson 4 folder selected

Message moved from Inbox

Message moved from Sent Items folder

Number of items in the Lesson 4 folder

PAUSE. LEAVE Outlook open to use in the next exercise.

MANAGING JUNK MAIL

The Bottom Line

Nearly every day, the average inbox receives *spam*—unwanted junk mail messages from advertisers and con artists. Aside from the nuisance factor, many junk mail messages are designed to plant viruses on your computer or lure you into divulging your identity information. In this section, you'll learn to spot and manage junk mail messages.

Viewing Message Properties

Having your mailbox flooded with ads is annoying, but falling prey to someone who is misrepresenting himself in a spam message is downright dangerous. Some spammers format and design their messages to look as though they are coming from someone else. You can spot most of these "spoofing" messages by examining the message header to ensure that its properties are in keeping with the content of the message. The message header is text that is encoded into every e-mail message. Though not visible when reading the actual message, it contains detailed information about the sender, the sender's domain, and the sender's e-mail service. In this exercise, you'll examine a message header's properties.

STEP BY STEP   **View Message Properties**

GET READY. LAUNCH Outlook if it is not already running.

1. If necessary, click the **Mail** button in the Navigation Pane to display the Inbox.
2. Double-click a message that you sent to yourself. The message window opens, displaying the selected message.
3. Click the **File** tab and click **Properties** in Backstage view. The Properties dialog box is displayed, as shown in Figure 3-8.

Figure 3-8

Properties dialog box

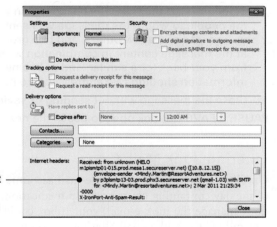

The Internet headers contain information about the person who sent the message

4. Click anywhere in the Internet Headers area at the bottom of the dialog box. The Internet Headers area can contain a lot of information that can be hard to read. To make it easier to locate the information you're looking for, it helps to copy the header information and paste it into a blank document or message window.
5. Press **Ctrl+A** to select all the information listed there. Press **Ctrl+C** to copy it. Click **Close** to close the Properties dialog box.
6. On the Message tab, click **Reply**. In the message area, press **Ctrl+V** to paste the information about the message header into your Reply message, as shown in Figure 3-9.

Figure 3-9

Reading a message header

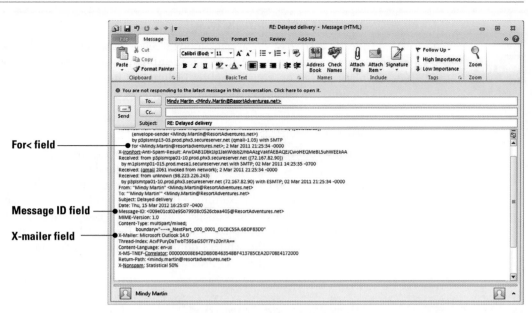

For< field

Message ID field

X-mailer field

7. Scroll through the information you've pasted in the Reply message area. Locate the *Message ID* field. This should end in the domain name of the sender. For example, if you received a message from PayPal asking to confirm your account settings, the domain name listed should match the paypal.com that the official PayPal site uses. If you see any other error in spelling, capitalization, or suffix, you know the message is a fake.

8. Locate the *X-mailer* field. This lists the e-mail software used by the sender. In most cases, a major corporation won't be sending messages from a webmail system, such as Hotmail or Yahoo Mail. They are more likely to use a business e-mail program like Outlook 2010.

9. Scroll through the message header again and locate the *for<* field. This field lists all the people to whom the message was sent. Now obviously you'll receive messages to you, to you and a few others, and to a group to which you belong. The key is to look at the message content in combination with the for< field. For example, messages from your bank (or a similar kind of business) containing supposedly confidential information shouldn't be addressed to a bulk mailing list.

10. Close the message without sending or saving.

PAUSE. LEAVE Outlook open to use in the next exercise.

Filtering Junk Mail

NEW to Office 2010

Unsolicited e-mail sent to many e-mail accounts is **spam** or junk e-mail. It arrives at all times of the day containing offers of cheap medication, knock-off jewelry, and bad stock tips. If you don't manage the junk e-mail, your Inbox could easily be buried in spam. Outlook 2010 has streamlined the junk e-mail filtering process to make it easier than ever to keep your Inbox free from spam. In this exercise, you'll explore Outlook's options for filtering junk e-mail and learn how to add someone to your Blocked Senders list.

STEP BY STEP | **Filter Junk Mail**

GET READY. LAUNCH Outlook if it is not already running.

1. If necessary, click the **Mail** button in the Navigation Pane to display the Inbox.

2. On the Home tab, click **Junk** in the Delete group. A list of options for handling junk mail is displayed.

3. Select **Junk E-mail Options**. The Junk E-mail Options dialog box is displayed, as shown in Figure 3-10.

Figure 3-10

Junk E-mail Options dialog box

Current security level

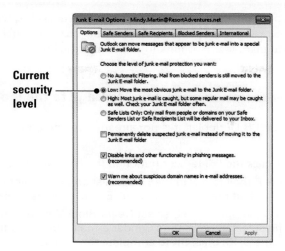

4. The default protection level is Low. If you click the High option, less junk e-mail will be delivered to your Inbox, but some messages that you want to see might be sent to the Junk E-mail folder as well. A higher setting will filter out more messages, but you'll find that more of the messages you want keep will get sent to the Junk E-mail folder. The question is whether the extra level of security is worth the hassle of hunting for messages in the Junk E-mail folder. There is no one right answer. If you are receiving a lot of junk messages, you'll want to use the High setting.

5. For now, you will leave the setting at Low so you don't miss any important messages. Click the Cancel button to close the dialog box and return to the main Outlook window.

6. If a message from a friend or coworker is in your Inbox, right-click the message in the message list. Point to Junk on the shortcut menu. A list of Junk E-mail options is displayed, as shown in Figure 3-11.

Figure 3-11

Selecting a Junk E-mail option

7. Click the Block Sender option. A message is displayed notifying you that the sender has been added to your Block Senders List, as shown in Figure 3-12.

Figure 3-12

Blocking a specific message

8. Click OK. The message moves from the Inbox to the Junk E-mail folder.

PAUSE. LEAVE Outlook open to use in the next exercise.

Increasing the level of protection decreases the amount of spam that will be directed to your Inbox. However, it increases the chance that a non-spam message will also be delivered to the Junk E-mail folder. If you choose to increase your protection level, check your Junk E-mail folder frequently.

Using Not Junk to Return a Specific Message to the Inbox

Outlook uses your filter settings to make a guess as to what is spam and what isn't. Sometimes a good message will slip into the Junk E-mail list. If this happens, you can easily move the message back to your Inbox and add the sender to your Safe Senders list, which will ensure that future messages don't get caught in the spam filter. In this exercise, you'll find a message in the Junk E-mail folder and mark it as Not Junk to return it to the Inbox.

STEP BY STEP   **Use Not Junk to Return a Specific Message to the Inbox**

GET READY. LAUNCH Outlook if it is not already running and complete the previous exercise.

1. If necessary, click the Folder List button in the Navigation Pane to display the mailbox.
2. Click the Junk E-mail folder in the Folder List and right-click on the message. Point to Junk in the shortcut menu. A list of Junk E-mail options is displayed as a fly-out menu.
3. In the Junk E-mail options list, select Never Block Sender. Outlook notifies you that it will move the selected message's Sender e-mail address to the Safe Senders List, as shown in Figure 3-13. Click OK to complete the process.

Figure 3-13

Using Never Block Sender to add a person to your Safe Senders List

4. Your friend's e-mail address is now considered safe, but the message remains in the Junk E-mail folder.
5. Right-click the message again and click Junk in the shortcut menu to open the list of options.
6. Click Not Junk. The Mark as Not Junk dialog box is displayed, as shown in Figure 3-14.

Figure 3-14

Mark as Not Junk dialog box

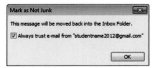

7. Click OK. The message moves back to the Inbox.

CLOSE Outlook.

Outlook's Junk E-mail options are outlined in Table 3-2 below.

Table 3-2

Junk E-mail Filtering Options

Option	Description
Block Sender	Add the sender to the Blocked Senders List. All future messages from this sender's e-mail address will go straight to the Junk E-mail folder.
Never Block Sender	Add the sender to the Safe Senders List. Future messages from this sender will be regarded as safe.
Never Block Sender's Domain	Add the sender's domain to the Safe Senders List. Future messages from anyone at the same domain will be considered safe.
Never Block this Group or Distribution List	Add the distribution list or contact group to the Safe Senders List. Future messages from the group will be considered safe.
Not Junk	Regardless of other settings, Not Junk marks the message as safe and returns it to the inbox.

As you receive messages from people you want to correspond with, add their e-mail addresses to the Safe Senders List. Messages from senders on the Safe Senders List are never directed to the Junk E-mail folder.

SOFTWARE ORIENTATION

Microsoft Outlook's Rules and Alerts Window

Message rules are displayed in the Rules and Alerts dialog box, as shown in Figure 3-15. You can refer to this figure as you work through this lesson and throughout the book.

Figure 3-15

Outlook's Rules and Alerts window

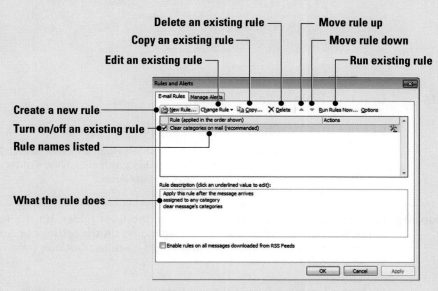

The rules that help you organize your messages are displayed in the Rules and Alerts window. In this window, you can edit existing rules, create new rules, enable rules, and disable rules.

CREATING AND RUNNING RULES

The Bottom Line

A **rule** defines an action that happens automatically when messages are received or sent. Rules can be created in a number of different ways. Using a template is the easiest method for creating a new rule. A **template** is an existing rule provided by Outlook that contains specific pieces of information that can be customized to create new rules. You also can create a rule from an existing message or copy an existing rule and edit one or more of the rule's components. If a rule is simple, you can create it quickly from scratch. In this section, you'll use a variety of methods to create rules.

Creating a Rule from a Template

One of the best ways to organize your mailbox is to move messages out of the Inbox and into folders that group related messages together. For example, you can place messages about your active projects in project folders and messages from vendors in separate vendor folders. Create and use as many folders as you need to keep yourself organized. Manually locating and moving a lot of messages can be time consuming and prone to errors. Instead, automate the process by creating a rule to move the messages for you. The simplest method of creating rules is to let the Rules Wizard helps you create a template from a template. A **wizard** consists of steps that walk you through completing a process in Microsoft Office applications. In this exercise, you'll use a template to create a rule for moving messages.

A rule consists of three parts: a condition, an action, and an exception. In simple terms, a rule says if A happens (the condition), then B (the action) occurs unless C (the exception). Table 3-3 describes these parts of a rule.

Table 3-3

Parts of a Rule

Part	Description
Condition	The **condition** identifies the characteristics used to determine the messages affected by the rule. Use caution when you define the conditions. If your conditions are too broad, the rule will affect more messages than intended. If your conditions are too narrow, the rule will not identify some of the messages that should be affected.
Action	The **action** determines what happens when a message meets the conditions defined in the rule. For example, the message can be moved, forwarded, or deleted.
Exception	The **exception** identifies the characteristics used to exclude messages from being affected by the rule.

STEP BY STEP   **Create a Rule from a Template**

GET READY. LAUNCH Outlook if it is not already running.

1. If necessary, click the **Mail** button in the Navigation Pane to display the mailbox. Right-click **Outlook Data Files** in the Folders List, and click **New Folder** in the shortcut menu. The Create New Folder dialog box is displayed.

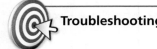

Troubleshooting For this exercise, you want to select the top-level folder. It's the folder that holds your Inbox, Sent Items folder, and so on. Depending on the settings on your computer and the type of e-mail account you have, this might be called Outlook Data Files, Personal Folders, or simply your e-mail address.

2. In the *Name* field, key **Lesson 5 Schedules**. If necessary, click **Outlook Data Files** in the *Select Where to Place the Folder* section. Click **OK** to create the folder and close the dialog box. You will create a rule to move messages into this folder.

3. Click the **File** tab. In Backstage view, click the **Manage Rules and Alerts** option. The Rules and Alerts window shown in Figure 3-15 is displayed. Click the **New Rule** button. The Rules Wizard window is displayed, as shown in Figure 3-16. Step 1 of this wizard involves choosing a template or blank rule.

Figure 5-16

Rules Wizard window with
default selections

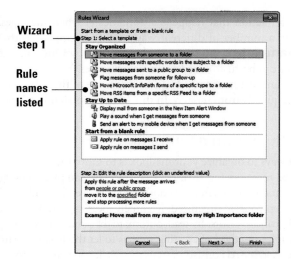

Wizard step 1

Rule names listed

Another Way
You can also open the Rules and Alerts window by clicking Rules on the Home tab and selecting Manage Rules and Alerts.

4. In the Stay Organized category of the Step 1 templates and rules list, click **Move messages with specific words in the subject to a folder**. This rule will move messages about the selected topic. The rule description in the lower area of the window changes, as shown in Figure 3-17.

Figure 3-17

Rules Wizard window with template to move messages selected

Template selected

Customized underlined text

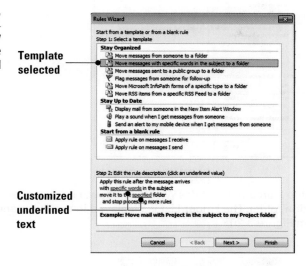

Troubleshooting To ensure that a rule looking for a specific subject moves the messages, the subject line must contain the exact words shown in the editing area of the Rules Wizard window.

5. In the Step 2 area, click **specific words**. The Search Text window is displayed, as shown in Figure 3-18.

Figure 3-18

Search Text window

Key specific words that must appear in the subject

List of words that must be in the subject to move the message

Click to add keyed text to the search list

Take Note   In this exercise, you will use a single phrase as the search text. To add more words or phrases to the search list, key the text into the Search Text window and click the Add button.

6. In the *Specify words or phrases to search for in the subject* field, key **Lesson 5 Schedule**. Click the **Add** button. The Lesson 5 Schedule phrase is enclosed by quotation marks and added to the search list for this rule. Click **OK** to close the Search Text window. The Rules Wizard window is displayed. The Lesson 5 Schedule search phrase is identified, as shown in Figure 3-19.

Figure 3-19

Rules Wizard window with the
search phrase identified

**Template
selected**

**Search text
specified as
"Lesson 5
Schedule"**

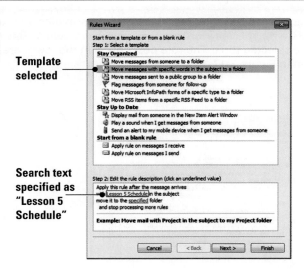

7. In the Step 2 area of the Rules Wizard window, click specified to identify the
destination folder. The Folder List is displayed in the Rules and Alerts window, as
shown in Figure 3-20.

Figure 3-20

Select the destination folder.

Outlook folders

8. Click the Lesson 5 Schedules folder in the Choose a Folder list, and click OK. The
specified destination folder is identified in the Rules Wizard window, as shown in
Figure 3-21.

Figure 3-21

Rules Wizard window with the
destination folder identified

**Outlook
folders**

**Template
customized**

**Click the Next button to
continue the Wizard**

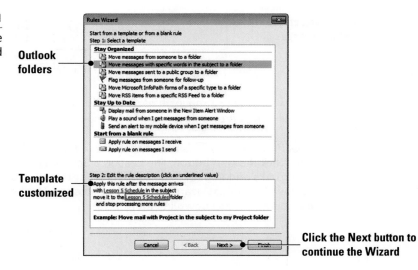

9. Click the **Next** button to continue to the next Wizard window. Under *Step 1: Select condition(s)*, you will see a list of conditions that can be added to the rule. You don't want to add conditions to this rule, so click the **Next** button to continue to the third Wizard window. Under *Step 1: Select action(s)*, you will see a list of actions that can be taken if the conditions are met. Without any conditions, you don't want to add actions to this rule, so click the **Next** button to continue to the next window of the Wizard. A list of exceptions to the rule is displayed, as shown in Figure 3-22.

Figure 3-22

Rules Wizard window with exceptions that can be added to the rule

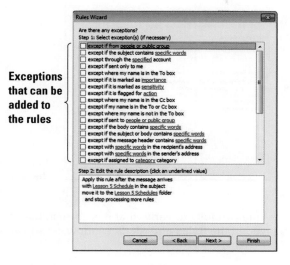

Exceptions that can be added to the rules

10. Click the second check box on the list: **except if the subject contains specific words**. Text is added to the rule description at the bottom of the Rules Wizard window.

11. In the rule description area at the bottom of the window, click **specific words**. The Search text window shown in Figure 3-18 is displayed.

12. In the *Specify words or phrases to search for in the subject* field, key **RE:**. Making RE: an exception prevents replies to the Lesson 5 Schedule messages from being moved to the destination folder. Click the **Add** button. The RE: text is enclosed by quotation marks and added to the search list for this rule. Click **OK** to close the Search Text window. The Rules Wizard window is displayed. The exception is added to the rule, as shown in Figure 3-23.

Figure 3-23

Rules Wizard window with exception added to the rule

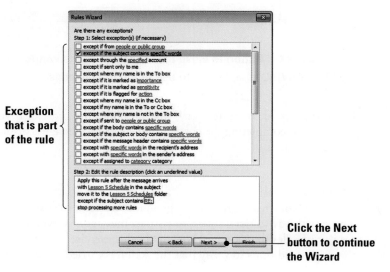

Exception that is part of the rule

Click the Next button to continue the Wizard

13. Click the Next button to continue the Wizard. The rule is displayed for your approval, as shown in Figure 3-24.

Figure 3-24

Rules Wizard window with rule displayed for approval

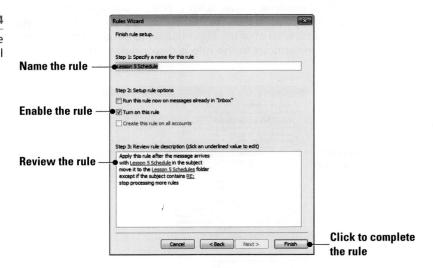

Name the rule

Enable the rule

Review the rule

Click to complete the rule

14. Examine the rule carefully to verify that it is correct. Click the Finish button. The new rule is displayed in the Rules and Alerts window, as shown in Figure 3-25.

Figure 3-25

Rules and Alerts window with the new rule displayed

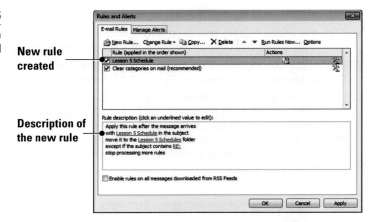

New rule created

Description of the new rule

15. Click the OK button to close the Rules and Alerts window.

PAUSE. LEAVE Outlook open to use in the next exercise.

Using the wizard to create a new rule simplifies the process. If you try to advance to the next step without completing the current step, an error message is displayed. It instructs you to finish the current step.

Testing a Rule

Whenever you create a rule, it is a good idea to test it to ensure that it works the way you expect. The easiest way to test a rule is to create a message that will meet the conditions of your rule to see if it handles the message properly. In this exercise, you'll send yourself a message that meets the rule's conditions to verify that the action is carried out as intended.

STEP BY STEP **Test a Rule**

GET READY. Before you begin these steps, be sure to complete the previous exercise creating a rule.

1. Click the New E-mail button on the Home tab. The Message window is displayed.
2. In the *To* field, key [your e-mail address].
3. In the *Subject* field, key Lesson 5 Schedule. When this message arrives, it will meet the condition defined in the Lesson 5 Schedule rule.
4. In the message area, key Lesson 5 Schedule rule test.
5. Click the Send button. The message is moved to the Outbox and sent when the computer is connected to the Internet.
6. Click the Lesson 5 Schedule folder. If necessary, click the Send/Receive All Folders button to receive the message. When the message arrives, the rule runs automatically and places the message in the Lesson 5 Schedules folder, as shown in Figure 3-26.

Figure 3-26

Rule moved the received message

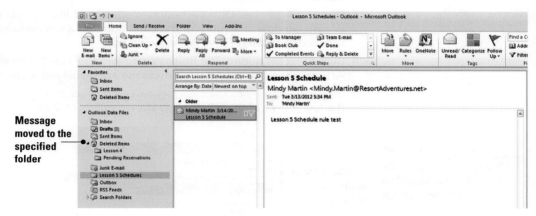

Message moved to the specified folder

PAUSE. LEAVE Outlook open to use in the next exercise.

After creating a rule, test the rule to verify that it works. For example, to test the rule created in the previous exercise, you sent a message with *Lesson 5 Schedule* as the subject to yourself. Over time, you might need to add conditions to the rule because not everyone who sends schedules to you uses the correct subject. You can add a condition such as the *Lesson 5 Schedule* phrase in the body of the message or add a condition identifying any message with the word *schedule* in the subject.

Creating a Rule from a Selected Message

Repeating the same action over and over is one of the most common reasons for creating a rule. For example, another common organization tool that requires repetitive tasks is categorizing messages. When you categorize messages, you assign messages about related topics a specific color code so that they are easy to locate. Automatically categorizing messages is a common organizational task that you can automate by creating a rule. The next time you select a message on which you plan to perform an often-repeated action, use the message to create a rule. In this exercise, you'll create a rule from an existing message. The rule will categorize messages by color.

STEP BY STEP **Create a Rule from a Selected Message**

USE the message you sent in the previous exercise.

1. If necessary, click the Mail button in the Navigation Pane to display the mailbox.
2. In the Navigation Pane, click the Lesson 5 Schedules folder. One message is in the folder. It is highlighted in the Message List.

3. Right-click the message. Point to Rules and select Create Rule on the shortcut menu. The Create Rule dialog box is displayed, as shown in Figure 3-27. The conditions of the selected message are displayed in the dialog box.

Figure 3-27

Create Rule dialog box

Conditions of the selected message

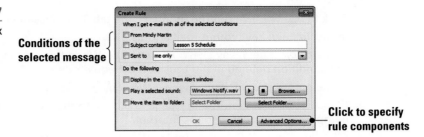

Click to specify rule components

4. Click the Subject contains check box. The field contains *Lesson 5 Schedule*, the subject of the selected message.

5. Click the Advanced Options button to specify additional rule components. The Rules Wizard window is displayed. The condition about the message's subject is already selected in the first Rules Wizard window.

6. Click the Next button. The Rules Wizard window lists the available actions for the rule. Actions based on the selected message are displayed at the top of the list.

7. Click the assign it to the category category check box. The selected action is moved to the lower area of the window, as shown in Figure 3-28.

Figure 3-28

Rules Wizard window with available actions based on the selected message

Characteristics of the selected message

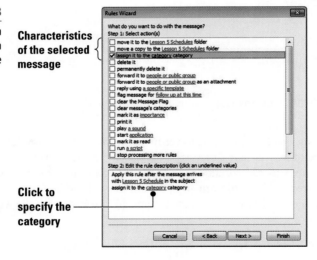

Click to specify the category

8. In the *Step 2: Edit the rule description* area, click the underlined category. The Color Categories dialog box is displayed, as shown in Figure 3-29.

Figure 3-29

Color Categories dialog box

Select the category

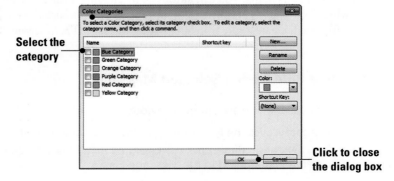

Click to close the dialog box

9. Click the Green Category check box. Click OK. When you complete the exercise and run the rule, messages that match the conditions you've outlined will be highlighted with green, making them easier to spot in a message list.

10. If a Rename Category window is displayed, click the No button. The Color Categories dialog box is closed, and you are returned to the Rules Wizard window.

Take Note   You can rename categories, but it isn't necessary in this lesson.

Another Way
You can also access the Rules and Alerts window by right-clicking a message, pointing to Rules, and selecting Manage Rules and Alerts.

11. The condition and action for the rule are complete. You don't want to identify any exceptions. Click the Finish button. The rule is saved. The Rules Wizard window is closed, and you are returned to the main Outlook window. In the following steps, you will rename and test the new rule.

12. On the Home tab, click Rules in the Move group and select Manage Rules and Alerts option. The Rules and Alerts window is displayed, as shown in Figure 3-30. The new rule you just created is identified as Lesson 5 Schedule (1). The name was inherited from the rule already applied to the message when you selected the message.

Figure 3-30

Rule created from a selected message

Click to change the rule's name

New rule created from a selected message

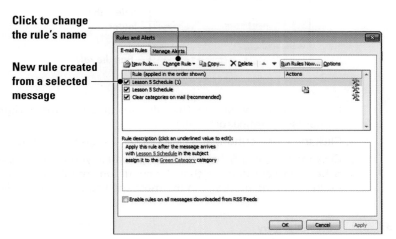

13. If necessary, select the Lesson 5 Schedule (1) rule. Click the Change Rule button, and click the Rename Rule option. The Rename dialog box is displayed, as shown in Figure 3-31.

Figure 3-31

Rename a Rule

14. In the *New name of rule* field, key Green Lesson 5 Schedule. Click OK. The Rename dialog box is closed. The name of the rule has been changed.

PAUSE. LEAVE Outlook open to use in the next exercise.

Running a Rule

Rules run automatically when new messages arrive. So, what happens to the mail that is already in your mailbox? You can run a rule manually. When you run a rule, it scans the mailbox as if it were new mail and applies the rule's actions on any messages that meet your conditions. In this exercise, you'll run a rule so that it processes your existing messages.

STEP BY STEP   **Test a Rule**

GET READY. LAUNCH Outlook if it is not already running.

1. If necessary, click the File tab to return to Backstage view. Click Manage Rules and Alerts. The Rules and Alerts window shown in Figure 3-15 is displayed.
2. Click the Run Rules Now button. The Run Rules Now dialog box is displayed.
3. In the *Select rules to run* section, click the Green Lesson 5 Schedule check box, as shown in Figure 3-32.

Figure 3-32

Run Rules Now dialog box

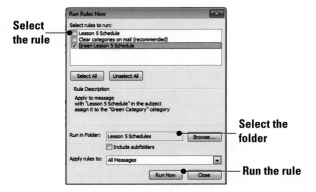

Click the Run Now button. The rule runs quietly in the background. In fact, there is no immediately noticeable effect.

4. Click the Close button, and click the OK button to return to the main Outlook window.
5. Click the Lesson 5 Schedule folder. Because you have a message in the Lesson 5 Schedule folder that matches the conditions of this rule, the Green Category has been assigned to the message in the message list, as shown in Figure 3-33.

Figure 3-33

Green Category assigned to a message

Green Category assigned

PAUSE. LEAVE Outlook open to use in the next exercise.

Creating a rule from a selected message has advantages. As you create the rule, the characteristics of the selected message are offered as rule components. This saves time and increases the rule's accuracy.

Creating a Rule by Copying an Existing Rule

Forwarding messages is another common task that can be performed by a rule. When many of the rule components are similar to an existing rule, you can copy the existing rule to create the new rule. In this exercise, you'll create a rule for forwarding messages by copying and modifying an existing rule.

STEP BY STEP   **Create a Rule by Copying an Existing Rule**

USE the message and the rule created in a previous exercise.

1. If necessary, click the Mail button in the Navigation Pane to display the mailbox.
2. On the Home tab, click the Rules command in the Move group. Select the Manage Rules and Alerts option from the menu that appears. The Rules and Alerts window shown in Figure 3-15 is displayed.

3. Click the Green Lesson 5 Schedule rule. Click the Copy button in the Manage Rules and Alerts window. The Copy Rule To dialog box is displayed, as shown in Figure 3-34. The Folder listing in this dialog box identifies the Inbox as being affected by the rule.

Figure 3-34

Copying a rule

Take Note   If your Outlook profile accesses more than one e-mail account, you can choose the Inbox to be affected by the rule. Refer to Outlook's Help for more information about Outlook profiles.

4. Click OK to accept the Folder listing and close the dialog box. A copy of the selected rule is created and added to the list of rules, as shown in Figure 3-35.

Figure 3-35

Copied rule created

Click to change the rule's name

Copy of rule is turned off

Copy of rule created

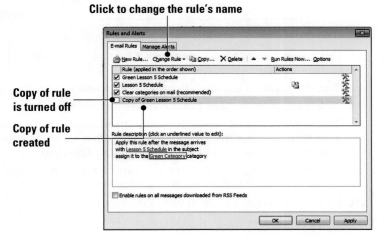

5. Select the Copy of Green Lesson 5 Schedule rule, if necessary. Click the Change Rule button, and click Rename Rule. The Rename dialog box is displayed.

6. In the *New name of rule* field, key Forward Lesson 5 Schedule. Click OK. The dialog box is closed, and the rule's name is changed.

7. With the Forward Lesson 5 Schedule rule selected, click the Change Rule button, and click the Edit Rule Settings option. The Rules Wizard window is displayed.

8. The condition about the message's subject is already selected. Click the Next button. The Rules Wizard window lists the available actions for the rule.

9. Click the assign it to the category category check box to deselect the action. Click the forward it to people or people group check box. The action is moved to the rule description in the lower area of the Rules Wizard window.

10. In the *Step 2: Edit the rule description* area, click the underlined people or people group text. The Rule Address dialog box is displayed.

Take Note   Throughout this chapter you will see information that appears in black text within brackets, such as [Press **Enter**] or [your e-mail address]. The information contained in the brackets is intended to be directions for you rather than something you actually type word for word. It will instruct you to perform an action or substitute text. Do **not** type the actual text that appears within brackets.

11. In the *To* field, key [the e-mail address of a friend or coworker]. Click the OK button to close the dialog box. The Rules Wizard window is updated, as shown in Figure 3-36.

Figure 3-36

Rule to forward messages

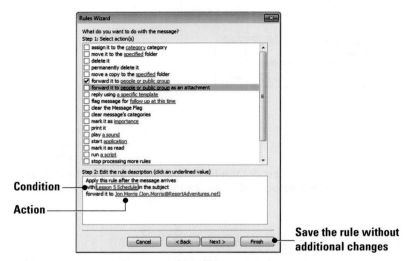

Condition

Action

Save the rule without additional changes

12. This rule does not have exceptions. Click the Finish button to save the rule and return to the Rules and Alerts window.

13. Click the Forward Lesson 5 Schedule check box to turn on the rule.

14. Click the Run Rules Now button. The Run Rules Now dialog box is displayed.

15. Click the Forward Lesson 5 Schedule check box. Click the Run Now button. Outlook looks through your mailbox for messages that meet the conditions you set and forwards them on to the e-mail address you specified in the Rule Address dialog box.

16. Click the Close button. Click OK to return to the main Outlook window. The forwarded message is listed in the Sent Items folder.

PAUSE. LEAVE Outlook open to use in the next exercise.

So far, you have created a rule to move a message, a rule to assign a category, and a rule to forward messages. Rather than creating three separate rules, you could create a single rule that performs all three actions.

When you combine actions into a single rule, keep in mind that you can't simply turn off individual actions. If you turn off a rule with several actions, none of the actions are performed. If one part of the rule or conditions is likely to change periodically, consider keeping that part as a unique rule.

Alternatively, if you do combine it into a single rule and conditions change, you can go in and manually alter the actions within a rule, but you'll have to remember to go back in and alter the actions again when conditions change. Although this is certainly doable, it is time consuming and could easily be forgotten. If an action is likely to change, it is better practice to leave it as a separate rule that you can simply turn on and off.

Let's put that in terms of a real-life situation. Suppose that Jon, the addressee of the forwarded messages you just created, goes on a two-week business trip followed by a two-week vacation in Hawaii. He asked you to stop forwarding schedules to him for four weeks. If the three actions were combined into one rule, you would need to create new rules or edit the combined rule so that the messages are still moved and categorized, but not forwarded to Jon. Then when Jon returns, you'll need to go back in and edit the rule again to add back the third step. If you keep the forwarded action in a separate rule, you just need to deselect the rule in the Rules & Alerts window to turn off the forwarding rule until Jon returns with a tan and too many vacation photos. When he gets back, just select the action again.

Creating a Rule from Scratch

Some rules are simple to write. You want to find messages that meet one condition and perform one action without exceptions. For example, a simple rule might be "Delete all the messages in the Green Category." As you learn in this exercise, you can quickly create simple rules like this from scratch. This is the best method to create simple rules with one condition, one action, and no exceptions.

 **STEP BY STEP**   **Create a Rule from Scratch**

USE the message you sent in the previous exercise.

1. If necessary, click the **Mail** button in the Navigation Pane to display the mailbox.
2. Click the **Rules** on the Home tab and click the **Manage Rules and Alerts** option. The Rules and Alerts window shown in Figure 3-15 is displayed.
3. Click the **New Rule** button. The Rules Wizard window is displayed, as shown in Figure 3-37.

Figure 3-37

Creating a rule from scratch

Select options in this category to write a rule from scratch ⎯●

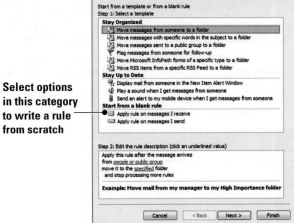

 **Another Way**
If you wanted to delete all messages from a specific sender instead, select the *from people or distribution list* condition in the *Step 1* area of this first Rules Wizard window. In the *Step 2* area, click *people or distribution list*. At the Rules Address page, you can key or click the sender's e-mail address into the *From* field and click OK to continue creating the rule.

4. In the *Start from a blank rule* section, click **Apply rule on messages I received**. This identifies when the rule will run automatically. Click the **Next** button to continue creating the rule.
5. In this Rules Wizard window, you identify the conditions of the rule. Click **with specific words** in the subject. This rule will identify messages about the selected topic.
6. In the *Step 2* area, click **specific words**. The Search Text window is displayed.
7. In the *Specify words or phrases to search for in the subject* field, key **Lesson 5 Schedule**. Click the **Add** button. The *Lesson 5 Schedule* phrase is enclosed by quotation marks and added to the search list for this rule.
8. Click **OK** to close the Search Text window. The Rules Wizard window is displayed. The *Lesson 5 Schedule* search phrase is identified. Click the **Next** button to continue creating the rule.
9. Available actions are listed in the Rules Wizard window. Click the **delete it** check box. You don't want to add any additional conditions, actions, or exceptions. Click the **Finish** button. The rule is complete: When a message arrives with Lesson 5 Schedule in the subject, delete it.
10. Select the **Lesson 5 Schedule (1)** rule, if necessary. Click the **Change Rule** button, and click **Rename Rule**. The Rename dialog box is displayed.
11. In the *New name of rule* field, key **Delete Lesson 5 Schedule**. Click **OK**. The dialog box is closed, and the rule's name is changed.
12. Click the **Delete Lesson 5 Schedule** check box to clear it. Click the **OK** button to close the Rules and Alerts window.

PAUSE. LEAVE Outlook open to use in the next exercise.

MANAGING RULES

Rules manage your messages. To manage your rules, change their sequence or turn them on or off. In this section, you'll change the order in which rules run, turn rules on and off, and delete rules.

Sequencing Rules

The sequence in which rules are processed can be important. For example, you can change the importance of a message before forwarding it to a coworker. Also, you want to forward a message before you delete it. In this exercise, you'll change the sequence of rules in the Rules and Alerts window.

STEP BY STEP   **Sequence Rules**

USE the rules you created in the previous exercises.

1. If necessary, click the Mail button in the Navigation Pane to display the mailbox.
2. Click the Rules on the Home tab and click the Manage Rules and Alerts option. The Rules and Alerts window shown in Figure 3-15 is displayed.
3. Click the Delete Lesson 5 rule. Click the Move Down button four times. The Delete Lesson 5 Schedule rule becomes last on the list of rules.
4. Click the Clear categories on mail (recommended) rule. Click the Move Up button two times. The sequence of your rules should match the rule sequence in Figure 3-38.

Figure 3-38

Sequenced rules

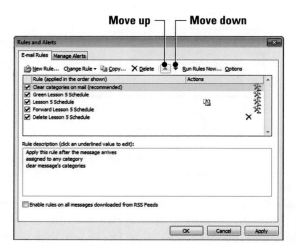

5. Click OK to save the changes and close the Rules and Alerts window.

PAUSE. LEAVE Outlook open to use in the next exercise.

The *Clear categories on mail (recommended)* rule is first on the list of rules. This clears the categories of the arriving message so you can apply your own category in the *Green Lesson 5 Schedule* rule.

Turning Off a Rule

In the Rules and Alerts window, the check box in front of the rule's name controls its status. A rule is either off or on. If a rule is on, the check box in front of the rule is checked. If a rule is off, the check box is empty. Turning off a rule rather than deleting it enables you to turn on the rule if you need it later. It also enables you to keep a rule turned off and run it at a time of your choice In this exercise, you'll turn off a rule.

STEP BY STEP | **Turn Off a Rule**

USE the rules you created in the previous exercises.

1. If necessary, click the Mail button in the Navigation Pane to display the Mailbox.
2. Click the Rules on the Home tab and click the Manage Rules and Alerts option. The Rules and Alerts window shown in Figure 3-15 is displayed.
3. Click the Delete Lesson 5 Schedule check box so the check box is empty.
4. Click OK to save the changes and close the Rules and Alerts window.

PAUSE. LEAVE Outlook open to use in the next exercise.

Deleting Rules

If you created a rule that you will not use again, delete it. This keeps your list of rules organized and reduces confusion caused by a long list of old rules that are not used. In this exercise, you'll delete a rule.

STEP BY STEP | **Delete Rules**

USE the rules you created in the previous exercises.

1. If necessary, click the Mail button in the Navigation Pane to display the mailbox.
2. Click the Rules on the Home tab and click the Manage Rules and Alerts option. The Rules and Alerts window shown in Figure 3-15 is displayed.
3. Click the Delete Lesson 5 Schedule rule. Click the Delete button. Click Yes in the dialog box to confirm the deletion.
4. Click OK to save the changes and close the Rules and Alerts window.

PAUSE. LEAVE Outlook open to use in the next exercise.

Use caution when deleting a rule rather than disabling it. You don't want to have to spend time re-creating a rule that you carelessly deleted.

SKILL SUMMARY

In This Lesson, You Learned How To:
Work with folders
Manage junk mail
Create and run rules
Manage rules

Knowledge Assessment

Fill in the Blank

Complete the following sentences by writing the correct word or words in the blanks provided.

1. Spam is stored in the _____ folder.

2. Messages are automatically moved to the _____ after they are sent.

3. To permanently remove deleted items from your Outlook data file, use the _____ tool.

4. Messages you send are stored in the _____ until your computer is connected to the Internet.

5. Messages from senders on the _____ are never delivered to the Junk E-mail folder.

6. The _____ contains messages you have written but not sent yet.

7. You should only _____ a rule if you are sure you won't need it again.

8. A(n) _____ is taken only if the conditions are met.

9. A(n) _____ provides structure for a rule.

10. A(n) _____ walks you through a process.

Multiple Choice

Select the best response for the following statements.

1. In a message header, the _____ field contains the sender's domain name.
   a. Message ID
   b. X-mailer
   c. Domain ID
   d. Sender ID

2. How do you remove an Outlook item from your computer?
   a. Delete the item and then delete again from within the Deleted Items folder
   b. Move the item to the Deleted Items folder
   c. Select the item and press the Delete key
   d. Delete the item and close Outlook

3. By default, where does e-mail arrive?
   a. Inbox
   b. Outbox
   c. Junk E-Mail
   d. Sent Items

4. How do you restore a folder?
   a. Delete the folder
   b. Archive the folder
   c. Move the folder from the Deleted Items folder to the Outlook Data Files in the Folder List
   d. Delete items from the folder

5. When you receive a junk e-mail message, select the message and click the _____ button in the Delete group.
   a. Spam
   b. Delete
   c. Block Sender
   d. Junk

6. Why would you change the sequence of your rules?
   a. Rules should be in alphabetic order
   b. Short rules should be processed first
   c. Some actions should be performed before others
   d. Rules should be processed in the order they were created

7. Why would you turn off a rule?
   a. The rule is no longer needed
   b. The rule should only be run periodically
   c. You don't want the rule to run automatically
   d. All of the above

8. What happens if a rule's conditions are too broad?
   a. The rule will affect more messages than intended
   b. The rule will affect fewer messages than intended
   c. The rule will not run
   d. The affected messages are deleted

9. What window enables you to add steps in a rule?
   a. Rules and Alerts
   b. Rules Wizard
   c. Steps
   d. New Rule

10. How does a rule identify the messages it affects?
    a. Actions
    b. Cues
    c. Conditions
    d. Phrases

Competency Assessment

Project 3-1: Create a Mail Folder

The Alpine Ski House is just a brisk walk away from Resort Adventures. Joe Worden, Mindy Martin's cousin, is the owner of the Alpine Ski House, which sells ski equipment. To attract and hold local customers when it isn't ski season, Joe started a ski club for local residents. During the off season, club members meet to hike, bike, and exercise together to stay in shape for skiing. As the ski club becomes more active and gains more members, Joe decides he needs to organize his ski club messages.

Create a folder to store ski club messages and send a message to the club about an upcoming hike

GET READY. LAUNCH Outlook if it is not already running.

1. Click the Folder List button in the Navigation Pane to display the Folder List.
2. On the Folder tab, click the New Folder button. The Create New Folder dialog box is displayed.
3. In the *Name* field, key Ski Club to identify the new folder.
4. Click Outlook Data Files folder at the top of the Navigation Pane to place the folder in the main level of folders.
5. Click the OK button to close the dialog box and create the folder.
6. Click the New E-mail button on the Home tab. The Message window is displayed.
7. In the *To* field, key your e-mail address. In the *Subject* field, key Ski Club Hike Saturday!

8. In the message area, key the following message:

Hi Ski Club members! [Press **Enter** twice.]

This is just a reminder. We'll be hiking the Mountain Dancer trail this Saturday. Meet in the Mountain Dancer camp site. Bring sandwiches for lunch and plenty of water for the hike. The weather forecast says it will be hot, hot, hot! Be sure you stay hydrated! [Press **Enter** twice.]

I'll see you Saturday at 9 AM! Call by Friday afternoon if you can't make it for the hike! [Press **Enter** twice.]

Joe Worden [Press **Enter**.]

Alpine Ski House [Press **Enter**.]

9. Click the Send button. The message is moved to the Outbox, and it is sent when your computer is connected to the Internet.

LEAVE Outlook open for the next project.

Project 3-2: Use Junk Mail Options

Add your own name to the Safe Senders List using the Never Block Sender option.

GET READY. LAUNCH Outlook if it is not already running.

1. Return to your Inbox if necessary. Click the Send/Receive All Folders button if the message you sent during Project 4-1 has not arrived yet. Select the message you just sent to yourself.

2. Click the Junk E-mail button on the Home tab and select Block Sender. Click OK. The message moves the selected message to the Junk E-mail folder and future messages sent to you from your own e-mail account will be blocked.

3. Open the Junk E-mail folder and right-click the message to yourself to open the shortcut menu.

4. Point to Junk E-mail on the shortcut menu and select Never Block Sender from the menu that appears. Click OK.

5. Right-click the message to yourself again and point to Junk E-mail on the shortcut menu. Select Not Junk from the shortcut menu to send the message back to the Inbox.

LEAVE Outlook open for the next project.

Proficiency Assessment

Project 3-3: Create Folders and Messages to Test Rules and Quick Steps

Jack Creasey owns a small Internet-based gift shop with a big name. World-Wide Importers sells a variety of crafted objects created by small crafters across the country and by one vendor in Canada, justifying the "World-Wide" portion of his company's name. Jack regularly receives pictures of crafted items from his suppliers and sends invoices to customers who buy his products. Jack decided to create rules to manage his messages automatically. First, he needs to create two folders and a message.

GET READY. LAUNCH Outlook if it is not already running.

1. If necessary, click the Mail button in the Navigation Pane to display the mailbox.

2. Right-click Outlook Data Files in the Folders List. Click New Folder in the shortcut menu. The Create New Folder dialog box is displayed.

3. In the *Name* field, key P5 Products. If necessary, click Outlook Data Files in the *Select where to place the folder* section. Click OK to create the folder and close the dialog box.

4. Right-click Outlook Data Files in the Folders List. Click New Folder in the shortcut menu. The Create New Folder dialog box is displayed.

5. In the *Name* field, key P5 Invoices. If necessary, click Outlook Data Files in the *Select where to place the folder* section. Click OK to create the folder and close the dialog box.

6. Click the New E-mail button on the Home tab. The Message window is displayed.

7. Click the *To* field. Key [your e-mail address].

8. Click the *Subject* field. Key New birdfeeder!

9. In the message area, key Take a look at this new birdfeeder! It's sure to be a big hit!

10. Click the Attach File button on the Ribbon. Navigate to the data folders for this lesson. Click the *Birdfeeder* file, and click the Insert button.

11. Click the Send button. The message is moved to the Outbox and sent when the computer is connected to the Internet.

12. Click the Send/Receive All Folders button on the Home tab.

LEAVE Outlook open for the next project.

@ The *Birdfeeder* file is available on the book companion website or in WileyPLUS.

Project 3-4: Create and Run a Rule that Moves Messages

Jack wants to create a rule that will automatically move messages about invoices into the P5 Invoices folder. To test the Invoice rule, Jack will send a message to himself with the word "Invoice" in the *Subject* field. Complete Project 5-1 before starting this project.

GET READY. LAUNCH Outlook if it is not already running.

1. Click the File tab. In Backstage view, click the Manage Rules and Alerts option to display the Rules and Alerts window.

2. Click the New Rule button. The Rules Wizard window is displayed.

3. In the Stay Organized category, click Move messages with specific words in the subject to a folder.

4. In the Step 2 area, click specific words. The Search Text window is displayed.

5. In the *Specify words or phrases to search for in the subject* field, key Invoice. Click the Add button. Click OK to close the Search Text window.

6. In the Step 2 area of the Rules Wizard window, click specified to identify the destination folder.

7. Click the P5 Invoices folder, and click OK.

8. Click the Finish button.

9. In the Rules and Alerts window, click Change Rule, and click the Rename Rule option. Key Move Invoices in the *New name of rule* field. Click OK.

10. Close the dialog boxes and return to the main Outlook window.

11. Create a message addressed to yourself. Use Invoice for the *Subject* field and Testing for the message body.

12. If necessary, click the Send/Receive All Folders button on the Home tab. The rule is run automatically when messages are received.

13. Click the P5 Invoices folder to verify that the received Invoice message was moved to the P5 Invoices folder.

LEAVE Outlook open for the next project.

Mastery Assessment

Project 3-5: Manage Rules

Jack has made several rules lately. Because he knows that it is important to keep his rules organized, he needs to go back and manage the rules in his Rules and Alerts dialog box. Complete Projects 5-1 and 5-3 before starting this project.

GET READY. LAUNCH Outlook if it is not already running.

1. Click the File tab. In Backstage view, click the Manage Rules and Alerts option to display the Rules and Alerts window.

2. Select the Green Lesson 5 Schedule rule and use the Move Up arrow to move this rule to the top.

3. Click the Lesson 5 Schedule rule and use the Move Down arrow to move it to the bottom of the list.

4. Select the rules you created in this Lesson. Select the Move Invoices rule to deselect it and click the Delete button. Click Yes to confirm.

5. Close the dialog box and return to the mailbox.

LEAVE Outlook open for the next project.

Project 3-6: Permanently Delete a Folder

Delete the Lesson 4 folder and empty the Deleted Items folder.

GET READY. LAUNCH Outlook if it is not already running.

1. If necessary, click the Folder List button in the Navigation Pane to display the complete list of Outlook folders.

2. Right-click the Lesson 4 folder created within the lesson. Click Delete folder from the shortcut menu. A warning dialog box is displayed.

3. Click Yes to close the warning dialog box.

4. Right-click the Deleted Items folder. Select Empty Folder from the list. Click Yes to confirm.

CLOSE Outlook.

INTERNET READY

Data management is essential for growing businesses. Hunting for messages is not only a nuisance, it costs money. In most businesses, efficiency is directly tied to profitability. Make a list of 10 file management tips that you can use to keep your mailbox organized.

Workplace *Ready*

ORGANIZING OUTLOOK ITEMS

Nicole Richards is an instructor at Forsyth College. Every session, a batch of new students registers for Nicole's classes. Nicole teaches several courses and many of her assignments require students to submit electronic files. The student messages from all the courses come directly to Nicole's e-mail account, so she uses Outlook to help her stay organized.

Every session, Nicole sets up a new e-mail folder for her classes. She sets up a mail folder for each student and places the student folders in the main course folder. Throughout the semester, she places the messages from each student in the folder she created for them. A few weeks after classes end, Nicole archives the class folders that are no longer needed.

Because she takes a bit of extra time at the beginning of each semester to get organized, she is able to keep up with her busy schedule and still have time for her students.

LESSON SKILL MATRIX

In This Lesson, You Will Learn The Following Skills:

Creating and Modifying Contacts

Sending and Receiving Contacts

Viewing and Deleting Contacts

Creating and Manipulating Contact Groups

Sending a Message to a Contact Group

Using Electronic Business Cards

KEY TERMS

- contact
- Contacts folder
- Contact Group
- duplicate contact
- electronic business cards
- message header
- spoofing

Like many business executives, Mindy Martin will tell you that *who* you know is just as important as *what* you know. Mindy refers to Outlook's contact information dozens of times every day. She calls, writes, and sends messages to suppliers, guests, and other business organizations. Direct contact with the right people can avoid problems or solve small problems before they become catastrophes. Mindy and John have decided to create an outdoor adventure video game based on some of their more popular programs. Mindy needs to set up contact information for her contacts in the software industry so that their information will be readily available. In this lesson, you will learn how to create contacts and Contact Groups, edit and modify contact information, and send a message to a Contact Group.

SOFTWARE ORIENTATION

Microsoft Outlook's Contacts Window

The main Contacts window displays basic information about the contacts in your Contacts folder, as shown in Figure 4-1.

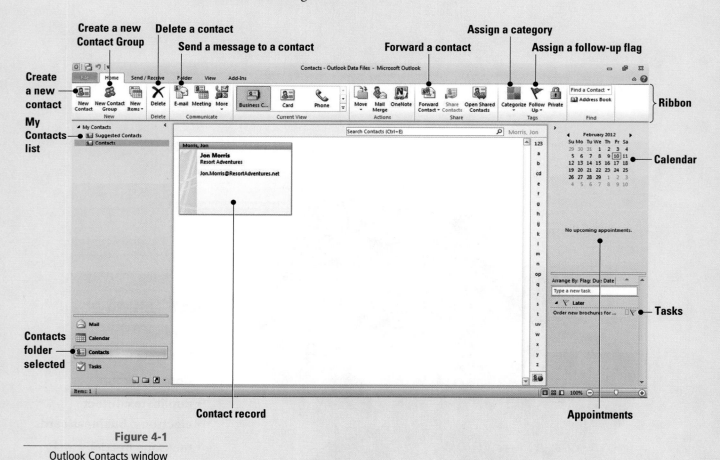

Figure 4-1

Outlook Contacts window

The Contacts folder enables you to organize and maintain information about the individuals and businesses you communicate with regularly. In this window, you can select a contact record, create a new contact record, view appointments, view tasks, send a message to a contact, call a contact, assign a contact to a category, and assign a follow-up flag to a contact.

CREATING AND MODIFYING CONTACTS

The Bottom Line

A **contact** is a collection of information about a person or company. Outlook's Contacts feature is an electronic organizer that you can use to create, view, and edit contact information. In this section, you'll learn a number of ways to create a contact and then modify contact information.

Creating a Contact from Scratch

You can use a variety of methods to create contacts. The most basic method of creating a contact is opening a new contact window and keying the necessary information. The blank Contact window has its own Ribbon and command groups. Once a contact has been created, their information is stored in the Outlook Address Book. In this exercise, you'll create a contact using the New Contact button on the Home tab.

STEP BY STEP   **Create a Contact from Scratch**

GET READY. Before you begin these steps, be sure to turn on or log on to your computer, and start Outlook 2010.

1. Click the **Contacts** button in the bottom section of the Navigation Pane to display the Outlook Contacts window shown in Figure 4-1.

Take Note   The Ribbon options look different in each of Outlook's tools. The Ribbon options now reflect the most commonly used commands for working with contacts.

2. Click **New Contact** on the Home tab. The Untitled—Contact window is displayed, as shown in Figure 4-2. The blank Contact window is ready to store data for a new contact.

Figure 4-2

Untitled—Contact window

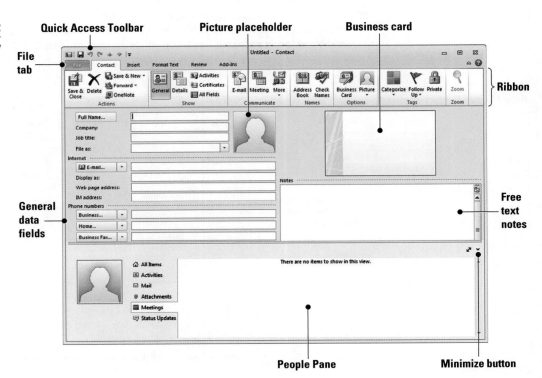

Quick Access Toolbar   Picture placeholder   Business card

File tab   Ribbon   General data fields   Free text notes   People Pane   Minimize button

3. Click the *Full Name* field, if your cursor isn't already positioned there. Key Gabe Mares and press Tab. The insertion point moves to the *Company* field. The *File as* field is automatically filled with *Mares, Gabe*, and *Gabe Mares* is displayed in the business card. The name of the window is changed to Gabe Mares—Contact.

4. In the *Company* field, key Wingtip Toys and press Tab. The insertion point moves to the *Job title* field. The company's name is added to the business card.

5. In the *Job title* field, key Sales Support Manager and press Tab. Gabe's job title is added to the business card. The insertion point moves to the *File as* field, highlighting the current value.

6. Click the dropdown arrow in the *File as* field. A short list of alternative ways of filing the contact is displayed. Some methods use the company name to file the contact. Other alternatives file the contact by the contact's first name. Release the mouse button to maintain the default selection, which files contacts by last name.

 **Troubleshooting** The e-mail addresses provided in these exercises belong to unused domains owned by Microsoft. When you send a message to these addresses, you will receive an error message stating that the message could not be delivered. Delete the error messages when they arrive.

7. Click the *E-mail* field. Key Gabe@wingtiptoys.com and press Tab. The *Display as* field is automatically filled, and Gabe's e-mail address is added to the business card.

8. You don't want to change the way Gabe's e-mail address is displayed, so press Tab. The insertion point moves to the *Web page address* field.

9. In the *Web page address* field, key www.wingtiptoys.com.

10. Below the *Phone numbers* heading, click the *Business* field. When you move the insertion point out of the *Web page address* field, the Web page address is automatically added to the business card. Key 6155551205 in the *Phone Numbers* field.

Take Note   It isn't necessary to key spaces or parentheses in phone numbers. Outlook automatically formats phone numbers when the insertion point leaves the field.

11. Click the minimize button in the top-right corner of the People Pane at the bottom of the Contact window. The People Pane collapses to a bar at the bottom of the Contact window and additional fields are displayed in the *Address* area of the Contact window.

12. Below the Addresses heading, click the *Business* field. Key 7895 First Street. Press Enter. Key Nashville, TN 76534. Press Tab. The business card is automatically updated and the Map It button is undimmed, as shown in Figure 4-3.

Figure 4-3

Gabe Mares—Contact window

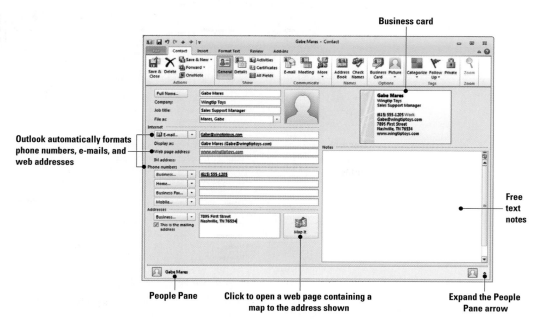

Business card

Outlook automatically formats phone numbers, e-mails, and web addresses

Notes

Free text notes

People Pane

Click to open a web page containing a map to the address shown

Expand the People Pane arrow

Take Note In a contact record, using the postal abbreviation for a state makes it easier to use the information in a mailing list or other data exports.

Troubleshooting If you press Tab in the *Address* field before keying at least two lines of text, the Check Address dialog box is displayed. Because Outlook expects at least two lines of text in an address, the text you have already keyed might be displayed in the wrong fields in the Check Address dialog box. Click the Cancel button to close the dialog box and continue keying the address.

13. In the Actions group on the Ribbon, click the Save & Close button. Gabe Mares' contact information is saved and stored in the Outlook Address Book, and you are returned to the main Contacts window.

PAUSE. LEAVE Outlook open to use in the next exercise.

Take Note You do not have to key information into every field. To save contact information, you should have a value in the *File As* field. If the *File As* field is empty when you try to save the contact, Outlook displays a warning message asking if you want to save the contact with an empty *File As* field. If you save the contact, it will be placed before any other contacts saved with a value in the *File As* field, because a blank is sorted as a value that occurs before any other value.

In the previous exercise, you keyed the basic information for a contact.

Creating a Contact from an Existing Contact

Often, you will have several contacts who work for the same company. Rather than keying the same data for a new contact, you can create the new contact from the existing contact. When you create a new contact for a person from the same company, the company name, File As, website, phone number, and address are carried over to the new contact. The name, job title, and e-mail address are not carried over to the new contact, because these fields will usually differ between contacts, even if they work for the same company. In this exercise, you'll learn how to create a new contact from an existing contact's record.

STEP BY STEP **Create a Contact from an Existing Contact**

GET READY. Before you begin these steps, be sure to complete the previous exercise.

1. Click the Contacts button in the Navigation Pane to open the Contacts window that now displays the Gabe Mares contact record.

2. Double-click the Gabe Mares contact record. The Gabe Mares Contact window is displayed.

3. In the Actions group on the Ribbon, click the Save & New arrow. In the dropdown list of options, click New Contact from Same Company. A new window titled Wingtip Toys— Contact is displayed.

4. Click the *Full Name* field if necessary. Key Diane Tibbott and press Tab. The insertion point moves to the *Company* field. The *File As* field is automatically filled with *Tibbott, Diane*, and *Diane Tibbott* is displayed in the business card. The name of the window is changed to Diane Tibbott—Contact.

5. Click the *Job title* field. Key Marketing Representative and press Tab. Diane's job title is added to the business card. The insertion point moves to the *File As* field, highlighting the current value.

6. Click the *E-mail* field. Key Diane@wingtiptoys.com and press Tab. The *Display As* field is automatically filled, and Diane's e-mail address is added to the business card.

7. In the Actions group on the Ribbon, click the Save & Close button. Diane Tibbott's contact information is saved and her Contact window closes. Close Gabe's contact record window to return to the main Contacts window.

Figure 4-4

Creating a contact from an existing contact

Original contact   **Newly created contact**

PAUSE. LEAVE Outlook open to use in the next exercise.

Creating a Contact from a Suggested Contact

NEW to Office 2010

One of the ways that Outlook 2010 helps you stay more organized is by recognizing when you send a message to someone who is not listed in your Address Book. Whenever you send a message to a new person, Outlook captures as much contact information as it can and saves it in the Suggested Contacts folder. You can easily save a suggested contact to your Address Book by just dragging it to the Contacts folder. In Lesson 2, you sent a message to someone@example.com. In this exercise, you'll create a contact using the suggested contact that Outlook created from that message.

STEP BY STEP   **Create a Contact from a Suggested Contact**

WileyPLUS Extra! features an online tutorial of this task.

GET READY. Before you begin these steps, be sure to have completed the Send a Message exercise in Lesson 2.

1. Click the **Contacts** button in the Navigation Pane to display the main Contacts window.
2. Click the **Suggested Contacts** folder in the My Contacts section of the Navigation Pane. The Suggested Contacts window opens and displays a business card for each person you've sent a message to who is not already listed in your Address Book, as shown in Figure 4-5.

Take Note   Depending on which exercises you've completed, you might see additional business cards.

Figure 4-5

Suggested Contacts folder

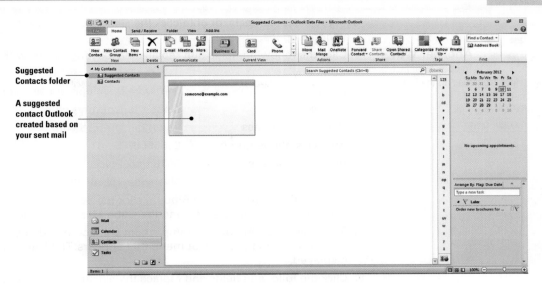

Figure 4-5

Suggested Contacts folder

3. Click the someone@example.com business card and drag it to the Contacts folder in the My Contacts section of the Navigation Pane.

4. Click the Contacts folder in the Navigation Pane. The someone@example.com business card appears at the beginning of available contacts because there is no name supplied yet.

PAUSE. LEAVE Outlook open to use in the next exercise.

Updating Contact Information

To keep the information in your Contacts list current, you often need to modify the information for existing contacts. After a contact has been created, you can modify the contact's information using either the main Contact window or the Outlook Address Book. You can modify an existing contact and save it as a new contact rather than overwriting the existing contact. In this exercise, you'll update the contact information in your Address Book and add contact information for a suggested contact.

STEP BY STEP | **Update Contact Information**

GET READY. Before you begin these steps, be sure to complete the preceding exercises and have Outlook open and running on your computer.

1. Click the Contacts button in the Navigation Pane to display the main Contacts window.

2. Double-click the Diane Tibbott contact record. The Diane Tibbott—Contact window is displayed.

3. Click the *Job title* field. Select the existing value, key Software Support Manager, and press Tab. Diane's job title is modified on the business card.

4. In the Actions group on the Ribbon, click the Save & Close button. The modified contact information is saved, and you are returned to the main Contacts window.

5. In the Find group on the Home tab, click Address Book. The Outlook Address Book window is displayed, as shown in Figure 4-6.

Figure 4-6

Outlook Address Book window

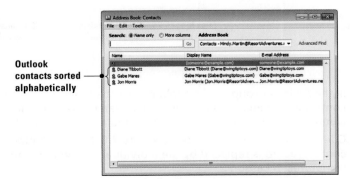

Outlook contacts sorted alphabetically

6. In the list of contacts, double-click the Gabe Mares contact. The Gabe Mares—Contact window opens.

7. Click the following fields and replace the existing values with the new values.

Company	**Tailspin Toys**
Job title	**Software Development Manager**
E-mail	**Gabe@tailspintoys.com**
Web page address	**www.tailspintoys.com**
Business phone number	**6155550195**
Business address	**5678 Park Place**
	Nashville, TN 76502

8. In the Actions group on the Ribbon, click the Save & Close button. The modified contact information is saved and the Gabe Mares—Contact window closes.

9. Right-click the someone@example.com contact record in the Address Book and select Properties from the shortcut menu that appears. The Untitled—Contact window is displayed.

10. Click the following fields and replace the existing values with the new values.

Name	**Susan Davis**
Company Name	**Example Company**

The name of the contact record window changes to Susan Davis—Contact.

11. Double-click the picture placeholder in the center of the window. The Add Contact picture dialog box is displayed. Navigate to the data files for this lesson and select the *Susan.jpg* file and click OK. The Add Contact picture dialog box closes and you return to the Susan Davis—Contact window.

12. Click the Expand People Pane arrow if necessary to see how the picture looks in all its locations, as shown in Figure 4-7.

Another Way
To open a contact, select Properties on the File menu.

The *Susan.jpg* file for this lesson is available on the book companion website or in WileyPLUS.

Figure 4-7

Susan Davis—Contact window

Updated title bar

Double-click to add an image to a contact

Updated contact information

Photo appears in default business card

Photo replaces the placeholder image

Expand the People Pane arrow

Click to open a web page containing a map to the address shown

Thumbnail of the photo appears in the bar and in the collapsed People Pane

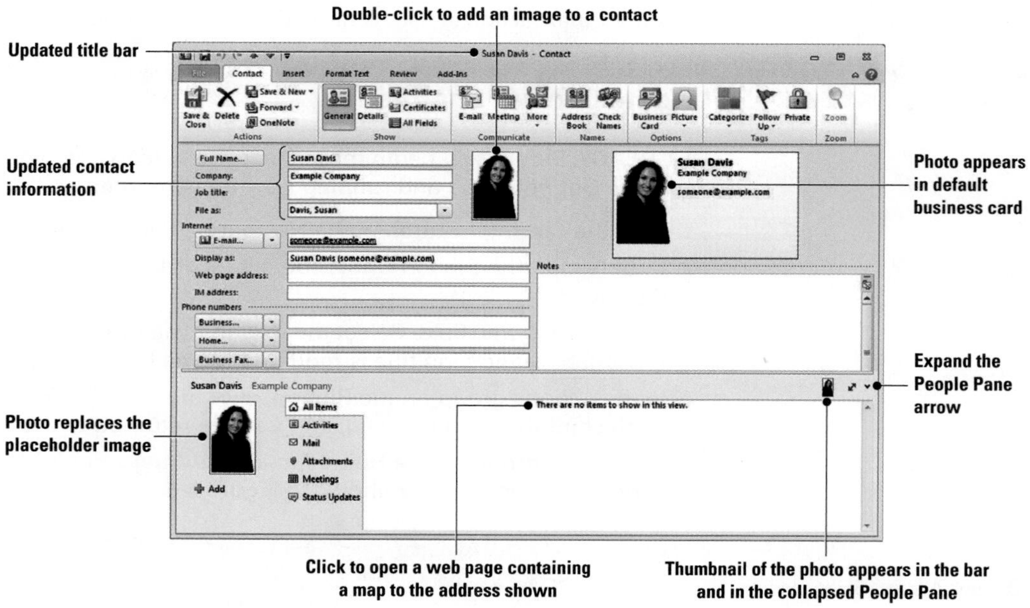

13. In the Actions group on the Ribbon, click the Save & Close button. The modified contact information is saved and the Susan Davis—Contact window closes. Close the Outlook Address Book to return to the main Contacts window.

14. Compare your Contacts folder to Figure 4-8. In your Contacts folder, Jon Morris's contact record is replaced by the individual with whom you exchanged digital signatures in Lesson 2.

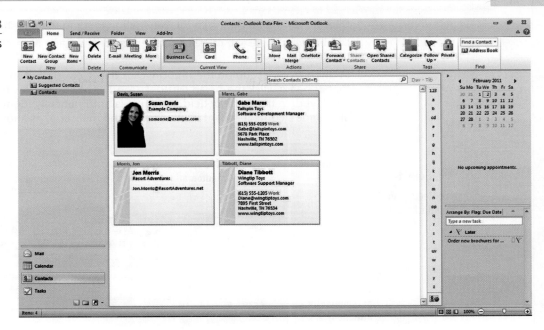

Figure 4-8

Modified contacts

PAUSE. LEAVE Outlook open to use in the next exercise.

In the previous exercise, you updated the information for three contacts. The following changes occurred.

- Gabe Mares left Wingtip Toys. He was hired by Tailspin Toys as the Software Development Manager. Most of his contact information has changed.

- Diane Tibbott was promoted to Gabe's previous position as Software Support Manager. Her e-mail address and phone number remain the same. Only her title has changed. The corner office with a view that came with the promotion is not part of her contact information.

- Susan Davis's name and company name were added to the contact that Outlook suggested for you.

SENDING AND RECEIVING CONTACTS

The Bottom Line

It is easy to exchange contact information via e-mail. You can send and receive contacts as attachments. Every time you send a message, you are also sending your contact information. In Outlook, you can create a contact for the sender of any message you receive, and you can create a contact from a message header.

Forwarding a Contact as an Attachment

You already know that you can send documents and files as attachments. You can also send contacts as attachments. These attachments can be formatted as Outlook contacts, business cards, or plain text. When you send a contact as an Outlook contact, recipients who use Outlook will be easily able to see all the information they need to add the contact to their records. However, if you are unsure what e-mail program the recipient uses, it is safest to send the contact as a business card. Recipients who have Outlook will see it as a contact record and everyone else will see it as an image of the business card. In this exercise, you learn how to send a contact as an attachment in Outlook 2010.

STEP BY STEP | **Forward a Contact as an Attachment**

GET READY. Before you begin these steps, be sure to complete the preceding exercises and have Outlook 2010 open and running on your computer.

1. Click the Contacts button in the Navigation Pane to display the main Contacts window.
2. Double-click the Gabe Mares contact record. The Gabe Mares—Contact window is displayed.
3. In the Actions group on the Ribbon, click the Forward button. In the dropdown menu that appears, click the As an Outlook Contact option. A new message window is displayed. In the *Subject* field, the topic is automatically identified as *FW: Gabe Mares*, and Gabe's contact record is attached to the message, as shown in Figure 4-9.

Figure 4-9

Sending a contact as an attachment

Subject automatically filled

Contact automatically attached

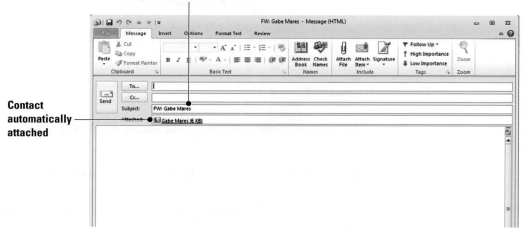

 Troubleshooting If a message is displayed stating that you must save the original item, click OK to continue.

4. In the message area, key **Gabe Mares' contact information is attached.**

Take Note Throughout this chapter you will see information that appears in black text within brackets, such as [Press **Enter**] or [next Friday's date]. The information contained in the brackets is intended to be directions for you rather than something you actually type word for word. It will instruct you to perform an action or substitute text. Do **not** type the actual text that appears within brackets.

5. In the *To* field, key [your e-mail address].

Take Note When you send contact information, any text in the *Notes* area of the contact record and items attached to the contact record are also sent. Before you send the contact record, delete any information in the *Notes* area and attachments that you don't want the recipient to see.

6. Click the Send button. The message is moved to the Outbox, and it is sent when your computer is connected to the Internet.
7. **CLOSE** the Gabe Mares—Contact window.

PAUSE. LEAVE Outlook open to use in the next exercise.

In the previous exercise, you sent contact information directly from the Contacts folder as an attachment to a message. This enables you to send contact information without keying it as text in a message.

Troubleshooting   If the recipient does not use Outlook 2007 or newer, the contact information might not be displayed correctly and the recipient might not be able to create a contact from the attachment.

Saving a Contact Received as a Contact Record

When you request contact information from a coworker's Contacts list, the coworker can send the information as a business card or a contact record in Outlook format. If the contact record is sent in Outlook format, you can open the attachment, view the information, and save it as a contact record. When you try to save a contact with an address that's already in your Address Book, Outlook automatically detects it as a **duplicate contact** and gives you an opportunity to add the new contact or to update the existing contact. However, once a duplicate is detected, you should always combine the information onto one record and delete the duplicate. This eliminates errors that can occur when one record is updated and the other is not. In this exercise, you learn how to save a received contact as a contact record and how to deal with duplicate contacts.

 **STEP BY STEP**   **Save a Contact Received as a Contact Record**

GET READY. Before you begin these steps, be sure that Microsoft Outlook is running and that you have completed the preceding exercises in this lesson.

1. Click the **Mail** button in the bottom section of the Navigation Pane to display the Inbox. If the *FW: Gabe Mares* message has not arrived yet, click the **Send/Receive All Folders** button on the Home tab.
2. Click the **FW: Gabe Mares** message. The message is displayed in the Reading Pane.

 Troubleshooting   If the Reading Pane is not visible, click Reset View on the View tab.

3. In the Reading Pane, double-click the **Gabe Mares** attachment. The attachment opens in the Gabe Mares—Contact window.
4. In the Actions group on the Ribbon, click the **Save & Close** button. Because you received this contact information at the same e-mail address used to send the contact information, the contact record is already in your Contacts list, and Outlook detects that this is a duplicate contact. The Duplicate Contact Detected window shown in Figure 4-10 is displayed. If the contact record was not a duplicate, the contact would be saved without any further action needed.

Figure 4-10

Duplicate Contact Detected window

Duplicate Contact Detected window

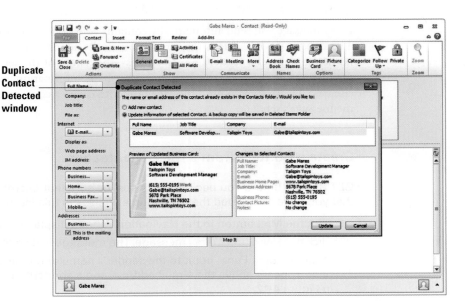

Take Note
As mentioned at the beginning of this exercise, creating duplicate contact records frequently leads to inaccurate information and is not a good practice. You are creating a duplicate record here only so that you can learn additional techniques for eliminating duplicate records in a later exercise.

5. You want to create a new contact, so select the Add new contact option at the top of the window and click the Add button at the bottom of the window. The Duplicate Contact Detected window is closed, the contact record is created, and you are returned to the Mail folder.

6. Click the Contacts button in the Navigation Pane to display the main Contacts window. Now, you have the original Gabe Mares contact record you created by keying the data and the Gabe Mares contact record you created from the attachment. Your Contacts folder should be similar to Figure 4-11. In your Contacts folder, Jon Morris's contact record is replaced by the individual with whom you exchanged digital signatures in Lesson 2.

Figure 4-11

Duplicate Contact record created

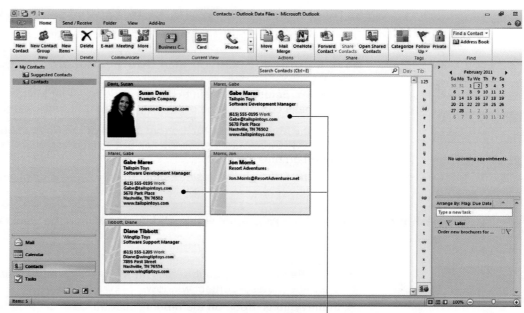

Duplicate contact records

PAUSE. LEAVE Outlook open to use in the next exercise.

Creating a Contact from a Message Header

Every message you send automatically contains your contact information in the message header. The **message header** is the text automatically added at the top of a message. The message header contains the sender's e-mail address, the names of the servers used to send and transfer the message, the subject, the date, and other basic information about the message. In this exercise, you'll learn how to use a message header to create a contact record in your Contacts list for the message's sender.

STEP BY STEP **Create a Contact from a Message Header**

GET READY. Before you begin these steps, be sure that Microsoft Outlook is running and that you have completed the preceding exercises in this lesson.

1. Click the Mail button in the Navigation Pane to display the Mail folder.

2. Click the FW: Gabe Mares message. The message is displayed in the Reading Pane.

3. In the Reading Pane, point to the sender's name or e-mail address. An information pane appears above the e-mail address and a shortcut menu appears below, as shown in Figure 4-12.

Figure 4-12

Outlook's sender information

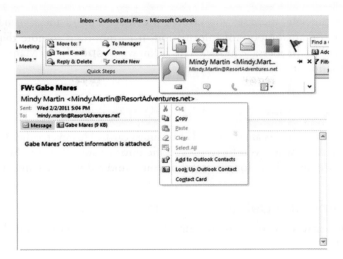

4. Click the **Add to Outlook Contacts** option on the shortcut menu. A Contact window containing the sender's name and e-mail address is displayed, as shown in Figure 4-13. Because you sent the *FW: Gabe Mares* message, it is your contact information in the Contact window.

Figure 4-13

Creating a contact from a message header

Data automatically entered from a message header

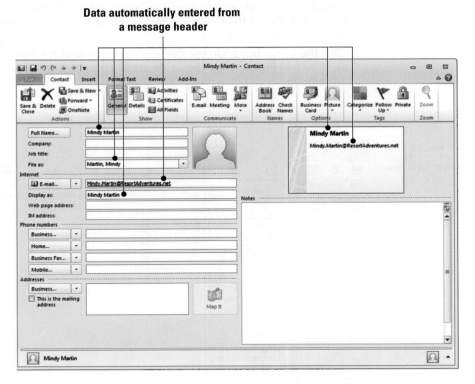

5. In the Actions group on the Ribbon, click the **Save & Close** button. The contact record is created, and you are returned to the Inbox.

6. Click the **Contacts** button in the Navigation Pane to display the Contacts window. Now, you have the original Gabe Mares contact record, the Gabe Mares contact record you created from the attachment, the contact record created when you received a digital signature in Lesson 2, Diane Tibbott's contact record created from Gabe's record, the Susan Davis contact created from Outlook's Suggested Contact folder, and your contact record created from a message header.

PAUSE. LEAVE Outlook open to use in the next exercise.

In the previous exercise, you created a contact from a message header. Although a message header contains important information, it is important to note that false information can be provided in the message header. This is known as **spoofing**. Many junk messages contain false information in the message header.

VIEWING AND DELETING CONTACTS

By default, contacts are displayed as business cards. However, other views are available. Selecting a different view lets you focus on specific information. Prevent clutter in your Contacts folder. When a contact is no longer useful or you found a duplicate contact, delete the contact record.

Viewing and Deleting Contacts

In this exercise, you'll explore some Contact window views and delete the duplicate contact record.

STEP BY STEP   **Viewing and Deleting Contacts**

GET READY. Before you begin these steps, be sure that Microsoft Outlook is running and that you have completed the preceding exercises in this lesson.

1. Click the **Contacts** button in the Navigation Pane to open the Contacts window, displaying the default Business Cards view of the Contacts records, as shown in Figure 6-9. This is the only view that displays any graphics on the business card, such as the contacts photo.

2. Click the **Cards** button in the Current View group of the Home tab. The view is modified as shown in Figure 4-14. The cards are lined up in narrow columns and any graphics are hidden.

Figure 4-14

The Contact List in Card view

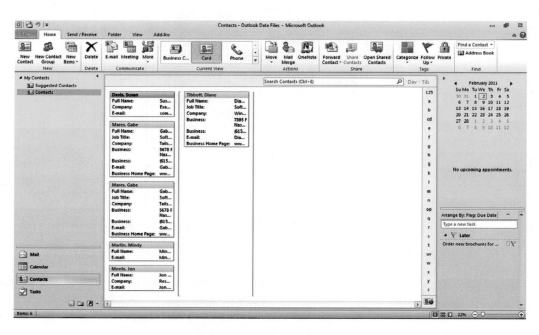

3. Click the **Phone** button in the Current View group of the Home tab. The view is modified as shown in Figure 4-15. Use this view if you need to call several contacts in your Contacts folder.

Figure 4-15

Contacts in Phone List view

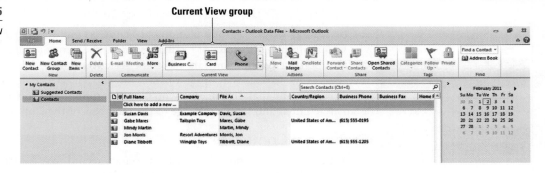

4. Click the **View** tab to see additional viewing options. In the Arrangement group, you can select to organize the list by category, company name, or location.

5. Click the **Categories** button. The view is modified to group the contacts by category. Use this view if you need to see all the contacts assigned to a specific color category.

6. Click the **Company** button in the Arrangement group in the View tab. The view is modified to group the contacts by company name, as shown in Figure 4-16. Use this view to see all the contacts working for a specific company.

Arrangement group

Resets view to its default settings

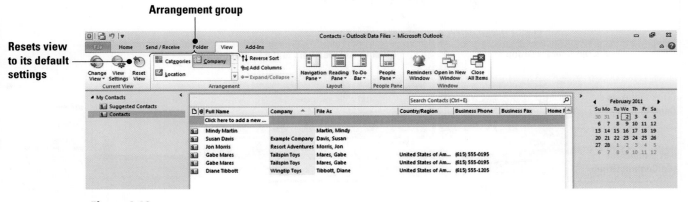

Figure 4-16

Contacts grouped by company name

7. Click the **Location** button in the Navigation Pane. The view is modified to group the contacts by country/region. Use this view to see contacts with an address in a particular area. This is more useful if your contacts are not located in the same geographic area.

8. Click the **Reset View** button in the Current View group to return the phone list to its default view.

9. Click **Change View** button in the Current Views group and select **Business Card** to return to the default view of the contacts.

10. Click the first **Gabe Mares** contact record. On the Home tab, click the **Delete** button. The contact record is moved to the Deleted Items folder. It will not be removed from your computer until the Deleted Items folder is emptied.

PAUSE. LEAVE Outlook open to use in the next exercise.

Another Way
To delete a contact record, right-click the contact and click Delete on the shortcut menu.

Because several views are available, select the view that targets the information you need to see. When you are viewing contact records, you can minimize clutter by deleting contacts that are no longer useful or duplicates that have been accidentally created.

CREATING AND MANIPULATING CONTACT GROUPS

The Bottom Line

A **Contact Group** is a group of individual contacts saved together as a single contact. A Contact Group simplifies the task of regularly sending the same message to a group of people. If you create a Contact Group, you can make one selection in the *To* field to send the message to all members of the Contact Group. In this section, you'll create a Contact Group, create notes to be stored with it, and make changes to who is in the group. Then you'll forward the Contact Group as an attachment and send a message to the members of the Contact Group.

Creating a Contact Group

To create a Contact Group, you create a contact record that is identified as a Contact Group. Then you select the members of the Contact Group and save the Contact Group. In this exercise, you'll create a Contact Group and add members to it.

STEP BY STEP **Create a Contact Group**

GET READY. Before you begin these steps, be sure that Microsoft Outlook is running and that you have completed the preceding exercises in this lesson.

1. Click the Contacts button in the Navigation Pane to display the Contacts window.

2. In the New group on the Home tab, click the New Contact Group button. The Untitled—Contact Group window is displayed, as shown in Figure 4-17. The Members button in the Show group on the Ribbon is selected.

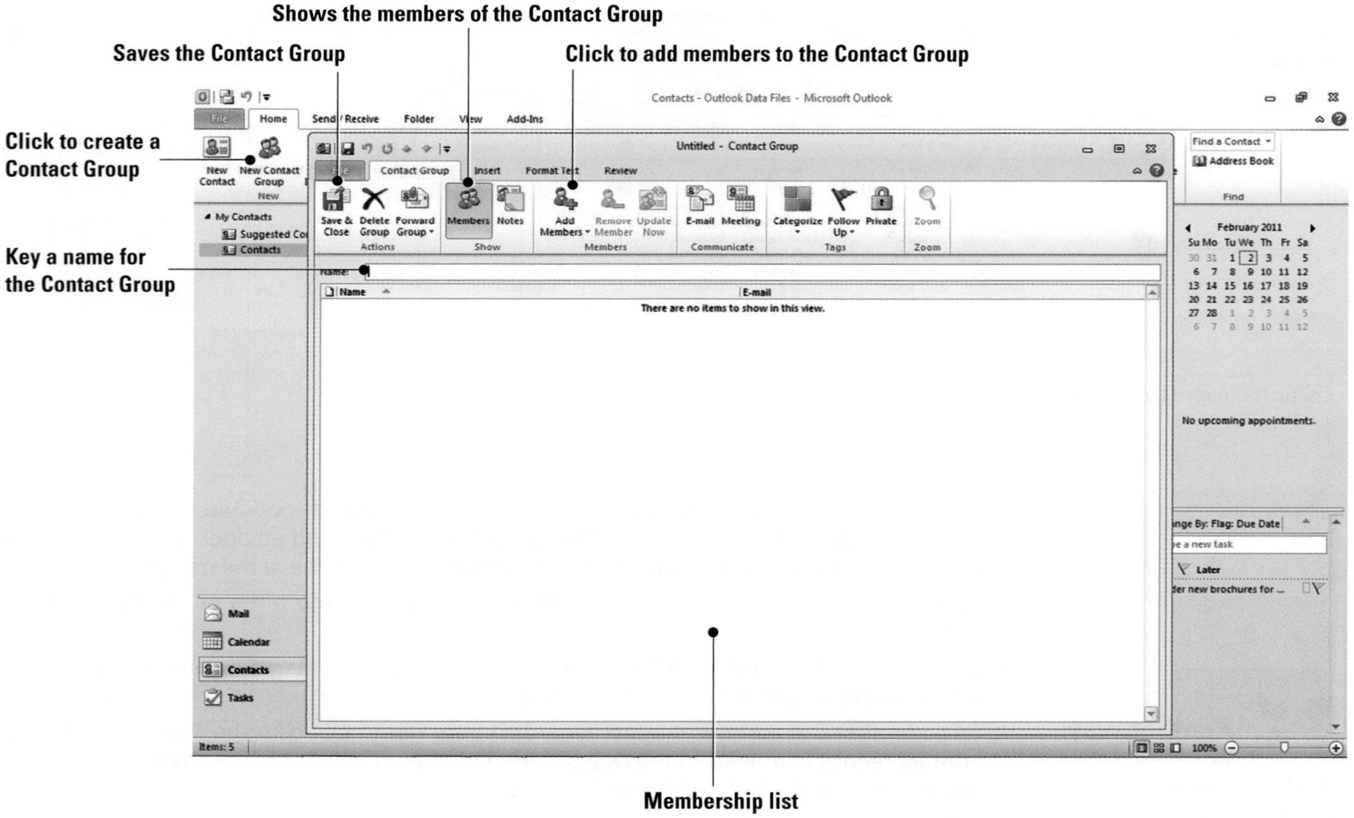

Shows the members of the Contact Group

Saves the Contact Group

Click to add members to the Contact Group

Click to create a Contact Group

Key a name for the Contact Group

Membership list

Figure 4-17

Untitled—Contact Group window

3. In the Members group on the Ribbon, click the Add Members button and select the From Outlook Contacts option. The Select Members: Contacts dialog box is displayed, as shown in Figure 4-18. The contacts in your Address Book are listed. The first contact is already selected.

Figure 4-18

Select Members: Contacts window

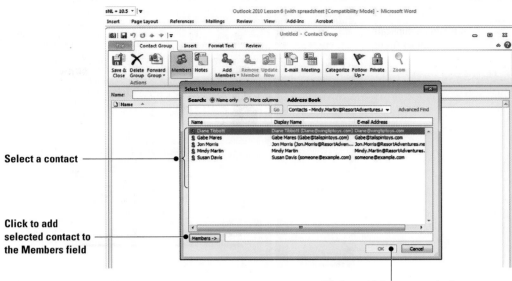

Select a contact

Click to add selected contact to the Members field

Click to add the contacts in the Members field to the Contact Group

4. Because the first contact you want to include in the Contact Group is already selected, click the **Members** button at the bottom of the dialog box. The contact's name is added to the *Members* field.

5. Click the second contact in the list, then click the **Members** button. The second contact is added to the *Members* field.

6. Repeat the actions in Step 5, to select and add the third, fourth, and fifth contacts from the list to the *Members* field.

7. Click **OK**. The Select Members: Contacts dialog box closes, and you return to the Untitled—Contact Group window, which now contains listings for the five contacts you added to this group.

8. Click the **Save & Close** button.

Take Note   When you view the Contact Group in the Contacts folder, the list of members is not visible. To see the list of members, open the contact record.

PAUSE. LEAVE Outlook open to use in the next exercise.

In the previous exercise, you created a Contact Group that contains all of your contacts. However, Contact Groups don't usually contain all of your contacts. Instead, they are typically limited to just the contacts working on a specific project.

Creating a Contact Group from an Existing Contact Group

You already know how to create a Contact Group from scratch, but you can also create a Contact Group by duplicating another group and then modifying it. In this exercise, you'll create a new Contact Group by duplicating an existing group.

STEP BY STEP   **Create a Contact Group from an Existing Contact Group**

GET READY. Before you begin these steps, be sure that Microsoft Outlook is running and that you have completed the preceding exercises in this lesson.

1. Click the **Contacts** button in the Navigation Pane to display the Contacts window.

2. Right-click the **General Announcements List** contact record and select **Copy** from the shortcut menu that appears.

3. Press **Ctrl+V**. A duplicate Contact Group record is displayed in the Contacts window, as shown in Figure 4-19.

Figure 4-19

Creating a duplicate
Contact Group

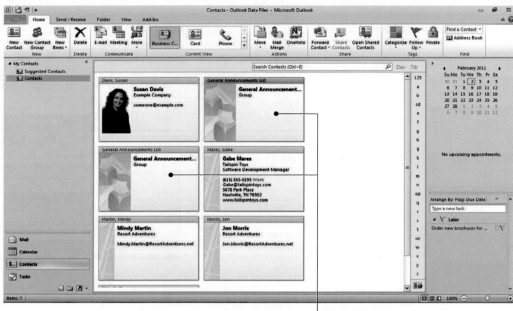

Duplicate Contact Groups

4. Double-click one of the General Announcements List contact records. The General Announcements list—Contact Group window is displayed.

5. Select the text in the *Name* field. Key **Wingtip Toys List**. This name is used to identify the name of the project this group is working on.

6. Click the **Save & Close** button. The Wingtip Toys List Contact Group is saved. The window is closed, and you are returned to the Contacts folder, with the Wingtip Toys List contact displayed, as shown in Figure 4-20.

Figure 4-20

Creating a Contact Group from
an existing Contact Group

PAUSE. LEAVE Outlook open to use in the next exercise.

In the previous exercise, you created a Contact Group for the Wingtip Toys project you are working on. However, because the Contact Group was created from a Contact Group that contained all of your contacts, you'll need to modify the Contact Group's membership to reflect the members of the project team.

Managing Contact Group Membership

Any Contact Group used over time will eventually require changes. In this exercise, you'll learn how to remove a member from a Contact Group list and edit the contact information.

STEP BY STEP | **Manage Contact Group Membership**

GET READY. Before you begin these steps, be sure that Microsoft Outlook is running and that you have completed the preceding exercises in this lesson.

1. Click the **Contacts** button in the Navigation Pane to display the default Contacts window.
2. Double-click the **Wingtip Toys List** contact. The Wingtip Toys List—Contact Group window is displayed.
3. Click Gabe's name in the lower area of the window. In the Members group on the Ribbon, click the **Remove Member** button. Gabe is removed from the Contact Group.
4. In the list of members, double-click your name. Your contact record is displayed.
5. Click the *Company* field. Key [the name of your company].
6. Click the **Save & Close** button in your Contact window. Your modified contact record is saved and closed.
7. Click the **Save & Close** button in the Contact Group window. The Contact Group is saved. The window is closed, and you are returned to the Contacts folder.

PAUSE. LEAVE Outlook open to use in the next exercise.

> **Another Way**
> To delete a contact from the group, click the contact and press Delete.

In the previous exercises, you created a Contact Group containing everyone who is working on the Outdoor Adventure software development project. During the weekly management meeting, Mindy and Jon decided to assign Katie Mathews, the resort's PR specialist, the role of lead liaison for the project.

In order for her to take the lead, she will need a copy of the Wingtip Toys Contact Group. Whenever you share Contact Groups with others, it is important to attach notes to the Contact Group so that there is no confusion about who is included and what has changed.

Using Contact Group Notes

You can use the Notes page to keep background information with a Contact Group. As Contact Groups change over time, it can be easy to forget what changes have been made. This is particularly important when the Contact Group list and information is forwarded to someone else. In this exercise, you'll use the Notes page to provide information about a Contact Group before sending it as an attachment to an e-mail message.

STEP BY STEP | **Use Contact Group Notes**

GET READY. Before you begin these steps, be sure that Microsoft Outlook is running and that you have completed the preceding exercises in this lesson.

1. Click the **Contacts** button in the Navigation Pane to display the default Contacts window.
2. Double-click the **Wingtip Toys List** contact. The Wingtip Toys List—Contact Group window is displayed with the Contact Group tab opened on the Ribbon.
3. Click the **Notes** button in the Contact Group tab to show the notes about a Contact Group. The Notes page for this Contact Group is displayed.
4. In the empty text area, key **The group includes everyone working on the Outdoor Adventure game project, including Susan Davis, an independent storyboard consultant.** Your screen should look similar to the one shown in Figure 4-21.

Figure 4-21

Adding notes to a Contact Group

Click to add or view notes

Include information about the members of the list

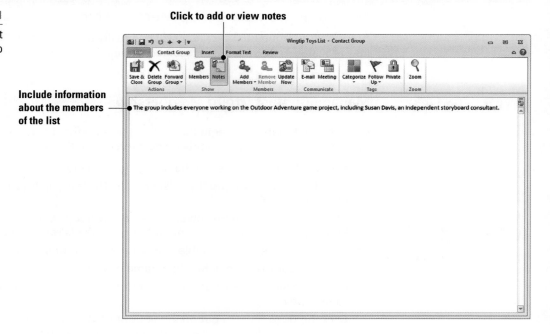

5. Click the Save & Close button in the Contact Group window. The Contact Group is saved. The window is closed, and you are returned to the Contacts folder.

6. Double-click the Wingtip Toys List contact record to open the Wingtip Toys List—Contact Group window again. Click the Notes button in the Contact Group tab to show the notes for this group.

7. Click the Save & Close button in the Contact Group window. The Contact Group is saved. The window is closed, and you are returned to the Contacts folder.

8. Double-click the Wingtip Toys List contact record to open the Wingtip Toys List—Contact Group window again. Click the Notes button in the Contact Group tab to show the notes for this group.

9. Click the Save & Close button in the Contact Group window. The Contact Group is saved. The window is closed, and you are returned to the Contacts folder.

PAUSE. LEAVE Outlook open to use in the next exercise.

In the previous exercise, you added an informative note about the Wingtip Toys List Contact Group. You are now ready to send the Contact Group to Katie.

Forwarding a Contact Group

Sending a Contact Group to someone as an e-mail attachment is just as easy as sending a contact. You can forward a Contact Group just by selecting the group's contact record and clicking Forward Contact in the Share group of the Contacts window's Home tab. In this exercise, you'll forward a Contact Group to an e-mail recipient.

STEP BY STEP   **Forward a Contact Group**

GET READY. Before you begin these steps, be sure that Microsoft Outlook is running and that you have completed the preceding exercises in this lesson.

1. Click the Contacts button in the Navigation Pane to display the default Contacts window.

2. Click the Wingtip Toys List contact record and then click Forward Contact in the Share group of the Home tab. In the dropdown menu that appears, select the As An Outlook Contact option. A new FW: Wingtip Toys List—Message window is displayed.

3. In the *To* field, key Katie.Mathews@ResortAdventures.net.

4. In the message area, key **Hi Katie, here is the Contact Group for the game project.** as shown in Figure 4-22.

Figure 4-22

Sending a Contact Group as an attachment

Contact Group attachment

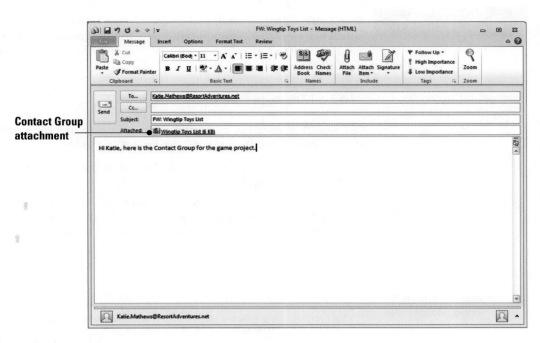

5. Click the **Send** button. The message is moved to the Outbox, and it is sent when your computer is connected to the Internet.
6. **CLOSE** the FW: Wingtip Toys List—Message window.

PAUSE. LEAVE Outlook open to use in the next exercise.

Deleting a Contact Group

Contact Groups are a great way to help you keep your contacts organized, but when you no longer need a Contact Group, you should delete it so you don't accidentally send messages to the group. Fortunately, deleting a Contact Group is just as easy as deleting a contact. In this exercise, you'll delete the General Announcements List Contact Group.

| STEP BY STEP | **Delete a Contact Group** |

GET READY. Before you begin these steps, be sure that Microsoft Outlook is running and that you completed the preceding exercises in this lesson.

1. Click the **Contacts** button in the Navigation Pane to display the main Contacts window.
2. Click the **General Announcements List** contact record. On the Home tab, click the **Delete** button. The Contact Group record is moved to the Deleted Items folder. It will not be removed from your computer until the Deleted Items folder is emptied.

PAUSE. LEAVE Outlook open to use in the next exercise.

Now that you've sent the Wingtip Toys List to Katie, you want to send a message to the members of the team to introduce Katie.

SENDING A MESSAGE TO A CONTACT GROUP

The Bottom Line

Sending an e-mail message to Contact Group is a simple process. By adding the Contact Group's name in the *To* field, any e-mail message will go to each member of the group. All you need to do to create a group e-mail is select the Contact Group in the Contacts window and click the E-mail button in the Communicate group. In this exercise, you'll create an e-mail message to be sent to a Contact Group.

STEP BY STEP **Send a Message to a Contact Group**

GET READY. Before you begin these steps, be sure that Microsoft Outlook is running and that you completed the preceding exercises in this lesson.

1. Click the Contacts button in the Navigation Pane to display the main Contacts window.
2. Click the Wingtip Toys List contact record.
3. In the Communicate group on the Home tab, click the E-mail button. A blank Message window is displayed. In the *To* field, the Wingtip Toys List contact is automatically entered, as shown in Figure 4-23. The rest of the fields are empty.

Figure 4-23

Message addressed to the Contact Group created

Click to close the message without sending it

Click to expand the Contact Group

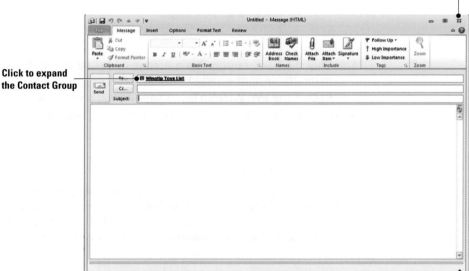

Another Way
You can also send a message to a Contact Group by typing the name of the group in the *To* field.

4. Click the plus sign (+) in the *To* field. A warning box is displayed stating that the group name will be replaced with the names of the group's members. Click OK. The individual addressees are displayed in the *To* field.

 **Troubleshooting** It is not necessary to expand the Contact Group in a message. You expanded the Contact Group in this exercise merely for demonstration purposes.

5. Click the Close button to close the message without sending it. Do not save changes to the message.

PAUSE. LEAVE Outlook open to use in the next exercise.

When you created the Wingtip Toys Contact Group, you included Gabe Mares. However, he works for Tailspin Toys now. In the previous exercise, you removed Gabe from the Contact Group. You also accessed and modified your contact record through the Contact Group. Finally, you created a message that could be sent to the members of the Contact Group.

SOFTWARE ORIENTATION

Microsoft Outlook's Edit Business Card Window

The default view in the Contacts window is the Business Card view, in which Outlook displays each of your contacts as a business card. By default, the text appears to the right of a wide, gray bar that borders the left side of the card, as shown in Figure 4-24.

Figure 4-24

Outlook's Edit Business Card window

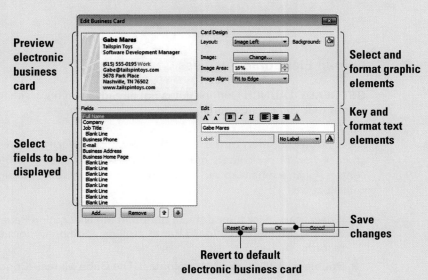

Use the Edit Business Card window to create an electronic business card that fits your company image. Refer to Figure 4-24 as you complete the following exercises.

USING ELECTRONIC BUSINESS CARDS

The Bottom Line

Electronic business cards are the digital version of paper business cards. They can be sent as attachments, used as signatures, and used to create a contact record. Because the default view in the Contacts window displays the electronic business cards, it is important to design an electronic business card that is memorable and easy to find when several electronic business cards are displayed on the screen. In this section, you'll edit a default business card by adding an image to it, send it to a coworker, and use it as a digital signature.

Editing an Electronic Business Card

The Edit Business Card window has four separate areas, as identified in Table 4-1. The four areas work together to provide a flexible tool that can create an amazing variety of customized business cards.

In this exercise, you'll customize the default Outlook contact record to create a unique electronic business card that is just as eye-catching as a paper business card.

Table 4-1

Edit Business Card window

Area	Description
Preview	View the effects of the changes you make.
Fields	Identify the fields you want to display on the electronic business card. Use the Add button to insert a new field. Select a field in the list and click the Remove button to delete a field. To move a field up or down on the card, select the field and click the Move Field Up (Up arrow) button or the Move Field Down (Down arrow) button.
Card Design	Insert and position a graphic or select a background color for the card. Position the image and define the amount of the card that can be used for the graphic. Although you can edit graphics in Outlook 2010, you cannot edit graphics in the Edit Business Card window.
Edit	Key the value to be displayed in the field. Limited text formatting options are available.

STEP BY STEP   **Edit an Electronic Business Card**

GET READY. LAUNCH Outlook if it is not already running. Use the Gabe Mares contact record that you created earlier.

Take Note   An electronic business card is created automatically when you create a contact. It is basically another view of the contact record. If you delete the electronic business card, you delete the contact. Changes made to the information on the electronic business card are changed for the contact as well.

1. If necessary, click the Contacts button in the Navigation Pane to display the Contacts window. Minimize the To-Do Bar to provide additional room to display your contact records.
2. Double-click the Gabe Mares contact. The Gabe Mares—Contact window is displayed.

Troubleshooting The e-mail addresses provided in these exercises belong to unused domains owned by Microsoft. When you send a message to these addresses, you will receive an error message stating that the message could not be delivered. Delete the error messages when they arrive.

 The *Bear Side* file is available on the book companion website or in WileyPLUS.

3. In the Options group on the Ribbon, click the Business Card button. The Edit Business Card window is displayed, as shown in Figure 4-24.
4. In the Card Design area in the upper right of the window, verify that Image Left is selected in the *Layout* field and Fit to Edge is selected in the *Image Align* field. This defines the position of the graphic. Currently, the graphic is the default gray bar.
5. Click the Change button. The Add Card Picture dialog box is displayed. Navigate to the data files for this lesson. Click the *Bear Side.jpg* image file and click OK. The bear image is added to the card preview.
6. In the Card Design area, click the *Image Area* field. Change the value to 25%. In the card preview, the image area widens to 25% of the card's width.
7. In the Card Design area, click the Image Align field. In the dropdown list, click Bottom Center. In the card preview, the image is resized and repositioned to appear at the bottom of the card.
8. In the Card Design area, click the Image Align field. In the dropdown list, click Fit to Edge. In the card preview, the image is resized and placed in its original position.

9. In the Fields area, click **Business Home Page** in the list of fields. Click the **Add** button. In the dropdown menu, point to Internet Address and then click **IM Address**. IM Address is added to the list of fields. The *IM Address* field is used for an instant messaging address.

10. With IM Address selected in the list of fields, click the empty field in the Edit area. Key **GabeTailspinToys**, as shown in Figure 4-25.

Figure 4-25

Modified Edit Business Card window

Value displayed in IM Address field

IM Address field added

Key information to be displayed in the selected IM Address field

11. Click **OK**. The Edit Business Card window is closed. Click the **Save & Close** button to return to the Contacts window. Gabe's business card is displayed, as shown in Figure 4-26.

Figure 4-26

Modified business card

PAUSE. LEAVE the Outlook Message window open to use in the next exercise.

Sending an Electronic Business Card

Electronic business cards can be shared with others by simply inserting one or more business cards in a message and clicking the Send button. Users of other e-mail applications can get the contact information from the .vcf files that Outlook automatically creates and attaches to the message when you insert the electronic business cards. In this exercise, you'll insert electronic business cards into an e-mail message and send them along with their .vcf file attachments to a colleague.

STEP BY STEP   **Send an Electronic Business Card**

USE the Gabe Mares contact record.

1. Click the **Mail** button in the Navigation Pane to display the Mail folder.
2. Click the **New E-mail** button on the Home tab. The Message window is displayed. By default, the Message tab is selected.

Take Note   Throughout this chapter you will see information that appears in black text within brackets, such as [Press **Enter**] or [your e-mail address]. The information contained in the brackets is intended to be directions for you rather than something you actually type word for word. It will instruct you to perform an action or substitute text. Do **not** type the actual text that appears within brackets.

3. In the *To* field key [your e-mail address].
4. In the *Subject* field key **Business cards attached**.
5. Click in the message area. Key **I attached the electronic business cards you requested.** Press **Enter** twice to add a bit of space between your text and the business card that you're about to attach.
6. Click the **Insert** tab. In the Include group, click the **Insert Business Card** button. A dropdown list is displayed.
7. Click **Other Business Cards** in the dropdown list. The Insert Business Card window is displayed, as shown in Figure 4-27. Click the **Gabe Mares** contact. A Preview pane at the bottom of the dialog box shows you an image of the business card you have chosen to send with the message.

Figure 4-27

Insert Business Card window

Click to attach business cards to a message

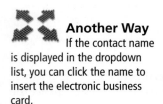

Another Way
If the contact name is displayed in the dropdown list, you can click the name to insert the electronic business card.

8. With the contact still selected, press **Ctrl**. This allows you to select multiple contacts. Click the **Diane Tibbott** contact. Click **OK**. The electronic business cards are inserted into the message. In the *Attached* field, the contact records are attached as .vcf files, as shown in Figure 4-28.

Figure 4-28

Electronic business cards
inserted into a message

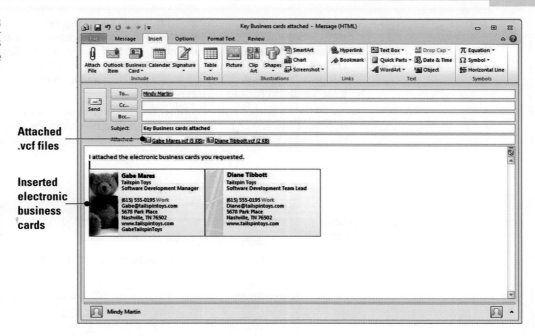

**Attached
.vcf files**

**Inserted
electronic
business
cards**

9. Click the Send button.

PAUSE. LEAVE Outlook open to use in the next exercise.

Creating a Contact from an Electronic Business Card

When you receive an electronic business card, Outlook allows you to add the contact record to your Contacts list either by using the .vcf file or by right-clicking on the business card itself. All the information on the electronic business card and the card's appearance are saved in your Contacts list. In this exercise, you'll create a contact record based on an electronic business card attached to a received e-mail message.

STEP BY STEP **Create a Contact from an Electronic Business Card**

USE the message you sent in the previous exercise.

1. Click the Mail button in the Navigation Pane to display the mailbox.
2. If the *Business cards attached* message has not arrived yet, click the Send/Receive All Folders button in the Send/Receive group of the Home tab.
3. Click the Key Business cards attached message in the message list to display it in the Reading Pane. The electronic business cards are displayed in the message body.

Troubleshooting If the Reading Pane Is not visible, click the Reading Pane button in the Layout group of the View tab and select Right.

4. Right-click the Gabe Mares electronic business card in the message body. Click the Add to Outlook Contacts option in the shortcut menu. A Gabe Mares—Contact window is displayed that contains the information from the electronic business card, including the preview image of the card.

5. Click the Save & Close button in the Actions group on the Ribbon. Because you received this contact information at the same e-mail address as was used to send the contact information, the contact record is already in your Contacts window. Therefore, Outlook detects that this is a duplicate contact, and the Duplicate Contact Detected window is displayed. If the contact record was not a duplicate, the contact would be saved with no further action needed.

6. You want to create a new contact for this exercise, so select the Add new contact option at the top of the window. The dialog box changes to show you the information that will be saved in the new contact record, as shown in Figure 4-29.

Figure 4-29

Duplicate Contact Detected window

Add new contact

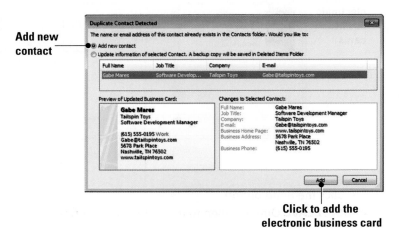

Click to add the electronic business card

Troubleshooting Normally, when you receive a duplicate record you will use the received information to update the contact in your *Contacts* folder. This exercise simply gives you the scenario for adding a new contact record. You can compare the information in your contact record with the information sent to you in the message. Before you update contact information, be sure that the new data is accurate.

7. Click the Add button at the bottom of the window. The Duplicate Contact Detected window is closed, the contact record is created, and you are returned to the Mail folder.

8. Click the Contacts button in the Navigation Pane to display the Contacts window. Now, you have the original Gabe Mares contact record and the Gabe Mares contact record you created from the electronic business card in the message.

9. In the Contacts window, click the first Gabe Mares contact record and click the Delete button in Home tab. The contact record is moved to the Deleted Items folder. It will not be removed from your computer until the Deleted Items folder is emptied.

PAUSE. LEAVE Outlook open to use in the next exercise.

Using an Electronic Business Card in a Signature

A signature can be added automatically in every message you send. Include your electronic business card in your signature to provide an easy way for the recipient to add the contact to the contacts window. In this exercise, you'll change settings to set an electronic business card as a default digital signature and send an e-mail to test it.

STEP BY STEP   **Use an Electronic Business Card in a Signature**

USE the Gabe Mares electronic business card you modified in a previous exercise.

1. Click the **Mail** button in the Navigation Pane to display the mailbox.

2. Click the **New E-mail** button on the Home tab to open the Message window with the Message tab selected.

3. Click the **Signature** button in the Include group on the Ribbon. In the dropdown list, click **Signatures**. The Signatures and Stationery window is displayed.

4. Click the **New** button to create a new signature. The New Signature dialog box is displayed.

5. To name the new signature, key **Gabe** into the *Type a name for this signature* field. Click **OK**. The New Signature dialog box is closed, and Gabe is highlighted in the *Select signature to edit* list box.

6. Click in the empty **Edit signature** box. Key the following text, pressing **Enter** to start each new line.

   Gabe Mares

   Software Development Manager

   Tailspin Toys

   Gabe@tailspintoys.com

Take Note   Outlook automatically recognizes the e-mail address as a link and formats it as a hyperlink.

7. Click the **Business Card** button above the Edit Signature box. The Insert Business Card window is displayed (refer to Figure 4-27).

8. Click the **Gabe Mares** contact record and click **OK**. The electronic business card is inserted into the signature, as shown in Figure 4-30.

Figure 4-30

Signature containing an electronic business card

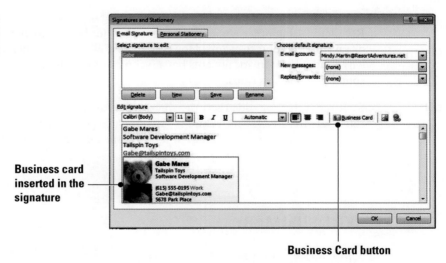

Business card inserted in the signature

Business Card button

9. Click **OK** to accept your changes and close the Signatures and Stationery window.

10. In the Message window, key [your e-mail address] in the *To* field.

11. In the *Subject* field, key **New Signature Test**.

12. In the message body, key **Testing new signature** and press **Enter**.

13. In the Include group on the Ribbon, click the **Signature** button and then click **Gabe** in the dropdown list of signatures that appears. The signature is inserted into the message, as shown in Figure 4-31.

Figure 4-31

Message containing Gabe's signature

Attachment containing information in the business card added automatically

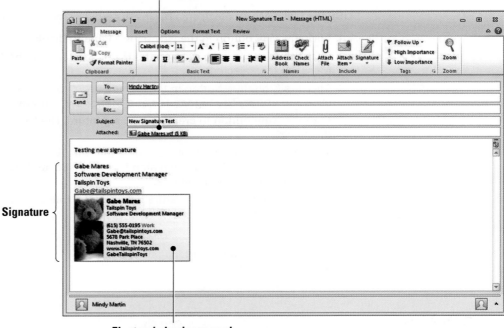

Signature

Electronic business card included in the signature

14. Click the **Send** button.

PAUSE. LEAVE Outlook open to use in the next exercise.

Recipients using other e-mail programs might not be able to view the electronic business card or save it as a contact record. However, almost all e-mail programs can read .vcf files. This is why Outlook automatically attaches a .vcf file containing the contact information to messages containing business cards.

Take Note

Remember that for added security some people avoid opening messages with attachments. You can delete the attachment before sending the message. Deleting the attachment doesn't remove the signature from the message, but prevents the recipient's spam filter from deleting your message simply because it has an attachment.

SKILL SUMMARY

In This Lesson, You Learned How To:
Create and modify contacts
Send and receive contacts
View and delete contacts
Create and manipulate contact groups
Send a message to a Contact Group
Use electronic business cards.

Knowledge Assessment

Multiple Choice

Select the best response for the following statements.

1. Which field should contain a value when you save a contact?
   a. Display as
   b. Full Name
   c. File As
   d. E-mail

2. How can you simplify the task of regularly sending messages to the same group of contacts?
   a. Resend the message to each contact.
   b. Use the bulk messaging feature.
   c. Set a predetermined time for sending the messages.
   d. Create a Contact Group.

3. _____ should be added to a Contact Group when it is modified or shared.
   a. the contact's name
   b. Notes
   c. protection
   d. track changes

4. A duplicate contact should be
   a. created for every contact.
   b. displayed before the original contact.
   c. deleted.
   d. modified.

5. When you key a phone number in a contact record,
   a. key the parentheses around the area code.
   b. don't key the area code.
   c. key a hyphen between each group of numbers.
   d. don't key spaces or hyphens in the number.

6. Which of the following is a way to send an e-mail message to a Contact Group?
   a. Key the group's name in the *To* field of an e-mail message window.
   b. Select a Contact Group from the Contacts window and click the E-mail button.
   c. Open the group's contact record and click the E-mail button.
   d. All of the above.

7. What value is not carried over to the new contact when you create a new contact record from the same company?
   a. Address
   b. E-mail address
   c. Website
   d. Phone number

8. What provides the information to create a contact from any message you receive?
   a. The attachment
   b. The subject
   c. The message header
   d. The *Subject* field

9. How many views are available in the Contacts feature?

   a. Four

   b. Three

   c. It depends on the number of contact records you have saved

   d. Five

10. What does a recipient need to save a contact received in Outlook format?

    a. Outlook 2007 or 2010

    b. Existing contact records

    c. Any e-mail program

    d. All of the above

Fill in the Blank

Complete the following sentences by writing the correct word or words in the blanks provided.

1. You can _____ a Contact Group to share it with someone else.

2. You can add explanatory information about a Contact Group on the _____ page of the contact record.

3. The default view in the Contacts folder is the _____ view.

4. When sending a message to a Contact Group, you can see which individuals will receive the message by clicking the _____ in the *To* field.

5. If you try to add a contact that already exists in your Contacts folder, Outlook detects a(n) _____.

6. Providing false information in a message header is called _____.

7. A(n) _____ is a group of individual contacts saved together as a single contact record.

8. You can add or delete individuals in a Contact Group using the _____ page.

9. Like documents and files, contact information can be sent as a(n) _____.

10. A(n) _____ is a collection of information about a person or company.

Competency Assessment

Project 4-1: Create Contacts from Scratch

Gabe Mares recently started a new job at Tailspin Toys. As part of the training program, he will be traveling to different divisions to examine their procedures. At his first stop in Pittsburgh, PA, Gabe collected contact information for the team leader.

GET READY. LAUNCH Outlook if it is not already running.

1. Click the Contacts button in the Navigation Pane to display the Contacts window.

2. Click New on the Standard toolbar. The Untitled—Contact window is displayed.

3. In the *Full Name* field, key Mandar Samant and press Tab.

4. In the *Company* field, key Tailspin Toys and press Tab.

5. In the *Job Title* field, key Software Development Team Lead and press Tab.

6. Click the *E-mail* field. Key Mandar@tailspintoys.com and press Tab.

7. In the *Web Page Address* field, key www.tailspintoys.com.

8. Below the Phone Numbers heading, click the *Business* field. Key 4125551117. Press Tab.

9. Below the Addresses heading, click the *Business* field. Key 4567 Broadway. Press Enter. Key Pittsburgh, PA 14202. Press Tab.

10. In the Actions group on the Ribbon, click the Save & Close button.

LEAVE Outlook open for the next project.

Project 4-2: Create a Contact from a Contact at the Same Company

While Gabe was in Pittsburgh, he interviewed a software developer in Mandar Samant's team. Although Gabe doesn't usually contact developers directly, he wants to save her contact information in case an opening occurs as a team leader.

GET READY. LAUNCH Outlook if it is not already running.

1. If necessary, click the Contacts button in the Navigation Pane to display the Contacts window.
2. Double-click the Mandar Samant contact. The Contact window is displayed.
3. In the Actions group on the Ribbon, click the Save & New arrow. In the dropdown list of options, click New Contact from Same Company.
4. Click in the *Full Name* field if necessary. Key Jamie Reding and press Tab.
5. In the *Job title* field, key Software Developer and press Tab.
6. In the *E-mail* field, key Jamie@tailspintoys.com and press Tab.
7. In the *Notes* field, key Potential team lead.
8. In the Actions group on the Ribbon, click the Save & Close button.
9. **CLOSE** the Mandar Samant contact record without saving changes.

LEAVE Outlook open for the next project.

Proficiency Assessment

Project 4-3: Modify Contact Information

Two months later, Jamie Reding was promoted to a team leader in the Pittsburgh office. Gabe modified her contact information.

GET READY. LAUNCH Outlook if it is not already running.

1. If necessary, click the Contacts button in the Navigation Pane to display the Contacts window.
2. Double-click the Jamie Reding contact. The Contact window is displayed.
3. Click the *Job title* field. Change her title to Software Development Team Lead and press Tab.
4. Click the *Notes* field. Change the text to Monitor her progress.
5. In the Actions group on the Ribbon, click the Save & Close button.

LEAVE Outlook open for the next project.

Project 4-4: Send a Contact as an Attachment

Gabe's manager asked for information about the team leader for a new project. Gabe sends Jamie's contact record.

GET READY. LAUNCH Outlook if it is not already running.

1. If necessary, click the Contacts button in the Navigation Pane to display the Contacts window.
2. Double-click the Jamie Reding contact. The Contact window is displayed.
3. In Actions group on the Ribbon, click the Forward button. Select the As an Outlook Contact option. If a message is displayed stating that you must save the original item, click OK to continue.
4. Click the To button. In the *Select Names: Contacts* window, click your contact record. Click the To button. Click OK.
5. Click in the message area. Key The contact information you requested is attached.
6. Click the Send button.
7. **CLOSE** Jamie Reding's contact record without saving changes.

LEAVE Outlook open for the next project.

Project 4-5: Create a Contact Group

Gabe sends several messages to the team leaders each day. To simplify the task, Gabe creates a Contact Group.

GET READY. LAUNCH Outlook if it is not already running.

1. If necessary, click the Contacts button in the Navigation Pane to display the Contacts window.
2. On the Home tab, click the New Contact Group button.
3. In the Members group on the Ribbon, click the Add Members button and select From Outlook Contacts.
4. Add all the Tailspin Toys employees to the *Members* field, including Gabe, and click OK.
5. Name the Contact Group Tailspin Team Leaders.
6. Click the Save & Close button.

LEAVE Outlook open for the next project.

Project 4-6: Modify a Contact Group

Gabe was not surprised to realize that the Tailspin Team Leaders Contact Group needs to be changed. Gabe needs to remove himself from the Contact Group and add Diane Tibbott. Diane just accepted the position of Software Development Team Lead for Tailspin Toys. She will work in the Nashville office with Gabe.

GET READY. LAUNCH Outlook if it is not already running.

1. If necessary, click the Contacts button in the Navigation Pane to display the Contacts window.
2. Use Gabe's contact record to create a new contact record from the same company for Diane Tibbott. Use the following information.

Full Name	Diane Tibbott
Job title	Software Development Team Lead
E-mail	Diane

3. Delete Diane Tibbott's outdated contact record from Wingtip Toys.
4. Open the Tailspin Team Leaders contact record.
5. Click Gabe Mares in the list of members and click the Remove Member button.
6. Click the Add Members button. In the Select Members: Contacts window, add Diane Tibbott to the *Members* field and click OK.
7. SAVE the changes to the Contact Group.

CLOSE Outlook.

INTERNET READY

Looking for a new job with better pay, the right amount of travel, better hours, and a larger office? Use the Internet. Research some companies that interest you. Create contact records for the Human Resources offices in those companies.

LESSON SKILL MATRIX

In This Lesson, You Will Learn The Following Skills:

Creating Appointments

Setting Appointment Options

Creating an Event

Printing Appointment Details

Creating a Meeting Request

Responding to a Meeting Request

KEY TERMS

- appointment
- banner
- Busy
- event
- Free
- iCalendar
- Out of Office
- private
- recurring appointment
- tasks
- Tentative
- mandatory attendee
- meeting
- meeting organizer
- meeting request
- optional attendee
- resource

As a marketing assistant, Terry Eminhizer knows the value of time. Terry manages her schedule and the schedules of two marketing representatives who are constantly on the road. Setting up travel arrangements, confirming appointments with clients, and generally smoothing out the bumps for the marketing representatives gives them more time to make bigger sales. Time is money. In this lesson, you'll create and manage appointments and events in Outlook.

SOFTWARE ORIENTATION

Microsoft Outlook's Appointment Window

The Appointment window displayed in Figure 5-1 enables you to schedule an appointment or event. Scheduled appointments and events are displayed on your calendar and in your To-Do Bar.

Figure 5-1

Outlook's Appointment window

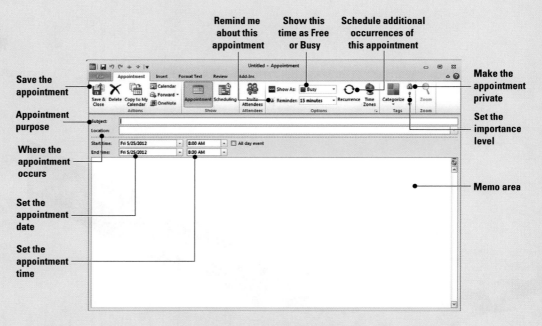

Use the Appointment window to create an appointment or event. Refer to Figure 5-1 as you complete the following exercises.

CREATING APPOINTMENTS

An **appointment** is a scheduled activity that does not require sending invitations to other people or resources. An appointment can occur once or occur at regular intervals. In this section, you'll create different kinds of appointments.

Creating a One-Time Appointment

Appointments can involve other people, but they do not require invitations sent through Outlook. Appointments can include activities such as doctor's appointments and picking up your daughter after soccer practice. In this exercise, you'll create a basic one-time appointment.

STEP BY STEP | **Create a One-Time Appointment**

Another Way
You can also select the date in the Appointment window. If the date is displayed in the monthly calendar, it is easier to select the date in the calendar. For appointments that occur several months in the future, it is easier to select the date in the Appointment window.

Another Way
You can key text in the Start time and End time fields rather than a date. Outlook translates the text into a date.

GET READY. Before you begin these steps, be sure to launch Microsoft Outlook.

1. Click the **Calendar** button in the Navigation Pane to display your Calendar. Click the **Month** button to display the Month view, if necessary.

2. Click [next Friday's date] on the monthly calendar.

3. On the Home tab, click the **New Appointment** button. The Appointment window in Figure 8-1 is displayed. The date selected in the monthly calendar is already displayed in the *Start time* and *End time* fields.

4. In the *Subject* field, key **Blood Drive**.

5. In the *Location* field, key **Van in the South parking lot**.

6. In the *Start time* fields, click the **Start time down arrow**. A list of possible starting times appears.

7. Select **2:00 PM**. By default, each appointment is 30 minutes long, so the time in the *End time* field changes to 2:30 PM.

8. You need to fill out forms before donating and eat a few cookies after donating, so give yourself a bit more time. Select an *End Time* of **3:00 PM**.

9. Click the **Save & Close** button in the Actions group on the Ribbon. The appointment is displayed on the calendar, as shown in Figure 5-2.

Figure 5-2

The appointment scheduled on the calendar

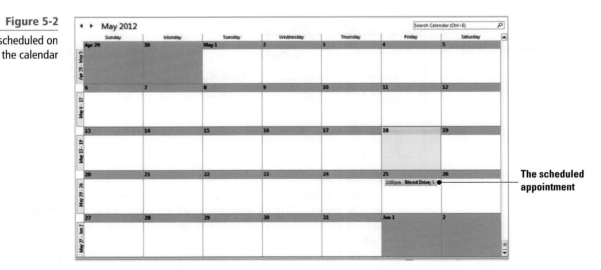

The scheduled appointment

PAUSE. LEAVE the Outlook Message window open to use in the next exercise.

By default, when you select a future date in the calendar, the displayed time of the appointment in the Appointment window will be the start of the workday.

Creating an Appointment from a Message

Sometimes, a message can lead to an appointment. For example, your son's cross-country running coach sends you a message about the awards banquet or you receive a message that a farewell lunch will be held Thursday for a coworker in your department. When you create an appointment from a message you received, the message text is saved automatically in the Appointment window's memo area. This stores the related message with the appointment. In this exercise, you'll simply use an e-mail message to create an appointment.

STEP BY STEP   **Create an Appointment from a Message**

GET READY. Before you begin these steps, be sure to launch Microsoft Outlook.

1. If necessary, click the Calendar button on the Navigation Pane to display the Calendar feature.
2. Click the New Items button in the Home tab. A list of available items is displayed
3. Click E-mail Message in the list to display a new Message window.

Take Note   Throughout this chapter you will see information that appears in black text within brackets, such as [Press Enter], or [next Friday's date]. The information contained in the brackets is intended to be directions for you rather than something you actually type word for word. It will instruct you to perform an action or substitute text. Do **not** type the actual text that appears within brackets.

4. In the *To* field, key [your e-mail address]. In the *Subject* field, key Vice President Duerr visiting Thursday afternoon. In the message area, key Vice President Bernard Duerr is visiting this division on Thursday. An employee meeting will be held in the company cafeteria from 2:00 PM to 4:00 PM. Attendance is mandatory. Click the Send button.
5. Return to your Inbox, if necessary. Click the Send/Receive button if the message has not arrived yet.
6. Click the Vice President Duerr visiting Thursday afternoon message to select it.
7. Click the Move button in the Move group on the Home tab. In the dropdown list, click Other Folder. The Move Items dialog box is displayed, as shown in Figure 5-3.

Figure 5-3

Move Items dialog box

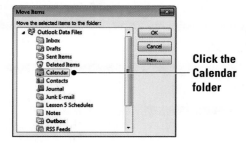

Click the Calendar folder

8. In the Move Items dialog box, click Calendar and then click OK. An Appointment window is opened. The message subject is displayed in the *Subject* field in the Appointment window. A link to the original message is displayed in the Memo area of the Appointment window.
9. Double-click the icon. The original message window is displayed. Close the message window.
10. In the Appointment window, key Company cafeteria into the *Location* field.
11. Key Thursday into the *Start time* field instead of a date. The date of the next available Thursday appears in the Start time date box. Key or select a *Start time* of 2:00 PM.
12. In the *End time* field, key an *End time* of 4:00 PM. The Appointment window should be similar to Figure 5-4.

Figure 5-4

Creating an appointment from a message

Subject created automatically from message subject —

Link to the original message used to create the appointment —

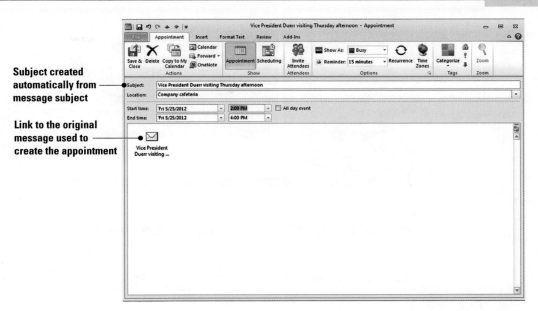

13. Click the Save & Close button in the Actions group on the Ribbon.
14. Click the Calendar button in the Navigation Pane to display the Calendar folder. The appointment created from the message is displayed.

PAUSE. LEAVE Outlook open to use in the next exercise.

Creating an Appointment from a Task

Tasks describe activities you have to do. Appointments tell you when activities are performed. Tasks frequently become appointments when the time to perform a task is scheduled. The task text is saved automatically in the Appointment window's memo area, storing the information with the appointment. In this exercise, you'll create an appointment from a task.

STEP BY STEP   **Create an Appointment from a Task**

GET READY. Before you begin these steps, be sure to launch Microsoft Outlook.

1. Click the Calendar button in the Navigation Pane to display the Calendar folder. Click the Month button to display the Month view, if necessary.
2. Click the View tab. Point to To-Do Bar and then click Normal. The To-Do Bar is displayed to the right of the monthly calendar, as shown in Figure 5-5. Your scheduled appointments are listed in the To-Do Bar. No tasks are displayed.

To-Do Bar

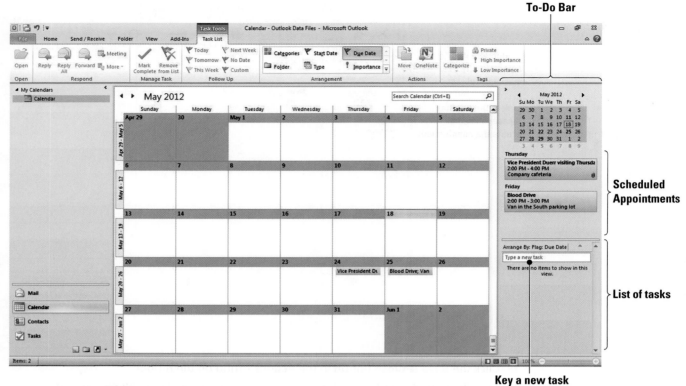

Figure 5-5

To-Do Bar displayed

3. Click the *Type a new task* field, and key **Lunch with Vice President Duerr**. Press **Enter**. The task is created.

4. Click the **Lunch with Vice President Duerr** task. Drag it to Thursday's date on the calendar. You already have an appointment for the employee meeting from 2:00 PM to 4:00 PM for that date.

5. Double-click the **Lunch with Vice President Duerr** item in the calendar. An Appointment window containing the task information is displayed.

6. Click the **All day event** check box to clear the check box. The time fields become available.

7. Key a Start time of **12:30 PM** and an End time of **1:45 PM**. The Appointment window should be similar to Figure 5-6.

Figure 5-6

Creating an appointment from a task

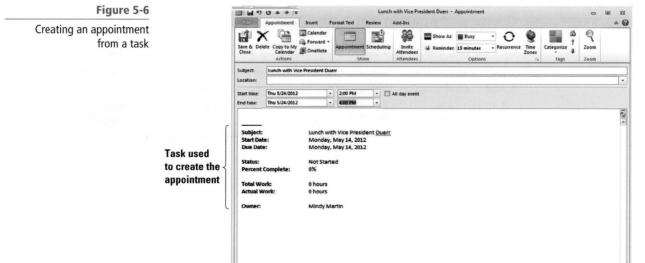

8. Click the Save & Close button in the Actions group on the Ribbon. The appointment created from the task is displayed on the calendar.

PAUSE. LEAVE Outlook open to use in the next exercise.

SETTING APPOINTMENT OPTIONS

Creating a basic appointment is one thing, but many appointments don't fit a cookie-cutter mold. For example, you might need to create an appointment that occurs every other Friday, mark an appointment as private, or forward an appointment on to a colleague. You can use Outlook's appointment options to customize the details of each appointment. In this section, you'll set some appointment options to create a recurring private meeting.

Creating and Customizing Appointments

Outlook offers many different kinds of options that you can use to set appointments. Appointment options are located in both the Options and Tags groups on the Appointment tab. The Time Zone option allows you to establish the time zone for an appointment, which can be very helpful when planning appointments with people in multiple time zones. The Show As option allows you to let others know whether you can be disturbed during a meeting. You can set the Reminder tool to give you an alert when an appointment approaches. In this exercise, you'll create an appointment and customize it with tools in the Options group.

STEP BY STEP | **Create and Customize an Appointment**

GET READY. Before you begin these steps, be sure to launch Microsoft Outlook.

1. Double-click [next Wednesday's date] on the monthly calendar. A new Appointment window is displayed.
2. In the *Subject* field, key **Customizing Appointment Options**.
3. In the *Location* field, key **Training Center**.
4. Click the **All day event** check box to clear the check box. Key a *Start time* of **1:00 PM** and an *End time* of **1:45 PM**.
5. Click the **Reminder dropdown arrow** in the Options group and select **1** hour from the list of available times that appears.
6. Click the **Show As down arrow** in the Options group and select Tentative.
7. Click the **Time Zone** button in the Options group on the Ribbon. A new Time Zone box appears next to the Start and End time boxes. The appointment is going to be conducted via a video feed from California, so select Pacific Time from the list, as shown in Figure 5-7.

Figure 5-7

Setting Appointment options

Time Zone boxes

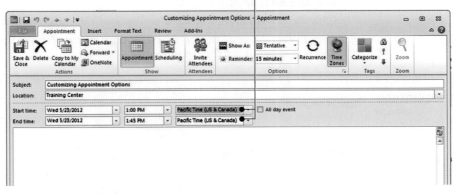

8. Click the Save & Close button in the Actions group on the Ribbon. The appointment created from the task is displayed on the calendar.

PAUSE. LEAVE Outlook open to use in the next exercise.

The *Show as* field in the Appointment window determines how the time is displayed on your calendar. When others look at your calendar, this tells them if you are available and how definite your schedule is for a specific activity. You can choose from four options displayed in Table 5-1.

Table 5-1

Show Time as Options

Show As	Description
Free	No activities are scheduled for this time period. You are available.
Busy	An activity is scheduled for this time period. You are not available for other activities.
Tentative	An activity is scheduled for this time period, but the activity might not occur. You might be available for other activities.
Out of Office	You are out of the office.

Scheduling a Recurring Appointment

A **recurring appointment** is an appointment that occurs at regular intervals. Recurring appointments are common in many calendars. Weekly soccer games, monthly lunch dates with an old friend, and semi-annual company dinners are examples of recurring appointments. Recurrences can be scheduled based on daily, weekly, monthly, and yearly intervals. In this exercise, you set a recurring appointment.

STEP BY STEP **Schedule a Recurring Appointment**

GET READY. Before you begin these steps, be sure to launch Microsoft Outlook.

1. Click the Calendar button in the Navigation Pane to display your Calendar. Click the Month button to display the Month view, if necessary.
2. Double-click the [third Monday of the month] on the monthly calendar. If the third Monday of this month has passed, click the third Monday of next month.

Take Note

In the Month view, double-click the lower part of the square to open a new Untitled—Event window. Double-clicking the top part of the square changes the calendar arrangement to Day view for the selected date.

3. In the *Subject* field, key Engineering Lunch.
4. In the *Location* field, key Conference Room B.
5. Click the All day event check box to clear the check box. Key a *Start time* of 12:15 PM and an *End time* of 1:15 PM.
6. Click the Memo area. Key New techniques and troubleshooting.
7. Click the Recurrence button in the Options group. The Appointment Recurrence dialog box is displayed, as shown in Figure 5-8.

Figure 5-8

Appointment Recurrence window

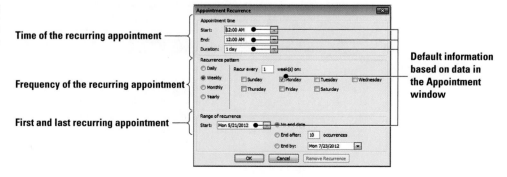

8. In the Appointment Recurrence dialog box, click Monthly in the Recurrence Pattern area. Selecting a different frequency changes the available patterns.

9. On the right side in the Recurrence Pattern area, click the radio button to select The third Monday of every 1 month(s). Because the date of the first recurring appointment was the third Monday of the month, the third Monday of every month is offered as a likely pattern (as is the selected date in each month), as shown in Figure 5-9.

Figure 5-9

Setting the recurrence pattern

Define how frequently the appointment will occur

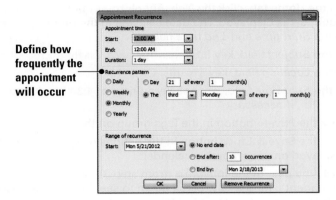

10. Click OK to set the recurrence pattern and return to the Appointment window. The recurrence pattern is displayed in the Appointment window, as shown in Figure 5-10.

Figure 5-10

Recurring appointment

Recurring pattern

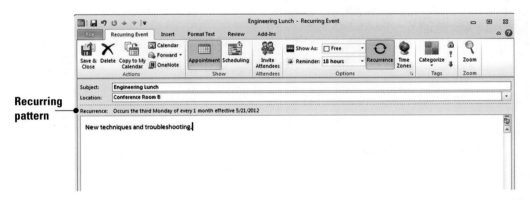

11. Click the Save & Close button in the Actions group on the Ribbon. The appointment is displayed on the monthly calendar. Click the Forward button at the top of the monthly calendar to verify that the recurring appointment is displayed in next month's calendar. Click the Back button at the top of the monthly calendar to return to the current month.

PAUSE. LEAVE the Outlook Message window open to use in the next exercise.

Marking an Appointment as Private

If you use your computer in a public place or just don't like the idea of someone looking over your shoulder and seeing the details about your appointments, you can also choose to mark an appointment as **private**. This feature blocks the details of an activity from a casual observer by showing only the subject line in the calendar with a lock icon. In this exercise, you'll mark an appointment as private.

STEP BY STEP　Mark an Appointment as Private

GET READY. Before you begin these steps, be sure to launch Microsoft Outlook.

1. Click the Calendar button in the Navigation Pane to display your Calendar. Click the Month button to display the Month view if necessary.
2. Click [next Friday's date] on the monthly calendar. The Blood drive is already scheduled for 2:00 PM on that date.
3. On the Home tab, click the New Appointment button. The Appointment window in Figure 5-1 is displayed. The date selected in the monthly calendar is already displayed in the *Start time* and *End time* fields.
4. In the *Subject* field, key Interview Rebecca Laszlo for receptionist.
5. In the *Location* field, key My office.
6. In the *Start time* field, key or select a time of 4:30 PM. Key or select an End time of 5:00 PM, if necessary.
7. Click the Private button in the Tags group on the Ribbon.
8. Click the Save & Close button in the Actions group on the Ribbon. The appointment is displayed on your monthly calendar.
9. Click [the date of the interview (from step 3)] on the calendar and click Day to display your agenda for the day. Scroll down to see the interview listing. Outlook displays a lock next to the private appointment, as shown in Figure 5-11.

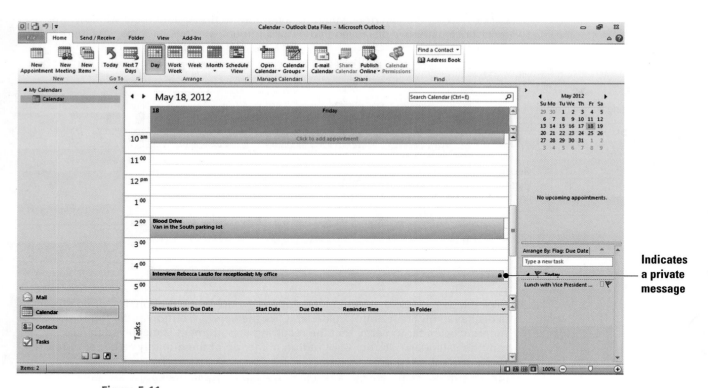

Indicates a private message

Figure 5-11

A private appointment

PAUSE. LEAVE Outlook open to use in the next exercise.

In the previous exercise, you marked an appointment as Private by clicking the Private button before saving the appointment. You also can open an existing appointment and click the Private button to turn on or off the Private feature for that appointment. Be sure to save the modified appointment after changing the Private status.

Take Note   Although marking appointments and events as private hides the details from the casual viewer, it does not ensure privacy. Any person who has Read privileges to your calendar could access the information by a variety of methods.

Forwarding an Appointment

Forwarding an appointment to someone allows you to invite someone to join you or notifies them of your schedule. You can forward an appointment as an attachment using the iCalendar file format. The **iCalendar (.ics)** format is interchangeable between most calendar and e-mail applications, which makes it a versatile tool. When you click on an iCalendar attachment, Outlook automatically adds the appointment to your calendar. In this exercise, you'll forward an appointment as an attachment.

 **Forward an Appointment**

WileyPLUS Extra! features an online tutorial of this task.

GET READY. Before you begin these steps, be sure to launch Microsoft Outlook.

1. Click the Calendar button in the Navigation Pane to display your Calendar. Click the Month button to display the Month view if necessary.

2. Select the Lunch with Vice President Duerr appointment and click the Forward down arrow. Select Forward as iCalendar. The FW: Lunch with Vice President Duerr message window is displayed with the appointment attached as an .ics file.

3. In the *To* field, key [your e-mail address].

4. In the message area, key Come and join us at McCarty's.

5. Right-click the .ics file and click Save As from the shortcut menu.

6. Save the file to the location where you store your solution files. Click Save.

Troubleshooting   It is important to save the file to a location that both you and the recipient can access. If you are on the same server, you can save it there. If not, you might try a website.

7. Click in the bottom of the message area. Click the Insert tab and click Picture. Navigate to the data files for this lesson. Click the iCalendar file and click Open. Outlook's stock iCalendar image is added to the message, as shown in Figure 5-12.

Figure 5-12

Sending an appointment as an attachment

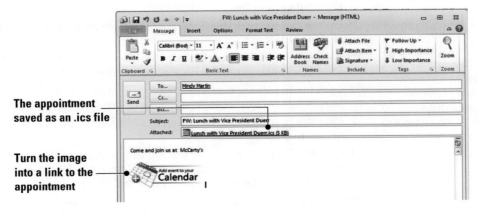

The appointment saved as an .ics file

Turn the image into a link to the appointment

8. Right-click the image and select Hyperlink. The Insert Hyperlink dialog box is displayed, as shown in Figure 5-13.

9. Select Existing File or Web Page, then use the Look In directory to navigate to the solution folder where you stored the appointment. Select the appointment and click OK.

Figure 5-13

Insert Hyperlink dialog box

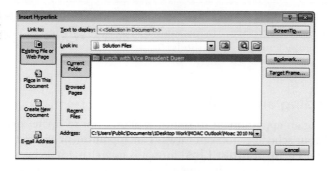

10. Click **Send**. The recipient can open the appointment from the attachment or the link.

PAUSE. LEAVE Outlook open to use in the next exercise.

CREATING AN EVENT

The Bottom Line

An **event** is an activity that lasts one or more days. In your calendar, an event is displayed as a **banner** text prominently displayed at the top of the day window that indicates an activity is going to require the entire day. For scheduling purposes, an event is displayed as free time, meaning that you are still available for appointments. In this exercise, you'll create an event in Outlook 2010.

STEP BY STEP   **Create an Event**

GET READY. Before you begin these steps, be sure to launch Microsoft Outlook.

1. Click the **Calendar** button in the Navigation Pane to display your Calendar. Click the **Month** button to display the Month view, if necessary.

2. On the Home tab, click the **New Appointment** button. The Appointment window in is displayed (refer to Figure 5-1).

3. In the *Subject* field, key **Anniversary**.

4. In the *Start time* field, key the date of your anniversary or a family member's anniversary.

5. Click the **All day event** check box to select the option. The time fields are dimmed.

6. Click the **Private** button in the Options group on the Ribbon.

7. Click the **Recurrence** button in the Options group on the Ribbon. The Appointment Recurrence window is displayed.

8. In the Appointment Recurrence window, click **Yearly** in the *Recurrence pattern* area. Selecting a different frequency changes the patterns available for selection on the right side in the Recurrence pattern area.

9. On the right side in the *Recurrence pattern* area, click the radio button to select **On [month] [date]**.

Another Way
The methods of creating new appointments from messages or tasks that you performed in the earlier exercises in this lesson can also be used to create events.

10. Click **OK** to set the recurrence pattern and return to the Appointment window. The recurrence pattern is displayed in the Appointment window.

11. Click the **Reminder dropdown list arrow**. Click the **1 week** option, to schedule Outlook to remind you one week in advance of the scheduled event.

12. Click the **Save & Close** button in the Actions group on the Ribbon. The appointment is added to your calendar.

13. Click the **Forward** button at the top of the monthly calendar to verify that the recurring event is displayed on the correct date. Click the **Back** button at the top of the monthly calendar to return to the current month.

PAUSE. LEAVE Outlook open to use in the next exercise.

PRINTING APPOINTMENT DETAILS

The Bottom Line

In Outlook 2010 it is easy to print out the details about an appointment or even print out a calendar. The Memo Style format allows you to print the selected appointment. You can use settings in the Print Options dialog box to select the print style and the range of dates to include.

Printing Appointment Details

In this section, you will print the details about one of your appointments.

STEP BY STEP **Print Appointment Details**

GET READY. Before you begin these steps, be sure to launch Microsoft Outlook.

1. Click the Calendar button in the Navigation Pane to display your Calendar. Click the Month button to display the Month view, if necessary.

2. Click File to open Backstage view and click Print in the navigation pane to open the print settings page.

3. Click the Print Options button. The Print dialog box is displayed, as shown in Figure 5-14.

Figure 5-14

Print dialog box

Available Calendar styles

Select the date range you want to print

Click to see a preview of the selected options

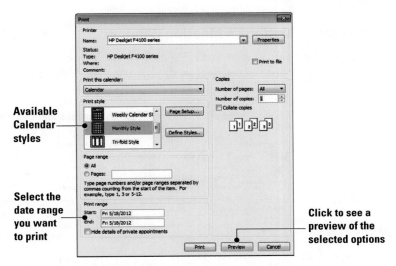

4. In the *Print Style* area, click Calendar Details Style.

5. In the *Start box* of the Print range area, key [next Friday's date].

Figure 5-15

Print preview of next Friday's schedule

6. In the *End* box, key [next Friday's date]. Click the Preview button. The Print settings page of Backstage view is displayed showing a preview of the new settings, as shown in Figure 5-15.

Click to open the Print options dialog box

Selected style

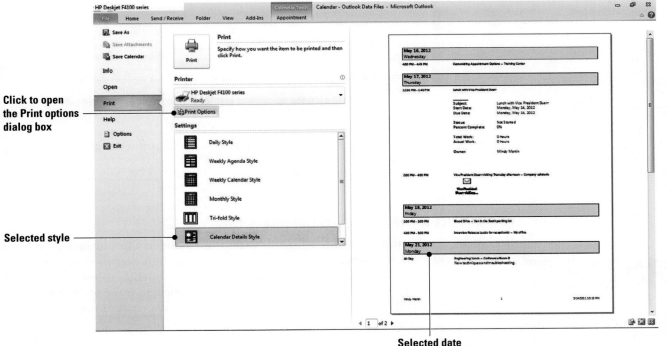

Selected date

Troubleshooting Notice that all the appointments for the week appear on the preview. Although you selected a specific date, the default for this style is to print the entire week. You can click the Define Style button in the Print options dialog box to edit the default style.

7. Click **Print** if you want to print the contact record using the default printer.
CLOSE Outlook.

SOFTWARE ORIENTATION

Microsoft Outlook's Meeting Window

The Meeting window displayed in Figure 5-16 enables you to create a meeting involving other people or resources. Scheduled meetings are displayed on your calendar.

Figure 5-16

Outlook's Meeting window

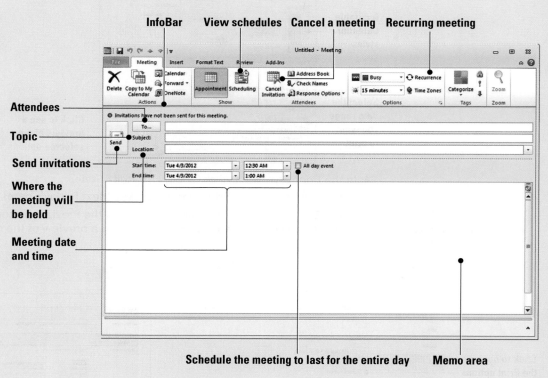

Use the Meeting window to create a meeting. Refer to Figure 5-16 as you complete the following exercises.

CREATING A MEETING REQUEST

The Bottom Line

In Outlook, a **meeting** is a scheduled appointment that requires sending invitations to other people or resources. A **resource** is an item or a location that can be invited to a meeting. Therefore, Outlook's Meeting window, shown in Figure 5-16, is very similar to the Appointment window. However, the Meeting window also includes the *To* field to invite attendees and the *Send* button to send the invitations. A meeting can occur once or at regular intervals.

Creating a One-Time Meeting

Meeting a goal often requires more than one person. Working with others to accomplish a goal usually requires meetings. Use Outlook to start planning a good meeting by selecting the right time, the right place, and the right people to accomplish the goal. A **meeting request** is an Outlook item that creates a meeting and invites attendees. In this exercise, you will start the process of creating a one-time meeting. In this exercise, you'll create a single meeting.

STEP BY STEP	**Create a One-Time Meeting**

GET READY. LAUNCH Outlook if it is not already running.

1. Click the Calendar button in the Navigation Pane to display the Calendar window.
2. Use the Date Navigator in the Navigation Pane to select [the third Monday of April].

WileyPLUS Extra! features an online tutorial of this task.

Troubleshooting Earlier you completed a recurring appointment for the Engineering Lunch is scheduled for 12:15 PM to 1:15 PM on the third Monday of every month. If you did not complete the busy times shown on your schedule will differ.

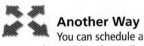

Another Way You can schedule a meeting from within the Mail and Contact features as well. Hover over a contact's name and click View More Options from the Contact Card. Select Schedule a Meeting from the option's dropdown menu.

3. On the Home tab, click New Meeting in the New group. The Meeting window shown in Figure 5-16 is displayed. Outlook selects a default time for the meeting and displays it adjacent to the existing 8:30 AM meeting.
4. Click the *Subject* field and key **Discuss Annual Convention**. In the *Location* field, key **Conference Room A**.

PAUSE. LEAVE the Meeting window open to use in the next exercise.

Inviting Mandatory and Optional Attendees

A **mandatory attendee** is a person who must attend the meeting. An **optional attendee** is a person who should attend the meeting, but whose presence is not required. When planning a meeting, you should always invite at least one mandatory attendee. If a mandatory attendee is not needed to accomplish a goal at the meeting, you might not need a meeting at all. When you select a meeting time, choose a time slot when all mandatory attendees are available. It is helpful to use the message area to provide information about the meeting, including an agenda. In this exercise, you will select the right people to make this meeting a success. You will add both a mandatory attendee and an optional attendee and write a brief note to the attendees.

STEP BY STEP	**Invite Mandatory and Optional Attendees**

Troubleshooting When creating messages you must send and receive the requests and responses from two different e-mail accounts. So, for the exercises in this lesson, you will need to either work with a friend or coworker or have access to a separate e-mail account.

GET READY. USE the meeting request you began in the preceding exercise. The mandatory attendee used in this exercise must have a different active e-mail account from you and be able to respond to your meeting invitation.

1. Click the Scheduling Assistant (or Scheduling) ibutton in the Show group on the Ribbon. Scheduling information is displayed, as shown in Figure 5-17.

Figure 5-17

Scheduling information

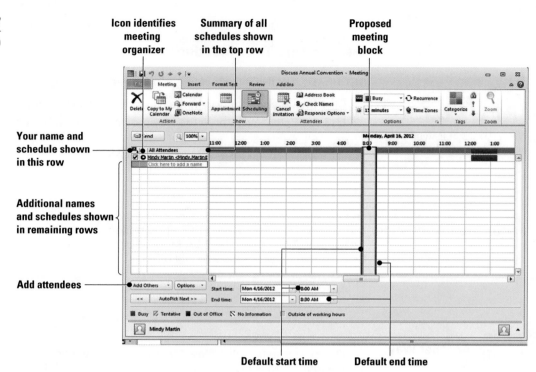

Troubleshooting If you are using Microsoft Exchange, the Scheduling button is called Scheduling Assistant and should include free/busy information for your contacts.

2. Click Add Others and then click Add from Address Book from the dropdown list that appears. The Select Attendees and Resources window appears, as shown in Figure 5-18.

Figure 5-18

Select Attendees and Resources: Contacts window

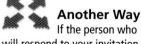

Another Way
If the person who will respond to your invitation is not in the address book, click the *Click here to add a name* text in the Meeting window. Key the desired e-mail address. Verify that the icon next to the keyed name is *Required Attendee*.

3. In the Search box, key [the name of the person or account that is acting as your mandatory attendee] for this lesson.

Troubleshooting If you have not sent messages to your mandatory attendee before now, create a contact record for the new user before completing this exercise, or key the new user's e-mail address directly into the *To* field.

4. Click [the name of your attendee] from the results list, then click Required to indicate that their attendance is mandatory. In this example, Mindy's mandatory attendee is Sara James.

5. Click Gabe Mares' contact information. Click the Optional button to indicate that his attendance is optional. Click OK to return to the Meeting window's Scheduling page. Your mandatory attendee and Gabe have been added to the list of attendees, as shown in Figure 5-19.

Figure 5-19

Attendees displayed

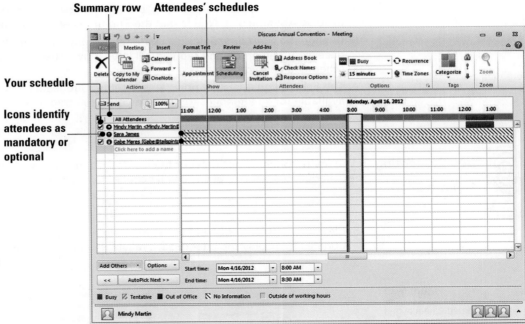

Another Way
You can also attach documents to the invitation before sending it. To attach documents, click the Insert tab and click the Attach File button in the Include group on the Ribbon.

6. Click the Appointment button in the Show group. In the message body, key: It's time to start planning for our annual convention. Bring the comments from last year's convention and we'll create our project plan during the meeting. Gabe, I hope you can join us. Press Enter twice and sign with your name.

PAUSE. Leave the meeting window open to use in the next exercise.

Determining When Attendees Can Meet

The scheduling page of a meeting shows your schedule for the selected day. If you are working on a Microsoft Exchange network, you can see when your attendees are free to attend your meeting and when they are busy. Ideally, you will be able to view this information for all of the attendees, but if you are inviting people outside of your Microsoft Exchange network, you will not have this information. In this exercise, you will examine the available scheduling information for the people you want to invite to the meeting, manually select a meeting time, and then let Outlook select a time for the meeting.

STEP BY STEP   **Determine When Attendees Can Meet**

GET READY. USE the meeting request you began in a previous exercise. The mandatory attendee used in this exercise must have an active e-mail account and be able to respond to your meeting invitation.

Take Note   The directions below require that you are operating on a Microsoft Exchange network. If you are not using Microsoft Exchange, take note of the Troubleshooting alerts throughout this exercise.

1. In the *Start time* field, key or select **9:00 AM**. Notice that the green and red vertical bars indicating the start and end time for the meeting moved to enclose the 9:00 AM to 9:30 AM time slot.

2. Click the red vertical line and drag it to the right so that the bars enclose the 9:00 AM to 10:00 AM time slot. Notice that the *End time* field changed to 10:00 AM.

3. Change the *Start time* field to **1:00 PM** and change the *End time* field to **2:00 PM**, if necessary. The green and red vertical lines move. The meeting time overlaps your scheduled appointment.

4. The Scheduling Assistant populates Meeting Suggestions pane with the best times available for all attendees to meet on your preferred date.

Troubleshooting   If you invite someone not on your Microsoft Exchange network, you will see the name on the Scheduling Assistant, but you will not see their schedule.

5. Click on **11:00 AM–12:00 AM** in the Meeting Suggestions pane and the schedule grid updates to display the attendees' availability at that time, as shown in Figure 5-20.

Figure 5-20

Updated schedule grid

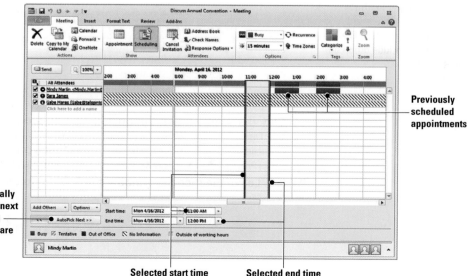

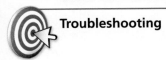

Troubleshooting If you are not using Microsoft Exchange, you will see an AutoPick Next button on the bottom left of the schedule grid. As with the Meeting Suggestions pane, the AutoPick Next button adjusts the schedule grid to show attendees' availability. Press the back arrow button (to the left of the AutoPick Next button) twice to jump back to 11:00 AM.

6. Click **Appointments** from the Show group on the Meeting tab to return to the Meeting window. The *To* field is automatically filled with the attendees' e-mail addresses, and the *Start time* and *End time* fields have been updated. Your Meeting window should resemble Figure 5-21.

Figure 5-21

Updated Meeting window

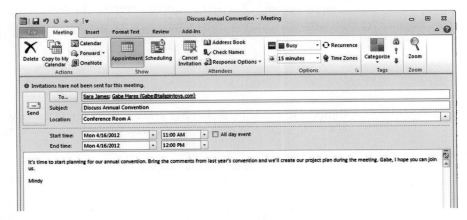

7. Click the **Send** button.

PAUSE. LEAVE Outlook open to use in the next exercise.

Sending a Meeting to a Contact Group

In Lesson 4, you discovered that creating a contact group is an efficient way to send frequent e-mails to a group of people. You also can use your contact groups to invite several people to your meeting at one time. In this exercise, you will send a meeting request to the contact group you created in Lesson 4.

STEP BY STEP | **Send a Meeting to a Contact Group**

GET READY. USE the Tailspin Team Leaders Contact Group you created in Lesson 4.

1. Click the **Calendar** button in the Navigation Pane to display the Calendar window.

2. Use the Date Navigator in the Navigation Pane to select [the third Monday of April].

3. On the Home tab, click **New Meeting** in the New group. The Meeting window shown in Figure 5-16 is displayed.

4. Click the *Subject* field and key **First Weekly Meeting**. In the *Location* field, key **Conference Room A**.

5. In the Meeting window, click the **To** button to open the Address Book. Select the **Tailspin Team Leaders Contact Group** you created in Lesson 4 and click the **Required** button to indicate that their attendance is mandatory.

6. Click **OK** to return to the Meeting window's Scheduling page. Click the **plus sign** in front of the contact group name. The Expand List dialog box is displayed asking if you want to replace the Contact Group name with the names of the individual members, as shown in Figure 5-22.

Figure 5-22

Expand List dialog box

Contact Group

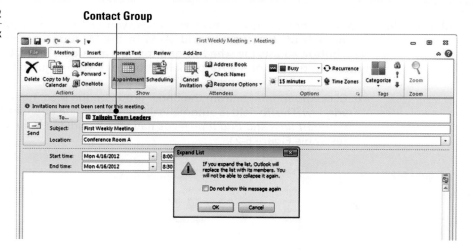

7. Click **OK** to close the dialog box and return to the Meeting window. The *To* field now shows the name of each of the Contact Group's members, as shown in Figure 5-23.

Figure 5-23

Meeting invitation to Contact Group

Expanded Contact Group attendees

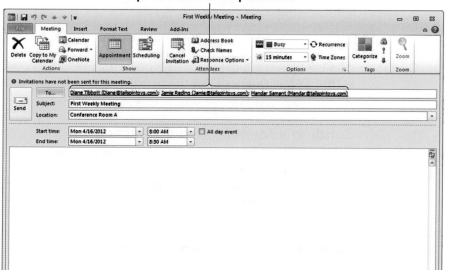

8. Change the *Start time* field to **2:00 PM** and change the *End time* field to **3:00 PM**, if necessary.

9. In the message body, key **Agenda: Create project plan**. Press **Enter**. **Assign project roles.** Press **Enter** twice and sign with [your name].

10. Click **Send**.

PAUSE. LEAVE Outlook open to use in the next exercise.

Creating a Meeting from a Message

Sometimes, a message can lead to a meeting. For example, when Gabe received the bug report in the weekly status update memo about Project Snow, he realized that there was a problem that needed to be addressed face-to-face in order to get to the bottom of it. When you create a meeting from a message you received, the message text is saved automatically in the Meeting Request window's message area. In this exercise, you'll reply to a message with a meeting request.

STEP BY STEP   **Create a Meeting from a Message**

GET READY. USE the Diane Tibbott contact record you created in Lesson 4.

1. From the Calendar folder, click the New Items button in the Home tab. A list of available items is displayed

2. Click E-mail Message in the list to display a new Message window.

3. In the *To* field, key [the e-mail address of the person or account that is acting as your mandatory attendee] for this lesson.

4. In the *Subject* field, key Latest bug report issues. In the message area, key Unfortunately, this week's bug report doesn't show much progress. We are still experiencing 20 glitches per unit. The cause is still unknown. Will send you the particulars later today. Click the Send button.

5. Return to your Inbox, if necessary. Click the Send/Receive All Folders button if the message has not arrived yet.

 Troubleshooting If you are not working with a friend or coworker on this lesson, switch to the mandatory attendee account that you are using.

6. In the mandatory attendee account, click the Latest bug report issues message. Click the Reply with Meeting button in the Respond group on the Home tab. The *Latest bug report issues—Meeting* request window is displayed with the contents of the original message, as shown in Figure 5-24.

Reply with a
Meeting button

Address
Book

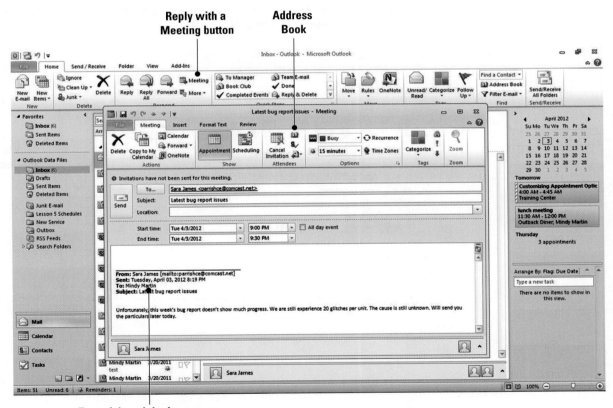

Text of the original message

Figure 5-24

Replying to a message with a meeting request

7. In the Meeting window, key Design Center 2 into the *Location* field.

8. Key Wednesday into the *Start time* field instead of a date. Key or select a start time of 9:00 AM.

9. In the *End time* field, key 11:00 AM.

10. Click High Importance in the Tags group.
11. Click the Address Book button in the Attendees group. Select Diane Tibbott, Jamie Reding, and Mandar Samant from the address book. Click Required and click OK.

PAUSE. LEAVE Outlook open to use in the next exercise.

Setting Response Options for a Meeting Request

By default, when you create a meeting in Outlook, there are two response options selected: Request Responses and Allow New Time Proposals. The Request Responses option adds response buttons to the meeting request. These buttons allow attendees to respond to the request letting you know whether they will attend. The Allow New Time Proposals option allows recipients to propose a different time to hold the meeting. As the meeting organizer, you still have final say about the meeting time; you also can choose to turn off one or both options. In this exercise, you'll reply to a message with a meeting request, but will not give anyone the option of changing the meeting time.

STEP BY STEP | **Set Response Options for a Meeting Request**

GET READY. USE the meeting request you starting in the preceding exercise.

1. In the *Latest bug report issues — Meeting* window, click the message area. Key This continuing problem is unacceptable. Bring all your data to this meeting. No one leaves until we have some answers.

2. In the Attendees group, click the Response Options button. A dropdown list is displayed, as shown in Figure 5-25.

Figure 5-25

Setting Response options

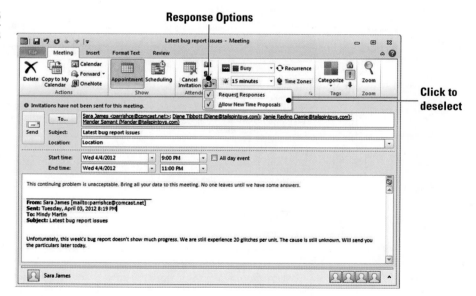

3. Click the Allow New Time Proposals option to deselect it.
4. Click Send. The meeting request is sent to your attendees and the meeting is added to your calendar.

PAUSE. LEAVE Outlook open to use in the next exercise.

RESPONDING TO A MEETING REQUEST

When you are invited to a meeting, you receive a meeting request in your Inbox. The meeting request can contain up to five options at the top of the message depending on the response options set by the meeting organizer. These meeting response options are used to let the meeting organizer know whether to expect you at the meeting, as shown in Table 5-2.

Table 5-2

Meeting Response Options

Detail Level	Description
Accept	Indicates that you have accepted the invitation and marks your calendar as busy.
Decline	Indicates that you will not attend the meeting and leaves your calendar free at the requested time.
Tentative	Indicates that you *might* attend the meeting, but does not commit you. Your calendar is marked as tentative with diagonal stripes.
Propose New Time	Indicates that you *might* be able to attend the meeting if the organizer were to change the time of the meeting to something that better fits your schedule.
Please Respond	Allows you to ask a question of the meeting organizer, perhaps asking for clarification, without accepting or declining the actual invitation. This link appears in the InfoBar, not at the top of the message.

Responding to a Meeting Request

Response options are set by the meeting organizer. The invitee must choose one of these options to let the meeting organizer know that invitee's intentions. In this exercise, you will tentatively accept a meeting invitation.

STEP BY STEP | **Respond to a Meeting Request**

GET READY. LAUNCH Outlook if it is not already running and complete the previous exercises. The mandatory attendee used in this exercise must have a different active e-mail account from yours and be able to respond to your meeting invitation.

1. In the mandatory attendee's account, click the **Mail** button in the Navigation Pane to display the Mail folder, if necessary.

2. Locate the Discuss Annual Convention message in the message list. If it has not arrived, click the **Send/Receive All Folders** button on the Home tab. The Discuss Annual Convention message is identified in the message list by the Meeting icon, shown in Figure 5-24, which resembles the New Meeting button on the Calendar's Home tab.

3. Click the **Discuss Annual Convention** message in the message list. The message is displayed in the Preview pane, as shown in Figure 5-26.

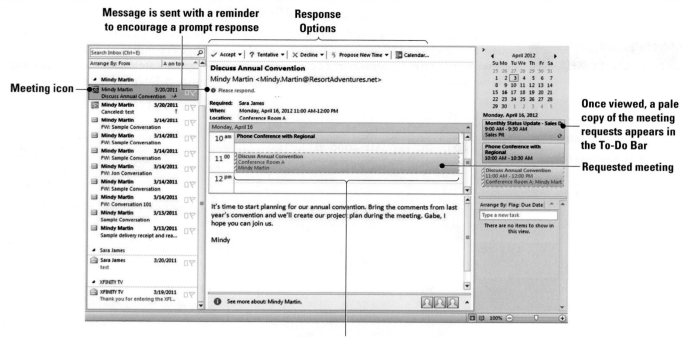

Message is sent with a reminder to encourage a prompt response

Response Options

Meeting icon

Once viewed, a pale copy of the meeting requests appears in the To-Do Bar

Requested meeting

Preview of your schedule for the requested time

Figure 5-26

Previewing a meeting request in the Reading Pane

4. Click the Tentative button. A dropdown list of options is displayed offering you the options to send your response now, add a comment before sending the response, or choose to not send a response, as shown in Figure 5-27.

Figure 5-27

Sending a Tentative response to a meeting request

Tentative response options

Click to send the default tentative response

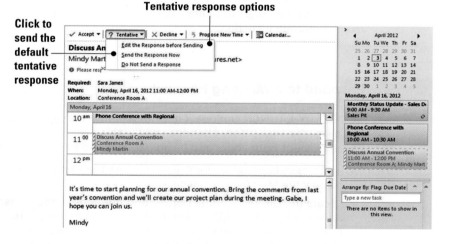

Another Way
You can also right-click on a meeting request in the message list to access the different response options.

5. Click the Send the Response Now option. Click OK. The meeting request is removed from your Inbox, and the meeting is added to your calendar.

LEAVE Outlook open to use in the next exercise.

Proposing a New Time for a Meeting

Meeting times are set by the **meeting organizer**, the person who creates the meeting and sends meeting invitations. In most cases, when a meeting invitation is received, an attendee can suggest a different time for the meeting that better fits the attendee's schedule as long as the organizer has enabled the setting on the meeting invitation. In this exercise, you will propose a new meeting time for a meeting invitation.

STEP BY STEP   Propose a New Time for a Meeting

GET READY. Before you begin these steps, complete the previous exercises. The mandatory attendee used in this exercise must have a different active e-mail account from yours and be able to respond to your meeting invitation.

1. In the mandatory attendee's account, click the Mail button in the Navigation Pane to display the Mail feature, if necessary.

2. Click the Deleted Items folder and locate the Discuss Annual Convention message. Because you already responded *Tentatively* to the meeting request, the message has been moved to the Deleted Items folder.

3. Double-click the Discuss Annual Convention deleted meeting request. The Discuss Annual Convention—Meeting window is displayed. Notice that the InfoBar reminds you that you have already responded to this request using the *Tentatively* option, as shown in Figure 5-28.

Figure 5-28

Discuss Annual Convention—
Message window

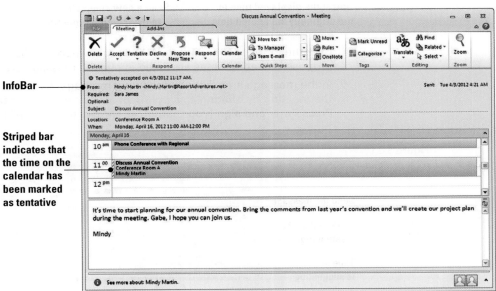

4. Click the Propose New Time button at the top of the message. The Propose New Time window is displayed, as shown in Figure 5-29. The meeting time is indicated with as a yellow bar.

Figure 5-29

Propose New Time: Discuss
Annual Convention window

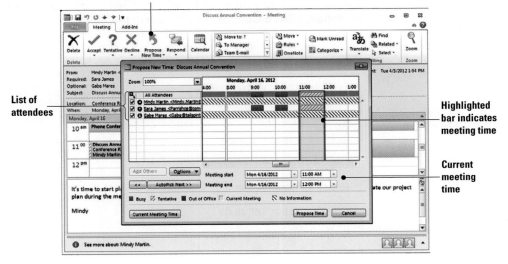

5. Verify that 11:00 is in the *Start time* field. Click the *End time* field. Key **12:30 PM**. The red line indicating the meeting's end time has moved to 12:30, as shown in Figure 5-30.

Figure 5-30

Proposing a new meeting time

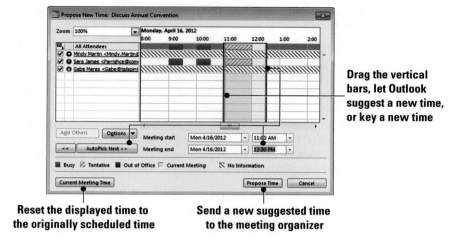

Drag the vertical bars, let Outlook suggest a new time, or key a new time

Reset the displayed time to the originally scheduled time

Send a new suggested time to the meeting organizer

6. Click the Propose Time button. A Message window is displayed. Both the current and proposed meeting times are listed above the message area.

7. In the message area, key the following message. Let's add 30 minutes and conclude the meeting by offering a sampling of foods available for the convention luncheon. Press Enter and sign [your name], as shown in Figure 5-31.

Figure 5-31

Updated meeting request

Send the message

Time sent by the meeting organizer

Time attendee is suggesting

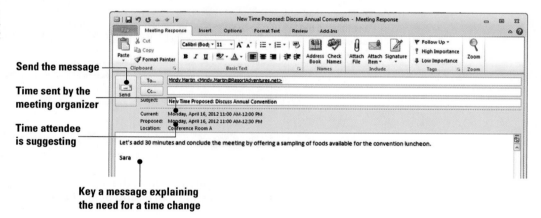

Key a message explaining the need for a time change

8. Click the Send button.

PAUSE. Switch to your e-mail account, if necessary. If someone else is responding to the invitation, **LEAVE** Outlook open to use in the next exercise.

SKILL SUMMARY

In This Lesson, You Learned How To:
Create appointments
Set appointment options
Create an event
Print appointment details
Create meeting requests
Respond to meeting requests

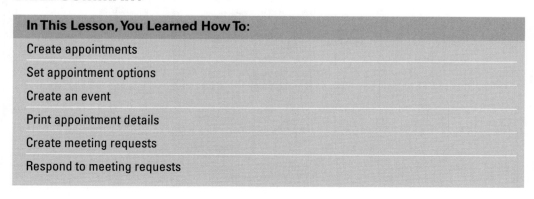

Knowledge Assessment

Multiple Choice

Select the letter beside the term that best completes each of the following statements.

1. A _____ appointment is one that occurs at regular intervals.
   a. recurring
   b. regular
   c. routine
   d. repeating

2. No activities are scheduled for a(n) _____ time period.
   a. Tentative
   b. Open
   c. Free
   d. Available

3. An activity that lasts one or more days is referred to as a(n) _____.
   a. extended activity
   b. session
   c. event
   d. All of the above

4. In Outlook, an activity that has to be performed is a(n) _____.
   a. duty
   b. task
   c. event
   d. chore

5. A(n) _____ is a scheduled activity that does not require sending invitations to other people or resources.
   a. private meeting
   b. solo meeting
   c. closed event
   d. appointment

6. The _____ feature protects the details of an activity from a casual observer.
   a. private
   b. secure
   c. encrypted
   d. lock

7. The _____ contains an option to print appointments from selected dates.
   a. Appointment Options dialog box
   b. Print Options dialog box
   c. Edit Settings box
   d. Layout dialog box

8. The _____ setting indicates that an activity is scheduled for this time period, but the activity might not occur.
   a. Show As: Possible
   b. Show As: Free
   c. Show As: Saved
   d. Show As: Tentative

9. A(n) _____ is text displayed at the top of a day to indicate an event.
   a. opener
   b. header
   c. flag
   d. banner

10. The _____ enables you to create a schedule.
    a. calendar
    b. appointment book
    c. weekly organizer
    d. ledger

True/False

Circle T if the statement is true or F if the statement is false.

T F **1.** A task cannot be used to create an appointment unless the task is private.

T F **2.** Marking an appointment as private ensures that users who can view your calendar cannot view the details of the private appointment.

T F **3.** Appointments require invitations sent through Outlook.

T F **4.** By default, each appointment is one hour long.

T F **5.** An event is displayed as a banner in your calendar.

T F **6.** You are not available for other activities when your time is displayed as Busy.

T F **7.** You can key text in the *Start time* and *End time* fields rather than a date.

T F **8.** Use the Appointment window to print an event.

T F **9.** A message is deleted automatically when it is used to create an appointment.

T F **10.** Recurrences can be scheduled based on daily, weekly, monthly, and yearly intervals.

Competency Assessment

Project 5-1: Schedule Vacation

Your boss has finally approved your vacation request for July. Now that it's official, it's time to add your vacation to the calendar.

GET READY. LAUNCH Outlook if it is not already running.

1. Click the **Calendar** button in the Navigation Pane to display the Calendar folder.
2. On the Home tab, click the **New Appointment** button. The Appointment window is displayed.
3. In the *Subject* field, key **Vacation**.
4. In the *Start time* field, key the [date of the first day] of your vacation.
5. In the *End time* field, key the [date of the last day] of your vacation.
6. Click the **All day event** check box to select the option. The time fields are dimmed.
7. Click the **Save & Close** button in the Actions group on the Ribbon. The appointment is added to your calendar.

LEAVE Outlook open for the next project.

Project 5-2: Create a One-Time Appointment

You have been selected to create a presentation about a new product your company will sell in the coming year. You will deliver the presentation at a company dinner on Wednesday. Schedule the time to prepare the presentation.

1. Click the **Calendar** button in the Navigation Pane to display the Calendar folder.
2. Click [next Monday's date] on the monthly calendar.

3. On the Home tab, click the New Appointment button. The Appointment window is displayed.

4. In the *Subject* field, key Prepare new product presentation.

5. In the *Start time* fields, key or select the time of 9:30 AM. Key or select the *End time* of 2:00 PM.

6. Click the Save & Close button in the Actions group on the Ribbon. The appointment is added to the calendar.

LEAVE Outlook open for the next project.

Proficiency Assessment

Project 5-3: Schedule a Recurring Appointment

Every week, you collect sales information to track the difference between sales goals and actual sales. Create a recurring appointment every Monday to gather the information and post the sales information for the managers to review.

GET READY. LAUNCH Outlook if it is not already running.

1. Click the Calendar button in the Navigation Pane to display the Calendar folder.

2. Click [next Tuesday's date] on the monthly calendar.

3. On the Home tab, click the New Appointment button. The Appointment window is displayed.

4. In the *Subject* field, key Prepare Sales Report.

5. In the *Start time* field, key or select 8:30 AM. Key or select an *End time* of 9:30 AM.

6. Click the Recurrence button in the Options group on the Ribbon. The Appointment Recurrence dialog box is displayed.

7. Click OK to accept the recurrence pattern and return to the Appointment window.

8. Click the Save & Close button in the Actions group on the Ribbon. The appointment is added to the calendar.

LEAVE Outlook open for the next project.

Project 5-4: Create an Appointment from a Message

A friend sent you a message about a concert in August. Create an appointment from the message.

GET READY. LAUNCH Outlook if it is not already running.

1. If necessary, click the Mail button in the Navigation Pane to display the Mail folder.

2. Click the New E-mail button on the Home tab to display the Message window.

3. In the *To* field, key [your e-mail address]. In the *Subject* field, key Concert! In the message area, key [the name of your favorite musical performer] is coming to [the name of the local concert hall]! Mark August 10 on your calendar! I've already bought our tickets! Click the Send button.

4. Return to your Inbox, if necessary. Click the Send/Receive button if the message has not arrived yet.

5. Double-click the Concert message to open it.

6. Click the Move to Folder button in the Actions group. In the dropdown list, click Other Folder. The Move Items dialog box is displayed.

7. In the Move Items dialog box, click Calendar, and then click OK. An Appointment window is opened.

8. Key August 10 in the *Start time* field. Key or select 7:00 PM.

9. Key or select an *End time* of 11:00 PM.

10. Click the Save & Close button in the Actions group on the Ribbon.

LEAVE Outlook open for the next project.

Project 5-5: Create and Print an Appointment from a Task

Last week, a coworker asked you to review a new marketing presentation. He finished the presentation yesterday. Turn the task into an appointment to review the presentation tomorrow after lunch.

GET READY. LAUNCH Outlook if it is not already running.

1. Display the *To-Do Bar*, if necessary.
2. Click the *Type a new task* field, and key **Review presentation for Gary Schare**. Press **Enter**. The task is created.
3. Click the **Review presentation for Gary Schare** task. Drag it to [tomorrow's date] on the calendar.
4. Double-click the **Review presentation for Gary Schare** item in the calendar. An Appointment window is displayed.
5. Click the **All day event** check box to clear the check box. The time fields become available.
6. Key or select a *Start time* of **3:30 PM** and an *End time* of **5:00 PM**.
7. Click the **Save & Close** button in the Actions group on the Ribbon. The appointment is added to the calendar.
8. Click the **File** tab and select **Print** in the Navigation Pane.
9. Click **Memo Style** in the Settings area and click **Print**.

LEAVE Outlook open for the next project.

Project 5-6: Mark an Appointment as Private

In Project 8-4, you created an appointment for the concert. Your taste in music might not be appreciated by everyone who views your calendar. Make the appointment private.

GET READY. LAUNCH Outlook if it is not already running.

1. Click the **Calendar** button in the Navigation Pane to display the Calendar folder.
2. Display **August** in the calendar.
3. Double-click the **Concert** appointment to open it.
4. Click the **Private** button in the Options group.
5. Click the **Save & Close** button in the Actions group. The private appointment is added to the calendar.

CLOSE Outlook.

INTERNET READY

Use the Internet to find some local events that you would like to attend. A local sports game or a concert performed by your favorite artist could be fun. Schedule the activities in your calendar.

Microsoft® Access® 2010

LESSON SKILL MATRIX

In This Lesson, You Will Learn The Following Skills:

Getting Started

Working in the Access Window

Using the On-Screen Tools

Using the Backstage View

Using the Microsoft Office Access Help Button

Defining Data Needs and Types

KEY TERMS

- **Backstage view**
- **badges**
- **Connection Status menu**
- **database**
- **database management system (DBMS)**
- **datasheet**
- **data type**
- **desktop**
- **dialog box launcher**
- **field**
- **File tab**
- **form**
- **groups**
- **KeyTip**
- **normal forms**
- **normalization**
- **objects**
- **primary key**

- query
- Quick Access Toolbar
- record
- redundant data
- relational database
- report
- Ribbon
- tab
- table

The School of Fine Art in Poughkeepsie, New York, is the brainchild of two professional artists—Shaun Beasley, a printmaker, and Jane Clayton, a sculptor. Last year, the new private high school opened with an enrollment of 12 students and with Jane and Shaun as the only full-time instructors. All academic and business records were maintained manually by the founders. This year, however, you were hired as an executive assistant to help them manage an increasing amount of information. Enrollment is climbing, new full-time faculty members are being hired, and the school is receiving scholarship funds from local patrons. With the help of an Access database, you will organize the school's academic and business data. In this lesson, you will learn basic database concepts and how to define data needs and types.

SOFTWARE ORIENTATION

Microsoft Access' Opening Screen

Before you begin working in Microsoft Access, you need to be familiar with the primary user interface. In the next section, you will be asked to open a new blank database in Access. When you do so, a screen appears that is similar to the one shown in Figure 1-1.

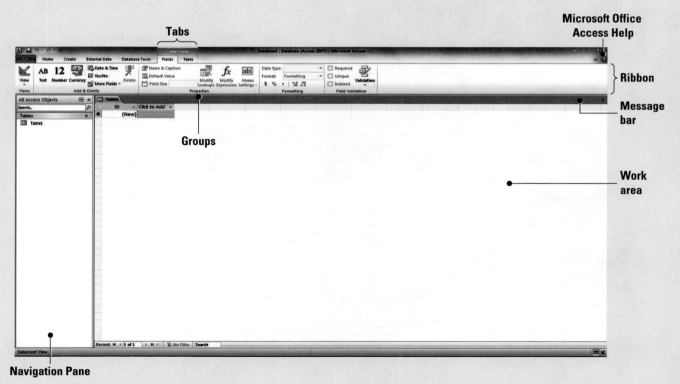

Figure 1-1

Opening screen for new blank Access database

When you create a blank database in Microsoft Access, the opening screen provides you with a workspace in which to build a database. Understanding the screen elements helps orient you to important tools and information. The elements and features of your screen may vary if default settings have been changed or if other preferences have been set. Use Figure 1-1 as a reference throughout this lesson as well as the rest of this book.

GETTING STARTED

The Bottom Line

A **database** is a tool for collecting and organizing information. For example, as a database, a phone book organizes a large amount of data—names, addresses, and phone numbers—so you can access it by name in alphabetic order. Even a grocery list is a simple type of database. A computerized **database management system (DBMS)**, such as Microsoft Office Access, enables you to easily collect large volumes of data organized into categories of related information. This type of database allows you to store, organize, and manage your data, no matter how complex it is, and then retrieve and present it in various formats and reports. As with any program, however, the first tasks are the most basic. This section shows you how to start Access and open an existing database.

Starting Access

The **Backstage view** appears when you start Access. From here, you can create a new blank database, create a database from a template, or open a recent database (if you have already created one). You can also access Microsoft Office Online for featured content and more information about the 2010 Microsoft Office system and Office Access 2010. In this exercise, you learn to start Access from the Microsoft Office menu.

 Ref

You learn to use Backstage view in a later section of this lesson.

STEP BY STEP **Start Access**

GET READY. Before you begin these steps, be sure to turn on and/or log on to your computer.

1. On the Windows taskbar, click the **Start button** and click **All Programs**. A menu of installed programs appears.
2. Click **Microsoft Office**. Another menu appears as shown in Figure 1-2.

WileyPLUS Extra! features an online tutorial of this task.

Figure 1-2

Start button and Microsoft Office menu

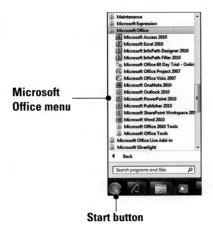

Microsoft Office menu

Start button

3. Click **Microsoft Access 2010**. Access opens displaying the Backstage view, as shown in Figure 1-3.

Search Office.com for templates

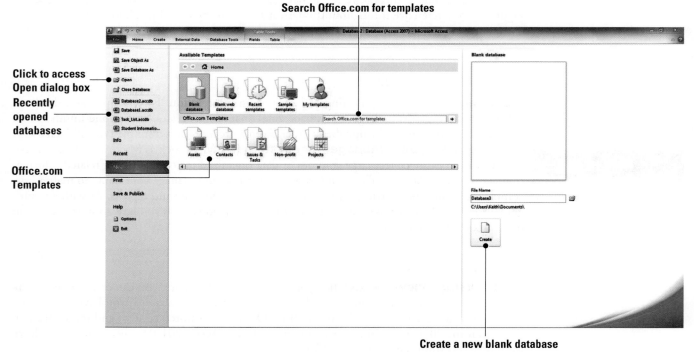

Click to access
Open dialog box
Recently
opened
databases

Office.com
Templates

Create a new blank database

Figure 1-3

Backstage view

PAUSE. LEAVE Microsoft Access open to use in the next exercise.

 **Another Way**
When Office was installed on your computer, a shortcut icon might have been added to the Start menu or to your **desktop**—the screen you see when you start Windows. Click the shortcut to start Access without having to go through the Start menu.

Opening an Existing Database

When you open an existing database, you access not only your previously entered and saved data, but also the elements you created to organize that data. In this exercise, you open a database that is in the beginning stages of development.

The Open command displays the Open dialog box used to find and open files wherever they may be located—on the desktop, in a folder on your computer, on a network drive, or on a CD or other removable media. The Look in box lists the available locations, such as a folder, drive, or Internet location. Click the location, and the folders will be displayed in the folder list. From this list, you can double-click the folder you want to open. When you find the file you want, double-click the filename to open it or click it once to select it and then click the Open button.

STEP BY STEP **Open an Existing Database**

GET READY. The blank database in Backstage view should be on the screen from the previous exercise.

1. Click the **Open** command on the left side of the Backstage View screen. The Open dialog box appears, as shown in Figure 1-4.

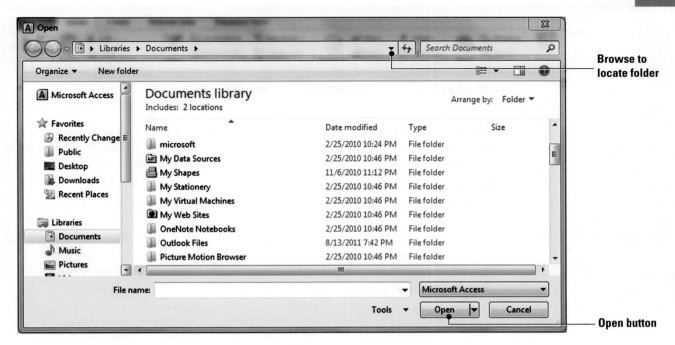

Figure 1-4

Open dialog box

Take Note

Another Way
Press Ctrl+O to display the Open dialog box.

@ The *Student Information* file for this lesson is available on the book companion website or in WileyPLUS.

If the database you want to use is listed under the Close Database command on the left panel of the Backstage view, simply click to open it.

2. Navigate to the data files for this lesson and select *Student Information*.

3. Click the Open button in the Open dialog box, as shown in Figure 1-4. The existing database opens, as shown in Figure 1-5.

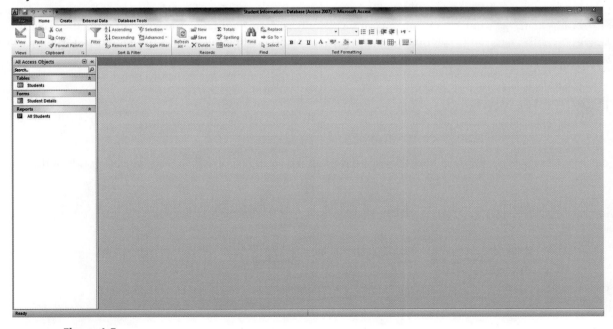

Figure 1-5

Existing database open in Access

Troubleshooting As part of the Office Access 2010 security model, when you open a database outside of a trusted location, a tool called the Message Bar appears to warn you that certain content has been disabled. If you know you can trust the database, click Enable Content.

PAUSE. LEAVE the database open to use in the next exercise.

Clicking the Open button opens the database for shared access in a multi-user environment so that you and other users can read and write to the database. If you click the arrow next to the Open button, other options are available on the menu as shown in Figure 1-6:

- **Open:** Opens with default access.
- **Open Read-Only:** Opens with only viewing ability and not editing ability. Others can still read and write.
- **Open Exclusive:** Opens so that the database is only available to you. Others will receive a message that the file is already in use.
- **Open Exclusive Read-Only:** Opens with only viewing ability and not editing ability. Others can only view and not edit the database.
- **Show previous versions:** Locates earlier copies of the database (if ones exist) before the latest modification.

Another Way
You can also display the Open dialog box by clicking Recent in the Backstage view.

Figure 1-6

Open button menu

Take Note Each time you start Access, you open a new instance of Access. You can only have one database open at a time in a single instance of Access. In other words, you cannot start Access, open one database, and then open another database without closing the first database. However, you can open multiple databases at the same time by opening another instance of Access. For example, to have two Access databases open, start Access and open the first Access database, and then start a new instance of Access and open the second database.

WORKING IN THE ACCESS WINDOW

The Bottom Line

The Access 2010 Window user interface was designed to help you find the commands you need quickly so that you can successfully perform your tasks. You will start using the Navigation Pane and exploring the Ribbon across the top right away. Also in this lesson, you will practice using other on-screen tools and features, such as the Backstage view and Access Help.

SOFTWARE ORIENTATION

Navigation Pane

By default, the Navigation Pane, shown in Figure 1-7, appears on the left side of the Access screen each time you create or open a database.

Figure 1-7

Navigation Pane

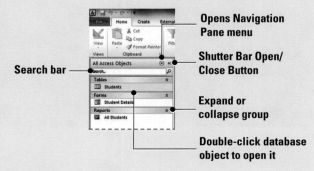

The Navigation Pane enables you to open, copy, and delete tables and other database **objects**. It also lists all the objects in your database, including: **tables**—the most basic database object that stores data in categories; **queries**—allow you to search and retrieve the data you have stored; **forms**—control data entry and data views, and provide visual cues that make data easier to work with; and **reports**—present your information in ways that are most useful to you. You learn more about managing database objects such as forms, queries, and reports in later lessons of this book. For now, just familiarize yourself with the Navigation Pane. Use Figure 1-7 as a reference throughout this lesson as well as the rest of this book.

Using the Navigation Pane

Before you can create a database, you need to understand its most basic elements. This section introduces you to some of the elements in a database that help you organize data and navigate using the Navigation Pane, object tabs, and different views.

STEP BY STEP **Use the Navigation Pane**

USE the database from the previous exercise.

1. In the Navigation Pane, double-click **Students** to display the table in the Access work area, as shown in Figure 1-8.

Double-click object in Navigation Pane to display it in the work area

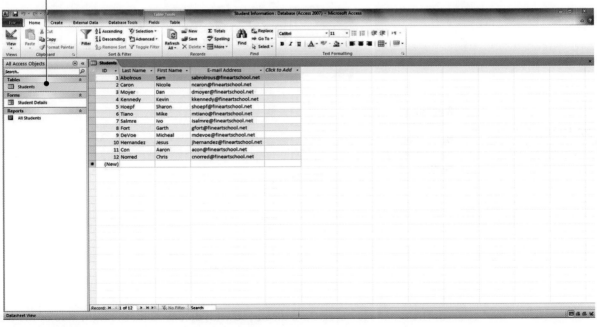

Figure 1-8

Table open in Access work area

Take Note The Navigation Pane replaces an older tool, the Database window, which appeared in earlier versions of Access.

2. Click the down arrow next to All Access Objects at the top of the Navigation Pane to display the menu, as shown in Figure 1-9.

Figure 1-9

Navigation Pane menu

Categories

Groups that relate to the selected category

3. Click Tables and Related Views. The default group in this category is All Tables, which appears in the menu at the top of the Navigation Pane. Notice the Students table and all other objects related to it are displayed under the Students header.

4. Click the down arrow next to All Tables at the top of the Navigation Pane to display the menu again, and click Object Type to return to the original view.

5. Right-click in the white area of the Navigation Pane to display a shortcut menu. Click View By and then Details, as shown in Figure 1-10.

Figure 1-10

Navigation Pane shortcut menu

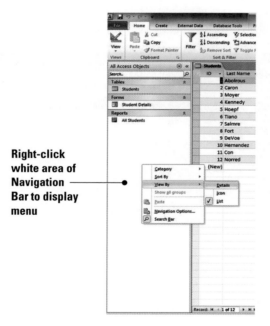

Right-click white area of Navigation Bar to display menu

6. The database objects are displayed with details. Click the right side of the Navigation Pane and drag to make it wider so all the information can be read, as shown in Figure 1-11.

Figure 1-11

Widen the Navigation Pane

Click and drag to enlarge
Navigation Pane

Database objects with
details displayed

7. If the search bar does not appear at the top of the Navigation Pane, right-click on the Tables header of the Navigation Pane. On the shortcut menu, click Search Bar. A search bar is now displayed at the top of the Navigation Pane. You can toggle the search bar display by clicking the Search Bar option.

8. Display the Navigation Pane shortcut menu, click View By and then List to display the database objects in a list.

9. Click the Shutter Bar Open/Close Button to collapse the Navigation Pane. Notice it is not entirely hidden, as shown in Figure 1-12.

Figure 1-12

Navigation Pane collapsed

Navigation
Pane
collapsed

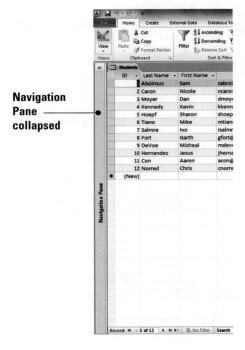

10. Click the Shutter Bar Open/Close Button to expand the Navigation Pane again.

PAUSE. LEAVE the database open to use in the next exercise.

The Navigation Pane divides your database objects into categories, and those categories contain groups. The default category is Tables and Related Views, which groups the objects in a database by the tables to which they are related. You can change the category to Object Type, which groups database objects by their type—tables, forms, reports, and so on.

Using Object Tabs

When you create a database in Access, all the objects in that database—including forms, tables, reports, and queries—are displayed in a single window separated by tabs. Tabs help keep open objects visible and accessible. To move among the open objects, click a tab. To close a tab, click its Close button. You can also right-click a tab to display the shortcut menu where you can save, close, close all, or switch views. In this exercise, you practice opening and displaying object tabs.

STEP BY STEP **Use Object Tabs**

USE the database you used in the previous exercise.

1. In the Navigation Pane, double-click **Student Details**. A new object tab opens to display the form, as shown in Figure 1-13.

Object tabs —

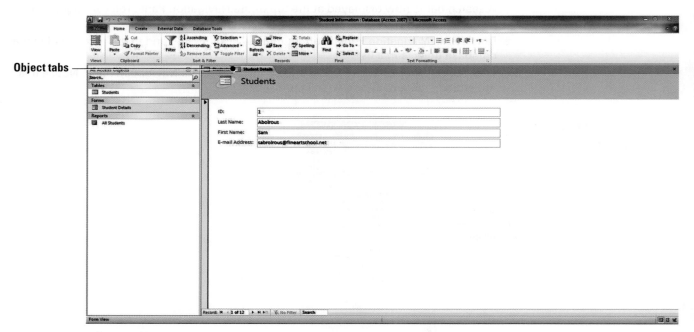

Figure 1-13

Tab with form

2. In the Navigation Pane, double-click **All Students**. A new object tab opens to display the report, as shown in Figure 1-14.

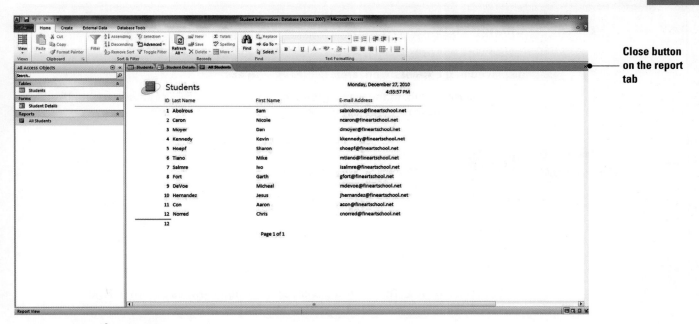

Close button on the report tab

Figure 1-14

Tab with report

3. Click the Close button on the Report tab to close it.
4. Right-click the Student Details tab to display the shortcut menu shown in Figure 1-15.

Figure 1-15

Tab shortcut menu

Right-click tab to display shortcut menu

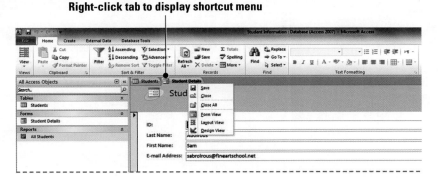

5. Click Close to close the form.

PAUSE. LEAVE the database open to use in the next exercise.

Changing Views

Each database object can be viewed several different ways. The main views for a table are Datasheet View and Design View. Datasheet View can be used to perform most table design tasks, so you will probably use it most often. A **datasheet** is the visual representation of the data contained in a table or of the results returned by a query. A query is simply a question you can ask a table or another query.

To change the view, click the View button's down arrow and then choose a view from the menu. When you change views, the commands available on the **Ribbon** change to match the tasks you will be performing in that view. You learn more about the Ribbon in the next section.

STEP BY STEP Change Views

USE the database you used in the previous exercise. The Students table should be displayed in the Access work area.

1. On the Home tab, in the Views group, click the View button's down arrow to display the menu shown in Figure 1-16.

Figure 1-16

View menu for a table

2. Click Design View. The table is displayed in Design View, as shown in Figure 1-17. Notice that the Design tab is now displayed on the Ribbon.

Contextual design commands

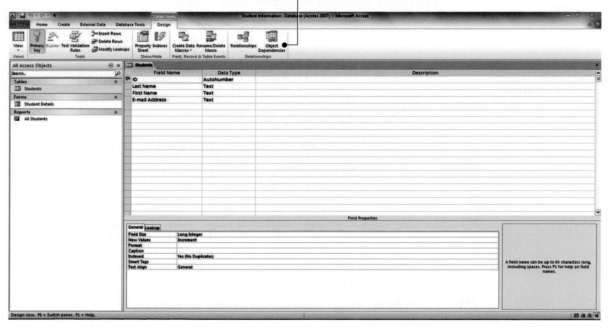

Figure 1-17

Table in Design View

3. On the Design tab, in the Views group, click the View button's down arrow, and then click Datasheet View.

4. Click the Fields tab under the Table Tools tab on the Ribbon to display the contextual commands for that view, as shown in Figure 1-18.

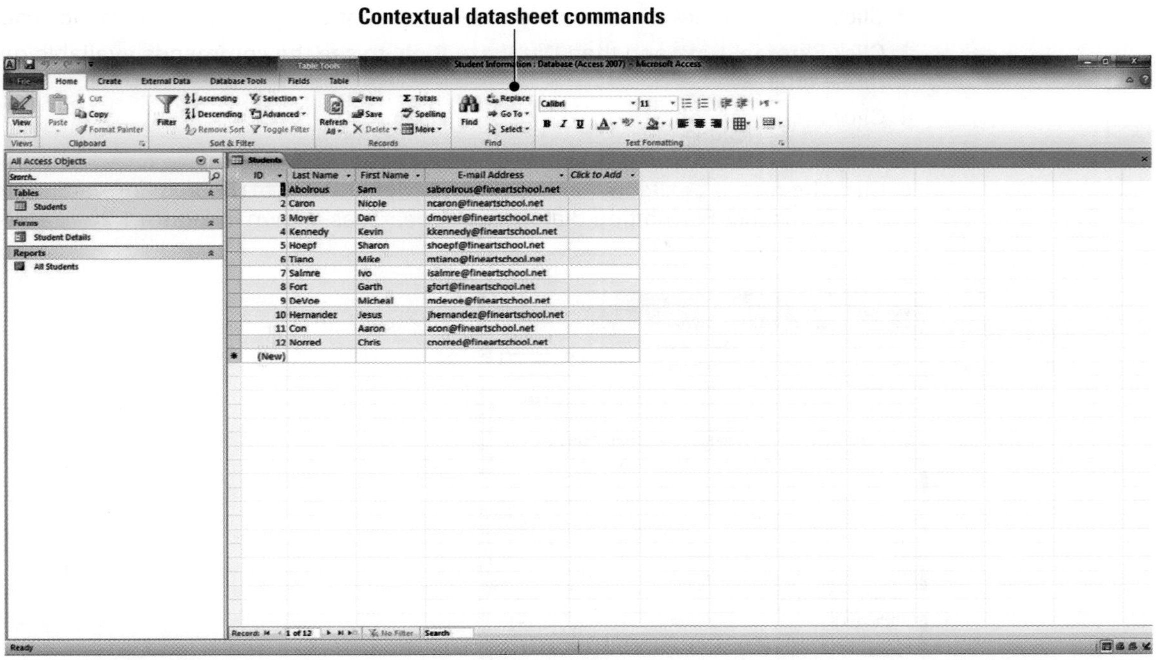

Contextual datasheet commands

Figure 1-18

Table in Datasheet View

PAUSE. LEAVE the database open to use in the next exercise.

USING THE ON-SCREEN TOOLS

The Bottom Line

Access has many tools to help with your database needs. In this section, you explore the Ribbon, which displays common commands in **groups** arranged by tabs. You'll also learn about other on-screen tools to help you get your work done faster, such as the **Quick Access Toolbar** and KeyTips.

Using the Ribbon

The Ribbon is located across the top of the screen and contains tabs and groups of commands. It is divided into five tabs, or areas of activity. Each tab contains groups of related commands. The Ribbon is contextual, which means it offers you commands related to the object that you are working on or the task that you are performing.

Some groups have a **dialog box launcher**, which is a small arrow in the lower-right corner of the group that you click to launch a dialog box that displays additional options or information. Some commands on the Ribbon have small arrows pointing down. These arrows indicate that a menu is available that lists more options from which you can choose.

In the next exercise you practice using the Ribbon.

STEP BY STEP   **Use the Ribbon**

USE the database you used in the previous exercise.

1. Click the **Home** tab to make it active. As shown in Figure 1-19, the Ribbon is divided into groups of commands.

Figure 1-19

The Ribbon

2. Click Create to make it the active tab. Notice that the groups of commands change.

3. Click External Data and then Database Tools to see the commands available on those tabs.

4. Click the Home tab.

5. Click the ID column header to select it.

6. Click the dialog box launcher in the lower-right corner of the Text Formatting group. The Datasheet Formatting dialog box appears, as shown in Figure 1-20.

Figure 1-20

Datasheet formatting dialog box

7. Click Cancel to close the dialog box.

8. Double-click the Home tab. Notice the groups are hidden to give you more screen space to work with your database.

9. Double-click Home again to display the groups.

PAUSE. LEAVE the database open to use in the next exercise.

NEW to Office 2010

New to Access 2010 is the ability to customize the Ribbon to have greater control over the commands that appear on it by turning off tabs and groups you rarely use, moving and/or duplicating groups from one tab to another, creating custom groups, and even creating custom tabs.

Using the Quick Access Toolbar

The Quick Access Toolbar contains the commands that you use most often, such as Save, Undo, and Redo.

Located on the Quick Access Toolbar is the Customize Quick Access Toolbar button that presents you with a menu that allows you to quickly add commonly used commands to the Quick Access Toolbar, as shown in Figure 1-21. You can also use this menu to choose an option to show the Quick Access Toolbar above or below the Ribbon, or click the More Commands button to open the Customize screen in the Access Options dialog box, as shown in Figure 1-22.

Figure 1-21

Customize Quick Access Toolbar menu

Customize Quick Access Toolbar button and menu

Figure 1-22

Customize the Quick Access
Toolbar screen of the Access
Options dialog box

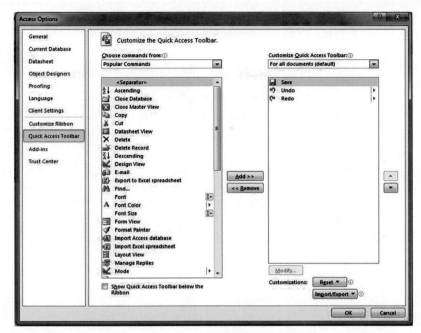

Use this dialog box to customize the Quick Access Toolbar by adding buttons from a greater variety of commands that you need the most so they are always just one click away.

In this exercise, you use the Customize Quick Access Toolbar menu to place the toolbar below the Ribbon.

STEP BY STEP **Use the Quick Access Toolbar**

USE the database you used in the previous exercise.

1. On the Quick Access Toolbar, click the Customize Quick Access Toolbar button. A menu appears.
2. Click Show Below the Ribbon. The toolbar is moved.
3. Click the Customize Quick Access Toolbar button again. Click Show Above the Ribbon.

PAUSE. LEAVE the database open to use in the next exercise.

Using KeyTips

When you press the Alt key, small letters and numbers called **KeyTips** appear on the Ribbon in small square labels, called **badges**. To execute a command using KeyTips, press the Alt key then press the KeyTip or sequence of KeyTips that corresponds to the command you want to use. Every command on the Ribbon has a KeyTip. You display KeyTips in the next exercise.

STEP BY STEP **Use KeyTips**

USE the database you used in the previous exercise.

1. Press **Alt**. Letters and numbers appear on the Ribbon to let you know which key to use to access commands or tabs. See Figure 1-23.

KeyTips

Figure 1-23

KeyTips

2. Press **C** to activate the Create tab.

3. Press **P** to display the Application Parts menu.

 Ref   You learn more about Application Parts in Lessons 2.

4. Press **Alt** to remove the KeyTips.

PAUSE. LEAVE the database open to use in the next exercise.

Take Note   Shortcut keys are keys or combinations of keys pressed together to perform a command. Shortcut keys provide a quick way to give commands without having to move your hands off the keyboard and reach for a mouse. Keyboard shortcuts from previous versions of Access that begin with Ctrl are the same. However, those that begin with Alt are different and require the use of KeyTips.

SOFTWARE ORIENTATION

Introducing the Backstage View

NEW to Office 2010

In Office 2010, Microsoft introduces the Backstage view. The Backstage view is on the File **tab** and contains many of the commands that were on the File menu in previous versions of Microsoft Access. The Backstage view enables you to do things to a database file including creating a new database, creating a database from a template, opening an existing database, and performing many database maintenance tasks. The Backstage view is the default view when you first open Microsoft Access. See Figure 1-24.

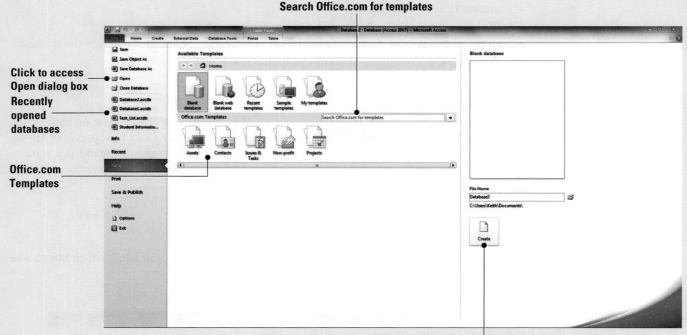

Figure 1-24

Backstage view

USING THE BACKSTAGE VIEW

The **File tab** on the Ribbon accesses the Backstage view—a menu of commands that you use for the common tasks performed with your database files—such as opening, saving, and printing. It also contains commands for managing and publishing your database.

Using the Backstage View

The File tab opens the Backstage view (Figure 1-24), a menu of basic commands and tabs for opening, saving, and printing files, as well as more advanced options. You can click commands to view related dialog boxes, as well as tabs to view more options within the Backstage view window.

The following is an overview of the commands and tabs in the Backstage view:

- **Save Object As:** Save the current object (such as a table, query, form, or report) as a new object.
- **Save Database As:** Save the current database object as a new object or save the database in another format that is compatible with earlier versions of Access.
- **Open:** Open an existing database.
- **Close Database:** Close the open database.
- **Info:** Compact and repair the database and encrypt the database with a password to restrict access.
- **Recent:** View a list of recently accessed databases.
- **New:** Create a new database from scratch or from available templates.
- **Print:** Quick print straight to the printer, open a dialog box from which to choose print options, or preview your document before printing.
- **Save & Publish:** Save the database to a document management server for sharing, or package the database and apply a digital signature.
- **Help:** View Microsoft Office support resources, the Options menu, and check for updates.
- **Options:** View the Options menu to customize language, display, and other settings.
- **Exit:** Exit the Access application.

You practice using the Backstage view in the next exercise.

STEP BY STEP   **Use the Backstage View**

1. **USE** the database you used in the previous exercise.

   Click the **File** tab. Backstage view opens, displaying a menu of commands and tabs down the left side of the window, as shown in Figure 1-25.

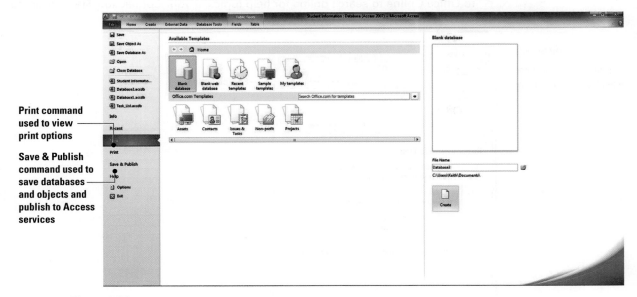

Print command used to view print options

Save & Publish command used to save databases and objects and publish to Access services

Figure 1-25

Backstage view's Print and Save & Publish commands

2. Click the Save & Publish command to view the options available.

3. Click the Print command to view more options.

4. Click the File tab again to remove the menu.

PAUSE. LEAVE the database open to use in the next exercise.

USING THE MICROSOFT OFFICE ACCESS HELP BUTTON

The Bottom Line

If you have questions, Microsoft Access Help has answers. In fact, you can choose whether you want to use the help topics on your computer that were installed with Office, or if you are connected to the Internet, you can choose to use the help that is available online. Either way, you can key in search words, browse help topics, or choose a topic from the Table of Contents to get your answers. In this exercise, you use the Help button to access the Help information installed on your computer with Access 2010.

Using the Help Button and Connection Status Command

The **Connection Status menu** in the lower-right corner of Access Help lets you choose between the help topics that are available online and the help topics installed in your computer offline. If you are usually connected to the Internet, you might prefer to set the Connection Status to Show content from Office Online to get the most updated help available. But there may be times when you can't or don't want to be online; in those instances you can choose Show content only from this computer to get offline help topics. You practice using Access Help and the Connection Status menu in the next exercise.

STEP BY STEP **Use the Help Button and Connection Status Command**

Take Note

When you rest the mouse pointer over a command on the Ribbon, a ScreenTip appears displaying the name of the command. Access 2010 also has Enhanced ScreenTips, which give more information about the command, as well as a Help button you can click to get more help.

USE the database you used in the previous exercise.

1. Click the Microsoft Office Access Help button. 🔲 The Access Help dialog box appears, as shown in Figure 1-26. Notice the Search button and Search menu button. The Search menu is used to specify the scope of topics you want to search, such as All Access, Access Templates, Access Training, and so on. Also notice the Connection Status command in the lower-right corner indicates that Access is set to Connected to Office Online to search online for help topics. If your Connection Status is set to Offline, the screen will look different.

Figure 1-26

Access Help dialog box when connected to Office online

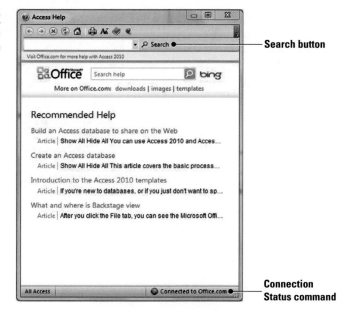

Search button

Connection Status command

2. Click the Connection Status button. A menu appears, as shown in Figure 1-27.

Figure 1-27

Access Help dialog box and
Connection Status menu

3. Click Show content only from this computer. Access Help appears, as shown in Figure 1-28.

Figure 1-28

Access Help dialog box
when Offline

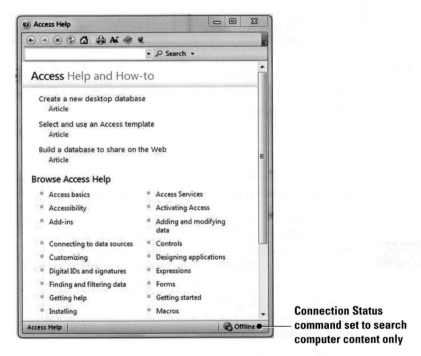

Connection Status
command set to search
computer content only

4. Key ribbon in the text box and click Search. A list of possible topics appears.

5. Click the Customize the Ribbon link in the search results that appear. The help topic appears.

6. Click the Show Table of Contents button ![button]. The Table of Contents pane appears.

7. Click the Getting started option in the Table of Contents pane to expand it and then click the What's new in Microsoft Access link. The text for the topic appears in the window.

8. Click the Home button  and then the Access basics link that appears. The text for the topic appears in the window, as shown in Figure 1-29.

Figure 1-29

Access Help with Table of Contents and topics displayed

Show/Hide Table of Contents button

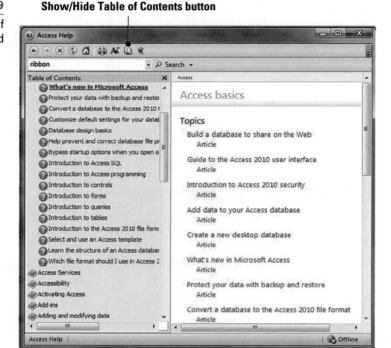

Another Way
The Access Help button is positioned in some dialog boxes and ScreenTips for quick access to context-related help. Click it wherever you see it to launch Access Help.

9. Click the Home button.

10. Click the Close button to close Microsoft Access Help.

STOP. CLOSE the database.

The Bottom Line

DEFINING DATA NEEDS AND TYPES

To create a database that achieves your goals and provides you with up-to-date, accurate information, you need to spend time planning and designing it.

When planning a database, the first step is to consider the purpose of your database. You need to design the database so that it accommodates all your data processing and reporting needs. You should gather and organize all the information that you want to include, starting with any existing forms or lists, and think about the reports and mailings you might want to create using the data.

Once you have decided how the information will be used, the next step is to categorize the information by dividing it into subjects such as Products or Orders, which become the tables in your database. Each table should only contain information that relates to that subject. If you find yourself adding extra information, create a new table.

In a database table, data is stored in rows and columns—similar in appearance to a spreadsheet. Each row in a table is called a **record**. Each column in a table is called a **field**. For example, if a table is named "Student List," each record (row) contains information about a different student and each field (column) contains a different type of information, such as last name or email address.

To create the columns within the table, you then need to determine what information you want to store in the table—such as Color, Year, or Cost. Break each piece of information into the smallest useful part—for example, use First Name and Last Name instead of just Name if you want to sort, search, calculate, or report using the separate pieces of information.

For each table, you will choose a primary key. A **primary key** is a column that uniquely identifies each row, such as Item Number.

Defining Table Fields

To define table fields, you establish which data needs to be stored in the table. Planning is an important part of creating a database. In this exercise, you open a database that is further along in the process of being developed to see what a more advanced database looks like.

Define Table Fields

@ The *Student Data* file for this lesson is available on the book companion website or in WileyPLUS.

OPEN the *Student Data* database from the data files for this lesson.

1. On the Student List form, click the ID for record 5 to display the Student Details dialog box for Sharon Hoepf, as shown in Figure 1-30.

Figure 1-30

Student Details

WileyPLUS Extra! features an online tutorial of this task.

2. Click the Guardian Information tab and then the Emergency Information tab. Each of the fields on these tabs is an example of the type of information that could be contained in a database table.
3. Click Close to close the Student Details dialog box.

PAUSE. LEAVE the database open to use in the next exercise.

(X) Ref   You learn more about defining and modifying a primary key in Lesson 3.

Defining and Modifying Data Types for Fields

When designing the database, you set a **data type** for each field (column) that you create to match the information it will store. A data type controls the type of data a field will contain—whether it is text, number, date/time, or some other type. When defining table fields, it is important to define them as specifically as possible. For example, if you are using a number, you should determine whether you need to use the Currency or Number data type. Or, if you need to store large amounts of text, you may need to use the Memo data type instead of Text. Sometimes you may also need to modify data types for preexisting fields. In this exercise, you practice reviewing and modifying data types.

When you create a new field in a table and then enter data in it, Office Access 2010 automatically tries to detect the appropriate data type for the new column. For example, if you key a price, such as $10, Access recognizes the data as a price, and sets the data type for the field to Currency. If Access doesn't have enough information from what you enter to guess the data type, the data type is set to Text.

NEW to Office 2010

New to Access 2010 is the calculated data type. The calculated data type creates a new field that can store formulas and expressions, which can perform logical, text, or mathematical calculations on existing fields within the same table and make it easy to add the calculated field to a form, query, or report. For example, you can easily create a calculated field named *FullName* that concatenates the *First Name* and *Last Name* fields into one string. Then, the *FullName* field can easily be added to a form, query, or report without having to create a new expression within the object.

Take Note

Most database management systems can store only a single value in a field, but with Microsoft Office Access 2010, you can create a field that holds multiple values, which may be appropriate in certain situations.

STEP BY STEP | **Review and Modify Data Types for Fields**

USE the database you used in the previous exercise.

1. Close the Student List form.
2. In the Navigation Pane, in the Supporting Objects group, double-click the Students table to open it.
3. Click the Date of Birth field header.
4. On the Ribbon, click the Fields tab. Notice in the Formatting group that the Data Type is Date/Time.
5. Click the down arrow in the Format box to display the menu of formatting options for that type, as shown in Figure 1-31.

Figure 1-31

Format options for Date/Time data type

6. Click the Last Name header. Notice that the Data Type is Text and that no formatting options are available for that data type.
7. Scroll to the right and click the Address header.
8. In the Data Type box, click the down arrow and click Text to modify the data type. When a warning message appears, click Yes.

Take Note

Be aware that changing a data type might cut off some or all of the data in a field, and in some cases may remove the data entirely.

9. Scroll to the far right and click the Click to Add <Click to Add ⌄> column header. In the Data Type box, click Yes/No.
10. Click the down arrow in the Format box to display the menu of formatting options for the Yes/No data type, as shown in Figure 1-32.

Figure 1-32

Format options for Yes/No data type

11. Click outside the menu to close it.

PAUSE. LEAVE the database open to use in the next exercise.

Access provides eleven different data types, each with its own purpose. The list in Table 1-1 describes the types of data that each field can be set to store.

Table 1-1

Types of data stored in fields

Data Type	Example	Description
Text	Last Name: Zimmerman Street: 6789 Walker Street	The most common data type for fields. Can store up to 255 characters of text, numbers, or a combination of both.
Memo	Comments: Student will make monthly payments on the 15th of each month of $247.	Stores large amounts of text—up to 64,000 characters of text, numbers, or a combination (although if you use that much space, your database will run slowly).
Number	Age: 19	Stores numeric data that can be used in mathematical calculations.
Date/Time	Birthday: December 1, 1987	Stores date and/or time data.
Currency	Registration Fee: $50.00	Stores monetary data with precision to four decimal places. Use this data type to store financial data and when you don't want Access to round values.
AutoNumber	Student ID: 56	Unique values created by Access when you create a new record. Tables often contain an *AutoNumber* field used as the primary key.
Yes/No	Insurance: Yes	Stores Boolean (true or false) data. Access uses 1 for all Yes values and 0 for all No values.
OLE Object	Photo	Stores images, documents, graphs, and other objects from Office and Windows-based programs.
Hyperlink	Web addresses	Stores links to websites, sites or files on an intranet or Local Area Network (LAN), and sites or files on your computer.
Attachment	Any supported type of file	You can attach images, spreadsheet files, documents, charts, and other types of supported files to the records in your database, much like you attach files to email messages.
Calculated	FullName: John Derenzo	Stores an expression based on two or more fields within the same table.

Take Note   The Number data type should only be used if the numbers will be used in mathematical calculations. For numbers such as phone numbers, use the Text data type.

 Ref   You learn more about multivalued fields in Lesson 4.

Defining Database Tables

Tables are the most basic organizational element of a database. Not only is it important to plan the tables to hold the type of data you need, but also to plan how the tables and information will be connected.

STEP BY STEP   **Define Database Tables**

USE the database you used in the previous exercise.

1. On the Database Tools tab, in the Relationships section, click Relationship to display a visual representation of the relationship between the Students and Guardians tables, as shown in Figure 1-33.

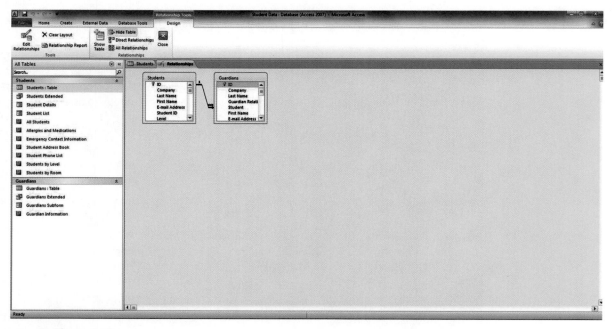

Figure 1-33

Relationship between tables

2. Close the Relationships tab.
3. Close the Students tab.

STOP. CLOSE the database.

In a simple database, you might only have one table, but most databases will have more. The tables you include in a database will be based on the data available. For example, a database of students might have a table for contact information, one for grades, and one for tuition and fees.

In database applications like Access, you can create a relational database. A **relational database** stores information in separate tables that are connected or linked by a defined relationship that ties the data together.

 Ref   You learn more about table relationships in Lesson 3.

An important principle to consider when planning a database is to try to record each piece of information only once. Duplicate information, or **redundant data**, wastes space and increases the likelihood of errors. Relationships among database tables help ensure consistency and reduce repetitive data entry.

As you create each table, keep in mind how the data in the tables are related to each other. Enter test data and then add fields to tables or create new tables as necessary to refine the database. The last step is to apply data normalization rules to see if your tables are structured correctly and make adjustments as needed. **Normalization** is the process of applying rules to your database design to ensure that you have divided your information items into the appropriate tables.

Database design principles include standards and guidelines that can be used to determine if your database is structured correctly. These are referred to as **normal forms**. There are five normal forms, but typically only the first three are applied, because that is usually all that is required. The following is a summary of the first three normal forms:

- **First Normal Form (1NF)**: Break each field down into the smallest meaningful value, remove repeating groups of data, and create a separate table for each set of related data.
- **Second Normal Form (2NF)**: Each nonkey column should be fully dependent on the entire primary key. Create new tables for data that applies to more than one record in a table and add a related field to the table.
- **Third Normal Form (3NF)**: Remove fields that do not relate to, or provide a fact about, the primary key.

Data can be brought into an Access database in a number of ways, including linking and importing. When defining tables, you have to decide whether data should be linked to or imported from external sources. When you import data, Access creates a copy of the data or objects in the destination database without altering the source. Linking lets you connect to data from another source without importing it, so that you can view and modify the latest data in both the source and destination databases without creating and maintaining two copies of the same data. Any changes you make to the data in the source are reflected in the linked table in the destination database, and vice versa.

SKILL SUMMARY

In This Lesson, You Learned How To:
Get started
Work in the Access window
Use the on-screen tools
Use the Backstage view
Use the Microsoft Office Access help button
Define data needs and types

Knowledge Assessment

Matching

Match the term in Column 1 to its description in Column 2.

Column 1	Column 2
1. record	a. most basic database object; stores data in categories
2. field	b. database object that presents information in a format that is easy to read and print
3. redundant data	c. duplicate information in a database
4. primary key	d. row in a database table
5. database	e. database object that enables stored data to be searched and retrieved
6. table	f. column in a database that uniquely identifies each row
7. query	g. database object that simplifies the process of entering, editing, and displaying data
8. report	h. column in a database table
9. form	i. kind of information a field contains
10. data type	j. tool for collecting and organizing information

True/False

Circle T if the statement is true or F if the statement is false.

T F 1. Any list you make for a specific purpose can be considered a simple database, even a grocery list.

T F 2. By default, the Navigation Pane appears on the right side of the Access screen each time you create or open a database.

T F 3. Forms, queries, and reports are examples of database objects.

T F 4. The dialog box launcher contains the commands that you use most often, such as Save, Undo, and Redo.

T F 5. When you press the Shift key, small letters and numbers called KeyTips appear on the Ribbon.

T F 6. The Connection Status menu lets you choose between the help topics that are available online and the help topics installed in your computer offline.

T F 7. In a database table, data is stored in rows and columns—similar in appearance to a spreadsheet.

T F 8. Each field in a table must be designated for a particular data type.

T F 9. An important principle to consider when planning a database is to try to record each piece of information as many times as possible for easy access.

T F 10. Normalization is the process of applying rules to your database design to ensure that you have divided your information items into the appropriate tables.

Competency Assessment

Project 1-1: Personalizing Access

When working in Access or another Microsoft Office application, it is useful to personalize your copy of the software. Personalizing your software helps credit you as the creator of the Access database or other Office application.

GET READY. LAUNCH Access if it is not already running.

1. Click the File tab.
2. Click the Options button to display the Access Options dialog box.

Take Note

Throughout this lesson you will see information that appears in black text within brackets, such as [Press **Enter**], or [your e-mail address]. The information contained in the brackets is intended to be directions for you rather than something you actually type word-for-word. It will instruct you to perform an action or substitute text. Do **not** type the actual text that appears within brackets.

3. In the *Personalize your copy of Microsoft Office* section of the dialog box, key [your name] in the User name box and key [your initials] in the Initials box.
4. Click OK to close the dialog box.

LEAVE Access open for the next project.

Project 1-2: Using the Navigation Pane

As a busy editor at Lucerne Publishing, you use Access to organize and manage your task list.

GET READY. LAUNCH Access if it is not already running.

@ The *task_list* file for this lesson is available on the book companion website or in WileyPLUS.

1. **OPEN** *task_list* from the data files for this lesson.
2. Click the Shutter Bar Open/Close Button to display the Navigation Pane.
3. Click the Contacts group header in the Navigation Pane to display those database objects.
4. Click the Supporting Objects group header to display those database objects.
5. In the Supporting Objects group, double-click Tasks to open that table.
6. In the Tasks group, double-click Tasks By Assigned To to open that report.
7. In the Navigation Pane, click the Tasks Navigation header to display the menu and then click Object Type.
8. **CLOSE** the database.

LEAVE Access open for the next project.

Proficiency Assessment

Project 1-3: Understanding Database Design

You work at Margie's Travel, a full-service travel agency that specializes in providing services to senior citizens. You plan to create a database of tours, cruises, adventure activities, group travel, and vacation packages geared toward seniors, but first you want to learn more about database design.

GET READY. LAUNCH Access if it is not already running.

1. Open Access Help.
2. Search for database design.
3. Read the article about database design basics.

4. **OPEN** a new Word document.

5. List the steps that should be taken when designing a database with a short description of each.

6. **SAVE** the document as *database_design* and then **CLOSE** the file.

LEAVE Access open for the next project.

Project 1-4: Planning Table Fields

You are a volunteer for the Tech Terrace Neighborhood Association that holds an annual March Madness 5K Run. In the past, all data has been kept on paper, but you decide it would be more efficient to create a database. Decide what fields would make sense for a table holding data about the runners.

GET READY. LAUNCH Access if it is not already running.

1. Think about what fields would be useful in a database table that contains information about the runners in an annual 5K road race.

2. **OPEN** a new Word document.

3. In the document, key a list of the names of at least six possible field names.

4. **SAVE** the document as *race_fields* and keep the file open.

LEAVE Access open for the next project.

Mastery Assessment

Project 1-5: Planning Data Types for Fields

Now that you have decided what fields to use in a database table containing information about runners in an annual 5K road race, you need to determine what data type should be used for each field.

USE the document you used in the previous project.

1. Beneath the name of each possible field name for the table about runners in the annual 5K road race, key the data type that would be used with a short explanation of why you chose that type.

2. **SAVE** the document as *data_type* and then **CLOSE** the file.

LEAVE Access open for the next project.

Project 1-6: What's New in Microsoft Access 2010

Your supervisor at Margie's Travel has suggested that you research what's new in Access 2010 before you begin to create a database.

GET READY. LAUNCH Access if it is not already running.

1. Open the Backstage view and access the Help menu.

2. Use Access Help to locate the article "What's New in Microsoft Access."

3. Read the overview.

CLOSE Access.

INTERNET READY

On the Help menu in the Backstage view there is a Getting Started option, as shown in Figure 1-34. Use Access Help to find out what this section offers and how to get the latest online content while working in Office 2010 by turning on automatic updates.

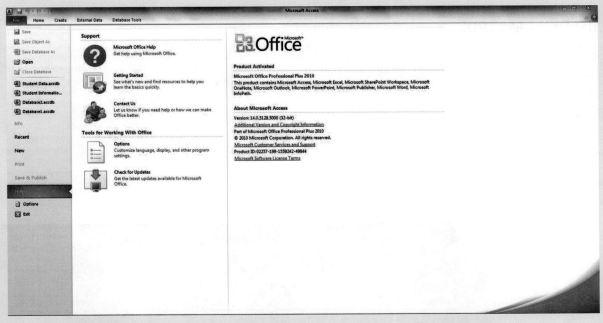

Figure 1-34

Backstage view Help menu

Workplace *Ready*

WORKING WITH TEMPLATES IN ACCESS

In today's business world, it can be overwhelming to keep up with the different types of data that a company needs to collect, organize, and report. Sales invoices, client contacts, employee files, vendor information—the list seems endless. You can customize the templates available in Access to meet your business needs and save the time it would take to create database objects from scratch.

In your position as the technical support director for the A. Datum Corporation, you are responsible for coordinating technical support for the company. You can streamline your work by downloading an Access template to use as a starting point and then modifying it to track critical data. Using the Issues database, you can set up, organize, and track technical service requests submitted by people in your organization. You can then assign, prioritize, and follow the progress of issues from start to finish.

The database template contains various predefined tables—such as Issues and Contacts—that you can use to enter data. Such tables may be functional just as they are. But, as you work, chances are that you will need to create tables that are more specific to the needs of your company.

The Issues database template, like all others in Microsoft Office Access 2010, also includes predesigned forms, reports, and queries that can be used as they are. This not only saves time, but also enables you to see a complete database system developed by professionals so you can be sure you are capturing essential business information in a logical and efficient manner.

2 Create Database Tables

LESSON SKILL MATRIX

In This Lesson, You Will Learn The Following Skills:

Creating a Database

Creating a Table

Saving a Database Object

KEY TERMS

- **Application Parts**
- **Quick Start**
- **template**

As an assistant curator at the Baldwin Museum of Science, you are responsible for the day-to-day management of the insect collection, including duties such as sorting and organizing specimens, as well as supervising the mounting and labeling of the insects. The insect collection catalog has never been transferred to an electronic database. Because you have experience with database management, part of your responsibility is to create a database to store the information about the specimens and collections, as well as museum exhibits and events, a task perfectly suited to Access 2010. In this lesson, you learn how to create a blank database and how to use a template to create a database. You also learn how to create a table from a template, how to create a table by copying the structure from another table, and how to save a database object.

SOFTWARE ORIENTATION

Getting Started with Microsoft Access

The New tab in the Backstage view, shown in Figure 2-1, provides options for creating a database. This is the default view after starting Access. The Backstage view is also where you can create a new, blank database. Use this figure as a reference throughout this lesson as well as the rest of this book.

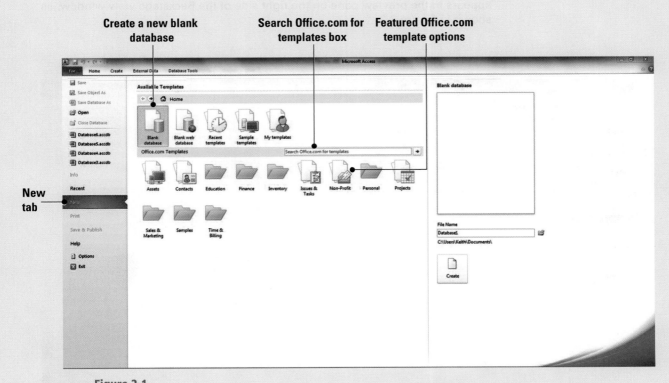

Figure 2-1

New tab in Backstage view

CREATING A DATABASE

The Bottom Line

In Microsoft Office Access 2010, the process of creating a new database is easier than ever. You can create a database using one of the many available **templates** (ready-to-use databases that contain all of the tables, queries, forms, and reports needed for performing specific tasks) or by creating a new blank database.

Using a Template to Create a Database

Access offers a variety of templates to help get you started. Some templates are immediately available for your use since they are built into Access, while you can easily download others from Office.com. Microsoft or users have created the templates found at Office.com. User-submitted templates have a specific thumbnail associated with them, as outlined in Figure 2-4. Built-in and Office.com templates are available that can be used to track issues, manage contacts, or keep a record of expenses. Some templates contain a few sample records to help demonstrate their use. You can use templates as is, or you can customize them to better suit your purposes. In this exercise, you use one of the many available templates to create a database.

STEP BY STEP   **Use a Template to Create a Database**

GET READY. Before you begin these steps, be sure that you are logged on to the Internet. **LAUNCH** Microsoft Access to display the Backstage view.

1. In the center of the Backstage view window, in the *Search Office.com for Templates* box, key **Personal** and press **Enter** on the keyboard.

2. In the list of Office.com Personal templates that appears in the middle of the Backstage view results pane, click **Home inventory**. A preview of the selected template appears in the preview pane on the right side of the Backstage view window, as shown in Figure 2-2.

Information about selected template displayed

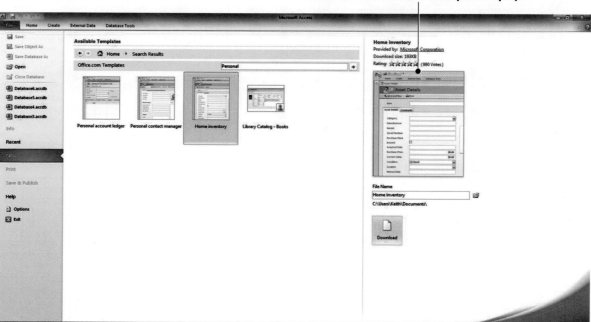

Figure 2-2

Office.com Personal templates

3. In the Office.com templates search box, key **Education** and press **Enter** on the keyboard.

4. In the list of Office.com Education templates that appears, click **Faculty**. Your screen should look similar to Figure 2-3.

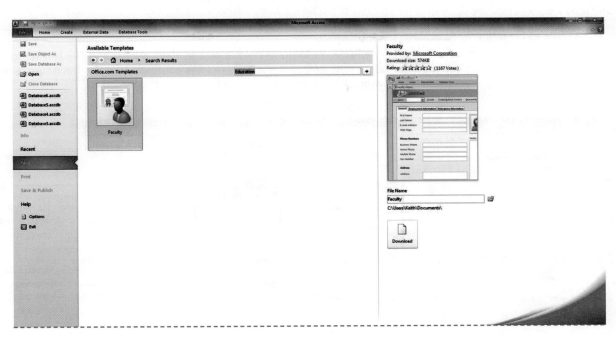

Figure 2-3

Office.com Faculty template

5. In the Office.com templates search box, key in **Assets** and press **Enter** on the keyboard. Your screen should look similar to Figure 2-4.

Office.com
user-submitted template

Office.com
Microsoft template

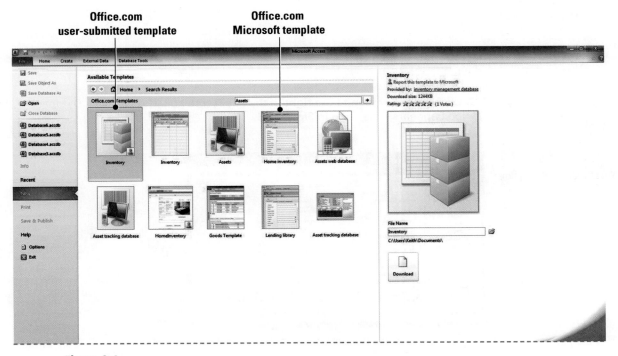

Figure 2-4

Office.com Assets templates

6. In the list of Office.com Business templates in the middle, click **Asset tracking database**.

Take Note

Throughout this lesson you will see information that appears in black text within brackets, such as [Press **Enter**], or [your e-mail address]. The information contained in the brackets is intended to be directions for you rather than something you actually type word-for-word. It will instruct you to perform an action or substitute text. Do **not** type the actual text that appears within brackets.

7. In the preview pane on the right of the Backstage view, click in the **File Name** box and key [your initials] at the end of the suggested file name, so that the file name is now **Assets XXX** (where XXX is your initials), as shown in Figure 2-5.

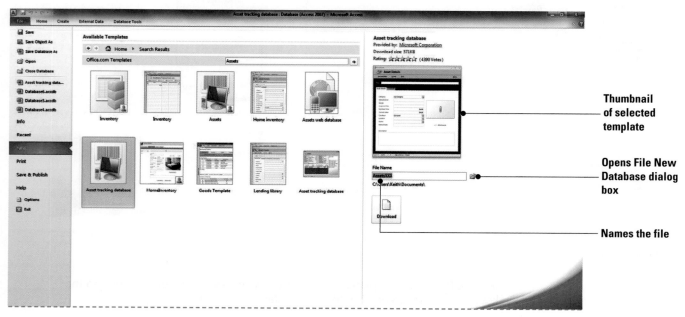

Figure 2-5

File Name box and folder icon

Take Note

If you do not add an extension to your database file name, Access does it for you—for example, *AccessXXX.accdb*.

8. Click the **folder** icon to the right of the File Name box. The File New Database dialog box appears, as shown in Figure 2-6.

Figure 2-6

File New Database dialog box

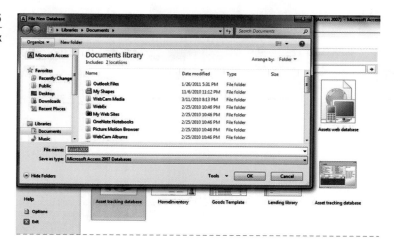

9. Navigate to the location where you want to save the file and click **OK**.

Take Note

You should save your files in a separate directory from where your data files are stored. This will ensure that you don't overwrite the original data files with your updated files. Check with your instructor to see if she wants you to save your work on a flash drive or in a particular network directory.

10. Click the Download button at the bottom of the Preview pane. The Downloading Template dialog box opens and indicates that the template is being downloaded, as shown in Figure 2-7. When the download is complete, the dialog box closes.

Figure 2-7

Downloading Template dialog box

11. Access creates and then opens the AccessXXX database. Getting Started and Access 2007 Help windows may appear, which contain helpful videos and links about using the Asset tracking database. Close these windows, if necessary, to return to the AccessXXX database with the Asset List table active, as shown in Figure 2-8. Click to place the insertion point in the first cell of the *Item* field and key Canon EOS Rebel 300D.

Access 2007 on the title bar specifies format of databases created with Access 2010, not the version

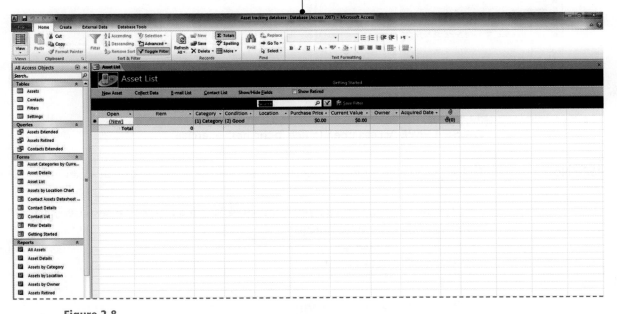

Figure 2-8

Assets template database

Take Note

When you open an Access database template that was created in Access 2007 (such as the Asset tracking database), Access may open the Access 2007 Help menu as well.

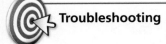 **Troubleshooting** If you are asked to enable the content, click the Enable Content button on the Security Warning Message Bar. By default, Access blocks potentially harmful content that might contain viruses or present other security issues. This content should only be enabled if the database is downloaded from a trustworthy site, like Microsoft Office Online.

12. Click the Shutter Bar Open/Close Button, if necessary, to display the Navigation Pane, as shown in Figure 2-9, to see all the objects in the database.

Shutter Bar
Open/Close Button

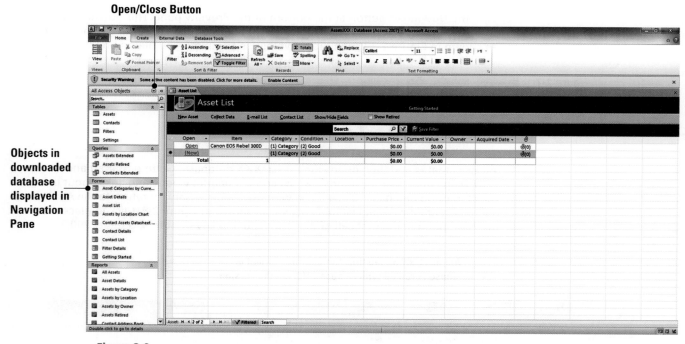

Objects in
downloaded
database
displayed in
Navigation
Pane

Figure 2-9

Assets database with
Navigation Pane displayed

13. CLOSE the database.

PAUSE. LEAVE Access open to use in the next exercise.

Take Note   Unless you choose a different folder, Access uses the following default locations to store your databases:

- Microsoft Windows Server 2008, Microsoft Windows 7, and Microsoft Windows Vista—c:\Users\user name\Documents

- Microsoft Windows Server 2003 or Microsoft Windows XP—c:\Documents and Settings\user name\My Documents

Creating a Blank Database

If you have existing data, you may decide that it is easier to create a blank database rather than using a template, because it would require a lot of work to adapt your existing data to the template's defined data structure. When you create a new blank database, Access opens a database that contains a table where you can enter data, but it creates no other database objects. By default, Access creates a primary key field named "ID" for all new datasheets, and it sets the data type for the field to AutoNumber. In this exercise, you create a new blank database.

STEP BY STEP   **Create a Blank Database**

GET READY. The Backstage view should be on the screen from the previous exercise.

1. Click the Blank database icon in the Available Templates section of Backstage view. A Blank database thumbnail image appears in the Preview pane, as shown in Figure 2-10.

Blank Database pane

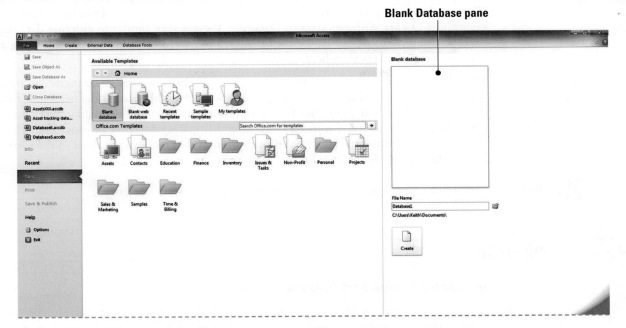

Figure 2-10

Blank database pane

2. In the File Name box below the thumbnail, key **Blank Database XXX** (where XXX is your initials).

3. If you want to save the file in a location other than the one shown beneath the File Name box, click the folder icon to the right of the File Name box and browse to a different location.

4. Click the **Create** button to create the blank database in your chosen location. Access creates the database, and then opens an empty table named Table1 in Datasheet View, as shown in Figure 2-11.

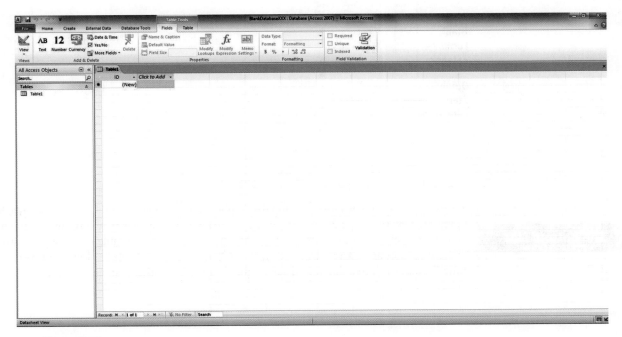

Figure 2-11

New blank database

PAUSE. LEAVE the database open to use in the next exercise.

 Ref You learn more about defining and modifying a primary key in Lesson 3.

With the insertion point in the first empty cell of your new, blank database, you can begin keying to add data. Entering data in Datasheet View is very similar to entering data into an Excel worksheet, except that data must be entered in related rows and columns, starting at the upper-left corner of the datasheet.

The table is structured through rows and columns, which become meaningful as you enter appropriate data. Anytime you add a new column to the table, Access defines a new field for that column's data. You do not need to format your data by including blank rows or columns, as you might do in an Excel worksheet, because that just wastes space in your table. The table merely contains your data. All visual presentation of that data will be done in the forms and reports that you design later.

 Ref   You learn more about creating forms and reports in Lessons 5 and 6.

SOFTWARE ORIENTATION

Templates Group and Application Parts

The Templates group on the Create tab contains the Application Parts gallery that you can use to insert predefined templates consisting of objects like tables, forms, and reports into a preexisting database. Use Figure 2-12 as a reference throughout this lesson as well as the rest of this book.

Figure 2-12

Application Parts gallery

Application Parts button accesses gallery

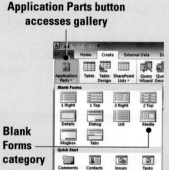

Blank Forms category

Quick Start category

CREATING A TABLE

The Bottom Line

It is easy to create a new table by using the Application Parts gallery and Quick Start. **Application Parts** are new to Access 2010 and consist of predefined templates that you can add to an existing database to help extend its functionality. Another way to create a table is to copy the structure of an existing table and paste it into the database. You can copy a database object and paste it into the same database or into a different database that is open in another instance of Access.

Using the Application Parts Gallery and Quick Start

Application parts vary from a single table to a collection of database objects like tables, forms, and reports. The Application Parts gallery consists of two categories, Blank Forms and Quick Start. The Blank Forms category contains a collection of form parts that allows you to add predefined forms to a database. The **Quick Start** category of these templates contains a collection of predefined objects arranged by parts for tracking things such as comments, contacts, and issues. In this exercise, you will quickly create a table using the Application Parts Gallery and Quick Start.

STEP BY STEP   **Create a Table Using the Application Parts Gallery and Quick Start**

USE the database that is open from the previous exercise.

1. On the Create tab, in the Templates group, click the Application Parts button to display the gallery shown in Figure 2-13.

Figure 2-13

Application Parts gallery

2. In the Quick Start section of the gallery, click Comments. Click Yes on the Microsoft Access dialog box that appears asking to close all open objects before instantiating this application part to close the empty table that appeared when you created the blank database in the previous exercise, and return to the Blank database screen with the Comments table open.

3. In the Navigation Pane, double-click Comments to display the newly created table with fields for comments, as shown in Figure 2-14. Close the Comments table by clicking on the Comments table close button.

Comments table tab

New table object named Comments in Navigation Pane

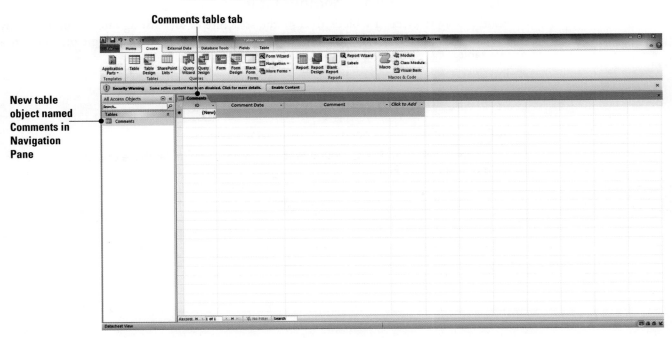

Figure 2-14

New Comments table for comments

4. On the Application Parts menu, click Contacts. In the Create Relationship dialog box that appears, select the There is no relationship radio button then click Create. A new table is created along with supporting forms and report objects, as shown in Figure 2-15.

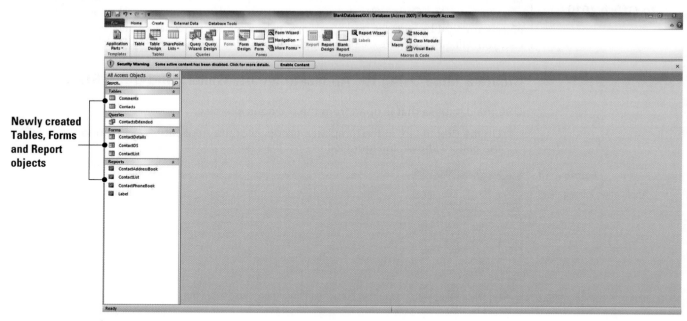

Newly created Tables, Forms and Report objects

Figure 2-15

New table, forms, and reports for contacts

PAUSE. LEAVE the database open to use in the next exercise.

Creating a Table from Another Table

Another way to create a table is to copy the structure of an existing table using the Copy and Paste commands. In this exercise, you copy the structure of an existing table to create a new table.

STEP BY STEP | **Create a Table from Another Table**

USE the database that is open from the previous exercise.

1. On the Navigation Pane, right-click the Comments table database object to display the menu shown in Figure 2-16.

Figure 2-16

Database object menu

Right-click to display menu

Another Way
You can also copy a database object by selecting it in the Navigation Pane and pressing Ctrl+C. Or on the Home tab, in the Clipboard group, you can click the Copy button.

2. Click **Copy**.

3. Right-click in a blank area of the Navigation Pane and, in the shortcut menu that appears, click **Paste** (see Figure 2-17).

Figure 2-17

Shortcut menu

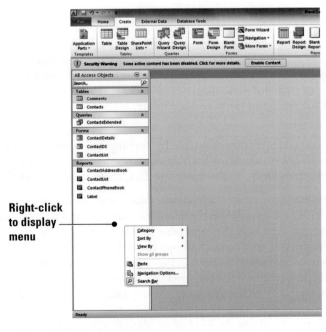

Right-click to display menu

Another Way
You can also paste a database object by selecting the destination location in the Navigation Pane and pressing Ctrl+V. Or on the Home tab, in the Clipboard group, you can click the Paste button.

4. The Paste Table As dialog box appears, as shown in Figure 2-18. Notice the default name, **Copy Of Comments**, in the Table Name box.

Figure 2-18

Paste Table As dialog box

5. In the Paste Options section, select the Structure Only radio button, to paste only the table's structure, rather than pasting a copy of the table's data along with its structure.

6. Click OK.

7. The new table appears at the end of the list of database table objects in the Navigation Pane, as shown in Figure 2-19.

Figure 2-19

New table copied from existing table

New copied table appears at the end of the list of database objects

8. Double-click Copy Of Comments to open the new table. Notice that the structure of the new table is the same as the table from which it was copied.

PAUSE. CLOSE the database.

LEAVE Access open for the next project.

When you create a copy of a table by copying and pasting, you have the option of re-creating just the table's structure, or both its structure and data. To paste just the structure of the table, click Structure Only. To also paste the data, click Structure and Data.

As you learned in Lesson 1, a relational database stores information in separate tables that are connected or linked by a defined relationship that ties the data together. When you add a new table to an existing database, that new table stands alone until you relate it to your existing tables. For example, say you need to track orders placed by a distributor. To do that, you add a table named Distributor Contacts to a sales database. To take advantage of the power that a relational database can provide—to search for the orders placed by a given contact, for example—you must create a relationship between the new table and any tables that contain the order data.

 Ref   You learn more about defining table relationships in Lesson 3.

SAVING A DATABASE OBJECT

The Bottom Line

Access automatically saves data that you have entered any time you add an Application Part like a Quick Start template, move to a new record, close an object or database, or quit the application. But you will need to save the design of a table, or any other database object, after it is created. Additionally, using the Save Object As command in the Backstage view, you can create a duplicate of a database object (like a table, query, or report) by specifying an alternate name.

Saving a Table

When you save a new table for the first time, give it a name that describes the information it contains. You can use up to 64 characters (letters or numbers), including spaces. For example, you might name a table Orders 2011, Clients, Tasks, Inventory Parts, or Comments. In this exercise, you save a database table and then use the Save Object As command to create a duplicate of the same table.

STEP BY STEP   **Save a Table**

GET READY. The Backstage view should be on the screen from the previous exercise.

1. If necessary, click the New command, then click the Blank database icon; a Blank Database thumbnail appears in the Preview pane.
2. In the Blank database preview's File Name box, keep the default name.
3. If you want to save the file in a location other than the one shown beneath the File Name box, click the folder icon and browse to a different location.
4. Click the Create button. A new blank database appears with the default table labeled Table1 displayed, as shown in Figure 2-20.

Figure 2-20

New blank database with default table

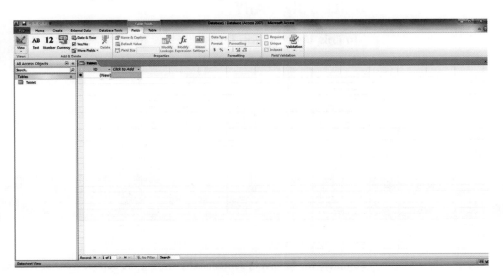

5. Click to place the insertion point in the cell under the Click to add field and key Sample Data.
6. Right-click on the Table1 tab to display the shortcut menu, as shown in Figure 2-21.

Figure 2-21

Shortcut menu

Right-click to display menu

7. Click Save. The Save As dialog box appears, as shown in Figure 2-22.

Figure 2-22

Save As dialog box

Another Way
You can also save a table by pressing Ctrl+S. You do not need to save new data that you enter. Access automatically saves a record when you move to a different record or close the object or database.

Access also automatically saves changes to your data whenever you quit the program. However, if you have made changes to the design of any database objects since you last saved them, Access asks whether you want to save these changes before quitting.

8. In the Table Name box, key Sample Table.
9. Click **OK** to close the dialog box and return to the table, which now is labeled Sample Table.
10. Click the **File** tab to display the Backstage view.
11. Click **Save Object As** to display the Save As dialog box.
12. In the Table Name box, key **Backup of Sample Table**.
13. Click **OK**.
14. Click the **Home** tab.
15. Notice the new table object named Backup of Sample Table in the Navigation Pane.
16. **CLOSE** the database.
CLOSE Access.

SKILL SUMMARY

In This Lesson, You Learned How To:
Create a database
Create a table
Save a tatabase object

Knowledge Assessment

Fill in the Blank

Complete the following sentences by writing the correct word or words in the blanks provided.

1. You can create a database using one of the many templates available or by creating a new _____ database.

2. By default, Access creates a(n) _____ field named "ID" for all new datasheets.

3. Entering data in Datasheet View is very similar to entering data in a(n) _____.

4. The _____ contains predefined templates included in two categories, Blank Forms and Quick Start.

5. One way to create a table is to copy the _____ of an existing table and paste it into the database.

6. When you add a new table to an existing database, that new table stands alone until you _____ it to your existing tables.

7. You can use up to _____ characters (letters or numbers), including spaces, to name a database object.

8. Several options for creating a database are provided on the _____ tab in the Backstage view.

9. The _____ category in the Application Parts gallery contains a collection of predefined database objects for tracking comments, contacts, and issues.

10. After you add _____ to a table, you should save its design.

Multiple Choice

Select the best response for the following statements.

1. In Access, a template is
   a. A database to manage contacts
   b. Where a database is stored
   c. Two tables linked together
   d A ready-to-use database

2. When you create a new blank database, Access opens a database that contains
   a. One of each type of database object
   b. A table
   c. Sample data
   d. A template

3. To save a database file in a location other than the default, click the
   a. Folder icon
   b. Blank database icon
   c. File name button
   d. Help button

4. The table structure is created when you
   a. Format the data
   b. Enter data
   c. Insert blank rows and columns
   d. Switch to Design View

5. The Templates group commands are located on which tab?
   a. Home
   b. Create
   c. Database Tools
   d. Datasheet

6. To copy a table, you must first select it in
   a. The Clipboard
   b. Microsoft Office Online
   c. The Navigation Pane
   d. Datasheet View

7. When you paste a table, which dialog box is displayed?
   a. Table Structure
   b. Copy Table
   c. Paste Data
   d. Paste Table As

8. After you have created a table or other database object, you should
   a. Save it with a descriptive name
   b. Copy it to create a backup
   c. Link it to an external data source
   d. Insert a blank column at the end

9. When you quit the program, Access automatically
   a. Creates a link between all tables
   b. Leaves the Navigation Pane open
   c. Saves the data
   d. Renames the file

10. Which is *not* a way to create a new database table?
   a. Use Quick Start
   b. Choose Create on the Table menu
   c. Copy the structure of another table
   d. Create a new blank database

Competency Assessment

Project 2-1: Contacts Database

You want to use Access to store, organize, and manage the contact information for the wholesale coffee suppliers used by Fourth Coffee, where you work as a buyer for the 15 stores in the northeast region. Use a template to create a database for the contacts.

GET READY. LAUNCH Access if it is not already running.

1. Open Backstage view and in the Office.com Templates section of the New tab, select the Contacts category.
2. On the next screen that displays, select the Call Tracker template.
3. Key Call tracker XXX (where XXX is your initials) in the File Name box.
4. If necessary, click the folder icon and choose a different location for the file.
5. Click Download (or click Create if not logged on to the Internet) to create and open the database.
6. Close the Access 2007 Help window that appears.
7. Click the Shutter Bar Open/Close Button to open the Navigation Pane.
8. Click the Supporting Objects header to display the database objects in that group.
9. Right-click the Customers table under the Customers header to display the menu and click Copy.
10. Right-click in the white area of the Navigation Pane and click Paste on the menu.
11. In the Paste Table As dialog box, key Customers structure.
12. Click the Structure Only radio button.
13. Click OK.
14. **CLOSE** the *Call trackerXXX* database.

LEAVE Access open for the next project.

Project 2-2: Database for Restaurants

As a regional manager for a franchise restaurant chain, you want to keep track of restaurant locations and customer comments. You decide to create a database to store the necessary information.

GET READY. LAUNCH Access if it is not already running.

1. In the Backstage view's New tab, click the Blank Database icon.
2. In the Blank Database pane on the right, key Restaurants XXX (where XXX is your initials) in the File Name box.
3. If necessary, click the folder icon and choose a different location for the file.
4. Click the Create button.
5. Right-click the Table1 tab and click Save.
6. In the Save As dialog box, key Locations.
7. Click OK.

LEAVE Access open for the next project.

Proficiency Assessment

Project 2-3: Adding Tables

You need to add some tables to the database that you just created for information about the restaurants.

USE the database that is open from the previous project.

1. Use the Application Parts gallery to create a table for comments.
2. In the Create Relationship window that appears, click the Cancel button.
3. Rename the table *Uptown Comments*.
4. Copy the structure of the Uptown Comments table to create a new table.
5. Name the new table *Downtown Comments*.
6. **CLOSE** the database.

LEAVE Access open for the next project.

Project 2-4: Nutrition Tracker

You have become health conscious and want to track your activity, exercise, and food logs using Access.

GET READY. LAUNCH Access if it is not already running.

1. If necessary, log on to the Internet.
2. In the *Search Office.com For Templates* box, search for, download, and save the Nutrition template with the file name *Nutrition XXX* (where XXX is your initials).
3. Key your information in the My Profile form that is displayed to see your body mass index and recommended calorie consumption. (If the My Profile form is not displayed, open it first.)
4. Click OK.
5. Open the Tips table to view the tips stored in the database.
6. Explore the other useful forms and information available.
7. **CLOSE** the database.

LEAVE Access open for the next project.

Mastery Assessment

Project 2-5: Northwind Traders

You have just joined the sales force at Northwind Traders. To familiarize yourself with the information available in the company database, open the file and browse through the objects.

GET READY. LAUNCH Access if it is not already running.

1. In the Sample templates category, download the Northwind database using the name *Northwind 2010 XXX* (where XXX is your initials).
2. Enable the content.
3. Log in as a sales representative, Jan Kotas, by selecting that name from the Select Employee drop-down menu and clicking the Log In button.
4. Open the Navigation Pane and open each group to view all the objects that are part of the database.
5. **CLOSE** the database.

LEAVE Access open for the next project.

Project 2-6: Customer Service Database

Southridge Video has a large membership of customers that rent new release and film library movies, as well as video games. As the store manager, customer complaints are directed to you. Create an Access database for the purpose of tracking customer service issues.

GET READY. LAUNCH Access if it is not already running.

1. Choose an Application Parts template to create a database called *Southridge XXX* (where XXX is your initials) that will store information about customer service issues. Make no changes to the default Application Parts template.
2. **CLOSE** the database.

LEAVE Access open for the next project.

INTERNET READY

If you want to read more about Access templates, you can explore the Office Online website. Search Access Help for "Access templates." Click the search results link titled "Introduction to the Access 2010 templates," as shown in Figure 2-23, to read more about the templates that are included with Access 2010 and on Office.com.

Figure 2-23

Search results for Access templates

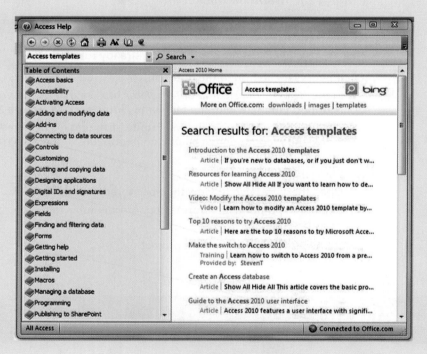

LESSON SKILL MATRIX

In This Lesson, You Will Learn The Following Skills:

Navigating among Records

Entering, Inserting, Editing, and Deleting Records

Working with Primary Keys

Finding and Replacing Data

Attaching and Detaching Documents

Sorting and Filtering Data and Setting Field Viewing Options within a Table

Understanding Table Relationships

KEY TERMS

- ascending
- composite key
- descending
- filter
- foreign key
- innermost field
- outermost field
- referential integrity
- sort
- wildcard

Fourth Coffee is a national chain of coffee shops. A new store recently opened in your neighborhood. You were able to get a part-time job working in the office, helping the office manager organize data on the computer. In addition to being a traditional neighborhood coffee shop, the store has also started selling coffees to companies for use at their business sites. It is your job to manage the inventory, customers, and order tables in Access. In this lesson, you learn to navigate among records; enter, edit, and delete records; find and replace data; sort and filter data; attach and detach documents; and define, modify, and print table relationships.

NAVIGATING AMONG RECORDS

The Bottom Line

Database tables are usually large, but contain useful information that can be manipulated in different ways. When a table contains many records and fields, it is important to be able to navigate among them.

Navigating Using the Keyboard

Access users who prefer using the keyboard to navigate records can press keys and key combinations to move among records in Datasheet View. In Datasheet View, you can navigate among records using the up, down, left, and right arrow keys to move to the field you want. You can also use the Tab key to move from field to field in a record and from the last field in a record to the first field of the next record. If you prefer to use the mouse, you can move among records by clicking the navigation buttons, which you'll do in a later exercise. However, in this exercise, you use the keyboard to navigate among records.

STEP BY STEP

Use the Keyboard to Navigate among Records

GET READY. Before you begin these steps, be sure to turn on and/or log on to your computer and start Access.

 The *Fourth Coffee* file for this lesson is available on the book companion website or in WileyPLUS.

WileyPLUS Extra! features an online tutorial of this task.

1. **OPEN** *Fourth Coffee* from the data files for this lesson.
2. Click the File tab, then click the Save Database As command. The Save As dialog box appears. Key Fourth Coffee XXX (where XXX is your initials) in the File name box. Find the location where you will save the solution files for this lesson and click Save.
3. In the Navigation Pane, double-click Coffee Inventory: Table to open the table.
4. Notice that the first cell of the first record is selected.
5. Press the Down Arrow key to move down to the next row. Notice that the cell is selected.
6. Press the Right Arrow key to move to the Product Name field.
7. Press the Tab key to move to the next cell.
8. Press the Tab key to move to the next cell.
9. Press the Tab key to move to the next row.
10. Press Ctrl+Down Arrow to move to the first field of the last record.

PAUSE. LEAVE the database open to use in the next exercise.

Table 3-1 lists keys and key combinations for moving among records.

Table 3-1

Keyboard Commands for Navigating Records

Commands	Results
Tab or Right Arrow	Moves cursor to the next field
End	Moves cursor to the last field in the current record
Shift+Tab or Left Arrow	Moves cursor to the previous field
Home	Moves cursor to the first field in the current record
Down Arrow	Moves cursor to the current field in the next record
Ctrl+Down Arrow	Moves cursor to the current field in the last record
Ctrl+End	Moves cursor to the last field in the last record
Up Arrow	Moves cursor to the current field in the previous record
Ctrl+Up Arrow	Moves cursor to the current field in the first record
Ctrl+Home	Moves cursor to the first field in the first record

Using Navigation Buttons

Access users who prefer to use the mouse can move among records by clicking the navigation buttons. In this exercise, you use the mouse to navigate among records.

The record navigation buttons are displayed at the bottom of the screen in Datasheet View. Click the First, Previous, Next, Last, and New (blank) Record buttons to go to those records. Key a record number into the Current Record box and press Enter to go to that record. Key data into the Search box to find a match in the table. The Filter Indicator shows whether a filter has been applied to the table, which will be covered later in this lesson.

STEP BY STEP   **Use Navigation Buttons**

USE the database open from the previous exercise.

1. Click the **First record** button, shown in Figure 3-1. The selection moves to the first record.

Figure 3-1

Record navigation buttons

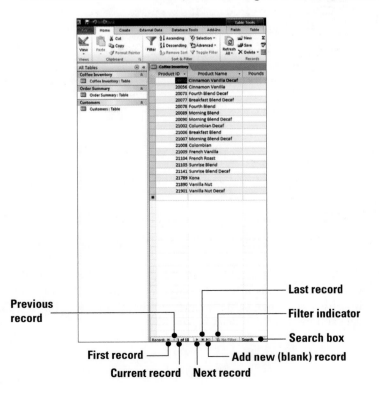

2. Click the Next record button. The selection moves to the next record.

3. Select and then delete the number 2 in the Current Record box. Key 5 and press Enter. The selection moves to the fifth record.

4. Click the Search box to position the insertion point. Key sunrise into the Search box. Notice that the selection moves to the first occurrence of the word Sunrise.

5. Press Enter. The selection moves to the next occurrence of the word Sunrise.

6. Click the New (blank) record button. The insertion point moves to the first column and last row of the table.

PAUSE. LEAVE the database open to use in the next exercise.

SOFTWARE ORIENTATION

Records Group, Record Selector Box, and Record Shortcut Menu

There are a few ways you can enter record data, delete data from individual fields of records, and insert and delete entire records, using the Records group, Record Selector box, and commands in the Record Shortcut menu, as shown in Figure 3-2. Refer to this figure as a reference throughout this lesson as well as the rest of this book.

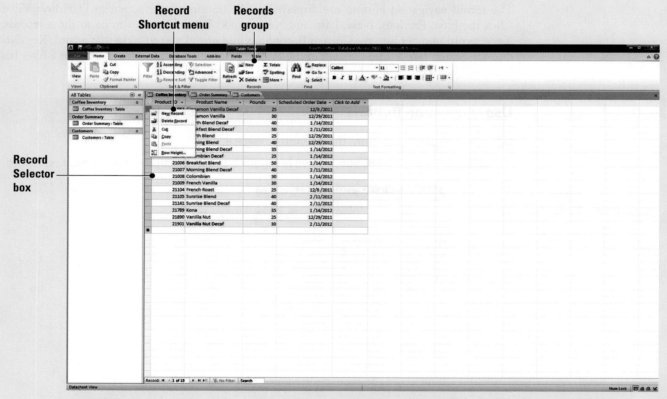

Figure 3-2

Records group, Record Selector box, and Record Shortcut menu

Use the commands in the Records group and the Record Shortcut menu, as well as the Record Selector box (a blank square to the left of a record), to assist you in entering record data and inserting and deleting records.

ENTERING, INSERTING, EDITING, AND DELETING RECORDS

The Bottom Line

Keeping a database up-to-date and useful is an ongoing process. You can easily enter data by positioning the insertion point in the table cell where you want to add data and begin keying. To insert a new record, select any record in the table and click the New button on the Home tab in the Records group. You can also click the Record Selector box then right-click the selected record and select New Record from the shortcut menu. A new record is added to the end of the table. Select existing data to edit or delete it.

Entering, Editing, and Deleting Records

To enter new data, in Datasheet View, position the insertion point in the first empty cell of a record and begin keying the data. After you enter data and move to a new field, Access automatically saves the data in the table. Each field in a table is formatted with a specific data type, so you must enter that kind of data in the field. If you do not, you will get an error message. To delete information from an individual field of a record, highlight the field data and press the Delete key or click the Delete button on the Home tab in the Records group. If you change your mind after you delete information from a field, you can undo the action by clicking the Undo button on the Quick Access Toolbar. In this exercise, you enter a new record as well as edit and delete existing records.

You can delete an entire record or several records at once from a database. Just select the row or rows using the Record Selector box and press the Delete key or click the Delete button on the Home tab in the Records group. You can also right-click and select Delete Record from the shortcut menu. After you delete a record, you cannot undo it.

STEP BY STEP **Enter, Edit, and Delete Records**

USE the database you used in the previous exercise.

1. The insertion point should be positioned in the first field of the new, blank row at the bottom of the datasheet, as shown in Figure 3-3. Notice the asterisk in the Record Selector box, which indicates that this is a new record, ready for data.

Figure 3-3

Blank record in Datasheet View

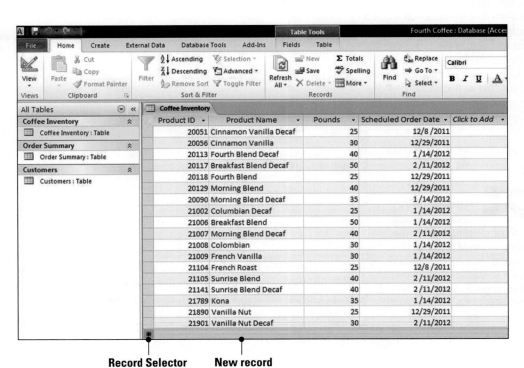

2. Key **21905** and press **Tab**. Notice that the asterisk has changed to a pencil icon, as shown in Figure 3-4, indicating that the record is being edited.

Figure 3-4

Entering data into a record

Indicates that the record is being edited ——

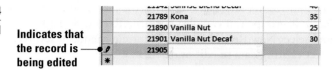

3. Key **Hazelnut** and press **Tab**.
4. Key **30** and press **Tab**.
5. Key **02112012** and press **Enter**.
6. Highlight **sunrise** in the Search box and key **Kona** to locate the Kona record.
7. Select **Kona** in the record to position the blinking insertion point there. Key **Hawaiian** and press **Tab**.
8. Click the **Undo** button on the Quick Access Toolbar.
9. Press **Tab**. Key **12292010** and press **Tab**.
10. Click the **Record Selector** box to the left of the Product ID field of the first record, 20051.
11. On the Home tab, in the Records group, click the **Delete button drop-down arrow**. Select **Delete Record** from the menu, as shown in Figure 3-5.

Figure 3-5

Delete menu

Another Way
An easy way to select an entire record is to click the Record Selector box. If you need to select other records above or below it, you can drag the mouse up or down to include those in the selection. To delete one or more selected records, right-click the Select All button and choose Delete Record from the shortcut menu.

Delete button and menu

12. A dialog box appears, as shown in Figure 3-6, asking if you are sure you want to delete the record. Click **Yes**.

Figure 3-6

Confirm deletion dialog box

Another Way
To delete a record without selecting it, place the cursor in one of the fields of a record and click the Delete menu on the Home tab in the Records group. Select Delete Record from the menu.

13. Notice that the Undo button on the Quick Access Toolbar is not available because you cannot undo a deletion. Close the table.

PAUSE. LEAVE the database open to use in the next exercise.

WORKING WITH PRIMARY KEYS

The Bottom Line

As you learned in Lesson 1, a primary key is a column that uniquely identifies a record or row in a table. Customer IDs, serial numbers, or product IDs usually make good primary keys. Each table should have a primary key, and some tables might have two or more. When you divide information into separate tables, the primary keys help Access bring the information back together again.

Defining a Primary Key

You can define a primary key for a field in Design View by selecting the row that contains the field for which you want to assign a primary key and clicking the Primary Key button on the Design tab in the Tools group on the Ribbon. When you create a new database, Access creates a primary key field named "ID" by default and sets the data type for the field to AutoNumber. If you don't have a field in an existing database that you think will make a good primary key, you can use a field with the AutoNumber data type. It doesn't contain factual information (such as a telephone number) about a record and it is not likely to change. In this exercise, you define a primary key.

Once a primary key is defined, you can use it in other tables to refer back to the table with the primary key. When a primary key from one table is used in another table, it is called the **foreign key.** The foreign key is used to reference the data from the primary key to help avoid redundancy.

You can modify a primary key by deleting it from one field and adding it to another field. To remove a primary key in Design View, select the row and click the Primary Key button on the Design tab in the Tools group on the Ribbon to remove it.

STEP BY STEP | **Define a Primary Key**

USE the database you used in the previous exercise.

1. In the Navigation Pane, double-click Order Summary: Table to open the table.
2. On the Home tab, in the Views group, click the View button drop-down arrow, and from the menu that appears, select Design View.
3. Click the Row Selector box beside the Order ID row to select the row.
4. On the Design tab, in the Tools group, click the Primary Key button. The Primary Key button is highlighted in orange and appears to be pushed in. A key icon appears on the Order ID row to designate the field as a primary key, as shown in Figure 3-7.

Another Way
To add or remove the primary key from a field, you can also select the row, right-click, and select Primary Key from the shortcut menu.

Figure 3-7

Primary Key

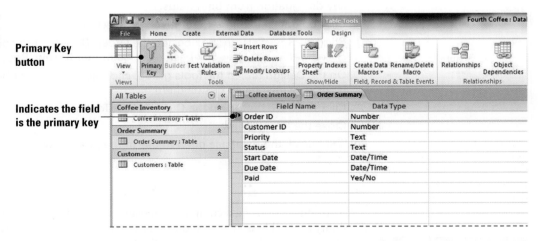

Primary Key button

Indicates the field is the primary key

PAUSE. LEAVE the table open to use in the next exercise.

Defining and Modifying a Multifield Primary Key

In some cases, you may want to use two or more fields that, together, provide the primary key of a table. In Design View, select the rows you want to designate as primary keys and click the Primary Key button. To remove multiple primary keys, select the rows and click the Primary Key button. In this exercise, you practice defining and modifying a multifield primary key.

Two or more primary keys in a table are called the **composite key.** Composite keys are useful in unique situations when a combination of data from two fields needs to provide a unique identifier in a table.

STEP BY STEP | **Define and Modify a Multifield Primary Key**

USE the database open from the previous exercise.

1. Press and hold the Ctrl key.
2. Click the Row Selector box beside the Paid row. Continue to hold down the Ctrl key and click the Order ID Row Selector box. Both fields should be selected, as shown in Figure 3-8. If not, continue to hold the Ctrl key and click the Paid Row Selector box again.

Figure 3-8

Primary Key row and another row selected

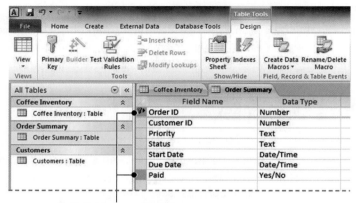

Both fields are selected

3. On the Design tab, in the Tools group, click the Primary Key button. A key icon should be displayed beside both of the two selected fields.
4. With the rows still selected, click the Primary Key button again to remove the primary key designation from both fields.
5. Click on any field name to remove the selection.
6. Click the Row Selector box beside the Order ID row. Press and hold the Ctrl key and click the Row Selector box beside the Customer ID row. Both fields should be selected.
7. On the Design tab, in the Tools group, click the Primary Key button. Both rows should have a key displayed beside them.
8. Click the Save button on the Quick Access Toolbar.
9. Close the Design View.

PAUSE. LEAVE the database open to use in the next exercise.

FINDING AND REPLACING DATA

The Bottom Line

A big advantage of using a computer database rather than paper and pencil for recordkeeping is the ability to quickly search for and/or replace data. These features may be accessed from the Find and Replace dialog box. The Find and Replace commands in Access work very much like those in Word or other Office applications you might have used. You can use the Find command to search for specific text in a table or to move quickly to a particular word or number in the table. The Replace command can be used to automatically replace a word or number with another.

In the Find and Replace dialog box, key the text or numbers that you want to search for into the Find What box and click Find Next to locate the record containing the data. If you want to replace the data, key the new data into the Replace With box and click Replace or Replace All.

Take Note   When replacing data, it is usually a good practice to click Replace instead of Replace All so that you can confirm each replacement to make sure that it is correct.

Finding and Replacing Data

The Find and Replace dialog box searches only one table at a time; it does not search the entire database. The Look In menu allows you to choose to search by field or to search the entire table. By default, Access searches the field that was selected when you opened the Find and Replace dialog box. If you want to search a different field, select the field while the dialog box is open; you don't have to close it first. In the next exercise, you find and replace table data.

Remember these points when finding and replacing data in Access 2010:

- In the Match menu, you can specify where you want Access to look in a field. Select Any Part of Field for the broadest search.
- Sometimes Access selects the Search Fields As Formatted check box. When it does, do not clear the check box, or your search probably will not return any results.
- Click the Match Case box to search for text with the same uppercase and/or lowercase capitalization of text.
- You can use **wildcard** characters such as a question mark or asterisk to find words or phrases that contain specific letters or combinations of letters. Key a question mark (?) to represent a single character—for example, keying *b?t* will find *bat, bet, bit,* and *but.* Key an asterisk (*) to represent a string of characters—for example, *m*t* will find *mat, moment,* or even *medium format.*
- If you key a wildcard character in the Replace With box, Access will insert that character just as you keyed it.

STEP BY STEP   **Find and Replace Data**

USE the database open from the previous exercise.

1. Open the **Customers** table.
2. On the Home tab, in the Find group, click the **Find** button. The Find and Replace dialog box appears with the Find tab displayed.
3. Click the **Replace** tab in the Find and Replace dialog box.
4. Key **Elm** into the Find What box.
5. Key **Little Elm** into the Replace With box.
6. Click the **down arrow** beside the Look In menu and select **Current document**, so that the entire table will be searched **instead** of just the Customer ID field.
7. Click the **down arrow** beside the Match menu and select **Any Part of Field** if it isn't already selected to broaden the search. See Figure 3-9.

Figure 3-9

Find and Replace dialog box

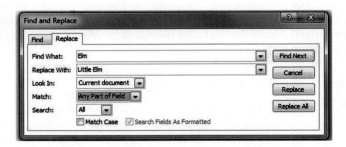

8. Click the **Find Next** button. Access searches the table and finds and selects the word *Elm*.

9. Click the **Replace** button. Access replaces *Elm* with *Little Elm*.

10. Click the **Find Next** button. Access finds *Elm* in the new text that was just inserted.

11. Click **Find Next** again. Access displays a message saying that no more occurrences of the word have been found. Click **OK**.

12. Click **Cancel** to close the Find and Replace dialog box.

13. Press the **down arrow** to remove the selection and allow Access to save the change.

14. Close the table.

PAUSE. LEAVE the database open to use in the next exercise.

Another Way
To open the Find tab in the Find and Replace dialog box using the keyboard, press Ctrl+F. To open the Replace tab, press Ctrl+H.

Take Note
If you want to use the Find and Replace dialog box to search for characters that are used as wildcards, such as a question mark, you must enclose that character in brackets, for example [?]. Follow this rule when searching for all wildcard characters except exclamation points (!) and closing brackets (]).

ATTACHING AND DETACHING DOCUMENTS

The Bottom Line
Access 2010 allows you to attach documents, such as Word documents or photo files, to records in a database. For example, the human resources department of a large company could keep a photo, a resume, and employee evaluation documents with each employee record. These attached files can also be easily detached, if necessary. The Attachments dialog box allows you to manage the documents attached to records.

Take Note
You cannot attach files to databases created in versions of Access prior to Access 2007. You cannot share attachments with a database created in these prior versions of Access.

Attaching and Detaching Documents

Before you can start attaching documents, you must create a field in a table and format it with the Attachment data type. You can add the field in Datasheet View or in Design View. Access displays a paper clip icon in the header row and in every record in the field along with a number in parentheses indicating the number of attached files in the field. In this exercise, you create a new field and format it with the Attachment data type, then remove the attachment from your database records.

Double-click the record in the Attachments field to display the Attachments dialog box where you can add, remove, open, or save multiple attachments, such as images, documents, and spreadsheets, for a single record. You can save attached files to your hard disk or network drive so that you can save changes to documents there before saving them to the database.

Take Note
You can attach a maximum total of 2 gigabytes of data, but each individual file cannot exceed 256 megabytes in size.

Another Way
You can also right-click in the Attachments field to display a shortcut menu. Select Manage Attachments from the menu to display the Attachments dialog box.

If the program that was used to create the attached file is installed on your computer, you can open and edit the file using that program. For example, if you open a Word resume that is attached to a record, the Word program starts and you view the document in Word. If you do not have the program that was used to create a file, Access prompts you to choose a program you do have to view the file.

| STEP BY STEP | **Attach and Detach Documents** |

USE the database open from the previous exercise.

1. Open the Order Summary table.
2. Click the header row of the Due Date field to select it.
3. In the Add & Delete group on the Table Tools Fields contextual tab, click the More Fields button. The More Fields menu appears.
4. Click Attachment under Basic Types, as shown in Figure 3-10. The Attachment field is inserted in the table.

Figure 3-10

More Fields menu

The *invoice 100* file for this lesson is available on the book companion website or in WileyPLUS.

5. Double-click the first row of the Attachments field. The Attachments dialog box appears.
6. Click the Add button. Navigate to the data files for this lesson and select *Invoice100.docx*. Click Open. The document appears in the Attachments dialog box, as shown in Figure 3-11.

Figure 3-11

Attachments dialog box

7. Click OK. The number of attachments in the first record changes to 1, as shown in Figure 3-12.

Figure 3-12

Attachments field displaying the number of attachments

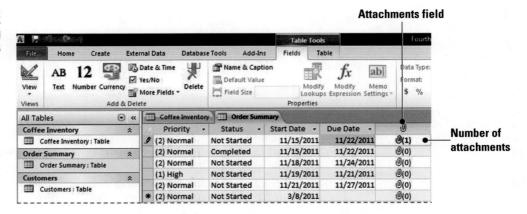

8. Double-click the attachment number in the Attachment field. The Attachments dialog box appears.

9. Click the Open button. The attachment, an invoice document, opens in Microsoft Word.

10. Click the Close button to close the invoice document.

11. Click the Access button on the taskbar, if necessary, to return to Access.

12. In the Attachments dialog box, click the Remove button, and click OK. The attachment is removed from the record.

13. Close the Order Summary table.

PAUSE. LEAVE the database open to use in the next exercise.

Take Note   Once a field has been set to the Attachment data type, it cannot be converted to another data type.

SORTING AND FILTERING DATA AND SETTING FIELD VIEWING OPTIONS WITHIN A TABLE

The Bottom Line

It is often helpful to display data in order, display similar records, or hide and freeze certain fields without affecting the preexisting data. Sorting allows you to order records. For example, an office contact list that displays employees in alphabetical order by last name would help the user find information for a particular employee quickly. If you wanted to view only the records of employees in a particular department, you could create a filter to display only those records. You could also hide or freeze certain fields. For example, in a table that has several fields, you can hide or freeze fields to help you concentrate on certain data.

SOFTWARE ORIENTATION

Sort & Filter Group

The Sort & Filter group is located on the Home tab in the Ribbon (Figure 3-13). Use the Sort & Filter group of commands to sort and filter records in tables.

Figure 3-13

Sort & Filter group

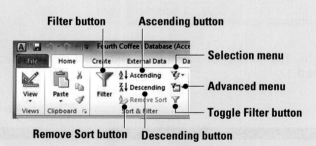

Sorting Data within a Table

To **sort** data means to arrange it alphabetically, numerically, or chronologically. Sorting within a table displays all the records in the table in the order that you select. You can easily sort by one or more fields to achieve the order that you want. Access can sort text, numbers, or dates in ascending or descending order. **Ascending** order sorts data from beginning to end, such as from A to Z, 1 to 10, and January to December. **Descending** order sorts data from the end to the beginning, such as from Z to A, 10 to 1, and December to January. In this exercise, you sort data using multiple fields and then remove the sort.

To sort text, numbers, dates, or other data types in a column, you first need to select the column. Then click the Ascending or Descending button in the Sort & Filter group of the Home tab. You can also right-click a selected column and choose a Sort command from the shortcut menu. The available sort commands in the shortcut menu vary depending on the type of data in the column, as shown in Table 3-2.

Table 3-2

Sort Commands on the Shortcut Menu

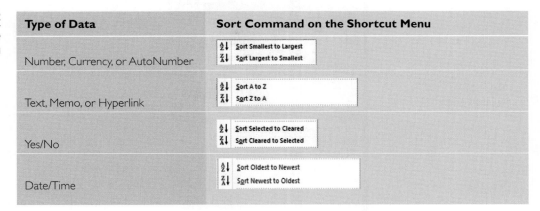

Type of Data	Sort Command on the Shortcut Menu
Number, Currency, or AutoNumber	↕↓ Sort Smallest to Largest ↕↓ Sort Largest to Smallest
Text, Memo, or Hyperlink	↕↓ Sort A to Z ↕↓ Sort Z to A
Yes/No	↕↓ Sort Selected to Cleared ↕↓ Sort Cleared to Selected
Date/Time	↕↓ Sort Oldest to Newest ↕↓ Sort Newest to Oldest

You can also sort records on multiple fields. When you are using multiple fields, determine which order you want them to be sorted in. The primary sort field is called the **outermost field**. A secondary sort field is called an **innermost field**. For example, if you want to sort a contact list so that each employee's last name is sorted primarily and first name is sorted secondarily, Last Name would be the outermost field and First Name would be the innermost field. In your completed sort, Wright, David, would be listed before Wright, Steven, in an A to Z (ascending) sort. When designating the sort order, however, you select the innermost field first and choose the type of sort you want from the shortcut menu. Then select the outermost field and select the type of sort that you want.

After you sort one or more columns, Access inserts sort arrows in the header row to show that the field is sorted. These sort commands remain with the table until you remove them. When you want to remove a sort order, click the Remove Sort button from the Sort & Filter group on the Home tab. This removes the sorting commands from all the fields in the table. In a table with more than one sorted field, you cannot remove just one sort.

STEP BY STEP   **Sort Data within a Table**

USE the database you used in the previous exercise.

1. Open the **Customers** table.
2. Click the header row of the Customer ID field to select it.
3. Right-click in the field to display the shortcut menu, shown in Figure 3-14. Select **Sort Largest to Smallest**.

Figure 3-14

Shortcut menu

↕↓ Sort Smallest to Largest
↕↓ Sort Largest to Smallest
    Copy
    Paste
    Field Width
    Hide Fields
    Unhide Fields
    Freeze Fields
    Unfreeze All Fields
    Find...
    Insert Field
    Modify Lookups
    Modify Expression
    Rename Field
    Delete Field

4. The data is sorted and an arrow is inserted in the header row, as shown in Figure 3-15, indicating that the data is displayed in sort order.

Figure 3-15

Sorted column

Sort arrow

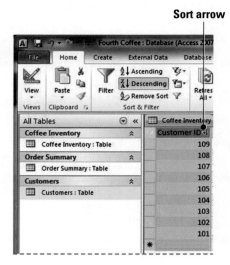

5. On the Home tab, in the Sort & Filter group, click the Remove Sort button. The sort is removed from the Customer ID field.

6. Select the First Name field. On the Home tab, in the Sort & Filter group, click the Ascending button. The data in the First Name field is sorted in ascending order.

7. Select the Last Name field. On the Home tab, in the Sort & Filter group, click the Ascending button. The data in the Last Name field is sorted in ascending order.

8. On the Home tab, in the Sort & Filter group, click the Remove Sort button. The sort is removed from both the First Name and Last Name fields.

9. Close the table. If a dialog box appears asking if you want to save changes to the table, click No.

PAUSE. LEAVE the database open to use in the next exercise.

Filtering Data within a Table

A **filter** is a set of rules for determining which records will be displayed. When you apply a filter, Access displays only the records that meet your filter criteria; the other records are hidden from view. Once the filtered records are displayed, you can edit and navigate the records just as you would without a filter applied. Filters remain in effect until you close the object. You can switch between views, and the filter settings will stay in effect. To make the filter available the next time you open the object, save the object before closing it. In this exercise, you practice creating filters in several different ways.

STEP BY STEP | **Apply a Filter**

USE the database you used in the previous exercise.

1. Open the Coffee Inventory table.

2. Select the Product Name field. On the Home tab, in the Sort & Filter group, click the Filter button. A menu appears.

3. Point to Text Filters. A second menu appears. Select Contains, as shown in Figure 3-16.

Figure 3-16

Filter menu with Contains selected

4. The Custom Filter box appears. Key Decaf, as shown in Figure 3-17, and click OK. Access filters the database to display only the records containing the word Decaf. A filter icon is displayed in the header row of the field, as shown in Figure 3-18.

Figure 3-17

Custom filter box

Figure 3-18

Filtered records

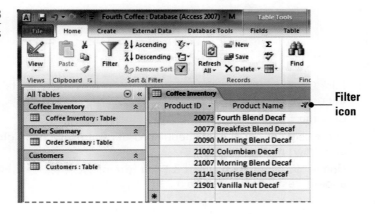

5. Click the Toggle Filter button in the Sort & Filter group to display the records without the filter.

6. In the second record in the Product Name field, double-click the word Decaf to select it.

7. Right-click the word Decaf to display the shortcut menu. Select Does Not Contain "Decaf," as shown in Figure 3-19. Notice that the records are filtered to show only those that do not contain the word Decaf.

Figure 3-19

Shortcut menu with Does
Not Contain "Decaf"
option selected

8. Click in the Pounds field of the first record.

9. On the Home tab, in the Sort & Filter group, click the Filter button.

10. Click the check boxes to remove the check marks beside 30, 35, 40, and 50, as shown in Figure 3-20. Only the check mark beside 25 should remain.

Figure 3-20

Filter menu selected
to show only 25 in the
pounds column

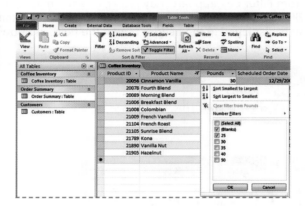

11. Click OK. Access filters the records to show only those containing the number 25 in the pounds field.

12. Click the Toggle Filter button.

13. In the second row of the Scheduled Order Date field, highlight 1/14/2012 by clicking and dragging the mouse.

14. On the Home tab, in the Sort & Filter group, click the Selection button. A menu appears, as shown in Figure 3-21.

Figure 3-21

Selection button and menu

Selection button and menu

15. Select On or After 1/14/2012. The data is filtered to show only those records with content in the Scheduled Order Date field that matches the filter selection.

16. In the seventh row of the Pounds field, select 30.

17. On the Home tab, in the Sort & Filter group, click the Selection button. Select Less Than or Equal to 30. The records are filtered.

PAUSE. LEAVE the database open to use in the next exercise.

Take Note   Only one filter can be applied per column. When you apply a filter to a column that is already filtered, the previous filter is removed and the new filter is applied.

Removing a Filter

After applying a filter, you may need to return to records not displayed by the filter. The Toggle Filter button lets you switch between viewing the filtered records and viewing the table without the filter. Note that the purpose of this button changes accordingly—when the records are filtered the button is used to remove the filter, and when the filter is removed the button is used to apply the filter. When you are finished using the filter, you can permanently remove it. In this exercise, you permanently remove the filter you previously applied.

STEP BY STEP   **Remove a Filter**

USE the table you used in the previous exercise.

1. Select the **Pounds** field. On the Home tab, in the Sort & Filter group, click the **Filter** button. A menu appears.
2. Select **Clear Filter from Pounds**, as shown in Figure 3-22.

Figure 3-22

Removing filter from the pounds column

3. On the Home tab, in the Sort & Filter group, click the **Advanced Filter Options** button. A menu appears.
4. Select **Clear All Filters** from the menu, as shown in Figure 3-23.

Figure 3-23

Advanced filter Options button and menu

Advanced filter Options button

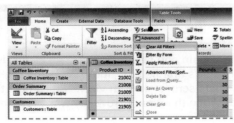

5. Save and close the table.

PAUSE. LEAVE the database open to use in the next exercise.

Freezing/Unfreezing and Hiding/Unhiding Fields

Sometimes you may need to change the view of a table's data to more efficiently find the information you're looking for. For example, it may be helpful to freeze First Name and Last Name fields so you can keep them fixed on the screen and then horizontally scroll and view other pertinent fields, like E-mail or Telephone Number to get a better view of your data. You can also hide those fields that may distract you from getting a better view of the data. For example, if you're interested in viewing just a person's name and telephone number, you may decide to hide all fields except First Name, Last Name, and Phone Number. In this exercise, you practice freezing and unfreezing fields, as well as hiding and unhiding them.

STEP BY STEP   **Freeze/Unfreeze and Hide/Unhide Fields**

USE the database you used in the previous exercise.

1. Open the **Customers** table.
2. Select the **Last Name** field. On the Home tab, in the Records group, click the **More** button. A menu appears, as shown in Figure 3-24.

Figure 3-24

More button menu

More button menu

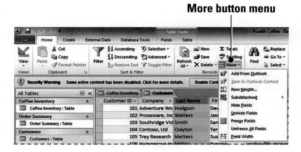

3. Select **Freeze Fields**. Notice that the Last Name field moves to the first field position in the table.
4. Click the **Restore Down** button in the top, right corner of the application window, as shown in Figure 3-25. The Restore Down button now becomes the Maximize button. Press the **Right Arrow** key to scroll the table's fields to the left, and stop when you reach the ZIP/Postal Code field. Notice that the Last Name field stays fixed as the other fields scroll.

Restore down button

Figure 3-25

Restore down button

5. Click the **More** button again and select **Unfreeze All Fields**. Notice how the Last Name field remains in the table's first field position. Press the **Right Arrow** key several times until the Last Name field scrolls off from view. Notice how the Last Name field moved with the other fields when the Right Arrow key was pressed several times.

Take Note   Fields can be rearranged in Datasheet View by clicking on the field name headers and dragging them to where you want to move them.

6. Click the **Maximize** button on the application window.
7. Select the **Customer ID** field. Click the **More** button and select **Hide Fields**. Notice the Customer ID field is now hidden from view, as shown in Figure 3-26.

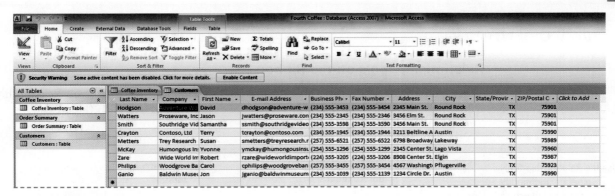

Figure 3-26

Hidden Customer ID field

8. Click the **More** button and select **Unhide Fields**. The Unhide Columns dialog box should appear as shown in Figure 3-27. Notice the check mark is missing from the Customer ID check box, signifying that it's hidden.

Figure 3-27

Unhide Columns dialog box

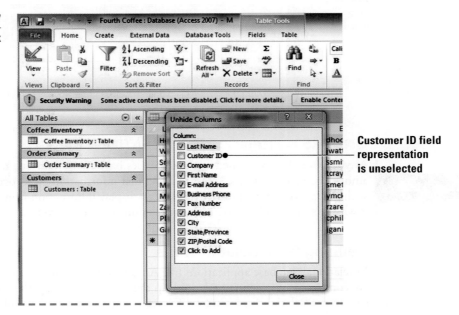

Customer ID field representation is unselected

9. Deselect the check boxes next to all the other field representations except Last Name and Business Phone, and then click the **Close** button in the Unhide Columns dialog box. Notice the only fields now displayed in Datasheet View are the Last Name and Business Phone fields.

10. Close the Customers table without saving the changes to the layout.

PAUSE. LEAVE the database open to use in the next exercise.

Take Note You can save your table so it retains your formatting the next time you open it.

Take Note To select more than one field to freeze or hide, hold down the shift key while selecting adjacent fields.

Another Way
You can also access the Hide/Unhide and Freeze/ Unfreeze options from the shortcut menu that appears after you right-click a field name.

SOFTWARE ORIENTATION

Relationship Tools on the Ribbon

When you click the Relationships button on the Database Tools tab, the Relationship window appears and the Relationship Tools are displayed in the Ribbon (Figure 3-28).

Figure 3-28

Use the Relationship Tools to define and modify table relationships

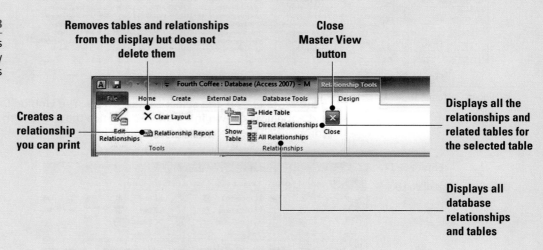

Removes tables and relationships from the display but does not delete them

Close Master View button

Creates a relationship you can print

Displays all the relationships and related tables for the selected table

Displays all database relationships and tables

UNDERSTANDING TABLE RELATIONSHIPS

The Bottom Line

As you have already learned, most databases have more than one table. Creating relationships among these tables allows Access to bring that information back together again through objects such as reports and queries so that you can display information from several tables at once. This is why it is a good idea to define table relationships before you start creating reports and queries.

Defining Table Relationships

In relational database applications like Access, you can store information in separate tables that are connected by a defined relationship that ties the data together. You define a table relationship in the Relationships window. To create that relationship, you place common fields in tables and define the relationships between the tables. Common fields used in different tables do not have to have the same names, but they usually do. They must have the same data type, though. In this exercise, you use a table that already has a primary key field to create a relationship with another table.

You can create three types of relationships in Access tables: one-to-one, one-to-many, and many-to-many.

In a one-to-one relationship, both tables have a common field with the same data. Each record in the first table can only have one matching record in the second table, and each record in the second table can have only one matching record in the first table. This type of relationship is not common because information related in this way is usually stored in the same table.

A one-to-many relationship is more common because each record in the first table can have many records in the second table. For example, in a Customers table and an Orders table, one customer could have many orders. The Customer ID would be the primary key in the Customers table (the one) and the foreign key in the Orders table (the many).

In a third type of relationship, called a many-to-many relationship, many records in the first table can have many records in the second table.

STEP BY STEP   **Define Table Relationships**

USE the database you used in the previous exercise.

1. On the Database Tools tab in the Relationships group, click the Relationships button. The Relationships View appears with the Customers table represented.

2. Click the Show Table button. The Show Table dialog box appears, as shown in Figure 3-29.

Figure 3-29

Show Table button and dialog box

3. Select Order Summary and click Add.

4. Click Close. The Customer table and Order Summary table are represented in Relationships View.

5. Click the Customer ID field in the Customers table and drag it to the Customer ID field of the Order Summary table and release the mouse button. The Customer ID field represents the common field between the two tables. The Edit Relationships dialog box appears, as shown in Figure 3-30.

Figure 3-30

Edit Relationships dialog box

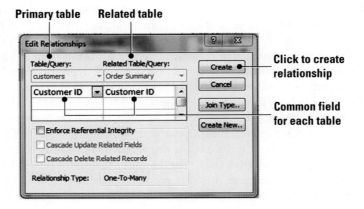

6. Select the *Enforce Referential Integrity* check box. Then select the *Cascade Update Related Fields* and *Cascade Delete Related Records* check boxes.

7. Click **Create**. A relationship line representing the one-to-many table relationship of the Customers and the Order Summary tables is displayed, as shown in Figure 3-31. You just created a one-to-many relationship between these tables using Customer ID, the common field. The one-to-many relationship type signifies that each customer record in the Customers table can have many order records in the Order Summary table.

Figure 3-31

One-to-many relationship

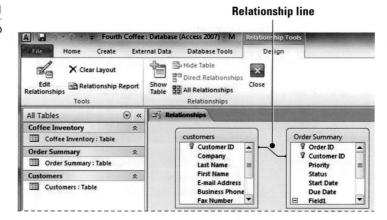

PAUSE. LEAVE the database open to use in the next exercise.

Modifying Table Relationships

A table relationship is represented by the line that connects the tables in the Relationship window. To modify the relationship, you can double-click the line to display the Edit Relationships dialog box or delete the line to delete the relationship. The Edit Relationships dialog box allows you to change a table relationship. You can change the tables on either side of the relationship or the fields on either side. You can also perform actions like enforcing referential integrity and choosing cascade options. In the next exercise, you delete the relationship you previously created, and then recreate and edit the relationship to enforce referential integrity.

Referential integrity is an option that you can select in the Edit Relationships dialog box to prevent orphan records. An orphan record is a record in one table that references records in another table that no longer exist. For example, when referential integrity is enforced, Access will not permit a Customer ID value as the foreign key in the Order Summary table that doesn't have a matching Customer ID value as the primary key in the Customers table. In this way, referential integrity ensures your tables contain logically related data. If an operation that violates referential integrity is performed once this option is selected, Access will display a dialog box with a message stating that referential integrity is being violated and therefore will not permit the operation. You can also choose one or both types of cascade options—cascade update related fields or cascade delete related fields—in the Edit Relationships dialog box once referential integrity has been selected. For example, if the cascade update related fields option is selected, Access will update the Customer ID value in the Order Summary table if the Customer ID value in the Customers table is updated. This ensures consistent Customer ID values in the related tables. Similarly, if the cascade delete related fields option is selected, Access will delete all Customer ID records from the Order Summary table if the related Customer ID record is deleted from the Customers table, therefore preventing orphaned records. When you enforce referential integrity between tables, the line connecting the tables becomes thicker. The number 1 is also displayed on the line on the one side of the relationship and an infinity symbol (∞) appears on the other side, to represent the "many" fields that can be included in this side of the relationship.

To remove a table relationship, you must delete the relationship line. You can select the line by pointing to it and clicking it. When the relationship line is selected, it appears thicker. Press the Delete key to delete the line and remove the relationship or right-click the line to display the delete menu.

STEP BY STEP   **Modify Table Relationships**

USE the database you used in the previous exercise.

1. Right-click the center section of the relationship line connecting the two tables. A menu appears, as shown in Figure 3-32.

Figure 3-32

Edit/Delete menu

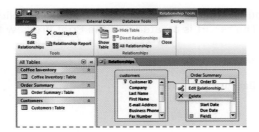

2. Select **Delete**. A message appears asking if you are sure you want to delete the relationship. Click **Yes**. The line disappears.

3. Select the **Customer ID** field in the first table. Drag the mouse to the Customer ID field in the second table and release the mouse button. The Edit Relationships dialog box appears.

4. Click the **Create** button. A line appears, creating the relationship.

5. Double-click the center section of the relationship line. The Edit Relationships dialog box appears again, listing the tables and the Customer ID fields on each side.

6. Click the **Enforce Referential Integrity** box and click **OK**. The line appears thicker, with the number 1 beside the first table and the infinity symbol (∞) beside the second, as shown in Figure 3-33.

Figure 3-33

Relationship displaying enforced referential integrity

Relationship line with the number 1 on the "one" side

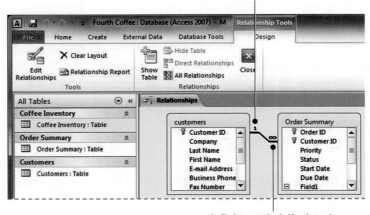

Infinity symbol displayed on the "many" side

PAUSE. LEAVE the database open to use in the next exercise.

Printing Table Relationships

You may want to print a table relationship to save for your records or to discuss with a colleague. The Relationship Report command makes this easy. When you choose to print the relationship report, the Print Preview tab will appear with options for viewing and printing the report. After you make any changes to the layout of the report, click the Print button to start printing. After printing the report, you can choose to save it. In this exercise, you view and print table relationships without saving the relationship report.

STEP BY STEP **Print Table Relationships**

USE the database you used in the previous exercise.

1. In the Tools group of the Relationship Tools Design tab, click the Relationship Report button. The report is created and the Print Preview tab appears, as shown in Figure 3-34.

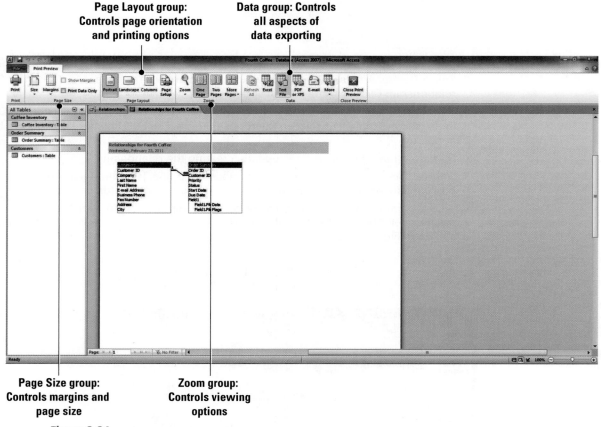

Page Layout group: Controls page orientation and printing options

Data group: Controls all aspects of data exporting

Page Size group: Controls margins and page size

Zoom group: Controls viewing options

Figure 3-34

Print preview of Relationship Report

2. Click the Print button. The Print dialog box appears, allowing you to select the printer you want to use.

3. Click OK to keep the default settings and print the report.

4. Click the Close button to close the Relationships for FourthCoffee tab. A message appears asking if you want to save changes to the report. Click No.

5. Close the Relationships tab.

STOP. CLOSE the database.

SKILL SUMMARY

In This Lesson, You Learned How To:
Navigate among records
Enter, insert, edit, and delete records
Work with primary keys
Find and replace data
Attach and detach documents
Sort and filter data and set field view options within a table
Understand table relationships

Knowledge Assessment

Matching

Match the term in Column 1 to its description in Column 2.

Column 1	Column 2
1. foreign key	a. prevents orphan records, to ensure that records do not reference other records that no longer exist
2. composite key	b. sorts data from beginning to end
3. outermost field	c. sorts data from end to beginning
4. referential integrity	d. to arrange data alphabetically, numerically, or chronologically
5. wildcards	e. a primary key from one table that is used in another table
6. ascending order	f. a set of rules for determining which records will be displayed
7. descending order	g. the secondary sort field in a multifield sort
8. filter	h. two or more primary keys in a table
9. sort	i. characters used to find words or phrases that contain specific letters or combinations of letters
10. innermost field	j. the primary sort field in a multifield sort

True/False

Circle T if the statement is true or F if the statement is false.

T   F   1. You can use the Navigation buttons to search for data in a table.

T   F   2. You can enter any kind of data into any field.

T   F   3. After you enter data and move to a new field, Access automatically saves the data for you in the table.

T   F   4. After you delete a record, you can click the Undo button to bring it back.

T   F   5. The Find and Replace dialog box searches all the tables in a database at one time.

T   F   6. An AutoNumber field will usually make a good primary key.

T   F   7. Before you can attach a document, there must be a field in a table formatted with the Attachment data type.

T   F   8. The outermost field is the primary sort field in a multifield sort.

T   F   9. The Toggle Filter button lets you permanently remove a filter and switches you back to the original view.

T   F   10. In a one-to-many relationship, each record in the first table can have many records in the second table.

Competency Assessment

Project 3-1: Charity Event Contacts List

You are working as an intern for Woodgrove Bank. Part of your job is helping your supervisor organize a charity event. Use an Access table to create a contacts list that your supervisor will use to make calls to local businesses requesting sponsorships and donations for the event.

GET READY. LAUNCH Access if it is not already running.

1. **OPEN** the *Charity Event* database.

2. **SAVE** the database as *Charity EventXXX* (where XXX is your initials).

3. Open the Contacts table.

4. Enter the records shown in the following table:

ID	Company	Last Name	First Name	Business Phone
17	Trey Research	Tiano	Mike	469-555-0182
18	Fourth Coffee	Culp	Scott	469-555-0141
19	Wingtip Toys	Baker	Mary	972-555-0167
20	Margie's Travel	Nash	Mike	972-555-0189

5. Click the View menu and choose Design View.

6. Select the ID row. On the Design tab, on the Tools menu, click the Primary Key button.

7. Save the design of the table and return to Datasheet View.

8. On the Home tab, in the Find group, click the Find button. The Find and Replace dialog box appears. Key 0177 into the Find What box.

9. Select Contents from the Look In menu and select Any Part of Field in the Match menu.

10. Click the Replace tab. Key 0175 into the Replace With box.

11. Click Find Next and then click Replace.

12. Click Cancel to close the dialog box.

13. Select the Lucern Publishing record.

14. On the Home tab, in the Records group, click the Delete button. Click Yes to delete the record.

15. **CLOSE** the database.

LEAVE Access open for the next project.

The *Charity Event* file for this lesson is available on the book companion website or in WileyPLUS.

Project 3-2: Angels Project Wish List

The four kindergarten classes at the School of Fine Art have adopted one boy and one girl "angel" from the community. Children from the classes may purchase holiday gifts for their angels. As an office assistant at the school, you are working with the Angel Project staff to organize information about each angel.

GET READY. LAUNCH Access if it is not already running.

@ The *Angels* file for this lesson is available on the book companion website or in WileyPLUS.

1. **OPEN** *Angels* from the data files for this lesson.
2. **SAVE** the database as *Angels XXX*, where XXX is your initials.
3. Open the List table.
4. Select the Gender field. On the Home tab, in the Sort & Filter group, click the Ascending button.
5. Select the Age field. On the Home tab, in the Sort & Filter group, click the Descending button.
6. On the Home tab, in the Sort & Filter group, click the Remove Sort button.
7. In the Gender field, select the M in the first record.
8. On the Home tab, in the Sort & Filter group, click the Selection button and select Equals "M."
9. On the Home tab, in the Sort & Filter group, click the Toggle Filter button.
10. Select the Wants field. On the Home tab, in the Sort & Filter group, click the Filter button. Select Text Filters from the menu, select Contains from the next menu, and key Bike in the Custom Filter dialog box and press Enter.
11. On the Home tab, in the Sort & Filter group, click the Advanced Filter Options button and select Clear All Filters from the menu.

LEAVE Access open for the next project.

Proficiency Assessment

Project 3-3: Angel Project Contact Information

GET READY. LAUNCH Access if it is not already running.

1. The Angel database should be open on your screen.
2. Open the Contact Information table.
3. Enter the following new records:

ID	Last Name	First Name	Parent's Name	Address	City	State	Zip Code	Home Phone
15	Wright	Steven	Kevin	2309 Monroe Ct	Marietta	GA	34006	770-555-0142
16	Cook	Cathan	Patrick	1268 Oak Dr	Marietta	GA	34006	770-555-0128

4. Switch to Design View. Remove the primary key from the Home Phone field and define the ID field as the primary key.
5. Save the design and return to Datasheet View.
6. Select the ID field and sort it in ascending order.
7. On the Database Tools tab, in the Relationships group, click the Relationships button.
8. Create a one-to-one relationship between the ID field of the List table and the ID field of the Contact Information table.
9. Save the Relationships View and close it.
10. **CLOSE** the tables and the database.

LEAVE Access open for the next project.

Project 3-4: Wingtip Toys Inventory Table

Wingtip Toys, a small manufacturer of wooden toys, has kept most of its records on paper for the last 20 years. The business has recently expanded, and you have been hired to help the company transfer its entire inventory and other administrative data to Access 2010. Edit the table to include all the latest handwritten data you've found.

GET READY. LAUNCH Access if it is not already running.

@ The *Wingtip Toys* file for this lesson is available on the book companion website or in WileyPLUS.

1. **OPEN** the *Wingtip Toys* database and save it as *Wingtip XXX*, where XXX is your initials.
2. Open the Inventory table.
3. On the Home tab, in the Find group, click the Replace button to display the Find and Replace dialog box. Change the following prices:

   Find all 14.99 and replace with 29.99

   Find all 16.99 and replace with 34.99

   Find all 15.99 and replace with 30.99

   Find all 24.99 and replace with 34.99
4. Delete the following records from the database:

   ID = 13

   ID = 19

   ID = 16
5. Edit the following records:

   ID = 30, change the number of items in stock to 3

   ID = 28, change the number of items in stock to 6

   ID = 6, change the number of items in stock to 4
6. Select the In Stock field and create a filter to display all the records with a value less than or equal to 10 in the field.
7. Remove the filter.
8. Close the table.
9. **CLOSE** the database.

LEAVE Access open for the next project.

Mastery Assessment

Project 3-5: Soccer Roster

As coach of your son's soccer team, you have created a database in which to store information about the team. Enter, edit, and delete records to update it.

GET READY. LAUNCH Access if it is not already running.

@ The *Soccer* file for this lesson is available on the book companion website or in WileyPLUS.

1. **OPEN** the *Soccer* database from the data files for this lesson.
2. **SAVE** the database as *Soccer XXX*, where *XXX* is your initials.
3. Open the Roster table.
4. Enter the following record for a new player:

   Eric Parkinson, 806-555-0170, uniform number 9
5. One player has quit the team, Russell King. Replace his data with this data for the following new player:

   George Jiang, 806-555-0123, uniform number 4
6. In the Size field, enter XS for each player, except for uniform numbers 4, 6, and 7, which should be size S.

@ The *Medical Alert* file for this lesson is available on the book companion website or in WileyPLUS.

7. Create an Attachment field and attach the Word document *Medical Alert.docx* to the record for Garrett Young.
8. Define the Uniform field as the primary key.
9. Save the table design and **CLOSE** the database.

LEAVE Access open for the next project.

Project 3-6: Donations Table

Donations are starting to come in for Woodgrove Bank's charity event. Track the donation commitments received.

GET READY. LAUNCH Access if it is not already running.

1. **OPEN** the *CharityEvent XXX* database you created in Project 3-1.
2. Open the Donations table.
3. Create a filter to display the items in the Needs field without Commitments from a company.
4. Remove the filter.
5. Use Find and Replace to find each occurrence of the word Company in the Needs field and replace it with the word Volunteer.
6. Create a relationship between the ID field in the Contacts table and the Committed Company ID in the Donations table.
7. Print the relationship.
8. Close the relationship without saving.
9. Close the tables.
10. **CLOSE** the database.

CLOSE Access.

INTERNET READY

Search the Internet for at least five coffee shops in your area or a favorite city of your choice. Draw a table on paper or in a Word document with fields for the Company Name, Location, Phone Number, and Hours of Operation. Insert data for the five coffee shops you found. If you feel ready for a challenge, create the table in a new database.

4 Modify Tables and Fields

LESSON SKILL MATRIX

In This Lesson, You Will Learn The Following Skills:

Modifying a Database Table

Creating Fields and Modifying Field Properties

KEY TERMS

- **multivalued field**
- **properties**
- **Quick Start field**
- **validation rule**
- **validation text**

Erin's Travel is a full-service travel agency that specializes in sports-event travel packages. The company offers both individual and group travel packages to many of the leading sports events throughout the country. The travel packages can be customized to include plane tickets, event tickets, event transportation, hotel accommodations, official event souvenirs, and on-site staff assistance. As an assistant event coordinator, you are responsible for gathering information about a variety of events; you use Access to store the necessary data. In this lesson, you learn how to modify table properties, rename a table, delete a table, modify field properties, and create and modify fields—including multivalue and attachment fields.

MODIFYING A DATABASE TABLE

The Bottom Line

After a table has been created, you may need to modify it. You can make many changes to a table—or other database object—using its property sheet. You can also rename or delete a table, but keep in mind that such a change could possibly break the functionality of the database, because in a relational database the various components work together.

Modifying Table Properties

You can set properties that control the appearance or behavior characteristics for an entire table in the table's property sheet. Sometimes it's necessary to describe the purpose of a table by modifying the table's Description property since others who view your table may require more information about its purpose. Other table properties are more advanced and used less often. In this exercise, you modify the description property for a table.

STEP BY STEP	**Modify Table Properties**

GET READY. Before you begin these steps, be sure to launch Microsoft Access.

 The *Events* file for this lesson is available on the book companion website or in WileyPLUS.

1. **OPEN** the *Events* database from the data files for this lesson.
2. **SAVE** the database as *EventsXXX* (where *XXX* is your initials).
3. Click the Close 'Event List' button to close the form that displays.
4. In the Navigation Pane, double-click Events to open that table.
5. On the Home tab, in the Views group, click the Views button and then click Design View.
6. On the Design tab, in the Show/Hide group, click Property Sheet. The Property Sheet pane appears on the right of the Access window, as shown in Figure 4-1.

WileyPLUS Extra! features an online tutorial of this task.

Property sheet pane

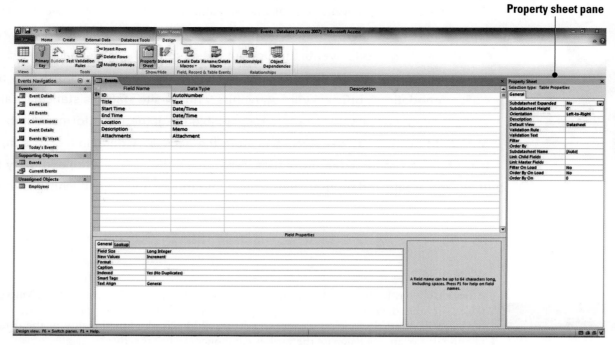

Figure 4-1

Property sheet pane

7. Place the insertion point in the property box for Description.

8. Press Shift+F2 to open the Zoom box, shown in Figure 4-2, to provide more space.

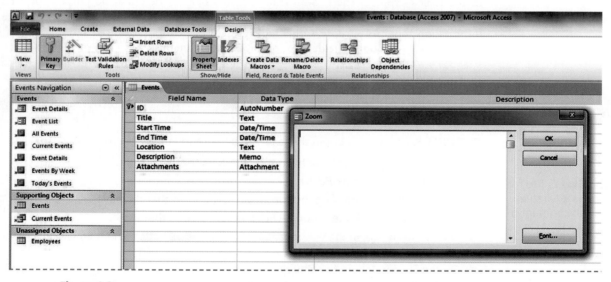

Figure 4-2

Zoom dialog box

9. Key Most popular events for 2012.

10. Click OK.

Another Way
You can also press Alt+Enter to display the property sheet for an object.

11. Click the Close button on the Property Sheet pane to close it.

12. Click the File tab and click Save to save the design changes you've made to the table.

PAUSE. LEAVE the database open to use in the next exercise.

To set the properties for a table, open the table in Design View. On the Design tab, in the Show/Hide group, click Property Sheet. Click the box for the property you want to set and key a setting for the property. Table 4-1 lists the available table properties and what they control.

Table 4-1

Table Properties

Table Property	Use This Table Property To
Subdatasheet Expanded	Specify whether to expand all subdatasheets when you open the table.
Subdatasheet Height	Specify whether to expand to show all available subdatasheet rows (default) when opened or to set the height of the subdatasheet window to show when opened.
Orientation	Set the view orientation, according to whether your language is read left-to-right or right-to-left.
Description	Provide a description of the table.
Default View	Set Datasheet, PivotTable, or PivotChart as the default view when you open the table.
Validation Rule	Supply an expression that must be true whenever you add a record or change a record.
Validation Text	Enter text that appears when a record violates the Validation Rule expression.
Filter	Define criteria to display only matching rows in Datasheet View.
Order By	Select one or more fields to specify the default sort order of rows in Datasheet View.
Subdatasheet Name	Specify whether a subdatasheet should appear in Datasheet View, and, if so, which table or query should supply the rows in the subdatasheet.
Link Child Fields	List the fields in the table or query used for the subdatasheet that match this table's primary key field(s).
Link Master Fields	List the primary key field(s) in this table that match the child fields for the subdatasheet.
Filter On Load	Automatically apply the filter criteria in the Filter property (by setting to Yes) when the table is opened in Datasheet View.
Order By On Load	Automatically apply the sort criteria in the Order By property (by setting to Yes) when the table is opened in Datasheet View.
Order By On	Provide an alternate method to the Order By On Load property by automatically applying the sort criteria in the Order By property when set to -1 (Yes).

Renaming a Table

To rename a table or other database object, you must first close it. In the Navigation Pane, locate and right-click the object that you want to rename, and then click Rename on the shortcut menu that appears. Or, select the table in the Navigation Pane, press F2, key a new name, and press Enter. Think carefully before you rename a table. If existing database objects, such as queries or reports, use data from that table, the name modification might break the functionality of the database. In this exercise, you create a new table and then rename it using the shortcut menu.

STEP BY STEP   **Rename a Table**

USE the database that is open from the previous exercise.

1. On the Create tab, in the Tables group, click the **Application Parts** button and click **Comments** to create a new table.
2. In the Create Relationship dialog box that appears, select **There is no relationship** and then click **Create**.

3. Open the Comments table and right-click Comments in the Navigation Pane to display the shortcut menu shown in Figure 4-3. Select Rename and a dialog box appears that states *You can't rename the database object 'Comments' while it's open,* as shown in Figure 4-4. Close the dialog box.

Figure 4-3

Rename command on table shortcut menu

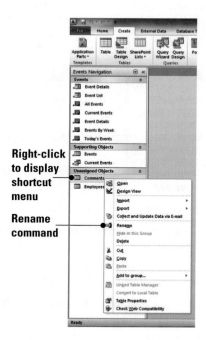

Right-click to display shortcut menu

Rename command

Figure 4-4

Can't rename table dialog box

4. Close the Comments table. The table closes.
5. Right-click Comments in the Navigation Pane to display the shortcut menu.
6. Click Rename. The table name is now selected for renaming, as shown in Figure 4-5.

Figure 4-5

Table name selected for renaming

Key new table name

7. Key Event Comments and press Enter. The table has been renamed.

PAUSE. LEAVE the database open to use in the next exercise.

Deleting a Table

Deleting an entire table is not a complex process; however, remember that when you delete an entire table you might break the functionality of your database. Although you will be asked to confirm the deletion of a table, you can always undo the action.

To delete a table or other database object like a report, form, or query, right-click it in the Navigation Pane and click Delete. Or, select the table in the Navigation Pane and press Delete.

 Ref

Another way to remove data is to delete information from individual records or delete entire records from a table, as you learned in Lesson 3.

SOFTWARE ORIENTATION

Field Properties

Some field properties are available in Datasheet View, but to access the complete list of field properties you must use Design View. An example of field properties for a table in Design View is shown in Figure 4-6.

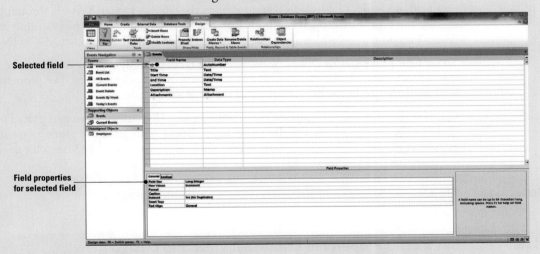

Figure 4-6

Field properties

Use this figure as a reference throughout this lesson as well as the rest of this book.

CREATING FIELDS AND MODIFYING FIELD PROPERTIES

The Bottom Line

A field has certain defining characteristics such as a name that uniquely identifies the field within a table, and a data type that's chosen to match the information to be stored. Every field also has an associated group of settings called **properties** that define the appearance or behavior of the field. In this section, you learn how to create fields and modify field properties.

Access uses the field property settings when you view and edit data. For example, the Format, Input Mask, and Caption properties affect how your information appears in table and query datasheets. In addition, any controls on new forms and reports that are based on the fields in the table inherit these same property settings by default.

Setting Field Properties

You can control the appearance of information, prevent incorrect entries, specify default values, speed up searching and sorting, and control other appearance or behavior characteristics by setting or modifying field properties. For example, you can format numbers to make them easier to read or you can define a validation rule that must be satisfied for information to be entered in a field. In this exercise, you set the *Required* field property in Datasheet View and Field Size property in Design View.

To set a field property in Datasheet View, open the table in Datasheet View. Click in the field for which you want to set the property. In the Field Validation group on the Table Tools Fields contextual tab, select the Unique check box to require the values in the field to be unique for all the records in the table. Or, select the Required check box to make this a required field, where all instances of this field must contain a value. In the Properties group, select the Field Size property box to define the text length for a field, which limits the number of characters allowed for input. You can also select other field properties like Name and Caption, where you can modify a preexisting field or specify a new field name and the associated caption for that field. The field name is what Access uses to reference the field behind the scenes and when you view the field names in Design View. The caption is what appears as column names in tables, and as labels in queries, forms, and reports. Keep in mind that Access will show field names as the column names and labels when no caption property value is specified.

You can set a few of the available field properties in Datasheet View, but to access all of the available field properties (Table 4-2), you must open the table in Design View. For example, you can modify the Field Size property in both Datasheet and Design Views, but can only modify the Smart Tags property—which allows actions to occur when field data is clicked—in Design View.

To set field properties in Design View, open the table in Design View. In the upper portion of the table design grid, click the field for which you want to set properties. The properties for this field are displayed in the lower portion of the table design grid.

Click the box for the field property you want to set. Alternatively, you can press F6 and then move to the property by using the arrow keys. Type a setting for the property or, if an arrow appears at the right side of the property box, click the arrow to choose from a list of settings for the property.

Take Note   The maximum number of characters you can enter into a field is 255.

STEP BY STEP   **Set a Field Property in Datasheet View and Design View**

USE the database that is open from the previous exercise.

1. Double-click the **Events** table in the Navigation Pane to open the table in Datasheet View, if it is not already open.
2. Click the **Location** column header to select that field.
3. Click the **Required** check box in the Field Validation group on the Table Tools Fields contextual tab, as shown in Figure 4-7. This setting determines that all instances of the *Location* field must contain a value.

Field Validation group with Required check box selected

Figure 4-7

Table Tools Tab

4. On the Home tab, in the Views group, click the **View** button and click **Design View**.

5. In the Field Name column in the upper portion of the table design grid, click in the *Title* cell.

6. In the Field Size row in the lower portion of the table design grid, select **150** in the property box and key **175** to change the maximum number of characters you can enter in the *Title* field.

PAUSE. LEAVE the database open to use in the next exercise.

Table 4-2

Available Field Properties.

Field Property	Use This Field Property To
Field Size	Set the maximum size for data stored as a Text, Number, or AutoNumber data type.
Format	Customize the way the field appears when displayed or printed.
Decimal Places	Specify the number of decimal places to use when displaying numbers.
New Values	Set whether an *AutoNumber* field is incremented or assigned a random number.
Input Mask	Display editing characters to guide data entry.
Caption	Set the text displayed by default as the column name in tables and labels for forms, reports, and queries.
Default Value	Automatically assign a default value to a field when new records are added.
Validation Rule	Supply an expression that must be true whenever you add or change the value in this field.
Validation Text	Enter text that appears when a value violates the Validation Rule.
Required	Require that data be entered in a field.
Allow Zero Length	Allow entry (by setting to Yes) of a zero-length string ("") in a *Text, Memo,* or *Hyperlink* field.
Indexed	Speed up access to data in this field by creating and using an index.
Unicode Compression	Compress text stored in this field when a large amount of text is stored.
IME Mode	Specify an Input Method Editor, a tool for using English versions of Windows.
IME Sentence Mode	Specify the type of data you can enter by using an Input Method Editor.
SmartTags	Attach a smart tag to this field.
Append Only	Allow versioning (by setting to Yes) of a *Memo* field.
Text Format	Choose Rich Text to store text as HTML and allow rich formatting. Choose Plain Text to store only text.
Text Align	Specify the default alignment of text within a control.
Precision	Specify the total number of digits allowed, including those both to the right and the left of the decimal point.
Scale	Specify the maximum number of digits that can be stored to the right of the decimal separator.

Setting Data Validation Rules

Validation rules help to ensure that your database users enter the proper types or amounts of data. A **validation rule** is an expression that limits the values that can be entered in the field. The maximum length for the Validation Rule property is 2,048 characters. For example, if the field contains a date, you can require that the date entered in the field be later than June 4, 1977. **Validation text** specifies the text in the error message that appears when a user violates a validation rule. For example, the error message could say "Please enter a date that is later than

June 4, 1977." The maximum length for the Validation Text property is 255 characters. In this exercise, you modify the Validation Rule and Validation Text properties for the *End Time* field.

Data can be validated in several ways, and you will often use multiple methods to define a validation rule. Each of the following can be used to ensure that your users enter data properly:

- **Data types:** When you design a database table, you define a data type for each field in the table, and that data type restricts what users can enter. For example, a *Date/Time* field accepts only dates and times, a *Currency* field accepts only monetary values, and so on.
- **Field sizes:** Field sizes provide another way to validate text. For example, if you create a field that stores first names, you can set it to accept a maximum of 15 characters. This can prevent a malicious user from pasting large amounts of text into the field. It could also prevent an inexperienced user from mistakenly entering a first, middle, and last name in a field designed only to hold a first name.
- **Table properties:** Table properties provide very specific types of validation. For example, you can set the Required property to Yes, and, as a result, force users to enter a value in a field.
- **Field properties:** You can also use field properties, such as the Validation Rule property to require specific values, and the Validation Text property to alert your users to any mistakes. For example, entering a rule such as >1 and <100 in the Validation Rule property forces users to enter values between 1 and 100. Entering text such as "Enter values between 1 and 100" in the Validation Text property tells users when they have made a mistake and how to fix the error.

Another Way
As you already learned in this lesson, you can also use the Input Mask property to validate data by forcing users to enter values in a specific way.

STEP BY STEP **Set Data Validation Rules**

USE the database that is open from the previous exercise.

1. In the Field Name column in the upper portion of the table design grid, click the End Time cell.
2. Click the Validation Rule property box in the lower portion of the table design grid to display the Expression Builder button (...) on the far right of the cell, as shown in Figure 4-8.

Figure 4-8

Expression Builder button

Click to open the Expression Builder

3. Click the **Expression Builder** button to display the Expression Builder dialog box, as shown in Figure 4-9.

Figure 4-9

Expression Builder dialog box

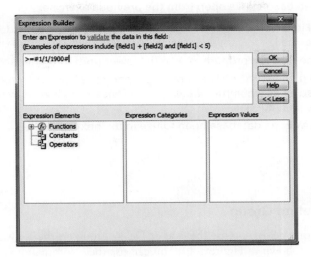

4. Select the number **1900** and replace it by keying **2012**.
5. Click **OK**.
6. Click the **Validation Text** property box in the lower portion of the table design grid.
7. Select the number **1900** and replace it by keying **2012**. The property boxes should look like those shown in Figure 4-10.

Figure 4-10

Modified Validation field properties

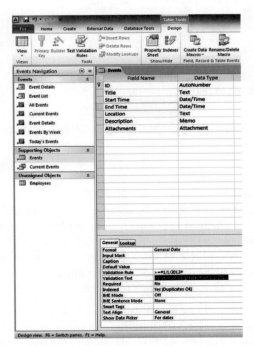

PAUSE. LEAVE the database open to use in the next exercise.

Entering Captions

The *Caption property* field specifies the text displayed by default as column names in tables and in labels for forms, reports, and queries. The maximum length for the Caption property is 255 characters. If you don't specify a caption to be displayed, the field name is used as the label. In this exercise, you set the Caption property for the *Location* field.

STEP BY STEP   Enter Captions

USE the database that is open from the previous exercise.

1. In the Field Name column in the upper portion of the table design grid, click the Location cell.
2. Click the Caption property box in the lower portion of the table design grid.
3. Key **To be announced**. The caption property has now been set to *To be announced* and will display as a column name in table Datasheet View, as well as in labels for forms, reports, and queries.

PAUSE. LEAVE the database open to use in the next exercise.

SOFTWARE ORIENTATION

Add & Delete Group

When creating fields, you use the Add & Delete group on the Table Tools Fields contextual tab, which is shown in Figure 4-11. You can use these commands to add fields with associated data types, add *Quick Start* fields, insert lookup columns, and delete columns.

Figure 4-11

Add & Delete group

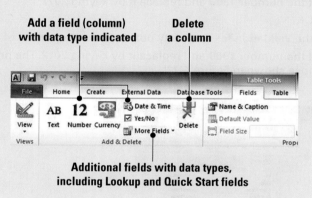

Use this figure as a reference throughout this lesson as well as the rest of this book.

Creating Fields

Fields can be created in different ways. You can add fields to a table in Design View, or add fields in Datasheet View using the Click to Add column and Add & Delete Group. Sometimes it is easier to choose from a predefined list of fields than to manually create a field. Access includes a quick and easy way for you to add fields to a table using the Add & Delete group on the Table Tools Fields contextual tab, which includes a collection of fields with associated data types and built-in *Quick Start* fields that can save you considerable time. In this exercise, you add fields to a table by using a combination of the Click to Add column and the Add & Delete group.

The last column in a table in Datasheet View has a Click to Add column, which you can use to add a field simply by keying information in that column. Rename the field by right-clicking the column head, choosing Rename Field from the menu, and keying a new name. Access will try to automatically determine the field data type by the data entered.

NEW to Office 2010

A **Quick Start field** is a predefined set of characteristics and properties that describes a field, including a field name, a data type, and a number of other field properties. *Quick Start* fields are new to Access 2010 and allow you to quickly add commonly used single fields or several related ones. For example, using *Quick Start* fields, you can choose from a variety of fields including "Status" to quickly add a field named Status with built-in options like Not Started, In Progress, and so on, or you can choose the "Address" Quick Start to quickly include related fields like City, State, and Zip Code.

To create a new field, you can simply choose from commonly used fields in the Add & Delete group, or click the More Fields button to access a menu with a greater variety of field types. To create a new field using Quick Start, click the More Fields button and then choose a Quick Start field from the menu, as shown in Figure 4-12.

Figure 4-12

More Fields button menu

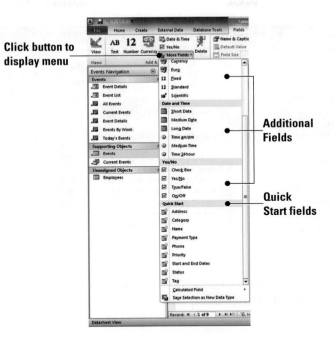

STEP BY STEP   **Create Fields**

USE the database that is open from the previous exercise.

1. On the Home tab, in the Views group, click the View button and click Datasheet View. Save the table, if required. If you get a message about data integrity, click Yes.

Take Note   Whenever you add or modify field validation rules for fields that contain data, the data may violate these new rules. You can allow Access to test the data against the rules and inform you if there are any violations.

2. Scroll to the right of the Events table to display the last column and click in the **first cell below the Click to Add header**, as shown in Figure 4-13. You are going to add a new field in which you can indicate whether or not events will have on-site staff.

Figure 4-13

Click to Add column

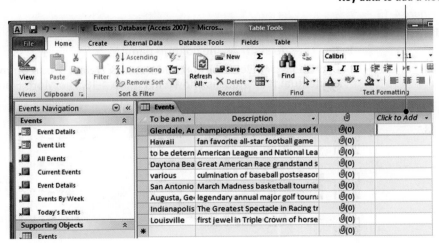

3. Key **Yes** and press **Enter**. A new field named Field1 is added, and the Click to Add column becomes the last column in the table, as shown in Figure 4-14.

Figure 4-14

New field created

New field created

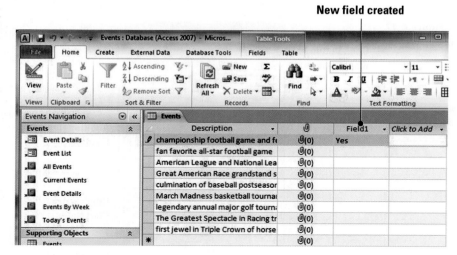

4. Right-click the **Field1** column header to display the shortcut menu and click **Rename Field**, as shown in Figure 4-15.

Right-click to display menu

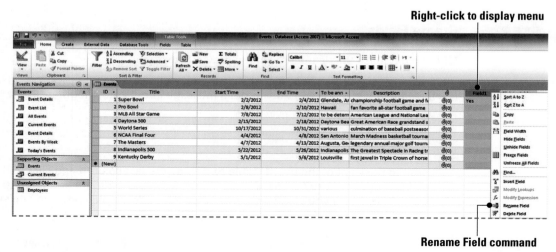

Rename Field command

Figure 4-15

Column shortcut menu

5. Key **On-site staff?** as the column name.

6. Click the **More Fields** button in the Add & Delete group on the Table Tools Fields contextual tab, which is shown in Figure 4-16. The More Fields menu appears.

Figure 4-16

More Fields button and menu

More Fields button displays menu with categories when clicked.

7. In the Yes/No category, click **Check Box**. A new field with check boxes is created in the table, as shown in Figure 4-17.

Figure 4-17

Check box field created

Check box field created for Yes/No values

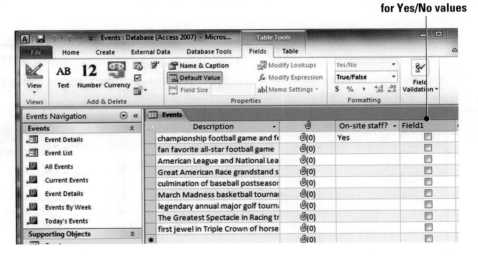

8. Click the **Name & Caption** button in the Properties group, which is shown in Figure 4-18. The Enter Field Properties dialog box appears.

Figure 4-18

Name & Caption button in Properties group

Name & Caption button

9. Key Souvenirs in the Name box and press Enter. Notice the column has been renamed Souvenirs.

10. Scroll to the right of the Events table to display the last column and click in the first cell below the Click to Add header.

11. Click the More Fields button in the Add & Delete group on the Table Tools Fields contextual tab to view the More Fields menu.

12. In the Quick Start category, click Status. A new *Quick Start* field named Status, in which you now have options to indicate the status of the event, appears to the right of the *Souvenirs* field, as shown in Figure 4-19.

Status field created

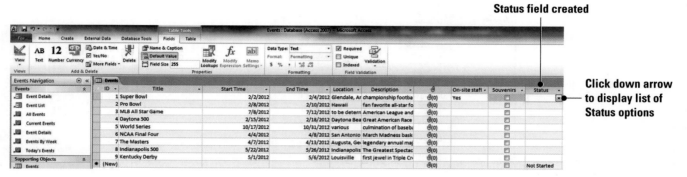

Click down arrow to display list of Status options

Figure 4-19

Status field created

13. Click the Status field drop-down arrow button to view the available options, and click Not Started, as shown in Figure 4-20.

Click down arrow to display list of Status options

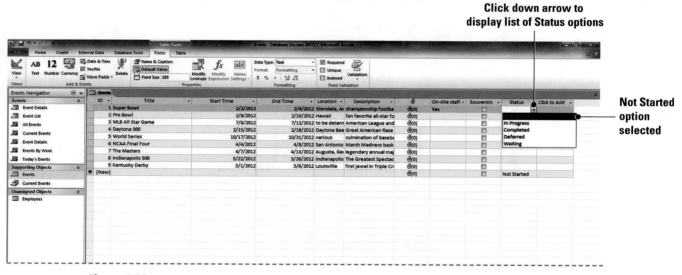

Not Started option selected

Figure 4-20

Status field drop-down box options

14. Click Close to close the Field Templates pane.

PAUSE. LEAVE the database open to use in the next exercise.

Deleting a Field

Before you delete a column from a datasheet, remember that doing so deletes all the data in the column and that the action cannot be undone. For that reason, you should back up the table before you delete the column. Before you can delete a primary key or a lookup field, you must first delete the relationships for those fields.

Another Way
You can also quickly add fields by accessing the Click to Add column menu on the right side of the Click to Add column header.

To delete a field in Datasheet View, select the column, right-click, and then click Delete Field from the shortcut menu. Or, on the Table Tools Fields contextual tab in the Add & Delete group, click the Delete button. You will see a confirmation message asking if you are sure you want to delete the column and all the data. Sometimes you may see an additional confirmation message warning you about potential issues when deleting fields. You should always be cautious when deleting fields from a table.

Creating Multivalued Fields

In Office Access 2010, it is possible to create a **multivalued field** that lets you select more than one choice from a list, without having to create a more advanced database design. You can create a field that holds multiple values, such as a list of employees that you have assigned to a particular event. Use the Lookup Wizard to create multivalued fields. The Lookup Wizard guides you through the process of creating a field or lookup column that can "look up" data that exists in one or more tables to automate the complexity of manually relating tables. In this exercise, you create a multivalued field using the Lookup Wizard in Datasheet View.

Another Way
You can also delete a field in Design View by selecting the field (row) that you want to delete and clicking Delete Rows on the Table Tools Design contextual tab, in the Tools group.

Use a multivalued field when you want to store multiple selections from a list of choices that is relatively small. It is also appropriate to use a multivalued field when you will be integrating your database with Windows SharePoint Services, software that allows for information sharing and collaboration—for example, by exporting an Access table to a SharePoint site or linking to a SharePoint list that contains a multivalued field type.

Take Note   You can also create lookup columns that allow for a single selection of a value.

STEP BY STEP   **Create a Multivalued Field**

USE the database that is open from the previous exercise.

1. Place the insertion point in the first cell of the table. Click the More Fields button in the Add & Delete group on the Table Tools Fields contextual tab, then click the Lookup & Relationship button. The Lookup Wizard appears, as shown in Figure 4-21.

Figure 4-21

Lookup Wizard

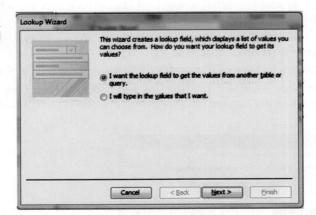

2. Click **Next >** to accept the default setting (*I want the lookup field to get the values from another table or query*) and display the next screen in the Lookup Wizard, as shown in Figure 4-22. Notice you have a choice of two tables to provide the values for the lookup field you're creating. The first table, Employees, should already be selected for you.

Figure 4-22

Lookup Wizard, second screen

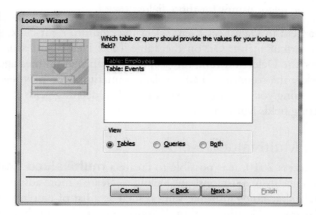

3. Click **Next >** to accept the default settings and display the next screen in the Lookup Wizard, as shown in Figure 4-23. The Available Fields scroll box contains all the fields of the Employees table, two of which you will select since they contain the values you want to eventually look up.

Figure 4-23

Lookup Wizard, third screen

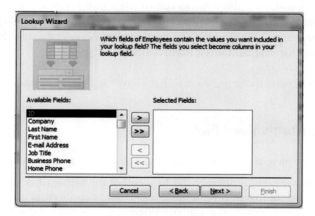

4. In the Available Fields list, select **Last Name**, then click the **>** button to move it to the Selected Fields box.

5. In the Available Fields list, select **First Name**, then click the **>** button to move it to the Selected Fields box.

6. Click **Next >** to accept your settings and display the next screen in the Lookup Wizard.

7. Click the **down arrow** in the first box and click **Last Name**, as shown in Figure 4-24. This will sort the Lookup column in alphabetical order by Last Name.

Figure 4-24

Lookup Wizard, fourth screen

8. Click **Next >** to accept your selection and to display the next screen in the Lookup Wizard, as shown in Figure 4-25.

Figure 4-25

Lookup Wizard, fifth screen

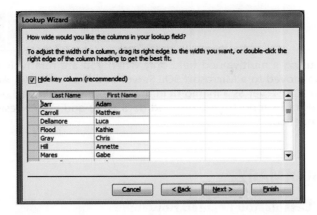

9. Click **Next >** to accept the default selection and to hide the primary key column to ensure only relevant and meaningful data displays in the lookup column later. The final screen of the Lookup Wizard displays, as shown in Figure 4-26.

Figure 4-26

Lookup Wizard, final screen

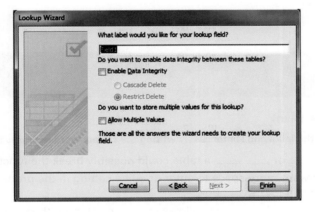

Another Way
You can also modify the Allow Multiple Values property in the Lookup Field Properties sheet in table Design View.

10. In the *What label would you like for your lookup field?* box, key **Coordinator**. This will create a new label named Coordinator for your column.

11. Select the **Allow Multiple Values** check box to allow for the multiple selection of values.

12. Click the **Finish** button. A new column named Coordinator appears after the *ID* field. Click the **down arrow** in the first cell to display the list of names, as shown in Figure 4-27.

Figure 4-27

Lookup column list

Click down arrow to display list of names

Check boxes allow multiple selections

13. Click Flood/Kathie and Mares/Gabe on the list and then click OK to choose those multiple values for the field.

STOP. CLOSE the database.

 **Troubleshooting**   Consider using a multivalued field only when you are relatively sure that your database will not be moved to a Microsoft SQL Server at a later date. An Access multivalued field is upsized to SQL Server as a memo field that contains a delimited set of values. Because SQL Server does not support a multivalued data type, additional design and conversion work might be needed.

SKILL SUMMARY

In This Lesson, You Learned How To:
Modify a database table
Create fields and modify field properties

Knowledge Assessment

Fill in the Blank

Complete the following sentences by writing the correct word or words in the blanks provided.

1. _____ or _____ a table could possibly break the functionality of the database.
2. If you want more space to enter or edit a setting in the property box, press Shift+F2 to display the _____ box.
3. Using the _____ field allows you to select more than one choice.
4. _____ specifies the text in the error message that appears when users violate a validation rule.
5. The _____ property field specifies the text displayed by default as column names in tables and in labels for forms, reports, and queries.
6. When creating fields, use the commands in the _____ group on the Table Tools Fields contextual tab.
7. A(n) _____ is a predefined set of characteristics and properties that describes a field.
8. Creating multivalued fields can be accomplished by using the _____ Wizard.
9. The _____ Quick Start includes fields for city, state, and zip.
10. To create a new field, you would use the _____ _____ group.

Multiple Choice

Select the best response for the following statements or questions.

1. To rename a table or other database object, first
   a. Save it
   b. Close it
   c. Rename it
   d. Open it

2. If you delete a database table,
   a. You cannot undo the action.
   b. Click Undo to restore the table.
   c. It is still available in the Navigation Pane.
   d. The data is transferred to the Clipboard.

3. A complete list of field properties is available in
   a. The Navigation Pane
   b. Datasheet View
   c. Design View
   d. All of the above

4. Which of the following is *not* a field property?
   a. Column Template
   b. Field Size
   c. Caption
   d. Allow Zero Length

5. A name that is listed in the column is called:
   a. caption
   b. title
   c. heading
   d. headline

6. The Append Only property applies only to a field that is set to
   a. Memo
   b. Number
   c. Currency
   d. Text

7. Which of the following is *not* a way to validate data?
   a. Data type
   b. Field sizes
   c. Filtering
   d. Field properties

8. The Caption field property is used for which field?
   a. Text
   b. Attachment
   c. Date/Time
   d. All of the above

9. Which type of field allows you to select more than one choice from a list?
   a. Attachment
   b. Multivalued
   c. Caption
   d. Validation

10. An example of a validation rule is:
    a. >M for male or F for female
    b. =M for male or F for female
    c. <M for male or F for female
    d. none of the above

Competency Assessment

Project 4-1: Home Inventory

You decide to use Access to create a home inventory database for insurance purposes. To include all the information you want, you need to add several fields to the existing table.

GET READY. LAUNCH Access if it is not already running.

@ The *Home Inventory* file for this lesson is available on the book companion website or in WileyPLUS.

1. **OPEN** the *Home inventory* database from the data files for this lesson.
2. **SAVE** the database as *Home inventory XXX* (where *XXX* is your initials).
3. Close the Home Inventory List form that is open.
4. In the Navigation Pane, double-click the Assets table to open it.
5. Horizontally scroll to the end of the table and click in the cell below the Click to Add header.
6. On the Table Tools Fields contextual tab, in the Add & Delete group, click the More Fields button and click Yes/No in the Yes/No category. A column named Field1 is created.
7. On the Table Tools Fields contextual tab, in the Properties group, click the Name & Caption button.
8. Key Insured to rename the Field1 column.
9. Click in the cell below the Click to Add header.
10. On the Table Tools Fields contextual tab, in the Add & Delete group, click the More Fields button and click Attachment in the Basic Types category to create an attachment field.
11. **CLOSE** the database.

LEAVE Access open for the next project.

Project 4-2: Customer Service

You are employed in the customer service department at City Power & Light. Each call that is received is recorded in an Access database. Because you know how to modify tables and fields, your supervisor asks you to add a lookup column to the Calls table to record the customer service representative who receives the call.

GET READY. LAUNCH Access if it is not already running.

@ The *Customer service* file for this lesson is available on the book companion website or in WileyPLUS.

1. **OPEN** *Customer service* from the data files for this lesson.
2. **SAVE** the database as *Customer service XXX* (where *XXX* is your initials).
3. Close the Case List form that is open.
4. In the Navigation Pane, double-click the Calls table to open it. Place the insertion point in the first cell of the table, if necessary.
5. On the Table Tools Fields contextual tab, in the Add & Delete group, click the More Fields button and then click the Lookup & Relationship button. The Lookup Wizard appears.
6. Click Next > to display the next screen in the Lookup Wizard.
7. Select Table: Employees and click Next >.
8. In the Available Fields list, select First Name, then click the > button to move it to the Selected Fields box.
9. In the Available Fields list, select Last Name, then click the > button to move it to the Selected Fields box.

10. Click **Next >** to display the next screen in the Lookup Wizard.

11. Click the **down arrow** in the first box and click **Last Name**.

12. Click **Next >** to display the next screen in the Lookup Wizard.

13. Click **Next >** again to display the final screen in the Lookup Wizard.

14. In the *What label would you like for your lookup field?* box, key **Service Rep**.

15. Click the **Finish** button. A new column named Service Rep appears as the second column of the table.

16. Click the **down arrow** and choose **Clair/Hector** from the list.

17. **LEAVE** the database open for the next project.

LEAVE Access open for the next project.

Proficiency Assessment

Project 4-3: Modify Field Properties

Your supervisor at City Power & Light asks you to make some modifications to the field properties in the Calls table of the customer service database.

USE the database that is open from the previous project.

1. Switch to Design View.

2. Display the *Lookup* field properties for the *Service Rep* field.

3. Change the Allow Multiple Values property to **Yes** and confirm the change.

4. Display the *General* field properties for the *Call Time* field.

5. Change the Validation Rule property so that the value must be **greater than 1/1/2000**.

6. Change the Validation Text property to say **Please enter a value that is greater than 1/1/2000**.

7. Display the *General* field properties for the *Caller* field.

8. Change the Field Size property to **60**.

9. Display the *General* field properties for the *Notes* field.

10. Change the Allow Zero Length property to **Yes**.

11. Change the Append Only property to **Yes**.

12. Save the table. If a data integrity message appears, click **No**.

13. **CLOSE** the database.

LEAVE Access open for the next project.

Project 4-4: Modify Database Tables

You work as the operations manager at Alpine Ski House and decide to increase your efficiency by using Access to plan the annual race events. You have started to create a database to manage the events sponsored by the company, but need to modify the tables.

GET READY. LAUNCH Access if it is not already running.

@ The *Alpine* file for this lesson is available on the book companion website or in WileyPLUS.

1. **OPEN** *Alpine* from the data files for this lesson.

2. **SAVE** the database as *Alpine XXX* (where *XXX* is your initials).

3. Close the Event List form that is open.

4. Delete the Nordic Events table and confirm the action.

5. Rename the World Cup table to Championships.

6. Open the Events table and switch to Design View.

7. Display the property sheet.

8. In the Description property box, key Annual events.

9. **CLOSE** the database.

LEAVE Access open for the next project.

Mastery Assessment

Project 4-5: Changing List Items

You are the owner of Coho Vineyard & Winery, a growing company that is converting all of its data from spreadsheets to Access. You created a table using the Assets table template, but need to make some modifications before you enter information in the database.

GET READY. LAUNCH Access if it is not already running.

@ The *Coho* file for this lesson is available on the book companion website or in WileyPLUS.

1. **OPEN** *Coho* from the data files for this lesson.

2. **SAVE** the database as *Coho XXX* (where *XXX* is your initials).

3. Open the Red Wine table and create a new *Lookup* field as the last field in the table that uses the *Country* field in the Countries table. Specify an ascending sort order for the records in this field.

4. Rename the field Origin.

5. Rename the *Current Value* field to Market Value.

6. Rename the *Acquired Date* field to Acquisition Date.

7. Create a *Yes/No* field as the last field in the table named *Stocked* with a caption named In Stock?

8. **SAVE** the table.

9. **CLOSE** the database.

LEAVE Access open for the next project.

Project 4-6: Lending Library

You have an extensive personal library that friends and family frequently ask to share. To keep track of all your books, you decide to use Access to create a lending library database.

GET READY. LAUNCH Access if it is not already running.

@ The *Lending library* file for this lesson is available on the book companion website or in WileyPLUS.

1. **OPEN** *Lending library* from the data files for this lesson.

2. **SAVE** the database as *Lending library XXX* (where *XXX* is your initials).

3. Modify the fields of the Assets table by: Requiring a value for Acquired Date, Purchase Price, Current Value, and Model; Modifying the field size for Model to 10; Modifying the validation rule for Acquired Date to only allow for values after 12/31/1999, and the validation text to "Value must be greater than 12/31/1999"; Modifying the Append Only property for Comments to "No."

4. **CLOSE** the database.

CLOSE Access.

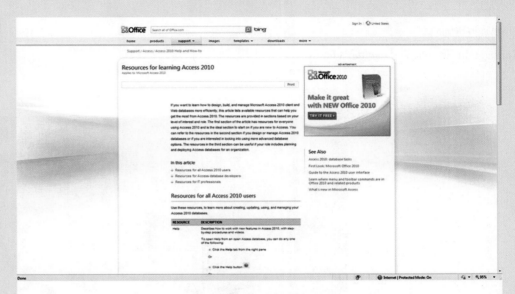

INTERNET READY

A number of online resources can provide solutions to challenges that you might face during a typical workday. Search the Microsoft website for Resources for learning Access 2010, shown in Figure 4-28. This web page is a place where you can find information on how to use Microsoft Access efficiently to perform typical business tasks and activities. Many links to resources are made available here, including links to self-paced training courses, online discussion groups, and Access Power Tips. Explore the resources and content this page has to offer to discover tools or solutions that could be useful on the job and ways you could use Access to be more productive.

Figure 4-28

Access Resource website

5 Create Forms

KEY TERMS

- **Blank Form tool**
- **common filters**
- **filter**
- **filter by form**
- **Form Design button**
- **Form tool**
- **Form Wizard**
- **Themes**

You are the owner of the Graphic Art Institute, a small fine-arts gallery dedicated to presenting challenging and contemporary visual arts and educational programs. The current exhibition is successfully under way; you are now calling for submissions for the next exhibition—a juried art show featuring photographic work from the local region. The competition is open to all regional artists who use photographic processes in their work. This particular event will be open to digital submissions. As each submission is received, you will enter the artist and image information into an Access database for easy retrieval. In this lesson, you learn how to create forms using a variety of methods; how to apply a Theme to a form; and how to sort and filter data within a form.

SOFTWARE ORIENTATION

Forms Group

The Forms group (Figure 5-1) is located on the Create tab in the Ribbon and can be used to create a variety of forms.

Figure 5-1

Forms group

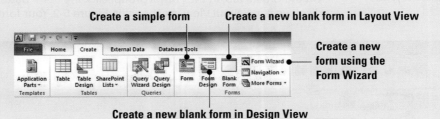

Create a simple form

Create a new blank form in Layout View

Create a new form using the Form Wizard

Create a new blank form in Design View

Use this figure as a reference throughout this lesson as well as the rest of this book.

CREATING FORMS

The Bottom Line

A form is a database object that you can use to enter, edit, or display data from a table or query. Forms can be used to control access to data by limiting which fields or rows of data are displayed to users. For example, certain users might need to see only certain fields in a table. Providing those users with a form that contains just those fields makes it easier for them to use the database. Think of forms as windows through which people see and reach your database in a more visually attractive and efficient way.

You can create forms in several different ways, depending on how much control you want over the form's design. Forms that include all fields in a table can be quickly created through a single mouse-click by using the Form tool, or you can control the number of fields you'd like to include on the form as well as the layout of the form by using the Form Wizard. You have the most flexibility with the amount and placement of fields on the form by using Layout or Design View, with Design View giving you the greatest control over field placement and properties. Finally, you can quickly apply a chosen theme to the form to modify its color and font scheme using the Themes command. In this section, you practice creating forms using a variety of these skills.

Creating a Simple Form

You can use the **Form tool** to create a form with a single mouse-click. When you use this tool, all the fields from the underlying data source are placed on the form. Access creates the form and displays it in Layout View. You can begin using the new form immediately, or you can modify it in Layout View or Design View to better suit your needs. In this exercise, you create a simple form by using the Form tool.

To use the Form tool to create a simple form, first click in the Navigation Pane on the table that contains the data you want to see on the form. On the Create tab, in the Forms group, click Form.

To save your form design, click the File tab and click Save. Key a name in the Form Name box and click OK. After you save your form design, you can run the form as often as you want. The design stays the same, but you see current data every time you view the form. If your needs change, you can modify the form design or create a new form that is based on the original.

STEP BY STEP   **Create a Simple Form**

GET READY. Before you begin these steps, be sure to **LAUNCH** Microsoft Access.

The *Graphic Art* file for this lesson is available on the book companion website or in WileyPLUS.

1. **OPEN** the *Graphic Art* database from the data files for this lesson.
2. **SAVE** the database as *Graphic Art XXX* (where *XXX* is your initials).
3. In the Navigation Pane, click the Photo Exhibit table. This is the table for which you will create a form.
4. On the Create tab, in the Forms group, click the Form button. Access creates the form and displays it in Layout View, as shown in Figure 5-2. Your form may be slightly different.

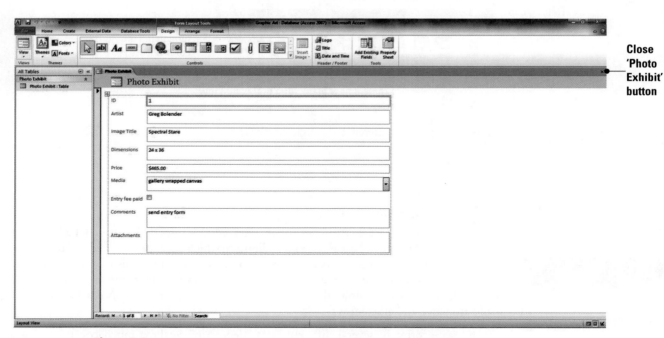

Figure 5-2

Simple form

5. Click the File tab and click Save. The Save As dialog box appears, as shown in Figure 5-3.

Figure 5-3

Save As dialog box

Take Note   You can use the record navigation buttons at the bottom of a form to navigate among the form's records, just as you used them to navigate among records in a table in Lesson 3.

6. Click **OK** to accept the Photo Exhibit form name suggested by Access. The form name appears in the Navigation Pane.
7. Click the **Close** button on Photo Exhibit to close the form.
8. **LEAVE** the database open.

PAUSE. LEAVE Access open to use in the next exercise.

Creating a Form in Design View

When you click the **Form Design button**, a new blank form is created in Design View. Design View gives you a more detailed view of the structure of your form than Layout View. The form is not actually running when it is shown in Design View, so you cannot see the underlying data while you are making design changes. In this exercise, you create a new blank form in Design View and manually add fields to it.

You can fine-tune your form's design by working in Design View. To switch to Design View, right-click the form name in the Navigation Pane and then click Design View. You can also use the View button on the Home tab on the Ribbon. You can add new controls—used to enter, edit, and find information—and fields to the form by adding them to the design grid. Plus, the property sheet gives you access to a large number of properties that you can set to customize your form.

STEP BY STEP   **Create a Form in Design View**

USE the database that is open from the previous exercise.

1. On the Create tab, in the Forms group, click the **Form Design** button. A new blank form is created in Design View, as shown in Figure 5-4.

Figure 5-4

New blank form in Design View

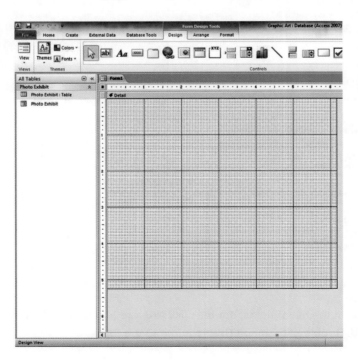

2. On the Form Design Tools Design contextual tab, in the Tools group, click the Add Existing Fields button. The Field List pane appears, as shown in Figure 5-5.

Figure 5-5

Field List pane

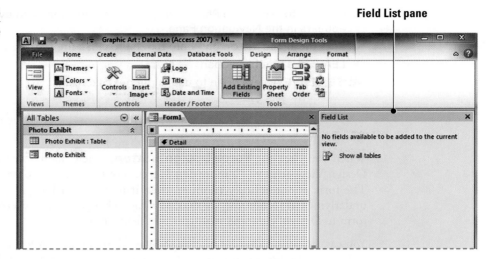

3. Click the Show all tables link, then the expand button to the left of the table name, as shown in Figure 5-6. The available fields display from the Photo Exhibit table, as shown in Figure 5-7.

Another Way
You can also display the Field List pane by clicking Alt+F8.

Figure 5-6

Field List pane with Show all tables link and expand button

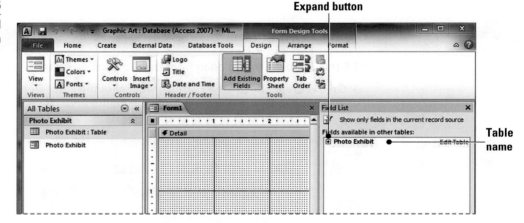

Figure 5-7

Field List pane with available fields

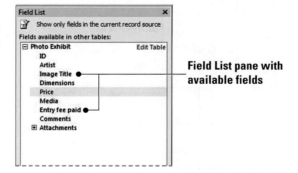

4. In the list of fields, double-click Artist to add it to the form.

5. Double-click Image Title to add it to the form.

6. Double-click **Price** to add it to the form. Your form should look similar to Figure 5-8.

Figure 5-8

Fields inserted in Design View

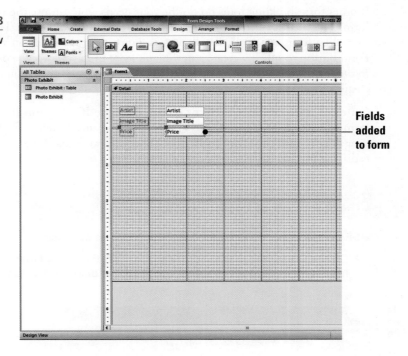

Fields
added
to form

Another Way
You can also click
the field name and drag it onto
the form to add a field.

7. Click the **File** tab and click **Save**.

8. In the Save As dialog box, key **Photo Label**, and click **OK**.

9. On the Design menu, in the Views group, click the lower half of the **View** button and click **Form View** to display the form in Form View, as shown in Figure 5-9.

Figure 5-9

Form View

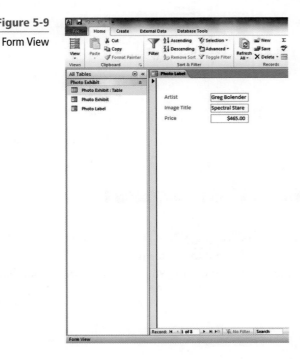

10. Click the **Close** button on Photo Label to close the form.

11. **LEAVE** the database open.

PAUSE. LEAVE the database open to use in the next exercise.

Creating a Form in Layout View

If other form-building tools do not fit your needs, you can use the Blank Form tool to create a form. The **Blank Form tool** creates a new form in Layout View. This can be a very quick way to build a form, especially if you plan to put only a few fields on your form. Click the Blank Form button to quickly create a new blank form in Layout View; you can make design changes to the form while viewing the underlying data. In this exercise, you use the Blank Form tool to create a form in Layout View.

On the Create tab, in the Forms group, click the Blank Form button. Access opens a blank form in Layout View and displays the Field List pane. To add a field to the form, double-click it or drag it onto the form. In Layout View, you can make design changes to the form while it is displaying data.

STEP BY STEP   **Create a Form in Layout View**

USE the database that is open from the previous exercise.

1. On the Create tab, in the Forms group, click the Blank Form button. A new blank form is created in Layout View, with the Field List displayed, as shown in Figure 5-10.

Figure 5-10

New blank form in Layout View

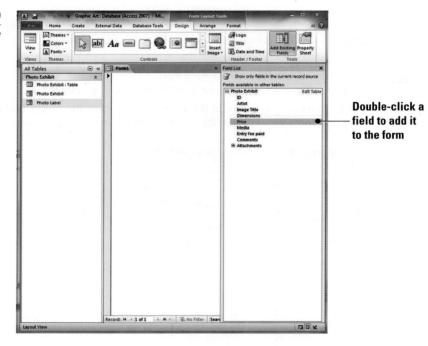

2. In the list of fields, double-click Image Title to add it to the form.
3. Double-click Dimensions to add it to the form.
4. Double-click Media to add it to the form. Your form should look similar to Figure 5-11.

Figure 5-11

Fields inserted in Layout View

5. Click the File tab and click Save.

6. In the Save As dialog box, key Image Info, and click OK.

7. Click the Close button to close the Field List.

8. Click the Close button on Image Info to close the form.

9. **LEAVE** the database open.

PAUSE. LEAVE the database open to use in the next exercise.

Take Note   To add more than one field at a time, press Ctrl and click several fields; then, drag them all onto the form at once.

Using the Form Wizard

Another method of building a form is to use the **Form Wizard** tool. The Form Wizard allows you to select the fields that will appear on the form, choose the form layout (which determines the positioning of controls, objects, and data on a form), and also choose a predefined style, if desired. In this exercise, you use the Form Wizard to create a datasheet form. A datasheet form looks very similar to the table upon which it is based and provides a way to enter data using columns and rows.

STEP BY STEP   **Use the Form Wizard**

USE the database that is open from the previous exercise.

1. On the Create tab, in the Forms group, click the Form Wizard button, shown in Figure 5-12.

Figure 5-12

Form Wizard button in Forms group

Form Wizard button

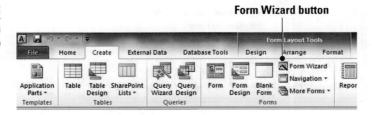

2. The Form Wizard displays, as shown in Figure 5-13.

Figure 5-13

Form Wizard

Click to move selected field

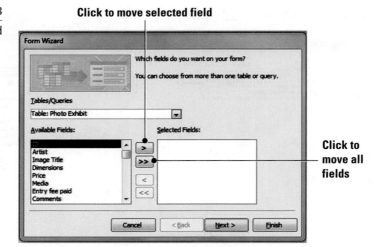

Click to move all fields

3. Click the >> button to move all the fields from the Available Fields box to the Selected Fields box.
4. Click the Next > button to move to the next screen in the Form Wizard, shown in Figure 5-14.

Figure 5-14

Form Wizard, next screen

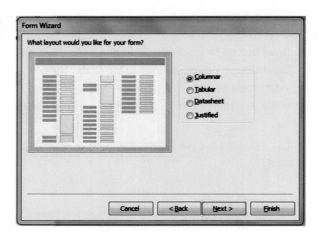

5. Click Datasheet as the layout for the form. Form layouts help determine the positioning of controls, objects, and data on a form.
6. Click the Next > button to move to the final screen in the Form Wizard, as shown in Figure 5-15.

Figure 5-15

Form Wizard, final screen

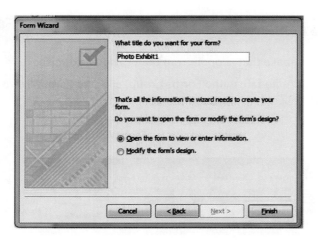

7. Key Photo Details as the title of the form.

8. Click the Finish button. A datasheet form appears, as shown in Figure 5-16.

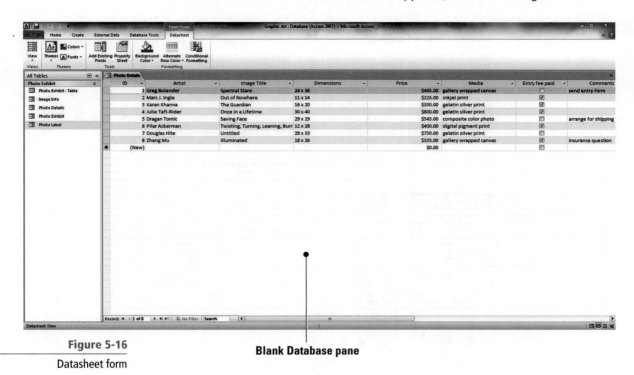

Figure 5-16

Datasheet form

Blank Database pane

9. Click the Close button on Photo Details to close the form.

PAUSE. LEAVE the database open to use in the next exercise.

Take Note
To include fields from more than one table on your form, do not click Next or Finish after you select the fields from the first table on the first screen of the Form Wizard. Instead, repeat the steps to select another table, and click any additional fields that you want to include on the form before continuing.

Applying a Theme

The **Themes** command applies a predefined color and font scheme to a form or report. A theme modifies a form by controlling the color and fonts of its text. In this exercise, you apply a Theme to a form.

To apply a theme, first switch to Layout View. On the Form Layout Tools Design contextual tab, in the Themes group, click the Themes button to view a gallery of theme styles from which to choose. You can point to each option to see the name of that format and a live preview before it's applied to the form.

STEP BY STEP   **Apply a Theme**

USE the database that is open from the previous exercise.

1. Double-click the Image Info form in the Navigation Pane to open it.

2. On the Home tab, in the Views group, click the lower half of the View button, and click Layout View on the View menu.

3. On the Form Layout Tools Design contextual tab, in the Themes group, click the Themes button, shown in Figure 5-17.

Figure 5-17

Themes button

Themes button accesses Themes gallery

4. A gallery of themes appears, as shown in Figure 5-18.

Figure 5-18

Themes gallery

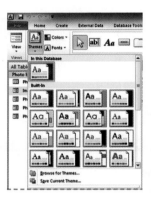

5. Click the Couture theme (fourth row, first column) to apply it to the form. Notice how the form's text has changed, shown in Figure 5-19.

Figure 5-19

Form in Layout View with Couture theme applied

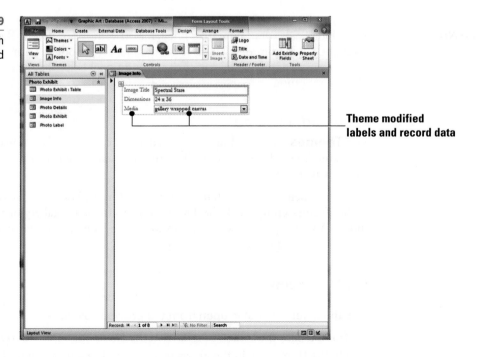

Theme modified labels and record data

6. Click the Close button on Image Info to close the form.

PAUSE. LEAVE the database open to use in the next exercise.

SORTING AND FILTERING DATA WITHIN A FORM

The Bottom Line

Sorting data in a form can help make it much more effective and easy to use. Sorting helps users review and locate the records they want without having to browse the data. To find one or more specific records in a form, you can use a filter. A **filter** limits a view of data to specific records without requiring you to alter the design of the form. You also can use a tool called filter by form to filter on several fields in a form or to find a specific record.

Sorting Data within a Form

Data can be sorted in the Form View of a form. The order that is chosen when a form is designed becomes that object's default sort order. But when viewing the form, users can sort the records in whatever way is most useful. You can sort the records in a form on one or more fields. In this exercise, you sort data in a form in ascending order.

STEP BY STEP | **Sort Data within a Form**

USE the database that is open from the previous exercise.

1. Double-click the Photo Label form in the Navigation Pane to open it in Form View.
2. Right-click the Price field to display the shortcut menu shown in Figure 5-20.

Figure 5-20

Price field shortcut menu

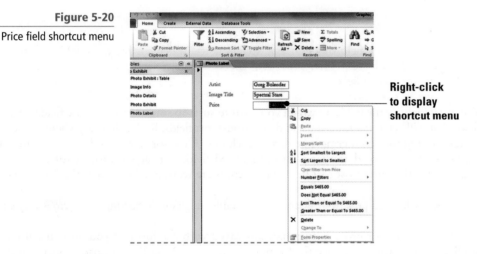

3. Click **Sort Smallest to Largest**. The form is sorted by price from smallest to largest. The record with the smallest price is displayed first, as shown in Figure 5-21.
4. Click the Next record button on the record navigator at the bottom of the form. Continue clicking through all the records to see the records in order according to price.
5. On the Home tab, in the Sort & Filter group, click the Remove Sort button.
6. Click the Close button on Photo Label to close the form.

PAUSE. LEAVE the database open to use in the next exercise.

Another Way
You can also sort on a field by selecting it and clicking the Ascending or Descending button on the Home tab in the Sort & Filter group.

Figure 5-21

Form sorted by price

Take Note   You cannot sort on a field that contains attachments. When sorting on a field with the Yes/No data type, a value of "Yes," "True," or "On" is considered "Selected"; a value of "No," "False," or "Off" is considered "Cleared."

You must identify the fields on which you want to sort. To sort on two or more fields, identify the fields that will act as the innermost and outermost sort fields. Right-click anywhere in the column corresponding to the innermost field, and click one of the sort commands. The commands vary based on the type of data that is in the selected field. Repeat the process for each sort field, ending with the outermost sort field. The records are rearranged to match the sort order.

 Ref   You already learned how to sort data within a table in Lesson 3. Sorting in a form is very similar.

The last-applied sort order is automatically saved with the form. If you want it automatically applied the next time you open the form, make sure the Order By On Load property of the form is set to Yes. Remember that you cannot remove a sort order from just a single field. To remove sorting from all sort fields, on the Home tab, in the Sort & Filter group, click Remove Sort.

Filtering Data within a Form

Common filters are built into every view that displays data. The filters available depend on the type and values of the field. When you apply the filter, only records that contain the values that you are interested in are included in the view. The rest are hidden until you remove the filter. In this exercise, you filter form data using common filters.

Filters are easy to apply and remove. Filter settings remain in effect until you close the form, even if you switch to another view. If you save the form while the filter is applied, it will be available the next time you open the form. To permanently remove a filter, on the Home tab, in the Sort & Filter group, click the Advanced button and click Clear All Filters.

STEP BY STEP | **Filter Data with Common Filters**

USE the database that is open from the previous exercise.

1. Double-click the Photo Exhibit form in the Navigation Pane to open it in Form View.
2. Right-click the Media field to display the shortcut menu and click Text Filters, as shown in Figure 5-22.

Figure 5-22

Media field text filters

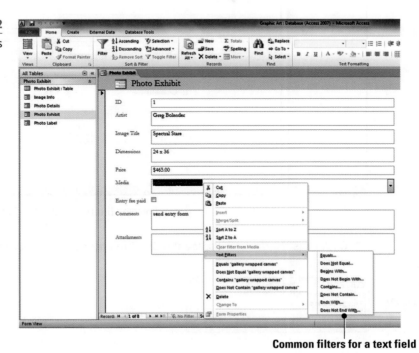

Common filters for a text field

3. Click Contains . . . to display the Custom Filter dialog box, as shown in Figure 5-23.

Figure 5-23

Custom Filter dialog box

4. In the *Media contains* box, key print, and click OK.
5. Click the Next record button on the record navigator at the bottom of the form. Continue clicking to see the five records that contain the word "print" in the *Media* field.
6. Right-click the Price field to display the shortcut menu and click Number Filters, as shown in Figure 5-24.

Figure 5-24

Price field number filters

Figure 5-24

Price field number filters

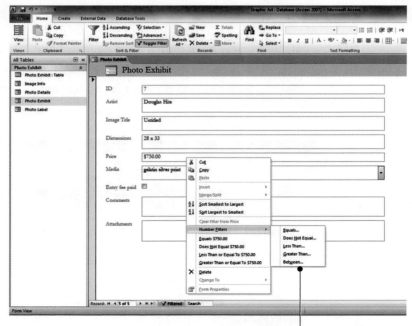

Common filters for a number field

7. Click **Less Than . . .** to display the Custom Filter dialog box shown in Figure 5-25.

Figure 5-25

Custom Filter dialog box

8. In the *Price is less than or equal to* box, key **500**, and click **OK**.
9. Click the **Next record** button on the record navigator at the bottom of the form. Continue clicking to see the three photos that use print media and are less than $500.
10. On the Home tab, in the Sort & Filter group, click the **Advanced Filter Options** button to display the menu shown in Figure 5-26.

Figure 5-26

Advanced Filter Options button menu

11. Click **Clear All Filters**.

PAUSE. LEAVE the database open to use in the next exercise.

 Ref

You already learned how to filter data within a table in Lesson 3. Filtering in a form using common filters is very similar.

Using Filter by Form

Although only a single filter can be in effect for any one field at any one time, you can specify a different filter for each field that is present in the view. In addition to the ready-to-use filters for each data type, you can also filter a form by completing an action called filter by form. **Filter by form** is useful when you want to filter several fields in a form or if you are trying to find a specific record. Access creates a blank form that is similar to the original form, you then complete as many of the fields as you want. When you are done, Access finds the records that contain the specified values. In this exercise, you filter by form.

To use filter by form, open the form in Form View and make sure the view is not already filtered by verifying that either the Unfiltered or the dimmed No Filter icon is present on the record selector bar. On the Home tab, in the Sort & Filter group, click Advanced, and then click Filter by Form. Click the down arrow in a field to display the available values.

Enter the first set of values on the Look for tab, then click the Or tab and enter the next set of values. Each time you click the Or tab, Access creates another Or tab so you can continue to add additional filter values. Click the Toggle Filter button to apply the filter. The filter returns any record that contains all of the values specified on the Look for tab, or all of the values specified on the first Or tab, or all of the values specified on the second Or tab, and so on.

STEP BY STEP   **Use Filter by Form**

USE the database that is open from the previous exercise.

1. On the Home tab, in the Sort & Filter group, click the Advanced Filter Options button and click Filter by Form. A form filter appears, as shown in Figure 5-27.

Figure 5-27

Form filter

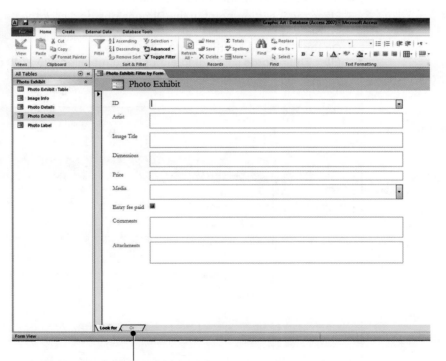

Click or tab to add additional filter values

2. Place the insertion point in the Dimensions box and click the down arrow on the right to display the list of options shown in Figure 5-28.

Figure 5-28

Form filter field options

Figure 5-28

Form filter field options

Click to see available field values

3. Click 30 × 40.

4. Click the Or tab at the bottom of the form.

5. Place the insertion point in the Dimensions box, click the down arrow, and then click 12 × 28.

6. On the Home tab, in the Sort & Filter group, click the Toggle Filter button to apply the filter. The records containing either the dimensions 30 × 40 or 12 × 28 are displayed, as shown in Figure 5-29.

Figure 5-29

Form filter results

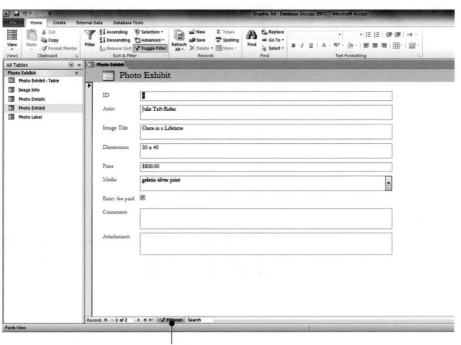

Indicates the form is filtered

7. Click the Next record button on the record navigator at the bottom of the form to see the second record in the form filter results.

8. On the Home tab, in the Sort & Filter group, click the Toggle Filter button again to remove the filter.

9. On the Home tab, in the Sort & Filter group, click the Advanced button and click Clear All Filters.

10. Click the File tab and click Close Database.

STOP. LEAVE Access open for use in the projects.

Take Note

If you want a field value to operate as a filter that is independent of other field values, you must enter that value on the Look for tab and each Or tab. In other words, the Look for tab and each Or tab represents an alternate set of filter values.

SKILL SUMMARY

In This Lesson, You Learned How To:
Create forms
Sort and filter data within a form

Knowledge Assessment

Matching

Match the term in Column 1 to its description in Column 2.

Column 1	Column 2
1. Form Wizard	a. useful when you want to filter on several fields in a form or if you are trying to find a specific record
2. Form Design button	b. creates a simple form with a single mouse-click
3. Theme command	c. applies a predefined combination of colors and fonts that you select for a form or report
4. Blank Form button	d. quickly creates a new blank form in Design View
5. form	e. allows you to select fields for the form, choose the form layout, and also choose a predefined style
6. filter by form	f. limits a view of data to specific records without requiring you to alter the design of the form
7. sorting	g. built into every view that displays data
8. Form tool	h. database object that you can use to enter, edit, or display data from a table or a query
9. common filters	i. helps users review and locate records without having to browse the data
10. filter	j. quickly creates a new blank form in Layout View

True/False

Circle T if the statement is true or F if the statement is false.

T F 1. The Forms group is located on the Home tab in the Ribbon.

T F 2. Forms can be used to control access to data, such as which fields or rows of data are displayed.

T F 3. After you save your form design, you can run the form as often as you want.

T F 4. Layout View gives you a more detailed view of the structure of your form than Design View.

T F 5. Using the Blank Form tool is a very quick way to build a form, especially if you plan to put only a few fields on your form.

T F 6. To access the Theme options, first switch to Form View.

T F 7. You cannot remove a sort order from just a single field.

T F 8. The filters available depend on the field's data type and values.

T F 9. To filter by form, first switch to Design View.

T F 10. When using the Form Wizard, you can only include fields from one table.

Competency Assessment

Project 5-1: Form Wizard

As a travel agent at Erin's Travel, you need an easy way to input data about events into the database. You decide to use the Form Wizard to create a datasheet form that has a preformatted style.

GET READY. LAUNCH Access if it is not already running.

@ The *Travel Events* file for this lesson is available on the book companion website or in WileyPLUS.

1. **OPEN** *Travel Events* from the data files for this lesson.

2. **SAVE** the database as *Travel Events XXX* (where *XXX* is your initials).

3. On the Create tab, in the Forms group, click the Form Wizard button.

4. Click the >> button to move all the fields from the Available Fields box to the Selected Fields box.

5. Click the Next > button to move to the next page in the Form Wizard.

6. Click Datasheet as the layout for the form.

7. Click the Next > button to move to the final page in the Form Wizard.

8. Key Event Details as the title of the form.

9. Click the Finish button to create a datasheet form.

10. On the Home tab, in the Views group, click the lower half of the View button, and click Form View.

11. Click the Close button on Event Details to close the form.

12. **CLOSE** the database.

LEAVE Access open for the next project.

Project 5-2: Used Games Forms

You are the manager at Southridge Video. To expand the store, you have recently started taking used games in trade. You store information about each title in an Access database. You decide to create some forms to help you use the database more efficiently.

GET READY. LAUNCH Access if it is not already running.

@ The *Games inventory* file for this lesson is available on the book companion website or in WileyPLUS.

1. **OPEN** *Games inventory* from the data files for this lesson.

2. **SAVE** the database as *Games inventory XXX* (where *XXX* is your initials).

3. In the Navigation Pane, double-click Games: Table to open the table.

4. On the Create tab, in the Forms group, click the Form button to create a simple form and display it in Layout View.

5. Click the File tab and click Save.

6. In the Save As dialog box, click OK to accept the Games form name suggested by Access.

7. Click the Close button for Games to close the form.

8. On the Create tab, in the Forms group, click the Form Design button to create a new blank form in Design View.

9. On the Form Design Tools Design contextual tab, in the Tools group, click the Add Existing Fields button to display the Field List pane.

10. Click the Show all tables link in the Field List pane.

11. Click the + next to Games to list the available fields.

12. Double-click Title to add it to the form.

13. Double-click Rating to add it to the form.

14. Double-click Platform to add it to the form.

15. Click the File tab and click Save.

16. In the Save As dialog box, key Game Rating, and click OK.

17. Click the Close button to close the Field List.

18. On the Design contextual tab, in the Views group, click the lower half of the View button and click Form View to display form in Form View.

19. Click the Close button for Game Rating to close the form.

20. **LEAVE** the database open for the next project.

LEAVE Access open for the next project.

Proficiency Assessment

Project 5-3: Sort and Filter Games

A customer comes into Southridge Video and asks about game publishers and the availability of a particular game. Sort and filter data in the forms you created to get the information that you need.

USE the database that is open from the previous project.

1. In the Navigation Pane, double-click the Games form to open it.

2. Right-click the Publisher field to display the shortcut menu.

3. Click Sort A to Z to sort the form by publisher name in alphabetic order.

4. Navigate to record 3, titled Marvel: Ultimate Alliance.

5. Right-click the Title field and click Contains "Marvel: Ultimate Alliance."

6. Click the Next record button on the record navigator at the bottom of the form to see all the versions of the game with that name.

7. On the Home tab, in the Sort & Filter group, click the Remove Sort button.

8. **CLOSE** the database.

LEAVE Access open for the next project.

Project 5-4: Toy Inventory

Your brother owns Wingtip Toys and recently started keeping a list of the store inventory in an Access database. He wants to add a form to the database and asks for your help. Add a simple form and then show him how to sort and apply filters.

GET READY. LAUNCH Access if it is not already running.

1. **OPEN** *Toy inventory* from the data files for this lesson.

2. Save the database as *Toy inventory XXX* (where *XXX* is your initials).

3. Open Inventory: Table.

@ The *Toy Inventory* file for this lesson is available on the book companion website or in WileyPLUS.

4. Use the Form tool to create a simple form.

5. Format it using the Trek theme option (last row, first column).

6. Save the form as Inventory.

7. Sort the form's *In Stock* field from Largest to Smallest.

8. Sort the *Description* field from A to Z.

9. Run a filter that finds all the records where the *Price* field is between $50 and $100.

10. Clear all sorts and filters.

11. Create a filter by form to find all the records that have two items in stock.

12. Close the form and **CLOSE** the database.

LEAVE Access open for the next project.

Mastery Assessment

Project 5-5: Red Wines

The Coho Vineyard has started a monthly wine club. Each month features a red wine hand picked for its unique label and diverse style. Information about the monthly club selections is stored in an Access database; you will create forms so that you can retrieve the data in a useful way.

GET READY. LAUNCH Access if it is not already running.

@ The *Red Wine* file for this lesson is available on the book companion website or in WileyPLUS.

1. **OPEN** the *Red Wine* database from the data files for this lesson.

2. Save the database as *Red Wine XXX* (where *XXX* is your initials).

3. Create a simple form that contains all the fields in the Club Selections table and name it Club Wines.

4. Use the Form Design button to create a form named Wine Details that looks like the one shown in Figure 5-30 when displayed in Form View.

Figure 5-30

Wine Details form

5. **CLOSE** the database.

LEAVE Access open for the next project.

Project 5-6: Personal Contacts

Your address book is becoming outdated, and you decide to transfer all the current information about friends and family to an Access database. Input the data and then create forms to manage it efficiently.

GET READY. LAUNCH Access if it is not already running.

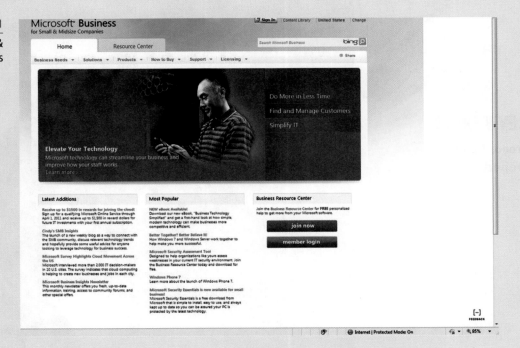

The *Personal Contacts* file for this lesson is available on the book companion website or in WileyPLUS.

1. **OPEN** *Personal Contacts* from the data files for this lesson.

2. **SAVE** the database as *Personal Contacts XXX* (where *XXX* is your initials).

3. Input as much contact information as you have about at least five friends or family members.

4. Create a simple form named Friends/Family using the Form tool. Apply the BlackTie theme.

5. Create a form named Birthday Contacts using the Form Wizard. Include the following fields: First Name, Last Name, E-mail Address, Home Phone, Mobile Phone, and Birthday. Use the Columnar layout. Keep all other default settings.

6. **CLOSE** the database.

STOP. CLOSE Access.

INTERNET READY

Microsoft has numerous online resources available to provide solutions, services, and support for whatever business needs you may have. If you are a small or midsized business, a helpful site is the Microsoft Business for Small & Midsize Companies. Here, you can find advice, products, tools, and information tailored to small and midsized businesses. Search the Microsoft site for Small & Midsize Companies, shown in Figure 5-31. Explore the resources offered on the site. In the Latest Editions section, choose a topic about which you would like to know more, and read an article that interests you.

Figure 5-31

Microsoft Business for Small & Midsize Companies

6 Create Reports

Alpine Ski House is a small mountain lodge that features cross-country skiing in the winter and hiking in the summer. As an administrative assistant for Alpine Ski House, you take care of many of the administrative duties for the innkeepers, including reservations, billing, and recordkeeping. You have recently started using Access to keep track of customers and reservations at the lodge. In this lesson, you learn three different ways to create reports for the lodge, how to apply auto formats to reports, and how to sort and filter report data.

SOFTWARE ORIENTATION

Reports Group

The Reports group (Figure 6-1) is located on the Create tab in the Ribbon. Use the Reports group of commands to create reports.

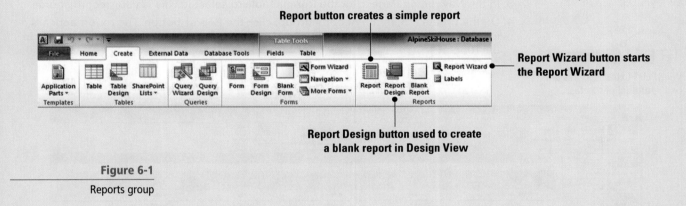

Figure 6-1

Reports group

CREATING REPORTS

The Bottom Line

A **report** is a database object that is used to organize and display data pulled from tables and queries. You can create a report using the Report button, the Report Wizard, or Design View, depending on the amount of customization desired. After creating a report, you can instantly apply a Theme to create a professional look. You can also sort and filter data in a report to display the records to suit your needs.

Creating a Simple Report

You can use Access 2010 to create simple or complex reports. When creating a complex report, you might spend quite a bit of time choosing which fields you want to include from various tables or queries. That is fine when you need such a report, but when you need a simple display of all the fields in a table or query, you can use the Report button to create a simple report. In this exercise, you use the Report button to create a simple report.

Reports are commonly used as formatted hard copies of table or query data. You can modify a report's design, but you cannot add or edit data in a report. The purpose of a report is to allow users to view data, not edit it. For example, a supervisor might ask you to create a sales report that is filtered to show only one region's sales. The supervisor does not need to edit the data, just view it.

A report's **record source** is the table or query that provides the data used to generate a report. Before you can create a report, you need to define the record source by clicking in the Navigation Pane on the table or query on which you want to base the report. Then, click the Report button and a report is generated based on the table or query you selected.

You can modify a report's design, print, or save and close a report. You should save a report's design if you are likely to use it again. To save a report, click the Save button on the File tab or in the Quick Access Toolbar. If you click the Close button without saving, Access will display a dialog box asking if you want to save it. Once it is saved, the report is listed in the Navigation Pane. You can open it and modify it in the future or create a new report based on the original. The next time you run the report, the design will be the same, but the data will be different if the data in the table or query has been updated.

STEP BY STEP **Create a Report**

 The *Alpine Ski House* file for this lesson is available on the book companion website or in WileyPLUS.

WILEY PLUS EXTRA

WileyPLUS Extra! features an online tutorial of this task.

GET READY. Before you begin these steps, be sure to turn on and/or log on to your computer and start Access.

1. **OPEN** *Alpine Ski House* from the data files for this lesson.
2. Save the database as *Alpine Ski House XXX* (where *XXX* is your initials).
3. In the Navigation Pane, click the Rooms table to select it. This is your record source.
4. On the Create tab, in the Reports group, click the Report button. The report appears in Layout View, as shown in Figure 6-2. Notice the Report Layout tools that appear in the Ribbon.

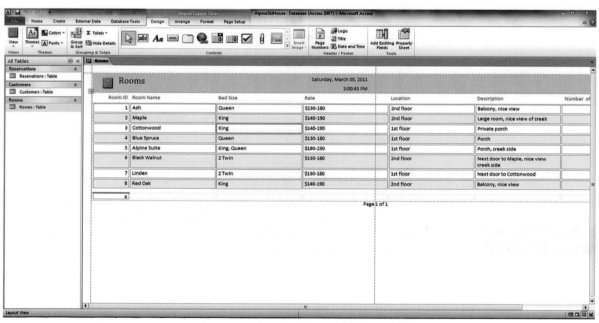

Figure 6-2

Simple report

5. Click the Room ID header to select it. Position the pointer over the right border until you see a double-sided arrow. Click and drag to the left, resizing the column to remove excess white space.

6. Resize the other columns until your screen looks similar to Figure 6-3.

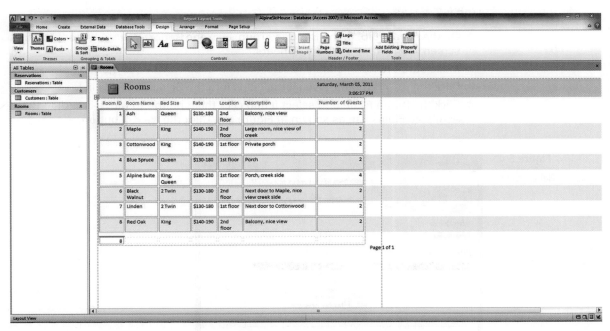

Figure 6-3

Report with resized columns

7. Click the **Save** button on the Quick Access Toolbar. The Save As dialog box appears with Rooms in the Report Name box. Click **OK**. Notice that the Rooms report is listed in the Navigation Pane.

8. Click the **Close** button to close the Rooms report.

PAUSE. LEAVE the database open to use in the next exercise.

Using the Report Wizard

You are probably already familiar with the way a "wizard" works. The Report Wizard displays a series of questions about the report you want and then it creates the report for you based on your answers. The Report Wizard knows what makes a good report, so the questions are designed to help you create a professional report with little effort. The Report Wizard is usually the easiest way to create a report when you want to choose which fields to include. It guides you through a series of questions and then generates a report based on your answers. If you want to skip steps such as Sorting or Grouping in the Report Wizard, click the Next button to go to the next screen. You can click the Finish button anytime it is available to create the report with the choices you have specified. In this exercise, you use the Report Wizard to create a report based on the Rooms table.

The Report Wizard allows you to include fields from more than one table or query. You can click the double right arrow button (>>) to include all the fields in the report or click the single right arrow button (>) to move them one at a time. Likewise, you can click the double left arrow button (<<) to move all the fields out of the report or the single left arrow button (<) to move them one at a time.

You can specify group levels, such as grouping all of the first-floor rooms together and all of the second-floor rooms together if creating a room report. You can also choose up to four fields on which to sort data in ascending or descending order. On the layout screen, you can choose from various layouts such as stepped, block, or outline, all of which indent fields and records in different ways to make the report clearer to read. You can also choose to display the report in portrait or landscape orientation. Access provides a wide variety of design styles from which to choose. On the last screen, you can key a name for the report and choose to preview or modify the report.

STEP BY STEP   **Use the Report Wizard**

USE the database you used in the previous exercise.

1. On the Create tab, in the Reports group, click the Report Wizard button. The first screen of the Report Wizard appears.
2. Make sure the Rooms table is selected in the Tables/Queries menu.
3. Click the >> button to move all the fields into the Selected Fields list.
4. Click the Room ID field to select it and click the < button to move it back to the Available Fields list, as shown in Figure 6-4. Click the Next > button.

Figure 6-4

The Report Wizard Fields screen

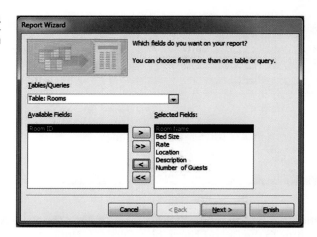

5. Click the Location field to select it and click the > button to add it as a grouping level, as shown in Figure 6-5.

Figure 6-5

The Report Wizard Grouping screen

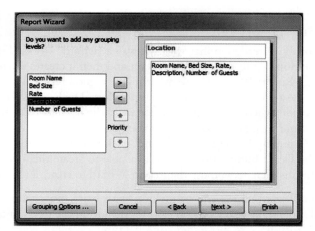

6. Click the Next > button.
7. Select Room Name from the fields menu to sort in ascending order, as shown in Figure 6-6, and click the Next > button.

Figure 6-6

The Report Wizard Sort screen

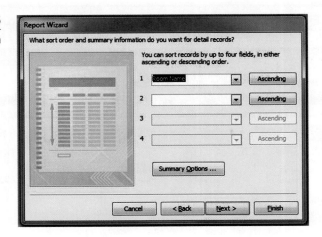

8. In the Layout section, click the **Outline** button. In the Orientation section, click the **Landscape** button, as shown in Figure 6-7. Click **Next >**.

Figure 6-7

The Report Wizard Layout screen

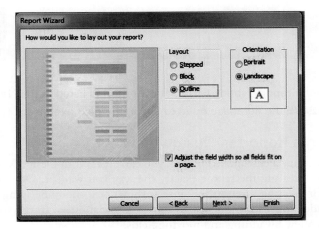

9. Key **Rooms Wizard** as the title of the report, as shown in Figure 6-8.

Figure 6-8

The Report Wizard Title screen

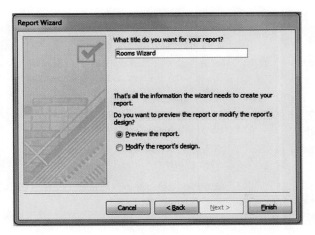

10. Click **Finish.** The Rooms Wizard report appears on the screen, as shown in Figure 6-9.

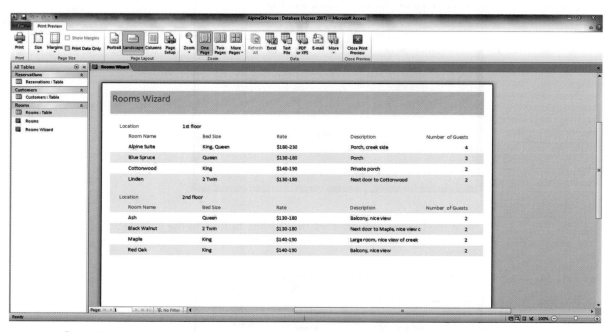

Figure 6-9

The Report Wizard report

11. Close the report. Notice that the new report is listed in the Navigation Pane.

PAUSE. LEAVE the database open to use in the next exercise.

Creating a Report in Design View

When you want a customized report, you can create it in Design View, which offers you many options for creating the report exactly the way you want it. Design View gives you the most options for creating a report, because it shows you the underlying structure of the report. It also provides you with more design tools and capabilities. In this exercise, you create a report in Design View by adding and moving fields.

In the previous exercise, you created a very basic report in Design View.

In Design View, a report is displayed on a design grid with sections. Table 6-1 lists the sections.

Table 6-1

Design View Sections

Section Name	Description
Report header	This section is printed once at the beginning of every report. This is a good place to include a logo, a date, or information that might normally appear on a cover page.
Page header	This section is printed at the top of every page of a report, so it would be good place to include the report title.
Group header	This section is printed at the beginning of a group. It is a good place to include the group name.
Detail	This section includes the body of the report. It is printed once for every row in a record source.
Group footer	This section is printed at the end of a group. It may include summary information for the group.
Page footer	This section is printed at the bottom of every page of a report, so it would be a good place to include information such as a page number.
Report footer	This section is printed once at the end of every report. This is a good place for report totals.

To add fields to the report design, you can display the Field List pane by clicking the Add Existing Fields button. Double-click a field in the Field List to add it to the design grid, or you can drag the field to a location on the grid. If you need to move a field on the grid, click the field to select it and then position the pointer on the border until you see a four-sided arrow. Then, drag to the new location. To change the size of a field, click and drag a selection handle.

To see what your report will look like, click the View button on the Views group and select Report from the menu.

STEP BY STEP	**Create a Report in Design View**

USE the database you used in the previous exercise.

1. If necessary, click the **Rooms** table in the Navigation Pane to select it.
2. On the Create tab, in the Reports group, click the **Report Design** button. A new blank report is displayed in Design View, as shown in Figure 6-10.

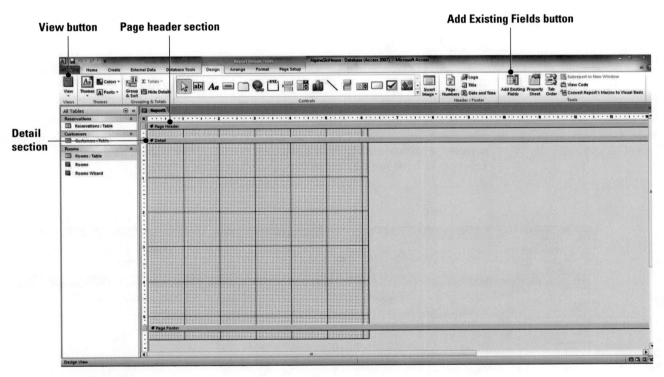

Figure 6-10

New blank report in Design View

3. If the Fields List is not already displayed, on the Design tab, in the Tools group, click the **Add Existing Fields** button. The Show all tables link appears.
4. Click the **Show all tables link** then the **plus (+)** box beside Rooms to display the fields in the table, as shown in Figure 6-11.

Figure 6-11

Fields List pane

5. Double-click **Room ID**. The field is inserted onto the design grid.

6. Double-click **Room Name**, **Bed Size**, and **Rate**.

7. Click the **Close** button on the Field List pane.

8. Click the **Bed Size** label. The border around the label changes to orange, indicating it is selected. Position the insertion point over the top of the border, as shown in Figure 6-12, until the pointer changes to a four-sided arrow. ⊹

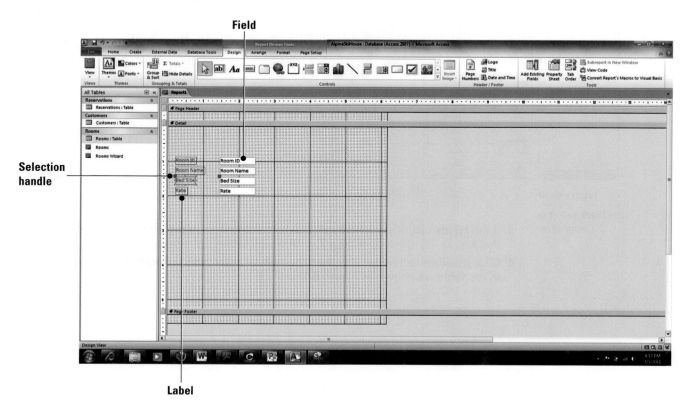

Figure 6-12

Bed Size label selected

9. Click and drag the label to position it about one-half inch to the right of the *Room ID* field and release the mouse button. The field is moved along with the label.

10. In the same manner, move the Rate label and field to position it below the *Bed Size* field, as shown in Figure 6-13.

Figure 6-13

Moved fields

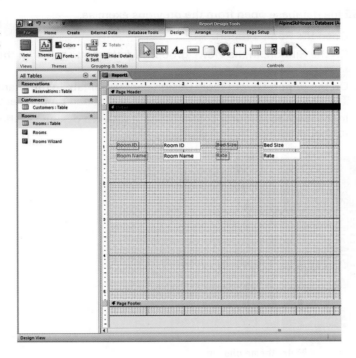

11. Click the **Room ID** field to select it. Position the mouse pointer on the square handle in the middle of the right-side border. Click and drag the field to the left to decrease the size by about one-quarter inch.

12. On the Ribbon, in the Views group, click the bottom-half of the **View** button and select **Report View** from the menu. The report is shown in Report View. Scroll down to see all the records.

13. Click the **Save** button on the Quick Access Toolbar.

14. Key **Report Design** in the Report Name box and click **OK**.

15. Close the report.

PAUSE. LEAVE the table open to use in the next exercise.

Take Note   You can add more than one field to a report design at once. Hold down the Ctrl key and click the fields you want, and then drag the selected fields onto the report.

APPLYING A THEME

The Bottom Line

A theme applies a set of predefined fonts, colors, and design to a report. You can apply a theme to any report in Layout View. The Themes gallery displays a variety of designs. After you click the design you want, it is applied to the report. This instant formatting can quickly give your report the professional look you want.

Applying a Theme

To apply a theme, on the Report Layout Tools Design contextual tab, in the Themes group, click the Themes button to display the Themes gallery. You can select a design from the list displayed, or browse for saved themes. You can also customize and then save a theme based on the current report. You can click the Colors button and choose a color scheme from the menu to update the currently applied theme's colors, and even create new theme colors. You can also click the

Fonts button and choose a font scheme to update the currently applied theme's fonts and create new theme fonts. In this exercise, you apply a theme to the Rooms report, and modify the fonts.

Apply a Theme

USE the database open from the previous exercise.

1. Open the Rooms report.

2. On the Ribbon, in the Views group, click the bottom-half of the View button. Select Layout View from the menu.

3. On the Report Layout Tools Design contextual tab, in the Themes group, click the Themes button. The Themes gallery of predefined report themes appears.

4. In the sixth row, fourth column, click the Metro design, as shown in Figure 6-14. The format is applied to the report.

Figure 6-14

Themes gallery with Metro theme chosen

Metro theme chosen

5. In the Themes group, click the Fonts button. Select Newsprint from the menu, as shown in Figure 6-15, and click OK. The new Font theme is applied.

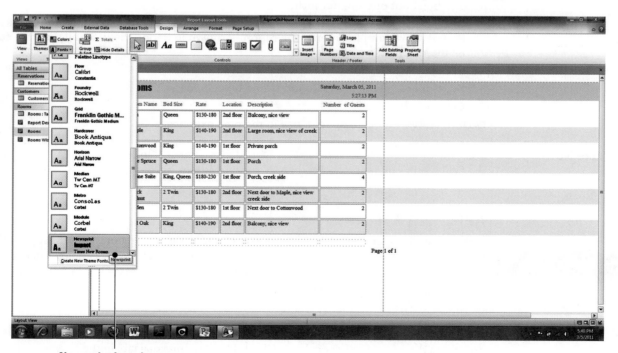

Newsprint font chosen

Figure 6-15

Fonts menu with Newsprint font chosen

6. **SAVE** the report.

PAUSE. LEAVE the report open to use in the next exercise.

WORKING WITH REPORTS

Reports help group and summarize data in different ways. However, after a report is created, you can use Layout View as well as Report View to help locate data. For example, you can use Layout View to easily sort field data one at a time, or perform more complex sorts using the Group, Sort, and Total pane. You can also use Layout View to filter data and view only those records based on the criteria you specify, and use Report or Layout View to find data based on any term you specify.

Sorting Data within a Report

Sorting organizes data into a particular sequence, such as alphabetic order or from smallest to largest numbers. For example, you can sort a customer list in alphabetic order by last name or by customer ID number. You can sort data by clicking the buttons on the Ribbon, right-clicking and choosing commands from the shortcut menu, or by using the Group, Sort, and Total pane. In this exercise, you sort data within a report by using the Ribbon, shortcut menu, and the Group, Sort, and Total pane.

Sorting data in a report is similar to sorting in a table. In Layout View, select the field you want to sort and click the Ascending or Descending button on the Home tab, in the Sort & Filter group. Click the Remove Sort button to remove the sort orders. You can sort as many fields as you like one at a time.

 Ref Lesson 3 has more information about sorting in a table.

You can also easily sort data by right-clicking in a field and choosing the type of sort you want from the shortcut menu. The sort commands in the shortcut menu vary depending on the type of data in the field. For text, you will choose Sort A to Z or Sort Z to A; for numbers, you will choose Sort Smallest to Largest or Sort Largest to Smallest; and for dates, you will choose Sort Oldest to Newest or Sort Newest to Oldest.

 Ref Lesson 5 has more information about sorting in a form.

The Group, Sort, and Total pane gives you more sorting options. You can use the pane to specify the sort order or to view the results of sorting using the shortcut menu. To specify a sort, click the Add a Sort button and select a field from the pop-up menu. Click the drop-down menu to specify the type of sort you want. Click the More Options button to display additional commands for creating detailed sorts. Click the Less Options button to return to the basic sorting options.

To delete a sort in the Group, Sort, and Total pane, click the Delete button at the end of the sort line.

 Ref Lesson 7 has more information about sorting in a query.

STEP BY STEP **Sort Data within a Report**

USE the report open from the previous exercise.

1. On the Home tab in the Views group, click the bottom-half of the View button. Select Layout View from the menu.

2. Click the **Room Name** header.

3. On the Home tab, in the Sort & Filter group, click the **Ascending** button. The column is sorted in ascending alphabetic order.

4. On the Home tab, in the Sort & Filter group, click the **Remove Sort** button. The Sort is removed.

5. Right-click the Room Name header. The shortcut menu appears.

6. Select Sort Z to A, as shown in Figure 6-16. The column is sorted.

Figure 6-16

Shortcut menu

Click Sort Z to A to sort
in descending order

7. On the Home tab, in the Sort & Filter group, click the Remove Sort button. The Sort is cleared.

8. On the Report Layout Tools Design contextual tab, in the Grouping & Totals group, click the Group & Sort button. The *Group, Sort, and Total* pane appears at the bottom of the screen, as shown in Figure 6-17.

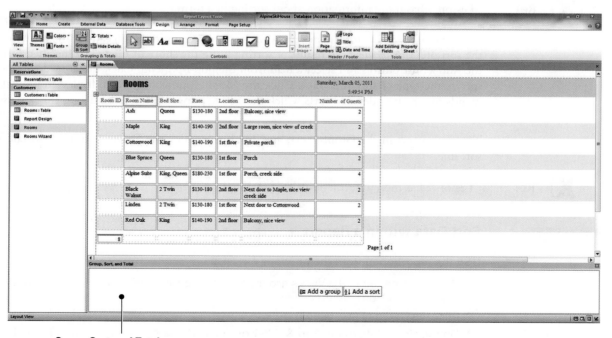

Group, Sort, and Total pane

Figure 6-17

Group, Sort, and Total pane

9. Click the **Add a Sort** button in the *Group, Sort, and Total* pane.

10. Click the **Room Name** field in the fields list. Notice that the field was sorted in ascending order by default and a line was added describing the sort.

11. Click the **down arrow** beside *with A on top* and select **with Z on top** from the menu, as shown in Figure 6-18. The field is sorted in descending order.

Field Name menu

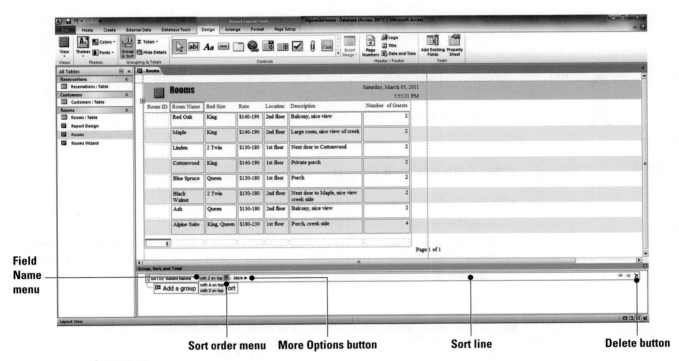

Sort order menu   More Options button   Sort line   Delete button

Figure 6-18

Sort displayed in the Group, Sort, and Total pane

12. Click the **More Options** button in the Sort line. Notice the options available for customizing a sort.

13. Click the **Delete** button. The sort is cleared.

14. On the Formatting tab, in the Grouping & Totals group, click the **Group & Sort** button. The *Group, Total, and Sort* pane is removed.

15. **SAVE** the report.

PAUSE. LEAVE the database open to use in the next exercise.

Filtering Data within a Report

A filter displays only data that meet the criteria you have specified and hides the rest. It does not modify the table data or the design of the report. After you remove a filter, all the records are displayed again. Filtering data in Layout View of a report is very similar to filtering data in a table. You can apply common filters using the commands on the Sort & Filter group or by right-clicking a field and choosing a filter from the shortcut menu. The filters available on the shortcut menu vary depending on the type of data in the field. Only one filter can be applied to a field at a time. However, you can specify a different filter for each field. In this exercise, you filter a report using a custom filter, and filter by selection.

You can toggle between filtered and unfiltered views using the Toggle Filter button. To remove a filter from a field, right-click in the field and select the Clear filter from field name command. To remove all filters permanently, select the Clear All Filters command on the Advanced menu in the Sort & Filter group.

Take Note

If you save a report (or other object) while a filter is applied, it will be available the next time you open the report. If you want to open the report and see the filter already applied, set the Filter On Load property setting to Yes.

You can also filter by selection in a report. If you want to view only the reservations for 12/13/11, select that date in the *Check-in* field and click the Selection button. That date will appear in the menu, so that you can choose Equals 12/13/11, Does Not Equal 12/13/11, and so on. You can also access these commands on the shortcut menu by right-clicking the value.

Take Note   If you need to apply a filter that is not in the common filters list, you can write an advanced filter using the Advanced Filter/Sort command on the Advanced menu. You need to be familiar with writing expressions, which are similar to formulas, and be familiar with the criteria that you specify when designing a query.

 Ref   Lesson 3 has more information about filtering records in a table.

 Ref   Lesson 5 has more information about filtering data within a form.

STEP BY STEP   **Filter Data within a Report**

USE the database you used in the previous exercise.

1. Click the **Location** header to select it.
2. On the Home tab, in the Sort & Filter group, click the **Filter** button. A menu appears.
3. Point to Text Filters. A second menu appears. Select **Begins with . . .** as shown in Figure 6-19. The Custom Filter box appears.

Figure 6-19

Text Filters menu

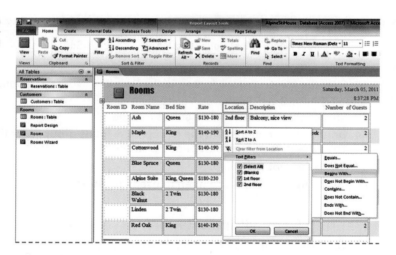

4. Key **1** into the Custom Filter box and click **OK**. The data is filtered to show only the rooms on the first floor.
5. Click the **Remove Filter** button. The report returns to its unfiltered state.
6. In the *Bed Size* field, click **King** in the second row.
7. On the Home tab, in the Sort & Filter group, click the **Selection** button. Select **Equals "King"** from the menu. The data is filtered to show only the rooms with King-sized beds.

8. Right-click the Bed Size header. A shortcut menu appears. Notice that the Equals "King" filter and the other filters from the Selection menu are also available in the shortcut menu, shown in Figure 6-20.

Figure 6-20

Shortcut menu

9. Select Clear filter from Bed Size from the menu. The filter is cleared.

10. **SAVE** and close the table.

PAUSE. LEAVE the database open to use in the next exercise.

Finding Data within a Report

When you want to quickly locate records in a report, you can use the Find command, which searches all the records of the report for any term you specify. Sometimes you may need to quickly find records within a report while in Report View or Report Layout View. To accomplish this, you can use the Find command in the Find group on the Home tab. In this exercise, you locate data in Report View by using the Find command.

 Ref

Lesson 3 has more information about the Find command.

The Find command was overviewed for tables in Lesson 3. Like the Find command in table Datasheet View, once clicked, the Find dialog box appears where you can enter search criteria, set options for where you'd like Access to look for the data, and set data matching and other search options. You can quickly locate records that match your search term and view multiple occurrences; however, remember that you cannot modify record data from within a report, so you cannot replace the record data that is found.

 **Another Way**
You can also access the Find command by pressing Ctrl+F on the keyboard.

Take Note   You cannot use the Find command when you're in Report Design View.

Take Note   You can also use the Find command in tables, forms, and queries.

STEP BY STEP   **Find Data within a Report**

USE the database open from the previous exercise.

1. Open the Rooms report.

2. On the Ribbon, in the Views group, click the bottom-half of the View button. Select Report View from the menu.

3. On the Home tab, in the Find group, click the Find button. The Find dialog box appears, as shown in Figure 6-21.

Figure 6-21

Find dialog box

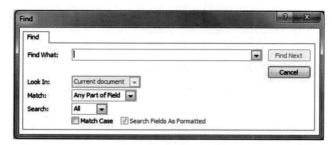

4. Key King in the Find What drop-down box and select Current document in the Look In drop-down box.

5. Click the Find Next button. Access highlights the first occurrence of 'King' in the report. Continue clicking the Find Next button until Access reports that it has finished searching the records.

6. Close the table. **CLOSE** the database.

STOP. CLOSE Access.

SKILL SUMMARY

In This Lesson, You Learned How To:
Create reports
Apply a theme
Work with reports

Knowledge Assessment

Matching

Match the term in Column 1 to its description in Column 2.

Column 1	Column 2
1. report	a. organizes data in a particular order
2. record source	b. displays data that meets the criteria you have specified and hides the rest
3. Report Wizard	c. a list of available fields for adding to a report
4. Field List pane	d. a database object that is used to organize and display data from tables and queries
5. Detail	e. locates data in an open object like a table, query, or report
6. theme	f. the table or query that provides the data used to generate a report
7. Sort	g. the way a report is displayed in Design View
8. Filter	h. guides you through a series of questions and then generates a report based on your answers
9. design grid	i. the section of a report that includes the body of the report
10. Find command	j. a predefined format that you can apply to any report in Layout View

True/False

Circle T if the statement is true or F if the statement is false.

T F 1. A simple report contains all the records in a table or query.

T F 2. You can edit the data in a report.

T F 3. Click the Report button to define a record source.

T F 4. In the Report Wizard, you can skip steps such as Sorting or Grouping by clicking the Next button.

T F 5. You can drag a field from the Field List pane to the design grid to add it to the report.

T F 6. Layout View gives you the most options for creating a report, because it shows you the underlying structure of the report.

T F 7. Templates resize column widths for you.

T F 8. You can save a filter with a report.

T F 9. You can use the Group, Sort, and Total pane to specify sort order or view the results of sorting using the shortcut menu.

T F 10. The Toggle Filter button removes a filter permanently.

Competency Assessment

Project 6-1: Soccer Team Report

You need a copy of the soccer team's roster that you can print and take with you to work. Create a simple report and apply a theme.

GET READY. LAUNCH Access if it is not already running.

@ The *SoccerTeam* file for this lesson is available on the book companion website or in WileyPLUS.

1. **OPEN** the *SoccerTeam* database.
2. Save the database as *SoccerTeamXXX* (where *XXX* is your initials).
3. Click the Roster table to select it.
4. On the Create tab, in the Reports group, click the Report button. A new report is created.
5. Resize each field so that all fields fit on one page.
6. On the Report Layout Tools Design contextual tab, in the Themes group, click the Themes button.
7. Select the purple format in the seventh row, third column named Opulent.
8. Click the Save button on the Quick Access Toolbar. The Save As dialog box appears with the name Roster in it. Click OK to accept that name for the report.
9. Close the report.
10. **CLOSE** the database.

LEAVE Access open for the next project.

Project 6-2: Fourth Coffee Inventory Report

In your job at Fourth Coffee, you are responsible for maintaining the coffee inventory. Create a report to view the inventory and prepare for the next order.

GET READY. LAUNCH Access if it is not already running.

@ The *Coffee* file for this lesson is available on the book companion website or in WileyPLUS.

1. **OPEN** *Coffee* from the data files for this lesson.
2. **SAVE** the database as *CoffeeXXX* (where *XXX* is your initials).
3. Click the Coffee Inventory Table in the Navigation Pane to select it.

4. On the Create tab, in the Reports group, click the Report Wizard button. The first Report Wizard screen appears.

5. Click the double arrow >> to move all the fields to the Selected Fields list and click Next.

6. On the grouping screen, click the Scheduled Order Date field, click the >, and click Next.

7. On the sorting screen, click the active down arrow on the menu, select Pounds, and click Next.

8. Keep the defaults as is on the layout screen and click Next.

9. Click Finish. The report is created.

10. Close the report.

11. **CLOSE** the database.

LEAVE Access open for the next project.

Proficiency Assessment

Project 6-3: Alpine Ski House Reservations Report

Every week is different at the Alpine Ski House. Sometimes the lodge is full of guests, and sometimes only a few rooms are occupied. Create a report to show the innkeepers what to expect in the coming weeks.

GET READY. LAUNCH Access if it is not already running.

@ The *Alpine House* file for this lesson is available on the book companion website or in WileyPLUS.

1. **OPEN** the *Alpine House* database.

2. **SAVE** it as *Alpine House XXX* (where *XXX* is your initials).

3. Use the Report Wizard to create a report using the *Room, Check-in Date,* and *Check-out Date* fields.

4. Group the report by Room and sort it in ascending order by Check-in Date.

5. Use stepped layout and portrait orientation.

6. Name the report December Reservations and finish the wizard.

7. Switch to Layout View and increase the width of the *Room* field.

8. Apply the Foundry theme.

9. Save and close the table.

10. **CLOSE** the database.

LEAVE Access open for the next project.

Project 6-4: Wingtip Toys Design View Report

The manufacturing department at Wingtip Toys needs summary information about each toy in inventory. Create a report in Design View that will display the requested information.

GET READY. LAUNCH Access if it is not already running.

@ The *Wingtip Toys* file for this lesson is available on the book companion website or in WileyPLUS.

1. **OPEN** *Wingtip Toys* and save it as *Wingtip Toys XXX* (where *XXX* is your initials).

2. Click the Inventory table in the Navigation Pane to select it.

3. On the Create tab, in the Reports group, click the Report Design button.

4. On the Design tab, in the Tools group, click the Add Existing Fields button. The Field List pane appears.

5. Position the fields from the Inventory table onto the design grid, as shown in Figure 6-22. Adjust field widths as shown.

Figure 6-22

Wingtip Toys report in Design View

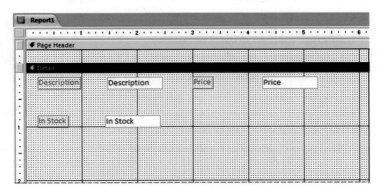

6. Save the report as Toy Summary.
7. Close the report.

LEAVE the database open for the next project.

Mastery Assessment

Project 6-5: Filter, Sort, and Find Records in a Wingtip Toys Report

A large order was recently filled, and now the inventory at Wingtip Toys is quite low on some items. Create a report that displays this information.

The *Wingtip Toys XXX* database should be open.

GET READY. LAUNCH Access if it is not already running.

1. Define the Inventory table as the record source for a new report.
2. Create a simple report.
3. Apply the Equity theme to the new report.
4. Sort the report in ascending order by the *Description* field.
5. Click the first row of the In Stock field, which contains the number 10.
6. Filter by selection to display the toys with 10 or fewer items in stock.
7. Click the In Stock field header and sort the field in ascending order.
8. Clear all sorts.
9. Clear all filters.
10. Find and cycle through all occurrences of the word Car.
11. Save the report as Inventory.
12. Close the report.
13. **CLOSE** the database.

LEAVE Access open for the next project.

Project 6-6: Angel Project Report

The school Angel Project has begun. Information for the boy angels needs to be distributed to the boys in the kindergarten classes, and the girl angels' information needs to be distributed to the girls. Create a report with filters that displays the boy and girl information separately.

GET READY. LAUNCH Access if it is not already running.

@ The *Angel Project* file for this lesson is available on the book companion website or in WileyPLUS.

1. **OPEN** the *Angel Project* database.
2. Save the database as ***Angel Project XXX*** (where *XXX* is your initials).
3. Define the List table as the record source for a new report.
4. Use the Report Wizard to create a report with all the fields.
5. Skip the grouping and sorting screens, and choose a tabular, portrait layout.
6. Name the report ***Angel Needs and Wants***.
7. Switch to Layout View and adjust field widths as necessary so that all data fits on the screen and on one page, and apply the Trek theme.
8. Display the *Group, Sort, and Total* pane.
9. Sort the report in ascending order by Age.
10. Create a filter to show only the information for the males.
11. Toggle the filter and create a new filter to show only the information for the females.
12. Save and close the report.
13. **CLOSE** the database.

CLOSE Access.

INTERNET READY

Search the Internet for at least five dream vacation packages and create a database table that lists each hotel's location, name, cost, and favorite amenities or activities. After creating the table, use the Report Wizard to create a professional-looking report that displays your data.

Create and Modify Queries 7

LESSON SKILL MATRIX

In This Lesson, You Will Learn The Following Skills:

Creating a Query

Modifying a Query

Sorting and Filtering Data within a Query

KEY TERMS

- field list
- parameter query
- query criterion
- select query

You work for Northwind Traders, a mountain-climbing apparel company dedicated to producing high-quality and technically innovative products. The company has a program called industry friends that offers discount purchasing privileges for employees and other outdoor professionals and friends who qualify. As operations coordinator, you are responsible for approving applications for the program and entering related information into the database. You often need to pull specific data from the database. In this lesson, you learn how to create queries from a single table—including a simple query and a find duplicates query—and how to create queries from multiple tables, including a find unmatched query; how to modify a query by adding a table, removing a table, and adding criteria to a query; and how to sort and filter data within a query.

SOFTWARE ORIENTATION

Queries Group

The Queries group (Figure 7-1) on the Create tab contains the commands used to create queries. The Query Wizard button launches the Query Wizard, which helps you create a simple query, a crosstab query, a find duplicates query, or a find unmatched query. The Query Design button creates a new, blank query in Design View. Use this figure as a reference throughout this lesson as well as the rest of this book.

Figure 7-1

Queries group

Launches the Query Wizard

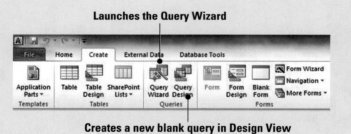

Creates a new blank query in Design View

CREATING A QUERY

The Bottom Line

A query is a set of instructions used for working with data. Creating a query is like asking the database a question. Running a query performs these instructions and provides the answers. The results that a query returns can be sorted, grouped, or filtered. A query can also create, copy, delete, or change data. A **select query** is the most basic type of Access query. It creates subsets of data that you can use to answer specific questions or to supply data to other database objects. The data is displayed in Datasheet View without being changed. A query is a powerful and versatile database tool. Queries differ from sort or filter commands because they can be saved for future use and can extract data from multiple tables or other queries.

Creating a Query from a Table

A query can get its data from one or more tables, from existing queries, or from a combination of the two. The tables or queries from which a query gets its data are referred to as its record source. When one table provides the information that you need, you can create a simple select query using the Query Wizard. You can also use a query to find records with duplicate field values in a single table. In this exercise, you create a simple select query that searches the data in a single table.

To create a simple select query, on the Create tab, in the Queries group, click the Query Wizard button. Click Simple Query Wizard and then click OK. Specify the table you want to use as the record source and the fields that you want to show. Name the query and click Finish. When you close the query, it is automatically saved.

To run a query after it has been created, simply double-click it in the Navigation pane to open it in Datasheet View and see the results.

STEP BY STEP   **Create a Simple Query**

GET READY. Before you begin these steps, be sure to **LAUNCH** Microsoft Access.

@ The *Northwind* file for this lesson is available on the book companion website or in WileyPLUS.

1. **OPEN** the *Northwind* file from the data files for this lesson.
2. **SAVE** the database as *Northwind XXX* (where *XXX* is your initials).
3. On the Create tab, in the Other group, click the Query Wizard button. The New Query dialog box appears, as shown in Figure 7-2.

Figure 7-2

New Query dialog box

WILEY PLUS EXTRA

WileyPLUS Extra! features an online tutorial of this task.

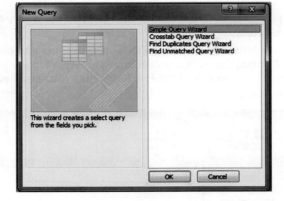

4. Click Simple Query Wizard and then click OK. The Simple Query Wizard appears, as shown in Figure 7-3.

Figure 7-3

Simple Query Wizard, screen 1

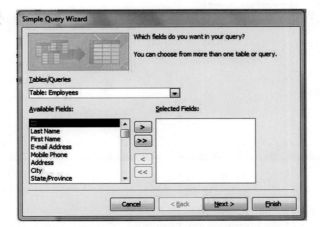

5. In the Tables/Queries drop-down list, Table: Employees should be selected by default. If it is not, select it.
6. Under Available Fields, double-click Last Name, First Name, E-mail Address, Mobile Phone, and Position to move them to the Selected Fields box.

Take Note
To remove a field from the Selected Fields box, double-click the field. This moves it back to the Available Fields box.

7. Click the **Next >** button. The second screen in the Simple Query Wizard appears, as shown in Figure 7-4.

Figure 7-4

Simple Query Wizard, screen 2

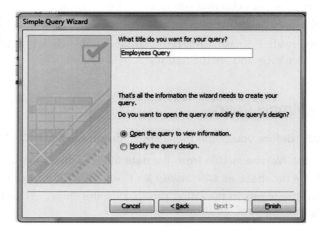

8. Name the query **Employees Contact Query**. *Open the query to view information* should be selected.

9. Click the **Finish** button to accept the default selections and complete the query. The Employees Contact Query is displayed, as shown in Figure 7-5. The results show all of the records, but show only the five fields that you specified in the query wizard.

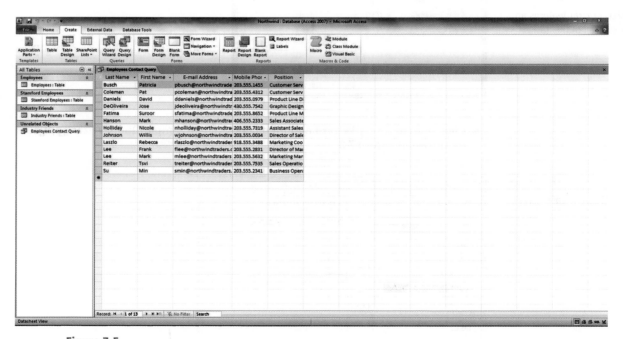

Figure 7-5

Simple select query

10. Click the **Close** button on the Employees Contact Query window to close the query.
PAUSE. LEAVE Access open to use in the next exercise.

Creating a Find Duplicates Query

As a general rule, duplicate data should be eliminated from a database whenever possible to reduce costs and increase accuracy. The first step in this process is finding duplicate data. Two or more records are considered duplicates only when all the fields in your query results contain the same values. If the values in even a single field differ, each record is unique. In this exercise, you use the Find Duplicates Query Wizard to find duplicate records.

You can also use the Find Duplicates Wizard to find records that contain *some* matching field values. You should include the field or fields that identify each record uniquely, typically the primary key. The query returns matching records where the values in the specified fields match character for character.

STEP BY STEP   **Create a Find Duplicates Query**

USE the database that is open from the previous exercise.

1. On the Create tab, in the Other group, click the Query Wizard button. The New Query dialog box appears.

2. Click Find Duplicates Query Wizard and then click OK. The *Find Duplicates Query Wizard* appears, as shown in Figure 7-6.

Figure 7-6

Find Duplicates Query
Wizard, screen 1

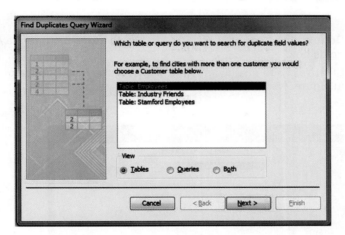

3. Click Table: Industry Friends and then click Next >. The next screen in the Find Duplicates Query Wizard appears, as shown in Figure 7-7.

Figure 7-7

Find Duplicates Query
Wizard, screen 2

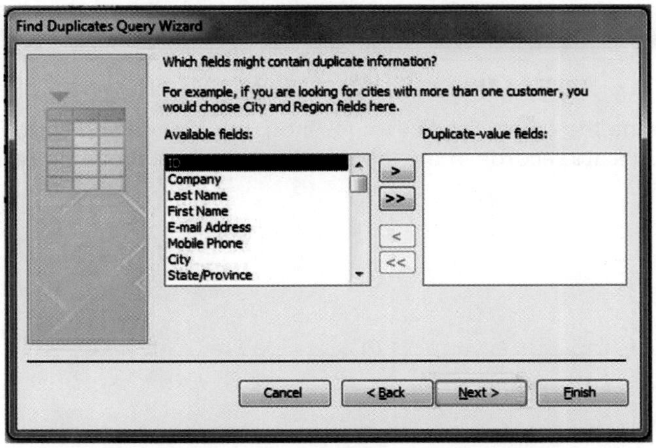

4. Double-click **Last Name**, **First Name**, and **E-mail Address** to move them to the Duplicate-value fields box. These are the fields that you think may include duplicate information.

5. Click **Next >** to display the next screen in the Find Duplicates Query Wizard, shown in Figure 7-8. This screen asks you if you want to show the other fields of the duplicate record besides just the ones with the duplicate data.

Figure 7-8

Find Duplicates Query Wizard, screen 3

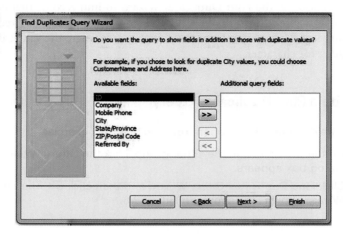

6. Double-click **Company** and **Referred By** to move them to the Additional query fields box.

7. Click **Next >** to display the final screen in the Find Duplicates Query Wizard, shown in Figure 7-9.

Figure 7-9

Find Duplicates Query Wizard, final screen

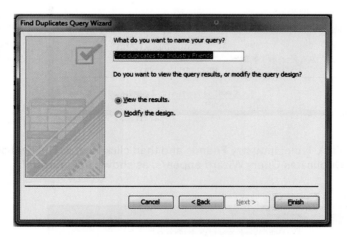

8. Name the query **Duplicates for Industry Friends** and click **Finish**. The query showing duplicate records in the table is displayed, as shown in Figure 7-10.

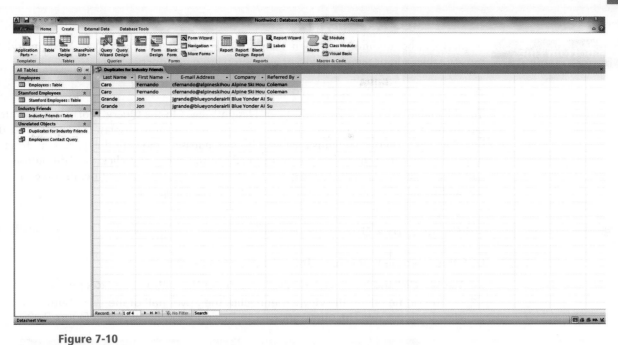

Figure 7-10

Duplicates for Industry
Friends query

9. Click the **Close** button in the Duplicates for Industry Friends tab to close the query.

PAUSE. LEAVE Access open to use in the next exercise.

SOFTWARE ORIENTATION

Design Tab

By switching to Design View, you can access all the tools needed to modify your query on the Query Tools contextual Design tab, shown in Figure 7-11. Use this figure as a reference throughout this lesson as well as the rest of this book.

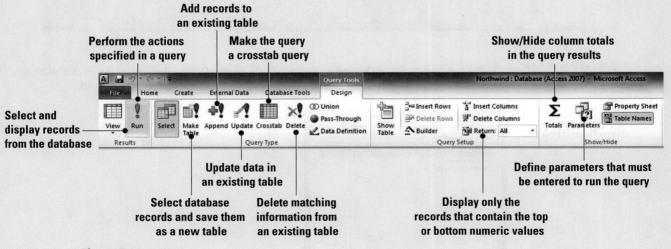

Figure 7-11

Design tab

MODIFYING A QUERY

The Bottom Line

A query can be modified in Design View, regardless of how it was created. You can add or remove a table, add or remove fields, or add criteria to refine query results.

Adding a Table to a Query

To add a table to a query, you must be in Design View. On the Query Tools Design contextual tab, in the Query Setup group, click the Show Table button to display the Show Table dialog box. There is a tab that contains the tables in the database, a tab with the queries, and a tab that displays both. Select the object you want to add to the query, and click the Add button. If you add a second copy of a table to the query, it is indicated by a "1" in the title. In this exercise, you add additional tables to a query using the Show Table dialog box.

STEP BY STEP | **Add a Table to a Query**

USE the database that is open from the previous exercise.

1. Double-click the **Industry Friends Query** in the Navigation pane to open it.
2. On the Home tab, in the Views menu, click the lower half of the **View** button and then click **Design View**. The query appears in Design View, as shown in Figure 7-12.

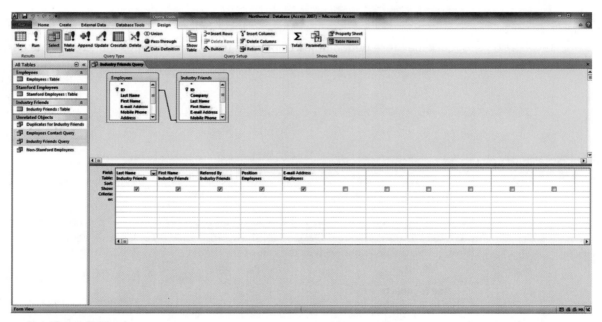

Figure 7-12

Query in Design View

3. On the Query Tools Design contextual tab, in the Query Setup group, click the **Show Table** button to display the Show Table dialog box, shown in Figure 7-13.

Figure 7-13

Show Table dialog box

4. Click **Industry Friends** and click the **Add** button. A second copy of the Industry Friends table is added to the query, as indicated by the "1" in the title, as shown in Figure 7-14.

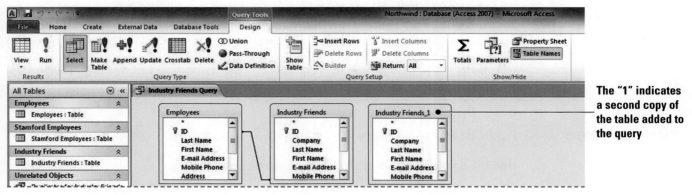

The "1" indicates a second copy of the table added to the query

Figure 7-14

Second copy of table in a query

5. Click **Stamford Employees** and click the **Add** button. The table is added to the query.

6. Click the **Close** button on the Show Table dialog box.

PAUSE. LEAVE the database open to use in the next exercise.

Removing a Table from a Query

To remove a table from a query, first open the query in Design View. In the upper part of query Design View, select the table you want to remove by clicking anywhere in its field list—a **field list** is a window that lists all the fields in the underlying record source or database object—then press the Delete key. The table is removed from the query, but it is not deleted from the database. In this exercise, you remove a table from a query.

STEP BY STEP | **Remove a Table from a Query**

USE the database that is open from the previous exercise.

1. Click anywhere in the **Industry Friends_1** field list.

2. Press the **Delete** key to remove the table.

3. Click anywhere in the **Stamford Employees** field list.

4. Press the **Delete** key to remove the table.

5. Click the **Close** button on the Industry Friends tab to close the query. If a message asks you if you want to save the changes, click **Yes**.

PAUSE. LEAVE the database open to use in the next exercise.

Adding Criteria to a Query

Not all queries must include criteria, but if you are not interested in seeing all the records that are stored in the underlying record source, you can add criteria to a query when designing it. A **query criterion** is a rule that identifies the records that you want to include in the query result. A criterion is similar to a formula. Some criteria are simple and use basic operators and constants. Others are complex and use functions, special operators, and include field references. Criteria can look very different from each other, depending on the data type of the field to which they apply and your specific requirements. You can also run a **parameter query**, in which the user interactively specifies one or more criteria values. This is not a separate query; it extends the flexibility of another type of query, such as a select query, by prompting the user for a value when it is run. In this exercise, you add criteria to queries to display certain records, use the Show check box, and create and run a parameter query that will prompt the user for a city name and display matching records.

To specify one or more criteria to restrict in the records returned in the query results, open the query in Design View. Select the field and type the condition that you want to specify in the Criteria row. To see the results, switch to Datasheet View. The results will show each field, including the one where the criterion was specified.

Sometimes, you may want to show only certain fields from the records that match the criterion to get a more concise view of the resulting data. In this case, deselect the Show row check box above the Criteria row for those fields you don't want to display in the results. The fields that you choose not to show, except the field with the criterion, will be removed from Design View after you switch to Datasheet View.

STEP BY STEP   **Add Criteria to a Query**

USE the database that is open from the previous exercise.

1. In the Navigation pane, double-click the Employees Contact Query to open it.
2. On the Home tab, in the Views group, click the lower half of the View button and click Design View.
3. In the Criteria row of the Position field, key Like "*Manager*" as shown in Figure 7-15.

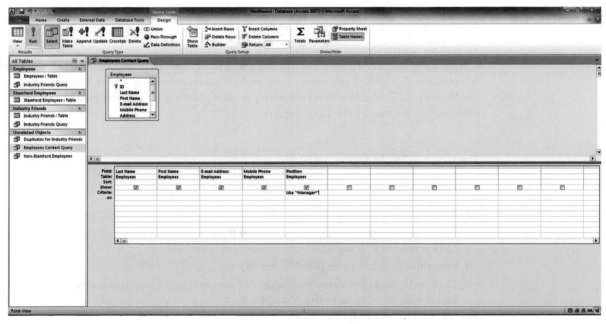

Figure 7-15

Query criterion

4. On the Query Tools Design contextual tab, in the Results group, click the lower half of the View button and click Datasheet View. The query results display all records with "Manager" in the position field, as shown in Figure 7-16.

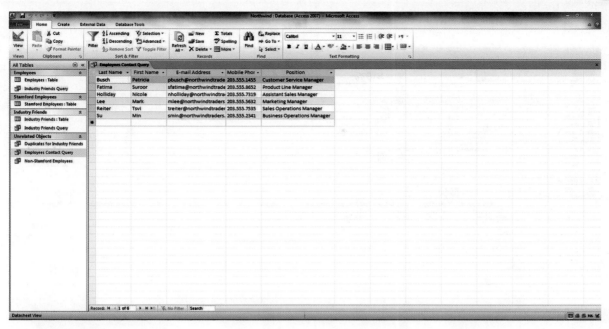

Figure 7-16

Results with query criteria applied

5. On the Home tab, in the Views group, click the lower half of the View button, and click Design View.

6. In the Show row, under the First Name field, click the Show check box to deselect it, as shown in Figure 7-17. The First Name field data will not appear in the query results.

Figure 7-17

Show check box deselected for First Name field

7. On the Home tab, in the Views group, click the lower half of the View button and click Datasheet View. Notice that the First Name field doesn't appear.

8. Click the Close button on the Employees Contact Query tab to close the query. When prompted to save, click Yes.

9. In the Navigation pane, double-click the Non-Stamford Employees Query to open it.

10. On the Home tab, in the Views group, click the lower half of the View button and click Design View.

11. In the Criteria row of the City field, key [City?] as shown in Figure 7-18.

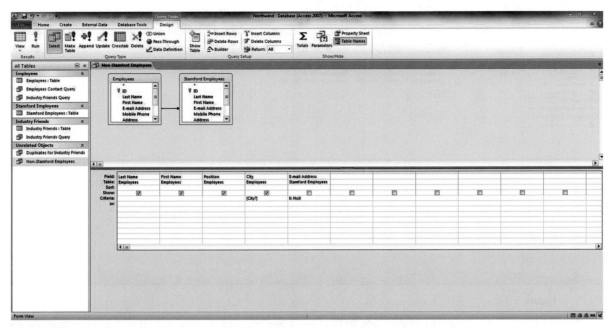

Figure 7-18

Parameter query criteria

12. On the Home tab, in the Views group, click the lower half of the View button and click Datasheet View. The prompt appears in the Enter Parameter Value dialog box, as shown in Figure 7-19.

Figure 7-19

Parameter query prompt dialog box

13. Key Darien in the City? box.

14. Click OK. The records for non-Stamford employees who live in Darien are displayed in the results, as shown in Figure 7-20.

Figure 7-20

Parameter query result

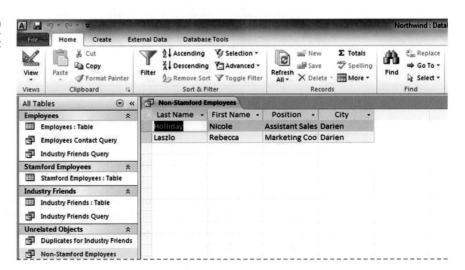

PAUSE. LEAVE the database open to use in the next exercise.

Table 7-1 shows some sample criteria and explains how they work. Table 7-2 shows the query results that are returned when specific criterion is used.

Table 7-1

Criteria Examples

Criteria	Description
>25 and <50	This criterion applies to a *Number* field, such as Inventory. It includes only those records where the *Inventory* field contains a value greater than 25 and less than 50.
DateDiff ("yyyy", [BirthDate], Date()) > 21	This criterion applies to a *Date/Time* field, such as BirthDate Only records where the number of years between a person's birth date and today's date is greater than 21 are included in the query result.
Is Null	This criterion can be applied to any type of field to show records where the field value is null.

Table 7-2

Query Result Examples

To Include Records That ...	Use This Criterion	Query Result
Exactly match a value, such as Manager	"Manager"	Returns records where the given field is set to Manager.
Do not match a value, such as Chicago	Not "Chicago"	Returns records where the given field is set to a value other than Chicago.
Begin with the specified string such as B	Like B*	Returns records for the given field where the value starts with "B," such as Boston, Bakersfield, and so on.
Do not begin with the specified string, such as B	Not Like B*	Returns records for the given field where the value starts with a character other than "B."
Contain the specified string, such as Sales	Like "*Sales*"	Returns records for the given field that contain the string "Sales."
Do not contain the specified string, such as Sales	Not Like "*Sales*"	Returns records for the given field that do not contain the string "Sales."

SORTING AND FILTERING DATA WITHIN A QUERY

The Bottom Line

Sorting and filtering data within a query allows you to display only the records you want and/ or only in a particular order.

Sorting Data within a Query

Sorting data in a query can help organize data efficiently and make it easier for users to review and locate the records they want without having to browse the data. Data can be sorted in the Datasheet View of a query. Right-click the field on which you want to sort and click the sort order you want—ascending or descending—from the shortcut menu. The records are rearranged to match the sort order. In this exercise, you sort data using Datasheet View of a query.

To sort by more than one field, on the Home tab, in the Sort & Filter group, click the Advanced button and click Advanced Filter/Sort to open up a tab where you can specify more than one field to sort by and the sort order.

STEP BY STEP   **Sort Data within a Query**

USE the database that is open from the previous exercise.

1. In the Navigation pane, double-click the Industry Friends Query to open it.
2. Right-click the Referred By field to display the shortcut menu shown in Figure 7-21.

Figure 7-21

Shortcut menu

3. Click Sort A to Z. The field is sorted in alphabetic order from A to Z, as shown in Figure 7-22.

Figure 7-22

Sorted query

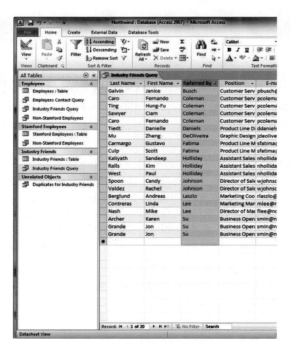

4. On the Home tab, in the Sort & Filter group, click the Remove Sort button.
5. On the Home tab, in the Sort & Filter group, click the Advanced button to display the menu shown in Figure 7-23.

Figure 7-23

Advanced menu

6. Click Advanced Filter/Sort. An Industry Friends QueryFilter1 tab appears, as shown in Figure 7-24.

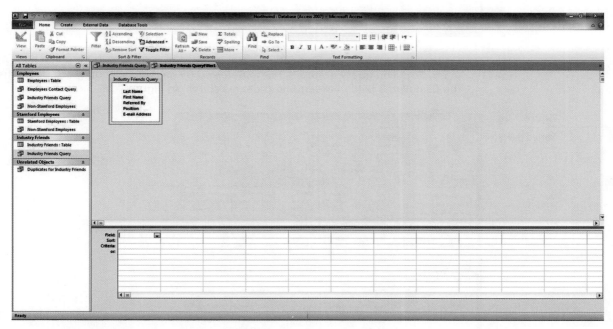

Figure 7-24

Industry Friends QueryFilter1 tab

7. Click the Field cell in the first column, click the down arrow, and click Referred By on the drop-down menu.
8. Click the Sort cell in the first column, click the down arrow, and click Ascending on the drop-down menu.
9. Click the Field cell in the second column, click the down arrow, and click Last Name on the drop-down menu.
10. Click the Sort cell in the second column, click the down arrow, and click Ascending on the drop-down menu. Your screen should look similar to Figure 7-25.

Figure 7-25

Advanced sort criteria

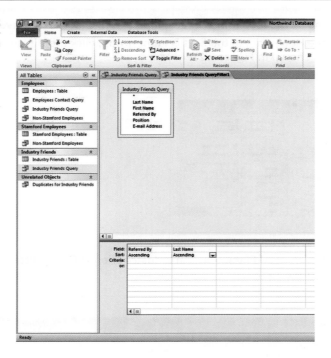

11. On the Home tab, in the Sort & Filter group, click the Advanced button and click Apply Filter/Sort. The query is sorted by the *Referred By* field in ascending order and then by the *Last Name* field in ascending order, as shown in Figure 7-26.

Figure 7-26

Sorted query

12. On the Home tab, in the Sort & Filter group, click the Remove Sort button.

PAUSE. LEAVE the database open to use in the next exercise.

Take Note   The same tab is used to perform an advanced filter for the query.

Take Note   You can also sort using the sort cell in Query Design View.

Filtering Data within a Query

A filter limits a view of data to specific records without requiring you to alter the design of the underlying query. If the criteria are temporary or change often, you can filter the query result instead of frequently modifying the query criteria. A filter is a temporary criterion that changes the query result without altering the design of the query. In this exercise, you filter data within a query.

To filter data within a query, click the field you want to filter. On the Home tab, in the Sort & Filter group, click the Filter button. The filters available depend on the type and values of the field. When you apply the filter, only records that contain the values that you are interested in are included in the view. The rest are hidden until you remove the filter by clicking the Toggle Filter button.

STEP BY STEP | **Filter Data within a Query**

USE the database that is open from the previous exercise. The Industry Friends Query should be open.

1. Click the **Position** header to select the field.

2. On the Home tab, in the Sort & Filter group, click the **Filter** button. A menu appears on the field, as shown in Figure 7-27.

Figure 7-27

Filter menu

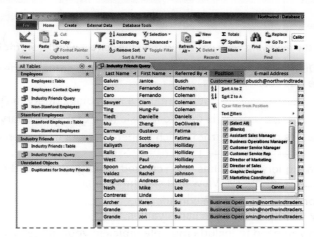

3. Click **Text Filters** and click **Contains** on the submenu. A Custom Filter dialog box appears, as shown in Figure 7-28.

Figure 7-28

Custom Filter dialog box

4. In the Position contains box, key **Marketing** and click **OK**. The records are filtered to show only those containing the word "Marketing" in the *Position* field, as shown in Figure 7-29.

Figure 7-29

Filtered query

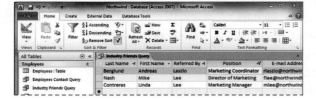

5. On the Home tab, in the Sort & Filter group, click the **Toggle Filter** button to remove the filter.

6. Click the **Close** button on Industry Friends Query to close the query and click **Yes** to save changes when prompted.

CLOSE the database.

SKILL SUMMARY

In This Lesson, You Learned How To:
Create a query
Modify a query
Sort and filter data within a query

Knowledge Assessment

Fill in the Blank

Complete the following sentences by writing the correct word or words in the blanks provided.

1. The Queries group on the _____ tab contains the commands used to create queries.

2. The _____ button creates a new, blank query in Design View.

3. A(n) _____ is the most basic type of Access query.

4. The tables or queries from which a query gets its data are referred to as its _____.

5. To run a query after it has been created, double-click it in the Navigation pane to open it in _____ View and see the results.

6. Two or more records are considered _____ only when all the fields in your query results contain the same values.

7. When you need to include multiple tables in your query, use the _____ Wizard to build a query from a primary table and a related table.

8. A _____ can get data from one or more tables.

9. By switching to _____ View, you can access all the tools needed to modify your query.

10. A(n) _____ is a window that lists all the fields in the underlying record source or database object.

Multiple Choice

Select the best response for the following statements or questions.

1. Creating a query is like
   a. Sorting the data
   b. Asking the database a question
   c. Creating a new table
   d. Opening an existing database

2. The results that a query returns can be
   a. Sorted
   b. Grouped
   c. Filtered
   d. All of the above
   e. None of the above

3. When one table will provide the information that you need, you can create a
   a. Record source
   b. Simple select query
   c. Query criterion
   d. Parameter query

4. Which query cannot be created using the Query Wizard?
   a. Parameter query
   b. Simple query
   c. Find duplicates query
   d. Find unmatched query

5. Queries are different from sort or filter commands because they can be
   a. Applied to multiple fields
   b. Saved
   c. Modified
   d. Used on forms

6. A query can get its data from
   a. One or more tables
   b. Existing queries
   c. A combination of a and b
   d. All of the above
   e. None of the above

7. To find records that contain matching field values, you can create a query using which wizard?
   a. Find Matching
   b. Matching Fields
   c. Duplicate Records
   d. Find Duplicates

8. Before creating a query from multiple tables, you must first ensure that the tables have
   a. Unmatched records
   b. A defined relationship
   c. A filter applied
   d. No related records

9. To add a table to a query, you must be in what view?
   a. SQL
   b. Datasheet
   c. PivotTable
   d. Design

10. A rule that identifies the records that you want to include in the query result is called a
    a. Parameter query
    b. Query criterion
    c. Select query
    d. Field list

Competency Assessment

Project 7-1: Create a Games Select Query

As the manager at Southridge Video, you have stored information in an Access database about each used game that the store has taken in trade. Now that you know how to create queries, you decide to create a select query to list the title, rating, and category, which are the fields that you most often need to view.

GET READY. LAUNCH Access if it is not already running.

@ The *Games* file for this lesson is available on the book companion website or in WileyPLUS.

1. **OPEN** *Games* from the data files for this lesson.
2. **SAVE** the database as *Games XXX* (where *XXX* is your initials).
3. On the Create tab, in the Queries group, click the Query Wizard button to display the New Query dialog box.
4. Click Simple Query Wizard and then click OK.
5. In the Tables/Queries drop-down list, Table: Games should be selected.
6. Under Available Fields, double-click Title, Rating, and Category to move them to the Selected Fields box.
7. Click the Next > button. The second screen in the Simple Query Wizard appears.
8. Name the query Games Query. *Open the query to view information* should be selected.
9. Click the Finish button.
10. Click the Close button in the Games Query tab to close the query.
11. **LEAVE** the database open for the next project.

LEAVE Access open for the next project.

Project 7-2: Create a Find Duplicates Query

You have taught the night manager at Southridge Video how to enter used game information into the database, but you have not yet developed a reliable system for determining if the game has already been entered. You are concerned there may be duplicate records. Create a find duplicates query to determine if there are duplicates.

USE the database that is open from the previous project.

1. On the Create tab, in the Queries group, click the Query Wizard button.
2. In the New Query dialog box, click Find Duplicates Query Wizard, and then click OK.
3. Click Table: Games and then click Next >. The next screen in the Find Duplicates Query Wizard appears.
4. Double-click Title, Platform, and Publisher to move them to the Duplicate-value fields box.
5. Click Next > to display the next screen in the Find Duplicates Query Wizard.
6. Double-click Category to move it to the Additional query fields box.
7. Click Next > to display the final screen in the Find Duplicates Query Wizard.
8. Name the query Duplicates for Games and click Finish to display the query showing duplicate records in the table.
9. Click the Close button on the Duplicates for Games tab to close the query.
10. **CLOSE** the database.

LEAVE Access open for the next project.

Proficiency Assessment

Project 7-3: Creating Queries

Information about each selection for the Coho Vineyard monthly wine club is stored in an Access database. Information about red wine and white wine is stored in separate tables. In your position as customer service rep, you are asked to create two queries from both tables.

GET READY. LAUNCH Access if it is not already running.

@ The *Club Wines* file for this lesson is available on the book companion website or in WileyPLUS.

1. **OPEN** *Club Wines* from the data files for this lesson.
2. **SAVE** the database as *Club Wines XXX* (where *XXX* is your initials).
3. Open the Red Wines: Table.
4. Start the Query Wizard and choose Simple Query Wizard.
5. In the Tables/Queries drop-down list, click Table: Red Wines.
6. Move the Bottled, Label, and Type fields to the Selected Fields box.
7. Click the Next > button.
8. Click the Next > button and name the query Red Wines Query.
9. Click the Finish button.
10. Start the Query Wizard and choose Simple Query Wizard.
11. In the Tables/Queries drop-down list, click Table: Red Wines.
12. Move the Bottled, Label, and Type fields to the Selected Fields box.
13. Click the Next > button.
14. Click the Next > button and name the query White Wines Query.
15. Click the Finish button.
16. Review the information in both queries and then close.
17. **LEAVE** the database open for the next project.

LEAVE Access open for the next project.

Project 7-4: Creating Parameter Queries

A red wine and a white wine should be selected for each month. The manager has asked you to create queries for specific wines within both queries.

USE the database that is open from the previous project.

1. Open the Red Wines Query in Design View.
2. In the Criteria row of the Label field, key [Label?].
3. Click the Run button and key Chateau Piganeau in the parameter query prompt dialog box then click OK.
4. Save and close the query.
5. Repeat steps 1-2 for the White Wines Query.
6. Click the Run button and key Le Muse in the parameter query prompt dialog box then click OK.
7. Save and close the query.
8. **CLOSE** the database.

LEAVE Access open for the next project.

Mastery Assessment

Project 7-5: Create a Query

In your job as a travel agent at Erin's Travel, a client has asked you to provide a list of all the travel packages available to sporting events that start in the month of April or May. You will add criteria to a query to get this information from the database.

GET READY. LAUNCH Access if it is not already running.

@ The *Sports Events* file for this lesson is available on the book companion website or in WileyPLUS.

1. **OPEN** *Sports Events* from the data files for this lesson.
2. Save the database as *Sports Events XXX* (where *XXX* is your initials).
3. Open the Events query and switch to Design View.
4. Add criteria that will query the database and display all fields for all events that start between 4/1/2012 and 5/31/2012.
5. Use the Show row to hide the *Start Time* and *End Time* fields.
6. Run the query.
7. Close the query and save the design when prompted.
8. **CLOSE** the database.

LEAVE Access open for the next project.

Project 7-6: Create a Parameter Query

Your brother, who owns Wingtip Toys, wants to be able to pull data from his toy inventory and asks for your help in creating a query. He wants to be able to query the database for toys for specific ages when prompted, so you show him how to create a parameter query.

GET READY. LAUNCH Access if it is not already running.

@ The *Toys* file for this lesson is available on the book companion website or in WileyPLUS.

1. **OPEN** *Toys* from the data files for this lesson.
2. **SAVE** the database as *Toys XXX* (where *XXX* is your initials).
3. Create a simple query named Inventory Query that contains all the available fields, except the *ID* field.
4. Create a parameter query on the *For Ages* field that gives you the prompt shown in Figure 7-30 when the query is run.

Figure 7-30

Enter Parameter Value prompt

5. Query the database for all the toys for ages 10–14 years.
6. Close the query and save when prompted.
7. **CLOSE** the database.

CLOSE Access.

INTERNET READY

Blogs can be a fun way to pass time, but they can also be a great source of business information. If you enjoy blogs, check out some of the business-related blogs available, such as The Small Business Blog from Microsoft, shown in Figure 7-31. The URL for this blog is: *http://blogs.technet .com/b/smallbusiness/*. Search for information on mail merges or another topic of interest to you and see what you can find.

Figure 7-31

The Small Business Blog from Microsoft

Component	Requirement
Computer and processor	500 MHz or faster processor.
Memory	256 MB RAM; 512 MB recommended for graphics features, Outlook Instant Search, and certain advanced functionality.[1,2]
Hard disk	3.0 GB available disk space.
Display	1024×576 or higher resolution monitor.
Operating system	Windows XP (must have SP3) (32-bit), Windows 7, Windows Vista with Service Pack (SP) 1, Windows Server 2003 R2 with MSXML 6.0 (32-bit Office only), Windows Server 2008, or later 32- or 64-bit OS.
Graphics	Graphics hardware acceleration requires a DirectX 9.0c graphics card with 64 MB or more video memory.
Additional requirements	Certain Microsoft® OneNote® features require Windows® Desktop Search 3.0, Windows Media® Player 9.0, Microsoft® ActiveSync® 4.1, microphone, audio output device, video recording device, TWAIN-compatible digital camera, or scanner; sharing notebooks requires users to be on the same network.
	Certain advanced functionality requires connectivity to Microsoft Exchange Server 2003, Microsoft SharePoint Server 2010, and/or Microsoft SharePoint Foundation 2010.
	Certain features require Windows Search 4.0.
	Send to OneNote Print Driver and Integration with Business Connectivity Services require Microsoft .NET Framework 3.5 and/or Windows XPS features.
	Internet Explorer (IE) 6 or later, 32-bit browser only. IE7 or later required to receive broadcast presentations. Internet functionality requires an Internet connection.
	Multi-Touch features require Windows 7 and a touch-enabled device.
	Certain inking features require Windows XP Tablet PC Edition or later.
	Speech recognition functionality requires a close-talk microphone and audio output device.
	Internet Fax not available on Windows Vista Starter, Windows Vista Home Basic, or Windows Vista Home Premium.
	Information Rights Management features require access to a Windows 2003 Server with SP1 or later running Windows Rights Management Services.
	Certain online functionality requires a Windows LiveTM ID.
Other	Product functionality and graphics may vary based on your system configuration. Some features may require additional or advanced hardware or server connectivity; **www.office.com/products.**

[1] 512 MB RAM recommended for accessing Outlook data files larger than 1 GB.

[2] GHz processor or faster and 1 GB RAM or more recommended for OneNote Audio Search. Close-talking microphone required. Audio Search is not available in all languages.

Glossary

A

absolute cell reference   A reference that does not change when a formula is copied or moved.

action   A button or text block programmed to perform a specific action, such as jumping to a slide or starting a program.

action button   A graphic that serves as a hyperlink to jump to a location or perform an action.

active cell   A cell that is highlighted or outlined by a bold black line.

address book   Stores names and e-mail addresses.

alignment   A setting that refers to how text is positioned between the margins.

annotate   To write or draw on a slide during a presentation.

Application Parts   A gallery that you can use to insert predefined templates consisting of objects like tables, forms, and reports into a preexisting database.

appointment   A scheduled activity that does not require sending invitations to other people or resources.

argument   A component of a function that is enclosed in parentheses.

array   Used to build single formulas that produce multiple results or that operate on a group of arguments.

Ascending   A sort order that sorts data from beginning to end, such as A to Z or 0 to 99. (*See also* Sort.)

aspect ratio   The relationship of width to height in a picture or shape.

assistant   In an organization chart, a person who reports directly to a superior.

attachment   File sent as part of an e-mail message.

attribute   File characteristic such as size, subject, or sender.

audio   A sound or music clip.

authentication   The process of verifying that people and products are who and what they claim to be.

Auto fill   An option that automatically fills cells with data and/or formatting.

AutoComplete   A command that automatically completes the text of the current date, day of the week, and month.

AutoCorrect   A feature that replaces commonly misspelled words with the correct spelling or replaces symbols and abbreviations with specific text strings.

AutoFilter   A built-in set of filtering capabilities.

AutoPreview   Displays the first three lines of every message in the message list.

axis   A line bordering the chart plot area as a frame of reference for measurement.

B

Backstage view   The view that opens when you click the File tab; it contains commands for managing files, setting program options, and printing.

Backstage   A view that enables you to easily navigate and customize different features that you frequently use in Excel.

badges   Small square labels that contain KeyTips.

balloons   Shaded blocks of text used for comments appearing on the right side of the document.

banner   Text displayed at the top of a day to indicate an event.

block style   A format style that aligns text along the left margin.

blog   An online interactive location maintained by companies, instructors, and individuals who post information, events, news, and more, where anyone can leave comments.

bookmark   A location or a selection of text that you name and identify for future reference.

boundary   The line between rows or columns.

broadcast   To deliver a presentation live in real time via a network or Internet connection.

building blocks   Built-in reusable content **such as** text, graphics, and objects **that** can be easily managed and inserted in a document for a quick format.

bulleted list   Groups of items or phrases that present related ideas.

busy   An activity is scheduled for this time period. You are not available for other activities.

C

Calendar group   A group of related calendars that are grouped together for easy viewing.

Calendar Snapshot   A picture of your calendar at a specific moment.

caption   A few descriptive words providing readers with information regarding a figure, table, or equation.

Categorized Mail Standard Search Folder   Displays messages with an assigned color category.

cell   A box on the grid identified by the intersection of a column and a row.

character styles   A style that is applied to individual characters or words that users have selected.

character   A letter, number, punctuation mark, or symbol.

chart   A graphical representation of numeric data in a worksheet.

chart area   An entire chart and all its elements.

chart sheet   A sheet that contains only a chart.

clip art   A collection of media files available to insert in Microsoft Office documents that can include illustrations, photographs, video, or audio content.

Clip Organizer   A tool supplied within Microsoft Office that collects and stores clip art, photos animations, videos, and other types of media to use in your documents.

columns   Vertical blocks of text in which text flows from the bottom of one column to the top of the next.

column heading   The identifying letter of a column.

column width   The left-to-right width of a column.

command group   Task-specific groups divided among the command tabs appropriate to the work a user is currently performing.

command tab   Task-oriented tabs that are organized on the Ribbon.

command   A button, list, or other clickable option on the Ribbon.

common filters   Popular filters available as context menu commands, depending on the type and values of the field.

comparison operator   A sign, such as greater than (>) or less than (<), that is used to compare two values.

composite key   Two or more primary keys used in a table.

compress   Reduces the size of an object.

condition   Identifies the characteristics used to determine the messages affected by a rule.

conditional formatting   Automatic formatting based on established criteria.

conditional formula   A formula in which the result is determined by the presence or absence of a particular condition.

Connection Status menu   A menu that lets users determine whether the Help screen displays content available at Office Online, or only those help topics currently installed on the computer.

constant   A number or text value that is entered directly into a formula.

constrain   To force a drawing object into a particular shape or alignment.

contact   Collection of information about a person or company.

Contact Group   Group of individual contacts saved together as a single contact.

Contacts folder   Electronic organizer that enables you to create, view, and edit contact information.

content controls   Individual programs within Word that allow you to add information in a document, such as a header or footer.

contiguous   Adjacent to one another. For example, slides 1 and 2 are contiguous.

Coordinated Universal Time (UTC)   The time standard used by Outlook, which is based on International Atomic Time.

copy   A command in Word that places a duplicate copy of selected text in the Clipboard.

copy pointer   A tool that allows users to drag a cell or range of cells to a new location.

criteria   Specifications that allot what data type users want to use in a cell or range of cells and how users want that data used, formatted, or displayed.

crop   The process of trimming the horizontal or vertical edges of a picture to get rid of unwanted areas.

current slide   The slide that is currently being edited.

custom show   A group of slides in a presentation that can be shown separately from the entire presentation.

cut   To remove data from a worksheet that is still available in the Clipboard for use.

D

data labels   Text that provides additional information about a data marker, which represents a single data point or value that originates from a worksheet cell.

data marker   A bar, area, dot, slice, or other symbol in a chart that represents a single data point or value that originates from a worksheet cell.

data series   All the data points for a particular category of plotted information.

data type   The kind of information a field contains—whether text, number, date/time, or some other type.

database management system (DBMS)   A system for managing data that allows the user to store, retrieve, and analyze information.

database   A collection of information that is organized so that you can retrieve information quickly.

datasheet   A visual representation of the data contained in a table or of the results returned by a query.

default   A predefined setting. You can accept Excel's default option settings or you can change them.

default settings   Standard settings installed by an application as presets so that the application has the same settings each and every time it is accessed.

Definitive Command   A command that closes Backstage view and returns the user to a workbook.

Deleted Items folder   Deleted items are held in this folder until the folder is emptied. Emptying this folder removes the items from your computer.

descending   A sort order that sorts data from the end to the beginning, such as Z to A or 99 to 0. (*See also* Sort.)

descending order   An arrangement in which data appear alphabetically from Z to A.

desktop shortcut   An icon placed on the Windows desktop that launches an application, opens a folder, or opens a file.

desktop   The first screen you see after you start the computer.

dialog box   A box that prompts the user for additional information when executing a command.

dialog box launcher   A small arrow in the lower-right corner of a group that you click to launch a dialog box.

distribution list   *see Contact Group.*

Document properties   Document information that identifies who created the document, when it was created, how large the file is, and other important information about the workbook.

document theme   A predefined set of colors, fonts, lines, and fill effects.

Drafts folder   Outlook messages you write but haven't sent are stored in this folder.

drop cap   A large initial letter that drops down two or more lines at the beginning of a paragraph to indicate that a new block of information is beginning and to give interest to newsletters or magazine articles.

drop-down arrow   A small, downward-pointing arrow next to some tools on the Ribbon.

drop-down list   A list that appears once a drop-down arrow is clicked, allowing you to choose from available options.

duplicate contact   Contact records containing the same information.

duplicate value   Occurs when all values in a row are an exact match for all the values in another row.

E

electronic business card   Digital version of paper business cards. They can be sent as attachments, used as signatures, and used to create a contact record.

embedded chart   A chart that is placed on a worksheet rather than on a separate chart sheet.

embedded object   A picture or other object inserted into a document that becomes part of the document. Compare to *linked object.*

embedded   Data that has been placed in a destination application so that it can be edited with the tools of its original source applications.

encrypting   Scrambling data in a way that can only be reconverted by an authorized user who has the password.

endnote   A citation in a document placed at the end of the document in which the citation is located.

event   An activity that lasts one or more days.

exception   Identifies the characteristics used to exclude messages from being affected by a rule.

external reference   A cell or range on a worksheet in another Excel workbook, or a defined name in another workbook.

F

Fast Command   A command that provides quick access to common functions and is located on the left navigation pane.

feature   The different components that make up Outlook: Calendar, Contacts, Mail.

field   A column in a database table.

field list   A window that lists all the fields in the underlying record source or database object.

fields   A placeholder where Word inserts content in a document. Word automatically uses fields when specific commands are activated, such as those for inserting dates, page numbers, and a table of contents.

File tab   A tab that displays the Backstage view and contains a menu of commands that you can use for the common tasks performed with your database files—such as opening, saving, and printing.

fill handle   A small black square in the lower-right corner of a selected cell.

filter by form   A tool that creates a blank form similar to the original; useful for filtering on several fields in a form or to find a specific record.

filter   A restriction that Excel uses to determine which worksheet rows to display.

first-line indent   A setting that inserts a one-half inch of blank space between the left margin and the first line of the paragraph; one-half inch is the default setting for this indent.

floating object   An image or other object positioned precisely on the page, allowing the text to wrap around it in one of several available formats. Compare to *inline object.*

fly-out   A menu or pane that opens floating above the main window instead of docked to a fixed place on the screen and which changes the way every other pane appears.

folder   Common name for Outlook components.

font   A set of typefaces used to display characters, numbers, and symbols.

font theme   A combination of two fonts to be applied to headings and text as part of a theme.

footer   A line of text that appears at the bottom of each page in a document.

footnote   A citation in a document placed at the bottom of the page in the document on which the citation is located.

foreign key   A primary key from one table that is used in another table.

form   A database object that simplifies the process of entering, editing, and displaying data.

Form Design button   A tool that creates a new blank form in Design view.

Form tool   A tool that creates a simple form that includes all the fields from the underlying data source.

Form Wizard   A form-building tool that allows you to choose the form fields, style, and layout.

Format Painter   A tool to copy character and paragraph formatting.

formula   An equation that performs calculations, such as addition, subtraction, multiplication, and division, on values in a worksheet.

formula bar   A bar located between the Ribbon and the worksheet in which users can edit the contents of a cell.

free   No activities are scheduled for this time period. You are available.

freeze   To keep certain rows or columns visible while the rest of a worksheet scrolls.

function   A predefined formula that performs a calculation.

G

gallery   A dropdown window containing multiple options within a group.

Go To   A command in the scroll box that enables users to browse by field, endnote, footnote, comment, section, page, edits, headings, graphics, or tables.

gridlines   A tool that provides a grid of vertical and horizontal lines that help you align graphics and other objects in a document or slide.

gridlines   The lines that display around worksheet cells.

group   A set of related tools on the Ribbon.

group schedule   Displays scheduling information for several people. Requires Microsoft Exchange 2000 or a more recent version of Microsoft Exchange.

group worksheets   A feature that allows users to enter and edit data on several worksheets at the same time or apply formatting to multiple worksheets.

groups   Related commands within the tabs on the Ribbon.

guides   Nonprinting vertical and horizontal lines that you can move or copy to align objects on a slide.

H

Handout Master   The master that controls the layout and elements of handouts.

handout   A printed copy of a presentation.

hanging indent   A setting that begins the first full line of text in a paragraph at the left margin; all the remaining lines in the paragraph are indented one-half inch from the left margin.

header   Information such as a date, slide number, or text phrase that appears at the top of each page of a presentation's handouts or notes.

header row   The first row of the table that is formatted differently and should be repeated for tables that continue beyond one page.

Help system   A system in Excel 2010 that is rich in information, illustrations, and tips that can help users complete any task as they create a worksheet and workbook.

hide   To make a worksheet invisible.

horizontal alignment   A setting that refers to how text is positioned between the left and right margins.

hotkey   Another name for a Keytip.

hyperlink   A block of text or a graphic that when mouse-clicked takes the user to a new location to an internal or external page. that opens another file or a web page when users click it.

Hypertext Markup Language (HTML)   Formatting language that enables you to format text and insert items such as horizontal lines, pictures, and animated graphics for viewing on the World Wide Web (web).

hyphenation   A dash that is used to join words and separate syllables of a single word; by default hyphenation is turned off in Word so that words appear on a single line.

I

I-beam   The large "I" created when users place the cursor near the insertion point.

I-beam pointer   The mouse pointer when over a text box or editable text area, appearing as a curly capital I. If you click when the I-beam pointer is displayed, the insertion point moves to that spot.

iCalendar (.ics)   An updatable calendar format that is interchangeable between most calendar and e-mail applications, making it a versatile tool.

import   Bring information into a file from an external source.

Inbox folder   By default, new messages are placed in this folder when they arrive.

indent   A blank space inserted between text and the left or right margin.

indent level   The distance of a paragraph of text from the placeholder's left border.

InfoBar   Banner containing information added automatically at the top of a message.

ink   The annotations created with the pen and highlighter tools during a slide show.

inline object   An image or other object that moves along with the text that surrounds it. Compare to *floating object*.

innermost field   A secondary sort field in a multifield sort.

insertion point   The blinking point at the upper-left side of the document where you will begin creating your text.

Instant Search   Outlook's enhanced search tool that includes two features that you can use to filter through the results: Search Suggestions List and the Search Contextual tab.

Internet Calendar Subscription   A calendar format that can be downloaded and updated.

item   A record stored in Outlook.

J

Junk E-Mail folder   Messages identified as spam are placed in this folder when they arrive.

K

key tips   A letter or number that appears next to an onscreen tool when the Alt key is pressed; keying that letter or number activates the associated tool.

keyword   A word or phrase that describes a subject or category on which you can search.

keywords   Words assigned to document properties that make organizing and finding documents easier.

L

label   Text entered in a worksheet that is used to identify numeric data.

landscape orientation   A format commonly used for brochures, graphics, tables, and so on that orients text across the longer dimension of the page.

landscape orientation   A page orientation that is wider than it is tall.

Large Mail   A standard Search Folder that displays messages larger than 100 kilobytes.

lassoing   To drag an imaginary box around a group of objects to select them.

layout master   The slide master for a particular slide layout.

layout   A predefined arrangement of placeholders for text or objects (such as charts or pictures).

leaders   A tool identified with symbols such as dotted, dashed, or solid lines that fill the space before tabs.

legend   A box that identifies the patterns or colors that are assigned to the data series or categories in a chart.

legend keys   A key that appears to the left of legend entries and identifies the color-coded data series.

line spacing   The amount of space between lines of text in a paragraph.

linked object   A picture or other object inserted into a document by creating a connection between the document and picture file but **not combining** them in the same file. Compare to *embedded object.*

lookup functions   Functions used to find information stored in a table in an Excel worksheet.

M

mandatory attendee   A person who must attend a meeting.

margins   The blank borders that occupy the top, bottom, and sides of a document.

mathematical operator   An element that specifies a calculation to be performed.

meeting   A scheduled activity that requires sending invitations to other people or resources.

meeting organizer   The person who creates the meeting and sends meeting invitations.

meeting request   Outlook item that creates a meeting and invites attendees.

menu   A list of options.

merged cells   Cells created by combining two or more adjacent horizontal or vertical cells.

message header   Text automatically added at the top of a message. The message header contains the sender's e-mail address, the names of the servers used to send and transfer the message, the subject, the date, and other basic information about the message.

Microsoft Office Button   Accesses the commands to open, save, print, and finish a document.

Microsoft Outlook Calendar Sharing Service   A service set up by Microsoft that allows you to share calendars with other Outlook users.

Mini toolbar   A small toolbar that appears when the mouse pointer is placed on a selected text object; provides commands for working with the text.

mixed punctuation   A style that requires a colon after the salutation and a comma after the closing.

mixed reference   A reference in which one component is absolute and one is relative.

monospace   A font in which all of its characters take up the same amount of horizontal space.

move pointer   A tool that allows users to drag a cell or range of cells to a new location, replacing any existing data in the destination cells.

multi-selection   A Word feature that enables users to select multiple items of the text that are not adjacent.

multivalued field   A field that allows you to select more than one value from a list.

N

name   A meaningful and logical identifier that a user can apply to make it easier to understand the purpose of a cell reference, constant, formula, or table.

Name box   Located below the Ribbon at the left end of the formula bar. When the user keys a cell location in this box and presses Enter, the cursor moves to that cell.

natural series   A formatted series of text or numbers.

Navigation Pane   A tool that appears in the left side of the window when you select its command in the Show command group.

negative indent   A setting that extends paragraph text into the left margin.

non-contiguous   Not adjacent to one another. See *contiguous.*

non-printing characters   Symbols for certain formatting commands that can help users create and edit documents.

normal forms   The standards and guidelines of database design that can be used to determine if a database is structured correctly.

Normal view   PowerPoint's default view, suited for editing individual slides; includes the Slide pane, Notes pane, and Slides/Outline pane.

normalization   The process of applying rules to a database design to ensure that information is divided into the appropriate tables.

note   Additional information associated with a slide.

Notes Page view   A view that displays a single slide and its associated notes.

numbered list   A group of steps, procedures, or actions that are listed in numerical order.

O

objects   Elements in a database, such as tables, queries, forms, and reports.

Office Clipboard   A location that collects and stores up to 24 copied or cut items, which are then available to be used in the active workbook and in other Microsoft Office programs.

open punctuation   A style that requires no punctuation after the salutation or the closing.

operand   An element that identifies the value to be used in a calculation.

optional attendee   A person who should attend the meeting but whose presence is not required.

order   The way in which objects stack up on a slide as you create them.

organization chart   A diagram that shows the relationships between personnel or departments in an organization.

orientation   The direction that material appears on a page when printed. See *portrait* and *landscape.*

orphan   The first line of a paragraph that appears alone at the bottom of a page.

out of office   An automatic reply notification that you are not in the office during this time period.

Outbox folder   Outgoing messages are held in this folder until you are connected to the Internet. When an Internet connection is detected, the message is sent.

outermost field   The primary sort field in a multifield sort.

Outlook Data file   File containing stored Outlook data. It is identified by the .pst extension.

overlay mode   Displays calendars on top of each other.

overlay stack   Several calendars are displayed on top of each other.

P

page break   A divider that breaks a worksheet into separate pages for printing.

Page Break Preview   A command on the View tab to control where page breaks occur.

paragraph styles   A style in which the formats are applied instantly to all text in the paragraph where the insertion point is located, whether or not text is selected.

parameter query   A query in which the user interactively specifies one or more criteria values.

paste   A command that pastes text from the Clipboard to a new location in the original document or new document.

Paste Special   A function that performs irregular cell copying.

pattern   A repeating pattern of lines in a certain color (the foreground color) on a background of another color (the background color).

People Pane   Displays all the e-mails, meetings, and attachments related to the selected person.

plain text   Text without any formatting.

plot area   The area bounded by the axes of a chart.

point size   A measurement that refers to the height of characters with one point equaling approximately $1/12$ of an inch.

portrait orientation   A format commonly used for business documents in which text extends across the shorter length of the document.

presentation tools   The tools and commands that are active during Slide Show view.

Presenter view   A viewing mode that allows the presenter to see notes on one screen while the audience views slides on another screen.

Preview   A tool that enables users to visually check your document for errors before printing.

primary key   The column in a database that uniquely identifies each row.

Print options   Options to customize and manipulate a workbook for printing, such as margins, orientation, scale, and collation.

print   To send a document to a printer.

Print Preview   A window that displays a full-page view of a worksheet just as it will be printed.

private   Feature that protects the details of an activity from a casual observer, but does not ensure privacy.

properties   Controls the appearance or behavior characteristics for objects and related parts like fields and controls.

proportional space   A font in which the horizontal spacing varies.

Q

query   A database object that enables stored data to be searched and retrieved.

query criterion   A rule that identifies the records that you want to include in the query result.

Quick Access Toolbar   A toolbar at the top left of the screen that contains the commands that you use most often, such as Save, Undo, Redo, and Print.

Quick Start   A collection of predefined objects that you can add to your database arranged by parts for tracking things such as comments, contacts, and issues.

Quick Start field   A predefined set of characteristics and properties that describes a field, including a field name, a data type, and a number of other field properties.

Quick Style   Built-in formatting for text, graphics, SmartArt diagrams, charts, WordArt, pictures, tables, and shapes.

R

Reading Pane   Displays the text of a selected e-mail message.

Really Simple Syndication (RSS)   A method that allows you to subscribe to content from a variety of websites offering the service.

record   A row in a database table.

record source   Tables or queries from which a query gets its data.

recurring appointment   An appointment that occurs at regular intervals.

redo   A command that repeats a user's last action.

redundant data   Duplicate information in a database.

reference   A component of a formula that identifies a cell or a range of cells on a worksheet.

referential integrity   A rule that prevents orphaned records.

relational database   A group of database tables that are connected or linked by a defined relationship that ties the information together.

relative cell reference   A reference that changes "relative" to the location where it is copied or moved.

replace   A command that enables users to replace one word or phrase with another.

report   A database object that presents information in a format that is easy to read and print.

reset   To restore a picture or other formatted object to its default settings.

resetting   Discards all formatting changes you made to a picture, including changes to contrast, color, brightness, and style.

resource   An item or a location that can be invited to a meeting.

restore   Make an item available for use. For example, moving an item out of the Deleted Items folder restores it for use.

Ribbon   A broad band that runs across the top of the window that organizes tools from the Menu toolbar into an easy-to-use interface.

Rich Text Format (RTF)   Formatting system that uses tags to format text.

row   Cells that run from left to right on the grid and are identified by numbers.

row heading   The identifying number of a row.

row height   The top-to-bottom height of a row.

rule   Defines an action that happens automatically when messages are received or sent.

rulers   Horizontal and vertical measures that help you position objects on a slide or document.

S

sans serif   A font that does not have the small line extensions on its characters.

Save As   A dialog box that will save a document in a specific format.

Save   A button in the Quick Access Toolbar that saves an existing document.

scale   The process of increasing or decreasing an original picture's height and width by the same percentage.

scaling   Shrinking or stretching printed output to a percentage of its actual size.

scope   The location within which Excel recognizes an item without qualification.

Screen Clippings   An image capture of only a part of your computer screen that you have selected.

screenshot   An image capture of the entire current display on your computer screen.

ScreenTip   A pop-up box that gives a command's name and descriptive text when you point at its button on the Ribbon.

scroll bar   A tool that allows the user to move up or down within the document.

scroll box   A tool that allows users to move horizontally and vertically through a document more quickly than the scroll buttons, or to see a **ScreenTip** displaying a user's position in the document.

scroll buttons   A tool that allows users to move up or down one line at a time, or more quickly if users click and hold the button.

Search Folder   A virtual folder that searches your e-mail folders to locate items meeting the saved search criteria.

secondary address book   The address book for an additional Contacts folder.

section   A grouping of contiguous slides.

section break   A tool used to create layout or formatting changes in a portion of a document.

select query   The most basic type of Access query, it creates subsets of data, displayed in Datasheet view, that can be used to answer specific questions or to supply data to other database objects.

select   To click in an area to make it active.

selecting text   Highlighting text.

sensitivity   Suggests how the recipient should treat the message and the type of information in the message. Sensitivity settings include normal, personal, private, and confidential.

Sent Items folder   Items are automatically moved to this folder after they have been sent.

serif   A font that has small lines at the beginning and end of characters and that is usually used with large amounts of text.

settings   An option that enables users to set document properties.

shapes   Figures such as lines, rectangles, block arrows, equation shapes, flowcharts, stars and banners, and callouts that you can add to your document or drawing campus.

shortcut menu   A menu that appears when you right-click an area or object.

side-by-side mode   Displays two or more calendars next to each other in the Calendar folder.

signature   Text or images that may be automatically placed at the end of outgoing messages.

SkyDrive   An online file storage service provided by Microsoft where you can store up to **25GB** of documents and pictures for free.

slide master   A slide that stores information about the formats applied in a presentation, such as theme, fonts, layouts, and colors.

Slide Show view   A view that allows the user to preview a presentation on the screen as it will appear to the audience.

SmartArt diagram   A visual representation of information.

SmartArt graphics   Graphical illustrations available within Word from a list of various categories, including List diagrams, Process diagrams, Cycle diagrams, Hierarchy diagrams, Relationship diagrams, Matrix diagrams, and Pyramid diagrams.

sort   To arrange data alphabetically, numerically, or chronologically.

spam   Unsolicited e-mail sent to many e-mail accounts.

spoofing   Providing false information in a message header.

string   Any sequence of letters or numbers in a field.

style   A set of formatting attributes that users can apply to a cell or range of cells more easily than setting each attribute individually.

subject   Topic of a message.

subordinates   In an organization chart, persons or departments who are subordinate to another person or department.

T

tab leader   The symbols that appear in a table of contents between a topic and the corresponding page number.

tab   Component of the navigation pane that a user can click to access groups of related functions and commands.

table   A range of cells in a worksheet that can be used by a lookup function.

table of contents   An ordered list of the topics in a document, along with the page numbers on which they are found. Usually located at the beginning of a long document.

tables   An arrangement of data made up of horizontal rows and vertical columns.

tabs   Eight areas of activity on the Ribbon that contain groups or collections of related Word commands.

template   A ready-to-use database slide, or document that contains all of the tables, queries, forms, and reports needed for performing a specific task.

tentative   An activity is scheduled for this time period, but the activity might not occur. You might be available for other activities.

text box   A container that holds text on a slide.

Text Effects   A new font command group that adds a distinctive appearance, such as outlines, shadows, glows, or reflections, to selected text.

text pane   The fly-out pane that allows you to key information for a SmartArt diagram.

texture   A graphic that repeats to fill an image, creating the appearance that the surface is a certain material, such as marble, wood, or paper.

Theme   A predefined combination of colors and fonts that you can select to apply to a form or report.

theme   A scheme of complementing colors.

thumbnail   A small picture of a slide or document page.

time zone   A geographic area using the same standard time.

timings   The amount of time assigned to each slide before it automatically advances to the next.

title   Descriptive text that is automatically aligned to an axis or centered at the top of a chart.

top-level shape   In an organization chart, the person or department at the head of the organization.

U

undo   A command that allows users to cancel or undo their last command or action.

unhide   To make a worksheet visible again.

Unread Mail   Standard Search Folder that displays unread messages.

V

validation rule   An expression that limits the values that can be entered in the field.

validation text   The text in the error message that appears when users violate a validation rule.

vertical alignment   A setting that refers to how text is positioned between the top and bottom margins of the page.

video   A movie, animated graphic, or motion video clip.

views   The ways in which presentation content can be displayed onscreen, such as Normal view, Slide Sorter view, or Slide Show view.

W

watermarks   Built-in text that display lightly behind the document's main text conveying the sensitivity of the document, such as, *confidential*, *draft*, or *urgent*.

widow   The last line of a paragraph that appears at the top of a page.

wildcard   Characters used to find words or phrases that contain specific letters or combinations of letters.

Wizard   A feature that guides you through steps for completing a process in Microsoft Office applications.

Word Wrap   A tool that automatically wraps text to the next line as it reaches the right margin.

WordArt   A feature used to turn text into a formatted graphic.

work week   The hours or days you work in a calendar week.

workbook   A spreadsheet file.

worksheet   Sheets similar to pages in a document or spreadsheet which you can enter information or organize numerical data that can be then analyzed or manipulated.

Z

zoom   A feature that allows users to make a worksheet appear bigger (zoom in) or smaller (zoom out).

Credits

Index